of

ess and
Management

The most authoritative and up-to-date reference
books for both students and the general reader.

Oxford Paperback Reference

ABC of Music
Accounting
Allusions
Animal Behaviour
Archaeology
Architecture and Landscape
    Architecture
Art and Artists
Art Terms
Arthurian Legend and
    Literature*
Astronomy
Battles*
Better Wordpower
Bible
Biology
British History
British Place-Names
Buddhism
Business and Management
Card Games
Catchphrases
Celtic Mythology
Chemistry
Christian Art
Christian Church
Chronology of English
    Literature
Century of New Words
Classical Literature
Classical Myth and Religion
Classical World*
Computing
Contemporary World History
Countries of the World
Dance
Dynasties of the World
Earth Sciences
Ecology
Economics
Encyclopedia
Engineering*
English Etymology
English Folklore
English Grammar
English Language
English Literature
English Surnames
Euphemisms
Everyday Grammar
Finance and Banking
First Names
Food and Drink
Food and Nutrition
Foreign Words and Phrases
Geography
Humorous Quotations
Idioms
Internet

Islam
Kings and Queens of Britain
Language Toolkit
Law
Law Enforcement*
Linguistics
Literary Terms
Local and Family History
London Place-Names
Mathematics
Medical
Medicinal Drugs
Modern Design
Modern Quotations
Modern Slang
Music
Musical Terms
Musical Works
Nicknames
Nursing
Ologies and Isms
Philosophy
Phrase and Fable
Physics
Plant Sciences
Plays*
Pocket Fowler's Modern English
    Usage
Political Quotations
Politics
Popes
Proverbs
Psychology
Quotations
Quotations by Subject
Reverse Dictionary
Rhymes*
Rhyming Slang
Saints
Science
Scientific Quotations
Shakespeare
Ships and the Sea
Slang
Sociology
Space Exploration
Statistics
Superstitions
Synonyms and Antonyms
Weather
Weights, Measures, and Units
Word Histories
World History
World Mythology
World Place-Names
World Religions
Zoology

*forthcoming

A Dictionary of

Business and Management

FOURTH EDITION

OXFORD
UNIVERSITY PRESS

OXFORD
UNIVERSITY PRESS

Great Clarendon Street, Oxford OX2 6DP

Oxford University Press is a department of the University of Oxford.
It furthers the University's objective of excellence in research, scholarship,
and education by publishing worldwide in

Oxford New York

Auckland Cape Town Dar es Salaam Hong Kong Karachi
Kuala Lumpur Madrid Melbourne Mexico City Nairobi
New Delhi Shanghai Taipei Toronto

With offices in

Argentina Austria Brazil Chile Czech Republic France Greece
Guatemala Hungary Italy Japan Poland Portugal Singapore
South Korea Switzerland Thailand Turkey Ukraine Vietnam

Oxford is a registered trade mark of Oxford University Press
in the UK and in certain other countries

Published in the United States
by Oxford University Press Inc., New York

First published 1990 as *A Concise Dictionary of Business*
Second edition 1996
Third edition 2002
Fourth edition 2006

British Library Cataloguing in Publication Data

Data available

Library of Congress Cataloging in Publication Data

Data available

Typeset by Market House Books Ltd.
Printed in Great Britain
on acid-free paper by
Clays Ltd, St Ives plc
Reading, Berkshire

ISBN 978-0-19-280648-2

4

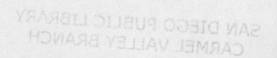

Contents

Preface

A Dictionary of Business and Management is the fourth edition of *A Concise Dictionary of Business*, first published in 1990. The original edition was prepared on the assumption that it would be of use to students of all kinds of business courses, ranging from GCSE Business Studies to degree and postgraduate business subjects, as well as to business people and their professional advisers (lawyers, bankers, accountants, managers, insurers, etc.)

Although both sales and feedback suggest that the book succeeded admirably in this remit, subsequent editions were enlarged to reflect changes in business practice and culture. The second edition paid greater attention to such matters as business strategy and marketing, while the third brought the book into the 21st century with a special emphasis on the use of the Internet in commerce.

In this fourth edition coverage of management terms and theory has been greatly increased to reflect the growing emphasis on human resources and organizational behaviour now found in MBAs and business courses at all levels. Several hundred new entries have been added to explain the concepts, vocabulary, and jargon associated with current theories of leadership, motivation, and team building. The book has also been fully updated to include the latest changes from such fast-moving fields as law, taxation, accounting, finance, and computing. We have added feature spreads on a number of key topics and there is an appendix of useful websites.

J.L. 2006

Note: An asterisk (*) placed before a term in a definition indicates that this term can be found as an entry in the dictionary and will provide further information. Synonyms and abbreviations are usually found within brackets immediately following a headword.

Credits

Editor of the fourth edition
Jonathan Law (Market House Books Ltd)

Editors of the previous editions
John Pallister MA, PhD (Cardiff Business School)
Alan Isaacs BSc, PhD (Market House Books Ltd)

Market House Books Ltd staff
Jessica Foote
Sandra McQueen
Anne Stibbs

Contributors

Graham Betts
Barry Brindley BA
Peter Chadwick BA, MSc,
    University of Gloucestershire
Leslie de Chernatony PhD
    City University Business School
Farooq Chudri MA
    Bristol Business School
Joan Gallagher MA,
    Personnel Consultant
Nicholas Hand MSc, Bcomm
    University of Greenwich
Ian Holden BSc, MBA,
Peter Lafferty MSc
Catherine Law MA, ACA

Clive Longhurst ACII
Gary Owen, MSc, FFIS
    University of Greenwich
Edward Philips LLB, BCL,
    University of Buckingham
John Smullen BSc, MA, MSc, MBA
    University of Greenwich
Stefan Szymanski BA, MSc, PhD,
    London Business School
R. M. Walters MA, FCA,
    Chartered Accountant
S. L. Williams MA,
    University of Buckingham
Matthew Wright MA, MPhil

A1 A description of property or a person that is in the best condition. In marine insurance, before a vessel can be insured, it has to be inspected to check its condition. If it is "maintained in good and efficient condition" it will be shown in *Lloyd's Register of Shipping as 'A' and if the anchor moorings are in the same condition the number '1' is added. This description is also used in life assurance, in which premiums are largely based on the person's health. After a medical examination a person in perfect health is described as 'an A1 life'.

AA Abbreviation for *Advertising Association.

AAP Abbreviation for *affirmative action programme.

abandonment The act of giving up the ownership of something covered by an insurance policy and treating it as if it has been completely lost or destroyed. If the insurers agree to abandonment, they will pay a total-loss claim (see ACTUAL TOTAL LOSS; CONSTRUCTIVE TOTAL LOSS). This often occurs in marine insurance if a vessel has run aground in hazardous waters and the cost of recovering it would be higher than its total value and the value of its cargo. It also occurs during wartime when a vessel is captured by the enemy. If the owner wishes to declare a vessel and its cargo a total loss, **notice of abandonment** is given to the insurer; if, subsequently, the vessel or its cargo are recovered, they become the property of the insurer.

ABB Abbreviation for *activity-based budgeting.

abbreviated accounts A shorter form of *annual accounts that may be filed with the *Registrar of Companies by a company qualifying as a small or medium-sized company under the UK Companies Act (1985; amended 2004). The use of abbreviated accounts can cut costs and save

time. It can also minimize the information made available to others, especially business rivals. See also SUMMARY FINANCIAL STATEMENT.

ABC 1. Abbreviation for *Audit Bureau of Circulation. **2.** Abbreviation for *activity-based costing.

ABC classification (ABC ranking) A method of ranking items held in *inventory enabling particular attention to be given to those that, if incorrectly managed, will be most damaging to the effectiveness or the efficiency of an operation. Items are categorized according to their value of usage, i.e. their individual value multiplied by their usage rate. In most cases *Pareto's Rule then applies, so that approximately 20% of the items accounts for approximately 80% of the value of the stock held; these items are classified as Class A items. Class B covers the 30% of items that represent the next 10% of value. Class C covers the remaining 50%, which accounts for the remaining 10% of value. In *material requirements planning (MRP), ranking is used to categorize inventory by its impact value, i.e. whether or not production will stop if this item is out of stock.

ABI Abbreviation for *Association of British Insurers.

ability to pay The principle that taxes should be levied on the basis of taxpayers' ability to pay. This normally leads to the view that as income or wealth increases, its marginal utility (its value to its owner) decreases so that higher rates of tax can be levied on the higher slices. A typical *progressive tax of this sort is UK *income tax. Compare BENEFIT TAXATION; FLAT TAX; REGRESSIVE TAX.

abnormal loss See NORMAL LOSS.

abnormal return A rate of return for taking a particular risk that is greater than that required by the market. The excess return is usually measured as being relative to that which the *capital asset pricing model or the *arbitrage pricing theory requires. See also ACTIVE MANAGEMENT; ANOMALY; EFFICIENT MARKETS HYPOTHESIS.

above par See PAR VALUE.

above-the-fold Originally denoting an advertisement displayed above the fold in printed media; in computer terms it indicates that a *banner advertisement or other content on a web page is displayed without the need to scroll. This is likely to give higher *clickthrough, but note that the location of the 'fold' within the *web browser is dependent on the screen resolution of a user's own computer.

above-the-line **1.** Denoting those entries printed above the horizontal line on a company's *profit and loss account that separates the entries that establish the profit (or loss) from the entries showing how the profit is distributed. Prior to the introduction of Financial Reporting Standard (FRS) 3, Reporting Financial Performance, in October 1992, it was understood that any exceptional items that were within the ordinary activities of the business were shown above the line, while any extraordinary items that were outside the ordinary activities of the business were shown below it. There was, however, criticism that the definitions of extraordinary and exceptional items could be manipulated to improve the *earnings per share figure. For example, if a building was sold for a large profit it could be interpreted as being exceptional and included in the earnings per share, whereas if it was sold at a loss it could be interpreted as being extraordinary and not included in the earnings per share. Since the introduction of FRS 3, both exceptional and extraordinary items are shown above the line and are included in the earnings per share. **2.** Denoting advertising expenditure on mass media advertising, including press, television, radio, and posters. It is traditionally regarded as all advertising expenditure on which a commission is payable to an *advertising agency. **3.** Denoting transactions concerned with revenue, as opposed to capital, in national accounts. Compare BELOW-THE-LINE.

ABP Abbreviation for *Associated British Ports.

absence culture An *organizational culture in which a certain degree of *absenteeism has come to be accepted as the norm. In companies with such a culture it may become routine for managers and workers to take occasional days off 'sick' when there is no justification for this.

absenteeism Absence from work for which there is no legitimate reason; it is often self-certified sick leave lasting for one day at a time. Most prevalent in large organizations, it can be a major problem. In order to combat it some organizations have introduced flexible working hours, increased annual leave, introduced personal days leave in addition to normal holiday entitlement, and devised incentive schemes for full attendance. High rates of absenteeism can be linked to low levels of *job satisfaction and an *absence culture in the workplace.

absolute cost advantage The cost advantage enjoyed by a country in producing certain goods, compared to costs in other countries. The costs of producing similar products vary between different countries because certain resources, such as labour, raw materials, and energy, will be cheaper in some countries than in others. Multinational enterprises are able to take advantage of these cost differences by buying components or products from countries that have these advantages. For example, a motor-vehicle manufacturer in an economy with high labour costs may purchase certain components from another country with significantly lower labour costs. Compare COMPETITIVE ADVANTAGE.

absolute performance standard A standard set at the theoretical limit of performance. For example, in manufacturing, the theoretical quality standard of 'zero defects', which it is impossible to improve on, might be set as the absolute performance standard. Such standards may be achievable in practice or may form an ideal against which an organization may judge its progress.

absorption (cost absorption; overhead absorption) An accounting process, used in *absorption costing, in which the *overhead of an organization is charged to the production of that organization by the use of *absorption rates.

PRODUCTION MEASURE	ABSORPTION RATE
units, weight, or volume	rate per unit, weight, or volume
direct labour hours	rate per direct labour hour
machine hours	rate per machine hour
direct labour cost	% on direct labour cost
direct material cost	% on direct material cost
prime cost	% on prime cost
standard hours	rate per standard hour

Absorption rate

absorption costing (full absorption costing; total absorption costing) The *cost accounting system in which the *overheads of an organization are charged to the production by means of the process of *absorption. Costs are first apportioned to *cost centres, where they are absorbed using *absorption rates. Although this method has the advantage of simplicity, it involves an essentially *arbitrary allocation of costs; for this reason the system of *activity-based costing is now widely preferred. *Compare* MARGINAL COSTING.

absorption rate (overhead absorption rate; recovery rate) The rate or rates calculated in an *absorption costing system in advance of an accounting period for the purpose of charging the *overheads to the *production of that period. Absorption rates are calculated for the accounting period in question using the following formula:

budgeted overhead/budgeted production.

In absorption costing production may be expressed in a number of different ways; the way chosen to express production will determine the absorption rate to be used. The seven major methods of measuring production, together with their associated absorption rate, are given in the table above. The rate is used during the accounting period to obtain the absorbed overhead by multiplying the actual production achieved by the absorption rate.

These rates have been used by accountants for over a century and they are still widely applied. Many, however, would argue that they cannot provide the accurate *cause-and-effect allocations of costs that modern managers require; for this a system of *activity-based costing must be used. *See also* TRADITIONAL COSTING SYSTEM.

abstract of title A document used in conveyancing land that is not registered to show how the vendor derived good title. It consists of a summary of certain documents, such as conveyances of the land, and recitals of certain events, such as marriages and deaths of previous owners. The purchaser will check the abstract against title deeds, grants of probate, etc. This document is not needed when registered land is being conveyed, as the land certificate shows good title.

ACA Abbreviation for Associate of the *Institute of Chartered Accountants.

ACAS Abbreviation for *Advisory Conciliation and Arbitration Service.

ACC Abbreviation for *Agricultural Credit Corporation Ltd.

ACCA Abbreviation for Associate of the Association of Chartered Certified Accountants. *See* CHARTERED CERTIFIED ACCOUNTANT.

accelerated depreciation A rate of *depreciation of assets that is faster than the useful-life basis normally used to calculate depreciation. For example, a computer may be expected to have a useful life of four years when it is purchased; however, as a result of new product innovation, it is replaced after two years. If the useful-life basis had been used, the full cost would not have been charged to the accounts until the end of the fourth year; by accelerating the depreciation the full charge would be made earlier, reflecting the short life cycle of high-technology products. In the USA, the accelerated depreciation may be used to gain tax advantages.

acceptable use policy (AUP) The rules of permitted behaviour on a particular portion of the Internet.

acceptance 1. The signature on a *bill

of exchange indicating that the person on whom it is drawn accepts the conditions of the bill. **2.** A bill of exchange that has been so accepted. Acceptances are divided into two categories: *banker's acceptances and trade acceptances. **3.** Agreement to accept the terms of an offer; for example, the agreement of an insurance company to provide a specified insurance cover or of a trader to accept a specified parcel of goods at the offer price.

acceptance credit A means of financing the sale of goods, particularly in international trade. It involves a commercial bank or merchant bank extending credit to a foreign importer, whom it deems creditworthy. An acceptance credit is opened against which the exporter can draw a *bill of exchange. Once accepted by the bank, the bill can be discounted on the *money market or allowed to run to maturity. In return for this service the exporter pays the bank a fee known as an **acceptance commission**.

acceptance number The number of sample units specified in a sampling plan that must conform to the specifications if the batch is to be accepted. *See* ACCEPTANCE SAMPLING.

acceptance sampling A *statistical process-control technique that uses inspection of a SAMPLE from a batch to decide whether to accept or reject the whole batch. In deciding the level of sampling, a balance has to be struck between achieving the desired quality levels and the cost of undertaking the sampling.

acceptance supra protest (acceptance for honour) The acceptance or payment of a *bill of exchange, after it has been dishonoured, by a person wishing to save the honour of the drawer or an endorser of the bill.

accepting house An institution specializing in accepting or guaranteeing *bills of exchange. A service fee is charged for guaranteeing payment, enabling the bill to be discounted at preferential rates on the *money market. The decline in the use of bills of exchange has forced the accepting houses to widen their financial activities, many of whom have returned to their original role as *merchant banks.

Accepting Houses Committee A committee representing the *accepting houses in the City of London. Members of the committee are eligible for finer discounts on bills bought by the Bank of England, although this privilege has been extended to other banks.

acceptor The drawee of a *bill of exchange after acceptance of the bill, i.e. the acceptor has accepted liability by signing the face of the bill.

accessibility The degree to which a market segment can be reached and served.

access lag A delay caused by the limited data-transmission speed between the user and the Internet.

access provider A company providing services to enable an organization or individual to access the Internet. Access providers are divided into *Internet service providers and *on-line service providers.

accident analysis The use of analytical techniques drawn from *ergonomics to identify the causes of accidents, to recognize potential hazards in the workplace, and to create action plans for reducing the risks of injury and system damage. *See* ACCIDENT PRONENESS.

accident insurance An insurance policy that pays a specified amount of money to the policyholder in the event of the loss of one or more eyes or limbs in any type of accident. It also pays a sum to the dependants of the policyholder in the event of his or her death. These policies first appeared in the early days of railway travel, when passengers felt a train journey was hazardous and they needed some protection for their dependants if they were to be killed or injured.

accident proneness The propensity of an individual to suffer (or cause) more than an average number of accidents. This is of particular interest in *industrial and organizational psychology, which is anxious to analyse the causes of accidents in the workplace in order to reduce their occurrence and their inevitable costs. There is, however, some doubt as to whether such a condition does in fact exist, or whether some people are simply the unlucky statistics that go to make up a *normal distribution of accident frequency.

On the other hand, it is not hard to imagine that accidents are more likely to occur at work (or anywhere else) if concentration is distracted by such extraneous factors as fatigue, illness, emotional preoccupation, or stress. Machine operators, for example, have certain skills at processing the information perceived by their senses so that an appropriate response is initiated. In addition to this skill, the personal qualities of the operator must also be involved in the smooth operation of the machine. If the operator is aware that his or her skill with the machine is less than it should be, this is not necessarily a recipe for accidents to occur; the intelligent operator will, under these circumstances, work more slowly, more cautiously, and with greater concentration. It is often, in fact, the more highly skilled operator, many of whose responses are automatic, who is more easily distracted by extraneous factors and thus more accident prone. Although organizational psychologists have been unable to provide a rigorous treatment of accident proneness, much valuable work has been done in analysing those activities that have high inherent risks and those environmental conditions (e.g. poor lighting, inappropriate room temperature) that increase the chances of accidents happening. Human error can be greatly reduced by improved design of equipment and work systems and through training programs and other administrative interventions.

accommodation bill A *bill of exchange signed by a person (the accommodation party) who acts as a guarantor. The accommodation party is liable for the bill should the *acceptor fail to pay at maturity. Accommodation bills are sometimes known as **windbills** or **windmills**. *See also* KITE.

accommodation endorser A person or a bank that endorses a loan to another party; for example, a parent company may endorse a bank loan to a subsidiary. The endorser becomes a guarantor and is secondarily liable in case of default. Banks may endorse other banks' acceptance

notes, which can then be traded on the secondary market.

accord and satisfaction A device enabling one party to a *contract to avoid an obligation that arises under the contract, provided that the other party agrees. The accord is the agreement by which the contractual obligation is discharged and the satisfaction is the *consideration making the agreement legally operative. Such an agreement only discharges the contractual obligation if it is accompanied by consideration. For example, under a contract of sale the seller of goods may discharge the contractual obligation by delivering goods of different quality to that specified in the contract, provided there is agreement with the buyer (the accord) and the seller offers a reduction in the contract price (the satisfaction). The seller has therefore 'purchased' the release from the obligation. Accord and satisfaction refer to the discharge of an obligation arising under the law of tort.

account **1.** A statement of indebtedness from one person to another. A provider of goods or services may render an account to a client or customer (*see* SALES INVOICE). **2.** A named segment of a *ledger recording transactions relevant to the person or the matter named. *See* BOOKS OF ACCOUNT. **3.** An account maintained by a *bank or a *building society in which a depositor's money is kept. *See* CHEQUE ACCOUNT; CURRENT ACCOUNT; DEPOSIT ACCOUNT; SAVINGS ACCOUNT. **4.** A period during which dealings on the *London Stock Exchange were formerly made without immediate cash settlement. Up to the end of each account, transactions were recorded but no money changed hands. Settlement of all transactions made within an account was made ten days after the account ended. This practice changed in 1996 when the account system was abandoned. **5.** In an advertising, marketing, or public-relations agency, a client of the agency from whom a commission or fee is derived, in return for the services. **6.** *See* ANNUAL ACCOUNTS.

accountability An obligation to give an account. For limited companies, it is assumed that the directors of the company are accountable to the shareholders and that this responsibility is discharged, in part, by the directors providing an annual report and accounts (*see* ANNUAL AC-COUNTS). In an accountability relationship there will be at least one principal and at least one agent. This forms the basis of an *agency relationship.

accountant A person who has passed the accountancy examinations of one of the recognized accountancy bodies and completed the required work experience. Each of the bodies varies in the way they train their students and the type of work expected to be undertaken. For example, accountants who are members of the Chartered Institute of Public Finance and Accountancy generally work in local authorities, the National Health Service, or other similar public bodies, while members of the Chartered Institute of Management Accountants work in industry (*see* MANAGEMENT ACCOUNTING). Wherever accountants work, their responsibilities centre on the collating, recording, and communicating of financial information and the preparation of analyses for decision-making purposes. *See also* CHARTERED ACCOUNTANT; CHARTERED CERTIFIED ACCOUNTANT.

account executive The person in an advertising, marketing, or public-relations agency responsible for implementing a client's business. This involves carrying out the programme agreed between the agency and client, coordinating the activities, and liaising with the client.

accounting code (cost code; expenditure code; income code) In modern accounting systems, a numerical reference given to each account to facilitate the recording of voluminous accounting transactions by computer.

accounting concepts (accounting principles; fundamental accounting concepts) The basic theoretical ideas devised to support the activity of accounting. As accounting developed largely from a practical base, it has been argued that it lacks a theoretical framework. Accountants have therefore tried to develop such a framework; although various concepts have been suggested, few have found universal agreement. However, four are often deemed to be fundamental:

- the *going-concern concept assumes that the business is a going concern

until there is evidence to the contrary, so that assets are not stated at their break-up value;
- the *accruals concept involves recording income and expenses as they accrue, as distinct from when they are received or paid;
- the *consistency concept demands that accounts be prepared on a basis that clearly allows comparability from one period to another;
- the *prudence concept calls for accounts to be prepared on a conservative basis, not taking credit for profits or income before they are realized but making provision for losses when they are foreseen.

These four principles were laid down in *Statement of Standard Accounting Practice (SSAP) 2, Disclosure of Accounting Policies; they are also recognized in the EU's *Fourth Accounting Directive and the UK Companies Acts together with a fifth principle, the *accounting entity concept. SSAP 2 has now been superseded by *Financial Reporting Standard (FRS) 18, which was issued in December 2000: this states that the consistency concept and the prudence concept should no longer be regarded as fundamental. FRS 18 also identifies four key objectives of financial information that can be regarded as fundamental principles: *comparability, *relevance, *reliability, and *understandability.

accounting entity (entity; business entity; reporting entity) The unit for which accounting records are maintained and for which *financial statements are prepared. The **accounting entity concept** (or **entity concept** or **separate entity concept**) is the principle that financial records are prepared for a distinct unit or entity regarded as separate from the individuals that own it. This will often be an incorporated *company, whose treatment as a separate accounting entity is required by law. For sole traders and partnerships accounts are also prepared to reflect the transactions of the business as an accounting entity, not those of the owner(s) of the business. Changing the boundaries of the accounting entity can have a significant impact on the accounts themselves, as these will reflect the purpose of the accounts and for whom they are prepared.

accounting event A transaction or change (internal or external) recognized by the accounting recording system. Events are recorded as debit and credit entries. For example, when a sale is made for cash the double entry for the sales transaction would be debit bank, credit sales (*see* DOUBLE-ENTRY BOOK-KEEPING).

accounting package *See* BUSINESS SOFTWARE PACKAGE.

accounting period 1. (financial period; period of account) The period for which a business prepares its accounts. Internally, management accounts may be produced monthly or quarterly. Externally, *financial statements are produced for a period of 12 months, although this may vary when a business is set up or ceases or if it changes its accounting year end. *See* ACCOUNTING REFERENCE DATE. **2. (chargeable account period)** A period in respect of which a *corporation tax assessment is raised. It cannot be more than 12 months in length. An accounting period starts when a company begins to trade or immediately after a previous accounting period ends. An accounting period ends at the earliest of:
- 12 months after the start date,
- at the end of the company's period of account,
- the start of a winding-up,
- on ceasing to be UK resident.

accounting policies The specific accounting bases adopted and consistently followed by an organization in the preparation of its *financial statements. These bases will have been determined by the organization to be the most appropriate for presenting fairly its financial results and operations; they will concentrate on such specific topics as pension schemes, *goodwill, research and development costs, and *foreign exchange. Under *Statement of Standard Accounting Practice 2 and its successor, *Financial Reporting Standard 18, companies are required to disclose their accounting policies in their *annual accounts.

accounting principles *See* ACCOUNTING CONCEPTS.

accounting rate of return (ARR) An *accounting ratio that expresses the profit of an organization before interest and taxation, usually for a year, as a percentage of the capital employed at the end of the period. Variants of the measure include using profit after interest and taxation, equity capital employed, and the average of opening and closing capital employed for the period. Although ARR can be used to forecast return on an investment project, *discounted cash flow measures are acknowledged to be superior for this purpose.

accounting ratio (financial ratio) A ratio calculated from two or more figures taken from the *financial statements of a company in order to provide an indication of the financial performance and position of that company. Ratios may be expressed as a percentage (e.g. *return on capital employed), in days (e.g. *debtor collection period), or as a multiple (e.g. *rate of turnover). *See* FINANCIAL-STATEMENT ANALYSIS; RATIO ANALYSIS.

accounting records The records kept by a company to comply with the Companies Act (1985), which requires companies to keep accounting records sufficient to show and explain their transactions and to prepare accounts that give a true and fair view of their activities. Accounting records take the form of manual or computerized ledgers, journals, and the supporting documentation.

accounting reference date (ARD) The date at the end of an **accounting reference period**, i.e. the financial year for a company, as notified to the *Registrar of Companies. For companies incorporated after 1 April 1990, it is normally taken as the last day of the month in which the anniversary of incorporation falls. Companies wishing to change their ARD must notify Companies House in advance.

Accounting Standards Board (ASB) The recognized body for setting accounting standards in the UK. It was established in 1990 to replace the **Accounting Standards Committee (ASC)** following the recommendations contained in the *Dearing Report. Under the Companies Act (1985), companies (except *small companies and *medium-sized companies) must state whether their accounts have been prepared in accordance with the relevant accounting standards and give details and reasons for any material departures from those standards. The ASB issues Financial Reporting Exposure Drafts (FREDs), *Financial Reporting Standards (FRS), and through its offshoot, the Urgent Issues Task Force, reports known as Abstracts. The ASB is a subsidiary of the *Financial Reporting Council.

accounting technician A person qualified by membership of an appropriate body (such as the *Association of Accounting Technicians) to undertake tasks in the accountancy field without being a fully qualified *accountant.

account management group 1. A group within an advertising, marketing, or public-relations agency responsible for planning, supervising, and coordinating all the work done on behalf of a client. In large agencies handling large accounts the group might consist of an account director, account manager, account or media planner, and *account executive. 2. A group in the sales department of an organization that is responsible for managing the relationship with existing clients.

account of profits A legal remedy available as an alternative to *damages in certain circumstances, especially in breach of *copyright cases. The person whose copyright has been breached sues the person who breached it for a sum of money equal to the gain made as a result of the breach.

account payee only Words printed between two vertical lines in the centre of a UK cheque that, in accordance with the Cheque Act (1992), make the cheque non-transferable. This is to avoid cheques being endorsed and paid into an account other than that of the payee, although it should be noted that banks may argue in some circumstances that they acted in good faith and without negligence if an endorsed cheque is honoured by the bank. In spite of this most cheques are now overprinted 'account payee only' or 'A/C payee', and the words 'not negotiable' are sometimes added.

account reconciliation 1. A procedure for confirming that the balance in a chequebook matches the corresponding *bank statement. This is normally done by preparing a *bank reconciliation statement. 2. A procedure for confirming the reliability of a company's *accounting records by regularly comparing balances of transactions. An account reconciliation may be prepared on a daily, monthly, or annual basis.

account rendered An unpaid balance appearing in a *statement of account, details of which have been given in a previous statement.

accounts 1. The *profit and loss account, *balance sheet, and *cash-flow statements of a company. See ANNUAL ACCOUNTS. 2. See ACCOUNT; BOOKS OF ACCOUNT.

account sale A statement giving details of a sale made on behalf of another person or firm, often as an *agent. The account sale shows the proceeds of the sale less any agreed expenses, commission, etc.

Accounts Modernization Directive An EU directive (2003) that requires companies to publish information that provides a "balanced and comprehensive" analysis of their development and performance during the financial year. This should include not only key financial performance indicators but also, where appropriate, non-financial indicators, including information relating to environmental and employee matters. The directive, which is binding on publicly listed companies for financial years beginning on or after 1 January 2005, has necessitated changes to the UK regulations on the *directors' report and the *operating and financial review.

accounts payable (trade creditors) The amounts owed by a business to suppliers (e.g. for raw materials). Accounts payable are classed as *current liabilities on the balance sheet, but distinguished from *accruals and other non-trade creditors (such as HM Revenue and Customs).

accounts receivable (trade debtors) The amounts owing to a business from customers for invoiced amounts. Accounts receivable are classed as *current assets on the balance sheet, but distinguished from prepayments and other non-trade debtors. A *provision for bad debts is often shown against the accounts receivable balance in line with the *prudence concept. This provision is based on the company's past history of bad debts and its current expectations. A general provision is often based on a percentage of the total credit sales, for example 2% of credit sales made during the period.

accrual (accrued charge; accrued expense; accrued liability) An estimate in the accounts of a business of a liability that is not supported by an invoice or a request for payment at the time the accounts are prepared. An accrual is a *current liability on the *balance sheet and will be charged under expenses in the *profit and loss account. Expenses are accrued as set out in the *accruals concept outlined in Statement of Standard Accounting Practice 2. An example of an accrual would be telephone expenses, which are billed in arrears. At the end of the accounting period, if no bill has been received, an estimate (based on past bills) would be made and credited to an accruals account; the corresponding debit would be made to the telephone expense account. The telephone expense account is then cleared to the profit and loss account.

accrual accounting A system of accounting in which *revenue is recognized when it is earned and expenses are recognized as they are incurred. Accrual accounting is a basic *accounting concept used in the preparation of the *profit and loss account and *balance sheet of a business. It differs from *cash accounting, which recognizes transactions when cash has been received or paid. In preparing *financial statements for an *accounting period using accrual accounting, there will inevitably be some estimation and uncertainty in respect of transactions. The reader of the financial statements therefore cannot have the same high level of confidence in these statements as in those using cash accounting.

accruals concept One of the four fundamental *accounting concepts laid down in *Statement of Standard Accounting Practice (SSAP) 2, Disclosure of Accounting Policies; it is also recognized in the Companies Act (1985) and the EU's *Fourth Accounting Directive. It requires that revenue and costs are recognized as they are earned or incurred, not as money is received or paid. Income and expenses

should be matched with one another, as far as their relationship can be established or justifiably assumed, and dealt with in the *profit and loss account of the period to which they relate. *Accruals and *prepayments are examples of the application of the accruals concept in practice. For example, if a rates bill for both a current and future period is paid, that part relating to the future period is carried forward as a current asset (a prepayment) until it can be matched to the future periods.

The importance of the accruals concept was reaffirmed in *Financial Reporting Standard 18, which has now superseded SSAP 2.

accrued benefits Benefits due under a *defined-benefit pension scheme in respect of service up to a given time. Accrued benefits may be calculated in relation to current earnings or protected final earnings. *Statement of Standard Accounting Practice 24 and *Financial Reporting Standard 17, Retirement Benefits, contain regulations on accounting for pension costs in financial accounts. From January 2005 listed companies have to comply with *International Accounting Standard 19, Employee Benefits.

accrued benefits method An actuarial method used in accounting for pension costs in which the actuarial value of liabilities relates at a given date to:

- the benefits, including future increases promised by the rules, for the current and deferred pensioners and their dependants;
- the benefits that the members assumed to be in service on the given date will receive for service up to that date only.

Allowance may be made for expected increases in earnings after the given date, and for additional pension increases not promised by the rules. The given date may be a current or future date. The further into the future the adopted date lies, the closer the results will be to those obtained by a prospective benefits valuation method.

accrued charge *See* ACCRUAL.

accrued income scheme An arrangement that applies in the UK when the owner of interest-bearing securities disposes of them. The interest accrued between the date of the last interest payment and the date of disposal is regarded, for tax purposes, as the income of the transferor. The transferee is able to deduct this sum from taxable income. The scheme does not apply to non-residents or if the transfer is part of a trade. Exemption also applies to individuals (husband and wife being regarded as one) if the total nominal value of the securities held does not exceed a certain amount.

accumulated depreciation (aggregate depreciation) The total amount of the *depreciation written off the cost price or valuation of a *fixed asset since it was brought into the balance sheet of an organization.

accumulated dividend A *dividend that has not been paid to a holder of *cumulative preference shares and is carried forward (i.e. accumulated) to the next accounting period. It represents a liability to the company. The Companies Act requires that where any fixed cumulative dividends on a company's shares are in arrears, both the amount of the arrears and the period(s) in arrears must be disclosed for each class of shares.

accumulated profits The amount showing in the *appropriation of profits account that can be carried forward to the next year's accounts, i.e. after paying dividends, taxes, and putting some to reserve.

accumulating shares Additional *ordinary shares issued to holders of ordinary shares in a company, instead of a dividend. Accumulating shares are a way of replacing annual income with capital growth; they avoid income tax but not capital gains tax. Usually tax is deducted by the company from the declared dividend, in the usual way, and the net dividend is then used to buy additional ordinary shares for the shareholder.

accumulation trust See DISCRETIONARY TRUST.

accumulation unit A unit in a *unit trust or an *investment trust in which dividends are ploughed back into the trust, after deducting income tax, enabling the value of the unit to increase. It is usually linked to a life-assurance policy.

achievement motivation theory A theory that establishes a relationship between personal characteristics, social background, and achievement. A person with a strong need for achievement tends to exhibit such characteristics as:
- regarding the task as more important than any relationship;
- having a preference for tasks over which they have control and responsibility;
- needing to identify closely, and be identified closely, with the successful outcomes of their actions;
- seeking tasks that are sufficiently difficult to be challenging, to be capable of demonstrating expertise, and to gain recognition from others, while also being sufficiently easy to be capable of achievement;
- avoiding the likelihood and consequences of failure;
- requiring feedback on achievements to ensure that success is recognized;
- needing opportunities for promotion.

The need for achievement is based on a combination of *intrinsic motivation (drives from within the individual) and *extrinsic motivation (pressures and expectations exerted by an organization, peers, and society). Achievement is also clearly influenced by education, social awareness, cultural background, and values. See MOTIVATION.

acid-test ratio See LIQUID RATIO.

ACII Abbreviation for Associate of the *Chartered Insurance Institute.

ACIS Abbreviation for Associate of the *Institute of Chartered Secretaries and Administrators.

ACMA Abbreviation for Associate of the Chartered Institute of Management Accountants. See ACCOUNTANT; MANAGEMENT ACCOUNTING.

ACORN Acronym for A Classification of Residential Neighbourhoods. This directory classifies 56 different types of neighbourhoods in the UK, assuming that people living in a particular neighbourhood will have similar behaviour patterns, disposable incomes, etc. It is used by companies to provide target areas for selling particular products or services (e.g. swimming pools, double glazing, etc.) or alternatively to exclude areas (particularly finance and insurance-related) from a sales drive. It is also used extensively for selecting representative samples for questionnaire surveys. *See also* GEOGRAPHIC INFORMATION SYSTEM.

acquisition accounting The accounting procedures followed when one company is taken over by another. The *fair value of the purchase consideration should, for the purpose of consolidated financial statements, be allocated between the underlying net tangible and intangible assets, other than *goodwill, on the basis of the fair value to the acquiring company. Any difference between the fair value of the consideration and the aggregate of the fair values of the separable net assets (including identifiable intangibles, such as patents, licences, and trademarks) will represent goodwill. The results of the acquired company should be brought into the *consolidated profit and loss account from the date of acquisition only.

Acquisition accounting and *merger accounting were covered by *Statement of Standard Accounting Practice (SSAP) 23, Accounting for Acquisitions and Mergers, until September 1994, when the Accounting Standards Board issued *Financial Reporting Standard 6, Acquisitions and Mergers, and Financial Reporting Standard 7, Fair Values in Acquisition Accounting, which replaced SSAP 23. The relevant *International Accounting Standard is IAS 22, Business Combinations.

acquisition cost The average cost of acquiring a prospect or a customer. This is often calculated for setting marketing budgets in direct marketing. *See* ALLOWABLE MARKETING COST.

acquisition-development-retention (ADR framework) A measurement of a firm's activities derived from its website and based on its impact on the acquisition, development, and retention of customers.

Acrobat (Adobe Acrobat) A software application produced by Adobe Inc., used for producing and viewing electronic documents. The file format, known as **PDF** (portable document format), allows an exact reproduction of printed text, including fonts. It is widely used for Internet

publication of official documents (e.g. annual accounts).

across the network Denoting a TV advertisement or programme series that is broadcast across all ITV regions simultaneously.

ACT 1. Abbreviation for *advance corporation tax. **2.** Abbreviation for *Association of Corporate Treasurers.

active management 1. A management style characterized by high levels of involvement in both task-related activities, such as initiating structures and setting goals, and interpersonal activities, such as listening, motivating, and providing feedback. *See* RELATIONSHIP-MOTIVATED; TASK-MOTIVATED. *See also* BLAKE–MOUTON MANAGERIAL GRID. **2.** A method of *portfolio management in which individual investments are selected with an eye to earning *abnormal returns. The general academic view is that this approach runs counter to the *efficient markets hypothesis and is therefore unlikely to be successful. The strategies of *diversification and following a market index are thought more likely to provide greater returns. *Compare* PASSIVE MANAGEMENT.

active partner A partner who has contributed to the business capital of a *partnership and who participates in its management. All partners are deemed to be active partners unless otherwise agreed. *Compare* SLEEPING PARTNER.

Active Server Page (ASP) A type of HTML page (denoted by an .asp file name) that includes *scripts (small programs) that are processed on a *web server before the web page is served to the user's *web browser. The main use of such programs is to process information supplied by the user in an on-line form. A query may then be run to provide specific information to the customer, such as delivery status of an order or a personalized web page. ASP is a Microsoft technology.

active stocks The stocks and shares that have been actively traded on a particular market on a given day.

Active X A programming language standard developed by Microsoft that enables complex customer applications to be written. Active X components are standard controls that can be incorporated into websites and automatically downloaded for users. Examples include graphics and animation, a calculator form for calculating interest on a loan, and a control for drawing graphs of stock exchange prices.

activity In *activity-based costing systems, any operation performed within an organization that causes *costs to be incurred. Examples of activities therefore include processing an order, writing a letter, designing a product, and visiting a customer. The number of activities identified as such will vary from organization to organization. Activity-based costing is founded on the recognition that resources generate costs, activities consume resources, and *cost objects (products, services, or customers) consume activities.

For purposes of *cost allocation, activities may be divided into several different categories:

- **Batch-level activities**, i.e. those activities that are performed each time a batch of goods is handled or processed. The cost incurred depends on the number of batches run rather than on the number of units in the batch. The cost is not therefore dependent on the volume of units. *See* BATCH COSTING.
- **Product-sustaining-level activities**, i.e. activities relating to specific products that must be carried out regardless of how many units are produced and sold.
- **Unit-level activities**, i.e. activities that must be performed for each unit of production.
- **Customer-level activities**, i.e. activities that are carried out for a customer but are not related to a specific product.

See also FACILITY-SUSTAINING ACTIVITY.

activity analysis In *activity-based costing, the identification and description of *activities in an organization. Each department will determine the key activities, how many people work on the activities, and what resources are required to perform the activities. Some activities may be performed in a number of different departments.

activity-based budgeting (ABB) Establishing the activities that incur costs in each function of an organization, defining the relationships between activities, and using the information to decide how much resource should be allowed for each activity in the *budget. ABB also attempts to determine how well a particular section of the budget is being managed and to explain any variances from budgeted expenditure.

activity-based costing (ABC; activity costing) A system of costing proposed by Professors Johnson and Kaplan in their book *Relevance Lost: The Rise and Fall of Management Accounting* (1987), in which they questioned accounting techniques based on *absorption costing. Their method recognizes that costs are incurred by each activity that takes place within an organization and that products (or customers) should bear costs according to the activities they use. *Cost drivers are identified, together with the appropriate *activity cost pools, which are used to charge costs to products. Adherents of activity-based costing maintain that it provides accurate *cause-and-effect allocations of costs that cannot be obtained from *traditional costing systems.

activity-based management The use made by the management of an organization of *activity-based costing. The identification of activities and *cost drivers encourages the management to review how projected cost levels compare with the activity levels achieved.

activity cost pool (cost pool) In *activity-based costing, a collection of *indirect costs grouped according to the activity involved. To identify the costs of each activity, cost pool managers will have to ask questions such as:

- What staff are involved with the activity?
- What machinery, equipment, vehicles, and computers are used by staff?
- What materials are used for the activity?

Each activity cost pool has one or more relevant *activity measures (or *cost drivers) that are used in allocating costs: for some common examples, see the table on p. 13.

The size of a particular cost pool will vary widely from one organization to another. For example, a cost pool for order processing may include hundreds of staff in a large organization, whereas a smaller organization may not have a separate cost

ACTIVITY COST POOL	ACTIVITY MEASURE
Order processing	Number of orders
Product design	Number of product designs
Deliveries	Number of deliveries
Other costs not included	Not applicable

Activity cost pool. Some common cost pools with relevant activity measures.

pool for this activity as it involves only one or two staff. Note that some costs may not be included in any activity cost pool, usually because they are too minor or too difficult to allocate in this way.

activity measure In *activity-based costing systems, a measure of the volume or rate of *activity in an *activity cost pool used as a basis for allocating costs. Ideally, the activity measure chosen will be such that any rise or fall in the measure correlates closely with a rise or fall in the total cost of the activity. The terms activity measure and *cost driver are therefore often used synonymously (*see also* ALLOCATION BASE). Examples of activity measures include *direct labour hours, *machine hours, number of deliveries, units of output, and number of production run set-ups. In a large international organization there may be thousands of activity measures, whereas a smaller organization may identify only 20–30 such measures. It is important to state that there is no optimal number of activity measures for an organization. Note also that managers often identify more than one activity measure for each activity.

Some activity measures, such as labour hours, are very closely related to the volume of production, whereas others, such as the number of orders, are not.

activity-on-arrow (AOA) One of two alternative conventions for the visual representation of network diagrams (*see* NETWORK MODELLING). In AOA the activities, which make up the network, are depicted as arrows, with durations attached. The direction of the arrow indicates the direction of time. *Compare* ACTIVITY-ON-NODE.

activity-on-node (AON) One of two alternative conventions for the visual representation of network diagrams (*see* NETWORK MODELLING). In AON the activities, which make up the network, are located on nodes, with the lines in between simply indicating the logical sequence. *Compare* ACTIVITY-ON-ARROW.

activity ratio A ratio used in *management accounting consisting of the *production achieved for an accounting period divided by the production level regarded as achievable for that period.

activity sampling (work sampling) A technique in which a large number of observations are made over a period of a group of machines, processes, or workers. Each observation records what is happening at that instant; the percentage of observations recorded for a particular activity enables the total time during which that activity is occurring to be predicted. Traditionally carried out by industrial engineers using manual recording systems, this technique used to be dependent on the correct calculation of the number of observations required to give statistically valid data. Increasing use of on-line computerized data now enables managers to account for every second of their staff's time. The technique is particularly suitable for such processes as phone selling, customer services, etc. It can, however, also be applied in manufacturing systems and to groups, e.g. by requiring teams to bar-code themselves into a work area.

act of God A natural event that is not caused by any human action and cannot be predicted. It is untrue (as is sometimes thought) that insurance policies covering homes and businesses exclude acts of God. In fact, both cover such natural events as storms, lightning, and floods. However, some contracts exclude liability for damage arising from acts of God (*see* FORCE MAJEURE).

act of war Anything that causes loss or damage as a result of hostilities or conflict. Such risks are excluded from all insurance policies (except life assurances). In marine and aviation insurance only, any extra premium may be paid to include war risks.

actual product A product's design, parts, quality level, features, brand name, packaging, and other attributes that combine to deliver a product with specified benefits.

actuals 1. (physicals) Commodities that can be purchased and used, rather than goods traded on a *futures contract. **2.** In futures contracts or forward dealing, the commodity underlying a contract. **3.** Expenses or receipts that have actually occurred, as opposed to targets, budgets, or other projections.

actual total loss The complete destruction or loss of an insured item or one that has suffered an amount of damage that makes it cease to be the thing it originally was. For example, a motor car would be an actual total loss if it was destroyed, stolen and not recovered, or damaged so badly that the repair cost exceeded its insured value. See also CONSTRUCTIVE TOTAL LOSS.

actuarial method A method used in *lease accounting to apportion rentals on the basis of compound *interest; it is also used in accounting for pensions to determine the charge to the *profit and loss account.

actuary A person trained in the application of statistics and probability theory to questions of commercial risk. Some are employed by insurance companies to calculate probable lengths of life and advise insurers on the amounts that should be put aside to pay claims and the amount of premium to be charged for each type of risk. Actuaries also advise on the administration of pension funds; the *government actuary is responsible for advising the government on state pension schemes. See also INSTITUTE OF ACTUARIES.

adapted marketing mix An international *marketing strategy for adjusting the elements of the *marketing mix of a product for each international target market. This strategy will add to the costs but is undertaken in the hope of attracting a larger market share and return.

adaptive customization The provision of the same basic product to all customers, who have the capability to filter out or alter various attributes of the item. Adaptive customization is often used with Internet software.

adaptive expectations In economic theory, a hypothesis explaining how economic agents form forecasts or expectations of the future values of certain economic variables by adjusting past values of the variable.

adaptive exponential smoothing A *quantitative forecasting technique in which averages derived from historical data are smoothed by a coefficient, which is allowed to fluctuate with time in relation to changes in the demand pattern. The larger the coefficient, the greater the smoothing effect.

ad click See CLICKTHROUGH.

ad concept testing Obtaining the reactions of target customers to preliminary versions of a number of alternative approaches to an advertisement. See CONCEPT TEST.

added value See VALUE ADDED.

additional voluntary contribution (AVC) Additional pension-scheme contributions that employees can make, at their discretion, in order to increase the benefits available from their pension fund on retirement. Additional voluntary contributions can be paid into an employers' scheme or to a scheme of the employee's choice (a free-standing AVC).

add-on A supplementary accessory, replacement part, or a premium version of a product or service sold to a customer. See also CROSS-SELLING.

ad hoc mail survey A questionnaire sent to selected individuals with no prior contact or warning by a marketing research organization.

ad hocracy A form of management that is reluctant to plan and tends only to respond to urgent problems. Ad-hocratic managements focus on individual projects or problems rather than the progress of an enterprise as a whole.

adjudication The judgement or decision of a court, especially in *bankruptcy proceedings.

adjustable-rate mortgage (ARM) A *mortgage in which the interest rate is adjusted at periodic intervals, usually to reflect the prevailing rate of interest in the *money markets. Borrowers are sometimes protected by a *cap, or ceiling, above which the interest rate is not allowed to rise.

adjustable-rate preferred stock (ARP) Stock or cumulative preference shares in the USA whose dividends are linked to Treasury Bill interest rates. Minimum and maximum rates are specified by the application of a *collar. **Convertible adjusted-rate preferred stock** can be converted to common stock at a fixed price at specified dates.

adjusted present value A calculation of the *all-equity net present value of an investment or project that is then adjusted to allow for any other impacts, for example any tax concessions on financing. *See also* NET PRESENT VALUE; PRESENT VALUE.

adjuster *See* LOSS ADJUSTER.

adjusting entries Entries made at a *balance-sheet date under an *accrual accounting system to ensure that the income and expenditure of the business concerned are included in the correct period. Examples of adjustments include those made for *depreciation, *payments in advance, *accruals, and closing stock (items that will not be sold until future periods).

adjusting events Events that occur between a balance-sheet date and the date on which *financial statements are approved, providing additional evidence of conditions existing at the balance-sheet date. For example, a valuation of a property held at the balance-sheet date that provides evidence of a permanent diminution in value would need to be adjusted in the financial statements. Such events include those that, because of statutory or conventional requirements, are reflected in financial statements. The traditional UK practice is set out in *Statement of Standard Accounting Practice 17, Accounting for Post Balance Sheet Events, which requires that such material events should be reflected in the actual account balances in the financial accounts, where they purport to give a *true and fair view. In 2004 SSAP

17 was replaced by *Financial Reporting Standard 21, Events After the Balance Sheet, which includes a stricter definition of adjusting events based on that in *International Accounting Standard 10. *Compare* NON-ADJUSTING EVENTS.

adjustment bond A *bond issued in exchange for existing bonds when a business in financial difficulties is being restructured.

administered VMS (AVMS; administered strategic alliance) A VERTICAL MARKETING SYSTEM in which a powerful *channel captain (quite often a major retailing chain) coordinates marketing activities at all levels in the channel, including planning and management, even though it does not directly own the other channel members. *Compare* CONTRACTUAL VMS; CORPORATE VMS.

administration order **1.** An order made in a county court for the administration of the estate of a judgement debtor (*see* JUDGEMENT CREDITOR). The order normally requires the debtor to pay all debts by instalments; so long as he does so, the creditors referred to in the order cannot enforce their individual claims by other methods without the leave of the court. Administration orders are issued when the debtor has multiple debts but it is thought that *bankruptcy can be avoided. **2.** An order of the court under the Insolvency Act (1986) made in relation to a company in financial difficulties with a view to securing its survival as a going concern or, failing that, to achieving a more favourable realization of its assets than would be possible on a *liquidation. While the order is in force, the affairs of the company are managed by an *administrator. With effect from September 2003, a company, the directors of a company, or the holder of a qualifying floating *charge over the company's assets can appoint an administrator without obtaining a court order.

administrative management (classical school of management) The traditional view of *management that centres on how a business should be organized and the practices an effective manager should follow. The two major contributors to this school of thought were Henri Fayol (1930) and Max Weber (1922). Fayol's 14 principles of management are still relevant, while Weber's bureaucracy model still has some relevance in medium and large organizations.

administrative receiver A *receiver appointed by a secured creditor who holds a floating *charge covering the whole, or substantially all, of a company's assets. The administrative receiver has the power to sell the assets that are secured by the charge or to carry on the company's business. With certain exceptions, an administrative receiver cannot be appointed in respect of any floating charge created after September 2003 (*see* ADMINISTRATION ORDER).

administrator 1. Any person appointed by the courts, or by private arrangement, to manage the property of another. **2.** Any person appointed by the courts to take charge of the affairs of a deceased person, who died without making a will. This includes collection of assets, payment of debts, and distribution of the surplus to those persons entitled to inherit, according to the laws of intestacy (*see* INTESTATE). The administrator must be in possession of *letters of administration as proof of the authority vested by the courts. **3.** Any person appointed by the courts to implement an *administration order or undertake the duty of an *administrative receiver.

adoption of innovations It has been suggested that those consumers who eventually accept an innovation can fall into the five groups shown in the diagram below. Understanding each of these groups should help a company in devising effective marketing strategies.

- **Innovators** – the first to buy and use new products, i.e. they put the innovation on show to create the image of being venturesome. They are likely to communicate with and persuade others to try the product. This group is defined as the first 2½% to adopt the new product.
- **Early adopters** – tend to be opinion leaders and to adopt new ideas early but carefully. This group is defined as the next 13½% of the adopting consumers.
- **Early majority** – people regarded as being deliberate in their decisions, who are rarely leaders. These form the next 34% of the adopting consumers.
- **Late majority** – sceptics who only adopt an innovation after most other people have tried it. These form the next 34% of the adopting consumers.
- **Laggards** – the most tradition-bound, who are suspicious of changes and innovations. They tend only to adopt the innovation when it has become widely accepted (i.e. no longer an innovation).

The innovators are clearly critical to the process of adoption. Without their support an innovation is unlikely to be successful. *See also* PRODUCT LIFE CYCLE.

adoption process The mental and behavioural stages through which an individual passes before making a purchase or placing an order. The stages are: awareness→interest→evaluation→trial, and finally adoption of the product or service.

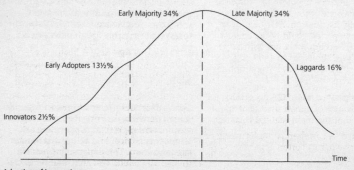

Adoption of innovations

ADR 1. Abbreviation for *acquisition-development-retention (framework). **2.** Abbreviation for *American depositary receipt.

ad referendum (Latin: to be further considered) Denoting a contract that has been signed although minor points remain to be decided.

ADSL Abbreviation for *a*symmetric *d*igital *s*ubscriber *l*ine; a method of high-speed digital transmission using existing copper telephone lines, employed especially in *broadband Internet connections. It requires a special ADSL transceiver and configuration of the connection.

ADST Abbreviation for *approved deferred share trust.

ad tracking research Marketing research that takes periodic measurements of the impact of an advertising campaign. While the goal of most advertising is to increase sales (and activity), there are many factors that can affect sales. Moreover, some advertisers judge the effectiveness of advertising by other criteria. The variables tracked are: unaided brand awareness, aided brand awareness, advertising awareness, playback, and proven recall.

ad valorem (Latin: according to value) Denoting a tax, duty, or commission that is calculated as a percentage of the total invoice value of goods or services. *VAT is an *ad valorem* tax.

advance A payment on account or a loan.

advance corporation tax (ACT) Formerly, an advance payment of *corporation tax, payable when a company made a *qualifying distribution. ACT paid in an *accounting period could be set against the gross corporation tax due for the period. ACT was abolished in 1999. Larger companies must now pay corporation tax in instalments.

advance postcard (APC) A postcard sent in advance of a mail shot advising the recipient that the main mailing is coming.

adventure A commercial undertaking of a speculative nature, often associated with overseas trading.

adverse balance A deficit on an ac-

count, especially a *balance of payments account.

adverse opinion An opinion expressed in an *auditors' report to the effect that the financial statements do not give a *true and fair view of the organization's activities. This situation usually arises when there is a disagreement between the auditor and the directors, and the auditor considers the effect of the disagreement so material or pervasive that the financial statements are seriously misleading. *See* AUDIT OPINION.

adverse selection In the market for insurance products and loans, the tendency for the most risky customers to be the most likely to demand products that exempt them from disclosing their status. To reduce their exposure to large claims on this basis, sellers often raise premiums generally or exclude high-risk customers from such products. *See also* ASYMMETRIC INFORMATION; MORAL HAZARD.

adverse variance *See* VARIANCE.

advertising A communication that is paid for by an identified sponsor with the object of promoting ideas, goods, or services. It is intended to persuade and sometimes to inform. The two basic aspects of advertising are the message and the medium. The media that carry advertising range from the press, television, cinema, radio, and posters to company logos on apparel. Advertising creates awareness of a product, extensive advertising creates confidence in the product, and good advertising creates a desire to buy the product. Advertising is a part of an organization's total marketing communications programme (i.e. its promotion mix). *See* ABOVE-THE-LINE; BELOW-THE-LINE; CONSUMER ADVERTISING; TRADE ADVERTISING.

advertising agency A business organization specializing in planning and handling *advertising on behalf of clients. A full-service agency provides a range of services to clients, including booking advertising space, designing and producing advertisements, devising media schedules, commissioning research, providing sales promotion advice, and acting as a marketing consultant. The departments within an agency include research, planning, creative design, media bookings, production, and accounts. Most advertising agents work on the basis of a commission on the total sums spent by the client.

advertising allowance A price concession given by a manufacturer of a product to a retailer to allow him to pay for local advertising. It is an effective way of advertising both the product and the retail outlet.

advertising appeal The central theme or idea behind an advertising message. Essentially its purpose is to tell potential buyers what the product offers and why the product is or should be appealing to them. To be meaningful, the appeal must be distinctive and credible.

Advertising Association (AA) An organization representing the interests of advertisers, *advertising agencies, and the media. Founded in 1926, it collects and assesses statistics on advertising expenditure as well as running an annual programme of seminars and training courses for people working in advertising, marketing, and sales promotion.

advertising awareness A part of *ad tracking research in which consumers are asked whether they have seen or heard of any advertising for brands in a product category (e.g. coffee or mortgages) in the recent past (7 days, 14 days, 30 days, etc.).

advertising brief An agreement between an *advertising agency and a client on the objectives of an advertising campaign. It is important that the client knows exactly what the objectives are, helps to plan the overall strategy, and sets the budgets. Once the brief has been agreed the agency can prepare and evaluate the advertisements themselves and develop the media plan.

advertising evaluation An attempt to measure the effectiveness of an advertising campaign. Generally this involves an assessment of the communications and sales effects of the advertisement as well as copy testing. This testing can be done before or after an advertisement is broadcast or published. Testing before would include direct rating, portfolio tests, and laboratory tests. Testing after would include recall tests (aided and unaided) as well as recognition tests. With communi-

cation and sales effectiveness, clearly the intention is to make consumers aware of and interested in the product, leading to the act of buying and producing satisfaction. It is recognized, however, that some potential buyers are unlikely to follow this course, particularly if the advertising is ineffective and the product does not meet the buyers' needs.

advertising network 1. A network that offers advertisers the ability to target specific audiences over the *Internet and to monitor results through DART (Dynamic Advertising Reporting and Targeting) technology. 2. A collection of independent websites of different companies and media networks, each of which has an arrangement with a single advertising broker to place *banner advertisements.

advertising objective (communication goal) A specific communications (advertising) task to be achieved, with a specific target audience, during a specific period. In the context of marketing, the objectives will be to gain attention, to be understood, to be believed, and to be remembered (i.e. to inform, persuade, compare, and remind).

advertising rates The basic charges made by the advertising media for use of their services or facilities.

advertising schedule A list of planned or booked advertisements showing details of the media involved, sizes, timing, and costs.

Advertising Standards Authority (ASA) An independent body set up and paid for by the advertising industry to ensure that its system of self-regulation works in the public interest. The ASA must have an independent chairman, who appoints individuals to serve on the council, two-thirds of which must be unconnected with the advertising industry. The ASA maintains close links with central and local government, consumer organizations, and trade associations. All advertising, apart from television and radio commercials, which are dealt with by the Independent Broadcasting Authority (IBA), must conform to the **British Code of Advertising Practice** (BCAP), which is administered by the ASA. The Code's requirement that adverts be legal, decent, honest, and truthful applies not only to what it said in an advertisement, but also what is shown. If it is claimed that one bar of chocolate contains ½ pint of milk, then the chocolate bar must contain that amount of milk. If the advertisement makes no claim, but shows a ½ pint bottle or carton of milk, then the chocolate must still contain this amount of milk. The ASA controls the contents of advertisements by continuous monitoring of publications and by dealing with complaints from members of the public.

advertising theme An *advertising appeal used in several different advertisements to give continuity to an advertising campaign. For example, Visa credit cards are advertised as the "most widely accepted card", while the theme of American Express card advertising is "the card has no spending limits".

advice note A note sent to a customer by a supplier of goods to advise him that an order has been fulfilled. The advice note may either accompany the goods or be sent separately, thus preceding the *sales invoice and any *delivery note. The advice note refers to a particular batch of goods, denoting them by their marks and numbers (if more than one package); it also details the date and method of dispatch.

advise fate A request by a collecting bank wishing to know, as soon as possible, whether a cheque will be paid on its receipt by the paying bank. The cheque is sent direct and not through the Bankers' Clearing House, asking that its *fate should be advised immediately.

Advisory Conciliation and Arbitration Service (ACAS) A UK government body set up in 1975 to mediate in industrial disputes in both the public and private sectors. Its findings are not binding on either side, but carry considerable weight. Its members, who are appointed by the Secretary of State for Trade and Industry, include employers and trade unionists as well as academics and other independent persons. ACAS does not, itself, carry out arbitrations but may recommend an arbitration to be held by the *Central Arbitration Committee or other

bodies. Since 1998 ACAS has also appointed arbitrators to give binding decisions in cases of alleged unfair dismissal.

advocacy promotion A firm's attempt to build customer goodwill and develop a better public image by promoting causes that are not naturally tied in to its products. A breakfast cereal producer supporting the WWF might be an example.

affective commitment *See* ORGANIZATIONAL COMMITMENT.

affective component One of three main components of the *attitudes a person (potential customer) can have regarding an object or phenomenon. The affective component is concerned with the customer's emotional reactions and involves such questions as: Is this brand good or bad? Is it desirable? Is it likeable? It also involves such judgements as: 'I love BMWs'; 'The Japanese are not competent to make luxury cars'. While the former emotional response may be based upon 10 years' experience of BMWs, the latter may be based upon little cognitive information. The affective component of an attitude need not be based on experience.

affective engineering *See* KAIZEN ENGINEERING.

affidavit A sworn written statement by a person (the deponent), who signs it in the presence of a commissioner for oaths. It sets out facts known to the deponent. In certain cases, particularly proceedings in the Chancery division of the High Court, evidence may be taken by affidavit rather than by the witness appearing in person.

affiliate networks A reciprocal arrangement between a company and third-party websites in which traffic is directed to the company from these sites through *banner advertisements, links, and incentives. In return for linking to the *destination site the third-party site typically receives a percentage of any resulting sale.

affiliates program (syndicated selling) A system that pays a percentage of the sales revenue from an on-line computer purchase to the website that suggested the purchase. This differs from a sponsorship program in that payment is dependent on an actual sale taking place during the referred visit.

affinity card A *credit card issued to members of a particular group (such as a club, college, etc.) or to supporters of a particular charity; the credit-card company pledges to make a donation to the charity or organization for each card issued and may also donate a small proportion of the money spent by card users. In the UK, affinity cards are sometimes called **charity cards**.

affirmation of contract Treating a *contract as being valid, rather than exercising a right to rescind it for a good reason. Affirmation can only occur if it takes place with full knowledge of the facts. It may take the form of a declaration of intention, be inferred from such conduct as selling goods purchased under the contract, or allowing time to pass without seeking a remedy.

affirmative action programme (AAP) A programme adopted by an organization to correct former policies that discriminated against women and ethnic, or other, minorities, particularly in respect of employment. In the USA such programmes are required of all organizations with federal contracts. See DISCRIMINATION.

affordable method The method of setting a company's communications budget (including advertising) at a level the management thinks it can afford, rather than on the level of sales, profits, or the amount spent by competitors.

afghani (AF) The standard monetary unit of Afghanistan, divided into 100 puli.

afloat Denoting goods, especially commodities, that are on a ship from their port of *origin to a specified port of destination; for example, 'afloat Rotterdam' means the goods are on their way to Rotterdam. The price of such goods will usually be between the price of spot goods and goods for immediate shipment from origin.

African Development Bank A regional bank, based on the model of the *International Bank for Reconstruction and Development (World Bank), created by independent African nations in 1964 to provide long-term development loans.

Membership was originally restricted to African countries but was widened in 1989.

after date The words used in a *bill of exchange to indicate that the period of the bill should commence from the date inserted on the bill, e.g. '... 30 days after date, we promise to pay ...'. *Compare* AFTER SIGHT; AT SIGHT.

after-hours deals Transactions made on a financial market after its official close at the end of its mandatory quote period. These deals are recorded as part of the next day's trading and referred to as **early bargains**.

after market *See* SECONDARY MARKET.

after-sales service Maintenance of products by the manufacturers or their agents after purchase. This often takes the form of a guarantee (*see* WARRANTY), which is effective for a stated period during which the service is free in respect of both parts and labour, followed by a maintenance contract for which the buyer of the product has to pay. Efficient and effective after-sales service is an essential component of good marketing policy, especially for such consumer durables as cars and computers; in the case of exported goods it is of overriding importance.

after sight The words used in a *bill of exchange to indicate that the period of the bill should commence from the date on which the drawee is presented with it for acceptance, i.e. has sight of it. *Compare* AFTER DATE; AT SIGHT.

AG Abbreviation for *Aktiengesellschaft. It appears after the name of a German, Austrian, or Swiss company, being equivalent to the British abbreviation plc (i.e. denoting a public limited company). *Compare* GMBH.

age allowance The *personal allowance available to taxpayers aged 65 and over. The age allowance for taxpayers aged 65–74 is £7090 and for those 75 and over is £7220, for 2005–06. There is an income limit of £19,500 for age allowance. The allowance is reduced at a rate of £1 off the allowance for every £2 by which the income exceeds the income limit, until the basic personal allowance is reached.

age analysis A listing of debtors' accounts (i.e. the amounts owing to a business), usually produced monthly, which analyses the age of the debts by splitting them into such categories as those up to one month old, two months old, and more than two months old. As a basic part of the credit control system, the analysis should be regularly examined so that any appropriate follow-up action may be taken.

age and life-cycle segmentation The process of dividing the consumer market into different age and life-cycle groups, e.g. 30–39 years old, married, two children under 10 years old, etc. See MARKET SEGMENTATION.

age discrimination See DISCRIMINATION.

ageing schedule A breakdown of *accounts receivable by time period.

agency agreement 1. An agreement between a customer and a bank allowing the customer to bank cheques at a branch of that bank, usually for logistical reasons. The cheques thus enter the clearing system, although the customer does not have an account with that bank. A charge is made by the bank for this service. **2.** Any agreement between an agent and a principal. See AGENCY RELATIONSHIP.

agency fee 1. In advertising, a sum of money paid for services provided based on a negotiated fee, as opposed to a commission. **2. (facility fee)** An annual fee paid to an agent for the work and responsibility involved in managing a loan after it has been signed.

agency loan A loan available for local-government authorities, public organizations, etc., from the *European Investment Bank.

agency relationship A relationship in which a principal engages an agent to perform some service on his or her behalf; this involves delegating authority by the principal. As it has to be assumed that the agent will not always act in the best interests of the principal, the principal incurs costs in monitoring and controlling the behaviour of the agent. In turn, the agent will incur bonding costs in convincing the principal that the interests of the principal will not be harmed. The agent may also take decisions that do not always maximize the welfare of the principal; these decisions can result in what is called a residual loss. The sum of the monitoring and bonding costs together with the residual loss form the **agency costs**. Even in an unregulated economy managers may choose to provide financial statements, examined by independent auditors, to shareholders and creditors in order to reduce agency costs. By supplying informative financial statements to external parties on the basis of information held by them, managers may avoid costly disputes and more expensive mechanisms for controlling their actions. These aspects of an agency relationship are sometimes referred to as **agency theory**. The so-called **agency problem** that arises when shareholders and managers have different interests and *asymmetric information was brought into sharp focus by the collapse of the US companies Enron and World Cons in 2002. See also GOAL DIVERGENCE; SIGNALLING HYPOTHESIS.

agenda The list of items to be discussed at a business meeting. For the *annual general meeting or an *extraordinary general meeting of a company, the agenda is usually sent to shareholders in advance. See also ORDER OF BUSINESS.

agent 1. Any person appointed by another (the *principal) to act on his or her behalf. See AGENCY RELATIONSHIP. **2.** In *contract law, a person appointed by a principal to negotiate a contract between the principal and a third party. If an agent discloses the principal's name (or at least the existence of a principal) to the third party in the transaction, the agent is not normally liable on the contract. An **undisclosed principal**, whose existence is not revealed by the agent to a third party, may still be liable on the contract, but in such cases the agent is also liable. However, an undisclosed principal may not be entitled to the benefit of a contract if the agency is inconsistent with the terms of the contract or if the third party has expressed a wish to contract with the agent personally.

In law, agents are either **general agents** or **special agents**. A general agent is one who has authority to act for the principal in all business of a particular kind, or who acts for the principal in the course of the agent's usual business or profession. A special agent is authorized to act only for a special purpose that is not in the ordinary course of the agent's business or profession. The principal of a general agent is bound by acts of the agent that are incidental to the ordinary conduct of the agent's business or the effective performance of the agent's duties, even if the principal has imposed limitations on the agent's authority. But in the case of a special agent, the principal is not bound by acts that are not within the authority conferred. In either case, the principal may ratify an unauthorized contract. A commercial (or mercantile) agent selling goods on behalf of the principal sometimes agrees to protect the principal against the risk of the buyer's insolvency. Such an agent is called a *del credere agent. **3.** A software program that can assist computer users to perform such tasks as finding particular types of information, for example, the best price for a product.

agent de change A stockbroker or securities house on the Paris Bourse (*see* BOURSE).

age of consent The age at which a person can enter into a legally binding *contract. It is set at 18 years by the Family Law Reform Act (1969). A contract entered into by someone below this age is not always capable of being enforced.

aggregate demand The sum of demands for all the goods and services in an economy at any particular time. Made a central concept in *macroeconomics by J. M. Keynes (1883–1946), it is usually defined as the sum of consumers' expenditure (*see* CONSUMPTION), *investment, government expenditure, and imports less exports. Keynesian theory proposes that the free market will not always maintain a sufficient level of aggregate demand to ensure *full employment and that at such times the government should seek to stimulate aggregate demand. However, many macroeconomists have questioned the feasibility of such policies and this remains a critical issue in macroeconomics. *See also* AGGREGATE SUPPLY.

aggregate planning An approach to planning that enables overall output levels and the appropriate resource input mix to be set for related groups of products over the near to medium term. Thus the aggregate plan for a car factory would consider the total number of units produced per month, but would not be concerned with the scheduling of individual models, colours, standards of finish, engine sizes, etc. It would be concerned with the labour and machine hours available in a given period but not with what each machine would be doing at a particular time. Aggregate planning assumes that the product/service mix remains stable over the period of the plan and that the capacity remains fixed, i.e. that problems cannot be solved by bringing new plant on stream within the timescale of the plan. Aggregate planning may also seek to influence demand through such variables as price, advertising, and the product mix.

aggregate supply The total supply of all the goods and services in an economy. J. M. Keynes made *aggregate demand the focus of macroeconomics; however, since the 1970s many economists have questioned the importance of aggregate demand in determining the health of an economy, suggesting instead that governments should concentrate on establishing conditions to encourage the supply of goods and services. This could entail *deregulation, encouraging *competition, and removing restrictive practices in the labour market.

aggregator A firm that collates and presents information about an individual's bank accounts, investments, insurance policies, etc. so that the person concerned can manage all his or her financial affairs via a single website.

AGM Abbreviation for *annual general meeting.

agora (*plural* **agorot**) A monetary unit of Israel, worth one hundredth of a *sheqel.

agreed bid A *takeover bid that is supported by a majority of the shareholders of the target company, whereas a **hostile bid** is not welcomed by the majority of the shareholders of the target company.

Agricultural Credit Corporation Ltd (ACC) A corporation established in 1964 to extend the availability of medium-term bank credit for buildings, equipment, livestock, and working capital to farmers, growers, and co-operatives. The ACC offers a guarantee to the farmer's bank for such loans and promises to repay the bank should the farmer fail to do so. In return for this service the farmer pays a percentage charge to the ACC.

Agricultural Mortgage Corporation Ltd (AMC) A corporation established to grant loans to farmers against mortgages on their land by the Agricultural Credits Act (1928). The AMC offers loans for periods of 5 to 30 years. The capital of the corporation is supplied by the Bank of England, the commercial banks, and by the issue of state-guaranteed debentures. The corporation's loans are irrevocable except in cases of default and are usually made through the local branches of the commercial banking system.

agricultural property relief An *inheritance tax relief available on the transfer of agricultural property when certain conditions are met. Since March 1992 the relief has been at a rate of 100% or 50%. The 100% rate applies if the transferor has vacant possession of the property or the right to vacant possession within the following 12 months; it may also apply if the property was let after 31 August 1995. Otherwise the 50% rate applies.

AGV Abbreviation for *automated guided vehicle.

AIDA A 19th-century acronym used in communications for attention, interest, desire, and action. AIDA is a model for a hierarchy of communication effects often regarded as a useful guideline in creating advertisements.

aided brand awareness One of the variables used in *ad tracking research; usually a researcher will ask respondents to indicate whether they are aware of various brands not mentioned in an unaided brand awareness question. Aided awareness is not regarded as a powerful indicator of future sales.

aided recall test See RECALL TEST.

aids to trade The formal study of commerce recognizes four aids to trade: advertising, banking, insurance, and transport.

AIM Abbreviation for *Alternative Investment Market.

AIO dimensions See LIFESTYLE.

air consignment note See AIR WAYBILL.

air date The date of first transmission of a commercial or an advertising campaign on television.

air freight 1. The transport of goods by aircraft, either in a scheduled airliner or chartered airliner carrying passengers (an all-traffic service) or in a freight plane (an all-freight service). Air cargo usually consists of goods that have a high value compared to their weight. **2.** The cost of transporting goods by aircraft. It is usually quoted on the basis of a price per kilogram.

airspace 1. The space that lies above a state's land and sea territory and is subject to its exclusive jurisdiction. **2.** The space above a piece of land. The owner of the land is entitled to the ownership and possession of the airspace above the land. This is not exclusive, however, and is limited by the reasonable and necessary use of that airspace by any neighbours as well as for the flight of aircraft.

airtime 1. The amount of time allocated to an advertisement on radio or television. **2.** The time of transmission of an advertisement on radio or television.

air waybill (air consignment note) A document made out by a consignor of goods by *air freight to facilitate swift delivery of the goods to the consignee. It gives the name of the consignor and the loading airport, the consignee and the airport of destination, a description of the goods, the value of the goods, and the marks, number, and dimensions of the packages.

Aktb Abbreviation for *Aktiebolaget*. It appears after the name of a Swedish joint-stock company.

Aktiengesellschaft A German, Austrian, or Swiss public limited company. See AG.

ALCO Abbreviation for *asset and liability management committee.

algorithm A set of well-defined rules for solving a problem in a finite number of steps. Algorithms are extensively used in computer science. The steps in the algorithm are translated into a series of instructions that the computer can understand. These instructions form the computer program.

alienation A feeling of detachment that causes employees to believe that their work is neither a relevant nor an important part of their life. Because conflicts and disputes, leading to underperformance, can be caused by alienation, managers need to be aware of its existence and its causes if they are to improve relationships within a workforce. Some of the principal causes of alienation are:

- **powerlessness** – the inability to influence work conditions, quality, volume, etc.;
- **meaninglessness** – an absence of recognition of the contribution made by the individual to the output of work;
- **isolation** – the absence of human interaction during working hours; this may result from the nature of the location or a psychological gap between individuals and their supervisors and managers;
- **low self-esteem** – a reflection of the lack of value placed on individuals by an organization and its managers;
- **loss of identity with the organization** – the absence of pride in working for the organization, reinforced by the feeling that the individual's personal commitment is not recognized either financially or psychologically;
- **lack of prospects** – a feeling of frustration at being trapped in a situation that offers little prospect of advancement;
- **lack of equality** – a result of strict differentiation between the grades and levels in a hierarchical organization.

Only by addressing these causes can managers achieve groups of people who feel pride in their work, supported by solving their problems, and rewarded for their skills and effort. *See* MOTIVATION; ORGANIZATIONAL COMMITMENT.

alienation of assets The sale by a borrower of some or all of the assets that form the actual or implied security for a loan. It is therefore common practice to include a clause in the document setting up a loan, which restricts the disposal of the borrower's assets to specific circumstances.

alienative contract *See* PSYCHOLOGICAL CONTRACT.

all-equity net present value A calculation of *net present value made as if the firm, project, or investment were funded entirely by equity. In such cases, the *discount rate is the discount rate for equity. *See also* ADJUSTED PRESENT VALUE; PRESENT VALUE.

Allfinanz *See* BANCASSURANCE.

all-inclusive income concept A concept used in drawing up a *profit and loss account, in which all items of profit and loss are included in the statement to arrive at a figure of earnings; this is the approach adopted in the UK and the USA. Although it is claimed that this basis gives the fullest picture of the operation of an enterprise, it does lead to a volatility in earnings figures as one-off costs, such as redundancies and sale of assets, will be included.

allocated quantity A quantity of an item held in stock that has already been allocated to an end use and is not therefore available to meet other requirements.

allocation base In *management accounting, the basis that is used to allocate costs to *cost objects. In a *traditional costing system there may be a single allocation base for each cost object, whereas in an *activity-based costing system there may be many such bases. In practice the term allocation base is often used synonymously with *activity measure or *cost driver. *See* COST ALLOCATION.

allonge An attachment to a *bill of exchange to provide space for further endorsements when the back of the bill itself has been fully used. With the decline in the use of bills of exchange it is now rarely needed.

all-or-nothing option *See* BINARY OPTION.

allotment A method of distributing previously unissued shares in a limited company in exchange for a contribution of capital. An application for such shares will often be made on the *flotation of a public company or on the privatization of a state-owned industry. The company accepts the application by dispatching a **letter of allot-**

ment to the applicant stating how many shares have been allotted; the applicant then has an unconditional right to be entered in the *register of members in respect of those shares. If the number of shares applied for exceeds the number available (oversubscription), allotment is made by a random draw or by a proportional allocation. An applicant allotted fewer shares than applied for, is sent a cheque for the unallotted balance (an application must be accompanied by a cheque for the full value of the shares applied for). *See also* MULTIPLE APPLICATION.

allotted shares Shares distributed by *allotment to new shareholders (allottees).

allowable capital loss *See* CAPITAL LOSS.

allowable marketing cost The amount that can be spent on marketing while preserving the required profit margin. It is often calculated by deducting the cost of goods, the cost of fulfilment, and the desired profit from the total expected sales revenue. For example, if a company's sales revenue is £30,000, cost of producing goods is £15,000, cost of distribution, etc. is £3000, and the required profit is £7500, then the allowable marketing cost would be £4500. Companies engaged in direct marketing activity often maintain cost control in this fashion.

allowance 1. Money paid to an employee for expenses incurred in the course of business. **2.** A deduction from an invoice for a specified purpose, such as substandard quality of goods, late delivery, etc. **3.** A price reduction or rebate given to a customer or intermediary on a large order or for some other specific reason. **4.** An agreed time used in *work measurement; it is added to the basic time in calculating the standard time (*see* STANDARD PERFORMANCE) for a particular job. These allowances provide time for rest, relaxation, and the workers' personal needs (e.g. toilet breaks). **5.** Promotional money paid by manufacturers to retailers in return for an agreement to feature the manufacturer's product in some way. **6.** An allowance against tax. *See* CAPITAL ALLOWANCES; INCOME TAX ALLOWANCES.

all-risks policy An insurance policy covering personal possessions against many risks but not, of course, all risks. A policy of this kind does not list the risks covered; instead it lists only the exclusions. Such wide cover often merits very high *premiums and items covered on this basis often include jewellery, photographic or electronic equipment, and other valuables.

alpha coefficient A measure of the expected return on a particular share compared to the expected return on shares with a similar *beta coefficient. It identifies the *specific risk associated with a share as opposed to the *systematic risk associated with securities of the same class.

alpha-release stage The first stage of testing a product or service in which *lead users, often company employees and loyal customers, test a new version. *See* BETA VERSION.

alteration of share capital An increase, reduction, or any other change in the *authorized share capital of a company. If permitted by the *articles of association, a limited company can increase its authorized capital as appropriate. It can also rearrange its existing authorized capital (e.g. by consolidating 100 shares of £1 into 25 shares of £4 or by subdividing 100 shares of £1 into 200 of 50p) and cancel unissued shares. These are reserved powers, passed – unless the articles of association provide otherwise – by an ordinary resolution.

alternate director A person who can act temporarily in place of a named director of a company in his or her absence. An alternate director can only be present at a meeting of the board of directors if the *articles of association provide for this eventuality and if the other directors agree that the person chosen is acceptable to undertake this role.

alternative evaluation The stage in the process of *decision making in which the buyer uses information to evaluate the alternative brands available.

Alternative Investment Market (AIM) A market of the *London Stock Exchange that opened in June 1995 to replace the Unlisted Securities Market, with the object of allowing small growing companies to raise capital and have their shares traded in a market, without the expense of a full market listing. Since its formation over 600 smaller companies have traded their shares on this market and the number of institutions investing in the market is increasing.

Altman's Z score *See* Z SCORE.

amalgamation The combination of two or more companies. The combination may be effected by one company acquiring others, by the merging of two or more companies, or by existing companies being dissolved and a new company formed to take over the combined business. The relevant accounting standards are *Financial Reporting Standard 6, Acquisitions and Mergers, and *International Accounting Standard 22, Business Combinations. *See also* ACQUISITION ACCOUNTING; MERGER ACCOUNTING.

ambulance stocks High performance stocks recommended by a broker to a client whose portfolio has not fulfilled expectations. They either refresh the portfolio – and the relationship between broker and client – or they confirm the client's worst fears.

AMC Abbreviation for *Agricultural Mortgage Corporation Ltd.

American depositary receipt (ADR) A receipt issued by a US bank to a member of the US public who has bought shares in a foreign country. The certificates are denominated in US dollars and can be traded as a security in US markets. The advantages of ADRs are the reduction in administration costs and the avoidance of stamp duty on each transaction.

American option *See* OPTION.

American terms A quotation of an exchange rate in terms of how many US dollars can be exchanged for one unit of another currency. *Compare* EUROPEAN TERMS.

amongst matter The position of an advertisement within a newspaper or magazine so that it is amongst editorial material.

AMOP Abbreviation for *Association of Mail Order Publishers.

amortization 1. The process of treating as an expense the annual amount deemed to waste away from a fixed asset. The concept is particularly applied to leases, which are acquired for a given sum for a specified term at the end of which the lease will have no value. It is customary to divide the cost of the lease by the number of years of its term and treat the result as an annual charge against profit. While this method does not necessarily reflect the value of the lease at any given time, it is an equitable way of allocating the original cost between periods. *Compare* DEPRECIATION.

*Goodwill may also be amortized. *Financial Reporting Standard 10, Goodwill and Intangible Assets, requires the writing-off of goodwill to the *profit and loss account in regular instalments over the period of its economic life. However, non-amortization is an option in exceptional circumstances. **2.** The repayment of debt by a borrower in a series of instalments over a period. Each payment includes interest and part repayment of the capital. **3.** The spreading of the *front-end fee charged on taking out a loan over the life of a loan for accounting purposes. **4.** In the USA, another word for *depreciation.

amortization schedule A schedule that summarizes the dates on which specified amounts must be paid in the repayment of a loan.

amortized cost That part of the value of an asset that has been written off; it represents the *accumulated depreciation to date.

amortizing loan A loan in which the repayment is made in more than one instalment.

amortizing mortgage A *mortgage in which all the principal and all the interest has been repaid by the end of the mortgage agreement period. Although equal payments may be made during the term of the mortgage, the sums are divided, on a sliding scale, between interest payments and repayments of the principal. In the early years most of the payments go towards the interest charges, while in later years more repays the sum borrowed, until this sum is reduced to zero with the last payment. *Compare* BALLOON MORTGAGE.

amounts differ The words stamped or written on a cheque or bill of exchange by a banker who returns it unpaid because the amount in words differs from that in figures. Banks usually make a charge for returning unpaid cheques.

AMPS Abbreviation for *auction market preferred stock.

AMSO Abbreviation for *Association of Market Survey Organizations.

analysis of variance (ANOVA; variance analysis) 1. A commonly used method for examining the statistically significant differences between the means of two or more POPULATIONS. In its simplest form (**one-way analysis of variance**), it involves only one dependent variable (metric measurement level) and one or more independent variables (non-metric). For example, a researcher may be interested in establishing if there is a statistically significant difference in the average amount spent on alcohol per week between two samples of population (say, male and female). Here, the dependent variable is the amount spent and the independent variable is the gender of the participants. **2.** In *standard costing and *budgetary control, the analysis of *variances in order to seek their causes. The total *profit variance or *production cost variance is analysed into sub-variances based on such factors as *direct labour, *direct materials, fixed and variable *overheads, and sales in order to indicate the major reasons for the difference between budgeted figures and actual figures.

analytical estimating A *work measurement technique enabling an estimate of the time required to carry out the elements of a job to be produced at a defined level of performance. This level is based on previous knowledge, e.g. *standard performance and *synthetic standard times, and experience of the elements concerned.

anchor services *Internet service providers that form the basis of e-commerce websites by attracting traffic or providing credibility.

ancillary credit business A business involved in credit brokerage, debt adjusting, debt counselling, debt collecting, or the operation of a credit-reference agency (*see* COMMERCIAL AGENCY).

- **Credit brokerage** includes the effecting of introductions of individuals wishing to obtain credit to persons carrying on a consumer-credit business.
- **Debt adjusting** is the process by which a third party negotiates terms for the discharge of a debt due under consumer-credit agreements or consumer-hire agreements with the creditor or owner on behalf of the debtor or hirer. The latter may also pay a third party to take over an obligation to discharge a debt or to undertake any similar activity concerned with its liquidation.
- **Debt counselling** is the giving of advice (other than by the original creditor and certain others) to debtors or hirers about the liquidation of debts due under consumer-credit agreements or consumer-hire agreements.
- A **credit-reference agency** collects information concerning the financial standing of individuals and supplies this information to those seeking it.

The Consumer Credit Act (1974) provides for the licensing of ancillary credit businesses and regulates their activities.

Andean Community *See* MERCOSUR.

andon *See* VISIBLE CONTROL.

anergy *See* SYNERGY.

angel An investor in a high-risk enterprise. Traditionally, the term was applied to the financial backers of stage productions but it is now used increasingly for investors in e-business.

Annual Abstract of Statistics An annual publication of the *Office for National Statistics giving UK industrial, vital, legal, and social statistics. *Compare* MONTHLY DIGEST OF STATISTICS.

annual accounts (annual report; report and accounts) The *financial statements of an organization, generally published annually. In the UK, incorporated bodies have a legal obligation to publish annual accounts and file them at Companies House. Annual accounts consist of a *profit and loss account, *balance sheet, *cash-flow statement (if required), and *statement of total recognized gains and losses, together with supporting notes and the *directors' report and *auditors' report. Companies falling into the legally defined *small companies and *medium-sized companies categories may file *abbreviated accounts and may also enjoy *audit exemption. Some bodies are regulated by other statutes; for example, many financial institutions and their accounts will have to comply with their own regulations. Non-incorporated bodies, such as partnerships, are not legally obliged to produce accounts but may do so for their own information, for their banks if funding is being sought, and for HM Revenue and Customs for taxation purposes. *See also* ANNUAL RETURN; PUBLISHED ACCOUNTS.

annual general meeting (AGM) An annual meeting of the shareholders of a company, which must be held every year; the meetings may not be more than 15 months apart. Shareholders must be given 21 days' notice of the meeting. The usual business transacted at an AGM is the presentation of the audited accounts, the appointment of directors and auditors, the fixing of their remuneration, and recommendations for the payment of dividends. Other business may be transacted if notice of it has been given to the shareholders. *See also* AGENDA; ORDER OF BUSINESS.

annual hours work plan A contractual arrangement in which staff agree to work a certain number of hours per year, rather than per week or month. This is particularly useful when there is a significant fluctuation in the demand for a product or service; it avoids the costs of overtime, part-time, or casual working, etc., to cover the peaks.

annually compounding yield (annual percentage yield) The annual *rate of return on an investment calculated on the assumption that interest payments are reinvested at the yield rate.

annual percentage rate (APR) The annual equivalent *rate of return on a loan or investment in which the rate of interest specified is chargeable or payable more frequently than annually. Most investment institutions are now required by law to specify the APR when the interest intervals are more frequent than annual. Similarly those charge cards that advertise monthly rates of interest (say, 2%) must state the equivalent APR; in this case it would be $[(1.02)^{12} - 1] = 26.8\%$.

annual plan A short-term plan that describes a company's current situation, its objectives, strategy, action programme, and budgets for the year ahead, together with the controls included in the plan.

annual report *See* ANNUAL ACCOUNTS.

annual return A document that must be filed with the *Registrar of Companies within seven months of the end of the relevant accounting period (ten months for private companies). Information required on the annual return includes the address of the registered office of the company and the names, addresses, nationality, and occupations of its directors and secretary: details of the share capital and shareholders must also be included. The *directors' report must be annexed to the return, as must the *annual accounts (or *abbreviated accounts) and the *auditors' report (unless exempt from statutory audit).

annuitant A person who receives an *annuity.

annuity 1. A contract in which a person pays a premium to an insurance company, usually in one lump sum, and in return receives periodic payments for an agreed period or for the rest of his or her life. An annuity has been described as the opposite of a life assurance as the policyholder pays the lump sum and the insurer makes the regular payments. Annuities form the basis for private pensions in most developed countries. *See also* ANNUITY CERTAIN; DEFERRED ANNUITY. **2.** A payment made on such a contract.

annuity certain An *annuity in which payments continue for a specified period irrespective of the life or death of the person covered. In general, annuities cease on the death of the policyholder unless they are annuities certain.

anomaly An opportunity for *abnormal returns in financial markets. If markets are efficient there should be no anomalies (*see* EFFICIENT MARKETS HYPOTHESIS), and the assumption that this will indeed be the case dictates the pricing of many financial obligations, notably derivatives (*see* ARBITRAGE-FREE CONDITION).

anonymous file transfer protocol A protocol that allows Internet users to retrieve documents, files, and other forms of data from anywhere on the net.

ANOVA Acronym for *analysis of variance.

ANSI Abbreviation for American National Standards Institute. This organization is the US equivalent of the *British Standards Institution or the Deutsche Industrie-normen (DIN).

Ansoff matrix *See* PRODUCT-MARKET STRATEGY.

ante-date To date a document before the date on which it is drawn up. This is not necessarily illegal or improper. For instance, an ante-dated cheque is not in law invalid. *Compare* POST-DATE.

anticipatory inventory *See* INVENTORY.

antidilution clause A term in a *warrant designed to protect the share price (and dividends per share) against such actions as *scrip issues.

anti-trust laws Laws passed in the USA, from 1890 onwards, making it illegal to do anything in *restraint of trade, set up monopolies, or otherwise interfere with free trade and competition.

Anton Piller order *See* SEARCH ORDER.

AOA Abbreviation for *activity-on-arrow.

AON Abbreviation for *activity-on-node.

APACS Acronym for *Association for Payment Clearing Services.

APC Abbreviation for *advance postcard.

APCIMS Abbreviation for *Association of Private Client Investment Managers and Stockbrokers.

APEX Acronym for Advance-Purchase Excursion: a form of return airline ticket offered at a discount to the standard fare, provided that bookings both ways are made a specified number of days in advance, with no facilities for stopovers or cancellations. APEX fares are also available for some long-distance rail journeys.

appellant A person or organization that appeals against the decision of a court. The party resisting the appeal is called the **respondent**.

applet A small program in the *Java programming language that can be incorporated in a web page to add additional features, such as sound or graphics.

application for listing The process by which a company applies to a stock exchange for its securities to be traded on that exchange. In obtaining the listing a company will be required to abide by the rules of the exchange. The advantage for a company in obtaining a listing is that it will be able to raise funds by issuing shares on the stock exchange and the marketability of the shares it issues will attract investors. *See also* FLOTATION; LISTING REQUIREMENTS.

application form A form, issued by a newly floated company with its *prospectus, on which members of the public apply for shares in the company. *See also* ALLOTMENT; MULTIPLE APPLICATION; PINK FORM.

application service provider (ASP) A supplier that brings together all the hardware and software needed to operate an e-commerce supply chain, provides the software on a central server, and permits customers access to the systems through browser software and an Internet link.

application services market A market in which expensive and complex software is located on a remote computer server and users, instead of installing the software themselves, access the server and pay a usage fee when running these programs.

applications software Computer programs that are designed for a particular purpose or application. For example, accounts programs, games programs, and educational programs are all applications software. *Compare* SYSTEMS SOFTWARE. *See* BUSINESS SOFTWARE PACKAGE.

applied research **1.** *See* RESEARCH AND DEVELOPMENT COSTS. **2.** In *marketing research, research aimed at solving a specific business problem, such as obtaining a better understanding of the market, determining why a particular strategy or tactic failed, or reducing the uncertainty in making management decisions.

appraisal *See* PERFORMANCE APPRAISAL. *See also* ECONOMIC APPRAISAL; FINANCIAL APPRAISAL.

a

appraisal costs *See* COST OF QUALITY. *See also* ENVIRONMENTAL COSTS.

appreciation 1. An increase in the value of an asset, through inflation, a rise in market price, or interest earned. The directors of a company have an obligation to adjust the nominal value of land and buildings and other assets in balance sheets to take account of appreciation. *See* ASSET STRIPPING. **2.** An increase in the value of a currency with a *floating exchange rate relative to another currency. *Compare* DEPRECIATION; DEVALUATION.

apprentice A young employee who signs a contract (an **indenture** or **articles of apprenticeship**) agreeing to be trained in a particular skill for a set amount of time by a specific employer. During this time the wages will be relatively low but on completion of the apprenticeship they increase to reflect the increased status of the employee and to recognize the skills acquired.

appropriation 1. An allocation of the net profit of organizations in its accounts. Some payments may be treated as expenses and deducted before arriving at net profit; other payments are deemed to be appropriations of profit, once that profit has been ascertained. Examples of the former are such normal trade expenses as wages and salaries of employees, motor running expenses, light and heat, and most interest payments on external finance. Appropriations of the net profit include dividends or scrip dividends to shareholders, transfers to reserves, and amounts for taxation. In the case of partnerships, appropriations include salaries, interest on capital, and profit. *See also* ACCUMULATED PROFITS. **2.** The allocation of payments to a particular debt out of several owed by a debtor to one creditor. The right to make the appropriation belongs first to the debtor but if the debtor fails to do so, the creditor is entitled to. **3.** A document identifying a particular batch of goods to be supplied in fulfilment of a forward contract for a commodity. In some cases, for example, a forward contract may call for goods to be shipped in six months' time. At the time the contract is made the goods may not be identifiable. As the period for shipment approaches the supplier will notify the customer exactly which parcel of goods he is going to ship against the contract by identifying them (e.g. by the marks and numbers on the packages) in an appropriation.

approved deferred share trust (ADST) A trust fund set up by a British company, and approved by HM Revenue and Customs, that purchases shares in that company for the benefit of its employees. Tax on dividends is deferred until the shares are sold and is then paid at a reduced rate. *See also* EMPLOYEE SHARE OWNERSHIP TRUST; SHARE INCENTIVE SCHEME.

APR Abbreviation for *annual percentage rate.

a priori segmentation The process of dividing markets on the basis of hunches, assumptions, or custom by the management of an organization, rather than by marketing research. *See* MARKET SEGMENTATION.

APT Abbreviation for *arbitrage pricing theory.

aptitude test A type of selection test intended to assess a candidate's promise, trainability, and potential rather than testing previously acquired competence. An intelligence test is often used as a measure of aptitude.

arbitrage The entering into a set of financial obligations to obtain profits with no risk, usually by taking advantage of differences in interest rates, exchange rates, or commodity prices between one market and another. Arbitrage is non-speculative because an arbitrageur will only switch from one market to another if the rates or prices in both markets are known and if the profit to be gained outweighs the costs of the operation. Thus, a large stock of a commodity in a user country may force its price below that in a producing country; if the difference is greater than the cost of shipping the goods back to the producing country, this could provide a profitable opportunity for arbitrage. Similar opportunities arise with *bills of exchange and foreign currencies. A person or firm that engages in arbitrage is known as an **arbitrageur**.

arbitrage-free condition (no-arbitrage condition) The assumption, important in financial modelling, that there are no opportunities for risk-free excess returns in financial markets and no market *anomalies. These premises inform many aspects of finance, notably option pricing.

arbitrage pricing theory (APT) A model proposed by Stephen Ross in 1976 for calculating security returns in terms of the *arbitrage-free condition. It is an alternative to the *capital asset pricing model (CAPM). APT assumes a number of different *systematic risk factors without, however, definitively identifying the various types of risk. In setting *discount rates for decisions or valuations, companies therefore generally prefer to base their calculations on the CAPM.

arbitrary allocation A *cost allocation in which the *allocation base used is not likely to give accurate costs. For example, the cost of a lecture is not significantly dependent on the number of students: a class of 10 students requires one lecturer for (say) one hour as does a class of 200 students. Therefore using the number of students as an allocation base would result in an arbitrary allocation. The system of *activity-based costing is based on the idea that arbitrary allocations should be avoided and replaced with *cause-and-effect allocations.

arbitration The determination of a dispute by an arbitrator or arbitrators rather than by a court of law. Any civil (i.e. noncriminal) matter may be settled in this way; commercial contracts often contain **arbitration clauses** providing for this to be done in a specified way. Various industries and chambers of commerce have set up tribunals for dealing with disputes in their particular trades or business. The judgement of the arbitrator may be either binding or indicative. The current legal framework for arbitration is provided by the Arbitration Act (1996), which repealed part of the Arbitration Act (1950) and the whole of the Arbitration Acts of 1976 and 1979.

arbs Abbreviation for arbitrageurs, i.e. dealers specializing in *arbitrage.

architectural innovation An innovation that creates an improvement in the ways in which components, at least some of which may not in themselves be innovative, are put together. Examples include flexible manufacturing systems and networked computer systems. *Compare* COMPONENT INNOVATION.

archive A store for documents and magnetic disks or tapes containing records that are seldom used. Most computer users maintain an archive holding copies of disks or tapes containing vital information. If the original disk or tape becomes damaged, the archive copy is used to reinstate the information.

ARD Abbreviation for *accounting reference date.

arithmetic mean (arithmetic average) An average obtained by adding together the individual numbers concerned and dividing the total by their number. For example, the arithmetic mean of 7, 20, 107, and 350 is 484/4 = 121. This value, however, gives no idea of the spread of numbers. *Compare* GEOMETRIC MEAN; MEDIAN; WEIGHTED AVERAGE. *See also* NORMAL DISTRIBUTION.

ARM Abbreviation for *adjustable-rate mortgage.

arm's length   1. Denoting a transaction in which the parties to the transaction are or behave as if they are unrelated parties. For example, a transaction between two subsidiaries of the same parent organization could only be said to be at arm's length if it could be shown that the deal had been carried out at current market prices with no preference of any kind being shown in the trading terms. **2.** Denoting an investment portfolio in which the owner is not aware of the asset composition or the transactions entered into. *See* BLIND TRUST.

ARP Abbreviation for *adjustable-rate preferred stock.

ARR Abbreviation for *accounting rate of return.

arrangement   1. A method of enabling a debtor to enter into an agreement with any creditors (either privately or through the courts) to discharge his or her debts by partial payment, as an alternative to bankruptcy. This is generally achieved by a **scheme of arrangement**, which involves applying the assets and income of the debtor in proportionate payment to the creditors. For instance, a scheme of arrangement may stipulate that the creditors will receive 20 pence for every pound that is owed to them. This is sometimes also known as **composition**. Once a scheme of arrangement has been agreed a **deed of arrangement** is drawn up, which must be registered with the Department of Trade and Industry within seven days. **2.** *See* VOLUNTARY ARRANGEMENT. **3.** A transaction or sale arranged by an intermediary, as in the case of an estate agent selling a mortgage as an agent for a bank.

arrears A liability that has not been settled by the due date. For example, *cumulative preference shares entitle the shareholders to receive an annual fixed dividend. If this is not paid, the dividend is said to be in arrears and this fact must be disclosed in the notes to the financial statements.

articled clerk A trainee solicitor. The Law Society lays down provisions regulating the training of solicitors. All trainees are now graduates and will have taken professional examinations. They are then required to be articled to (i.e. to sign an agreement to learn from) a qualified solicitor for two years before being admitted as solicitors themselves.

article of incorporation In the USA, an official document that details a company's existence. It is similar to the UK *memorandum of association.

articles of apprenticeship *See* APPRENTICE.

articles of association The document that governs the running of a company. It sets out voting rights of shareholders, conduct of shareholders' and directors' meetings, powers of the management, etc. Either the articles are submitted with the *memorandum of association when application is made for incorporation or the relevant model articles contained in the Companies Regulations (Tables A to F) are adopted. Table A contains the model articles for companies limited by shares. The articles constitute a contract between the company and its members but this applies only to the rights of shareholders in their capacity as members. Therefore directors or company solicitors (for example) cannot use the articles to enforce their rights. The articles may be altered by a *special resolution of the members in a general meeting.

articles of partnership *See* PARTNERSHIP AGREEMENT.

articulated accounts Accounts prepared under the *double-entry bookkeeping system, in which the retained earnings figure on the *profit and loss account equals the increase in net worth of the business on the *balance sheet, subject to any other increases, such as an injection of new capital.

artificial person An entity that is recognized by the law as a **legal person**, i.e. one having legal rights and duties distinct from the individuals who comprise it. For example, a company is a person in the sense that it can sue and be sued, hold property, etc., in its own name. It is not, however, an individual or natural person. *See* CORPORATION.

ASA Abbreviation for *Advertising Standards Authority.

ASA model Abbreviation for *attraction-selection-attrition model.

ASB Abbreviation for *Accounting Standards Board.

ascending tops A series of market peaks, each of which represents a higher level of prices than its predecessor. In *chartist analysis such a series is seen as a sign of a *bull market. *Compare* RISING BOTTOMS. *See also* DOUBLE TOP.

ASCII Acronym for American Standard Code for Information Interchange. This is a standard code adopted by many computer manufacturers to simplify the transfer of information between computers. The code represents the numbers, letters, and symbols used in computing by a standard set of numbers. For example, the capital letter A is represented by the number 65, B is represented by the number 66, and so on. Many computers can convert their output to ASCII code, in which form it can be transferred to, and recognized by, other computers. ASCII is based on coding with 7 bits and provides 2^7 (i.e. 128) distinct numbered characters. Other characters with values from 129 to 256 (based on 8 bits) form an extended character set (known as **extended ASCII**). *See also* UNICODE.

ASEAN Abbreviation for *Association of South East Asian Nations.

A shares In the USA, the most important class of *ordinary shares. A shares usually have greater voting power than *B shares and may carry various other privileges.

ASP 1. Abbreviation for *application service provider. **2.** Abbreviation for *Active Server Page.

as per advice Words written on a *bill of exchange to indicate that the drawee has been informed that the bill is being drawn on him.

aspirational groups *See* CONSUMER GROUPS.

assay A chemical test to determine the purity of a sample of metal or to determine the content of an alloy. In the UK assays are carried out by official Assay Offices, the marks of which appear in the *hallmarks of silver and gold articles.

assented stock A security, usually an ordinary share, the owner of which has agreed to the terms of a *takeover bid. During the takeover negotiations, different prices may be quoted for assented and **non-assented stock.**

assertiveness training Training courses designed to help employees to develop their abilities, exercise initiative, present themselves convincingly, translate ideas into action, and generally maximize their potential. Assertiveness training aims to raise trainees' self-esteem to enable them to accept that as individuals they have a right to express themselves, to be listened to, and to be taken seriously.

assessment The method by which a tax authority raises a bill for a particular tax and sends it to the taxpayer or his or her agent. The assessment may be based on figures already agreed between the authority and the taxpayer or it may be an estimate by the tax authorities. The taxpayer normally has a right of appeal against an assessment within a specified time limit. *See also* SELF-ASSESSMENT; DEFERRED ASSET.

assessment centre A part of the personnel department of an organization that uses a range of tests in selecting new employees and considering current employees for promotion. The tests include questionnaires, interviews, and practical exercises that attempt to identify the skills and qualities required for a particular job as well as the character traits of the individual. The overall purpose of the assessment centre is to provide an organization with a process of assessment that is consistent, free of prejudice, and fair.

assessor *See* LOSS ASSESSOR.

asset Any object, tangible or intangible, that is of value to its possessor. In most cases it either is cash or can be turned into cash; exceptions include prepayments, which may represent payments made for rent, rates, or motor licences, in cases in which the time paid for has not yet expired. *Tangible assets include land and buildings, plant and machinery, fixtures and fittings, trading stock, investments, debtors, and cash; *intangible assets include *goodwill, patents, copyrights, and trademarks.

asset and liability management committee (ALCO) A senior management committee of a bank or financial institution that has overall responsibility for setting and overseeing risk-control policies in relation to the balance sheet (*see* ASSET–LIABILITY MANAGEMENT; GAP ANALYSIS). In some cases it will also be responsible for general management policy.

asset-backed fund A fund in which the money is invested in tangible or corporate assets, such as property or shares, rather than being treated as savings loaned to a bank or other institution. Asset-backed funds can be expected to grow with inflation in a way that bank savings cannot. *See also* EQUITY-LINKED POLICY; UNIT-LINKED POLICY.

asset-backed security A bond or note whose *collateral is the cash flows from a pool of financial obligations such as mortgages, car loans, or credit-card receivables. *See* SECURITIZATION.

asset cover A ratio that provides a measure of the solvency of a company; it consists of its *net assets divided by its *debt. Those companies with high asset cover are considered the more solvent.

asset deficiency The condition of a company when its *liabilities exceed its *assets. Although each particular circumstance must be interpreted in its own context, the financial viability of an organization with an asset deficiency must be in question.

asset financing Funding arranged by using assets as collateral. Examples of asset financing are *factoring and *hire purchase agreements.

asset–liability gap See GAP.

asset–liability management The management of assets and liabilities in order to influence the *credit risk, *interest-rate risk, and *liquidity risk of a bank. See ASSET AND LIABILITY MANAGEMENT COMMITTEE; GAP ANALYSIS.

asset management 1. The management of the financial assets of a company in order to maximize the return on the investments. 2. An investment service offered by banks and some other financial institutions. In the UK some private banks offer an asset management service for wealthy customers. See also PORTFOLIO.

asset stripping The acquisition of a firm for a price that is well below its total *asset value, and the subsequent sale of these assets. This may occur either because a particular asset, such as property, is valued in the firm's balance sheet at well below its potential market price, or because the firm has been poorly managed, in which case the low share price does not reflect the true value of the firm. After acquisition the assets of the firm are sold to third parties for significantly more than the purchase price of the assets. Because little or no consideration is given to the interests of other stakeholders, such as employees, suppliers, or customers, the practice is viewed critically.

asset turnover See CAPITAL TURNOVER.

asset valuation 1. An assessment of the value at which the *assets of an organization, usually the *fixed assets, should be entered into its balance sheet. The valuation may be arrived at in a number of ways; for example, a revaluation of land

and buildings would often involve taking professional advice. 2. The assessment of the value of assets, most usually by a *present value calculation.

asset value (per share) (break-up value) The total value of the assets of a company less its liabilities, divided by the number of ordinary shares in issue. This represents in theory, although probably not in practice, the amount attributable to each share if the company was wound up. The true value of the assets may well not be the total of the values shown by a company's balance sheet, since it is not the function of balance sheets to value assets. It may, therefore, be necessary to substitute the best estimate that can be made of the market values of the assets (including goodwill) for the values shown in the balance sheet. If there is more than one class of share, it may be necessary to deduct amounts due to shareholders with a priority on winding up before arriving at the amounts attributable to shareholders with a lower priority. The asset value per share is also known as the **net asset value (NAV)**. See also BALANCE-SHEET ASSET VALUE; BOOK VALUE.

assignment The act of transferring, or a document (a **deed of assignment**) transferring, property to some other person. Examples of assignment include the transfer of rights under a contract or benefits under a trust to another person. See also ASSIGNMENT OF LEASE.

assignment of copyright See COPYRIGHT.

assignment of insurable interest Assigning to another party the rights and obligations of the *insurable interest in an item of property, life, or a legal liability to be insured. This enables the person to whom the interest is assigned to arrange insurance cover, which would not otherwise be legally permitted.

assignment of lease The transfer of a *lease by the tenant (assignor) to some other person (assignee). Leases are freely transferable at common law although it is common practice to restrict assignment by conditions (covenants) in the lease. An assignment that takes place in breach of such a covenant is valid but it may entitle the landlord to put an end to the lease and re-enter the premises. An assignment of a legal lease must be by deed. An assignment puts the assignee into the shoes of the assignor, so that there is 'privity of estate' between the landlord and the new tenant. This is important with regard to the enforceability of covenants in the lease (see COVENANT). An assignment transfers the assignor's whole estate to the assignee, unlike a sub-lease (see HEAD LEASE).

assignment of life policies Transfer of the legal right under a *life-assurance policy to collect the proceeds. Assignment is only valid if the life insurer is advised and agrees; life assurance is the only form of insurance in which the assignee need not possess an *insurable interest. In recent years policy auctions have become a popular alternative to surrendering *endowment assurances. In these auctions, a policy is sold to the highest bidder and then assigned to him or her by the original policyholder.

assisted stock replenishment A system making use of *electronic-point-of-sale data to generate stock replenishment orders. Using the previous week's sales for each item, new stock can be delivered in advance and reviews of current sales enable extra items to be supplied at short notice.

Associated British Ports (ABP) A statutory corporation set up by the Transport Act (1981) to administer the 19 ports previously controlled by the British Transport Docks Board. ABP now administers 21 ports and is controlled by Associated British Ports Holding plc.

Association for Payment Clearing Services (APACS) An association set up by the UK banks in 1985 to manage payment clearing and overseas money transmission in the UK. The Association has four main Interest Groups: the Card Payments Group, the Electronic Commerce Group, and the Liquidity Managers Group. APACS also has four operating companies under its aegis: **BACS Payment Schemes Ltd**, which is responsible for automated interbank clearing payment and settlement services in the UK; **Voca Ltd**, which physically processes direct debit and direct credit payments; **Cheque and Credit Clearing Co. Ltd**, which operates a bulk clearing system for interbank cheques and paper credits; and **CHAPS**, which provides electronic funds transfer in sterling and euros.

Association of Accounting Technicians An association set up in 1980 by the *Consultative Committee of Accountancy Bodies (CCAB) to provide a second-tier accounting qualification. This qualification can enable an individual to obtain subsequently a full CCAB qualification.

Association of British Insurers (ABI) A trade association representing some 380 insurance companies offering any class of insurance business, whose members transact over 95% of the business of the British insurance market. It was formed in 1985 by a merger the British Insurance Association, the Accident Offices Association, the Fire Offices Committee, the Life Offices Association, and the Industrial Life Offices Association.

Association of Chartered Certified Accountants (ACCA) The professional association for *chartered certified accountants. It was formed in 1938 as the Association of Certified and Corporate Accountants, as a result of the amalgamation of the Corporation of Accountants (Glasgow; 1891) and the London Association of Accountants (1904). In 1941 the Institute of Certified Public Accountants joined the association. It was known as the **Chartered Association of Certified Accountants** from 1984 until 1996, when it adopted its present name.

Association of Corporate Treasurers (ACT) An organization set up to encourage and promote the study and practice of treasury management in companies. A small organization in relation to the professional accounting bodies, it has become influential in the field of corporate treasurership. Fellows of the Association are designated FCT and members as MCT.

Association of Mail Order Publishers (AMOP) A trade association set up for publishers involved in selling by mail-order (see MAIL-ORDER HOUSE).

Association of Market Survey Organizations (AMSO) An association of 27 of the largest UK survey research organizations. Member companies adhere to a strict code of conduct to ensure the highest standards of marketing research.

Association of Private Client Investment Managers and Stockbrokers (APCIMS) A representative body for private-client investment managers and stockbrokers, formed in June 1990. It aims to improve the environment and expand the market in which private-investors' business is transacted. The association represents 95% of eligible firms with a network of over 400 offices throughout the UK and Ireland. It publishes a directory of private-client stockbrokers, with details of members and the services they provide. It is run by an elected committee with a small permanent secretariat based in London, assisted by specialist practitioner committees.

Association of South East Asian Nations (ASEAN) A political and economic grouping of certain nations of South East Asia, formed in 1967 and currently comprising: Thailand, Malaysia, Singapore, Philippines, Indonesia, Brunei, Laos, Myanmar (Burma), Vietnam, and Cambodia. The countries are very diverse – for example, the per capita income of Singapore is some 300 times that of Vietnam – and interests often diverge accordingly. Although ASEAN is committed to strengthening economic ties, progress has been limited. There has also been political, technological, and cultural cooperation. There are regular consultations between ASEAN and the major industrialized countries.

assurance *Insurance against an eventuality (especially death) that must occur. See LIFE ASSURANCE.

assured The person named in a life-assurance policy to receive the proceeds in the event of maturity or the death of the *life assured. As a result of the policy, the person's financial future is 'assured'.

AST Abbreviation for *automated screen trading.

asymmetric information 1. The situation in which managers have superior information to shareholders regarding the state of the shareholders' investment. *See* AGENCY RELATIONSHIP; SIGNALLING HYPOTHESIS. **2.** The situation in which the purchaser of an insurance contract knows more about the nature of the risks than the seller of the contract (*see* ADVERSE SELECTION).

at A monetary unit of Laos, worth one hundredth of a *kip.

at and from Denoting a marine hull insurance cover that begins when the vessel is in dock before a voyage, continues during the voyage, and ends 24 hours after it has reached its port of destination.

at best (market order) An instruction to a broker to buy or sell shares, stocks, commodities, currencies, etc., as specified, at the best available price. It must be executed immediately irrespective of market movements. *Compare* AT LIMIT.

at call Denoting money that has been lent on a short-term basis and must be repaid on demand. *Discount houses are the main borrowers of money at call.

ATII Abbreviation for Associate of the *Chartered Institute of Taxation (formerly Associate of the Taxation Institute Incorporated), a professional qualification achieved by passing the Institute's examination. Most members with the qualification are partners or senior employees of accountancy or solicitors' firms, working mainly in the tax field. Some members work in banks, HM Revenue and Customs, insurance, industry, or commerce.

at limit (limit order) An instruction to a broker to buy or sell shares, stocks, commodities, currencies, etc., as specified, at a stated limiting price (i.e. not above a stated price if buying or not below a stated price if selling). When issuing such an instruction the principal should also state for how long the instruction stands, e.g. for a day, a week, etc. *Compare* AT BEST.

ATM Abbreviation for *automated teller machine.

atmosphere An aspect of the environment designed to create or reinforce a buyer's inclination to buy a particular product. In large supermarkets, for example, the smell of freshly baked bread is extracted from the bakery and directed into the store to increase bread sales.

at par *See* PAR VALUE.

at sight The words used on a *bill of exchange to indicate that payment is due on presentation. *Compare* AFTER DATE; AFTER SIGHT.

ATT Abbreviation for Associate of the Association of Tax Technicians, a qualification undertaken by employees working in taxation at a level below that of members of the *Chartered Institute of Taxation. The Association was set up in 1989 under the sponsorship of the Institute.

attachment The procedure enabling a *judgement creditor to secure payment of the amount due from a debtor. The judgement creditor obtains a further court order (the *garnishee order) to the effect that money or property due from a third party to the debtor must be frozen and paid instead to the judgement creditor to satisfy the amount due.

attest To bear witness to an act or event. The law requires that some documents are only valid and binding if the signatures on them have been attested to by a third party. This also requires the third party's signature on the document. For instance, the signature of the purchaser of land under a contract must be attested to by a witness.

attitude The way in which a person views and evaluates something or someone. Attitudes determine whether people like or dislike things – and therefore how they behave towards them.

Attitude is traditionally divided into cognitive, behavioural, and *affective components, although the main emphasis now tends to fall on defining attitude in terms of affect – the person's feelings towards the object, brand, etc. Is the brand good or bad? Is it likeable? The importance of the cognitive and behavioural components is

still accepted, but they are no longer regarded as critical components.

attitude research An investigation into the *attitudes of people towards an organization or its products. Attitude research is important to advertising specialists in planning campaigns. For example, it might reveal a 'Buy British' attitude among respondents, which would present a marketing and advertising problem to a US manufacturer.

attraction-selection-attrition model (ASA model) A theory holding that: (1) individuals are attracted to organizations whose members are similar to themselves in terms of personality, values, interests, and other attributes; (2) organizations are more likely to select those who possess knowledge, skills, and abilities similar to the ones their existing members possess; and (3) over time, those who do not fit in well are more likely to leave. Owing to these three factors, the personal characteristics of those who work for an organization are likely to become more similar over time, leading to the consolidation of *organizational culture.

attribute A characteristic of a product or service that can be measured by a rating having only two possible states, e.g. good or bad, acceptable or not acceptable, etc. *Compare* VARIABLE.

at warehouse Delivery terms for goods that are available for immediate delivery, in which the buyer pays for delivery of the goods, including the cost of loading them onto the road or rail transport. *Compare* EX WAREHOUSE.

auction A method of sale in which goods, securities, rights, etc. are sold in public to the highest bidder. Auctions are

ATTITUDE

COGNITIVE COMPONENT	AFFECTIVE COMPONENT	BEHAVIOURAL COMPONENT
(thoughts/ knowledge)	(feelings/ emotions)	(motive/ behaviour tendencies)

Attitude. The components of attitude.

used for any property for which there are likely to be a number of competing buyers, such as houses, second-hand and antique furniture, works of art, etc., as well as for certain commodities, such as tea, bristles, wool, furs, etc., which must be sold as individual lots, rather than on the basis of a standard sample or grading procedure. In most auctions the goods to be sold are available for viewing before the sale and it is usual for the seller to put a *reserve price on the articles offered, i.e. the articles are withdrawn from sale unless more than a specified price is bid. The auctioneer acts as agent for the seller in most cases and receives a commission on the sale price. An auctioneer is an agent of the seller, who must have the authority of the seller to sell, and must know of no defect in the seller's title to the goods, without promising that a buyer will receive good title for a specific object. An advertisement that an auction will be held does not bind the auctioneer to hold it. It is illegal for a dealer (a person who buys at auction for subsequent resale) to offer a person a reward not to bid at an auction. *See also* DOUBLE AUCTION; DUTCH AUCTION; VIRTUAL AUCTION.

auction enabler An on-line service that helps an auction house run an effective physical auction.

auction market preferred stock (AMPS) A US floating rate preferred stock whose dividend is set by *Dutch auction.

audience data syndicated services Research companies that collect, package, and sell data on media audiences to a variety of firms.

audience research Research to establish readership, audience, and circulation data, which is vital information in *advertising. Research into television audiences is undertaken by *BARB (Broadcasters' Audience Research Board), into radio audiences by JICRAR (*Joint Industry Committee for Radio Audience Research), and into national readership by JICNAR (*Joint Industry Committee for National Readership) and the *Audit Bureau of Circulation.

audimeter An electromechanical device used to record the channel that a television set is tuned to (if any). The informa-

tion collected enables the marketing research company to say how many sets were tuned to a particular programme and for how long the television was on; it does not show how many persons were viewing or the length of time for which they were viewing.

audioconferencing A national and international telephone service enabling several users in different places to conduct a business meeting over the telephone. Connections can be made between callers in several different countries. Details are available from British Telecom. *See also* VIDEOCONFERENCING.

audio response device A output device, connected to a computer, that produces human speech. These devices are used, for example, in computerized telephone enquiry systems. They work by storing words, syllables, or phrases in the computer and linking them together to form more-or-less recognizable speech.

audit An independent examination of, and the subsequent expression of opinion on, the financial statements of an organization. This involves the auditor in collecting evidence by means of compliance tests (tests of control) and substantive tests (tests of detail). *External audits (i.e. audits performed by an auditor external to the organization) are required under statute for limited companies by the Companies Act and for various other undertakings, such as housing associations and building societies, by other Acts of Parliament. *Internal audits are performed by auditors within an organization, usually an independent department, such as an internal-audit department. Internal auditors examine various areas, including financial and non-financial concerns, with emphasis on ensuring that internal controls are working effectively. Internal auditors may assist the external auditor of an organization. Non-statutory audits can be performed at the request of the owners, members, or trustees of an undertaking, for example. Financial statements other than the annual accounts may also be audited; for example, summaries of sales made by an organization. *See also* AUDIT OPINION; AUDITOR; AUDITORS' REPORT; STATUTORY AUDIT.

Audit Bureau of Circulation (ABC) An organization to which most newspaper, magazine, and periodical publishers belong. Its function is to collect and audit sales figures from publishers regularly and to publish monthly circulation figures in its quarterly *Circulation Review*, a publication of great value to advertisers. A newspaper, magazine, or periodical must have been publishing for a minimum of six months before joining the ABC.

audit evidence The evidence required by an auditor on which to base an *audit opinion on the *financial statements of the company whose accounts are being audited. Sources of information include the accounting systems and the underlying documentation of the enterprise, its tangible assets, management and employees, its customers, suppliers, and any other third parties who have dealings with, or knowledge of, the enterprise or its business. The evidence will be obtained by means of **compliance tests** (tests to determine the effectiveness of a company's control procedures) and **substantive tests** (tests of the accuracy and completeness of accounting records and financial statements). Techniques involved in gathering the evidence include inspection, observation, enquiry, analysis, and *computer-assisted audit techniques.

audit exemption The exemption from *statutory audit by a registered auditor that can be claimed by certain *small companies. Companies with a turnover of not more than £1 million and a balance-sheet total of not more than £1.4 million may be totally exempt from audit. Companies with a turnover in the range £1 million to £5.6 million (and a balance-sheet total of not more than £2.8 million) may claim exemption from the audit requirement but still need a *reporting accountant's report. The **audit exemption report** must state that the accounts are, in the opinion of the accountant, in agreement with the accounting records kept by the company and that the accounts have been drawn up in a manner consistent with the provisions of the Companies Act (1985). Also, the accountant must report that, on the basis of the information contained in the accounting records, the company is entitled to the exemption on the basis of size. The audit exemption report was formerly known as a **compilation report**.

Further details of audit exemptions are available at the Department of Trade and Industry website at www.dti.gov.uk

audit fee (auditors' remuneration) The amount payable to an auditor for an audit; this has to be approved at the *annual general meeting of a company. In the *financial statements, audit fees must be distinguished from fees payable to the auditor for non-audit work.

audit opinion An opinion contained in an *auditors' report. It expresses a view as to whether or not the *financial statements audited have been prepared consistently using appropriate accounting policies, in accordance with relevant legislation, regulations, or applicable accounting standards. The opinion also has to state that there is adequate disclosure of information relevant to the proper understanding of the financial statements. If the auditors are satisfied on these points, and if any departure from legislation, regulations, or applicable accounting standards has been justified and adequately explained in the financial statements, an unqualified opinion will be given. If the scope of the auditors' examination has been limited, or the auditors disagree materially with the treatment or disclosure of a matter in the financial statements, or they do not comply with relevant accounting or other requirements, a qualified opinion will be issued. *See* ADVERSE OPINION.

auditor A person or firm appointed to carry out an *audit of an organization. In the UK, since the Companies Act (1989) an external auditor must be a registered auditor or a member of a *Recognized Supervisory Body and be eligible for appointment under the rules of that body. The supervisory bodies are required to have rules designed to ensure that persons eligible for appointment as company auditors are either individuals who hold the appropriate qualification or firms controlled by properly qualified persons. These bodies must also ensure that eligible persons continue to maintain the appropriate level of competence and must monitor and enforce compliance with their rules. These rules do not apply to internal auditors.

auditors' remuneration *See* AUDIT FEE.

auditors' report (audit report) A report by the auditors appointed to audit the accounts of a company or other organization. Auditors' reports may take many forms depending on who has appointed the auditors and for what purposes. Some auditors are engaged in an internal audit while others are appointed for various statutory purposes. The auditors of a limited company are required to form an opinion as to whether the *annual accounts of the company give a *true and fair view of its profit or loss for the period under review and of its state of affairs at the end of the period; they are also required to certify that the accounts are prepared in accordance with the requirements of the Companies Act (1985). The auditors' report is technically a report to the members of the company and it must be filed together with the accounts with the Registrar of Companies under the Companies Act (1985). Under this Act, the auditors' report must also include an audit of the *directors' report with respect to consistency.

audit software Computer programs used by an auditor to examine an enterprise's computer files. Utility programs may be used, for example, for sorting and printing data files. Package or tailor-made programs may be used to interrogate the computer-based accounting system of a client. More sophisticated *computer-assisted audit techniques (CAATs) include the use of embedded audit facilities, in which program codes and additional data are incorporated into the client's computerized accounting system to facilitate a continuous review of the system.

audit trail (paper trail) The sequence of documents, computer files, and other records examined during an *audit, showing how a transaction has been dealt with by an organization from start to finish. Documents will require cross-referencing so the trail is not broken. For example, a sales transaction can be traced from the item of stock sold, to the invoice, through the sales day book, to the sales account, and finally to the bank account. *See also* COMPUTER-ASSISTED AUDIT TECHNIQUES.

augmented product Additional consumer services and benefits sold with a core product. The augmented product can be critical to the success of the core product. For example, a camcorder (the core product) may be marketed with a warranty, quick repair service, freephone number for problems, and possibly free lessons on how to use the device.

AUP Abbreviation for *acceptable use policy.

aurar The plural of *eyrir.

Australian Stock Exchange (ASX) The stock exchange based in Sydney, which in 1987 superseded the exchanges in Brisbane, Adelaide, Hobart, Melbourne, and Perth. It abolished fixed-rate commissions in 1984 and adopted fully automated trading in October 1990. The most important market index is now the S&P ASX200, covering the top 200 shares on the exchange, although the All-Ordinaries share index, covering some 500 shares, is still quoted.

authentication In e-commerce, *see* SECURITY.

authoritarian leader A leader who makes all major decisions himself or herself and takes a highly dominant role in interactions with subordinates. Experimental studies of *leadership style have found that work groups with authoritarian leaders tend to be more discontented than those with *democratic leaders or *laissez-faire leaders and to be less productive than such groups when the leader is absent.

authorized auditor An individual granted authorization by the Board of Trade or the Secretary of State to be the auditor of a company, under the Companies Act (1967). Authorizations were granted to individuals not otherwise eligible to act as auditors on the basis of their experience. The power to grant authorizations ended in April 1978. Under the Companies Act (1989) an authorized auditor is eligible for appointment as an auditor of an unlisted company but is not qualified to be the auditor of any other company.

authorized investments Formerly, certain legally authorized investments considered suitable for trust funds, as set out in the Trustees Investment Act (1961).

A much wider *general power of investment for trustees was introduced in 2000.

authorized minimum share capital
In the UK, the statutory minimum of £50,000 for the share capital of a public company. There is no minimum share capital for private companies.

authorized share capital (nominal share capital; nominal capital; registered capital) The maximum amount of share capital that may be issued by a company, as detailed in the company's *memorandum of association. The authorized share capital must be disclosed on the face of the *balance sheet or alternatively in the notes to the accounts. See also AUTHORIZED MINIMUM SHARE CAPITAL; ISSUED SHARE CAPITAL.

automated answer The response to a routine, non-special-case query that can be answered quickly by computer or other device without special handling.

automated guided vehicle (AGV) A self-propelled vehicle guided by cables set in the floor, by radio or microwave transmitters, by onboard computer, or by optical guidance systems. AGVs are used to transport materials or components without human intervention. They are most often used in manufacturing plants, especially if these involve hazardous chemicals or structures, where AGVs can form an integrated part of the process design, replacing conveyor belts, etc.

automated screen trading (AST) Electronic dealing in securities using visual-display units to display prices and the associated computer equipment to enter, match, and execute deals. The system does away with the need for face-to-face trading on a formal stock-exchange floor, and even dispenses with telephone dealing. It potentially reduces or eliminates paperwork.

automated teller machine (ATM) A computerized machine usually attached to the outside wall of a High-Street bank or building society that enables customers to withdraw cash from their *current accounts, especially outside normal banking hours. The machines may also be used to pay in cash or cheques, effect transfers, and obtain statements. They are operated by *cash cards or *multifunctional cards in conjunction with a *PIN. ATMs are often known colloquially as **cash dispensers**.

automatic debit transfer See GIRO.

automatic identification A means of identifying a product mechanically and entering the data obtained automatically into a computer. The most widely used method involves *bar codes. Other methods include *optical character recognition (OCR), magnetic ink character recognition (MICR), magnetic stripes, and voice systems.

automatic response system A software program designed to answer frequently asked questions (see FAQ) without human intervention.

automatic stabilizers Adjustments to fiscal policy that occur automatically during *business cycles and smooth the path of economic growth. For example, in a *recession the government will pump money into the economy by paying more in unemployment benefit without a change in policy. Automatic stabilizers counterbalance the feedback effect of changes in economic activity, although in practice their effectiveness is limited.

automatic vending Selling products by means of vending machines.

autonomous work groups (AWGs) Small work units within an organization that are given considerable responsibility for organizing their activities and achieving results without guidance from management. Advocates of AWGs argue that improvements in performance can be attained if employees are highly motivated and fully involved in the direction and control of their work.

autorespond e-mail A system enabling an answer to a query sent by e-mail to be automatically retrieved from a stored database; the answer is sent to the receiver without human intervention. See FAQ.

available market The consumers who have interest in, sufficient income to buy, and access to a particular product or service. See also QUALIFIED AVAILABLE MARKET.

aval 1. A third-party guarantee of payment on a *bill of exchange or promissory note; it is often given by a bank. **2.** A signature on a bill of exchange that endorses or guarantees the bill.

AVC Abbreviation for *additional voluntary contribution.

average 1. A single number used to represent a set of numbers; mean. *See* ARITHMETIC MEAN; GEOMETRIC MEAN; MEDIAN; WEIGHTED AVERAGE. **2.** A partial loss in *marine insurance (from French: *avarie*, damage). In **general average (GA)**, a loss resulting from a deliberate act of the master of the ship (such as throwing overboard all or part of the cargo to save the ship) is shared by all the parties involved, i.e. by the shipowners and all the cargo owners. *See* AVERAGE ADJUSTER; AVERAGE BOND. In a **particular average (PA)**, an accidental loss is borne by the owners of the particular thing lost or damaged, e.g. the ship, an individual cargo, etc. Cargo can be insured either **free of particular average (FPA)** or **with average (WA)**. An FPA policy covers the cargo against loss by perils of the sea, fire, or collision and includes cover for any contribution payable in the event of a general average. A WA policy gives better cover as it also includes damage by heavy seas and sea-water damage. In addition, marine cargo can be covered by an *all-risks policy. *See also* FREE OF ALL AVERAGES; INSTITUTE CARGO CLAUSES. **3.** A method of sharing losses in property insurance to combat underinsurance. This is usually applied in an **average clause** in a fire insurance policy, in which it is stated that the sum payable in the event of a claim shall not be more than the proportion that the insured value of an item bears to its actual value.

average adjuster A person who handles marine insurance claims on behalf of the insurers. If there is a claim that involves general *average and contributions have to be made by all the parties involved it is the average adjuster who is responsible for apportioning payment.

average bond A promise to pay general *average contributions, if required. If a general-average loss occurs during a marine voyage the carrier has a right to take part of the cargo as payment of the cargo owners' contribution to the loss. As an alternative to the possibility of losing part of the cargo, the cargo owner may take out an average bond with insurers, who agree to pay any losses arising in this way.

average clause *See* AVERAGE.

average cost 1. The average cost per unit of output calculated by dividing the total costs, both *fixed costs and *variable costs, by the total units of output. **2.** (**AVCO; weighted-average cost**) A method of valuing units of *raw material or *finished goods issued from stock; it involves recalculating the unit value to be used for pricing the issues after each new consignment of raw materials or finished goods has been added to the stock. The average cost is obtained by dividing the total stock value by the number of units in stock. Because the issues are at an average cost, it follows that the valuation of the closing stock should be made on the same average cost basis. The method may also be used in *process costing to value the work in process at the end of an accounting period.

average life A somewhat artificial measure sometimes used to compare bonds of different duration and different repayment schedules. It is calculated as the average of the periods for which funds are available, weighted by the amounts available in each of these periods.

average order cost In *direct-mail selling, the total cost of orders, divided by the total number of orders.

average order value In *direct-mail selling, the total value of orders received, divided by the total number of orders.

average stock A method of accounting for stock movements that assumes goods are taken out of stock at the average cost of the goods in stock. *See* BASE STOCK; FIFO COST; LIFO COST; STOCK.

average variable cost An average taken over a specified period of the variable cost of producing units of production (*see* AVERAGE COST). The variable costs (such as the cost of raw materials, direct labour, machine time, etc.) of producing a unit are those that vary directly with the number of units produced. As they are likely to change from time to time it may be convenient for budgeting purposes to take an average.

averaging Adding to a holding of particular securities or commodities when the price falls, in order to reduce the average cost of the whole holding. **Averaging in** consists of buying at various price levels in order to build up a substantial holding of securities or commodities over a period. **Averaging out** is the opposite process, of selling a large holding at various price levels over a long period.

aviation broker A broker who arranges chartering of aircraft, air-freight bookings, insurance of air cargo and aircraft, etc.

aviation insurance The insurance of aircraft, including accident or damage to aircraft, insurance of air cargo, loss of life or injury while flying, and loss or damage to baggage.

AVMS Abbreviation for administered vertical marketing system. *See* ADMINISTERED VMS.

avo A monetary unit of Macao, worth one hundredth of a *pataca.

avoidable costs Costs that will not be incurred if a particular course of action is not taken. For example, if a specific product is not produced, certain material and labour costs may be avoided. *Variable costs are often avoidable costs, whereas *fixed costs, such as business rates, are not avoidable in the short term. *See also* RELEVANT COST.

AWGs Abbreviation for *autonomous work groups.

BAA A public limited company floated on the London Stock Exchange in 1987 and formed from the former **British Airports Authority**. It owns and operates London airports (Heathrow, Gatwick, and Stansted) as well as Aberdeen, Edinburgh, Prestwick, and Glasgow airports. It is responsible for the construction and maintenance of buildings, fire and security services, passenger services, and terminal management.

baby boom A major increase in the annual birthrate following World War II, which lasted until the early 1960s. The 'baby boomers', now moving into advanced middle age, are a prime target for marketers, particularly as their own offspring will now have ceased to be a financial drain on them. *See also* GREY MARKET.

backdate **1.** To put an earlier date on a document than that on which it was compiled, in order to make it effective from that earlier date. **2.** To agree that salary increases, especially those settled in a pay award, should apply from a specified date in the recent past.

back door One of the methods by which the *Bank of England injects cash into the *money market. The bank purchases Treasury bills at the market rate rather than by lending money directly to the discount houses (the front door method) when it acts as *lender of last resort.

back-end load The final charge made by an *investment trust or *unit trust when an investor sells shares in the fund. *Compare* FRONT-END LOAD.

backer A person or organization that invests in a new company or project and may require a share in the equity of the company.

backflush accounting A method of costing a product based on a management philosophy that includes having the minimum levels of *inventory available; in these circumstances, the valuation of stocks becomes less important, making the complex use of *absorption costing techniques unnecessary. Backflush accounting works backwards; after the actual costs have been determined they are allocated between inventory and *cost of sales to establish profitability. There is no separate accounting for *work in progress.

back freight The cost of shipping goods back to the port of destination after they have been overcarried. If the master overcarried the goods for reasons beyond his control, the shipowner may be responsible for paying the back freight. If delivery was not accepted in reasonable time at the port of destination and the master took the goods on or sent them back to the port of shipment, the back freight would be the responsibility of the cargo owner.

backlog An accumulation of unfulfilled orders held by a firm. This may result from an inability to cope with the demand for a product during a particular period or it may be a deliberate policy to even out an irregular demand, avoid having to hold excessive stocks, or the necessity to increase short-term production capacity by paying overtime rates.

back office *See* FRONT OFFICE–BACK OFFICE.

back-to-back credit (countervailing credit) A method used to conceal the identity of the seller from the buyer in a credit arrangement. When the credit is arranged by a British finance house, the foreign seller provides the relevant documentation. The finance house, acting as an intermediary, issues its own documents to the buyer, omitting the seller's name and so concealing the seller's identity.

back-to-back loan One loan of a matching pair of loans in different currencies: A lends to B and B lends to A where the loans are of the same value. The back-to-back loan was a precurser of the *currency swap and can be used to avoid currency restrictions.

back-to-back swaps Two *swaps that have been combined, sometimes as a method of winding up a swap position.

back-up credit An alternative source of funds arranged if an issue of *commercial paper is not fully taken up by the market. Back-up credit is provided by a bank for a fee or by the deposit of credit balances at the bank of the issuer. The back-up is often a stand-by facility provided by the bank, which may be drawn upon if the paper is not placed.

backwardation 1. The difference between the spot price of a commodity, plus any *carrying costs, and the forward price, when the spot price is the higher. **2.** A situation that occasionally occurs on s stock exchange when a market maker quotes a buying price for a share that is lower than the selling price quoted by another market maker. However, with prices now displayed on screens, this situation does not now last long.

backward channel A channel of distribution for recycling, in which the customary flow from producer to ultimate user is reversed. For example, bottles, cans, and paper are now returned to the producer for recycling.

backward integration *See* INTEGRATION.

BACS Abbreviation for Bankers Automated Clearing System. *See* ASSOCIATION FOR PAYMENT CLEARING SERVICES.

bad debt An amount owed by a debtor that is unlikely to be paid; for example, due to a company going into liquidation. The full amount should be written off to the *profit and loss account of the period or to a *provision for bad debts as soon as it is foreseen, on the grounds of prudence. Bad debts subsequently recovered either in part or in full should be written back to the profit and loss account of the period (or to a provision for bad and doubtful debts).

badges of trade The criteria that distinguish trading from investment for taxation purposes. They were set out by the Royal Commission on the Taxation of Profits and Income in 1954. Dealing on the *commodity markets is normally regarded as trading and profits are subject to income tax or corporation tax; dealing on security markets is often (but not always) treated as investment and profits are subject to lower taxation by the capital-gains tax.

baht (B) The standard monetary unit of Thailand, divided into 100 satang.

bailment A delivery of good from the **bailor** (the owner of the goods) to the **bailee** (the recipient of the goods), on the condition that the goods will ultimately be returned to the bailor. The goods may thus be hired, lent, pledged, or deposited for safe custody. A delivery of this nature is usually also the subject of a contract; for example, a contract with a bank for the deposit of valuables for safekeeping. Nonetheless, in English law a bailment retains its distinguishing characteristic of a business relationship that arises outside the law of contract and is therefore not governed by it.

bailout Financial aid given to an economy or a company that is approaching collapse.

baiza A monetary unit of Oman, worth one hundredth of a *rial.

balance concentration The practice of consolidating the bank accounts of a group of companies in order to minimize overdraft costs.

balanced scales Measurement scales in marketing research, with the same number of positive and negative (or favourable and unfavourable) categories, i.e. there is no mid-point. They are therefore made up of even number categories – 4, 6, 8, 10, etc.

balanced scorecard (BSC) An approach to management that integrates both financial and non-financial *performance measurement in a framework proposed by Professors Kaplan and Norton. The BSC was first reported in the *Harvard Business Review* in 1992 and has since been adopted by a wide range of organizations. It is considered one of the most significant recent developments in management accounting. The approach looks at performance from four interrelated dimensions:

- The **financial perspective**—how do we measure financial performance? Possible performance measures include *operating profits, *return on capital employed, and *unit costs.
- The **customer perspective**—how do we measure customer satisfaction? Possible performance measures include customer profitability, customer satisfaction, and market share.
- The **internal business-process perspective**—what must we excel at? Possible measures include time to develop new products, defect rates, and product returns.
- The **learning and growth perspective**—how can we continue to improve and create value? Possible measures include employee satisfaction and employee productivity.

The balanced scorecard approach requires managers to identify both lagging and leading measures. **Lagging measures** are financial measures that show the impact of decisions made in the past, whereas **leading measures** are non-financial measures relating to the customer, internal business-process, and learning and growth perspectives. The latter are the drivers of future financial performance.

balance of payments The accounts setting out a country's transactions with the outside world. They are divided into various sub-accounts, notably the **current account** and the **capital account**. The former includes the trade account, which records the balance of imports and exports (see BALANCE OF TRADE). Overall, the accounts must always be in balance. A deficit or surplus on the balance of payments refers to the level of purchases or sales of the currency by the national government, usually through its central bank. The conventions used for presenting balance-of-payments statistics are those recommended by the *International Monetary Fund.

balance of trade The accounts setting out the results of a country's trading position. It is a component of the *balance of payments, forming part of the *current account. It includes *visibles (i.e. imports and exports in physical merchandise) but not *invisible earnings and expenditure (receipts and expenditure on such services as insurance, finance, freight, and tourism).

balance sheet A statement of the total assets and liabilities of an organization at a particular date, usually the last day of the *accounting period. The first part of the statement lists the fixed and current assets and the liabilities, whereas the second part shows how they have been financed; the totals for each part must be equal. Under the UK Companies Act the balance sheet is one of the primary statements to be included in the *annual accounts of a company. The Companies Act requires that the balance sheet of a company must give a *true and fair view of its state of affairs at the end of its financial year, and must comply with statute as to its form and content. A balance sheet does not necessarily value a company, as some assets may be given an unrealistic value and important *intangible assets may be omitted altogether (see ASSET VALUE (PER SHARE); BOOK VALUE). It can be difficult to compare the balance sheets of companies from different countries as they may disclose different information.

balance-sheet asset value The value of an asset as represented on the *balance sheet. For tangible fixed assets this is the cost less accumulated depreciation (although freehold land is generally not subject to depreciation). *Intangible assets are shown at cost less *amortization. Current assets are valued at the lower of cost and *net realizable value. Under the alternative accounting rules given in the Companies Act (1985), the historical cost of certain assets (for example, buildings and stocks) may be replaced by current cost. See also BOOK VALUE; NET BOOK VALUE.

balancing charge The charge that may be assessable to *corporation tax on the disposal of an asset when the proceeds realized on the sale of the asset exceed the *written-down value, for tax purposes. The balancing charge amounts to the difference between the proceeds and the written-down value. For example, if the written-down value is £23,000 and the proceeds on disposal were £30,000, there would be a balancing charge of the difference of £7000. The balancing charge is deducted from the other allowances for the period. If the charge exceeds the allowances available, the net amount is added to the profit for the period and assessed to tax.

balboa (B) The standard monetary unit of Panama, divided into 100 centésimos.

Baldridge Award (Malcolm Baldridge National Quality Award; MBNQA) An annual award, named after a US Secretary of State for Commerce, given to companies in the USA that have "excelled in quality management and quality achievement". There are three categories of winners: manufacturing, service, and small business, with up to two awards in each category. The award is based on performance against a set of criteria now used by a wide range of companies as a benchmark for their own *total quality management systems, regardless of whether they enter for the award. The first-level categories are: leadership, information and analysis, strategic planning, human resource development and management, process management, business results, and customer focus and satisfaction.

balloon A large sum repaid as an irregular instalment of a loan repayment. **Balloon loans** are those in which repayments are not made in a regular manner, but are made, as funds become available, in balloons.

balloon mortgage A *mortgage in which one or more large payments may be made as part of the repayment profile; it is also called a **non-amortizing mortgage**. With a balloon mortgage a lump sum often has to be repaid at the end of the term to cover the remaining debt.

ballot A random selection of applications for an oversubscribed *new issue of securities (*see also* FLOTATION). The successful applicants may be granted the full number of securities for which they have applied or a specified proportion of their applications. Applicants not selected in the ballot have their applications and cheques returned.

Baltic Exchange A former commodity and freight-chartering exchange in the City of London. It took its name from the trade in grain with Baltic ports, which was the mainstay of the business in the 18th century. Its activities, including the Baltic International Freight Futures Exchange (BIFFEX), are now undertaken by the *London International Financial Futures and Options Exchange.

ban (*plural* **bani**) A monetary unit of Romania and Moldova, worth one hundredth of a *leu.

bancassurance (Allfinanz) The combination of traditional loan and savings bank products with such assurance products as *life assurance and pensions. It is now common for major UK banks to provide this combined service and the practice is spreading worldwide.

Bancogiro *See* GIRO.

band **1.** A trading range, set by upper and lower limits, of a commodity or currency. For example, the ERM II (*see* EUROPEAN MONETARY SYSTEM) now sets a band against a central rate of conversion to the euro of ± 15%. **2.** Four ranges of maturities set by the Bank of England to influence short-term interest rates in the money market. They are set on *Treasury bills, *local authority bills, and eligible bank bills (*see* ELIGIBLE PAPER); band 1 is from 1 to 14 days, band 2 from 15 to 33 days, band 3 from 34 to 63 days, and band 4 from 64 to 91 days.

banded pack A special offer of goods in which two or more related (or sometimes unrelated) items are bound together to form a single pack. This pack is offered at a lower price than the combined price of the individual items. Banded packs are sometimes offered with the slogan 'buy one, get one free'. *See* PRICE-BUNDLING STRATEGY.

bandwagon effect The phenomenon by which success breeds success; in business terms, the higher the market share the easier it is to make additional sales.

bandwidth In computer systems, the limit on the amount of data that can be sent through a particular channel. As a result of the increase in computer processing power, many systems now offer the option of transmitting text, voice, still pictures, and full video. Transmission systems installed only a few years ago, to deal with simple text applications, do not now have the bandwidth to carry all the data that is available. *See* BROADBAND.

bangtail A type of envelope usually having an attached perforated 'tail', which can be used as a response note or order form. Known as a two-in-one type of letter, it is normally used as part of one-piece mailer or self-mailer in *direct marketing. This arrangement reduces the costs of *direct-mail selling.

bank A commercial institution that takes deposits and extends loans. Banks are concerned mainly with making and receiving payments on behalf of their customers, accepting deposits, and making short-term loans to private individuals, companies, and other organizations. However, they also provide money transmission services and in recent years have diversified into many areas of financial services. In the UK, the banking system comprises the *Bank of England (the central bank), the *commercial banks, *merchant banks, branches of foreign and Commonwealth banks, the *National Savings Bank, and the National Girobank (*see* GIRO). The first (1990) *building society to become a bank in the UK was the Abbey National (now Abbey), after its public *flotation; many other building societies have now followed this precedent. In other countries banks are also usually supervised by a central bank.

bank account *See* ACCOUNT; CHEQUE ACCOUNT; CURRENT ACCOUNT; DEPOSIT ACCOUNT; LOAN ACCOUNT; POSTAL ACCOUNT; SAVINGS ACCOUNT.

bank advance *See* BANK LOAN.

bank bill A bill of exchange issued or guaranteed (accepted) by a bank. It is more acceptable than a trade bill as there is less risk of non-payment and hence it can be discounted at a more favourable rate, although to some extent this depends on the bank's credit rating.

bank certificate A certificate, signed by a bank manager, stating the balance held to a company's credit on a specified date. It may be asked for during the course of an audit.

bank charge The amount charged to a customer by a bank, usually for a specific transaction, such as paying in a sum of money by means of a cheque or withdrawing a sum by means of an automated teller machine. However, modern practice is to provide periods of commission-free banking by waiving most charges on personal current accounts. Business customers invariably pay tariffs in one form or another.

bank deposit A sum of money placed by a customer with a bank. The deposit may or may not attract interest and may be instantly accessible or accessible at a time agreed by the two parties. Banks may use a percentage of their customers' deposits to lend on to other customers; thus most deposits may only exist on paper in the bank's books. Money on deposit at a bank is usually held in a *savings account, a *deposit account, or a *current account.

bank draft (banker's cheque; banker's draft) A cheque drawn by a bank on itself or its agent. A person who owes money to another buys the draft from a bank for cash and hands it to the creditor who need have no fear that it might be dishonoured. A bank draft is used if the creditor is unwilling to accept an ordinary cheque.

banker's acceptance A *time draft that promises to pay a certain sum and has been accepted by a bank. It is a form of promissory note, widely used in international trade; once signed and dated it can be traded before its maturity. *See also* THIRD-COUNTRY ACCEPTANCE.

Bankers Automated Clearing System *See* ASSOCIATION FOR PAYMENT CLEARING SERVICES.

banker's cheque *See* BANK DRAFT.

banker's order *See* STANDING ORDER.

banker's reference (status enquiry) A report on the creditworthiness of an individual supplied by a bank to a third party, such as another financial institution or a bank customer. References and status enquiries are often supplied by specialist credit-reference agencies, who keep lists of defaulters, bad payers, and people who have infringed credit agreements. References must be very general and recent legislation has given new rights to the subjects of such reports, which restrict their value even further.

Bank for International Settlements

(BIS) An international bank that fosters cooperation among central banks and other agencies in pursuit of monetary and financial stability. The BIS was originally established in 1930 as a financial institution to coordinate the payment of war reparations between European central banks. It was hoped that the BIS, with headquarters in Basle, would develop into a European central bank but many of its functions were taken over by the *International Monetary Fund (IMF) after World War II. Since then the BIS has fulfilled several roles including acting as a trustee and agent for such international groups as the OECD, the European Monetary System, and the IMF. The frequent meetings of the BIS directors have been a useful means of cooperation between central banks, especially in combating short-term speculative monetary movements. The BIS also sets *capital adequacy ratios for banks in European countries. The original members were France, Belgium, West Germany, Italy, and the UK but now most European central banks are represented as well as the USA, Canada, and Japan. The London agent is the Bank of England, whose governor is a member of the board of directors of the BIS.

Bank Giro *See* GIRO.

bank guarantee An undertaking given by a bank to settle a debt should the debtor fail to do so. A bank guarantee can be used as a security for a loan but the banks themselves will require good cover in cash or counter-indemnity before they issue a guarantee. A guarantee has to be in writing to be legally binding. Such guarantees often contain indemnity clauses, which place a direct onus on the guarantor. This onus leaves the guarantor liable in law in all eventualities.

Bank Holidays Public holidays in the UK, when the banks are closed. They are New Year's Day, Easter Monday, May Day (the first Monday in May), Spring Bank Holiday (the last Monday in May), August Bank Holiday (last Monday in August), and Boxing Day. In Scotland, Easter Monday is replaced by 2 January and the August Bank Holiday is on the first Monday in August. In Northern Ireland St Patrick's Day (17 March) and the Battle of the Boyne (12 July) are added. In the Channel Islands Liberation Day (9 May) is included. Bank Holidays have a similar status to Sundays in that *bills of exchange falling due on a Bank Holiday are postponed until the following day and also they do not count in working out *days of grace. Good Friday and Christmas Day are also public holidays, but payments falling due (including *bills of exchange) on these days are payable on the preceding day. When Bank Holidays fall on a Sunday, the following day becomes the Bank Holiday.

banking The activities undertaken by banks; this includes personal banking (non-business customers), commercial banking (small and medium-sized business customers), and corporate banking (large international and multinational corporations). In the UK most banking for both business and personal customers is undertaken through the High-Street banks, known as **branch banking** (*see also* COMMERCIAL BANK).

Banking Acts (1979; 1987) UK Acts of Parliament defining a bank as a taker of deposits and investing supervision of *deposit-taking institutions in the *Bank of England. The Acts created safeguards to ensure that only fit and proper persons should be allowed to be managers, directors, or controllers of banks. The Acts also stipulate that the paid-up capital reserves of such an institution should be not less than £1 million. The only exceptions to this limit are authorized *building societies, municipal and school banks, and some central or international development banks. The UK legislation was made necessary by the First Banking Directive of the European Community (now the European Union). *See also* LICENSED DEPOSIT TAKER.

Banking Ombudsman *See* FINANCIAL OMBUDSMAN SERVICE.

bank loan (bank advance) A specified sum of money lent by a bank to a customer, usually for a specified time, at a specified rate of interest. In most cases banks require some form of security for loans, especially if the loan is to a commercial enterprise. *See also* LOAN ACCOUNT; OVERDRAFT; PERSONAL LOAN.

bank mandate A document given by a customer of a bank to the bank, requesting that the bank should open an account in the customer's name and honour cheques and other orders for payment drawn on the account. The mandate specifies the signatures that the bank should accept for transactions on the account and also contains specimens of the signatures.

banknote An item of paper currency issued by a central bank. Banknotes developed in England from the receipts issued by London goldsmiths in the 17th century for gold deposited with them for safekeeping. These receipts came to be used as money and their popularity as a *medium of exchange encouraged the goldsmiths to issue their own banknotes, largely to increase their involvement in banking and, particularly, moneylending. Now only the Bank of England and the Scottish and Irish banks in the UK have the right to issue notes. Originally all banknotes were fully backed by gold and could be exchanged on demand for gold; however, since 1931 the promise on a note to "pay the bearer on demand" simply indicates that the note is legal tender. *See also* PROMISSORY NOTE.

Bank of England The central bank of the UK. It was established in 1694 as a private bank by London merchants in order to lend money to the state and to deal with the national debt. It came under public ownership in 1946 with the passing of the Bank of England Act. The Bank of England acts as the government's bank, providing loans through ways and means advances and arranging borrowing through the issue of *gilt-edged securities. The bank helps to implement the government's financial and monetary policy as directed by the Treasury. Since May 1997 its *Monetary Policy Committee has had sole authority for setting the *base rate, which was formerly a joint decision of the Chancellor of the Exchequer and the Governor of the Bank of England (although the Chancellor retains the right to overrule the Governor in exceptional circumstances). It formerly had wide statutory powers to supervise the banking system, including the commercial banks, but these supervisory powers have now passed to the *Financial Services Authority. The bank, however, retains its responsibility

for systemic stability and that of *lender of last resort.

The Bank Charter Act 1844 divided the bank into an issue department and a banking department. The issue department is responsible for the issue of banknotes and coins as supplied by the *Royal Mint. The banking department provides banking services (including accounts) to commercial banks, foreign banks, other central banks, and government departments. The bank manages the national debt, acting as registrar of government stocks. It also manages the *exchange equalization account. The bank is controlled by a governor, two deputy governors, and a court (board) of 16 directors.

Bank of England Stock Register The register of holders of government stocks (*see* GILT-EDGED SECURITY) maintained by the *Bank of England. Purchases and sales of government stocks made by stockbrokers and banks are recorded on this register. Income tax on interest paid on these stocks is deducted at source, unlike stocks on the *National Savings Stock Register.

Bank of Japan The Japanese central bank, which controls monetary policy but does not regulate Japanese banks.

bank rate *See* BASE RATE.

bank reconciliation statement A statement that reconciles the bank balance in the books of an organization with the *bank statement. Differences may be due to cheques drawn by the organization but not yet presented to the bank, bank charges deducted from the account not yet notified to the organization, and payments made to the bank but not yet recorded by the organization. Bank reconciliations are usually performed weekly or monthly and are a form of internal control check.

bankruptcy The state of individuals who are unable to pay their debts and against whom a **bankruptcy order** has been made by a court. The order deprives bankrupts of their property, which is then used to pay their debts. See feature BANKRUPTCY LAW on p. 51.

Bankruptcy Reform Act (1978) A US law that brought about major changes to bankruptcy law after 40 years of the previ-

BANKRUPTCY LAW

Bankruptcy proceedings are started by a **bankruptcy petition**, which may be presented to the court by
  (1) a creditor or creditors;
  (2) a person affected by a *voluntary arrangement to pay debts set up by the debtor under the Insolvency Act (1986);
  (3) the Director of Public Prosecutions; or
  (4) the debtor.
The grounds for a creditors' petition are that the debtor appears to be unable to pay a debt for which a statutory demand has been made or that a court has ordered him or her to pay. The debt must amount to at least £750. The grounds for a petition by a person bound by a voluntary arrangement are that the debtor has not complied with the terms of the arrangement or has withheld material information. The Director of Public Prosecutions may present a petition in the public interest under the Powers of Criminal Courts Act (1973). The debtor may also present a petition on the grounds of being unable to pay his or her debts.

Once a petition has been presented, the debtor may not dispose of any property. The court may halt any other legal proceedings against the debtor. An interim receiver may be appointed. This will usually be the *official receiver, who will take any necessary action to protect the debtor's estate. A special manager may be appointed if the nature of the debtor's business requires it.

The court may make a **bankruptcy order** at its discretion. Once this has happened, the debtor is an undischarged bankrupt, who is deprived of the ownership of all property and must assist the official receiver in listing it, recovering it, protecting it, etc. The official receiver becomes manager and receiver of the estate until the appointment of a **trustee in bankruptcy**. The bankrupt must prepare a statement of affairs for the official receiver within 21 days of the bankruptcy order. A **public examination** of the bankrupt may be ordered on the application of the official receiver or the creditors, in which the bankrupt will be required to answer questions about his or her affairs in court.

Within 12 weeks the official receiver must decide whether to call a **meeting of creditors** to appoint a trustee in bankruptcy. The trustee's duties are to collect, realize, and distribute the bankrupt's estate. The trustee may be appointed by the creditors, the court, or the Secretary of State and must be a qualified *insolvency practitioner or the official receiver. All the property of the bankrupt is available to pay the creditors, except for the following:
  • equipment necessary for him or her to continue in employment or business;
  • necessary domestic equipment;
  • income required for the reasonable domestic needs of the bankrupt and his or her family.
The court has discretion whether to order sale of a house in which a spouse or children are living.

All creditors must prove their claims to the trustee. Only unsecured claims can be proved in bankruptcy. When all expenses have been paid, the trustee will divide the estate. Legislation sets out the order in which creditors will be paid (*see* PREFERENTIAL CREDITOR).

The bankruptcy may end automatically after two or three years, but in some cases a court order is required. The bankrupt is discharged and receives a certificate of discharge from the court.

ous legislation. The reforms made it easier to file petitions, amended the previous absolute rule giving priority to secured creditors in all cases, and gave federal bankruptcy judges more powers to hear cases. The reforms also added a clause covering tests for ability to pay under chapter 13 of the Bankruptcy Act. Under *chapter 11 a firm can apply to the court for protection from its creditors while it undergoes a reorganization in an attempt to pay its debts.

bank statement A regular record, issued by a bank or building society, showing the credit and debit entries in a customer's cheque account, together with the current balance. The frequency of issue will vary with the customer's needs and the volume of transactions going through the account. Cash dispensers enable customers to ask for a statement whenever one is needed.

bank transfer (bank giro credit; BGC) A method of making payments in which the payer may make a payment at any branch of any bank for the account of a payee with an account at any branch of the same or another bank.

banner advertisement (banner ad) Typically, a rectangular graphic displayed on a web page for purposes of brand building or driving traffic to a site. It is normally possible to perform a *clickthrough to access further information from another website. Banners may be static or animated.

Banque de France The central bank of France. Established in 1800 and nationalized in January 1946, it was granted operational independence in 1993 as a preparation for European Monetary Union. It is now linked to the *European Central Bank.

banques d'affaires The French name for an *investment bank.

BARB Acronym for Broadcasters' Audience Research Board: a joint system for researching BBC and commercial television audiences, established in 1981. The board is responsible for commissioning television audience research, both quantitative (how many watched a particular programme) and qualitative (whether or not

they liked the programme). The data is collected by on-line *audimeters attached to the TV sets of some 3000 private households in the UK. Regional panels vary in size (up to 350 households), according to the size of the population in a television area. The data is downloaded daily. The meter records accurately when the TV is switched on, but does not indicate who is actually watching. Thus the research is supplemented by push button handsets for each member of the household aged over four years, to record when they started and finished watching.

barbell A *portfolio made up predominantly of short- and long-term obligations, notably in bonds. Its name derives from the idea of such a portfolio being 'weighted' at both ends like a barbell or dumb-bell.

bar chart (bar diagram) A chart that presents statistical data by means of rectangles (i.e. bars) of differing heights. For example, the sales figures for a range of products for an accounting period may be presented in this way, the different sizes of the bars enabling the users to see at a glance how each product has performed during the period.

bar code (universal product code; UPC) A code, consisting of an array of parallel rectangular bars and spaces, printed on a package for sale in a retail outlet. When an optical scanner (**bar-code reader**) reads the bar code at the checkout till (see ELECTRONIC POINT OF SALE), the price and description of the goods are displayed on the till screen and the computer-controlled stock record is simultaneously reduced. This also enables the retailer to compile sales volume information.

bareboat charter (demise charter) A form of *chartering a ship in which the expenses incurred during the period of the charter are paid by the hirer, including the hiring of the master and crew, the provision of fuel and stores, etc. All the hirer gets is the ship.

bargain 1. A transaction on the London Stock Exchange. The bargains made during the day are included in the Daily Official List. **2.** A sale made at a specially low price, either as a means of sale promotion or to clear old stock.

barometer stock A security whose performance and price is regarded as an indicator of the overall health of the market. It will be a widely held *blue chip with a stable price record.

barratry Any act committed wilfully by the master or crew of a ship to the detriment of its owner or charterer. Examples include scuttling the ship and embezzling the cargo. Illegal activities (e.g. carrying prohibited persons) leading to the forfeiture of the ship also constitute barratry. Barratry is one of the risks covered by *marine insurance policies.

barrel 1. A unit of capacity used in the oil industry equal to 42 US gallons (35 Imperial gallons). **2.** A unit of capacity used in the brewing industry equal to 36 Imperial gallons.

barrier option See IN-BARRIER OPTION; OUT-BARRIER OPTION.

barriers to entry Factors that prevent competitors from entering a particular market. These factors may be innocent, e.g. an absolute cost advantage on the part of the firm that dominates the market, or deliberate, such as high spending on advertising to make it very expensive for new firms to enter the market and establish themselves. Other entry barriers may result from a firm's technological advantage, often protected by patents, or from a firm's existing access to end users as a result of its control of the distribution network. Barriers to entry reduce the level of competition in a market, i.e. they make it less contestable, thereby by enabling incumbents to charge higher-than-competitive prices. See also LIMIT PRICE.

If a particular market for a product is dominated by a large multinational corporation, barriers to entry for smaller firms may be formidable: the multinational may be able to produce the product more cheaply because of *economies of scale, the existing product may have built up a strong *brand loyalty, the multinational may control the supply of raw material, or own the patent rights to all or part of the production process.

barriers to exit Factors that make it difficult for a company to leave a market that is no longer profitable or that has ceased to provide an acceptable return on capital. For example, the workforce producing the product may not be redeployable, the plant and machinery producing it may be unsaleable, the product may have a niche in the company's product range that would affect sales of the whole range if it was withdrawn, etc.

BARS Abbreviation for *behaviourally anchored rating scales.

barter A method of trading in which goods or services are exchanged without the use of *money. It is a cumbersome system, which severely limits the scope for trade. Money, used as a medium of exchange, enables individuals to trade with each other at much greater distance and through whole chains of intermediaries, which are inconceivable in a barter system. The modern equivalent of barter is known as *countertrading.

base currency The currency used as the basis for an exchange rate, i.e. a foreign currency rate of exchange is quoted per single unit of the base currency, usually US dollars.

base date See BASE YEAR.

base metals The metals copper, lead, zinc, and tin. Compare PRECIOUS METALS. See also LONDON METAL EXCHANGE.

base rate 1. The rate of interest used as a basis by banks for the rates they charge their customers. In practice most customers will pay a premium over base rate on loans and will receive below the base rate on deposits with banks. **2.** An informal name for the rate at which a country's *central bank lends to the banking system, which effectively controls the lending rate throughout the banking system. The abolition of the *minimum lending rate in 1981 heralded a loosening of government control over the banking system, but the need to increase interest rates in the late 1900s (to control inflation and the *balance of payments deficit) led to the use of this term in this sense. In 1997 sole responsibility for setting the base rate was given to the Bank of England. The base rate is more formally known as the **bank rate**.

base stock A certain volume of stock, assumed to be constant in that stock levels are not allowed to fall below this level.

When the stock is valued, this proportion of the stock is valued at its original cost. This method is not normally acceptable for financial accounting purposes.

base-weighted index *See* INDEX NUMBER.

base year (base date) The first of a series of years in an index. The value of the index in that year is often denoted by the number 100, enabling percentage rises (or falls) to be seen at a glance. For example, if a price index indicates that the current value is 190, this will only be meaningful if it is compared to an earlier figure. This may be written: 190 (base year 1987 = 100), making it clear that there has been a 90% increase in prices since 1987.

BASIC Acronym for Beginner's All-purpose Symbolic Instruction Code. BASIC is a popular language used especially to program small computers. It is easy to learn and has been extensively used in teaching programming. A disadvantage is that, over the years, many different versions (dialects) of the language have developed and this has restricted the transfer of programs between different machines. A widely used form, **Visual Basic**, was developed by Microsoft and launched in 1990. This allows the user to produce applications by dragging and dropping controls (e.g. buttons or dialogue boxes) and defining their properties.

basic rate of income tax A rate of income tax between the starting rate and the higher rate. In the UK it is 22%, which is applied to that part of *taxable income in the band £2091 to £32,400 (2005–06). *See also* HIGHER RATE OF INCOME TAX; STARTING RATE OF INCOME TAX.

basing-point pricing A pricing strategy in which the seller designates a particular city as a basing point and charges all customers the freight cost from that city to the customer's location, regardless of the city from which the goods are actually shipped. This strategy tends to be the case in large countries, such as the USA and Australia.

basis of assessment The basis upon which personal income or business profits are assessed in the UK for each *fiscal year. The individual rules for each income-

tax *schedule identify the profits or income to be assessed in that year. These rules are complex and the advice of a tax expert should be sought. The basis of assessment does not necessarily equate to the actual tax year. In the case of a partnership that has been trading for many years, the profits for the year to 30 April 2006, i.e. those arising during the period 1 May 2005 to 30 April 2006, will form the basis of the assessment for the tax year 2006–07. This is known as the *current-year basis of assessment. Other income received during the year, e.g. building society interest received, is assessed on an actual basis and so for 2006–07 the basis of assessment will be the tax year, i.e. the interest received during the year 6 April 2006 to 5 April 2007.

basis point (point) One hundredth of one per cent; this unit is often used in finance when prices involve fine margins. *See also* TICK.

basis swap A *swap in which the payments are based on two variable interest rates. The swap may be either in a single currency or across currencies. *See* CROSS-CURRENCY INTEREST-RATE SWAP; INTEREST-RATE SWAP.

basket of currencies A group of selected currencies used to establish a value for some other unit of currency.

Basle Convergence Accord An agreement reached in 1988 by the *Group of Ten (G10), and enacted through the *Bank for International Settlements, concerning *capital adequacy regulations for banking in G10 countries. It suggested that banks should have specific liabilities to cover a minimum of 8% of their *capital at risk. Capital at risk was defined in terms of a set of multipliers to be attached to a number of different asset classes and multiplied by their balance-sheet worth. The **Basle Market Risk Amendment** (1996) allowed the use of internal risk models based on *value-at-risk in the calculation of a bank's capital at risk. *See also* BASLE TWO.

Basle Two An accord, implemented in 2004, that supplants the *Basle Convergence Accord of 1988. It establishes a new framework for defining *capital at risk and risk weightings, based to a greater extent than previously on credit ratings and internal models. There are also additional requirements for disclosure of risk-related information.

batch costing A form of costing in which the unit costs are expressed on the basis of a batch produced. This is particularly appropriate where the cost per unit of production would result in an infinitesimal unit cost and where homogeneous units of production can conveniently be collected together to form discrete batches. *See* BATCH PRODUCTION.

batch-level activities *See* ACTIVITY.

batch processing A method of processing data, using a computer, in which the programs to be executed are collected together into groups, or batches, for processing. All the information needed to execute the programs is loaded into the computer at the start so that it can work without further intervention. This contrasts with interactive processing, in which information is fed into the computer during processing. Batch processing is used for such tasks as preparing payrolls, maintaining inventory records, and producing reports.

batch production A manufacturing process in which medium to high volumes of similar items are made in batches, rather than continuously, with the product moving from process to process in batches. The key to batch production is the careful scheduling of work to ensure good utilization of capacity and to minimize the capital locked up in work in progress. Examples in which batch production are used include small engineering works and book printers. *See also* BATCH COSTING. *Compare* CONTINUOUS PROCESSING.

bath-tub curve (failure-rate curve) A graph, having the outline shape of a bath tub, in which the failure rate of a piece of machinery is plotted against time (on the horizontal axis). The graph has three phases: a burn-in or start-up phase, during which faults related to installation and assembly are likely to show up quickly; a normal phase, during which the machine will be reliable as long as it is maintained and used within its design parameters; and a wear-out phase, during which the machinery reaches the end of its design

life and parts begin to fail at a rate that makes it uneconomical to repair. The extent of each phase will vary, e.g. a piece of electronic equipment might function perfectly until the moment that it fails. In practical terms, it has no wear-out phase.

baud A unit that measures the rate at which information is transmitted along a communications link. In normal computer usage, it is equivalent to bits per second (*see* BINARY NOTATION). Thus, a 300-band communications link sends 300 bits of information per second.

B2B Abbreviation for business-to-business; denoting direct Internet trading between commercial organizations.

BBA Abbreviation for *British Bankers Association.

BBS Abbreviation for *bulletin board system.

BCAP Abbreviation for British Code of Advertising Practice. *See* ADVERTISING STANDARDS AUTHORITY.

BCG matrix *See* BOSTON MATRIX.

bear A dealer on a stock exchange, currency market, or commodity market who expects prices to fall. A **bear market** is one in which a dealer is more likely to sell securities, currency, or goods than to buy them. A bear may even sell securities, currency, or goods without having them. This is known as selling short or establishing a **bear position**. The bear hopes to close (or cover) such a short position by buying in at a lower price the securities, currency, or goods already sold. The difference between the purchase price and the original sale price represents the successful bear's profit. A concerted attempt to force prices down by one or more bears by sustained selling is called a **bear raid**. In a **bear squeeze**, sellers force prices up against someone known to have a bear position that has to be covered. *Compare* BULL.

bear closing The purchase of securities, currency, or commodities to close an open *bear position. Bear closing can have the effect of firming up a weak market.

bearer A person who presents for payment a cheque or *bill of exchange marked "pay bearer". As a bearer cheque or bill does not require endorsement it is considered a high-risk form of transfer.

bearer security (bearer bond) A security for which proof of ownership is possession of the security certificate; this enables such bonds to be transferred from one person to another without registration. This is unusual as most securities are registered, so that proof of ownership is the presence of the owner's name on the security register. *Eurobonds are bearer securities, enabling their owners to preserve their anonymity, which can have taxation advantages. Bearer bonds are usually kept under lock and key, often deposited in a bank. Dividends are usually claimed by submitting coupons attached to the certificate.

bear hug An approach to the board of a company by another company indicating that an offer is about to be made for their shares. If the target company indicates that it is not against the merger, but wants a higher price, this is known as a **teddy bear hug**.

bear note *See* BULL NOTE.

bear spread A position in the bond market that is long in short-dated securities and short in longer dated securities; it is intended to take advantage of a fall in commodity or security prices. *Compare* BULL SPREAD.

bed and breakfast An operation on the London Stock Exchange in which a shareholder sold a holding one evening and made an agreement with the broker to buy the same holding back again when the market opened the next morning. The object was to establish a loss, which could be set against other profits for calculating capital gains tax. In the event of an unexpected change in the market, the deal was scrapped. Tax changes have made such operations far less attractive, as the time between sale and repurchase must now be more than 30 days for the shareholder to benefit in this way.

behavioural indicators *See* PERFORMANCE MEASUREMENT.

behaviourally anchored rating scales (BARS) A measure used in evaluating the job performance of employees. It involves disaggregating a particular job into its key tasks, identifying a range of possible behaviours that can be displayed by an employee undertaking each task, placing these behaviours on a scale ranging from ineffective to excellent performance, and assessing the jobholder against these scales for each of the tasks. This allows a total profile of job performance to be created for each employee, covering the various dimensions of his or her work. Involving jobholders themselves in the creation of performance scales can afford the BARS method greater validity. *Compare* BEHAVIOURAL OBSERVATION SCALE; MIXED-STANDARD SCALE. *See also* CRITICAL INCIDENT TECHNIQUE.

behavioural observation scale (BOS) A measure used in evaluating the performance of employees, often as part of a formal *performance appraisal. BOS involves a process of identifying the key tasks of a particular job and evaluating how frequently employees exhibit the required behaviour for effective performance. The scores for each of these observed behaviours can then be totalled to produce an overall performance measure. *Compare* BEHAVIOURALLY ANCHORED RATING SCALES; MIXED-STANDARD SCALE. *See also* CRITICAL INCIDENT TECHNIQUE.

behavioural segmentation The process of dividing a market (*see also* MARKET SEGMENTATION) into groups based upon the consumer's knowledge of a product, attitude to it, use for it, or response to it.

behavioural theories of leadership *See* LEADERSHIP THEORIES.

Beige Book The report on the current economic climate prepared by the US Federal Reserve Board ahead of one of the meetings (held eight times a year) of the *Federal Open Market Committee.

bellwether security In the USA, a security considered to be a good guide to the direction in which the market is moving.

below par *See* PAR VALUE.

below-the-line **1.** Denoting entries below the horizontal line on a company's *profit and loss account that separates the entries that establish the profit (or loss) from the entries that show how the profit is distributed or where the funds to finance the loss have come from. **2.** Denoting advertising expenditure in which no commission is payable to an advertising agency. For example, direct mail, exhibitions, point-of-sale material, and free samples are regarded as below-the-line advertising. **3.** Denoting transactions concerned with capital, as opposed to revenue, in national accounts. *Compare* ABOVE-THE-LINE.

benchmarking The process of identifying the best practice in relation to products and processes, both within an industry and outside it, with the object of using this as a guide and reference point for improving the practice of one's own organization. Benchmarking can take place within an organization, when it may form part of a *total quality management (TQM) exercise; in relation to direct competitors, although such organizations may be unwilling to divulge the details of their practices; or in relation to organizations in totally different fields, in which case the main value of the practice is that it forces people to look outside their established patterns of behaviour.

Most of the early work in benchmarking was carried out in manufacturing but the technique is now applied in a wide range of organizations. Typical areas in which benchmarking can be expected to bring benefits to an organization include:

- **Customer satisfaction**. An organization wishing to improve some aspect of its performance (e.g., its website) might ask customers how this compares with that of competitors. By identifying and making improvements the company can expect to improve sales in the long run.
- **Cost reduction**. The benchmarking exercise may identify an area in which the organization has higher costs than competitors. Potential savings may be identified, such as reducing the number of suppliers or making better use of technology. Benchmarking can be applied to all departments.
- **Increased efficiency and effectiveness**. Benchmarking can help to streamline processes and identify ways of delivering a better service.

Before introducing benchmarking an organization will have to identify the costs of the exercise and the potential benefits and cost savings. The most significant cost will be the management time.

benchmark job A job that is used as a guide or reference point in setting remuneration packages for other jobs. To be suitable for this purpose a job should be well known within the industry, have a level of pay that is generally considered fair, and occupy a key point on the *job evaluation scale that is being used. Benchmark jobs play a key role in the *classification method and *factor-comparison method of job evaluation.

beneficial interest The right to the use and enjoyment of property, rather than to its bare legal ownership. For example, if property is held in trust, the trustee has the legal title but the beneficiaries have the beneficial interest in equity. The beneficiaries, not the trustee, are entitled to any income from the property and will be taxed on this income and any chargeable gain arising if the property is sold.

beneficiary 1. A person for whose benefit a *trust exists. **2.** A person who benefits under a will. **3.** A person who receives money from the proceeds of a *letter of credit. **4.** A person who receives payment at the conclusion of a transaction, e.g. a retailer who has been paid by a customer by means of a *credit card.

benefit segmentation The process of dividing a market (*see* MARKET SEGMENTATION) according to the specific benefits consumers seek from a product. For example, some car buyers want comfort and reliability from their car, while others look for style and speed. A car manufacturer, therefore, has to decide which benefits to offer.

benefits in kind Benefits other than cash arising from employment. The UK tax legislation seeks to assess all earnings to tax, whether they be in the form of cash or in kind. The treatment of benefits depends on the level of total earnings, including the value of any benefits, and whether the employee is a director of a company. The general rule is to value benefits at their cash equivalent although some specific benefits (e.g. company cars) are subject to specific valuation rules. For employees earning less than £8500, the benefits are only assessable if they are living accommodation or if they are capable of being turned into cash, such as credit tokens. For all *directors or higher-paid employees (i.e. employees with total earnings, including benefits, in excess of £8500) the benefits must be reported on form P11D by the employer at the end of the *fiscal year. This form will include details of company cars and associated fuel provided by the employer, beneficial loans, mobile telephones or laptop computers, medical insurance provided by the employer, subscriptions paid, and any costs paid on the employee's behalf. These benefits will be assessed to tax. This often takes the form of a restriction to the *income tax code. See also FRINGE BENEFITS.

benefit taxation A form of taxation in which taxpayers pay tax according to the amounts of benefit that they receive from the system. Such a system of taxation is, in practice, very difficult to apply unless specific charges are made for specific services, as with metered water charges. Compare ABILITY TO PAY.

Benelux An association of countries in western Europe, consisting of Belgium, the Netherlands, and Luxembourg. Apart from geographical proximity these countries have particularly close economic interests, recognized in their 1947 *customs union. In 1958 the Benelux countries joined the *European Economic Community.

Berne Union The informal name for the International Union of Credit and Investment Insurers, an association of credit insurers from the main industrial countries. Its main function is to facilitate an exchange of information, especially over credit terms. The *Export Credits Guarantee Department of the UK government is a member.

beta coefficient A measure of the volatility of a share. A share with a high beta coefficient is likely to respond to stock market movements by rising or falling in value by more than the market average. It is thus a measure of the *systematic risk associated with a particular security. See also ALPHA COEFFICIENT; CAPITAL ASSET PRICING MODEL.

beta version A preliminary version of a product or service often provided free. The purpose of releasing the beta version is to allow selected customers to preview the product and provide valuable feedback to the organization. See also ALPHA-RELEASE STAGE.

BEXA Abbreviation for *British Exporters Association.

BGC Abbreviation for bank giro credit. See BANK TRANSFER.

bid **1.** The price at which a buyer is willing to close a deal. If the seller has made an *offer that the buyer considers too high, the buyer may make a bid at a lower price (or on more advantageous terms). Having received a bid, the seller may accept it, withdraw, or make a counteroffer. **2.** The price or yield at which a buyer indicates that he or she is willing to buy a financial obligation. See BID PRICE. **3.** An approach by one company to buy the share capital of another. See TAKEOVER BID.

bid–offer spread The difference between an *offer price and the *bid price.

bid price The price at which a *market maker will buy shares: the lower of the two figures quoted on the screens of the *Stock Exchange Automated Quotations System, the higher being the *offer price. Some dealers prefer to rely on the figure quoted, others prefer to haggle over the price.

bid rate Short for *London Inter Bank Bid Rate (LIBID).

BIFFEX Acronym for Baltic International Freight Futures Exchange. See BALTIC EXCHANGE.

bifurcation The divestment of part of a business to improve the strategic focus of the remaining part.

Big Bang The upheaval on the *London Stock Exchange (LSE) when major changes in operation were introduced on 27 October, 1986. The major changes enacted on that date were: (a) the abolition of LSE rules enforcing a dual-capacity system; (b) the abolition of fixed commission rates charged by *stockbrokers to their clients. The measures were introduced by the LSE in return for an undertaking by the government (given in 1983) that they would not prosecute the LSE under the Restrictive Trade Practices Act. Since 1986 the Big

Bang has also been associated with the *globalization and modernization of the London securities market.

Big Board Colloquial name for the *New York Stock Exchange, on which the stocks of the largest corporations in the USA are traded. *Compare* LITTLE BOARD.

Big Four 1. The major High-Street or *commercial banks in the UK: Barclays (now incorporating the Woolwich), Lloyds TSB, HSBC (formerly Midland), and NatWest (now owned by the Royal Bank of Scotland). In terms of market capitalization the four were joined in the 1990s by Abbey National (now Abbey) and the Halifax (now HBOS following its merger with the Bank of Scotland), which changed their status from *building societies to banks. **2.** The four largest firms of accountants in the world, i.e. Deloitte and Touche, Ernst and Young, KPMG, and Price WaterhouseCooper. **3.** In Japan, the four largest securities houses: Daiwa, Nikko, Nomura, and Yamaichi.

bilateral bank facility A *facility provided by a bank to a corporate customer. The agreement is restricted to the two parties, which enables a relationship to develop between the bank and the customer (*see* RELATIONSHIP BANKING). *Compare* SYNDICATED BANK FACILITY.

bilateral contract A contract that creates mutual obligations, i.e. both parties undertake to do, or refrain from doing, something in exchange for the other party's undertaking. The majority of contracts are bilateral in nature. *Compare* UNILATERAL CONTRACT.

bilateral monopoly A situation in which a *monopoly seller bargains with a monopoly buyer (*see* MONOPSONY). The classic application of bilateral monopoly is to the negotiation of wages between a union and a firm. The most famous solution (1950) is that stated by John Nash, which suggests that both sides will settle for the wage that maximizes the benefits from cooperation.

bilateral netting 1. An agreement between two counterparties that mutual obligations will be settled by a single payment. **2.** A method of reducing bank charges in which two related companies

offset their receipts and payments with each other, usually monthly. In this way a single payment and receipt is made for the period instead of a number, which saves on both transaction costs and paperwork. *See also* MULTILATERAL NETTING.

bilateral trade agreement An agreement on trade policy between two countries, usually concerning a reduction in tariffs or other protective barriers. Although bilateral deals tend to fragment world trade, governments are attracted by their relative simplicity. The USA, in particular, has used such deals in free-trade agreements with Mexico and Canada and to hasten the resolution of problems with particular trading partners, notably Japan and other Asian countries.

bill broker (discount broker) A broker who trades in *bills of exchange.

billion Formerly, one thousand million (10^9) in the USA and one million million (10^{12}) in the UK; now it is almost universally taken to be one thousand million.

bill-me-later A facility offered by some suppliers of goods or services, who agree to give their customers credit by sending an invoice after the goods have been delivered. This facility eases an organization's *cash flow.

bill of entry A detailed statement of the nature and value of a consignment of goods prepared by the shipper of the consignment for *customs entry.

bill of exchange An unconditional order in writing, addressed by one person (the drawer) to another (the drawee) and signed by the person giving it, requiring the drawee to pay on demand or at a fixed or determinable future time a specified sum of money to or to the order of a specified person (the payee) or to the bearer. If the bill is payable at a future time the drawee signifies *acceptance, which makes the drawee the party primarily liable upon the bill; the drawer and endorsers may also be liable upon a bill. The use of bills of exchange enables one person to transfer to another an enforceable right to a sum of money. A bill of exchange is not only transferable but also negotiable, since, if a person without an enforceable right to the money transfers a bill to a *holder in due course, the latter obtains a good title to it. If the drawee or acceptor of the bill is a bank, the bill is known as a *bank bill or in the USA as a *banker's acceptance. If it is a trader, it is called a **trade acceptance**. These bills have a standard 90 days to maturity and their attractiveness will depend on whether they are eligible for rediscounting at the central bank. *See* ACCOMMODATION BILL; BILLS IN A SET; DISHONOUR.

bill of lading A document acknowledging the shipment of a consignor's goods for carriage by sea. It is used primarily when the ship is carrying goods belonging to a number of consignors (a general ship). In this case, each consignor receives a bill issued (normally by the master of the ship) on behalf of either the shipowner or a charterer under a charterparty. The bill serves three functions: it is a receipt for the goods; it summarizes the terms of the contract of carriage; and it acts as a document of title to the goods. A bill of lading is also issued by a shipowner to a charterer who is using the ship for the carriage of his or her own goods. In this case, the terms of the contract of carriage are in the charterparty and the bill serves only as a receipt and a document of title. During transit, ownership of the goods may be transferred by delivering the bill to another if it is drawn to bearer or by endorsing it if it is drawn to order. It is not, however, a negotiable instrument. The bill gives details of the goods; if the packages are in good order a **clean bill** is issued; if they are not, the bill will say so (*see* DIRTY BILL OF LADING). *See also* CONTAINERIZATION.

bill of materials (BOM) 1. A document listing all the materials required to produce a range of products, including all the components and their relevant quantities, the order in which they are assembled, and the *work centres that perform the assembly. The BOM is one of the main inputs into the *material requirements planning (MRP) system; in fact, the success of MRP depends on accurate BOMs. Their reliability has been improved by the use of *computer-aided design systems linked to *inventory status records. **2.** *See* BILL OF QUANTITIES.

bill of quantities (bill of materials) A document drawn up by a quantity surveyor showing in detail the materials and parts required to build a structure (e.g. factory, house, office block), together with the price of each component and the labour costs. The bill of quantities is one of the tender documents that goes out to contractors who wish to quote for carrying out the work.

bill of sale 1. A document by which a person transfers the ownership of goods to another. Commonly the goods are transferred conditionally, as security for a debt, and a **conditional bill of sale** is thus a mortgage of goods. The mortgagor has a right to redeem the goods on repayment of the debt and usually remains in possession of them; the mortgagor may thus obtain false credit by appearing to own them. An **absolute bill of sale** transfers ownership of the goods absolutely. The Bills of Sale Acts (1878; 1882) regulate the registration and form of bills of sale. **2.** A document recording the change of ownership when a ship is sold; it is regarded internationally as legal proof of ownership.

bill of sight A document that an importer, who is unable fully to describe an imported cargo, gives to the Customs and Excise authorities to authorize them to inspect the goods on landing. After the goods have been landed and the importer supplies the missing information the entry is completed and the importer is said to have **perfected the sight**.

bill of sufferance A document issued by the Customs and Excise enabling goods to be landed in the absence of detailed documentation, subject to the Customs being able to examine the goods at any time.

bill rate (discount rate) The rate on the *discount market at which *bills of exchange are discounted (i.e. purchased for less than they are worth when they mature). The rate will depend on the quality of the bill and the risk the purchaser takes. First-class bills, i.e. those backed by banks or well-respected finance houses, will be discounted at a lower rate than bills involving greater risk.

bills in a set One of two, or more usually three, copies of a foreign bill of exchange. Payment is made on any one of the three, the others becoming invalid on the payment of any one of them. All are made out in the same way, except that each refers to the others. The first copy is called the **first of exchange**, the next is the **second of exchange**, and so on. The duplication or triplication is to reduce the risk of loss in transit.

bills payable 1. The amounts owed by a business to its *creditors, such as trade suppliers. **2.** An item that may appear in a firm's accounts under current liabilities, summarizing the *bills of exchange being held, which will have to be paid when they mature.

bills receivable 1. The amounts owed to a business by its *debtors, i.e. its customers. **2.** An item that may appear in a firm's accounts under current assets, summarizing the *bills of exchange being held until the funds become available when they mature.

bill stuffer Any type of promotional material inserted into an envelope with an invoice or statement in order to save on postage. *See also* FREE RIDE.

BIM Abbreviation for *British Institute of Management.

BIMBO Acronym for buy-in management buy-out: a form of *management buy-out in which management invests in the venture together with outsider venture capitalists, who have more managerial control than is usual with a management buy-out.

binary notation A way of writing numbers using two symbols only. The symbols are usually written as 0 and 1, and called **binary digits** or **bits**. These bits are usually grouped in eights, called *bytes. Numbers written in binary notation are generally much longer than their decimal equivalents. For example, the binary number 1111 is equivalent to the decimal number 15. In a binary number the columns from the right represent 'units', 'twos', 'fours', 'eights', and so on. Binary notation is used in computing because digital computers represent numbers in terms of the presence (1) or absence (0) of an electrical pulse.

binary option (all-or-nothing option; cash-or-nothing option; digital option) An *exotic option in which the payoff is either a given value or nothing.

bin card (store card) A card attached to each site or bin in which individual items of *stock are stored to record the receipts, issues, and balances of each item of stock in units. The bin card balance should indicate the physical stock available at any time; regular reconciliations with the physical quantities should be made to ensure accuracy.

bingo card (reader service card) A reply card bound into a publication, which readers can complete to request further information or samples from companies that have either advertised or been referred to in the publication.

binomial process A process consisting of several stages, at each one of which there are two possible outcomes with separate probabilities. In finance, models based on binomial processes are used to consider the value of financial obligations, most notably certain option-pricing models. They are also sometimes used in decision making.

biodata In *personnel selection, items of biographical information about the candidates for a job that can be objectively assessed, e.g. qualifications, years of experience, positions of responsibility, etc. Each candidate is scored on the answers given and those whose total scores fall below a certain level are eliminated. This can be an effective way of selecting a short list. *See* STANDARD APPLICATION BLANK.

biological assets *Assets that are living plants or animals, such as trees in a plantation or orchard, cultivated plants, sheep and cattle, etc. The term was introduced in *International Accounting Standard 41, Agriculture, which became operative for annual financial statements covering periods beginning on or after 1 January 2003.

birr (Br) The standard monetary unit of Ethiopia, divided into 100 cents.

BIS Abbreviation for *Bank for International Settlements.

bit Abbreviation for binary digit. *See* BINARY NOTATION.

BlackBerry *Trademark* A type of *PDA. First released in 1999, it became very popular with business people and others because it can be used for wireless e-mail.

black box An element in a system that is effectively opaque to those observing it. Inputs enter one end of the box and emerge, transformed, at the other. In terms of controlling the system, this may be perfectly adequate, however complex the processes might be within the element. The black box may be used as a way of representing the unobservable psychological processes that underlie a consumer's decision making. Researchers must focus on the input to and the output from the black box, as they are unable to observe the processes within it.

black economy Economic activity that is undisclosed, as to disclose it would render the earnings involved liable to taxation or even cause those engaged to be imprisoned (if they are claiming state benefits and have lied about their earnings). The black economy is thought to be significant in many countries, largely due to the benefits of evading tax. Earnings made in the black economy do not appear in national statistics.

black knight A person or firm that makes an unwelcome *takeover bid for a company. *Compare* GREY KNIGHT; WHITE KNIGHT.

blackleg **1.** An employee who refuses to join a trade union. **2.** An employee who refuses to strike when an official strike has been declared.

black market An illegal market for a particular good or service. It can occur when regulations control a particular trade (as in arms dealing) or a particular period (as in wartime). *Compare* GREY MARKET.

Black Monday Either of the two Mondays on which the two largest stock market crashes of the 20th century occurred. The original Wall Street crash occurred on Monday, 28 October 1929, when the *Dow Jones Industrial Average fell by 13%. On Monday, 19 October 1987, the Dow Jones Average lost 23%. In both cases Black Monday in the USA triggered heavy stock market falls around the world.

Black Wednesday Wednesday, 16 September 1992, when sterling left the Exchange Rate Mechanism, which led to a 15% fall in its value against the Deutschmark (*see* EUROPEAN MONETARY SYSTEM). Because of the improved economic performance of the UK following the event, it is also known as **White Wednesday**.

Blake–Mouton managerial grid A model in which the *leadership style of a manager is described on two dimensions: concern for production and concern for people. Leadership behaviour is measured on a 9-point scale along each dimension, so that there are a total of 81 possible styles. These range from laissez-faire (production 1, people 1) to authoritarian (production 9, people 1) and country club (production 1, people 9), with the optimum score (production 9, people 9) representing true team leadership. The Blake–Mouton grid has often been used as the basis for organizational interventions designed to improve the performance of managers on both dimensions (a **grid organizational development**). It was devised by the US psychologists Robert R. Blake and Jane S. Mouton. *See also* RELATIONSHIP-MOTIVATED; TASK-MOTIVATED.

blank bill A *bill of exchange in which the name of the payee is left blank.

blank cheque *See* CHEQUE.

blank endorsed *See* ENDORSEMENT.

blanket policy An insurance policy that covers a number of items but has only one total sum insured and no insured sums for individual items. The policy can be of any type, e.g. covering a fleet of vehicles or a group of buildings.

blank transfer A share transfer form in which the name of the transferee and the transfer date are left blank. The form is signed by the registered holder of the shares so that the holder of the blank transfer has only to fill in the missing details to become the registered owner of the shares. Blank transfers can be deposited with a bank, when shares are being used as a security for a loan. A blank transfer can also be used when shares are held by *nominees, the beneficial owner holding the blank transfer.

blind testing A marketing-research technique in which unidentified products are tested by consumers in order to determine their preference. It is often used to test a new product against an established product, especially one with a strong market position.

blind trust A trust that administers the private financial affairs of a person in public office without informing him or her of the transactions entered into, so that there can be no conflict of interest. *See also* ARM'S LENGTH.

blocked account A bank account from which money cannot be withdrawn for any of a number of reasons, the most likely being that the affairs of the holder of the account are in the hands of a receiver owing to *bankruptcy, or *liquidation in the case of a company. A bank account held in another country may be blocked owing to *exchange controls (*see* BLOCKED CURRENCY).

blocked currency A currency that cannot be removed from a country as a result of *exchange controls. Trading usually takes place in such currencies at a discount through brokers specializing in blocked-currency trading, who convert it to other funds for importers and exporters with blocked currency accounts.

Bloomberg A US-based financial information service.

blow-in card A loose card (usually providing reply facilities) inserted into a publication for advertising purposes.

blue chip Colloquial name for any of the ordinary shares in the most highly regarded companies traded on a stock market. Originating in the USA, the name comes from the colour of the highest value chip used in poker. Blue-chip companies have a well-known name, a good growth record, and large assets. The main part of an institution's equity portfolio will consist of blue chips.

blue-collar worker A manual worker, normally one working on the shop floor, as opposed to an office worker, who is known as a *white-collar worker. The blue collar refers to the blue overalls often worn in factories and the white collar to the normal office attire of a white shirt and a tie.

blueprinting The detailed modelling of the production process for a new product

or service, using *flow charts, *computer-aided design, or trial plants.

blue-sky law In the USA, a law providing for state regulation and supervision for issuing investment securities in that state. It includes broker licensing and the registration of new issues.

Board of Customs and Excise A small number of higher civil servants responsible for collecting and administering customs and excise duties and *VAT. The Commissioners of Customs were first appointed in 1671 by Charles II; the Excise department, formerly part of the Inland Revenue Department, was merged with the Customs in 1909. The Customs and Excise have an investigation division responsible for preventing and detecting evasions of revenue laws and for enforcing restrictions on the importation of certain goods (e.g. arms, drugs, etc.). Their statistical office compiles overseas trade statistics from customs import and export documents. In September 2004 the Board merged with the *Board of Inland Revenue, thereby bringing it under the direct control of the Treasury.

board of directors *See* DIRECTOR.

Board of Inland Revenue A small number of higher civil servants responsible to the Treasury for the administration and collection of the principal direct taxes in the UK, but not the indirect VAT and excise duties. They are responsible for income tax, capital gains tax, corporation tax, inheritance tax, petroleum revenue tax, and stamp duties. The agency responsible for collecting *National Insurance contributions became an executive office of the Inland Revenue in April 1999. Under the Taxes Management Act (1970), they are under a duty to appoint inspectors and collectors of taxes who, in turn, act under the direction of the board. They also advise on new legislation and prepare statistical information. In September 2004 the Board of Inland Revenue and the *Board of Customs and Excise merged to form **HM Revenue and Customs**.

body corporate A *corporation consisting of a body of persons legally authorized to act as one person, while being distinct from that person. For example, the shareholders of a company are separate from the company. *See* ARTIFICIAL PERSON.

BOGOF Acronym for *buy one get one free*.

boilerplate A copy intended for use in making other copies. It is sometimes used to describe a group of instructions that is incorporated in different places in a computer program or the detailed standard form of words used in a contract, guarantee, etc.

boiler room A colloquial name for a *bucket shop that specializes in selling securities over the telephone.

bolívar (B) The standard monetary unit of Venezuela, divided into 100 céntimos.

boliviano ($b) The standard monetary unit of Bolivia, divided into 100 centavos.

BOM Abbreviation for *bill of materials.

bona fide In good faith, honestly, without collusion or fraud. A bona fide purchaser for value without notice is a person who has bought property in good faith, without being aware of prior claims to it (for example, that it is subject to a trust). The purchaser will not be bound by those claims, unless (if the property is land) they were registered.

bona vacantia Goods without an apparent owner. An example could be the possessions of a person with no living relatives who has died intestate. The Crown is entitled to any personal property without an apparent owner. The prerogative may also be extended to real estate by the doctrine of **escheat**, the return of ownerless land to the superior landowner.

bond An IOU issued by a borrower to a lender. Bonds usually take the form of *fixed-interest securities issued by governments, local authorities, or companies. However, bonds come in many forms: with fixed or variable rates of interest, redeemable or irredeemable, short- or long-term, secured or unsecured, and marketable or unmarketable. Fixed-interest payments are usually made twice a year but may alternatively be credited at the end of the agreement (typically 5 to 10 years). The borrower repays a specific sum of money plus the face value (par) of the bond. Most bonds are unsecured and do not grant shares in an organization (*see*

DEBENTURE). Bonds are usually sold against loans, mortgages, credit-card income, etc., as marketable securities. A discount bond is one sold below its face value; a premium bond is one sold above par. *See also* EUROBOND; INCOME BOND; PREMIUM BONDS. *Compare* NOTE.

bonded goods Imported goods on which neither customs duty nor excise have been paid although the goods are dutiable. They are stored in a *bonded warehouse until the duty has been paid or the goods re-exported.

bonded warehouse A warehouse, usually close to a sea port or airport, in which goods that attract customs duty or excise are stored after being imported, pending payment of the duty or the re-export of the goods. The owners of the warehouse are held responsible for ensuring that the goods remain in bond until the duty is paid; they may only be released in the presence of a customs officer.

bond note A document, signed by an officer of the Customs and Excise, that enables goods to be released from a bonded warehouse, usually for re-export.

bond risk The *risk associated with holding bonds, which falls into two categories. In *interest-rate risk, the value of a bond falls if the rate of interest rises; in *credit risk, the rating of the bond may deteriorate, payments may be delayed, or the bond may default.

bond washing *See* DIVIDEND STRIPPING.

bonus 1. An extra payment made to employees by management, usually as a reward for good work, to compensate for something (e.g. dangerous work) or to share out the profits of a good year's trading. **2.** An extra amount of money additional to the proceeds, which is distributed to a policyholder by an insurer who has made a profit on the investment of a life-assurance fund. Only holders of *with-profits policies are entitled to a share in these profits and the payment of this bonus is conditional on the life assurer having surplus funds after claims, costs, and expenses have been paid in a particular year. **3.** Any extra or unexpected payment. *See also* NO-CLAIM BONUS; REVERSIONARY BONUS; TERMINAL BONUS.

bonus dividend A *dividend issued to a shareholder in addition to those expected. Typically, two dividends are issued each year. If an additional dividend is paid to shareholders, perhaps because of a takeover, this is known as a bonus dividend.

bonus rate The total rate of return on a *with-profits policy, including the *terminal bonus or any other bonuses paid by the insurance company.

bonus shares (bonus issue) Shares issued to the existing shareholders of a company following a *scrip issue. The number of shares received depends on the level of the shareholding prior to the bonus issue. The number of bonus shares is usually one share for a specified number of shares held before the issue. For example, if the specified number is four this would be denoted as a 1:4 bonus issue. It is also possible to have a 2:1 bonus, when two shares are issued for every one held.

book **1.** The totality of the purchases and sales that make up the *position of a trader on financial markets. The terms **long book**, **short book**, and **open book** are used synonymously with *long position, *short position, and *open position. **2.** To record an item in the accounts, usually a sale. **3.** Short for *book value.

book-keeping The keeping of the *books of account of a business. The records kept enable a *profit and loss account and the *balance sheet to be compiled. Most firms now use *business software packages of programs to enable the books to be kept by computer.

book of prime entry A book or record in which certain types of transaction are recorded before becoming part of the *double-entry book-keeping system. The most common books of prime entry are the *day book, the *cash book, and the *journal.

books of account The *ledgers, *journals, and other accounting records in which a business records its transactions. If the business is a limited company the accounting records must show in sufficient detail the position of the company at any time. See STATUTORY BOOKS.

book value **1.** See NET BOOK VALUE.

2. (net asset value) The value of a company calculated as that of its total assets less *intangible assets and *liabilities. The information required to calculate the book value is all in the *balance sheet. However, it can be very misleading to measure value on this basis, as assets (stocks, buildings, land) are historical accounting figures. The book value of a company is often compared to its *market value, particularly as a means of valuing intangible assets (see INTELLECTUAL CAPITAL). Coca-Cola and Dell Computers are examples of companies whose book value is 10% or less of the market value. The **market-to-book ratio** is calculated by taking current market price per share and dividing by the book value per share. This ratio indicates management's success in creating value for its shareholders, with a high ratio being preferred. The ratio can be compared over time and against other companies. See also NET ASSETS; NET WORTH.

boom The part of the *business cycle that follows a recovery, in which the economy is working at full capacity. Demand, prices, and wages rise, while unemployment falls. If government control of the economy is not sufficiently tight a boom can lead to a recession and ultimately to a slump.

bootstrap **1.** A *leveraged buy-out, especially one involving a *two-tier tender offer to shareholders of the target company. Multiple price offers are not permitted in the UK, but they are in some other countries, notably Germany and the USA. **2.** A company that is started up with very little capital, the intention being that costs will be met out of operating revenues. **3.** A technique enabling a computer to load a program of instructions. Before computer hardware can function, a program must be loaded into it. However, as a program is needed in the computer to enable it to load a program, preliminary instructions are stored permanently in the computer making it possible for longer programs to be accepted.

borrowing costs Costs that are incurred when an organization borrows money. Interest payments are an example of borrowing costs. In accounting, borrowing costs may be recognized as an expense when incurred or capitalized as part of the cost of an asset. For listed companies in the EU, the treatment of borrowing costs is now governed by *International Accounting Standard 23, Capitalization of Borrowing Costs.

borsa An Italian stock exchange.

Börse A German stock exchange.

BOS Abbreviation for *behavioural observation scale.

Boston matrix (BCG matrix) A means of analysing and categorizing the performance of business units in large diversified firms by reference to market share and growth rates. It was developed by the Boston Consultancy Group (BCG), a leading firm of strategic consultants. Four main categories are displayed in a two-dimensional matrix, which seeks to identify those business units that generate cash and those that use it, and then to relate the position of the business units to the formulation of an overall business strategy. The Boston matrix has also been applied to a company's product range so that an overall product development strategy can be implemented.

Market Share

		High	Low
Market Growth Rate	High	STAR	QUESTION MARK
	Low	CASH COW	DOG

Boston matrix

- **Cash Cows**: mature businesses or products with a high market share but low growth rate. Typically, most fixed investment has already been made and a substantial cash flow is generated, the surplus being used to develop and support other businesses or products requiring higher levels of investment and marketing support.
- **Stars**: businesses or products with a high rate of growth, which are often able to generate sufficient cash to fund the high investment necessary to meet increasing demand. As the market matures, such businesses or products should be managed in order to become future cash cows.

- **Question Marks** (or **Problem Children**): although operating in a growth market, the low market share is likely to mean that these business units are unable to sustain the required level of investment needed in order to try and turn them into stars. Competitor pressures may result in such a business or product becoming a dog.
- **Dogs**: the combination of low growth rate and market share is typical of these businesses and products, which operate in mature markets. Firms frequently face strategic decisions regarding whether to continue to support dogs or to implement a divestment strategy. *Barriers to exit would also need to be considered.

bottleneck *See* CAPACITY.

bottom An old mercantile name for a ship, which still occurs in references to shipments of cargo being "made in one bottom" (i.e. in the same ship) and in bottomry bonds (*see* HYPOTHECATION).

bottom fishing The practice of seeking out very low-priced shares to invest in, or of waiting until the market as a whole is low before investing, in the hope of making a profit when prices rise.

bottom line The profit figure used as the earnings figure in the *earnings-per-share calculation of a company. The introduction of *Financial Reporting Standard (FRS) 3, Reporting Financial Performance, in October 1992 amended the regulations in *Statement of Standard Accounting Practice 3, Earnings per Share, to include *extraordinary items in the bottom-line earnings figure. Further changes to the calculation and disclosure of earnings per share were introduced by FRS 14, Earnings per Share, and its successor FRS 22, Earnings Per Share. These have reduced the significance of the concept. *See also* ABOVE-THE-LINE.

bottomry bond *See* HYPOTHECATION.

bottom-up design An approach to product design based on research into the specific requirements of users, rather than on general design principles or existing models. *Compare* TOP-DOWN DESIGN.

bottom-up planning An approach to planning based on an awareness of what is feasible at the shop-floor level. Ideally, planning an organizational strategy should be an iterative process involving both a strategic awareness of market requirements and an operational awareness of organizational capabilities. Just as operations must be able to respond to opportunities identified by marketing, so marketing and the strategic decision makers should be able to respond to improved capabilities generated by operations.

bought day book *See* PURCHASE DAY BOOK.

bought deal 1. A method of raising capital for acquisitions or other purposes, used by listed companies as an alternative to a *rights issue or *placing. The company invites *market makers or banks to bid for new shares, selling them to the highest bidder, who then sells them to the rest of the market in the expectation of making a profit. Bought deals originated in the USA and are becoming increasingly popular in the UK, although they remain controversial as they violate the principle of *pre-emption rights. *See also* VENDOR PLACING. **2.** A *management buy-out or one in which the finance is obtained from a single institution.

bought ledger *See* PURCHASE LEDGER.

bought note *See* CONTRACT NOTE.

bounce back A technique for increasing sales by 'bouncing back' a further promotional offer to customers when fulfilling an order given in response to an earlier promotion.

boundaryless organization An organization in which there has been a concerted attempt by managers to break down (1) the internal barriers that separate different levels in the hierarchy, different functions (e.g. manufacturing and marketing), and different departments; and (2) the external barriers between the organization and its suppliers, customers, and even its competitors. Becoming boundaryless normally involves the creation of cross-functional teams, *delayering, and *empowerment of employees.

bounded rationality The type of rationality that most people (or organizations) resort to when faced with complex decisions in fast-moving, real-life situations

where perfect information is unavailable. Given these constraints, decision makers will be content to find an alternative that gives satisfactory profits rather than one that maximizes profits. The concept of bounded rationality is thus a corrective to the assumption of many economic theories that economic agents make ideally rational decisions to optimize their self-interest. *See* SATISFICING BEHAVIOUR.

bourse The French name for a *stock exchange (from the French *bourse*, purse). 'The Bourse' usually refers to the stock exchange in Paris (*see* PARIS BOURSE), but some other stock markets are also known by this name, e.g. the Bourse de Genève, the Bourse de Luxembourg, and the Bourse de Montréal. In Belgium, the term denotes foreign-exchange dealing.

boutique 1. An office, usually with a shop front and located in a shopping parade, that offers financial advice to investors, often on a walk-in basis. **2.** Specialist investment bankers, who cover a particular sector of the market, e.g. management buy-outs, acquisitions, etc.

box spread A combination of call and put *options held at the same *exercise price.

boycott To refuse to supply a customer or potential customer with one's products or to refuse to buy the products of a particular supplier, usually for commercial rather than political reasons. *Compare* EMBARGO.

BPR Abbreviation for *business process re-engineering.

bracket indexation A change in the upper and lower limits of any particular *taxation bracket in line with an index of inflation. This is needed in times of inflation to avoid fiscal drag (the tax system collecting unduly large amounts of tax).

BRAD Acronym for *British Rates and Data*.

brainstorming A group discussion in order to invoke ideas and solve business problems. No idea is rejected, no matter how irrelevant it appears, until it has been thoroughly discussed and evaluated. A major rule of brainstorming is that the discussion of ideas should not be inhibited. *Compare* DELPHI TECHNIQUE.

branch accounting An accounting system in which each department or branch of a business is established as a separate *cost centre or *budget centre. The net profit per branch may be added together to arrive at the profit for the whole business. **Branch accounts** may be prepared to show the performance of both a main trading centre (i.e. the head office) and subsidiary trading centres (i.e. branches) but with all the accounting records being maintained by head office. Alternatively, **separate entity branch accounts** are prepared in which branches maintain their own records, which are later combined with head-office records to prepare accounts for the whole business.

brand (brand name) A tradename used to identify a specific product, manufacturer, or distributor. The sale of most branded products began in the UK at the turn of the century; some, such as Bovril (Trademark) and Horlicks (Trademark), were mid-Victorian when manufacturers wanted to distinguish their goods from those of their competitors. As consumers became more sophisticated, manufacturers placed more emphasis upon promoting their brands directly to consumers (rather than to distributors), spending considerable sums on advertising the high quality of their products. Manufacturers believe that if they invest in the quality of their brands they will build up a **brand image**, to which consumers will respond by asking for their goods by their brand names and by being willing to pay a premium for them (*see* BRAND LOYALTY). Manufacturers also believe they will be less susceptible to demands from distributors for extra discounts to stock their brands. For some products (e.g. perfumes and alcoholic drinks), considerable effort has been devoted to promoting brands to reflect the personality of their likely purchasers; marketing research has indeed shown that for these products consumers can be persuaded to buy brands that enhance the image they have of themselves. *See* BRAND VALUE; GENERIC PRODUCT; OWN BRAND.

brand equity The value of a *brand beyond its functional purpose, based on the extent to which it commands *brand loyalty (expressed as repeat buying), name awareness, perceived quality, and strong brand associations, as well as other assets, such as patents, trademarks, and channel relationships. Market share and profit margins can be greater as a result of the *goodwill associated with the brand equity.

brand extension Using a successful brand name to launch a new or modified product in a separate category. A successful brand helps a company enter new product categories more easily. For example, a car manufacturer may use a brand name to launch a lawn mower. Brand extensions do not always work, however, as one manufacturer of canned foods found with the unsuccessful launch of a pet food.

brand image *See* BRAND.

brand loyalty Support by consumers for a particular *brand or product. Brand loyalty is usually the result of continued satisfaction with a product or its price and is reinforced by effective and heavy advertising. Strong brand loyalty, which is often subjective or subconscious, reduces the impact of competitive brand promotions and **brand switching** unless it is for an improved product.

brand manager (product manager) The executive responsible for the overall marketing and promotion of a particular branded product. Responsibilities range from setting objectives for the product to managing and coordinating its sale. Brand managers emerged in the 1930s at Proctor and Gamble but are now employed by most producers of consumer goods.

brand mark A unique symbol that is part of a brand. Most well-known brands are associated with a brand name and a symbol that uniquely conjures up the image of the product or service.

brand switching *See* BRAND LOYALTY.

brand value The value of a *brand name to a company as a reflection of the *market penetration the brand has achieved and the *brand loyalty it has acquired. The brand values of a company's range of products may be of importance in a *takeover bid; they may be shown in a company's balance sheets as *intangible assets.

breach of contract A failure by a party to a *contract to perform the obligations in that contract or an indication of an intention not to do so. An indication that a contract will be breached in the future is called **repudiation** or an **anticipatory breach**; it may be either expressed in words or implied from conduct. Such an implication arises as the only reasonable inference from a person's acts in this respect. For example, an anticipatory breach occurs if a person contracts to sell a car to A but sells and delivers it to B before the delivery date agreed with A. The repudiation of a contract entitles the injured party to treat the contract as discharged and to sue immediately for *damages for the loss sustained. The same procedure only applies to an actual breach if it constitutes a **fundamental breach**, i.e. a breach of a major term (see CONDITION) of the contract. In either an anticipatory or an actual breach, the injured party may, however, decide to affirm the contract instead (see AFFIRMATION OF CONTRACT). When an actual breach relates only to a minor term of the contract (a warranty) the injured party may sue for damages but has no right to treat the contract as discharged. The process of treating a contract as discharged by reason of repudiation or actual breach is sometimes referred to as *rescission. Other remedies available under certain circumstances for breach of contract are an *injunction and *specific performance.

breach of trust The contravention by a *trustee of the duties imposed by a *trust. If one of several trustees agrees to a breach of trust by a co-trustee, this also constitutes a breach of trust.

breach of warranty See WARRANTY.

breakeven analysis (cost-volume-profit analysis; CVP analysis) The technique used in *management accounting in which costs are analysed according to *cost behaviour characteristics into *fixed costs and *variable costs and compared to sales revenue in order to determine the level of sales volume, sales value, or production at which the business makes neither a profit nor a loss (see BREAKEVEN POINT). The technique is also used in decision making to assist management to determine such questions as the profit or loss likely to arise from any given level of production or sales, the impact on profitability of changes in the fixed or variable costs, and the levels of activity required to generate a desired profit. Breakeven analysis may either be carried out by drawing a *breakeven chart or by calculation. For example, the formula for determining the level of activity required to generate a desired profit is:

(total fixed costs + desired level of profit)/contribution per unit of production.

See also CONTRIBUTION.

breakeven chart (breakeven graph) A graph on which an organization's total costs, analysed into *fixed costs and *variable costs, are drawn over a given range of activity, together with the sales revenue for the same range of activity. The point at which the sales-revenue curve crosses the total-cost curve is known as the *breakeven point (expressed either as sales revenue or production/sales volume). The breakeven chart, like *breakeven analysis, may also be used to determine the profit or loss likely to arise from any given level of production or sales, the impact on profitability of changes in the fixed or variable costs, and the levels of activity required to generate a required profit.

breakeven point The level of production, sales volume, percentage of capacity, or sales revenue at which an organization makes neither a profit nor a loss. The breakeven point may either be determined by the construction of a *breakeven chart or by calculation. The formulae are:

breakeven point (units) = total fixed costs/contribution per unit,

breakeven point (sales) = (total fixed cost × selling price per unit)/contribution per unit.

See also CONTRIBUTION.

break-forward (Boston option) A contract on the money market that combines the features of a *forward-exchange contract and a currency option. The forward contract can be undone at a previously agreed rate of exchange, enabling the consumer to be free if the market moves favourably.

breaking a leg (lifting a leg) Closing out one part of an arbitrage or spread transaction, while leaving the other part open. *See also* LEG; STRADDLE.

breaking bulk The practice of *bulk buying products, commodities, etc., and selling smaller quantities to users or consumers. This operation is often performed by a *wholesaler although it may be done by a *retailer.

breakout In *chartist analysis, a movement in the market price of a security above or below the limits within which it has recently fluctuated. When a security's price moves to a level above the usual price ceiling or below the usual price floor, this is thought to herald a continuing move in the same direction. *See also* RESISTANCE LEVEL.

break-up value 1. The value of the assets of an organization on the assumption that it will not continue in business. On this assumption the assets are likely to be sold piecemeal and probably in haste. **2.** The *asset value per share of a company.

bribery and corruption Offences relating to the improper influencing of people in positions of trust. The offences commonly grouped under this expression are now statutory. Under the Public Bodies Corrupt Practices Act (1889), amended by the Prevention of Corruption Act (1916), it is an offence corruptly to offer to a member, officer, or servant of a public body any reward or advantage to do anything in relation to any matter with which that body is concerned; it is also an offence for a public servant or officer to corruptly receive or solicit such a reward. The Prevention of Corruption Act (1906) amended the 1916 Act is wider in scope. Under this Act it is an offence corruptly to give or offer any valuable consideration to an agent to do any act or show any favour in relation to a principal's affairs.

bricks-and-clicks *See* CLICKS-AND-MORTAR.

bridging loan A loan taken on a short-term basis to bridge the gap between the purchase of one asset and the sale of another. It is particularly common in the property and housing market.

Britannia coins A range of four British *gold coins (£100, £50, £25, and £10 denominations). They were introduced in October 1987 for investment purposes, in competition with the *Krugerrand. Although all sales of gold coins attract VAT, Britannia coins are dealt in as bullion coins.

British Airports Authority *See* BAA.

British Bankers Association (BBA) A London-based organization that represents the views of all the banks recognized in the UK. Founded in 1919, it is regarded as the banks' trade association. It established model contracts for financial instruments and publishes daily market interest rates in major currencies. It collects and publishes London Inter Bank Offer Rate Quotes, which are the basis for many financial contracts expressed on BBA terms.

British Code of Advertising Practice (BCAP) *See* ADVERTISING STANDARDS AUTHORITY.

British Exporters Association (BEXA) An association, formerly the British Export Houses Association (BEHA), that puts UK suppliers in touch with Association members, who trade and finance trade throughout the world.

British Insurance and Investment Brokers Association (BIBA) A trade association for insurance brokers registered with the *Insurance Brokers Registration Council and investment brokers registered under the Financial Services Act (1986). Formed in 1977 as the British Insurance Brokers Association by the amalgamation of a number of insurance broking associations, it changed to its current name in 1988 to widen its membership to include investment advisers. It provides public relations, free advice, representation in parliament, and a conciliation service for consumers.

British Rates and Data **(BRAD)** A monthly publication listing addresses, cover price, circulation, frequency, rate cards, copy and cancellation requirements, and advertising representatives for national and provincial newspapers, consumer, trade, technical, and professional publications, and for television and radio stations.

British Standard 5750 A quality assurance standard applied to processes and procedures, rather than to products. The standard specifies processes capable of producing outputs that will satisfy the requirements of customers for high and consistent quality; these are formalized, documented, and inspected. Subsequent periodic inspections are then made to ensure that the certified procedures are being adhered to. At its inception, a BS 5750 accreditation was an order-winning criterion providing a competitive advantage. Now, in many industries, it is impossible to trade without it. *Compare* ISO 9000.

British Standards Institution (BSI Group) An institution founded in 1901, which received a royal charter in 1929. Its function is to formulate technical standards for building, engineering, chemical, textile, and electrical products, etc., ensuring that they maintain a specified quality. Products certified by the BSI are entitled to use the **Kitemark** logo as a symbol of reliability. Manufacturers who use the Kitemark do so under licence on condition that products are subject to regular inspection. The BSI also operates the European Union's CE certification scheme in the UK for products that come under the relevant EU directives. Apart from maintaining quality and safety standards in this way, the BSI attempts to ensure that the design of goods is restricted to a sensible number of patterns and sizes for one purpose, to avoid unnecessary variety. In this work the BSI collaborates closely with the *International Standards Organization.

A subdivision of the group, **BSI Management Systems**, provides quality assessments of management systems worldwide and advises organizations on how to improve their efficiency, health and safety record, and environmental sustainability.

British Technology Group (BTG) An organization formed in 1981 by the merger of the National Enterprise Board (NEB) and the National Research and Development Corporation (NRDC). Its purpose is to encourage technological development by providing finance for new scientific and engineering products and processes discovered through research at UK universities, research councils, and government research establishments. It was privatized in 2000.

British Telecom The British Telecommunications Corporation was formed in 1981 as a public corporation to control the UK telephone and telecommunications system, which had previously been the responsibility of the Post Office. In 1984 this corporation became British Telecommunications plc, when 51% of the shares were sold to the public. British Telecom then lost its monopoly to run telecommunications throughout the UK.

British Waterways A board set up under the Transport Act (1962) to provide services and facilities for UK inland waterways. Its responsibilities extend over approximately 2000 miles of waterways and 90 reservoirs.

broadband Describing communications in which a wide range of frequencies can be transmitted at the same time. Broadband *Internet access allows much greater transmission rates than are possible with a traditional *modem. The most popular method is to use *ADSL.

broadbanding Adoption of an organizational pay structure that consists of a small number of broad pay 'bands', usually four or five in total. This allows greater scope for rewarding individual employees on the basis of performance, skill level, and market value without moving them into a different pay band or changing their job titles. *See also* DELAYERING.

broad money An informal name for M3 or any wide definition of the *money supply). *Compare* NARROW MONEY.

broker An agent who brings two parties together, enabling them to enter into a contract to which the broker is not a principal. The broker's remuneration consists of a **brokerage**, usually calculated as a percentage of the sum involved in the contract but sometimes fixed by a tariff. Brokers are used because they have specialized knowledge of certain markets or to conceal the identity of a principal, in addition to introducing buyers to sellers. *See* AVIATION BROKER; BILL BROKER; COM-

MODITY BROKER; INSURANCE BROKER; SHIP-BROKER; STOCKBROKER.

brokerage The commission earned by a *broker.

broker/dealer 1. An agent for buyers and sellers who also trades on his or her own account. 2. A member of the *London Stock Exchange who, since the *Big Bang, has functioned both as a stockbroker and a jobber, but only in a single capacity in one particular transaction. *See* MARKET MAKER.

brownfield development A housing or industrial development within an existing urban area. *Compare* GREENFIELD DEVELOPMENT.

brown goods Televisions, hi-fi equipment, etc., which were formerly often housed in wood or imitation wood cabinets. *Compare* WHITE GOODS.

browser *See* WEB BROWSER.

BSC Abbreviation for *balanced scorecard.

B shares In the USA, a category of less important *ordinary shares. B shares are usually distinguished from *A shares by their limited voting power.

BSI Group *See* BRITISH STANDARDS INSTITUTION.

BTEC Abbreviation for Business and Technology Education Council. *See* VOCATIONAL TRAINING.

BTG Abbreviation for *British Technology Group.

bubble A situation in which asset prices are seriously inflated. The unstable boom thus created may lead to a market crash. The most infamous example of this was the South Sea Bubble of 1720, which led to the collapse of the British share market and the bankruptcy of many investors. A more recent example was the so-called 'dot.com bubble' of 1999–2000.

bucket shop 1. A derogatory term for a firm of brokers, dealers, agents, etc., of questionable standing and frail resources, that is unlikely to be a member of an established trade organization. 2. A travel agent who provides a service for travellers who book late, require the lowest prices, and will accept a minimum standard of service.

budget 1. A financial or quantitative statement, prepared prior to a specified accounting period, containing the plans and policies to be pursued during that period. It is used as the basis for *budgetary control. Generally a *functional budget is drawn up for each functional area within an organization, but in addition it is also usual to produce a *capital budget, a *cash-flow budget, stock budgets, and a *master budget, which includes a budgeted profit and loss account and balance sheet. 2. **(the Budget)** In the UK, the government's annual budget, which is presented to parliament by the Chancellor of the Exchequer (traditionally, but not always, on a Tuesday in March). It contains estimates for the government's income and expenditure, together with the tax rates and the fiscal policies designed to meet the government's financial goals for the succeeding fiscal year.

budgetary control The process by which *financial control is exercised within an organization. *Budgets for income and expenditure for each *function of the organization are prepared in advance of an accounting period and are then compared with actual performance to establish any *variances. Individual function managers are made responsible for the *controllable costs within their budgets, and are expected to take remedial action if the adverse *variances are regarded as excessive.

budget centre A section or area of an organization under the responsibility of a manager for which *budgets are prepared; these budgets are compared with actual performance as part of the *budgetary control process. A budget centre may be a *function, department, section, individual, *cost centre, or any combination of these that the management wishes to treat as a budget centre. It is usual to produce regular financial statements on the basis of each budget centre so that each budget-centre manager is aware of its budgeted and actual performance and any *variances that arise.

budget committee The committee responsible for the operation of the *budgetary control process within an organization. The membership and responsibilities of the committee vary between organizations, but a typical committee might comprise a chief executive as chairman, the functional managers as members, and a financial manager as committee secretary or budget director. The committee is responsible for ensuring the formulation of the budgets according to the directives and policies communicated by the board of *directors, scrutinizing the various budgets for coordination and acceptability, and ultimately submitting the budgets (or budget revisions) to the board of directors for approval.

budget cost allowance The amount of budgeted expenditure that a *cost centre or *budget centre is allowed to spend according to its budget, having regard to the level of activity (or other basis of cost incurrence) actually achieved during the *budget period. The budget cost allowance is usually based on the level of activity achieved and whether the cost item is classified as a *fixed cost or a *variable cost.

budget deficit The excess of government expenditure over government income, which must be financed either by borrowing or by printing money. Keynesians have advocated that governments should run budget deficits during *recessions in order to stimulate *aggregate demand. Monetarists and new classical macroeconomists, however, argue that budget deficits simply stimulate *inflation and crowd out private investment. Most economists now agree that, at least on average, governments should seek a balanced budget and that persistent deficits should be eliminated, either by reducing expenditure or increasing taxation. In some cases a **budget surplus** can be used during a *boom to collect more revenue than is being spent.

budgeted capacity The productive *capacity available in an organization for a budget period as expressed in the *budget for that period. It may be expressed in terms of *direct labour hours, *machine hours, or *standard hours.

budgeted cost A cost included in a *budget representing the cost expected to

be incurred by a *budget centre, *cost centre, *cost unit, product, process, or job.

budgeted revenue The income level included in a *budget representing the income that is expected to be achieved during that budget period.

budget manual A manual setting out the administrative procedures and operations that should be applied in the operation of the *budgetary control system. It covers guidelines for the operation of the *budget committee and the *budget centres and includes such information as levels of responsibility, budget timetable, budget preparation, and budget-revision procedures.

budget period A period for which a *budget is prepared and during which it is intended to apply. It is usual for the budget period to be a year, but it is often broken down into shorter control periods, such as a month or a quarter. The budget periods should coincide with the *accounting periods adopted by the organization.

budget slack The surplus that arises when managers preparing a budget overestimate costs or underestimate revenues. Most organizations would want to eliminate budget slack but some managers may be motivated to create it to improve their performance evaluations. In certain cases, slack may be deliberately created by organizations to protect against uncertainty in the environment: for example, a company may hold excess stocks of a product to make sure that customers can always order the quantities they need. However, managers who create excessive slack in this way can be seen as inefficient.

budget surplus *See* BUDGET DEFICIT.

buffering The practice of isolating the operations within an organization from the effects of environmental uncertainty. This can be achieved either by holding *inventory or by the design of the organization's systems. While a degree of stability may be appropriate in some situations, management theory now favours a close relationship between operations and the ultimate customers, to ensure that the process is both effective in meeting the customers' needs and commercially efficient. *See* JUST IN TIME.

buffer inventory *See* INVENTORY.

buffer stock A stock of a commodity owned by a government or trade organization and used to stabilize the price of the commodity. Usually the manager of the buffer stock is authorized to buy the commodity in question if its price falls below a certain level, which is itself reviewed periodically, to enable producers to find a ready market for their goods at a profitable level. If the price rises above another fixed level, the buffer stock manager is authorized to sell the commodity on the open market. Thus, producers are encouraged to keep up a steady supply of the commodity and users are reassured that its price has a ceiling. This arrangement is often effective, but may collapse during a boom or slump. *See also* UNITED NATIONS CONFERENCE ON TRADE AND DEVELOPMENT.

bug An error in a computer program, or a malfunction in a computer system. To **debug** a program is to find and correct all bugs.

Building Societies Act (1986) A UK Act of Parliament regulating the activities of *building societies. It widened their powers to include making unsecured loans and offering a range of financial services, such as providing foreign exchange, buying and selling shares, managing unit-trust schemes and personal-equity plans, arranging and giving advice on insurance, etc. The Act subjected building societies to a new regulatory agency, the Building Societies Commission, and additionally allowed societies to issue shares and become public limited companies, subject to the agreement of their members.

Building Societies Ombudsman *See* FINANCIAL OMBUDSMAN SERVICE.

building society Traditionally, a financial institution that accepts deposits, upon which it pays interest, and makes loans for house purchase or house improvement secured by *mortgages. They developed from the *Friendly Society movement in the late 17th century and were non-profit-making with mutual status. These institutions can be found in the UK, Australia, South Africa, Ireland, and New Zealand. The US *savings and loan associations are broadly similar organizations.

In the UK, the *Building Societies Act (1986) greatly widened the range of services they are permitted to offer; this has enabled them to compete with the commercial banks in many areas. They offer cheque accounts, which pay interest on all credit balances, cash cards, credit cards, loans, money transmission, foreign exchange, and valuation and conveyancing services. The distinction between banks and building societies is fast disappearing; indeed many building societies have obtained the sanction of their members to become *public limited companies. This means that they become profit-making banks, owned by their shareholders, instead of non-profit-making societies owned by subscribing members. These changes have led to the merger of many building societies to provide a national network that can compete with the *Big Four banks. Competition is well illustrated in the close relationship of interest rates between banks and building societies as they both compete for the market's funds. Moreover, the competition provided by the building societies has forced the banks into offering free banking services, paying interest on current accounts, and Saturday opening. Similar changes have taken place in all the other countries that have building societies. The UK building societies are now regulated by the *Financial Services Authority.

built-in obsolescence *See* OBSOLESCENCE.

built-in software Computer programs that are built into a computer and available automatically when the computer is switched on. Examples include the *word processors, *spreadsheets, and graphics programs that are built into most desktop terminals.

bulk buying The buying of products or commodities in sufficiently large quantities to take advantage of bulk discounts or other quantity discounts. *See also* BREAKING BULK.

bulk carrier A ship in which the cargo is carried in bulk, rather than in bags, containers, etc. Bulk cargoes are usually homogeneous and capable of being loaded by gravity; examples include ores, coal, wheat, etc.

bull A dealer on a financial market who expects prices to rise. A **bull market** is one in which prices are rising or expected to rise, i.e. one in which a dealer is more likely to be a buyer than a seller, even to the extent of buying without having made a corresponding sale, thus establishing a **bull position** or a **long position**. A bull with a long position hopes to sell these purchases at a higher price after the market has risen. *Compare* BEAR.

bulldog bond A fixed-interest *bond issued in the UK by a foreign borrower.

bullet 1. A security offering a fixed interest and maturing on a fixed date. **2.** The final repayment of a loan, which consists of the whole of sum borrowed. In a **bullet loan**, interim repayments are interest-only repayments, the principal sum being repaid in the final bullet. *Compare* AMORTIZING LOAN.

bulletin board system (BBS) A computer accessory enabling users of a network to send and reply to messages.

bullion Gold, silver, or some other precious metal used in bulk, i.e. in the form of bars or ingots rather than in coin. Central banks use gold bullion in the settlement of international debts. In the **London bullion market**, bullion brokers act as agents for both buyers and sellers and also trade as principals.

bull note A bond whose redemption value is linked to a market index or a commodity price (e.g. the price of gold). Thus, a holder of a bull note will receive on redemption an amount greater than the principal of the bond if the relevant index or price has risen (but less if it has fallen). With a **bear note** the reverse happens. Bull and bear notes are therefore akin to an ordinary bond plus an *option, providing opportunities for hedging and speculating.

bull spread The simultaneous buying and selling of options on the same commodity or security to take advantage of an anticipated rise in the price of the *underlying. *Compare* BEAR SPREAD.

bundling The marketing ploy of giving away a relatively cheap product with a relatively expensive one to attract customers; for example, incorporating one or more CD-ROMs with the software package supplied with a computer. *See* PRICE-BUNDLING STRATEGY.

burden In the USA, another word for *overheads.

bureaucracy A hierarchical administrative system designed to deal with large quantities of work in a routine manner, largely by adhering to a set of strict and impersonal rules; it is characterized by its permanence and stability, its body of experience and precedent, and its absence of a reliance on individuals. Bureaucracies have sprung up all over the world in the public and private sectors of an economy, in government, and in the service industries. It is generally believed to be the only viable structure for large sophisticated organizations. However, the modern strategies of *downsizing, *business process re-engineering, and *total quality management have to some extent undermined the inevitability of its structures.

bureaucratic leader A leader who depends on his or her position in a clearly defined hierarchy to influence followers, who adheres to established rules and procedures, and who is generally inflexible and suspicious of change. *Compare* CHARISMATIC LEADER. *See also* LEADERSHIP STYLES.

Bureau of Customs The US equivalent of the British Board of Customs and Excise (now part of HM Revenue and Customs). It is a part of the Department of the Treasury.

bureaupathology (red-tape syndrome) The manifestations of exaggerated bureaucratic behaviour (*see* BUREAUCRACY). They include resistance to change, an obsessive reliance on rules and regulations, and an individual incapability of responding to unpredictable events. The bureaupath tends to believe the policies and procedures of an organization constitute an end in themselves, rather than a means to an end.

bureausis A reaction against bureaucratic behaviour (*see* BUREAUCRACY; BUREAUPATHOLOGY) by an individual (usually a client). The individual demands personal attention and refuses to abide by the rules and procedures followed by an organization.

burnout A work-related condition of emotional exhaustion in which interest in work, personal achievement, and efficiency decline sharply and the sufferer is no longer capable of making decisions. The condition is brought on by the unrelenting stress of pressure at work and is frequently experienced by individuals in jobs involving considerable involvement with people, who derive a major part of their self-esteem from their work, and have few interests outside it.

burnout turnaround The process of restructuring a company that is in trouble by producing new finance to save it from liquidation, at the cost of diluting the shareholding of existing investors.

burn rate The rate at which a new company or project uses up its funding before cash begins to come in from its trading activities. It is frequently used to evaluate high-tech or venture capital investments.

business analysis A means by which the current performance of a firm is evaluated as part of the strategic planning process. It should include an analysis of its current market performance in terms of *market share, by product or service category, a *SWOT analysis of the firm (including major competitors), and a *PESTLE analysis of the environmental factors most likely to affect the firm's performance over the future planning period.

Business and Technology Education Council (BTEC) See VOCATIONAL TRAINING.

business buyer behaviour (industrial buyer behaviour) The shaping of business decisions by the purchaser of raw materials, components, industrial equipment, and services for an organization. The amount of time devoted to the process will depend on a number of factors, including the importance of the decision, the cost to the organization of the decision, the alternative products or services available, and the purchasing officer's experience. Three situations are recognized:

- **straight rebuy** – a familiar product (e.g. stationery, electricity) is bought from a regular supplier;

- **modified rebuy** – looking around for a product with improved performance, perhaps reflecting dissatisfaction with current suppliers;
- **new-task buying** – the buyer, on behalf of the organization, is attempting to fulfil a need or solve a problem that has not been previously encountered.

The higher the risk factor involved in a purchase (e.g. new production equipment, an innovative robotic machine), the larger will be the team forming the *decision-making unit (DMU) involved.

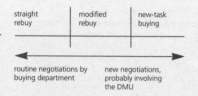

Business buyer behaviour

business combination The combining of two or more companies by means of acquisition or merger. See INTEGRATION. See also ACQUISITION ACCOUNTING; MERGER ACCOUNTING.

business cycle (trade cycle) The process by which investment, output, and employment in an economy tend to move through a recurrent cycle of upturn, prosperity, downturn, and *recession. The cycle does not describe a regular pattern in either length or amplitude. Cycles in the immediate postwar period were of historically low amplitude, while those of the late 1970s and 1980s had greater amplitude and involved much deeper recessions. The reasons for the business cycle remain little understood. See also KONDRATIEFF CYCLE.

business entity See ACCOUNTING ENTITY.

Business Expansion Scheme See ENTERPRISE INVESTMENT SCHEME.

business games Exercises used in personnel training in which teams of employees compete against one another in attempting to solve typical business or management problems. The games, which often involve role play, encourage participants to develop their problem-solving and decision-making abilities, to modify their ideas and attitudes, and to bond with other team members. *See also* TEAM-BUILDING EXERCISES.

business-interruption policy (conse-quential-loss policy; loss-of-profits policy) An insurance policy that pays claims for financial losses occurring if a business has to stop or reduce its activities as a result of a fire or any other insurable risk. Claims can be made for lost profit, rent, rates, and other unavoidable overhead costs that continue even when trading has temporarily ceased.

business judgement rule The rule that the courts will not generally interfere in the conduct of a business. For example, the courts will not substitute their judgement for that of the directors of a company unless the directors are acting improperly. The rule is often invoked when directors are accused of acting out of self-interest in *takeover bids.

business market All the organizations that buy goods and services to use in the production of other products and services or for the purpose of reselling or renting them to others at a profit.

business marketing research *See* IN-DUSTRIAL MARKETING RESEARCH.

Business Monitor A government publication produced by the *Business Statistics Office giving information and data on production, services and distribution, civil aviation, car registrations, and cinema audiences.

business name *See* REGISTERED NAME.

business plan **1.** A detailed plan setting out the objectives of a business over a stated period, often three, five, or ten years. A business plan is drawn up by many businesses, especially if the business has passed through a bad period or if it has had a major change of policy. For new businesses it is an essential document for raising capital or loans. The plan should quantify as many of the objectives as possible, providing monthly *cash flows and production figures for at least the first two years, with diminishing detail in subsequent years; it must also outline its strategy and the tactics it intends to use in achieving its objectives. Anticipated

*profit and loss accounts should form part of the business plan on a quarterly basis for at least two years, and an annual basis thereafter. For a group of companies the business plan is often called a **corporate plan**. See feature CHECKLIST FOR A BUSINESS PLAN on pp. 78–79. **2.** A forecast of the activity volumes and cash flows relating to a specific project within an organization.

business portfolio The collection of businesses and products that make up a company.

business process re-engineering (BPR; process innovation) An approach to the restructuring of organizations that seeks to introduce a fundamental and radical reassessment of the organizational processes. Rather than adjusting or improving on existing methods, BPR asks what the organization is trying to achieve, what are its core processes, and what are its predominant competencies. Based on the answers to these questions, it attempts to plan the most efficient, effective, and direct ways of achieving these ends. It has been argued that BPR simply updates the aims and techniques of *method study; however, while the underlying principles may be the same, the potential of the BPR approach can be significantly enhanced by the use of *information technology. Multiple-access databases, *local area networks, etc., allow parallel and simultaneous processing of tasks that would have been performed sequentially in traditional systems. This, in turn, permits much closer links between those who use the outputs from processes and those who produce the outputs. Modern technology also enables information to be shared across functions as well as geographically, so that organizational learning takes place more rapidly and more uniformly. However, experience shows that radical process innovation of this kind can be difficult to implement in practice, not least because of employee resistance. Employees may be concerned about losing their jobs, which will affect morale.

business promotion A *sales promotion designed to generate business leads, stimulate purchase, reward business customers, and motivate the salesforce.

CHECKLIST FOR A BUSINESS PLAN

The business

The following information about the nature and objectives of the business
should be given:

Personal details For the founder, proprietor, partners, or directors state each
person's name, address, age, and profession if it is relevant to the business.
Some details of their background and experience should also be given.

Structure of the business State whether the business is or will be set up as a
sole trader, a partnership, or a limited company.

Business activities Describe the product or service the business will offer for
sale and to what extent (if at all) it will manufacture the product.

Commencement date State the date on which trading will start (for a new
business) and why this date has been selected.

Objectives State what the business is expected to achieve in general terms of
sales and profitability, referring to a more detailed analysis later in the plan.

History A new business will probably have no history; however, something
should be said of how it came into being. A restructured business or a business
seeking new capital will have a history and this should be given here, paying
special attention to any mergers or takeovers.

Personnel

State the number of employees (other than directors, partners, etc). For all
senior personnel give names, ages, qualifications, position, and salary. If no
staff are currently employed but some will be required, state the numbers you
propose to recruit and their salaries as accurately as possible. An overall plan of
staff requirements, together with any further recruitment or redundancies,
should be given. If this requires considerable detail it should be given in an
appendix.

The product(s) or service(s) in relation to the market

Product or service details Provide details of all products and their proposed sale
prices. Explain your pricing policy, taking into account the price and quality of
competing products or services.

Market details State the nature of the market; whether it is growing, declining,
static, or seasonal. Give brief details of any market testing undertaken and
profiles of intended customers. If substantial orders, or letters stating an intent
to place substantial orders, have been received, attach copies. State if any
market research has been undertaken.

The competition Give the names of major competitors, their pricing policy,
strengths, weaknesses, etc. Explain how the company's products or services
will be better than those of competitors and any other ideas you have about
overcoming competition.

Proposed marketing methods Give details of how you propose to market your
products or services and the cost of doing so. Include in your budgeted
expenditure a figure for advertising. If advertising and PR are important to your
sales plan, give details in an appendix.

Suppliers Give details of your principal suppliers as well as alternative sources
of supply. Give a brief account of the advantages in using the chosen supplier. If
you have any letters from suppliers that could be of interest, attach copies.

The premises

Property type State whether offices and any manufacturing or storage units
will be leased or bought. If the premises are to be leased, state the length of the
lease, whether there is an option to renew, the present rent, and the frequency
of rent reviews. Mention should also be made of who bears responsibility for

internal and external repairs. If you own the premises, state the purchase price and when they were bought. If a valuer's report has been obtained, enclose a copy. If the property is freehold, state its *written-down value. In both leasehold and freehold property state the amounts payable in rates.
Specifications State the overall size of the premises and how they are (or will be) subdivided, e.g. production space, storage space, retailing space, office space. If appropriate, supply a plan.

Equipment required
If the business manufactures or is intended to manufacture its product(s), it may be useful to give a brief outline here of the process involved.
Manufacturing equipment Give details of equipment already owned, including the purchase price, *depreciation, and current value. Also give financial details of any manufacturing equipment currently hired, leased, or borrowed. Add a note about the cost of servicing equipment.
General trading equipment Give details of any equipment owned for trading purposes, e.g. cash tills, company vans or cars, including the depreciation, present value, and purchase price. Mention any such items leased or borrowed, stating the rent paid and terms of leasing.
Equipment on hire purchase Give details of any equipment currently being bought on hire purchase, together with the date and terms of the contract.
Equipment required Give details of all equipment you intend to buy, either to begin trading or to increase existing production. State the prices, leasing arrangements, and source of funds.

Sales forecasts
The business plan should state how sales are to be achieved, with details of any distribution network. Discounts and agency fees should be stated and a breakdown of the sale price in the form of a pie chart is often useful. Provide a detailed forecast of sales either on a monthly basis, if this is feasible, or on a quarterly or annual basis. The sales forecasts should be projected as far into the future as possible (certainly three years but longer if a sensible forecast can be made). These figures will form the basis of the all-important *cash-flow projections.

Financial summary
Source of funds For an existing business the *capital structure should be given. This may consist of shares, loan stock, and debt. The long-term debt may consist of *debentures, while the short-term debt may be in the form of bank loans. For a new business, the intended capital structure should be outlined together with a list of shareholders, stock and debenture holders, etc. For a business seeking new capital, state your requirements precisely and explain what form of security you can offer.
Cash-flow projection This is probably the most important part of the business plan. If the plan is to be credible, it is essential that the cash-flow projection should not contain any estimates that cannot be substantiated as fair and likely. For a convincing business plan the cash-flow projection might cover the first three years in detail and the next two years in less detail. If an outline projection for ten years can be provided the picture becomes increasingly credible.
Projection of profits Give an estimate of the profit over at least three years. This should be realistic, even if it shows that the venture is unlikely to be profitable in its initial year (or two).

For a restructured business or a business seeking new capital the supporting documents should also include copies of the *balance sheets and *profit and loss accounts for at least the past three years.

b

business property relief An *inheritance tax relief available on certain types of business property. For an interest in an unlisted business, including a partnership share, the relief is 100%. Land or buildings owned and used in a company under the control of the donor, or a partnership in which the donor was a partner, attract 50% relief. A majority controlling interest in a listed company also attracts 50% relief.

business rates The local tax paid in the UK by businesses. It is based on a local valuation of the property occupied by the business and the **Uniform Business Rate** (**UBR**) set by central government.

business reply service A service offered by the Post Office enabling a company to supply its customers with a prepaid business reply card, envelope, or label (either first- or second-class postage) so that they can reply to direct-mail shots, ask for follow-up literature, pay bills promptly, etc., free of postal charges.

business segments Separately identifiable parts of the business operations of a company or group whose activities, assets, and results can be clearly identified. Companies are obliged to disclose in their annual report and accounts certain financial information relating to business segments (see SEGMENTAL REPORTING). Although *Statement of Standard Accounting Practice 25 provides guidance as to what comprises a business segment, many inconsistencies appear in the information provided by companies. Standard setters have recognized that companies are not keen to improve segmental reporting because they fear they could suffer some competitive disadvantage.

business software package One of a wide range of *software programs sold in packages to enable computers to be used for a variety of business uses. They range in complexity and expense from those suitable for an individual PC to large systems operated on a mainframe or a network. A typical package would include one or more of: book-keeping programs, which provide facilities for keeping sales, purchase, and nominal ledgers; accounting packages, enabling balance sheets, budgetary control, and sale and purchase

analysis to be undertaken automatically (see SPREADSHEET); payroll packages, dealing with wages, salaries, PAYE, National Insurance, pensions, etc.; and *database management systems to maintain company records. Business software packages may also include more general software, such as a *spreadsheet program and a word-processing application. The programs comprising the package are designed to work together and use each other's data. See also AUDIT SOFTWARE.

Business Statistics Office A department of the *Office for National Statistics. It collects statistics of British businesses and publishes *Business Monitors*.

business strategy An overall longer-term policy for a firm that coordinates the separate functional areas of a business. It defines the business objectives, analyses the internal and external environments, and determines the direction of the firm. Each firm operates in a competitive environment and seeks to formulate a strategy that will provide it with an advantage over its rivals: design, quality, innovation, and branding are examples of ways in which competitive advantages may be established. Some firms may seek to diversify into new markets, either through *internal growth (i.e. by expanding their existing products or introducing new ones) or by *external growth through mergers, takeovers, joint ventures, or strategic partnerships (see DIVERSIFICATION). Each of these methods carries different levels of risk.

business structure The formal structure of a business. At the simplest level is a *sole proprietor, a small business run by a single owner. A *partnership is a business owned and controlled by two or more persons through a *partnership agreement; it is widely used by professional practices, such as accountants and solicitors, including the largest firms. A *private limited company is one in which the liability of the owners is restricted to their shareholdings and the shares are not available to a wider public. A *public company (plc), on the other hand, offers its shares for sale to the public and often has a very diverse ownership. A *co-operative is a business in which the ownership and control is held equally by its worker members.

business system The distinctive system of a nation's business organizations. The interaction of economic factors and social institutions within different countries has evolved in different ways. Business systems acquired their distinctive characteristics at an early stage of the industrialization process and they have subsequently developed and adapted to their environment. This helps to explain why the business systems in, say, Britain, Germany, and Japan have developed in different ways, as a result of such institutional factors as the system of government, the financial system, education and training, and industrial relations.

business-to-business marketing Marketing aimed at selling a product for any use other than personal consumption. The buyer may be a manufacturer, a reseller, a government body, a non-profit-making institution, or any organization other than an ultimate consumer.

busted bond (old bond) A bond issued by a government or corporation that has already defaulted on the loan on which the bonds are based. Busted bonds are now collectors' items, especially those from prerevolutionary Russia and those issued by US railroad companies. Occasionally promises are made to honour Russian or Chinese bonds.

butterfly A strategy used by dealers in traded *options. It involves simultaneously purchasing and selling call or put options at different *exercise prices. A butterfly is most profitable when the price of the underlying security fluctuates within narrow limits but the losses from the strategy are limited. Compare STRADDLE.

butut A monetary unit of the Gambia, worth one hundredth of a *dalasi.

buy-back 1. The buying back by a company of its shares from an investor, who put venture capital up for the formation of the company. The shares are bought back at a price that satisfies the investor, which has to be the price the company is willing to pay for its independence. The buy-back may occur if the company is pub-

licly floated or is taken over. **2.** The buying back by a corporation, especially in the USA, of its shares to reduce the number on the market, either to increase the return on those shares still available or to remove threatening shareholders. **3.** Action by a developing country's government to reduce some or all of its debt to overseas banks by buying back that debt at the market price or at a substantial discount. The attraction for the banks is the removal of a damaging and negative debt, which may already have been provided for in its balance sheet. The advantage to the country in debt is a return to creditworthiness and the possibility of acquiring new loans.

buy earnings To invest in a company that has a low *yield but whose earnings are increasing, so that a substantial capital gain can be expected.

buyer 1. A person who makes a purchase of a product or service. Quite often, this person will be different from both the 'influencer' of the buying decision and the 'user' of the product or service (see CONSUMER BUYING BEHAVIOUR). For example, a mother may – on the advice of a friend – make a purchase, which is consumed by her child. **2.** A person in an organization's *buying centre (or *decision-making unit) with formal authority to select the supplier and arrange the terms of purchase. See BUSINESS BUYER BEHAVIOUR.

buyers' market A market in which the supply exceeds the demand, so that buyers can force prices down. At some point, however, sellers will withdraw from the market if prices fall too low; when this happens the supply will fall off and prices will begin to rise again. Compare SELLERS' MARKET.

buyers over A market in securities, commodities, etc., in which the sellers have sold all they wish to sell but there are still buyers. This is clearly a strong market, with an inclination for prices to rise. Compare SELLERS OVER.

buygrid The three classes of industrial buying: rebuying, which usually entails reordering from existing suppliers; modified rebuying, which involves reassessing existing policy, often seeking improved quality; and new-task buying, in which an organization buys something it has not bought before. *See* BUSINESS BUYER BEHAVIOUR.

buy-in The purchase of a holding of more than 50% in a company by (or on behalf of) a group of executives from outside the company, who wish to run the company.

buying centre All the individuals and units that participate in the business buying process for an organization.

buying forward Buying commodities, securities, foreign exchange, etc., for delivery at a date in the future in order to establish a *bull position or to cover a forward *bear sale. *See* FORWARD DEALING.

buying in The buying of securities, commodities, etc., by a broker because the original seller has failed to deliver. This invariably happens after a rise in a market price (the seller would be able to buy in himself if the market had fallen). The broker buys at the best price available and the original seller is responsible for any difference between the buying-in price and the original buying price, plus the cost of buying in. *Compare* SELLING OUT.

buy-out **1.** An option, open to a member of an *occupational pension scheme on leaving, of transferring the benefits already purchased to an insurance company of his or her own choice. **2.** *See* LEVERAGED BUY-OUT. **3.** *See* MANAGEMENT BUY-OUT.

buy-to-let The purchase of a residential or other property as an investment for the income it will produce on letting.

BV Abbreviation for *Besloten Vennootschap*.

It appears after the name of a Dutch company, being equivalent to the British abbreviation Ltd (denoting a private limited company). *Compare* NV.

by-product A product from a process that has secondary economic significance compared to the *main product of the process. For example, while the primary reason for cracking oil is to produce petroleum, other products produced as a result of the process, such as lubricating oil, paraffin, and other distillates, are by-products. *See also* PROCESS COSTING.

by-product pricing Setting the price for *by-products in order to make the price of the main product more competitive. For example, in producing processed meats, chemicals, or oil there are often by-products, which – if they had to be disposed of – would make the main product uncompetitive. The producer therefore attempts to sell these by-products at the best possible price in order to keep the main product competitive.

byte A unit of information in a computer, consisting of a group of binary digits, that represents a number or character. Most small computers use a byte with 8 binary digits; larger computers use a byte with 16 digits. Byte and character are often used synonymously. For example, a floppy disk holding 180 000 bytes will store 180 000 characters. (However, slightly less than 180 000 characters are available to the user because some disk space is needed by the computer to index and lay out the data on the disk.)

C A language used to program computers. It was developed in the mid-1970s by the Bell laboratories in the USA. An extension of C, called C++, is widely used.

CA 1. Abbreviation for *chartered accountant. **2.** Abbreviation for *Consumers' Association.

CAATs Abbreviation for *computer-assisted audit techniques.

cabbage letter A letter used in *direct-mail selling, which contains illustrations, making it a hybrid between a letter and a leaflet.

CAD 1. Abbreviation for *cash against documents. **2.** Abbreviation for *computer-aided design.

Cadbury Code A UK code of best practice concerning appropriate senior management remuneration, produced by the 1992 **Cadbury Committee** on the financial aspects of *corporate governance. The Code includes the provisions that *non-executive directors should be appointed for specified terms and reappointment should not be automatic, that such directors should be selected through a formal process, and that both their selection and their appointment should be a matter for the board as a whole. *See also* GREENBURY REPORT; HAMPEL COMMITTEE.

cafeteria plan In the USA, an agreement that permits employees to select a fringe benefit from a variety of such benefits (including cash); under the tax code, the benefit is not included in the gross income of the participants solely because the participants are required to choose from a variety of benefits.

calculative contract *See* PSYCHOLOGICAL CONTRACT.

call 1. A demand from a company to its shareholders to pay a specified sum on a specified date in respect of their *partly paid shares (*see also* CALLED-UP SHARE CAPITAL). **2.** A notification that redeemable

shares or bonds should be presented for repayment.

callable bonds Fixed-rate bonds, usually *convertibles, in which the issuer has the right, but not the obligation, to redeem (call) the bond during the life of the bond. A grace period during which the borrower is unable to call the bond will usually be included in the terms of the agreement. *Compare* PUTTABLE BONDS.

call bird A low-priced article used in the retail trade to encourage members of the public to come into a shop, in the hope that purchases for higher-priced goods will follow.

call centre An office whose sole purpose is to handle large numbers of incoming or outgoing telephone calls. It may be used for telephone sales, to carry out marketing research (*see* CENTRAL LOCATION TELEPHONE INTERVIEWING), or by large organizations wishing to deal with all enquiries centrally rather than in local branches. There is a growing trend for major UK organizations to site their call centres in other English-speaking countries where labour is cheaper (e.g. India).

called-up share capital When the *issued share capital of a company consists of *partly paid shares, that part of the share capital that has been paid in by subscribers. *Compare* PAID-UP SHARE CAPITAL; RESERVE CAPITAL.

call money 1. Money put into the money market that can be called at short notice (*see also* MONEY AT CALL AND SHORT NOTICE). **2.** *See* OPTION MONEY.

call-of-more option *See* OPTION TO DOUBLE.

call option *See* OPTION.

callover A meeting of commodity brokers and dealers at fixed times during the day in order to form a market in that commodity. The callover has traditionally been used for trading in futures, in fixed quantities on a standard contract, payments being settled by differences through a *clearing house. Because traders usually form a ring around the person calling out the prices, this form of market is often called **ring trading**. It has been largely superseded by *automated screen trading systems. *See also* OPEN OUTCRY; PIT.

call record sheets Marketing research interviewers' logs, listing the number of contacts or interviews conducted and their results.

call report A salesperson's periodic report listing the number of sales calls made, the sales concluded, and any other relevant activities. The call reports will usually be examined by a sales manager.

CAM Abbreviation for *computer-aided manufacturing.

campaign An organized course of action, carefully planned to achieve set objectives, especially in advertising, sales, public relations, or marketing.

Campaign A weekly magazine that gives details of new advertising campaigns, job vacancies, personnel moves in advertising agencies, and general advertising gossip. It is now possible to read the entire magazine on-line.

cancellation The right to cancel a commercial contract after it has been entered into. The right to cancel exists generally for contracts concluded at a distance (*see* DISTANCE SELLING), such as mail order and Internet sales when the contract is with a *consumer, and in particular in such sectors as time-share sales and consumer credit.

cancellation price The lowest price at which the manager of a *unit trust may offer to redeem units on a particular day. The cancellation price is calculated on the basis of a formula laid down by the *Securities and Investment Board.

c & f Abbreviation for cost and freight. It is the basis of an export contract in which the seller pays the cost of shipping the goods to the port of destination but not the cost of insuring the goods once they have been loaded onto a ship or aircraft. It is, in other respects, similar to a *c.i.f. contract. *Compare* FREE ON BOARD.

c & m Abbreviation for *care and maintenance.

candlestick chart A type of graph used by *chartists in which each trading period is represented by a separate histogram. The blocks of the diagram represent the opening and closing prices, while the high and low periods are represented by vertical lines from the opening and closing prices, which in the case of the highs resemble candlewicks.

cannibalization A market situation in which increased sales of one brand results in decreased sales of another brand within the same *product line, usually because there is little differentiation between them. For instance, two drinks marketed by the same manufacturer and packaged in almost the same colour could cause increased sales of one to be achieved at the expense of decreased sales of the other.

cap A ceiling on a charge; for example, an interest-rate cap would set a maximum interest rate to be charged on a loan, regardless of prevailing general interest-rate levels. A lender would charge a fee for including a cap at the outset to offset this risk. Caps may also limit annual increases to a certain level. *Compare* FLOOR. *See also* COLLAR.

CAP Abbreviation for *Common Agricultural Policy.

capacity (system capacity) The highest sustainable output from an operating system in units per given time. A system's overall capacity is determined by the capacity of its 'narrowest' part, i.e. the **bottleneck**. For example, if a car assembly line can produce 120 cars per hour but the paint shop can only handle 100 cars in an hour, the overall capacity of the plant is 100. Identifying capacity in terms of services can be particularly difficult. For example, students per year provides an insufficient measure of the capacity of a university, as it fails to take into account the quality or effectiveness of the teaching. *See also* BUDGETED CAPACITY; DESIGNED CAPACITY; EFFECTIVE CAPACITY.

capacity requirements plan (CRP) Part of the second phase of *material requirements planning, which produces daily or weekly estimates of the workload on key machines and processes in each department of a plant. This enables proactive adjustment of capacity to be made, if possible, or feedback into the *master production schedule, so that adjustments can be made.

cap and collar mortgage A *mortgage in which the variable interest rate paid by the borrower cannot rise above or fall below specified levels; such a mortgage may be granted for the first few years of a loan. See also CAPPED MORTGAGE.

CAPAR Abbreviation for *computer-assisted panel research.

CAPI Abbreviation for *computer-aided personal interview.

capital 1. The total value of the assets of a person less liabilities. **2.** The amount of the proprietors' interests in the assets of an organization, less its liabilities. **3.** The money contributed by the proprietors to an organization to enable it to function; thus *share capital is the amount provided by way of shares and the *loan capital is the amount provided by way of loans. However, the capital of the proprietors of companies not only consists of the share and loan capital, it also includes retained profit, which accrues to the holders of the ordinary shares. See also RESERVE CAPITAL. **4.** In economic theory, the man-made factor of production, usually either machinery and plant (**physical capital**) or money (**financial capital**). However, the concept can be applied to a variety of other assets, such as *human capital or *intellectual capital. Capital is generally used to enhance the productivity of other factors of production (e.g. combine harvesters enhance the productivity of land; tools enhance the value of labour) and its return is the reward following from this enhancement. In general, the rate of return on capital is called *profit.

capital account 1. An account in the financial records of a limited company showing the total amounts for each class of share capital, for example the *preference share capital and the *ordinary share capital. **2.** An account or series of accounts showing the interests of each partner in the net assets of a partnership. This account records the partners' capital contributions, goodwill valuation, and revalu-

ations. In sole tradership accounts, the capital account records the interest the sole trader holds in the net assets of the business. See also CURRENT ACCOUNT. **3.** An account recording *capital expenditure on such items as land and buildings, plant and machinery, etc. **4.** A budgeted amount that can only be spent on major items, especially in public-sector budgeting. Compare REVENUE ACCOUNT. **5.** That part of the *balance of payments account that shows flows of money between currencies for investment purposes.

capital adequacy ratio The proportion of a bank's total assets that is held in the form of *shareholders' equity and certain other defined classes of capital. It is a measure of the bank's ability to meet the needs of its depositors and other creditors. The minimum international requirement is 8% but some countries may require banks to have a higher ratio.

capital allocation The allocation of investment capital to particular units within an organization on the basis of possible losses, which are calculated by *value-at-risk techniques. This is particularly common in financial institutions. Capital allocation may also be related to the funding structure of units and is often used as a basis for the calculation of *shareholder value or *Economic Value Added. See also RISK-ADJUSTED RETURN ON CAPITAL.

capital allowances Allowances against UK income tax or corporation tax available to a business, sole trader, partnership, or limited company that has spent capital on *plant and machinery used in the business. Capital allowances are also given on *industrial buildings and some agricultural and commercial buildings. The level of allowances varies according to the different categories of asset. Plant and machinery qualifies for a 25% *writing-down allowance and small to medium-sized businesses may claim a *first-year allowance on certain assets. An allowance of 4% calculated by the *straight-line method is available on industrial buildings, with no initial allowance. An allowance of 6% is also available for certain long-life assets expected to last for 25 years or more. The allowances are treated as an expense in the computation of taxable profit and the capital allowance period reflects the period during which the accounts are prepared. The estimated cost to the government of providing capital allowances under corporation tax and income tax has been estimated at about £19,000 million annually (2003–04).

capital asset *See* FIXED ASSET.

capital asset pricing model (CAPM) A statistical model to explain the expected or average return on an investment. It assumes that this return will be composed of the *risk-free rate of return and a *risk premium. The risk premium is related to those *systematic risks that cannot be avoided. Formally, the CAPM is based on the equation:

$$E(R_i) = R_f + \beta_i[E(R_m) - R_f],$$

where $E(R_i)$ is the expected/average return on the assets in portfolio i, R_f is the risk-free rate of return, $E(R_m)$ is the expected/average return on all assets, and B_i is the *beta coefficient of the asset or the portfolio i. The beta is the percentage that the return in i will change with a 1% change in R_m. The CAPM is a measure of the risk in the asset or the portfolio. It is the basis for calculating the required return on an investment and is frequently used to calculate the discount rate for a *net present value calculation.

capital at risk A measure of worst-case losses in excess of the average that is used in banking to calculate both capital requirements and certain performance measures, such as *risk-adjusted return on capital (RAROC). It is usually based on the *value-at-risk methodology. *See also* BASLE CONVERGENCE ACCORD.

capital bond National Savings Capital Bond; a type of UK bond, introduced by the Department of *National Savings in 1989, that offers a guaranteed rate of return over a five-year period. Tax is not deducted at source from the interest. The bonds may be bought in units of £100; the maximum holding is £1 million.

capital budget The sums allocated by an organization for future *capital expenditure. The capital budget may well encompass a longer period than the next accounting period.

capital budgeting The process by which an organization appraises a range of different investment projects with a view to determining which is likely to give the highest financial return. The approaches adopted include *net present value, the *internal rate of return, the *profitability index, and the *payback period method.

capital commitments (commitments for capital expenditure) Firm plans, usually approved by the board of directors in the case of companies, to spend sums of money on *fixed assets. Capital commitments must by law be shown by way of a note in the company accounts.

capital consumption The total depreciation in the value of the capital goods in an economy during a specified period. It is difficult to calculate this figure, but it is needed as it has to be deducted from the *gross national product (GNP) and the *gross domestic product (GDP) to obtain the net figures.

capital-conversion plan An *annuity that converts capital into income. Capital-conversion policies are often used to provide an income later in life for a person who might be liable to capital gains tax if his or her capital is not reinvested in some way.

capital employed Either the sum of the *shareholders' equity in a company and its long-term debt or the *fixed assets of a company plus its *net current assets. Although this term is neither legally defined nor required to be disclosed in a *balance sheet, it is an important element of *ratio analysis, particularly in the calculation of *return on capital employed.

capital expenditure (capital costs; capital investment; investment costs; investment expenditure) The expenditure by an organization of a significant amount for the purchase or improvement of a *fixed asset; the amount expended would warrant the item being depreciated over an estimated useful life of a reasonably extended period. Capital expenditure is not charged against the profits of the organization when it takes place, but is regarded as an investment to be capitalized in the *balance sheet as a fixed asset and subsequently charged against profits by depreciating the asset over its estimated useful life. Relief against taxation is available through *capital allowances.

capital formation See FIXED CAPITAL FORMATION.

capital gain The gain on the disposal of an asset calculated by deducting the cost of the asset from the proceeds received on its disposal. Under *capital gains tax legislation the *chargeable gain may be reduced by *taper relief (or by *indexation if the asset was purchased prior to 6 April 1998). Capital gains by companies are adjusted by indexation and are chargeable to *corporation tax.

capital gains tax (CGT) A UK tax on *capital gains. Most countries have a form of income tax under which they tax the profits from trading and a different tax to tax substantial disposals of assets either by traders for whom the assets are not trading stock (e.g. a trader's factory) or by individuals who do not trade (e.g. sales of shares by an investor). The latter type of tax is a capital gains tax. In the UK, capital gains tax is charged on the total amount of *chargeable gains accruing to a person in a fiscal year after deducting any allowable *capital losses. The rate of tax is 10%, 20%, or 40% depending on the taxpayer's marginal rate of income tax. *Taper relief may be available to reduce a chargeable gain, as may *indexation if the asset was purchased before 6 April 1998.

capital gearing See GEARING.

capital goods Long-term man-made factors of production, such as factories and machinery.

capital growth An increase in the value of invested capital. Investment in *fixed-interest securities or bonds provides income but limited capital growth (which may be improved in index-linked *gilt-edged securities). To have a chance of making substantial capital growth it is necessary to invest in equities (see ORDINARY SHARE), the value of which should increase more rapidly than *inflation. Investing in equities is thus said to be a hedge against inflation. See GROWTH STOCKS.

capital-intensive Denoting a technique of production that requires a high ratio of capital to labour costs. Compare LABOUR-INTENSIVE.

capital investment See INVESTMENT.

capitalism An economic system in which the *factors of production are privately owned and individual owners of *capital are free to make use of it as they see fit; in particular, for their own profit. In this system the market and the profit mechanism will play a major role in deciding what is to be produced, how it is to be produced, and who owns what is produced. See also FREE COMPETITION; PRIVATE ENTERPRISE.

capitalization 1. The act of providing *capital for a company or other organization. **2.** The structure of the capital of a company or other organization, i.e. the extent to which its capital is divided into share or loan capital and the extent to which share capital is divided into ordinary and preference shares. See also THIN CAPITALIZATION. **3.** The conversion of the reserves of a company into capital by means of a *scrip issue. **4.** The accounting practice of treating *capital expenditure as a fixed asset on the balance sheet rather than charging it against profits when it occurs.

capitalization issue See SCRIP ISSUE.

capitalization of borrowing costs See BORROWING COSTS.

capitalized value 1. The value at which an asset has been recorded in the balance sheet of a company or other organization, usually before the deduction of *depreciation. **2.** The capital equivalent of an asset that yields a regular income, calculated at the prevailing rate of interest. For example, a piece of land bringing in an annual income of £1000, when the prevailing interest rate is 10%, would have a notional capitalized value of £10,000 (i.e. £1000/0.1). This may not reflect its true value.

capital lease In the USA, a lease that does not legally constitute a purchase although the leased asset should be recorded as an asset on the lessee's books if any one of the following four criteria is met:
- the lease transfers ownership of the property to the lessee at the end of the lease term;

- a **bargain purchase option** exists; i.e. an option exists enabling the lessee to buy the leased property at the end of the lease for a minimal amount or to renew the lease for a nominal rental (a **bargain renewal option**);
- the lease term is 75% or more of the life of the property;
- the *present value of minimum lease payments equals or exceeds 90% of the fair value of the property.

See also FINANCE LEASE.

capital loss (**allowable capital loss**) The excess of the cost of an asset over the proceeds received on its disposal. Both individuals and companies may set capital losses against *capital gains to establish tax liability. *Indexation is not permitted to create or increase a capital loss.

capital maintenance concept 1. The **financial capital maintenance concept** is that the capital of a company is only maintained if the financial or monetary amount of its *net assets at the end of a financial period is equal to or exceeds the financial or monetary amount of its net assets at the beginning of the period, excluding any distributions to, or contributions from, the owners. **2.** The **physical capital maintenance concept** is that the physical capital is only maintained if the physical productive or operating capacity, or the funds or resources required to achieve this capacity, is equal to or exceeds the physical productive capacity at the beginning of the period, after excluding any distributions to, or contributions from, owners during the financial period.

capital market A market in which long-term *capital is raised by industry and commerce, the government, and local authorities. The money comes from private investors, insurance companies, pension funds, and banks and is usually arranged by *issuing houses and *merchant banks. *Stock exchanges are also part of the capital market in that they provide a market for the shares and loan stocks that represent the capital once it has been raised. It is the presence and sophistication of their capital markets that distinguishes the industrial countries from the *developing countries, in that this facility for raising industrial and commercial capital is either absent or rudimentary in the latter.

capital movement The transfer of capital between countries, either by companies or individuals. Restrictions on *exchange controls and capital transfers between countries have been greatly reduced in recent years. Capital movements seeking long-term gains are usually those made by companies investing abroad, for example to set up a factory. Capital movements seeking short-term gains are often more speculative, such as those taking advantage of temporarily high interest rates in another country or an expected change in the exchange rate.

capital profit *See* CAPITAL GAIN.

capital rationing The situation that arises when managers have insufficient money to invest in all projects with a positive *net present value. The term **soft capital rationing** is used of situations in which a company sets its own limits on the amount of money available for investment in projects; if there are external constraints on money available for investments, the term **hard capital rationing** is used. Whenever capital rationing exists, managers need to rank potential investments so that net present value can be maximised (*see* PROFITABILITY INDEX).

capital redemption reserve A reserve created if a company purchases its own shares in circumstances that result in a reduction of share capital. It is a reserve that cannot be distributed to the shareholders and thus ensures the maintenance of the capital base of the company and protects the creditors' buffer (which gives creditors confidence to invest in the company, e.g. as suppliers or debenture holders). *See also* PERMISSIBLE CAPITAL PAYMENT.

capital reserves *See* UNDISTRIBUTABLE RESERVES.

capital risk The risk, in a lending operation, that the capital amount of the investment may be less than its *par value, even at maturity.

capital share *See* INVESTMENT TRUST; SPLIT-CAPITAL INVESTMENT TRUST.

capital stock In the USA, the equity shares in a corporation. The two basic types of capital stock are *common stock and *preferred stock.

capital structure (financial structure)
The balance between the assets and liabilities of a company, the nature of its assets, and the composition of its borrowings. The assets may be fixed (tangible or intangible) or current (stock, debtors, or creditors); the borrowings may be long- or short-term, fixed or floating, secured or unsecured. Ideally the assets and liabilities should be matched. *See also* GEARING.

capital surplus In the USA, the difference between the *par value of a share and its *issue price. It is the equivalent of a *share premium in the UK.

capital transfer tax (CTT) A tax introduced into the UK in 1974 to replace estate duty. In 1986 sweeping changes to capital transfer tax were made and the name was changed to *inheritance tax.

capital turnover (asset turnover) The ratio of the sales of a company or other organization to its *capital employed (i.e. its assets less current liabilities). It is presumed that the higher this ratio, the better the use that is being made of the assets in generating sales. *See also* RATE OF TURNOVER.

CAPM Abbreviation for *capital asset pricing model.

capped mortgage A *mortgage in which the variable interest rate paid by the borrower cannot rise above a specified level, usually for the first few years of the loan. The interest rate can, however, be reduced if interest rates fall generally. *See also* CAP AND COLLAR MORTGAGE.

captive audience An audience that is unlikely to be able to escape being exposed to an advertising message in toto. Examples include cinema audiences and conference audiences.

captive finance company A finance company controlled by an industrial or commercial company.

captive insurance company An insurance company that is totally owned by another organization and insures only, or mostly, the parent company's risks. In this way the parent organization is able to obtain insurance cover (particularly those classes that are compulsory by law) without having to pay premiums to an organization outside its trading group.

captive market A group of purchasers who are obliged to buy a particular product as a result of some special circumstance, such as the absence of an alternative supplier or product.

captive-product pricing Setting a price for products that have to be used with a main product, such as blades for a razor or film for a camera.

CAR Abbreviation for *compound annual return.

carat **1.** A measure of the purity (fineness) of gold. Pure gold is defined as 24 carat; 14-carat gold contains 14/24ths gold, the remainder usually being copper. **2.** A unit for measuring the weight of a diamond or other gemstone, equal to 0.2 gram.

care and maintenance (c & m) Denoting the status of a building, machinery, ship, etc., that is not currently in active use, usually as a result of a fall in demand, but which is being kept in a good state of repair so that it can be brought back into use quickly, if needed.

career anchor A pattern of skills, interests, and values developed in the early stages of a person's career, when that person begins to recognize his or her abilities and the aspects of work that he or she enjoys most. Career anchors help to guide subsequent decisions about jobs and careers. The term was introduced by US organizational theorist Edgar H. Schein.

cargo insurance An insurance covering cargoes carried by ships, aircraft, or other forms of transport. On a *free on board (FOB) contract the responsibility for insuring the goods for the voyage rests with the buyer. The seller's responsibility ends once the goods have been loaded onto the ship or aircraft (or train in the case of free on rail (FOR) contracts). On a *c.i.f. contract, insurance is the responsibility of the seller up to the port of destination. On a *c & f contract, the seller arranges the shipment and pays the freight but the buyer is responsible for the insurance during the voyage (as in an FOB contract). *See also* AVERAGE; FLOATING POLICY; OPEN COVER.

Caribbean Community and Common Market (CARICOM) An association of Caribbean states established in 1973 to further economic cooperation, coordinate foreign policy, and provide common services in health, education, and communications. The members are Antigua and Barbuda, the Bahamas, Barbados, Belize, Dominica, Grenada, Guyana, Haiti, Jamaica, Montserrat, St Christopher and Nevis, St Lucia, St Vincent and the Grenadines, Suriname, and Trinidad and Tobago.

carriage cost The cost of delivering goods within the UK. **Carriage forward** means that the cost of delivery has to be paid by the buyer. **Carriage paid** or **carriage free** means that they are paid by the seller.

carried down (c/d) In book-keeping, describing an amount that is to be transferred as the opening balance in the next period.

carried forward (c/f) In book-keeping, describing the total of a column of figures that is to be the first item in the corresponding column on the next page.

carrier A person or firm that carries goods or people from place to place, usually under a contract and for a fee. A **common carrier**, who has to have an A licence in the UK, provides a public service and must carry any goods or people on regular routes; must charge a reasonable rate; and is liable for all loss or damage to goods in transit. A **limited carrier**, who requires a B licence, carries only certain types of goods (e.g. liquid chemicals in tankers), and may refuse to carry anything else. A **private carrier**, with a C licence, carries only his or her own goods.

carrying amount The balance-sheet value of an asset or liability. For example, a *fixed asset, such as a building, will be shown at the historical cost less the accumulated *depreciation to date, using the *historical-cost convention. Under alternative accounting rules it can be shown at the revalued amount less the accumulated depreciation to date.

carrying costs (holding costs) 1. The costs of maintaining an inventory, including any *opportunity costs, protective measures, wastage, etc. **2.** The costs of holding a particular financial *position.

carry-over The quantity of a *commodity that is carried over from one crop to the following one. The price of some commodities, such as grain, coffee, cocoa, and jute, which grow in annual or biannual crops, is determined by the supply and the demand. The supply consists of the quantity produced by the current crop added to the quantity in the hands of producers and traders that is carried over from the previous crop. Thus, in some circumstances the carry-over can strongly influence the market price.

car tax An excise duty levied in the UK on motor cars at the wholesale stage. It applies to both home-produced and imported cars and is additional to VAT.

cartel An association of independent companies formed to regulate the price and sales conditions of the products or services they offer. A cartel may be national or international, although some countries, including the UK and the USA, have legislation forbidding cartels to be formed on the grounds that they are *monopolies that function against the public interest. The International Air Transport Association is an example of an international price-fixing cartel that is regarded as acceptable because of fears that price-cutting of fares between airlines would jeopardize safety.

cascade shareholdings A form of *pyramiding in which a holding company has a controlling interest in a company that in turn has a controlling interest in further companies, and so on.

CASE Abbreviation for *computer-assisted self-explication.

case of need An endorsement written on a *bill of exchange giving the name of someone to whom the holder may apply if the bill is not honoured at maturity.

cash *Legal tender in the form of banknotes and coins that are readily acceptable for the settlement of debts.

cash accounting 1. An accounting scheme for *value added tax enabling a *taxable person to account for VAT on the basis of amounts paid and received during the period of the VAT return. Relief for bad debts is automatically available under this scheme. In order to qualify for the scheme, expected turnover should not exceed £660,000 in the next 12 months. A business already in the scheme is allowed a 25% tolerance limit above this threshold. **2. (cash-flow accounting)** A system of accounting that records only the cash payments and receipts relating to transactions made by a business, rather than when the money is earned or when expenses are incurred, as in *accrual accounting. UK legislation does not permit this system of accounting to be used for *published accounts.

cash against documents (CAD) **1.** The simultaneous exchange of assets and payment. **2.** Payment terms for exported goods in which the shipping documents are sent to a bank, agent, etc., in the country to which the goods are being shipped, and the buyer then obtains the documents by paying the invoice amount in cash to the bank, agent, etc. Having the shipping documents enables the buyer to take possession of the goods when they arrive at their port of destination; this is known as **documents against presentation**. *Compare* DOCUMENTS AGAINST ACCEPTANCE.

cash and carry **1.** A wholesaler, especially of groceries, who sells to retailers and others with businesses at discounted prices on condition that they pay in cash, collect the goods themselves, and buy in bulk. **2.** An operation that is sometimes possible on the futures market (*see* FUTURES CONTRACT), especially the *London Metal Exchange. In some circumstances the spot price of a metal, including the cost of insurance, warehousing, and interest for three months, is less than the futures-market price for delivery in three months. Under these conditions it is possible to buy the spot metal, simultaneously sell the forward goods, and make a profit in excess of the yield the capital would have earned on the money market.

cash book The *book of prime entry in which are recorded receipts into and payments out of the organization's bank account (*compare* PETTY CASH). The cash book, unlike most other books of prime entry, is also an *account, as its balance shows the amount due to or from the bank.

cash budget *See* CASH FLOW.

cash card A plastic card enabling customers of UK banks and building societies to obtain cash from *automated teller machines, in conjunction with a *personal identification number. Many cash cards also function as *cheque cards and *debit cards.

cash cow *See* BOSTON MATRIX.

cash crop A crop that is sold for money as opposed to one that is consumed by the producer. In tropical and subtropical areas, cocoa, coffee, sugar and bananas are common cash crops. In cooler areas cash crops include grain and some vegetables. *Compare* SUBSISTENCE CROP.

cash cycle In manufacturing industry, the interval between an outlay of cash to buy raw materials and the receipt of payment for the manufactured goods produced from them.

cash deal A transaction (either buying or selling) on the *London Stock Exchange in which settlement is made immediately, i.e. usually on the following day.

cash discount A *discount receivable or allowable for settling an invoice for cash, or within a specified period. In the *profit and loss account, discounts receivable are classed as revenue; discounts allowable as expenditure.

cash dispenser *See* AUTOMATED TELLER MACHINE.

cash dividend A *dividend paid in cash rather than shares. Cash dividends are paid net of income tax, credit being given to the shareholder for the tax deducted.

cash flow **1.** The movement of cash in and out of a business. A **cash-flow statement** shows the inflows and outflows of cash and cash equivalents for a business over an accounting period under various set headings. In the UK, *Financial Reporting Standard 1 requires certain companies to publish a cash-flow statement in their annual accounts. A **cash-flow projection** (or **cash budget**) sets out all the expected payments and receipts in a given period. This is different from the projected profit and loss account and, in times of cash shortage, may be more important. It is on the basis of the cash-flow projection that managers may arrange appropriate financing facilities and may also arrange for employees and creditors to be paid at appropriate times. *See also* DISCOUNTED CASH FLOW; FREE CASH FLOW. **2.** The net income from a particular transaction after all cash expenses have been met (noncash expenses such as depreciation being specifically excluded from the calculation).

cash flow at risk A measure of the risks to a firm's cash flows, calculated by applying the concept of *value-at-risk.

cash inflows The cash receipts of a business. Cash inflows arise from transactions such as sales of trading stock, receipts from debtors for credit sales, and disposals of *fixed assets.

cashless society A society in which modern electronic credit and debit cards can be substituted for cash in all or nearly all purchases. *See* ELECTRONIC FUNDS TRANSFER AT POINT OF SALE.

cash management The planning, monitoring, and execution of a firm's policy regarding *liquidity.

cash management account A bank account in which deposits are invested by the bank, usually on the *money market; it is, however, a cheque account and the client is able to obtain loans if required.

cash on delivery (COD) Terms of trade in which a supplier will post goods to a customer, provided the customer pays the postman or delivery man the full invoice amount when they are delivered. It was extensively used in mail order (*see* MAILORDER HOUSE), but the use of telephone ordering using credit cards has reduced the amount of COD business.

cash-or-nothing option *See* BINARY OPTION.

cash outflows The cash payments made by a business. Cash outflows arise from transactions such as purchase of materials, *direct labour costs, *overheads, and payment of taxes and dividends.

cash price The price at which a seller is prepared to sell goods provided that payment is received immediately in cash, i.e.

no credit or commission to a credit-card company has to be given. This is invariably below the price that includes a *hire-purchase agreement.

cash ratio (liquidity ratio) The ratio of the cash reserve that a bank keeps in coin, banknotes, etc., to its total liabilities to its customers, i.e. the amount deposited with it in current accounts and deposit accounts. Because cash reserves earn no interest, bankers try to keep them to a minimum, consistent with legal reserve requirements.

cash refund offer An offer to refund all or part of the purchase price of a product to consumers who send 'proof of purchase' to the manufacturer.

CASI Abbreviation for *computer-aided self-interview.

casting vote A second or deciding vote. It is common practice to give the chairman of a meeting a second vote to be used to resolve a deadlock. In the case of a company meeting, the chairman is generally given this right by the articles of association, but has no common-law right to a casting vote.

CAT Abbreviation for *computer-assisted trading.

catalogue 1. A book, brochure, computer disk, or website containing details of items for sale, as used in *catalogue marketing. *See also* ELECTRONIC CATALOGUE. **2. (directory)** A structured listing of registered websites in different categories. Yahoo! and Excite are the best known examples of catalogues. The distinction between a *search engine and a catalogue has become blurred since many sites now include both facilities as part of a portal service.

catalogue marketing *Direct marketing by means of print, DVD, or electronic catalogues mailed to selected customers, made available in stores, or presented online. *See also* CATALOGUE STORE.

catalogue store A retail operation that sells a wide selection of fast-moving goods at discount prices. The selling medium is a *catalogue, with very little stock on display. The stores are not designed for the comfort of the customer, but the simple

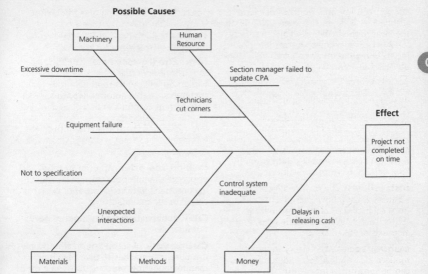

Possible Causes

Machinery

Human Resource

Excessive downtime

Section manager failed to update CPA

Technicians cut corners

Effect

Equipment failure

Project not completed on time

Not to specification

Control system inadequate

Unexpected interactions

Delays in releasing cash

Materials

Methods

Money

Cause–effect diagram

premises enable prices to be kept competitive.

catastrophe risk A *risk in which the potential loss is of the greatest size, such as the explosion of a nuclear power station or a major earthquake.

catching bargain (unconscionable bargain) An unfair *contract, often one in which one party has been taken advantage of by the other. Such a contract may be set aside or modified by a court.

category killer (category discounter) An exceptionally aggressive off-price retailer that offers branded merchandise in clearly defined product categories at heavily discounted prices. Their predatory pricing strategy and ability to decimate much of the competition in their sector explains the name.

CATI Abbreviation for *computer-assisted telephone interviewing.

CAT standard A set of minimum standards, which applies to *ISAs that meet the terms laid down by the government. An ISA that complies with these terms bears a CAT mark giving assurance under

three headings: Charges, Access, and Terms. The assurances are that there will be either no charges or reasonable charges, easy access to funds at any time, and no unfair terms hidden in the small print. It also guarantees that any increases required as a result of a change of base rate will be made within one calendar month. CAT marking does not, of course, guarantee that a particular ISA will be profitable.

causal quantitative models Techniques used to forecast such future trends as demand for a product, based on establishing a causal relationship between two or more variables. For example, average temperature, time of year, and a local demographic profile can be used to predict ice-cream sales in an area. The reliability of the techniques is dependent on the correct identification of significant variables. Mathematical techniques, using *regression analysis, are used to establish a functional relationship between variables.

cause-and-effect allocation A *cost allocation in which the *allocation base is a significant determinant of the cost. To ensure that *indirect costs are accurately assigned to *cost objects, managers need to use cause-and-effect allocations rather than the *arbitrary allocations sometimes used in *traditional costing systems. *See* ACTIVITY-BASED COSTING.

cause–effect diagram (fish-bone diagram; Ishikawa diagram) A diagram that, by working back from a given problem, is used to identify the main categories of possible causes of the problem and then to generate detailed lists of specific possible causes. Attributed to Kaoru Ishikawa, the technique is one of a set taught to members of quality circles or quality-improvement teams within the *total quality management process. The method involves four steps: (1) identifying the problem or effect to be analysed; (2) identifying the main classes of possible causes using categories appropriate to the process under review; (3) identifying possible detailed causes under each of these categories; (4) recording these possible causes on the diagram to enable them to be discussed and clarified.

cautious shift *See* CHOICE-SHIFT EFFECTS.

caveat A proviso or qualification that limits liability by putting another party on notice. For example, a retailer may sell goods subject to the caveat that no guarantee of their suitability for a particular purpose is given. The purchaser in these circumstances has no remedy against the retailer should the goods in fact turn out to be unsuitable for that particular purpose.

caveat emptor (Latin: let the buyer beware) A maxim implying that the purchaser of goods must take care to ensure that they are free from defects of quality, fitness, or title, i.e. that the risk is borne by the purchaser and not by the seller. If the goods turn out to be defective, the purchaser has no remedy against the seller. The rule does not apply if the purchaser is unable to examine the goods, if the defects are not evident from a reasonable examination, or if the seller has behaved fraudulently. Some measure of protection for the unwary purchaser is afforded by a number of statutes, including the Unfair Contract Terms Act (1977), the

Sale of Goods Act (1979), and the Consumer Protection Act (1987).

CAVIAR Cinema and Video Industry Audience Research: a media audience-research operation that covers cinema audience profiles, viewing of video films, and newspaper reading habits.

CBI Abbreviation for *Confederation of British Industry.

CBT Abbreviation for *computer-based training.

CCA Abbreviation for *current-cost accounting.

c.c.c. Abbreviation for *cwmni cyfyngedig cyhoeddus: the Welsh equivalent of plc.

CD Abbreviation for *certificate of deposit.

CDC Group A body set up by the UK government in 1948 (as the **Commonwealth Development Corporation**) to provide investment capital for private-sector businesses in the developing world. CDC is owned by the government but operationally independent. It invests through third-party fund managers rather than directly in businesses.

cedi The standard monetary unit of Ghana, divided into 100 pesewas.

cell-based manufacturing A process design that identifies the common manufacturing characteristics in batches of apparently different products and groups of machinery to enable their common features to be organized in a way that provides some of the benefits of line production.

cellular layout A process design in which equipment used to make similar parts is grouped together. It is often associated with *job-design programmes aiming to overcome the perceived demotivating influence of conventional line production by putting staff together in relatively autonomous teams.

cellular network Any of the networks enabling mobile telephones to connect to the main telephone system. Originally established in the UK jointly by British Telecom and Securicor (as Cellnet), it consists of a number of adjacent cells, each containing a transmit/receive station connected to the main telephone network and reached by the mobile subscriber using a battery-operated portable radiotelephone. As subscribers move from one geographical cell to another (e.g. by car), they are automatically switched to receive signals from the new area.

census An official count of a population for demographic, social, or economic purposes. In the UK, population censuses have been held every ten years since 1801 and since 1966 supplementary censuses have been held halfway through the ten-year period. A **census of distribution**, quantifying the wholesale and retail distribution, has been carried out approximately every five years since 1950. A **census of production**, recording the output of all manufacturing, mining, quarrying, and building industries, together with that of all public services, has been held every year since 1968.

census tract A small geographical area (about 1200 households) in which the population has many socio-economic characteristics in common. The term is of US origin.

cent 1. A monetary unit of American Samoa, Antigua and Barbuda, Australia, the Bahamas, Barbados, Belau, Belize, Bermuda, the British Virgin Islands, Brunei, Canada, the Cayman Islands, Dominica, East Timor, Ecuador, El Salvador, Fiji, Grenada, Guam, Guatemala, Guyana, Hong Kong, Jamaica, Kiribati, Liberia, Malaysia, the Marshall Islands, Micronesia, Namibia, Nauru, New Zealand, Puerto Rico, Saint Kitts and Nevis, Saint Lucia, Saint Vincent and the Grenadines, Singapore, the Solomon Islands, Taiwan, Trinidad and Tobago, Tuvalu, the USA, the Virgin Islands, and Zimbabwe, worth one hundredth of a *dollar. **2.** A monetary unit of Andorra, Austria, Belgium, Bosnia and Hercegovina, Finland, France, French Guiana, Germany, Greece, Guadeloupe, Ireland, Italy, Kosovo, Luxembourg, Madeira, Martinique, Mayotte, Monaco, Montenegro, The Netherlands, Portugal, Réunion, San Marino, and Spain, worth one hundredth of a *euro. **3.** A monetary unit of Ethiopia, worth one hundredth of a *birr. **4.** A monetary unit of Kenya, Somalia, Tanzania, and Uganda, worth one

hundredth of a *shilling. **5.** A monetary unit of South Africa, worth one hundredth of a *rand. **6.** A monetary unit of Mauritius, the Seychelles, and Sri Lanka, worth one hundredth of a *rupee. **7.** A monetary unit of Swaziland, worth one hundredth of a *lilangeni. **8.** A monetary unit of Surinam and the Netherlands Antilles, worth one hundredth of a *guilder. **9.** A monetary unit of Sierra Leone, worth one hundredth of a *leone. **10.** A monetary unit of Malta, worth one hundredth of a *lira. **11.** A former monetary unit of The Netherlands, worth one hundredth of a guilder (until 2002).

centavo 1. A monetary unit of Bolivia, worth one hundredth of a *boliviano. **2.** A monetary unit of Brazil, worth one hundredth of a *real. **3.** A monetary unit of Argentina, Chile, Colombia, Cuba, the Dominican Republic, Mexico, and the Philippines, worth one hundredth of a *peso. **4.** A monetary unit of El Salvador, worth one hundredth of a *colón. **5.** A monetary unit of Guatemala, worth one hundredth of a *quetzal. **6.** A monetary unit of Honduras, worth one hundredth of a *lempira. **7.** A monetary unit of Nicaragua, worth one hundredth of a *córdoba. **8.** A monetary unit of Peru, worth one hundredth of a *new sol. **9.** A monetary unit of Cape Verde, worth one hundredth of an *escudo. **10.** A monetary unit of Mozambique, worth one hundredth of a *metical. **11.** A monetary unit of São Tomé e Príncipe, worth one hundredth of a *dobra. **12.** A former monetary unit of Portugal and Madeira, worth one hundredth of an escudo (until 2002).

centesimo (*plural* **centesimi**) A former monetary unit of Italy and San Marino, worth one hundredth of a lira (until 2002).

centésimo 1. A monetary unit of Panama, worth one hundredth of a *balboa. **2.** A monetary unit of Uruguay, worth one hundredth of a *peso.

centime 1. A monetary unit of Benin, Burkina-Faso, Burundi, Cameroon, the Central African Republic, Chad, Comoros, Congo, Congo-Brazzaville, Côte d'Ivoire, Djibouti, Equatorial Guinea, Gabon, Guinea, Liechtenstein, Madagascar, Mali, Niger, Rwanda, Senegal, Switzerland, Tahiti, and Togo, worth one hundredth of a *franc. **2.** A monetary unit of Algeria, worth one hundredth of a *dinar. **3.** A monetary unit of Haiti, worth one hundredth of a *gourde. **4.** A monetary unit of Morocco, worth one hundredth of a *dirham. **5.** A former monetary unit of Andorra, Belgium, France, Luxembourg, and Monaco, worth one hundredth of a franc (until 2002).

céntimo 1. A monetary unit of Costa Rica, worth one hundredth of a *colón. **2.** A monetary unit of Paraguay, worth one hundredth of a *guaraní. **3.** A monetary unit of Venezuela, worth one hundredth of a *bolívar. **4.** A monetary unit of Peru, worth one hundredth of a *new sol. **5.** A former monetary unit of Spain and Andorra, worth one hundredth of a peseta (until 2002).

Central Arbitration Committee A committee set up by the Employment Protection Act (1975) to arbitrate on matters voluntarily submitted to it through the *Advisory Conciliation and Arbitration Service by the parties to a trade dispute. It also determines claims for statutory recognition of trade unions under the Employment Relations Act (1999) and adjudicates on issues arising from the European Works Council Directive.

central bank A bank that provides financial and banking services for the government of a country and its commercial banking system as well as implementing the government's monetary policy. The main functions of a central bank are: to manage the government's accounts; to accept deposits and grant loans to the commercial banks; to control the issue of banknotes; to manage the public debt; to help manage the exchange rate when necessary; to influence the interest rate structure and control the money supply; to hold the country's reserves of gold and foreign currency; to manage dealings with other central banks; and to act as lender of last resort to the banking system. Examples of major central banks include the *Bank of England in the UK, the *Federal Reserve Bank of the USA, and the *European Central Bank established in 1998.

central bank discount rate The rate of interest charged by a *central bank for discounting *eligible paper.

Centrale de Livraison de Valeurs Mobilières (CEDEL) A settlement service for *eurobonds in Luxembourg. It is owned by a consortium of international banks. *See also* EUROCLEAR.

centralization The process or situation in which decision making is confined to the top managers of an organization. *Compare* DECENTRALIZATION.

central location telephone interviewing A marketing-research technique in which interviewers make telephone calls from a *call centre to interview respondents. In recent years this has been the fastest growth area in marketing research; it is seen as a quick and cheap way of reaching opinion leaders and other groups.

Central Statistical Office *See* OFFICE FOR NATIONAL STATISTICS.

centre-of-gravity method A method of calculating the ideal location for warehousing facilities by calculating the transport costs to each of the outlets to be served by the facility. The centre of gravity is the location giving the lowest total transport costs.

certain annuity (terminable annuity) A form of investment contract that pays fixed sums at scheduled intervals to an individual after he or she attains a specified age; it runs for a specified number of years.

certainty equivalent method In *capital budgeting, a method of risk analysis in which a particularly risky return is expressed in terms of the *risk-free rate of return that would be its equivalent.

certificate of damage A certificate issued by a dock or wharfage company when it takes in damaged goods. The certificate, signed for or on behalf of the dock surveyor, states the nature of the damage and the cause, if known.

certificate of deposit (CD) A negotiable certificate issued by a bank in return for a term deposit of up to five years. They originated in the USA in the 1960s. From 1968, a sterling CD was issued by UK banks. They were intended to enable the *merchant banks to attract funds away from the *clearing banks with the offer of competitive interest rates. However, in 1971 the clearing banks also began to issue CDs as their negotiability and higher average yield had made them increasingly popular with the larger investors.

A secondary market in CDs has developed, made up of the *discount houses and the banks in the interbank market. They are issued in various amounts between £10,000 and £50,000, although they may be subdivided into units of the lower figure to facilitate negotiation of part holdings. *See also* ROLL-OVER CD.

certificate of incorporation The certificate that brings a company into existence; it is issued to the shareholders of a company by the *Registrar of Companies. It is issued when the *memorandum and *articles of association have been submitted to the Registrar of Companies, together with other documents that disclose the proposed registered address of the company, details of the proposed directors and company secretary, the nominal and issued share capital, and the capital duty. The statutory registration fee must also be submitted. Until the certificate is issued, the company has no legal existence.

certificate of insurance A certificate giving abbreviated details of the cover provided by an insurance policy. In a *motor-insurance policy or an *employers' liability insurance policy, the information that must be shown on the certificate of insurance is laid down by law and in both cases the policy cover does not come into force until the certificate has been delivered to the policyholder.

certificate of origin A document that states the country from which a particular parcel of goods originated. In international trade it is one of the shipping documents and will often determine whether or not an import duty has to be paid on the goods and, if it has, on what tariff. Such certificates are usually issued by a chamber of commerce in the country of origin.

certificate of quality A certificate to provide proof that goods to be traded in a *commodity market comply with an agreed standard.

certificate of value A statement made in a document certifying that the transaction concerned is not part of a transaction (or series of transactions) for which the amount involved exceeds a certain value. The statement is made in relation to stamp duty, denoting that either it is not payable or it is payable at a reduced rate.

certificate to commence business A document issued by the *Registrar of Companies to a public company on incorporation; it certifies that the nominal value of the company's share capital is at least equal to the authorized minimum of £50,000. Until the certificate has been issued, the company cannot do business or exercise its borrowing powers.

certified accountant *See* CHARTERED CERTIFIED ACCOUNTANT.

certified check *See* MARKED CHEQUE.

certified stock (certificated stock) Stocks of a commodity that have been examined and passed as acceptable for delivery in fulfilment of contracts on a futures market (*see* FUTURES CONTRACT).

cesser clause A clause in a charterparty (*see* CHARTERING), inserted when the charterer intends to transfer to a shipper the right to have goods carried. It provides that the shipowner is to have a lien over the shipper's goods for the freight payable under the charterparty and that the charterer's liability for freight ceases on shipment of a full cargo.

CET Abbreviation for *Common External Tariff.

CFC Abbreviation for Common Fund for Commodities. *See* UNITED NATIONS CONFERENCE ON TRADE AND DEVELOPMENT.

CFTC Abbreviation for *Commodity Futures Trading Commission.

CGT Abbreviation for *capital gains tax.

chaebol A large, often family-owned, conglomerate in South Korea. The Hanbo Business Group, which collapsed in 1997 with debts of $US 6 billion, is an example of a *chaebol*.

chain stores *See* MULTIPLE SHOPS.

chairman (chairwoman; chairperson; chair) The most senior officer in a company, who presides at the *annual general meeting of the company and usually also at meetings of the board of directors. He or she may combine the roles of chairperson and *managing director, especially in a small company of which he or she is the majority shareholder; alternatively, he or she may be a figurehead, without executive participation in the day-to-day running of the company. He or she is often a retired managing director. In the USA the person who performs this function is often called the **president**.

chairman's report (chairperson's report; chairwoman's report) A report by the chair of a company in the annual report and accounts (see ANNUAL ACCOUNTS), addressed to the *members of the company, giving an overview of the company's activities during the financial period. These statements are not prescribed by regulation and often present a favourable view of the activities and prospects of an organization. The report often also gives a survey of what can be expected in the coming year. It is signed by the chairperson, who usually reads it at the *annual general meeting.

chamber of commerce In the UK, a voluntary organization, existing in most towns, of commercial, industrial, and trading businessmen who represent their joint interests to local and central government. The London Chamber of Commerce is the largest such organization in the UK; it also fulfils an educational role, running several commercial courses, for which it also sets examinations. Most UK chambers of commerce are affiliated to the Association of British Chambers of Commerce. *Compare* CHAMBER OF TRADE.

chamber of trade An organization of local retailers set up to protect their interests in local matters. They are a much narrower organization than a *chamber of commerce and most in the UK are affiliated to the *National Chamber of Trade (NTC).

change agent A group or individual whose purpose is to bring about a change in existing practices of an organization that have become entrenched routines. In many instances this role is fulfilled by outside management consultants as they are regarded as more objective and therefore their advice is more acceptable to those affected by the changes.

change management A systematic approach to dealing with both planned and unplanned change in the organization. A major part of change management is dealing with fear of or *resistance to change in the workforce. The best strategy for dealing with such resistance is usually one of communication, participation, encouragement, and support.

channel captain (channel leader) The most powerful member in the *distribution channel of goods. The channel consists of the manufacturer, wholesaler, and retailer, the channel captain usually being the manufacturer. There are, however, exceptions, most notably when the retailer is a major department store or chain, whose buying power enables it to become the channel captain. The channel captain controls the distribution channel and can insist that products should be made to their own specifications. *See also* CHANNEL CONFLICT.

channel conflict A disagreement between members of a *distribution channel. Horizontal channel conflict can occur among retailers, if one retailer feels another is competing too vigorously through pricing or is using advertising to invade unauthorized sales territory. Vertical conflict occurs between retailers and their suppliers when either side feels dominated by the other. Conflict can arise when a manufacturer creates a new channel, such as direct e-commerce.

channel cooperation Cooperation between members of a *distribution channel as a result of harmonious marketing objectives and strategies. Problems can emerge when specific channel members have too much power or act negatively. Restriction of lines, limits on the number of new products, or the demand for promotional bonuses (typically a powerful retailer demanding cash for a promotion) by retailers and wholesalers can limit competition.

chaos theory A set of mathematical models according to which simple equations and initial conditions give rise to complicated paths for variables. Some of these models have been applied to financial markets.

CHAPS Acronym for Clearing House Automatic Payment System. *See* ASSOCIATION FOR PAYMENT CLEARING SERVICES.

chapter 7 In the USA, the statute of the Bankruptcy Reform Act (1978) that refers to liquidation proceedings. It provides for a trustee appointed by the court to make a management charge, secure additional financing, and operate the business in order to prevent further loss. The intention of the statute, which is based on fairness and public policy, is to accept that honest debtors may not always be able to discharge their debts fully and to give them an opportunity to make a fresh start both in their business and personal lives. *Compare* CHAPTER 11; CHAPTER 13.

chapter 11 In the USA, the statute of the Bankruptcy Reform Act (1978) that refers to the reorganization of partnerships, corporations, and municipalities, as well as sole traders, who are in financial difficulties. Unless the court rules otherwise, the debtor remains in control of the business and its operations. By allowing activities to continue, debtors and creditors can enter into arrangements, such as the restructuring of debt, rescheduling of payments, and the granting of loans. *Compare* CHAPTER 7; CHAPTER 13.

chapter 13 In the USA, the statute of the Bankruptcy Reform Act (1978) that refers to debt restructuring and provides for individuals to repay creditors over time. *Compare* CHAPTER 7; CHAPTER 11.

characteristics of easy movement *See* PRINCIPLES OF MOTION ECONOMY.

characteristics of services operations *See* SERVICE.

charge 1. A legal or equitable interest in land, securing the payment of money. It gives the creditor in whose favour the charge is created (the **chargee**) the right to payment from the income or proceeds of sale of the land charged, in priority to claims against the debtor by unsecured creditors. **2.** An interest in company property created in favour of a creditor (e.g. as a *debenture holder) to secure the amount owing. Most charges must be registered by the *Registrar of Companies (*see*

also REGISTER OF CHARGES). A **fixed charge** is attached to specific fixed assets (e.g. premises, plant and machinery) and while in force prevents the company from dealing freely in those assets without the consent of the lender. A **floating charge** is not immediately attached to any specific asset but 'floats' over all the company's assets, to which it will not attach until **crystallization**, i.e. until some event (typically winding-up) causes it to become fixed. Before crystallization, the company may deal freely with such assets; this type of charge is suitable for *current assets, whose values must necessarily fluctuate. If the company goes into liquidation, fixed-charge holders are paid before *preferential creditors, who are paid before floating-charge holders.

A charge can also be created upon shares. For example, the articles of association usually give the company a lien in respect of unpaid calls, and company members may, in order to secure a debt owed to a third party, charge their shares, either by a full transfer of shares coupled with an agreement to retransfer upon repayment of the debt or by a deposit of the share certificate.

chargeable assets All forms of property, wherever situated, that are not specifically designated as exempt from tax on *capital gains. **Exempt assets** include motor cars, National Savings Certificates, foreign currency for private use, betting winnings, life-insurance policies for those who are the original beneficial owners, works of art of national importance given for national purposes, principal private residences, *gilt-edged securities, certain low-value items, and investments under *personal equity plans and *Individual Savings Accounts.

chargeable event Any transaction or event that gives rise to a liability to income tax or to capital gains tax.

chargeable gain In the UK, that part of a *capital gain arising as a result of the disposal of an asset that is subject to taxation. Non-chargeable gains include:
- gains resulting from proceeds that are taxable under *income tax;
- gains from exempt assets (*see* CHARGEABLE ASSETS);
- gains covered by other exemptions and

reliefs (e.g. personal exemption from capital gains tax of £8500 for 2005–06 for a tax year);

- gains not charged in full or at all owing to the system of *taper relief (or *indexation in the case of company assets).

chargeable transfer Certain lifetime gifts that are transfers of value not covered by any of the exemptions and are therefore liable to *inheritance tax. If such a lifetime gift is not a *potentially exempt transfer, it is a chargeable transfer. If the gift is a potentially exempt transfer, but death occurs within seven years, then that potentially exempt transfer becomes a chargeable transfer.

charge account (credit account) An account held by a customer at a retail shop that allows him or her to pay for any goods purchased at the end of a stated period (usually one month).

charge card A plastic card entitling the holder to purchase goods or services either up to a prescribed limit or (in some cases) without limit, provided that payment in full is made at regular intervals (usually monthly). Some charge cards are issued by retailers and may only be used in that retailer's outlets (see also STORE CARD). However, most charge cards are issued by banks (e.g. American Express, Diners' Club), which have a wide acceptability similar to *credit cards, although they do not have the facility to roll over credit from month to month. Charge cards are issued to businesses and to individuals, who have convinced the issuers of their probity and resources. They are therefore more prestigious than other forms of credit card.

charges forward An instruction to the effect that all carriage charges on a consignment of goods will be paid by the consignee after receipt.

charges register **1.** See LAND REGISTRATION. **2.** See REGISTER OF CHARGES.

charismatic leader A leader who inspires his or her followers through personal magnetism and highly developed communication skills. Charismatic leaders tend to be confident, visionary, and change-oriented and may display eccentric or unusual behaviour. Compare BUREAU-CRATIC LEADER. See also LEADERSHIP STYLE; POWER STYLES; TRANSFORMATIONAL LEADERSHIP.

charitable trust A trust set up for a charitable purpose that is registered with the *Charity Commission. Charitable trusts do not have to pay income tax if they comply with the regulations of the Charity Commissioners.

Charity Commission The government department that acts as both an adviser to, and an investigator of, charities. It is responsible to the Home Secretary and is governed by the Charities Act (1993).

chartered accountant (CA) A qualified member of the *Institute of Chartered Accountants in England and Wales, the Institute of Chartered Accountants of Scotland, or the Institute of Chartered Accountants in Ireland. These were the original bodies to be granted royal charters. Other bodies of accountants now have charters (the *Association of Chartered Certified Accountants, the Chartered Institute of Management Accountants, and the Chartered Institute of Public Finance and Accountancy) but their members are not known as chartered accountants. Most firms of chartered accountants are engaged in public practice concerned with auditing, taxation, and other financial advice; however, many trained chartered accountants fulfil management roles in industry.

Chartered Association of Certified Accountants See ASSOCIATION OF CHARTERED CERTIFIED ACCOUNTANTS.

chartered bank A bank in the USA that is authorized to operate as a bank by a charter granted either by its home state (state-chartered bank) or by the federal government (nationally chartered bank). In Canada, a similar charter is granted to banks by the Comptroller of Currency. The use of charters dates back to the use of Royal Charters, which predated Acts of Parliament.

chartered certified accountant (CCA) A member of the *Association of Chartered Certified Accountants. The Association's members are trained in industry, in the public sector, and in the offices of practising accountants. Membership is granted on the basis of completion of the

Association's examinations and of sufficient relevant work experience. Members are recognized by the UK Department of Trade and Industry as qualified to audit the accounts of companies. They may be associates (ACCA) or fellows (FCCA) of the Association and, although they are not *chartered accountants, they fulfil much the same role. Chartered certified accountants were known as **certified accountants** until 1996. In the USA the equivalent is a **certified public accountant (CPA)**.

chartered company *See* COMPANY.

Chartered Institute of Management Accountants *See* ACCOUNTANT; MANAGEMENT ACCOUNTING.

Chartered Institute of Marketing (CIM) A professional organization founded in 1911 as the Sales Managers' Association. Its goals are to promote the principles and practices of marketing throughout industry, to provide services for members and registered students, and to uphold professional standards in the field. The Institute received a Royal Charter in 1989.

Chartered Institute of Personnel and Development (CIPD) A professional organization for personnel managers in the UK, founded in 1913. The Institute, an independent and non-political body, aims to encourage and assist the development of personnel management by promoting investigation and research and establishing standards of qualification and performance. Previously known as the **Institute of Personnel Management (IPM)**, it received the Royal Charter in 2000.

Chartered Institute of Public Finance and Accountancy *See* ACCOUNTANT.

Chartered Institute of Public Relations (CIPR) The professional organization, established in 1948, for UK public relations consultancies. It is the largest such organization in Europe.

Chartered Institute of Taxation A professional institute for those engaged in working within the taxation field, in accountancy practices, legal firms, banks, and in commerce. An Associate of the Institute is designated *ATII and a Fellow *FTII. Until 1994 it was known as the **Institute of Taxation**. *See also* ATT.

Chartered Insurance Institute (CII) An association of insurers and brokers in the insurance industry. Its origins date back to 1873; its first Royal Charter was granted in 1912. It provides training by post and at its own college, examinations leading to its associateship diploma (ACII) and fellowship diploma (FCII), and sets high standards of ethical behaviour in the industry.

Chartered Management Institute (CMI) The principal UK professional body for managers, formed in 1992 from a merger of the British Institute of Management and the Institute of Industrial Managers. Its purpose is to promote high professional standards among managers and to provide information and other benefits for its members. It was awarded a Royal Charter in 2002.

chartered secretary *See* INSTITUTE OF CHARTERED SECRETARIES AND ADMINISTRATORS.

chartered surveyor *See* ROYAL INSTITUTION OF CHARTERED SURVEYORS.

chartering Hiring the whole of a ship or aircraft. The hirer is called the **charterer** and the document setting out the terms and conditions of the contract is called the **charterparty**. In a *time charter the ship or aircraft is hired for a specified period, usually with the owner operating it and the charterer paying fuel and stores costs. However, in a *bareboat charter (or demise charter), which is a form of time charter, the charterer pays for all crew expenses. In a *voyage charter, the ship or aircraft is hired for a single voyage between stated ports to carry a stated cargo and the owner pays all the expenses of running the ship. In an **open charter** the charterer may use the ship or aircraft to carry any cargo to any port.

chartist An *investment analyst who uses charts of prices and volumes in an attempt to predict what will happen in financial markets. Most chartist analysis is based on the assumption that history repeats itself and that the movements of share prices conform to a small number of repetitive patterns.

chase demand strategy (variable output plan) An approach to aggregate planning that attempts to match supply and output with fluctuating demand. Depending on the product or service involved, the approach can incur costs by the ineffective use of capacity at periods of low demand, by the need to recruit or lay off staff, by learning-curve effects, and by a possible loss of quality. The advantages include low storage costs and greater ability to respond to the needs of the customer. *Compare* LEVEL OUTPUT STRATEGY.

chat room A website at which users of the Internet can engage in interactive, real-time, text-based discussions. Chat rooms can be confined to a specific topic or can be free ranging.

chattels All property of whatever kind, excluding freehold land and anything permanently affixed to freehold land. Interests in land (e.g. leaseholds) are **chattels real**. **Chattels personal** are all movable and tangible articles of property. Chattels include timber growing on land (whether freehold or leasehold) and articles of personal use.

cheap money (**easy money**) A monetary policy of keeping *interest rates at a low level. This is normally done to encourage an expansion in the level of economic activity by reducing the costs of borrowing and investment. It was used in the 1930s to help recovery after the Depression and during World War II to reduce the cost of government borrowing. *Compare* DEAR MONEY.

check The US spelling of *cheque.

check digit A digit often appended at the end of a string of digits; it is used for carrying out a check to verify the accuracy of a sequence or a customer number.

cheque A preprinted form on which instructions are given to an account holder (a bank or building society) to pay a stated sum to a named recipient. It is the most common form of payment of debts of all kinds (*see also* CHEQUE ACCOUNT; CURRENT ACCOUNT).

In a **crossed cheque** two parallel lines across the face of the cheque indicate that it must be paid into a bank account and not cashed over the counter (a **general crossing**). A **special crossing** may be used in order to further restrict the negotiabil-

ity of the cheque, for example by adding the name of the payee's bank. An **open cheque** is an uncrossed cheque that can be cashed at the bank of origin. An **order cheque** is one made payable to a named recipient 'or order', enabling the payee to either deposit it in an account or endorse it to a third party, i.e. transfer the rights to the cheque by signing it on the reverse. In a **blank cheque** the amount is not stated; it is often used if the exact debt is not known and the payee is left to complete it. However, the drawer may impose a maximum by writing 'under £...' on the cheque. In the USA the word is spelled **check**. *See also* MARKED CHEQUE; RETURNED CHEQUE; STALE CHEQUE.

cheque account An account with a bank or building society on which cheques can be drawn. The US name for such an account is a **checking account**. *See* CURRENT ACCOUNT.

cheque card A plastic card issued by a retail bank to its customers to guarantee cheques drawn on the customer's current account up to a specified limit. The card carries the account number, the name of the customer, and has to be signed by the customer. The card number must be written on the reverse of the cheque that it is guaranteeing. Many cheque cards have now been replaced by *multifunctional cards, which also function as *cash cards and *debit cards.

chetrum A monetary unit of Bhutan, worth one hundredth of a *ngultrum.

Chicago Board of Trade (**CBOT**) A US exchange for trading in commodities and *financial futures. It started in 1848, trading in grain. A screen-based trading system was introduced in 2000.

Chicago Mercantile Exchange (**CME**) The prime US futures and options market. It was instituted in 1919 as a market for commodity futures but in 1972 opened the **International Monetary Market**, the world's first market for *financial futures.

chief executive The person with responsibility for ensuring that an organization functions efficiently if it is non-profit-making and makes a profit acceptable to the shareholders if it is profit-making. Although the term was formerly more common in North America than the UK, it is now sometimes used in place of *managing director in the UK.

Chinese wall A notional information barrier between the parts of a business, especially between the market-making part of a stockbroking firm and the broking part. It would clearly not be in investors' interests for brokers to persuade their clients to buy investments from them for no other reason than that the market makers in the firm, expecting a fall in price, were anxious to sell them.

CHIPS Acronym for *Clearing House Inter-Bank Payments System.

choice criteria The critical attributes made use of by a consumer in evaluating alternative products. Choice criteria can include the colour of the packaging, the perceived taste of the product, expectations related to the brand (e.g. the reliability of a make of car), etc.

choice-shift effects The finding that after participating in a group discussion, individuals tend to advocate more extreme positions and call for riskier courses of action than they would have done had they not taken part in the discussion. This phenomenon is also known as the **risky shift**. More recently, certain experimental conditions have been found that lead group discussion to inhibit risk (a so-called **cautious shift**); as a result, the term 'choice-shift effect' is now sometimes applied to both effects.

chon A monetary unit of North Korea and South Korea, worth one hundredth of a *won.

chooser option An *option in which the holder has the freedom to decide, up to a specified point before expiry, whether it is a put or a call option.

chose in action A right of proceeding in a court of law to obtain a sum of money or to recover damages. Examples include rights under an insurance policy, a debt, and rights under a contract. A chose in action is a form of property and can be assigned, sold, held in trust, etc. *See also* CHOSE IN POSSESSION.

chose in possession Moveable chattels that a person possesses. Examples include

goods, merchandise, etc. All assets are either choses in possession or *choses in action.

churning **1.** The practice by a broker of encouraging an investor to change investments frequently in order to earn excessive commissions. **2.** The practice by a bank, building society, insurance broker, etc., of encouraging a householder with an endowment *mortgage to surrender the policy and to take out a new one when seeking to increase a mortgage or to raise extra funds, instead of topping up the existing mortgage. The purpose is to increase charges and commissions at the expense of the policyholder. **3.** A government policy of paying a benefit to a wide category of persons and taxing it so that those paying little or no taxes receive it while the well-off return it through the tax system. There have been suggestions that a higher child benefit is suitable for churning.

c.i.f. Abbreviation for *cost, insurance, and freight*. It is the basis of an export contract in which the seller pays the cost of shipping the goods to the port of destination and of insuring the goods up to this point. On a c.i.f. contract, the seller sends the documents giving title to the goods to the buyer, usually through a bank. These documents include the *bill of lading, the *insurance policy, the commercial invoice, and sometimes such additional documents as a *certificate of origin, quality certificate, or export licence. In order to obtain the goods the buyer is obliged to pay for the documents when they are presented. It is said that with a c.i.f. contract the buyer is paying for documents rather than goods, because provided the documents are in order, there is an obligation to pay for them even if the goods themselves have been lost at sea during the voyage. In these circumstances the buyer would hold the insurance policy which would provide recompense for the lost goods. *Compare* C & F; C.I.F.C.I.; FREE ON BOARD.

c.i.f.c.i. Abbreviation for *cost, insurance, and freight plus commission and interest*. A price quoted c.i.f.c.i. is a *c.i.f. price, which also includes an agreed commission payable by the seller to the buyer and the interest charged by the seller's bank for negotiating the documents.

CII Abbreviation for *Chartered Insurance Institute.

CIM **1.** Abbreviation for *CompuServe Information Manager. **2.** Abbreviation for *Chartered Institute of Marketing.

CIMS Abbreviation for *computer-integrated manufacturing system.

CIPD Abbreviation for *Chartered Institute of Personnel and Development.

CIPR Abbreviation for *Chartered Institute of Public Relations.

circuit breakers Measures put in place by the major stock and derivatives exchanges to prevent very large market movements; for example, suspending trading on a particular market when certain extreme price fluctuations take place. These provisions were first instituted after the major stock market crash on *Black Monday 1987.

circuity of action The return of a *bill of exchange, prior to maturity, to the person who first signed it. Under these circumstances it may be renegotiated, but the person forfeits any right of action against those who put their names to it in the intervening period.

circular A notice or advertisement in any form distributed by post or by hand to large numbers of individuals or households.

circular letter of credit *See* LETTER OF CREDIT.

circulating assets *See* CURRENT ASSETS.

circulation **1.** The distribution of a publication. **2.** The number of copies sold per issue of a publication.

CIS Abbreviation for *CompuServe.

CIT Abbreviation for *critical incident technique.

City The district of London that contains the Stock Exchange, the Bank of England, Lloyds, and the head offices of many financial institutions. Occupying the so-called **Square Mile** on the north side of the River Thames between Waterloo Bridge and Tower Bridge, the City has been an international merchanting centre since medieval times. Although many institutions remain in the square mile, others have mi-

grated eastwards, to the Docklands area or westwards to former newspaper offices in Fleet Street.

City Call A financial information service provided by British Telecom over the telephone in the UK. It gives nine bulletins of updated information each day.

City Code on Takeovers and Mergers A code first laid down in 1968, and subsequently modified, giving the practices to be observed in company takeovers (*see* TAKEOVER BID) and *mergers. It is administered by a panel (the **Takeover Panel**) including representatives from major financial and business institutions. The code does not have the force of law but the panel can admonish offenders and refer them to their own professional bodies for disciplinary action. The *Financial Services Authority may also, at the request of the panel, take enforcement action against a person who contravenes the code.

The code attempts to ensure that all shareholders, including minority shareholders, are treated equally, are kept advised of the terms of all bids and counterbids, and are advised fairly by the directors of the company receiving the bid on the likely outcome if the bid succeeds. Its many other recommendations are aimed at preventing directors from acting in their own interests rather than those of their shareholders, ensuring that the negotiations are conducted openly and honestly, and preventing a spurious market arising in the shares of either side.

City Group for Smaller Companies (CISCO) *See* QUOTED COMPANIES ALLIANCE.

civil law **1.** The law applied by the civil courts in the UK, as opposed to ecclesiastical, criminal, or military law. It is, thus, the law that regulates dealings between private citizens that are not subject to interference by the state. Its chief divisions include the law of contract, torts, and trusts. **2.** Roman law. **3.** The law generally in force on the Continent, which has its basis in Roman law.

CIX Abbreviation for *Commercial Internet Exchange.

class action A legal action in which a

person sues as a representative of a class of persons who share a common claim.

classical school of management *See* ADMINISTRATIVE MANAGEMENT.

classical system of corporation tax
A system of taxing companies in which the company is treated as a taxable entity separate from its own shareholders. The profits of companies under this system are therefore taxed twice, first when made by the company and again when distributed to the shareholders as dividends. *Compare* IMPUTATION SYSTEM.

classification method A method of *job evaluation in which jobs are placed in certain predefined categories on the basis of job title, *job description, and comparison with *benchmark jobs. It is mainly associated with large hierarchical organizations such as the civil service and local government. *Compare* FACTOR-COMPARISON METHOD; JOB-COMPONENT METHOD; POINT METHOD; RANKING METHOD.

classified advertising The form of *advertising that consists of small typeset or semi-display advertisements grouped together in such categories as cars for sale, furniture for sale, flats to let, etc., usually in a paper or magazine. They are usually inserted by direct contact between the advertiser and the advertising department of the publication.

Classified Directories UK trade directories (known colloquially as **Yellow Pages** because they are printed on yellow paper) issued by British Telecom for each business area. Businesses are listed by trade.

claused bill of lading *See* DIRTY BILL OF LADING.

clawback 1. Money that a government takes back from members of the public by taxation, especially through the *higher rate of income tax, having given the money away in benefits, such as retirement pensions. Thus the money is clawed back from those who have no need of the benefit (because they are paying higher-rate taxes). **2.** An agreement requiring the sponsors of a project to repay past profits in the event of a shortfall in later periods. This may be a condition in *project financing.

Clayton Act A US *anti-trust law passed in 1914; it placed restrictions on mergers and acquisitions that limited competition and debarred individuals from holding directorships on the boards of competing companies.

clean bill of lading *See* BILL OF LADING.

clean floating A government policy allowing a country's currency to fluctuate without direct intervention in the foreign-exchange markets. In practice, clean floating is rare as governments are frequently tempted to manage exchange rates by direct intervention by means of the official reserves, a policy sometimes called **managed floating** (*see also* MANAGED CURRENCY). However, clean floating does not necessarily mean that there is no control of exchange rates, as they can still be influenced by the government's monetary policy.

clean price The price of a *gilt-edged security excluding the accrued interest since the previous dividend payment. Interest on gilt-edged stocks accrues continuously although dividends are paid at fixed intervals (usually six months). Prices quoted in newspapers are usually clean prices, although a buyer will normally pay for and receive the accrued income as well as the stock itself.

clear days The full days referred to in a contract, i.e. not including the days on which the contract period starts or finishes.

cleared balance A balance on a bank account, excluding any receipts that do not yet represent *cleared value.

cleared for fate Denoting the date on which the payer's bank has confirmed that funds are available to provide value for a transfer in accordance with the instructions given in a cheque, etc. *See* CLEARING CYCLE.

cleared value Denoting the time at which a credit to a customer's bank account becomes available to him. The *cleared balance is used for calculating interest and for establishing the undrawn balance of an agreed overdraft facility. *See also* CLEARING CYCLE.

clearing bank 1. In the UK, a bank that

is a member of the central clearing system, to enable passage and clearance of cheques. It is often used as an alternative description for the major High-Street banks. **2.** In the USA, a bank that settles federal, agency, and corporate securities for its customers.

clearing cycle The process by which a payment made by cheque, etc., through the banking system is transferred from the payer's to the payee's account. Historically, in the UK the average time for the clearing cycle to be completed was three days, although by 1994 this had been reduced to two days in many cases. However, with this reduction in the cycle, the payee's bank may not have received confirmation from the payer's bank that funds are available to provide value, *cleared for fate.

clearing house A centralized and computerized system for settling indebtedness between members. The best-known in the UK is the *Association for Payment Clearing Services (APACS), which enables the member banks to offset claims against one another for cheques and orders paid into banks other than those upon which they were drawn. Similar arrangements exist in some commodity exchanges, in which sales and purchases are registered with the clearing house for settlement at the end of the accounting period. See LONDON CLEARING HOUSE.

Clearing House Inter-Bank Payments System (CHIPS) A US bankers' *clearing house for paying and accepting funds. It is an electronic system operated through terminals in bank branches. Participating banks must be members of the New York Clearing House Association or affiliates of it, for example foreign banks operating in the USA can only take part through selected correspondents among the 12 New York Clearing Houses. Outside New York, similar transactions are undertaken through Fedwire, a clearing system for members of the *Federal Reserve System.

Clearing Houses Automated Payment System (CHAPS) See ASSOCIATION FOR PAYMENT CLEARING SERVICES.

clickable Denoting a company or organization that operates on the *Internet. See E-COMMERCE.

clicks-and-mortar (bricks-and-clicks) A business model that combines *e-commerce with the use of physical premises such as retail outlets or warehouses.

clickstream A record of the path a user takes through a website. Clickstreams enable website designers to assess how their site is being used.

clickthrough (ad click) The act of clicking on a *banner advertisement with the mouse, to direct a user to a web page that contains further information.

clickthrough fee (prospect fee) A payment made to a company for traffic generated by a link on the company's website, typically by means of a *banner advertisement.

clickthrough rate The percentage of visitors to a website who click on a particular *banner advertisement. Clickthrough rates of 1% or 2% are common for standard nonpersonalized advertisements.

click-tracking Java Software that can be used to track the movements of individual users of a website. See JAVA.

client account A bank or building society account operated by a professional person (e.g. a solicitor, stockbroker, agent, etc.) on behalf of a client. A client account is legally required for any company handling investments on a client's behalf; it protects the client's money in case the company becomes insolvent and makes dishonest appropriation of the client's funds more difficult. For this reason money in client accounts should be quite separate from the business transactions of the company or the professional person.

close company A company resident in the UK that is under the control of five or fewer *participators or any number of participators who are also directors. There is also an alternative asset-based test, which applies if five or fewer participators, or any number who are directors, would be entitled to more than 50% of the company's assets on a winding-up. The principal consequences of being a close company are that certain payments made to shareholders can be treated by HM Revenue and Customs as a *distribution, as can loans or quasi-loans. Close investment companies do not qualify for the reduced rate of *corporation tax. In the USA close companies are known as **closed companies**.

closed economy A theoretical model of an economy that neither imports nor exports and is therefore independent of economic factors in the outside world. No such economy exists, although the foreign sector of the US economy is relatively small and most economic decisions are taken by the US government independently of the rest of the world.

closed-ended questions Questions on a questionnaire that ask the respondent to choose from a list of answers, e.g. asking which of a list of brands they have recently bought. *Compare* OPEN-ENDED QUESTION.

closed indent *See* OPEN INDENT.

closed shop Any organization in which there is an agreement between the employers and a trade union that only members of that union will be taken on as employees. Under the Employment Protection (Consolidation) Act (1978), as amended by the Employment Acts (1980, 1982, and 1988), all employees are free to join a trade union or not, as they wish. If an employer takes action, short of dismissal, against an employee to enforce membership of a union, the employee can complain to an *employment tribunal, which can order the employer to pay him compensation. Dismissal for failure to belong to a trade union is automatically unfair (*see* UNFAIR DISMISSAL).

closed system A system that is unaffected by influences from outside its boundaries. While a real system that is totally immune to outside influences is hard to imagine, the concept can be useful as a theoretical model.

close investment holding company A *close company that does not exist wholly or mainly as a trading company, a property company letting to third parties, or a holding company of a trading company.

closely held corporation In the USA, a public corporation that has only a limited number of stockholders and consequently few of its shares are traded.

close price The price of a share or commodity when the margin between the bid and offer prices is narrow.

closing The step in the selling process in which the salesperson asks the customer for an order.

closing balance The debit or credit balance on a ledger at the end of an *accounting period, which will be carried forward to the next accounting period. A debit closing balance (such as an *accrual) will be carried forward to the credit side of a ledger and a credit closing balance (such as a prepayment) will be carried forward to the debit side of a ledger.

closing deal A transaction on a financial market that closes a long or short position or terminates the liability of an *option holder.

closing out The final (or closing) results of either a direct mailing or direct response advertisement. For example, a 5% response rate indicates that 5% of those approached have responded positively to a mailing or advertising campaign.

closing prices The buying and selling prices recorded on a financial market at the end of a day's trading. *See* AFTER-HOURS DEALS.

closing signal A sign given by a prospective buyer indicating that a decision has been arrived at to make a purchase.

closing stock The *stock remaining within an organization at the end of an *accounting period as *raw materials, *work in progress, or *finished goods. It is necessary to establish the level of closing stocks so that the cost of their creation is not charged against the profits of the period (*see* OPENING STOCK). Closing stocks are therefore valued and deducted from the costs of the period and appear as *current assets in the *balance sheet.

club deal *See* SYNDICATED BANK FACILITY.

cluster sampling A method of selecting a *sample in which the members of the sample are chosen from one or more groups (clusters), rather than from the *population as a whole. This technique is often used when random sampling from the whole population would be impractical or expensive. In auditing, for example, groups of, say, invoices are chosen at random by the auditor and then each item in each group is examined in detail. In marketing research, clusters of respondents are often chosen according to their geographical areas in order to reduce travelling costs. *See also* SYSTEMATIC SAMPLING.

cluster theory A marketing theory stating that customers with similar demographic or other characteristics are also likely to share buying preferences.

CMEA Abbreviation for *Council for Mutual Economic Assistance.

CMI Abbreviation for *Chartered Management Institute.

CNAR Abbreviation for compound net annual rate. *See* COMPOUND ANNUAL RETURN.

coaster A small cargo ship that makes short trips around the coast of the UK from port to port.

COBOL Acronym for *Co*mmon *B*usiness-*O*riented *L*anguage. This language is widely used to program computers for business applications, such as invoice and payroll production. It is an easy-to-learn *high-level language that uses a limited number of English words. Programs written in COBOL can be run on different computers, provided that the standard version has been used. Because it was designed to make program writing easy, COBOL occupies considerable amounts of computer memory, making it more popular on larger systems than on microcomputers. However, microcomputer versions of COBOL are available.

co-branding An arrangement between two or more companies in which they agree to display joint *content and perform joint promotions using brand logos or *banner advertisements. The aim is to strengthen the bands by making them appear complementary. This is a reciprocal arrangement, which can occur without payment.

COD Abbreviation for *cash on delivery.

code of conduct A statement setting out the guidelines regarding the ethical principles and acceptable behaviour expected of a professional organization or company. For example, the Market Research Society has a professional code of conduct and utility companies have customer charters.

coding notice A document issued by the HM Revenue and Customs as part of the PAYE system showing the amount of *income tax allowances to be set against an individual's taxable pay. The total of allowances is reduced to a code by dropping the last digit and adding a letter depending on the taxpayer's circumstances.

coemption The act of buying up the whole stock of a commodity. *See* CORNER.

coercive contract *See* PSYCHOLOGICAL CONTRACT.

cognitive dissonance A state of mental conflict caused by a difference between a consumer's expectations of a product and its actual performance. As expectations are largely formed by advertising, dissonance may be reduced by making only realistic and consistent claims about a product's performance. Cognitive dissonance can increase if the buyer feels anxious about the decision, particularly if new information has been received about the product or service. The more negative the new information, the greater the dissonance.

cognitive processes The broad range of mental activities, including perception, learning, memory, thinking, information processing, and reasoning, that involve the interpretation of stimuli and the organization of thoughts and ideas. These processes have relevance to the *attitudes of potential customers and their evaluation of the flow of information provided for them by advertising and other communications seeking to persuade them to make purchases. *See also* HUMAN INFORMATION PROCESSING.

cognitive theories of leadership *See* LEADERSHIP THEORIES.

cohort effect Any effect associated with being a member of a group born at roughly the same time and bonded by common life experiences (e.g. growing up in the 1980s). The effect is of great interest to advertisers and others involved in marketing. In large organizations, cohorts are often defined by entry date and can retain some common characteristics (size, cohesiveness, competition) that affect the organization.

coinsurance The sharing of an insurance risk between several insurers. An insurer may find a particular risk too large to accept because the potential losses may be out of proportion to their claims funds. Rather than turning the insurance away, the insurer can offer to split the risk with a number of other insurers, each of whom would be asked to cover a percentage of the risk in return for the same percentage of the premium. The policyholder deals only with the first or leading insurer, who issues all the documents, collects all the premiums, and distributes shares to the others involved. A coinsurance policy includes a schedule of all the insurers involved and shows the percentage of the risk each one is accepting.

A policyholder can also become involved in coinsurance. In this case, a reduction of the premium by an agreed percentage is given, in return for an acceptance by the policyholder that all payments of claims are reduced by the same proportion.

cold calling A method of selling a product or service in which a sales representative makes calls, door-to-door, by post, or by telephone, to people who have not previously shown any interest in that product or service. In view of the high cost of maintaining a salesforce, many companies direct their sales representatives to those potential customers who are favourably disposed to the supplier (either as an existing customer or by replying to a press advertisement). When companies wish to extend their market to new customers, the sales representative must be willing to call on a large number of people, many of whom will show no interest in the product. The primary objective in cold calling is to establish a favourable relationship quickly, enabling the representative to explain the benefits of their product or service before being dismissed.

collaborative customization The tailoring of a product to meet a customer's unique requirements, based on a dialogue between the seller and the customer. *See* CUSTOMIZATION.

collar An arrangement in which both the maximum (*cap) and minimum (*floor) rate of interest payable on a loan are fixed in advance.

collateral A form of *security, especially an impersonal form of security, such as life-assurance policies or shares, used to secure a bank loan. In some senses such impersonal securities are referred to as a secondary security, rather than a primary security, such as a guarantee.

collateralize In the USA, to pledge assets to secure a debt. If the borrower defaults on the terms and conditions of the agreement the assets will be forfeited.

collecting bank (remitting bank) The bank to which a person who requires payment of a cheque (or similar financial document) has presented it for payment.

collective bargaining Bargaining between employers and employees over wages, terms of employment, etc., when the employees are represented by a trade union or some other collective body.

collective effort model In psychology, a model proposing that working on tasks as part of a group tends to weaken individual *motivation by (1) lowering the individual's expectancy that his or her actions can lead to the attainment of goals and (2) reducing the subjective value of these goals to the individual. *See* SOCIAL LOAFING; SUCKER EFFECT. *See also* PATH-GOAL LEADERSHIP MODEL; VALENCE-INSTRUMENTALITY-EXPECTANCY THEORY.

collectivism An economic system in which much of the planning is carried out by a central government and the means of production is owned by the state. This system was formerly common in eastern Europe and the developing world but has now been generally replaced by free-market systems

Collector of Taxes A civil servant responsible for the collection of taxes for which assessments have been raised by *Inspectors of Taxes and for the collection of tax under *PAYE.

collusion 1. An agreement between two or more parties in order to prejudice a third party, or for any improper purpose. Collusion to carry out an illegal, not merely improper, purpose is punishable as a conspiracy. In a business context, collusion may consist of an agreement to suppress competition by price fixing, conditions of sale, etc. *See* RESTRICTIVE TRADE PRACTICES. **2.** In legal proceedings, a secret agreement between two parties as a result of which one of them agrees to bring an action against the other in order to obtain a judicial decision for an improper purpose. **3.** A secret agreement between the parties to a legal action to do or to refrain from doing something in order to influence the judicial decision. For instance, an agreement between the plaintiff and the defendant to supress certain evidence would amount to collusion. Any judgement obtained by collusion is a nullity and may be set aside.

collusive duopoly A form of *duopoly in which producers collude with each other in a price-fixing agreement, thus forming a virtual *monopoly, and negotiate a profit-sharing arrangement.

colón (¢) (*plural* **colónes**) **1.** The standard monetary unit of Costa Rica, divided into 100 céntimos. **2.** The standard monetary unit of El Salvador, divided into 100 centavos.

colophon A publisher's identifying emblem on a book or other published material. It was formerly an inscription at the end of the book giving the title, date of publication, and the printer.

column inches (column centimetres) A measurement of area of typeset matter equal to the width of a column of type in a newspaper or magazine multiplied by its depth. Column centimetres are now replacing column inches in practice, although most *public relations consultancies still refer to column inches when measuring the coverage their activities have achieved.

COM Abbreviation for *computer output microfilm.

combined-transport bill of lading *See* CONTAINERIZATION.

COMECON Acronym for *Council for Mutual Economic Assistance.

comedian *See* RELATIONSHIP ROLES.

COMEX Acronym for *Commodity Exchange Inc. of New York.

command economy (planned economy) An economy in which the activities of firms and the allocation of productive resources is determined by government direction rather than market forces.

commercial An advertisement on television or radio.

commercial agency (credit-reference agency) An organization that gives a credit reference on businesses or persons. They specialize in collating information regarding debtors, bankruptcies, and court judgements in order to provide a widely based service to their clients. *See also* ANCILLARY CREDIT BUSINESS; CREDIT RATING.

commercial bank A privately owned bank that provides a wide range of financial services, both to the general public and to firms. The principal activities are operating cheque current accounts, receiving deposits, taking in and paying out notes and coin, and making loans. Additional services include trustee and executor facilities, the supply of foreign currency, the purchase and sale of securities, insurance, a credit-card system, and personal pensions. They also compete with the *finance houses and *merchant banks by providing venture capital and with *building societies by providing mortgages.

The main banks with national networks of branches in the UK are the so-called *Big Four (the Royal Bank of Scotland group, including NatWest; Barclays, including Woolwich; Lloyds TSB, and HSBC), together with Abbey, HBOS (Halifax/Bank of Scotland), and Alliance and Leicester. They are also known as **High-Street banks**, **joint-stock banks**, or **retail banks**.

commercial bill Any *bill of exchange other than a *Treasury bill. *See* BANK BILL; TRADE BILL.

commercial code Any of a number of codes used to reduce the cost of sending cables. However, the international use of Telex and fax has reduced the need for cables and writing in commercial codes.

commercial credit company A US finance house that gives credit to businesses rather than individuals.

Commercial Internet Exchange (CIX)
A US-based organization of commercial Internet service providers.

commercialization The stage in the development of a new product during which a decision is made to embark on its full-scale production and distribution. *See* NEW PRODUCT DEVELOPMENT.

commercial law *See* MERCANTILE LAW.

commercial loan selling A transaction involving two banks and one business customer. Bank A grants a loan to the customer and then sells that loan agreement to Bank B. Bank A makes a profit on the sale; Bank B has a loan book it would not otherwise achieve; and the customer borrows at a favourable rate. Commercial loan selling is common in the USA.

commercial online services Companies that offer online information, entertainment, shopping, and other services to subscribers who pay the company a monthly fee. They make use of their own dedicated networks and operate their own computers, which are connected to the Internet, thus offering somewhat better security than the Internet itself.

commercial paper A relatively low-risk short-term (maturing at 60 days or less in the US but longer in the UK) unsecured form of borrowing. Commercial paper is often regarded as a reasonable substitute for Treasury bills, certificates of deposit, etc. The main issuers are large creditworthy institutions, such as insurance companies, bank trust departments, and pension funds. In the UK, sterling commercial paper was first issued in 1986. Commercial paper is now available in Australia, France, Hong Kong, the Netherlands, Norway, Singapore, Spain, Sweden, and elsewhere. *See also* EURO-COMMERCIAL PAPER; EURONOTE.

commission A payment made to an intermediary, such as an agent, salesman, broker (*see also* BROKERAGE), etc., usually calculated as a percentage of the value of the goods sold. Sometimes the whole of the commission is paid by the seller (e.g. an estate agent's commission in the UK) but in other cases (e.g. some commodity markets) it is shared equally between buyer and seller. In *advertising, the com-

mission is the discount (usually between 10% and 15%) allowed to an *advertising agency by owners of the advertising medium for the space or time purchased on behalf of their clients. A **commission agent** is an agent specializing in buying or selling goods for a principal in another country for a commission.

commission broker In the USA, a stock-exchange dealer who executes orders to buy or sell securities on payment of a fee or a commission based on the value of the deal.

commission disclosure The disclosure of commissions on insurance and investment business. Until the mid 1990s this was covered by a 'maximum commissions agreement' in the UK, resulting in the practice of **soft disclosure**. This meant that there was no need to make customers explicitly aware of commissions and charges, provided they were within the maximum limits set and the customer did not specifically ask for detailed information. In 1991, the *Office of Fair Trading objected that this practice was uncompetitive and amounted to an illegal price-fixing cartel. It was recommended that the industry move to a practice of **hard disclosure**. Initially, this took the form of disclosing the percentage of the commission charge rather than a strict monetary disclosure. But since 1995 there has been a practice of hard disclosure of the monetary value of commissions, expenses, charges and early surrender value to customers at the point of purchase.

commitment *See* ORGANIZATIONAL COMMITMENT.

commitment fee An amount charged by a bank to keep open a line of credit or to continue to make unused loan facilities available to a potential borrower. *See* FIRM COMMITMENT.

commitments for capital expenditure *See* CAPITAL COMMITMENTS.

committed costs Costs, usually *fixed costs, that the management of an organization have a long-term responsibility to pay. Examples include rent on a long-term lease and depreciation on an asset with an extended life.

committed facility An agreement between a bank and a customer to provide funds up to a specified maximum at a specified *interest rate (in the UK this is usually based upon an agreed margin over the *London Inter Bank Offered Rate) for a certain period. The total cost will be the interest rate plus the *mandatory liquid asset cost. The agreement will include the conditions that must be adhered to by the borrower for the facility to remain in place. *Compare* UNCOMMITTED FACILITY. *See also* REVOLVING BANK FACILITY.

commodity 1. A *good regarded in economics as the basis of production and exchange. **2.** Any raw material or primary product. **3.** A raw material traded on a *commodity market, such as grain, coffee, cocoa, wool, cotton, jute, rubber, pork bellies, or orange juice (sometimes known as *soft commodities) or base metals and other solid raw materials (known as *hard commodities). In some contexts soft commodities are referred to as **produce**.

commodity broker A *broker who deals in *commodities, especially one who trades on behalf of principals in a *commodity market (*see also* FUTURES CONTRACT). The rules governing the procedure adopted in each market vary from commodity to commodity and the function of brokers may also vary. In some markets brokers pass on the names of their principals, in others they do not, and in yet others they are permitted to act as principals. Commodity brokers, other than those dealing in metals, are often called **produce brokers**.

commodity exchange *See* COMMODITY MARKET.

Commodity Exchange Inc. of New York (COMEX) A *commodity market in New York that specializes in trading in metal *futures contracts and *options.

Commodity Futures Trading Commission (CFTC) A US government body set up in 1975 in Washington to regulate trading in commodity futures (*see* FUTURES CONTRACT). Its remit was extended to cover other forms of *derivatives trading in the early 1990s.

commodity market A market in which *commodities are traded. The main *terminal markets in commodities are in Lon-

don, New York, and Chicago, but in some commodities there are markets in the country of origin. Some commodities are dealt with at auctions (e.g. tea), each lot being sold having been examined by dealers, but most dealers deal with goods that have been classified according to established quality standards (*see* CERTIFIED STOCK). In these commodities both *actuals and futures (*see* FUTURES CONTRACT) are traded on **commodity exchanges**, in which dealers are represented by *commodity brokers. Many commodity exchanges offer *option dealing in futures, and settlement of differences on futures through a *clearing house. As commodity prices fluctuate widely, commodity exchanges provide users and producers with *hedging facilities with outside speculators and investors helping to make an active market, although amateurs are advised not to gamble on commodity exchanges.

The fluctuations in commodity prices have caused considerable problems in developing countries, from which many commodities originate, as they are often important sources of foreign currency, upon which the economic welfare of the country depends. Various measures have been used to restrict price fluctuations but none have been completely successful. *See also* INTERNATIONAL PETROLEUM EXCHANGE; LONDON COMMODITY EXCHANGE; LONDON INTERNATIONAL FINANCIAL FUTURES AND OPTIONS EXCHANGE; LONDON METAL EXCHANGE.

Common Agricultural Policy (CAP) A policy set up by the *European Economic Community to support free trade within the Common Market and to protect farmers in the member states. The *European Commission fixes a **threshold price**, below which cereals may not be imported into the European Union (EU), and also buys surplus cereals at an agreed **intervention price** in order to help farmers achieve a reasonable average price, called the **target price**. Prices are also agreed for meats, poultry, eggs, fruit, and vegetables, with arrangements similar to those for cereals. The European Commission is also empowered by the CAP to subsidize the modernization of farms within the community. The common policy for exporting agricultural products to non-member countries is laid down by the CAP. In the UK, the Intervention Board for Agricultural Produce is responsible for the implementation of EU regulations regarding the CAP. Important reforms designed mainly to eliminate surpluses and to uphold environmental and production standards were agreed in 1984, 1988, 1999, and 2003.

Common Budget The fund, administered by the *European Commission, into which all levies and customs duties on goods entering the European Union are paid and from which all subsidies due under the *Common Agricultural Policy are taken.

common carrier *See* CARRIER.

Common External Tariff (CET) The tariff of import duties payable on certain goods entering any country in the European Union from non-member countries. Income from these duties is paid into the *Common Budget.

Common Fisheries Policy A fishing policy agreed between members of the European Community (EC) in 1983. An earlier agreement of 1971 introduced the principle of free access to European Community waters and a single fishing market. The key elements resulting from the 1983 agreement were: the setting of a Total Annual Catch (TAC) for the Community, which aimed to ensure conservation of stocks; a national TAC allocation; schemes for fleet restructuring; and negotiation with 'third party' nations. A radical reform of the policy imposing severe cuts in fishing quotas was agreed in 2002.

common law 1. The law common to the whole of the UK, as opposed to local law. **2.** Case law as opposed to legislation, i.e. the law that has evolved by judicial precedent rather than by statute. For instance, the rules relating to the formation of contracts is a product of the common law, and is not contained in any Act of parliament. **3.** The law of the UK as opposed to foreign law. In this sense, the common law would include case law as well as legislation.

Common Market *See* EUROPEAN ECONOMIC COMMUNITY; EUROPEAN UNION.

common stock The US name for *ordinary shares.

Commonwealth Development Corporation *See* CDC GROUP.

communication The result of any action (physical, written, or verbal) that conveys meanings between two individuals. In the context of marketing, the marketer wants the communication, in the form of a promotional message, to gain attention and to be understood, believed, and remembered. *See* ADVERTISING OBJECTIVE.

communication adaptation A global communication strategy for adapting advertising messages for local markets.

communication goals *See* ADVERTISING OBJECTIVE.

communication ring A shared communication structure on the Internet. Individuals in a communication ring can send messages to all the members of the ring, a subgroup of the ring, or each other. Examples include e-mail lists and instant messaging 'buddy lists' (of friends and acquaintances).

communication timing The manner in which an Internet communication is scheduled, determining whether it is real-time or stored.

community of users The group of people who visit and use a particular site on the Internet.

community of values A network of users or contributors to an Internet site, who share knowledge, expertise, or similar outlooks.

commutation The right to receive an immediate cash sum in return for accepting smaller annual payments at some time in the future. This is usually associated with a pension in which certain life-assurance policyholders can, on retirement, elect to take a cash sum from the pension fund immediately and a reduced annual pension.

Companies Acts Legislation governing the activities of companies. In the UK, the first Companies Act was passed in 1844; the current comprehensive legislation is contained in the 1985 Companies Act. The Companies Act (1989) incorporated various EU directives into UK law.

Companies House (Companies Registration Office) The office of the *Registrar of Companies, formerly in London but now in Cardiff. It contains a register of all UK private and public companies, their directors, shareholders, and balance sheets. All this information has to be provided by companies by law and is available to any member of the public for a small charge.

company A corporate enterprise that has a legal identity separate from that of its members; it operates as one single unit, in the success of which all the members participate. An **incorporated company** is a legal person in its own right, able to own property and to sue and be sued in its own name. A company may have limited liability (a *limited company), so that the liability of the members for the company's debts is limited. An *unlimited company is one in which the liability of the members is not limited in any way.

A **registered company**, i.e. one registered under the Companies Acts, is much the most common type of company. A company may be registered either as a *public limited company or a private company. A public limited company must have a name ending with the initials 'plc' and have an authorized share capital of at least £50,000, of which at least £12,500 must be paid up. A private company is any registered company that is not a public company. The shares of a private company may not be offered to the public for sale. Unregistered companies include *joint-stock companies, in which the members pool their stock, **chartered companies**, formed under Royal Charter, and **statutory companies**, formed by special Act of Parliament (e.g. the privatized utilities).

There are legal requirements placed on companies to make certain financial information regarding their activities public. Such information normally comprises a *profit and loss account and *balance sheet and is included with other financial and non-financial information in an annual report and accounts (*see* ANNUAL ACCOUNTS). The term company is often used more widely to refer to any association of persons, such as a *partnership, joined together for the purpose of conducting a business, although legally there are significant differences. *See also* ARTIFICIAL PERSON; CORPORATION.

company and individual brand strategy A branding approach that focuses on the company name and individual brand name.

company doctor 1. An executive or accountant with wide commercial experience, who specializes in analysing and rectifying the problems of ailing companies. He or she may either act as a consultant or may be given executive powers to implement the policies recommended. **2.** A medical doctor employed by a company, either full-time or part-time, to look after its staff, especially its senior executives, and to advise on medical and public-health matters.

company formation The procedure to be adopted for forming a company in the UK. The subscribers to the company must send to the *Registrar of Companies a statement giving details of the registered address of the new company together with the names and addresses of the first directors and secretary, with their written consent to act in these capacities. They must also give a declaration (**declaration of compliance**) that the provisions of the Companies Acts have been complied with and provide the *memorandum of association and the *articles of association. Provided all these documents are in order the Registrar will issue a *certificate of incorporation and a *certificate to commence business. In the case of a *public limited company additional information is required.

company limited by guarantee An incorporated organization in which the liability of members is limited by the *memorandum of association to amounts that they have agreed to undertake to contribute in the event of winding up. *See* LIMITED COMPANY.

company limited by shares An incorporated organization in which the liability of members is limited by the *memorandum of association to the amounts paid, or due to be paid, for shares. *See* LIMITED COMPANY.

company seal A seal with the company's name engraved on it in legible characters, often used to authenticate share certificates and other important documents issued by the company or affixed to contracts. Until recent reforms in English company law, certain types of contract were not binding unless made under seal.

company secretary An *officer of a company. The appointment is usually made by the directors. The secretary's duties are mainly administrative, including preparation of the agenda for directors' meetings. However, the modern company secretary has an increasingly important role, which may include managing the office and entering into contracts on behalf of the company. Duties imposed by law include the submission of the annual return and the keeping of minutes. The secretary of a public company is required to have certain qualifications, set out in the Companies Act (1985). *See* INSTITUTE OF CHARTERED SECRETARIES AND ADMINISTRATORS.

comparability The accounting principle that financial information for a company should be comparable with financial information for other similar companies. Comparability is one of the most important characteristics of useful financial information. The concept is defined in the Accounting Standards Board's Statement of Principles and in *Financial Reporting Standard 18, Accounting Policies.

comparable worth The view that jobs should be paid equally when the work requires equal training, skills, and responsibilities, and that this principle should override differences in job titles, status, or accepted market rates. The doctrine is mainly associated with the feminist point that jobs traditionally considered 'male' tend to be better paid than those considered 'female', even where the behavioural demands of these jobs are very similar.

comparative parity method A method of setting a promotional budget in which the marketer tries to match the expenditure of competitors. *Compare* AFFORDABLE METHOD.

comparison advertising Advertising that compares one brand, either directly or indirectly, with other brands. This is quite often used in car advertising, by comparing the availability of a range of features on competitors'models in the same price bracket. *See also* KNOCKING COPY.

compensable job factor In *job evaluation, any of a range of factors that are held to determine the value of a job to the organization and hence the level of remuneration paid to the job holder. These factors usually include the skills, training, and experience required to perform the job adequately and its behavioural demands in terms of effort, responsibility, and decision making. *See* FACTOR-COMPARISON METHOD; POINT METHOD.

compensation for loss of office A payment made by a company to a director, senior executive, or consultant who is forced to retire before the expiry of a service contract, as a result of a merger, takeover, or any other reason. This form of **severance pay** (*see also* REDUNDANCY) may be additional to a retirement pension or in place of it; it must also be shown separately in the company's accounts. Because these payments can be very large, they are known as **golden handshakes**. *See also* GOLDEN PARACHUTE.

compensation fund A fund set up by the *London Stock Exchange, to which member firms contribute. It provides compensation to investors who suffer loss as a result of a member firm failing to meet its financial obligations.

competency Any of the skills, talents, and traits required to be able to perform a particular task to a given standard. The assessment of competencies is central to various key aspects of human resources management: setting standards of performance that can be expected from employees and appraising them against such standards; assessing the training and development needs of individual employees; and identifying the skills, abilities, and characteristics needed when recruiting and selecting new employees.

competition Rivalry between suppliers providing goods or services for a market. The consensus of most economic theory is that competition is beneficial for the public, largely because it brings prices down. Governments usually pursue policies aimed at increasing competition in markets, although there may sometimes be a conflict between policies that increase competition and those that promote the national interest.

Competition Commission A commission established in 1948 as the Monopolies and Restrictive Practices Commission, renamed the **Monopolies and Mergers Commission** in 1973, and given its present name in 1999 under the Competition Act (1998). It investigates questions referred to it relating to monopolies and mergers, and its Appeals Tribunal hears appeals against decisions by the *Office of Fair Trading and utility regulators relating to anticompetitive trade practices.

competitive advantage An advantage over competitors gained by offering consumers greater value, either by means of lower prices or by providing greater benefits and better servicing facilities that could justify higher prices. This may be achieved by creative advertising, increased product performance, or superior distribution methods.

competitive devaluation The *devaluation of a country's currency to make its economy more competitive in international trade, rather than to correct an ongoing disequilibrium in the exchange rate.

competitive exclusion The diversion of on-line traffic away from competitors by companies holding exclusive partnership deals with popular websites on the Internet.

competitiveness 1. The ability of an economy to supply increasing *aggregate demand and maintain exports. A loss of competitiveness is usually signalled by increasing imports and falling exports. Competitiveness is often measured in a narrower sense by comparing relative inflation rates. For instance, if the sterling–dollar exchange rate remains constant, but prices rise faster in the UK than in the US, UK goods will become relatively more expensive, reflecting a loss in competitiveness; this in turn may lead to a falling demand for exports. **2.** The ability of an organization to compete successfully with its commercial rivals. See COMPETITIVE ADVANTAGE; COMPETITOR ANALYSIS.

competitive strategy A strategy that strongly positions a company against competitors and gives that company the strongest possible strategic advantage.

competitor analysis The gathering of data about a competitor's products and prices in order to identify actual or future sources of *competitive advantage. An understanding of a competitor's objectives, strategies, strengths, and weaknesses will help an organization to develop its own strategy. The analysis should reveal which competitors to attack and which to avoid. See BENCHMARKING; SWOT.

competitor-centred company A company mainly motivated by its competitors' actions and reactions. Its principal preoccupation is tracking its competitors' market shares and trying to find strategies to increase its own share compared to its competitors' shares.

competitor intelligence Information gathered by a company so that it is informed of what the competition is doing or is planning.

completion The conveyance of land in fulfilment of a contract of sale. The purchaser will have obtained an equitable interest in the land at the date of the *exchange of contracts but will not become the full legal owner until completion. If the seller refuses to complete, the court may grant a decree of *specific performance. The date on which completion must take place is stated in the contract of sale.

completion risk The inherent risk in *project financing schemes that a construction project will not be completed. Compare SUPPLY RISK; TECHNOLOGICAL RISK.

complex buying behaviour *Consumer buying behaviour in situations in which a considerable amount of technical information has to be assessed and significant differences exist between brands. For example, in buying a new personal computer the buyer has to consider the relative merits of 'Pentium 4 chip' and '1 gig of RAM'; to do so means evaluating a large amount of data.

compliments slip (comp slip) A slip of paper with the words 'With the compliments of…' printed on it, followed by the name and address of the firm sending it. It is enclosed with material sent to another person or firm to identify the sender, when a letter is not necessary.

component innovation An innovation

that creates an improvement in the capabilities of the individual components in a system, e.g. more powerful processors in computers. *Compare* ARCHITECTURAL INNOVATION.

composite rate A special rate of tax that applied to banks and building societies from 1951 to 1991. This rate of tax was used to deduct tax from interest payments. The main disadvantage of the tax was that non-taxpayers were unable to reclaim the tax deducted from the interest paid to them. The change in 1991 resulted in tax being paid at basic rate, which could be reclaimed. A provision was also introduced enabling non-taxpayers to elect to have the interest paid gross.

composition *See* ARRANGEMENT.

compound annual return (CAR) The total return available from an investment or deposit in which the interest is used to augment the investment. The more frequently the interest is credited, the higher the CAR.

CAR = 1 + (nominal rate/number of times interest paid per annum)

The CAR is usually quoted on a gross basis. The return, taking into account the deduction of tax at the basic rate on the interest, is known as the **compound net annual rate (CNAR)**.

compound interest *See* INTEREST.

compound net annual rate (CNAR) *See* COMPOUND ANNUAL RETURN.

comprehensive income tax An income tax for which the tax base consists not only of income but also of *capital gains as well as other accretions of wealth, such as legacies. Although this is not a tax currently levied in the UK, tax theorists find it attractive since sometimes clear distinctions between income, capital gains, etc., are difficult to sustain. *See also* SINGLE-TAX SYSTEM.

compressed working week A work pattern that is becoming increasingly common and that involves the reallocation of work time into fewer and longer blocks during the week. The total length of work time remains unchanged, but each shift or period of work is lengthened. Typically, this means that the same basic

hours are worked in four and a half days a week or nine days out of ten in a fortnight.

compression The process of reducing the size of a digital file to enable it to occupy less storage space or to transmit more rapidly.

comptroller The title of the financial director in some companies or chief financial officer of a group of companies. The title is more widely used in the USA than in the UK. *See also* CONTROLLER.

Comptroller of the Currency A US Treasury Department official, appointed by the president, who is responsible for the regulation of the national banking system.

compulsory liquidation (compulsory winding-up) The *liquidation of a company by a court. A petition must be presented both at the court and the registered office of the company. Those by whom it may be presented include: the company, the directors, a creditor, an official receiver, and the Secretary of State for Trade and Industry. The grounds on which a company may be wound up by the court include: a special resolution of the company that it be wound up by the court; that the company is unable to pay its debts; that the number of members is reduced below two; or that the court is of the opinion that it would be just and equitable for the company to be wound up. The court may appoint a *provisional liquidator after the winding-up petition has been presented; it may also appoint a *special manager to manage the company's property. On the grant of the order for winding-up, the official receiver becomes the *liquidator and continues in office until some other person is appointed, either by the creditors or the members. *Compare* CREDITORS' VOLUNTARY LIQUIDATION; MEMBERS' VOLUNTARY LIQUIDATION.

compulsory purchase The compulsory acquisition of land by the state when it is required for some purpose under the Town and Country Planning legislation. Compensation is paid on the basis of market value. *Compare* REQUISITIONING.

compulsory purchase annuity An annuity that must be purchased with the fund built up from certain types of pension arrangements. When retirement age is reached, a person who has been paying premiums into this type of pension fund is obliged to use the fund to purchase an annuity to provide an income for the rest of his or her life. The fund may not be used in any other way (except for a small portion, which may be taken in cash).

Compumailer A machine that turns continuous stationery into personalized letters and envelopes, enclosing one inside the other. It also seals the envelopes ready for mailing. Compumailers are frequently used by direct mailing organizations.

CompuServe (CIS) One of the principal US-based on-line information services.

CompuServe Information Manager (CIM) The official off-line reader and system navigator for *CompuServe.

computer An electronic tool that manipulates information in accordance with a predefined sequence of instructions. Computers have a simple 'brain', called the **central processing unit (cpu)**, that can do arithmetic and take decisions based on the results, and a **memory**, which stores the instructions and information. Strictly speaking, all other parts of a computer system are peripheral devices, but in practice all computers have at least: an input device, such as a keyboard, by means of which the information is fed in; an output device, such as a screen or printer, which displays the results of their work; and extra memory in the form of magnetic disks or magnetic tape, called backing store. Inside a computer, both information and instructions are represented by binary numbers (*see* BINARY NOTATION) and all processing is done using these numbers. A computer needs to be given detailed instructions, called a program, before it can perform even the simplest task. The art of composing these instructions is called **computer programming**. The general term for the programs that a computer needs in order to operate is *software, while the computer and devices attached to it are called *hardware.

Traditionally, computers have been classified into three types according to size. The largest is the *mainframe, used typically for large-scale corporate data processing; and the smallest is the *personal computer, designed for a single user. Between these extremes is the *minicomputer. These distinctions have become blurred, as minicomputers and personal computers become more powerful. Moreover, mainframe and minicomputers have been replaced in many situations by groups of personal computers linked to form *local area networks.

computer-aided design (CAD) The use of computers to produce designs and to manipulate them rapidly. In many cases it can replace the need to produce expensive prototypes. In conjunction with live data, CAD can also be used for testing complex projects; for example, nuclear tests in the Pacific provided data enabling computer simulations to test future weapons. In conjunction with *virtual reality, CAD can allow potential customers to view new products at an early stage, before significant amounts of capital have been expended on plant, etc. CAD is also linked to *material requirements planning systems permitting rapid costing of new models to be made together with the appropriate *bills of materials.

computer-aided manufacturing (CAM) The use of computers to control industrial processes, such as brewing, chemical manufacture, oil refining, and steel making. They are also used to control automatic machines that can be programmed to carry out different tasks, especially in the car-manufacturing industry. CAM is often used with *computer-integrated manufacturing as well as *computer-aided design.

computer-aided personal interview (CAPI) A method of interviewing in which researchers use laptop computers to conduct personal interviews and transmit the resulting data over the Internet. This dramatically reduces the time of the research process. It also allows on-screen presentation of stimuli to the respondent, reduces respondent fatigue, helps generate good-quality data, and allows fast collation of data from different geographical locations. Pioneered by Research International, UK, it has become a widely used method for data collection. It is essential that the interviewer should be proficient in the use of the laptop if the respondent is not to become irritated and uncooperative.

computer-aided self-interview (CASI) A method of interviewing in which the respondent interacts directly with the computer instead of through the interviewer. In theory, it is similar to a self-completion questionnaire and offers the same advantages (privacy and reduced interviewer bias). It is also called a **computerized self-administered questionnaire (CSAQ)**.

computer-assisted audit techniques (CAATs) Techniques developed by auditors for performing audit tests on computer systems and the data they hold. There are two main categories of technique. (1) The auditor creates a set of input data to be processed by the computer programs; the results are then checked against the expected results. (2) Computer *audit software is used by the auditor to select data from a number of files. Various operations are then performed on the data and the results are transferred to a special audit file to be printed out in a required format.

computer-assisted panel research (CAPAR) A method of conducting panel research remotely. Panel members transmit details of specific purchases using barcode scanners over the telephone to a host computer in which the information is accumulated. Television audience measurement is also conducted by this method.

computer-assisted self-explication (CASE) An on-line Internet system that asks visitors structured questions about their preferences and uses this information to produce rankings and recommendations on products and services for both consumers and producers.

computer-assisted telephone interviewing (CATI) A system in which a telephone interviewer conducts a sales or marketing interview, using a computer and a computerized questionnaire. This system reduces the number of errors as the interviewer keys in the respondent's answers as they are given and the computer follows a complex questionnaire routing efficiently, enabling the required statistics to be extracted automatically.

computer-assisted trading (CAT) The use of computers by brokers and traders

on a market, such as a stock exchange or foreign-exchange market, to facilitate trading by displaying prices, recording deals, etc.

computer-based training (CBT) The use of computers in training. Exercises are shown on the screen and participants have to key in answers to questions, which are assessed by the computer.

computer-integrated manufacturing system (CIMS) A system bringing together *computer-aided design, *computer-aided manufacturing, *flexible manufacturing systems, and outputs from integrated information processing systems. These systems are dependent on the adoption of common operating systems and transparent communications networks. Their success often depends on cultural and political issues rather than technical capabilities, as they often cut across traditional roles and power structures.

computer output microfilm (COM) A system that produces computer output on microfilm or microfiche. The information is recorded on film either by a camera that photographs a miniature screen displaying the computer output, or by a laser beam recorder, which writes directly onto the film. COM is used where there is a large volume of output, particularly where immediate reference is not required.

concealed unemployment *See* HIDDEN UNEMPLOYMENT.

concentrated segmentation (niche marketing) A comparatively small segment of a market that has been identified, usually by a small company, in which to concentrate their efforts. For example, a company might decide to offer a service converting cine films to video tapes; as long as this activity does not threaten the profitability of the manufacturers of either video tapes or cine films, it can establish a profitable niche in the market.

concentration The degree to which an industry is dominated by a small group of firms and thus closed to competitive pressure.

concept test A technique used in *marketing research to assess the reactions of consumers to a new product or a proposed change to an existing product (*see* NEW PRODUCT DEVELOPMENT). Before an organization invests in production facilities for a new product it writes a **concept statement** describing the proposed product and commissions a market researcher to interview a small number of potential consumers either in *group discussion or *depth interview. Respondents are shown the concept statement and their reactions are explored in detail. The results of these interviews help the organization to understand what it should do with the proposed product if it is to be successful.

concert-party agreements Secret agreements between apparently unconnected shareholders to act together to manipulate the share price of a company or to influence its management. The Companies Act (1981) laid down that the shares of the parties to such an agreement should be treated as if they were owned by one person, from the point of view of disclosing interests in a company's shareholding.

conciliation *See* ADVISORY CONCILIATION AND ARBITRATION SERVICE; MEDIATION.

concurrent control (real-time control) An approach to controlling the performance of an operating system that attempts to bring together the monitoring of performance, comparison with parameters, and taking action stages. Thus in *total quality management members of staff take responsibility for the quality of every stage of a process as they are performing it, in contrast to a *feedback control system, in which the quality would not be inspected until the process had been completed. In some specialist environments the use of electronic data-capture has enabled the feedback cycle to become very short. Processes can be adjusted within milliseconds, thus minimizing any cost penalties. *See also* FEEDFORWARD CONTROL.

concurrent engineering (interactive engineering; simultaneous engineering) An approach to the design and introduction of new products that aims to shorten lead times and reduce costs by running development stages in parallel. In traditional systems, each stage in development is discrete, i.e. production planning can only

begin when the product design has been finalized. In concurrent engineering, production planning will start as soon as there is a reasonable level of confidence in the likely outcome of the preceding phase. In this way, not only is each stage able to start earlier but it is also able to provide feedback that helps to optimize the preceding stage. This approach has been facilitated by the development of *computer-integrated manufacturing systems. Full exploitation may require application of *business process re-engineering techniques.

condition **1.** A major term of a contract that, if unfulfilled, constitutes a fundamental *breach of contract and may invalidate it. *Compare* WARRANTY. **2.** A provision that does not form part of a contract but either suspends the contract until a specified event has happened (**condition precedent**) or brings it to an end in specified circumstances (**condition subsequent**). An example of a condition precedent is an agreement to buy a particular car if it passes its MOT test; an example of a condition subsequent is an agreement that entitles the purchaser of goods to return them if they prove unsatisfactory.

conditional bid *See* TAKEOVER BID.

conditionality The terms under which the *International Monetary Fund (IMF) provides balance-of-payments support to member states. The principle is that support will only be given on the condition that it is accompanied by steps to solve the underlying problem. Programmes of economic reform are agreed with the member; these emphasize the attainment of a sustainable balance-of-payments position and boosting the supply side of the economy. Lending by commercial banks is frequently linked to IMF conditionality.

conditional sale agreement A contract of sale under which the price is payable by instalments and ownership does not pass to the buyer (who is in possession of the goods) until specified conditions relating to the payment have been fulfilled. The seller retains ownership of the goods as security until being paid in full.

Confederation of British Industry (CBI) An organization that lobbies for

British business on matters of concern, chiefly to the UK government but also to the European Union and other international bodies. Its objective is to help create and sustain the conditions in which British business can compete and prosper. The CBI was formed from a merger of several other employers' organizations in 1965 and now represents some 250 000 UK companies. Its ruling body is the CBI Council, which meets on a quarterly basis in London. There are also 12 regional councils.

conference lines *See* SHIPPING CONFERENCE.

conferencing *See* AUDIOCONFERENCING; VIDEOCONFERENCING.

confidence indicators *See* PERFORMANCE MEASUREMENT.

confidentiality clause A clause in a contract of employment that details certain types of information the employee will acquire on joining the firm that may not be passed on to anyone outside the firm.

confirmation note A document confirming the main facts and figures of a deal between two parties, usually a deal that has been agreed verbally or by telephone. The *London code of conduct recommends that the dealer records the telephone calls and that both parties send confirmation notes.

confirmed letter of credit *See* LETTER OF CREDIT.

confirming house An organization that purchases goods from local exporters on behalf of overseas buyers. It may act as a principal or an agent, invariably pays for the goods in the exporters' own currency, and purchases on a contract that is enforceable in the exporters' own country. The overseas buyer, who usually pays the confirming house a commission or its equivalent, regards the confirming house as a local buying agent, who will negotiate the best prices on its behalf, arrange for the shipment and insurance of the goods, and provide information regarding the goods being sold and the status of the various exporters.

conflict management The control of conflict within an organization. There are three main philosophies of conflict management:

- **traditionalists** hold that all conflict is bad and potentially destructive for an organization;
- **behaviourists** see conflict as inevitable in an organization and attempt to harness it in a positive way;
- **interactionists** see conflict as essential to the survival of an organization and as something that should be encouraged.

See also CHANGE MANAGEMENT; DIVERSITY MANAGEMENT.

conflict of interests A situation that can arise if a person (or firm) acts in two or more separate capacities and the objectives in these capacities are not identical. The conflict may be between self-interest and the interest of a company for which a person works or it could arise when a person is a director of two companies, which find themselves competing. The proper course of action in the case of a conflict of interests is for the person concerned to declare any interests, to make known the way in which they conflict, and to abstain from voting or sharing in the decision-making procedure involving these interests.

Confravision *See* VIDEOCONFERENCING.

confused positioning A *positioning error that leaves consumers with a confused image of a company, its products, or brands.

conglomerate A diverse group of companies, usually managed by a *holding company. There is usually little integration and few transactions between each of the subsidiaries, often because their activities and products are unrelated. This form of business structure is generally disliked by investors because conglomerates may lack a clear strategic focus and the overall value of the group can undervalue the combined individual values of the operating subsidiaries.

conjoint analysis A statistical method that attempts to determine the relative importance consumers attach to salient *attributes and the utilities they attach to the levels of attributes. The technique is based on the premise that products and services are made up of features or attributes that vary according to the identified preferences of consumers. The more dominant the interest in a particular attribute of a product, the higher will be the utility value given to it by actual or potential purchasers. It is widely used in marketing for various purposes, including concept identification of new products, competitive analysis, market segmentation, pricing, advertising, and distribution. *See also* UTILITY THEORY.

connected person In the context of the Companies Act (disclosure requirements for directors and connected persons), a director's spouse, child, or stepchild (under 18 years of age), a body corporate with which a director is associated, a trustee for a trust that benefits a director or connected person, or a partner of a director.

consequential-loss policy *See* BUSINESS-INTERRUPTION POLICY.

conservatism A prudent and not overoptimistic view of the state of affairs of a company or other organization. Because it is regarded as imprudent to distribute to shareholders profits that may not materialize, it is a general principle of accounting not to anticipate profits before they are realized but to anticipate losses as soon as they become foreseeable. *See also* PRUDENCE CONCEPT.

consideration 1. A tangible benefit that is exchanged as part of a *contract. It is essential if a contract (other than a deed) is to be valid. It usually consists of a promise to do or not to do something or to pay a sum of money. 2. The money value of a contract for the purchase or sale of securities on the *London Stock Exchange, before commissions, charges, stamp duty, and any other expenses have been deducted.

consignee 1. Any person or organization to whom goods are sent. 2. An agent who sells goods, usually in a foreign country, on *consignment on behalf of a principal (consignor).

consignment 1. A shipment or delivery of goods sent at one time. 2. Goods sent **on consignment** by a principal (consignor) to an agent (consignee), usually in a foreign country, for sale either at an agreed price or at the best market price. The

agent, who usually works for a commission, does not normally pay for the goods until they are sold and does not own them, although usually having possession of them. The final settlement, often called a **consignment account**, details the cost of the goods, the expenses incurred, the agent's commission, and the proceeds of the sale.

consignment note A document accompanying a consignment of goods in transit. It is signed by the *consignee on delivery and acts as evidence that the goods have been received. It gives the names and addresses of both consignor and consignee, details the goods, usually gives their gross weight, and states who has responsibility for insuring them while in transit. It is not a negotiable document (*compare* BILL OF LADING) and in some circumstances is called a **way bill**.

consignment stock Stock held by one party (the dealer) but legally owned by another; the dealer has the right to sell the stock or to return it unsold to its legal owner. Because it can be difficult to distinguish between the commercial realities of the transaction and the legal agreement, consignment stock is sometimes used as a means of *creative accounting.

consignor 1. Any person or organization that sends goods to a *consignee. 2. A principal who sells goods on *consignment through an agent (consignee), usually in a foreign country.

consistency concept One of the four fundamental *accounting concepts laid down in *Statement of Standard Accounting Practice (SSAP) 2, Disclosure of Accounting Policies; it is also recognized in the Companies Act (1985) and the EU's *Fourth Accounting Directive. The concept requires consistency of treatment of like items within each accounting period and from one period to the next; it also requires that *accounting policies are consistently applied. Under *Financial Reporting Standard 18, Accounting Policies, which has now replaced SSAP 2, the consistency concept is no longer recognized as a fundamental principle. Rather, an entity is required to implement those policies that are judged most appropriate to its circumstances for the purpose of giving a *true and fair view. *Comparability is therefore held to be a more important characteristic of financial statements than consistency.

consolidated accounts *See* CONSOLIDATED FINANCIAL STATEMENTS.

consolidated annuities *See* CONSOLS.

consolidated balance sheet The *balance sheet of a group providing the financial information contained in the individual financial statements of the parent company of the group and its subsidiary undertakings, combined subject to any necessary *consolidation adjustments. It must give a *true and fair view of the state of affairs of a group as at the end of the financial year, and its form and content should comply with Schedule 4 of the Companies Act (1989). If the balance sheet formats require the disclosure of the balances attributable to group undertakings (creditors, debtors, investments), the information should be analysed to show the amounts attributable to parent and fellow subsidiary undertakings of the parent company, and amounts attributable to unconsolidated subsidiaries.

consolidated financial statements (**consolidated accounts**; **group accounts**; **group financial statements**) The financial statements of a group of companies obtained by *consolidation. These are required by the Companies Act and *Financial Reporting Standard 2, Accounting for Subsidiary Undertakings. The information contained in the individual financial statements of a group of undertakings is combined into consolidated financial statements, subject to any *consolidation adjustments. The consolidated accounts must give a *true and fair view of the profit or loss for the period and the state of affairs as at the last day of the period of the undertakings included in the consolidation. Subsidiary undertakings within the group may be excluded from consolidation and the parent company itself may be exempt from preparing consolidated accounts.

Accountants also need to be aware of *International Accounting Standard 27, Consolidated and Separate Financial Statements, and *International Financial Reporting Standard 3, Business Combinations.

Consolidated Fund The Exchequer account, held at the Bank of England and controlled by the Treasury, into which taxes are paid and from which government expenditure is made. It was formed in 1787 by the consolidation of several government funds.

consolidated goodwill The difference between the *fair value of the consideration given by an acquiring company when buying a business and the aggregate of the fair values of the separable net assets acquired. *Goodwill is generally a positive amount. Under *Financial Reporting Standard 10, Goodwill and Intangible Assets, goodwill should normally be capitalized on the *balance sheet and *amortized to the *profit and loss account over a period not exceeding 20 years. The international accounting standards relevant to the treatment of consolidated goodwill are *International Financial Reporting Standard 3, Business Combinations, *International Accounting Standard (IAS) 36, Impairment of Assets, and IAS 38, Intangible Assets.

consolidated profit and loss account A combination of the individual *profit and loss accounts of the members of a *group of organizations, subject to any consolidation adjustments. The consolidated profit and loss account must give a *true and fair view of the profit and loss of the undertakings included in the consolidation. A parent company may be exempted, under section 230 of the Companies Act, from publishing its own profit and loss account if it prepares group accounts. The individual profit and loss account must be approved by the directors, but may be omitted from the company's annual accounts. In such a case, the company must disclose its profit or loss for the financial year and also state in its notes that it has taken advantage of this exemption.

consolidation 1. An increase in the *nominal price of a company's shares, by combining a specified number of lower-price shares into one higher-priced share. For example five 20p shares may be consolidated into one £1 share. In most cases this can be done by an ordinary resolution at a general meeting of the company.

2. The inclusion of one or more subsidiary companies in a parent company's financial statements. *See* CONSOLIDATED FINANCIAL STATEMENTS.

Consols Government securities that pay interest but have no redemption date. The present bonds, called **consolidated annuities** or **consolidated stock**, are the result of merging several loans at various different times going back to the 18th century. Their original interest rate was 3% on the nominal price of £100; some now pay 2½% and therefore stand at a price that makes their annual *yield comparable to long-dated *gilt-edged securities, e.g. at £31 they yield about 8%.

consortium A combination of two or more businesses formed on a temporary basis, often to quote for and carry out a single large project. The purpose of forming a consortium may be to eliminate competition between the members or to pool skills, not all of which may be available to the individual companies. *See also* CONSORTIUM RELIEF.

consortium relief A modified form of *group relief applying to consortia. A consortium is held to exist if 20 or fewer companies each own at least 5% of the ordinary share capital of the consortium company and together hold at least 75% of the ordinary shares of the consortium company. Losses can be surrendered between the consortium members and the consortium company. The loss that can be surrendered is restricted to the proportion of the claimant's profits that corresponds with the surrendering company's interest in the consortium. From 1 April 2000 members of a consortium no longer have to be resident in the UK to qualify for relief.

constant-dollar plan The US name for *pound cost averaging, i.e. the investment of a specified sum of money at regular intervals in the acquisition of assets. It is sometimes called **dollar-cost averaging**.

constant sum scales Scales used in marketing research asking the respondent to divide (usually) 100 points between two or more attributes based on their importance to the respondent. For example, the respondent may be asked to allocate points to the attributes speed, comfort, fuel consumption, and reliability by a car manufacturer. If the average scores of all respondents are: speed 10, comfort 10, fuel consumption 30, and reliability 50, the manufacturer will have useful information to assist the engineering and design departments.

constraint A factor of production, a shortage of which prevents an organization achieving higher levels of performance. A constraint results from the impact of a limiting factor (or principal budget factor), which must be eliminated or reduced before the constraint is removed. For example, at various times a shortage of skilled labour, materials, production capacity, or sales volume may constitute a limiting factor. Constraints are also brought into the statement of problems in *linear programming. *See* THEORY OF CONSTRAINTS.

constructive dismissal A situation that arises when an employer's behaviour towards an employee is so intolerable that the employee is left with no option but resignation. In these circumstances the employee can still claim compensation for *wrongful dismissal.

constructive total loss A loss in which the item insured is not totally destroyed but is so severely damaged that it is not financially worth repairing. The Marine Insurance Act (1906) defines a constructive total loss as one in which "the subject matter insured is reasonably abandoned on account of its actual total loss appearing to be unavoidable, or because it could not be preserved from actual total loss without an expenditure which would exceed its value when the expenditure had been incurred."

consular invoice An export invoice that has been certified in the exporting country by the consul of the importing country. This form of invoice is required by the customs of certain countries (especially South American countries) to enable them to charge the correct import duties. A *certificate of origin may also be required. The fee charged by the consul for this or any other commercial service is called the **consulage**.

Consultative Committee of Accountancy Bodies (CCAB) A committee set up in 1970 by the six main accountancy bodies to foster closer cooperation. It plays an active part in many financial accounting and reporting issues.

consumable materials Materials that are used in a production process although, unlike *direct materials, they do not form part of the *direct cost of sales. Examples are cooling fluid for production machinery, lubricating oil, and sanding discs. In circumstances in which direct materials of small value are used, such as cotton or nylon thread or nails and screws, they are sometimes treated in the same way as consumable materials.

consumer A private individual acting otherwise than in the course of a business. Consumers are often given special legal protection when entering into contracts, for example by having a right to avoid certain unfair terms or to cancel the contract (*see* CONSUMER PROTECTION; DISTANCE SELLING).

consumer advertising The *advertising of goods or services specifically aimed at the potential end-user, rather than at an intermediary in the selling chain. *Compare* TRADE ADVERTISING.

consumer buying behaviour The buying behaviour of individuals and households who buy goods and services for personal consumption. A number of different people, playing different roles, have been identified in the decision to make a specific purchase:

- **initiator**, the person who first suggests or thinks of the idea of buying a particular product or service;
- **influencer**, a person whose views or advice influences the buying decision;
- **decider**, the person who ultimately makes the decision to buy (or any part of it); this decision includes whether to buy, what to buy, how to buy, and where to buy;
- **buyer**, the person who makes the actual purchase;
- **user**, the person who uses the produce or service.

It is usual to regard a consumer's decision to make a specific purchase as having five stages:

problem recognition
↓
information search
↓
evaluation of alternatives
↓
choice
↓
post purchase experience

This model emphasizes that the decision process is sequential and combines both mental and physical activities. In broad terms, the first four of these stages constitute the decision phase. This is followed by the actual purchase, and the subsequent experience of using the newly acquired product. If this experience is positive it can act as a reinforcement to make further similar purchases. A negative experience will encourage a change to another product or supplier.

consumer credit Short-term loans to the public for the purchase of goods. The most common forms of consumer credit are credit accounts at retail outlets, personal loans from banks and finance houses, *hire purchase, and *credit cards. Since the *Consumer Credit Act (1974), the borrower has been given greater protection, particularly with regard to regulations establishing the true rate of interest being charged when loans are made (*see* ANNUAL PERCENTAGE RATE). The Act also made it necessary for anyone giving credit in a business (with minor exceptions) to obtain a licence. *See* CONSUMER-CREDIT REGISTER.

Consumer Credit Act (1974) A UK Act of Parliament aimed at protecting the borrower in credit agreements, loans, and mortgages. The Act requires full written details of the true interest rate (i.e. *annual percentage rate) to be quoted; a *cooling-off period to be given, during which borrowers may change their minds and cancel agreements; and all agreements to be in writing. The Act does not cover overdrafts.

Consumer Credit Protection Act (1968) The US equivalent of the UK

*Consumer Credit Act (1974). The Act is enforced by the Federal Reserve Bank.

consumer-credit register The register kept by the *Office of Fair Trading, as required by the Consumer Credit Act (1974), relating to the licensing or carrying on of consumer-credit businesses or consumer-hire businesses. The register contains particulars of undetermined applications, licences that are in force or have at any time been suspended or revoked, and decisions under the Act and any appeal from them. The public is entitled to inspect the register on payment of a fee.

consumer durable *See* CONSUMER GOODS.

consumer goods Goods that are purchased by members of the public. **Consumer durables** are consumer goods, such as cars, refrigerators, and television sets, whose useful life extends over a relatively long period. The purchase of a consumer durable falls between *consumption and *investment. **Consumer non-durables** or **disposables** are goods that are used up within a short time after purchase. They include food, drink, newspapers, etc.

consumer groups The groups to which consumers belong and which influence their behaviour. These groups can be small primary groups, such as the family or a work group, or they can be larger secondary groups, such as professional associations or trade unions. **Reference groups** serve as direct (face-to-face) or indirect points of reference, providing comparisons that help to form a person's attitudes or behaviour. Within these groups are **aspirational groups**, to which people would like to belong; quite often, the aspiring person assumes the values, attitudes, and even the dress of the group. **Opinion leaders** are important within reference groups, because their special skills, knowledge, or personality enables them to influence others.

consumer instalment loan The US name for *hire purchase.

consumerism An organized movement of citizens and government agencies to improve the rights and power of buyers in relation to sellers.

consumer market The market for

*consumer goods, as opposed to the industrial market, in which buyers of goods are not the end users.

consumer non-durable *See* CONSUMER GOODS.

consumer-oriented marketing A principle of enlightened marketing holding that a company should view and organize its marketing activities from the point of view of the consumers of its products and services.

consumer preference The way in which consumers in a free market choose to divide their total expenditure in purchasing goods and services. Using a limited number of assumptions, an individual's preferences can be built up into a utility function (*see* CONSUMER THEORY). Applying *price theory to the utility functions of individuals enables a model to be constructed of the behaviour of markets in an economy.

Consumer Price Index **(CPI) 1.** In the UK, the usual name for the **Harmonized Index of Consumer Prices (HICP)**, a measure of price level introduced in 1997 to enable comparisons within the EU. In 2003 the Chancellor of the Exchequer announced that government inflation targets would subsequently be based on the CPI rather than the *Retail Price Index. **2.** In the USA, the measure of price level calculated monthly by the Bureau of Labor Statistics. It is commonly known as the cost-of-living index and gives the cost of specific consumer items compared to the base year of 1967.

consumer profile A profile of a typical consumer of a product, in terms of age, sex, social class, and other characteristics. *See also* CONSUMER GROUPS.

consumer promotion A sales promotion designed to stimulate consumer purchasing. It may offer samples, coupons, rebates, price reductions, premiums, patronage rewards, displays, contests, sweepstakes, etc.

consumer protection The protection, especially by legal means, of consumers. It is the policy of current UK legislation to protect consumers against unfair contract terms. In particular they are protected by the Unfair Contract Terms Act (1977) and the Sale of Goods Act (1979) against terms that attempt to restrict the seller's implied undertakings including a right to sell the goods, that the goods conform with either description or sample (*see* TRADE DESCRIPTION), and that they are of merchantable quality and fit for their particular purpose. Consumers are further protected in these respects by the Unfair Terms in Consumer Contracts Regulations (1999). There is also provision for the banning of unfair consumer trade practices in the Fair Trading Act (1973), which established the *Office of Fair Trading. Consumers (including individual businesspeople) are also protected when obtaining credit by the Consumer Credit Act (1974). *See also* CONSUMER-CREDIT REGISTER. There is provision for the imposition of standards relating to the safety of goods under the Consumer Protection Act (1987), which also makes the producer of a product liable for any damage it causes (*see* PRODUCTS LIABILITY).

consumer relationship-building promotion A sales promotion that promotes a product's *positioning and includes a selling message.

consumer research Any form of *marketing research undertaken among the final consumers of a product or service. For example, a manufacturer supplying man-made fibres to a shirt factory might undertake consumer research, interviewing purchasers of shirts, in order to establish the merits, or otherwise, of the fibres. *Compare* INDUSTRIAL MARKETING RESEARCH.

Consumers' Association (CA) A UK charitable organization formed in 1957 to provide independent and technically based guidance on the goods and services available to the public. The Consumers' Association tests and investigates products and services and publishes comparative reports on performance, quality, and value in its monthly magazine *Which?*. It also publishes *Holiday Which?* and *Gardening From Which?* as well as various books, including *The Legal Side of Buying a House*, *Starting Your Own Business*, and *The Which? Book of Saving and Investing*. The US equivalent is the **Consumer Advisory Council**.

consumers' expenditure *See* CONSUMPTION.

consumer theory The theory explaining the choices made by individuals and households in terms of the concept of utility. Consumers are assumed to be able to order their preferences (*see* CONSUMER PREFERENCE) in such a way that they can choose a basket of goods that maximize their utility, subject to the constraint that their income is limited. The application of *price theory and demand theory to this problem forms the basis of *microeconomics (together with the theory of the firm) and also of *macroeconomics.

consumption 1. The using up of *consumer goods and services for the satisfaction of the present needs of individuals, organizations, and governments. **2.** The amount of money spent by the whole of an economy on consumer goods and services. Economists contrast this amount of money (sometimes called **consumers' expenditure**) with the amount spent on *investment, which provides for future consumption. In most economies about 80% of national income is spent on consumption, the balance going to investment. However, the distinction between consumption and investment is not always clear as some goods, such as consumer durables, provide for both present and future consumption.

containerization The use of large rectangular containers for the shipment of goods. Goods are packed into the containers at the factory or loading depot and transported by road in these containers to the port of shipment, where they are loaded direct onto the ship without unpacking. At the port of destination they can again be transported by road to the final user. It is usual for such shipments to be covered by a **container bill of lading** (**combined-transport bill of lading**).

contango 1. *See* FORWARDATION. **2.** The former practice of carrying the purchase of stocks and shares over from one account day on the London Stock Exchange to the next.

contempt of court An act that hinders the course of justice or that constitutes disrespect to the lawful authority of the court. Contempt may be divided into acts committed in court (for instance, unseemly behaviour or refusing to answer a question as a witness) and acts committed out of court (such as intimidating a witness or refusing to obey a court order). Contempt of court is punishable by fine or imprisonment or both.

content In website design, the text, graphical information, and design features that constitute a web page. Good content is the key to attracting customers to a website and retaining their interest or achieving repeat visits.

content analysis A technique used to study written material (often advertising copy) to reduce it to meaningful units, using carefully applied rules. It provides an objective and systematic description of a communication's content.

contingencies Potential gains and losses known to exist at the balance-sheet date although the actual outcomes will only be known after one or more events have occurred (or not occurred). Depending on the nature of a particular contingency, it may be appropriate to include it in the financial statements or to show it as a *note to the accounts; *Financial Reporting Standard 12 provides guidance on the appropriate accounting treatment. Generally, accountants apply the *prudence concept and will disclose information on *contingent losses more readily than on *contingent gains.

contingency insurance An insurance policy covering financial losses occurring as a result of a specified event happening. The risks covered by policies of this kind are various and often unusual, such as a missing documents indemnity, the birth of twins, or *pluvial insurance.

contingency plan A plan that is formulated to cope with some event or circumstances that may occur in the future. For example, the contingency may be an increase in sales, in which case the plan would include means of increasing production very quickly.

contingency theories of leadership In *industrial and organizational psychology, various models stating that the performance of a leader will depend not only on his or her qualities or methods but also on certain key aspects of the work situation. The leader will be most effective when his or her *leadership style is best suited to the characteristics of the group (e.g. level of experience) and the nature of the group task (e.g. whether clearly structured or not). One of the earliest and most influential of such theories, that of Fred Fiedler, proposes that *task-motivated leaders will be most successful in very favourable or very unfavourable situations and that *relationship-motivated leaders will be most successful when the situation is not so extreme. Some other models suggest that it may be easier for the leader to alter the work situation to suit his or her style than vice versa. See LEADERSHIP THEORIES. See also SITUATIONAL LEADERSHIP THEORY; TANNENBAUM–SCHMIDT CONTINUUM; VROOM–YETTON–JAGO MODEL.

contingency theory of management accounting The theory that there is no single *management accounting system acceptable to all organizations or any system that is satisfactory in all circumstances in a single organization. Consequently, accounting systems are contingent upon the circumstances that prevail at any time; they must be capable of development in order to take into consideration such factors as changes in the environment, competition, organizational structures, and technology.

contingent agreement See EARN-OUT AGREEMENT.

contingent annuity (reversionary annuity) An annuity in which the payment is conditional on a specified event happening. The most common form is an annuity purchased jointly by a husband and wife that begins payment after the death of one of the parties (see JOINT-LIFE AND LAST-SURVIVOR ANNUITIES).

contingent asset A possible asset that arises from past events and whose existence will be confirmed only by the occurrence of one or more uncertain future events, which are not wholly in the control of the accounting entity. Under *Financial Reporting Standard 12, an entity should not recognize a contingent asset unless the appropriate economic events can be expected. Compare CONTINGENT LIABILITY. See also CONTINGENT GAIN.

contingent consideration A payment that is contingent on a particular factor or factors occurring. The concept often used in relation to *earn-out agreements.

contingent gain A gain that depends upon the outcome of some contingency. For example, if a company is making a substantial legal claim against another organization, the company has a contingent gain (depending upon the successful outcome of the claim). *Compare* CONTINGENT LOSS. *See also* CONTINGENT ASSET.

contingent interest *See* VESTED INTEREST.

contingent liability 1. A possible obligation that arises from past events, whose existence will be confirmed only by the occurrence of one or more uncertain future events not wholly within an entity's control. **2.** A present obligation that arises from past events in which either the amount of the obligation cannot be measured reliably or it is not probable that a transfer of economic benefits will be required to settle the obligation. Under *Financial Reporting Standard 12, an entity should not recognize a contingent liability. *Compare* CONTINGENT ASSET. *See also* CONTINGENT LOSS.

contingent loss A loss that depends upon the outcome of some contingency. For example, if there is a substantial legal claim for damages against a company, there is a contingent loss (depending on the outcome of the claim). *Compare* CONTINGENT GAIN. *See also* CONTINGENT LIABILITY.

contingent reinforcement In management and leadership, the use of rewards and penalties to motivate followers and achieve compliance with organizational goals and norms. Reliance on contingent reinforcement is a hallmark of *transactional leadership. The term is associated with behaviouristic schools of psychology that emphasize the correlation of stimulus and response. *Compare* HUMAN RELATIONS THEORY.

contingent time off (job and finish) A *job-design practice in which staff are allowed to go home as soon as an agreed amount of work, to an agreed standard, has been completed.

contingent worker A worker who has a conditional arrangement with an employer, such as a temporary, agency, or casual worker. Contingent workers tend to be employed by organizations when they have temporary need for a particular service, technology, or skill at a particular time and place.

continual access Twenty-four-hours-a-day, seven-days-a-week access. Sometimes referred to as 24/7.

continuance commitment *See* ORGANIZATIONAL COMMITMENT.

continuation An arrangement between an investor and a stockbroker in which the broker reduces the *commission for a series of purchases by that investor of the same stock over a stated period.

continuity The commissioning and scheduling of advertisements to appear evenly within a given period.

continuity programs Special services and benefits extended to important customers to encourage them to make further purchases. Airline 'frequent flyer' programs are an example.

continuity series A marketing method in which a customer is offered a series of similar products over an extended period.

continuous improvement The ongoing process of improving an organization's goods or services, with the aim of increasing customer satisfaction. In a highly competitive environment, organizations need to search actively for ways of reducing costs, improving quality, and eliminating waste. *See also* ITERATIVE DESIGN; KAIZEN; KANSEI ENGINEERING; TOTAL QUALITY MANAGEMENT.

continuous-operation costing A system of costing applied to industries in which the method of production is *continuous processing; examples include electricity generation and bottling. Because the product is homogeneous, this costing system is essentially a form of *average costing in which the unit cost is obtained by dividing the total production cost by the number of units produced. *Compare* PROCESS COSTING.

continuous processing A process in which very high volumes are produced on dedicated plant continuously, e.g. cement production or electricity generation. The plant usually involves very high capital expenditure. Unplanned shut-downs are very costly, typically involving a major refurbishment, for example to replace cracked furnace linings. Most continuous processes are largely self-controlling or are monitored by computer (*see* COMPUTER-AIDED MANUFACTURING) with only minor operator involvement. The product is often made to stock and is therefore vulnerable to market fluctuations. *Compare* BATCH PRODUCTION. *See* PROCESS CHOICE.

contra A book-keeping entry on the opposite side of an account to an earlier entry, with the object of cancelling the effect of the earlier entry. *See also* PER CONTRA.

contra accounts Accounts that can be offset, one against the other. For example, if Company A owes money to Company B and Company B also owes money to Company A, the accounts can be offset against each other, enabling both debts to be settled by one payment.

contraband Illegally imported or exported goods, i.e. goods that have been smuggled into or out of a country.

contract A legally binding agreement. Agreement arises as a result of an *offer and *acceptance, but a number of other requirements must be satisfied for an agreement to be legally binding:

- there must be a *consideration (unless the contract is by deed);
- the parties must have an intention to create legal relations;
- the parties must have capacity to contract (i.e. they must be competent to enter a legal obligation, by not being a minor, mentally disordered, or drunk);
- the agreement must comply with any formal legal requirements;
- the agreement must be legal;
- the agreement must not be rendered void either by some common-law or statutory rule or by some inherent defect.

In general, no particular formality is required for the creation of a valid contract. It may be oral, written, partly oral and partly written, or even implied from conduct. However, certain contracts are valid only if made by deed (e.g. transfers of shares in statutory companies, transfers of shares in British ships, legal *mortgages, certain types of *lease) or in writing (e.g. *hire-purchase agreements, *bills of exchange, *promissory notes, contracts for the sale of land made after 21 September 1989), and certain others, though valid, can only be enforced if evidenced in writing (e.g. guarantees, contracts for the sale of land made before 21 September 1989). *See also* SERVICE CONTRACT.

Certain contracts, though valid, may be liable to be set aside by one of the parties on such grounds as misrepresentation or the exercise of undue influence. *See also* AFFIRMATION OF CONTRACT; BREACH OF CONTRACT.

contract costing A costing technique applied to *long-term contracts, such as civil-engineering projects, in which the costs are collected by contract. A particular problem of long-term projects is the determination of annual profits to be taken to the profit and loss account when the contract is incomplete. This requires the valuation of *work in progress at the end of the financial year.

contract for service A contract undertaken by a self-employed individual. The distinction between a contract for service (self-employed) and a *service contract (employee) is fundamental in establishing the tax position. With a contract for service the person may hire and pay others to carry out the work, will be responsible for correcting unsatisfactory work at their own expense, and may make losses as well as profits.

contract guarantee insurance An insurance policy designed to guarantee the financial solvency of a contractor during the performance of a contract. If the contractor becomes financially insolvent and cannot complete the work the insurer makes a payment equivalent to the contract price, which enables another contractor to be paid to complete the work. *See also* CREDIT INSURANCE.

contracting out *See* STATE EARNINGS-RELATED PENSION SCHEME.

contract manufacturing A joint venture in which a company contracts with a manufacturer, generally in a foreign market, to produce a particular product for the company to sell or distribute.

contract note 1. A document containing details of a contract sent from one counterparty to the contract to the other. **2.** A document sent by a stockbroker or commodity broker to a client as evidence that the broker has bought (in which case it may be called a **bought note**) or sold (a **sold note**) securities or commodities in accordance with the client's instructions. It will state the quantity of securities or goods, the price, the date (and sometimes the time of day at which the bargain was struck), the rate of commission, the cost of the transfer stamp and VAT (if any), and the amount due and the settlement date.

contract of employment *See* SERVICE CONTRACT.

contract of service *See* SERVICE CONTRACT.

contractual VMS A *vertical marketing system in which independent firms at different levels of production and distribution contract to join together to obtain more economies or greater sales impact than they could achieve alone. *Compare* ADMINISTRATIVE VMS; CORPORATE VMS.

contra proferentem A rule of interpretation primarily applying to documents. If any doubt or ambiguity arises in the interpretation of a document, the rule requires that the doubt or ambiguity should be resolved against the party who drafted it or who uses it as a basis for a claim against another. For instance, a plaintiff who sues for breach of a written contract can expect that any ambiguity in the terms of the contract will be resolved against him. The expression derives from the Latin: *verba chartarum fortuis accipiuntur contra proferentum*, the words of a contract are construed more strictly against the person proclaiming them.

contribution 1. The amount that, under *marginal-costing principles, a given

transaction produces to cover fixed overheads and to provide profit. The **unit contribution** is normally taken to be the selling price of a given unit of merchandise, less the variable costs of producing it. Once the total contributions exceed the fixed overheads, all further contribution represents pure profit. The **total contribution** is the product of the unit contribution and the number of units produced. This is based on the assumptions that the marginal cost and the sales value will be constant. **2.** The sharing of claim payments between two or more insurers who find themselves insuring the same item, against the same risks, for the same person. As that person is not entitled to claim more than the full value of the item once, each insurer pays a share. For example, if a coat was stolen from a car, it might be insured under both a personal-effects insurance and a motor policy. As the policyholder is only entitled to the value of the coat (and cannot profit from the theft), each insurer contributes half of the loss.

contribution income statement The presentation of an *income statement or *profit and loss account using the *marginal costing layout. In such a treatment the *fixed costs are not charged to the individual products produced as in *absorption costing but are treated as a deduction from the total *contribution of all the products. A simplified contribution income statement is shown below.

contributory Any person who is liable to contribute towards the assets of a company on liquidation. The list of contributories will be settled by the liquidator or by the court. This list will include all shareholders, although those who hold fully paid-up shares will not be liable to pay any more.

contributory pension A *pension in which the employee as well as the em-

	PRODUCT A	PRODUCT B	TOTAL
Sales revenue	2000	5000	7000
Variable costs	1400	2900	4300
Contribution	600	2100	2700
Total Fixed costs			1200
Total profit			1500

Contribution income statement. A simplified example.

ployer contribute to the pension fund. *Compare* NON-CONTRIBUTORY PENSION.

control The ability to direct the financial and operating policies of another undertaking with a view to gaining economic benefits from its activities. One company is said to control another company if it holds more than 50% of that company's share capital, voting power, distributable income, or net assets in a winding-up. If one company has control in this sense over another, the two companies should produce *consolidated financial statements.

control accounts Accounts in which the balances are designed to equal the aggregate of the balances on a substantial number of subsidiary accounts. Examples are the sales ledger control account (or total debtors account), in which the balance equals the aggregate of all the individual debtors' accounts, the purchase ledger control account (or total creditors account), which performs the same function for creditors, and the stock control account, whose balance should equal the aggregate of the balances on the stock accounts for each item of stock. This is achieved by entering in the control accounts the totals of all the individual entries made in the subsidiary accounts. The purpose is twofold: to obtain total figures of debtors, creditors, stock, etc., at any given time, without adding up all the balances on the individual records, and to have a crosscheck on the accuracy of the subsidiary records.

control chart A graphical representation of the statistically derived performance limits (normally ±2 *standard deviations), which is used in *statistical process control. By recording samples on a control chart, it is possible to identify the trends and to take remedial action before performance goes outside the limits. *See also* CONCURRENT CONTROL; FEEDFORWARD CONTROL.

controllability concept The principle that managers should only be held responsible for *controllable costs and *controllable investment. This concept is often difficult to apply in practice. Many costs are not easily classified as either controllable or uncontrollable and others are clearly only partially controllable. For example, the manager at a building society branch is not responsible for advertising costs, staff salaries, or interest rates on savings or loans. *See* CONTROLLABLE CONTRIBUTION.

controllable contribution The sales revenue of a division less those costs that are controllable by the divisional manager (*see* CONTROLLABLE COSTS). Controllable contribution is the most appropriate measure of a divisional manager's performance. In practice, however, it can be difficult to distinguish between controllable costs and *uncontrollable costs. Where a division is a *profit centre, *depreciation is not a controllable cost, as the manager is not responsible for investment decisions. However, the manager of an investment centre is responsible for investments and therefore depreciation is a controllable cost.

controllable costs Costs identified as being controllable and therefore able to be influenced by a particular level of management. Information about those costs is therefore directed to the correct management personnel in the appropriate *operating statements. In any system of responsibility accounting, managers can only be regarded as responsible for those costs over which they have some control.

controllable investment The *capital employed that is controllable by a divisional manager. When calculating *performance measures for a division it is important to ensure that only those assets and liabilities that a manager can influence are included. *See* CONTROLLABLE CONTRIBUTION.

controllable turnover *See* LABOUR TURNOVER RATE.

controllable variance In *standard costing or *budgetary control, a *variance that is regarded as controllable by the manager responsible for that area of an organization. The variance occurs as a result of the difference between the *budget cost allowance and the actual cost incurred for the period. *See also* CONTROLLABLE COSTS.

controlled foreign company A foreign company in which a UK-resident company or individual has a 25% stake or more. The UK resident can be charged to UK tax in respect of profits from the controlled foreign company if the rate of tax paid by the foreign company is significantly less than the rate that would be payable in the UK. The tax rules applying to controlled foreign companies are very complex and are currently being reexamined as it has been argued that they contravene EU law.

controller In the USA, the chief accounting executive of an organization. The controller will normally be concerned with financial reporting, taxation, and auditing but will leave the planning and control of finances to the *treasurer. *See also* COMPTROLLER.

controlling interest An interest in a company that gives a person or another company control of it. To have a controlling interest in a company, a shareholder would normally need to own or control more than half the voting shares. However, in practice, a shareholder might control the company with considerably less than half the shares, if the other shares were divided among a large number of different holders. For legal purposes, a director is said to have a controlling interest in a company if he or she alone, or together with his or her spouse, minor children, and the trustees of any settlement in which he or she has an interest, owns more than 20% of the voting shares in a company or in a company that controls that company. *See also* MINORITY INTEREST; PARTICIPATING INTEREST.

control process A process that helps an organization to determine whether or not its objectives are being achieved and whether or not adjustments need to be made to meet them. A good control system should help managers to determine why goals and objectives are not being met; knowing the cause of failure will help to decide the corrective actions. Control activities should relate directly to tactical and operational plans; in turn, these will affect and influence the organization's long-term strategic plans.

convenience product A consumer product that customers usually buy frequently, immediately, and with a minimum of comparison and buying effort.

convenience store A store that trades primarily on the convenience it offers to customers. The products stocked may be influenced by local tastes or ethnic groups and the stores are often open long hours as well as being conveniently placed for customers in residential areas. They are often members of a multiple chain.

conventional distribution channel A channel consisting of one or more independent producers, wholesalers, and retailers, each a separate business seeking to maximize its own profits even at the expense of profits for the system as a whole.

convergence The general trend in which computers, telecommunications, and the broadcast media have become increasingly interdependent and have assumed similar functions for many business and other purposes. *See* INFORMATION TECHNOLOGY.

Long-term strategic goals and plans are set

Managers determine short-term tactical and operational objectives and plans

Control standards are established in line with objectives

Performance is measured

Comparisons are made between performance and standards

Corrective action is taken; the standard is changed or performance is continued

Control process. Steps in the control system of an organization.

conversational systems See INTERACTIVE.

conversion The tort (civil wrong) equivalent to the crime of theft. It is possible to bring an action in respect of conversion to recover damages, but this is uncommon.

conversion cost The costs incurred in a production process as a result of which raw material is converted into finished goods. The conversion costs usually include *direct labour and *manufacturing overheads but exclude the costs of *direct material itself.

convertible 1. A *bond or preferred stock that can be changed into other securities, usually equity, on predetermined conditions. 2. A government security in which the holder has the right to convert a holding into new stock instead of obtaining repayment.

convertible adjusted-rate preferred stock See ADJUSTABLE-RATE PREFERRED STOCK.

convertible revolving credit A *revolving credit that can be converted by mutual agreement into a fixed-term loan.

convertible term assurance A *term assurance that gives the policyholder the option to widen the policy to become a *whole life policy or an *endowment assurance policy, without having to provide any further evidence of good health. All that is required is the payment of the extra premium. The risks of AIDS has meant that policies of this kind are no longer available, as insurers are not now prepared to offer any widening of life cover without evidence of good health.

conveyancing The transfer of ownership of land from the person currently holding title to a new owner. See also ELECTRONIC CONVEYANCING.

cookie A small text file stored on an end-user's computer (quite often without the user's knowledge) to enable websites to identify the user. It enables a company to identify a previous visitor to a site and may be used to build up a profile of that visitor's behaviour. A particular use of cookies in e-commerce is to store information for a 'shopping basket' of items from different pages on a website.

cooling-off period 1. The 14 days that begins when a life-assurance policy, credit agreement, etc., is effected, during which new policyholders, borrowers, etc., can change their minds. During this period any policies or agreements entered into can be cancelled with a full refund of any premiums, arrangement fees, etc. 2. The time that must elapse after a failed *takeover bid before a new bid can be made.

co-operative 1. **(worker co-operative)** A type of business organization sometimes adopted in labour-intensive industries, such as agriculture, and often associated with socialist systems. Agricultural co-operatives have been encouraged in the developing countries, where individual farmers are too poor to take advantage of expensive machinery and large-scale production. In this case several farms pool resources to jointly purchase and use agricultural machinery. The principle has sometimes been extended to other industries, as when factory employees arrange a worker buy-out in order to secure threatened employment. The overall management of such co-operatives is usually vested in a committee of the employee-owners. 2. **(consumer co-operative)** A movement launched in 1844 by 28 Rochdale weavers who combined to establish retail outlets where members enjoyed not only the benefits of good-quality products at fair prices but also a share of the profits (a dividend) based on the amount of each member's purchases.

copyright The exclusive right to reproduce or authorize others to reproduce artistic, dramatic, literary, or musical works. It is conferred by the Copyright Act (1988), which also extends to sound broadcasting, cinematograph films, television broadcasts, and computer programs. In EU countries copyright lasts for the author's lifetime plus 70 years from the end of the year of death (or from the end of the year of publication, if later); it can be assigned or transmitted on death. The principal remedies for breach of copyright (see PIRACY) are an action for *damages and account of profits or an *injunction. It is a criminal offence to make or deal in articles that infringe a copyright.

copy testing The process of measuring

the communication effect of an advertisement, either before or after it is printed or broadcast. The advertising copy is usually tested on likely buyers of the product or service.

copywriter A person who writes the text for advertisements or other promotional material. Copywriters are usually employed by an *advertising agency, although in the case of highly technical advertising matter they are often employed by the company manufacturing or distributing the product.

córdoba (C$) The standard monetary unit of Nicaragua, divided into 100 centavos.

core competency *See* CORE SKILL.

core job characteristics The five characteristics that have been identified by *job characteristics theory as inducing the critical psychological states required for *motivation at work:

- **skill variety** – the degree to which the job includes different activities drawing on several skills and abilities;
- **task identity** – the extent to which a person is able to complete a task from start to finish;
- **task significance** – the degree to which a person carrying out a task perceives it to be important to the organization and its clients;
- **autonomy** – the degree to which a person has discretion as to how and when the task will be done;
- **feedback** – the extent to which the person receives feedback on the quality of performance from the task itself.

These core job characteristics are important to the psychological well-being of the individual. If they are lacking, then *job satisfaction (and hence motivation) may well suffer unless a programme of *job enlargement or *job enrichment is instituted.

core product The problem-solving service or core benefit that a consumer is really buying when purchasing a product.

core skill (core competency) Any distinctive capability that endows a particular business with a competitive advantage over its rivals. The degree to which the business can exploit this unique competence varies according to the extent to which it can be imitated by rival firms. Some skills, such as technologies or processes, may be protected by patents; others may have been built up by reputation or by marketing expertise.

core strategy The identification of a group of customers for whom a firm has a differential advantage prior to *positioning itself in that market.

corner The situation in which an individual or organization succeeds in establishing a controlling influence over the supply of a particular good or service. It will then force the price up until further supplies or substitutes can be found. This objective has often been attempted, but rarely achieved, in international *commodity markets. Because it is undesirable and has antisocial effects, 'cornering the market' in this way is now generally prevented by government restrictions on monopolies and antitrust laws.

corporate anorexia A malaise that affects businesses after a severe cost-cutting phase. The firm's ability to expand production to maintain its competitive position in the market may, for example, be compromised by a misguided pressure to reduce costs by *downsizing, resulting in the elimination of personnel who made a long-term contribution to the company's viability.

corporate bond A bond issued by a private corporation.

corporate brand licensing A form of licensing enabling a firm to rent a corporate trademark or logo made famous in one product or service category to use in a related category.

corporate brand strategy A brand strategy designed to make a company's name the dominant brand identity for all of its products.

corporate culture *See* ORGANIZATIONAL CULTURE. *See also* CORPORATE IMAGE.

corporate finance 1. The branch of financial economics concerned with business funding, decision making, and mergers and acquisitions. 2. An activity in investment and merchant banks in which advice and funding for mergers and acquisitions, etc., is provided to large corporations. **3.** Loans made to large companies by banks.

corporate governance The manner in which organizations, particularly limited companies, are managed and the nature of *accountability of the managers to the owners. This topic has been of increased importance since the publication of the Cadbury Report (1992), which set out guidance in a Code of Practice (the *Cadbury Code). There is now a stock-exchange requirement for listed companies to state their compliance with this Code. In particular, the Cadbury Report issued guidelines separating the roles of the chairman of a company and its chief executive, in order to reduce the power of one director. A wider role was also given to *non-executive directors.

corporate image The image that a company projects of itself. To gain a benevolent image for the way a company treats its employees or the environment, for example, can be as important to its sales as its individual brand images. In recent years there has been an increase in advertising to create an acceptable corporate image. For example, Shell has spent considerable sums advertising its concern for the unspoilt countryside.

corporate modelling The use of simulation models to assist the management of an organization in carrying out planning and decision making. A budget is an example of a corporate model.

corporate plan See BUSINESS PLAN.

corporate raider A person or company that buys a substantial proportion of the equity of another company (the target company) with the object of either taking it over or of forcing the management of the target company to take certain steps to improve the image of the company sufficiently for the share price to rise enough for the raider to sell the holding at a profit.

corporate restructuring A change in the *business strategy of a company by *diversification into new areas, which it considers more attractive. Alternatively, following poor performance, it may seek to withdraw from an area by *divestment

or closure of parts of its business, which it no longer considers to be part of its future strategic focus. *See also* DOWNSIZING; RIGHT-SIZING.

corporate social reporting *See* SOCIAL RESPONSIBILITY REPORTING.

corporate venturing The provision of *risk capital by one company, either directly or by means of a venture-capital fund, for another company. This may be undertaken as a means of obtaining information about the company requiring venture capital or its market, of taking a first step towards acquiring the company, or of moving into a new market cheaply and without needing to acquire the relevant expertise and personnel.

Corporate Venturing Scheme (CVS) A scheme designed to encourage established companies to invest in the ordinary shares of companies of the same kind as those qualifying under the *enterprise investment scheme; the scheme encourages the investing and qualifying companies to form mutually beneficial corporate venturing relationships. Companies investing through the CVS may obtain *corporation tax relief (at 20%) on the amount invested provided that the shares are held for at least three years after issue or, if later, three years after the trade for which the money was raised begins. Investing companies also obtain relief for most allowable losses on the shares and deferral of corporation tax when a chargeable gain from the disposal of CVS shares is reinvested in a new CVS investment.

corporate VMS A *vertical marketing system that combines successive stages of production and distribution under single ownership in order to establish channel leadership. *Compare* ADMINISTERED VMS; CONTRACTUAL VMS.

corporate website A site set up by a company on the *World Wide Web, which carries information and other features designed to answer customer's questions, build customer relationships, and generate interest in the company, rather than to sell its products or services directly. The website handles interactive communications initiated by the consumer.

corporation A succession of persons or

body of persons authorized by law to act as one person and having rights and liabilities distinct from the individuals forming the corporation. The *artificial person may be created by Royal Charter, statute, or common law. The most important type is the registered *company formed under the Companies Act. **Corporations sole** are those having only one individual forming them; for example, a bishop, the sovereign, the Treasury Solicitor. **Corporations aggregate** are composed of more than one individual, e.g. a limited company. They may be formed for special purposes by statute; the BBC is an example. Corporations can hold property, carry on business, bring legal actions, etc., in their own name. Their actions may, however, be limited by the doctrine of *ultra vires. *See also* PUBLIC CORPORATION.

corporation tax (CT) Tax charged on the total profits of a company *resident in the UK arising in each *accounting period. The rate of corporation tax depends on the level of profits of the company. The small companies rate of 19% currently applies to companies with total profits of £300,000 or less; since 2002 very small companies with total annual profits of £10,000 or less pay no CT. Full-rate corporation tax of 30% applies to companies with total profits of over £1.5 million. There is a *marginal relief for those companies with total profits between £300,000 and £1.5 million or between £10,000 and £50,000. Large companies pay corporation tax in instalments: other companies pay CT nine months after the end of the company's chargeable accounting period.

correspondent bank A bank in a foreign country that offers banking facilities to the customers of a bank in another country. These arrangements are usually the result of agreements, often reciprocal, between the two banks. The most frequent correspondent banking facilities used are those of money transmission.

corruption The introduction of errors into computer data through mechanical accident or malfunction. All forms of electronic or magnetic data storage are vulnerable to corruption, which can occur for no discernable reason. Corruption can also occur when data is sent over telephone lines between communicating computers.

corset 1. A restriction of the movements of currency exchange values imposed by certain formal market mechanisms. **2.** A government restriction on the growth of bank deposits and thus indirectly on bank lending and the money supply.

cosmetic customization The practice of presenting a standard product in different ways for different audiences without actually changing the product. *See* CUSTOMIZATION.

cost 1. An expenditure, usually of money, for the purchase of goods or services. **2.** An expenditure, usually of money, incurred in achieving a goal, e.g. producing certain goods, building a factory, or closing down a branch. *See also* CURRENT COST; ECONOMIC COSTS; FIXED COST; HISTORICAL COST; MARGINAL COST; OPPORTUNITY COST; REPLACEMENT COST.

cost accounting The techniques used in collecting, processing, and presenting financial and quantitative data within an organization to ascertain the cost of the *cost centres, the *cost units, and the various operations. Cost accounting is now regarded as a division of *management accounting, which also incorporates the techniques of planning, decision making, and control.

cost allocation The process of assigning costs to one or more *cost objects when it is not possible to trace a cost directly. *Indirect costs (overheads) always have to be assigned to cost objects using cost allocations. The basis on which costs are assigned to cost objects is called the *allocation base or *cost driver. The purposes of cost allocation can be briefly summarized as follows:
• to provide information for decisions: an example would be deciding whether or not to replace a machine;
• to set selling prices;
• to measure profits accurately (product profitability and customer profitability);
• to motivate management or employees.
Broadly, two types of systems can be used to assign indirect costs to cost objects: *traditional costing systems and *activity-based costing. Traditional costing systems focus on product costs and are often criticized for relying on *arbitrary allocations.

Activity-based costing systems use *cause-and-effect allocations.

cost and freight *See* C & F.

cost assignment (cost attribution) The procedures by which direct or indirect costs are charged to or made the responsibility of particular *cost centres, and ultimately charged to the products manufactured or services provided by the organization. Procedures used to achieve cost attribution include *absorption costing, *activity-based costing, and *marginal costing. *See also* COST ALLOCATION; COST TRACING.

cost behaviour The changes that occur to total costs as a result of changes in activity levels within an organization. The total of the *fixed costs tends to remain unaltered by changes in activity levels in the short term, whereas the total of the *variable costs tends to increase or decrease in proportion to activity. There are also some costs that demonstrate *semi-variable cost behaviour, i.e. they have both fixed and variable elements. The study of cost behaviour is important for *breakeven analysis and also when considering decision-making techniques.

cost-benefit analysis A technique used in *capital budgeting that takes into account the estimated costs to be incurred by a proposed investment and the estimated benefits likely to arise from it. In a *financial appraisal the benefits may arise from an increase in the revenue from a product or service, from saved costs, or from other cash inflows, but in an *economic appraisal the economic benefits, such as the value of time saved or of fewer accidents resulting from a road improvement, often require to be valued.

cost centre The area of an organization for which costs are collected for the purposes of cost ascertainment, planning, decision making, and control. Cost centres are determined by individual organizations; they may be based on a function, department, section, individual, or any group of these. Cost centres are of two main types: **production cost centres** in an organization are those concerned with making a product, while **service cost centres** provide a service (such as stores, boil-

erhouse, or canteen) to other parts of the organization.

cost classification The process of grouping expenditure according to common characteristics. Costs are initially divided into *capital expenditure and *revenue expenditure. In a production organization the revenue expenditure is classified sequentially to enable a product cost to build up in the order in which these costs tend to be incurred. Revenue costs would normally include:
- direct material,
- direct labour,
- direct expenses,
- production overheads,
- administration overheads,
- selling overheads,
- distribution overheads,
- research overheads.

cost control The techniques used by various levels of management within an organization to ensure that the costs incurred fall within acceptable levels. Cost control is assisted by the provision of financial information to management by the accountant and by the use of such techniques as *budgetary control and *standard costing, which highlight and analyse any variances.

cost convention The custom used as a basis for recording the costs to be charged against the profit for an accounting period. The cost convention used may be based on *historical cost, *current cost, or *replacement cost.

cost driver In a system of *activity-based costing, any factor such as number of units, number of transactions, or duration of transactions that drives the costs arising from a particular *activity. When such factors can be clearly identified and measured, they will be used as a basis for allocating costs to cost objects. The term cost driver is therefore effectively synonymous with both *activity measure and *allocation base and the literature often uses them interchangeably. *See also* ACTIVITY COST POOL; COST ALLOCATION.

cost effectiveness 1. Achieving a goal with the minimum of expenditure. 2. Achieving a goal with an expenditure that makes the achievement viable in commercial terms.

cost function A formula or equation that represents the way in which particular costs behave when plotted on a graph. For example, the most common cost function represents the total cost as the sum of the *fixed costs and the *variable costs in the equation $y = a + bx$, where y is the total cost, a is the total fixed cost, b is the variable cost per unit of production or sales, and x is the number of units produced or sold.

cost, insurance, and freight *See* C.I.F..

cost minimization The behavioural assumption that an individual or firm will seek to purchase a given amount of goods or inputs at the least cost, other things being equal. By making certain assumptions, there will exist a single cost-minimizing combination of inputs for any level of output. Thus, assuming that firms or *entrepreneurs choose to minimize costs, their behaviour can be predicted. It can be shown that the profit-maximizing level of output for a firm is also cost minimizing; however, it need not be assumed that firms actually maximize profits, which is a different behavioural assumption.

cost object Any item for which a separate measurement of *costs is desired. This may be a product, a service, a customer, or a specific operation associated with any of these (e.g., designing a new product, processing a mortgage application, making a telephone call to a customer). The number of cost objects identified and the frequency of measuring the costs will vary between organizations; a product cost will normally be calculated on a weekly or monthly basis, whereas the cost of processing a mortgage application may only be calculated on an annual basis.

cost of capital The return, expressed in terms of an interest rate, that an organization is required to pay for the capital used in financing its activities. This will vary according to the type or types of capital employed (e.g., *equity capital, *loan capital, or some mixture of the two). One approach to establishing the cost of capital is therefore to compute a unique *weighted average cost of capital for each organization, based on its particular mix of capital sources. The cost of capital is often used as

a *hurdle rate in *discounted cash flow calculations.

cost of funds 1. The cost to banks of borrowing in the principal *money markets, which determines their rates of interest when lending to their customers. **2.** The cost to an organization of raising additional *loan capital.

cost of goods manufactured (manufacturing cost of finished goods) The total *production cost of the *finished goods transferred from the production facility of an organization during an accounting period. It is made up of the total expenditure for the period on *direct materials, *direct labour, *direct expenses, and *manufacturing overheads adjusted by the opening and closing stocks of raw materials and the *work in progress at the beginning and end of the period.

cost of quality The total costs of ensuring good quality or rectifying poor quality. Ultimately, by improving quality managers will reduce costs and improve profits. Four categories of costs are useful for this analysis:

- **prevention costs**. These are the costs incurred in preventing mistakes. Examples include training, quality planning, process controls, and market research. Expenditure in this area is seen as an investment.
- **appraisal costs**. These include the costs of inspecting parts from suppliers, inspecting and testing products in manufacture, and performing quality audits.
- **internal failure costs**. These are the costs incurred when a product does not conform to quality standards. Examples include the costs of scrap, repairs to defective products, and downtime. They are incurred before the customer receives the product.
- **external failure costs**. These are the costs incurred when the customer receives a poor quality product. Examples include the costs of investigating complaints, of replacing products returned by the customer, and warranty charges. If the customer is dissatisfied and finds a new supplier, the total cost will be much higher.

See also ENVIRONMENTAL COSTS.

cost of sales (cost of goods sold; COGS)
A figure representing the cost to an organization of supplying goods or services for sale, excluding administration and other general overheads. In a sales organization, it is the *opening stock at the beginning of an accounting period plus the purchases for the period, less the closing stock at the end of the period. In a manufacturing organization, the purchases for the period would be replaced by the *production cost of finished goods for the period. In a service providing organization, the cost of sales would be calculated as *direct costs adjusted by the opening and closing values of *work in progress. The cost of sales figure is deducted from the sales revenue to obtain the *gross profit for the period.

cost per enquiry (CPE) A commonly used method of calculating costs in *direct marketing in which the total cost of the mailing is divided by the number of resultant enquiries received. For example, if 1000 enquiries were generated by a mailing operation costing £5000, the CPE would be £5 (i.e. 5000/1000).

cost per mille (CPM) The cost of an advertisement per thousand people who will see or hear it.

cost per order (CPO) The total cost of a mailing divided by the total number of orders received.

cost per product The cost needed to generate a visit to a website. For advertising on the web it is the cost per *banner advertisement divided by the *click-through rate.

cost per targeted mille (CPTM) The cost of an advertisement per targeted thousand people who will see or hear it.

cost-plus contract A contract entered into by a supplier in which the goods or services provided to the customer are charged at cost plus an agreed percentage markup. This method of pricing is very common if the cost of producing the commodity is unknown or if its production will involve significant research work. However, because simple cost-plus contracts do not encourage suppliers to minimize their costs, there has been a move away from this type of contract in UK government orders with private industry.

cost-plus pricing An approach to establishing the selling price of a product or service in a commercial organization, in which the total cost of the product or service is estimated and a percentage *mark-up is added in order to obtain a profitable selling price. A variation to this approach is to estimate the costs to a particular stage, say the costs of production only, and then to add a percentage mark-up to cover both the other overheads (including administration, selling, and distribution costs) and the profit margin. This approach to costing is very different from *target costing. Compare FULL COST PRICING; MARGINAL COST PRICING.

cost-plus transfer prices *Transfer prices set by *cost-plus pricing, which include a mark-up to provide a profit for the supplying division. When *variable costs rather than full costs are used in this calculation, the mark-up will need to be higher to cover both the *fixed costs and a profit margin. This method involves a problem for managers, as cost-plus transfer pricing does not identify the output levels that will maximize prices.

cost-push inflation An increase in the prices of goods or services caused by increases in the cost of inputs (especially wages and raw materials). As an explanation of *inflation, cost-push theories became popular in the 1970s when they appeared to explain the rapid inflation of that period, which followed on from very rapid rises in wages and the increases in oil prices. However, the theory is also widely criticized as: (a) it describes only changes in relative prices (e.g. oil) rather than rises in the general price level (which is how inflation is defined); and (b) most economists would now agree that price rises can only continue if there is an accompanying increase in the *money supply.

cost tracing The process of assigning *direct costs to the relevant *cost objects. Compare COST ALLOCATION.

cost unit A unit of production for which the management of an organization wishes to collect the costs incurred. In some cases the cost unit may be the final item produced, for example a chair or a light bulb, but in other more complex products the cost unit may be a sub-assembly, for example an aircraft wing or a gear box. Cost units may also be expressed as batches of items, particularly when the unit cost of the individual product would be very small; for example, the cost unit for a manufacturer of pens might be the cost per thousand pens. *See also* COST OBJECT.

Council for Mutual Economic Assistance (CMEA; COMECON) A former organization of Soviet-bloc countries formed in 1949 to promote the economic interdependence of its member states. The members were Bulgaria, Cuba, Czechoslovakia, German Democratic Republic (GDR), Hungary, Mongolia, Poland, Romania, USSR, and Vietnam. COMECON was replaced in 1991 by an organization designed to help those economies integrate with the rest of Europe.

counterbid 1. A bid made in an auction that exceeds a bid already made (which then becomes the **underbid**). **2.** A second bid made in reply to a *counteroffer.

counteroffer A reply made to a *bid. If a seller makes an *offer of goods on specified terms at a specified price, the buyer may accept it or make a bid against the offer. Sellers who find the bid unacceptable may make a counteroffer, usually on terms or at a price that are a compromise between those in the offer and bid. If the buyers still find the counteroffer unacceptable they may make a *counterbid.

counterparty A person who is a party to a contract.

counterparty risk The *risk that either of the parties to a contract (counterparties) will fail to honour their obligations under the contract. In such organized markets as the *London International Financial Futures and Options Exchange this risk is reduced by the *London Clearing House (now LCH.Clearnet) becoming counterparty to the contract, i.e. the buyer contracts to buy from LCH and the seller contracts to sell to LCH (*see* NOVATION). The risk of default by either the buyer or the seller is thus assumed by LCH, the buyer and seller being left with the greatly reduced counterparty risk that LCH will fail. The risk is, however, greater in over-the-counter transactions.

countertrading The practice in international trading of paying for goods in a form other than by hard currency. For example, a South American country wishing to buy aircraft may countertrade (usually through a third party) by paying in coffee beans.

countervailing credit *See* BACK-TO-BACK CREDIT.

countervailing duty An extra import duty imposed by a country on certain imports. It is usually used to prevent *dumping or to counteract export subsidies given by foreign countries.

country risk The *risk of conducting transactions with, or holding assets of entities within, a particular country arising from political or economic events within that country. *See* POLITICAL CREDIT RISK; TRANSFER CREDIT RISK.

coupon 1. One of several dated slips attached to a *bond, which must be presented to the agents of the issuer or the company to obtain an interest payment or dividend. They are usually used with *bearer securities; the **coupon yield** is the *yield provided by a bearer bond. **2.** The rate of interest paid by a fixed-interest bond. The annual payment is a percentage of the bond's nominal value. **3.** (**coupon security**) A general name for bonds and notes on US Treasury Markets. **4.** A fixed-rate payment on an interest or currency swap.

coupon stripping A financial process in which the *coupons are stripped off a *bearer bond and then sold separately as a source of cash, with no capital repayment; the bond, bereft of its coupons, becomes a *zero-coupon bond and is also sold separately.

coupon yield *See* COUPON.

covenant 1. A promise made in a deed, which may or may not be under seal. Such a promise can be enforced by the parties to it as a contract, even if the promise is gratuitous: for example, if A covenants to pay B £100 per month, B can enforce this promise even without having done anything in return. Covenants were formerly used to minimize income tax, by transferring income from higher rate taxpayers to non-taxpayers (such as children or charities). However, since the Finance Act (1988), and the introduction of the *gift aid system covenants can no longer be used for tax planning in this way.

Covenants may be entered into concerning the use of land, frequently to restrict the activities of a new owner or tenant (e.g. a covenant not to sell alcohol or run a fish-and-chip shop). Such covenants may be enforceable by persons deriving title from the original parties. This is an exception to the general rule that a contract cannot bind persons who are not parties to it. **2.** An undertaking in a loan agreement the breaching of which will make the loan repayable immediately. *See also* EVENT OF DEFAULT; RATIO COVENANT.

cover 1. The security provided by *insurance or *assurance against a specified risk. **2.** *See* DIVIDEND COVER. **3.** Collateral given against a loan or credit, as in option dealing. **4.** A *hedge purchased to safeguard an *open position. **5.** Money set aside from income to meet potential bad debts or losses.

CPA 1. Abbreviation for certified public accountant. **2.** Abbreviation for critical-path analysis. *See* NETWORK MODELLING. **3.** Abbreviation for *customer profitability analysis.

CPE Abbreviation for *cost per enquiry.

CPM Abbreviation for *cost per mille.

CPO Abbreviation for *cost per order.

CPP accounting Abbreviation for *current purchasing power accounting.

CPTM Abbreviation for *cost per targeted mille.

craft union *See* TRADE UNION.

crash 1. A rapid and serious fall in the level of prices in a market. **2.** A breakdown of a computer system. A program is said to crash if it terminates abnormally. A computer is said to crash either if it suffers a mechanical failure, or if one of the programs running on it misbehaves in a way that causes the computer to stop. Generally, the computer must then be switched off, any necessary repairs made, and restarted.

crawling peg (adjustable peg; sliding peg) A method of exchange-rate control

that accepts the need for stability given by fixed (or pegged) exchange rates, while recognizing that fixed rates can be prone to serious misalignments, which in turn can cause periods of financial and economic upheaval. Under crawling-peg arrangements, countries alter their pegs by small amounts at frequent intervals, rather than making large infrequent changes. This procedure provides flexibility and, in conjunction with the manipulation of interest rates, reduces the possibility of destabilizing speculative flows of capital. However, it is exposed to the criticism made against all fixed-rate regimes, that they are an inefficient alternative to the free play of market forces. At the same time, the crawling peg loses a major advantage of fixed rates, which is to inject certainty into the international trading system and more stable inflationary expectations. The rates may move as frequently as daily under a crawling-peg policy.

creative accounting Misleadingly optimistic, though not illegal, forms of accounting. This can occur because there are a number of accounting transactions that are not subject to regulations or the regulations are ambiguous. Companies sometimes make use of these ambiguities in order to present their financial results in the best light possible. In particular, companies often wish to demonstrate increasing accounting profits and a strong balance sheet. Examples of transactions in which creative accounting has taken place concern *consignment stocks and *repurchase agreements. In these contexts, creative accounting will involve the separation of legal title from the risks and rewards of the activities, the linking of several transactions to make it difficult to determine the commercial effect of each transaction, or the inclusion in an agreement of *options, which are likely to be exercised. Such policies are sometimes referred to as *off-balance-sheet finance or *window dressing. Creative accounting is now less prevalent than it was in the 1980s. This is due both to a number of scandals that have raised the profile of *corporate governance and the responsibilities of auditors, and to the activities of the *Accounting Standards Board, which has addressed some of the worst abuses.

credit **1.** The reputation and financial standing of a person or organization. **2.** The sum of money that a trader or company allows a customer before requiring payment. **3.** The funding of members of the public to purchase goods and services with money borrowed from finance companies, banks, and other money lenders. **4.** An entry on the right-hand side of an *account in double-entry book-keeping, usually showing a sale or a liability. **5.** A payment into an account.

credit account *See* CHARGE ACCOUNT.

credit balance A balancing amount of an account in which the total of credit entries exceeds the total of debit entries. Credit balances represent revenue, liabilities, or capital.

credit brokerage *See* ANCILLARY CREDIT BUSINESS.

credit call A national or international telephone call that is charged to the caller's credit card.

credit card A plastic card issued by a bank or finance organization to enable holders to obtain credit in shops, hotels, restaurants, petrol stations, etc. The retailer or trader receives monthly payments from the credit-card company equal to its total sales in the month by means of that credit card, less a service charge. Customers also receive monthly statements from the credit-card company, which may be paid in full within a certain number of days with no interest charged, or they may make a specified minimum payment and pay interest on the outstanding balance. Credit cards may be used to obtain cash either at a bank or its ATMs. *See also* CHARGE CARD; DEBIT CARD; GOLD CARD.

credit control Any system used by an organization to ensure that its outstanding debts are paid within a reasonable period. It involves establishing a **credit policy**, *credit rating of clients, and chasing accounts that become overdue. *See also* FACTORING.

credit crunch A period during which lenders are unwilling to extend credit to borrowers. *See also* CREDIT SQUEEZE.

credit guarantee **1.** A type of insurance provided by credit guarantee associations, government institutions, or lenders to enable small firms to obtain credit from banks. **2.** *See* CREDIT INSURANCE.

credit insurance **1.** An insurance policy that continues the repayments of a particular debt in the event of the policyholder being financially unable to do so because of illness, death, redundancy, or any other specified cause. **2. (credit guarantee)** A form of insurance against losses arising from bad debts. This is not usually undertaken by normal insurance policies but by specialists known as factors (*see* FACTORING). *See also* BERNE UNION; EXPORT CREDITS GUARANTEE DEPARTMENT.

credit line **1.** The extent of the credit available to a borrower or the user of a *credit card as set down in the initial credit agreement. **2.** The facility for borrowing money over a given period to a specified extent.

credit note A document expressing the indebtedness of the organization issuing it, usually to a customer. When goods are supplied to a customer an invoice is issued; if the customer returns all or part of the goods the invoice is wholly or partially cancelled by a credit note.

creditor One to whom an organization or person owes money. The *balance sheet of a company shows the total owed to creditors and a distinction has to be made between creditors who will be paid during the coming accounting period and those who will not be paid until later than this.

creditor–days ratio A ratio that gives an estimate of the average number of days' credit taken by an organization before the creditors are paid. It is calculated by the formula:

(trade creditors × 365)/annual purchases on credit.

creditors' committee A committee of creditors of an insolvent company or a bankrupt individual, which represents all the creditors. They supervise the conduct of the administration of a company or the bankruptcy of an individual or receive reports from an administrative *receiver.

creditors' ledger *See* PURCHASE LEDGER.

creditors' voluntary liquidation (CVL)
The winding-up of a company by special
resolution of the members when it is insolvent. A **meeting of creditors** must be
held within 14 days of such a resolution
and the creditors must be given seven
days' notice of the meeting. The creditors
also have certain rights to information before the meeting. A *liquidator may be appointed by the members before the
meeting of creditors or at the meeting by
the creditors. If two different liquidators
are appointed, the creditors' nominee is
usually preferred. CVLs, also known as
creditors' voluntary winding-ups, are the
most common form of liquidation in use
in the UK. *Compare* MEMBERS' VOLUNTARY
LIQUIDATION.

credit rating An assessment of the creditworthiness of an individual or a firm, i.e.
the extent to which they can safely be
granted credit. Traditionally, banks have
provided confidential trade references (*see*
BANKER'S REFERENCE), but recently **credit-
reference agencies** (also known as **rating
agencies**) have grown up, which gather information from a wide range of sources,
including the county courts, bankruptcy
proceedings, hire-purchase companies,
and professional debt collectors. This information is then provided as a **credit reference**, for a fee, to interested parties. The
consumer was given some protection from
such activities in the *Consumer Credit
Act (1974), which allows an individual to
obtain a copy of all the information held
by such agencies relating to that individual, as well as the right to correct any discrepancies. There are also agencies that
specialize in the corporate sector, giving
details of a company's long-term and
short-term debt. This can be extremely important to the price of the company's
shares on the market, its ability to borrow,
and its general standing in the business
community. Credit ratings for the debt instruments of large corporations are provided by such organizations as Moody's
Investor Service and Standard and Poor.
See also ANCILLARY CREDIT BUSINESS.

credit risk The *risk that a counterparty
will default or delay payment on an obligation or that the value of a flow of payments will decline due to an adverse
movement in the counterparty's *credit

rating. *See also* POLITICAL CREDIT RISK;
TRANSFER CREDIT RISK.

credit sale agreement *See* HIRE PUR-
CHASE.

credit squeeze A government measure,
or set of measures, to reduce economic activity by restricting the money supply.
Measures used include increasing the interest rate (to restrain borrowing), controlling moneylending by banks and others,
and increasing down payments or making
other changes to hire-purchase regulations.

credit transfer An electronic system of
settling a debt by transferring money
through a bank or post office. The payer
completes written instructions naming
the receiver and giving the receiver's address and acount number. Several receivers may be listed and settled by a
single transaction. The popularity of this
system in the UK led the banks to introduce a credit-clearing system in 1961 and
the Post Office to do so in 1968. *See also*
GIRO.

creditworthiness An assessment of a
person's or a business's ability to pay for
goods purchased or services received.
Creditworthiness may be presented in the
form of a *credit rating.

creeping takeover The accumulation
of a company's shares, by purchasing
them openly over a period on a stock exchange, as a preliminary to a takeover (*see*
TAKEOVER BID). There are regulations governing this process and stipulating the
maximum number of shares that can be
acquired before formal notification must
be made and a bid undertaken.

CREST An electronic share settlement
system created by the Bank of England for
the securities industry that began operation in 1996. Using CREST, shares are registered electronically, purchases and sales
are settled instantaneously on the due
date, and the dividends can be paid electronically direct to the shareholder's bank.
Paper certificates and associated paperwork have been abolished for those who
join CREST. As with paper shares, the
company register of shareholders provides
proof of ownership. Those wishing to retain paper certificates are able to do so.

critical event In critical-path analysis, an event – i.e. the start and/or completion of an activity – that lies on a critical path (*see* NETWORK MODELLING).

critical incident technique (CIT) An analytical technique used to identify those factors that are critical to the success or failure of individuals or systems in a given setting. People with first-hand experience (e.g. factory supervisors) are asked to describe incidents in which behavioural or other factors had a critical effect. These findings are then collated and analysed. The technique has mainly been used to devise rating scales for *employee evaluation (*see* BEHAVIOURALLY ANCHORED RATING SCALES; BEHAVIOURAL OBSERVATION SCALE) but is also used in *accident analysis, analysis of customer complaints, and various other applications.

critical mass A threshold number of users or customers needed for the sustainable growth of a product or service. Critical mass is required for the success of many on-line communities and for competing standards.

critical-path analysis (CPA) *See* NETWORK MODELLING.

critical success factors The strengths and weaknesses that most affect an organization's success. These are measured relative to those of its competitors.

CRM systems *See* CUSTOMER RELATIONSHIP MANAGEMENT SYSTEMS.

crore In India, Pakistan, and Bangladesh, 100 *lakhs, i.e. 10 million. It usually refers to a number of rupees.

cross-border listing The practice of listing shares in a company on the stock exchanges of different countries in order to create a larger market for the shares.

cross-currency interest-rate swap A *swap of two different interest rates in two different currencies. This usually involves swapping a fixed rate for a floating rate (or vice versa); if both rates are floating it is known as a *basis swap. *See* CURRENCY SWAP; INTEREST-RATE SWAP.

crossed cheque *See* CHEQUE.

cross-holding A situation in which two or more companies hold shares in each

other in order to cement business ties and forestall takeovers.

crossing the chasm A common problem in new-product marketing in which there is a gap between the use of a technology by *early adopters and its adoption by more pragmatic mainstream consumers.

cross-selling The practice of selling related products and services to existing customers. For example, a car dealer may also offer its customers servicing of the vehicle, valeting, re-upholstering, etc. An insurance broker may also offer motor-car insurance to its house-insurance customers. Businesses often cross-sell as part of their customer loyalty and retention strategy. Research evidence suggests that the greater the number of different products or services a customer buys from the same vendor, the lower the defection rate.

crown jewel option A form of *poison pill in which a company, defending itself against an unwanted *takeover bid, writes an *option that would allow a partner or other friendly company to acquire one or more of its best businesses at an advantageous price if control of the defending company is lost to the unwelcome predator. The granting of such an option may not always be in the best interests of the shareholders of the defending company.

CRP Abbreviation for *capacity requirement plan.

cruzeiro *See* REAL.

crystallization *See* CHARGE.

CT Abbreviation for *corporation tax.

CTT Abbreviation for *capital transfer tax.

C2 Principles A code of best practice, established by Thomas Dunfee and David Hess of the University of Pennsylvania, describing how a company and its employees should deal with any attempt to make or solicit improper payments.

cultural environment Institutions and other forces that affect society's basic values, perceptions, preferences, and behaviours.

cum- *See* EX-.

cum-new Denoting a share that is offered for sale with the right to take up any *scrip issue or *rights issue. *Compare* EX-NEW.

cumulative preference share A type of *preference share that entitles the owner to receive any dividends not paid in previous years. Companies are not obliged to pay dividends on preference shares if there are insufficient earnings in any particular year. Cumulative preference shares guarantee the eventual payment of these dividends in arrears before the payment of dividends on ordinary shares, provided that the company returns to profit in subsequent years.

cumulative preferred stock In the USA, stock in which the dividends accumulate if not paid out in a particular financial period.

currency **1.** Any kind of money that is in circulation in an economy. **2.** Anything that functions as a *medium of exchange, including coins, banknotes, cheques, *bills of exchange, promissory notes. etc. **3.** The money in use in a particular country. *See* FOREIGN EXCHANGE. **4.** The time that has to elapse before a bill of exchange matures.

currency future A *financial futures contract in which a currency for forward delivery is bought or sold at a particular exchange rate.

currency option A contract giving the right either to buy or to sell a specified currency at a fixed exchange rate within a given period. The price agreed is called the *exercise price or strike price. This is the price at which the buyer has the right to buy or sell the currency.

currency risk *See* EXCHANGE-RATE EXPOSURE.

currency swap A *swap in which specified amounts of one currency are exchanged for another currency at agreed principles over time. In an ordinary currency swap both currencies bear interest at a fixed rate: if both currencies bear interest at a floating rate the transaction is known as a *basis swap and if one rate is floating and the other fixed it is a *cross-currency interest-rate swap.

current account **1.** An active account at a bank or building society into which deposits can be paid and from which withdrawals can be made by cheque (*see also* CHEQUE ACCOUNT). Building societies usually make no charges and pay interest on balances maintained in a current account. Banks, in order to remain competitive, have been obliged to follow the same practice for most non-business accounts. **2.** The part of the *balance of payments account that records non-capital transactions. It includes trade in visibles and invisibles. **3.** An account in which intercompany or interdepartmental balances are recorded. **4.** An account recording the transactions of a partner in a partnership that do not relate directly to his or her capital in the partnership (*see* CAPITAL ACCOUNT).

current assets (**circulating assets; circulating capital; floating assets**) The assets of an organization that are constantly changing their form and are circulating from cash to goods and back to cash again. Cash is used to purchase raw materials, which become work in progress when issued to a production department. The work in progress becomes finished goods, which once they are sold, become debtors or cash from an accounting point of view. Debtors are ultimately changed into cash when they pay, thus completing the cycle. *Compare* FIXED ASSET.

current cost **1.** A cost calculated to take into consideration current circumstances of cost and performance levels. **2.** The sum that would be required at current prices to purchase or manufacture an asset. This may be the replacement cost or the historical cost adjusted for inflation by means of an appropriate price index. **3.** (**constant dollar**) In the USA, the method of converting historical cost to current cost and then adjusting to constant purchasing power by using the average *Consumer Price Index for the current year.

current-cost accounting (**CCA**) A form of accounting in which the approach to capital maintenance is based on maintaining the operating capability of a business. Assets are valued at their *value to the business, which is the loss that a business would suffer if it were to be deprived of the use of the asset. This may be the *replacement cost of the asset, its *net realizable value, or its *economic value to the business. Current-cost accounting ensures that a business maintains its operating capacity by separating holding gains from *operating profits, thereby preventing them from being distributed to shareholders. The current-cost accounting profit figure is derived by making a number of adjustments to the *historical-cost accounting profit and loss account: these are the cost of sales adjustment, *depreciation adjustment, monetary *working-capital adjustment, and the *gearing adjustment. The current-cost reserve in the balance sheet is used to 'collect' the current cost adjustments. This method of accounting was widely used in the UK in the late 1970s and early 1980s, when inflation was high; it was not popular, however, and as inflation has reduced it has been largely abandoned. *Statement of Standard Accounting Practice 16, Current Cost Accounting, was issued in 1980 but withdrawn in 1988.

current liabilities Amounts owed by a business to other organizations and individuals that should be paid within one year from the balance-sheet date. These generally consist of trade creditors, *bills of exchange payable, amounts owed to group and related companies, taxation, social-security creditors, proposed dividends, accruals, deferred income, payments received on account, bank overdrafts, and short-term loans. Any long-term loans repayable within one year from the balance-sheet date should also be included. Current liabilities are distinguished from long-term liabilities on the balance sheet.

current marketing situation The section of a marketing plan that describes a target market and a company's position in it.

current purchasing power accounting (constant purchasing power accounting; CPP accounting) A form of accounting that measures profit after allowing for the maintenance of the purchasing power of the shareholders' capital. The *Retail Price Index is used to adjust for general price changes to ensure that the shareholders' capital maintains the same monetary purchasing power. There is no requirement to

allow for the maintenance of the purchasing power of the loan creditors' capital. Current purchasing power accounting was covered by the provisional *Statement of Standard Accounting Practice 7, issued in 1974 but withdrawn in 1978.

current ratio (working-capital ratio) The ratio of the *current assets of a business to the *current liabilities, expressed as x:1 and used as a test of liquidity. For example, if the current assets are £250,000 and the current liabilities are £125,000 the current ratio is 2:1. There is no simple rule of thumb, but a low ratio, e.g. under 1:1, would usually raise concern over the liquidity of the company. Too high a ratio, e.g. in excess of 2:1, may indicate poor management of *working capital; this would be established by calculating the *stock turnover ratio and *debtor collection period ratio. Care must be taken when making comparisons between companies to ensure that any industry differences are recognized. The *liquid ratio is regarded as a more rigorous test of liquidity.

current-year basis The *basis of assessment for tax purposes in the UK in which tax is charged in a *fiscal year on profits arising in the accounts for the period ending in that tax year. Compare PRECEDING-YEAR BASIS.

current yield See YIELD.

curriculum vitae (Latin: the course of one's life) An account of one's education, qualifications, and career prepared by a candidate for a job and given to a prospective employer. It should be typed and give full details. It is usual to add a section on outside interests. In the USA it is often called a **resumé**.

customer acquisition costs See ACQUISITION COST.

customer agent A software package or on-line shopping service that goes to different websites to compare prices and terms of sale on behalf of a customer.

customer capital See INTELLECTUAL CAPITAL.

customer-centred company A company that focuses on customer developments in designing its *marketing strategies and on delivering superior value to its target customers.

customer coalitions Groups of customers working together to obtain preferential prices for specific goods or services or to ensure high quality service by the provider.

customer database An organized collection of comprehensive information about individual customers or prospects, including geographic, demographic, and psychographic data as well as information about buying behaviour. *See also* LIVE-MARKETING DATABASE.

customer delivered value The difference between total customer value and the total customer cost of a marketing offer. It can be regarded as 'profit' to the customer.

customer-level activities *See* ACTIVITY.

customer lifetime value *See* LIFETIME VALUE.

customer perspective *See* BALANCED SCORECARD.

customer processing technology The technology that either provides the immediate interface between an organization and its customers (e.g. a bank *automated teller machine) or facilitates human interaction with customers. Direct interaction between the customer and the organization has traditionally been a low-technology activity. Increasingly, *information technology is being used to make that interaction more efficient; for example, by giving salespersons up-to-date product information and allowing them to transmit orders instantly. This both speeds the back-office operation and makes customers feel that they have received a more customized and responsive service.

customer profitability analysis (CPA) The analysis of profits by customer. In the past, management accounting reports focused exclusively on product profitability, but in recent years it has become clear that managers need to understand both product and customer profitability. Typically, organizations that introduced CPA in the 1990s discovered that a small number of customers accounted for most of the profit; identifying profitable customers can

therefore be very important. *See also* LIFETIME VALUE.

customer relationship management systems (CRM systems) Computer applications that integrate a company's information about its customers with the knowledge of how best to use this information.

customer service The services an organization offers to its customers, especially of industrial goods and expensive consumer goods, such as computers or cars. Customer services cover a wide variety of forms, including after-sales servicing, such as a repair and replacement service, extended guarantees, regular mailings of information, and, more recently, freephone telephone calls in case of complaints. The appeal of a company's products are greatly influenced by the customer services it offers.

customer value A consumer's assessment of the overall capacity of a product to satisfy his or her needs.

customer value analysis An analysis undertaken to determine what benefits target customers value and how they rate the relative value of various competitors' offers.

customer value delivery system The system made up of the value chains of a company and its suppliers, distributors, and ultimately its customers, who work together to deliver value to customers.

customization The design and development of a product to meet the specific requirements of a single customer. Because of the high cost and time required to produce a unique product, most firms prefer to provide a product that consists of a set of standard features, some of which have been modified. Many cars, for example, are available in several different body styles, colours, and trim combinations. In addition, optional extras are specified to enable buyers to customize their purchases.

custom of the trade A practice that has been used in a particular trade for a long time and is understood to apply by all engaged in that trade. Such customs or practices may influence the way in which a term in a contract is interpreted and courts will generally take into account established customs of a trade in settling a dispute over the interpretation of a contract.

Customs and Excise *See* BOARD OF CUSTOMS AND EXCISE.

customs entry The record kept by the Customs of goods imported into or exported from a country. In the UK a *bill of entry is used for either imports (**entry in**) or exports (**entry out**). If no duty is involved with a consignment it is given **free entry**.

customs invoice An invoice for goods imported or exported, which is prepared especially for the customs authorities.

customs tariff A listing of the goods on which a country's government requires customs duty to be paid on being imported into that country, together with the rate of customs duty applicable. For the UK the Customs Tariff is published by the *Stationery Office.

customs union A union of two or more states to form a region in which there are no import or export duties between members but goods imported into the region bear the same import duties. The *European Union is an example.

CVL Abbreviation for *creditors' voluntary liquidation.

CVS Abbreviation for *Corporate Venturing Scheme.

cwmni cyfyngedig cyhoeddus (c.c.c.) Welsh for *public limited company.

cwo Abbreviation for cash with order.

cybermediaries Intermediaries who bring together buyers and sellers on the Internet or those who need and those who supply particular information or services.

cycle The medium-term wavelike rise and fall of the sales of a product, resulting from changes in general economic and competitive activity.

cycle inventory *See* INVENTORY.

cycle time The length of time required from the placing of an order by a customer to the delivery of the product or service. In companies using *just-in-time techniques, this should be equivalent to the time taken from start to finish of the manufacturing process. Reducing cycle times is very important for just-in-time companies; some ways in which this can be done include reducing set-up times, improving quality to reduce time spent on inspection and replacing faulty parts, and preventative maintenance to reduce machine downtime.

DA Abbreviation for *deposit account.

D/A Abbreviation for *documents against acceptance.

Daily Official List *See* OFFICIAL LIST.

***daimyo* bond** A *bearer security issued on the Japanese markets and in the *eurobond market by the *World Bank.

daisy chain The buying and selling of the same items several times over, for example stocks and shares. This may be done to 'inflate' trading activity (that is, the sale of the same items are being included in the sales figure more than once).

dalasi (D) The standard monetary unit of the Gambia, divided into 100 bututs.

damages Compensation, in monetary form, for a loss or injury, breach of contract, tort, or infringement of a right. Damages refers to the compensation awarded, as opposed to damage, which refers to the actual injury or loss suffered. The legal principle is that the award of damages is an attempt, as far as money can, to restore injured parties to the position they were in before the event in question took place; i.e. the object is to provide restitution rather than profit. See feature ASSESSMENT OF DAMAGES on p. 151.

dandy note A delivery order issued by an exporter and countersigned by the Board of Customs and Excise, authorizing a bonded warehouse to release goods for export.

danger money *See* OCCUPATIONAL HAZARD.

dangling debit An accounting practice in which companies wrote off *goodwill to *reserves and created a goodwill account, which was deducted from the total of shareholders' funds. This treatment is no longer permitted in the UK.

data The information that is processed, stored, or produced by a computer.

database An organized collection of information held on a computer. A special computer program, called a **database management system** (**DBMS**), is used to organize the information held in the database according to a specified schema, to update the information, and to help users find the information they seek. There are two kinds of DBMS: simple DBMS, which are the electronic equivalents of a card index; and programmable DBMS, which provide a programming language that allows the user to analyse the data held in the database. On large computer systems, other programs can generally communicate with the DBMS and use its facilities. The term **data bank** is used for a collection of databases. *See also* DATA WAREHOUSING; MANAGEMENT INFORMATION SYSTEM.

databased marketing Marketing based on extensive use of computerized databases of customers. The databases usually contain customers' names, addresses, phone numbers, past purchases, and other data. These databases can be owned by the company doing the marketing (e.g. a bank's own customers) or they can be purchased from companies who supply consolidated lists.

data capture The insertion of information into a computerized system. For example, information about the sale of an item (the item sold, the sales price, and discount given, date and location of sale, etc.) is taken into the accounting system either at the point of sale in a retail organization by an electronic till or by keyboarding into the system when the invoice is prepared. This information is then readily available and up-to-date; it can also be used to adjust stock levels.

data file A *file on a computer system that contains *data, as opposed to one that contains a program. A data file is usually subdivided into records and fields.

data flow chart (**data flow diagram**) A chart that illustrates the way in which

ASSESSMENT OF DAMAGES

Damages are not assessed in an arbitrary fashion but are subject to various judicial guidelines. The general principle is that the claimant is entitled to full compensation for his or her losses. The purpose of damages in tort is to put the claimant in the position that he or she would have been in had the tort not been committed. The purpose of damages in contract is to put the claimant in the position that he or she would have been in had the contract been performed. In either case the claimant must take all reasonable steps to mitigate his or her losses. Damages can be further classified as liquidated or unliquidated, general or specific, and substantial, nominal, or exemplary.

Liquidated and unliquidated damages

Damages capable of being quantified in monetary terms are known as **liquidated damages**. In particular, liquidated damages include instances in which a genuine pre-estimate can be given of the loss that will be caused to one party if a contract is broken by the other party. If the anticipated breach of contract occurs this will be the amount, no more and no less, that is recoverable for the breach. Liquidated damages must be distinguished from any penalties specified in a contract as payable on its breach (which do not usually constitute a genuine estimate of the likely loss). Another form of liquidated damages is that expressly made recoverable under a statute. These may also be known as **statutory damages** if they involve a breach of statutory duty or are regulated or limited by statute. **Unliquidated damages** are those fixed by a court rather than those that have been estimated in advance.

General and specific damages

General damages represent compensation for general damage, which is the kind of damage the law presumes to exist in any given situation. They are recoverable even without being specifically claimed and are awarded for the usual or probable consequences of the wrongful act complained of. For example, in an action for medical negligence, pain and suffering is presumed to exist, therefore if the action is successful, general damages would be awarded as compensation even though not specifically claimed or proved. Loss of earnings by the injured party, however, must be specifically claimed and proved, in which case they are known as **specific damages**.

Prospective damages are awarded to a plaintiff, not as compensation for any loss suffered at the time of a legal action but in respect of a loss it is reasonably anticipated will be suffered at some future time. Such an injury or loss may sometimes be considered to be too remote and therefore not recoverable.

Substantial, nominal, and exemplary damages

Substantial damages are awarded to provide compensation when actual damage has been caused. By contrast, **nominal** and **contemptuous damages** are awarded for trifling amounts – usually when the court is of the opinion that although the plaintiff's rights have been infringed no real loss has been suffered, or, that although actual loss has resulted, the loss has been caused in part by the conduct of the plaintiff. The prospect of receiving only nominal or contemptuous damages prevents frivolous actions being brought. The award is usually accompanied by an order that each party bears their own legal costs.

Exemplary damages, on the other hand, are punitive damages awarded not merely as a means of compensation but also to punish the party responsible for the loss or injury. This usually occurs when the party causing the damage has done so wilfully or has received financial gain from the wrongful conduct. Exemplary damages will be greater than the amount that would have been payable purely as compensation.

specified data is handled by a computer program. Its purpose is to specify the data, to show where it is used or changed, where it is stored, and which reports use it.

data processing (DP) The class of computing operations that manipulate large quantities of information. In business, these operations include book-keeping, printing invoices and mail shots, payroll calculations, and general record keeping. Data processing forms a major use of computers in business, and many firms have full-time data-processing departments.

data protection Safeguards relating to personal data, i.e. personal information about individuals that is stored on a computer or "relevant manual filing systems". Legislation to prevent the potential misuse of such data has now been enacted in many countries. See feature DATA PROTECTION ACT (1998) on p. 153.

Datastream A UK financial information provider.

data warehousing Computer technology enabling data from multiple operational processing systems to be brought together into a single source, which can then be accessed and interrogated. The data can be both current and historical. Warehousing differs from previous *management information systems in that designers do not need to think about what questions might be asked of the system. The data is held in detail, rather than prespecified categories; it is therefore possible to ask questions and to relate variables that may never have seemed relevant before, without having to interrupt ongoing operational processes. *See also* DECISION SUPPORT SYSTEM; EXPERT SYSTEM.

dated security A stock that has a fixed *redemption date.

date stamp A date stamped on the packaging of prepacked perishable food to indicate either the date by which it must be sold by a retailer (**sell-by date**) or the date by which it must be consumed by the consumer (**consume-by date**). This is a legal requirement for prepacked perishable food sold in the UK.

dawn raid An attempt by one company or investor to acquire a significant holding in the equity of another company by instructing brokers to buy all the shares available in that company as soon as the stock exchange opens, usually before the target company knows that it is, in fact, a target. The dawn raid may provide a significant stake from which to launch a *takeover bid. The conduct of dawn raids is now restricted by the *City Code on Takeovers and Mergers.

day book A specialized *book of prime entry recording specific transactions. For example, the *sales day book records invoices for sales, the *purchase day book records invoices received from suppliers. Day-book entries are transferred to memorandum *ledgers, such as the debtors' ledger and the creditors' ledger, while totals of entries are transferred to the *nominal ledger control accounts, such as the debtors' ledger control account and the creditors' ledger control account.

day order An order to a stockbroker, commodity broker, etc., to buy or sell a specified security or commodity. The order is valid for the day on which it is given and automatically becomes void at the close of trading on that day.

days of grace (**grace period; period of grace**) **1.** The interval between the establishment of a loan and the first due date for repayment. **2.** Time given to defaulters to satisfy their obligations (*see* GRACE AND NOTICE PROVISION). **3.** The extra time allowed for payment of a *bill of exchange or insurance premium after the actual due date. With bills of exchange the usual custom is to allow 3 days of grace (not including Sundays and *Bank Holidays) and 14 days for insurance policies.

DBM Abbreviation for *disk-by-mail.

DBMS Abbreviation for database management system. *See* DATABASE.

DB scheme Abbreviation for *defined-benefit pension scheme.

DCF Abbreviation for *discounted cash flow.

DCI Abbreviation for *direct computer interviewing.

DC scheme Abbreviation for *defined-contribution pension scheme.

DATA PROTECTION ACT (1998)

In the UK the principles of data protection, the responsibilities of data controllers, and the rights of data subjects are now governed by the Data Protection Act (1998), which came into force on 1 March 2000. As compared to the Data Protection Act (1984), the 1998 Act extends the operation of protection beyond computer storage, replaces the system of registration with one of notification, and demands that the level of description by data controllers under the new Act is more general than the detailed coding system previously required. Under the 1998 Act, the eight principles of data protection are:

(1) The information to be contained in personal data shall be obtained, and personal data shall be processed, fairly and lawfully.
(2) Personal data shall be held only for specified and lawful purposes and shall not be used or disclosed in any manner incompatible with those purposes.
(3) Personal data held for any purpose shall be relevant to that purpose and not excessive in relation to the purpose(s) for which it is used.
(4) Personal data shall be accurate and, where necessary, kept up to date.
(5) Personal data held for any purpose shall not be kept longer than necessary for that purpose.
(6) Personal data shall be processed in accordance with the rights of data subjects.
(7) Appropriate technical and organizational measure shall be taken against unauthorized and unlawful processing of personal data and against accidental loss or destruction of, or damage to, personal data.
(8) Personal data shall not be transferred to a country or territory outside the European Union unless that country or territory ensures an adequate level of protection for the rights and freedoms of data subjects in relation to the processing of personal data.

Data controllers must now notify their processing of data (unless they are exempt) with the **Information Commissioner** via the telephone, by requesting, completing, and returning a notification form, or by obtaining such a form from the website http://www.dpr.gov.uk/notify/1.html. Notification is renewable annually; a data controller who fails to notify his or her processing of data, or any changes that have been made since notification, commits a criminal offence.

The Information Commissioner can seek information from and ultimately take enforcement action against data controllers for noncompliance with their full obligations under the 1998 Act. Appeals against decisions of the Commissioner may be made to the **Data Protection Tribunal**. Apart from non-notification, strict liability criminal offences under the 1998 Act include:
- obtaining, disclosing (or bringing about the disclosure), or selling (or advertising for sale) personal data, without consent of the data controller;
- obtaining unauthorized access to data;
- asking another person to obtain access to data;
- failing to respond to an information and/or enforcement notice.

Data subjects have considerable rights conferred on them under the 1998 Act. They include:
- the right to find out what information is held about them;
- the right to seek a court order to rectify, block, erase, and destroy personal details if these are inaccurate, contain expressions of opinion, or are based on inaccurate data;
- the right to prevent processing where such processing would cause substantial unwarranted damage or substantial distress to themselves or anyone else;
- the right to prevent the processing of data for direct marketing;
- the right to compensation from a data controller for damage or damage and distress caused by any breach of the 1998 Act.

dead-cat bounce A temporary recovery on a stock exchange, after a substantial fall. It does not imply a reversal of the downward trend.

dead freight *Freight charges incurred by a shipper for space reserved but not used.

deads Mail that the Royal Mail has been unable to deliver to the addressee on at least two occasions. Sometimes this is due to their death, but more often because they have moved away.

deadweight cargo Any cargo, such as minerals and coal, for which the *freight is charged on the basis of weight rather than volume.

deadweight debt A debt that is incurred to meet current needs without the security of an enduring asset. It is usually a debt incurred by a government; the national debt is a deadweight debt incurred by the UK government during the two World Wars.

deadweight tonnage *See* TONNAGE.

dealer **1.** A trader of any kind. **2.** A person who deals as a principal on a financial market rather than as a broker or agent.

dealer brand Any product on which a middleman, usually a retailer, puts its own brand name. For example, St Michael is the dealer brand for Marks and Spencer's products.

Dearing Report The report of a committee set up under the chairmanship of Sir Ronald Dearing to examine the setting of accounting standards. The report, published in 1988, led to the establishment of the *Accounting Standards Board and the *Financial Reporting Council in 1990.

dear money (tight money) A monetary policy in which loans are difficult to obtain and only available at high rates of interest. *Compare* CHEAP MONEY.

death-valley curve A curve on a graph showing how the venture capital invested in a new company falls as the company meets its start-up expenses before its income reaches predicted levels. This erosion of capital makes it difficult for the company to interest further investors in providing additional venture capital. *See also* MAXIMUM SLIPPAGE.

debenture **1.** The most common form of long-term loan taken by a company. It is usually a loan repayable at a fixed date, although some debentures are *irredeemable securities; these are sometimes called *perpetual debentures. Most debentures also pay a fixed rate of interest, and this interest must be paid before a *dividend is paid to shareholders. Most debentures are also secured on the borrower's assets, although some, known as **naked debentures** or *unsecured loan stock, are not. In the USA debentures are usually unsecured, relying only on the reputation of the borrower. In a *secured debenture, the bond may have a fixed *charge (i.e. a charge over a particular asset) or a floating charge. If debentures are issued to a large number of people (for example in the form of **debenture stock** or **loan stock**) trustees may be appointed to act on behalf of the debenture holders. There may be a premium on redemption and some debentures are *convertible, i.e. they can be converted into ordinary shares on a specified date, usually at a specified price. The advantage of debentures to companies is that they carry lower interest rates than, say, overdrafts and are usually repayable a long time into the future. For an investor, they are usually saleable on a stock exchange and involve less risk than *equities. **2.** A *deed under seal setting out the main terms of such a loan. **3.** A form of bank security covering corporate debt, either fixed or floating; in either case the bank ranks as a preferred creditor in the event of liquidation.

debit An entry on the left-hand side of an *account in double-entry book-keeping, showing an amount owed by the organization keeping the book. In the case of a bank account, a debit shows an outflow of funds from the account.

debit balance The balance of an account whose total *debit entries exceed the total of the *credit entries. Debit balances represent expenditure and *assets.

debit card A plastic card issued by a bank or building society to enable its customers with cheque accounts to pay for goods or services at certain retail outlets by using the telephone network to debit their cheque accounts directly. It is also known as a **payment card**. The retail outlets need to have the necessary computerized input device, into which the card is inserted; the customer may be required to tap in a *personal identification number before entering the amount to be debited. Most debit cards also function as *cheque cards and *cash cards. In the USA these cards are sometimes called **asset cards**.

debit note A document sent by an organization to a person showing that the recipient is indebted to the organization for the amount shown in the debit note. Debit notes are rare as invoices are more regularly used; however, a debit note might be used when an invoice would not be appropriate, e.g. for some form of intercompany transfer other than a sale of goods or services.

debt 1. A sum owed by one party to another. In commerce, it is usual for debts to be settled within one month of receiving an invoice, after which *interest may be incurred. **2.** Any funding instrument other than equity, such as a *bond, *bill of exchange, or *promissory note. *See also* DEBENTURE.

debt adjusting *See* ANCILLARY CREDIT BUSINESS.

debt collection agency An organization that specializes in collecting the outstanding debts of its clients, charging a commission for doing so. Because of the historical stigma attached to the phrase 'debt collection', these agencies prefer to be called **commercial collection agencies**. *See also* ANCILLARY CREDIT BUSINESS.

debt counselling *See* ANCILLARY CREDIT BUSINESS.

debt discounting The purchase of a *debt from a trader, especially an exporter at a discount. *See* DEBT COLLECTION AGENCY; FORFAITING.

debt–equity ratio A ratio used to examine the financial structure or *gearing of a business. The long-term debt, normally including *preference shares, of a business is expressed as a percentage of its equity. A business may have entered into an agreement with a bank that it will maintain a certain debt–equity ratio; if it

breaches this agreement the loan may have to be repaid. The debt–equity ratio is now sometimes expressed as the ratio of the debt to the sum of the debt and the equity. *See* GEARING RATIOS.

debt-for-equity swap A transaction in which debt is swapped for equity. It often accompanies the reorganization of companies in *financial distress.

debt instrument A document used to raise non-equity finance consisting of a *promissory note, *bill of exchange, or any other legally binding *bond.

debtor One who owes money to another. In *balance sheets, debtors are those who owe money to the organization and a distinction has to be made between those who are expected to pay their debts during the next accounting period and those who will not pay until later.

debtor collection period (average collection period) The period, on average, that a business takes to collect the money owed to it by its trade debtors. If a company gives one month's credit then, on average, it should collect its debts within 45 days. The **debtor collection period ratio** is calculated by dividing the amount owed by trade debtors by the annual sales on credit and multiplying by 365. For example if debtors are £25,000 and sales are £200,000, the debtors collection period ratio will be:

(£25,000 × 365)/£200,000 = 46 days approximately.

debtors' ledger *See* SALES LEDGER.

debt rescheduling A negotiation concerning outstanding loans in which the debtor has repayment difficulties. The rescheduling can take the form of an entirely new loan or an extension of the existing loan repayment period, deferring interest or principal repayments. When debt rescheduling concerns less developed countries, the new agreement may involve a lowering of interest rates or an offer of an aid package of foreign investment to the country to offset some of the existing debt. In the late 1980s the major UK commercial banks wrote off or made provision for nearly £10 billion of debt to less developed countries — often Latin American countries who had simply stopped repaying their earlier loans. Subsequently a wide range of rescheduling schemes were adopted, including some in which the debt, or part of it, was converted into internal aid programmes.

debt restructuring The adjustment of a debt, either as a result of legal action or by agreement between the interested parties, to give the debtor a more feasible arrangement with the creditors for meeting the financial obligations. The management may also voluntarily restructure debt, for example by replacing long-term debt with short-term debt.

debt service ratio (DSR) The proportion of annual export earnings needed to service a country's external debts, including both interest payments and repayment of principal. The DSR is an important statistic, indicating the severity of a country's indebtedness. The effect of rescheduling programmes can be examined by comparing pre- and post-rescheduling DSRs.

debt swap The exchange of an outstanding loan to a third party between one bank and another. The loans are usually to governments of countries in the developing world and are often expressed in the local currency.

debug *See* BUG.

decentralization The delegation of decision-making responsibilities to the subunits of an organization. The advantages claimed for decentralization are that local managers are more aware of immediate problems, are better motivated, and have greater control over local circumstances. The disadvantages of decentralization are the possibility of wasteful competition between subunits, the duplication of certain services and functions, and the loss of central control and access to information. *See* DIVISIONALIZATION.

deceptive advertising *See* MISLEADING ADVERTISING.

decider *See* CONSUMER BUYING BEHAVIOUR; DECISION-MAKING UNIT.

decimal currency A currency system in which the standard unit is subdivided into 100 parts. Following the example of the USA in 1792, most countries have introduced a decimal system. However, it was not until 15 February, 1971 that decimalization was introduced in the UK, following the recommendations of the Halesbury Committee of 1961.

decision making The act of deciding between two or more alternative courses of action. In the running of a business, accounting information and techniques are used to facilitate decision making, especially by the provision of decision models, such as *discounted cash flow, *critical-path analysis, *marginal costing, and *breakeven analysis.

decision-making unit (DMU) The informal group of individuals within an organization that decides which items the organization should buy. Commercial buying is undertaken by a group of people, rather than by individuals; it is important for the seller to discover the composition of this group within each of his potential customers, and to recognize that membership changes periodically. The group's composition varies according to the cost and complexity of the item being bought, but might comprise: the company's purchasing manager, the proposed user of the item (the **internal user**), the **influencer** (one or more people, such as the production scheduler, indirectly associated with the use of the item), and the **decider** (one or more people, such as a director, who authorize the purchase).

decision model A model that simulates the elements or variables inherent in a business decision, together with their relationships to each other and the constraints under which they operate; the purpose of the model is to enable a solution to be arrived at in keeping with the objectives of the organization. For example, a *linear programming decision model may arrive at a particular production mix that, having regard to the constraints that exist, either minimizes costs or maximizes the *contribution. Other decision models include *decision trees and *discounted cash flow.

decision support system (DSS) A computer system specifically designed to assist managers in making unstructured or semistructured decisions, i.e. the nature of the problem requiring a decision is not known in advance. A language subsystem has to be included in the DSS to allow managers to communicate easily with the system. A problem processing subsystem, such as a *spreadsheet, is also required. Typically, a system of this type has a store of internal data and is able to access external data. A **group decision support system** (**GDSS**) is designed to facilitate group decision making. *See also* DATA WAREHOUSING; EXPERT SYSTEM; MANAGEMENT INFORMATION SYSTEM.

decision table A table used to aid decision making. The table shows the problems requiring actions to be considered and estimated probabilities of outcomes. Where probabilities are difficult to estimate, the maximax and maximin criteria are often used, the former leading to the selection of the option with the greatest maximum outcome, the latter to the selection of the action with the greatest minimum outcome.

decision trees Diagrams that illustrate the choices available to a decision maker and the estimated outcomes of each possible decision. Each possible decision is shown as a separate branch of the tree, together with each estimated outcome or each decision and the subjective *probabilities of these outcomes actually occurring. From this information the *expected

values for each outcome can be determined, which can provide valuable information in decision making. For an example see the diagram below.

deck cargo Cargo that is carried on the deck of a ship rather than in a hold. This may increase the insurance premium – depending on the nature of the cargo.

declaration of compliance *See* COMPANY FORMATION.

declaration of dividend A statement in which the directors of a company announce that a *dividend of a certain amount is recommended to be paid to the shareholders. The liability should be recognized as soon as the declaration has been made and the appropriate amount is included under *current liabilities on the *balance sheet.

declaration of solvency A declaration made by the directors of a company seeking voluntary liquidation that it will be able to pay its debts within a specified period, not exceeding 12 months from the date of the declaration. It must contain a statement of the company's assets and liabilities, and a copy must be sent to the Registrar of Companies. A director who participates in a declaration of solvency without reasonable grounds will be liable

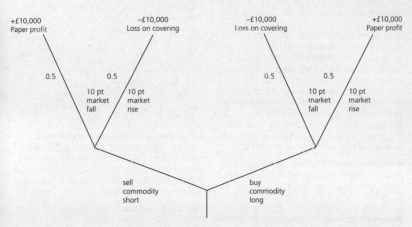

Decision tree. A decision tree showing the outcome of a speculative sale and purchase of a commodity, assuming that there is an equal probability of a 10 point market rise and a 10 point market fall. It is assumed that there is a stop loss order to cover after an adverse market movement of 10 points, but profits are allowed to run.

to a fine or imprisonment on conviction. *See* MEMBERS' VOLUNTARY LIQUIDATION.

decline stage The stage in a *product life cycle when the sales of the product begin to fall, because of such factors as reduced popularity, obsolescence, and market saturation.

decreasing term assurance A form of *term assurance in which the amount to be paid in the event of the death of the *life assured reduces with the passage of time. These policies are usually arranged in conjunction with a cash loan or mortgage and are designed to repay the loan if the *life assured dies. As the amount of the loan decreases with successive repayments the sum assured reduces at the same rate.

deductible The amount deducted from a claim in an *excess policy; whereas 'excess' is the usual word in motor-vehicle and householders' policies, 'deductible' is used in large commercial insurances. It is an amount that is deducted from every claim that is paid. If a claim is made for a figure below the deductible no payment is made. Deductibles are usually applied to policies in return for a premium reduction.

deductions at source A method of tax collection in which a person paying income to another deducts the tax on the income and is responsible for paying it to the authorities. Tax authorities have found that, in general, it is easier to collect tax from the payer rather than the recipient of income, especially if paying the tax is made a condition of the payer's obtaining tax relief for the payment. The payee receives a credit against any tax liability for the tax already suffered. Examples of this in the UK tax system are *PAYE, share dividends, interest on government securities, deeds of covenant, trust income, and sub-contractors in the building industry.

deduplication The removal of names and addresses that appear in a customer or prospect list more than once. Duplicate records often occur because data is collated from a variety of sources. Furthermore, names and addresses are not always listed in exactly the same way and details are often incomplete. Good deduplication software, usually known as de-duping soft-ware, should be able to identify and flag these anomalies.

deed A document that has been signed, sealed, and delivered. The seal and the delivery make it different from an ordinary written agreement. The former use of sealing wax and a signet to effect the seal is now usually replaced by using a small paper disc; delivery may now be informal, i.e. by carrying out some act to show that the deed is intended to be operative. Some transactions, such as conveyances of land, must be carried out by deed to be effective.

deed of arrangement *See* ARRANGEMENT.

deed of assignment *See* ASSIGNMENT.

deed of covenant A former legal document enabling a person to obtain tax relief on annual payments to a charity. From 2000 it was replaced by the *gift aid system.

deed of partnership A *partnership agreement drawn up in the form of a deed. It covers the respective *capital contributions of the partners, their entitlement to interest on their capital, their profit-sharing percentages, agreed salary, etc.

deed of variation A written *deed that identifies the specific provisions of a will to be varied. It must be signed by any person who would otherwise have benefited from the will as originally drawn. No payment or inducement must pass between the *beneficiaries in order to encourage them to enter into the variation. In order to apply, the deed must have been executed within two years of the testator's death and must have been filed within six months of the deed being executed.

deed poll A *deed having a straight edge at the top, as opposed to an *indenture. A deed poll was used when only one party was involved in an action, e.g. when a person declared a wish to be known by a different name. Deeds commonly now have straight edges and are used for all purposes.

deep discount A loan stock issued at a discount of more than 15% of the amount on redemption or, if less, at a discount of more than 1/2% for each completed year between issue and redemption. The discount will be treated as income accruing over the life of the stock. For example, a **deep-discount bond** might be a four-year loan stock issued at £95 for every £100 nominal (the discount exceeds ½% per annum) or a 25-year loan stock issued at £75 for every £100 nominal (the discount exceeds 15% in total). On **deep-discount securities** the discount is normally chargeable to tax. There are new proposals to tax all discounts.

deep-gain security A security issued at a *deep discount or redeemed at a premium. The terms of the issue mean that the amount of discount or premium cannot be allocated evenly over the life of the bond.

deep-line strategy *See* FULL-LINE STRATEGY.

deep market A market in which a large number of transactions can take place without moving the price of the underlying commodity, currency, or financial instrument. *Compare* THIN MARKET.

de facto (Latin: in fact) Denoting that something exists as a matter of fact rather than by right. For example, a plaintiff may have de facto control of a property. This compares to **de jure** (Latin: in law), which denotes that something exists as a matter of legal right. For example, a planning authority may have acted de jure in refusing a planning application. In international law, one government may recognize another de facto, i.e. acknowledge that it is in control of the country even though it has no legal right to be. De jure recognition acknowledges that it has a legal right to govern. The basis of the distinction, however, is more political than legal.

defalcation Embezzlement of property belonging to another party.

default 1. Failure to do something that is required by law, especially failure to comply with the rules of legal procedure. **2.** Failure to comply with the terms of a contract. A seller defaults by failing to supply the right quality goods at the time contracted. A buyer defaults by failing to take up documents or pay for goods according to contract. Before taking legal action

against a defaulter a **default notice** must be served on him or her. **3.** Failure to make required payments, as on a mortgage or other loan.

defended takeover bid A *takeover bid for a company in which the directors of the target company oppose the bid.

defender strategy A competitive strategy in which a business concentrates on its existing products or services and attempts to protect (rather than expand) its market share by offering superior quality, low prices, and strong customer service. Such a policy requires firm cost control and is usually only successful in an established, stable market where there is little scope for innovation. *Compare* PROSPECTOR STRATEGY.

defensive interval ratio A ratio that demonstrates the ability of a business to satisfy its current debts by calculating the time for which it can operate on current liquid assets, without needing revenue from the next period's sales. Current assets less stock is divided by the projected daily operational expenditure less non-cash charges. Projected daily operational expenditure is calculated by dividing by 365 the total of the *cost of sales, operating expenses, and other cash expenses.

defensive security A stable *security that is expected to have relatively good performance in periods of recession or downturn in financial markets.

deferred annuity An *annuity in which payments do not start at once but either at a specified later date or when the policyholder reaches a specified age.

deferred asset An *asset the realization of which is likely to be considerably delayed.

deferred credit (deferred liability) Income received or recorded before it is earned, under the *accruals concept. The income will not be included in the *profit and loss account of the period but will be carried forward on the *balance sheet until it is matched with the period in which it is earned. A common example of a deferred credit is a government grant. The grant is shown as a separate item or under *creditors in the balance sheet, and an annual amount is transferred to the profit and loss account until the deferred credit balance is brought to nil.

deferred debit (deferred asset; deferred expense) An item of expenditure incurred in an accounting period but, under the *accruals concept, not matched with the income it will generate. Instead of being treated as an operating cost for that period, it is treated as an *asset with the intention of treating it as an operating cost to be charged against the income it will generate in a future period. An example is rent paid for a period beyond the end of the accounting period.

deferred income *See* DEFERRED CREDIT.

deferred ordinary share **1.** A type of *ordinary share, formerly often issued to founder members of a company, in which dividends are only paid after all other types of ordinary share have been paid. They often entitle their owners to a large share of the profit. **2.** A type of share on which little or no dividend is paid for a fixed number of years, after which it ranks with other ordinary shares for dividend.

deferred-payment agreement *See* HIRE PURCHASE.

deferred pricing A situation in which a transaction is agreed upon before the price of the transaction is settled.

deferred rebate A rebate offered by a supplier of goods or services to customers on the understanding that further goods and services are purchased from the same supplier. The rebate is usually paid periodically, after the supplier has seen that he has the customer's continued support. Some shipping companies offer a deferred rebate to shippers.

deferred taxation A sum set aside for tax in the accounts of an organization that will become payable in a period other than that under review. It arises because of timing differences between tax rules and accounting conventions. The principle of **deferred-tax accounting** is to reallocate a tax payment to the same period as that in which the relevant amount of income or expenditure is shown. Historically, the most common reason for this timing difference is because the percentages used for the calculation of *capital al-

lowances have differed from those used for *depreciation.

deficit financing The creation of a government *budget deficit for the purpose of expanding economic activity by fiscal policy.

defined-benefit pension scheme (DB scheme) An occupational pension scheme in which the rules specify the benefits to be received on retirement and the scheme is funded accordingly. The benefits are normally calculated on a formula incorporating years of service and salary levels (*see* FINAL SALARY SCHEME). Accounting for pension costs poses a number of difficulties for accountants; the basic regulations are set out in *Statement of Standard Accounting Practice 24, although *Financial Reporting Standard 17, Retirement Benefits, and *International Accounting Standard 19, Employee Benefits, should also be consulted.

In recent years rising costs have led many companies to close their existing DB schemes to new employees, who are obliged to join *defined-contribution pension schemes.

defined-contribution pension scheme (DC scheme) A pension scheme in which the benefits are based on the value of the contributions paid in by each member. The rate of contribution is normally specified; the amount of pension an individual will receive will depend on the size of the fund accumulated and the annuity that can be obtained from it at the date of retirement. *Compare* DEFINED-BENEFIT PENSION SCHEME.

deflation The situation in which there is a general decrease in prices, especially when this is accompanied by falling levels of output, employment, and trade. Because of these associations, advocates of anti-inflationary policies usually now prefer the term *disinflation. *Compare* INFLATION.

defunct company A company that has been wound up and has therefore ceased to exist.

degearing The process in which some of the fixed-interest loan stock of a company is replaced by *ordinary share capital. *See* GEARING.

de-industrialization A substantial fall in the importance of the manufacturing sector in the economy of an industrialized nation as it becomes uncompetitive with its neighbours. This may result from bad industrial relations, poor management, inadequate investment in capital goods, or short-sighted government economic policies. In many cases each of these factors contributes to de-industrialization.

de jure *See* DE FACTO.

delayering The removal of layers of middle management (usually) from organizational structures, in order to bring an organization closer to the customer and generally to be more flexible and responsive. The process is facilitated by increased use of *information technology, which allows hierarchies of sequential decision making to be replaced by less bureaucratic procedures. *See also* BROADBANDING.

del credere agent A selling *agent who guarantees to pay for any goods sold on behalf of a principal if the customer fails to do so. An extra commission is charged for covering this risk.

delegatus non potest delegare
(Latin: a delegate cannot further delegate) The rule that a person to whom a power, trust, or authority is given to act on behalf, or for the benefit of, another, cannot delegate this obligation unless expressly authorized to do so. For instance, an auditor who has been appointed to audit the accounts of a company cannot delegate the task to another unless expressly allowed to do so. If express authorization has not been granted the auditor will have acted *ultra vires*.

delivered price (freight-allowed price) A quoted price that includes the cost of packing, insurance, and delivery to the destination given by the buyer (sometimes within a specified area).

delivery date 1. The day in the month that commodities on a futures contract have to be delivered. **2.** The maturity date for foreign exchange in a forward exchange contract. **3.** The date that a buyer of securities receives the relevant certificates.

delivery month The month in which the *underlying of a futures contract must be handed over to the buyer. A month is specified but usually any day within that month will fulfil the contract obligations.

delivery note A document, usually made out in duplicate, that is given to the consignee of goods when they are delivered to him. The consignee, or his representative, signs one copy of the delivery note as evidence that the goods have been received. *See also* ADVICE NOTE.

delivery order A written document from the owner of goods to the holder of the goods (e.g. a warehouse company) instructing them to release the goods to the firm named on the delivery order or to the bearer (if made out to 'bearer'). A delivery order backed by a dock or warehouse *warrant may be accepted by a bank as security for a loan.

Delphi technique A *qualitative forecasting technique that seeks to eliminate the effects of personal relationships and domination by strong personalities. A coordinator sends a written question to each relevant expert, who then replies in writing. The replies are edited and summarized. On the basis of the summary, new questions are issued to the experts, who again reply in writing. The cycle is repeated until the coordinator is satisfied that the process has provided an objective assessment of the issue in question (e.g. the likely sales of a new product).

demand curve A curve on a graph relating the quantity of a good demanded to its price. Economists usually expect the demand curve to slope downwards, i.e. an increase in the price of a good brings a lower level of demand.

demand deposit An instant-access checking account (i.e. current account) in the USA.

demand-pull inflation A rise in prices caused by an excess of demand over supply in the economy as a whole. When the labour force and all resources are fully employed extra demand will only disappear as a result of rising prices. *Compare* COST-PUSH INFLATION.

demarcation dispute An industrial dispute between trade unions or between members of the same union regarding the allocation of work between different types of tradesmen or workers.

demarketing The process of discouraging consumers from either buying or consuming a particular product, such as cigarettes. It may also be used if a product is found to be faulty and the producers do not wish to risk their reputation by continuing to sell it.

demerger A business strategy in which a large company or group of companies splits up so that its activities are carried on by two or more independent companies. Alternatively, subsidiaries of a group are sold off. Demerging was popular in the late 1980s when large *conglomerates became unfashionable. One of the main reasons for demerging is to improve the value of the company's shares, particularly if one part of a group's value can be better reflected by a separate share quotation.

Deming Prize A prize instituted in 1951 by the Union of Japanese Scientists and Engineers, in honour of W. Edwards Deming, one of the leading *total quality management theorists, who introduced the idea that quality control should be a strategic activity led by senior management. The prize is given to companies that can demonstrate successful "company-wide quality control", using *statistical process control techniques. Assessment is made in ten categories: policy, organization and management, education and dissemination, assembling and disseminating information on quality, analysis, standardization, control, quality assurance, results, and future plans.

demise charter See CHARTERING.

democratic leader A leader who maintains an egalitarian atmosphere within the group and who is prepared to delegate planning, decision making, and other responsibilities to followers. Experimental studies of *leadership style have found that work groups with democratic leaders tend to be more flexible, innovative, and highly motivated than those with *authoritarian leaders or *laissez-faire leaders.

demographic segmentation Dividing a market into groups based on such demographic variables as age, sex, family size, family life cycle, income, occupation, education, religion, race, or nationality (*see also* MARKET SEGMENTATION). While demographic segmentation has been popular in marketing, it is now used together with benefit, life-stage, and life-cycle segmentation to try to produce more predictable market information. See also GEODEMOGRAPHIC SEGMENTATION.

demography The study of human populations, including their size, composition (by age, sex, occupation, etc.), and sociological features (birth rate, death rate, etc.).

demurrage **1.** Liquidated *damages payable under a charterparty (*see* CHARTERING), at a specified daily rate for any days (**demurrage days**) required for completing the loading or discharging of cargo after the *lay days have expired. **2.** Unliquidated damages to which a shipowner is entitled if, when no lay days are specified, the ship is detained for loading or unloading beyond a reasonable time. **3.** Liquidated damages included in any contract to compensate one party if the other is late in fulfilling his obligations. This occurs frequently in building contracts. Even if the loss caused by the delay is less than the demurrage, the demurrage must be paid in full.

demutualization The act by which a *mutual, such as a *building society, changes its status to that of a public limited company. In recent decades this has been seen in the retail financial services industry worldwide.

denationalization See PRIVATIZATION.

department A discrete section of an organization under the responsibility of a **department manager**; separate costs and, where appropriate, income are allocated or apportioned to the department for the purposes of costing, performance appraisal, and control.

Department for Work and Pensions A UK government department formed in 2001 from parts of the former Department of Education and Employment and the Department of Social Security. It is responsible for helping unemployed people back into work and for administering unemployment benefit and other *social security payments, including state pensions.

Department of Education and Skills
The UK government department formed in 2001 from part of the former Department of Education and Employment. It is responsible for all state education services and encourages lifelong learning and the training of workers in industry.

Department for International Development The UK government department responsible for providing economic, technical, and other assistance to overseas countries with the goals of eradicating extreme poverty and promoting sustainable development.

Department of Trade and Industry (DTI) The UK government department responsible for: international trade policy; the promotion of exports; consumer and competition policy; policy on scientific research and technical innovation; company legislation and the Companies Registration Office (see COMPANIES HOUSE); weights and measures legislation; patents and the *Patent Office; the insolvency service; and national policy regarding all forms of energy.

department store A retail organization that carries a wide variety of products – typically clothing, home furnishings, and household goods; each department is managed by specialist buyers or merchandisers. Historically, department stores have occupied large multistorey buildings in city centres.

dependent demand The situation arising when the demand for one product is derived from or depends on the demand for other items. If a car manufacturer, for example, knows how many vehicles to produce in a month, this will fix how many engines, wheels, doors, seats, etc., have to be ordered. Compare INDEPENDENT DEMAND.

depletion The using up of an *asset, especially a mineral asset. For example, a quarry is depleted by the extraction of stone. See also WASTING ASSET.

deposit 1. A sum of money paid by a buyer as part of the sale price of something in order to reserve it. Depending on the terms agreed, the deposit may or may not be returned if the sale is not completed. **2.** A sum of money left with an organization, such as a bank, for safekeeping or to earn interest or with a broker, dealer, etc., as a security to cover any trading losses incurred. **3.** A sum of money paid as the first instalment on a *hire-purchase agreement. It is usually paid when the buyer takes possession of the goods.

deposit account (DA) An *account with a bank or building society from which money cannot be withdrawn without notice and on which interest is paid. See also SAVINGS ACCOUNT.

deposit-taking institution An institution whose main function is to take deposits. This is the basis of the legal definition of a bank as laid down in the *Banking Acts (1979; 1987). In the UK regulation of deposit-taking institutions was transferred from the Bank of England to the *Financial Services Authority in 2001. See also FINANCIAL INSTITUTION; LICENSED DEPOSIT TAKER.

depreciation **1.** The diminution in value of a *fixed asset due to *wear and tear or *obsolescence over an accounting period. A **provision for depreciation** can be computed by means of a number of generally accepted techniques, including the *straight-line method, the *diminishing-balance method, the *sum-of-the-digits method, the *production-unit method, and the *revaluation method. The depreciation reduces the book value of the asset and is charged against income of an organization in the income statement or *profit and loss account. In the UK, Financial Reporting Standard 15 deals with the subject of depreciation in the accounts. **2.** A fall in the value of a currency with a *floating exchange rate relative to other currencies. Depreciation can refer both to day-to-day movements and to long-term realignments in value. For currencies with a *fixed exchange rate a *devaluation or *revaluation of currency is required to change the relative value. Compare APPRECIATION.

depreciation rate The percentage rate used in the *straight-line method and *diminishing-balance method of *depreciation in order to determine the amount of depreciation that should be written off a *fixed asset and charged against income or the profit and loss account.

depression (slump) An extended or severe period of *recession. Depressions occur infrequently. The most recent Great Depression occurred in the 1930s; prior to that they occurred in the periods 1873–96, 1844–51, and 1810–17. Depressions are usually associated with falling prices (*see* DEFLATION) and large-scale involuntary unemployment. They are often preceded by major financial crashes, e.g. the Wall Street crash of 1929. *See also* BUSINESS CYCLE.

depth interview An unstructured interview that explores a marketing issue for purposes of *marketing research. The interviewer, a specialist acting on behalf of a client, will have previously compiled a topic guide that identifies the points to be explored; the respondent is part of a *sample chosen to match certain criteria (e.g. if the problem concerned tea all respondents would be tea drinkers). The interview is conducted informally and the interviewer adopts a passive role; he encourages the respondent to talk and ask questions, while ensuring that all the points on the topic guide are covered. After a minimum of ten such interviews, the interviewer reports back to his client with his marketing recommendations. Depth interviews are a qualitative procedure (*see* QUALITATIVE MARKETING RESEARCH).

depth of product line The number of different items in a line of products. For example, a soap manufacturer may have eight brands of soap in the bar soap line.

deregulation The removal of controls imposed by governments on the operation of markets. Many economists and politicians believe that during the mid-20th century governments imposed controls over markets that had little or no justification. Since the 1980s many governments have followed a deliberate policy of deregulation. However, most economists still argue that certain markets should be regulated, particularly if *market failure is involved.

derivative A financial instrument, the price of which has a strong relationship

with an *underlying commodity, currency, economic variable, or financial instrument. The different types of derivatives are *futures contracts, forwards (*see* FORWARD DEALING), *swaps, and *options. They are traded on **derivative markets** or *over the counter (OTC). The market-traded derivatives are standard, while the OTC trades are specific and customized. The main market-traded derivatives are futures and options.

derivative action A legal action brought by a shareholder on behalf of a company, when the company cannot itself decide to sue. A company will usually sue in its own name but if those against whom it has a cause of action are in control of the company (i.e. directors or majority shareholders) a shareholder may bring a derivative action. The company will appear as defendant so that it will be bound by, and able to benefit from, the decision. The need to bring such an action must be proved to the court before it can proceed.

descriptive research Marketing research aimed at providing good descriptions of marketing problems, situations, or markets. Descriptive research explores the market potential for a product, the demographics of a market, and the attitudes of consumers. Most marketing research in the UK is of this type.

descriptive statistics (univariate statistics) The branch of statistics that provides marketing researchers with a summary of the available data. Usually a single variable is analysed alone, such as the mean age of the consumers of a product or the consumption level of a type of food.

design & build A contract used in the construction industry to cover a situation in which one company takes the responsibility for both the design and building of a major building, such as a school or office block. It brings together the usually separated activities of architectural design and building construction in order to achieve greater integration to meet the client's needs.

Designated Professional Body (DPB) A professional body registered with the *Financial Services Authority as having statutory responsibility for regulating its profession. The DPBs are the Association of Chartered Certified Accountants, the Institute of Actuaries, the Institute of Chartered Accountants in England and Wales, the Institute of Chartered Accountants in Ireland, the Institute of Chartered Accountants of Scotland, the Law Society, the Law Society of Northern Ireland, and the Law Society of Scotland. The DPBs were formerly known as **Recognized Professional Bodies (RPBs)**.

designed capacity The maximum theoretical output of an *operating system in units per time, taking no account of such operational limitations as staffing decisions, set-up times, unforeseeable failures, maintenance, etc. *Compare* EFFECTIVE CAPACITY.

desirable products Products that give both high immediate satisfaction and high long-run benefits.

deskilling The process of removing the requirement for individual skills as part of an operating system. Techniques to improve the efficiency of systems tend to simplify and standardize procedures, so that they can be repeated at minimum cost. Computers and information technology can also play a role in replacing human decision making. Deskilling can result in a loss of motivation on the part of employees.

desk research A *marketing research study using mainly external published data and material but also including some internal reports, company records, etc. *See also* OFF-THE-PEG RESEARCH.

desktop publishing (DTP) An application of computers that enables small companies and individuals to produce reports, advertising, magazines, etc., to near-typeset quality. Modern systems, which simulate many of the functions of professional typesetting systems, consist of a *personal computer, using DTP software, and a *laser printer. The software is designed to format text into pages using a wide range of different typefaces. A common feature is the ability to preview each page on the computer's screen before it is printed and to import pictures and diagrams into the page.

destination site Any website visited following a click on a *hyperlink, especially one visited following a *click-through on a *banner advertisement.

Deutschmark (DM) Formerly, the standard monetary unit of Germany, divided into 100 Pfennige. It was subsumed into the euro for all purposes other than cash transactions in 1999 and abolished in 2002.

devaluation A reduction in the value of a currency relative to gold or to other currencies. Governments engage in devaluation when they feel that their currency has become overvalued, for example through high rates of inflation making exports uncompetitive or because of a substantially adverse *balance of trade. The intention is that devaluation will make exports cheaper and imports dearer, although the loss of confidence in an economy forced to devalue invariably has an adverse effect. Devaluation is a measure that need only concern governments with a *fixed exchange rate for their currency. With a *floating exchange rate, devaluation or revaluation takes place continuously and automatically (*see* DEPRECIATION; REVALUATION OF CURRENCY).

developing countries Countries that often have abundant natural resources but lack the capital and entrepreneurial and technical skills required to develop them. The average income per head and the standard of living in these countries is therefore far below that of the industrial nations.

The developing countries, in which nearly 80% of the world's population lives, are characterized by mainly agricultural economies from which poverty, hunger, and disease have not been eliminated. Many depend on a single product for their exports and are therefore vulnerable in world markets. Some have developed small low-technology companies, but market mechanisms (particularly distribution) do not exist.

development costs *See* RESEARCH AND DEVELOPMENT COSTS.

development stage The stage in the development of a new product during which the concept is transformed into a prototype and the basic marketing strategy is developed. *See* NEW PRODUCT DEVELOPMENT.

dial-in direct Denoting an Internet connection accessed by dialing into a computer through a telephone line.

diary method A procedure for collecting purchase data and the media habits of consumers; it requires respondents to complete a written report (in a diary) of their behaviour. This is either collected by or mailed to a marketing research company weekly or monthly.

diary panel A group of shops and shoppers who keep a regular record of all purchases or purchases of selected products, for the purpose of *marketing research.

dichotomous question A question that asks the respondent to choose between two answers, generally 'yes' or 'no'.

dies non (Latin: short for *dies non juridicus*, a non-juridical day) A day on which no legal business can be transacted; a non-business day.

difference option An *option that pays the difference between the price of two assets. The buyer's profit will depend on how the price differential at the *exercise date compares with the price differential at the time of purchase.

differential analysis (incremental analysis) An assessment of the impact on costs and revenues of specific management decisions. Such an analysis will focus on identifying the **differential** (or **incremental**) cash flows, i.e. those costs or revenues that will change as a result of a specific decision. In decision making, the **differential costs** are the only *relevant costs. See also OUT-OF-POCKET COSTS.

differential pricing A method of pricing a product in which the same product is supplied to different customers, or different market segments, at different prices. This approach is based on the principle that to achieve maximum market penetration the price charged should be what a particular market will bear. For example, the prices charged for similar motor vehicles in the UK market have been higher than those charged in the rest of Europe.

differentiated culture See ORGANIZATIONAL CULTURE.

differentiated marketing (multiple market segmentation) **1.** Marketing in which provision is made to meet the special needs of certain consumers. For example, weight watchers require diet drinks and left-handed people require left-handed scissors. **2.** A marketing exercise in which the marketer selects more than one target market and then develops a separate marketing mix for each. The differentiation strategy for each of these target markets is a strategy in which the marketer offers a product that is unique in the industry, provides a distinct advantage, or is otherwise set apart from competitors' brands in some way other than price.

diffusion of innovation See ADOPTION OF INNOVATIONS.

digital brand (on-line brand) A brand identity of a product or company on-line that differs from the traditional brand.

digital option See BINARY OPTION.

digital television A form of television in which information is received and displayed using digitized signals rather than analog signals. This provides better pictures and sound quality and also allows a large number of services to operate. In the UK there are plans to complete the switch to digital television by 2012.

digital whiteboard An area on a computer screen that can be written or drawn on by several users, enabling them to participate in audio- and video-conferencing as well as joint document creation.

digitizing The translation of text, illustrations, etc., into digital form.

dilapidations Disrepair of leasehold premises. The landlord may be liable to repair certain parts of domestic premises (e.g. the structure and exterior, and the sanitary appliances) under the Landlord and Tenant Act (1985) if the lease is for less than seven years. Otherwise, the lease will usually contain a covenant by either the landlord or the tenant obliging them to keep the premises in repair. Under the Landlord and Tenant Act (1985), a landlord cannot enforce a repairing covenant against a tenant by ending the lease prematurely unless a notice is first served specifying the disrepair and giving time for the repairs to be carried out. If there is no covenant in the lease, the tenant is under a common-law duty not to damage the premises and must keep them from falling down.

diluted earnings per share *See* FULLY DILUTED EARNINGS PER SHARE.

dilution of equity An increase in the number of ordinary shares in a company without a corresponding increase in its assets or profitability. The result is a fall in the value of the shares as a result of this dilution. The percentage of the equity held by an individual shareholder (and hence his or her voting power) will also be reduced.

diminishing-balance method (reducing-balance method) A method of computing the *depreciation of a *fixed asset in an accounting period, in which the percentage to be charged against income is based on the depreciated value at the beginning of the period (*see* NET BOOK VALUE). This has the effect of reducing the annual depreciation charge against profits year by year. The annual percentage to be applied to the annual depreciated value is determined by the formula:

rate of depreciation = $1 - (S/C)^{1/N}$,

where N is the estimated life in years, S is the estimated scrap value at the end of its useful life, and C is the original cost.

dinar **1.** (DA) The standard monetary unit of Algeria, divided into 100 centimes. **2.** The standard monetary unit of Bahrain (BD), Iraq (ID), Jordan (JD), and Kuwait (KD), divided into 1000 fils. **3.** (TD) The standard monetary unit of Tunisia, divided into 1000 millimes. **4.** (Din.) The standard monetary unit of Serbia, divided into 100 paras. **5.** (LD) The standard monetary unit of Libya, divided into 1000 dirhams. **6.** (SD) The standard monetary unit of Sudan. **7.** A monetary unit of Iran, worth one hundredth of a *rial.

dinkie Denoting an affluent couple without children who may be expected to be extensive purchasers of consumer goods. The word is formed from *double-income no-kids*.

direct-action advertising *See* DIRECT-RESPONSE TV ADVERTISING.

direct computer interviewing (DCI) A form of interviewing in which the respondent interacts directly with a computer programmed to ask questions and accept responses. This interactive process often encourages respondents to give information that they may be unwilling to disclose to an interviewer.

direct costs **1.** Product costs that can be directly traced to a product or *cost unit. They are usually made up of *direct materials costs (which can be charged directly to the product by means of materials requisitions), *direct labour costs (charged by means of time sheets, time cards, or computer direct data entries), and *direct expenses (which are subcontract costs charged by means of an invoice from the subcontractor). The total of direct materials, direct labour, and direct expenses is known as the **prime cost** or **direct cost of sales**. **2.** Departmental or *cost centre overhead costs that can be traced directly to the appropriate parts of an organization, without the necessity of *cost allocation. For example, the costs of a maintenance section that serves only one particular cost centre should be charged directly to that cost centre. *Compare* INDIRECT COSTS.

direct customer dialogue Two-way communication between a firm and its customers without the services of intermediaries.

direct debit A form of *standing order given to a bank by an account holder to pay regular amounts from his cheque account to a third party. Unlike a normal standing order, however, the amount to be paid is not specified; the account holder trusts the third party to claim from his bank an appropriate sum. In the USA this system is known as **reverse wire transfer**.

direct expense Expenditure that would not have been incurred had a particular product not been produced, excluding the costs of direct labour and materials. Direct expenses are included in the *direct cost of an item.

direct exporting A form of the export trade in which a domestic producer sells products directly to foreign buyers. Other than transportation, there are no other intermediaries.

direct foreign investment Investment

of capital by a government, company, or other organization in production (assembly or manufacturing facilities) and marketing operations that are located in a foreign country.

direct investment *See* FOREIGN INVESTMENT.

directive 1. A legislative decision by the European Union's Council of Ministers and Parliament, which is binding on member states but allows them to decide how to enact the required legislation. *See* ACCOUNTS MODERNIZATION DIRECTIVE; FINANCIAL SERVICES DIRECTIVE; FOURTH ACCOUNTING DIRECTIVE; INVESTMENT SERVICES DIRECTIVE; SECOND BANKING DIRECTIVE; SEVENTH ACCOUNTING DIRECTIVE; WORKING HOURS. 2. An instruction to carry out certain money-market operations, particularly instructions given by the US Federal Reserve Open Market Committee.

direct labour Workers directly concerned with the production of a product, service, or *cost unit, such as machine operators, assembly and finishing operators, etc. *Compare* INDIRECT LABOUR.

direct labour cost (direct wages) Expenditure on wages paid to those operators who are directly concerned with the production of a product, service, or *cost unit. It is one of the *cost classifications making up the *direct cost of a cost unit; it is quantified as the product of the time spent on each activity (collected by means of time sheets or job cards) and the rate of pay of each operator concerned. A percentage of the direct labour cost is sometimes used as a basis for absorbing production overheads to the cost unit in *absorption costing.

direct letter of credit *See* LETTER OF CREDIT.

Direct Mail Accreditation and Recognition Centre (DMARC) A regulatory body that offers an accreditation scheme for companies involved in *direct-mail selling in the UK. It guarantees that its members will abide by a code of conduct and adopt certain ethical and professional standards. DMARC accreditation is a condition for membership of the *Direct Marketing Association UK.

direct-mail selling (direct-mail marketing) A form of *direct marketing in which sales literature or other promotional material is mailed directly to selected potential purchasers. The seller may be the producer of the products or a business that specializes in this form of marketing. The seller may build up his own list of potential customers or he may buy or rent a list (*see* LIST RENTING). *See also* MAIL-ORDER HOUSE.

direct marketing Selling by means of dealing directly with consumers rather than through retailers. Traditional methods include mail order (*see* MAIL-ORDER HOUSE), *direct-mail selling, *cold calling, *telephone selling, and door-to-door calling. More recently telemarketing, direct radio selling, magazine and TV advertising, and on-line computer shopping have been developed. *See also* DIRECT-RESPONSE TV ADVERTISING; HOME SHOPPING CHANNELS.

Direct Marketing Association UK (DMA) A trade association for marketers and suppliers in the *direct-marketing industry, formed in 1992 from a merger of several similar bodies.

direct materials Materials that are directly incorporated in the final product or *cost unit of an organization. For example, in the production of furniture, direct materials would include wood, glue, and paint. *Compare* INDIRECT MATERIALS.

direct materials cost Expenditure on *direct materials. It is one of the *cost classifications that make up the *direct cost of a *cost unit and is ascertained by collecting together the quantities of each material used on each product by means of materials requisitions and multiplying the quantities by the cost per unit of each material. A percentage on direct materials cost is sometimes used as a basis for absorbing production overheads to the cost unit in *absorption costing.

director A person appointed to carry out the day-to-day management of a company. A public company must have at least two directors, a private company at least one. The directors of a company, collectively known as the **board of directors**, usually act together, although power may be conferred (by the *articles of association) on one or more directors to exercise executive powers; in particular there is often a managing director with considerable executive power.

The first directors of a company are usually named in its articles of association or are appointed by the subscribers; they are required to give a signed undertaking to act in that capacity, which must be sent to the *Registrar of Companies. Subsequent directors are appointed by the company at a general meeting, although in practice they may be appointed by the other directors for ratification by the general meeting. Directors may be discharged from office by an *ordinary resolution with special notice at a general meeting, whether or not they have a *service contract in force. They may be disqualified for *fraudulent trading or *wrongful trading or for any conduct that makes them unfit to manage the company.

Directors owe duties of honesty and loyalty to the company (fiduciary duties) and a duty of care; their liability in *negligence depends upon their personal qualifications (e.g. a chartered accountant must exercise more skill than an unqualified person). Directors need no formal qualifications. Directors may not put their own interests before those of the company, may not make contracts (other than service contracts) with the company, and must declare any personal interest in work undertaken by the company. Their formal responsibilities include:

- presenting to members of the company, at least annually, the accounts of the company and a *directors' report;
- keeping a register of directors, a register of directors' shareholdings, and a register of shares;
- calling an *annual general meeting;
- sending all relevant documents to the Registrar of Companies;
- submitting a statement of affairs if the company is wound up (*see* LIQUIDATOR).

*Directors' remuneration consists of a salary and in some cases **directors' fees**, paid to them for being a director, and an expense allowance to cover their expenses incurred in the service of the company. Directors' remuneration must be disclosed in the company's accounts and shown separately from any pension payments or *compensation for loss of office. *See also*

DIRECTORS OR HIGHER-PAID EMPLOYEES; EXECUTIVE DIRECTOR; NON-EXECUTIVE DIRECTOR; SHADOW DIRECTOR.

directors' interests *See* REGISTER OF DIRECTORS' INTERESTS.

directors or higher-paid employees Under UK tax law, a higher-paid employee is defined as one earning more than £8500 per annum. This amount, which has remained unaltered since it was set in 1979, includes remuneration together with benefits and reimbursed expenses. An employer must account to HM Revenue and Customs, on form P11D, for all the benefits received by a higher-paid employee or director (for whom there is no earnings limit). These benefits are assessed at the cost to the employer, although special rules apply to certain benefits, e.g. company cars. *See* BENEFITS IN KIND.

directors' remuneration (directors' emoluments) The amounts received by directors from their office or employment, including all salaries, fees, wages, perquisites, and other profit as well as certain expenses and benefits paid or provided by the employer, which are deemed to be remuneration or emoluments.

directors' report An annual report by the directors of a company to its shareholders, which forms parts of the accounts required to be filed with the Registrar of Companies under the Companies Act (1985). The information that must be given includes the principal activities of the company, a fair review of the developments and position of the business with likely future developments, details of research and development, significant issues on the sale, purchase, or valuation of assets, recommended dividends, transfers to reserves, names of the directors and their interests in the company during the period, employee statistics, and any political or charitable gifts made during the period. The Department for Trade and Industry issued new regulations for the directors' report in 2005; these require a more comprehensive review of the company's performance and a description of the principal risks and uncertainties affecting its future.

directory *See* CATALOGUE.

direct placing A *placing of shares in a company direct to investors, without recourse to underwriters to back the deal or to public subscription.

direct quote (reciprocal exchange rate) An exchange rate expressed in terms of the number of units of domestic currency corresponding to one unit of the foreign currency. In EU countries, for example, a direct quote for the US dollar might be €0.63. *Compare* INDIRECT QUOTE.

direct-response TV advertising (DRTV advertising; direct-action advertising) A television advertisement designed to stimulate immediate purchase or encourage some other direct response. Television spots, typically 60 to 120 seconds long, attempt to describe a product or service, persuade viewers of its merits, and provide a free phone number for ordering or for further information. *See also* HOME SHOPPING CHANNELS.

direct taxation Taxation, the effect of which is intended to be borne by the person or organization that pays it. Economists distinguish between direct taxation and *indirect taxation. The former is best illustrated by *income tax, in which the person who receives the income pays the tax and his income is thereby reduced. The latter is illustrated by *VAT, in which the tax is paid by traders but the effects are borne by the consumers who buy the trader's goods. In practice these distinctions are rarely clear-cut. For example, *corporation tax is a direct tax but there is evidence that its incidence can be shifted to consumers by higher prices or to employees by lower wages.

direct write-off method In the USA, the procedure of writing off bad debts as they occur instead of creating a provision for them. Although this practice is unacceptable for financial reporting purposes, it is the only method allowed for tax purposes.

dirham 1. (DH) The standard monetary unit of Morocco, divided into 100 centimes. 2. (Dh) The standard monetary unit of the United Arab Emirates, divided into 100 fils. 3. A Qatari monetary unit, worth 10 dinars and one hundredth of a *riyal. 4. A Libyan monetary unit, worth one

thousandth of a *dinar. 5. A Kuwaiti monetary unit, worth one tenth of a *dinar.

dirty bill of lading (foul or claused bill of lading) A *bill of lading carrying a clause or endorsement by the master or mate of the ship on which goods are carried to the effect that the goods (or their packing) arrived for loading in a damaged condition.

disbursement 1. A payment by a bank under a facility or other agreement. 2. A payment made by an agent, often a professional such as a solicitor, on behalf of a client.

discharge To release a person from a binding legal obligation by agreement, by the performance of an obligation, or by law. For example, the payment of a debt discharges the debt; similarly, a judicial decision that a contract is frustrated discharges the parties from performing it.

disclaimer A clause in a contract that reduces potential liability. For instance, a liquidator of a company may disclaim its lease to avoid liability for the rent.

disclosure 1. The obligation, in contract law, that each party has to the other to disclose all the facts relevant to the subject matter of the contract. *See* UTMOST GOOD FAITH. 2. The obligation, in company law, that a company has to disclose all relevant information and results of trading to its shareholders and other interested parties. The information is normally given in the *directors' report and the *annual accounts.

discontinuous innovation An entirely new product introduced to the market to perform a function that no previous product has performed. Such a product requires new consumption or usage patterns to be developed. The introduction of the home personal computer, for example, illustrates how new marketing systems had to be established. In addition to new retailers, consumers had to be encouraged to buy and use PCs. *Compare* DYNAMICALLY CONTINUOUS INNOVATION.

discount 1. A deduction from a *bill of exchange when it is purchased before its maturity date. The party that purchases (discounts) the bill pays less than its face value and therefore makes a profit when it matures. The amount of the discount consists of interest calculated at the *bill rate for the length of time that the bill has to run. *See* DISCOUNT MARKET. **2.** A reduction in the price of goods below list price, for buyers who pay cash (**cash discount**), for members of the trade (*see* TRADE DISCOUNT), for buying in bulk (**bulk** or **quantity discount**), for retailers who advertise a manufacturer's product (**promotional discount**), etc. **3.** The amount by which the market price of a security is below its *par value. A £100 par value loan stock with a market price of £95 is said to be at a 5% discount. **4.** To convert a *future value into a *present value, as by the *discounted cash flow method.

discount broker *See* BILL BROKER.

discounted cash flow (DCF) A method used in *capital budgeting, *capital expenditure appraisal, and decision appraisal that predicts the future stream of cash flows, both inflows and outflows, over time and discounts them, using a *cost of capital rate or *hurdle rate, to *present values in order to determine whether the project or decision is likely to be financially sensible. A number of appraisal approaches use the DCF principle, namely *net present value, *internal rate of return, and the *profitability index. Most computer spreadsheet programs now include a DCF appraisal routine.

discounted payback method A method of *capital budgeting in which managers calculate the time required before the forecast discounted cash inflows from an investment will equal the initial investment expenditure (*see* DISCOUNTED CASH FLOW). This method is similar to the *payback period method but makes some allowance for the *time value of money. Despite theoretical problems, it is widely used in practice.

discounted value *See* PRESENT VALUE.

discount factor (present-value factor) A factor that, when multiplied by a particular year's predicted cash flow, brings the cash flow to a *present value. The factor takes into consideration the number of years from the inception of the project and the *hurdle rate that the project is expected to earn before it can be regarded as

feasible. The factor is computed using the formula:

$$\text{discount factor} = 1/(1 + r)^t,$$

where r is the hurdle rate required and t is the number of years from project inception.

In practice there is little necessity to compute discount factors when carrying out appraisal calculations as they are readily available in discount tables. Most computer spreadsheet programs now include a *discounted cash flow routine, which also obviates the need for using discount factors.

discount house 1. A company or bank on the *discount market that specializes in discounting *bills of exchange, especially *Treasury bills. **2.** *See* DISCOUNT STORE.

discounting 1. The application of *discount factors to each year's cash flow projections in a *discounted cash flow appraisal calculation. **2.** The process of selling a *bill of exchange before its maturity at a price below its face value.

discount market In the UK, the part of the *money market consisting of banks, *discount houses, and *bill brokers. By borrowing money at short notice from commercial banks or discount houses, bill brokers are able to discount bills of exchange, especially Treasury bills, and make a profit.

discount rate 1. The *hurdle rate of interest or *cost of capital rate applied to the *discount factors used in a *discounted cash flow appraisal calculation. The discount rate may be based on the cost-of-capital rate adjusted by a risk factor based on the risk characteristics of the proposed investment in order to create a hurdle rate that the project must earn before being worthy of consideration. Alternatively, the discount rate may be the interest rate that the funds used for the project could earn elsewhere. **2.** *See* BILL RATE. **3.** The interest rate charged by the US Federal Reserve Banks when lending to other banks.

discount store A retail organization that regularly sells standard merchandise (national brands) at lower prices than supermarkets, etc., by accepting lower margins and selling a higher volume. In the UK, several major grocery retailers operate in this way.

discretionary account (DA) An account placed with a stockbroker, securities house, commodity broker or other authorized investment manager in which they are empowered to carry out transactions on this account without referring back for approval to the principal. Principals normally set parameters for their accounts, but with a discretionary account the broker has more discretion, only reporting back on purchases, sales, profits and losses, and the value of the portfolio.

discretionary costs (managed costs) Costs incurred as a result of a managerial decision; the extent of these costs is consequently subject to managerial discretion. A characteristic of such costs is that they are often for a specified amount or subject to a specific formula, such as a percentage of sales revenue. Examples include advertising and research expenditure.

discretionary order 1. An order given to a stockbroker, commodity broker, etc., to buy or sell a stated quantity of specified securities or commodities, leaving the broker discretion to deal at the best price. **2.** A similar order given to a stockbroker in which the sum of money is specified but the broker has discretion as to which security to buy for his client.

discretionary trust 1. A *trust in which the shares of each beneficiary are not fixed by the *settlor in the trust deed but may be varied at the discretion of some person or persons (often the trustees). In an **exhaustive discretionary trust** all the income arising in any year must be paid out during that year, although no beneficiary has a right to any specific sum. In a **nonexhaustive discretionary trust** (or **accumulation trust**), income may be carried forward to subsequent years and no beneficiary need receive anything. Such trusts are useful when the needs of the beneficiaries are likely to change, for example when they are children. *Compare* INTEREST-IN-POSSESSION TRUST. **2.** In the USA, an *investment trust in which the managers can decide what investments to make.

discriminating monopoly A *monop-

oly in which the supplier's products or services are sold to consumers at different prices; by dividing the market into segments and charging each market segment the price it will bear, the monopolist increases profits. An example is the different domestic and industrial tariffs operated by suppliers of electricity in many countries.

discriminating tariff A *tariff that is not imposed equally by a country or group of countries on all its trading partners. The abolition of discriminating tariffs is one of the purposes of the *World Trade Organization.

discrimination The practice of treating some people less favourably than others on grounds unrelated to merit, normally because they belong to a particular group or category. In the UK, it is illegal to discriminate on grounds of sex, race, disability, religious or other belief, or sexual orientation. From December 1996 age discrimination will also be unlawful. **Indirect discrimination** is deemed to occur where a provision, criterion, or practice is applied to everyone but the result is to put one group at a particular disadvantage. *See* EQUAL PAY.

disguised observation The research process of monitoring people, objects, or occurrences when the people do not know they are being watched. This can only take place in public, where people can reasonably expect to be observed.

dishonour 1. To fail to pay a cheque when the account of the drawer does not have sufficient funds to cover it. When a bank dishonours a cheque it marks it 'refer to drawer' and returns it to the payee through his or her bank. **2.** To fail to accept a *bill of exchange (**dishonour by non-acceptance**) or to fail to pay a bill of exchange (**dishonour by non-payment**). **3.** To fail to honour any other financial obligation.

disinflation A fall in the rate of *inflation, especially one that is not accompanied by falls in output and employment. *See* DEFLATION.

disintermediation 1. The elimination of such middlemen as brokers and bankers from financial transactions. Disintermediation has been a consequence of new technology, deregulation, and *globalization. Although it enables both parties to a transaction to save costs on commissions and fees, these savings have to be offset by the increase in the *credit risk. **2.** The elimination of a layer of intermediaries from a marketing channel or the displacement of traditional resellers by radically new types of intermediaries.

disinvestment The reducing of investment in an activity, asset, company, or location.

disk-by-mail (DBM) In marketing research, an interviewing method in which a respondent is sent a disk containing the questionnaire through the post. This has to be completed using a personal computer. The disk is then returned to the researcher for processing. Completed questionnaires can also be returned by e-mail. The dangers of importing computer viruses must be taken into account by researchers.

dismissal procedure The standard course of action that should be followed by employers in all cases of dismissal except those involving gross misconduct by the employee or the dismissal of a group of employees. It therefore applies in cases of redundancy, early retirement, and non-renewal of a fixed-term contract. The standard procedure has three steps: (1) a written statement is given to the employee explaining the reasons for dismissal; (2) a formal meeting is held between employer and employee; (3) a second meeting is held to consider any appeal by the employee. If the employer does not follow this procedure and the case goes to an *employment tribunal, any compensation awarded to the employee may be increased by up to 50%. *See also* UNFAIR DISMISSAL; WRONGFUL DISMISSAL.

dispatching rules Rules used to decide the priorities for fulfilling orders. Examples include:
- **first-come-first-served (FCFS)**;
- **first-in-first-out (FIFO)** – often seen as a fair rule, especially by the customer, but in practice it leads to overall inefficiency;
- **earliest-due-date (EDD) first** – the job due out first is processed first: this ig-

nores arrival times and processing times;
- **shortest processing time (SPT) first** – an ideal method for getting small jobs out of the way and minimizing work in progress, but it can make large jobs late and it ignores due dates and arrival times;
- **longest processing time (LPT) first** – this tends to increase work in progress and to make short jobs late;
- **truncated shortest processing time (TSPT)** – jobs that have been waiting longer than a predetermined time are given priority (if no work has been waiting long, SPT rules apply);
- **critical ratio (CR)** – this is the ratio of the time until the due date to the processing time: jobs with the lowest CR are processed first.

display advertising Advertising, such as a full-page or quarter-page advertisement, often containing a logo or illustration, rather than simple *classified advertising.

disposable income 1. The income a person has available to spend after payment of taxes, National Insurance contributions, and other deductions, such as pension contributions. **2.** In national income accounts, the total value of income of individuals and households available for consumer expenditure and savings, after deducting income tax, National Insurance contributions, and remittances overseas.

disposables *See* CONSUMER GOODS.

disposals account An account used to record the disposal of a fixed *asset. The original cost (a debit entry), *accumulated depreciation (a credit entry), and the amount received (credit entry) are transferred to the account, the balancing figure being any profit (debit entry) or loss (credit entry) on disposal.

disproportionate stratified sampling A sampling method in which the size of the *sample drawn from a particular stratum is not proportional to the relative size of that stratum. For example, a stratum could be large supermarkets, which may only account for 20% of all grocery stores – although they account for 80% of grocery sales. In this case, a disproportionate sample would be used to represent the large supermarkets to reflect their sales (i.e. 80%) rather than the number of stores. *Compare* PROPORTIONATE STRATIFIED SAMPLING. *See* STRATIFIED SAMPLING.

distance selling The sale of goods or services to a consumer in which the parties do not meet, such as sale by mail order, telephone, digital TV, e-mail, or the Internet. The EU distance selling directive implemented from October 2000 in the UK by the Consumer Protection (Distance Selling) Regulations 2000 contains the relevant law. In particular, consumers have rights to certain information about the contract to be entered into and, in many cases, the right to cancel the contract within a certain period, often seven working days from the day after receipt of the goods. The right applies whether the goods are defective or not, but it does not apply in certain important categories (such as auctions, betting, goods specifically made for a consumer, and food that will deteriorate).

distrain To seize goods as a security for the performance of an obligation, especially the seizure of goods by a landlord because a tenant is in arrears with his rent.

distributable profits (distributable reserves) The profits of a company that are legally available for distribution as *dividends. They consist of a company's accumulated realized profits after deducting all realized losses, except for any part of these net realized profits that have been previously distributed or capitalized. *Public companies, however, may not distribute profits to such an extent that their net assets are reduced to less than the sum of their *called-up share capital and their *undistributable reserves.

distributed processing A system of processing data in which several computers are used at various locations within an organization instead of using one central computer. The computers may be linked to each other in a *local area network, allowing them to cooperate, or they may be linked to a larger central computer, although a significant amount of the processing is done without reference to the central computer.

distribution **1.** A payment by a company from its *distributable profits, usually by means of a *dividend. **2.** The allocation of goods to consumers by means of wholesalers and retailers. **3.** The division of property and assets according to law, e.g. of a bankrupt person or a deceased person or on the winding-up of a company (*see* LIQUIDATION).

distribution bond An *investment bond issued by an insurance policy, in which the investment is a mixture of *fixed-interest securities and ordinary shares.

distribution centre A large highly automated warehouse designed to receive goods from various suppliers, take orders, fulful them efficiently, and deliver goods to customers as quickly as possible.

distribution channel The network of firms necessary to distribute goods or services from the manufacturers to the consumers; the channel therefore consists of manufacturers, distributors, wholesalers, and retailers.

distribution overhead (distribution cost; distribution expense) The *cost classification that includes the costs incurred in delivering a product to the customers. Examples include postage, transport, packaging, and insurance.

distribution to owners In the USA, a payment of a *dividend to shareholders (stockholders).

distributor An intermediary, or one of a chain of intermediaries (*see* DISTRIBUTION CHANNEL), that specializes in transferring a manufacturer's goods or services to the consumers.

distributor brand *See* OWN BRAND.

diversification **1.** Movement by a manufacturer or trader into a wider field of products. This may be achieved by buying firms already serving the target markets or by expanding existing facilities. It is often undertaken to reduce reliance on one market, which may be diminishing (e.g. tobacco), to balance a seasonal market (e.g. ice cream), or to provide scope for general growth. **2.** The spreading of an investment *portfolio over a wide range of assets to avoid serious losses if a recession is localized to one sector of the market.

diversity management Management that embraces the challenges of managing a workforce that is heterogeneous in terms of culture, ethnicity, religious belief, and political affiliation. The growing diversity of the workforce in most countries today means that many former assumptions about shared attitudes, values, and cultural norms no longer apply. Successful diversity management requires that managers acknowledge cultural differences in the workforce, understand the ways in which these can translate into different work-related attitudes (e.g. in terms of attitudes toward authority or individual competitiveness), and accept this diversity as an asset rather than a liability to the organization.

divestment A *business strategy in which a part of a business is sold off. It may be motivated either by a firm's decision to focus on certain aspects of its operation by selling those parts that no longer fit, or by the need to reduce costs and improve the profitability of the business by selling unprofitable parts. Competitors may seek to increase their market position by buying a divested business, or other companies may purchase a divested business as part of a *diversification strategy.

dividend **1.** The distribution of part of the earnings of a company to its shareholders. The dividend is normally expressed as an amount per share on the *par value of the share. Thus a 15% dividend on a £1 share will pay 15p. However, investors are usually more interested in the **dividend yield**, i.e. the dividend expressed as a percentage of the share value; thus if the market value of these £1 shares is now £5, the dividend yield would be 1/5 × 15% = 3%. The size of the dividend payment is determined by the board of directors of a company, who must decide how much to pay out to shareholders and how much to retain in the business; these amounts may vary from year to year. In the UK it is usual for companies to pay a dividend every six months, the largest portion (the **final dividend**) being announced at the company's AGM together with the annual financial results. A smaller **interim dividend** usually accompanies the interim

statement of the company's affairs, six months before the AGM. In the USA dividends are usually paid quarterly. *See also* DIVIDEND COVER; YIELD.

Interest payments on *gilt-edged securities are also sometimes called dividends although they are fixed.

2. A payment made by a *co-operative society out of profits to its members. It is usually related to the amount the member spends and is expressed as a number of pence in the pound.

dividend cover The number of times a company's *dividends to ordinary shareholders could be paid out of its *net profits after tax in the same period. For example, a net dividend of £400,000 paid by a company showing a net profit of £1M is said to be covered 2½ times. Dividend cover is a measure of the probability that dividend payments will be sustained (low cover might make it difficult to pay the same level of dividends in a bad year's trading) and of a company's commitment to investment and growth (high cover implies that the company retains its earnings for investment in the business). Negative dividend cover is unusual, and may be a sign that a company is in difficulties. In the USA, the dividend cover is expressed as the **pay-out ratio**, the total dividends paid as a percentage of the net profit. *See also* PRICE–DIVIDEND RATIO.

dividend mandate A document in which a shareholder of a company notifies the company to whom dividends are to be paid.

dividend stripping (bond washing) The practice of buying *gilt-edged securities after they have gone ex-dividend (*see* EX-) and selling them cum-dividend just before the next dividend is due. This procedure enables the investor to avoid receiving dividends, which in the UK are taxable as income, and to make a tax-free *capital gain. This activity has mainly been indulged in by high-rate taxpayers but has now become of little interest since the rules regulating the taxation of accrued interest were changed.

dividend waiver A decision by a major shareholder in a company not to take a dividend, usually because the company cannot afford to pay it.

dividend warrant The cheque issued by a company to its shareholders when paying *dividends. It states the tax deducted and the net amount paid.

dividend yield See DIVIDEND.

divisionalization 1. The splitting up of a large organization into separate divisions, based on the products or services provided or on the geographical location of a particular plant. Although some management functions are repeated separately in each division, and economies of scale are not maximized, many large organizations that encompass a diversity of activities are structured in this way. Because decision making is decentralized to the divisional managers, a swift response to a change in markets is possible. Coordination between divisions is achieved by a central management. See DECENTRALIZATION. **2.** The process of transforming the subsidiary organizations in a group into divisions of a single integrated company.

DJIA Abbreviation for *Dow Jones Industrial Average.

DMA Abbreviation for *Direct Marketing Association UK.

DMARC Abbreviation for *Direct Mail Accreditation and Recognition Centre.

DMU Abbreviation for *decision-making unit.

DNI framework The keywords digital, networked, individuals that represent the fundamental forces shaping Internet marketing.

DNS Abbreviation for *Domain Name System.

dobra (Db) The standard monetary unit of São Tomé e Príncipe, divided into 100 centavos.

dock receipt (wharfinger's receipt) A receipt for goods given by a dock warehouse or wharf, acknowledging that the goods are awaiting shipment. A more formal document is a **dock warrant** or wharfinger's warrant (see WARRANT), which gives the holder title to the goods.

documentary bill A *bill of exchange attached to the shipping documents of a consignment of goods. These documents

include the *bill of lading, insurance policy, dock warrant, invoice, etc.

documentary credit See LETTER OF CREDIT.

document merge The process of combining two or more documents to produce a single document. This is a common operation in word processing (see WORD PROCESSOR). An example is the combining of data produced by a *spreadsheet program into a document produced by a word processing program.

documents against acceptance (D/A) A method of payment for goods that have been exported in which the exporter sends the shipping documents with a *bill of exchange to a bank or agent at the port of destination. The bank or agent releases the goods when the bill has been accepted by the consignee. Compare CASH AGAINST DOCUMENTS.

documents against presentation (D/P) See CASH AGAINST DOCUMENTS.

dog See BOSTON MATRIX.

dollar The standard monetary unit of American Samoa (US$), Antigua and Barbuda (EC$), Australia ($A), the Bahamas (B$), Barbados (BDS$), Belau (US$), Belize (BZ$), Bermuda (Bd$), the British Virgin Islands (US$), Brunei (B$), Canada (Can$), the Cayman Islands (CI$), Dominica (EC$), East Timor (US$), Ecuador (US$), El Salvador (US$), Fiji (F$), Grenada (EC$), Guam (US$), Guatemala (US$), Guyana (G$), Hong Kong (HK$), Jamaica (J$), Kiribati ($A), Liberia (L$), Malaysia (M$; called a ringgit), the Marshall Islands (US$), Micronesia (US$), Namibia (N$), Nauru ($A), New Zealand ($NZ), Puerto Rico (US$), Saint Kitts and Nevis (EC$), Saint Lucia (EC$), Saint Vincent and the Grenadines (EC$), Singapore (S$), the Solomon Islands (SI$), Taiwan (NT$), Trinidad and Tobago (TT$), Tuvalu ($A), the USA (US$), the Virgin Islands (US$), and Zimbabwe (Z$), in all cases divided into 100 cents.

dollarization The adoption by a country of the US dollar in place of its own currency, usually as a means of controlling inflation and interest-rate volatility. Partial dollarization is said to occur when a country gives the US dollar equal status to its own currency or pegs its currency one-to-one with the dollar.

dollar stocks US or Canadian securities.

domain name A registered address for an organization or an individual for use on the Internet. Domain names are hierarchical with the parts separated by full stops, known as dots. The highest hierarchical part is called the **top-level domain**; this identifies the nature of the site:

.gov	a government department
.com	a commercial company
.org	a non-commercial organization
.edu	an educational establishment
	etc.

The domain may also identify the country in which the organization is situated:

.uk	the United Kingdom
.fr	France etc.

The **subdomain** identifies the organization and sometimes department of an organization or an individual in it:

jsmith.ucsd.edu
    identifies John Smith at the University of California, San Diego campus.
jsmith.ford.co.uk
    identifies John Smith at the Ford Motor Company in the UK.

The **Domain Name System** (DNS) is the Internet system in which the domain name is given a unique numeric Internet Protocol (IP) address (e.g. 162.18.2.3). When the domain name is keyed into the Internet to access a website the name is automatically translated into its numeric equivalent to enable it to be used by the Internet routing software. The **Domain Name Service** is the Internet system that implements the Domain Name System and retains in its databases both the domain name and its IP address, which can be accessed by the user. *See also* UNIFORM RESOURCE LOCATOR.

domain strategy The branding and positioning of a firm to enable its website to be found easily, especially the *domain name and subdomains chosen.

domicile (domicil) 1. The country or place of a person's permanent home, which may differ from that person's nationality or place where they are a *resident. Domicile is determined by both the physical fact of residence and the continued intention of remaining there. For ex-

ample, a citizen of a foreign country who is resident in the UK is not necessarily domiciled there unless there is a clear intention to make the UK a permanent home. In order to prove that the **domicile of origin** has been relinquished in favour of the **domicile of choice**, tangible changes have to be made. Links with the domicile of origin must be severed and active steps taken to become involved with the country that is the domicile of choice, e.g. by making a will under its laws. Under the common law, it is domicile and not residence or nationality that determines a person's civil status. Whether a person is domiciled in the UK may affect their liability to UK taxation. A corporation may also have a domicile, which is determined by its place of registration. **2.** In banking, an account is said to be domiciled at a particular branch and the customer will usually treat that branch as his or her main banking contact. Computer technology, however, now allows customers to use other branches as if their account was domiciled there.

dông (D) The standard monetary unit of Vietnam, divided into 10 hào.

donor A person making a gift or transferring property to another person (the **donee**).

donor list A list of all those who have donated to a particular charity. Lists of this type are of great importance to direct-marketing agencies specializing in marketing for charities.

door-to-door retailing Selling door-to-door, office-to-office, or at home-sales parties. Originally started in the USA with the Fuller Brush Company, this is now a popular method of marketing. In the UK cosmetics and plastic containers are widely marketed at home-sale parties. The Japanese market is the largest direct-sales market with some $25 billion sales, mainly because most Japanese cars are sold door-to-door.

dormant company A company that has had no significant accounting transactions for the accounting period in question. Such a company need not appoint auditors.

DOS *See* MS-DOS.

double auction An *auction in which both bids and offers are competitive. An example is an *open outcry market, in which buyers and sellers shout out the prices at which they are willing to trade. *See* CALLOVER.

double bottom In *chartist analysis, the situation in which the prices of a security fall, then rise, then fall again to the same level, producing a 'W' pattern on a graph. This pattern is thought to indicate that the security has much support at the price at the bottom of the W. *Compare* DOUBLE TOP. *See* SUPPORT LEVEL.

double declining balance method A method of *depreciation in which the historical cost (or revalued amount) of an *asset less its estimated residual value (*see* NET RESIDUAL VALUE) is divided by the number of years of its estimated useful life and the resulting amount is multiplied by two to give the depreciation figure. For example, in the first year an asset costing £12,000 with an estimated residual value of £2000 and an estimated useful life of 10 years would have a depreciation charge of £2000, i.e. 2 × [(£12,000 − £2000)/10].

double-entry book-keeping A method of recording the transactions of a business in a set of *accounts, such that every transaction has a dual aspect and therefore needs to be recorded in at least two accounts. For example, when a person (debtor) pays cash to a business for goods purchased, the cash held by the business is increased and the amount due from the debtor is decreased by the same amount; similarly, when a purchase is made on credit, the stock is decreased and the amount owing to creditors is increased by the same amount. This double aspect enables the business to be controlled because all the *books of accounts must balance.

double option A combination of a put *option and a call option. It is less flexible, since the put and call cannot be separated.

double taxation Taxation that falls on the same source of income in more than one country. Taxation is normally levied on a person's worldwide income in the country of residence but, in addition, most countries also levy a charge on income that arises within that country whether it is from interest or a business. As a result a large number of treaties (**double-taxation agreements**) have been concluded between countries to ensure that their own residents are not doubly taxed. The agreements also attempt to cover fiscal evasion.

As a result there are several different kinds of relief from double taxation available: (1) relief by agreement, providing for exemption, in whole or in part, of certain categories of income; (2) credit agreement, in which tax charged in one country is allowed as a credit in the other; (3) deduction agreement, in which the overseas income is reduced by the foreign tax paid on it; (4) if there is no agreement the UK tax authorities will allow the foreign tax paid as a credit up to the amount of the corresponding UK liability.

See UNILATERAL RELIEF.

double top In *chartist analysis, a pattern of fluctuation in the price of a security, in which a rise is followed by a fall, then a second rise to the same level. This pattern is thought to indicate that the security is meeting resistance to a move to a higher level. *Compare* DOUBLE BOTTOM. *See also* ASCENDING TOPS; RESISTANCE LEVEL.

doubtful debts Money owed to an organization, which it is unlikely to receive. A provision for doubtful debts may be created, which may be based on specific debts or on the general assumption that a certain percentage of debtors' amounts are doubtful. As the doubtful debt becomes a *bad debt, it may be written off to the provision for doubtful debts or alternatively charged to the *profit and loss account if there is no provision. *See* PROVISION FOR BAD DEBTS.

Dow Jones Industrial Average (DJIA) An index of security prices issued by Dow Jones & Co. (a US firm providing financial information), used on the New York Stock Exchange. It is a narrowly based index, having 30 constituent companies. The index was founded in 1884, based then on 11 stocks (mostly in railways), but was reorganized in 1928 when it was given the value of 100. Its lowest point was on 2 July 1932, when it reached 41. In 2005 it exceeded 10,900. Dow Jones also publishes other indices, and the DJIA is now just one of a number of US stock price indices.

download To retrieve electronic information, such as a web page or e-mail, from another location, such as a *web server.

downsizing A reduction in the size of an organization, especially by cutting the number of direct employees. The main purpose of downsizing is to improve profitability by reducing costs, although there may also be gains in both focus and flexibility. Apart from the damage to staff morale, the main danger is that the loss of experienced employees will lead to loss of customers and 'business memory'. *Compare* RIGHTSIZING.

downstream **1.** To borrow funds for use by a subsidiary company at the better rates appropriate to the parent company, which would not have been available to the subsidiary company. *Compare* UP-STREAM. **2.** Denoting the respondent bank (**downstream bank**) in an arrangement with a *correspondent bank. **3.** Denoting a later stage in the production process or *value chain.

down time The period during which a computer is out of action, usually because of a fault or for routine maintenance work.

DP Abbreviation for *data processing.

D/P Abbreviation for documents against presentation. *See* CASH AGAINST DOCU-MENTS.

DPB Abbreviation for *Designated Professional Body.

drachma (Dr) Formerly, the standard monetary unit of Greece, divided into 100 lepta. It was subsumed into the *euro for all purposes except cash transactions in 2001 and abolished in 2002.

draft **1.** *See* BANK DRAFT. **2.** Any order in writing to pay a specified sum, e.g. a *bill of exchange. **3.** A preliminary version of a document, before it has been finalized.

dragon bond A foreign *bond issued in the Asian bond markets.

dragon markets A colloquial name for those markets and economies in the Pacific basin that developed rapidly in the 1980s and early 1990s, notably Indonesia, Malaysia, the Philippines, and Thailand.

They enjoyed dynamic growth and high savings ratios until 1997, when the region suffered a severe financial and economic crisis.

dram (AMD) The standard monetary unit of Armenia, divided into 100 louma.

drawback The refund of import duty by the Customs and Excise when imported goods are re-exported. Payment of the import duty and claiming the drawback can be avoided if the goods are stored in a *bonded warehouse immediately after unloading from the incoming ship or aircraft until re-export.

drawdown **1.** The drawing of funds against a *credit line. *See also* FLEXIBLE DRAWDOWN. **2.** The movement of a customer's funds from one account to another account, which may be in another bank.

drawee **1.** The person on whom a *bill of exchange is drawn (i.e. to whom it is addressed). The drawee will accept it (*see* AC-CEPTANCE) and pay it on maturity. **2.** The bank on whom a cheque is drawn, i.e. the bank holding the account of the individual or company that wrote it. **3.** The bank named in a *bank draft. *Compare* DRAWER.

drawer **1.** A person who signs a *bill of exchange ordering the *drawee to pay the specified sum at the specified time. **2.** A person who signs a cheque ordering the drawee bank to pay a specified sum of money on demand.

drawings *Assets (cash or goods) withdrawn from an unincorporated business by its owner. If a business is incorporated, drawings are usually in the form of *dividends or *scrip dividends. Drawings are shown in a **drawings account**, which is used, for example, by the partners in a *partnership.

drip-feed To fund a new company in stages rather than by making a large capital sum available at the start.

drop-date A specified date upon which direct-mailing envelopes will be delivered to the Royal Mail for distribution.

drop-dead fee A fee paid by an individual or company that is bidding for another company to the organization lending the money required to finance the bid. The fee is only paid if the bid fails and the loan is not required. Thus, for the price of the drop-dead fee, the bidder ensures that the interest charges are only incurred if the money is required. It is sometimes called a **termination fee**.

drop lock A bond initially issued with a variable rate of interest which becomes a fixed-rate bond if the index or rate falls below a trigger at a coupon reset date.

drop ship A method of processing orders in *direct marketing in which the marketers pass orders to manufacturers to deliver the goods direct to the consumer.

DRTV advertising Abbreviation for *direct-response TV advertising.

dry test A test in which consumers are asked to order a particular product before it has been manufactured. The manufacturer will only proceed with production if the response rate is sufficiently high to ensure a specified profit. If the desired level of response is not reached, the product is not manufactured. In such cases compensation is often offered.

DSR Abbreviation for *debt service ratio.

DSS Abbreviation for *decision support system.

DTP Abbreviation for *desktop publishing.

dual-capacity system A system of trading on a stock exchange in which the functions of *stockjobber and *stockbroker are carried out by separate firms. In a **single-capacity system** the two functions can be combined by firms known as *market makers. Dual capacity existed on the *London Stock Exchange prior to October, 1986 (*see* BIG BANG), since when a single-capacity system has been introduced.

dual distribution A method of using two separate distribution channels to market a product. For example, a manufacturer may sell a product over the Internet as well as by direct-response television.

dual-rate transfer prices *Transfer prices that are set at different levels for the supplying and receiving divisions of an organization. The dual prices method charges a low price, say a price based on the *marginal cost, to the buying division,

while at the same time crediting a high price, say a price based on *full cost pricing, to the selling division. The idea is that this will encourage a buying division to buy within the organization without penalizing the selling division. However, this is only likely to be beneficial to the organization as a whole if the selling division has sufficient spare capacity to supply the buying division's needs. A compensating entry to eliminate unrealized profits is required in the books of the head office when the divisional results are consolidated. Managers rarely use this method in practice as it can lead to confusion.

due date The date on which a debt is due to be settled, such as the maturity date of a *bill of exchange.

dummy name A method of tracking the usage of a proprietary mailing list in *list renting by inserting a unique name in the list. For example, if a list is rented for using once only the presence of this name would indicate if it has been used on more than one occasion.

dump 1. To transfer the contents of a computer's main memory onto a backing memory. This provides a back-up copy of the main memory for security reasons. 2. A printout of the contents of computer memory, or of a *file, used to diagnose such problems as *crashes.

dumping The selling of goods abroad at prices below their marginal cost, which implies that the seller is making a loss. It has often been argued that developing countries wishing to establish an industry should use tariffs and quotas to ensure a monopoly for producers at home, while selling goods cheaply overseas. However, this practice inevitably leads to claims of dumping by other countries. The *General Agreement on Tariffs and Trade allows countries to prevent dumping by imposing tariffs on goods that are being dumped, although it is always difficult to establish conclusively that a particular price level constitutes dumping. Dumping is prohibited in the EU.

duopoly A market in which there are only two producers or sellers of a particular product or service and many buyers. The profits in such an imperfect form of competition are in practice usually less than could be achieved if the two suppliers merged to form a *monopoly but more than if the two allowed competition to force them into *marginal costing. *See also* COLLUSIVE DUOPOLY.

durables *See* CONSUMER GOODS.

duration driver A measure of the amount of time required to perform an *activity when this is a significant *cost driver. Duration drivers provide a more accurate basis for allocating costs than the number of transactions when there is a significant variation in the time required to complete an activity. For example, if all deliveries are completed in 10 minutes then it is simple (and accurate) to use the number of deliveries as a cost driver. If one delivery requires 10 minutes and another two hours, then using time for deliveries as the cost driver will improve the accuracy of the costing system. However, duration drivers are often seen as more expensive to measure and record than transaction drivers.

dustbin checkers *See* GARBOLOGISTS.

Dutch auction An *auction sale in which the auctioneer starts by calling a very high price and reduces it until a bid is received.

Dutch disease The deindustrialization of an economy as a result of the discovery of a natural resource, so named because it occurred in Holland after the discovery of North Sea gas. The discovery of such a resource lifts the value of the country's currency, making manufactured goods less competitive; exports therefore decline and imports rise.

duty A government tax on certain goods or services. *See* EXCISE DUTY; IMPORT DUTY; STAMP DUTY; TARIFF.

duty of care *See* NEGLIGENCE.

dynamically continuous innovation
The development of new products that are different from previously available products but that do not strikingly change buying or usage patterns. Thus the company remains in the same product and markets but continues to improve the products. This needs to be done dynamically (to save time and increase effectiveness), as well as continuously, because of the effect of the *product life cycle. *Compare* DISCONTINUOUS INNOVATION.

E & OE Abbreviation for errors and omissions excepted. These letters are often printed on invoice forms to safeguard the sender in case an error has been made in the recipient's favour.

EAP Abbreviation for *employee assistance programme.

ear The advertising space at the top left or right corner of a newspaper's front page.

early adopter *See* ADOPTION OF INNOVATIONS.

early bargains *See* AFTER-HOURS DEALS.

early majority *See* ADOPTION OF INNOVATIONS.

early payment A reduction offered as reward for payment of an invoice before a specified date.

EARN Acronym for *Euro Area Reference Note.

earnings before interest and tax *See* EBIT; EBITDA.

earnings per share (eps) The *profit in pence attributable to each *ordinary share in a company, based on the consolidated profit for the period, after deducting *minority interests and *preference share dividends. This profit figure is divided by the weighted average number of equity shares in issue during the period. The eps may be calculated on a **net basis** or a **nil basis**. Using the net basis, the tax charge includes any variable elements of tax, such as unrelieved overseas tax arising from the payment or proposed payment of dividends (*see* OVERSEAS-INCOME TAXATION). The nil basis excludes such items from the tax charge. The eps should be shown on the face of the *profit and loss account, both for the period under review and for the corresponding previous period. The basis of calculating the earnings per share should be disclosed on the face of the

profit and loss account or in the notes to the accounts.

Earnings per share was seen as an important measure of performance in the 1950s and 1960s but its significance has since declined. In recent years the UK and international standard setters have worked together to agree a common approach to eps. This resulted in the issuing of *Financial Reporting Standard (FRS) 22, Earnings Per Share, to replace the earlier FRS 14 in 2004. This requires the disclosure of both basic eps and *fully diluted earnings per share on the profit and loss account. *See also* BOTTOM LINE.

earnings retained *See* RETAINED EARNINGS.

earnings yield *See* YIELD.

earn-out agreement (contingent contract) An agreement to purchase a company in which the purchaser pays a lump sum at the time of the acquisition, with a promise to pay more (a *contingent consideration) if certain criteria, usually specified earnings levels, are met for a specified number of years. This method of acquisition has been popular in 'people' businesses, in particular advertising agencies. The agreement provides a means of retaining the previous owners in the business, with a motivation to maintain the company's profitability.

easement A right, such as a right of way, right of water, or right of support, that one owner of one piece of land (the dominant tenement) may have over the land of another (the servient tenement). The right must benefit the dominant tenement and the two pieces of land must be reasonably near each other. The right must not involve expenditure by the owner of the servient tenement and must be analogous to those rights accepted in the past as easements. An easement may be granted by *deed or it may be acquired by prescription (lapse of time, during which it is exercised without challenge); it may also be acquired of necessity (for example, if A sells B a piece of land that B cannot reach without crossing A's land) or when 'continuous and apparent' rights have been enjoyed with the part of the land sold before it was divided. Existing easements over the land of third parties pass with a conveyance of the dominant tenement.

easy money *See* CHEAP MONEY.

e-banking *See* HOME BANKING.

Ebay The largest on-line auction house on the Internet. *See* VIRTUAL AUCTION.

EBIT Abbreviation for *e*arnings *b*efore *in*terest and *t*ax, the *profit of a company as shown on the *profit and loss account, before deducting the variables of interest and tax. This figure, which is used in calculating many ratios, enables better comparisons to be made with other companies.

EBITDA Abbreviation for *e*arnings *b*efore *i*nterest, *t*axation, *d*epreciation, and *a*mortization. This figure is frequently cited by investment analysts since it represents a *cash-flow vision of shareholders' return.

e-business A company that engages in *e-commerce.

EC Abbreviation for European Community. *See* EUROPEAN ECONOMIC COMMUNITY; EUROPEAN UNION.

ECB Abbreviation for *European Central Bank.

ECGD Abbreviation for *Export Credits Guarantee Department.

ecocentric management Management that treats environmental issues as a core business concern, rather than an *externality. Recognizing the relationship that the firm has with the natural environment, it regards taking full account of the environmental impact it produces as part of management's responsibility.

e-commerce (electronic commerce) The use of the *Internet to buy and sell goods and services. At the simplest level, a company will probably have a website that provides details of products and contacts.

economic appraisal A method of *capital budgeting that makes use of *discounted cash flow techniques to determine a preferred investment. However, instead of using annual projected cash flows in the analysis, the technique discounts over the project's life the expected annual *economic costs and *economic benefits. It is mainly used in the assessment of governmental or quasi-governmental projects, such as road, railway, and port developments.

economic batch quantity A refinement of the *economic order quantity to take into account circumstances in which the goods are produced in batches. The formula is:

$$Q = [2cdr/h(r-d)]^{1/2},$$

where Q is the quantity to be purchased or manufactured, c is the cost of processing an order for delivery, d is the demand in the period for that stock item, h is the cost of holding a unit of stock, and r is the rate of production.

economic benefits The projected benefits revealed by an *economic appraisal. Economic benefits are usually gains that can be expressed in financial terms as the result of an improvement in facilities provided by a government, local authority, etc. For example, the economic benefits arising from the construction of a new or improved road might include lower vehicle operating costs, time savings for the road users, and lower accident costs as a result of fewer accidents. In each case the savings would be in economic terms, that is, excluding the effect of taxes and subsidies within the economy. *See* ECONOMIC COSTS.

economic costs The projected costs revealed by an *economic appraisal. Economic costs differ from financial costs in that they exclude the transfer payments within the economy, which arise when an investment is made. In the construction of a road, for example, the economic costs exclude taxes and import duties on the materials and plant used in its construction, while any subsidies made are added back to the costs. *See* ECONOMIC BENEFITS.

economic duress Historically, in *contract law, a claim that a contract was voidable for duress could only be successful if a threat to the person (i.e. physical duress) had induced the contract. Now, however, a contract may be voidable for economic duress. The essential elements are that an illegitimate threat has been made (e.g. to breach an existing contract or to commit a tort) and that the injured party has no practical alternative to agreeing to the terms set out by the person making the threat.

economic environment Factors that affect the buying power and spending patterns of consumers. These factors include income distribution, changes in purchasing power as a result of inflation, the state of the country's economy, etc. While the economic environment can be influenced extensively by government activity, companies need to monitor these changes in order to predict their sales estimates.

economic good *See* GOOD.

economic growth The expansion of the output of an economy, usually expressed in terms of the increase of national income. Nations experience different rates of economic growth mainly because of differences in population growth, investment, and technical progress.

economic order quantity (EOQ) A decision model, based on differential calculus, that determines the optimum order size for purchasing (sometimes called the **economic purchase quantity**) or manufacturing (**economic manufacturing quantity**) an item of stock. The optimum order quantity is that which equates the total ordering and total *carrying costs. The formula used is:

$$Q = \sqrt{(2cd/h)},$$

where Q is the quantity to be purchased or manufactured, c is the cost of processing an order for delivery, d is the demand in the period for that stock item, and h is the cost of holding a unit of stock. *See also* ECONOMIC BATCH QUANTITY.

economic sanctions Action taken by one country or group of countries to harm the economic interest of another country or group of countries, usually to bring about pressure for social or political change. Sanctions normally take the form of restrictions on imports or exports, or on financial transactions. They may be applied to specific items or they may be comprehensive trade bans. There is considerable disagreement over their effectiveness. Critics point out that they are easily evaded and often inflict more pain on those they are designed to help than on the governments they are meant to influence. They can also harm the country that imposes sanctions, through the loss of export markets or raw material supplies. In addition the target country may impose retaliatory sanctions. *See also* EMBARGO.

Economic Trends A monthly publication of the UK *Office for National Statistics devoted to economic statistics.

economic value The *present value of expected future *cash flows. For example, the economic value of a *fixed asset would be the present value of any future revenues it is expected to generate, less the present value of any future costs related to it.

Economic Value Added (EVA) A performance measure used to evaluate a company's **economic profit** (i.e., the value added to a company by its activities in a given time period). It is the calculation of a company's net *operating profit after taxes, minus a *cost of capital charge for the investment or capital employed in the business. The Stern Stewart consulting organization registered EVA as a tradename in the 1990s. In 1997 *The Economist* magazine reported that more than 300 firms worldwide had adopted it, including Coca-Cola and AT&T.

economies of scale (scale effect) Reductions in the average cost of production, and hence in the unit costs, when output is increased. If the average costs of production rise with output, this is known as **diseconomies of scale**. Economies of scale can enable a producer to offer his product at more competitive prices and thus to capture a larger share of the market. **Internal economies of scale** occur when better use is made of the factors of production and by using the increased output to pay for a higher proportion of the costs of marketing, financing, and development, etc. Internal diseconomies can occur when a plant exceeds its optimum size, requiring a disproportionate unwieldy administrative staff. **External economies** and diseconomies arise from the effects of a firm's expansion on market conditions and on technological advance.

economies of scope *See* SCOPE ECONOMIES.

economy, efficiency, and effectiveness The primary performance measures for an *operating system. In order for a system to be effectively managed, it is necessary to have feedback. **Economy** requires feedback on the cost of the inputs to a system. **Efficiency** measures how successfully the inputs have been transformed into outputs. **Effectiveness** measures how successfully the system achieves its desired outputs. Because effectiveness involves the subjective reaction of the customer, it is the most difficult to measure.

ECP Abbreviation for *euro-commercial paper.

ECSC Abbreviation for *European Coal and Steel Community.

ECU Abbreviation for *European Currency Unit.

EDI Abbreviation for *electronic data interchange.

editorial advertisement An advertisement in a newspaper or magazine written in the form of an editorial feature. Such advertisements must, however, be clearly labelled 'advertisement'.

EDSP Abbreviation for Exchange Delivery Settlement Price. *See* SETTLEMENT PRICE.

EDX Abbreviation for European Derivatives Exchange. *See* LONDON STOCK EXCHANGE.

EEA Abbreviation for *European Economic Area.

EEC Abbreviation for *European Economic Community.

effective annual rate The total interest paid or earned in a year expressed as a percentage of the principal amount at the beginning of the year.

effective capacity The capacity of a system in units per time, taking into account such factors as staffing decisions (e.g. whether to run 24 hours a day, 7 days a week, or to operate one 8-hour shift, 5

days a week), set-up times, maintenance, and an allowance for unforeseeable failures. *Compare* DESIGNED CAPACITY.

effective tax rate The average tax rate that is applicable in a given circumstance. In many cases the actual rate of tax applying to an amount of income or to a gift may not, for various reasons, be the published rate of the tax; these reasons include the necessity to gross up, the complex effects of some reliefs, and peculiarities in scales of rates. The effective rate is therefore found by dividing the additional tax payable as a result of the transaction by the amount of the income, gift, or whatever else is involved in the transaction.

effective yield *See* GROSS REDEMPTION YIELD.

efficiency 1. **(technical efficiency)** A measure of the ability of an organization to produce the maximum output of acceptable quality with the minimum of time, effort, and other inputs. One company is said to be more efficient than another if it can produce the same output as the other with less inputs, irrespective of the price factor. *See* ECONOMY, EFFICIENCY, AND EFFECTIVENESS. 2. **(economic efficiency)** A measure of the ability of an organization to produce and distribute its product at the lowest possible cost. A firm can have a high technical efficiency but a low economic efficiency because its prices are too high to meet competition.

efficiency ratio A ratio that measures the efficiency of labour or an activity over a period by dividing the *standard hours allowed for the production by the actual hours taken. It is usually expressed as a percentage, using the formula:

(standard hours allowed × 100)/actual hours worked.

efficient markets hypothesis A central theory of modern finance holding that transactors in financial markets cannot make *abnormal returns on the basis of exploiting information, since market prices incorporate all available information. The economist Eugene Fama defined three categories of market efficiency: **weak-form efficiency**, in which only historical information is incorporated into the market prices; **semi-strong-form efficiency**, in which all publicly available information, past or present, is incorporated; and **strong-form efficiency**, in which all public or private information is incorporated. *See also* ACTIVE MANAGEMENT; ANOMALY.

EFTA Acronym for *European Free Trade Association.

EFTPOS Abbreviation for *electronic funds transfer at point of sale.

EGM Abbreviation for *extraordinary general meeting.

EIB Abbreviation for *European Investment Bank.

EIS Abbreviation for *Enterprise Investment Scheme.

elective resolution A form of *resolution for private *companies introduced by the Companies Act (1989). It can be passed by the members in general meeting provided that (1) at least 21 days' written notice has been given, stating the terms of the resolution, and (2) it is approved by all members entitled to attend and vote, whether in person or by proxy.

electronic banking *See* HOME BANKING.

electronic catalogue 1.. An on-line *catalogue of goods for purchase. **2..** An interactive *videotex system in which consumers see products on their home TV screens, using touch-tone phones to control the sequence and to place orders.

electronic commerce *See* E-COMMERCE.

electronic conveyancing (e-conveyancing) The transfer of land by electronic means instead of by paper documents. The framework for such conveyancing has been set in place by the Electronic Communications Act (2000) and the Land Registration Act (2002). Although electronic conveyancing is not yet a reality, the land registers are already kept in electronic form and it is possible to discharge mortgages of registered land electronically. *See* LAND REGISTRATION.

electronic data interchange (EDI) The use of electronic data-transmission networks to move information. For example, EDI can be used for orders, invoices, and payments to suppliers, customers, banks,

etc., without recourse to hard copy. EDI is dependent on users having compatible technology and systems that are transparent to the other members of the network.

electronic funds transfer at point of sale (EFTPOS) The automatic debiting of a purchase price from the customer's bank or credit-card account by a computer link between the checkout till and the bank or credit-card company. The system can only work when the customer has a *debit card or *credit card recognized by the retailer. In the increasingly widely used 'chip and PIIN' system the transaction is ratified by use of the customer's *personal identification number (PIN), rather than by signature of a printed voucher.

electronic mail *See* E-MAIL.

electronic mail survey (EMS) A relatively easy, low cost, and fast method of conducting marketing surveys in which potential respondents are sent the questionnaire by group mail. Respondents e-mail the completed questionnaires back to the researchers. Evidence suggests that e-mail surveys produce a faster but lower response rate than mail (postal) surveys.

electronic mall *See* VIRTUAL MALL.

electronic marketspace *See* MARKETSPACE.

electronic point of sale (EPOS) A computerized method of recording sales in retail outlets, using a laser scanner at the checkout till to read *bar codes printed on the items' packages. Other advantages over conventional checkout points include a more efficient use of checkout staff time, the provision of a more detailed receipt to the customer, and real-time stock control, enabling rapid replenishment of stock and minimizing the stock that has to be held. In consumer goods sales, the data can also be used to produce consumer profiles for marketing purposes.

electronic shopping (e-shopping) The buying of goods or services over the Internet, using either a computer or an Internet television.

electronic signature An item of data incorporated into or associated with an electronically transmitted document or contract for use in establishing the authenticity of the communication. Under the Electronic Communications Act (2000) electronic signatures are recognized in legal proceedings and as having legal effect. An electronic signature can be purchased from such bodies as the Post Office and Chamber of Commerce on production of relevant identification documents.

electronic transfer of funds (ETF) The transfer of money from one bank account to another by means of computers and communications links. Banks routinely transfer funds between accounts using computers; ETF is also used in *home banking services. In the USA, the Electronic Transfer of Funds Act (1978) limits customer liability for unauthorized transfers to $50M. *See also* ELECTRONIC FUNDS TRANSFER AT POINT OF SALE.

eligibility Criteria that determine which bills the Bank of England will discount, as *lender of last resort. Such bills are known as *eligible paper.

eligible list A listing of the names of banks entitled to discount acceptances at the Bank of England.

eligible paper **1.** Treasury bills, short-dated gilts, and any first-class security, accepted by a British bank or an accepting house and thus acceptable by the *Bank of England for rediscounting, or as security for loans to discount houses. The Bank of England's classification of eligible paper influences portfolios because of the ability to turn them into quick cash, and thus reinforces the Bank's role as *lender of last resort. **2.** Acceptances by US banks available for rediscounting by the *Federal Reserve System.

eligible reserves Cash held in a US bank plus the money held in its name at its local *Federal Reserve Bank.

e-mail (electronic mail) Software that enables messages (e.g. letters, memos, documents) between individuals or from individuals to groups to be exchanged by computer. Its operation can be restricted to a *local area network or it can be open to a wide area network, such as the *Internet, by means of telephone lines. Messages are held in a **mailbox**, access to which is usually controlled by a user

identification and password. In recent years e-mails have replaced letters and faxes in many business communications.

emalengeni The plural of *lilangeni.

embargo A ban on some or all of the trade with one or more countries. A trade embargo is a form of *economic sanction. Prominent examples include the international ban on trade in arms with South Africa and on certain high-technology products with the Eastern bloc. Full embargos are rare and difficult to apply in practice.

embezzlement A form of theft in which an employee dishonestly appropriates money or property given to him or her on behalf of an employer. The special offence of embezzlement ceased to exist in 1969.

EMCF Abbreviation for *European Monetary Cooperation Fund.

EMI Abbreviation for *European Monetary Institute.

emoluments Amounts received from an office or employment including all salaries, fees, wages, perquisites, and other profits as well as certain expenses and benefits paid or provided by the employer, which are deemed to be emoluments. *See also* DIRECTORS' REMUNERATION.

emotional appeal The attempt by advertising to stir up negative or positive emotions to motivate a purchase. Much marketing and advertising is geared to creating fear, guilt, shame, love, pride, or joy in the potential customer rather than evoking dispassionate appraisal on the basis of objective criteria.

emotional selling proposition (ESP) The unique associations established by consumers with particular products. Many car marques evoke an emotional response that ensures their continual success, even though other makers offer superior performance at the same price.

employee assistance programme (EAP) A confidential personal counselling service funded by an employer. EAPs provide professional counsellors with whom employees can discuss their work and non-work-related problems, which may be emotional, financial, or legal or related to alcohol or drug misuse.

employee buy-out *See* MANAGEMENT BUY-OUT.

employee empowerment *See* EMPOW-ERMENT.

employee evaluation A formal assessment of an employee's performance in his or her job, as measured by certain objective indicators (e.g. sales figures, absenteeism) or by more subjective rating procedures. The employee may be evaluated in absolute terms or by comparison with others doing similar work, as in the *paired comparison method. The results are usually presented to the employee as part of his or her *performance appraisal.

employee participation 1. The encouragement of motivation in a workforce by giving shares in the company to employees. Employee shareholding (*see* EM-PLOYEE SHARE OWNERSHIP PLAN) can be an important factor in improving industrial relations. **2.** The appointment to a board of directors of a representative of the employees of a company, to enable the employees to take part in the direction of the company. *See* PARTICIPATIVE DECISION MAKING.

employee report A simplified version of the statutory annual report and accounts of a company prepared for the employees of the company (*see* ANNUAL ACCOUNTS). Although this is a voluntary practice, such documents should comply with section 240 of the Companies Act relating to *non-statutory accounts. Employee reports were particularly popular in the 1930s and the 1970s.

employee share ownership plan (ESOP) A method of providing the employees of a company with shares in the company. The ESOP buys shares in its sponsoring company, usually with assistance from the company concerned. The shares are ultimately made available to employees, usually directors, who satisfy certain performance targets. The advantage claimed for ESOPs is that they do not involve dilution of the sponsoring company's share capital by the creation of new shares. In the USA these are known as **employee stock option plans**. *See also*

EMPLOYEE SHARE OWNERSHIP TRUST; SHARE INCENTIVE SCHEME; SHARE OPTION.

employee share ownership trust (ESOT) A trust set up by a UK company, under the provisions introduced in 1989, to acquire shares in the company and distribute them to the employees. The company's payments to the trust are tax-deductible. The trust deed sets out the specified period of employment and all those employees who fulfil the requirements must be included in the class of beneficiaries of the trust. *See also* APPROVED DEFERRED SHARE TRUST; EMPLOYEE SHARE OWNERSHIP PLAN; SHARE INCENTIVE SCHEME.

employers' liability insurance An insurance policy covering an employer's legal liability to pay compensation to any of his employees suffering or contracting injury or disease during the course of their work. This type of insurance is compulsory by law for anyone who employs another person (other than members of their own family) under a contract of service. A *certificate of insurance must be displayed at each place of work, confirming that employer's liability insurance is in force and giving details of the policy number and the insurer's name and address. *See also* PUBLIC-LIABILITY INSURANCE.

employment agency An organization that introduces suitable potential employees to employers, charging the employer a fee, usually related to the initial salary, for the service. Employment agencies also provide temporary staff, in which they are the employers, the temporary staff member being charged out at an hourly rate. Employment agencies that specialize in finding suitable managers and executives for a firm, or finding suitable jobs for executives who want a change, are often known as **head hunters**. Such agencies will often provide a short list of candidates in order to save their client's time in personnel selection. Employment agencies run by the government are called *job centres.

employment costs The expenditure incurred in employing personnel. It includes salaries, wages, bonuses, incentive payments, employer's National Insurance contributions, and employer's pension scheme contributions.

employment protection The safeguarding of an employee's position with regard to his employment. According to the Employment Protection (Consolidation) Act (1978), an employer must give an employee, within 13 weeks of the start of the employment, a contract stating the rate of pay, hours of work, holiday entitlement, details of sick pay and pension scheme (if any), and the length of notice to be given by either side to terminate the contract. *See also* DISCRIMINATION; REDUNDANCY; UNFAIR DISMISSAL.

employment tribunal Any of the bodies established under the UK employment protection legislation to hear disputes between employers and employees or trade unions relating to statutory terms and conditions of employment. For example, the tribunals hear complaints concerning *unfair dismissal, *redundancy, *equal pay, and *maternity rights. Tribunals may also hear complaints from members of trade unions concerning unjustifiable disciplining by their union. The tribunal usually consists of a legally qualified chairperson and two independent lay members; they are appointed by the Secretary of State for Trade and Industry. It differs from a civil court in that it cannot enforce its awards (this must be done by separate application to a court) and it can conduct its proceedings informally. Strict rules of evidence need not apply and the parties can present their own case or be represented by anyone they wish at their own expense; legal aid is not available. The tribunal has wide powers to declare a party in breach of a contract of employment, to award compensation, and to order the reinstatement or re-engagement of a dismissed employee. Until 1998 employment tribunals were known as **industrial tribunals**.

empowerment In *human-resource management, the giving of increased responsibility and a measure of control to employees in their working lives. The concept is based on the view that people need personal satisfaction and fulfilment in their work and that responsibility and control increase satisfaction. Employees like empowerment because an increase in responsibility usually leads to greater rewards and enhanced prospects. On the other hand, it has been criticized because staff are asked to become more accountable without being given more authority. Empowerment also has the added advantage that it enables potential talents to be identified and developed, either by the employing organization or the individual.

In general, empowerment is a motivational strategy, or part of a process of re-engineering organizational structures to remove layers of management (*see* DELAYERING) to make the system respond more rapidly to customers' requirements.

EMS **1.** Abbreviation for *electronic mail survey. **2.** Abbreviation for *European Monetary System.

EMU Abbreviation for European Monetary Union. *See* EUROPEAN MONETARY SYSTEM.

EMV Abbreviation for *expected monetary value.

encourager *See* RELATIONSHIP ROLES.

encryption The encoding of electronic data so that it can be transmitted without interception. With the growing use of the *Internet for commercial purposes, there has been an ongoing need for secure encryption methods, notably in the transmission of credit card details. *See* SECURITY.

encumbrance (incumbrance) A charge or liability, such as a *mortgage or registered judgement, to which land is subject.

end-of-day sweep An automatic transfer of funds from one bank account held by a company to another of its bank accounts, usually one that pays interest on deposits. The sweep takes place at the end of every day, or at the end of the day when certain conditions are met.

endorsement (indorsement) **1.** A signature on the back of a *bill of exchange or cheque, making it payable to the person who signed it. A bill can be endorsed any number of times, the presumption being that the endorsements were made in the order in which they appear, the last named being the holder to receive payment. If the bill is **blank endorsed**, i.e. no endorsee is named, it is payable to the bearer. In the case of a **restrictive endorsement** of the form "Pay X only", it ceases to be a *negotiable instrument. A **special**

endorsement, when the endorsee is specified, becomes payable **to order**, which is short for 'in obedience to the order of'. **2.** A signature required on a document to make it valid in law. **3.** An amendment to an *insurance policy or cover note, recording a change in the conditions of the insurance. **4.** Another term for a guarantee.

endowment assurance An assurance policy that pays a specified amount of money on an agreed date or on the death of the *life assured, whichever is the earlier. As these policies guarantee to make a payment (either to the policyholder or his or her dependants) they offer both life cover and a reasonable investment. A *with-profits policy will also provide bonuses in addition to the sum assured. These policies are often used in the repayment of an *endowment mortgage or as a form of saving.

endowment mortgage A *mortgage in which repayment of the principal is made principally by means of an *endowment assurance policy. In the UK in the 1980s and 1990s, many first-time home buyers were encouraged to take out this form of mortgage (which earns the mortgagor's agent an immediate commission from the life cover provider). However, with the subsequent poor performance of investments on the stock exchange, many endowment mortagees, rather than looking forward to a profit from the life fund once the principal has been repaid, are facing a shortfall in the principal at the end of the mortgage's life.

Engel's law The law stating that the lower a family's income the greater is the proportion spent on food. As the income rises the family's spending is spread across a wider range of goods and services, such as housing, transport, consumer goods, leisure activities, etc. It was stated by the German statistician Ernst Engels (1821–96).

enlightened marketing A marketing philosophy holding that a company's marketing should support the best long-run performance of the marketing system; its five principles are consumer-oriented marketing, innovative marketing, value marketing, sense-of-mission marketing, and societal marketing.

enquiry (inquiry) An initial request from a potential purchaser for information regarding the quality, price, delivery date, etc., of a particular product. This may be the standard practice in some trades and commercial markets or it may be a consumer's response to an advertisement, sales promotion, or *direct marketing approach.

enquiry test (inquiry test) A method of testing the response to an advertisement or a particular medium by comparing the number of enquiries received as a result of it.

Enterprise Investment Scheme (EIS) An investment scheme in the UK that replaced the **Business Expansion Scheme** (BES) on 1 January 1994. Its purpose is to help certain types of small higher-risk unlisted trading companies to raise capital. Individuals who invest between £500 and £200,000 in eligible shares in any one year are entitled to a tax relief of 20% of the amount subscribed. This contrasts with the relief given under the BES, in which a higher-rate taxpayer received full tax relief. Gains on the sale of shares issued under the scheme are exempt from capital gains tax. Investors may hold paid directorships of the companies concerned. *See also* CORPORATE VENTURING SCHEME.

enterprise zone An area, designated as such by the government, in which its aim is to restore private-sector activity by removing certain tax burdens and by relaxing certain statutory controls. Benefits, which are available for a 10-year period, include: exemption from rates on industrial and commercial property; 100% allowances for corporation- and income-tax purposes for capital expenditure on industrial and commercial buildings; exemption from industrial training levies; and a simplified planning regime.

entity concept *See* ACCOUNTING ENTITY.

entrepôt trade Trade that passes through a port, district, airport, etc., before being shipped on to some other country. The entrepôt trade may make use of such a port because it is conveniently situated on shipping lanes and has the warehouses and customs facilities required for re-export or because that port is the centre of the particular trade concerned and facilities are available there for sampling, testing, auctioning, breaking bulk, etc. Much entrepôt trade used to pass through London, but since the decline of the London docks other European ports, such as Rotterdam, have taken its place. Singapore and Hong Kong are also centres of the entrepôt trade.

entrepreneur An individual who undertakes (from the French *entreprendre* to undertake) to supply a good or service to the market for profit. The entrepreneur will usually invest capital in the business and take on the risks associated with the investment. In most modern capitalist economies the initiative of entrepreneurs is regarded as an important element in creating a society's wealth; governments are therefore led to establish conditions in which they will thrive.

entry A record made in a book of account, register, or computer file of a financial transaction, event, proceeding, etc. *See also* DOUBLE-ENTRY BOOK-KEEPING.

entry-level criteria *See* ORDER-QUALIFYING CRITERIA.

enumeration district A geographical area of approximately 150 households corresponding to the census breakdown of Great Britain, used for the segmentation of consumer markets using data lists.

environmental accounting *See* GREEN REPORTING; SOCIAL RESPONSIBILITY REPORTING.

environmental audit (green audit) An *audit of the impact of the activities of an organization on the environment. Its purpose is usually to ensure that the organization has clear environmental policies, that its operations comply with the stated environmental policies, and that its policies are subject to regular review. Environmental audits may be conducted internally or externally by environmental consultants. Areas covered by a green audit include energy usage, wastage and recycling procedures, conservation of raw materials, and adopting cleaner technologies. *See also* GREEN REPORTING; SOCIAL AUDIT; SOCIAL RESPONSIBILITY REPORTING.

environmental costs The *costs of making sure that a company's activities do not damage the environment or that any such damage is put right. There are many types of environmental costs and these are often difficult to identify as they are hidden in *overheads. Measuring environmental costs is now an important issue for many companies, as national regulations become more stringent and penalties or fines more severe. It is useful to classify environmental costs into four categories:

- **environmental appraisal costs**. These are the costs of activities performed to monitor environmental effects that a firm is responsible for. Examples include the costs arising from inspection of products and contamination testing.
- **environmental prevention costs**. These are the costs of activities performed to prevent the production of waste that could cause damage to the environment. Examples include the costs of recycling products, training staff, and carrying out environmental studies.
- **environmental internal failure costs**. These are the costs of activities that have to be performed when contaminants and waste have been produced by a company but not discharged into the environment. Examples include treating toxic waste and maintaining pollution equipment.
- **environmental external failure costs**. These are the costs incurred by a company if it discharges waste into the environment. Examples include the costs of cleaning up oil spills or cleaning a polluted river. A company may also incur fines or other penalties or lose sales if it acquires a poor environmental reputation.

See also COST OF QUALITY.

environmental management perspective A management outlook in which a firm takes aggressive action to affect the people and forces controlling its marketing environment, rather than simply watching them and reacting to them.

environmental scanning An examination of the environment of a business in order to identify its marketing opportunities, competition, etc.

EOQ Abbreviation for *economic order quantity.

EPOS Abbreviation for *electronic point of sale.

EPP Abbreviation for *executive pension plan.

eps Abbreviation for *earnings per share.

EQA Abbreviation for *European Quality Award.

equal employment opportunity legislation Laws that prevent *discrimination in job selection or in the performance of job duties after employees have been hired. The law lays down that equal employment opportunities must be available in all organizations. It is a company's responsibility to ensure that hiring, promotion, and dismissal are nondiscriminatory.

equal pay The requirement of the Equal Pay Act (1970), expressing the principle of **equal opportunities**, that men and women in the same employment must be paid at the same rate for like work or work rated as equivalent. Work is rated as equivalent when the employer has undertaken a study to evaluate his employees' jobs in terms of the skill, effort, and responsibility demanded of them and the woman's job is given the same grade as the man's or when an independent expert appointed by an *employment tribunal evaluates the two jobs as of equal value.

equipment trust certificate In the USA, a document setting out the details of a loan used to fund the purchase of equipment. The holder of the certificate has a secured interest in the asset in the event of a corporate default.

equitable apportionment The process of sharing common costs between *cost centres in a fair manner, using a basis of apportionment that reflects the way in which the costs are incurred by the cost centres.

equitable interest An interest in, or ownership of, property that is recognized by *equity but not by the *common law. A beneficiary under a trust has an equitable interest. Any disposal of an equitable interest (e.g. a sale) must be in writing. Some equitable interests in land must be registered or they will be lost if the legal title to the land is sold. Similarly, equitable interests in other property will be

lost if the legal title is sold to a bona fide purchaser for value who has no notice of the equitable interest. In such circumstances the owner of the equitable interest may claim damages from the person who sold the legal title.

equity 1. A beneficial interest in an asset. For example, a person having a house worth £250,000 with a mortgage of £100,000 may be said to have an equity of £150,000 in the house. *See also* NEGATIVE EQUITY. **2.** The net assets of a company after all creditors (including the holders of *preference shares) have been paid off. **3.** The amount of money returned to a borrower in a mortgage or hire-purchase agreement, after the sale of the specified asset and the full repayment of the lender of the money. **4.** The ordinary share capital of a company (*see* EQUITY CAPITAL). **5.** The system of law developed by the medieval chancellors and later by the Court of Chancery. It is distinguished from the *common law, which was developed by the king's courts, having originated from the residual jurisdiction delegated by the king to the chancellor. A citizen dissatisfied by the common law could petition the chancellor, who might grant relief on an ad-hoc basis. In time this developed into a complementary but separate system of law providing remedies unavailable at common law, such as specific performance of a contract rather than damages. Until 1873 equity was applied and administered by the Court of Chancery, and equitable remedies were not available in the common law courts (and vice versa). However, the Judicature Acts (1873; 1875) merged the two systems so that any court may now apply both common law and equity. If the two sets of rules contradict each other, the equitable rule prevails. Equity has been particularly important in the development of the law of trusts, land law, administration of estates, and alternative remedies for breach of contract. *See also* NEGATIVE EQUITY.

equity accounting The practice of showing in a company's accounts a share of the undistributed profits and a share of the net assets of another company in which it holds a share of the *equity (usually a share of between 20% and 50%). The share of profit shown by the equity-

COST CLASSIFICATION	WORK IN PROGRESS (UNITS)	DEGREES OF COMPLETION (%)	EQUIVALENT UNITS
direct materials	3000	100	3000
direct labour	3000	50	1500
overheads	3000	50	1500

Equivalent units. A simple example.

holding company is usually equal to its share of the equity in the other company. Although none of the profit may actually be paid over, the company has a right to this share of the undistributed profit.

equity capital The part of the *share capital of a company owned by ordinary shareholders, although for certain purposes, such as *pre-emption rights, other classes of shareholders may be deemed to share in the equity capital and therefore be entitled to share in the profits of the company or any surplus assets on winding up. *Compare* NON-EQUITY SHARE.

equity dilution *See* DILUTION OF EQUITY.

equity dividend cover A ratio that shows how many times the *dividend to ordinary shareholders can be paid out of the profits of a company available for distribution. The higher the cover, the greater the certainty that dividends will be paid in the future.

equity finance Finance raised from shareholders in the form of *ordinary shares and reserves, as opposed to *non-equity shares and to borrowing.

equity gearing *See* GEARING.

equity-linked policy An insurance or assurance policy in which a proportion of the premiums paid are invested in equities. The surrender value of the policy is therefore the selling price of the equities purchased; as more premiums are paid the portfolio gets larger. Although investment returns may be considerably better on this type of policy than on a traditional endowment policy, the risk is greater, as the price of equities can fall dramatically reducing the value of the policy. With *unit-linked policies, a much wider range of investments can be achieved and the risk is correspondingly reduced.

equity share capital *See* EQUITY CAPITAL.

equity theory A cognitive theory of *motivation, based on the work of J. Stacey Adams, which claims that employees will be motivated if they believe that they are fairly treated in the workplace. The theory proposes that employees form an estimate of how the total benefits they receive from a job (pay, status, interest) compare with their total input (effort, skill, experience); this ratio is then compared with that of other people doing similar work. If the latter comparison is unfavourable, motivation will suffer.

equivalent units (effective units) Unfinished units of production that remain in a process at the end of a period as *work in progress (or process). Degrees of completion are assigned to each cost classification, which, when applied to the number of units in work in progress, give an equivalent number of completed units. For example, if the number of units of work in progress is, say, 3000 units to the following degrees of completion, the effective units are given in the table above.

The equivalent units have an impact on the valuation of opening and closing work in process.

ERDF Abbreviation for *European Regional Development Fund.

ergonomics (human factors) The discipline that draws on human physiology and psychology in order to design jobs, equipment, and work environments that are safe and efficient. For example, such human characteristics as size, reach, and flexibility must match the machines and tools that people have to use.

ERG theory (existence, relatedness, and growth theory) A theory of human *motivation that focuses on three groups of needs that form a hierarchy: **existence needs** (physical and material wants); **relatedness needs** (the desire for interpersonal relationships and for deeper relationships with the important people in one's life);

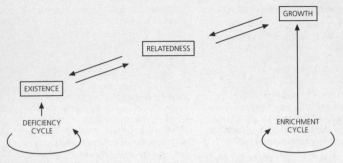

ERG theory. The existence, relatedness, and growth theory of motivation.

and **growth needs** (desires to be creative and productive). The theory suggests that these needs change their position in the hierarchy as circumstances change (see diagram above). A need does not have to be fully satisfied for upward movement to occur; a downward movement can occur when a need is not satisfied. In the deficiency cycle at the bottom of the hierarchy the individual can become obsessed with satisfying existence needs. The enrichment cycle leads a person to learn and grow, generally in multiple environments (i.e. work, home, etc.). The theory, which was developed from *Maslow's motivational hierarchy by the US organizational psychologist Clayton P. Alderfer (1940–), has been widely applied to issues of workplace motivation and consumer behaviour.

ERM Abbreviation for Exchange Rate Mechanism. *See* EUROPEAN MONETARY SYSTEM.

errors and omissions excepted *See* E & OE.

escalation clause A clause in a contract authorizing the contractor to increase the price in specified conditions of all or part of the services or goods he has contracted to supply. Escalation clauses are common in contracts involving work over a long period in times of high inflation. The escalation may refer to either or both labour and materials and may or may not state the way in which the price is permitted to escalate. An escalation clause does not convert a contract into a *cost-plus contract, but it represents a move in that direction.

escalation of commitment Increasing the resources available to an unsuccessful venture in the hope of recovering past losses. This is sometimes called a **creeping commitment**. This policy is often adopted in *new product development when the company continues to pour in funds, irrespective of the likelihood of success, in an attempt to recover some of its investment. It is known colloquially as throwing good money after bad.

escape clause A clause in a contract releasing one party from all or part of the contractual obligations in certain specified circumstances.

escrow A *deed that has been signed and sealed but is delivered on the condition that it will not become operative until some stated event happens. It will become effective as soon as that event occurs and it cannot be revoked in the meantime. Banks often hold escrow accounts, in which funds accumulate to pay taxes, insurance on mortgaged property, etc.

escudo 1. The standard monetary unit of Cape Verde (CV Esc), divided into 100 centavos. **2.** The former monetary unit of Portugal and Madeira, divided into 100 centavos. It was subsumed into the *euro for all purposes other than cash transactions in 1999 and abolished in 2002.

ESOP Abbreviation for *employee share ownership plan (or, in the USA, employee stock option plan).

ESOT Abbreviation for *employee share ownership trust.

ESP Abbreviation for *emotional selling proposition.

estate **1.** The sum total of a person's assets less his or her liabilities (usually as measured on his or her death for the purposes of *inheritance tax). **2.** A substantial piece of land, usually attached to a large house.

estate in land The length of time for which a piece of land will be held; for example, a life estate would last only for the life of the owner. *See* FEE SIMPLE.

estoppel **1.** A rule of evidence by which a person is prevented from denying that a certain state of affairs exists, having previously asserted that it does. **2. (promissory estoppel)** The rule that if a person has declared that the strict legal rights under a contract will not be insisted upon, they cannot be insisted upon later if the other party has relied on that declaration. The strict legal rights may, however, be enforced on giving reasonable notice, if this would not be inequitable. **3. (proprietary estoppel)** The rule that if one person allows or encourages another person to act to his or her detriment in respect of land, he or she will not later be able to refuse to grant something that he or she allowed the other person to expect. For example, if A encourages B to build a garage, which can only be reached by driving over A's land, saying that a right of way will be granted, A will not later be able to refuse to do so.

ETF Abbreviation for *electronic transfer of funds.

ethernet A high-speed *local area network, working at up to 10 million *bits per second.

ethical behaviour Behaviour judged to be good, just, right, and honourable, based on principles or guides from a specific ethical theory. However, ethical theories may vary from person to person, country to country, or company to company. Ethical realism accepts that although morality does not apply internationally, the ethical values of a trading partner should be respected.

ethical dilemmas The moral quandaries that can occur in running a business. While not confronting the law, most of these dilemmas arise as a result of conflict between what the businessperson sees as necessary in the interests of the business and his or her personal ethical values. These dilemmas may be related to entrepreneurial activities (Does the product or service offered conflict with one's social responsibility?), to one's behaviour to competitors (Have the claims for the superiority of one's product or service overstepped the limits of fair competition?), to one's shareholders (Are they earning a fair return on their capital?), and most of all, perhaps, to one's customers (Does the product or service offer fair value for money?).

ethical indicators *See* PERFORMANCE MEASUREMENT.

ethical investment (socially responsible investment) An investment made in a company not engaged in an activity that the investor considers to be unethical, such as armaments or tobacco, or an investment in a company of which the investor approves on ethical grounds, e.g. one having a good environmental employment record.

ethnic segmentation Recognizing the special strengths or needs of an ethnic community in offering it appropriate products and services using an appropriate marketing approach. *See* MARKET SEGMENTATION.

ethnocentrism Belief, often unconscious, in the superiority of one's own ethnic group or the universality of one's own culture-bound practices and preferences. In a global economy, such assumptions may be particularly dangerous in the fields of marketing and advertising.

EU Abbreviation for *European Union.

Euratom Abbreviation for *European Atomic Energy Community.

Eurex An electronic derivatives exchange formed by a merger of the Deutsche Terminbörse and the Swiss Options and Financial Futures Exchange in 1998. The electronic system on which trading occurs is accessible in 700 locations worldwide.

euro The currency unit of the European Monetary Union, divided into 100 cents (see EUROPEAN MONETARY SYSTEM). In January 1999 it was adopted for all purposes except cash transactions by Austria, Belgium, Finland, France, Germany, Ireland, Italy, Luxembourg, The Netherlands, Portugal, and Spain; Greece followed suit in 2001. Euro-denominated notes and coins were issued in January 2002 and the national currencies were withdrawn after a short period of dual circulation. The EU countries that adopted the euro have become known collectively as the *euro-zone. The euro is also legal tender in Andorra, Bosnia and Hercegovina, French Guiana, Guadeloupe, Kosovo, Madeira, Martinique, Mayotte, Monaco, Montenegro, Réunion, San Marino, and the Vatican City.

Euro-ad An advertisement designed to be used in all countries of the European Union. Certain products, particularly those that have been in use for long enough for national traditions to build up, are not suitable for multinational advertisements. Food is an example: there would be no point in advertising tinned baked beans in France. On the other hand, advertisements for cars, a more recent product, can have an equal appeal in all European countries.

Euro Area Reference Note (EARN) A euro-denominated bond first issued by the *European Investment Bank in 1999 to establish a market in euro-denominated securities.

Eurobanks Financial intermediaries that deal in the *eurocurrency market.

eurobond A *bond issued in a *eurocurrency, which is now one of the largest markets for raising money (it is much larger than the UK stock exchange). The reason for the popularity of the eurobond market is that *secondary market investors can remain anonymous, usually for the purpose of avoiding tax. For this reason it is difficult to ascertain the exact size and scope of operation of the market. Issues of new eurobonds normally take place in London, largely through syndicates of US and Japanese investment banks; they are *bearer securities, unlike the shares registered in most stock exchanges, and interest payments are free of any *withholding taxes. There are various kinds of eurobonds. An ordinary bond,

called a **straight**, is a fixed-interest loan of 3 to 8 years duration; others include **floating-rate notes**, which carry a variable interest rate based on the *London Inter Bank Offered Rate; and perpetuals, which are never redeemed. Some carry *warrants and some are *convertible.

euro certificate of deposit (Euro CD) A *certificate of deposit denominated in a *eurocurrency. London is the main issuing centre.

eurocheque A cheque drawn on a European bank, which can be cashed at any bank or bureau de change in the world that displays the European Union sign (of which there are some 200 000). It can also be used to pay for goods and services in shops, hotels, restaurants, garages, etc., that display the EU sign (over 4 million). The cheques are blank and are made out for any amount as required. They have to be used with a **Eurocheque Card**, which guarantees cheques up to a stated limit. In most cases, a commission of 1.25% is added to the value of the cheque and there may be a cheque charge by the bank on which they are drawn.

Euroclear The world's largest provider of domestic and cross-border settlement and related services for bond, equity, and investment-fund transactions. Based in Brussels, it was set up in 1968 by a number of banks.

euro-commercial paper (ECP) *Commercial paper issued in a *eurocurrency, the market for which is centred in London. It provides a quick way of obtaining same-day funds by the issue of unsecured notes, for example in Europe for use in New York.

eurocredit A loan in a *eurocurrency.

eurocurrency A foreign currency deposit at a bank located outside the country where the currency is issued as a legal tender. For example, dollars deposited in a bank in Switzerland are *eurodollars, yen deposited at a US bank are euroyen, etc. The deposit need not be held at a European bank or in Europe. Eurocurrency is used for lending and borrowing; the **eurocurrency market** often provides a cheap and convenient form of liquidity for the financing of international trade and investment. The main borrowers and lenders are the commercial banks, large companies, and the central banks. By raising funds in eurocurrencies it is possible to secure more favourable terms and rates of interest, and sometimes to avoid domestic regulations and taxation. The deposits and loans were initially on a short-term basis but increasing use is being made of medium-term loans, particularly through the raising of *eurobonds. This has to some extent replaced the syndicated loan market, in which banks lent money as a group in order to share the risk.

eurodeposit A deposit using the currency of another country, i.e. a transaction in the *eurocurrency market.

eurodollars Dollars deposited in financial institutions outside the USA. The eurodollar market evolved in London in the late 1950s when the growing demand for dollars to finance international trade and investment coincided with a greater supply of dollars. The prefix 'euro' indicates the origin of the practice but it now refers to all dollar deposits made anywhere outside the USA. *See also* EUROCURRENCY.

euroequity An *equity issue made on a stock exchange outside the country of the issuing company but denominated in the currency of that country.

euromarket **1.** A market that emerged in the 1950s for financing international trade. Its principal participants are *commercial banks, large companies, the *central banks of members of the EU, and (from 1999) the European Central Bank. Its main business is in *eurobonds, *euro-commercial paper, *euronotes, and *euroequities issued in *eurocurrencies. The largest euromarket is in London, but there are smaller ones in Paris, Brussels, and Frankfurt. **2.** The European Union, regarded as one large market for goods.

Euronext NV A holding company, set up in September 2000, incorporating the Amsterdam, Brussels, and Paris futures and options exchanges. It acquired the *London International Financial Futures and Options Exchange (LIFFE) and the Bolsa de Valores de Lisboa e Porto in 2002. It provides a market and clearing system for traded *derivatives.

euronote A form of *euro-commercial paper consisting of short-term negotiable *bearer notes. They may be in any currency but are usually in dollars or euros. The **euronote facility** is a form of *note issuance facility set up by a syndicate of banks, which underwrites the notes.

European Atomic Energy Community (Euratom) The organization set up by the six members of the *European Coal and Steel Community in 1957; the *European Economic Community was established at the same time. Euratom was formed to create the technical and industrial conditions necessary to produce nuclear energy on an industrial scale. Its controlling bodies were absorbed into the *European Commission in 1967.

European Central Bank (ECB) The central bank of the *European Union, established on 1 July 1998 to direct the single monetary policy needed for European Monetary Union (EMU; *see* EUROPEAN MONETARY SYSTEM). From that date it superseded the *European Monetary Institute and the *European Monetary Cooperation Fund. The bank became fully functional on 1 January 1999 when the single European currency (*see* EURO) was launched. The president, vice-president, and board members are appointed by the participating governments but the bank is otherwise entirely independent. Its main objective is achieving and maintaining price stability. Based in Frankfurt-am-Main, Germany, it works closely with the governors of the central banks of the participating states.

European Coal and Steel Community (ECSC) The first of the European Communities (EC), founded in 1953. The ECSC created a common market in coal, steel, iron ore, and scrap between the original six members of the EC (Belgium, France, West Germany, Italy, Luxembourg, and the Netherlands). These six countries, in 1957, signed the Treaty of Rome setting up the *European Economic Community.

European Commission The single executive body formed in 1967 (as the Commission of the European Communities) from the three separate executive bodies of the *European Coal and Steel Community, the *European Atomic Energy Community, and the *European Economic Community. It now consists of 30 Commissioners: two each from France, Germany, Spain, Italy, and the UK; and one each from Austria, Belgium, Cyprus, the Czech Republic, Denmark, Estonia, Finland, Greece, Hungary, Ireland, Latvia, Lithuania, Luxembourg, Malta, the Netherlands, Poland, Portugal, Slovakia, Slovenia, and Sweden. There are plans to reduce the membership to one Commissioner per country, with further reductions from 2009. The Commissioners accept joint responsibility for their decisions, which are taken on the basis of a majority vote. The Commission initiates and implements EU legislation and mediates between member governments. The Commissioners are backed by a staff of some 16 000 civil servants.

European Community *See* EUROPEAN ECONOMIC COMMUNITY; EUROPEAN UNION.

European Currency Unit (ECU) A former currency medium and unit of account created in 1979 to act as the reserve asset and accounting unit of the *European Monetary System (EMS). The value of the ECU was calculated as a weighted average of a basket of specified amounts of *European Union currencies. Fluctuations in the value of the ECU in terms of the currencies of the member states were controlled by the EMS. The ECU also acted as the unit of account for all EU transactions. ECU reserves were not allocated to individual countries but held in the *European Monetary Cooperation Fund. With the introduction of the *euro in January 1999 the ECU ceased to exist. The initial value of the euro against other currencies was set at one ECU.

European Derivatives Exchange London *See* LONDON STOCK EXCHANGE.

European Economic Area (EEA) The organization formed in 1992 between the members of the *European Union and the members of the *European Free Trade Association (EFTA) except Switzerland. The EEA was intended to come into force in 1993, with the single market of the EU, but owing to Switzerland's rejection of the plan, this was delayed until 1994. The EEA is controlled by a committee of EU and EFTA members and meetings of ministers.

European Economic Community (EEC; Common Market) The European common market set up by the six member states of the *European Coal and Steel Community (ECSC) in 1957. At the same time the *European Atomic Energy Community (Euratom) was set up. The European Parliament and the European Court of Justice were formed in accordance with the Treaty of Rome in 1957. The treaty aimed to forge a closer union between the countries of Europe by removing the economic effects of their frontiers. This included the elimination of customs duties and quotas between members, a common trade policy to outside countries, the abolition of restrictions on the movement of people and capital between member states, and a *Common Agricultural Policy. In addition to these trading policies, the treaty envisaged a harmonization of social and economic legislation to enable the Common Market to work. The **European Community (EC)** was created in 1967, when the controlling bodies of the EEC, ECSC, and Euratom were merged to form the Commission of European Communities (*see* EUROPEAN COMMISSION) and the Council of European Communities. The UK, Ireland, and Denmark joined the EC in 1973, Greece joined in 1981, and Portugal and Spain became members in 1986, making a total of 12 nations. In 1993 the European Community became the *European Union, which has since been joined by a further 13 nations. *See also* EUROPEAN MONETARY SYSTEM.

European Free Trade Association (EFTA) A trade association formed in 1960 between Austria, Denmark, Norway, Portugal, Sweden, Switzerland, and the UK. Finland, Iceland, and Liechtenstein joined later while the UK, Denmark, Portugal, Austria, Finland, and Sweden left on joining the *European Union (or its earlier forms). EFTA is a looser association than the EU, dealing only with trade barriers rather than generally coordinating economic policy. All tariffs between EFTA and EU countries were abolished finally in 1984. EFTA is governed by a council in which each member has one vote; decisions must normally be unanimous and are binding on all member countries. In 1992 the *European Economic Area (EEA) was formed to facilitate the movement of goods, services, capital, and labour between all EU and EFTA countries with the exception of Switzerland. EFTA has also signed economic cooperation treaties with some former eastern bloc countries.

European Investment Bank (EIB) A bank set up under the Treaty of Rome in 1958 to finance capital-investment projects in the *European Economic Community (EEC). It grants long-term loans to private companies and public institutions for projects that further the aims of the Community. The members of the EIB are the member states of the *European Union, all of whom have subscribed to the Bank's capital; however, most of the funds lent by the bank are borrowed on the EU and international capital markets. The bank is non-profit-making and charges interest at a rate that reflects the rate at which it borrows. Its headquarters are in Luxembourg.

European Monetary Cooperation Fund (EMCOF) A fund organized by the *European Monetary System in which members of the *European Union deposited reserves to provide a pool of resources to stabilize exchange rates and to finance *balance of payments support. In return for depositing 20% of their gold and gross dollar reserves, member states were given access to a wide variety of credit facilities, denominated in ECU, from the fund. It ceased operations with the introduction of the *euro in 1999.

European Monetary Institute (EMI) An organization set up by the Maastricht Treaty in 1991 in order to coordinate the economic and monetary policy of members of the *European Union until the achievement of European Monetary Union (EMU; *see* EUROPEAN MONETARY SYSTEM). It was superseded by the *European Central Bank in July 1998.

European Monetary System (EMS) A system of exchange-rate stabilization involving the countries of the *European Union, which began operations in 1979. There were two elements: the **Exchange Rate Mechanism (ERM)**, under which participating countries committed themselves to maintaining the values of their currencies within agreed limits, and a *balance of payments support mechanism, organized through the *European Monetary Cooperation Fund. The ERM operated by giving each currency a value in ECUs and drawing up a parity grid giving exchange values in ECUs for each pair of currencies. If market rates differed from the agreed parity by more than a permitted percentage, the relevant governments had to take action to correct the disparity. In 1992 the UK pound and the Italian lira were forced out of the ERM and the Spanish peseta also fell below its floor value; some of the currencies remaining within the system were subsequently allowed wider (plus or minus 15%) fluctuations.

Although some saw the EMS as no more than a mechanism to facilitate monetary cooperation, the view that its ultimate goal should be **European Monetary Union (EMU)**, with a single European currency and a *European Central Bank, gained ground in the 1980s and 1990s. The decision to create a single currency was part of the Maastricht Treaty of 1991. In June 1998 11 EU countries – all the then member states except Denmark, Greece, Sweden, and the UK – committed themselves to monetary union. Their currencies were then locked together irrevocably and the European Central Bank was established to direct the single monetary policy essential for EMU. The *euro was launched for all purposes except cash transactions in January 1999. Euro bank notes and coins came into circulation in January 2002 and the national currencies were withdrawn after a short transitional period. A new exchange-rate mechanism, known as **ERM II**, was established in January 1999 to link the currencies of other EU states to the euro (with fluctuation rates of plus or minus 15% as the basic rule). Its initial members were Denmark and Greece; the latter adopted the euro in 2001. In mid-2004 three of the new accession states – Estonia, Lithuania, and Slovenia – joined ERM II, with others announcing plans to follow suit in due course. Countries must participate in ERM II for a minimum of two years before adopting the euro.

European option *See* OPTION.

European Quality Award (EQA) An award instituted in 1992 by the European Foundation for Quality Management. It is given to companies that can demonstrate excellence in their management of quality and that their approach to *total quality management has contributed to the satisfaction of customers, employees, and other stakeholders. The nine first-level categories of the EQA model are: leadership, policy and strategy, people management, resources, processes, customer satisfaction, people satisfaction, impact on society, and business results.

European Regional Development Fund (ERDF) A fund used by the European Union to allocate money for specific projects in member states for work on the infrastructure, usually in regions of high unemployment or social deprivation. Each country has a quota and has to undertake works approved by the EU before grant aid is given.

European terms The quotation of foreign-exchange rates in terms of how many units of a currency can be exchanged for one US dollar. *Compare* AMERICAN TERMS.

European Union (EU) The 25 nations that have joined together to form an economic community (EC), with some common monetary, political, and social aspirations. The EU was created in 1993 from the European Community (EC), which itself grew from the European Coal and Steel Community, the European Atomic Energy Community, and the *European Economic Community. The 12 nations of the EC (Belgium, Denmark, France, Germany, Greece, Ireland, Italy, Luxembourg, the Netherlands, Portugal, Spain, and the UK) were joined by Austria, Sweden, and Finland in 1995 and by (Greek) Cyprus, the Czech Republic, Estonia, Hungary, Latvia, Lithuania, Malta, Poland, Slovakia, and Slovenia in May 2004. Its executive body is the *European Commission, which was formed in 1967 with the Council of the European Communities. EU policy emerges from a dialogue between the Commission, which initiates and implements the policy, and the Council, which takes the major policy decisions. The European Parliament, formed in 1957, exercises democratic control over policy, and the European Court of Justice imposes the rule of law on the EU, as set out in its various treaties. Although a draft EU Constitution, proposing the creation of an EU president and foreign minister, was published in 2004, its future is now uncertain following rejection by the electorates of France and the Netherlands. *See also* SINGLE MARKET; SOCIAL CHAPTER.

Europort Any of the main European ports, especially Rotterdam.

eurosecurities Financial instruments traded on *euromarkets, notably *eurocommercial paper, *euronotes, *eurobonds, and *euroequities.

eurozone The 12 member countries of the European Union that have adopted the *euro as their currency, namely Austria, Belgium, Finland, France, Germany, Greece, Ireland, Italy, Luxembourg, The Netherlands, Portugal, and Spain. *See* EUROPEAN MONETARY SYSTEM.

EV Abbreviation for *expected value.

EVA Abbreviation for *Economic Value Added.

evaluation of training An assessment of the effectiveness of personnel training programs. Ideally, such a review should be carried out at four levels:
(1) **reaction** – What did the trainees themselves think of the programme? This involves collecting data directly from trainees about their reaction to the length, depth, pace, difficulty, and usefulness of the training.
(2) **learning** – How much new knowledge has been acquired by the trainees? This can be assessed by testing trainees on the information content of the course.
(3) **behaviour** – How has the program affected the behaviour of trainees? To answer this, supervisors must find evidence of new skills or positive behavioural traits that can be attributed directly to the programme.
(4) **results** – How has the effectiveness of the group or organization as a whole benefitted from the training? This involves relating the answers received for questions (1), (2), (3), and (4) to an agreed system of *performance measurement for the organization.

event of default In a loan agreement, a specified occurrence that will make the loan repayable immediately. The breaching of any *covenant clause will be an event of default. Events of default also include failure to pay, failure to perform other duties and obligations, false *representation and warranty, *material adverse change, bankruptcy, and *alienation of assets.

evergreen fund A fund that provides capital for new companies and supports their development for a period with regular injections of capital.

ex- (Latin: without) A prefix used to exclude specified benefits when a security is quoted. A share is described as **ex-dividend** (xd or ex-div) when a potential purchaser will no longer be entitled to receive the company's current dividend, the right to which remains with the vendor. Government stocks go ex-dividend 36 days before the interest payment. Similarly, **ex-rights**, **ex-scrip**, **ex-coupon**, **ex-capitalization** (**ex-cap**), and **ex-bonus** mean that each of these benefits belongs to the vendor rather than the buyer. **Ex-all** means that all benefits belong to the vendor. **Cum-** (Latin: with) has exactly the opposite sense, meaning that the dividend or other benefits belong to the buyer rather than the seller. The price of a share that has gone ex-dividend will usually fall by the amount of the dividend, while one that is **cum-dividend** will usually rise by this amount. However, in practice market forces usually mean that these falls and rises are often slightly less than expected.

ex-all See EX-.

ex ante (Latin) Before the event. The phrase is used, for example, of a budget that is prepared as an estimate and subsequently compared with actual figures. *Compare* EX POST.

ex-capitalization (ex-cap) See EX-.

Excel *Trademark* A widely used *spreadsheet program supplied by Microsoft.

excepted peril A *risk that is expressly excluded from an insurance policy. In the carriage of goods, excepted perils exclude *acts of God, *inherent vice, *negligence, and loss resulting from action of the Queen's enemies. *See also* INSURABLE RISK.

exceptional items Costs or income affecting a company's *profit and loss account that arise from the normal activities of the company but are of exceptional

magnitude, either large or small. Unlike *extraordinary items they are included in the calculation of the normal trading profit or loss. The rules are set out in *Financial Reporting Standard 3.

excess 1. An initial sum which the holder of an insurance policy must bear before any claim is met by the insurer. It is most often used in car insurance, e.g. the first £50 of any claim has to be borne by the insured party. **2.** A bank or other financial institution's margin of assets over liabilities. *See also* EXCESS RESERVES. **3.** *See* EXCESS SHARES.

excess capacity The part of the output of a plant or process that is not currently being utilized but which, if it could be, would reduce the average cost of production. The excess capacity is thus the amount by which the present output must be increased to reduce the average cost per unit to a minimum.

excess policy An insurance policy in which the insured is responsible for paying a specified sum (the **excess**) of each claim and cannot make claims of a lower value than this excess. For example, a £100 excess on a motor-insurance policy means that the insured has to pay the first £100 of any claim and cannot make a claim on the policy for less than £100. This arrangement enables the insurer to offer the insurance at a lower premium than would otherwise be the case as he avoids the administrative cost of small claims and also makes a saving on claims paid out. *See also* DEDUCTIBLE; FRANCHISE.

excess reserves Higher reserves than required, held by banks. This usually undesirable state occurs as a result of poor demand for loans or high interest rates. Banks often sell excess reserves to one another.

excess shares Shares not taken up by other shareholders in a *rights issue, for which an invitation to purchase is sent to shareholders with their standard letters of *allotment.

exchange 1. The trading of goods, stocks, shares, commodities, paper currencies, or other financial instruments. **2.** The place in which such trading occurs, e.g. a stock exchange or commodities exchange. This may not necessarily have a physical location. **3.** An agreement to swap, as in *exchange of contracts.

exchange control Restrictions on the purchase and sale of foreign exchange. It is operated in various forms by many countries, in particular those who experience shortages of *hard currencies; sometimes different regulations apply to transactions that would come under the capital account of the *balance of payments. There has been a gradual movement toward dismantling exchange controls by many countries in recent years. The UK abolished all form of exchange control in 1979.

Exchange Delivery Settlement Price (EDSP) *See* SETTLEMENT PRICE.

exchange equalization account An account set up in 1932 and managed by the *Bank of England on behalf of the government. It contains the official gold and foreign-exchange reserves (including *Special Drawing Rights) of the UK and is used to manage the value of sterling. Although all *exchange controls were abolished in 1979, the Bank of England still makes use of this account to help to stabilize rates of exchange.

exchange of contracts A procedure adopted in the sale and purchase of land in which both parties sign their copies of the contract, having satisfied themselves as to the state of the property, etc., and agreed that they wish to be bound. There need be no physical exchange of documents; the parties or their advisers can exchange contracts by agreeing to do so orally (for example, by telephone). From that moment the contract is binding and can normally be enforced by specific performance. Contracts for the sale of land must be in writing.

exchange offer A proposal to debt or equity holders that they should exchange their existing securities for new securities, the terms of which are usually less favourable. It is a mechanism for capital restructuring in situations of *financial distress.

exchange rate *See* RATE OF EXCHANGE.

exchange-rate exposure (currency risk; exchange-rate risk; foreign-exchange rate

risk) The risk associated with uncertain exchange rates.

Exchange Rate Mechanism (ERM) *See* EUROPEAN MONETARY SYSTEM.

exchange-traded option (exchange option; listed option) An option traded on one of the institutional markets, such as the *London International Financial Futures and Options Exchange, as opposed to one sold on the *over-the-counter market; such options have standard terms and conditions.

Exchequer The account held by the *Bank of England for all government funds.

Exchequer stocks *See* GILT-EDGED SECURITY.

excise duty A duty or tax levied on certain goods consumed within a country, such as alcoholic drinks and tobacco products, unlike customs duty, which is levied on imports. In the UK, both excise and customs duties are collected by the *Board of Customs and Excise.

exclusive distribution **1.** The use by a manufacturer of a single retailer or wholesaler in a particular market for a particular product. **2.** A situation in which a distributor carries the products of one manufacturer and not those of competing manufacturers; this may give the distributor the exclusive right to distribute the company's products in other territories. *See* EXCLUSIVE TERRITORY.

exclusive economic zone *See* TERRITORIAL WATERS.

exclusive territory **1.** An area, defined by geographical boundaries or population, assigned by a manufacturer to a retailer, wholesaler, or other dealer with the understanding that no other distributors will be allowed to sell the manufacturer's products in that area. **2.** A practice used by some manufacturers in which intermediaries may only sell their products within a designated geographical area.

executive director (working director) A *director of a company who is also an employee (usually full-time) of that company. An executive director will often have a specified role in the management of the company, such as finance director, marketing director, production director, etc. By contrast a *non-executive director is involved in planning and policy-making, but not in the day-to-day management of the company.

executive pension plan (EPP) A pension for a senior executive or director of a company in which the company provides a tax-deductible contribution to the premium. An executive pension plan may be additional to any group pension scheme provided by the company, as long as the pension limit of two-thirds of the working salary is not exceeded.

executive share option scheme An approved *share option scheme that entitles a specified class of directors or employees to purchase shares in the company in which they are employed. *See* SAVINGS RELATED SHARE OPTION SCHEME.

executor A person named in a will of another person to gather in the assets of that estate, pay liabilities, and distribute any residue to the beneficiaries in accordance with the instructions contained in the will.

exempt gilts In the UK, government *gilt-edged securities that pay interest gross, unlike ordinary gilts, on which tax is deducted from interest payments. These gilts are of particular interest to foreign buyers and others, such as institutions, who do not pay income tax.

exempt private company A family company that was exempt from filing its *financial statements with the *Registrar of Companies. The exempt private company was created by the Companies Act (1948) and abolished by the Companies Act (1967). The *small companies and *medium-sized companies' filing exemptions replace it to some extent.

exempt supplies Supplies of goods or services in the categories of items that are identified as exempt from *value added tax, as given in the Value Added Tax Act (1994). The main categories are: land (including rent), insurance and financial services, postal services, betting, charities (except on their business activities), education (non-profit-making), trade unions and professional bodies, sport, cultural

services, health services, burial and cremation.

exempt transfers Transfers resulting in no liability to *inheritance tax. These are:
- the first £3000 transferred in any tax year;
- gifts to a spouse;
- normal expenditure out of income;
- small gifts, up to £250, to any number of individuals;
- marriage gifts, up to £5000 for each parent and £2500 for grandparents of the parties to the marriage, but limited to £1000 for other gifts;
- gifts to charities;
- gifts for national purposes;
- gifts for public benefit;
- gifts to political parties;
- certain transfers to employee trusts.

See also POTENTIALLY EXEMPT TRANSFER.

exempt unit trust A *unit trust in which only institutional investors who are not subject to taxation are allowed to invest, i.e. it is restricted to charities and pension funds.

exercise To make use of the right to carry out a transaction on previously agreed terms, mainly in the *options market.

exercise date The date on which the holder of an *option can exercise the right to implement the option contract. It is normally after three, six, or nine months.

exercise notice Formal notification from the *taker of an *option to the *writer expressing an intention to exercise the option to buy (for a call option) or sell (for a put option) at the *exercise price on the *exercise date.

exercise price (strike price; striking price) The price per share at which a traded *option entitles the owner to buy the *underlying in a call option or to sell it in a put option.

ex factory *See* EX WORKS.

ex gratia (Latin: as of grace) Denoting a payment made out of gratitude, moral obligation, kindness, etc., rather than to fulfil a legal obligation. When an ex gratia payment is made, no legal liability is admitted by the payer.

ex gratia pension A pension paid by an

POSSIBLE OUTCOMES (£)	SUBJECTIVE PROBABILITY (P)	PRODUCT (£ × P)
3000	0.5	1500
4000	0.3	1200
6000	0.2	1200
	1.0	EMV = 3900

Expected monetary value. In this simple example the EMV of a project is calculated as £3900.

employer although there is no legal, contractual, or implied commitment to provide it.

ex growth (of a share or a company) Having had substantial growth in the past but now not holding out prospects for immediate growth of earnings or value.

exhibition list A list of visitors to an exhibition. Such lists are often used as a data source for *direct marketing to business customers.

Eximbank *See* EXPORT-IMPORT BANK.

existence needs *See* ERG THEORY.

exit charge The charge to *inheritance tax made when an asset is taken out of a *discretionary trust.

exit interview An interview in which an employee who has handed in his or her resignation is questioned by personnel staff. Such interviews can be useful to the employer because they provide a means of finding out the reasons why the employee is leaving, which may be helpful in designing policies that can help to retain staff (e.g. by improving promotion opportunities or job satisfaction).

exit value The *net realizable value of an asset, i.e. its market price at the date of a balance sheet less the selling expenses. Exit values are effectively *break-up values and are not consistent with the *going-concern concept, which assumes that a business is continuing to trade.

ex-new Describing a share that is offered for sale without the right to take up any *scrip issue or *rights issue. *Compare* CUM-NEW.

exotic options (exotics) Options that have unusual features, particularly in relation to their *exercise price, payoff formula, or *underlying. Examples include *binary options and *exploding options.

expected monetary value (EMV) In

decision making, the sum of the products of the outcomes in monetary terms and the probabilities of these outcomes arising. In *decision trees subjective probability estimates are assigned to each possible outcome. In the EMV, the outcomes are expressed in terms of money. In the example given in the table above, the EMV is 3900. *Compare* EXPECTED VALUE.

expected value (EV) A statistical measure of central value often used in decision making. It is the sum of the possible outcomes in quantitative terms, such as units of output or sales, weights, or volumes, multiplied by the respective probabilities of these outcomes arising. *Compare* EXPECTED MONETARY VALUE.

expenditure The costs or expenses incurred by an organization. They may be *capital expenditure or *revenue expenditure. Although expenditure is usually incurred by an outlay of money, expenditure may also arise in accounting by the acknowledgement of a liability, for example rent accrued due, which is regarded as expenditure in the period accrued although it will not be paid until a later date.

expenditure tax *See* SALES TAX.

expense 1. A sum spent for goods or services, which therefore no longer represents an asset of the purchasing organization. Expenses are normally shown as charge against profit in the *profit and loss account. **2.** A sum of money spent by an employee during the course of his work. The employee records this expenditure in an **expense account**, for refund by the company and submission to HM Revenue and Customs on a P11D form for assessment of any taxable element.

expense account 1. An account, opened in either the cost ledger or the nominal ledger, for each *expenditure heading in which the costs of an organization are recorded before being totalled and transferred to the *profit and loss account at the end of an accounting period. **2.** The amount of money that certain staff members are allowed to spend on personal expenses in carrying out their activities for an organization.

experience curve A relationship between the costs of production and cumulative output, showing that efficiency increases with the repetition of the process. As experience increases, costs fall, adding to the competitive advantage of a firm. This may be a continuous process as improvements are regularly made to the manufacture of a product over its life cycle.

experiencing focus groups *Focus groups that enable a client to listen to consumers' thoughts and feelings regarding specific products and services.

experimental marketing research The gathering of primary data by selecting matched groups of subjects, giving them different treatments, controlling related factors, and checking for differences in group responses.

expert system A computer application used to solve problems in a particular area of knowledge. The system uses the computer's ability to store, organize, and retrieve large amounts of information and is programmed to make decisions of the type that would be made by an expert in the field. Typically, an expert-system program asks questions of the user, who chooses one of several possible answers. This leads to other questions, and eventually to a conclusion. A common successful use is in basic medical diagnosis, but expert systems can also be designed for analysis of company results, review of loan applications, buying stocks and shares, and other financial purposes.

expiry date 1. The date on which a contract expires. **2.** The last day on which an *option expires. In a European option the option must be taken up or allowed to lapse on this date. In an American option the decision can be taken at any time up to the expiry date.

exploding option An *exotic option in which exercise is automatic if the price of

the *underlying reaches the *exercise price.

exploratory focus groups *Focus groups that aid in the precise definition of a problem, in pilot testing, in generating hypotheses for testing, or suggesting concepts for further *marketing research.

exploratory research Preliminary *marketing research to clarify the exact nature of a problem to be solved. Quite often sales managers recognize that there is a problem but do not understand the dimensions of the problem. In these circumstances preliminary research is conducted with small numbers of potential customers to define the nature of the problem.

exponential smoothing See ADAPTIVE EXPONENTIAL SMOOTHING.

Export Credits Guarantee Department (ECGD) A UK government department that operates under the Export and Investment Guarantees Act (1991). It encourages exports from the UK by making export credit insurance available to exporters and guaranteeing repayment to UK banks that provide finance for exports on credit terms of two years or more. It also insures British private investment overseas against war risk, expropriation, and restrictions on the making of remittances. Some sections of the ECGD were privatized in 1991, including short-term credit insurance.

Export-Import Bank (Eximbank) A US bank established by the US government to foster trade with the USA. It provides export guarantees and guarantees loans made by commercial banks to US exporters.

export incentive An incentive offered by a government to exporters. They can include subsidies, grants, tax concessions, credit facilities, etc.

export licence A licence required before goods can be exported from a country. Export licences are only required in the UK for certain works of art, antiques, etc., and certain types of arms and armaments.

exports Goods or services sold to foreign countries. Export selling may be achieved by using international marketing middlemen (**indirect exporting**) or by a company's own overseas branch or sales representatives or by a company's *agents abroad (**direct exporting**). In terms of the *balance of payments, goods are classified as *visibles, while such services as banking, insurance, and tourism are treated as invisibles. The UK has traditionally relied on its invisibles to achieve its trade balance as it tends to spend more on imports than it receives in exports. *See also* EXPORT CREDITS GUARANTEE DEPARTMENT.

ex post (Latin) Short for *ex post facto*: after the event. This abbreviation is used, for example, to refer to the collection of financial data for transactions after they have been effected. *Compare* EX ANTE.

exposure The degree of *risk involved in holding a particular *position on a financial market.

ex quay Delivery terms for goods in which the seller pays all freight charges up to the port of destination, unloading onto the quay, and loading onto road or rail vehicles. Thereafter all transport charges must be paid by the buyer.

ex ship (**free overboard**; **free overside**) Delivery terms for goods shipped from one place to another. The seller pays all charges up to the port of destination, including unloading from the ship. All subsequent charges, e.g. lighterage, loading charges, etc., are paid by the buyer.

extended ASCII *See* ASCII.

extended community An Internet community that is larger and more extensive than a *personal community.

extended guarantee A servicing and maintenance cover that a manufacturer offers to a customer for a specified additional amount of time beyond the original guarantee. Extended guarantees usually have to be paid for.

extended marketing mix An addition to the traditional *marketing mix of product, price, place, and promotion (the four Ps) to include three further Ps, when marketing services, i.e.:

- **physical evidence** – the tangible elements of a service that enable consumers to evaluate it;

- **people** – an evaluation of the personnel providing the service (e.g. knowledge, competence, politeness);
- **process** – an evaluation of the overall experience provided by the service to ensure that all the elements of which it consists operate effectively together.

extended trial balance A *trial balance that gives a vertical listing of all the *ledger account balances with three additional columns for adjustments, *accruals, and *payments in advance, and a final two columns (each containing a debit and a credit side) that show the entries in the *profit and loss account and the *balance sheet.

extendible bond issue A *bond, the maturity of which can be extended at the option of all the parties.

extension risk The *risk associated with an agreement that permits one of the partners to extend its term, so that payments take place later than expected. It is the opposite of *prepayment risk.

extension service An alliance partner to an *anchor service on the Internet; if, for example, the anchor service is an airline, an extension service might be provided by a firm of travel agents.

external audit An *audit of an organization carried out by an auditor who is external to, and independent of, the organization. An example would be a *statutory audit carried out on behalf of the shareholders of a limited company. *Compare* INTERNAL AUDIT.

external environment The institutions and people outside a business organization that affect it; these include national and local government, trade unions, competitors, customers, suppliers, etc. The external environment is one of the contingency factors that has to be taken into account in designing an organization.

external failure costs *See* COST OF QUALITY. *See also* ENVIRONMENTAL COSTS.

external growth The means by which a business can grow by merger, takeover, or joint ventures, rather than by growing organically through its own internal development (*see* BUSINESS STRATEGY). External growth is widely used by companies as it can offer greater speed in achieving its corporate objectives than internal development. Typically firms can increase their market share by merging with or taking over a competitor in the same field (horizontal diversification). In mature or declining markets, restructuring of combined operations can lead to cost savings. Alternatively, a company may seek to gain greater control of its supply chain by expanding through merging or taking over a supplier or distributor (vertical integration). Unrelated external expansion may take place when a firm buys into a market in which it has no existing expertise; often the time taken to develop a significant presence on its own account is considered to be too long and risky, compared to buying an established business. Although great benefits may accrue from external growth, it also carries high risks, since the expected gains may often be slow to appear as a result of the restructuring and organizational changes involved as well as the high costs of financing the merger or takeover. *Joint ventures, often between rival firms, sometimes between companies from different countries, are becoming a more common form of external growth. In such cases, the parties bring complementary strengths (technology, operations, marketing) and share the risks of the venture, although differences in company and country culture may cause difficulties.

externality A cost or benefit to an economic agent that is not matched by a compensating financial flow. For example, siting a railway station close to a housing estate represents an externality to householders on that estate. It is an external economy if the householders benefit from shorter journey times to work (and consequent rising house prices) and an external diseconomy if the noise of trains keeps them awake at night. In relation to businesses, externalities can be defined as those economic effects of a business that are not recorded in its accounts as they do not arise from individual transactions of the business. For example, local overcrowding may arise because a large number of employees have been attracted to the neighbourhood, thus incurring extra costs for roads, schools, health care, etc. It is usually argued that governments should take steps to internalize external diseconomies, such as pollution, by means of taxation or other penalties. *See also* FREE RIDE; MARKET FAILURE.

external link A web link that takes the user to a different, usually independent, website.

extranet An *intranet extended beyond a company to its customers, suppliers, collaborators, or even competitors. Like an intranet, an extranet is password-protected to prevent access by general Internet users.

extraordinary general meeting (EGM) Any general meeting of a company other than the *annual general meeting. Most company's articles give the directors the right to call an EGM whenever they wish. Members have the right to requisition an EGM if they hold not less than 10% of the paid-up share capital; a resigning auditor may also requisition a meeting. Directors must call an EGM when there has been a serious loss of capital. The court may call an EGM if it is impracticable to call it in any other way. Those entitled to attend must be given 14 days' notice of the meeting (21 days if a special resolution is to be proposed). *See also* AGENDA; ORDER OF BUSINESS.

extraordinary items Costs or income affecting a company's *profit and loss account that do not derive from the normal activities of the company, are not expected to recur, and, if undisclosed, would distort the normal trend of profits. Such items are disclosed after the normal trading profit or loss has been shown. A wider defination of ordinary activities was introduced by *Financial Reporting Standard 3, Reporting Financial Performance, with the result that virtually all previously extraordinary items are now treated as *exceptional items.

extraordinary resolution A *resolution submitted to a general meeting of a company; 14 days' notice of such a resolution is required, and the notice should state that it is an extraordinary resolution. 75% of those voting must approve the resolution for it to be passed.

extrapolation *See* INTERPOLATION.

extrinsic motivation An incentive to

do something that arises from factors outside the individual, such as rewards or punishments. The promise of a bonus if one meets agreed performance targets is an obvious example of such *motivation. *Compare* INTRINSIC MOTIVATION. *See* EXTRINSIC REWARD.

extrinsic reward A positive outcome that is obtained by performing work but which is separate from and not inherent to the work task. The most obvious extrinsic rewards are the pay and benefits that workers receive in return for work, though others might include praise from superiors and a sense of career progression. *Compare* INTRINSIC REWARD. *See* EXTRINSIC MOTIVATION.

ex warehouse Delivery terms for goods that are available for immediate delivery, in which the buyer pays for the delivery of the goods but the seller pays for loading them onto road or rail transport. *Compare* AT WAREHOUSE.

ex works (ex factory) Delivery terms for goods in which the buyer has to pay for transporting them away from the factory that made them. In some cases, however, the seller will pay for loading them onto road or rail transport.

eyrir (*plural* **aurar**) A monetary unit of Iceland, worth one hundredth of a *króna.

faa Abbreviation for *free of all averages.

face value 1. The value printed on a banknote or coin. **2.** *See* PAR VALUE.

facility An agreement between a bank and a company that grants the company a line of credit with the bank. This can either be a *committed facility or an *uncommitted facility.

facility-sustaining activity In *activity-based costing, an *activity that is performed to sustain the organization as a whole. Examples include security, safety, maintenance, and plant management. It is not possible to identify these costs with particular products.

fact book A file containing information on the history of a product, including data on sales, distribution, competition, customers, and relevant marketing research undertaken, as well as a detailed record of the product's performance in relation to the marketing effort made on its behalf.

factor 1. A firm that engages in *factoring. **2.** An individual or firm that acts as an agent (often called a **mercantile agent**) in certain trades, usually receiving a **factorage** (commission or fee) based on the amount of sales achieved. Unlike some other forms of agent, a factor takes possession of the goods and sells them in his own name.

factor-comparison method A method of *job evaluation in which jobs are compared with each other in terms of *compensable job factors. These may include skill, effort, decision making, working conditions, and responsibility for people, finance, or equipment. Ideally, all factors should be present in all the jobs being evaluated to some degree, so that each job can be scored under each factor heading. The total scores across factors can then determine the sorting of jobs into a set of pay grades, usually by comparison with a number of *benchmark jobs. *Compare* CLASSIFICATION METHOD; HAY METHOD; JOB-COMPONENT METHOD; POINT METHOD; RANKING METHOD.

factoring The buying of the trade debts of a manufacturer, assuming the task of debt collection and accepting the credit risk, thus providing the manufacturer with working capital. **With service factoring** involves collecting the debts, assuming the credit risk, and passing on the funds as they are paid by the buyer. **With service plus finance factoring** involves paying the manufacturer up to 90% of the invoice value immediately after delivery of the goods, with the balance paid after the money has been collected. This form of factoring is clearly more expensive than with service factoring. In either case the factor, which may be a bank or finance house, has the right to select its debtors. *See also* UNDISCLOSED FACTORING.

factors of production The resources required to produce economic goods. They are land (including all natural resources), labour (including all human work and skill), *capital (including all money, assets, machinery, raw materials, etc.), and entrepreneurial ability (including organizational and management skills, inventiveness, and the willingness to take risks). For each of these factors there is a price, i.e. rent for land, wages for labour, interest for capital, and profit for the entrepreneur.

factory costs (factory expenses) The expenditure incurred by the manufacturing section of an organization. Factory costs include *direct materials, *direct labour, *direct costs, and *manufacturing overheads but not mark-up or profit.

factory overhead *See* MANUFACTURING OVERHEAD.

factory shop (factory outlet) A retailing operation owned and operated by a manufacturer to sell the manufacturer's surplus, discontinued, or irregular goods.

facultative reinsurance A form of

*reinsurance in which the terms, conditions, and reinsurance premium is individually negotiated between the insurer and the reinsurer. There is no obligation on the reinsurer to accept the risk or on the insurer to reinsure it if it is not considered necessary. The main differences between facultative reinsurance and *coinsurance is that the policyholder has no indication that reinsurance has been arranged. In coinsurance, the coinsurers and the proportion of the risk they are covering are shown on the policy schedule. Also, coinsurance involves the splitting of the premium charged to the policyholder between the coinsurers, whereas the reinsurers charge entirely separate reinsurance premiums.

fad A fashion that enters the market quickly, is adopted with great enthusiasm, peaks early, and declines rapidly. Fashion clothing and many novelty products fall into this category.

failure mode and effect analysis (FMEA) A technique for analysing how systems might fail and what the consequences of that failure would be. Primarily used to calculate and predict risks for safety and insurance purposes, FMEA identifies all the ways in which it is possible for each component to fail and then follows through the consequence of each type of failure. From this data it is possible to develop preventive maintenance and contingency plans.

failure-rate curve *See* BATH-TUB CURVE.

fair average quality *See* FAQ.

fair presentation The requirement that *financial statements should not be misleading. 'Fair presentation' is the US and *International Accounting Standards equivalent of the British requirement that financial statements give a *true and fair view.

fair trade The policy of benefiting producers in developing countries by buying such commodities as rice and coffee directly from them at a guaranteed price. In the UK, consumer demand for fairly traded products has grown rapidly in recent years.

fair value The amount of money for which it is assumed an asset or liability

could be exchanged in an *arm's length transaction between informed and willing parties. The concept is essential in *acquisition accounting.

fall-back price *See* COMMON AGRICULTURAL POLICY.

fallen angel A security in the US market that has dropped below its original value; it may be sold for its increased *yield.

falsification of accounts A dishonest entry in a firm's *books of account, made by an employee with the object of covering up the theft of goods or money from the firm.

family brand A group of brand names for the products of a company, all of which contain the same word to establish their relationship in the minds of the consumers. *See also* PRODUCT LINE.

family life cycle The six stages of family life based on demographic data: (1) young single people; (2) young couples with no children; (3) young couples with youngest child under six years; (4) couples with dependent children; (5) older couples with no children at home; (6) older single people. These groups have been useful in marketing and advertising for defining the markets for certain goods and services, as each group has its own specific and distinguishable needs and interests.

Fannie Mae Colloquial name in the USA for the *Federal National Mortgage Association (FNMA).

FAO Abbreviation for *Food and Agriculture Organization.

FAPA Abbreviation for Fellow of the Association of Authorized Public Accountants.

faq 1. Abbreviation for fair average quality. This is a trade description of certain commodities that are offered for sale on the basis that the goods supplied will be equal to the average quality of the current crop or recent shipments rather than on the basis of a specification or quality sample. **2.** Abbreviation for free alongside quay. *See* FREE ALONGSIDE SHIP. **3.** Abbreviation for frequently asked questions. Standard answers to such questions are often prepared and made available in e.g. information and instruction manuals or in the form of *automated answers.

fas Abbreviation for *free alongside ship.

FASB Abbreviation for *Financial Accounting Standards Board.

fast food Food served in restaurants or other outlets with limited and standardized menus. They are often takeaway or self-service establishments offering the same quality of product throughout the country or, in some cases, internationally.

fast-moving consumer goods (FMCG) Products that move off the shelves of retail shops quickly, which therefore require constant replenishing. Fast-moving consumer goods include standard groceries, etc., sold in supermarkets as well as records and tapes sold in music shops.

fate Whether or not a cheque or bill has been paid or dishonoured. A bank requested by another bank to *advise fate of a cheque or bill is being asked if it has been paid or not.

FATFML Abbreviation for *Financial Action Task Force on Money Laundering.

fault trees An analytical technique used to provide a model of the way components interact during the course of the failure of a system.

favourable variance See VARIANCE.

fax A widely used method of communication between businesses, linked to the international telephone system. Use of a fax machine enables messages, copies of documents, diagrams, plans, etc., to be sent for the cost of a telephone call of equal duration (approximately 30–60 seconds per A4 page). The system operates worldwide. In recent years it has been increasingly replaced by *e-mail.

FCA Abbreviation for Fellow of the *Institute of Chartered Accountants.

FCCA Abbreviation for Fellow of the Association of Chartered Certified Accountants. See CHARTERED CERTIFIED ACCOUNTANT.

FCII Abbreviation for Fellow of the *Chartered Insurance Institute.

FCIS Abbreviation for Fellow of the *Institute of Chartered Secretaries and Administrators.

FCMA Abbreviation for Fellow of the Chartered Institute of Management Accountants. See ACCOUNTANT; MANAGEMENT ACCOUNTING.

FCPA Abbreviation for *Foreign Corrupt Practices Act (1977).

FCT Abbreviation for Fellow of the *Association of Corporate Treasurers.

FDIC Abbreviation for *Federal Deposit Insurance Corporation.

feasibility study An investigation to determine which of a range of decisions is likely to give a satisfactory return in a *financial appraisal or *economic appraisal of the alternatives.

FED Abbreviation for the *Federal Reserve System.

Federal Deposit Insurance Corporation (FDIC) A corporation that provides *deposit insurance for US banks through the Bank Insurance Fund. It operates throughout the *Federal Reserve System and also for other banks outside it (see STATE BANKS).

federal funds rate The highly volatile and sensitive interest rate charged between member banks of the *Federal Reserve System. As the overnight rate paid on federal funds, it is a key indicator of money-market interest rates. Every transaction can alter the level at which the rate is fixed.

Federal Home Loan Banks Twelve regional organizations in the USA that supply credit for *savings and loans associations (the US equivalent of *building societies) and other organizations providing domestic mortgages. They are independent organizations but since 1989 they have been supervised by a five-member **Federal Housing Finance Board**. The same legislation made it a duty for district banks to provide cheap mortgage finance for borrowers on low incomes.

Federal Home Loan Mortgage Corporation (FHLMC) A corporation established in the USA in 1970 to buy mortgages from *savings and loan associations in order to resell them in the secondary market packaged as securities. The stock of the corporation is held by the *Federal Home Loan Banks. The FHLMC is usually referred to in market reports as **Freddie Mac**.

Federal National Mortgage Association (FNMA) A government sponsored privately owned company formed in the USA to trade in *mortgages, guaranteed by the Federal Housing Finance Board (*see* FEDERAL HOME LOAN BANKS). It is the largest source of housing finance in the USA. FNMA is often referred to in market reports as **Fannie Mae**.

Federal Open Market Committee (FOMC) The policy committee of the *Federal Reserve System, which sets the level of money and credit in the US banking system. Its members, the governors of the Federal Reserve Board and the presidents of the 12 *Federal Reserve Banks (seven of whom cannot vote on policy), meet monthly and regulate the money supply by instructing the federal banks to buy or sell securities.

Federal Reserve Bank Any of the 12 banks that together form the *Federal Reserve System in the USA; they are situated in Boston, New York, Philadelphia, Cleveland, Richmond, Atlanta, Chicago, St Louis, Minneapolis, Kansas City, Dallas, and San Francisco. They provide *central bank services and are involved with the Federal Reserve Board of Governors in developing and enacting monetary policy, as well as regulating local commercial and savings banks. Each Federal Reserve Bank is owned by the local banks in its district.

Federal Reserve System (FED) The organization, consisting of the 12 *Federal Reserve Banks, that functions as the *central bank of the USA. Created by the Federal Reserve Act (1913), the system controls monetary policy, regulates the cost of money and the money supply to local banks, and supervises international banking by means of its agreement with the central banks of other countries. The system is administered centrally by the **Federal Reserve Board**, based in Washington DC.

Federal Trade Commission (FTC) US government agency established in 1915 by the Federal Trade Commission Act (1914) to promote free and fair competition in interstate commerce and to prevent unfair methods of competition. Its wide brief covers takeovers, mergers, cartels, price fixing, and fraudulent advertising.

Fed funds (Federal funds) Non-interest-bearing deposits held at the US *Federal Reserve System that are traded between member banks.

FEDMA Abbreviation for Federation of European Direct Marketing Associations.

fedwire A high-speed electronic link in the USA between the 12 *Federal Reserve Banks and the Treasury, used to move large sums of money for themselves and their customers. The transactions are often completed within minutes of being initiated.

feedback Information or opinions about the performance of a product, system, intervention (e.g. a *management development or training program), or employee. Important sources of feedback include clients and customers, users of a product or system, and an employee's supervisors or fellow workers. Regular and reliable feedback is essential to *employee evaluation and *performance appraisal, and its absence may be detrimental to *job satisfaction (*see* CORE JOB CHARACTERISTICS). Feedback also plays a key role in modern management philosophies of *continuous improvement, such as *total quality management. *See* MULTISOURCE FEEDBACK.

feedback control A method for controlling the performance of an *operating system by monitoring outputs and comparing them with the system's design parameters. Because the approach is based on past activities it is essentially reactive. Although it may allow adjustments to be made to avoid problems in the future, it cannot avoid the cost of the original divergence from targets. *Compare* CONCURRENT CONTROL; FEEDFORWARD CONTROL.

feedforward control An approach to controlling the performance of an *operating system that attempts to forecast a future state and to take the necessary action before problems arise. For example, in a *statistical process control system the operation may remain in control, but knowledge of the system enables the operator to extrapolate trends in control data and to take the action necessary to avoid the system becoming out of control. The success of this approach is dependent on the ability to predict the consequences of a particular event. *Compare* CONCURRENT CONTROL; FEEDBACK CONTROL.

fee simple The most usual freehold *estate in land. Although all land in England is theoretically held by the Crown, the owner of a fee simple (or his or her heirs) will own the land forever and may dispose of it as they wish both during the lifetime of the owner and by will. The land will revert to the Crown only if the owner dies without leaving a will and with no surviving relatives. This is the only type of freehold estate that can now exist in common law, as opposed to in equity.

fen A monetary unit of China worth one hundredth of a *yuan.

FHLMC Abbreviation for *Federal Home Loan Mortgage Corporation.

FIA Abbreviation for Fellow of the *Institute of Actuaries.

fiat money Money that a government has declared to be legal tender, although it has no intrinsic value and is not backed by reserves. Most of the world's paper money is now fiat money.

fictitious asset An *asset shown in a balance sheet that does not exist. The asset may have been inadvertently left on the books despite having ceased to exist or no longer having any value (as with *goodwill), alternatively, it may be shown as part of a deliberate fraud.

fidelity guarantee An insurance policy covering employers for any financial losses they may sustain as a result of the dishonesty of employees. Policies can be arranged to cover all employees or specific named persons. Because of the nature of the cover, insurers require full details of the procedure adopted by the organization in recruiting and vetting new employees and they usually reserve the right to refuse to cover a particular person without giving a reason.

fiduciary Denoting a person who holds property in trust or as an executor. Persons acting in a fiduciary capacity do so not for their own profit but to safeguard the interests of some other person or persons.

fiduciary deposit Funds deposited in a bank and managed for the benefit of the depositor by the bank.

fiduciary issue Banknotes issued by a central bank without backing in gold, the value of the issues relying entirely on the reputation of the issuing bank.

fiduciary loan A loan that is made on trust, rather than against some security.

field experiments Marketing tests conducted outside the laboratory in a real market environment. *See* TEST MARKETING.

field sales manager A district or regional sales manager (so called because his or her main concern is the control of salespeople in the field). The primary task of the field sales manager is to motivate and supervise sales personnel. Depending on the organization, the field sales manager may also be involved in setting salesforce objectives, designing the strategy, and recruiting, selecting, training, and evaluating the field sales personnel.

field selling Non-retail selling that takes place outside the employer's place of business, usually on the prospective customer's premises. The sales personnel involved are the company's personal link with customers and can bring back to the company much needed information about the customers.

FIFO cost Abbreviation for *first in first out cost.

file In computer technology, a collection of related information held on backing store that is treated as a unit. A file may contain data of any kind.

file server *See* SERVER; LOCAL AREA NETWORK.

file transfer protocol *See* FTP.

fillér A monetary unit of Hungary worth one hundredth of a *forint.

fils **1.** A monetary unit of the United Arab Emirates, worth one hundredth of a *dirham. **2.** A monetary unit of Bahrain, Iraq, Jordan, and Kuwait, worth one thousandth of a *dinar. **3.** A monetary unit of Yemen, worth one hundredth of a *riyal.

FIMBRA Abbreviation for Financial Intermediaries, Managers and Brokers Regulatory Association Ltd. *See* PERSONAL INVESTMENT AUTHORITY.

final accounts The *annual accounts produced at the end of a company's financial year as opposed to any interim accounts produced during the year.

final dividend *See* DIVIDEND.

final invoice An invoice that replaces a *proforma invoice for goods. The proforma invoice is sent before all the details of the goods are known. The final invoice contains any missing information and states the full amount still owing for the goods.

final salary scheme An occupational pension scheme in which payments are determined by the employee's final salary. *See* DEFINED-BENEFIT PENSION SCHEME.

finance **1.** The practice of manipulating and managing money. **2.** The capital involved in a project, especially the capital that has to be raised to start a new business. **3.** A loan of money for a particular purpose, especially by a *finance house. **4.** An academic discipline within the general field of economics dealing with funding, financial markets, and the funding implications for managing businesses.

Finance Act The annual UK Act of Parliament that changes the law relating to taxation, giving the rates of income tax, corporation tax, etc., proposed in the preceding *Budget.

finance bill A *bill of exchange used for short-term credit. It cannot be sold on to another party in the same way as a *banker's acceptance.

finance company A company that provides finance, normally in the form of loans. As it tends to finance ventures with a high risk factor, the cost of borrowing is likely to be higher than that made by a clearing bank.

finance house An organization, many of which are owned by *commercial banks, that provides finance for *hire-purchase or *leasing agreements. A consumer, who buys an expensive item (such as a car) from a trader and does not wish to pay cash, enters into a hire-purchase contract with the finance house, who collects the deposit and instalments. The finance house pays the trader the cash price in full, borrowing from the commercial banks in order to do so. The finance house's profit is the difference between the low rate of interest it pays to the commercial banks to borrow and the high rate it charges the consumer.

finance lease A lease in which the lessee acquires all the financial benefits and risks attaching to ownership of whatever is being leased. In accounting, it is as if the business owned the assets. *Compare* OPERATING LEASE.

finance vehicle An entity set up by a company to obtain some financial benefit. The setting up of overseas companies to lower tax liabilities is a prime example of a finance vehicle.

financial accounting The branch of accounting concerned with classifying, measuring, and recording the transactions of a business. At the end of a period, usually a year but sometimes less, a *profit and loss account, a *balance sheet, a *statement of total recognized gains and losses, and a *cash-flow statement are prepared to show the performance and position of the business. Financial accounting is primarily concerned with providing a *true and fair view of the activities of a business to parties external to it. To ensure that this is done correctly considerable attention will be paid to *accounting concepts and to any requirements of legislation, accounting standards, and (where appropriate) the regulations of the *stock exchange. Financial accounting can be separated into a number of specific activities, such as conducting *audits, *taxation, book-keeping, and *insolvency. **Financial accountants** need not be qualified, in that they need not belong to an accountancy body, although the majority of those working in public practice will be. *Compare* MANAGEMENT ACCOUNTING.

Financial Accounting Standards Board (FASB) The US body that sets accounting standards. Owing to its close relationship with the *Securities and

Exchange Commission, companies that wish for a market listing have to comply with its standards.

Financial Action Task Force on Money Laundering (FATFML) An organization founded in 1989 by the *Organization for Economic Cooperation and Development to curtail the practice of *laundering money, chiefly by persuading individual governments to legislate against it.

financial adviser 1. Anyone who offers financial advice to someone else, especially one who advises on *investments. *See also* INDEPENDENT FINANCIAL ADVISER. **2.** An organization, usually a merchant bank, who advises the board of a company during a takeover (*see* TAKEOVER BID).

financial appraisal The use of financial evaluation techniques to determine which of a range of possible alternatives is preferred. Financial appraisal usually refers to the use of *discounted cash flow techniques but it may also be applied to any other approaches used to assess a business problem in financial terms, such as *ratio analysis, *profitability index, or risk analysis. *Compare* ECONOMIC APPRAISAL.

financial control (financial management) The actions of the management of an organization taken to ensure that the costs incurred and revenue generated are at acceptable levels. Financial control is assisted by the provision of financial information to management by the accountant and by the use of such techniques as *budgetary control and *standard costing, which highlight and analyse any *variances.

financial crisis A collapse in the price of financial obligations, which may lead to a collapse in the economy. The major financial crisis in the history of world finance took place after the Wall Street Crash of 1929. This crisis led to a widespread failure in the US banking system and the interwar recession. Recent years have seen a number of financial crises, notably in Russia, South-East Asia, and Latin America. These crises have had major impacts on the economies of the countries that suffered them, but the impacts have not spread to the international economy.

financial distress The situation in which the activity of a business is influenced by the possibility of impending insolvency. The costs of distress can be divided into those related to bankruptcy and those incurred without bankruptcy. The costs of bankruptcy are those directly incurred in winding up or restructuring the business. The costs short of bankruptcy are those arising from a sudden change in suppliers' and customers' behaviour, prompted by their concerns over dealing with a potentially insolvent firm. They also include costs engendered by the diversion of managerial focus and conflicts between stakeholders, notably managers, debt holders, and shareholders. As a firm increases the level of its debt or *gearing, so the costs of financial distress will rise (and hence the cost of funding). The costs of financial distress are an important factor in determining the firm's level of gearing.

financial futures A *futures contract in currencies, interest rates (*see* INTEREST-RATE FUTURES), or other financial assets. The contract is a standard one, which is exchange-traded. Until about 1970 trading in financial futures did not exist, although futures and options were dealt in widely on *commodity markets. However, instantaneous trading across the world coupled with accelerated international capital flows combined to produce great volatility in interest rates, stock-market prices, and currency exchanges. The result has been an environment in which organizations and individuals responsible for managing large sums need a financial futures and options market both to manage risks effectively and as a source of additional profit. In the UK financial futures and options are traded on the *London International Financial Futures and Options Exchange (LIFFE). *See also* HEDGE; INDEX FUTURES; PORTFOLIO INSURANCE.

financial gearing *See* GEARING; DEBT–EQUITY RATIO.

financial institution An organization whose core activity is to provide financial services or advice in relation to financial products. Financial institutions include state bodies, such as central banks, and private companies, such as banks, savings and loan associations, and also financial markets. At one time there was a clear distinction and regulatory division between *deposit-taking institutions, such as banks, and non-deposit-taking institutions, such as brokers or life-insurance companies. This is no longer the case; brokers and other companies now often invest funds for their clients with banks and in the money markets.

financial instrument A contract involving a financial obligation. Examples are stocks, bonds, loans, and derivatives.

Financial Intermediaries, Managers and Brokers Regulatory Association Ltd (FIMBRA) *See* PERSONAL INVESTMENT AUTHORITY.

financial intermediary 1. An institution, be it a bank, building society, finance house, insurance company, investment trust, etc., that holds funds borrowed from lenders in order to make loans to borrowers. **2.** In the *Financial Services Act (1986), a person or organization that sells insurance but is not directly employed by an insurance company (e.g. a broker, insurance agent, bank). *See also* INDEPENDENT INTERMEDIARY.

financial investment *See* INVESTMENT.

financial leverage *See* GEARING.

financial management *See* FINANCIAL CONTROL.

financial modelling The construction and use of planning and decision models based on financial data to simulate actual circumstances in order to facilitate decision making within an organization. The financial models used include *discounted cash flow, *economic order quantity, *decision trees, *learning curves, and *budgetary control.

Financial Ombudsman Service (FOS) A UK body set up to deal with complaints in relation to financial services and products. It was established by the *Financial Services and Markets Act (2000) to replace a number of separate complaint schemes: the Banking Ombudsman; Building Societies Ombudsman; Insurance Ombudsman; Investment Ombudsman; and Pensions Ombudsman.

financial perspective *See* BALANCED SCORECARD.

financial planning The formulation of short-term and long-term plans in financial terms for the purposes of establishing goals for an organization to achieve, against which its actual performance can be measured.

financial report The *financial statements of a company. *See also* ANNUAL ACCOUNTS.

Financial Reporting Council (FRC) A UK body set up in 1990, following the recommendation of the *Dearing Report, to promote good financial reporting. There are five operating bodies: the *Financial Reporting Review Panel, the *Accounting Standards Board, the Auditing Practices Board, the Professional Oversight Board for Accountancy, and the Accountancy Investigation and Discipline Board. Its members are appointed by the Secretary of State for Trade and Industry.

Financial Reporting Review Panel (FRRP) An operating body of the *Financial Reporting Council, which acts as its sole director. The panel investigates departures from the accounting requirements of the Companies Acts and is empowered to take legal action to remedy any such departures. Its remit covers the financial reports of public companies and large private companies.

Financial Reporting Standard (FRS) Any of a series of standards issued by the *Accounting Standards Board. Many of the more recent FRSs have the aim of harmonizing UK practice with the standards published by the *International Accounting Standards Board. See box on p. 217.

financial risk The *risk that an organization will not be able to meet its monetary commitments, notably any debt-related payments.

financials A shorthand term for the *financial statements of an organization.

Financial Services Act (1986) A UK act of parliament that came into force in April 1988. Its main objectives were to regulate investment business, providing investors with greater protection, and to promote competition in the savings industry. These objectives were to be achieved by means of the *Securities and Investment Board and its *Self-Regulating Orga-

---

FINANCIAL REPORTING STANDARDS

1. Cash Flow Statements, issued 1991, revised 1996
2. Accounting for Subsidiary Undertakings, issued 1992, amended 2004
3. Reporting Financial Performance, issued 1992
4. Capital Instruments, issued 1993, now superseded by FRS 25 below
5. Reporting the Substance of Transactions, issued 1994, amended 1994, 1998, 2003
6. Acquisitions and Mergers, issued 1994
7. Fair Values in Acquisition Accounting, issued 1994
8. Related Party Transactions, issued 1995
9. Associates and Joint Ventures, issued 1997
10. Goodwill and Intangible Assets, issued 1997
11. Impairment of Fixed Assets and Goodwill, issued 1998
12. Provisions, Contingent Liabilities and Contingent Assets, issued 1998
13. Derivatives and Other Financial Instruments: Disclosures, issued 1998
14. Earnings Per Share, issued 1998, now superseded by FRS 22 below
15. Tangible Fixed Assets, issued 1999
16. Current Tax, issued 1999
17. Retirement Benefits, issued 2000, revised 2002
18. Accounting Policies, issued 2000
19. Deferred Tax, issued 2000
20. Share-based Payment, issued 2004
21. Events After the Balance Sheet Date, issued 2004
22. Earnings Per Share, issued 2004
23. The Effects of Change in Foreign Exchange Rates, issued 2004
24. Financial Reporting in Hyperinflationary Economies, issued 2004
25. Financial Instruments: Disclosures and Presentation, issued 2004
26. Financial Instruments: Measurement, issued 2004
27. Life Assurance, issued 2004
28. Corresponding Amounts, issued 2005
29. Financial Instruments: Disclosures, issued 2005

---

nizations. It provided legislation for many of the recommendations of the *Gower Report. In 2000 the Act was superseded by the *Financial Services and Markets Act.

Financial Services and Markets Act (2000) Legislation, implemented in November 2001, establishing a regulatory framework for UK banking, insurance, and investment. Under the terms of the Act, the *Financial Services Authority became the key regulator, taking over functions from the Bank of England, the Building Societies Commission, and the Treasury. However, the Bank of England still retains a regulatory interest where systemic risk to the UK financial system is concerned. *See also* FINANCIAL OMBUDSMAN SERVICE.

Financial Services Authority (FSA) An independent, nongovernmental body that regulates the financial services industry in the UK. It was set up in 1997 and given statutory powers by the Financial Services and Markets Act (2000). The FSA is financed by the industry and its board, which consists of a chairman, a chief executive officer, three managing directors, and 11 nonexecutive directors (including the deputy chairman), is appointed by the Treasury. The Financial Services and Markets Act specifies four statutory objectives for the FSA:

- to maintain market confidence;
- to promote public understanding of the financial system;
- to ensure a satisfactory degree of consumer protection;
- to reduce the extent to which it is possible for a business carried on by a regu-

lated person to be used for a purpose connected with financial crime.

Financial Services Compensation Scheme A body established under the UK *Financial Services and Markets Act (2000) to provide compensation to customers of insolvent businesses or to those who have incurred losses as a result of bad financial advice.

Financial Services Directive An EU directive (1996) on the regulation of financial services. It is based on the principle that a firm authorized to undertake business in one EU state under local regulations should be able to conduct business in any other member state. It also provides for the harmonization of minimum standards.

Financial Services Modernization Act (1999) (Gramm–Leach–Bliley Act) Legislation enacted in the USA that removed the restrictions on banks undertaking securities business that had been imposed by the *Glass–Steagall Act (1933). It also empowered companies to set up financial holding companies to supply banking, insurance, and investment services.

financial-statement analysis Analysis of the *financial statements of a company to assess its position and performance. The standard analysis will consider the business from the perspectives of managerial performance, liquidity, and stock-exchange performance. *See* ACCOUNTING RATIO; RATIO ANALYSIS.

Financial Statement and Budget Report (FSBR) The document published by the Chancellor of the Exchequer on Budget Day. It summarizes the provisions of the *Budget as given in the Chancellor's speech to the House of Commons. It is sometimes known as the **Red Book**.

financial statements The annual statements summarizing a company's activities over the last year. They consist of the *profit and loss account, *balance sheet, *statement of total recognized gains and losses, and, if required, the *cash-flow statement, together with supporting notes.

Financial Statistics A monthly publication of the UK *Office for National Sta-

tistics giving a full account of financial statistics.

Financial Times Share Indexes A number of share indexes published by the *Financial Times* as a barometer of share prices on the London Stock Exchange. See feature THE FINANCIAL TIMES SHARE INDEXES on p. 219.

financial year 1. Any year connected with finance, such as a company's *accounting period or a year for which budgets are made up. **2.** In the UK, a specific period relating to *corporation tax, i.e. the 12 months beginning on 1 April in one year and ending on 31 March in the next year. Corporation-tax rates are fixed for specific financial years by the Chancellor in the Budget; if a company's accounting period falls into two financial years the profits have to be apportioned to the relevant financial years to find the rates of tax applicable. *Compare* FISCAL YEAR.

financier A person who finances a business deal or venture or who makes arrangements for such a deal or venture to be financed by a merchant bank or other *financial institution. The term often implies a hands-on approach, in addition to providing finance.

fine paper *See* FIRST-CLASS PAPER.

fine trade bill A *bill of exchange that is acceptable to the Bank of England as security, when acting as *lender of last resort. It will be backed by a first-class bank or finance house.

fine tuning The implementation of economic policy, in particular monetary and fiscal policy, by means of small, incremental policy changes. Doubt has been cast on any real possibility of fine-tuning economies, given their lack of short-term forecastability. Critics argue that, if an economy is impossible to forecast in detail, then it follows that it is also impossible to determine appropriate short-term incremental policies.

finished goods stock (finished goods inventory) The value of goods that have completed the manufacturing process and are available for distribution to customers. In any accounting period there will be *opening stock of finished goods at the beginning of the period and *closing stock

THE FINANCIAL TIMES SHARE INDEXES

The **Financial Times-Stock Exchange** (**FTSE**) **Actuaries Share Indexes** are calculated by the Institute of Actuaries and the Faculty of Actuaries as weighted arithmetic averages for 10 broad sectors of the market (general industrial, cyclical consumer goods, etc.), which are further divided into 34 industry subsectors. They are widely used by investors and portfolio managers.

The widest measure of the market is provided by the **FTSE Actuaries All-Share Index** of over 700 shares and fixed-interest stocks, which includes a selection from the financial sector. Calculated after the end of daily business, it covers over 98% of the market and some 90% of turnover by value.

For many years the **Financial Times Ordinary Share Index** (**FT 30**) was the main day-to-day market barometer. It records the movements of 30 leading industrial and commercial shares, chosen to be representative of British industry rather than of the Stock Exchange as a whole; it therefore excludes banks, insurance companies, and government stocks. The index, which started from a base of 100 in 1935, is an unweighted geometric average, calculated hourly during the day and closing at 4.30 pm.

The FT 30 continues to be published but has been superseded as the main indicator of market activity by the **Financial Times-Stock Exchange 100 Share Index** (**FTSE 100** or **Footsie**), a weighted arithmetic index representing the price of 100 securities with a base of 1000 on 3 January 1984. This index is calculated minute-by-minute and its constituents, whose membership is by market capitalization above £1 billion, are reviewed quarterly.

In 1992 the UK index series was extended to create two further real-time indexes, the **FTSE 250**, comprising companies capitalized between £150 million and £1 billion, and the **FTSE 350**, which aggregates the FTSE 100 and the FTSE 250. Both are based on 31 December 1985 and are calculated both inclusive and exclusive of investment companies. The FTSE 350 is the source for the **FTSE 350 Supersectors**, a series of 18 indexes based on industry baskets that provide an instant view of industry performance across the market. The baskets correspond roughly to sectors defined by markets in New York and Tokyo.

There are also several indexes for smaller companies. The **FTSE SmallCap Index** covers over 350 companies capitalized between £20 million and £150 million; it is calculated at the end of the day's business, both including and excluding investment trusts. The **FTSE Fledgling Index** covers all those companies that are too small to be included in the SmallCap Index but that meet the other criteria for inclusion in the UK index series. The mainly smaller companies on the London Stock Exchange's *Alternative Investment Market are covered by the **FTSE AIM Index**.

The **Financial Times Government Securities Index** measures the movements of government stocks (gilts).

Several indexes now measure the performance of companies resident and incorporated in the European Union. These include the **Euro-Top 100 Index** of the 100 most highly capitalized EU companies, the **FTSE Euro 100 Index** of *eurozone companies, and the **FTSE New EU Index**, which covers the markets of the ten countries that joined the EU in May 2004. In 2003 FTSE Ltd launched the Eurofirst Index series in conjunction with the cross-border derivatives exchange Euronext NV; the most important of these is the **FTSE Eurofirst 300 Index** of blue-chip European companies.

The **FTSE All-World Index** was launched in 1987 and now covers over 2700 share prices from 48 countries. With sectors for the developed world and the emerging economies, it is calculated daily and published in sterling, euros, US dollars, and yen.

of finished goods at the end of the period. Methods of valuing finished goods stock are covered by Statement of Standard Accounting Practice 9 and may include *first-in-first-out cost or *average cost methods.

finite capacity loading *Loading based on the assumption that capacity is finite, i.e. cannot be increased. This parameter aligns load to the available capacity, enabling realistic lead times to be calculated. Compare INFINITE CAPACITY LOADING.

fire insurance An insurance policy covering financial losses caused by damage to property by fires. Most fire insurance policies also include cover for damage caused by lightning and explosions of boilers or gas used for domestic purposes. On payment of an additional premium, fire insurers are usually prepared to widen the cover to include such special perils as those arising from various weather-related or man-made causes.

firewall 1. In a conglomerate, a barrier created between the organization, funding, and ownership of one business entity and those of other entities in the group, so that problems experienced by the one do not affect others. **2.** A system usually inserted between a *local area network and the *Internet to filter incoming traffic, to try to eliminate viral infection, and to restrict the access of *hackers to the system. It may create a bottleneck in the transmission of data to and from the system.

firm 1. Any business organization. **2.** A business partnership.

firm commitment 1. An undertaking by a bank to lend up to a maximum sum over a period at a specified rate; a *commitment fee usually has to be paid by the borrower, which is not returned if the loan is not taken up. **2.** In the USA, an agreement in which an underwriter of a flotation assumes the risk that not all the securities issued will be sold, by guaranteeing to buy all the excess securities at the offer price. **3.** Any binding commitment to enter into an agreement.

firm offer An offer to sell goods that remains in force for a stated period. For example, an "offer firm for 24 hours" binds the seller to sell if the buyer accepts the offer within 24 hours. If the buyer makes a lower *bid during the period that the offer is firm, the offer ceases to be valid. An offer that is not firm is usually called a *quotation.

firm order An order to a broker (for securities, commodities, currencies, etc.) that remains firm for a stated period or until cancelled. A broker who has a firm order from a principal does not have to refer back if the terms of the order can be executed in the stated period.

firmware Computer programs or data that are stored in a memory chip. These are often built into a computer to make it unnecessary to load the programs or data from disk or from the keyboard. Wordprocessing programs, for example, on read-only memory (ROM) chips are built into some business computer systems. Firmware is also used where absolute reliability is required, for example in air-traffic control.

first-class paper (fine paper) A *money-market instrument that is backed by a bank with a high credit rating.

first-in-first-out cost (FIFO cost) A method of valuing units of *raw material or *finished goods issued from stock based on using the earliest unit value for pricing the issues until all the stock received at that price has been used up. The next latest price is then used for pricing the issues, and so on. Because the issues are based on a FIFO cost, the valuation of closing stocks is described as being on the same FIFO basis. The method may also be used in *process costing to value the work in process at the end of an accounting period. Compare LAST-IN-FIRST-OUT COST; NEXT-IN-FIRST-OUT COST.

first-loss policy A property insurance policy in which the policyholder arranges cover for an amount below the full value of the items insured and the insurer agrees not to penalize him for under-insurance. The main use of these policies is in circumstances in which a total loss is virtually impossible. For example, a large warehouse may contain £2.5M worth of wines and spirits but the owner may feel that no more than £500,000 worth could be stolen at any one time. The solution is a first-loss policy that deals with all claims up to £500,000 but pays no more than this

221

fixed capital formation

figure if more is stolen. First-loss policies differ from *coinsurance agreements with the policyholders because the insured is not involved in claims below the first-loss level and the premiums are not calculated proportionately. In the above example, the premium might be as much as 80–90% of the premium on the full value.

first mortgage debenture A *debenture with the first charge over property owned by a company. Such debentures are most commonly issued by property companies.

first notice day 1. The date on which a seller in a futures market contract gives notice of an intention to deliver according to the terms of a particular *futures contract. **2.** The date on which the buyer is notified of such an arrangement.

first of exchange See BILLS IN A SET.

first preferred stock In the USA, *preferred stock with prior rights where dividends are concerned or in the event of liquidation.

first-tier market The main market on which the equity of large companies is traded. There is customarily a high level of regulation and supervision in such markets. Compare SECOND-TIER MARKET.

first-year allowance In the UK, a special *capital allowance against *corporation tax that is granted in the year of purchase of an asset in place of the standard *writing-down allowance of 25%. Various first-year allowances have been made available at various times. In 2000–03, for example, small businesses that invested in computer and Internet technology were able to claim 100% first-year allowances. A 100% allowance is currently available to businesses that invest in energy-saving technology.

fiscal agent 1. A third party who acts on behalf of a bond issuer to pay subscribers to the issue and generally assist the issuer. **2.** An agent for one of the national *financial institutions in the USA who acts as an adviser, for example, to the National Mortgage Association for its debt securities. **3.** In the USA, an agent empowered to collect taxes, revenues, and duties on behalf of the government. For example, the *Federal Reserve Banks perform this function for the US Treasury.

fiscal drag The deflationary impact on a country's economy of a steady increase in tax revenues. Because most developed countries have progressive rates of taxation, the proportion of national income paid in taxes rises as national income grows.

fiscal year In the UK, the year beginning on 6 April in one year and ending on 5 April in the next year. The 2005–06 fiscal year therefore runs from 6 April 2005 to 5 April 2006. *Income tax, *capital gains tax, and annual allowances for *inheritance tax are all computed for fiscal years and the UK Budget estimates refer to the fiscal year. In the USA the fiscal year now runs from 1 October to the following 30 September. The fiscal year is sometimes called the **tax year** or **year of assessment**. Compare FINANCIAL YEAR.

fish-bone diagram See CAUSE–EFFECT DIAGRAM.

fixed asset (capital asset) An asset of a business intended for continuing use, rather than a short-term *current asset (such as stock). Fixed assets must be classified in a company's *balance sheet as intangible, tangible, or investments. Examples of *intangible assets include *goodwill, *patents, and *trademarks. Examples of tangible fixed assets include land and buildings, plant and machinery, fixtures and fittings. Fixed assets must be written off to the *profit and loss account over their useful economic life; this is effected by the *amortization of intangible fixed assets and the *depreciation of tangible fixed assets. An investment included as a fixed asset is shown at its purchase price, market value, or directors' valuation, or using the equity method of accounting (see EQUITY ACCOUNTING).

fixed capital The amount of an organization's *capital that is tied up in its *fixed assets.

fixed capital formation An investment over a given period, as used in the national income accounts. It consists primarily of investment in manufacturing and housing. **Gross fixed capital formation** is the total amount of expenditure on investment, while **net fixed capital formation** includes a deduction for the *depreciation of existing capital.

fixed charge 1. *See* CHARGE. **2.** The part of an expense that remains unchanged, irrespective of the amount of the commodity or service used or consumed. For example, in the UK both the electricity and gas industries operate tariffs consisting of a fixed charge, which remains unchanged irrespective of the consumption of energy, and a variable charge, based on the energy consumed.

fixed cost (fixed expense) An item of expenditure that remains unchanged, in total, irrespective of changes in the levels of production or sales. Examples are business rates, rent, and some salaries. *Compare* SEMI-VARIABLE COST; VARIABLE COST.

fixed debenture A *debenture that has a *fixed charge as security. *Compare* FLOATING DEBENTURE.

fixed exchange rate A *rate of exchange between one currency and another that is fixed by government and maintained by that government's economic policy and its buying or selling its currency to support or depress it. *Compare* FLOATING EXCHANGE RATE.

fixed-for-fixed Denoting a *currency swap in which both parties pay a fixed rate of interest.

fixed-for-floating Denoting an *interest-rate swap or *cross-currency interest-rate swap in which one party pays a fixed rate, while the other pays a floating rate.

fixed-interest security A type of *security that gives a fixed stated interest payment. They include *gilt-edged securities, *bonds, *preference shares, and *debentures; as they entail less risk than *equities they offer less scope for capital appreciation. They do, however, often give a better *yield than equities.

The prices of fixed-interest securities tend to move inversely with the general level of interest rates, reflecting changes in the value of their fixed yield relative to the market. Fixed-interest securities tend to be particularly poor investments at times of high and increasing inflation as their value does not adjust to changes in the price level. To overcome this problem some gilts now give index-linked interest payments.

fixed overhead cost The elements of the *indirect costs of an organization's product that, in total, remain unchanged irrespective of changes in the levels of production or sales. Examples include administrative salaries, sales personnel salaries, and rent.

fixed-price tender A bid to undertake an activity for a given price. *See* TENDER.

fixed production overhead The elements of an organization's *manufacturing overheads that, in total, remain unchanged irrespective of changes in the level of production or sales. Examples include factory rent, depreciation of machinery using the *straight-line method, and the factory manager's salary.

fixed-rate loan A loan on which the interest rate is fixed at the start of the loan.

fixed-rate mortgage A *mortgage in which the rate of interest paid by the borrower is fixed, usually for the first few years of the loan.

fixed spot A television advertising spot for which a premium is paid (normally 15%) to ensure that it is transmitted in a preselected commercial break during a particular programme.

fixtures and fittings Items normally forming part of the setting in which an organization conducts its business, as distinct from the *plant and machinery it uses in conducting the business.

flag of convenience The national flag of a small country, such as Panama, Liberia, Honduras, or Costa Rica, flown by a ship that is registered in one of these countries, although the ship is owned by a national of another country. The practice of registering ships in these countries, and sailing them under flags of convenience, grew up in the post-war years and still continues. The object for the shipowners is to avoid taxation and the more stringent safety and humanitarian conditions imposed on ships and their crews by the larger sea-going nations.

flash report In the USA, a management report that highlights key data for corrective action.

flat tax (proportional tax) A tax with a single rate (as opposed to one in which the rate of tax increases with the size of the *tax base) and with no reliefs or exemptions apart from a standard personal allowance. In recent years a flat rate of income tax has been introduced in Russia and a number of Eastern European economies. The advantages claimed for such a system are that it is very simple to understand and operate, thereby reducing administrative costs for both government and business, that it eliminates many forms of tax avoidance, that the abolition of the higher-rate tax bands encourages enterprise and wealth creation, and that the raising of the threshold at which people begin to pay tax benefits the lowest earners (who also gain from the elimination of poverty traps). Opponents argue that it denies governments flexibility in setting tax policy and offends against the *ability to pay principle by shifting the burden of tax from the wealthiest to those on middle incomes. *Compare* PROGRESSIVE TAX; REGRESSIVE TAX. *See also* SINGLE-TAX SYSTEM.

flat yield *See* YIELD.

fleet rating A single special premium rate quoted by an insurer for covering the insurance on a number of ships or vehicles owned by one person or company, rather than considering each one individually. The fleet need not consist of identical vehicles or vessels but common ownership is essential. A common method of fleet rating is to examine the claims history of the fleet against the total premium. In this way one fleet member may have several claims (which would individually merit a premium adjustment) but if the rest of the fleet is claim-free no adjustment need be made. Insurers vary on the minimum number constituting a fleet.

flexibility The ability to adapt an *operating system to respond to changes in the environment. Increasingly seen as a source of competitive advantage in a rapidly changing market, it is an area of *operations management in which Japanese practices have had a major impact. Flexibility has two dimensions: how quickly and how far an organization can change. Changes may be called for in terms of the product or service, i.e. the

flexibility to introduce new products; mix flexibility is the ability to provide a wide range or mix of products; volume flexibility is the ability to produce different volumes to suit demand; delivery flexibility is the ability to change (usually advance) the delivery date.

flexible budget A budget that takes into account the fact that values for income and expenditure on some items will change with changing circumstances. Consequently, in a flexible budget the *budget cost allowances for each variable cost item will change to allow for the actual levels of activity achieved. A budget that has been adjusted in this way is known as a **flexed budget**.

flexible drawdown The *drawdown in stages of funds available under a credit agreement.

flexible manufacturing system (FMS) An automated and computerized production line that can be reprogrammed to produce more than one product line. Use of a flexible manufacturing system enables companies to lower costs and vary production quickly in response to changes in consumer demand. The ability to reprogramme machines by means of software rather than the physical set-up makes FMS particularly applicable to handling batches of a fairly small range of products.

flexible mortgage A *mortgage on a property in which the lender (mortgagee) allows a measure of flexibility in the repayments made by the borrower (mortgagor). In some flexible mortgages the borrower may overpay on the nominal repayments in order to pay off the debt more quickly. Others permit underpayments or even a repayment holiday for one instalment. Some flexible mortgages offer loans including all these concessions.

flexible working Employees who have children aged under 6 or a disabled child aged under 18 now have the legal right to request a change in their working hours and conditions, including the option of working from home. Although employers have no obligation to grant such a request, they are legally obliged to consider it seriously and to give a written explanation for any refusal.

flexitime (flexihours) A system of working, especially in offices, in which employees are given a degree of flexibility in the hours they work. Provided they work an agreed number of hours per day, they may start or finish work at different times. The object is usually to reduce time spent in rush-hour travelling or to adjust work schedules to other demands, such as responsibility for children.

flier *See* FREE-STANDING STUFFER.

flight to quality A movement of investors into safer assets in times of uncertainty. Government securities, *blue-chip stocks, short-term government debt, gold, and US investments all typify the type of assets that are bought at such times.

flip-flop FRN A perpetual *floating-rate note (i.e. one without redemption), which can be converted into a short-term note of up to four years' maturity and back again into a perpetual FRN.

float **1.** In the USA, the proportion of a corporation's stocks that are held by the public rather than the corporation. **2.** Money created as a result of a delay in processing cheques, e.g. when one account is credited before the paying bank's account has been debited. **3.** Money set aside as a contingency fund or an advance to be reimbursed. **4.** *See* SLACK TIME. **5.** *See* FLOTATION.

floater A colloquial name for a *floating-rate note.

floating charge *See* CHARGE.

floating debenture A *debenture that has a floating *charge as security. *Compare* FIXED DEBENTURE.

floating debt **1.** The part of the national debt that consists primarily of short-term *Treasury bills. *Compare* FUNDED DEBT. *See also* FUNDING OPERATIONS. **2.** Short-term borrowing (i.e. for less than one year). **3.** Debt with a floating rate of interest.

floating exchange rate A *rate of exchange between one currency and others that is permitted to float according to market forces. Most major currencies and countries now have floating exchange rates but governments and central banks intervene, buying or selling currencies

when rates become too high or too low. *Compare* FIXED EXCHANGE RATE.

floating policy An insurance policy that has only one sum insured although it may cover many items. No division of the total is shown on the policy and the policyholder is often able to add or remove items from the cover without reference to the insurers, provided that the total sum insured is not exceeded. Cover for contractors' plant and machinery is often arranged on this basis, because it enables them to purchase specialist equipment for a particular contract, without having to contact the insurers on every occasion.

floating-rate certificate of deposit (FRCD) A certificate of deposit with a variable interest rate, normally for interbank lending purposes. Commonly bearing a one-year maturity, these certificates have interest rates that may be adjusted (e.g. every 90 days); they are usually expressed in eurodollars at a rate linked to LIBOR.

floating-rate interest An *interest rate on certain bonds, certificates of deposit, etc., that changes with the market rate in a predetermined manner, usually in relation to the *base rate.

floating-rate loan A loan that does not have a fixed interest rate throughout its life. Floating-rate loans can take various forms but they are all tied to a short-term market indicator; in the UK this is usually the *London Inter Bank Offered Rate.

floating-rate note (FRN) A *eurobond with a *floating-rate interest, usually based on the *London Inter Bank Offered Rate. They first appeared in the 1970s and have a maturity of between 7 and 15 years. They are usually issued as negotiable *bearer bonds. A **perpetual FRN** has no *redemption. *See also* FLIP-FLOP FRN.

floating warranty A guarantee given by one person to another that induces this other person to enter into a contract with a third party. For example, a car dealer may induce a customer to enter into a hire-purchase contract with a finance company. If the car does not comply with the dealer's guarantee, the customer may recover damages from the dealer, on the basis of the hire-purchase contract, even though the dealer is not a party to that contract.

floor 1. (trading floor) The area in a financial market set aside for face-to-face dealing between *floor traders. With the increased use of *automated screen trading, floor trading has become less frequent. *See also* PIT. **2.** The minimum interest rate on a financial obligation. *Compare* CAP. *See also* COLLAR.

floor trader A member of a stock exchange, commodity market, Lloyd's, etc., who is permitted to enter the dealing room of these institutions and deal with other traders, brokers, underwriters, etc. Each institution has its own rules of exclusivity, but in many, computer dealing is replacing or has replaced face-to-face floor trading.

florin (Af) The standard monetary unit of Aruba, divided into 100 cents.

flotation The process of launching a public company for the first time by inviting the public to subscribe in its shares (also known as 'going public'). It applies both to private and to previously nationalized share issues, and can be carried out by means of an *introduction, *issue by tender, *offer for sale, *placing, or *public issue. After flotation the shares can be traded on a stock exchange. Flotation allows the owners of the business to raise new capital or to realize their investments.

flotation cost The total cost incurred by a company in offering its securities to the public.

flotsam 1. Items from a cargo or ship that is itself floating on the sea after a shipwreck. In British waters, it can be claimed by the ship's owners for 366 days after the shipwreck; thereafter it belongs to the Crown. *Compare* JETSAM. **2.** In *marine insurance, items or rights that are lost as a result of breach of *warranty. In such cases the policyholder has no right to make an insurance claim.

flow chart A chart used to provide a model for the flow of material, information, or people through a system. The primary purpose of a flow chart is to identify the activities taking place within a system and to enable this information to be presented graphically. Flow charts can be used in the initial design layout of a process, to diagnose problems, or to optimize existing processes by, for example, identifying duplication of effort or elements in which no value is added. The principles of flow charting now form the basis for a range of computer packages enabling production and service environments to be simulated with 'what-if' scenarios. There are a number of conventional symbols used in flow charts. The important ones are the process box, which indicates a process taking place, and the decision lozenge, which indicates where a decision is needed.

flurry A burst of activity on a speculative market, especially on a financial market.

flying picket *See* PICKETING.

flyposting *See* POSTER.

FMCG Abbreviation for *fast-moving consumer goods.

FMEA Abbreviation for *failure mode and effect analysis.

FMS Abbreviation for *flexible manufacturing systems.

FNMA Abbreviation for *Federal National Mortgage Association.

FOB Abbreviation for *free on board.

FoC Abbreviation for father of chapel. This is the person in charge of a trade-union chapel, usually a unit of the union within a particular printing or publishing firm.

focused strategy A business strategy in which firms seek to divest themselves of all but their core activities, using the funds so raised to enhance their *core skills. This strategy is a reaction to the trend towards *diversification and the development of *conglomerates.

focus group An exploratory research group of 8 to 12 participants, led by a moderator, who meet for an in-depth discussion on one particular topic or concept. The participants are generally chosen for their relevance to the particular topic or concept. By skilful use of probes and other interviewing devices, the group members are encouraged to respond in depth to the moderator. These group discussions largely depend for their success on the moderator, who must establish the right atmosphere in order to gain the maximum involvement and cooperation of all the group members. Focus groups are useful in the early stages of developing methods to understand the nature of business or organizational problems and for suggesting issues that should be covered in a questionnaire survey. Discussions are usually recorded and observed through see-through mirrors (with the full knowledge of the group members). Normally, these groups last for between one and three months.

focus-group facility A facility belonging to a marketing research agency consisting of a conference room with a separate observation room. The facility could have audiovisual recording equipment, enabling observers to see and hear what is happening in the conference room, and sometimes see-through mirrors. See FOCUS GROUP.

focus-group moderator A person appointed by a marketing research agency on behalf of a client to lead a *focus group. This person may need a background in psychology or sociology or, at least, in marketing.

follow-the-leader strategy A pricing strategy in which an organization sets prices at the level established by the market leader. This strategy is especially common in organizations in weak competitive positions. It applies to both price increases and reductions.

follow-up The last step in the *selling process, in which the salesperson follows up the customer after the sale to ensure satisfaction and in the hope of achieving repeat business.

FOMC Abbreviation for *Federal Open Market Committee.

Food and Agriculture Organization (FAO) A specialized agency of the United Nations with its headquarters in Rome. It is responsible for organizing world agriculture, especially in developing countries, to improve nutrition and avoid famine.

footprint The physical space occupied by a commercial organization. A retailer, for example, with many stores may wish to shrink its footprint if profits are falling, by selling off some of its premises.

FOOTSIE See FINANCIAL TIMES SHARE INDEXES.

FOQ Abbreviation for free on quay. See FREE ALONGSIDE SHIP.

FOR Abbreviation for free on rail. See FREE ON BOARD.

forbearance The position taken by a lender who chooses not to exercise his or her legal right of *foreclosure when a borrower defaults. Instead, the lender may renegotiate the terms of the loan.

forced sale A sale that has to take place because it has been ordered by a court or because it is necessary to raise funds to avoid bankruptcy or liquidation.

forced saving A government measure imposed on an economy with a view to increasing savings and reducing expenditure on *consumer goods. It is usually implemented by raising taxes, increasing interest rates, or raising prices.

forced scale In marketing research, a rating scale that does not include a "no opinion" or "no knowledge" category; it therefore requires respondents to indicate their position on the attitude scale.

force-field analysis An analytical technique, usually presented graphically (see diagram); it is used to identify all the positive forces and all the negative forces acting on a problem.

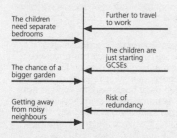

Force-field analysis. A simple force-field diagram analysing whether or not to move house

force majeure (French: superior force) An event outside the control of either party to a contract (such as a strike, riot, war, act of God) that may excuse either party from fulfilling his contractual obligations in certain circumstances, provided that the contract contains a force majeure clause. If one party invokes the *force majeure* clause the other may either accept that it is applicable or challenge the interpretation. In the latter case an *arbitration would be involved.

forecasting The art of estimating future demand for goods or services by anticipating how buyers are likely to react under given sets of conditions. See QUALITATIVE FORECASTING TECHNIQUES; QUANTITATIVE FORECASTING TECHNIQUES.

foreclosure The legal right of a lender of money if the borrower fails to repay the money or part of it on the due date. The lender must apply to a court to be permitted to sell the property that has been held as security for the debt. The court will order a new date for payment in an order called a foreclosure nisi. If the borrower again fails to pay, the lender may sell the property. This procedure can occur when a mortgagor fails to pay the mortgagee (bank, building society, etc.) the mortgage instalments, in which the security is the house in which the mortgagor lives. The bank, etc., then forecloses the mortgage, dispossessing the mortgagor. See feature MORTGAGE LAW on p. 352.

foreign bill See INLAND BILL.

foreign bond A bond held by a resident of one country that is denominated in the currency of another country and issued by a non-domestic creditor. See BULLDOG BOND; YANKEE BOND.

Foreign Corrupt Practices Act (1977) (FCPA) A US statute that prohibits a company from using bribes to obtain business in another country or to prevent the restriction of its business. The **Foreign Corrupt Practices Amendment**, which tightens the regulations, was enacted in 1997.

foreign currency cross-rate A mechanism whereby an exchange rate can be calculated between two currencies for which no direct rate of exchange exists. The US dollar, which is customarily used as the vehicle currency in foreign-exchange trading, is the common denominator of such calculations. Thus, there

may not be a direct rate between, say, the Barbados dollar and the Argentine peso. A cross-rate is calculated by divided the $US rate for the peso by the $US rate for the Barbados dollar, showing how many Barbados dollars are needed to purchase one peso.

foreign exchange (FX) The currencies of foreign countries, as bought and sold on a *foreign-exchange markets. Firms or organizations require foreign exchange to purchase goods from abroad or for purposes of investment or speculation.

foreign-exchange broker A *broker who specializes in arranging deals in foreign currencies on the *foreign-exchange markets. Most transactions are between commercial banks and governments. Foreign-exchange brokers do not normally deal direct with the public or with firms who require foreign currencies for buying goods abroad (who buy from commercial banks).

foreign-exchange dealer A person who buys and sells *foreign exchange on a *foreign-exchange market, usually as an employee of a *commercial bank. Banks charge fees or commissions for buying and selling foreign exchange on behalf of their customers; dealers may also be authorized to speculate in forward exchange rates.

foreign-exchange market An international market in which foreign currencies are traded. It consists primarily of foreign-exchange dealers employed by *commercial banks (acting as principals) and foreign-exchange brokers (acting as intermediaries). Although tight *exchange controls have been abandoned by many governments, including the UK government, the market is not entirely free in that it is to some extent manipulated by governments. Currency dealing has a *spot market for delivery of foreign exchange within two days and a forward-exchange market (see FORWARD-EXCHANGE CONTRACT) in which transactions are made for foreign currencies to be delivered at agreed dates in the future. This enables dealers, and their customers who require foreign exchange in the future, to hedge their purchases and sales. Options and futures on forward-exchange rates can also be traded on various world markets, both *over-the-counter (OTC) and on exchanges.

foreign investment Investment in the domestic economy by foreign individuals or companies. Foreign investment takes the form of either **direct investment** in productive enterprises or investment in financial instruments, such as a portfolio of shares. Countries receiving foreign investment tend to have a mixed attitude towards it. While the creation of jobs and wealth is welcome, there is sometimes antagonism on the grounds that the country is being 'bought by foreigners'. Similarly, there may be resentment in the country whose nationals invest overseas, especially if there is domestic unemployment. Nevertheless, foreign investment is increasingly important in the economy of the modern world.

foreign sector The part of a country's economy that is concerned with external trade (imports and exports) and capital flows (inward and outward).

foreign trade multiplier The mutually beneficial effect on national income that occurs when one country buys another's exports. The rise in employment and income levels in the exporting country will enable workers there to spend more on products from the other country.

foreign trade zone *See* FREE PORT.

forensic accounting 1. Accounting undertaken in relation to proceedings in a court of law. In such circumstances accountants may be called on to provide expert evidence. **2.** Accounting that sets out to determine the nature of past business activity, often on the basis of partial documentation.

FOREX *See* FOREIGN EXCHANGE.

forfaiting A form of *debt discounting for exporters in which a forfaiter accepts at a discount, and without recourse, a *promissory note, *bill of exchange, *letter of credit, etc., received from a foreign buyer by an exporter. Maturities are normally from one to three years. Thus the exporter receives payment without risk at the cost of the discount.

forfeited share A partly paid share in a

company that the shareholder has to forfeit because of a failure to pay a subsequent part or final payment. Such shares must be sold or cancelled by a public company but a private company is not regulated in this respect.

forgery The legal offence of making a false instrument in order that it may be accepted as genuine, thereby causing harm to others. Under the Forgery and Counterfeiting Act (1981), an instrument may be a document or any device (e.g. magnetic tape) on which information is recorded. An instrument is considered false, for example, if it purports to have been made or altered by someone who did not do so, on a date or at a place when it was not, or by someone who does not exist. It is also an offence to copy or use a false instrument knowing it to be false or to make or possess any material meant to be used to produce such specified false instruments as money, cheques, share certificates, cheque cards, credit or debit cards, passports, or registration certificates.

for information only Denoting a quotation given to provide a client with a guide to current market prices. It cannot be treated as a firm offer either to buy or to sell at the quoted price.

forint (Ft) The standard monetary unit of Hungary, divided into 100 fillér.

formation expenses The expenses incurred on setting up a company. According to the Companies Act, these expenses must not be treated as an asset of the company.

Form 10-K An annual report supplied to the US *Securities and Exchange Commission (SEC) by companies listed on the national stock exchanges, detailing financial and other information on the operations of the business. The form must be filed within 90 days of the end of a company's financial year.

Form 10-Q A quarterly submission by publicly listed companies to the US *Securities and Exchange Commission (SEC). The information it required is less detailed than that on *Form 10-K and does not have to be audited.

FORTRAN Acronym for *fo*rmula *tr*anslation, a computer programming language. The first *high-level language to gain widespread acceptance for mathematical and scientific work, FORTRAN has been dominant in this field since the 1950s. A vast amount of software has been written in it, forming an investment that ensures its continued popularity despite advances in programming language design.

forwardation A situation in a *commodity market in which spot goods can be bought more cheaply than goods for forward delivery, enabling a dealer to buy spot goods and carry them forward to deliver them against a forward contract. *Compare* BACKWARDATION.

forward-dated *See* POST-DATE.

forward dealing Dealing in commodities, securities, currencies, freight, etc., for delivery at some future date at a price agreed at the time the contract (called a **forward contract**) is made. This form of trading enables dealers and manufacturers to cover their future requirements by hedging their more immediate purchases (*see* HEDGE). Strictly, a forward contract differs from a *futures contract in that the former cannot be closed out by a matching transaction, whereas a futures contract can, and often is. However, this distinction is not always adhered to and the terms are sometimes used synonymously.

forward delivery Terms of a contract in which goods are purchased for delivery at some time in the future (*compare* SPOT GOODS). Commodities may be sold for forward delivery up to one year or more ahead, often involving shipment from their port of origin.

forward differential *See* FORWARD POINTS.

forward-exchange contract An agreement to purchase *foreign exchange at a specified date in the future at an agreed exchange rate. In international trade, with floating rates of exchange, the forward-exchange market provides an important way of eliminating risk on future transactions that will require foreign exchange. *See also* FINANCIAL FUTURES; FOREIGN-EXCHANGE MARKET.

forwarding agent *See* SHIPPING AND FORWARDING AGENT.

forward integration *See* INTEGRATION.

forward margin *See* FORWARD POINTS.

forward points (forward differential; forward margin) The amount to be added to or deducted from the spot foreign-exchange rate to calculate the forward-exchange rate.

forward price The fixed price at which a given amount of a commodity, currency, or a financial instrument is to be delivered on a fixed date in the future. A forward contract differs from a *futures contract in that each forward deal stands alone.

forward-rate agreement (FRA) 1. A contract between two parties that determines the rate of interest that will apply to a future loan or a deposit, which may or may not materialize. **2.** A specified amount of a specified currency to be exchanged on an agreed future date at a specified rate of exchange.

FOS Abbreviation for *Financial Ombudsman Service.

foul bill of lading *See* DIRTY BILL OF LADING.

founders' shares Shares issued to the founders of a company. They often have special rights to dividends. *See also* DEFERRED ORDINARY SHARE.

four-plus cover An advertising campaign in which a particular advertisement is exposed to the public at least four times. It is based on the theory that four exposures is the most likely to persuade a person to buy a particular product.

Fourth Accounting Directive An EU directive (1978) concerning the harmonization of company law and accounting practices in member states. It recognized five *accounting concepts as fundamental: the *accounting entity concept, the *accruals concept, the *consistency concept, the *going-concern concept, and the *prudence concept.

FPA Abbreviation for free of particular average. *See* AVERAGE.

FRA Abbreviation for *forward-rate agreement.

FRAC Abbreviation for *f*requency, *re*-cency, *a*mount, and *c*ategory. A method of scoring based on a customer's behavioural data. It is normally used in *databased marketing to provide easy access to that customer's transactional information. Frequency refers to time elapsed between purchases. Recency is the date of the last purchase. Amount is the average value of that customer's purchases. Category refers to the category of the product in which the customer is interested. Each customer is given a score based on these parameters, which can be used to divide customers into groups. A company may use this information at both tactical and strategic levels in its direct marketing effort.

fractional banking A banking practice that some governments impose on their banks, calling for a fixed fraction between cash reserves and total liabilities. If governments increase the ratio of reserves to deposits, this indicates a tighter credit policy.

fragmentation culture *See* ORGANIZATIONAL CULTURE.

fragmented industry An industry characterized by having many opportunities to create competitive advantages although each advantage is small.

franc 1. (F) The standard monetary unit of various former French colonies and some French dependencies: Benin (Communauté Financière Africaine franc; CFAF), Burkina-Faso (CFAF), Burundi (FBu), Cameroon (CFAF), the Central African Republic (CFAF), Chad (CFAF), Comoros (CF), Congo-Brazzaville (CFAF), the Democratic Republic of Congo (CoF), Côte d'Ivoire, (CFAF), Djibouti (DF), Equatorial Guinea (CFAF), French Polynesia (FPF), Gabon (CFAF), Guinea (GF), Guinea-Bissau (CFAF), Madagascar (FMG), Mali (CFAF), New Caledonia (FPF), Niger (CFAF), Rwanda (RF), Senegal (CFAF), and Togo (CFAF). In all countries it is divided into 100 centimes. **2. (Swiss franc)** the standard monetary unit of Switzerland and Liechtenstein, divided into 100 centimes. **3.** The former standard monetary unit of France, most French dependencies, Monaco, and (with the peseta) Andorra **(French franc)**; of Belgium **(Belgian franc)**; and of Luxembourg **(Luxembourg franc)**. In each case it was subsumed into the euro for all purposes other than cash transactions in January 1999 and abolished in 2002.

franchise 1. A licence given to a manufacturer, distributor, trader, etc., to enable them to manufacture or sell a named product or service in a particular area for a stated period. The holder of the licence **(franchisee)** usually pays the grantor of the licence **(franchisor)** a royalty on sales, often with a lump sum as an advance against royalties. The franchisor may also supply the franchisee with a brand identity as well as finance and technical expertise. Franchises are common in the fast-food business, petrol stations, travel agents, etc. **2.** A clause in an insurance policy, often a marine-insurance policy, that excludes the payment of claims up to a specified level but agrees to pay in full all claims above it. For example, a £25 franchise would mean that insurers would not deal with claims below £25 but a claim for £26 would be met in full. Franchise clauses are used by insurers to avoid administratively expensive small claims, while still providing the policyholder with full cover for larger claims. *See also* EXCESS POLICY.

franco (French: free) Export delivery terms in which the seller of goods pays for all transport and insurance to the buyer's warehouse, even when this is in a foreign country. In some countries the term **rendu** is used.

franked investment income A concept formerly used in the *imputation system of taxation that was discontinued when *advance corporation tax was abolished in 1999. Dividends and distributions from UK companies received by other companies were regarded as 'franked', i.e. exempt from further corporation tax charges.

Frankfurt Stock Exchange (Frankfurt Wertpapierbörse) The oldest and largest of eight regional stock exchanges in Germany. It first recorded trading in 1820 and was subsequently recognized as a centre for dealing in bonds. Trading is now on four markets, including the Neuer Markt launched in 1997 for companies involved in Internet trading. The main market indicator is the Deutsche Aktienindex (Dax index).

franking machine A machine supplied by the Post Office to businesses who wish to frank their own mail. Instead of taking mail to a post office and using gummed stamps, the business uses the machine to produce slips of paper that state the postage and the date. The machine records the amount of money spent, which has to be remitted to the Post Office.

fraud A false representation by means of a statement or conduct, in order to gain a material advantage. A contract obtained by fraud is voidable on the grounds of fraudulent *misrepresentation. If a person uses fraud to induce someone to part with money he or she would not otherwise have parted with, this may amount to theft. *See also* FRAUDULENT CONVEYANCE; FRAUDULENT PREFERENCE; FRAUDULENT TRADING.

fraudulent conveyance The transfer of property to another person with the aim of putting it beyond the reach of creditors. For example, if a man transfers his house into the name of his wife because he realizes that his business is about to become insolvent, the transaction may be set aside by the court under the provisions of the Insolvency Act (1986).

fraudulent preference Putting a creditor of a company into a better position than he would have been in, at a time when the company was unable to pay its debts. If this occurs because of an act of the company within six months of winding-up (or two years if the preference is given to a person connected with the company), an application to the court may be made to cancel the transaction. The court may make any order that it thinks fit, but no order may prejudice the rights of a third party who has acquired property for value without notice of the preference.

fraudulent trading Carrying on business with intent to defraud creditors or for any other fraudulent purpose. This includes accepting money from customers when the company is unable to pay its debts and cannot meet its obligations under the contract. Such conduct is a criminal offence. The liquidator of a company may apply to the court for an order against any person who has been a party to fraudulent trading to make such contributions to the assets of the company as the court thinks fit. 'Fraudulent' in this context implies actual dishonesty or real moral blame. *Compare* WRONGFUL TRADING.

FRC Abbreviation for *Financial Reporting Council.

FRCD Abbreviation for *floating-rate certificate of deposit.

Freddie Mac Colloquial name in the USA for the *Federal Home Loan Mortgage Corporation (FHLMC).

free alongside ship (fas) The basis of an export contract in which the seller pays for sending the goods to the port of shipment but not for loading them onto the ship. The seller must cover all insurance up to this point and any lighterage required. This may be the same as **free on quay (FOQ)** or **free alongside quay (faq)** as long as the ship can reach the dock. If it is unable to, the buyer has to pay for lighterage.

free asset ratio The ratio of the market value of an insurance company's assets to its liabilities.

free capital 1. Capital in the form of cash. *See also* LIQUID ASSETS. 2. The shares in a public company that are available to the general public, i.e. those not held by controlling shareholders. In the USA it is known as the **free float**.

free cash flow A measure of the cash that a company is generating or consuming. Free cash flow is often defined as after-tax *operating profit less net *capital expenditure:

> free cash flow = revenues – operating expenses + depreciation – taxes – capital expenditure costs

However, there is no precise definition of free cash flow: another equation might include changes in *working capital. Making comparisons between companies on this basis is not very useful if they are using different definitions. Free cash flow is not determined in accordance with *generally accepted accounting principles (GAAP) and should be considered in addition to, not as a substitute for, financial measures determined in accordance with GAAP.

Free cash flow is important for managers as a positive cash flow can be used to pay dividends, acquire other companies, or invest in new opportunities. It is also an important measure of a company's ability to reduce debt. The value of a company can be calculated as the sum of the future discounted free cash flows (see DISCOUNTED CASH FLOW).

free competition (free economy) An economy in which the market forces of supply and demand control prices, incomes, etc., without government interference. In such an economy *private enterprise is dominant, the public sector being very small. See COMPETITION.

free depreciation A method of granting tax relief to organizations by allowing them to charge the cost of *fixed assets against taxable profits in whatever proportions and over whatever period they choose. This gives businesses considerable flexibility, enabling them to choose the best method of *depreciation depending on their anticipated cash flow, profit estimates, and taxation expectations.

free docks The basis of an export contract in which the exporter pays to deliver the goods to the shipping dock, but the buyer arranges and pays for loading and shipping.

free economy See FREE COMPETITION.

free enterprise See PRIVATE ENTERPRISE.

free fall See FREE-STANDING STUFFER.

Freefone A telephone service provided to businesses by British Telecom in which the business pays for incoming calls. A customer dials 0800/0808 and asks to be connected to a specified Freefone number, knowing that he or she will not have to pay for the call (although certain mobile operators may charge for access to Freefone). This service is much used by *mail-order houses.

freehold An *estate in land that is now usually held in *fee simple. Land that is not freehold will be *leasehold land.

free in and out Denoting a selling price that includes all costs of loading goods

(into a container, road vehicle, ship, etc.) and unloading them (out of the transport).

free issue See SCRIP ISSUE.

free-keeper A small gift given as a reward for placing an order by mail. Normally the gift can be kept even if the buyer returns the goods ordered.

free list A list, issued by the Customs and Excise, of the goods that can be imported into the UK without paying duty.

free lunch Economists' jargon for a nonexistent benefit. It derives from a 19th-century tavern that advertised free food, it being clearly understood that anyone attempting to exploit this offer without buying a drink would be thrown out. The phrase is now used to reflect the economist's belief that wherever there appears to be a free benefit, someone, somewhere, always pays for it. See also FREE RIDE.

freely callable Describing a bond that the issuer may choose to redeem at any time from the issue date. See CALLABLE BONDS.

free market 1. A market that is free from government interference, prices rising and falling in accordance with supply and demand. 2. A security that is widely traded on a stock exchange, there being sufficient stock on offer for the price to be uninfluenced by availability. 3. A *foreign-exchange market that is free from influence on rates by governments, rates being free to rise and fall in accordance with supply and demand.

free of all averages (faa) Denoting a marine insurance that covers only a total loss, general *average and particular average losses being excluded.

free of capture Denoting a *marine insurance in which capture, seizure, and mutiny are excluded. This usually applies to policies taken out in wartime.

free of particular average (FPA) See AVERAGE.

free on board The basis of an export contract in which the seller pays for sending the goods to the port of shipment and loading them on to the ship or aircraft. The seller also pays for the insurance up to this point. Thereafter the transport and insurance charges have to be paid by the buyer. If the goods are to travel by rail rather than by ship, the equivalent terms are **free on rail** (**FOR**).

free on quay (FOQ) *See* FREE ALONGSIDE SHIP.

free overside (free overboard) *See* EX SHIP.

free port A port, such as Bremerhaven, Gdansk, Rotterdam, or Singapore, that is free of customs duties. The area around the port, known as a **foreign trade zone** or **free zone**, specializes in *entrepôt trade, as goods can be landed and warehoused before re-export without the payment of customs duties.

Freepost A UK business reply service provided by the Post Office. Members of the public reply to advertisements and the advertiser pays the cost of postage after the reply is delivered.

free ride The situation in which an economic agent benefits from the expenditure of others without making a contribution. A free ride is a type of *externality and a source of market imperfection. An important example of free riding in financial markets is when small investors benefit from the monitoring of firms carried out by institutional investors.

freesheets Local newspapers and magazines that are published and distributed without charge. As they are entirely dependent upon advertising revenue they must ensure high circulation and low costs to survive. For this reason, the advertising to editorial ratio is exceptionally high.

free-standing stuffer (free-fall; flier) A promotional item distributed by being inserted into a newspaper or a magazine.

free trade The flow of goods and services across national frontiers without the interference of laws, tariffs, quotas, or other restrictions. Since World War II, under the auspices of GATT and the World Trade Organization, trade barriers have continuously, if slowly, fallen.

free trade agreement An agreement to abolish tariffs between two or more countries. Notable examples are the agreement to set up the *European Free Trade

Association (EFTA) in 1960 and the *North American Free Trade Agreement (NAFTA), concluded in 1994 between the USA, Canada, and Mexico.

freeze-out Pressure applied to minority shareholders of a company that has been taken over, to sell their stock to the new owners.

freezing injunction An order of the court preventing the defendant from dealing with specified assets. Such an order will be granted in cases in which the plaintiff can show that there will be a substantial risk that any judgement given against the defendant will be worthless, because the defendant will sell assets to avoid paying it. It is usually granted to prevent assets leaving the jurisdiction of the English courts, but may in exceptional circumstances extend to assets abroad. It was formerly called a **Mareva injunction** after the 1975 case *Mareva Compania Naviera SA* v *International Bulkcarriers SA.*

free zone *See* FREE PORT.

freight **1.** The transport of goods by sea (**sea freight**) or air (**air freight**). **2.** The goods so transported. **3.** The cost of shipping goods for a particular voyage by sea or by air. Freight is charged on the basis of weight (*see* DEADWEIGHT CARGO) or the volume occupied, described as **weight or measurement**. Usually the rate is quoted per tonne or per cubic metre, the freight paid being whichever is the greater amount. Air freights are usually quoted on the basis of per kilo or per 7000 cubic centimetres, whichever is the greater. Certain cargoes are charged on an *ad valorem basis, expressed as a percentage of the *free on board (FOB) value. Freight is normally paid when the goods are delivered for shipment but in some cases it is paid at the destination (**freight forward**).

freight-absorption pricing A geographic pricing strategy in which a company absorbs all or part of the freight charges in delivering the goods in order to capture the business.

freight-allowed price *See* DELIVERED PRICE.

freight forward Denoting a shipment of goods in which the *freight is payable by the buyer at the port of destination.

freight insurance A form of marine or aviation insurance in which a consignor or a consignee covers loss of sums paid in *freight for the transport of goods.

freight note An invoice from a shipowner to a shipper showing the amount of *freight due on a shipment of goods.

freight release An endorsement on a *bill of lading made by a shipowner or his agent, stating that *freight has been paid and the goods may be released on arrival. Sometimes the freight release is a separate document providing the same authority.

frequency 1. The number of times the average person in a target market is exposed to an advertising message during a given period. **2.** The number of times an advertisement is repeated in a given medium (television, radio, etc.) within a given period, usually a month. **3.** In statistics, a measurement of the likelihood of a particular event occurring.

frequency marketing Special services and benefits extended to customers who make frequent purchases from the same seller.

frictional unemployment A minimal level of *unemployment that will occur in even the most efficient economy. Frictional unemployment exists because of lags between workers leaving one job and taking up another and because there are times of the year when many new workers (such as school and college leavers) enter the labour market; in these circumstances there is some delay in finding them all jobs.

friction-free capitalism A term coined by the US founder of Microsoft, Bill Gates (1955–), to refer to the enhanced efficiency of markets resulting from the widespread use of the Internet; this is held to have abolished such traditional market imperfections as physical distance, lack of information, lack of choice, and local regulation.

Friendly Society A UK non-profit-making association registered as such under the Friendly Society Acts (1896–1992). Mutual insurance societies of this kind date back to the 17th century and remained widespread until the introduction of National Insurance in 1946, after which many closed. Those that remain offer a range of personal assurance and insurance benefits relating to sickness, pensions, and unemployment. The 1992 Act created a new framework for Friendly Societies, enabling them to extend their services and to compete with other organizations. The Act also established the Friendly Society Commission, to regulate their activities. In 2001 the Commission's responsibilities passed to the *Financial Services Authority.

fringe benefits 1. Non-monetary benefits offered to the employees of a company in addition to their wages or salaries. They include company cars, expense accounts, the opportunity to buy company products at reduced prices, private health plans, canteens with subsidized meals, luncheon vouchers, cheap loans, social clubs, etc. Some of these benefits, such as company cars, do not escape the tax net. *See* BENEFITS IN KIND. **2.** Benefits, other than dividends, provided by a company for its shareholders. They include reduced prices for the company's products or services, Christmas gifts, and special travel facilities. *See* SHAREHOLDERS' PERKS.

FRN Abbreviation for *floating-rate note.

front door *See* BACK DOOR.

front-end fee A charge levied by a lender when a loan is set up or when the first payment of the loan is taken.

front-end load The initial charge made by a *unit trust, life-assurance company, or other investment fund to pay for administration and commission for any introducing agent. The investment made on behalf of the investor is, therefore, the total initial payment less the front-end load. *Compare* BACK-END LOAD.

front office–back office The division between those elements of an *operating system that are transparent to the customer and with which they can interact (**front office**), and those that are hidden (**back office**). In the service sector there is a trade-off between the benefits that accrue from close and open relationships with the customer and the greater ease with which operations can be controlled when they are out of sight. Application of information technology to many service operations has allowed the customer to experience what appears to be a customized service, while at the same time allowing standardization of procedures.

front running The generally illegal practice by brokers or intermediaries of dealing on advance information provided by their brokers and investment analysis department, before their clients have been given the information. *See also* CHINESE WALL.

frozen assets Assets that for one reason or another cannot be used or realized. This may happen when a government refuses to allow certain assets to be exported. *See* FREEZING INJUNCTION.

FRRP Abbreviation for *Financial Reporting Review Panel.

FRS Abbreviation for *Financial Reporting Standard.

frugging (fund raising under the guise of research) The unethical practice of deliberate deception by fund raisers masquerading as market researchers. Respondents are often invited to take part in a survey as a lead-in to a presentation, or as an attempt to obtain information that could be used for donor leads or mailing lists. *Compare* SUGGING.

frustration of contract The termination of a *contract as a result of an unforeseen event that makes its performance impossible or illegal. A contract to sell an aircraft could be frustrated if it crashed before the contract was due to be implemented. Similarly an export contract could be frustrated if the importer was in a country that declared war on the country of the exporter.

FSA Abbreviation for *Financial Services Authority.

FSBR Abbreviation for *Financial Statement and Budget Report.

FTC Abbreviation for *Federal Trade Commission.

FTII Abbreviation for Fellow of the *Chartered Institute of Taxation. In order to achieve this qualification a thesis on an aspect of UK taxation has to be submitted

and accepted as being of the appropriate standard.

FTP (file transfer protocol) The protocol that controls the way that files move across the *Internet from one computer to another. An **ftp site** is a site at which a number of files are available for download and to which files may be uploaded. Such sites may be private or public.

FT-SE See feature THE FINANCIAL TIMES SHARE INDEXES on p. 219.

fulfilment The process of dealing with an order from its receipt to delivery of the goods.

full consolidation The method of accounting in which the whole impact of subsidiaries is incorporated into group accounts (*see* CONSOLIDATED FINANCIAL STATEMENTS). If a subsidiary undertaking is less than 100% owned, the percentage pertaining to the *minority interest must be adjusted for. This method of consolidation is generally adopted in the UK.

full cost pricing An approach to setting selling prices that attempts to ensure that the price of a good or service is based on all the costs incurred in its supply, including *overheads. It usually involves an *absorption approach to the costing of units. *Compare* COST-PLUS PRICING; MARGINAL COST PRICING.

full-cost transfer prices *Transfer prices that are set by *full cost pricing but do not include a profit margin for the supplying division. This method is widely used in practice. However, there can be problems for managers if they do not have accurate cost information, which may lead to poor decision making.

full employment The state in which all the economic resources of a country (and more specifically, its labour force) are fully utilized.

full-line strategy (deep-line strategy) A strategy that involves a company in offering a large number of variations of its products. Companies employing a full-line strategy are seeking both a high market share and market growth. Leading detergent manufacturers offer up to 15 brands of their detergents.

full listing A description of a company

whose shares appear on the *Official List of the *main market of the *London Stock Exchange. *See* LISTING REQUIREMENTS.

full-text retrieval The ability to obtain a full copy of an article or document from a newspaper, journal, or organizational source by means of the *Internet.

fully diluted earnings per share The *earnings per share (eps) for a company that takes into account not only the number of shares in issue but also those that may be issued as a result of such factors as convertible loans and options or warranties. *Financial Reporting Standard 22, issued in 2004, requires that diluted earnings per share be disclosed on the face of the profit and loss account as well as basic earnings per share. The US equivalent is **primary earnings per share**.

fully paid share A *share on which the full nominal or *par value has been paid by the shareholder (plus any premium). *Compare* PARTLY PAID SHARE. *See also* PAID-UP SHARE CAPITAL.

function A section or department of an organization that carries out a discrete activity, under the control of a manager or director. It is the section of the business for which *functional budgets are produced. Examples of separate functions are production, sales, finance, and personnel.

functional budget A financial or quantitative statement prepared for a *function of an organization; it summarizes the policies and the level of performance expected to be achieved by that function for a *budget period.

functional discount A price reduction offered by the seller of goods to those trade channel members that perform certain functions, such as selling, storing, and record keeping. *See also* TRADE DISCOUNT.

functional leader In the social psychology of groups, any group member who performs the functions associated with the role of leader, whether he or she has a formal leadership role or not. These functions may be either goal-oriented (e.g. suggesting solutions to problems, inciting action) or relationship-oriented (e.g. reducing conflict, raising morale).

functional strategy The contribution

to the overall organizational objectives made by individual functions. Functional strategy is particularly concerned with the management of functions to achieve the optimum outputs and to maximize systems synergy.

function costing The technique of collecting the costs of an organization by *function and presenting them to the functional management in operating statements on a regular basis.

functions of money In economics, money fulfils the functions of acting as a *medium of exchange, a *unit of account, and a store of value. None of the functions occur in an economy based on barter.

fund **1.** A resource managed on behalf of a client by a *financial institution. **2.** A separate pool of monetary and other resources used to support designated activities.

fundamental term A term in a *contract that is of such importance to the contract that to omit it would make the contract useless. Fundamental terms cannot be exempted from a contract, whereas lesser terms, known as conditions and *warranties, can be exempted by mutual consent.

funded debt **1.** The part of the national debt that the government is under no obligation to repay by a specified date. This consists mostly of *Consols. *Compare* FLOATING DEBT. *See also* FUNDING OPERATIONS. **2.** Borrowing with a maturity in excess of a year.

funded pension scheme A pension scheme that pays benefits to retired people from a pension fund invested in securities. The profits produced by such a fund are paid out as pensions to the members of the scheme.

funding Paying short-term debt by arranging long-term borrowing. *See* FUNDING OPERATIONS.

funding operations **1.** The replacement of short-term fixed-interest debt (*floating debt) by long-term fixed-interest debt (*funded debt). This is normally associated with the government's handling of the National Debt through the operations of the Bank of England. The bank buys

Treasury bills and replaces them with an equal amount of longer-term government bonds, thus lengthening the average maturity of government debt. This has the effect of tightening the monetary system, as Treasury bills are regarded by the commercial banks as liquid assets while bonds are not. **2.** A change in the *gearing of a company, in which short-term debts, such as overdrafts, are replaced by longer-term debts, such as *debentures.

fund manager (investment manager) An employee of one of the larger institutions, such as an insurance company, *investment trust, or *pension fund, who manages its investment fund. The fund manager decides which investments the fund shall hold, in accordance with the specified aims of the fund, e.g. high income, maximum growth, etc.

fund of funds A *unit trust belonging to an institution in which most of its funds are invested in a selection of other unit trusts owned by that institution. It is designed to give maximum security to the small investor by spreading the investment across a wide range.

fund supermarket An Internet facility that provides private investors with a range of advice and investment opportunities.

fungible issue 1. A *bond issued on the same terms and conditions as a bond previously issued by the same company. It has the advantage of having paperwork consistent with the previous bond and of increasing the depth of the market of that particular bond (see DEEP MARKET; THIN MARKET). The *gross redemption yield on the fungible issue will probably be different from that of the original issue, which is achieved by issuing the bond at a discount or a premium. **2.** Any security that is interchangeable with another of the same class.

fungibles 1. Interchangeable goods, securities, etc., that allow one to be replaced by another without loss of value. *Bearer securities and banknotes are examples. **2.** Perishable goods the quantity of which can be estimated by number or weight.

Futures and Options Exchange (London FOX) The principal European exchange for soft commodities. A successor to the *London Commodity Exchange, which it replaced in 1987, it merged in 1996 with the *London International Financial Futures and Options Exchange, becoming a separate department within this exchange (**LIFFE Commodity Products**).

futures contract An agreement to buy or sell a fixed quantity of a particular commodity, currency, or security for delivery at a fixed date in the future at a fixed price. Unlike an *option, a futures contract involves a definite purchase or sale and not an option to buy or sell; it therefore may entail a potentially unlimited loss. However, **futures** provide an opportunity for those who must purchase goods regularly to *hedge against changes in price and for speculators to make large profits. In London, futures are traded in a variety of markets. *Financial futures are traded on the *London International Financial Futures and Options Exchange, whose commodity department (LIFFE Commodity Products) deals with shipping and with cocoa, coffee, and other foodstuffs; the *London Metal Exchange with metals; and the *International Petroleum Exchange with oil. In many cases actual goods (see ACTUALS) do not pass between dealers in these **futures markets**, a bought contract being cancelled out by an equivalent sale contract, and vice versa; money differences arising as a result are usually settled through a *clearing house. In some futures markets only brokers are allowed to trade; in others, both dealers and brokers are permitted to do so. See also FORWARD DEALING.

future value The value that a sum of money (the *present value) invested at compound interest will have in the future. If the future value is F, and the present value is P, at an annual rate of interest r, compounded annually for n years, $F = P(1 + r)^n$. Thus a sum with a present value of £1000 will have a future value of £1973.82 at 12% p.a., after six years.

FX Abbreviation for *foreign exchange.

G3; G7; G8; G10 *Abbreviations for* *Group of Three; *Group of Seven; Group of Eight (*see* GROUP OF SEVEN); *Group of Ten.

GA Abbreviation for general average. *See* AVERAGE.

GAAP Abbreviation for *generally accepted accounting principles.

GAAS Abbreviation for *generally accepted auditing standards.

GAB Abbreviation for *general arrangements to borrow.

gai atsu Foreign pressure on Japan to bring its trade and financial policies more in line with those of the rest of the developed world.

gaijin A foreign investor on the Japanese Stock Market.

gain sharing A form of output-based incentive that operates at company or workplace level. There are a variety of forms, including the Scanlon and Rucker plans and Improshare, but common to most is an attempt to link payment to a measure of *value added. Here, value added is calculated by removing labour costs and expenditure on raw materials, energy, and support services from the income derived from the sale of the finished product. If value added increases above a target level, then it is shared between workforce and company in accordance with a preset formula. The aim is to create a group incentive that reflects the contribution of the work force to business performance more directly than *profit-sharing schemes or *profit-related pay.

game theory A mathematical theory, developed by J. von Neumann (1903–57) and O. Morgenstern (1902–77) in 1944, concerned with predicting the outcome of games of strategy (rather than games of chance) in which the participants have incomplete information about the others' intentions. Under perfect competition there is no scope for game theory, as individual actions are assumed not to influence others significantly; under *oligopoly, however, this is not the case. Game theory has been increasingly applied to economics in recent years, particularly in the theory of industrial organizations. The theory was further elucidated by the economists John Nash, John Harsanyi, and Reinhard Selten, who received the Nobel Prize for Economics in 1994.

gaming contract A *contract involving the playing of a game of chance by any number of people for money. A **wagering contract** involves only two people. In general, both gaming contracts and wagering contracts are solid and no action can be brought to recover money paid or won under them.

Gantt chart A chart presenting a planned activity as a series of horizontal bands against a series of vertical lines representing dates (see illustration on p. 239). It can be used to measure progress on a project or to compare planned production in a period to actual production. It was invented by Henry L Gantt in 1917. *See also* SCHEDULE.

gap 1. (asset–liability gap) A measure of *interest-rate risk used in banking. It comprises the difference between rate-sensitive assets (i.e. loans) and rate-sensitive liabilities (i.e. deposits) within a particular range of repricing time periods. If short-term rate-sensitive assets are greater than short-term liabilities, the gap will lead to a situation in which an interest-rate fall will lower the profitability and value of a bank. *See also* MISMATCH. **2.** Any disparity between goals, expectations, or requirements on the one hand and the actual situation on the other, as between the predicted and actual performance of a business or business unit or between consumer expectations and the quality of goods or services supplied. *See* SERVQUAL; STRATEGIC GAP ANALYSIS.

gap analysis 1. A methodical tabulation

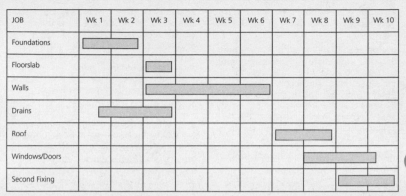

JOB	Wk 1	Wk 2	Wk 3	Wk 4	Wk 5	Wk 6	Wk 7	Wk 8	Wk 9	Wk 10
Foundations										
Floorslab										
Walls										
Drains										
Roof										
Windows/Doors										
Second Fixing										

Gantt chart. A Gantt chart showing the stages of building a house.

of all the known requirements of consumers in a particular category of products, together with a cross-listing of all the features provided by existing products to satisfy these requirements. Such a chart shows up any gaps that exist and therefore provides a pointer to any new products that could supply an unfulfilled demand. **2. (gap management)** The management of a bank's *interest-rate risk by monitoring and controlling *gaps between rate-sensitive assets and liabilities. *See also* ASSET–LIABILITY MANAGEMENT. **3.** *See* STRATEGIC GAP ANALYSIS.

garage To transfer assets and liabilities internationally in order to benefit from tax advantages.

garbologists (dustbin checkers) Marketing researchers who sort through people's dustbins to analyse household consumption patterns. This normally has to be done with the permission of the householder.

garden leave clause A clause in an employment contract that provides for a long period of notice, during which the employee will be remunerated in full but will not be required to attend at the workplace. The use of such clauses is increasing by employers wishing to safeguard trade secrets or prevent a highly skilled employee from leaving to work for a rival firm. An employee who has been headhunted could be required to serve 'garden leave' for a period of up to one year in

order to lawfully terminate his or her existing contract. Throughout this period the employee will be subject to all the normal contractual restraints. Management sees the use of such clauses as an expensive, but reliable and enforceable, alternative to traditional *restraint of trade clauses.

garnishee order An order made by a judge on behalf of a *judgement creditor restraining a third party (often a bank or an employer), called a **garnishee**, from paying money to the judgement debtor until sanctioned to do so by the court. The order may also specify that the garnishee must pay a stated sum to the judgement creditor, or to the court, from the funds belonging to the judgement debtor. *See* ATTACHMENT.

gatekeeper 1. A manager in a large company who controls the flow of information. It is the gatekeeper who decides what information shall be passed upwards to a parent company and downwards to a subsidiary. **2.** *See* RELATIONSHIP ROLES.

GATT Abbreviation for *General Agreement on Tariffs and Trade.

Gaussian distribution *See* NORMAL DISTRIBUTION.

gazump To raise the price of, or accept a higher offer for, land, buildings, etc., on which a sale price has been agreed but before the *exchange of contracts has taken place. The intending purchaser with whom the sale price had been agreed has no remedy, even though he or she may have incurred expenditure on legal fees, surveys, etc.

gazunder To reduce an offer on a house, flat, etc., immediately before exchanging contracts, having previously agreed a higher price. In a market in which house prices are falling, the unscrupulous buyer is aware that the seller will be extremely anxious to sell, having incurred legal expenses and perhaps having bought another property.

GDP Abbreviation for *gross domestic product.

GDP deflator The factor by which the value of GDP (see GROSS DOMESTIC PRODUCT) at current prices must be reduced (deflated) to express GDP in terms of the prices of some base year (e.g. 1980). The GDP deflator is thus a measure of *inflation.

GDSS Abbreviation for group decision support system. See DECISION SUPPORT SYSTEM.

gearing (capital gearing; equity gearing; financial gearing; leverage) The relative size of the funds provided to a company by its ordinary shareholders and the long-term funds with a fixed interest charge, such as *debentures and *preference shares. A company is said to be high geared when its fixed interest capital is dominant and low geared when its capital is predominantly in ordinary shares, especially in relation to other similar companies. A high-geared company is considered to be a speculative investment for the ordinary shareholder and will be expected to show good returns when the company is doing well. See also DEBT–EQUITY RATIO; FINANCIAL DISTRESS.

gearing adjustment In *current-cost accounting, an adjustment that reduces the charge to the owners for the effect of price changes on *depreciation, *stock, and *working capital. It is justified on the grounds that a proportion of the extra financing is supplied by the *loan capital of the business.

gearing ratios (leverage ratios) Ratios that express a company's capital *gearing. There are a number of different ratios that can be calculated from either the *balance sheet or the *profit and loss account. Ratios based on the balance sheet usually express *debt as a percentage of *equity, or as a percentage of debt plus equity (see DEBT–EQUITY RATIO). **Income gearing** is normally calculated by dividing the *profit before interest and tax by the gross interest payable to give the *interest cover.

geisha bond See SHOGUN BOND.

gender segmentation Dividing a market on the basis of gender, i.e. into male and female. See MARKET SEGMENTATION.

General Agreement on Tariffs and Trade (GATT) A trade treaty that operated from 1948 until 1995, when it was replaced by the *World Trade Organization (WTO). GATT was supported by 95 nations and a further 28 nations applied its rules de facto. Its objectives were to expand world trade and to provide a permanent forum for international trade problems. GATT was especially interested in extending *free trade, which it achieved in eight 'rounds': Geneva (1947), Annecy (1948), Torquay (1950), Geneva (1956), Dillon (1960–61), Kennedy (1964–67), Tokyo (1973–79), and Uruguay (1986–94).

general arrangements to borrow (GAB) The special arrangements made by the *Group of Ten (G10) to enable the *International Monetary Fund to increase its lending to members of G10. They came into effect in 1962 and were augmented in 1983 when Switzerland, though not a member of the IMF, joined the GAB, enabling it to extend its loan facilities to non-members.

general average (GA) See AVERAGE.

General Commissioners An unpaid local body of persons of good standing appointed by the Lord Chancellor (in Scotland by the Scottish Executive) to hear appeals against income tax, corporation tax, and capital gains tax assessments or matters of dispute arising from them. General Commissioners can appoint their own clerk, often a lawyer, who can advise them on procedure and legal matters. Compare SPECIAL COMMISSIONERS.

general crossing See CHEQUE.

general insurance Insurance cover against the occurrence of certain specified events. The most common examples of general insurance relate to the risks of fire, automobile damage or loss, and theft.

General Insurance Standards Council A UK regulatory body set up to oversee the insurance industry in 2000 but wound up in 2002 as a result of the *Financial Services Authority taking over the regulatory role in this sector.

generally accepted accounting principles (GAAP) In the USA, the rules, accounting standards, and *accounting concepts followed by accountants in measuring, recording, and reporting transactions. There is a requirement to state whether *financial statements conform with GAAP. In the UK the term is more loosely used but is normally taken to mean accounting standards and the requirements of company legislation and the *stock exchange.

generally accepted auditing standards (GAAS) In the USA, the broad rules and guidelines set down by the Auditing Standards Board of the American Institute of Certified Public Accountants (AICPA). In carrying out audit work for a client, a certified public accountant is also obliged to apply *generally accepted accounting principles.

general meeting A meeting that all the members of an association may attend. *See also* ANNUAL GENERAL MEETING.

general need description The stage in the business buying process in which a company describes the general characteristics and quantity required of an item it wishes to purchase. *See* BUSINESS BUYER BEHAVIOUR.

general obligation bond In the USA, a security in which the municipal department with the authority to levy taxes has unconditionally promised payment.

general offer An offer of sale made to the general public rather than to a restricted number of people. For example, an object displayed in a shop window with a price tag is a general offer; the shopowner must sell to anyone willing to pay the price.

general partner *See* PARTNERSHIP.

general power of investment A

power, introduced by the Trustee Act (2000), that allows trustees to make any kind of investment that they could make if they were absolutely entitled to the assets of the trust fund. Previously, trustees were only permitted to make certain *authorized investments. This much wider general power of investment may be expressly excluded in the trust instrument. There are still some restrictions on investments in land. In exercising the general power of investment, the trustees are required by the Act to consider criteria relating to the suitability of the proposed investment to the trust and to review the investments from time to time with the same criteria in mind.

general price level An index that gives a measure of the purchasing power of money. In the UK, the best-known measure is the *Retail Price Index; in the USA it is the *Consumer Price Index.

general strike *See* STRIKE.

general union *See* TRADE UNION.

generic advertising Advertising a type of product or service rather than a branded product or service. Wool and fabric conditioners are both products that have benefitted from generic advertising.

generic brand *See* GENERIC PRODUCT.

generic demand (primary demand) Demand for a class of products (e.g. cars, television sets, etc.), without regard to brand.

generic name The name of a class or category of products, such as videos or pens. Sometimes the name of an extensively promoted and successful brand comes to be used as a generic name; examples include Biro, Hoover, and Walkman, which are then often written without an initial capital letter.

generic product (generic brand) A product that carries neither a manufacturer's name nor a distributor's *brand. The goods are plainly packaged with stark lettering that simply lists the contents. These no-name brands offer no guarantees of quality and are produced and sold inexpensively.

Gensaki The market for the resale and repurchase of medium- and long-term government securities that provides a money market substitute in Japan.

geodemographic segmentation

*Marketing segmentation in which consumers are grouped according to demographic variables, such as income and age, and identified by a geographic variable, such as post code or zip code. The base data is obtained from the census data. Two principles are involved: (1) people who live in the same neighbourhood, defined by a census enumeration district, are likely to share similar buying habits; (2) neighbourhoods can be categorized in terms of their populations: two or more neighbourhoods with similar populations can be placed in the same category. *See* GEOGRAPHIC INFORMATION SYSTEM.

geographic information system (GIS)

A tool for interpreting data based on *geodemographic segmentation. It consists of a demographic database, digitized maps, and computer software. The main systems available are:

ACORN – the first to be marketed, it has 56 neighbourhood types classified into 12 groups.

Mosaic – identifies some 60 types of neighbourhood with a wide range of variables classified into 2 market groupings.

Pinpoint – has many of the features of both *ACORN* and Mosaic but claims to offer greater discrimination by focusing on individual postal sectors and so targets potential customers more closely. This system has 60 neighbourhood types, which are aggregated to 25, and finally reduced to 12 main types.

geography-based organization

An organizational structure in which a market area is divided into territories; marketing efforts are specialized and carried out by geographic area.

geometric mean

An average obtained by calculating the nth root of a set of n numbers. For example the geometric mean of 7, 100, and 107 is $\sqrt[3]{74\,900} = 42.15$, which is considerably less than the *arithmetic mean of 71.3.

Gesellschaft

The German name for a limited company. *See* AKTIENGESELL-SCHAFT; GESELLSCHAFT MIT BESCHRÄNKTER HAFTUNG.

Gesellschaft mit beschränkter Haftung (GmbH)

The German name for a private limited company. The letters GmbH after the name of a company is equivalent to Ltd in the UK. *Compare* AKTIENGESELLSCHAFT.

gift aid

A system enabling individuals and companies to donate money to charities and for the charities to recover the tax paid on these donations (thus increasing the value of the donation by 28% in 2005–06). The taxpayer must make a **gift aid declaration** to the charity, stating that the payment is to be treated as gift aid. This system was first introduced in 1990, but tax relief was subject to the donation being of a minimum value. From April 2000, however, the system was extended to gifts of any value, including regular and one-off payments. It replaced the *deed of covenant in favour of charities from that date, although existing covenants remain valid. There are equivalent arrangements whereby tax relief can be obtained on gifts of land, stocks and shares, or plant and machinery.

gifts *inter vivos*

Gifts made during an individual's lifetime. The treatment of such gifts, for *inheritance tax purposes, depends on the amount of the gift, the occasion of the gift, and the recipient of the gift. Small gifts can be covered by the small gifts exemption (if less than £250) or by the individual's annual exemption (if less than £3000). Additional gifts are exempt if they are given on the occasion of marriage. Any gift from one individual to another individual is a *potentially exempt transfer and only becomes liable to tax if the donor dies within seven years of making the gift. Gifts to some *discretionary trusts are chargeable to inheritance tax at lifetime rates, which is half the death rate. The level of charge is dependent on the size of the transfer to the discretionary trust and the amount of previous *chargeable transfers within the preceding seven years. *See also* EXEMPT TRANSFERS.

gift tax

A US federal tax on property given away, levied on the donor.

gift with reservation

A gift in which the donor retains some benefit from the asset given away. Examples include:

- ˙shares given away in which the donor continues to receive the dividends;
- property given by a parent to a child, although the parent continues to live in the property, rent-free.

HM Revenue and Customs has detailed rules to cover gifts with reservation to ensure that such gifts are not used as a means of avoiding tax.

gilt-edged market makers (gilts primary dealers) The *market makers approved and supervised by the Bank of England for dealing directly with the Bank in gilt-edged securities. They have to some extent taken over the role of the *government broker.

gilt-edged security (gilt) A *fixed-interest security or stock issued by the British government in the form of **Exchequer stocks** or **Treasury stocks**. Gilts are among the safest of all investments, as the government is unlikely to default on interest or on principal repayments. They may be irredeemable (*see* CONSOLS) or redeemable. **Redeemable gilts** are classified as: **long-dated gilts** or **longs** (not redeemable for 15 years or more), **medium-dated gilts** or **mediums** (redeemable in 5 to 15 years), or **short-dated gilts** or **shorts** (redeemable in less than 5 years).

Like most fixed-interest securities, gilts are sensitive not only to interest rates but also inflation rates. This led the government to introduce **index-linked gilts** in the 1970s, with interest payments moving in a specified way relative to inflation.

Most gilts are issued in units of £100. If they pay a high rate of interest (i.e. higher than the current rate) a £100 unit may be worth more than £100 for a period of its life, even though it will only pay £100 on *redemption.

gilt repos market A market in the sale and repurchase of *gilt-edged securities set up by the Bank of England in 1996. Its size relative to the money market has made it an attractive market for the implementation of monetary policy with regard to the liquidity of the banking system.

gilts primary dealers *See* GILT-EDGED MARKET MAKERS.

gilt strip A discount UK government stock that has been issued by the Bank of England since 1996. A bond can be divided into a set of payments, which are made by the state and sold at a discount.

gilt unit trust A *unit trust that invests in *gilt-edged securities only.

Ginnie Mae **1.** Colloquial US name for the *Government National Mortgage Association (GNMA). **2.** Colloquial US name for a mortgage-supported bond issued by the Government National Mortgage Association. A **Ginnie Mae pass-through** is a bond backed by mortgages guaranteed by the GNMA, entitling the buyer to part of a pool of residential mortgages. These securities are called 'pass-throughs' because the investor receives both the principal and interest from the bank or originating mortgage supplier, who retains no margin or profit.

giro **1.** A banking arrangement for settling debts that has been used in Europe for many years. In 1968 the Post Office set up the UK National **Girobank** (now Girobank plc) based on a central office in Bootle, Merseyside. Originally a system for settling debts between people who did not have bank accounts, it now offers many of the services provided by *commercial banks, with the advantage that there are more post offices, at which Girobank services are provided, than there are bank branches. Also the post offices are open for longer hours than banks. Girobank also offers banking services to businesses, including an automatic debit transfer system, enabling businesses to collect money from a large number of customers at regular intervals for a small charge. **Bank Giro** is a giro system operated in the UK, independently of Girobank, by the clearing banks. It has no central organization, being run by bank branches. The service enables customers to make payments from their accounts by credit transfer to others who may or may not have bank accounts. **Bancogiro** is a giro system in operation on the Continent, enabling customers of the same bank to make payments to each other by immediate book entry. **2.** A colloquial name for a payment made by the UK Department for Work and Pensions to a person in need of financial support.

glass ceiling Invisible artificial barriers

(sometimes generated by management) that can limit the career advancement of employees, particularly women and members of minority groups. The expectations and aspirations of all staff within an organization should be met equally. While standards of practice in this area are laid down by law in many countries, they are not always observed. *See* EQUAL EMPLOYMENT OPPORTUNITY LEGISLATION.

Glass–Steagall Act (1933) US legislation that separated commercial banking and securities operations by banks. It was introduced in the aftermath of the great stock-market crash of 1929 to lessen the likelihood of such panics occurring again. It has been extensively modified in recent years, most notably by the *Financial Services Modernization Act (1999).

global bond 1. A bond traded in a number of different markets. **2.** A single bond for the total amount of a new issue of bonds, issued on a temporary basis to the bank (normally the *paying agent) that has responsibility for distributing the actual bonds to investors. In due course the global bond, sometimes referred to as a **global bearer bond**, is exchanged for the actual bonds.

global custody Safekeeping, usually by banks, of securities held on behalf of clients. It can include full portfolio services, with valuation and reporting, settlement of trades, registration of ownership, use of specialized nominee companies, collection of domestic and foreign income, and tax accounting. These services span markets and securities in a number of countries.

global firm An organization that operates in more than one country. Global firms have research, production, marketing, and financial advantages in their costs and reputation that are not available to purely domestic competitiors.

global information system An organized collection of telecommunications equipment, computer software, data, and personnel designed to capture, store, update, manipulate, analyse, and display on computer a broad range of information about worldwide business activity.

globalization 1. The process that has

enabled investment in financial markets to be carried out on an international basis. It has come about as a result of improvements in technology and *deregulation; with globalization, for example, investors in London can buy shares or bonds directly from Japanese brokers in Tokyo rather than passing through intermediaries. *See also* DISINTERMEDIATION. **2.** The process by which the world economy has become dominated by powerful *multinational enterprises operating across national and geographical barriers. The emergence since the 1980s of a single world market in which companies can easily move their operations from one country to another to take advantage of factors such as lower labour costs has affected the ability of national governments to order their own economic affairs. The benefits and drawbacks of this process, and the extent to which it may be controlled or influenced, are the subject of much controversy. **3.** The internationalization of products and services by large firms (*see* GLOBALIZATION STRATEGY; GLOBAL PRODUCT).

globalization strategy (standardization strategy) A *marketing strategy that is standardized for use throughout the world. The strategy assumes that the behaviour of many consumers throughout the world has become very similar. It assumes that members of market segments require the same features and buy for the same reasons. It also anticipates that the cost savings obtained from production and marketing on a global scale will more than offset the lower sales achieved because the product has not been adapted for local markets. Part of the globalization strategy is to make use of these *economies of scale to support the development of new products.

global offering A security issued in a number of different markets at the same time.

global organization A form of international organization in which top corporate management and staff plan worldwide manufacturing or operational facilities, marketing policies, financial flows, and logistical systems. The global operating unit reports directly to the chief executive, rather than an international divisional head.

global product A product that is marketed throughout the world with the same *brand name, such as Coca Cola, Guinness, Levi, and McDonalds. The advantage of a global product is that it usually enables an advertisement or image to be used worldwide. However, one drawback is that some advertising slogans do not travel well. For example, "things come alive with Pepsi", when translated into Chinese, led the populace to believe that their ancestors would be brought back from the dead; the Vauxhall Nova encountered similar problems in Spain, where Nova means "no go"!

Globex A global round-the-clock futures and options trading system introduced by the *Chicago Mercantile Exchange, the Chicago Board of Trade, Marché à Terme Internationale de France, and *Reuters.

GmbH Abbreviation for *Gesellschaft mit beschränkter Haftung. Compare AG.

GNMA Abbreviation for *Government National Mortgage Association, often referred to colloquially as *Ginnie Mae.

gnomes of Zürich An unflattering term applied to Swiss bankers and financiers, alluding to their secrecy and speculative activity. It was popularized by the Labour politician George Brown during the sterling crisis of 1964.

GNP Abbreviation for *gross national product.

goal divergence The situation in which there is a disparity or conflict between the goals of those who should ideally be working together to achieve mutually beneficial outcomes. In business, goal divergence may arise between shareholders and managers, managers and workers, or between a manufacturer or service provider and its marketing channels. The creation of **goal convergence**, rather than divergence, is a major concern of agency theory (see AGENCY RELATIONSHIP).

goal setting The practice of setting individual performance targets for employees. To maximize performance and increase *motivation four general principles should be followed: (1) goals should

be challenging but realistic; (2) goals should be specific, not vague; (3) employees should have involvement in setting these goals; and (4) goals should be measurable. See also PERFORMANCE MEASUREMENT.

godfather offer A *tender offer pitched so high that the management of the target company is unable to discourage shareholders from accepting it.

going-concern concept One of four fundamental *accounting concepts recognized in *Statement of Standard Accounting Practice (SSAP) 2, Disclosure of Accounting Policies; it is also referred to in the Companies Act (1985) and the EU's *Fourth Accounting Directive. It is the assumption that an enterprise will continue in operation for the foreseeable future, i.e. that there is no intention or necessity to liquidate or significantly curtail the scale of the enterprise's operation. The implication of this principle is that assets are shown at cost, or at cost less depreciation, and not at their *break-up values; it also assumes that liabilities applicable only on liquidation are not shown. The **going-concern value** of a business is higher than the value that would be achieved by disposing of its individual assets, since it is assumed that the business has a continuing potential to earn profits. This assumption will underlie the preparation of *financial statements. If an auditor thinks that a business may not be a going concern, the *auditors' report should be qualified.

Under the terms of *Financial Reporting Standard 18, Accounting Policies, which replaced SSAP 2 in December 2000, users of financial statements may assume that the going-concern concept has been applied unless there is clear warning to the contrary.

going-rate pricing Setting the price of products largely by following competitors' prices rather than by basing them on company costs or demand.

gold card A *credit card that entitles its holder to various benefits (e.g. an unsecured overdraft, some insurance cover, a higher limit, lower interest rates) in addition to those offered to standard card holders. The cards are available only to those on higher-than-average incomes.

gold clause A clause in a loan agreement between governments stipulating that repayments must be made in the gold equivalent of the currency involved at the time either the agreement or the loan was made. The purpose is to protect the lender against a fall in the borrower's currency, especially in countries suffering high rates of inflation.

gold coins Coins made of gold ceased to circulate after World War I. At one time it was illegal to hold more than four post-1837 gold coins and there have been various restrictions on dealing in and exporting gold coins at various times. Since 1979 (Exchange Control, Gold Coins Exemption, Order) gold coins may be imported and exported without restriction, except that gold coins more than 50 years old with a value in excess of £8000 cannot be exported without authorization from the Department of Trade and Industry. *See also* BRITANNIA COINS; KRUGERRAND.

golden handcuffs Financial incentives offered to key staff to persuade them to remain with an organization.

golden handshake *See* COMPENSATION FOR LOSS OF OFFICE.

golden hello A payment made to induce an employee to take up employment. The tax treatment depends on the nature of the payment; in some cases the taxpayer has successfully argued that the payment should be tax-free. However, in 1991 the House of Lords ruled that a payment made to a well-known footballer by a football club, as an inducement to join a new club, was taxable.

golden parachute A clause in an employment contract, usually of a senior executive, that provides for financial and other benefits if this person is sacked or decides to leave as the result of a takeover or change of ownership.

golden share A share in a company that controls at least 51% of the voting rights. A golden share has been retained by the UK government in some *privatization issues to ensure that the company does not fall into foreign or other unacceptable hands.

Goldilocks economy A colloquial term for an economy that combines low inflation with steady economic growth. Such an economy is "not too hot, not too cold, but just right" – like the porridge in the story of *Goldilocks and the Three Bears*.

gold market The market for buying and selling gold, which can be traded as *bullion, as coins, or in the futures and forward markets.

gold reserves Reserves held in the form of gold by a country for intervention on foreign-exchange markets.

gold standard A former monetary system in which a country's currency unit was fixed in terms of gold. In this system a currency was freely convertible into gold and free import and export of gold was permitted. It formed the basis for stable prices, since it linked the money supply to the quantity of gold reserves in a country. The UK was on the gold standard from the early 19th century until it finally withdrew in 1931. Most other countries withdrew soon after. *See also* INTERNATIONAL MONETARY FUND.

gold tranche *See* RESERVE TRANCHE.

good A *commodity or *service that is regarded by economists as satisfying a human need. An **economic good** is one that is both needed and sufficiently scarce to command a price. A **free good** is also needed but it is in abundant supply and therefore does not need to be purchased; air is an example. However, a commodity or service that is free but has required an effort to produce or obtain is not a free good in this sense. *See also* CONSUMER GOODS.

good delivery Delivery on the terms specified by the contract.

Goodhart's law Originally, an economic theory stating that if a particular definition of the *money supply were to be used as the basis for monetary policy, the stability of its statistical relationship with spending on the economy would break down and the policy would prove ineffective. The law is now used more widely to highlight the problems of focusing on the value of any specific variable as an indicator. In simple terms, when a measure becomes a target, it ceases to be a good measure. The applications to *performance measurement in management accounting and other aspects of business are obvious.

goods-in-transit insurance An insurance policy covering property against loss or damage while it is in transit from one place to another or being stored during a journey. Policies often specify the means of transport to be used, which may include the postal service. Goods shipped solely by sea are not covered by this type of policy, in which case a *marine insurance policy would be used.

goodwill An *intangible asset reflecting a business's customer connections, reputation, and similar factors. It can be valued as the difference between the value of the separable net assets of a business and the total value of the business. *Purchased goodwill is the difference between the fair value of the price paid for a business and the aggregate of the fair values of its separable net assets. It may be written off to *reserves or recognized as an intangible asset in the balance sheet and written off by *amortization to the *profit and loss account over its useful economic life. Internally generated goodwill should not be recognized in the financial statements of an organization. The treatment of goodwill is governed by *Financial Reporting Standard 10. The relevant *International Accounting Standards are IAS22, Business Combinations; IAS36, Impairment of Assets; and IAS38, Intangible Assets.

gopik A monetary unit of Azerbaijan worth one hundredth of a *manat.

go private To take a listed company into private ownership, thus removing its shares from the stock exchange. *Compare* GO PUBLIC.

go public To apply to a stock exchange to become a *public limited company. *Compare* GO PRIVATE. *See* FLOTATION.

Gordon growth model A model used to value businesses or shares based on applying a *present-value formula to future dividends. It assumes that the value of shares is the present value of future dividends, which will grow at a fixed rate g, and is expressed in the formula:

$$P_t = D_i + 1/(r - g),$$

where P_t is the value of a share or business in time period t; $D_i + 1$ is the value of the dividend in time period t plus one time period; r is the appropriate present value discount rate; and g is the growth rate of dividends per time period. The formula will only work if r is greater than g, which will be the case for mature companies.

go slow A form of *industrial action in which employees work at a deliberately slow pace. *See also* WORK-TO-RULE.

gourde (G) The standard monetary unit of Haiti, divided into 100 centimes.

government actuary A government officer who works with a small team of *actuaries to produce detailed population projections on the basis of observed trends and to assess their implications for national planning and public expenditure. He or she provides a consulting service to government departments and the public sector, giving advice on social security schemes, superannuation arrangements, and on government supervision of insurance companies.

government broker The stockbroker appointed by the government to sell government securities on the London Stock Exchange, under the instructions of the *Bank of England. He is also the broker to the National Debt Commissioners. Until October 1986 (*see* BIG BANG) the government broker was traditionally the senior partner of Mullins & Co. Since then, when the Bank of England started its own gilt-edged dealing room, the government broker has been appointed from the gilt-edged division of the Bank of England, although some of his or her functions are now undertaken by the *gilt-edged market makers.

government grant An amount paid to an organization to assist it to pursue activities considered socially or economically desirable. Grants may be revenue-based, i.e. made by reference to a specified category of revenue expenditure. Revenue-based grants should be credited to the *profit and loss account in the same period as the revenue expenditure to which they relate. Capital-based grants are made by reference to specified categories of capital expenditure and should be credited to the profit and loss account over the useful economic life of the asset to which they relate. *Statement of Standard Accounting Practice 4, Accounting for Government Grants, gives guidance with respect to the treatment of grants.

government market The market consisting of national and local government units that purchase or hire goods and services for carrying out their main functions. This includes defence procurement, education requirements (school buildings, books, teachers), medical services, road building, etc.

Government National Mortgage Association (GNMA) A US government agency that guarantees payment on securities backed by mortgages granted by such national organizations as the Federal Housing Finance Board (*see* FEDERAL HOME LOAN BANKS. *See also* GINNIE MAE.

government security (**government stock**) *See* GILT-EDGED SECURITY.

Government Statistical Service (GSS) *See* OFFICE FOR NATIONAL STATISTICS.

Gower Report A report on the protection of investors delivered to the UK government in 1984 by Professor J. Gower. Many of its recommendations were adopted in the subsequent *Financial Services Act (1986).

grace and notice provision The provision in a loan agreement that a borrower who fails on the due date to meet either an interest obligation or capital repayment obligation or who fails to comply with an undertaking is not initially in default. The grace and notice provision is inserted into a loan agreement to avoid problems arising because of administrative mistakes, such as payments not being made on the correct day.

Gramm–Leach–Bliley Act *See* FINANCIAL SERVICES MODERNIZATION ACT (1999).

grandfathered activity A transaction or practice that may be continued by those already engaged in it, but that is forbidden to new participants by changes in the legal or regulatory framework.

granny bond An index-linked savings certificate (*see* NATIONAL SAVINGS). They were formerly only available to persons over retirement age, hence the name.

grant-in-aid Any grant from central government to a local authority for particular services, other than the rate-support grant.

grant of probate An order from the High Court in the UK authorizing the executors of a will to deal with and distribute the property of the deceased person. If the person died intestate or did not appoint executors, the administrator of the estate has to obtain *letters of administration.

graphical user interface (GUI) A method that enables a user to operate software without a keyboard or without needing to learn a command language. GUIs rely on graphically presented menus, button-bars, and icons, which are activated using a mouse.

graphic rating scale A technique for evaluating the performance of an employee that can be used as part of the formal appraisal process (*see* EMPLOYEE EVALUATION; PERFORMANCE APPRAISAL). It involves listing the desirable traits that the jobholder should possess (e.g. integrity, drive, reliability, etc.) and rating (on a 5–7 point scale) each employee for each of these traits. These trait scores can then be aggregated into overall performance scores.

graphics Any computer output except alphanumeric characters, especially the drawings, graphs, and symbols that can be produced on computers. Most *business software packages include a graphics program that can produce graphs, histograms, and piecharts. More powerful graphics programs are used for *computer-aided design and animation.

graphology The analysis of handwriting as a tool of *personnel selection. In theory, a person's handwriting is supposed to reveal aspects of their personality and character, so a company might use a graphologist to produce profiles of the candidates for a job based on handwriting samples. This method of profiling candidates has low validity but is nonetheless sometimes used by management.

green audit *See* ENVIRONMENTAL AUDIT.

Greenbury Report A report issued in 1995 by a committee under the chairmanship of Sir Richard Greenbury that developed a number of recommendations of the Cadbury Report on directors' remuneration (*see* CADBURY CODE). It stressed the importance of a *remuneration committee of *non-executive directors, the provision of information on remuneration policy in the annual report and accounts, and the restriction of notice and contract periods to less than one year. *See also* HAMPEL COMMITTEE.

green currencies The currencies of members of the European Union using artificial rates of exchange for the purposes of the *Common Agricultural Policy (CAP). Their object was to protect farm prices in the member countries from wide variations caused by fluctuations in the real rates of exchange. The need for green currencies was greatly reduced by the *European Monetary System and with the advent of the single European currency the term is now seldom used.

greenfield development A housing or industrial development on a virgin site in the country. *Compare* BROWNFIELD DEVELOPMENT.

greenmail (**greymail**) The purchase of a large block of shares in a company, which are then sold back to the company at a premium over the market price in return for a promise not to launch a bid for the company. This practice is not uncommon in the USA, where companies are much freer than in the UK to buy their own shares. Although the morality of greenmail is dubious, it can be extremely profitable.

green marketing Marketing products that benefit the environment. The ecological properties of products are important in order that companies produce ecologically safer products, including recyclable and biodegradable packing. Better pollution controls and more energy-efficient production processes and product performance also form a part of green marketing. *See* PRODUCT LIFE CYCLE.

green product A product that its manufacturers claim will not cause damage to the environment, especially a new product or formulation that is being launched to replace one that is said to cause environmental damage.

green reporting (**environmental accounting**) A report by the directors of a company that attempts to quantify the costs and benefits of that company's operations in relation to the environment. At present relatively few companies disclose such information in their *annual accounts and report. This is, however, a growing practice and reflects the concerns of many investors, consumers, and other stakeholders. New Zealand is one of several countries that have recently introduced legislation on green reporting. The European Union's *Accounts Modernization Directive, which is binding on publicly listed companies from 1 January 2005, states that company information should disclose the environmental impact of a business's activities "where appropriate". *See* OPERATING AND FINANCIAL REVIEW. *See also* ENVIRONMENTAL AUDIT; ENVIRONMENTAL COSTS; SOCIAL RESPONSIBILITY REPORTING.

greenshoe (**greenshoe option**) An option given by an issuer of securities to an *underwriter entitling the latter to buy and sell extra shares in an issue if there is high public demand. The term derives from the first company to provide such an arrangement, the Green Shoe Manufacturing Co.

Grey Book Regulations issued by the *Bank of England to the UK banking sector.

grey-hair investment *See* GREY WAVE.

grey knight In a takeover battle, a counter bidder whose ultimate intentions are undeclared. The original unwelcome bidder is the *black knight, the welcome counter bidder for the target company is the *white knight. The grey knight is an ambiguous intervener whose appearance is unwelcome to all.

greymail *See* GREENMAIL.

grey market 1. Any market for goods that are in short supply. It differs from a *black market in being legal. 2. A market in shares that have not been issued, although they are due to be issued in a short time. Market makers will often deal with investors or speculators who are willing to trade in anticipation of receiving an allotment of these shares or are willing to cover their deals after flotation. This type of grey market provides an indication of the market price (and premium, if any) after flotation. **3.** The market for goods or services created by older people with a comfortable disposable income and a willingness to spend.

grey wave (grey-hair investment) A company that is thought to be potentially profitable and ultimately a good investment, but that is unlikely to fulfil expectations in the near future. The fruits of an investment in the present should be available when the investor has grey hair.

grid organizational development *See* BLAKE–MOUTON MANAGERIAL GRID.

grievance procedure A standard course of action that should be followed by employees with a complaint against their employer. The procedure normally has three steps: (1) the employee submits a written statement setting out his or her complaint; (2) a formal meeting is held between employer and employee; (3) if the complaint is rejected, a second meeting should be held to consider any appeal by the employee. If the employee does not complete step (1) he or she cannot take the case to an *employment tribunal; if either side fails to complete steps (2) and (3) then the tribunal may vary any compensation awarded by up to 50%. The procedure does not apply in cases of collective grievance.

Groschen 1. A former monetary unit of Austria, worth one hundredth of a *Schilling (until 2002). **2.** A former German coin, worth 10 Pfennige (until 2002).

gross domestic product (GDP) The monetary value of all the goods and services produced by an economy over a specified period. It is measured in three ways:
(1) on the basis of expenditure, i.e. the value of all goods and services bought, including consumption, capital expenditure, increase in the value of stocks, government expenditure, and exports less imports;
(2) on the basis of income, i.e. income arising from employment, self-employment, rent, company profits (public and private), and stock appreciation;
(3) on the basis of the value added by in-

dustry, i.e. the value of sales less the costs of raw materials.
In the UK, statistics for GDP are published monthly by the government on all three bases, although there are large discrepancies between each measure. Economists are usually interested in the real rate of change of GDP to measure the performance of an economy, rather than the absolute level of GDP. *See also* GDP DEFLATOR; GROSS NATIONAL PRODUCT; NET NATIONAL PRODUCT.

gross income 1. The income of a person or an organization before the deduction of the expenses incurred in earning it. **2.** Income that is liable to tax but from which the tax has not been deducted. For many types of income, tax may be deducted at source (*see* DEDUCTIONS AT SOURCE) leaving the taxpayer with a net amount.

grossing up Converting a net return into the equivalent gross amount. For example, if a net dividend (*d*) has been paid after deduction of *r*% tax, the gross equivalent (*g*) is given by:

$$g = 100d/(100 - r).$$

gross interest The amount of interest applicable to a particular loan or deposit before tax is deducted. Interest rates may be quoted gross (as they are on government securities) or net (as in most building society deposits or bank deposits). The gross interest less the tax deducted at the basic rate of income tax gives the net interest. Any tax suffered is usually, but not always, available as a credit against tax liabilities.

gross investment *See* NET INVESTMENT.

gross margin *See* GROSS PROFIT.

gross margin ratio *See* GROSS PROFIT PERCENTAGE.

gross national product (GNP) The *gross domestic product (GDP) with the addition of interest, profits, and dividends received from abroad by UK residents and with those payments made from the UK to overseas residents deducted. The GNP better reflects the welfare of the population in monetary terms, although it is not as accurate a guide as to the productive performance of the economy as the GDP. *See also* NET NATIONAL PRODUCT.

gross profit (gross margin; gross profit margin) The difference between the sales revenue of a business and the *cost of sales. It does not include the costs of finance, administration, or distribution. *Compare* NET PROFIT.

gross profit percentage (gross margin ratio) A ratio of financial performance calculated by expressing the *gross profit as a percentage of sales. With retailing companies in particular, it is regarded as a prime measure of their trading success. The only ways in which a company can improve its gross margin ratio are to increase selling prices and/or reduce its *cost of sales.

gross receipts The total amount of money received by a business in a specified period before any deductions for costs, raw materials, taxation, etc. *Compare* NET RECEIPTS.

gross redemption yield (effective yield; yield to maturity) The internal rate of return of a bond bought at a specified price and held until maturity; it therefore includes all the income and all the capital payments due on the bond. The tax payable on the interest and the capital repayments are ignored.

gross tonnage (gross register tonnage) *See* TONNAGE.

gross weight **1.** The total weight of a package including its contents and the packing. The **net weight** is the weight of the contents only, i.e. after deducting the weight of the packing (often called the **tare**). **2.** The total weight of a vehicle (road or rail) and the goods it is carrying, as shown by a weighbridge. The **net weight** is obtained by deducting the tare of the vehicle.

grosz (*plural* **groszy**) A monetary unit of Poland worth one hundredth of a *zloty.

ground rent Rent payable under a lease that has been granted or assigned for a capital sum (premium). Normally, long leases on offices, flats, etc., are granted for such a premium, payable when the lease is first granted; in addition the leaseholder pays the landlord a relatively small annual ground rent. *See also* RENT.

group A parent undertaking and its subsidiary or subsidiaries. In UK tax law, two or more companies constitute a group where one company holds more than 50% of the shares in the other(s). This test is usually applied to the voting share capital only. Where there is a group of companies, the availability of the lower rates of corporation tax is restricted. Where the links between companies are made by share ownership of 75% or over, assets can be passed among the companies without a charge to *capital gains tax. *See* CONSOLIDATED FINANCIAL STATEMENTS; GROUP RELIEF. *See also* MEDIUM-SIZED GROUP; SMALL GROUP.

group accounts (group financial statements) *See* CONSOLIDATED FINANCIAL STATEMENTS.

group decision support system (GDSS) *See* DECISION SUPPORT SYSTEM.

group discussion A *marketing research technique that brings between six and eight respondents together for at least an hour to discuss a marketing issue under the guidance of an interviewer. It has been found that, once such a group is relaxed, it will fully explore issues in a manner that shows what is important to it, using its own rather than marketers' terminology. The interviewer, who is a specialist acting on behalf of a client, first draws up a **topic guide** that identifies the points to be explored. A *sample of respondents – who must not know one another – is recruited to match certain criteria (e.g. if the problem concerned tea all respondents would be tea drinkers). The group meets in the interviewer's home or in a hotel; with the discussion being tape-recorded, the interviewer describes the problem and then adopts a passive role, allowing the group to discuss their views and interjecting further questions only if some aspect of the problem is not being explored adequately. After a minimum of four group discussions, the interviewer will have sufficient material to write a report and recommend a particular action. Group discussions are a qualitative procedure (*see* QUALITATIVE MARKETING RESEARCH) frequently used to determine attitudes to particular products or advertisements. *See also* FOCUS GROUP.

group income A *dividend paid by one company in a group to another. The dividends received are not subject to *corporation tax.

group life assurance A *life-assurance policy that covers a number of people, usually a group of employees or the members of a particular club or association. Often a single policy is issued and premiums are deducted from salaries or club-membership fees. In return for an agreement that all employees or members join the scheme, insurers are prepared to ask only a few basic questions about the health of a person joining. However, with the advent of AIDS insurers are no longer prepared to waive all health enquiries, as they were some years ago.

Group of Eight (G8) The *Group of Seven plus Russia. Russia was admitted as a full member of this economic summit grouping in June 2002.

Group of Seven (G7) The seven leading Western industrial nations: namely, the USA, Japan, Germany, France, UK, Italy, and Canada. This group evolved from the first economic summit held in 1976 and now holds an annual meeting attended by heads of state. The original aim was to discuss economic coordination but the agenda has since broadened to include political issues. Since the 1980s increasing enthusiasm for international economic cooperation has sometimes led to collective action, for example on exchange rates as a result of meetings of G7 finance ministers. Since 1991 Russia has attended G7 meetings, initially as an observer but from 2002 as a full participant. *See* GROUP OF EIGHT.

Group of Ten (G10; the Paris Club) The ten prosperous industrial nations that agreed in 1962 to lend money to the *International Monetary Fund (IMF), namely Belgium, Canada, France, (West) Germany, Italy, Japan, The Netherlands, Sweden, UK, and the USA. They inaugurated *Special Drawing Rights. Switzerland, although not a member of the IMF, is a party to the *general arrangements to borrow, which the G10 countries established to provide additional credit facilities. Luxembourg is also an associate member.

Group of Thirty A group of economic

experts comprising individuals from central and commercial banks and finance ministries, as well as academic economists. The group was founded in 1979 by the Rockefeller Foundation to carry out research into international economic issues.

Group of Three (G3) The three largest Western industrialized economies, i.e. the USA, Germany, and Japan.

group registration Registration for *value added tax for a group of companies under common control. The business carried on by any group member is treated as that of the representative member. VAT is not charged on supplies between group members.

group relief Relief available to companies within a 75% group as a result of which *qualifying losses can be transferred to other group companies. The losses transferred are available to set against the other group members' profits chargeable to corporation tax, thus reducing the overall tax liability for the group. A 75% group, for group relief, exists if one company holds 75% or more of:
• the ordinary share capital, and
• the distributable income rights, and
• the rights to the net assets in a winding-up.
From 1 April 2000 members of a group no longer have to be resident in the UK to qualify for relief. *See also* CONSORTIUM RELIEF.

group roles Certain identifiable roles (i.e. coherent sets of behaviours) that tend to be adopted by the different members of a group, partly as a matter of personal inclination but also as a response to the expectations of others. These will include *relationship roles, such as the group encourager or comedian, as well as *task roles, such as the initiator or summarizer.

groupthink In group decision making, the tendency to drift into ill-conceived policies or decisions without adequate debate. This can be a result of various pressures, including the illusion of ingroup superiority and the wish to achieve consensus and avoid painful disagreements.

growth 1. An increase in the value of an asset. If growth is sought in an investment, it is an increase in its capital value

that is required. *See also* GROWTH STOCKS.
2. The expansion of an economy, usually expressed in terms of an increase of national income.

growth curve A curve on a graph in which a variable is plotted as a function of time. The curve thus illustrates the growth of the variable. This may be used to show the growth of a population, sales of a product, price of a security, etc.

growth fund A managed fund holding assets that are expected to grow in value and provide capital gains. In general, these funds are supposed to provide higher returns but with greater risks.

growth industry Any industry that is expected to grow faster than GDP.

growth needs *See* ERG THEORY.

growth rate The amount of change over a period in some of the financial characteristics of a company, such as sales revenue or profits. It is normally measured in percentage terms and can be compared to the *Retail Price Index, or some other measure of inflation, to assess the real performance of the company.

growth recession *See* RECESSION.

growth stage The stage in a *product life cycle during which a product's sales start climbing rapidly.

growth stocks Securities that are expected to offer the investor sustained *capital growth. Investors and investment managers often distinguish between growth stocks and income stocks. The former are expected to provide *capital gains; the latter, high income. The investor will usually expect a growth stock to be an ordinary share in a company whose products are selling well and whose sales are expected to expand, whose capital expenditure on new plant and equipment is high, whose earnings are growing, and whose management is strong, resourceful, and investing in product development and long-term research.

GSS Abbreviation for Government Statistical Service. *See* OFFICE FOR NATIONAL STATISTICS.

guaraní (₲) The standard monetary unit of Paraguay, divided into 100 céntimos.

guarantee **1.** *See* WARRANTY. **2.** A promise made by a third party (**guarantor**), who is not a party to a contract between two others, to accept liability if one of the parties fails to fulfil the contractual obligations. For example, a bank may make a loan to a person, provided that a guarantor is prepared to repay the loan if the borrower fails to do so. The banker may require the guarantor to provide some *security to support his guarantee. *See also* BANK GUARANTEE.

guaranteed bond (**guaranteed stock**) A *bond in which payments of principal or interest are guaranteed by a party other than the issuer. In the USA this is often a state.

guaranteed-income bond A bond issued by a life-assurance company that guarantees the purchaser a fixed income as well as a guaranteed return of capital at the end of the term or on prior death. *See also* SINGLE-PREMIUM ASSURANCE.

guarantor *See* GUARANTEE.

GUI Abbreviation for *graphical user interface.

guide price *See* COMMON AGRICULTURAL POLICY.

guilder **1.** The standard monetary unit of the Netherlands Antilles (NAf) and Surinam (Sf), divided into 100 cents. **2.** The former standard monetary unit of The Netherlands, divided into 100 cents. It was subsumed into the euro for all purposes other than cash transactions in January 1999 and abolished in 2002.

guinea A former British coin, originally made from gold from Guinea. First issued in 1663, it had various values; during most of the 18th century it stood at 21 shillings. Although it was replaced in 1817 by the sovereign, it persisted, not as a coin but as a unit of 21 shillings for charging for some professional services, until decimalization (1971).

habitual buying behaviour Consumer behaviour in the buying of cheap frequently purchased items, characterized by low consumer involvement and few significant *brand differences. Purchases are made out of habit, rather than a strong commitment to a brand. Generally, price and sales promotions are used to stimulate sales, as consumers tend to base their decisions on past behaviour and have no need for further information.

hacker An individual with a good understanding of the structure and operation of computer networks, who deliberately breaks into confidential systems. In many cases there are no malign intentions, although hackers can cause damage by inadvertently introducing viruses or commands that disrupt the proper working of the system. Those with more malign intentions are sometimes known as **crackers**.

halal Acceptable under Islamic law. The term is applied to those forms of banking and finance that avoid the religious prohibition against taking interest payments. *Compare* HARAAM. *See* ISLAMIC FINANCE.

halala A monetary unit of Saudi Arabia, worth one hundredth of a *riyal.

haler (*plural* **haleru** or **halers**) A monetary unit of the Czech Republic and Slovakia, worth one hundredth of a *koruna.

half-commission man A person who is not a member of a stock exchange but works for a *stockbroker, introducing clients in return for half, or some other agreed share, of the commission.

hallmark A series of marks (usually four) stamped on articles made of gold, silver, or platinum in the UK to indicate the maker, the hall or assay office making the mark, the quality of the metal, and the date of assay. Each of the four halls (London, Birmingham, Sheffield, and Edinburgh) have distinguishing marks (e.g. a leopard for London, an anchor for Birmingham). The quality of gold was indicated by a *carat mark (22, 18, 14, and 9 carats) until 1975, after which it was expressed in parts of gold per 1000 (e.g. 22 carat = 916, 14 carat = 585, 9 carat = 375). The quality mark for sterling silver (925 parts per 1000) in England is a lion (passant) and in Scotland a thistle or lion (rampant). Britannia silver (958) is indicated by a full-length figure of Britannia. Platinum is indicated by an orb. The date is indicated by a letter in a specifically shaped shield. Hallmarks on precious metals are accepted internationally and there are heavy penalties for forging them or selling articles made in the UK of these metals (except those exempt) without them. The future of hallmarks is, however, uncertain, owing to current moves to make the marking of precious metals consistent throughout the EU. Since January 1999 all articles made in the EU of gold, silver, or platinum must carry a numeral indication of purity (in parts per 1000) in addition to any hallmarks.

hall test A marketing research test conducted in a room or hall close to a shopping centre. Consumers, selected at random, are invited to come to the hall to participate in the test, which involves answering questions about their buying habits, purchases, etc.

halo effect *See* HORNS AND HALO EFFECT.

hammering An announcement on the *London Stock Exchange that a broker is unable to meet his obligations. It was formerly (until 1970) introduced by three blows of a hammer by a waiter and followed by the broker's name.

Hampel Committee A committee set up under the chairmanship of Sir Ronald Hampel to review the implementation of the *Cadbury Code and the recommendations of the *Greenbury Report. A report was issued in 1998 emphasizing that the primary duty of directors is to shareholders and that the recommendations of the two earlier reports should be treated as guidelines rather than prescriptive rules.

handbill A form of printed advertisement delivered into the hands of likely customers; handbills may also be attached to their cars or put through their letter boxes.

Hang Seng Index An arithmetically weighted index based on the capital value of 33 stocks on the Hong Kong Stock Exchange. It was first quoted in 1964 and takes its name from the Hang Seng Bank. The number of stocks, 33, was chosen because the bank was founded in 1933 and 33 is a lucky number in Chinese astrology.

hào A monetary unit of Vietnam, worth one tenth of a *đông.

haraam Forbidden by Islamic law. In financial contexts, this applies chiefly to lending or borrowing money at interest. Various schemes enable Muslims to take out loans, notably mortgages, without violating this principle of faith. *Compare* HALAL. *See* ISLAMIC FINANCE.

hard commodity *See* COMMODITY.

hard currency A currency that is commonly accepted throughout the world; they are usually those of the Western industrialized countries although other currencies have achieved this status, especially within regional trading blocs. Holdings of hard currency are valued because of their universal purchasing power. Countries with *soft currencies go to great lengths to obtain and maintain stocks of hard currencies, often imposing strict restrictions on their use by the private citizen.

hard dollars A fee paid to a US stockbroker, investment adviser, etc., for research, analysis, or advice, as opposed to **soft dollars**, which refers to the commission earned on purchases made.

hard sell The use of selling methods that emphasize the supposed virtues of a product, repeat its name, and attempt to force it upon the consumer by forceful and unsubtle means. *Compare* SOFT SELL.

hard systems Systems that consist entirely of non-human elements, e.g. machines. The behaviour of all the elements in the system should be predictable and amenable to mathematical or other scientific modelling methods. *Compare* SOFT SYSTEMS METHODOLOGY.

hardware The electronic and mechanical parts of a computer system; for example, the central processing unit, disk drive, screen, and printer. *Compare* SOFTWARE.

Harmonized Index of Consumer Prices (HICP) *See* CONSUMER PRICE INDEX.

harmonizer *See* RELATIONSHIP ROLES.

harvesting strategy Making a short-term profit from a particular product shortly before withdrawing it from the market. This is often achieved by reducing the marketing support it enjoys, such as advertising, on the assumption that the effects of earlier advertising will still be felt and the product will continue to sell.

haulage The charge made by a **haulier** (**haulage contractor**) for transporting goods, especially by road. If the goods consist of a large number of packages (e.g. 100 tonnes of cattlefood packed in 2000 bags each weighing 50 kilograms) there will be a separate charge for loading and unloading the vehicle.

Hawthorne studies Research conducted in the 1920s and 1930s at the Western Electric Company's Hawthorne plant in Chicago. The programme set out to explore the effects of physical working conditions on employee productivity but became known more for its major finding of the importance of the social dimension of workplace relations. Although output increased significantly after changes were made in working conditions, it was subsequently concluded that this owed more to the workers' sense that they were receiving special treatment than to the changes themselves. The Hawthorne studies laid the basis for the *human relations theory of management.

Hay method A *job evaluation system based on three core factors: know-how, problem solving, and accountability. The system, which is named after the US management expert Edward N. Hay, is essentially a combination of the *point method and the *factor-comparison method.

head hunter *See* EMPLOYMENT AGENCY.

head lease The main or first *lease, out

of which **sub-leases** may be created. For example, if A grants a 99-year lease to B and B then grants a 12-year lease of the same property to C, the 99-year lease is the head lease and the 12-year lease is a sub-lease.

Health and Safety Commission A UK government body appointed to look after the health, safety, and welfare of people at work; to protect the public from risks arising from work activities; and to control the use and storage of explosives and other dangerous substances. It is composed of representatives from trade unions, employers, and local authorities with a full-time chairman. The **Health and Safety Executive** is a statutory body that advises the Commission and enforces its policies through inspection of industrial and other premises.

hedge A financial transaction or position designed to mitigate the risk of other transactions or positions. For example, a manufacturer may contract to sell a large quantity of a product for delivery over the next six months. If the product depends on a raw material that fluctuates in price, and if the manufacturer does not have sufficient raw material in stock, an open position will result. This open position can be hedged by buying the raw material required on a *futures contract; if it has to be paid for in a foreign currency the manufacturer's currency needs can be hedged by buying that foreign currency forward or on an *option. Operations of this type do not offer total protection because the prices of *spot goods and futures do not always move together, but it is possible to reduce the vulnerability of an open position substantially by hedging.

Buying futures or options as a hedge is only one kind of hedging; it is known as **long hedging**. In **short hedging**, something is sold to cover a risk. For example, a fund manager may have a large holding of long-term fixed income investments and is worried that an anticipated rise in interest rates will reduce the value of the *portfolio. This risk can be hedged by selling interest-rate futures on a *financial futures market. If interest rates rise the loss in the value of the portfolio will be offset by the profit made in covering the futures sale at a lower price.

hedge fund A *unit trust that is subject to minimum regulation, typically a partnership or mutual fund that attempts to obtain gains by exploiting market anomalies. These funds are often high-return and are regarded as speculative. The hedge fund Long Term Capital Management got into serious trouble in 1998, raising concerns over the stability of the whole international financial system.

hedging against inflation Protecting one's cash flow, income, or capital against inflation by buying *equities or making other investments that are likely to rise with the general level of prices.

hereditament *Real property. Originally, it was property that would be inherited by the heir on intestacy. **Corporeal hereditaments** are physical real property, such as land, buildings, trees, and minerals. **Incorporeal hereditaments** are intangible rights, such as easements or profits à prendre, attached to land.

Herstatt risk *See* SETTLEMENT RISK.

Herzberg's two-factor theory *See* HYGIENE FACTORS; MOTIVATORS.

HICP Abbreviation for Harmonized Index of Consumer Prices. *See* CONSUMER PRICE INDEX.

hidden reserve Funds held in reserve but not disclosed on the balance sheet (they are also known as **off balance sheet reserves** or **secret reserves**). They arise when an asset is deliberately either undisclosed or undervalued. Such hidden reserves are permitted for some banking institutions but are not permitted for limited companies as they reduce profits and therefore the corporation tax liability of the company.

hidden tax *See* STEALTH TAX.

hidden unemployment (**concealed unemployment**) *Unemployment that does not appear in government statistics, which are usually based on figures for those drawing unemployment benefit (since 1996 known as jobseeker's allowance in the UK). In addition to these people there will be some who are doing very little productive work, although they are not registered as unemployed. These include workers on short time for whom their employers are expecting to be able to provide work shortly; workers who are not usefully employed, although their employers think they are; people who are not in full-time work but who do not qualify for the jobseeker's allowance for various reasons (including those drawing alternative benefits, such as income support or incapacity benefit); and others who choose not to claim benefit.

hierarchy of effects The steps in the persuasion process that lead a consumer to purchase a particular product. They are awareness, knowledge, liking, preference, conviction, and finally a decision to purchase.

hierarchy of needs *See* MASLOW'S MOTIVATIONAL HIERARCHY.

higher rate of income tax A rate of *income tax that is higher than the *basic rate of income tax. For 2005–06 higher-rate tax is payable on taxable income, after *personal allowances and other allowances, of £32,400 and over. The rate of tax is 40%.

high-involvement management An approach to management that emphasizes the need to develop *organizational commitment amongst employees, on the grounds that this will lead to improved *motivation, better performance, and a lower *labour turnover rate. It argues that employee commitment can be enhanced through training, incentives, sharing of information, and participation in decision making.

high-involvement product A product that involves the consumer in taking time and trouble before deciding on a purchase. This will include looking in several catalogues, shops, etc., to compare prices and the products themselves. High-involvement products include such major purchases as cars and houses, as well as computers, home entertainment systems, and many other domestic products. *Compare* LOW-INVOLVEMENT PRODUCT.

high-level language A type of computer-programming language. High-level languages are designed to reflect the needs of the programmer rather than the capabilities of the computer. They use abstract data and control structures, and symbolic

names for variables. There are a large number of high-level languages; *BASIC, *COBOL, *FORTRAN, and *C are examples.

high-street bank *See* COMMERCIAL BANK.

high yielder A stock or share that gives a high yield but is more speculative than most, i.e. its price may fluctuate.

HIP Abbreviation for *human information processing.

hire purchase (HP) A method of buying goods in which the purchaser takes possession of them as soon as an initial instalment of the price (a **deposit**) has been paid and obtains ownership of the goods when all the agreed number of subsequent instalments have been paid. A **hire-purchase agreement** differs from a **credit-sale agreement** and **sale by instalments** (or a **deferred payment agreement**) because in these transactions ownership passes when the contract is signed. It also differs from a contract of hire, because in this case ownership never passes. Hire-purchase agreements were formerly controlled by government regulations stipulating the minimum deposit and the length of the repayment period. These controls were removed in 1982. Hire-purchase agreements were also formerly controlled by the Hire Purchase Act (1965), but most are now regulated by the Consumer Credit Act (1974). In this Act a hire-purchase agreement is regarded as one in which goods are bailed in return for periodical payments by the bailee; ownership passes to the bailee if the terms of the agreement are complied with and the option to purchase is exercised.

A hire-purchase agreement often involves a *finance company as a third party. The seller of the goods sells them outright to the finance company, which enters into a hire-purchase agreement with the hirer.

histogram A graph of a frequency distribution constructed with rectangles, in which the areas of the rectangles are proportional to the frequencies.

historical cost The value of a unit of stock or other asset calculated on the basis of the original cost to the organization of purchasing or manufacturing it, rather than on the basis of its current value to the organization. *Compare* CURRENT COST.

historical-cost accounting A system of accounting based on the principle that assets should be valued at *historical cost. It is relaxed to some extent by such practices as the valuation of stock at the lower of cost and *net realizable value and, in the UK, revaluation of *fixed assets. The advantages of historical-cost accounting are that it is relatively objective, easy to apply, difficult to falsely manipulate, and suitable for audit verification. In times of high inflation, however, the results of historical-cost accounting can be misleading as profit can be overstated, assets understated in terms of current values, and *capital maintenance is only concerned with the nominal amount of the capital invested rather than its purchasing power. Because of these defects it is argued that historical-cost accounting is of little use for decision making, but attempts to replace it with such other methods as *current-cost accounting have failed.

Company legislation sets out the rules for the application of historical-cost accounting to *financial statements. Companies may also choose to use alternative accounting rules based on the **modified historical-cost convention**, in which certain assets are included at revalued amounts.

historical summary A voluntary statement appearing in the *annual accounts and report of some companies in which the main financial results are given for the previous five to ten years.

HM Revenue and Customs *See* BOARD OF CUSTOMS AND EXCISE; BOARD OF INLAND REVENUE.

HMSO Formerly, abbreviation for Her Majesty's *Stationery Office.

hockey-stick growth Very rapid exponential growth, in which a graph of, for example, revenue or visitors to a website against time is shaped like a hockey stick.

holder The purchaser of a financial obligation, i.e. a dealer who has a *long position in this obligation.

holding company (parent company) A company that holds shares in other com-

panies in a *group (usually, but not necessarily, its subsidiaries).

holding costs *See* CARRYING COSTS.

holdout A situation in which creditors refuse to agree to a particular reorganization proposal for a firm in *financial distress.

holiday and travel insurance An insurance policy covering a variety of risks for the duration of a person's holiday. Although policies vary, an average policy covers the policyholder's baggage and personal effects for all risks (*see* ALL-RISKS POLICY); compensation for delays while travelling to or from the holiday; refund of deposits lost if the holiday has to be cancelled for any of a number of specific causes; theft or loss of money, traveller's cheques, or credit cards; payment of medical expenses or costs of flying home in the event of illness or injury; and payment of legal compensation for injuring other people or damaging their property because of negligence.

holistic evaluation An evaluation of an advertising or marketing campaign as a whole, as distinct from an analysis of the results of its constituent parts.

holon *See* SOFT SYSTEMS METHODOLOGY.

home audit Marketing research conducted in the home by means of panels of householders who keep a diary on a regular basis recording the products they buy and when they buy them.

home banking Carrying out banking transactions by means of a home computer linked to a bank's computer via the Internet (**e-banking**) or by means of a telephone link to a call centre or a computerized system (**telephone banking**). This enables the account-holder to carry out certain operations – most commonly checking the balance held or transferring sums between accounts – at any time of the day or night without leaving the home or office. Although regular transfers, such as direct debits, can be arranged, paying in or drawing cheques is not possible in home banking (although it is using a *postal account). In the UK these services are now offered by all the High-Street banks but only a minority of account-holders make regular use of them. Home banking is, however, a growing trend among business customers.

home page A document, usually in graphical form, that acts as the entry point to a *World Wide Web server. Set out in a page format, it provides hypertext access to related menus and files.

home service assurance *See* INDUSTRIAL LIFE ASSURANCE.

home shopping channels A form of television direct marketing in which television programmes or entire channels are dedicated to selling goods and services. While still relatively small in money terms in the UK and Europe, in the USA it is estimated that more than $4 billion is spent on goods and services in this manner. *Compare* DIRECT-RESPONSE TV ADVERTISING.

honour policy A marine insurance policy that covers the risk of a person who has an interest in a voyage in circumstances in which the interest may be difficult to establish.

horizontal integration *See* INTEGRATION.

horizontal job enlargement *See* JOB ENLARGEMENT.

horizontal marketing systems A channel arrangement in which two or more companies, at one level, join together to follow a new marketing opportunity. Such *joint ventures have become more commonplace as companies combine their capital, production facilities, and marketing resources to compete in global markets.

horizontal mobility *See* MOBILITY OF LABOUR.

horizontal spread A combination of *options with different expiry dates, such as a long put option combined with a short put option.

horns and halo effect An effect in which one person's judgement of another is unduly influenced by a first impression; it may be either unfavourable (horns) or favourable (halo). The effects can be misleading when interviewing job applicants. For example, a well-qualified candidate who arrives late for an interview, for a good reason, may be passed over as a bad timekeeper, while a poorly qualified but punctual and well-groomed candidate may be offered the job.

hostile bid A *takeover bid that is unwelcome either to the board of directors of the target company or to its shareholders.

hot list The most up-to-date names on a mail-order buyer or enquirer list. Hot lists are of great value in *direct marketing.

hot money 1. Money that moves at short notice from one financial centre to another in search of the highest short-term interest rates, for the purposes of *arbitrage, or because its owners are apprehensive of some political intervention in the money market, such as a *devaluation. Hot money can influence a country's *balance of payments. **2.** Money that has been acquired dishonestly and must therefore be untraceable.

house brand *See* OWN BRAND.

household insurance 1. An insurance policy that covers the structure of a home (often called **buildings insurance**). **2.** An insurance policy covering the personal goods and effects kept inside a home (**contents policy**). A **comprehensive householder's policy** will cover both the buildings and the contents.

house journal A journal produced by a large organization for the benefit of its employees. It usually seeks to keep all levels of employees informed of the general policy of the company, to function as a forum for employees, and often to provide social news. It often helps to create a corporate identity, especially if employees are widely distributed geographically.

house list A direct-mail seller's own list of names of either current or lapsed customers, prospects, members, etc.

HP Abbreviation for *hire purchase.

HRM Abbreviation for *human-resource management.

hryvna The standard monetary unit of Ukraine, divided into 100 kopiykas.

HTML (hypertext markup language) The computer language used to write *hypertext. A particular feature of HTML is the use of tags to display *hyperlinks.

HTTP (hypertext transfer protocol) A standard protocol for the transmission of information on the World Wide Web. *See* HYPERTEXT; INTERNET.

hull insurance *Marine insurance or aircraft insurance covering the structure of a ship, boat, hovercraft, or aeroplane and the equipment maintained permanently on board.

human capital The skills, general or specific, acquired by an individual in the course of training and work experience. The concept was introduced by Gary Becker in the 1960s in order to point out that wages reflect in part a return on human capital. This theory has been used to explain large variations in wages for apparently similar jobs and why even in a *recession a firm may retain its workers on relatively high wages, in spite of involuntary *unemployment. *See also* INTELLECTUAL CAPITAL.

human factors *See* ERGONOMICS.

human information processing (HIP) The *cognitive processes involved in thinking, remembering, interpreting, and *decision making. The importance of HIP to business is that an understanding of the way in which people use information in the decision-making process should make it possible to determine the most appropriate information to be provided and the most suitable form.

human relations theory An approach to management based on the idea that employees are motivated not only by financial reward but also by a range of social factors (e.g. praise, a sense of belonging, feelings of achievement and pride in one's work). The theory, which developed from empirical studies carried out in the 1920s and 1930s (*see* HAWTHORNE STUDIES), holds that attitudes, relationships, and *leadership styles play a key role in the performance of an organization. *See* MOTIVATION; SELF-ACTUALIZATION.

human-resource accounting (human-asset accounting) An attempt to recognize the human resources of an organization, quantify them in monetary terms, and show them on the *balance sheet. A value is placed on such factors as the age and experience of employees as well as their future earning power for the company. Although this approach has aroused some interest, in practice considerable difficulty has been met in quantifying the value of human resources.

human-resource management (HRM) The management of people to achieve individual behaviour and performance that will enhance an organization's effectiveness. HRM encourages individuals to set personal goals and rewards, guiding them to shape their behaviour in accordance with the objectives of the organization that employs them.

HRM was traditionally called **personnel management** and involved such responsibilities as interviewing job applicants, providing training, and storing personal data on employees. However, current trends place a greater emphasis on the morale and *motivation of employees, which is increasingly seen as the key to competitiveness. Strategies for achieving enhanced *job satisfaction may include training employees to do more than one job and encouraging all the members of a workforce to accept responsibility (*see* EMPOWERMENT).

hundredweight **1.** (Abbreviation: cwt) A former unit of weight used in the UK, equal to 112 lbs; 20 cwt equal 1 long ton (2240 lbs). It has been largely replaced by metric units; many bags that used to contain 1 cwt of material now contain 50 kilos. 1 cwt = 50.8 kilograms. According to the Weights and Measures Act (1985) and the EU directive on metric measures adopted into British law in January 2000 it is no longer legal to use the hundredweight in trade. **2.** A unit of weight used in the USA, equal to 100 lbs; 20 hundredweights = 1 short ton (2000 lbs).

hurdle rate The rate of interest in a *capital budgeting study that a proposed project must exceed before it can be regarded worthy of consideration. The hurdle rate is often based on the *cost of capital or the *weighted average cost of capital, adjusted by a factor to represent the risk characteristics of the projects under consideration.

hybrid A synthetic financial instrument

formed by combining two or more individual financial instruments, such as a bond with a warrant attached.

hybrid marketing channels Two or more marketing channels set up by a single firm to reach one or more customer segments. In this form of multichannel distribution a variety of direct and indirect approaches are used to deliver the firm's goods to its customers.

hygiene factors In the two-factor theory of *motivation introduced by Frederick Herzberg, those aspects of the work situation that can cause dissatisfaction if they are lacking or inadequate but cannot by themselves create *job satisfaction. They include quality of supervision, job security, remuneration, and physical working conditions. *Compare* MOTIVATORS.

hyperinflation A very high rate of increase in the general price level. For accounting purposes, hyperinflation is defined in *International Accounting Standard 29. The appropriate accounting treatment in the UK is explained in *Financial Reporting Standard 24. *See also* INFLATION.

hyperlink A word, phrase, or image on a web page that is clickable and enables navigation to another page on the site or another site on the World Wide Web. Hyperlinks are generally indicated to the user by text highlighted by underlining and/or a different colour. *See* HYPERTEXT; INTERNET.

hypermarket A very large shop, usually having a selling area of at least 50 000 square feet (4645 square metres), that sells a wide range of products. Able to buy in bulk, hypermarkets are often located adjacent to towns and base their attraction on low prices and the convenience to car-owning consumers, who can make many of their purchases in one place where

parking facilities are provided. Hypermarkets are now widespread, especially in grocery and do-it-yourself retailing. *See also* SUPERMARKET; SUPERSTORE.

hypertext A document format used in multimedia and on the *Internet in which a page of text contains links, usually in the form of highlighted words or icons (*see* HTML). Selecting one of these *hyperlinks takes the user directly to related documents, enabling them to pursue a line of investigation without having to search for each item individually. Links could be to further documents directly relating to the initial search subject, to related subjects, or even to further specialist sources. The connections can therefore increase exponentially.

hypothecation **1.** An authority given to a banker, usually as a **letter of hypothecation**, to enable the bank to sell goods that have been pledged (*see* PLEDGE) to them as security for a loan. It applies when the bank is unable to obtain the goods themselves. The goods have often been pledged as security in relation to a documentary bill, the banker being entitled to sell the goods if the bill is dishonoured by non-acceptance or non-payment. **2.** A mortgage granted by a ship's master to secure the repayment with interest, on the safe arrival of the ship at her destination, of money borrowed during a voyage as a matter of necessity (e.g. to pay for urgent repairs). The hypothecation of a ship itself, with or without cargo, is called **bottomry** and is effected by a **bottomry bond**; that of its cargo alone is **respondentia** and requires a **respondentia bond**. The bondholder is entitled to a maritime *lien. **3.** The practice of reserving the revenue from a tax or duty for spending on a particular stated purpose; for example dedicating revenues received from the tax on tobacco products to health spending.

IA Abbreviation for *information acceleration.

IAP Abbreviation for Internet access provider. *See* ACCESS PROVIDER.

IAS Abbreviation for *International Accounting Standard.

IASB Abbreviation for *International Accounting Standards Board.

IBEL Abbreviation for *interest-bearing eligible liabilities.

IBF Abbreviation for *international banking facility.

IBNR claims reserve A reserve held by an insurance company for claims "incurred but not yet reported".

IBOR Abbreviation for Inter Bank Offered Rate. *See* INTERBANK MARKET.

IBRD Abbreviation for *International Bank for Reconstruction and Development.

ICC Abbreviation for *International Chamber of Commerce.

ICSA Abbreviation for *Institute of Chartered Secretaries and Administrators.

IDA Abbreviation for *International Development Association.

IDC Abbreviation for *industrial development certificate.

idea generation The systematic search for new product ideas. *See* NEW PRODUCT DEVELOPMENT.

idea screening Screening new-product ideas in order to identify and develop good ideas and drop poor ones as soon as possible.

identifiable assets and liabilities (separable assets and liabilities) Those *assets and *liabilities of a business that could be disposed of separately, i.e. without disposing of the business as a whole.

idle capacity The part of the *budgeted capacity within an organization that is unused. It is measured in hours using the same measure as production. Idle capacity can arise as a result of a number of causes in all of which the actual hours worked is less than the budgeted hours available. The reasons can include non-delivery of raw materials, shortage of skilled labour, or lack of sales demand.

idle time The time, usually measured in labour hours or machine hours, during which a production facility is unable to operate. *See also* IDLE CAPACITY; WAITING TIME.

IFA Abbreviation for *independent financial adviser.

IFAD Abbreviation for *International Fund for Agricultural Development.

IFC Abbreviation for *International Finance Corporation.

IFRS Abbreviation for *International Financial Reporting Standard.

ijarah *See* ISLAMIC FINANCE.

ijarawa-iktina *See* ISLAMIC FINANCE.

illegal contract A *contract prohibited by statute (e.g. one between traders providing for minimum resale prices) or illegal at common law on the grounds of *public policy. An illegal contract is totally void, but neither party (unless innocent of the illegality) can recover any money paid or property transferred under it, according to the maxim *ex turpi causa non oritur actio* (a right of action does not arise out of an evil cause). Related transactions may also be affected. A related transaction between the same parties (e.g. if X gives Y a promissory note for money due from him under an illegal contract) is equally tainted with the illegality and is therefore void. The same is true of a related transaction with a third party (e.g. if Z lends X the money to pay Y) if the original illegality is known to that party.

illegal partnership A *partnership formed for an illegal purpose and therefore disallowed by law. A partnership of more than 20 partners is illegal, except in the case of certain professionals, e.g. accountants, solicitors, and stockbrokers.

ILO Abbreviation for *International Labour Organization.

ILU Abbreviation for *Institute of London Underwriters.

IMA Abbreviation for *Institute of Management Accountants.

image A composite mental picture formed by people about an organization or its products. See BRAND; CORPORATE IMAGE.

IMF Abbreviation for *International Monetary Fund.

immediate annuity An *annuity contract that begins to make payments as soon as the contract has come into force.

immediate holding company A company that has a *controlling interest in another company, even though it is itself controlled by a third company, which is the *holding company of both companies.

immigrant remittances Money sent by immigrants from the country in which they work to their families in their native countries. These sums can be a valuable source of foreign exchange for the native countries.

impact day The first day on which a newly issued security may be traded by subscribers. Trading will reveal whether the market price of the security is above or below the *issue price.

Imperial units A system of units formerly widely used in the UK and the rest of the English-speaking world. It includes the pound (lb), quarter (qt), *hundredweight (cwt), and *ton (ton); the foot (ft), yard (yd), and mile (mi); and the gallon (gal), British thermal unit (btu), etc. These units have been largely replaced by metric units, although Imperial units persist in some contexts. In January 2000 an EU regulation outlawing the sale of goods in Imperial measures was adopted into British law; an exception was made for the sale of beer and milk in pints. Compare METRIC SYSTEM; US CUSTOMARY UNITS.

impersonal account A *ledger account that does not bear the name of a person or company, such as a *nominal account or *real account.

implied term A provision of a *contract not agreed to by the parties in words but either regarded by the courts as necessary to give effect to their presumed intentions or introduced into the contract by statute (as in the case of contracts for the sale of goods). An implied term may constitute either a *condition of the contract or a *warranty; if it is introduced by statute it often cannot be expressly excluded.

import deposit A method of restricting importation to a country, in which the importer is required to deposit a sum of money with the customs and excise authorities when goods are imported. It is sometimes used as an alternative to raising import duties.

import duty A tax or *tariff on import goods. Import duties can either be a fixed amount or a percentage of the value of the goods. They have been a major type of barrier used to protect domestic production against foreign competition and they have also been an important source of government revenue, especially in developing countries.

import entry form A form completed by a UK importer of goods and submitted to the Customs and Excise for assessment of the *import duty, if any. When passed by the Customs the form functions as a *warrant to permit the goods to be removed from the port of entry.

import licence A permit allowing an importer to bring a stated quantity of certain goods into a country. Import licences are needed when *import restrictions include *import quotas, currency restrictions, and prohibition. They also function as a means of exchange control, the licence both permitting importation and allowing the importer to purchase the required foreign currency.

import quota An *import restriction imposed on imported goods, to reduce the quantity of certain goods allowed into a country from a particular exporting country, in a stated period. The purpose may be to conserve foreign currency, if there is an unfavourable *balance of payments, or to protect the home market against foreign competition (*see* PROTECTIVE DUTY). Quotas are usually enforced by means of *import licences.

import restrictions Restrictions imposed on goods and services imported into a country, which usually need to be paid for in the currency of the exporting country. This can cause a serious problem to the importing country's *balance of payments, hence the need for restrictions, which include *tariffs, *import quotas, currency restrictions, and prohibition. Prohibition will also apply to preventing the importation of illegal goods (e.g. drugs, arms). The restrictions may also be imposed to protect the home industry against foreign competition (*see* PROTECTIVE DUTY) or during the course of political bargaining.

imports Goods or services purchased from another country. *See* IMPORT DUTY; IMPORT QUOTA; IMPORT RESTRICTIONS.

import surcharge An extra tax applied by a government on certain imports in addition to the normal *tariff. It is usually applied as a temporary measure by a government that is in difficulty with its *balance of payments, but does not wish to violate its international tariff agreements.

impression management *See* POWER STYLES.

imprest account A means of controlling *petty-cash expenditure in which a person is given a certain sum of money (float or imprest). When some of it has been spent, that person provides appropriate vouchers for the amounts spent and is then reimbursed so that the float is restored. Thus at any given time the person should have either vouchers or cash to a total of the amount of his float.

impulse buying The buying of a product by a consumer without previous intention and almost always without evaluation of competing brands. Impulse buying is encouraged by such factors as prominent shelf position; manufacturers are therefore keen to persuade retailers to give these advantages to their products.

imputation system Formerly, the UK system in which a company making a *qualifying distribution paid *advance corporation tax on the dividend paid; this amount could then be set against the gross *corporation tax for the accounting period. The shareholder receiving the dividend was treated as having suffered tax on the dividend. Advance corporation tax was abolished in 1999.

imputed cost A cost that is not actually incurred by an organization but is introduced into the *management accounting records in order to ensure that the costs incurred by dissimilar operations are comparable. For example, if rent is not payable by an operation it will be introduced as an imputed cost so that the costs may be compared with an operation that does pay rent.

IMRO Abbreviation for *Investment Management Regulatory Organization.

inactive buyer A customer of a *direct marketing company, who has not made a purchase for a specified time.

in-barrier option An *option that is eliminated if the price of the *underlying fails to pass a certain level. In such cases the premium paid for the option is partly reimbursed. *Compare* OUT-BARRIER OPTION.

in-basket test *See* WORK-SAMPLE TEST.

in bond Delivery terms for goods that are available for immediate delivery but are held in a *bonded warehouse. The buyer has to pay the cost of any Customs duty due, the cost of loading from the warehouse, and any further on-carriage costs.

incentive-compatible contract A contract designed to ensure mutually beneficial behaviour by the parties. So, for example, the employment contracts of a company's managers might incorporate a bonus system to make sure that their interests and those of the shareholders are congruent. *See* AGENCY RELATIONSHIP; GOAL DIVERGENCE.

incentive system A scheme in which rewards are offered to managers or other employees conditional on certain performance targets being met. Apart from cash bonuses, such rewards may include shares or share options (*see* SHARE INCENTIVE SCHEME), health insurance, gym membership, or corporate entertainment.

incestuous share dealing The buying and selling of shares in companies that belong to the same group, in order to obtain an advantage of some kind, usually a tax advantage. The legality of the transaction will depend on its nature.

inchoate instrument A *negotiable instrument in which not all the particulars are given. The drawer of an inchoate instrument can authorize a third party to fill in a specified missing particular.

incidence of taxation The impact of a tax on those who bear its burden, rather than those who pay it. For example, *VAT is paid by traders, but the ultimate burden of it falls on the consumer of the trader's goods or services. Again, a company may pay *corporation tax but if it then raises its prices or reduces its employees' wages to recoup the tax it may be said to have shifted the incidence.

income 1. Any sum that a person or organization receives either as a reward for effort (e.g. salary or trading profit) or as a return on investments (e.g. rents or interest). From the point of view of taxation, income has to be distinguished from *capital. *See* TOTAL INCOME. **2.** In economics, the flow of economic value attributed to an individual or group of individuals over a particular period. The total of income throughout an individual's life, minus expenditure, is equal to that person's wealth. Note that both income and wealth are generally considered to include more than simply money; for example, benefits in kind, services rendered by governments, and *human capital should all be included.

income and expenditure account An account, similar to a *profit and loss account, prepared by an organization whose main purpose is not the generation of profit. It records the income and expenditure of the organization and results in either a surplus of income over expenditure or of expenditure over income. Such an organization's accounts do not use the *accruals concept.

income bond 1. (National Savings In-come Bond)** A type of bond introduced by the Department for *National Savings in 1982. They offer monthly interest payments on investments between £500 and £1 million. Interest is taxable but not deducted at source. **2.** *See* GUARANTEED-INCOME BOND.

income distribution 1. The proportions of income paid to different sections of a community. *See* INCOME REDISTRIBUTION. **2.** The payment by a *unit trust of its half-yearly income to unit holders, in proportion to their holdings. The income distributed is the total income less the manager's service charge and income tax at the standard rate.

income in kind *See* BENEFITS IN KIND.

income redistribution The use of taxation to ensure that the incomes of the richer members of the community are reduced and those of the poorer members are increased. Tax theorists have tended to favour *progressive taxes for this purpose, combined with various forms of income support for the poorer members of the community.

income segmentation Dividing a market into different income groups.

income share *See* INVESTMENT TRUST; SPLIT-CAPITAL INVESTMENT TRUST.

income smoothing The manipulation by companies of certain items in their *financial statements so that they eliminate large movements in profit and are able to report a smooth trend over a number of years. The practice is pursued because of the belief that investors have greater confidence in companies that are reporting a steady increase in profits year by year. It is doubtful if any regulations can totally prevent this form of *creative accounting.

incomes policy A government policy aimed at controlling inflation and maintaining full employment by holding down increases in wages and other forms of income and prices by means of statute or *moral suasion.

income statement In the USA, the equivalent of a UK *profit and loss account.

income stock A stock or share bought

primarily for the steady and relatively high income it can be expected to produce. This may be a fixed-interest *gilt-edged security or an ordinary share with a good *yield record.

income tax (IT) A direct tax on an individual's income. In general, individuals can earn income without paying tax up to a threshold, with subsequent income giving rise to tax liabilities, usually at increasing rates as income increases (*progressive taxation).

In UK tax legislation income is not defined; amounts received are classified under various headings (see SCHEDULE), some of which are subdivided into cases. In order to be classed as income an amount received must fall under one of these headings (see SCHEDULE). There are some specific occasions when the legislation requires capital receipts to be treated as income for taxation purposes, e.g. when a landlord receives a lump sum on the granting of a lease. In the UK the importance of the distinction between income and capital has diminished since income and capital gains are now charged at essentially the same rate. (Prior to 6 April 1988 capital was charged at 30%, whereas the top rate of income tax was 60%.) The tax is calculated on the taxpayer's taxable income, i.e. gross income less any *income tax allowances and deductions. If the allowances and deductions exceed the gross income in a *fiscal year, no income tax is payable. In the UK, there are three tax-rate bands: a *starting rate of income tax of 10% on taxable earnings up to £2090, a *basic rate of income tax of 22% on taxable earnings between £2090 and £32,400, and a *higher rate of income tax at 40% on taxable earnings over £32,400 (2005–06 figures). See also PAYE.

income tax allowances Allowances that may be deducted from a taxpayer's gross income before calculating the liability to *income tax. Every individual who is a UK resident is entitled to a *personal allowance, the level of which will depend on his or her age (see AGE ALLOWANCE). After 5 April 2000 the former married couple's allowance was discontinued for all couples in which the elder spouse was under 65 on that date; it has been replaced by tax credits for working families

with children. If one spouse was born before 6 April 1935, the married couple's allowance is £5905 for 2005–06. This increases to £5975 if one spouse is aged 75 or over. There is also a registered blind person's allowance of £1610 (2005–06).

income tax code A code number issued by HM Revenue and Customs that takes account of the *personal allowance available to the taxpayer together with any other additional allowances to which he or she is entitled, e.g. age allowance. The code is used by the employer through the *PAYE scheme to calculate the taxable pay using tables supplied by the Revenue (now usually in the form of computer software). The income tax code can also be used to tax *benefits in kind, such as company cars, by reducing the code number and so collecting more tax each tax week or month. The code provides a means of ensuring that the tax due for the *fiscal year is deducted from the employee's earnings in equal weekly or monthly amounts.

income tax month See TAX MONTH.

income tax year See FISCAL YEAR.

income velocity of circulation See VELOCITY OF CIRCULATION.

incompatibility The inability of one computer to handle data and programs produced for a different type of computer.

inconvertible currency A currency that cannot be legally converted into other currencies. It is often the case that currencies are inconvertible for certain purposes, such as overseas investment. Currencies are most likely to be inconvertible where the underlying economy is weak or underdeveloped.

inconvertible paper money Paper money that cannot be converted into gold. Most paper money now falls into this category, although until 1931, in the UK, the Bank of England had an obligation to supply any holder of a bank note with the appropriate quantity of gold.

incorporated company See COMPANY.

Incorporated Society of British Advertisers Ltd (ISBA) A society founded in 1900 as the Advertisers Protection Society. It is open to any advertising company and is concerned with all matters relating to advertising, including *direct marketing, *public relations, and sponsorship.

Incoterms A glossary of terms used in international trade published by the *International Chamber of Commerce in Paris. It gives precise definitions to eliminate misunderstandings between traders in different countries.

increasing capital An increase in the number or value of the shares in a company to augment its authorized *share capital. If the *articles of association of the company do not permit this to be done (with the agreement of the members), the articles will need to be changed. A company cannot increase its share capital unless authorized to do so by its articles of association.

incremental analysis *See* DIFFERENTIAL ANALYSIS.

incremental cost of capital The overall cost of raising extra finance. For example, if extra debt is incurred, this increases the risk to equity and debt funders, who will in turn demand a higher rate of return on their investment. The concept is also applied to funding raised to implement specific decisions, and should reflect the risks involved in the activity. *See* COST OF CAPITAL.

indemnity **1.** An agreement by one party to make good the losses suffered by another, usually by payment of money, repair, replacement, or reinstatement. This is the function of *indemnity insurance. **2.** An undertaking by a bank's client, who has lost a document (such as a share certificate or bill of lading), that the bank will be held harmless against any consequences of the document's absence if it proceeds to service the documents that have not been mislaid. The bank usually requires a *letter of indemnity to make sure that it suffers no loss.

indemnity insurance Any insurance designed to compensate a policyholder for a loss suffered, by the payment of money, repair, replacement, or reinstatement. In every case the policyholder is entitled to be put back in the same financial position as he or she was immediately before the event insured against occurred. There must be no element of profit to the policy-holder nor any element of loss. Most – but not all – insurance policies are *indemnity contracts. For example, personal accident and life-assurance policies are not contracts of indemnity as it is impossible to calculate the value of a lost life or limb (as the value of a car or other property can be calculated).

indenture **1.** A *deed, especially one creating or transferring an estate in land. It derives its name from the former practice of writing the two parts of a two-part deed on one piece of parchment and separating the two parts by an irregular wavy line. The two parts of the indenture were known to belong together if the indented edges fitted together. A deed with a straight edge was known as a *deed poll. **2.** A document establishing the terms and conditions of a securities issue. **3.** *See* APPRENTICE.

independent demand The situation in which the demand for a product is independent of the production process, i.e. it is subject to market forces and therefore demand has to be forecast. When a car manufacturer produces a car, the number of wheels required is known before each unit can be sent out of the factory. However, the manufacturer does not know how many transmissions will fail, or whether individuals will buy their replacements from other suppliers. They cannot therefore predict accurately how many spares to produce. *Compare* DEPENDENT DEMAND.

independent financial adviser (IFA) A person defined under the *Financial Services Act (1986) as an adviser who is not committed to the products of any one company or organization. Such a person is licensed to operate by the *Financial Services Authority (before 2000 by one of the *Self-Regulating Organizations or *Recognized Professional Bodies). With no loyal ties except to the customer, the IFA is bound legally to give impartial advice. In practice, however, this may prove difficult as an IFA may deal with a limited range of products. Eight categories of IFA exist, grouped into four main areas: advising on investments; arranging and transacting life assurance, pensions, and unit trusts; arranging and transacting other types of investments; and management of investments. All licensed independent financial advisers contribute to a compensation fund for the protection of their customers.

independent intermediary A person who acts as a representative of a prospective policyholder in the arrangement of an insurance or assurance policy. In *life assurance and *pensions it is a person who represents more than one insurer and is legally bound to offer advice to clients on the type of assurance or investment contracts best suited to their needs. In general insurance the independent intermediary can represent more than six insurers and is responsible for advising clients on policies that best suit their needs. They must, themselves, have *professional indemnity insurance to cover any errors that they may make. Although, in both cases, intermediaries are the servants of the policyholder (and the insurer is therefore not responsible for their errors), they are paid by the insurer in the form of a commission, being an agreed percentage of the first or renewal premium paid by the policyholder.

independent retailer A small *retailer, generally owning between one and nine shops. They are now less important than *multiple shops in many areas of retailing.

index *See* FINANCIAL TIMES SHARE INDEXES; RETAIL PRICE INDEX.

indexation 1. The policy of connecting such economic variables as wages, taxes, social-security payments, annuities, or pensions to rises in the general price level (*see* INFLATION). This policy is often advocated by economists in the belief that it mitigates the effects of inflation. In practice, complete indexation is rarely possible, so that inflation usually leaves somebody worse off (e.g. lenders, savers) and somebody better off (borrowers). *See* RETAIL PRICE INDEX. **2.** The practice of adjusting the *chargeable gain from the sale of an asset to take account of inflation over the period of ownership of the asset. In the UK *corporation tax system an indexation factor derived from the rise in the *Retail Price Index during the period of ownership is applied to the cost, or 31 March 1982 value, of an asset. The indexed cost or value is then deducted from

the proceeds of sale on disposal of the asset, in order to establish the chargeable gain. Indexation was formerly also applied to gains chargeable to *capital gains tax, but in such cases it has been replaced by *taper relief from 6 April 1998. However, for assets acquired before that date, the indexation allowance is calculated to 5 April 1998 and this figure is used to calculate the chargeable gain in any subsequent disposal.

indexed security 1. A *security that has its coupon payment or redemption value adjusted for inflation. **2.** A security in which the coupon or the principal is related to the performance of a financial index.

index futures A *futures contract on a *financial futures market, such as the *London International Financial Futures and Options Exchange, which offers facilities for trading in futures and *options on a financial index. On the FTSE 100 Index (*see* FINANCIAL TIMES SHARE INDEXES) the trading unit is £25 per index point; thus if a futures contract is purchased when the index stands at 2400, say, the buyer is covering an equivalent purchase of equities of £60,000 (£25 × 2400). If the index rises 100 points the purchaser can sell a matching futures contract at this level, making a profit of £2500 (£25 × 100). *See also* PORTFOLIO INSURANCE.

index-linked gilts *See* GILT-EDGED SECURITY; INDEXATION.

index-linked savings certificates *See* INDEXATION; NATIONAL SAVINGS.

index number A number used to represent the changes in a set of values between a *base year and the present. If the index reflects fluctuations in a single variable, such as the price of a commodity, the index number can be calculated using the formula:

$$100 \ (p_n/p_0),$$

where p_0 represents the price in the base year and p_n represents the price in the current year. In practice many indices reflect variations in a combination of variables, such as the raw materials required to manufacture a product. In this situation it is necessary to produce an index that weights the important variables, e.g.

labour costs. These are known as **weighted aggregate indices**. If both costs and quantities have varied over a period, it is further necessary to find a way of using the same quantities for the numerator and denominator of the index. When the calculation uses base-year quantities as the fixed point, the resultant index is a **base-weighted** (or **Laspeyres'**) **index**, i.e.:

100(total cost of base year quantities at current prices/total cost of base year quantities at base year prices),

or

$$100(\Sigma p_n q_0 / \Sigma p_0 q_0),$$

where p represents the price and q represents the quantity. When the calculation uses current year quantities, it is known as a **current-weighted** (or **Paasche's**) **index**, i.e.:

100(total cost of current quantities at current prices/total cost of base year quantities at current prices),

or

$$100(\Sigma p_n q_n / \Sigma p_0 q_n).$$

See also FINANCIAL TIMES SHARE INDEXES; RETAIL PRICE INDEX.

Index of Industrial Production A UK index produced by the *Office for National Statistics to show changes in the volume of production of the main British industries and of the economy as a whole.

index tracking Setting up a *portfolio or investment product in such a way that it should provide the same returns as a particular market index. An **index fund** or **tracker fund** is one that has been weighted in the same proportions as a leading financial index.

indication of interest A mechanism whereby investors give indications of their possible reactions to the pricing of new share issues. This information is then used in establishing the *issue price.

indicative prices On a financial market, prices quoted as indicators of the likely prices at which market makers or dealers will trade. They are not explicit commitments to deal at those prices.

indicator A measurable variable that gives information regarding performance or prospects. Examples of macroeconomic indicators are price, money supply, income, imports, and exports. Most organizations will use a range of financial and other indicators to assess the performance of individuals, departments, or the company as a whole. *See* KEY PERFORMANCE INDICATORS; PERFORMANCE MEASUREMENT.

indirect costs (**indirect expenses**) Expenses that cannot be traced directly to a *product or *cost unit and are therefore *overheads (*compare* DIRECT COSTS). Some indirect product costs may, however, be regarded as *cost centre direct costs; the indirect cost centre costs are usually those costs requiring apportionment to cost centres in an *absorption costing system.

indirect discrimination *See* DISCRIMINATION.

indirect labour **1.** Employees of a contractor who carry out work for another organization. This organization employs the contractor to supply the labour for a particular task. For example, some councils use a contractor, and indirect labour, to collect refuse. **2.** The part of a workforce in an organization that does not directly produce goods or provide the service that the organization sells. Indirect labour includes office staff, cleaners, canteen workers, etc. *Compare* DIRECT LABOUR.

indirect materials Those materials that do not feature in the final product but are necessary to carry out the production, such as machine oil, cleaning materials, and consumable materials. *Compare* DIRECT MATERIALS.

indirect method The method used for a *cash-flow statement in which the operating profit is adjusted for non-cash charges and credits to reconcile it with the net cash flow from operating activities.

indirect quote The expression of an exchange rate in terms of the number of units of a foreign currency corresponding to a single unit of the domestic currency. For example, in the UK an indirect quote for the dollar might be $1.8 = £1. *Compare* DIRECT QUOTE.

indirect taxation Taxation that is intended to be borne by persons or organizations other than those who pay the tax (*compare* DIRECT TAXATION). The principal indirect tax in the UK is VAT, which is paid by traders as goods or services enter into the chain of production, but which is ultimately borne by the consumer of the goods or services. One of the advantages of indirect taxes is that they can be collected from comparatively few sources while their economic effects can be widespread.

individual marketing Tailoring products and marketing programmes to the needs and preferences of individual customers.

individual network value The value to a specific individual of belonging to and using a network.

individual retirement account (IRA) A US pension plan that allows annual sums to be set aside from earnings free of tax and accumulated in a fund, which pays interest. Basic-rate tax is payable once the saver starts to withdraw from the account, which must be done no later than the participant's 70th birthday. The concession is not available to employees in a company-pension scheme or profit-sharing scheme.

Individual Savings Account (ISA) A savings portfolio for small investors introduced in the UK in 1999. It replaced *personal equity plans (PEPs) and *Tax Exempt Special Savings Accounts (TESSAs); ISAs entitle individuals to save up to £7000 per year free of tax. The savings may be in the form of cash, shares, or life-assurance policies. ISAs are available in two main forms: **maxi-ISAs**, which must include shares, either exclusively or together with cash or assurance policies (or both), the whole package being supplied by one provider; and **mini-ISAs**, in which each component can be supplied by different providers, the maximum holding of shares and assurance policies being £4000 and of cash and assurance policies £3000 (the original provision for a separate assurance-policy component was ended from 6 April 2005). Savers can invest in either (a) one maxi-ISA or (b) one or two mini-ISAs in one year, but not both. ISAs can be cashed in at any time without loss of the tax relief, which includes exemption from personal income tax and capital gains tax. *See also* ISA MORTGAGE.

indorsement See endorsement.

industrial action Any form of coordinated action in an **industrial dispute** by employees, with or without the support of a trade union, that seeks to force employers to agree to their demands relating to wages, terms of employment, working conditions, etc. It may take the form of a *go slow, *overtime ban, *work-to-rule, *sit-down strike, or *strike.

industrial and organizational psychology (industrial psychology; organizational psychology) The application of psychological concepts to the issues and problems that arise in business, industry, and other organizational settings. An understanding of individual and group psychology is particularly relevant to such areas as *motivation, decision making, leadership (*see* LEADERSHIP THEORIES), team work, *human-resource management, and *personnel selection.

industrial bank **1.** A relatively small *finance house that specializes in *hire purchase, obtaining its own funds by accepting long-term deposits, largely from the general public. **2.** A US bank that specializes in industrial leasing.

industrial buildings Factories and ancillary premises used for manufacturing a product or for carrying on a trade in which goods are subjected to any process. For qualifying buildings there is a special category of *capital allowance, known as **industrial-buildings allowance**. The *writing-down allowance of 4% is calculated using the *straight-line method. The allowance is based on the cost of the building including the cost of preparing the land, but excluding the cost of the land itself. The same allowance is available for certain agricultural and commercial buildings, including some hotels. An allowance of 100% of building cost is available for qualifying buildings in a designated enterprise zone.

industrial buyer behaviour *See* BUSINESS BUYER BEHAVIOUR.

industrial democracy Any system in which workers participate in the management of an organization or in sharing its profits. *Participative decision making can improve *industrial relations and add to workers' *job satisfaction and *motivation. Various schemes have been tried, including worker directors on the boards of some nationalized industries, workers' councils, and *profit-sharing schemes.

industrial development certificate (IDC) A certificate required by an industrial organization wishing to build a new factory in the UK or to extend an existing one. An IDC has to accompany any application for planning permission for industrial property. The certificate is issued by the Department of the Environment.

industrial disability benefit Benefits paid by the Department for Work and Pensions in the UK to compensate for disablement resulting from an industrial accident or from certain diseases due to the nature of a person's employment. A weekly payment is made on a scale of disablement ranging from 14% to 100%. No benefit is paid for less than 14% disablement. Claimants have to submit to a medical examination. The payment is made if the claimant is still suffering disability 15 weeks or more after the accident or onset of the disease.

industrial dispute *See* INDUSTRIAL ACTION; TRADE DISPUTE.

industrial engineering The application of *work study techniques. It was traditionally regarded as a specialist function within organizations, with its own professional bodies. Increasingly, it is being taught as techniques to operations managers in organizations that take the more holistic approach associated with *total quality management.

industrial espionage Spying on a competitor to obtain *trade secrets by dishonest means. The information sought often refers to the development of new products, innovative manufacturing techniques, commissioned market surveys, forthcoming advertising campaigns, research plans, etc. The means used include a wide range of telephone- and computer-tapping devices, infiltration of the competitor's workforce, etc.

industrial estate *See* TRADING ESTATE.

industrial life assurance A *life-assurance policy, usually for a small amount, the premiums for which are paid on a regular basis (weekly or monthly) and collected by an agent of the assurance company, who calls at the policyholder's home. Records of the premium payments are kept in a book, which – together with the policy document – has to be produced to make a claim. This type of assurance began in industrial areas (hence its name), where small weekly policies were purchased to help pay the funeral expenses of the policyholder. This type of insurance is now more widely known as **home service assurance**. It is fast becoming obsolete, owing to its high costs and low revenues.

industrial marketing research (business marketing research) Any form of *marketing research undertaken among organizations that buy and add value to products and services but are not the final consumers. *Compare* CONSUMER RESEARCH.

industrial medicine The health care provided by employers for their employees. Apart from the provision of first aid and nursing care in larger organizations, its main aims are prophylactic: the prevention of accidents by providing adequate guards for machinery, the prevention of disease by controlling noxious fumes, dusts, etc., and the prevention of stress by providing the best possible working environment. In addition, regular check-ups are often provided to monitor the health of members of staff.

industrial product A product bought by individuals and organizations for further processing or for use in conducting a business.

industrial psychology *See* INDUSTRIAL AND ORGANIZATIONAL PSYCHOLOGY.

industrial relations The relationship between the management of an organization and its workforce. If industrial relations are good, the whole workforce will be well motivated to work hard for the benefit of the organization and its customers. The job satisfaction in such an environment will itself provide some of the rewards for achieving good industrial relations. If the industrial relations are bad, both management and workers will find the workplace an uncongenial environment, causing discontent, poor motivation, and a marked tendency to take self-destructive *industrial action.

industrial tribunal *See* EMPLOYMENT TRIBUNAL.

industrial union *See* TRADE UNION.

industry 1. An organized activity in which *capital and labour are utilized to produce *goods. **2.** The sector of an economy that is concerned with manufacture. **3.** A group of firms that offer a product or class of products that are close substitutes for each other. The set of all sellers of a product or service, e.g. the car industry or the steel industry.

inertia selling A form of selling in which unrequested goods are sent to a potential customer on a sale-or-return basis. This method is especially prevalent with book and CD clubs.

infant industry A new industry that may merit some protection against foreign competition in the short term. The argument in favour of providing protection, say in the form of a tariff on imported competitors' goods, is that it would provide a period during which the new industry could streamline its process and make the necessary economies in order for it to become truly competitive with all market producers.

infinite capacity loading *Loading based only on the due dates for deliveries, taking no notice of whether capacity is available. This parameter encourages a critical examination of the options available for expanding capacity, e.g. overtime, subcontracting. *Compare* FINITE CAPACITY LOADING.

inflation A general increase in prices in an economy and consequent fall in the purchasing value of money. *See also* HYPER-INFLATION; RETAIL PRICE INDEX.

inflation accounting A method of accounting that, unlike *historical-cost accounting, attempts to take account of the fact that a monetary unit (e.g. the pound sterling) does not have a constant value; because of the effects of inflation, successive accounts expressed in that unit do not necessarily give a fair view of the trend of profits. The principal methods of dealing with inflation have been *current-cost accounting and *current purchasing power accounting.

inflationary gap The difference between the total spending in an economy (both private and public) and the total spending that would be needed to maintain full employment in a given time period.

influencer *See* CONSUMER BUYING BEHAVIOUR; DECISION-MAKING UNIT.

infomediary An *intermediary business whose main source of revenue is obtained from capturing consumer information and developing detailed profiles of individual customers for use by third parties.

infomercial A television commercial, usually 30 minutes long, that has the appearance of being a programme. The product advertised is repeatedly demonstrated, together with a telephone number to enable the viewer to order. Infomercials are widely used in the USA.

infopreneurial industry The manufacture and sale of electronic office and factory equipment for the distribution of information. *See* INFORMATION TECHNOLOGY.

information acceleration (IA) A *virtual reality system designed to place a consumer in a virtual buying environment similar to one in which he or she normally makes purchase decisions.

information flow management *See* SUPPLY-CHAIN MANAGEMENT.

information goods Products with a high information content. Such products can be digitized and delivered on-line.

information practice statement A discrete statement that describes a particular use or practice regarding consumers' personal information and/or a choice offered to consumers about their personal information.

information search *See* CONSUMER BUYING BEHAVIOUR.

information technology (IT) The use of computers and other electronic means to process and distribute information. Information can be transferred between computers using cables, satellite links, or telephone lines and the cellular network (mobile phones). Networks of connected computers can be used to send *e-mail, to interrogate remote *databases using the *Internet, and to transmit sound, pictures, and moving images. These systems also enable *electronic transfer of funds between banks, as well as *home banking, automated screen trading in stocks and shares, and the buying of goods and services on-line. In doing so, they have played a major role in the *globalization of financial and other markets since the 1980s. The entertainment industry has seen a similar convergence of the broadcast media with computers and telecommunications.

informative advertising Advertising used to inform consumers about a new product or feature in order to build primary demand.

infrastructure The goods and services, usually requiring substantial investment, considered essential to the proper functioning of an economy. For example, roads, railways, sewerage, and electricity supply constitute essential elements of a community's infrastructure. Since the infrastructure benefits the whole of an economy, it is often argued that it should be funded, partly if not wholly, by the government by means of taxation.

inherent vice A defect or weakness of an item, especially of a cargo, that causes it to suffer some form of damage or destruction without the intervention of an outside cause. For example, certain substances, such as jute, when shipped in bales, can warm up spontaneously, causing damage to the fibre. Damage by this cause is excluded from most cargo insurance policies as an *excepted peril.

inheritance tax (IHT) A tax introduced in the Budget of 1986 to replace *capital transfer tax. Inheritance tax is chargeable on the death of an individual domiciled in the UK on all property, wherever it is situated. It is also charged on *potentially exempt transfers made within seven years of death. A non-UK domiciled individual is charged on death to inheritance tax on all UK property. Inheritance tax arises on lifetime *chargeable transfers at a lifetime rate, which is half the death rate of inheritance tax (see also EXEMPT TRANSFERS). The threshold at which inheritance tax takes effect was set at £275,000 for 2005–06,

£285,000 for 2006–07, and £300,000 for 2007–08. No tax is payable if the cumulative total of all chargeable transfers is less than the threshold. Above this amount, tax is payable on the excess at a single rate of 40%.

initial charge The charge paid to the managers of a *unit trust by an investor when units are first purchased. For most trusts the initial charge ranges between 5% and 6%, as laid down in the trust deed. *Money-market unit trusts and *exempt unit trusts have lower initial charges and in some cases no initial charge.

initial public offering (IPO) The first sale of shares by a *private limited company to the public. It can be difficult to set an *issue price that will be low enough to attract sufficient investors to take up the whole issue and yet high enough to give the company the maximum capital. An IPO is underpriced if the issue price is less than the market price and overpriced if the issue price is greater than the market price. *See* FLOTATION; OFFER FOR SALE; PUBLIC ISSUE.

initial yield The gross initial annual income from an asset divided by the initial cost of that asset. *Compare* GROSS REDEMPTION YIELD.

initiator 1. *See* TASK ROLES. **2.** *See* CONSUMER BUYING BEHAVIOUR.

injunction An order by a court that a person shall do, or refrain from doing, a particular act. This is an equitable remedy that may be granted by the High Court wherever "just and convenient". The county court also has a limited jurisdiction to grant injunctions. An **interlocutory injunction** lasts only until the main action is heard. **Interim injunctions**, lasting a short time only, may be granted on the application of one party without the other being present (an **ex parte interim injunction**) if there is great urgency. **Prohibitory injunctions** forbid the doing of a particular act; **mandatory injunctions** order a person to do some act. Failure to obey an injunction is contempt of court and punishable by a fine or imprisonment.

inland bill A *bill of exchange that is both drawn and payable in the UK. Any other bill is classed as a **foreign bill**.

Inland Revenue *See* BOARD OF INLAND REVENUE.

inland waterways *See* BRITISH WATERWAYS.

innominate terms (intermediate terms) Terms of a *contract that cannot be classified as a *condition or *warranty. The parties to a contract may label the terms of the contract as either conditions or warranties and those labels will usually be respected by the courts provided that the result is reasonable. Similarly, certain terms have traditionally been treated as conditions or warranties even though they have not been labelled as such (for example, time clauses in mercantile contracts are to be treated as conditions). Innominate terms are those that will not fit the above categories. The remedy for breach of an innominate term will depend on whether or not the breach is of a fundamental nature, i.e. that the injured party has been deprived of substantially the whole of the benefit of the contract. If the injured party has been so deprived, he or she will be entitled to treat the contract as repudiated and claim damages. If not, the injured party will be entitled to damages only. *See also* BREACH OF CONTRACT.

innovation Any new approach to designing, producing, or marketing goods that gives the innovator or his company an advantage over competitors. By means of *patents, a successful innovator can enjoy a temporary monopoly, although eventually competitors will find ways of supplying a valuable market. Some companies rely on bringing out new products based on established demand, while others develop technological innovations that open up new markets. *See* DISCONTINUOUS INNOVATION; DYNAMICALLY CONTINUOUS INNOVATION.

innovative marketing A principle of enlightened marketing that requires a company to seek real improvements in its products and its marketing.

innovators *See* ADOPTION OF INNOVATIONS.

input substitution The substitution of a cheaper raw material input for other inputs that have stayed the same price or become more expensive.

input tax *Value added tax paid by a *taxable person on purchasing goods or services from a VAT-registered trader. The input tax, excluding irrecoverable input VAT, is set against the *output tax in order to establish the amount of VAT to be paid to the tax authorities.

inquiry test *See* ENQUIRY TEST.

inscribed stock (registered stock) Shares in loan stock, for which the names of the holders are kept in a register rather than by the issue of a certificate of ownership. On a transfer, a new name has to be registered, which makes them cumbersome and unpopular in practice.

inside director In the USA, an employee of a company who has been appointed to the board of directors.

insider dealing (insider trading) Dealing in company securities with a view to making a profit or avoiding a loss while in possession of price-sensitive information that is not generally known (**insider information**). Under the UK Companies Securities (Insider Dealing) Act (1985) those who are or have been connected with a company (e.g. the directors, the company secretary, employees, and professional advisers) are prohibited from such dealing on or, in certain circumstances, off the stock exchange if they acquired the information by virtue of their connection and in confidence. The prohibition extends to certain unconnected persons to whom the information has been conveyed. Similar laws on insider dealing now operate in most developed countries.

insolvency The inability to pay one's debts when they fall due. In the case of individuals this may lead to *bankruptcy and in the case of companies to *liquidation. In both of these cases the normal procedure is for a specialist, a trustee in bankruptcy or a liquidator, to be appointed to gather and dispose of the assets of the insolvent and to pay the creditors. Insolvency does not always lead to bankruptcy and liquidation, although it often does. An insolvent person may have valuable assets that are not immediately realizable.

insolvency practitioner A person authorized to undertake insolvency administration as a *liquidator, provisional liquidator, *administrator, *administrative receiver, or nominee or supervisor under a *voluntary arrangement. Insolvency practitioners must be members of an approved professional body, such as the **Insolvency Practitioners Association** or the Institute of Chartered Accountants.

insolvency risk **1.** The *risk that a borrower may be unable to repay a debt. **2.** The risk that a *counterparty may be unable to honour a contract owing to insolvency. *See* COUNTERPARTY RISK.

inspection and investigation of a company An enquiry into the running of a company made by inspectors appointed by the Department of Trade and Industry. Such an enquiry may be held to supply company members with information or to investigate fraud, unfair prejudice, nominee shareholdings, or *insider dealing. The inspectors' report is usually published.

inspector general In the USA, the federal office that performs audit and investigative activities on federal agencies, making periodic reports to Congress.

Inspector of Taxes A civil servant responsible to HM Revenue and Customs for issuing tax returns and assessments, the conduct of appeals, and agreeing tax liabilities with taxpayers.

instalment One of a series of payments, especially when buying goods on *hire purchase, settling a debt, or buying a new issue of shares.

instalment sale The USA equivalent of a UK retail sale by hire purchase.

instant Of the current month. In commercial English it used to be common to refer to a date as, for example, the 5th instant, or more usually 5th inst., meaning the 5th of the current month. **Ultimo** refers to the previous month; for example, the 5th ultimo, or more usually the 5th ult., means the 5th of last month. **Proximo** refers to the next month; the 5th proximo, or 5th prox., means the 5th of next month.

Institute cargo clauses Clauses issued by the *Institute of London Underwriters that are added to standard *marine insurance policies for cargo to widen or restrict the cover given. Each clause has a wording agreed by a committee of insurance companies and *Lloyd's underwriters. By attaching particular clauses to the policy the insurers are able to create an individual policy to suit the clients' requirements.

Institute of Actuaries One of the two professional bodies in the UK to which *actuaries belong. To become an actuary it is necessary to qualify as a fellow of one or the other. The roots of the profession go back to 1756, when a Fellow of the Royal Society, James Dodson, produced the first table of premiums for life assurance, after having been turned down for an assurance policy on the grounds of his age. The Institute is in London; the other organization, the **Faculty of Actuaries**, is based in Edinburgh.

Institute of Chartered Accountants Any of the three professional accountancy bodies in the UK, the **Institute of Chartered Accountants in England and Wales (ICAEW)**, the **Institute of Chartered Accountants of Scotland (ICAS)**, and the **Institute of Chartered Accountants in Ireland (ICAI)**. The institutes are separate but recognize similar codes of practice. The largest is the England and Wales institute, with some 125 000 members, who are identified by the letters ACA or FCA (as are members of the Ireland institute; in Scotland members use the letters CA). The institutes ensure high standards of education and training in accountancy, provide qualification by examination, and supervise professional conduct in the service of clients and of the public. They are members of the Consultative Committee of Accountancy Bodies, whose Accounting Standards Committee is responsible for drafting accounting standards. *See also* CHARTERED ACCOUNTANT.

Institute of Chartered Secretaries and Administrators (ICSA) A professional body for secretaries and administrators in the UK. Founded in 1891 and granted a Royal Charter in 1902, the institute represents members' interests to government bodies on such matters as company law; publishes journals, reports, pamphlets, and papers; promotes the professional standing of members; and conducts the education and examination of members.

Institute of Directors A nonpolitical organization for directors of companies, founded in London in 1903. There are approximately 55 000 members in the UK and more than 65 000 worldwide. Membership has increased 50% over the past five years and includes directors from many sectors of the economy. The Institute encourages members to improve their standards of performance and represents the views of business leaders to government and other organizations. Members receive a variety of benefits including information, advice, training, conferences, and publications.

Institute of London Underwriters (ILU) An association of UK insurance companies that cooperate with each other in providing a market for *marine insurance and *aviation insurance. Although Lloyd's underwriters are not members of the institute, the two organizations work closely with each other. The ILU appoints agents to settle claims, provides certificates of insurance for cargo shippers insured by members, and is responsible for drawing up its own insurance contracts for the use of members; it also draws up the *Institute cargo clauses widely used in many marine and aviation policies.

Institute of Management (IM) *See* CHARTERED MANAGEMENT INSTITUTE.

Institute of Management Accountants (IMA) A US-based international accountancy body established in 1919 as the National Association of Cost Accountants.

Institute of Management Services An institution, founded in 1941, that is the professional and qualifying body for people in *management services. Its main aims are to create and maintain professional standards for the practice of management services; to provide a system of qualifying examinations; and to encourage research and development in management services.

Institute of Marketing *See* CHARTERED INSTITUTE OF MARKETING.

Institute of Personnel Management (IPM) *See* CHARTERED INSTITUTE OF PERSONNEL AND DEVELOPMENT.

Institute of Practitioners in Advertising (IPA) The professional organization, established in 1917, for UK advertising agencies. Its members handle some 95% of all UK advertising.

Institute of Public Relations (IPR) *See* CHARTERED INSTITUTE OF PUBLIC RELATIONS.

Institute of Sales Promotion (ISP) The professional organization for UK sales-promotion agencies. Its purpose is to raise the status of the role of sales promotion in the UK. The Institute was formed in 1978, following the reorganization of the Sales Promotion Executives Association, itself founded in 1969.

institutional advertisement An advertisement designed to promote the image of an organization, to stimulate *generic demand for a product (e.g. coffee), or to build goodwill for an industry.

institutional broker A securities firm or broker dealing with financial institutions.

institutional investor (institution) A large organization, such as an insurance company, unit trust, bank, trade union, or a pension fund of a large company, that has substantial sums of money to invest on a stock exchange, usually in the UK, in both gilts and equities. Institutions usually employ their own investment analysts and advisors; they are usually able to influence stock exchange sentiment more profoundly than private investors and their policies can often affect share prices. Because institutions can build up significant holdings in companies, they can also influence company policy, usually by making their opinions known at shareholders' meetings, especially during *takeover-bid negotiations.

insurable interest The legal right to enter into an insurance contract. A person is said to have an insurable interest if the event insured against could cause that person a financial loss. For example, anyone may insure their own property as they would incur a loss if an item was lost, destroyed, or damaged. If no financial loss would occur, no insurance can be arranged. For example, a person cannot insure a next-door neighbour's property.

The limit of an insurable interest is the value of the item concerned, although there is no limit on the amount of life assurance a person can take out on his or her own life, or that of a spouse, because the financial effects of death cannot be accurately measured.

Insurable interest was made a condition of all insurance by the Life Assurance Act (1774). Without an insurable interest, an insured person is unable to enforce an insurance contract (or life-assurance contract) as it is the insurable interest that distinguishes insurance from a bet or wager.

insurable risk (static risk) The possibility of suffering some form of loss or damage that can be described sufficiently accurately for a calculation to be made of the probability of its happening, on the basis of past records. Fire, theft, accident, etc., are all insurable *risks because underwriters can assess the probability of having to pay out a claim and can therefore calculate a reasonable *premium. If the risk is met so infrequently that no way of calculating the probability of the event exists, no underwriter will insure against it and it is therefore an **uninsurable risk**.

insurance A legal contract in which an insurer promises to pay a specified amount to another party, the *insured, if a particular event (known as the peril), happens and the insured suffers a financial loss as a result. The insured's part of the contract is to promise to pay an amount of money, known as the *premium, either once or at regular intervals. In order for an insurance contract to be valid, the insured must have an *insurable interest. It is usual to use the word 'insurance' to cover events (such as a fire) that may or may not happen, whereas *assurance refers to an event (such as death) that must occur at some time (*see also* LIFE ASSURANCE). The main branches of insurance are: *accident insurance, *fire insurance, *holiday and travel insurance, *household insurance, *liability insurance, *livestock and bloodstock insurance, loss-of-profit insurance (*see* BUSINESS-INTERRUPTION POLICY), *marine insurance, *motor insurance, *pluvial insurance, *private health insurance, and *property insurance. *See also* REINSURANCE.

insurance broker A person who offers advice on all insurance matters and arranges cover, on behalf of the client, with an *insurer. Insurance brokers act as intermediaries and their income comes from commission paid to them by insurers, usually in the form of an agreed percentage of the first premium or on subsequent premiums. Insurance brokers are regulated by the *Financial Services Authority. *See also* LLOYD'S.

Insurance Brokers Registration Council A statutory body established under the Insurance Brokers Registration Act (1977). It is responsible for the registration and training of insurance brokers and for laying down rules relating to such matters as accounting practice, staff qualifications, advertising, and the orderly conduct and discipline of broking businesses.

Insurance Ombudsman *See* FINANCIAL OMBUDSMAN SERVICE.

insurance policy A document that sets out the terms and conditions of an *insurance contract, stating the benefits payable and the *premium required. *See also* LIFE ASSURANCE.

insurance premium *See* INSURANCE; PREMIUM.

insurance tied agent An agent who represents a particular insurance company or companies. In life and pensions insurance, a tied agent represents only one insurer and is only able to advise the public on the policies offered by that one company. In general insurance (motor, household, holiday, etc.), a tied agent represents no more than six insurers, who are jointly responsible for the financial consequences of any failure or mistake the agent makes. In both cases the agent receives a commission for each policy that is sold and a further commission on each subsequent renewal of the policy. The commission is calculated as an agreed percentage of the total premium paid by the policyholder. The distinction between the two forms of insurance tied agent was a consequence of the Financial Services Act (1987) and the General Insurance Selling Code (1989) of the *Association of British Insurers.

insured A person or company covered

by an *insurance policy. In some policies that cover death, the alternative word *assured may be used for the person who receives the payment in the event of the assured's death.

insurer A person, company, syndicate, or other organization that underwrites an insurance risk.

intangible asset (invisible asset) An asset that can neither be seen nor touched. The most common of these are competencies, *goodwill, and *intellectual properties such as *patents, *trademarks, and copyrights. Goodwill is probably the most intangible and invisible of all assets as no document provides evidence of its existence and its commercial value is difficult to determine. However, it frequently does have very substantial value as the capitalized value of future profits, not attributable purely to the return on *tangible assets. While goodwill is called either an intangible asset or an invisible asset, such items as insurance policies and less tangible overseas investments are usually called invisible assets. Intangible assets are increasingly seen as the key to competitive advantage and the *market value of a firm (see also BOOK VALUE; INTELLECTUAL CAPITAL).

The accounting treatment for intangible assets has been a controversial topic. Under the Companies Act (1985) intangible assets is a main heading that should appear on the face of the balance sheet. The following subheadings are required but may be shown either on the face of the balance sheet or in the notes: *research and development costs; concessions, patents, licences, trademarks, and similar rights and assets; goodwill; payments on account. *Financial Reporting Standard 10, Goodwill and Intangible Assets, was issued in 1997; the relevant *International Accounting Standards are IAS 22, Business Combinations; IAS 36, Impairment of Assets; and IAS 38, Intangible Assets.

integrated accounts A single set of accounting records containing both the financial accounts and the cost accounts of an organization in an integrated form (see FINANCIAL ACCOUNTING; MANAGEMENT ACCOUNTING). This avoids the necessity of reconciling separate financial and cost books and at the same time ensures that both records are based on the same data.

integrated logistics management A physical distribution concept that recognizes the need for a firm to integrate its logistics system with those of its suppliers and customers. The aim is to maximize the performance of the entire distribution system.

integrated marketing communications Marketing communications in which all the elements of *promotional mix are coordinated and systematically planned to be in harmony with each other.

integration The combination of two or more companies under the same control for their mutual benefit, by reducing competition, saving costs by reducing overheads, capturing a larger market share, pooling resources, cooperating on research and development, enhancing competitive advantage, etc. In **horizontal** (or **lateral**) **integration** the businesses carry out the same stage in the *value chain or produce similar products or services; they are therefore competitors. In a monopoly, horizontal integration is complete, while in an oligopoly there is considerable horizontal integration. In **vertical integration** a company obtains control of its suppliers (sometimes called **backward integration**) or of the concerns that buy its products or services (**forward integration**). Conglomerate integration takes place between firms in different value chains.

integrative culture See ORGANIZATIONAL CULTURE.

intellectual capital A complex concept that includes human knowledge, information systems, brand names, and reputation. One popular definition is given by the equation:

intellectual capital = *human capital + structural capital + relationship capital

Here **human capital** includes knowledge, competences, and the experience and expertise of staff, **structural capital** includes information systems and databases, and **relationship** (or **customer**) **capital** includes customer relationships, *brands, and trademarks.

In accounting, intellectual capital is often treated as being synonymous with *intangible assets and valued in the same way, that is, by calculating the difference between the *market value of a company and its *book value. Measuring the intellectual capital is important if one is buying or selling a company or comparing the performance of one company with another. In some companies the book value is only a small percentage of the market value. For example, in 2002 Microsoft had a market capitalization of $250 billion with tangible assets valued at less than $70 billion. The intellectual capital of Microsoft was therefore valued at over $180 billion. Clearly, the balance sheet for Microsoft is not reporting the all-important intellectual capital of the company, which includes technology, patents, brands, and human knowledge.

intellectual property An *intangible asset, such as a copyright, *patent, *trademark, or design right. Intellectual property is an asset, and as such it can be bought, sold, licensed, or exchanged. Further, the intellectual property owner has the right to prevent the unauthorized use or sale of the property.

Examples of intellectual properties include inventions, literary and artistic works, names, images, designs used in commerce, and computer programs. *See also* ROYALTY.

intelligent terminal A computer terminal that is able to process data without the help of the computer to which it is connected. An example is a point-of-sale terminal that adds up the cost of the items purchased and also informs the main stock computer that they are no longer in stock.

intensive distribution A distribution strategy aimed at obtaining the maximum number of outlets to stock a product at the wholesale or retail level. Such products as sweets, chewing gum, disposable razors, soft drinks, and camera film are sold in numerous outlets (including supermarkets, newsagents, and petrol stations) to provide maximum brand exposure and consumer convenience.

interactive Denoting a computer system or application in which there is continuous two-way communication between the computer and its operator. The computer program prompts the operator when it needs information and stops running until the information is supplied. Interactive computer systems are also called **conversational systems**. *Compare* BATCH PROCESSING.

interactive banner advertisement A *banner advertisement that enables the user to enter information.

interactive design strategies *See* CONCURRENT ENGINEERING.

interactive engineering *See* CONCURRENT ENGINEERING.

interactive marketing Marketing by a service firm recognizing that perceived service quality depends heavily on the quality of buyer–seller interaction.

interbank market The wholesale *money market in which banks lend to and borrow from one another. The importance of the market is that it allows individual banks to adjust their liquidity positions quickly, covering shortages by borrowing from banks with surpluses. This reduces the need for each bank to hold large quantities of liquid assets, thus releasing funds for more profitable lending transactions. The **Inter Bank Offered Rate (IBOR)** is the rate of interest charged on interbank loans in a particular financial centre. *See* LONDON INTER BANK OFFERED RATE.

intercompany transactions (intra-group transactions) Transactions between the companies in a *group. These may be in the form of charges or the transfer of goods or services. It is important in the preparation of *consolidated financial statements that such transactions are eliminated or suitable adjustments made as they do not reflect transactions between the group and external parties. *See also* CONSOLIDATION.

inter-dealer broker A member of the *London Stock Exchange who is only permitted to deal with *market makers, rather than the public.

interdict An *injunction in Scottish law.

interest 1. The charge made for borrowing a sum of money. The *interest rate is the charge made, expressed as a percentage of the total sum loaned, for a stated period of time (usually one year). Thus, a rate of interest of 15% per annum means that for every £100 borrowed for one year, the borrower has to pay a charge of £15, or a charge in proportion for longer or shorter periods. In **simple interest**, the charge is calculated on the sum loaned only, thus $I = Prt$, where I is the interest, P is the principal sum, r is the rate of interest, and t is the period. In **compound interest**, the charge is calculated on the sum loaned plus any interest that has accrued in previous periods. In this case $I = P[(1 + r)^n - 1]$, where n is the number of periods for which interest is separately calculated. Thus, if £500 is loaned for two years at a rate of 12% per annum, compounded quarterly, the value of n will be $4 \times 2 = 8$ and the value of r will be $12/4 = 3\%$. Thus, $I = 500[(1.03)^8 - 1] = £133.38$, whereas on a simple-interest basis it would be only £120. These calculations of interest apply equally to deposits that attract income in the form of interest.

In general, rates of interest depend on the money supply, the demand for loans, government policy, the risk of nonrepayment as assessed by the lender, the period of the loan, and relative levels of foreign-exchange rates into other currencies.
2. A share of ownership. *See* CONTROLLING INTEREST; MINORITY INTEREST; PARTICIPATING INTEREST.

interest arbitrage Transactions between financial centres in foreign currencies that take advantage of differentials in interest rates between the two centres and the difference between the forward and spot exchange rates. In some circumstances it is possible to make a profit by borrowing money on domestic markets at fixed rates, buying a foreign currency, lending the foreign currency at fixed rates, and entering into a forward contract to buy domestic currency.

interest-bearing eligible liabilities (IBEL) Liabilities recognized by the Bank of England as being held by UK banks, e.g. net deposits. In times of strict monetary control the Bank of England requires other UK banks to deposit a percentage of these liabilities with it.

interest cover (fixed-charge–coverage ratio) A ratio showing the number of times interest charges are covered by earnings before interest and tax (*see* EBIT). For example, a company with interest charges of £12 million and earnings before interest and tax of £36 million would have its interest covered three times. The ratio is one way of analysing *gearing and reflects the vulnerability of a *company to changes in interest rates or profit fluctuations. A highly geared company, which has a low interest cover, may find that an increase in the interest rate will mean that it has no earnings after interest charges with which to provide a dividend to shareholders.

interest factors An individual's personal interests and likes or dislikes, as revealed in answers to a standardized questionnaire or derived from his or her hobbies, leisure activities, etc. In *personnel selection and vocational guidance, interest factors are seen as revealing stable personality traits and therefore as predictors of successful performance in a particular job or type of job. **Interest tests**, such as the Strong Interest Inventory and the Kuder Occupational Interest Survey, require participants to express their preferences among a range of activities, characteristics, and values; their answers can then be compared with the patterns of answers obtained from individuals who have proved successful in a particular occupation.

interest-in-possession trust A type of fixed-interest *trust in which there is an entitlement to the income generated by the trust assets. The *beneficiaries of an interest-in-possession trust, the life tenants, are entitled to the income arising for a fixed period or until their death. The capital in the trust then passes absolutely to the recipient known as the remainderman. *Compare* DISCRETIONARY TRUST.

interest-only yield *See* YIELD.

interest rate The amount charged for a loan, usually expressed as a percentage of the sum borrowed. Conversely, the amount paid by a bank, building society, etc., to a depositor on funds deposited, again expressed as a percentage of the sum deposited. *See* ANNUAL PERCENTAGE RATE; BASE RATE; LONDON INTER BANK BID RATE; LONDON INTER BANK OFFERED RATE.

interest-rate cycle The notion that the movement of interest rates is cyclical and related to the *business cycle. Historically, the variable path of inflation has modified any cyclical pattern in rates.

interest-rate exposure *See* INTEREST-RATE RISK.

interest-rate futures A form of *financial futures that enables investors, portfolio managers, borrowers, etc., to obtain protection against future movements in interest rates. Interest-rate futures also enable dealers to speculate on these movements. In the UK, interest-rate futures are dealt in on the *London International Financial Futures and Options Exchange, using contracts for three-month sterling, eurodollars, euros, etc., in the short term and long gilts, US Treasury bonds, euro bonds, etc., in the long term. For long gilts, for example, the standard contract is for £50,000 of nominal value and the *tick size is 0.01% of the nominal value. *See* HEDGE.

interest-rate guarantee An indemnity sold by a bank, or similar financial institution, that protects the purchaser against the effect of future movements in interest rates. It is similar to a *forward-rate agreement, but the terms are specified by the customer.

Interest-rate margin 1. The difference between the interest rate at which banks lend and the rate they pay on deposits. It is likely to be a major indicator of a bank's profitability. **2.** The amount charged to borrowers over and above the *base rate. This margin is the bank's profit on the transaction but has to take account of risk of loss or default by the borrower.

interest-rate option A form of *option enabling traders and speculators to *hedge themselves against future changes in interest rates. It is an option to purchase a specific debt instrument.

interest-rate policy The policy by which governments or central banks influence *interest rates. Higher rates of interest will reduce the demand for money, giving a downward impetus to output, employment and prices. Lower interest rates will have the opposite effect. Responsibility for interest-rate policy was restored to

the Bank of England by the UK government in 1997.

interest-rate risk (interest-rate exposure) The *risk arising from changes in interest rates. In recent decades the different forms of interest-rate risk have been the subject of much analysis, monitoring, and scrutiny. In the 1980s, for example, the *savings and loan associations (S & L) in the USA faced a major crisis as a result of continuing to offer fixed-rate loans despite a steadily climbing interest rate; this meant that their interest revenues remained at a constant level while their interest costs rose. The main forms of interest-rate risk are: the risk that interest-rate changes will impact on the value of fixed-interest assets and liabilities; the risk of mismatches in terms of the repricing of interest on assets and liabilities (as illustrated by the S & L example); *prepayment risk, in which a borrower repays an obligation, such as a mortgage, early; the risk that reinvestment may take place at lower rates; and the risk that, as rates rise, repayments will take longer than expected. *See* GAP.

interest-rate swap A form of dealing between banks, security houses, and companies in which institutions exchange interest-rate payments on a notional capital value. *Swaps can be in the same currency or cross-currency (*see* CROSS-CURRENCY INTEREST-RATE SWAP). If a swap is in the same currency it will usually involve a fixed interest payment in exchange for a floating interest payment; a swap involving two different floating rates is called a *basis swap. *See also* RATE ANTICIPATION SWAP.

interest-sensitive Denoting an activity that is sensitive to changes in the general level of interest rates. For example, the demand for consumer goods usually bought on some form of *hire-purchase basis is interest-sensitive because they cost more as interest rates rise.

interim accounts *See* INTERIM FINANCIAL STATEMENTS.

interim dividend A *dividend paid during a *financial year.

interim financial statements (interim accounts; interim report) *Financial statements issued for a period of less than a financial year. Although there are provisions under the Companies Act (1985) that refer to interim accounts in certain circumstances relating to the distribution of *dividends, there are no legal requirements obliging companies to produce interim accounts on a regular basis. However, *listed companies on the *London Stock Exchange are required to prepare a half-yearly report on their activities and *profit and loss during the first six months of each financial year. The interim financial statement must be either sent to the holders of the company's listed *securities or advertised in at least one national newspaper not later than four months after the end of the period to which it relates. A copy of the interim financial statements must also be sent to the Company Announcements Office and to the competent authority of each other state in which the company's shares are listed. The vast majority of companies choose to send the interim statement to shareholders with a brief announcement of the headline figures reported in the press. There is no requirement for the interim statements to be audited. Although the stock-exchange regulations require mainly profit information, there is a trend for the larger companies to also provide *balance sheet and *cash-flow statements. In the UK, the requirements only call for six-monthly financial statements, but some larger companies with interests in the USA follow the US practice of issuing reports quarterly.

intermarket spread swap Swapping securities in the hope of improving the spread between the yields of the securities.

intermediaries Firms in a distribution channel that help a company to find customers or make sales to them. Intermediaries include brokers, agents, dealers, wholesalers, and retailers that buy and resell goods.

intermediate-term See MEDIUM-TERM.

intermediate terms See INNOMINATE TERMS.

intermediation The activity of a bank, similar financial institution, broker, etc., in acting as an intermediary between the two parties to a transaction; the intermediary can accept all or part of the credit

risk or the other commercial risks. *Compare* DISINTERMEDIATION.

intermodalism A method of using more than one form of transport in the delivery of goods. In the USA, for example, an increasing number of manufacturers and *shipping and forwarding agents are delivering goods by combining low-cost long-haul rail transport with the flexibility of road transport to the final destination.

internal audit An *audit that an organization carries out on its own behalf, normally to ensure that its own internal controls are operating satisfactorily. Whereas an external audit is almost always concerned with financial matters, this may not necessarily be the case with an internal audit; internal auditors may also concern themselves with such matters as the observation of the safety and health at work regulations or of the equal opportunities legislation. It may also be used to detect any theft or fraud (*see also* INTERNAL CONTROL).

internal business-process perspective See BALANCED SCORECARD.

internal control The measures an organization employs to ensure that opportunities for fraud or misfeasance are minimized. Examples range from requiring more than one signature on certain documents, security arrangements for stock-handling, division of tasks, keeping of *control accounts, use of special passwords, handling of computer files, etc. It is one of the principal concerns of an *internal audit to ensure that internal controls are working properly so that the external auditors can have faith in the accounts produced by the organization. Internal control should also reassure management of the integrity of its operations.

internal control system A system of controls, both financial and non-financial, set up by the management of a company to carry out the business of the company in an orderly and efficient manner. The system should ensure that management policies are adhered to, assets are safeguarded, and the records of the company's activities are both complete and accurate. The individual components of an internal control system are the individual internal controls.

internal customer A unit, division, or individual employee who is the recipient of materials, products, information, or services from another unit in the same organization (the **internal supplier**). The concept encourages employees to treat their co-workers as though they were external customers or suppliers, thereby raising quality consciousness within the organization.

internal failure costs *See* COST OF QUALITY. *See also* ENVIRONMENTAL COSTS.

internal growth (organic growth) The means by which a business can grow using its own resources (*see* BUSINESS STRATEGY). A business will grow by increased *market penetration at the expense of its competitors, by *new product development, and by market development through seeking new applications and markets for existing products or services. All these means utilize a firm's *core competencies and while some may have a relatively short lead time (e.g. market penetration) others, notably product development, can involve significant lead times and development costs. Firms that have a successful record of innovation are usually more successful at internal growth, whereas others favour greater reliance on *external growth.

internal marketing Marketing in which a service firm trains and effectively motivates its customer-contact employees and the supporting service team to work together to provide customer satisfaction.

internal rate of return (IRR) An interest rate that gives a *net present value of zero when applied to the projected cash flow from an asset, liability, or financial decision. This interest rate, where the *present values of the cash inflows and outflows are equal, is the internal rate of return for a project under consideration, and the decision to adopt the project will depend on its size compared with the *cost of capital. The approximate IRR can be computed manually by interpolation but most computer *spreadsheet programs now include a routine enabling the IRR to be computed quickly and accurately. The IRR technique suffers from the possibility of multiple solution rates in some circumstances. If it suggests a differ-

ent decision to that obtained from *net present value it should be disregarded, because net present value is a superior decision tool.

Internal Revenue Code The federal tax law of the USA, which comprises the regulations applied to taxpayers.

Internal Revenue Service (IRS) In the USA, the branch of federal government responsible for collecting most types of taxes. The IRS administers the *Internal Revenue Code, investigates tax abuses, and makes criminal prosecution for tax fraud through the US tax court.

internal supplier *See* INTERNAL CUSTOMER.

internal user *See* DECISION-MAKING UNIT.

International Accounting Standard (IAS) Any of the accounting standards issued by the board of the International Accounting Standards Committee (IASC) between 1973 and 2001. In 2001 the IASC was replaced by the *International Accounting Standards Board (IASB), which announced that its accounting standards would be designated *International Financial Reporting Standards (IFRS). The IASB stated that all of the International Accounting Standards issued by the IASC would continue to be applicable unless and until they were amended or withdrawn by the new body. For years starting on or after 1 January 2005, listed companies in the EU are required to use adopted IASs in their consolidated accounts. See box on p. 284.

International Accounting Standards Board (IASB) An independent, privately funded body responsible for establishing and improving international accounting standards. It superseded the **International Accounting Standards Committee** (IASC) in 2001. According to the mission statement of the IASB, its objectives are:

- to develop, in the public interest, a single set of high-quality, understandable, and enforceable global accounting standards that require high-quality, transparent, and comparable information in financial statements and other financial reporting, thereby helping participants

INTERNATIONAL ACCOUNTING STANDARDS

1. Presentation of Financial Statements (revised 2003)
2. Inventories (revised 2003)
7. Cash Flow Statements
8. Accounting Policies, Changes in Accounting Estimates, and Errors (revised 2003)
10. Events After the Balance Sheet Date (revised 2003)
11. Construction Contracts
12. Income Taxes
14. Segment Reporting (revised 2003)
16. Property, Plant and Equipment (revised 2003)
17. Leases (revised 2003)
18. Revenue
19. Employee Benefits
20. Accounting for Government Grants and Disclosure of Government Assistance
21. The Effects of Changes in Foreign Exchange Rates (revised 2003)
23. Capitalization of Borrowing Costs
24. Related Party Disclosures (revised 2003)
26. Accounting and Reporting by Retirement Benefit Plans
27. Consolidated and Separate Financial Statements (revised 2003)
28. Investments in Associates (revised 2003)
29. Financial Reporting in Hyperinflationary Economies
30. Disclosures in the Financial Statements of Banks and Similar Financial Institutions
31. Interests In Joint Ventures (revised 2003)
32. Financial Instruments: Disclosure and Presentation
33. Earnings Per Share (revised 2003)
34. Interim Financial Reporting
36. Impairment of Assets
37. Provisions, Contingent Liabilities and Contingent Assets
38. Intangible Assets
39. Financial Instruments: Recognition and Measurement
40. Investment Property (revised 2003)
41. Agriculture

As indicated, 14 IASs were issued in revised form under the International Accounting Standards Board's Improvements Project in December 2003.

in the world's capital markets and other users make economic decisions;
- to promote the use and rigorous application of those standards;
- to bring about convergence of national accounting standards with *International Accounting Standards and *International Financial Reporting Standards.

The IASB has no authority to require compliance with its accounting standards. However, many countries (including the USA and member states of the EU) now require that statements of publicly traded companies are prepared in accordance with IASB standards. The organization is based in London.

International Bank for Reconstruction and Development (IBRD) A specialized agency working in coordination with the United Nations, established in 1945 to help finance post-war reconstruction and to help raise standards of living in developing countries, by making loans to governments or guaranteeing outside loans. It lends on broadly commercial terms, either for specific projects or for more general social purposes; funds are raised on the international capital markets. The Bank and its affiliates, the *International Development Association and the *International Finance Corporation, are often known collectively as the **World Bank**; it is owned by the governments of 184 countries. Members must also be members of the *International Monetary Fund. The headquarters of the Bank are in Washington, with a European office in Paris and a Tokyo office.

international banking facility (IBF) A banking facility in the USA that is authorized by the *Federal Reserve System to participate in *eurocurrency lending. Such facilities are exempt from reserve requirement and may have many other advantages usually associated with offshore banking.

International Chamber of Commerce (ICC) An international business organization that represents business interests in international affairs. It also conducts arbitrations and promotes business self-regulation. Its office is in Paris. *See also* INCOTERMS.

international commodity agreements Agreements between governments that aim to stabilize the price of commodities. This is often important for producing nations, for whom the revenue from commodity sales may make a major contribution to the national income. Methods tried include government-financed buffer stocks and the imposition of price limits between which the price of the commodity is allowed to fluctuate. Among the commodities for which agree-

ments have been made are coffee, sugar, wheat, cocoa, and tin.

International Datapost A parcel delivery service offered by Parcelforce Worldwide (part of Consignia). Guaranteed delivery is provided to 221 countries.

International Development Association (IDA) An affiliate of the *International Bank for Reconstruction and Development (IBRD) established in 1960 to provide assistance for poorer developing countries. It is funded by subscription and transfers from the net earnings of IBRD. The headquarters of the IDA are in Washington, with offices in Paris and Tokyo, administered by IBRD staff.

international division A division of an international marketing organization that handles all a firm's international activities. Marketing, manufacturing, research, planning, and specialist staff are organized into operating units according to geography or product groups, or organized as an international subsidiary responsible for its own sales and profitability.

International Finance Corporation (IFC) An affiliate of the *International Bank for Reconstruction and Development (IBRD) established in 1956 to provide assistance for private investment projects. Although the IFC and IBRD are separate entities, both legally and financially, the IFC is able to borrow from the IBRD and reloan to private investors. The headquarters of the IFC are in Washington. Its importance increased in the 1980s after the emergence of the debt crisis and the subsequent reliance on the private sector.

International Financial Reporting Standard (IFRS) Any of the accounting standards issued by the *International Accounting Standards Board (IASB) since its institution in 2001. For financial years starting on or after 1 January 2005 listed companies in the EU are required to follow IFRSs in their published accounts. See box on p. 286. *See also* INTERNATIONAL ACCOUNTING STANDARD.

International Fund for Agricultural Development (IFAD) A fund, proposed by the 1974 World Food Conference, that began operations in 1977 with the purpose of providing additional funds for agri-

---

INTERNATIONAL FINANCIAL REPORTING STANDARDS

There are currently seven IRFRs:

1. First-time Adoption of International Financial Reporting Standards
2. Share-based Payment
3. Business Combinations
4. Insurance Contracts
5. Non-current Assets Held for Sale and Discontinued Operations
6. Exploration for and Evaluation of Mineral Assets
7. Financial Instruments: Disclosures

---

cultural and rural development in developing countries. It has some 163 member states. The headquarters of IFAD are in Rome.

International Labour Organization (ILO) A special agency of the United Nations, established under the Treaty of Versailles in 1919, with the aim of promoting lasting peace through social justice. The ILO establishes international labour standards, runs a programme of technical assistance to developing countries, and attacks unemployment through its World Employment Programme. The ILO is financed by contributions from its member states. Its headquarters, The International Labour Office, is in Geneva.

International Monetary Fund (IMF) An international organization established in 1947 to enhance stability and convertibility in the international monetary system. The Fund assists any member experiencing short-term balance of payments difficulties by supplying the amount of foreign currency it wishes to purchase in exchange for the equivalent amount of its own currency. The member repays this amount by buying back its own currency in a currency acceptable to the Fund, usually within three to five years. High levels of borrowing are conditional on the implementation of IMF suggested policies for a country. The Fund is financed by subscriptions from its members, the amount determined by an estimate of their means. Voting power is related to the amount of the subscription. The head office of the IMF is in Washington. *See also* CONDITIONALITY.

International Monetary Market *See* CHICAGO MERCANTILE EXCHANGE.

international paper sizes See feature on p. 287.

International Petroleum Exchange (IPE) An exchange, founded in London in 1980, that deals in *futures contracts and *options (including traded options) in oil (gas oil, Brent crude oil, and heavy fuel oil) with facilities for making an exchange of futures for physicals (*see* ACTUALS). The exchange was formerly noted for its *open outcry system; however, its trading pits were closed on 7 April 2005, since when all markets have operated electronically.

International Securities Market Association (ISMA) The *eurobond market's trade association, founded in 1969. It is based in Zürich.

international security identification number (ISIN) An identification system for all securities issues on the international market.

International Standards Organization (ISO) An organization founded in 1946 to standardize measurements and other standards for industrial, commercial, and scientific purposes. The *British Standards Institution is a member.

International Telecommunication Union (ITU) A special agency of the United Nations founded in Paris in 1865 as the International Telegraph Union. It sets up international regulations for telegraph, telephone, and radio services; promotes international cooperation for the improvement of telecommunications; and is con-

INTERNATIONAL PAPER SIZES

International paper sizes are based upon a rectangle of paper with an area of one square metre, the sides of which are in the proportion $1:\sqrt{2}$. This geometrical relationship is used so that any lengthways halfing of the original rectangle of paper produces another rectangle of paper with the same geometric relationship. For example, the A series is shown below.

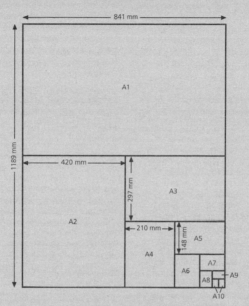

There are three series of international paper size; A, B, and C. A is the most common series, with A4 being the favoured size for business correspondence. The B series is often used for posters, wall charts, other large items and where circumstances dictate a size of paper intermediate between any two adjacent sizes of the A series. The C series is used mainly when it is necessary to fit an envelope inside another envelope. The range and sizes of the three series are as follows:

A series (mm)

A0	841×1189	A4	210×297	A8	52×74
A1	594×841	A5	148×210	A9	37×52
A2	420×594	A6	105×148	A10	26×37
A3	297×420	A7	74×105		

B series (mm)

B0	1000×1414	B4	250×353	B8	62×88
B1	707×1000	B5	176×250	B9	44×62
B2	500×707	B6	125×176	B10	31×44
B3	353×500	B7	88×125		

C series (mm)

C4	324×229	C5	229×162	C6	162×114

cerned with the development of technical facilities. It is responsible for the allocation and registration of radio frequencies for communications. Its headquarters are in Geneva.

International Union of Credit and Investment Insurers *See* BERNE UNION.

Internet (the Net) An international network of computers connected by modems, dedicated lines, telephone cables, and satellite links, with associated software controlling the movement of data. It offers facilities for accessing remote databases, transfer of data between computers, and *e-mail. In addition, there are high-level services. **MBONE** (multicast backbone service), for example, allows transmission to more than one destination and is used for *videoconferencing. The **World Wide Web** is a multimedia facility allowing pictures, sound, and video to be displayed. A particular feature of the Web is the availability of *hyperlinks between pages and documents.

Originally, the Internet was mainly used by the academic community, but the wider availability of personal computers has led to an enormous growth in the number of individual users. This has resulted in increasing commercial exploitation in such areas as electronic shopping, *home banking, advertising, and marketing research. Most businesses now have their own websites and companies are increasingly using the Internet to publish their annual accounts and other financial information. It is also possible for individuals and companies to file their tax returns on line. *See also* INFORMATION TECHNOLOGY.

Internet access provider (IAP) *See* ACCESS PROVIDER.

Internet exchanges Web-based bazaars, often shared by buyers, in which suppliers bid against requirements posted on the Internet.

Internet Explorer A *web browser introduced by Microsoft in 1995; it is now the most commonly used browser.

Internet marketing The application of the Internet and related digital technologies to achieve marketing objectives.

Internet relay chat (IRC) A communica-

tions tool that enables a text-based 'chat' to take place between different Internet users, who are logged on at the same time.

Internet service provider (ISP) A company that provides home or business users with a connection to access the Internet. Internet service providers can also host websites or provide a link from web servers to enable other companies and consumers access to a corporate website. *See also* ON-LINE SERVICE PROVIDER.

Internet tool Software that is used on the Internet. An example is a *web browser.

interpolation Estimation of the value of an unknown quantity that lies between two of a series of known values. For example, one can estimate by interpolation the population of a country at any time between known 10-year census figures. This would normally be done on a graph, the shape of the curve between known points enabling a good estimate to be made of the interpolated value. **Extrapolation** involves estimating an unknown quantity that lies outside a series of known values. Thus one could obtain a figure for the population of a country five years after its last census, by extending the population curve after the last known value.

intervention price *See* COMMON AGRICULTURAL POLICY.

interviewer error An error in marketing research that results from conscious or unconscious bias on the part of the interviewer. For example, the interviewer may guess incorrectly the age of the respondent or may assume that because someone is driving a car they own the car.

inter vivos gifts *See* GIFTS INTER VIVOS.

intestate A person who dies without having made a will. The estate, in these circumstances, is divided according to the rules of **intestacy**. The division depends on the personal circumstances of the deceased. If there is a spouse then there is a fixed statutory legacy, with the remainder being split between an *interest-in-possession trust for the remaining spouse and the children's absolute entitlement to the other half, if they are over 18. Where there is no surviving spouse the estate is divided between the children or

their issue. Where there are no children then the split is rather more complicated and can include parents, brothers and sisters, grandparents, uncles, and aunts.

in-the-money option An *option that would generate a gain if currently exercised. An option that would not generate a gain is an **out-of-the money option**. See IN-TRINSIC VALUE.

intraday limit 1. The maximum price movement in a single day's trading that is permitted by the rules of a particular financial market. **2.** The limit placed on a given trader's *exposure in a single day.

intranet A network within a single company or other organization that provides access to private information using the familiar tools of the Internet, such as *web browsers and e-mail. Only staff within the company or organization can access the intranet, which is usually protected by a password.

intrapreneur An executive or senior manager of a large firm who uses the entrepreneurial approach to management. In order to encourage entrepreneurship, it has become common for firms to encourage risk-taking and profit-orientated behaviour among its managers by organizing a business into a number of separate profit centres. Each centre is responsible for making a profit by intra-group trading and, where appropriate, by building up its external sales and clients. This approach has been used in the service departments of large companies, giving subsidiary companies the choice of using the internal services or of going outside to independent suppliers. This process of developing an internal market for services has also been applied by the public sector; for example, the UK National Health Service was encouraged to use this intrapreneurial approach in the 1990s. Critics, however, often suggest that decisions may then be taken too narrowly, rather than for the benefit of the whole organization; the internal market in the NHS was discontinued largely for this reason in 1999.

intrinsic motivation An incentive to do something that arises from factors within the individual, such as a need to feel useful or to seek *self-actualization.

Compare EXTRINSIC MOTIVATION. *See* INTRINSIC REWARD; MOTIVATION.

intrinsic reward A positive outcome of performing work that is integral to the work task itself, such as love of or pride in one's work, a sense of challenge or achievement, etc.

intrinsic value The difference between the market value of the *underlying in a traded *option and the *exercise price when the option is 'in the money'. Otherwise the intrinsic value is zero. *See also* TIME VALUE.

introduction A method of issuing new securities in which a broker or issuing house takes small quantities of the company's shares and issues them to clients at opportune moments. It is also used by existing public companies that wish to issue additional shares. *Compare* OFFER FOR SALE; PLACING.

introduction stage *See* PRODUCT LIFE CYCLE.

inventoriable costs Costs that can be included in the valuation of *inventory (raw materials, *work in progress, or finished goods). *See* INVENTORY VALUATION.

inventory 1. (**stock; stock-in-trade**) The products or supplies of an organization on hand or in transit at any time. For a manufacturing company the types of inventory are raw materials, work in progress, and finished goods. An inventory count usually takes place at the end of the *financial year to confirm that the actual quantities support the figures given in the *books of account. The differences between the inventories at the beginning and the end of a period are used in the calculation of *cost of sales for the *profit and loss account and the end inventory is shown on the *balance sheet as a *current asset. **2.** More broadly, the total accumulation of material resources within an *operating system (not only what is held deliberately in stock). It includes all the transformed resources that are locked up in the system, such as work in progress, scrap, rejects, etc. All operations have some inventory, which represents locked-up capital. The task of *operations is to ensure that levels are kept to the minimum without affecting the efficiency and effectiveness of the transformation process.

Inventory, in this sense, falls into a number of different categories:

- **Anticipatory inventory** is produced in periods of relatively low demand in anticipation of a later increase in demand. This is only possible if the goods are non-perishable and is only economically viable if the costs of storage are less than the costs of changing production levels to match demand.
- **Uncoupling inventory** is the amount of material held to decouple elements of the *transformation system, such as the raw-material supplier from the manufacturer, one machine from another, or the manufacturer from the customer. This provides an element of operational flexibility.
- Similar to uncoupling inventory is the **buffer inventory**, which protects against variations in supply, demand, and lead times. It represents a safety margin and is therefore directly related to the reliability of demand forecasting, etc.
- **Pipeline inventory** is that part of the inventory that is locked up in the system. Because all processes take time, the pipeline is a function of a *transformation system rather than performing a function within it. If organizations have to subcontract part of their products or if elements of the system are widely separated geographically, the amount of resource locked up in the pipeline can increase dramatically. Modern process-monitoring systems based on *information technology are designed to ensure that the pipeline inventory in particular is kept to a minimum.
- **Cycle inventory** is a function of the *economic order quantity (EOQ) calculation and represents a trade-off between minimizing the inventory and the costs of setting up and changing processes. *Just-in-time techniques are designed to rely on a minimum EOQ.

Clearly there is some overlap between these different types of inventory.

inventory control See STOCK CONTROL.

inventory effect The fact that the relationship between price and demand for a product is much more sensitive in the short term than the long term for nonperishable products. This is largely because consumers know that they can stock and safely store nonperishables during a sale.

inventory status record A data file containing up-to-date information on the status of every item, component, etc., controlled by the *material requirements planning system. This file contains the identification number, quantity in hand, safety stock level, quantity allocated, and procurement lead time of every item.

inventory valuation (stock valuation) The valuation of stocks of raw material, work in progress, and finished goods. According to *Statement of Standard Accounting Practice 9, stocks should be valued at the lower of cost or *net realizable value and the costs incurred up to the stage of production reached. This effectively means that finished goods and work in progress should include both fixed and variable production costs but exclude the selling and distribution costs. In the UK valuing stocks at cost, the *first-in-first-out cost, or the *average cost may be used, but not the *last-in-first-out cost or the *next-in-first-out cost. *Marginal cost may be used as a basis of stock valuation for *management accounting purposes but is unacceptable for *financial accounting.

investment 1. The purchase of capital goods, such as plant and machinery in a factory in order to produce goods for future consumption. This is known as **capital investment**; the higher the level of capital investment in an economy, the faster it will grow. **2.** The purchase of assets, such as securities, works of art, bank and building-society deposits, etc., with a primary view to their financial return, either as income or capital gain. This form of **financial investment** represents a means of saving. The level of financial investment in an economy, will be related to such factors as the rate of interest, the extent to which investments are likely to prove profitable, and the general climate of business confidence.

investment analyst A person employed by stockbrokers, banks, insurance companies, unit trusts, pension funds, etc., to give advice on the making of investments, especially investments in securities, commodities, etc. Many pay special attention to the study of *equities in the hope of being able to advise their employers to make profitable purchases of ordinary shares. To do this they use a variety of techniques, including a comparison of a company's present profits with its future trading prospects; this enables the analyst to single out the companies likely to outperform the general level of the market. This form of **technical analysis** is often contrasted with **fundamental analysis**, in which predicted future market movements are related to the underlying state of an economy and its expected trends. Analysts who rely on past movements to predict the future are called *chartists.

investment bank A US bank that fulfils many of the functions of a UK *merchant bank. It is usually one that advises on mergers and acquisitions and provides finance for industrial corporations by buying shares in a company and selling them in relatively small lots to investors. Capital provided to companies is usually long-term and based on fixed assets. In the USA, commercial banks were excluded from selling securities for many years but the law was relaxed in the late 1980s, when certain safeguards were introduced, including a ceiling on the value of transactions.

investment bond A single-premium life-assurance policy in which an investment of a fixed amount is made (usually over £1000) in an *asset-backed fund. Interest is paid at an agreed rate and at the end of the period the investment is returned with any growth. Investment bonds confer attractive tax benefits in some circumstances. See also SINGLE-PREMIUM ASSURANCE; TOP SLICING.

investment club A group of investors who, by pooling their resources, are able to make more frequent and larger investments on a stock exchange, often being able to reduce brokerage and to spread the risk of serious loss. The popularity of investment clubs has waxed and waned with the developments of investment vehicles and the value of stocks.

investment company See INVESTMENT TRUST.

investment-grade Describing a bond that has been given a relatively high credit rating by a major *rating agency, namely Baa and above by Moody's or BBB and above by Standard & Poor's or Fitch's. Lower-rated bonds may promise a higher yield but are inherently more speculative.

investment grant (**investment incentive**) A grant made to a company by a government to encourage investment in plant, machinery, buildings, etc. The incentives may take various forms, some being treated as a deduction for tax purposes, others being paid whether or not the company makes a profit.

investment income 1. A person's income derived from investments. **2.** The income of a business derived from its outside investments rather than from its trading activities.

Investment Management Regulatory Organization (**IMRO**) A former *Self-Regulating Organization set up in 1986 to regulate any institutions offering investment management. Its functions are now exercised by the *Financial Services Authority, into which it was absorbed in 2001.

investment manager See FUND MANAGER.

Investment Ombudsman See FINANCIAL OMBUDSMAN SERVICE.

investment portfolio See PORTFOLIO.

investment properties Properties owned by a company that holds investments as part of its business, such as an *investment trust or a property-investment company. Investment properties may also include properties owned by a company whose main business is not the holding of investments. Such properties are strictly defined by *Statement of Standard Accounting Practice 19, Accounting for Investment Properties, as being an interest in land and/or buildings:

(1) in respect of which construction work and development have been completed; and
(2) that is held for its investment potential, any rental income being negotiated at arm's length.

However, a property owned and occupied by a company for its own purposes is not an investment property, and a property let to and occupied by another company in the same group is not an investment property for the purposes of its own accounts or the *group accounts. Investment properties should not be depreciated annually unless they are held on a lease. If they are leased they should be depreciated on the basis set out in *Statement of Standard Accounting Practice 12, Accounting for Depreciation, at least over the period, when the unexpired term is 20 years or less. Investment properties should be included in the *balance sheet at their open-market value, movements being taken to the *investment revaluation reserve unless it is insufficient to cover a deficit, in which case it should be taken to the *profit and loss account.

investment revaluation reserve A *reserve created by a company with *investment properties, if these properties are included in the *balance sheet at open-market value. Changes in the value of investment properties should be disclosed as movements on the investment revaluation reserve, unless the total of the investment revaluation reserve is insufficient to cover a deficit, in which case the amount by which the deficit exceeds the amount in the investment revaluation reserve should be charged to the *profit and loss account. In the case of *investment trust companies and property *unit trusts it may not be appropriate to deal with these deficits in the profit and loss account; in these circumstances they should be shown prominently in the *financial statements.

Investment Services Directive (ISD) An EU directive (1993) providing a regulatory framework for securities dealing. It states that securities firms should be admitted by their domestic regulator before they are allowed to operate at a European level. A new ISD, which greatly strengthens the single market for financial services, has been passed by the European Parliament and is expected to be implemented in 2006.

investment tax credit In the USA, an incentive to investment in which part of the cost of an asset subject to depreciation is used to offset income tax falling due in the year of purchase.

investment trust (investment company)

A company that invests the funds provided by shareholders in a wide variety of securities. It makes its profits from the income and capital gains provided by these securities. The investments made are usually restricted to securities quoted on a stock exchange, but some will invest in unquoted companies. The advantages for shareholders are much the same as those with *unit trusts, i.e. spreading the risk of investment and making use of professional managers. Investment trusts, which are not usually *trusts in the usual sense, but private or public limited companies, differ from unit trusts in that in the latter the investors buy units in the fund but are not shareholders. Some investment trusts aim for high capital growth (**capital shares**), others for high income (**income shares**). See also ACCUMULATION UNIT; SPLIT-CAPITAL INVESTMENT TRUST; UNITIZATION.

invisible assets See INTANGIBLE ASSET.

invisible earnings (invisibles) The earnings from abroad that contribute to the *balance of payments as a result of transactions involving services, such as insurance, banking, shipping, and tourism (often known as **invisibles**), rather than the sale and purchase of goods. Invisibles can play an important part in a nation's current account, although they are often difficult to quantify. The UK relies on a substantial invisible balance in its balance of payments.

invitation to treat See OFFER.

invoice See SALES INVOICE.

invoice discounting A form of debt discounting in which a business sells its invoices to a *factoring house at a discount for immediate cash. The service does not usually include sales accounting and debt collecting.

IOU A written document providing evidence of a debt, usually in the form 'I owe you...'. It is not a *negotiable instrument or a *promissory note and requires no stamp (unless it does include a promise to pay). It can, however, be used as legal evidence of a debt.

IPA Abbreviation for *Institute of Practitioners in Advertising.

IPE Abbreviation for *International Petroleum Exchange.

IPO Abbreviation for *initial public offering.

IRA Abbreviation for *individual retirement account.

IRC Abbreviation for *Internet relay chat.

IRR Abbreviation for *internal rate of return.

irredeemable securities (irredeemables) Securities, such as some government loan stock (*see* CONSOLS) and some *debentures, on which there is no date given for the redemption of the capital sum. The price of fixed-interest irredeemables on the open market varies inversely with the level of interest rates.

irrevocable documentary acceptance credit A form of irrevocable confirmed *letter of credit in which a foreign importer of UK goods opens a credit with a UK bank or the UK office of a local bank. The bank then issues an irrevocable letter of credit to the exporter, guaranteeing to accept *bills of exchange drawn on it on presentation of the shipping documents. Once the letter of credit has been drawn up, the importer has to 'accept' that he or she will pay, by signing the acceptance.

irrevocable letter of credit *See* LETTER OF CREDIT.

IRS Abbreviation for *Internal Revenue Service.

ISA Abbreviation for *Individual Savings Account.

ISA mortgage A *mortgage in which the borrower repays only the interest on the loan to the lender, but at the same time puts regular sums into an *Individual Savings Account (ISA). When the ISA matures it is used to repay the capital. An ISA mortgage is similar to an *endowment mortgage, except that it does not provide any life-assurance cover and that ISA funds are untaxed.

ISBA Abbreviation for *Incorporated Society of British Advertisers Ltd.

ISD *See* INVESTMENT SERVICES DIRECTIVE.

Ishikawa diagram *See* CAUSE–EFFECT DIAGRAM.

ISIN Abbreviation for *international security identification number.

Islamic finance A system of finance that is bound by religious laws that prevent the taking of interest payments (*see* HALAL; HARAAM). Joint ventures in which the funder and the borrower share profits and risks are, however, acceptable. There are a number of different techniques by which this takes place. **Murabaha** is a good vehicle for temporary idle funds, which are used to purchase goods from a supplier for immediate sale and delivery to the buyer, who pays a predetermined margin over cost on a deferred payment date. The term can be as short as seven days. **Musharaka** transactions involve participation with other parties in trade financing, leasing, real estate, and industrial projects. Net profits are shared in proportions agreed at the outset. **Shirkah** is a partnership between a bank and a customer to share the risks and gains of a project. **Muqarada** is a joint venture by finance providers. **Ijarah** involves profit from rental income on real estate. **Ijarawaiktina** is leasing of large capital items, such as property or plant and machinery. Leasing is achieved by the equivalent of monthly rental payments, and at the expiry the lessee purchases the equipment.

ISO Abbreviation for *International Standards Organization.

ISO 9000 An EU-sponsored process quality standard, based largely on *British Standard 5750.

ISP 1. Abbreviation for *Institute of Sales Promotion. **2.** Abbreviation for *Internet service provider.

issue 1. The number of shares or the amount of stock on offer to the public at a particular time. *See also* NEW ISSUE; RIGHTS ISSUE; SCRIP ISSUE. **2.** The number of banknotes distributed by the Bank of England at a particular time.

issue by tender (sale by tender; tender offer) A type of *offer for sale in which an issuing house asks investors to tender for a new issue of shares or other securities, which are then allocated to the highest bidders. It is usual for the tender documents to state the lowest price acceptable. This method is not frequently employed. *Compare* PUBLIC ISSUE.

issued share A *share that has been allotted by the directors of a company to an applicant and paid for in part or in full by that applicant. *See* FULLY PAID SHARE; PARTLY PAID SHARE.

issued share capital (subscribed share capital) The amount of the *authorized share capital of a company for which shareholders have subscribed. *See also* CALLED-UP SHARE CAPITAL; PAID-UP SHARE CAPITAL.

issue price (offering price) The price at which a new issue of shares is sold to the public. Once the issue has been made the securities will have a market price, which may be above (at a premium on) or below (at a discount on) the issue price (*see also* STAG). In an *introduction or *public issue, the issue price is fixed by the company on the advice of its stockbrokers and bankers; in an *issue by tender the issue price is fixed by the highest price that can be ob-tained for the whole issue; in a *placing the issue price is negotiated by the issuing house or broker involved. *See also* INITIAL PUBLIC OFFERING; OFFER FOR SALE.

issuing house A financial institution, usually a *merchant bank or *investment bank, that specializes in the *flotation of private companies on a *stock exchange. In some cases the issuing house will itself purchase the whole issue (*see* UNDER-WRITER), thus ensuring that there is no un-certainty in the amount of money the company will raise by flotation. It will then sell the shares to the public, usually by an *offer for sale, *introduction, *issue by tender, or *placing.

IT 1. Abbreviation for *income tax. **2.** Ab-breviation for *information technology.

iterative design The practice of mak-ing *continuous improvements in the de-sign of a product on the basis of testing, expert evaluation, and consumer feed-back. *See also* KAIZEN; KANSEI ENGINEERING.

ITU Abbreviation for *International Telecommunication Union.

Java A programming language standard supported by Sun Microsystems that enables complex and graphical customer applications to be written and then accessed from a *web browser. An example might be a form for calculating interest on a loan.

jerque note A certificate issued by a UK customs officer to the master of a ship, stating that he is satisfied that the cargo on his ship has been correctly entered on the *manifest and that no unentered cargo has been found after searching the ship.

jetsam Items of a ship's cargo that have been thrown overboard and sink below the surface of the water. *Compare* FLOTSAM.

jettisons Items of a ship's cargo that have been thrown overboard to lighten the ship in dangerous circumstances. If the items are insured they constitute a general average loss (*see* AVERAGE).

jiao A monetary unit of China, worth one tenth of a *yuan.

JICNAR Abbreviation for *Joint Industry Committee for National Readership.

JICRAR Abbreviation for *Joint Industry Committee for Radio Audience Research.

JIT Abbreviation for *just in time.

job An identifiable discrete piece of work carried out by an organization. For costing purposes a job is usually given a *job number.

job analysis A detailed study of a particular job, the tools and equipment needed to do it, and its relation to other jobs in an organization. The analysis should also provide the information needed to say how the job should best be done and the qualifications, experience, or aptitudes of the person best suited to doing it. Data is usually collected by questioning those already doing or supervising the job and is subjected to various forms of interpreta-

tion by a **job analyst**. Accurate job analysis is crucial to effective *job evaluation, *employee evaluation, and *personnel selection. *See also* JOB DESCRIPTION; JOB DIMENSIONS.

job and finish *See* CONTINGENT TIME OFF.

jobber **1.** *See* STOCKJOBBER. **2.** A dealer who buys and sells commodities, etc., for his or her own account.

jobbing A type of process in which small numbers of products are made to order. It involves high levels of skill and the movement of resources to the product. Examples of jobbing include prototype engineering, cabinet making, etc.

jobbing backwards Looking back on a transaction or event and thinking about how one might have acted differently, had one known then what one knows now.

job centre plus A UK government agency that seeks work for those out of a job, assists employers to find suitable employees, and offers occupational advice on retraining. It also administers claims for and payments of *social security benefits.

job characteristics theory A theory that describes how *job design can affect motivation, performance, and job satisfaction. A number of specific *core job characteristics are held to induce high levels of motivation and performance.

job-component method A method of *job evaluation in which jobs are ranked according to a statistical analysis of the behavioural demands they impose. The data is usually obtained from employees' answers to a standardized questionnaire. *Compare* CLASSIFICATION METHOD; FACTOR-COMPARISON METHOD; POINT METHOD; RANKING METHOD.

job costing (**job order costing; specific order costing**) A costing process to assess the individual costs of performing each *job. It is important in organizations in which the production of different products is carried out, and also in service organizations, in which the cost is required of each service provided.

job description An official document that states the purpose of a specific job, together with tasks or duties involved, performance objectives, and the reporting relationships. It also provides information on the remuneration and working hours. In large organizations, a job description is usually arrived at through a formal process of *job analysis; it can then be used to compile a *personnel specification defining the skills and other attributes necessary to successful performance of the job. *See also* JOB DIMENSIONS; PERSONNEL SELECTION.

job design The process of putting together the various elements of work that constitute an *operating system, to form jobs that individuals will perform (*see* WORK STUDY). The process involves a balance between the needs of the individual to be healthy, safe, and motivated and the needs of the organization to be economic, efficient, and effective. There is no single solution: each compromise will reflect the strategy and management philosophy favoured by a particular organization.

job dimensions The general scope of a particular job in terms of the tasks or duties that are typically required, e.g. secretarial duties or responsibility for financial decisions. Most *job descriptions now cite the key dimensions of a job rather than attempting a comprehensive list of all the tasks that may be involved. The notion of job dimensions is sometimes extended to include the key *competencies, including personality traits, that are held to be essential to performance of a job.

job enlargement An approach to *job design that seeks to enhance staff motivation by increasing either (a) the number and variety of related tasks given to an individual (**horizontal job enlargement**) or (b) the complexity of the tasks and the autonomy and responsibility of the worker performing them (**vertical job enlargement**).

job enrichment An approach to *job design that aims to increase motivation and job satisfaction by giving workers a greater level of autonomous decision making and personal control. For example, production-line workers might be given responsibility for preventive maintenance of their work station and for running their own *statistical process control.

job evaluation An assessment of the work involved in a particular job, the responsibilities borne by the person who does it, and the skills, experience, or qualifications required, all with a view to evaluating the appropriate remuneration for the job and the differentials between it and other work in the same organization. Job evaluation enables different jobs to be compared with agreed common standards. These standards may be specific to an organization or an industry or they may be universal. Several procedures for job evaluation are in common use; *see* BENCHMARK JOB; CLASSIFICATION METHOD; FACTOR-COMPARISON METHOD; JOB-COMPONENT METHOD; POINT METHOD; RANKING METHOD.

job interview *See* SELECTION INTERVIEW.

job number A number assigned to each job where *job costing is in operation; it enables the costs to be charged to this number so that all the individual costs for a job can be collected.

job rotation An approach to *job design that reduces boredom, and thus increases motivation, by rotating staff through a range of jobs. This process can also increase the flexibility of a system by introducing an element of multiskilling. The key is to make use of rotation with a minimum of disruption and learning-curve effects, and to retain the element of freshness.

job satisfaction The sense of fulfilment and pride felt by people who enjoy their work and do it well. This feeling is enhanced if the significance of the work done and its value are recognized by those in authority (*see* EMPOWERMENT; MOTIVATION; SELF-ACTUALIZATION).

The factors that determine job satisfaction are investigated by *industrial and organizational psychology because it is widely accepted that a satisfied workforce is more productive and compliant than a dissatisfied force. The general conclusion is that to motivate and reassure employees, managers should encourage the sense of community felt by everyone in a successful organization, in addition to broadening their jobs (see JOB ENLARGEMENT; JOB ENRICHMENT) and praising their work.

An absence of job satisfaction has been blamed for *absenteeism, *accident proneness, high *labour turnover rates, poor *industrial relations, and a demotivated workforce that produces shoddy work (see ALIENATION).

Organizational psychologists have shown that apart from the human needs fulfilled by working, satisfaction is also related to the expectations aroused by the job: both the needs and the expectations require fulfilment if the job is to provide satisfaction. See also HYGIENE FACTORS; MOTIVATORS.

job sharing Dividing the work of one full-time employee between two or more part-time employees.

job specification See PERSONNEL SPECIFICATION.

joint account A bank or building-society account held in the names or two or more people, often husband and wife. On the death of one party the balance in the account goes to the survivor(s), except in the case of partnerships, executors' accounts, or trustees' accounts. Normally, any of the holders of a joint account is entitled to operate it alone.

joint and several liability A liability that is entered into as a group, on the understanding that if any of the group fail in their undertaking the liability must be shared by the remainder. Thus if two people enter into a joint and several guarantee for a bank loan, if one becomes bankrupt the other is liable for repayment of the whole loan.

Joint Industry Committee for National Readership (JICNAR) A committee formed in 1968 to run readership surveys, although continuous research and surveys have been undertaken since 1956. The committee comprises members of the *Institute of Practitioners in Advertising, the *Incorporated Society of British Advertisers Ltd, and the Newspaper and Periodical Contributors Committee. Its research is based on a stratified random sample involving 28 000 adult interviews

in a continuous survey lasting 12 months. The research covers all major UK publications and is published twice yearly. It is heavily dependent on demographic data, but it also includes regional variations, television viewing, cinema attendance, commercial radio audiences, and special interests.

Joint Industry Committee for Radio Audience Research (JICRAR) A committee composed of representatives of the *Institute of Practitioners in Advertising, the *Incorporated Society of British Advertisers Ltd, and independent radio companies. The committee provides information on the listening habits of radio audiences. Its research is based on *quota sampling of listeners aged 15 or over living in private households within a radio station's designated area. Samples of 300–1200 people, determined according to the population size of the area, record details of their radio listening (BBC or commercial) in 15-minute periods in specially designed seven-day diaries. Other data about the respondents' media habits is also collected.

joint investment A security purchased by more than one person. The certificate will bear the names of all the parties, but only the first named will receive notices. To dispose of the holding all the parties must sign the *transfer deed.

joint-life and last-survivor annuities Annuities that involve two people (usually husband and wife). A joint-life annuity begins payment on a specified date and continues until both persons have died. A last-survivor annuity only begins payment on the death of one of the two people and pays until the death of the other. Compare SINGLE-LIFE PENSION.

jointness of supply The situation in which the cost of supplying a good to the first user is the same, or nearly the same, as supplying it to many users. This is true of most digital goods.

joint-stock bank A UK bank that is a *public limited company rather than a private bank (which is a partnership). During the 19th century many private banks failed; the joint-stock banks became stronger, however, largely as a result of amalgamations and careful investment. In the 20th century, they became known as the *commercial banks or High-Street banks.

joint-stock company A *company in which the members pool their stock and trade on the basis of their joint stock. This differs from the earliest type of company, the merchant corporations or regulated companies of the 14th century, in which members traded with their own stock, subject to the rules of the company. Joint-stock companies originated in the 17th century; they are now rare.

joint supply (complementary supply) The supply of two or more separate commodities that are produced by the same process; examples include milk and butter, wool and mutton, and petrol and heavy oil. If the demand for one increases, the supply of the other will also increase, but its price will fall unless its demand also increases.

joint tenants Two or more persons who jointly own an interest in land. When one dies, the other(s) takes his share by right of survivorship. No one tenant has rights to any particular part of the property and no tenant may exclude another.

joint venture A commercial undertaking entered into jointly by two or more entities. Joint ventures are generally governed by the Partnership Act (1890) but they differ from *partnerships in that they are limited by time or by activity. Separate books are not usually kept and the joint venturers will have a profit- or loss-sharing ratio for the purpose of the joint venture only. Joint venturers often carry on their principal businesses independently of, and at the same time as, the joint venture. Joint ventures have become increasingly common as companies cooperate with each other in international markets, in order to share costs, exploit new technologies, or gain access to new markets.

journal 1. A *book of prime entry in which transfers to be made from one *account to another are recorded. It is used for transfers not recorded in any other of the books of prime entry, such as the *sales day book or the *cash book. **2.** Any *day book.

judgement creditor A person in whose favour a court decides, ordering a **judge-**ment debtor** to pay the sum that he or she is owed. If the judgement debtor fails to pay, the judgement creditor must return to the court asking for the judgement to be enforced. *See also* GARNISHEE ORDER.

judgemental sampling A form of *non-probability sampling in which a researcher selects a *sample from a population on the basis of his or her judgement, rather than by using statistical sampling techniques. For example, in marketing research an interviewer might interview a woman with a child because the questions relate to children's clothing. Such an approach can be valuable in *qualitative marketing research.

junk bond A *bond that offers a high rate of interest because it carries a higher than usual probability of default. The issuing of junk bonds to finance the takeover of large companies in the USA is a practice that has developed rapidly over recent years and has spread elsewhere. *See* LEVERAGED BUY-OUT.

just in time (JIT) An approach to manufacturing that aims to reduce stocks of raw materials and finished goods, queues and bottlenecks, excess transport, and levels of scrap and defective units. Whereas traditional systems isolate operations from the environment, for example by uncoupling *inventory, JIT recognizes that without protection processes can go wrong but, if they do, the reasons should be found and the process put right. It seeks to improve all performance variables, such as cost, quality, speed, dependability, and flexibility. The key elements of JIT are:
- respect for the contribution that employees can make;
- encouragement of personal responsibility and process ownership from a multi-skilled workforce that is proactive in problem solving;
- a demand-pull system in which material only flows when needed;
- *kanban;
- standardized product design;
- accelerated learning-curve effects;
- preventive rather than reactive maintenance;
- level scheduling;
- reduction of set-up times;
- efficient plant layout, eliminating places in which inventory can get lost;

- JIT purchasing involving close liaison with suppliers;
- *total quality management committed to *continuous improvement.

JIT has been facilitated by the advent of cheap computing power and *computer-aided manufacturing systems. It is easier to install JIT techniques from the outset, rather than attempting to introduce them piecemeal when a process is running.

K *See* KILOBYTE.

kaizen The Japanese concept of *continuous improvement that underlies both *total quality management and *just-in-time techniques. Its prime consideration is to ensure that problems are continuously sought out and rectified and that opportunities for improvement, in any aspect of the system, are exploited. Rather than concealing problems, staff are encouraged to bring them to the surface and to suggest solutions; a degree of employee *empowerment is therefore required. The aim of this approach is to prevent the large-scale change that may be required if a system is allowed to stagnate and then has to be brought back into line.

kamikaze pricing The practice of offering loans and transactions at exceptionally low rates to capture a larger share of the corporate banking market. It is used pejoratively to describe the practice of some Japanese banks and stockbrokers, and is named after the Japanese suicide pilots of World War II.

kanban A Japanese method of controlling the movement of materials through a *just-in-time system. Literally meaning 'visual record', *kanban* cards provide authority for a work station to produce or to transfer materials.

kangaroos An informal name for Australian shares, especially in mining, land, and tobacco companies, on the London Stock Exchange.

***Kansei* engineering (affective engineering)** An approach to product design and development in which a company seeks out users' emotional and aesthetic reactions to the product and attempts to incorporate these into subsequent models. *Kansei* is a Japanese word meaning 'psychological feeling'. *See* ITERATIVE DESIGN.

Kassenobligation A German term for a medium-term financial obligation, most notably in the form of three- to five-year federal government securities.

keelage A fee paid by the owners of a ship for being permitted to dock in certain ports and harbours.

keepwell A guarantee by a *holding company that it will maintain financial backing for a subsidiary for a stated period. The usual purpose is to enhance the creditworthiness of the subsidiary.

Keidanren The Japanese name for the Federation of Economic Organizations, which is the most powerful of the Japanese business organizations. It functions as the headquarters of the business community; its members are the major trade associations and the prominent companies.

keiretsu In Japan, a group of companies that have interlocking *cross-holdings. These are usually minor shareholdings to cement relationships and typically involve at least one financial institution. The *keiretsu* is now the main form of business organization in Japan. *Compare* ZAIBATSU.

Keogh plan A US savings scheme to create a pension plan for self-employed people, in which tax is deferred until withdrawals are made. It can be held at the same time as a corporate pension or *individual retirement account. Keogh plans originated with the Self-Employment Individuals Retirement Act (1982).

kerb market Any informal financial market, such as one for dealing in securities not listed on a stock exchange. The term derives from the former practice of trading on the street after the formal close of business of the London Stock Exchange.

keyed advertisement An advertisement designed to enable the advertiser to know where a respondent saw it, for instance by including a code number of a particular department in the return address.

key performance indicators (KPIs)
Specific measures of the performance of
an individual, team, or department in
defined **key performance areas (KPAs)**. In
the case of an individual employee, these
will be based on that person's *job description and may be specified in his or
her contract of employment. *See* EMPLOYEE
EVALUATION; PERFORMANCE MEASUREMENT.

key-person assurance An assurance
policy on the life of a key employee of a
company, especially the life of a senior executive in a small company, whose death
would be a serious loss to the company. In
the event of the key person dying, the
benefit is paid to the company. In order
that there should be an *insurable interest, a loss of profit must be the direct result of the death of the key person.

khoum A monetary unit of Mauritania,
worth one fifth of an *ouguiya.

kickback A colloquial term for an illegal
payment made to secure favourable treatment in the award of a contract.

killer bee A banker who assists a business in resisting predatory *takeover bids
by making the target company appear a
less attractive proposition.

kilobyte A measure of computer memory capacity, often abbreviated to K. One
kilobyte is 1024 *bytes, or characters; a
64K memory therefore holds $64 \times 1024 =$
65 536 bytes or characters.

kina (k) The standard monetary unit of
Papua New Guinea, divided into 100 toea.

kip (KN) The standard monetary unit of
Laos, divided into 100 at.

kite An informal name for an *accommodation bill. **Kite-flying** or **kiting** is the
discounting of a kite (accommodation bill)
at a bank, knowing that the person on
whom it is drawn will dishonour it

Kitemark *See* BRITISH STANDARDS INSTI-
TUTION.

kiting **1.** *See* KITE. **2.** An informal US
name for the dishonest practice of improving the apparent cash position in a company's accounts by paying a large cheque
on the last day of the accounting period
from one of its current accounts into a second current account. Because the first ac-

count will not have been debited, but the
second account will have been credited,
the overall cash position is temporarily
overstated. **3.** The act of changing a
cheque illegally by altering the amount to
be drawn. **4.** The practice of artificially
driving up the market price of a share.

knock-for-knock agreement An
agreement between motor insurers that
they will pay for their own policyholders'
accident damage without seeking any contribution from the other insurers, irrespective of blame but provided that the
relevant policies cover the risk involved.
The agreement works on the principle
that, having paid for their own policyholder's damage, insurer A refrains from
claiming the payment back from insurer
B, even though it may be clear that A's
client was to blame for the accident. On
another occasion the roles might be reversed; insurer B then refrains from claiming from A even though A's client was
responsible.
   Before the knock-for-knock agreement,
insurers found they were exchanging
roughly similar amounts in payment of
these claims. The agreement has cut down
the expensive administration of claim and
counterclaim, which has helped to reduce
the cost of premiums.

knocking copy Advertising copy that attacks a rival product.

knowledge management The creation and sharing of knowledge in an organization. Knowledge management is a
relatively new concept and there are
many different definitions. Successful
knowledge management initiatives will
typically lead to improved employee involvement, improved individual and organizational creativity, and enhanced
intrapreneurship and innovation.

knowledge worker An individual who
is employed to analyse and communicate
ideas and information.

kobo A monetary unit of Nigeria, worth
one hundredth of a *naira.

Kondratieff cycle A hypothesis, first
suggested by the economist Nikolai Kondratieff, that the international economy is
characterized by 50-year price cycles. The
term has also been used more generally to

support the notion that there are 50-year cycles in economic activity. *See* BUSINESS CYCLE.

kopeck A monetary unit of Russia and Belarus, worth one hundredth of a *rouble.

kopiyka A monetary unit of Ukraine, worth one hundredth of a *hryvna.

koruna (Kčs) The standard monetary unit of the Czech Republic and Slovakia, divided into 100 haleru.

KPAs Abbreviation for key performance areas. *See* KEY PERFORMANCE INDICATORS.

KPIs Abbreviation for *key performance indicators.

krona (Skr) The standard monetary unit of Sweden, divided into 100 öre.

króna (*plural* **krónor**; ISk) The standard monetary unit of Iceland, divided into 100 aurar.

krone (*plural* **kroner**) The standard monetary unit of Denmark (Dkr), the Faeroe Islands (Fkr), Greenland (Dkr), and Norway (Nkr), divided into 100 øre.

kroon (*plural* **krooni**; EEK) The standard monetary unit of Estonia, divided into 100 sents.

Krugerrand A South African coin containing 1 troy ounce of gold, minted since 1967 for investment purposes.

KSAOs Abbreviation for knowledge, skills, abilities, and other characteristics: attributes of an employee or job applicant that are assessed for such purposes as *personnel selection, *performance appraisal, and career development. In larger organizations, the KSAOs required for a particular job will be identified by a formal process of *job analysis and itemized in a *personnel specification.

kuna (*plural* **kune**) The standard monetary unit of Croatia, divided into 100 lipas.

kuru (*plural* **kuruş**) A monetary unit of Turkey, worth one hundredth of a *lira.

kwacha 1. (Mk) The standard monetary unit of Malawi, divided into 100 tambala. **2.** (k) The standard monetary unit of Zambia, divided into 100 ngwee.

kwanza (Nkz) The standard monetary unit of Angola, divided into 100 lwei.

kyat (k) The standard monetary unit of Myanmar (Burma), divided into 100 pyas.

laari A monetary unit of the Maldives, worth one hundredth of a *rufiyaa.

labor union US name for a *trade union.

labour costs (wages costs) Expenditure on wages paid to those operators who are both directly and indirectly concerned with the production of the product, service, or *cost unit. *See also* DIRECT LABOUR COST; INDIRECT COSTS.

labour-intensive Denoting an industry, company, production process, or project in which the remuneration paid to employees represents a high proportion of the total costs. *Compare* CAPITAL-INTENSIVE.

labour turnover rate The ratio, usually expressed as a percentage, of the number of employees leaving an organization or industry in a stated period to the average number of employees working in that organization or industry during the period. An important distinction is made between **uncontrollable turnover**, as by death, superannuation, or unavoidable redundancy, and **controllable turnover**. A high rate of controllable voluntary turnover (i.e. by resignation) can be a sign of low *job satisfaction in an organization; a high rate of controllable involuntary turnover (e.g. by dismissal for misconduct or poor performance or by retirement owing to work-related illness) is usually a sign that the organization has graver problems.

laches (Norman French *lasches*: negligence) Neglect and unreasonable delay in enforcing an equitable right. If a plaintiff with full knowledge of the facts takes an unnecessarily long time to bring an action (e.g. to set aside a contract obtained by fraud) the court will be of no assistance; hence the maxim "the law will not help those who sleep on their rights". No set period is given but if the action is covered by limitation-of-actions legislation, the period given will not be shortened. Other-

wise the time allowed depends on the circumstances.

laddered portfolio A *portfolio holding a range of fixed-interest bonds or other securities with fixed values in different maturities. *See also* BARBELL.

Lady Macbeth strategy A strategy used in takeover battles in which a third party makes a bid that the target company would favour, i.e. it appears to act as a *white knight, but subsequently changes allegiance and joins the original bidder.

laesio enormis (Latin: extraordinary injury) A doctrine of Roman law that is included in some European legal systems but not in English law. It states that the price given in a contract by way of *consideration must be fair and reasonable or the contract may be rescinded.

laggards *See* ADOPTION OF INNOVATIONS.

lagging measures *See* BALANCED SCORECARD.

LAIA Abbreviation for *Latin American Integration Association.

laissez-faire economy An economy in which government intervention is kept to a minimum and *market forces are allowed to rule. The term, attributed to the French merchant J. Gourlay (1712–59), is best translated as 'let people do as they think best'. *See* FREE COMPETITION.

laissez-faire leader A leader who effectively abdicates from the leadership role by allowing members of the group freedom of action and providing little guidance or structure. Experimental studies of *leadership style have found that work groups with laissez-faire leaders tend to be more apathetic and less productive than those with *authoritarian leaders or *democratic leaders.

lakh In India, Pakistan, and Bangladesh 100 000. It often refers to this number of rupees. *See also* CRORE.

lame duck A company that has national prestige and is a large employer of labour (especially in an area of high unemployment) or is a leader in a particular technology but, being unable to meet foreign competition, is unable to survive without government support.

LAN Abbreviation for *local area network.

land In law, the part of the earth's surface that can be owned, including all buildings, trees, minerals, etc., attached to or forming part of it. It also includes the airspace above the land necessary for its reasonable enjoyment. In law, a first-floor flat can constitute a separate piece of land, although it has no contact with the soil, just as a cellar may be a separate *estate in land.

land bank The amount of land a developer owns that is awaiting development.

land certificate A document that takes the place of a *title deed for registered land. It is granted to the registered proprietor of the land and indicates ownership. It will usually be kept in the *Land Registry if the land is subject to a mortgage.

land charges Incumbrances, such as contracts, payments, or other matters, to which *land is subject; they must either be dealt with before the land is sold or they will bind the purchaser. Formerly, they bound a purchaser who had notice of them. Now most of them must be registered if they are to remain effective, either under the Land Charges Act (1972; applicable to unregistered land) or under the Land Registration Act (1925; applicable to registered land).

Land Charges Register 1. The register of *land charges on unregistered land, kept at the *Land Registry. Charges are registered against the name of the estate owner. The kinds of charges that must be registered are set out in the Land Charges Act (1972) and include estate contracts, equitable easements, restrictive covenants, and Inland Revenue charges. Registration constitutes actual notice to any person of the existence of the charge. If the purchaser of the land is unable to discover the charge (for example, because it is registered against the name of an estate owner that does not appear on the title deeds available to the purchaser), compensation may be payable to the purchaser at public expense. If a charge is not registered it will not bind a purchaser for money or money's worth of a legal estate in the land, even if he had notice of the charge. Some charges, if not registered, will not bind the purchaser for value of any interest (whether legal or equitable) in the land. **2. (Local Land Charges Register)** A register kept by each London borough, the City of London, and each district council. Public authorities may register statutory restrictions on land, e.g. under town and country planning legislation. These are registered against the land itself, not the estate owner. If restrictions are not registered, the purchaser is still bound by them, but will be entitled to compensation.

landed Denoting an export price in which the exporter pays all the charges to the port of destination and also pays the *landing charges but not any dock dues or onward carriage charges to the importer's factory or warehouse. *Compare* c.i.f.; franco.

landfill tax A tax charge, introduced in the Finance Act (1996), on the commercial disposal of waste by way of landfill.

landing account An account prepared by a public warehousing company to the owner of goods that have recently been landed from a ship and taken into the warehouse. The account, which is usually accompanied by a *weight note, states the date on which the warehouse rent begins and also the quantity of goods and their condition (from the external appearance of the packages).

landing charges The charges incurred in disembarking a cargo, or part of it, from a ship at the port of destination.

landing order A document given to an importer by the UK Customs and Excise, enabling him to remove newly imported goods from a ship or quay to a *bonded warehouse, pending payment of duty or their re-export.

landlord and tenant The parties to a *lease. The landlord grants the lease to the tenant. The landlord may be the freehold owner of the land or may be a tenant of a superior landlord (*see* HEAD LEASE). The law of landlord and tenant is that governing the creation, termination, and regulation of leases. Many leases, both business and residential, are subject to statutory control. This means that the right of the landlord to end a lease and evict tenants may be restricted and the rent may be controlled. It is therefore essential to consider statutory rights when considering the relation between landlord and tenant, as well as those given by the lease.

land registration The system of registration of title introduced by the Land Registration Act (1925) and overhauled by the Land Registration Act (2002). Land is registered by reference to a map rather than against the name of any estate owner. Three registers are kept:
- the **property register**, which records the land and estate; it refers to a map and mentions any interests benefiting the land, e.g. *easements and restrictive *covenants;
- the **proprietorship register**, which sets out the name of the owner, the nature of the title (e.g. freehold or leasehold), and any restrictions on the way the land may be dealt with (e.g. if the land is subject to a trust);
- the **charges register**, which contains notice of rights adverse to the land, such as mortgages and *land charges as defined in the Land Charges Act (1972).

The owner's title is guaranteed by registration in most circumstances. Rights in registered land may be a registered interest, which amounts to ownership of the freehold or leasehold estate; an overriding interest, which binds a purchaser without needing to be registered; or a minor interest, which needs to be protected by an entry on the register (e.g. interest under a trust or restrictive covenant). The purpose of the system is to simplify conveyancing, so that instead of checking title deeds, a search of the register will reveal all relevant matters. Eventually, all land in England and Wales will be registered, enabling unregistered conveyancing to disappear; this process is now over 90% complete. *See also* ELECTRONIC CONVEYANCING; RECTIFICATION OF REGISTER; REGISTERED LAND CERTIFICATE.

Land Registry The official body that keeps the various land registers (*see* LAND REGISTRATION) and is responsible for implementing the policy of registering title to all land in England and Wales. The main registry is in Lincoln's Inn Fields in London, but there are also regional registries and information is now held electronically. Title information and a location plan for any registered land can be downloaded by the general public for a small fee (www.landreg.gov.uk). *See also* RECTIFICATION OF REGISTER.

land waiter A UK customs officer who examines goods at the ports for export or import and ensures that the correct taxes or duties are levied.

language laboratory A room used, especially by business people, to study a foreign language. The object is to acquire a proficiency in the spoken language as quickly as possible and to this end extensive use is made of recording equipment and prerecorded tapes or CDs. A supervisor can plug into recordings made by students, to monitor their progress and correct errors, especially of pronunciation.

Lanham Trademark Act (1947) A US law prohibiting brand names and trademarks from being confusingly similar to registered trademarks.

lapping In the USA, the fraudulent practice of concealing a shortage of cash by delaying the recording of cash receipts. In the UK it is referred to as **teeming and lading**. There are a number of variations, but essentially the cashier conceals the theft of cash received from the first customer by recording the cash received from the second customer as attributable to the first, and so on with subsequent customers. The cashier hopes to be in a position to replace the cash before the dishonesty is discovered. As such hopes are frequently based on attempts at gambling, the deception is often discovered.

laptop computer A small portable personal computer that can be operated from its own batteries, has a flat display screen that folds over the keyboard when not in use, and is generally suitable for use while travelling. Laptops usually have all the features of an equivalent desktop model but tend to be more expensive. Small versions of laptops are sometimes called **notebook computers**. *See also* PALMTOP COMPUTER; PDA.

lari The standard monetary unit of Georgia, divided into 100 tetri.

laser printer A type of high-speed printer used with computers. The characters to be printed are formed by a low-power laser, which alters the electrical charge on appropriate areas of the surface of a photoconductive rotating drum, as in *xerography. The drum is selectively coated with a toner powder, which is attracted by the charge produced by the laser but repelled by that on the rest of the drum. The powder is transferred to paper and fused into place by heated rollers. Laser printers are very fast and silent, producing high-quality lettering and graphics. They are often used with *desktop publishing equipment to produce reports, catalogues, and newsletters.

LASH Acronym for lighter *aboard ship*. This is a method of cargo handling in which cargo-carrying barges (lighters) are lifted on and off ocean-going ships by the ship's own crane, thus reducing to a minimum the need for port facilities.

Laspeyres' index *See* INDEX NUMBER.

last-in-first-out cost (LIFO cost) A method of valuing units of raw material or finished goods issued from stock by using the latest unit value for pricing the issues until all the quantity of stock received at that price is used up. The next earliest price is then used for pricing the issues, and so on. Because the issues are based on a LIFO cost, the valuation of closing stocks is described as being on the same LIFO basis. The method may also be used in *process costing to value the work in process at the end of an accounting period. This method of costing is not normally acceptable for stock valuation in the UK. *Compare* FIRST-IN-FIRST-OUT COST; NEXT-IN-FIRST-OUT COST.

last-survivor policy **1.** An *assurance policy on the lives of two people, the sum assured being paid on the death of the last to die. *See also* JOINT-LIFE AND LAST-SURVIVOR ANNUITIES. **2.** A contract (formerly called a **tontine**) in which assurance is arranged by a group of people, who all

pay premiums into a fund while they are alive. No payment is made until only one person from the group is left alive. At that point the survivor receives all the policy proceeds. Contracts of this kind are not available in the UK because of the temptation they provide to members to murder their fellows, in order to be the last survivor.

last trading day The last day on which commodity trading for a particular delivery period can be transacted.

late majority *See* ADOPTION OF INNOVATIONS.

lateral integration *See* INTEGRATION.

Latin American Integration Association (LAIA; ALADI) An economic grouping of South American countries with headquarters in Montevideo. It superseded the **Latin American Free Trade Area (LAFTA)** in 1981. Its members are Argentina, Bolivia, Brazil, Chile, Colombia, Cuba, Ecuador, Mexico, Paraguay, Peru, Uruguay, and Venezuela. *See also* MERCOSUR.

lats (*plural* **lati**) The standard monetary unit of Latvia, divided into 100 santimes.

laundering money Processing money acquired illegally (as by theft, drug dealing, etc.) so that it appears to have come from a legitimate source. This may be achieved by paying the illegal cash into a foreign bank and transferring its equivalent to a bank with a good name in a hard-currency area. There are now stringent controls on this activity.

LAUTRO Abbreviation for Life Assurance and Unit Trust Regulatory Organization. *See* PERSONAL INVESTMENT AUTHORITY.

lay days The number of days allowed to a ship to load or unload without incurring *demurrage. **Reversible lay days** permit the shipper to add to the days allowed for unloading any days he has saved while loading. Lay days may be calculated as *running days (all consecutive days), *working days (excluding Sundays and public holidays), or *weather working days (working days on which the weather allows work to be carried out).

laying off Suspending or terminating the employment of workers because there is no work for them to do. If the laying off involves a permanent termination of employment, *redundancy payments will be involved.

lay-off pay US for *redundancy payment.

LBO Abbreviation for *leveraged buy-out.

LCH Abbreviation for *London Clearing House.

LCM Abbreviation for *lower of cost or market.

lead The first named underwriting syndicate on a Lloyd's insurance policy. When a broker seeks to cover a risk he will first try to get a large syndicate to act as lead, which encourages smaller syndicates to cover a share of the risk. The premium rate is calculated by the lead; if others wish to join in the risk they have to insure at that rate. On a collective policy the lead insurer is the first insurer on the schedule of insurers; he issues the policy, collects the premiums, and distributes the proportions to the coinsurers.

lead bank See LEAD MANAGER.

leadership continuum theory See TANNENBAUM–SCHMIDT CONTINUUM.

leadership style The traits, behavioural tendencies, and characteristic methods of a person in a leadership position. An important dimension of leadership style is the extent to which the leader is willing to delegate responsibility and encourage input from followers; some key styles here are those of the *authoritarian leader, *democratic leader, and *laissez-faire leader. Another basic dimension is the extent to which a leader is *task-motivated (concerned with defining goals and the means to achieve them) or *relationship-motivated (concerned with supporting and encouraging subordinates). A distinction can also be drawn between the *charismatic leader, who relies on his or her personal qualities to inspire followers, and the *bureaucratic leader, who depends on his or her position in the hierarchy and an established set of rules and procedures. See TRANSACTIONAL LEADERSHIP; TRANSFORMATIONAL LEADERSHIP. See also POWER STYLES.

leadership theories In *industrial and organizational psychology, various theories that have been put forward to explain the successful or unsuccessful performance of leaders. Such theories tend to fall into three main categories:

- **Trait theories of leadership** focus on the role played by certain key personality traits in the leader. These usually include decisiveness, organizational ability, confidence, and communication skills.
- **Behavioural theories of leadership** focus on issues of *leadership style, notably the extent to which the leader can be described as *task-motivated or *relationship-motivated. *Contingency theories of leadership attempt to define the different leadership behaviours demanded by different situations.
- **Cognitive theories of leadership** focus on the ways in which followers' ideas and perceptions can affect the performance of their leaders.

See also PATH-GOAL LEADERSHIP MODEL; SITUATIONAL LEADERSHIP THEORY; TANNENBAUM– SCHMIDT CONTINUUM; VROOM–YETTON– JAGO MODEL.

leading and lagging **1.** Techniques often used at the end of a financial year to enhance a cash position and reduce borrowing. This is achieved by arranging for the settlement of outstanding obligations to be accelerated (leading) or delayed (lagging). **2.** The use of similar techniques to benefit from the expected change in a currency value.

leading indicators Key variables in a *time-series analysis that change in the same direction but in advance of company sales.

leading measures See BALANCED SCORECARD.

lead manager (lead bank) A bank or other financial institution chosen to underwrite a new issue of bonds or to head a *syndicated bank facility. It is usually chosen either because it has a close relationship with the borrower or because it has been successful in a competitive *bought deal contest. The lead manager is the main organizer of the transactions and takes a larger fee than the other institutions involved.

lead users The first users of a new product or service, who are asked to assess its advantages and disadvantages in relation to those of its competitors. They are often company employees, loyal customers, or people who have the relevant expertise.

leakage **1.** The loss of a liquid from a faulty container. **2.** An allowance for loss of a liquid in transit, due to evaporation or other causes.

lean back A period of cautious inaction by a government agency before intervening in a market. For example, a central bank might allow a lean-back period to elapse to allow exchange rates to stabilize, before intervening in the foreign exchange market.

learning and growth perspective *See* BALANCED SCORECARD.

learning curve A technique that takes into account the reduction in time taken to carry out production as the cumulative output rises. The concept is based on a doubling of output, so that a 70% learning curve means that the cumulative average time taken per unit falls to 70% of the previous cumulative average time as the output doubles. The cumulative average time per unit is measured from the very first unit produced. The formula for the learning curve is:

$$y = ax^{-b},$$

where y is the cumulative average time per unit of production, a is the time taken to produce the first unit, x is the cumulative number of units manufactured to date, and b is the learning coefficient.

lease A contract between the owner of a specific asset, the **lessor**, and another party, the **lessee**, allowing the latter to hire the asset. The lessor retains the right of ownership but the lessee acquires the right to use the asset for a specific period of time in return for the payment of specific rentals or payments. *Statement of Standard Accounting Practice 21, Accounting for Leases and Hire Purchase Contracts, classifies leases into *operating leases and *finance leases with differing accounting treatments.

leaseback (renting back) An arrangement in which the owner of an *asset (such as land or buildings) sells it to another party but immediately enters into a *lease agreement with the purchaser to obtain the right to use the asset. Such a

transaction is a method for raising funds and can affect the *financial statements of a company, depending on whether a *finance lease or an *operating lease is entered into.

leased department retailer An independent retailer who owns the merchandise stocked and displayed but who leases floor space from another (usually larger) retailer, often using their own retailing name. This arrangement is sometimes called a shop within a shop.

leasehold land Land held under a *lease. The land will eventually revert to the freehold owner, although there has been some statutory modification of this right to repossession (e.g. in the Rent Acts). This is the most common way for blocks of offices to be owned. The landlord maintains possession of the common parts and creates separate leases for each office. The ownership of each office may subsequently change as leases are assigned.

lease-purchase agreement A lease in which the payments go towards the purchase of the asset. *See also* HIRE PURCHASE.

leasing Hiring equipment, such as a car or a piece of machinery, to avoid the capital cost involved in owning it. In some companies it is advantageous to use capital for other purposes and to lease some equipment, paying for the hire out of income. The equipment is then an asset of the leasing company rather than the lessor. Sometimes a case can be made for leasing rather than purchasing, on the grounds that some equipment quickly becomes obsolete.

Least Preferred Co-worker Scale (LPC Scale) A measure used to identify the extent to which a leader is predominantly *task-motivated or *relationship-motivated. The participant is asked to think of the co-worker with whom he or she has had the most problems in the past and to rate this person on a series of dimensions, such as intelligent–unintelligent, honest–dishonest, and so on. A total score is then derived from these ratings. Leaders who score their least preferred co-worker relatively highly are assumed to be *relationship-motivated; those who are more critical are assumed to be *task-motivated. *See also* CONTINGENCY THEORIES OF LEADERSHIP; LEADERSHIP STYLE.

ledger A collection of *accounts of a similar type. Traditionally, a ledger was a large book with separate pages for each account; in modern systems they will usually consist of computer records. The most common ledgers are the *nominal ledger containing the *impersonal accounts, the *sales ledger containing the accounts of an organization's customers, and the *purchase ledger containing the accounts of an organization's suppliers.

leg One element in a complex set of financial transactions. *See* BREAKING A LEG; STRADDLE.

legal capital In the USA, the amount of stockholders' equity, which cannot be reduced by the payment of dividends. This is the value of a company's shares in the balance sheet.

legal person *See* ARTIFICIAL PERSON.

legal reserve The minimum amount of money that building societies, insurance companies, etc., are bound by law to hold as security for the benefit of their customers.

legal tender Money that must be accepted in discharge of a debt. It may be **limited legal tender**, i.e. it must be accepted but only up to specified limits of payment; or **unlimited legal tender**, i.e. acceptable in settlement of debts of any amount. Bank of England notes and the £2 and £1 coins are unlimited legal tender in the UK. Other Royal Mint coins are limited legal tender; i.e. debts up to £10 can be paid in 50p and 20p coins; up to £5 by 10p and 5p coins; and up to 20p by bronze coins.

lek (Lk) The standard monetary unit of Albania, divided into 100 qindars.

lempira (L) The standard monetary unit of Honduras, divided into 100 centavos.

lender of last resort A country's *central bank with responsibility for controlling its banking system. In the UK, the Bank of England fulfils this role, lending to *discount houses, either by repurchasing *Treasury bills, lending on other paper assets, or granting direct loans, charging the *base rate of interest. *Commercial

banks do not go directly to the Bank of England; they borrow from the discount houses.

lending multiple 1. The ratio of a bank's deposits to its highly liquid assets. **2.** In the UK housing market, a multiple of the borrower's income used to calculate the maximum amount that will be lent on a mortgage.

leone (Le) The standard monetary unit of Sierra Leone, divided into 100 cents.

lepton (*plural* **lepta**) A former monetary unit of Greece, worth one hundredth of a *drachma (until 2002).

lessee The party to a *lease contract who uses the asset and makes the lease payments.

lessor The party to a *lease contract who provides the asset and receives the lease payments.

letter of allotment *See* ALLOTMENT.

letter of comfort 1. A letter to a bank from the parent company of a subsidiary that is trying to borrow money from the bank. The letter gives no guarantee for the repayment of the projected loan but offers the bank the comfort of knowing that the subsidiary has made the parent company aware of its intention to borrow; the parent also usually supports the application, giving, at least, an assurance that it intends that the subsidiary should remain in business and that it will give notice of any relevant change of ownership. **2.** A letter by one party to a bank indicating a relationship that will make a second party more likely to repay a bank loan.

letter of credit (documentary credit) A letter from one banker to another authorizing the payment of a specified sum to the person named in the letter on certain specified conditions (*see* LETTER OF INDICATION). Commercially, letters of credit are widely used in the international import and export trade as a means of payment. In an export contract, the exporter may require the foreign importer to open a letter of credit at the importer's local bank (the issuing bank) for the amount of the goods. This will state that it is to be negotiable at a bank (the negotiating bank) in the exporter's country in favour of the exporter; often, the exporter (who is called the beneficiary of the credit) will give the name of the negotiating bank. On presentation of the shipping documents (which are listed in the letter of credit) the beneficiary will receive payment from the negotiating bank.

An **irrevocable letter of credit** cannot be cancelled by the person who opens it or by the issuing bank without the beneficiary's consent, whereas a **revocable letter of credit** can. In a **confirmed letter of credit** the negotiating bank guarantees to pay the beneficiary, even if the issuing bank fails to honour its commitments (in an **unconfirmed letter of credit** this guarantee is not given). A confirmed irrevocable letter of credit therefore provides the most reliable means of being paid for exported goods. However, all letters of credit have an expiry date, after which they can only be negotiated by the consent of all the parties.

A **circular letter of credit** is an instruction from a bank to its correspondent banks to pay the beneficiary a stated sum on presentation of a means of identification. It has now been replaced by *traveller's cheques.

Although the term 'letter of credit' is still widely used, in 1983 the International Chamber of Commerce recommended **documentary credit** as the preferred term for these instruments.

letter of hypothecation *See* HYPOTHE-CATION.

letter of indemnity 1. A letter stating that the organization issuing it will compensate the person to whom it is addressed for a specified loss. *See also* INDEMNITY. **2.** A letter written to a company registrar asking for a replacement for a lost share certificate and indemnifying the company against any loss that it might incur in so doing. It may be required to be countersigned by a bank. **3.** A letter written by an exporter accepting responsibility for any losses arising from faulty packing, short weight, etc., at the time of shipment. If this letter accompanies the *shipping documents, the shipping company will issue a clean *bill of lading, even if the packages are damaged, enabling the exporter to negotiate the

documents and receive payment without trouble.

letter of indication (letter of identification) A letter issued by a bank to a customer to whom a *letter of credit has been supplied. The letter has to be produced with the letter of credit at the negotiating bank; it provides evidence of the bearer's identity and a specimen of his or her signature. It is used particularly with a circular letter of credit carried by travellers, although *traveller's cheques are now more widely used.

letter of intent A letter in which a person formally sets out his or her intentions to do something, such as signing a contract in certain circumstances, which are often specified in detail in the letter. The letter does not constitute either a contract or a promise to do anything, but it does indicate the writer's serious wish to pursue the course set out.

letter of licence A letter from a creditor to a debtor, who is having trouble raising the money to settle the debt. The letter states that the creditor will allow the debtor a stated time to pay and will not initiate proceedings against the debtor before that time. *See also* ARRANGEMENT.

letter of regret A letter from a company, or its bankers, stating that an application for an allotment from a *new issue of shares has been unsuccessful.

letter of renunciation 1. A form, often attached to an *allotment letter, on which a person who has been allotted shares in a *new issue renounces any rights to them, either absolutely or in favour of someone else (during the **renunciation period**). **2.** A form on the reverse of some *unit-trust certificates, which the holder completes to dispose of the holding. The holder sends the completed certificate to the trust managers.

letter of set-off *See* SET-OFF.

letters of administration An order authorizing the person named (the *administrator) to distribute the property of a deceased person, who has not appointed anyone else to do so. The distribution must be in accordance with the deceased's will, or the rules of intestacy if he or she died *intestate.

leu (*plural* **lei**) The standard monetary unit of Romania (ROL) and Moldova (MLD), divided into 100 bani.

lev (BGL; *plural* **leva**) The standard monetary unit of Bulgaria, divided into 100 stotinki.

level output strategy An approach to *aggregate planning that aims to regulate production at a constant level, regardless of fluctuation in demand. It involves storing the product in times of low demand and is not therefore an option available to the providers of services. The benefits include maintaining a stable workforce and the optimum use of capacity. The disadvantages include the costs of storage and the difficulty of responding to major changes in demand. *Compare* CHASE DEMAND STRATEGY.

level scheduling *See* UNIFORM LOAD SCHEDULING.

leverage 1. A US word, now increasingly used in the UK, for *gearing. **2.** The use by a company of its limited assets to guarantee substantial loans to finance its business.

leveraged buy-out (LBO) The acquisition of one company by another through the use of borrowed funds. The intention is that the loans will be repaid from the cash flow of the acquired company. In the 1980s many takeovers in the USA were financed by the issue of *junk bonds in highly leveraged buyouts. *See also* BOOTSTRAP.

leveraged lease A *lease in which the lessor borrows as part of the finance of the asset to be leased.

leverage ratios *See* GEARING RATIOS.

liability 1. The funding of a business debt. *See* CURRENT LIABILITIES; DEFERRED CREDIT; LONG TERM LIABILITY; SECURED LIABILITY. **2.** An obligation to make a financial payment. *See* CONTINGENT LIABILITY. **3.** The acceptance of an insurance risk.

liability insurance A form of insurance policy that promises to pay any compensation and court costs the policyholder becomes legally liable to pay because of claims for injury to other people or damage to their property as a result of the policyholder's negligence. Policies often define the areas in which they will deal with liability, e.g. personal liability or employers' liability (*see* EMPLOYERS' LIABILITY INSURANCE).

LIBID Abbreviation for *London Inter Bank Bid Rate.

LIBOR Abbreviation for *London Inter Bank Offered Rate.

licence 1. Official permission to do something that is forbidden without a licence (e.g. sell alcohol or own a TV or a firearm). Licences may be required for social reasons or simply to enable revenue to be collected. Since the Consumer Credit Act (1974) all businesses involved with giving credit to purchasers of goods must be licensed by the Office of Fair Trading. **2.** *See* FRANCHISE. **3.** Formal permission to enter or occupy land. Such licenses are of three kinds. (a) The simplest gives the licensee the permission of the landowner to be on land (e.g. the right of a visitor to enter a house). It may be revoked at any time as long as the licensee is given time to leave. (b) **Contractual licences** are permissions to be on land in the furtherance of some contractual right (e.g. the right of the holder of a cinema ticket to be in the cinema). This type of licence has been used to get round the Rent Acts (which apply to leases only): a licence to occupy a flat or house may be granted, which is said to be revocable at any time. It has been held that if the licence gives the licensee exclusive possession of the property, it is in fact a lease, despite the fact that it is called a licence. The exact state of the law in this area is uncertain. It is also unclear whether a contractual licence can be made irrevocable and binding on those who were not a party to the contract (e.g. purchasers of the land). It was originally held that a licence could always be revoked, although damages might be payable. Recent cases have cast doubt on this proposition. (c) Licences coupled with an interest are those that go with a recognizable interest in the land of another. Such licences are irrevocable and assignable. They bind successors in title in the same way as the interest in land to which they relate. **4.** A *carrier's licence.

licensed brand A product or service using a registered brand name offered by the brand owner to a licensee for an agreed fee or royalty.

licensed dealer A dealer licensed under the *Financial Services Act (1986) to provide investment advice and deal in securities, either as an agent or principal. Licensed dealers are not members of the *London Stock Exchange and are not covered by its compensation fund.

licensed deposit taker A former category of financial institutions as defined by the Banking Act (1979), which distinguished between recognized banks, licensed deposit takers, and exempt institutions. To qualify for authorization, the licensed deposit taker had to satisfy the Bank of England that it conducted its business in a prudent manner. The Banking Act (1987), however, established a single category of *deposit-taking institutions eligible to carry out banking business.

licensing In international marketing, an agreement by which a company (the licensor) permits a foreign company (the licensee) to set up a business in the foreign market using the licensor's manufacturing processes, patents, trademarks, trade secrets, etc., in exchange for payment of a fee or royalty.

lien The right of one person to retain possession of goods owned by another until the possessor's claims against the owner have been satisfied. In a **general lien**, the goods are held as security for all the outstanding debts of the owner, whereas in a **particular lien** only the claims of the possessor in respect of the goods held must be satisfied. Thus an unpaid seller may in some contracts be entitled to retain the goods until receiving the price, a carrier may have a lien over goods being transported, and a repairer over goods being repaired. Whether a lien arises or not depends on the terms of the contract and usual trade practice. This type of lien is a **possessory lien**, but sometimes actual possession of the goods is not necessary. In an **equitable lien**, for example, the claim exists independently of possession. If a purchaser of the property involved is given notice of the lien it binds him; otherwise he will not be bound. Similarly a **maritime lien**, which binds a ship or cargo in connection with some maritime

liability, does not depend on possession and can be enforced by arrest and sale (unless security is given). Examples of maritime liens are the lien of a salvor, those of seamen for their wages and of masters for their wages and outgoings, that of a bottomry or respondentia bondholder (*see* HYPOTHECATION), and that over a ship at fault in a collision in which property has been damaged.

life annuity An *annuity that ceases to be paid on the death of a specified person, which may or may not be the *annuitant.

life assurance An *insurance policy that pays a specified amount of money on the death of the *life assured or, in the case of an *endowment assurance policy, on the death of the life assured or at the end of an agreed period, whichever is the earlier. Life assurance grew from a humble means of providing funeral expenses to a means of saving for oneself or one's dependants, with certain tax advantages. *With-profits policies provide sums of money in excess of the sum assured by the addition of *bonuses. *Unit-linked policies invest the premiums in funds of assets, by means of buying units in the funds. *See also* WHOLE LIFE POLICY.

Life Assurance and Unit Trust Regulatory Organization (LAUTRO) *See* PERSONAL INVESTMENT AUTHORITY.

life assured The person upon whose death a life-assurance policy makes an agreed payment. The life assured need not be the owner of the policy.

lifeboat 1. A fund set up to rescue dealers on an exchange in the event of a market collapse and the ensuing insolvencies. **2.** The rescue of a company that is in financial difficulty by new or restructured loans from its group of bankers.

life-cycle costing An approach to determining the total costs of a *fixed asset that takes into account all the costs likely to be incurred both in acquiring it and in operating it over its effective life. For example, the initial cost to an airline of an aircraft is only part of the costs relevant to the decision to purchase it. The operating costs over its effective life are also relevant and would therefore be part of the decision-making data. This is an aspect of *terotechnology.

life-cycle segmentation An approach to marketing that recognizes that consumers' needs change at different stages of their lives.

life office A company that provides *life assurance.

lifestyle The activities, interests, opinions, and values of individuals as they affect their mode of living. Lifestyle reflects more than social class or personality; it provides a profile of a person's whole pattern of behaviour and interaction with the world. Lifestyles are important in marketing because they influence the way in which people elect to make purchases. The technique for measuring lifestyle is part of *psychographic segmentation. It involves measuring primary characteristics, known as **AIO dimensions** (activities, interests, and opinions). Lifestyle classifications have been developed out of this, particularly the **Values and Lifestyles Typology** (**VALS**), which classifies consumers into nine lifestyle groups. VALS 2 classifies people into eight groups according to their consumption tendencies, i.e. how they spend their time and money.

lifestyle business A small business run by owners with a personal interest in the product. The business reflects their lifestyles and provides them with a comfortable income, but is not a growth venture. Compilers of reference books could fall into this category.

lifestyle format An advertising format that reflects a target market's *lifestyle.

lifestyle segmentation Segmentation of a market based on *lifestyles. More companies are segmenting their markets by lifestyles, as these are increasingly seen as good predictors of consumer behaviour. Most companies use off-the-shelf research-agency classifications, because of the high cost and complexity of developing their own. See MARKET SEGMENTATION.

lifetime transfers See POTENTIALLY EXEMPT TRANSFER.

lifetime value (**customer lifetime value**; **customer equity**) The future long-term profitability of a particular customer, i.e.

the amount by which the revenue received from this customer will exceed the cost of attracting, selling to, and servicing him or her. There is no clear agreement on how lifetime value can be measured. One technique is to forecast future cash flows for the customer, identify an appropriate *discount rate or *cost of capital, and then calculate the *net present value of the cash flows. This is a relatively simple calculation but it does involve managers making difficult assumptions. One key assumption is customer retention. Managers may not agree on how loyal a customer will be in the future and whether sales will increase or decrease. A company will always be looking at strategies for maximizing the lifetime value of customers. See also CUSTOMER PROFITABILITY ANALYSIS.

LIFFE Abbreviation for *London International Financial Futures and Options Exchange.

LIFO cost Abbreviation for *last-in-first-out cost.

lifting a leg See BREAKING A LEG.

light dues A levy on shipowners for maintaining lighthouses, beacons, buoys, etc., collected in the UK by HM Revenue and Customs on behalf of *Trinity House.

lighter A flat-bottomed cargo barge, usually without its own means of propulsion, that is towed by a tug for short distances, as between a ship and a quay or along a river from a port to a warehouse. The charge for transporting goods by lighter is the **lighterage**. See also LASH.

lilangeni (*plural* **emalangeni**; E) The standard monetary unit of Swaziland, divided into 100 cents.

LIMEAN Abbreviation for *London Inter Bank Mean Rate.

limit 1. The *maximum fluctuations (up or down) allowed in certain markets over a stated period (usually one day's trading; *see* INTRADAY LIMIT). In some volatile circumstances the market moves the limit up (or down). The movement of prices on the Tokyo Stock Exchange is limited in this way as it is on certain US commodity markets. In some markets, if the limit is reached trading is stopped for the day or for a cooling-off period. **2.** A restriction on a derivatives or commodity exchange on the number of contracts or positions one party can hold.

limitation of actions Statutory rules limiting the time within which civil actions can be brought. Actions in simple contract and tort must be brought within six years of the cause of action. There are several special rules, including that for strict liability actions for defective products, in which case the period is three years from the accrual of the cause of action or (if later) the date on which the plaintiff knew, or should have known, the material facts, but not later than ten years from the date on which the product was first put into circulation. The present UK law is contained in the Limitations Act (1980), the Latent Damage Act (1986), and the Consumer Protection Act (1987).

limited by guarantee *See* LIMITED COMPANY.

limited carrier *See* CARRIER.

limited company A *company in which the liability of the members in respect of the company's debts is limited. It may be **limited by shares**, in which case the liability of the members on a winding-up is limited to the amount (if any) unpaid on their shares. This is by far the most common type of registered company. The liability of the members may alternatively be **limited by guarantee**; in this case the liability of members is limited by the memorandum to a certain amount, which the members undertake to contribute on winding-up. These are usually societies, clubs, or trade associations. Since 1980 it has not been possible for such a company to be formed with a share capital, or converted to a company limited by guarantee with a share capital. *See also* PUBLIC LIMITED COMPANY.

limited-function wholesaler *See* LIMITED-SERVICE MERCHANT WHOLESALER.

limited liability *See* LIMITED COMPANY; LIMITED LIABILITY PARTNERSHIP.

limited liability partnership A legally recognized entity under the Limited Liability Partnership Act (2000). This type of business organization is intended to combine the flexibility of a traditional *partnership with the corporate notion of limited liability. Persons intending to set up a limited liability partnership must register it with *Companies House. There are also several disclosure requirements that are similar in nature to those required by companies. Much of the pressure for this change in the law was led by accountancy and audit partnerships, wishing to limit the liability of partners against claims for *negligence.

limited market A market for a particular security in which buying and selling is difficult, usually because a large part of the issue is held by very few people or institutions.

limited partner *See* PARTNERSHIP. *See also* LIMITED LIABILITY PARTNERSHIP.

limited recourse financing *See* PROJECT FINANCING.

limited-service merchant wholesaler (limited-function wholesaler) A wholesaler that offers less than full service for customers but charges lower prices than a full-service merchant wholesaler.

limited-service retailer A retailer that provides only a limited number of services to shoppers, but usually sells goods at a discount.

limit order *See* AT LIMIT.

limit price The highest price that established sellers in a market can charge for a product, without inducing a new seller to enter the market. The limit price is usually lower than the monopoly price but higher than the competitive price. Limit pricing enables established sellers to make higher profits than they would if they sold at the competitive price and it also ensures that new firms will not enter the market and drive the prices down to competitive levels.

line and staff management A system of management used in large organizations in which there are two separate hierarchies; the **line management** side consists of **line managers** with responsibility for deciding the policy of and running the organization's main activities (such as manufacturing, sales, etc.), while the **staff management**, and its separate **staff managers**, are responsible for providing such supporting services as warehousing, accounting, transport, personnel management, and plant maintenance.

linear cost function *Cost behaviour that, when plotted on a graph against activity levels, results in a straight line. For example, total fixed cost levels and variable costs per unit of activity will both result in a straight line horizontal to the *x*-axis when activity, production, or sales is plotted on the *x*-axis. Total variable costs will also result in a straight line and is thus a linear cost function.

linear depreciation *Depreciation charges that, when plotted on a graph against time on the *x*-axis, result in a straight line, as a constant amount per annum is written off the assets concerned. Both the *straight-line method of depreciation and the *rate per unit of production method, when the depreciation charge is plotted against production levels, result in linear depreciation.

linear programming A modelling technique that determines an optimal solution for attaining an objective by taking into consideration a number of *constraints. The objective function, often to optimize profits or minimize costs, is expressed as an equation and the constraints are also expressed in mathematical terms. Where only two products and few constraints are involved a solution may be obtained graphically. More than two products requires a computer program.

line extending Increasing a line of products by adding variations of an existing brand. For example, Coca Cola extended its line with Diet Coke. Line extending runs the risk of weakening the brand name. *Compare* LINE FILLING.

line filling Adding products to an existing line of products in order to leave no opportunities for competitors. Line filling can be horizontal or vertical. In horizontal line filling, a video manufacturer may produce machines with a variety of features, such as half-speed copying, multi-recording memory, etc., at the top end of the price range, and relatively cheap cost-effective machines at the opposite end; a competitor can therefore only compete on price. In vertical line-filling a manufacturer may produce a wide variety of brand names within a single product line; some detergent manufacturers do this. *Compare* LINE EXTENDING.

line management *See* LINE AND STAFF MANAGEMENT.

line production (mass production) A type of process in which high volumes of identical, or very similar, products are made in a set sequence of operations. It involves high capital expenditure and depends on efficient plant layouts and procedures, as well as good product design to minimize unit costs. The levels of skill required are not usually high. In recent years a number of organizations have experimented with systems that trade off the benefits of full line production in exchange for the increased levels of motivation following from giving staff more ownership of the product, e.g. through *cellular layout. The introduction of computerized control systems has enabled some manufacturers to produce apparently unique products without losing the benefits of the line process. For example, some Japanese car manufacturers have put together a relatively small range of standard components, trims, finishes, etc., to the customer's specification, which enables them to claim that no two of their cars are identical.

lipa A monetary unit of Croatia, worth one hundredth of a *kuna.

liquid assets (liquid capital; quick assets; realizable assets) Assets held in cash or in something that can be readily turned into cash with minimal capital loss (e.g. deposits in a bank current account, trade debts, marketable investments). The ratio of these assets to current liabilities provides an assessment of an organization's *liquidity or solvency. *See also* LIQUID RATIO; MANDATORY LIQUID ASSETS.

liquidation (winding-up) The distribution of a company's assets among its creditors and members prior to its dissolution. This brings the life of the company to an end. The liquidation may be voluntary (*see* CREDITORS' VOLUNTARY LIQUIDATION; MEMBERS' VOLUNTARY LIQUIDATION) or by the court (*see* COMPULSORY LIQUIDATION).

liquidation committee A committee set up by creditors of a company being wound up in order to consent to the *liquidator exercising certain of his powers. When the company is unable to pay its debts, the committee is usually composed of creditors only; otherwise it consists of creditors and *contributories.

liquidator A person appointed by a court, or by the members of a company or its creditors, to regularize the company's affairs in a *liquidation (winding-up). In the case of a *members' voluntary liquidation, it is the members of the company who appoint the liquidator. In a *creditors' voluntary liquidation, the liquidator may be appointed by company members before the **meeting of creditors** or by the creditors themselves at the meeting; in the former case the liquidator can only exercise his or her powers with the consent of the court. If two liquidators are appointed, the court resolves which one is to act. In a *compulsory liquidation, the court appoints a provisional liquidator after the winding-up petition has been presented; after the order has been granted, the court appoints the *official receiver as liquidator, until or unless another officer is appointed.

The liquidator is in a relationship of trust with the company and the creditors as a body; a liquidator appointed in a compulsory liquidation is an officer of the court, is under statutory obligations, and may not profit from the position. A liquidator must be a licensed *insolvency practitioner, according to the Insolvency Act (1986) as amended by the Insolvency Act (1994). On appointment, the liquidator assumes control of the company, collects the assets, pays the debts, and distributes any surplus to company members according to their rights. In the case of a compulsory liquidation, the liquidator is supervised by the court, the *liquidation committee, and the Department of Trade and Industry. The liquidator receives a *statement of affairs from the company officers and must report on these to the court.

liquid capital See LIQUID ASSETS.

liquid instrument A *negotiable instrument that the purchaser is able to sell before maturity.

liquidity The extent to which an organi-

zation's assets are liquid (see LIQUID ASSETS), enabling it to pay its debts when they fall due and also to move into new investment opportunities.

liquidity index A measure of a company's liquidity assessed by calculating the number of days it would take for current assets to be converted into cash.

liquidity premium The relative advantage of holding assets in liquid form. Investors are prepared to receive lower returns on *liquid assets, because they can easily be transferred into cash with little capital loss. Liquid assets are thus to some extent a hedge against uncertainty.

liquidity risk The risk, in lending operations, that an investment cannot be liquidated during its life without significant costs.

liquidity trap A situation in which investors hold on to cash because they are worried about the likelihood of a fall in the price of financial assets. J. M. Keynes argued that in these circumstances monetary policy becomes ineffective, because monetary expansion will not lower interest rates.

liquid market A financial market in which *spreads are narrow, there are many buyers and sellers, and large transactions do not have a marked impact on the market price.

liquid ratio (quick ratio) A ratio used for assessing the *liquidity of a company; it is the ratio of the *liquid assets (i.e. the *current assets less the *stock) to the *current liabilities. For example, a company has current assets of £250,000, including stock of £150,000, and liabilities of £120,000. This gives a liquid ratio of:

(£250,000 − £150,000)/£120,000 = 0.83,

i.e. 83% or 0.83:1. This may be interpreted as the company having 83 pence of liquid assets for every £1 of current liabilities. If, for some reason, the company was obliged to repay the current liabilities immediately there would be insufficient liquid assets to allow it to do so. The company might therefore be forced into a hurried sale of stock at a discount to raise finance. Although there is no rule of thumb, and there are industry differences, a liquid ratio significantly below 1:1 will give rise to concern. The liquid ratio is regarded as an acid test of a company's solvency and is therefore sometimes called the **acid-test ratio**.

lira 1. (IT) The standard monetary unit of Turkey, divided into 100 kuruş. **2.** (Lm) The standard monetary unit of Malta, divided into 100 cents and 1000 mils. **3.** (l; lit) Formerly, the standard monetary unit of Italy and San Marino, divided into 100 centesimi. It was subsumed into the *euro for all purposes except cash transactions in January 1999 and abolished in 2002.

lisente A monetary unit of Lesotho, worth one hundredth of a *loti.

listed company A company that has a listing agreement (*see* LISTING REQUIRE-MENTS) with a major stock exchange and whose shares have a quotation on that exchange. These companies were formerly called **quoted companies**.

listed option *See* EXCHANGE-TRADED OP-TION.

listed security 1. In general, a security that has a *quotation on a recognized *stock exchange. **2.** On the *London Stock Exchange, a security that has a quotation in the Official List of Securities of the *main market. *See also* FLOTATION; LIST-ING REQUIREMENTS; YELLOW BOOK.

listing requirements The conditions that must be satisfied before a security can be traded on a stock exchange. To achieve a quotation in the Official List of Securities of the *main market of the *London Stock Exchange, the requirements contained in a **listing agreement** must be signed by the company seeking quotation. The two main requirements of such a listing are usually:

- that the value of the company's assets should exceed a certain value;
- that the company publish specific finan-cial and operating information, both at the time of *flotation and regularly thereafter.

Listing requirements are generally more stringent the larger the market. For exam-ple, the main market in London demands considerably more information from com-panies than the *Alternative Investment Market. The listing requirements are set out in the *Yellow Book.

list price 1. The retail price of a con-sumer good as recommended by the man-ufacturer and shown on his price list. If no price-maintenance agreements apply, a discount on the list price may be offered by the retailer to attract trade. **2.** A sup-plier's price as shown on an invoice to a retailer or wholesaler, before deduction of any discounts.

list renting The practice of renting a list of potential customers to an organization involved in *direct-mail selling or to a charity raising funds. When the terms of hiring restrict the use of the list to one mail shot, it is usual for the owner of the list to carry out the mailing, so that the hirer cannot copy it for subsequent use.

lists closed The closing of the applica-tion lists for a *new issue on the London Stock Exchange, after a specified time or after the issue has been fully subscribed.

litas (*plural* **litai**) The standard monetary unit of Lithuania, divided into 100 centai.

litigation 1. The taking of legal action. The person who takes it is called a **litigant**. **2.** The activity of a solicitor when dealing with proceedings in a court of law.

Little Board The colloquial name for the American Stock Exchange, the New York market for smaller company stocks and bonds. *Compare* BIG BOARD.

live-marketing database An abbrevi-ated version of a full *customer database. A live-marketing database sacrifices some degree of customer information to enable marketing decisions to be made more quickly.

livery company One of some eighty chartered companies in the City of London that are descended from medieval craft guilds. Now largely social and charitable institutions, livery companies owe their name to the elaborate ceremonial dress (livery) worn by their officers. Several sup-port independent schools (e.g. Merchant Taylors, Haberdashers, Mercers) and al-though none are now trading companies, some still have some involvement in their trades (e.g. Fishmongers). In 1878 they joined together to form the City and Guilds of London Institute, which founded the City and Guilds College of the Imperial College of Science and Technology and has been involved in other forms of technical education.

livestock and bloodstock insurance
An insurance policy covering the owners against financial losses caused by the death of an animal. Policies may be widened to include cover for treatment fees for certain specified diseases or lost profits for stud animals. Insurances can be arranged to cover single animals or for whole herds.

Lloyd's A corporation of underwriters (**Lloyd's underwriters**) and insurance brokers (**Lloyd's brokers**) that developed from a coffee shop in Tavern Street in the City of London in 1689. It takes its name from the proprietor of the coffee shop, Edward Lloyd. By 1774 it was established in the Royal Exchange and in 1871 was incorporated by act of parliament. It now occupies a building in Lime Street (built in 1986 by Richard Rogers). As a corporation, Lloyd's itself does not underwrite insurance business; all its business comes to it from some 260 Lloyd's brokers, who are in touch with the public, and is underwritten by some 279 *syndicates of Lloyd's underwriters, who are approached by the brokers and who do not, themselves, contact the public.

The 20 000 or so Lloyd's underwriters must each deposit a substantial sum of money with the corporation and accept unlimited liability before they can become members. They are grouped into syndicates, run by a syndicate manager or agent, but most of the members of syndicates are **names**, underwriting members of Lloyd's who take no part in organizing the underwriting business, but who share in the profits or losses of the syndicate and provide the risk capital. Lloyd's has long specialized in marine insurance but now covers almost all insurance risks. In the period 1988 to 1994 Lloyd's lost some £8 billion. This brought severe hardship to many names and a number of changes to the way in which the organization is run, including allowing limited liability companies to become underwriters. *See also* LLOYD'S AGENT; LLOYD'S LIST AND SHIPPING GAZETTE; LLOYD'S REGISTER OF SHIPPING.

Lloyd's agent A person situated in a port to manage the business of Lloyd's members, keeping the corporation informed of shipping movements and accidents, arranging surveys, helping in the settlement of marine insurance claims, and assisting masters of ships. A Lloyd's agent will be found in every significant port in the world.

Lloyd's broker *See* LLOYD'S.

Lloyd's List and Shipping Gazette A daily newspaper published by Lloyd's, founded in 1734 and formerly known as **Lloyd's List**. It gives details of the movements of ships and aircraft, accidents, etc. **Lloyd's Loading List**, published weekly by Lloyd's, lists ships loading in British and continental ports, with their closing dates for accepting cargo. It also gives general news on the insurance market.

Lloyd's Register of Shipping A society formed by *Lloyd's in 1760 to inspect and classify all ocean-going vessels in excess of 100 tonnes. Ships are periodically surveyed by **Lloyd's surveyors** and classified according to the condition of their hulls, engines, and trappings. The society also provides a technical advice service. Its annual publication is called *Lloyd's Register of British and Foreign Shipping*. The Register enables underwriters to have instant access to the information they need to underwrite marine risks, even when the vessels may be thousands of miles away.

Lloyd's underwriter *See* LLOYD'S.

LME Abbreviation for *London Metal Exchange.

load 1. The cumulative amount of work assigned at any time to a work centre for processing in the future. **2.** *See* BACK-END LOAD; FRONT-END LOAD.

loading 1. The process of allocating jobs or orders to work centres within a production facility. If there is a range of jobs there could be a range of possible routes through the various work centres. Building up a profile of the load on each location enables approximate completion dates for each job to be estimated and bottlenecks in the system to be identified. Loading is based on average times and does not take into account job interference, etc. **Forward loading** begins with the present date and loads jobs forwards. **Backward loading** begins with the completion date and works backwards. *See* FINITE

CAPACITY LOADING; INFINITE CAPACITY
LOADING. **2.** The addition of a charge to
cover incidental expenses, administrative
costs, profit, etc., on an insurance policy,
bank account, or purchases of unit trusts.
See BACK-END LOAD; FRONT-END LOAD.

load line One of a series of lines marked
on the hull of a ship to show the extent to
which the hull may be immersed in the
water. Originally introduced by Samuel
Plimsoll MP in 1874 and running right
round the hull, the **Plimsoll Line** made a
great contribution to safety at sea. The
modern markings consist of a series of
lines, usually painted on the hull amid-
ships, applying to different conditions.
The line marked TF applies to tropical
fresh water, F fresh water, T tropical sea
water, S summer sea water, W winter sea
water and WNA winter in the North At-
lantic. Shipowners and masters who allow
vessels to be overloaded face heavy penalties.

loan Money lent on condition that it is
repaid, either in instalments or all at once,
on agreed dates and usually that the borrower pays the lender an agreed rate of interest (unless it is an **interest-free loan**). *See
also* BALLOON; BANK LOAN; BRIDGING LOAN;
BULLET; LOCAL LOAN; PERSONAL LOAN.

loan account An account opened by a
bank in the name of a customer to whom
it has granted a loan, rather than an
*overdraft facility. The amount of the loan
is debited to this account and any repayments are credited; interest is charged on
the full amount of the loan less any repayments. The customer's current account is
credited with the amount of the loan.
With an overdraft facility, interest is only
charged on the amount of the overdraft,
which may be less than the full amount of
the loan.

loanback An arrangement in which an
individual can borrow from the accumulated funds of his pension scheme. Usually
a commercial rate of interest has to be
credited to fund for the use of the capital.
Some life assurance companies offer loan
facilities on this basis of up to fifteen
times the annual pension premium.

loan-backed Describing an *asset-
backed security in which the assets are
portfolios of loans. For example, credit-

card portfolios or portfolios of unsecured
personal loans are loan-backed securities.

**loan capital (borrowed capital; debt cap-
ital)** Capital used to finance an organization that is subject to payment of interest
over the life of the loan, at the end of
which the loan is normally repaid. There
are different categories of loan capital:
*mortgage debentures are secured on
specific assets of the organization, while
convertible debentures may be converted
into equity according to the terms of the
issue.

loan creditor A person or institution
that has lent money to a business. For example, when a bank loan is obtained the
bank becomes a loan creditor.

Loan Guarantee Scheme A UK government scheme that guarantees 70% of a
company's overdraft for a 3% premium.
The bank must accept the risk for the balance of 30%. Its purpose is to support
small businesses.

loan note A form of loan stock (*see*
DEBENTURE) in which an investor takes a
note rather than cash as the result of a
share offer to defer tax liability. The yield
is often variable and may be linked to the
*London Inter Bank Offered Rate. Loan
notes are not usually marketable but are
usually repayable on demand.

loan-price ratio The ratio of the value
of a loan to the value of any *collateral.
This formula is often used to judge the
risk exposure for mortgages.

loan selling The sale of bank loans by
one bank to another. For example, the
debt of a developing country may be sold
at a discount to the market value in order
to reduce the burden of the debt on a particular bank. Loans to individuals may also
be sold in this way, from one financial institution to another, often without the
borrower knowing that the lender has
changed. *See also* EUROBOND.

loan stock *See* DEBENTURE.

local A person who has a seat on a financial market and who deals for his or her
own account.

local area network (LAN) A network of
microcomputers, printers, and other devices connected together in a localized

area, such as an office building. Individual microcomputers (**workstations**) are able to use data on their own local hard disk. In addition, they can access data and software held on a central shared unit (the **file server**), which also controls the operation of the network.

local authority bill A *bill of exchange drawn on a UK local government authority.

localization Altering the content of a product such as a website, computer program, etc., so that it is appropriate to users in a particular country or language group.

local loan A loan issued by a UK local government authority for financing capital expenditure.

location strategy The process of choosing where to locate a unit producing goods or services. This must take account of a range of variables to achieve the minimum cost that optimizes the overall strategy of the particular organization. There are three basic strategies. In a **product-based** strategy, independent facilities are used to produce each product in a company's range. This permits dedicated design and organization of facilities, which may vary from product to product. A **market-based** strategy gives priority to locating as close to customers as possible. This is clearly important in the case of services and for organizations offering a quick response to customer requirements, e.g. in fast-moving consumer goods. A **vertically differentiated** strategy locates different elements of the process at different sites, according to the economic characteristics of each element. These considerations are particularly important for transnational and global operations.

lockbox In the USA, a Postal Service box used for the collection of customer payments. The recipient's bank will arrange collection from these boxes throughout the day, deposit the funds, and provide a computer listing of the payments with the daily total. This method is effective for small number of payments with a high value as the bank's charges per item are relatively high.

lock-out A form of industrial action in which the employer refuses to allow employees access to their place of work unless they accept the employer's terms of employment.

lock-up An investment in assets that are not readily realizable or one that is specifically intended to be held for a long period – say, over ten years.

loco Denoting a price for goods that does not include any loading or transport charges; i.e. the goods are located in a specified place, usually the seller's warehouse or factory, and the buyer has to pay all the charges involved in loading, transporting, or shipping them to their destination. A **loco price** might be quoted in the form: £100 per tonne, loco Islington factory.

locus poenitentiae (Latin: an opportunity to repent) An opportunity for the parties to an illegal contract to reconsider their positions, decide not to carry out the illegal act, and so save the contract from being void. Once the illegal purpose has been carried out, no action in law is possible.

log file A file stored on a *web server that records every item *downloaded by users. **Log file analysers** are used to build a picture of the amount of usage of different parts of a website, based on the information contained in the log file.

logistics 1. See SUPPLY-CHAIN MANAGEMENT. **2.** The detailed planning of any complex operation.

logo (logtype) A brand name or company name written in a distinctive way.

Lombard rate 1. The rate of interest at which the German central bank, the Bundesbank, lends to German commercial banks, usually ½% above the *discount rate. **2.** The interest rate charged by a European commercial bank lending against security.

Lombard Street The street in the City of London that is the traditional centre of the *money market. Many commercial banks have offices in or near Lombard Street, as do many bill brokers and discount houses. The Bank of England is round the corner.

London acceptance credit A method of providing immediate cash for a UK exporter of goods. On shipment of the goods the exporter draws a *bill of exchange on the foreign buyer. The accepted bill is then pledged to a *merchant bank in London, which accepts an *accommodation bill drawn by the exporter. The acceptance can be discounted on the bank's reputation, to provide the exporter with immediate finance, whereas the foreign buyer's acceptance would be difficult, or impossible, to discount in London.

London approach The approach adopted by London banks to customers facing a cash-flow crisis. The key feature is that the banks remain supportive for as long as possible, decisions are made collectively, and all information and any money paid is shared between the lending banks on an equitable basis.

London Bankers' Clearing House Formerly, the organization that daily set off all cheques drawn for and against the *clearing banks in the UK. It was established in Lombard Street, in the City of London, in the 1770s. In 1985 it was superseded by the *Association for Payment Clearing Services.

London Bullion Market The world's largest market for gold and silver trading. Market makers mainly quote prices in US dollars per troy ounce for spot and forward delivery. It is operated by the London Bullion Market Association (LBMA), whose primary task is to ensure that refiners of gold and silver meet the required standards of quality. The Association maintains close links with the Bank of England, which is responsible for the supervision of the market and for publishing its code of conduct.

London Chamber of Commerce The largest *chamber of commerce in the UK. It provides the normal services of a chamber of commerce and in addition runs courses and examinations in business subjects.

London Clearing House (LCH) A *clearing house established in 1888 (known before 1991 as the International Commodities Clearing House). It provides futures and options markets with netting and settlement services as well as becoming a counterparty (*see* COUNTERPARTY RISK) to every transaction between its members.

In this capacity LCH takes the risk of its members defaulting, which it covers by collecting *margins from members; it also provides an independent guarantee from its shareholders and from the insurance market. Exchanges making use of LCH facilities include the *London Stock Exchange, the *London Metal Exchange, and the *International Petroleum Exchange. In 2003 LCH merged with the Continental clearing house Clearnet to form **LCH.Clearnet**; the new group serves markets across Europe and is the sole clearer for *Euronext NV.

London code of conduct A code issued by the Bank of England, that is applicable to all wholesale dealings not regulated by the rules of a recognized exchange. It is considered the best practice for company treasurers by the *Association of Corporate Treasurers.

London Commodity Exchange (LCE) A commodity exchange, which emerged in 1954 as a successor to the London Commercial Sale Rooms. In 1987 it became the *Futures and Options Exchange (London FOX), Europe's leading market for futures and options in soft commodities, and in 1996 it merged with the *London International Financial Futures and Options Exchange (LIFFE).

London Inter Bank Bid Rate (LIBID) The rate of interest at which banks borrow from each other on the London *interbank market. *See* LONDON INTER BANK OFFERED RATE.

London Inter Bank Currency Options Market A London-based *over-the-counter market in currency options.

London Inter Bank Mean Rate (LIMEAN) The median average between the *London Inter Bank Offered Rate (LIBOR) and the *London Inter Bank Bid Rate (LIBID).

London Inter Bank Offered Rate (LIBOR) The rate of interest at which banks lend to each other on the London *interbank market. The loans are for a minimum of £250,000 for periods from overnight up to five years. LIBOR is the most significant interest rate for international banks. It is also used as a benchmark for lending to bank customers and as a reference rate for many derivatives. *See also* LONDON INTER BANK BID RATE.

London International Financial Futures and Options Exchange (LIFFE) A *financial futures market opened in 1982, in London's Royal Exchange, to provide facilities within the European time zone for dealing in options and futures contracts, including those in government bonds, stock-and-share indexes, foreign currencies, and interest rates. In 1991 LIFFE moved into its own premises in the City of London. Until quite recently, trading was carried out chiefly by *open outcry among authorized floor traders. Electronic trading was introduced in 1989 but did not replace live *pit trading until 1998. The London Traded Options Market merged with LIFFE in 1992, when the words 'and Options' was added to its name, although the acronym remains unchanged. In 1996 LIFFE merged with the *Futures and Options Exchange, making it the only exchange in the world to provide futures and options contracts on financial, equity, and commodity products and equity indices. Since 2001, it has become part of the European derivatives business *Euronext NV, with markets in Amsterdam, Brussels, Lisbon, and Paris.

London Metal Exchange (LME) One of the world's largest non-ferrous metals exchanges, the total value of contracts each year being around $2000 billion. Established in 1877, it is now regulated by the UK *Financial Services Authority. The range of metals traded includes copper, aluminium, nickel, zinc, and lead. Dealings on the LME include *futures and *options contracts.

London rules A set of guidelines, approved by the Bank of England, relating to the treatment of distressed borrowers.

London Securities and Derivatives Exchange (OMLX) An exchange set up in 1990 to trade in *futures and *options in Swedish equities. Originating as a way of reducing liability to Swedish tax, it has remained in London after the tax it was set up to avoid was rescinded.

London Stock Exchange The market in London that deals in securities. Dealings in securities began in London in the 17th century. The name Stock Exchange

was first used for New Jonathan's Coffee House in 1773, although it was not formally constituted until 1802. The development of the industrial revolution encouraged many other share markets to flourish throughout the UK, all the remnants of which amalgamated in 1973 to form The Stock Exchange of Great Britain and Ireland. After the *Big Bang in 1986 this organization became the International Stock Exchange of the UK and Republic of Ireland Ltd (ISE) in an attempt to stress the international nature of the main UK securities market; it is now the London Stock Exchange plc. The reforms of 1986 included:

- allowing banks, insurance companies, and overseas securities houses to become members and to buy existing member firms;
- abolishing scales of commissions, allowing commissions to be negotiated;
- abolishing the division of members into jobbers and brokers, enabling a member firm to deal with the public, to buy and sell shares for their own account, and to act as *market makers;
- the introduction of the *Stock Exchange Automated Quotations System, a computerized dealing system that has virtually abolished face-to-face dealing on the floor of exchange.

The London Stock Exchange now has four core business areas:

- **equity markets** – the *main market for listed companies and the *Alternative Investment Market for unlisted securities;
- **trading services** – trading platforms that are used by broking firms around the world to buy and sell securities;
- **market information** – the provision of prices and news;
- **derivatives** – a recent diversification beyond the core equity markets. The London Stock Exchange created the **European Derivatives Exchange (EDX) London** in 2003.

long-dated gilt *See* GILT-EDGED SECURITY.

long hedging *See* HEDGE.

longitudinal design A marketing research design in which the views of a fixed population sample are measured over a period to show trends and changes in audiences. Many of the consumer panels, TV audience panels, and readership panels are of this type.

long lease A lease that has more than 50 years to run, as defined by the Companies Act (1985). *Compare* SHORT LEASE.

long position A *position held in securities, commodities, currencies, derivatives, etc., such that a rise in the market increases the value of the position. *Compare* SHORT POSITION.

long-range plan A plan that describes the principal factors and forces affecting an organization during the coming years, including long-term objectives, the chief marketing strategies used to attain them, and the resources required.

longs 1. *See* GILT-EDGED SECURITY. 2. Securities, commodities, currencies, etc., held in a *long position.

long-term bond A bond that does not mature in less than one year.

long-term contract A contract that falls into two or more accounting periods before being completed. Such a contract may be for the design, manufacture, or construction of a single substantial asset, for example in the construction or civil engineering industries. From an accounting point of view, there is a problem in determining how much profit can be reasonably allocated to each accounting period, although the contract is not complete. *Statement of Standard Accounting Practice (SSAP) 9, Stocks and Long Term Contracts, requires contracts to be assessed on an individual basis and shown in the *profit and loss account by recording turnover and related activity as the contract progresses. Where the outcome of the contract can be assessed with reasonable certainty, even though it is not complete, the part of the profit that can be attributed to the work performed by an accounting date may be recognized in the profit and loss account. Attributable profit is that part of the total profit currently estimated to arise over the duration of the contract, after allowing for estimated remedial costs, maintenance costs, and increases in costs not recoverable under the contract agreement. More recently, the Accounting Standards Board has proposed

the replacement of SSAP 9 with two international standards.

long-term debt Loans and debentures that are not due for repayment for at least ten years.

long-term liability A sum owed that does not have to be repaid within the next accounting period of a business. In some contexts a long-term liability may be regarded as one not due for repayment within the next three, or possibly ten, years.

long ton *See* TON.

loose insert An advertising leaflet distributed with another publication and usually inserted loosely within its pages.

loss adjuster A person appointed by an insurer to negotiate an insurance claim. The loss adjuster, who is independent of the insurer, discusses the claim with both the insurer and the policyholder, producing a report recommending the basis on which the claim should be settled. The insurer pays a fee for this service based on the amount of work involved for the loss adjuster, not on the size of the settlement. *Compare* LOSS ASSESSOR.

loss assessor A person who acts on behalf of the policyholder in handling a claim. A fee is charged for this service, which is usually a percentage of the amount received by the policyholder. *Compare* LOSS ADJUSTER.

loss leader A product or service offered for sale by an organization at a loss in order to attract customers. This practise was curbed in the UK by the Resale Prices Act (1976), although it still continues, especially in supermarkets.

loss-of-profits policy *See* BUSINESS-INTERRUPTION POLICY.

loss ratio The total of the claims paid out by an insurance company, underwriting *syndicate, etc., expressed as a percentage of the amount of premiums coming in in the same period. For example, if claims total £2M and premiums total £4M, the result is a 50% loss ratio. Insurers use this figure as a guide to the profitability of their business when they are reconsidering premium rates for a particular risk.

loss reliefs Relief available to sole traders, partnerships, and companies making losses, as adjusted for tax purposes. *Capital allowances can create a trading loss or can enhance it. Trading losses can be carried forward to set against future trading profits.

For sole traders and partnerships, trading losses can be set against other income for the year of the loss and for the previous year. Partners can decide individually how to use their share of the losses. Special rules apply to trading losses in the early years of a trade. These losses can be carried back three years to a period before the trade commenced. From 1991–92 it has been possible to set trading losses against capital gains if the loss cannot be used first by setting against other income during the year.

For companies, a trading loss can be set off against the profits of the previous 12-month period provided the company was carrying on the same trade during that period. *Capital losses can be set against capital gains in the same period. Any surplus capital loss that cannot be utilized during the current year must be carried forward to set against future capital gains. Capital losses cannot be set against other income, unlike trading losses. *See also* TERMINAL-LOSS RELIEF.

loti (*plural* **maloti**; MI) The standard monetary unit of Lesotho, divided into 100 lisente.

Lotus 1-2-3 *Trademark* A *spreadsheet program for personal computers originated by Lotus Development Corp. (now part of IBM). It provides statistical, database, and graph-drawing facilities.

lower of cost or market (LCM) A method of valuing a *current asset of an organization in which the value taken is either its purchase (or production) price or the cost of replacing it (by purchase or manufacture), whichever is the lower. The Companies Act (1985) requires that a current asset be valued at either its purchase (or production) price or its *net realizable value, whichever is the lower.

lower rate of income tax A former rate of *income tax below the *basic rate of income tax. In 1999 it was replaced with the *starting rate of income tax.

low-involvement product A product that involves the consumer in little or no trouble or deliberation when making a purchase. Such products are invariably cheap; manufacturers try to make them more interesting and appealing by means of advertising with the intention of developing a brand loyalty. *Compare* HIGH-INVOLVEMENT PRODUCT.

loyalty techniques Incentive schemes in which customers receive points for repeat purchases. These points can be converted into discounts, free products, or cash. Most supermarkets now operate schemes in which customers' points are recorded by means of plastic **loyalty cards**, which are swiped through the checkout till at the time of purchase. In **on-line incentive schemes** customers may receive points for visiting certain websites.

LPC Scale Abbreviation for *Least Preferred Co-worker Scale.

Ltd The usual abbreviation for limited. This (or the Welsh equivalent) must appear in the name of a private *limited company. *Compare* PLC.

luma A monetary unit of Armenia, worth one hundredth of a *dram.

lump sum **1.** A sum of money paid all at once, rather than in instalments. **2.** A sum of money paid for freight, irrespective of the size of the cargo. **3.** An insurance benefit, such as a sum of money paid on retirement or redundancy or to the beneficiaries on the death of an insured person. Retirement *pensions can consist of a lump sum plus a reduced pension. **4.** A form of *damages; a **lump-sum award** is given in tort cases.

Lutine Bell A bell that hangs in the underwriting room at *Lloyd's and is rung for ceremonial occasions and rarely to draw the attention of underwriters to an important announcement. It was formerly rung once if a ship sank and twice for good news. It was recovered from the *Lutine*, a ship that was insured by Lloyd's and sank in the North Sea in 1799, with a cargo of bullion (£1.4M value), most of which was lost.

lwei A monetary unit of Angola, worth one hundredth of a *kwanza.

M0; M1; M2; M3; M4; M5 *See* MONEY SUPPLY.

machine-down time The period during which a machine cannot be used, usually because of breakdown. If a machine is 'down', clearly production is not taking place, but it is customary in costing to attribute costs to the down time.

machine hour A measurement of production in terms of the time taken for a machine operation to complete a given amount of production.

machine hour rate An *absorption rate used in *absorption costing, obtained by the formula:

budgeted *cost centre overheads/
budgeted machine hours.

machine-idle time The period during which a machine is not being used. This is similar in effect to *machine-down time though it may be caused by lack of work rather than by a fault in the machine.

machine-readable Denoting any form of data that can be input directly into a computer. It includes data that has been stored on a magnetic medium (e.g. disks, tapes, etc.) and data that has been prepared for *OCR.

macroeconomics The branch of economics that studies economies as a whole rather than the behaviour of particular economic agents. Modern macroeconomics is largely concerned with the relationships between such factors as money supply, employment, interest rates, government spending, investment, and consumption and with the role, if any, that a government should play in a national economy. In recent economic thinking the distinction between macroeconomics and *microeconomics has become less clear cut than previously.

macroenvironment The broad sweep of the environment that creates the forces that shape every business and non-profit marketer. The physical environment, social and cultural forces, demographic make-up, economic climate, prevailing political beliefs, and current legal infrastructure are components of the macroenvironment. Generally, most companies have no control over these factors. *Compare* MICROENVIRONMENT.

MAD Abbreviation for *mean absolute deviation.

mad dog An informal name for a company with the potential to grow quickly, providing it can obtain substantial capital; risks are likely to be high. The information technology industry is an example of a sector that has included a number of mad dogs.

magnetic ink character recognition (MICR) A type of magnetic ink used on cheques and other documents to enable them to be automatically sorted and the characters to be read and fed into a computer.

Magnuson–Moss Warranty Act A US federal law requiring that guarantees provided by sellers should be made available to buyers before a purchase is made and that they specify who the warrantor is, what products (or parts of products) are covered, what the warrantor must do if the product is defective, how long the warranty applies, and the obligations of the buyer.

mailing list A list of names and addresses used in *direct-mail selling, advertising, fund raising, etc. *See also* LIST RENTING.

mail-order house A firm that specializes in selling goods direct to customers by post. Orders are obtained from an illustrated catalogue supplied by the firm or by agents, who introduce the catalogue. The low costs of selling, especially the absence of retail premises, enable the mail-order houses to offer goods at competitive prices. *See also* DIRECT-MAIL SELLING.

mail shot Selling, advertising, or fund-raising material sent to all the names on a mailing list.

mail survey Marketing research conducted by mail. As respondents have time to consider their answers, this form of research has advantages over both telephone surveys and face-to-face surveys. However, it does suffer from low returns.

mainframe The largest type of *computer, requiring an air-conditioned room and special staff to run it. Used by large organizations, such as banks, they can handle vast amounts of information with ease and calculate at high speed. They can also handle many users simultaneously (see TIME SHARING). *Compare* LOCAL AREA NETWORK; PERSONAL COMPUTER; MINICOMPUTER.

main market The premier market for the trading of *equities on the *London Stock Exchange. The *listing requirements are more stringent, and the liquidity of the market is greater, than on the *Alternative Investment Market. A company wishing to enter this market must have audited trading figures covering at least five years and must place 25% of its shares in public hands. The main market currently deals in over 2600 securities.

main product The product of a process that has the greatest economic significance. Other products of secondary economic importance are regarded as *by-products; however, if all products have equal economic significance they are regarded as joint products. *See also* PROCESS COSTING.

mainstream corporation tax (MCT) Formerly, the liability for corporation tax of a company for an accounting period after the relevant *advance corporation tax was deducted. Advance corporation tax was abolished in 1999. *See also* IMPUTATION SYSTEM.

maintenance margin The minimum *margin required in a brokerage account by a particular exchange or brokerage firm.

making a price On the *London Stock Exchange, the quoting by a *market maker of a selling price and a buying price for a particular security, usually without knowing whether the broker or other person asking for a price wishes to buy or sell. Having made a price, the market maker is bound to buy or sell at the prices quoted, though the quantity may be limited if the broker stipulates the quantity at the time of making the price.

Malcolm Baldridge National Quality Award (MBNQA) *See* BALDRIDGE AWARD.

mall intercept interviewing A form of interviewing in which shoppers are intercepted in the public areas of shopping centres and malls to be interviewed face-to-face. The population samples so selected are usually *judgement samples or convenience samples.

maloti *See* LOTI.

malpractice insurance *See* PROFESSIONAL INDEMNITY INSURANCE.

managed costs *See* DISCRETIONARY COSTS.

managed currency (managed floating) A currency in which the government influences the exchange rate. This control is exerted by the central bank buying and selling in the foreign-exchange market and by its overall economic policy. *See also* CLEAN FLOATING.

managed fund A fund, made up of investments in a wide range of financial obligations, that is actively managed by a life-assurance company to provide low risk investments for the smaller investor, usually in the form of *investment bonds, *unit trusts, or unit-linked saving plans (see UNIT-LINKED POLICY). The *fund managers will have a stated investment policy favouring a specific category of investments.

managed PEP *See* PERSONAL EQUITY PLAN.

managed unit trust *See* MANAGED FUND.

management 1. The running of an organization or part of it. Management has perhaps three main components: an organizational skill, an entrepreneurial sense, and an ability to get the best out of followers. The organizational skill, involving many traditional principles and techniques of management, is taught at col-

leges and business schools (*see* ADMINIS-
TRATIVE MANAGEMENT; SCIENTIFIC MANAGE-
MENT); the entrepreneurial sense,
recognizing and making use of opportunities, predicting market needs and trends,
and achieving one's goals by sustained
drive, skilful negotiation, and articulate
advocacy, is not so easily taught, although
contact with the market place in association with a successful entrepreneur will
encourage an inherent ability to develop.
The third component, the ability to motivate subordinates, has become an increasingly prominent part of management
theory and training (*see* LEADERSHIP STYLE;
LEADERSHIP THEORY; MOTIVATION), although the extent to which such leadership skills can be taught in the abstract
remains disputable. *See also* ACTIVE MAN-
AGEMENT; CHANGE MANAGEMENT; CONFLICT
MANAGEMENT; DIVERSITY MANAGEMENT;
HIGH-INVOLVEMENT MANAGEMENT; HUMAN-
RESOURCE MANAGEMENT; SALESFORCE MAN-
AGEMENT; SUPPLY-CHAIN MANAGEMENT;
TOTAL QUALITY MANAGEMENT.
2. The people involved in the running of
an organization. **Top management** includes the *chief executive (*see also* MANAG-
ING DIRECTOR) of an organization, his
deputy or deputies, the board of *directors, and the managers in charge of the divisions or departments of the
organization. **Middle management** consists
largely of the managers to whom top management delegates the day-to-day running
of the organization.

Management is traditionally broken
down into the categories formalized in
*line and staff management: the line man-
agers organize the production of the
goods or oversee the services provided by
the organization, while the staff management provides such support as personnel
management, transport management, service management, etc.

management accounting The techniques used to collect, process, and present financial and quantitative data within
an organization to help effective performance measurement, cost control, planning, pricing, and decision making to take
place. The major professional body of
management accountants in the UK is the
Chartered Institute of Management Accountants (CIMA).

management audit An independent
review of the management of an organization, carried out by a firm of *management consultants specializing in this type
of review. The review will cover all aspects
of running the organization, including the
control of production, marketing, sales,
finance, personnel, warehousing, etc.

management buy-in The acquisition
of a company by an outside team of managers, usually specially formed for the purpose, often backed by a venture-capital
organization. Their normal target is the
small family-owned company, which the
owners wish to sell, or occasionally an unwanted subsidiary of a public company.

management buy-out (MBO) The acquisition of a company or a subsidiary by
the existing management. It is frequently
used as a means of *divestment by companies seeking to focus on their core activities. The new owner-managers of the
buy-out frequently improve its performance as they usually are well aware of
any remedial action required and have a
serious incentive in the form of their
equity stake. Additional capital is provided
by financial institutions and venture capitalists and also in many cases by allowing
other employees to buy shares. In a few
instances, all employees have participated
in a buy-out; these are sometimes called
employee buy-outs. Some very large companies have been bought out by management, but many of these have suffered
from unrealistically high levels of debt (in
the form of loan capital), which has restricted their successful recovery and
longer-term viability.

management by exception **1.** A principle of management in which a management decision that cannot be made at one
level is passed up to the next level for a
decision; i.e. exceptional decisions are
passed up the management tree. **2.** The
principle used in *budgetary control in
which items of income or expenditure
that show no *variances or small variances require no action, whereas exceptional items showing adverse variances to
an unacceptable degree require action to
be taken.

management by objectives (MBO) A
management technique in which all levels

of management are encouraged to specify and agree quantitative and/or qualitative objectives to be achieved within a set period and to answer to higher levels of management for the actual performance achieved against these objectives.

management by walking around (MBWA) The practice by managers of spending a significant part of their time listening to staff problems and ideas while walking around an office or plant. The opportunity to communicate with managers can be seen as providing an important contribution to staff motivation.

management company A company that manages *unit trusts. Its fees, known as **management charges**, are usually stated in the agreement setting up the trust; they are paid by the unit holders.

management consultant A professional adviser who specializes in giving advice to organizations on ways for improving their efficiency and hence their profitability. They come into an organization as total outsiders, uninfluenced by either internal politics or personal relationships, and analyse the way the business is run. At the end of a period, during which two or more members of the consultant firm have spent a considerable time in the organization, they provide a detailed report, giving their suggestions for improving efficiency. Their advice usually spans board-level policy-making and planning, the use of available resources (department by department), the best use of manpower, and a critical assessment of industrial relations, production, marketing, and sales.

Management Consultancies Association (MCA) An association founded in 1956 to establish and maintain the professional standards of the management consultancy profession in the UK.

management contracting The practice in which a domestic firm supplies the management know-how to a foreign company that provides the capital in order to create a *joint venture; the domestic firm exports management services rather than products.

management development The process of ensuring that an organization has the appropriate management skills and competencies to meet its developing needs. Existing skills and abilities are assessed and actual or potential shortfalls are identified with the aim of ameliorating them. Various programmes and interventions may be used for this purpose, including training, *mentoring, or role-play and *team-building exercises.

management discussion and analysis (MD&A) In the USA, the section in the annual report to stockholders (*see* ANNUAL ACCOUNTS) and in *Form 10-K that is required by the *Securities and Exchange Commission. The purpose of the MD&A is to assist investors to understand the impact of changes in accounting and business activity that have affected comparisons with the results of previous years. Management should summarize and discuss, among other matters, the reasons for changes in the results of operations, capital resources, and liquidity. In the UK, the *operating and financial review is modelled to some extent on the MD&A.

management information system (MIS) An information system designed to provide financial and quantitative information to all the levels of management in an organization. Most modern management information systems provide the data from an integrated computer *database, which is constantly updated from all areas of the organization in a structured way. Access to the data is usually restricted to the areas regarded as useful to particular managers, access to confidential information is limited to top management. An MIS should run parallel to the configuration of the physical and organizational structures. The systematic application of *information technology has enabled MIS to drive these structures.

management letter A letter written by an auditor to the management of a client company at the end of the annual *audit to suggest any possible improvements that could be made to the company's accounting and internal control system or to communicate any other such information that the auditor believes would be of benefit to the client.

management services The department of an organization that is concerned with systematic attempts to improve its productivity and quality of output through such methods as *industrial engineering, *work studies, *systems analysis, and *business process re-engineering. Professionals in these fields qualify through the *Institute of Management Services.

managing director (MD) The company director responsible for the day-to-day running of a company. Second in the hierarchy only to the *chairman, if there is one, the managing director is the company's *chief executive, a title that is becoming increasingly popular in both the USA and the UK. In the USA the *president is often the equivalent of the MD. If a company has more than one MD, they are known as **joint managing directors**.

manat **1.** (AZM) The standard monetary unit of Azerbaijan, divided into 100 gopik. **2.** (TMM) The standard monetary unit of Turkmenistan, divided into 100 tenesi.

mandate **1.** A written authority given by one person (the **mandator**) to another (the **mandatory**) giving the mandatory the power to act on behalf of the mandator. It comes to an end on the death, mental illness, or bankruptcy of the mandator. **2.** A document instructing a bank to open an account in the name of the mandator (customer), giving details of the way it is to be run, and providing specimen signatures of those authorized to sign cheques, etc.

mandatory liquid assets Certain *liquid assets, the structure and nature of which is defined by regulatory requirement, that a bank is required to maintain on its balance sheet. Such a policy may be implemented as an instrument of monetary control or as a protection against 'runs' on particular banks. The regulatory trend is away from this type of control, since it often gives a market advantage to short-term government debt, which is a major part of the specified assets.

man-hour (person-hour) The amount of work done by one person in one hour. It is sometimes convenient in costing a job to estimate the number of man-hours it will take.

manifest A list of all the cargo carried by a ship or aircraft. It has to be signed by the captain (or first officer) before being handed to the customs on leaving and arriving at a port or airport.

manufacturer brand A *brand name created by a manufacturer. Kellogs and Polaroid are examples.

manufacturer's agent A commission agent who usually has a *franchise to sell a particular manufacturer's products in a particular country or region for a given period.

manufacturers' recommended price (MRP) *See* RECOMMENDED RETAIL PRICE.

manufacturing account (manufacturing statement) An accounting statement forming part of the internal final accounts of a manufacturing organization; for a particular period, it is constructed to show, inter alia, *direct cost of sales, *manufacturing overhead, total *production cost, and *cost of goods manufactured. In some cases a *manufacturing profit is also computed.

manufacturing cost of finished goods *See* COST OF GOODS MANUFACTURED.

manufacturing costs (manufacturing expenses) Items of expenditure incurred to carry out the manufacturing process in an organization. They include *direct materials, *direct labour, *direct expenses (such as subcontract costs), and *manufacturing overhead. *See* COST OF GOODS MANUFACTURED; COST OF SALES.

manufacturing overhead (factory overhead; production overhead) The costs of production that cannot be traced directly to the product or *cost unit. Apart from the *direct costs, all other costs incurred in the manufacturing process are the manufacturing overhead; examples include depreciation of machinery, factory rent and business rates, cleaning materials, and maintenance expenses.

manufacturing profit/loss (production profit/loss) The difference between the value of the goods transferred from a *manufacturing account to a *trading account at a price other than the *cost of goods manufactured, and the cost of goods manufactured. This difference is measured in organizations wishing to submit the production department to market prices; it involves crediting production according to some formula, such as a price per unit.

maquiladora (Spanish: twin-plant) The US practice of building factories that straddle the US–Mexican border, enabling US companies to take advantage of lower Mexican labour costs.

Mareva injunction *See* FREEZING INJUNCTION.

margin **1.** The *profit margin on sales of goods or services. It is often expressed as a percentage of revenue. *See* GROSS PROFIT; GROSS PROFIT PERCENTAGE; NET PROFIT; NET PROFIT PERCENTAGE. *See also* CONTRIBUTION; MARK-UP. **2.** The difference between the prices at which a *market maker or commodity dealer will buy and sell. This is also known as the *bid–offer spread and colloquially as a **haircut**. **3.** In banking, the difference between the rate of interest on funds lent and funds borrowed by a bank. **4.** Money or securities advanced by a client to a stockbroker or dealer to cover any possible losses the client may make. *See* MARGIN CALL.

marginal cost The additional cost incurred as a result of the production of one additional unit of production. In accounting, it usually equates to the variable costs per unit of production. The variable costs are usually regarded as the direct costs plus the variable overheads.

marginal costing (direct costing; variable costing) A costing and decision-making technique that charges only the *marginal costs to the *cost unit and treats the *fixed costs as a lump sum to be deducted from the total *contribution, in obtaining the profit or loss for the period. In some cases, *inventory valuation is also at marginal cost, although this approach does not conform to *Statement of Standard Accounting Practice 9 and is used for internal reporting purposes only. *Compare* ABSORPTION COSTING.

marginal cost pricing The setting of product selling prices based on the charging of *marginal costs only to the product. The approach is only likely to be used in exceptional circumstances, such as when competition is intensive, as its application to the complete range of products is likely to cause the business to make losses by its failure to cover its *fixed costs. *Compare* COST-PLUS PRICING; FULL COST PRICING.

marginal-cost transfer prices *Transfer prices set by *marginal cost pricing. When there is no market for the goods and services that are bought and sold between the divisions of an organization, the transfer price should be the marginal cost, which is normally assumed to be short-term *variable cost. Setting transfer prices equal to marginal costs helps managers to identify the output levels that will maximize profits. There can be problems if managers do not have accurate cost information.

marginal rate of tax The amount of extra tax that is incurred if a taxpayer earns £1 more than his or her current income. Under a *progressive tax regime, the marginal rate of tax rises as incomes rise. *See also* ABILITY TO PAY.

marginal relief (small companies relief) In the UK, relief available when the profits chargeable to *corporation tax of a company fall between the upper and lower limits for the financial year (currently between £300,000 and £1,500,000). Since 1999 marginal relief has also been available for very small companies whose total profits fall between £10,000 (currently the threshold for the starting rate of corporation tax) and £50,000.

marginal revenue The additional revenue that a producer will achieve by selling one additional unit of production.

margin call A call to a client from his commodity broker or stockbroker to increase his *margin, i.e. the amount of money or securities deposited with the broker as a safeguard. This usually happens if the client has an *open position in a market that is moving adversely for this position.

margin of safety The difference between the level of activity at which an organization breaks even and a given level of activity greater than the *breakeven point. The margin of safety may be expressed in the same terms as the breakeven point, i.e. sales value, number of units, or percentage of capacity.

margin of safety ratio The *margin of

safety expressed as a percentage of a given level of activity. For example, if the sales level achieved is £500,000 and the sales level breakeven point is £400,000, the margin of safety is £100,000 and the margin of safety ratio will be:

(£100,000 × 100)/£500,000 = 20%.

marine insurance The insurance of ships or their cargo against specified causes of loss or damage that might be encountered at sea. The definition has widened over the years to include the transit of cargo over land at each end of the voyage and the term 'vessel' now extends to include ships under construction or repair and drilling rigs.

marked cheque A cheque that the bank on which it is drawn has marked 'good for payment'. This practice has been replaced in the UK by *bank drafts, although it is still used in the USA, where such cheques are called **certified checks**.

marker barrel A standard oil price based on one barrel of Saudi Arabian oil or some other internationally recognized oil (e.g. North Sea Brent crude). It sets standard prices for oil in the rest of the world.

market 1. An arena in which buyers and sellers exchange goods and services, usually for money. It does not have to have a physical location. **2.** An organized gathering for trading in financial obligations, such as a stock exchange, commodity market, etc. **3.** The demand for a particular product or service, often measured by sales during a specified period.

marketable security A *security (stock, share, bond, etc.) that can be bought or sold on a *stock exchange. *Compare* NON-MARKETABLE SECURITIES.

Market and Opinion Research International (MORI) A marketing research organization engaged in a wide variety of research activities. It is best known for its social and political research and its MORI opinion polls.

market assessment The identification and evaluation of a market for a particular good or service to ascertain its size and to estimate the price that the product or service would command. *See also* MARKETING RESEARCH.

market-based transfer prices *Transfer prices that are based on market prices. When there is a perfectly competitive market for the goods and services that are bought and sold between divisions of an organization, the transfer price should be the market price. The transfer price may be slightly lower than the market price if the selling expenses are lower for interdivisional transfers, e.g. because there is no advertising cost for transfers between divisions. There is a problem for managers in that market prices may fluctuate.

market capitalization (market valuation) The value of a company obtained by multiplying the number of its issued shares by their *market price.

market-centred company A company that pays balanced attention to both customers and competitors in designing its marketing strategies.

market challenger A firm that is fighting to increase its market share. Generally, such a company is second in market share and aggressively challenging the *market leader.

market development A strategy by which an organization attempts to sell an existing product to new customers, usually by introducing the product in a new geographical area. *See* PRODUCT–MARKET STRATEGY.

market failure A situation in which a market does not operate efficiently. Factors that may cause market failure include the possession of *market power by transactors, *externalities, or information problems. *See also* EFFICIENT MARKETS HYPOTHESIS.

market follower A firm that is usually second to the *market leader in an industry and wants to hold its share without upsetting the status quo. Market followers do not want to challenge the leader, but can maintain their market share with much lower investment costs than the leader.

market forces The forces of supply and demand that in a *free market determine the quantity available of a particular product or service and the price at which it is offered. In general, a rise in demand will cause both supply and price to increase, while a rise in supply will cause both a fall in price and a drop in demand, although many markets have individual features that modify this simple analysis.

marketing The process of planning and executing the conception, pricing, promotion, and distribution of ideas, products, and services to create exchanges that will satisfy the needs of individuals and organizations. Marketing a product involves such tasks as anticipating changes in demand (usually on the basis of *marketing research), promotion of the product (see SALES PROMOTION), ensuring that its quality, availability, and price meet the needs of the market, and providing after-sales service. See also DIRECT MARKETING.

marketing audit A review of an organization's marketing capabilities based on a structured appraisal of a marketing department's internal strengths and weaknesses, which helps the company decide how best to respond to external opportunities and threats. Sales are analysed, the effectiveness of the *marketing mix is assessed, and, externally, the *marketing environment is monitored. When the marketing audit has been completed, a *marketing plan is drawn up based on its results.

marketing control The process of measuring and evaluating the results of *marketing strategies to ensure that corrective action can be taken to enable *marketing objectives to be attained. This is usually achieved by means of the *marketing plan.

marketing costs The costs incurred by an organization in carrying out its marketing activities. These would include sales promotion costs, salesmen's salaries, advertising, and point-of-sale promotional material, such as display stands.

marketing database An organized set of data about individual customers or prospective customers that can be used to generate and qualify customer leads, sell products and services, and maintain customer relationships.

marketing environment The combined influence of all the factors external to a company that could affect its sales. These factors include: cultural traditions, technological developments, competitors'

activity, government policies, and changes in distribution channels. The marketing environment cannot be controlled by the company and, because it may change frequently, requires constant monitoring.

marketing implementation The process that converts *marketing strategies and plans into action in order to accomplish *marketing objectives.

marketing information system (MIS) An organized set of procedures and methods by which pertinent, timely, and accurate information is continually gathered, analysed, and evaluated for use by marketing decision makers. Most systems are computerized and consist of a data-collection system and a *decision support system.

marketing intelligence system A network of diverse sources that provides data about the *marketing environment; it forms part of an organization's data-collection system. The data should include customers, sales personnel, suppliers, retailers, agencies, competitors' activities, and government bodies.

marketing intermediaries Firms that help a company to promote, sell, and distribute its products to final buyers. They include middlemen, wholesalers, retailers, distribution firms, marketing-service agencies, and financial intermediaries.

marketing logistics See LOGISTICS; PHYSICAL DISTRIBUTION.

marketing management The planning and implementation of programmes designed to create, build, and maintain sales of a product. This is achieved by the *marketing mix.

marketing mix The factors controlled by a company that can influence consumers' buying of its products. The four components of a marketing mix (often called the **four Ps**) are:
- the product — quality, branding, packaging, and other features;
- pricing — recommended retail price, discounts for large orders, and credit terms;
- promotion — see SALES PROMOTION;
- place — where to sell the product, which distributors and transport services to use, and desirable stock levels.

The potential profitability of a particular marketing mix and its acceptability to its market are assessed by *marketing research. *See also* EXTENDED MARKETING MIX.

marketing myopia A failure to define an organization's purpose in terms of its function from the consumers' point of view. For example, railway companies that define their markets in terms of trains, rather than transportation, fail to recognize the challenge of competition from cars, airlines, and buses. It is therefore necessary to define the needs of the consumer in more general terms rather than product-specific terms.

marketing objective A statement about the level of performance an organization, business unit, or operating unit intends to achieve. Objectives must be defined in measurable terms.

marketing plan A detailed statement (usually prepared annually) of how a company's *marketing mix will be used to achieve its *market objectives. A marketing plan is usually prepared following a *marketing audit.

marketing research The systematic collection and analysis of data to resolve problems concerning *marketing, undertaken to reduce the risk of inappropriate marketing activity. Data is almost always collected from a *sample of the target market, by such methods as observation, interviews, and audit of shop sales. Interviews (*see* OPEN-ENDED QUESTION; STRUCTURED INTERVIEW) are the most common technique, and can be carried out face-to-face, by telephone, or by post. When the results have been analysed (usually by computer), recommendations regarding the original problem can be made. *See also* QUALITATIVE MARKETING RESEARCH; QUANTITATIVE MARKETING RESEARCH.

Market research, which is often used synonymously with the preferred term 'marketing research', is more correctly used to refer to research with the restricted objective of discovering the size of the market for a particular brand or product.

marketing-service agency A marketing research firm, advertising agency, marketing consultancy firm, or other service provider that helps a company to promote its products in the market.

marketing strategy A plan identifying what marketing goals and objectives will be pursued to sell a particular product or product line and how these objectives will be achieved in the time available.

marketing website A site on the *World Wide Web created by a company to interact with consumers for the purpose of moving them closer to a purchase or other marketing outcome. The site is designed to handle interactive communication initiated by the company.

market leader The firm in a particular industry with the largest market share. The market leader usually dominates other firms in price changes, the introduction of new products, distribution coverage, and promotion spending. This firm may or may not be admired by other companies, but generally these companies accept the dominance.

market maker **1.** Any intermediary who creates a market for a financial obligation. **2.** A dealer in securities on the *London Stock Exchange who undertakes to buy and sell securities as a principal and is therefore obliged to announce buying and selling prices for a particular security at a particular time. Before October 1986 (*see* BIG BANG) this function was performed by a *stockjobber, who was then obliged to deal with the public through a *stockbroker. Since that date market makers have combined dealing in securities as principals with acting as agents, working for a commission. While this dual role may create a conflict of interest for market makers (*see* CHINESE WALL; FRONT RUNNING), it avoids the restrictive trade practice of the former system and reduces the cost of dealing in the market.

market manager An individual responsible for administering all the marketing activities of a company that relate to a particular market, including forecasting, product planning, and pricing.

market objectives The objectives to be fulfilled by a *marketing plan. Marketing objectives are determined by interpreting the relevant parts of a corporate plan (*see*

BUSINESS PLAN) in the light of a *marketing audit.

market order *See* AT BEST.

market orientation *See* PRODUCT ORIENTATION.

market overhang The situation in which sellers, worried by falling prices, prefer to postpone their sales until there is greater market demand. By reducing transactions, this behaviour can itself delay the hoped for recovery.

market penetration (penetration)
1. The process of entering a market to establish a new brand or product. Market penetration may be achieved by offering the brand or product at a low initial price to familiarize the public with its name. This is known as **market-penetration pricing**. **2.** The extent to which a product or an advertisement has been accepted by, or has registered with, the total number of possible users. It is usually expressed as a percentage. *Compare* MARKET SHARE. **3.** A marketing strategy based on low prices and extensive advertising to increase a product's market share. For penetration strategy to be effective the market will have to be large enough to be able to sustain low profit margins. *See* PRODUCT–MARKET STRATEGY.

market portfolio *See* MARKOWITZ MODEL.

market positioning *See* POSITIONING.

market power The ability of a transactor to influence market prices, owing to the very large share of the demand or supply in a particular market that this transactor controls. The major UK supermarkets are often said to possess market power of this kind.

market price The price of a raw material, product, service, security, etc., in an open market. In formal markets, such as a stock exchange, commodity market, foreign-exchange market, etc., there is often a *margin between the buying and selling price; there are, therefore, two market prices. In these circumstances the market prices often quoted are the average of the buying and selling price (*see* MIDDLE PRICE). *See also* MARKET VALUE.

market price to book ratio *See* BOOK VALUE.

market–product strategy *See* PRODUCT-MARKET STRATEGY.

market rate of discount *See* BILL RATE.

market research *See* MARKETING RESEARCH.

Market Research Society (MRS) A professional association in the UK for those who use survey techniques for marketing, social, and economic research. The MRS aims to maintain professional standards, to provide its members with training programmes and information about new techniques, and to represent the interests of its members to government and commerce.

market risk The *risk inherent in dealing on a market where prices may change. The obvious market risks are buying on a market that subsequently falls and selling on a market that rises; these risks can be reduced by hedging (*see* HEDGE), especially by means of *futures contracts or *options, but they can never be eliminated. These forms of market risk are the obverse of the market opportunities that provide speculators with the chance of making a profit.

market segmentation The division of a *market into homogeneous groups of consumers, each of which can be expected to respond to a different *marketing mix. There are numerous ways of segmenting markets, the more traditional being by age, sex, family size, income, occupation, and social class; more recently *geodemographic segmentation, which identifies housing areas in which people share a common lifestyle and will be more likely to buy certain types of products, has become more popular. Another frequently used method is *benefit segmentation. Once a segment has been identified, the marketer can then develop a unique marketing mix to reach it, for example by advertising only in the newspapers read by that market segment. Therefore, to be of practical value a market segment must be large enough to warrant the development costs.

market share The share of the total sales of all brands or products competing in the same market that is captured by one particular brand or product, usually expressed as a percentage. For example, if brands A, B, and C are the competing brands of a product and in a particular month they achieved sales of £48,000, £62,000, and £90,000, respectively, brand A's market share would be (48,000/(48,000 + 62,000 + 90,000)) × 100 = 24%.

market-skimming pricing Setting a high price for a new product in order to skim the maximum revenues, layer by layer, from the market segments willing to pay the high price. Using this high-price strategy, the company makes fewer but more profitable sales.

marketspace (electronic marketspace) A virtual marketplace, such as the Internet, in which no direct contact occurs between buyers and sellers.

market targeting The process of evaluating each market segment and selecting the most attractive segments to enter with a particular product or product line.

market testing *See* TEST MARKETING.

market timing An investment strategy based on the forecasting of changes in the direction of market prices. However, there is little evidence to suggest that investors can apply such a strategy systematically and even if it were possible, it would violate the *efficient markets hypothesis.

market-to-book ratio *See* BOOK VALUE.

market valuation *See* MARKET CAPITALIZATION.

market value **1. (market capitalization)** The value of a company obtained by multiplying the number of its issued ordinary shares by their *market price. This may differ widely from the *book value of the company. **2. (open market value; OMV)** The value of an asset if it were to be sold on the open market at its current *market price. When land is involved it may be necessary to distinguish between the market value in its present use and that in some alternative use; for example, a factory site may have a market value as a factory site, and be so valued in the company's accounts, which may be less than its market value as building land. *See* FAIR VALUE.

markings The official number of bargains that have taken place during a working day on the *London Stock Exchange.

marking to market The valuation of financial obligations according to current *market prices.

marking to model The valuation of financial obligations according to pricing models. This occurs when there is not a current market price for the obligation, for example in relation to derivatives sold on the *over-the-counter market.

markka (Fmk) The former standard monetary unit of Finland, divided into 100 penniä. It was absorbed into the euro for all purposes other than cash transactions in January 1999 and abolished in 2002.

Markowitz model A method of selecting the optimum investment *portfolio, devised by H. M. Markowitz (1927–   ) and for which he received the Nobel prize in Economics in 1990. It assumes that investors are interested in the average return on a risky investment and the standard deviation of those returns. Investors are risk-averse, which means they like higher returns and dislike higher standard deviations of returns. It concludes that investors should diversify as widely as possible and decide the level of risk and return they choose by the proportions they borrow, lend, and invest in risky assets.

mark-up The amount by which the cost of a service or product has been increased to arrive at the selling price. It is calculated by expressing the *profit as a percentage of the cost of the good or service. For example, if a product cost £8 and is sold for £12, the mark-up would be:

£4/£8 × 100 = 50%.

Note that the *margin is calculated by expressing the profit as a percentage of the selling price; in this case it would be:

£4/£12 × 100 = 33.3%.

The mark-up is widely used in retailing, both for setting prices and as a ratio for control and decision making. *See* GROSS PROFIT PERCENTAGE; NET PROFIT PERCENTAGE.

Maslow's motivational hierarchy (Maslow's hierarchy of needs) A model of human *motivation developed by the US psychologist Abraham Maslow (1908–70). It posits a hierarchy of human needs (or motives) with five levels: physiological needs, such as food and sleep; safety needs; love needs; esteem needs, such as competence and recognition; and meta needs, such as the needs for beauty, knowledge, and *self-actualization. Essentially, the higher levels of motivation come into play after the lower needs have been satisfied. Maslow developed this model largely as a reaction against behaviouristic theories of motivation, which focus on the role of physical and material rewards. It has proved widely influential in *human relations theory and other aspects of industrial and organizational psychology. *See also* ERG THEORY.

mass customization The ability to create tailored marketing messages or products for individual customers, or a group of similar customers (a bespoke service), while retaining the *economies of scale and the capacity of mass marketing or production.

mass marketing Marketing in which the same product, price, promotion, and distribution is used for all consumers in a particular market.

mass media *See* MEDIA.

mass production *See* LINE PRODUCTION.

mass service technology The type of technology used in labour-intensive service industries, with low customer contact, e.g. university teaching. *Compare* PROFESSIONAL SERVICE TECHNOLOGY.

master The captain of a merchant ship.

master production schedule (MPS) A schedule developed from firm orders or from forecasts of demand. The MPS is a key input into a *material requirements planning (MRP) system. The MPS identifies how many of each end product need to be produced and when they need to be produced by within each planning period. This data forms one of three key inputs enabling an MRP system to produce detailed timings for component manufacture and material purchases. It summarizes what the business plans to make and drives the operation in terms of what is assembled, what is made, and what is bought in. In addition it forms the basis for planning the utilization of labour and equipment and determines the requirements for materials and cash.

matched bargain A transaction in which a sale of a particular quantity of stock is matched with a purchase of the same quantity of the same stock. Transactions of this kind are carried out on the *London Stock Exchange by **matching brokers**.

matched sale–purchase agreement (MSP) A device used by the US Federal Reserve in which it sells money-market instruments for immediate effect and couples the sale with the forward purchase of the same instrument, to facilitate the distribution of reserves of the banking system.

material adverse change A clause in a loan agreement or bank facility stating that the loan will become repayable if there should a material change in the borrower's credit standing. The clause can be contentious because it is not always clear what constitutes a material change.

material fact **1.** Any important piece of information that a person seeking insurance must disclose to the insurer to enable the insurer to decide whether or not to accept the insurance and to calculate the premium. What is and what is not material may have to be decided by a court of law, but very often it is obvious. While a person cannot be penalized for not revealing facts that are not known or cannot reasonably be expected to be known, an insurance contract can become void if the facts have been deliberately concealed from the insurer if they could have influenced the acceptance of the risk, the premium charged, or the exceptions made. **2.** Relevant information about a company that must be made public in its *prospectus, if it is seeking a flotation on a stock exchange. **3.** Any information that could be provided by a witness in court proceedings and could influence the decision of the court.

materiality The extent to which an item of accounting information is material. Information is considered material if its omission from a *financial statement could influence the decision making of its users. Materiality is therefore not an absolute concept but is dependent on the size and nature of an item and the particular circumstances in which it arises.

material requirements planning (MRP) A computer-based information system that uses known orders and forecast orders to produce a commitment to manufacture a given number of products in a given period. MRP is often divided into two phases: MRPI produces the commitment to manufacture, while MRPII develops the concept to assess the financial implications of the material requirements.

materials cost The expenditure incurred by an organization on *direct materials or *indirect materials. The expenditure on direct materials is part of *direct cost of sales and that on indirect materials is a *manufacturing overhead.

materials management *See* SUPPLY-CHAIN MANAGEMENT.

maternity rights The rights of a woman when she is absent from work because of her pregnancy or confinement. The current law is contained in the Employment Rights Act (1996) as supplemented by the Maternity and Parental Leave Regulations (1999 and 2002). There are currently seven statutory rights:

(1) All pregnant employees are entitled to reasonable time off work, with pay, for antenatal care.

(2) An employee is entitled not to be dismissed because of pregnancy or any reason connected with it.

(3) A pregnant employee who meets certain qualifying conditions is entitled to receive **statutory maternity pay** from her employer for up to 26 weeks. Employers can recover 92% of such payments by setting the amount against their National Insurance payments.

(4) An employee who continues to be employed by her employer until the beginning of the 11th week before the expected week of confinement is entitled to **maternity leave** of at least 26 weeks. Additional maternity leave of up to 26 weeks from the end of ordinary maternity leave is also available to employees who have completed a minimum of 26 weeks' service by the 14th week before the expected week of confinement.

(5) An employee entitled to maternity leave is also entitled to return to work with her employer, provided that the employer employs more than five people.

(6) Throughout the maternity leave period the employee is entitled to continue to benefit from all contractual terms of her employment with the exception of remuneration (money payment).

(7) Pregnant women, and women who have recently given birth or who are breastfeeding, have the right to be offered any suitable alternative work, rather than being suspended on maternity-related health and safety grounds.

In the UK men enjoyed no statutory **paternity rights** until 1999, when an EU directive was adopted into British law entitling a parent of either sex to take a total of 13 weeks unpaid leave in the first five years of a child's life (but only four weeks in any one year). New fathers became entitled to two weeks' statutory paternity pay in April 2003. A growing number of companies now operate contractual schemes providing for a period of paid and/or unpaid paternity leave.

mate's receipt A document signed by the mate of a ship as proof that the goods specified in the document have been loaded onto his ship, especially if they have been delivered direct to the ship, rather than from a quayside warehouse. The mate's receipt functions as a document of title, which may be required as proof of loading in a *free on board (FOB) contract, pending the issue of the *bill of lading.

matrix organization A management structure in an organization in which some employees report to two (or more) managers in different departments. It is often used if two separate areas of the external environment demand management attention. For example, if a wholesaler of an organization's product requires extra credit, the distribution management and the finance management would both need to be consulted. In effect, this would involve the employees concerned in a multiple-authority structure rather than a simple chain of command (see diagram on p. 338).

maturity date The date on which a doc-

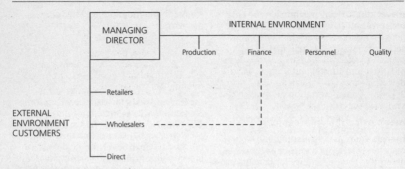

Matrix organization

ument, such as a *bond, *bill of exchange, or insurance policy, becomes due for payment. In some cases, especially for redeemable government stocks, the maturity date is known as the **redemption date**. *See also* REDEMPTION.

maturity stage *See* PRODUCT LIFE CYCLE.

maximum allowable cycle time The maximum time that can elapse between consecutive items leaving a production process, if the designated *capacity of the process is to be achieved.

maximum fluctuation The maximum daily price fluctuation that is permitted on a financial market. *See* LIMIT.

maximum investment plan (MIP) A unit-linked endowment policy marketed by a life-assurance company that is designed to produce maximum profit rather than life-assurance protection. It calls for regular premiums, usually over ten years, with options to continue. These policies normally enable a tax-free fund to be built up over ten years and, because of the regular premiums, *pound cost averaging can be used, linked to a number of markets. Such investment products are now largely obsolete, since there is now a general preference for separating the life assurance and investment elements of products.

maximum slippage The period between the date on which a new company expects to start earning income and the date up to which it can survive on its venture capital. After this date has passed, the company would be unable to raise further

funds and would sink into insolvency. *See also* DEATH-VALLEY CURVE.

MB Abbreviation for *megabyte.

MBA Abbreviation for Master of Business Administration.

MBNQA Abbreviation for Malcolm Baldridge National Quality Award. *See* BALDRIDGE AWARD.

MBO 1. Abbreviation for *management buy-out. **2.** Abbreviation for *management by objectives.

MBWA Abbreviation for *management by walking around.

MCA Abbreviation for *Management Consultancies Association.

MCT 1. Abbreviation for Member of the *Association of Corporate Treasurers. **2.** Abbreviation for *mainstream corporation tax.

MD Abbreviation for *managing director.

MDS Abbreviation for *multi-dimensional scaling.

mean *See* ARITHMETIC MEAN; GEOMETRIC MEAN. *Compare* MEDIAN.

mean absolute deviation (MAD) A measure of forecast error, for example when carrying out *adaptive exponential smoothing of time-series data. MAD is the average forecast error, either positive or negative, calculated as the sum of the absolute value of forecast error for all periods, divided by the total number of periods evaluated.

mean deviation In statistics, the *arithmetic mean of the deviations (all taken as positive numbers) of all the numbers in a set of numbers from their arithmetic mean. For example, the arithmetic mean of 5, 8, 9, and 10 is 8, and therefore the deviations from this mean are 3, 0, 1, and 2, giving a mean deviation of 1.5. *Compare* STANDARD DEVIATION.

mean price *See* MIDDLE PRICE.

means test Any assessment of the income and capital of a person or family to determine their eligibility for benefits provided by the state or a charity.

measurability The degree to which the size, purchasing power, and profitability of a market segment can be measured.

measured daywork A method of assessing wages in which a daily production target is set and a daily wage agreed on this basis. If the target is reached the worker receives the agreed daily wage; if it is not reached (or is exceeded) the worker is paid pro rata.

measurement tonnage *See* TONNAGE.

mechanical observation Observation techniques involving mechanical observers either in conjunction with, or in place of, human observers. Examples include the motion-picture or video camera, the *audimeter, the psychogalvanometer, the eye-camera, and the pupilometer. None of these would be used without the knowledge and permission of the respondent.

mechanistic organization An organization characterized by clearly specified roles and clear definitions of the rights and obligations of individuals within the hierarchical structure. Interaction and communication are largely vertical. This type of structure is appropriate if the environment is certain. *Compare* ORGANIC ORGANIZATION.

media (mass media) The means, such as television, radio, newspapers, and magazines, by which advertisers, politicians, etc., communicate with large numbers of members of the general public.

media analysis (media research; media planning; media selection) An investigation into the relative effectiveness and the relative costs of using the various advertising *media in an advertising campaign. Before committing an advertising budget it is necessary to carry out marketing research on potential customers, their reading habits, television-watching habits, how many times the advertisers wish the potential customers to see an advertisement, how great a percentage of the market they wish to reach, etc. These elements all need to be considered and balanced to plan a campaign that will effectively reach its target audience at a reasonable cost.

media equation The equation 'media = real life', indicating that users of Internet technology treat the media as they do real social interaction; in many ways they relate to the virtual world as they relate to the real world.

media impact The qualitative value of exposure through a given medium. For example, messages on TV are likely to create more impact than messages on the radio.

median A typical value that is identified by arranging a set of numbers in an ascending or descending scale and selecting the middle number (if there are an odd number in the set) or the arithmetic mean of the middle two numbers (if there are an even number). This can give a more representative average in some circumstances than an *arithmetic mean or a *geometric mean.

MECHANISTIC ORGANIZATION		ORGANIC ORGANIZATION

CERTAINTY ◄———————————————————————► UNCERTAINTY

EXTERNAL ENVIRONMENT

Mechanistic and organic organizations

media schedule A schedule identifying the media to be used for an advertising programme and the dates on which advertisements are to appear. Decisions have to be made on:
- reach (the percentage of market that would be expected to see the ad);
- frequency (how often the target market would see the ad);
- impact (qualitative value of the ad);
- major media to be used (TV, radio, newspapers, etc.);
- media vehicles (specific media to be used, e.g. *The Times* newspaper);
- media timing (the schedule of the appearance of the ads in the chosen media).

mediation The intervention of a neutral third party in an industrial dispute. The object is to enable the two sides to reach a compromise solution to their differences, which the mediator usually does by seeing representatives of each side separately and then together. If the mediator has power to make binding awards the process is known as *arbitration; if the mediator can only suggest means of settling the dispute it is known as **conciliation**. *See* ADVISORY CONCILIATION AND ARBITRATION SERVICE.

media vehicle A specific channel, such as a particular magazine, television show, or radio programme, within each general media type.

medical insurance *See* PRIVATE HEALTH INSURANCE.

medium-dated gilt *See* GILT-EDGED SECURITY.

medium of exchange A substance or article of little intrinsic value that is used to pay for goods or services. In primitive economies various articles, such as sea shells, have been used for this purpose but *money is now used universally.

mediums *See* GILT-EDGED SECURITY.

medium-sized company A company that is entitled to certain filing exemptions because it meets two out of three of the following criteria for the current and preceding year, or the two preceding financial years:
- the company's *net worth should not exceed £11.4 million;

- the *turnover should not exceed £22.8 million
- the average number of employees should not exceed 250.

These criteria have been increased in recent years, making it more attractive for *sole proprietors and *partnerships to become *limited companies.

In a company's first *financial year it need only meet the conditions for that year; in its second financial year it may claim the filing exemptions of a medium-sized company if it met the conditions in its first financial year. A *public limited company, a banking or insurance company, an authorized person under the Financial Services Act (1986), or a member of an ineligible group may not claim medium-sized company filing exemptions.

A medium-sized company must prepare full audited *financial statements for distribution to its shareholders but it may file *abbreviated accounts instead of full accounts with the *Registrar of Companies. Further details of filing exemptions can be obtained from the Department of Trade and Industry website at www.dti.gov.uk. There is a link to the *Companies House website. *See also* SMALL COMPANY.

medium-sized group A *group that meets two out of three of the following criteria for the current and preceding year, or the two preceding financial years:
- the group's *net worth should not exceed £11.4 million net or £13.68 million gross;
- its *turnover should not exceed £22.8 million net or £27.36 million gross;
- the average number of employees should not exceed 250.

If a group is in its first financial year, it may still qualify if it falls within these limits.

A group containing a public company, a banking or insurance company, or an authorized person under the Financial Services Act (1986) is ineligible for the exemptions for medium-sized groups.

Under the Companies Act, a parent company is not required to prepare *group accounts for a financial year in which the group headed by that parent qualifies as a medium-sized group. Further details of filing exemptions can be obtained from the Department of Trade and Industry website at www.dti.gov.uk. There is a link to the *Companies House website. *See also* SMALL GROUP.

medium-term (intermediate-term) Denoting a time period of medium duration, the extent of which will differ according to context. For example, in accounting 'medium-term' describes liabilities of between one and ten years, in money markets it means maturities of greater than a year, in bond markets a period of five to ten years, and in *eurobond markets one of two to seven years.

medium-term note (MTN) An unsecured note issued in a *eurocurrency with a maturity of about three to six years.

meeting of creditors *See* CREDITORS' VOLUNTARY LIQUIDATION; LIQUIDATOR. See also feature BANKRUPTCY LAW on p. 51.

megabyte (MB) A measure of computer memory capacity, equal to one thousand *kilobytes, or 1 024 000 bytes.

meltdown A disastrous and uncontrolled fall in share prices. *Black Monday has also been called Meltdown Monday, for example. The expression is, of course, derived from the disaster that results when the core of a nuclear reactor melts uncontrollably.

member bank A bank that belongs to a central banking or clearing system. In the UK a member bank is a *commercial bank that is a member of the *Association for Payment Clearing Services. In the USA it is a commercial bank that is a member of the *Federal Reserve System.

member firm A firm of brokers or *market makers that is a member of the *London Stock Exchange. Banks, insurance companies, and overseas securities houses can now become corporate members.

member of a company A shareholder of a company whose name is entered in the *register of members. Founder members (*see* FOUNDERS' SHARES) are those who sign the *memorandum of association; anyone subsequently coming into possession of the company's shares becomes a member.

member profile The accumulated information on a member of a *community of users. This information will include details of their lifestyle, buying habits, membership of clubs, etc.

membership group A group to which a person belongs that has a direct influence on that person's behaviour.

membership rules Qualifications or characteristics required for an individual to become part of a *community of users.

members' voluntary liquidation (members' voluntary winding-up) The winding-up of a company by a special resolution of the members in circumstances in which the company is solvent. Before making the winding-up resolution, the directors must make a *declaration of solvency. It is a criminal offence to make such a declaration without reasonable grounds for believing that it is true. When the resolution has been passed, a *liquidator is appointed; if, during the course of the winding-up, the liquidator believes that the company will not be able to pay its debts, a meeting of creditors must be called and the winding-up is treated as a members' *compulsory liquidation.

memorandum of association An official document setting out the details of a *company's existence. It must be signed by the first subscribers and must contain the following information:
- the company name;
- the address of the registered office;
- the objects of the company (*see* OBJECTS CLAUSE);
- the amount of *authorized share capital and its division;
- if applicable, a statement that the company is a public company;
- if applicable, a statement of limited liability;
- in the case of a *company limited by guarantee, the amount of the guarantee.

memorandum of satisfaction A document stating that a mortgage or charge on property has been repaid. It has to be signed by all the parties concerned and a copy sent to the *Registrar of Companies, if the mortgage or charge was made by a company.

mentoring The process in which a senior employee takes an active role in a junior colleague's development. The mentor usually provides support and encouragement as well as advice on how the mentee can develop his or her competencies to progress along a successful career path. In larger organizations, mentors are often formally assigned to those at an earlier stage of their career.

menu A list of choices displayed by a computer. When many options are available the user may be presented first with a main menu, from which more detailed menus can be selected. A well-designed menu system can make a complicated program simple to use.

mercantile agent *See* FACTOR.

mercantile law The commercial law, which includes those aspects of a country's legal code that apply to banking, companies, contracts, copyrights, insolvency, insurance, patents, the sale of goods, shipping, trademarks, transport, and warehousing.

merchandising The promotion by a retailer of selected products. Commonly used techniques include displays to encourage *impulse buying, free samples and gifts, and temporary price reductions. Merchandising policy is usually designed to influence the retailer's sales pattern and is influenced by such factors as the firm's *market, the speed at which different products sell, *margins, and service considerations. Sometimes merchandising is used to attract customers into the shop rather than to promote the product itself.

merchant A trader who buys goods for resale, acting as a principal and usually holding stocks. Typically a merchant sells goods in smaller lots than he buys and often exports goods or is involved in *entrepôt trade.

merchantable quality An implied condition respecting the state of goods sold in the course of business. Such goods should be as fit for their ordinary purpose as it is reasonable to expect, taking into account any description applied to them, the price (if relevant), and all the other relevant circumstances. The condition does not apply with regard to defects specifically drawn to the buyer's attention or defects that should have been noticed in an examina-

tion of the goods before the contract was made.

merchant bank A bank that formerly specialized in financing foreign trade, an activity that often grew out of its own merchanting business. This led them into accepting *bills of exchange and functioning as accepting houses. More recently they have tended to diversify into the field of *hire-purchase finance, the granting of long-term loans (especially to companies), providing venture capital, advising companies on flotations and *takeover bids, underwriting new issues, and managing investment portfolios and unit trusts. Many of them are old-established and some offer a limited banking service. Their knowledge of international trade makes them specialists in dealing with the large multinational companies. They are most common in Europe, but some merchant banks have begun to operate in the USA; the US equivalent in terms of current activity is known as an **investment bank**. Several UK merchant banks were taken over in the 1990s either by the commercial banks or by large overseas banks.

merchant wholesaler An independently owned business that functions as a wholesaler and takes title to the merchandise it handles, i.e. it takes goods into stock and supplies its customers from stock, rather than acting as an agent or distributor for a manufacturer.

Mercosur (**Southern Common Market**) An association of South American nations formed in 1991 with the aim of establishing a common market between member states and harmonizing their economic and social policies. The current members are Argentina, Brazil, Paraguay, Uruguay, and Venezuela; Bolivia has been invited to join in 2006–07 and Chile is an associate member. In 2004 Mercosur signed a cooperation agreement with the **Andean Community** (**CAN**), which comprises Bolivia, Colombia, Ecuador, Peru, and Venezuela. The ultimate goal is now the complete integration of the two blocs to form a continent-wide association on the model of the *European Union. *See also* LATIN AMERICAN INTEGRATION ASSOCIATION.

merger A combination of two or more

businesses on a relatively equal footing that results in the creation of a new reporting entity. The shareholders of the combining entities mutually share the risks and rewards of the new entity and no one party to the merger obtains control over another. Under *Financial Reporting Standard 6, Acquisitions and Mergers, to qualify as a merger a combination must satisfy four criteria:

• no party is the acquirer or acquired;
• all parties to the combination participate in the management structure of the new entity;
• the combining entities are relatively equal in terms of size;
• the consideration received by the equity shareholders of each party consists primarily of equity shares in the combined entity, any other consideration received being relatively immaterial.

Investment banks and other financial institution often have mergers and acquisitions (M&A) departments to provide financial and other forms of support for these activities.

In the UK, approval of the *Competition Commission may be required and the merger must be conducted on lines sanctioned by the City Code on Takeovers and Mergers. The recently issued *International Financial Reporting Standard 3, Business Combinations, will have a major impact on accounting for mergers and acquisitions.

merger accounting A method of accounting that treats two or more businesses as combining on an equal footing. It is usually applied without any restatement of *net assets to fair value and includes the results of each of the combined entities for the whole of the *accounting period, as if they had always been combined. It does not reflect the issue of shares as an application of resources at fair value. The difference that arises on *consolidation does not represent *goodwill but is deducted from, or added to, *reserves. The recently issued *International Financial Reporting Standard 3 prohibits merger accounting for all business combinations falling within its scope. *Compare* ACQUISITION ACCOUNTING.

merger relief Relief from adding to, or setting up, a *share premium account

when issuing shares at a premium if an issuing company has secured at least a 90% equity holding in another company. This relief applies if the issuing company is providing for the allotment of equity shares in the issuing company in exchange for the equity shares (or non-equity shares) in the other company or by the cancellation of any such shares not held by the issuing company. This relief is given under section 131 of the Companies Act (1985). *See* MERGER RESERVE.

merger reserve (merger capital reserve) A *reserve credited in place of a *share premium account when *merger relief is made use of. *Goodwill on consolidation may be written off against a merger reserve (unlike the share premium account).

mergers task force An office of the European Commission that oversees the regulation of *mergers.

merit bonus A *bonus granted to an employee as a reward for good work.

message board A website showing messages and information to visitors about a specific company or area of interest.

message source The source from which an advertising message proceeds. This can be a company, its brand name, the salesperson, or the actor in the advertisement who endorses a product.

meta search engine A *search engine that submits keywords typed by users to a range of other search engines in order to increase the number of relevant pages, since different search engines may have indexed different sites.

meta tags In an HTML file (*see* HYPERTEXT), tags containing text that is not displayed by the browser. This **meta text** may summarize the content of the site (**content meta tag**) and relevant keywords (**keyword meta tag**), which are matched against the keywords typed into *search engines.

Metcalfe's law The law that the value of a network of people using the same Internet site(s) increases with the square of the number of participants. This is strictly true only if all users belong to a *community of values.

methodological log A journal of detailed and time-sequenced notes on the investigative techniques used during a market-research enquiry, with special attention to biases or distortions each technique may have introduced.

method study A critical examination of existing and proposed ways of carrying out work, with the object of seeking methods that are more effective, more efficient, or cheaper. Normally a method study is carried out before *work measurement as there is no point in measuring an inappropriate method. *See also* WORK STUDY.

METI The Japanese Ministry for Economy, Trade and Industry, formerly known as MITI (Ministry for International Trade and Industry). This government body played a vital role in Japan's postwar economic boom.

metical (*plural* **meticais**; Mt) The standard monetary unit of Mozambique, divided into 100 centavos.

metrics for Internet marketing Measures that indicate the effectiveness of *Internet marketing activities in meeting customer, business, and marketing objectives.

metric system A system of measurement based on the decimal system. It was first formalized in France at the end of the 18th century and by the 1830s was being widely adopted in Europe. In the UK, bills for its compulsory adoption were defeated in 1871 and 1907 and *Imperial units remained supreme until 1963, when the yard was redefined as 0.9144 metre and the pound as 0.453 592 37 kilogram. The Metrication Board set up in 1969 failed to achieve its target of the **metrication** of British industry by 1975. However, the Weights and Measures Act (1985), the 1994 Amendment Order, and the 1994 Regulations took into account directives issued by the European Union. As a result certain traditional units such as the hundredweight, ton, pound, ounce, yard, foot, inch, gallon, bushel, square mile, cubic yard, and cubic foot were outlawed for purposes of trade. Finally, in January 2001, the UK adopted into law an EU directive making it illegal (with a few specified exceptions) to sell goods in any measures other than the gram, kilogram, millimetre, and metre. The pint (for milk and draught beer), the mile (for road traffic signs), and the acre (for land registration) are authorized without time limit. For all scientific purposes and many trade and industrial purposes the form of the metric system known as *SI units is now in use. In the USA metrication has been even slower than in the UK.

metric ton *See* TON.

metrology The scientific study of weights and measures. The subject has long been closely associated with trade and commerce, which is based on the exchange of measured quantities of goods or services for money or measured quantities of other goods or services. *See* IMPERIAL UNITS; METRIC SYSTEM; SI UNITS.

metropolitan statistical area (MSA) A geographic unit of the US Census Bureau consisting of: (1) a city with 50 000 or more inhabitants or (2) an urbanized area of at least 50 000 inhabitants and a total population of at least 100 000 (75 000 in New England).

mezzanine finance 1. Finance, usually provided by specialist financial institutions, that is neither pure equity nor pure debt. It can take many different forms and can be secured or unsecured; it usually earns a higher rate of return than pure debt but less than equity. Conversely, it carries a higher risk than pure debt, although less than equity. It is often used in *management buy-outs. **2.** A form of finance used by venture capitalists after *seed capital has been provided.

M-form Describing a type of organizational structure consisting of a relatively large number of relatively small semi-autonomous units, which are controlled mainly by the setting of financial targets from the centre. 'M' stands for 'multidivisional'. Recent years have seen a trend towards M-form and *N-form structures.

MFR Abbreviation for *minimum funding requirement.

MICR Abbreviation for *magnetic ink character recognition.

microcomputer *See* PERSONAL COMPUTER.

microcredit The lending of small sums of money on very low security, especially to small businesses or to small producers in the developing world.

microeconomics The analysis of economic behaviour at the level of individual market participants, chiefly individual businesses or consumers. For an individual or household microeconomics is concerned with the optimal allocation of a given budget, the labour supply choice, and the effects of taxation. For a business it is largely concerned with the production process, costs, and the marketing of output, dependent on the type of competition faced. *Compare* MACROECONOMICS.

microenvironment The environment close to a company, which affects its ability to serve its customers. This includes the company itself, firms in its market channel, customer markets, and competitors. *Compare* MACROENVIRONMENT.

micromarketing A form of target marketing in which companies tailor their marketing programmes to the needs of a narrowly defined geographic, demographic, psychographic, or behavioural market segment.

microprocessor In computer technology, an integrated circuit that contains on one chip the arithmetic, logical, and control functions of the central processing unit. Microprocessors are used as control systems in many devices, including car electronics and cameras, as well as in *personal computers.

middleman A person or organization that makes a profit by trading in goods as an intermediary between the producer and the consumer. Middlemen include agents, brokers, dealers, merchants, factors, wholesalers, distributors, and retailers. They earn their profit by providing a variety of different services, including finance, bulk buying, holding stocks, breaking bulk, risk sharing, making a market and stabilizing prices, providing information about products (to consumers) and about markets (to producers), providing a distribution network, and introducing buyers to sellers.

middle management *See* MANAGEMENT.

middle price (**mean price**) The average of the *offer price of a security, commodity, currency, etc., and the *bid price. It is the middle price that is often quoted in the financial press.

MIGA Abbreviation for *Multilateral Investment Guarantee Agency.

migrant worker A worker who has come from another country or region to work. Attracted by better wages in the country or region to which they have migrated, such workers may or may not bring their family with them. In many cases they will not have done so and will therefore be sending a substantial proportion of their earnings back to their native country. This can have an adverse effect on the *balance of payments of countries that attract substantial numbers of migrant workers and conversely can be advantageous to countries from which many workers migrate.

mil A monetary unit of Malta, worth one thousandth of a *lira.

milk round An annual visit to universities by the personnel managers of large companies seeking graduates to join their organizations.

millième A monetary unit of Egypt, worth one thousandth of a *pound.

millime A Tunisian monetary unit, worth one thousandth of a *dinar.

minicomputer A *computer that is less powerful than a *mainframe but more powerful than a *personal computer. It is unable to handle as many people or programs at the same time as a mainframe, but it is adequate for a wide range of business and scientific applications.

minimum funding requirement (**MFR**) In the UK, the legal requirement that the assets of an occupational pension should represent at least 90% of its liabilities at any time. Since the liabilities and assets of a fund relate to future obligations and returns, both depend on certain actuarial assumptions about the future and thus may fluctuate from year to year. The MFR was introduced as a provision of the Pensions Act (1995) and came into force in 1997.

minimum lending rate (**MLR**) Between 1971 and 1981, the minimum rate at which the Bank of England would lend to the *discount houses. This was a published figure; the present more informal *base rate does not have the same status.

minimum subscription 1. The minimum sum of money, stated in the *prospectus of a new company, that the directors consider must be raised if the company is to be viable. 2. The smallest bid required in terms of the number of new securities at issue.

minimum wage The minimum wage that an employer may pay an employee. In some countries there are statutory national minimum wages and in other countries there may be agreed minimum wages within certain industries. The UK introduced its first statutory minimum wage in 1999; the current (2005) rates are £5.05 per hour for those aged 22 or over and £4.25 for those aged 18–21, increasing to £5.35 and £4.45 respectively from October 2006.

minority interest The interest of individual shareholders in a company more than 50% of which is owned by a *holding company. For example, if 60% of the ordinary shares in a company are owned by a holding company, the remaining 40% will represent a minority interest. These **minority shareholders** will receive their full share of profits in the form of dividends although they will be unable to determine company policy as they will always be outvoted by the majority interest held by the holding company. *See* CONTROLLING INTEREST; PARTICIPATING INTEREST.

minority protection Remedies evolved to safeguard a minority of company members from the abuse of majority rule. They include just and equitable winding-up, applying for relief on the basis of *unfair prejudice, bringing a *derivative or representative action, and seeking an *inspection and investigation of the company.

mint A factory, owned by a government or a bank, in which coins and banknotes are manufactured. *See* ROYAL MINT.

mint par of exchange The rate of exchange between two currencies that were on the *gold standard. The rate was then determined by the gold content of the basic coin.

MIP 1. Abbreviation for monthly investment plan. 2. Abbreviation for *maximum investment plan.

MIPS Abbreviation for millions of instructions per second, used as a measure of computer power.

MIRAS Abbreviation for *mortgage interest relief at source.

mirror swap *See* OFFSETTING SWAP.

MIS 1. Abbreviation for *management information system. 2. Abbreviation for *marketing information system.

misdeclaration penalty A penalty of up to 15% of the *value added tax lost in understating the VAT liability or overstating the VAT refund due on the VAT return, when the amounts involved are material. The penalty will apply if the inaccuracy equals the lesser of £1 million and 30% of the total amount of tax due for the period of the VAT return. The penalty can be avoided if the *taxable person can show that there was reasonable excuse, that there had been a voluntary disclosure, or that the taxable person had reason to believe that their VAT affairs were under investigation by Customs and Excise. *See also* PERSISTENT MISDECLARATION PENALTY.

misfeasance 1. The negligent or otherwise improper performance of a lawful act. 2. An act by an officer of a company in the nature of a breach of trust or breach of duty, particularly if it relates to the company's assets.

misfeasance summons An application to the court by a creditor, contributory, liquidator, or the official receiver during the course of winding up a company. The court is asked to examine the conduct of a company officer and order restitution to be made if the officer is found guilty of breach of trust or duty.

misleading advertising (deceptive advertising) Advertising that, although not strictly untrue, leads consumers to less-than-accurate conclusions. Intentionally misleading consumers is an extreme form of misleading advertising and is against the advertising standards code of conduct (*see* ADVERTISING STANDARDS AUTHORITY).

mismatch 1. Any financial *position that is not perfectly *offset. 2. A *floating-rate note in which the coupon is paid monthly but the interest rate paid is that applicable to a note of longer maturity. **3.** The situation in which the assets (loans made) and liabilities (deposits taken) of a bank are not matched, typically because the bank borrows short-term and lends long-term. This is usually acceptable as long as deposits keep coming in. *See* ASSET–LIABILITY MANAGEMENT; GAP.

misrepresentation An untrue statement of fact, made by one party to the other in the course of negotiating a contract, that induces the other party to enter into the contract. The person making the misrepresentation is called the **representor**, and the person to whom it is made is the **representee**. A false statement of law, opinion, or intention does not constitute a misrepresentation; nor does a statement of fact known by the representee to be untrue. Moreover, unless the representee relies on the statement so that it becomes an inducement (though not necessarily the only inducement) to enter into the contract, it is not a misrepresentation. The remedies for misrepresentation vary according to the degree of culpability of the representor. If guilty of **fraudulent misrepresentation** (i.e. if the truth of a statement is not honestly believed, which is not the same as saying that it is known to be false) the representee may, subject to certain limitations, set the contract aside and may also sue for *damages. If guilty of **negligent misrepresentation** (i.e. if the statement is believed without reasonable grounds for doing so) the representee may also rescind (*see* RESCISSION) the contract and sue for damages. If the representor has committed merely an **innocent misrepresentation** (one reasonably believed to be true) the representee is restricted to rescinding the contract.

missionary sales personnel Salespersons who visit prospective customers, distribute information to them, and handle their questions and complaints but do not usually take orders from them. Sales personnel who perform these functions tend to be employed by an agency and are hired out to the selling company.

mission statement (**vision statement**) A statement that encapsulates the overriding purpose and objectives of an organization. It is used to communicate this purpose to all stakeholder groups, both internal and external, and to guide employees in their contribution towards achieving it. *See also* STRATEGIC INTENT.

mistake In law, a misunderstanding or erroneous belief about a matter of fact (**mistake of fact**) or a matter of law (**mistake of law**). In civil cases, mistake is particularly important in the law of *contract. Mistakes of law have no effect on the validity of agreements, and neither do many mistakes of fact. When a mistake of fact does do so, it may render the agreement void under common-law rules (in which case it is referred to as an **operative mistake**) or it may make it voidable, i.e. liable, subject to certain limitations, to be set aside under the more lenient rules of equity.

When both parties to an agreement are under a misunderstanding, the mistake may be classified as either a **common mistake** (i.e. a single mistake shared by both) or a **mutual mistake** (i.e. each misunderstanding the other). In the case of common mistake, the mistake renders the contract void only if it robs it of all substance. The principal (and almost the only) example is when the subject matter of the contract has, unknown to both parties, ceased to exist. A common mistake about some particular attribute of the subject matter (e.g. that it is an original, not a copy) is not an operative mistake. However, a common mistake relating to any really fundamental matter will render a contract voidable. In the case of mutual mistake, the contract is valid if only one interpretation of what was agreed can be deduced from the parties' words and conduct. Otherwise, the mistake is operative and the contract void. When only one party to a contract is under a misunderstanding, the mistake may be called a **unilateral mistake** and it makes the contract void if it relates to the fundamental nature of the offer and the other party knew or ought to have known of it. Otherwise, the contract is valid so far as the law of mistake is concerned, though the circumstances may be such as to make it voidable for *misrepresentation.

A deed or other signed document (whether or not constituting a contract) that does not correctly record what both parties intended may be rectified by the courts. When one signatory to a document was fundamentally (but not carelessly) mistaken as to the character or effect of the transaction it embodies, the signatory may plead the mistake as a defence to any action based on the document.

mitigation of damage Minimizing the loss incurred by the person who suffered the loss and is claiming *damages as a result of it. The injured party has a duty to take all reasonable steps to mitigate any loss and the courts will not, therefore, award damages to compensate for a loss that could have been avoided by reasonable action.

mixed economy An economy in which some goods and services are produced by the government and some by private enterprise. A mixed economy lies between a *command economy and a complete *laissez-faire economy. In practice, however, most economies are mixed; the significant feature is whether an economy is moving towards or away from a more laissez-faire situation. Although most Western economies retreated from laissez-faire policies in the post-war era, this trend has been reversed since the 1980s.

mixed-standard scale A measure used in evaluating the job performance of employees. An example of good, average, and poor behaviour is identified for each of the key elements of a job; supervisors are then asked to rate the performance of the employee in terms of whether it is better than, equal to, or worse than each of the identified behaviours. A total score is derived from these responses. *Compare* BEHAVIOURALLY ANCHORED RATING SCALES; BEHAVIOURAL OBSERVATION SCALE.

MMC Abbreviation for Monopolies and Mergers Commission. *See* COMPETITION COMMISSION.

MMDA Abbreviation for *money-market deposit account.

MNE Abbreviation for *multinational enterprise.

mobility of labour The extent to which workers are willing to move from one region or country to another (**geographical mobility**) or to change from one occupation to another (**occupational mobility**). In **horizontal mobility** there is no change of status, whereas in **vertical mobility** there is. An upward change in status will increase a worker's mobility, whereas a downward change will reduce it. The more highly skilled a worker, the less his occupational mobility will be, but he will often be highly geographically mobile. An unskilled worker will often be both occupationally and geographically mobile. In the UK, many government retraining schemes aim to increase occupational mobility; at the same time considerable effort goes into encouraging new industries into areas of high unemployment to reduce the need for geographical mobility.

mock auction An *auction during which a lot is sold to someone at a price lower than his highest bid, part of the price is repaid or credited to the bidder, the right to bid is restricted to those who have bought or agreed to buy one or more articles, or articles are given away or offered as gifts. Under the Mock Auction Act (1961) it is an offence to promote or conduct a mock auction.

mode *See* NORMAL DISTRIBUTION.

modem Abbreviation for *mo*dulator-*dem*odulator, a device that enables a computer to transmit and receive data by means of a communications link, such as a telephone line. The process of converting computer signals into a form suitable for transmission is called modulation. The reverse process, making the transmitted signals intelligible to the computer, is called demodulation. Modems provide access to the telephone network for *e-mail and for the *Internet.

moderator 1. An individual who supervises activities in Internet marketing research or in Internet chat rooms or discussions in order to maintain relevance and quality. **2.** *See* FOCUS-GROUP MODERATOR.

modified accounts The original name for what are now called *abbreviated accounts.

modified rebuy A situation in which a buyer is unhappy with current suppliers or products and is looking at competitors' products and prices rather than automatically rebuying the same product as before. *See* BUSINESS BUYER BEHAVIOUR.

modular design A design technique that aims to provide a variety of products using combinations of a small range of components. The end result is that customer choice is maximized while operational complexity is minimized.

monadic testing A technique used in marketing research in which consumers are presented with a product to test on its own, rather than being asked to compare it with a competing product (*see* PAIRED COMPARISONS).

monetary assets *Assets, such as *cash and *debtors, that have a fixed monetary exchange value and are not affected by a change in the price level. If there are no regulations requiring companies to account for changing price levels, monetary assets remain in the *financial statements at their original amounts. If the principle of accounting for changes in price levels is applied, the monetary assets will be indexed.

monetary control The use of the *central bank of a country by its government to control the *money supply. In the UK, the Bank of England acted in this way prior to 1997 but, as with the Federal Reserve Bank in the USA, it is now largely independent of government policy.

Monetary Policy Committee (MPC) The committee of *Bank of England officials and outside economic experts that has been responsible for setting interest rates in the UK since 1997. Prior to this date, interest rates were set by the Treasury.

monetary reform The revision of a country's currency by the introduction of a new currency unit or a substantial change to an existing system. Examples include decimalization of the UK currency (1971), the change from the austral to the peso in Argentina (1992), and the introduction of the *euro (1999–2002).

monetary system 1. The system used by a country to provide the economy with money for internal use and to control the exchange of its own currency with those of foreign countries. It also includes the system used by a country for implementing its **monetary policy**, i.e. its policy regarding the *money supply. **2.** A system

used to control the exchange rate of a group of countries. *See* EUROPEAN MONETARY SYSTEM.

monetary unit The standard unit of currency in a country. The monetary unit of each country is related to those of other countries by a *foreign exchange rate.

money A *medium of exchange that functions as a *unit of account, a store of value, and a means for deferred payment. Originally money enhanced economic development by enabling goods to be bought and sold without the need for barter. However, throughout history money has been beset by the problem of its debasement as a store of value as a result of *inflation. Now that the supply of money is a monopoly of the state, most governments are committed in principle to stable prices. The word 'money' is derived from the Latin *moneta*, which was one of the names of Juno, the Roman goddess whose temple was used as a mint.

money at call and short notice One of the assets that appears in the balance sheet of a bank. It includes funds lent to discount houses, money brokers, the stock exchange, bullion brokers, corporate customers, and increasingly to other banks. **At call money** is repayable on demand, whereas **short notice money** implies that notice of repayment of up to 14 days will be given. After cash, money at call and short notice are the banks' most liquid assets. They are usually interest-earning secured loans but their importance lies in providing the banks with an opportunity to use their surplus funds and to adjust their cash and liquidity requirements.

money broker In the UK, a *broker who arranges short-term loans in the *money market, i.e. between banks, discount houses, and dealers in government securities. Money brokers do not themselves lend or borrow money; they work for a commission arranging loans on a day-to-day and overnight basis. Money brokers also operate in the *eurobond markets.

money laundering *See* LAUNDERING MONEY.

moneylender A person whose business it is to lend money, other than pawnbrokers, friendly or building societies, corporate bodies with special powers to lend money, banks, or insurance companies. The Consumer Credit Act (1974) replaces the earlier Moneylenders Acts and requires all moneylenders to be registered, to obtain an annual licence to lend money, and to state the true *annual percentage rate (APR) of interest at which a loan is made.

money market **1.** The wholesale market for short-term loans and debt instruments. In the UK, *money brokers arrange for loans between the banks, the government, the discount houses, and the accepting houses, with the Bank of England acting as lender of last resort. The main items of exchange are *bills of exchange, *Treasury bills, and trade bills. The market has traditionally taken place in and around *Lombard Street in the City of London. Private investors, through their banks, can place deposits in the money market at a higher rate of interest than bank deposit accounts. These are considered to be safe investments. *See also* INTER-BANK MARKET. **2.** The *foreign-exchange market and the bullion market in addition to the short-term loan market.

money-market deposit account (MMDA) A high-yielding savings account introduced in the USA in 1982 to allow *deposit-taking institutions to compete with the money markets for savers' funds. As long as the account has a balance of more than $1000 there is no regulatory limit on the account. Balances below $1000 attract a lower rate of interest. Restrictions on the account apply to withdrawals (three a month) and transfers for bill payment (three a month).

money-market line An agreement between a bank and a company that entitles the company to borrow up to a certain limit each day in the *money markets, on a short-term basis (often overnight or in some cases up to one month). *See* UNCOM-MITTED FACILITY.

money-market unit trust (cash unit trust) A *unit trust that invests in money-market instruments in order to provide investors with a risk-free income.

money-purchase pension scheme A *defined-contribution pension scheme as opposed to a *defined-benefit pension scheme.

money supply (monetary stock) The quantity of money issued by a country's monetary authorities (usually the central bank). If the demand for money is stable, the widely accepted quantity theory of money implies that increases in the money supply will lead directly to an increase in the price level, i.e. to inflation. Since the 1970s most Western governments have attempted to reduce inflation by controlling the money supply. This raises two issues:
(i) how to measure the money supply;
(ii) how to control the money supply (*see* INTEREST-RATE POLICY).

In the UK various measures of the money supply have been used, from the very narrow M0 to the very broad M5. They are usually defined as:
M0 — notes and coins in circulation plus the banks' till money and the banks' balances with the Bank of England;
M1 — notes and coins in circulation plus private-sector current accounts and deposit accounts that can be transferred by cheque;
M2 — notes and coins in circulation plus non-interest-bearing bank deposits plus building society deposits plus National Savings accounts;
M3 — M1 plus all other private-sector bank deposits plus certificates of deposit;
M3c — M3 plus foreign currency bank deposits;
M4 — M1 plus most private-sector bank deposits plus holdings of money-market instruments (e.g. Treasury bills);
M5 — M4 plus building society deposits.

In some contexts the amount of money existing in an economy is called the **monetary stock**. To obtain the money supply the monetary stock has to be multiplied by the *velocity of circulation.

Monopolies and Mergers Commission (MMC) *See* COMPETITION COMMISSION.

monopoly A market in which there is only one seller (or producer). Governments usually try to eliminate monopolies as being against the public interest. In recent decades some of the services formerly regarded as natural monopolies, such as electricity and water supply, have been privatized to encourage competition and eliminate the monopolistic element. *See also* CARTEL; CORNER.

monopsony A market in which there is only a single buyer.

Monte Carlo simulation A *simulation in which random data are generated from specified distributions and used as an input into predictive or other models. In finance, such simulations are used to price complicated derivatives and portfolios and provide the basis for many *risk-management systems. Firms also employ them in their decision-making and capital-appraisal models.

Monthly Digest of Statistics A monthly publication of the UK *Office for National Statistics providing statistical information on industry, national income, and the UK population.

moonlighting Having two jobs, one a full-time daytime job, the other a part-time evening job. Often the second job is undertaken on a self-employed basis and income is not returned for tax purposes.

moral appeal An appeal in an advertisement or sales literature that is directed to the audience's sense of what is right and proper.

moral hazard The situation in which a person has no incentive to act honestly or with due prudence. The term is mainly used in the insurance world, where a typical example of a person exposed to moral hazard would be the owner of an insured car, who has little or no incentive to guard against theft. Moral hazard is closely associated with the concept of *adverse selection, as when a person purchasing health insurance declines to reveal his or her greater likelihood to need health treatment than the average.

moral suasion A regulatory body's use of argument and persuasion, rather than coercion or legislation, to influence the activities of those within its purview. The term is often applied to the efforts of the Federal Reserve Board (*see* FEDERAL RESERVE SYSTEM) to persuade its members to comply with its policies.

moratorium 1. An agreement between a creditor and a debtor to allow additional time for the settlement of a debt. **2.** A period during which one government permits a government of a foreign country to suspend repayments of a debt. **3.** A period during which all the trading debts in a particular market are suspended as a result of some exceptional crisis in the market. In these circumstances, not to call a moratorium would probably lead to more insolvencies than the market could stand. The intention of such a moratorium is, first, that firms should be given a breathing space to find out exactly what their liabilities are and, secondly, that they should be given time to make the necessary financial arrangements to settle their liabilities.

MORI Abbreviation for *Market and Opinion Research International.

mortality rate (death rate) The crude death rate, i.e. the number of deaths per 1000 of the average population in a given year. It can be subdivided into different rates for different age groups of the population and for different regions.

mortality table (life table) An actuarial table prepared on the basis of mortality rates for people in different occupations in different regions of a country. It provides life-assurance companies with the information they require to quote for life-assurance policies, annuities, etc.

mortgage An interest in property created as a security for a loan or payment of a debt and terminated on payment of the loan or debt. The borrower, who offers the security, is the **mortgagor**; the lender, who provides the money, is the **mortgagee**. *Building societies and banks are the usual mortgagees for house purchasers. In either case the mortgage is repaid by instalments over a fixed period (often 25 years), either of capital and interest (**repayment mortgage**) or of interest only, with other arrangements being made to repay the capital, for example by means of an *endowment assurance policy (this is known as an **endowment mortgage**). Business uses of the mortgage include using property to secure a loan to start a business. Virtually any property may be mortgaged (though land is the most common). See feature MORTGAGE LAW on p. 352.

mortgage-backed security A security in which cash flows derive from an under-

MORTGAGE LAW

Types of mortgage

Under the Law of Property Act (1925), which governs mortgage regulations in the UK, there are two types of mortgage, legal and equitable.

A **legal mortgage** confers a legal estate on the mortgagee (lender). Under the 1925 Act, the only valid mortgages are:

(a) a lease granted for a stated number of years, which terminates on repayment of the loan at or before the end of that period; and

(b) a deed expressed to be a *charge by way of legal mortgage.

All other mortgages are **equitable mortgages**, in which the mortgagee obtains an equitable interest in the property only. Such a mortgage may arise in two ways:

(1) If the mortgagor (borrower) has only an equitable, as opposed to a legal, interest in the property (for example, because he or she is a beneficiary under a trust of the property) he or she can only grant an equitable mortgage. Provided that the mortgage is created by deed, the rights of the parties are very similar to those under a legal mortgage.

(2) An equitable mortgage can also be created of a legal or equitable interest by an informal written agreement, e.g. the mortgagor hands the title deeds to the mortgagee as security for a loan. The great majority of mortgages are now of this kind. Such a mortgagee has the remedies of repossession and foreclosure only (see below).

Second mortgages

A second or subsequent mortgage may be taken out on the same property, provided that the value of the property is greater than the amount of previous mortgage(s). All mortgages of registered land are noted in the *register of charges on application by the mortgagee, and a charge certificate is issued. When mortgaged land is unregistered, a first legal mortgagee keeps the title deeds. A subsequent legal mortgagee and any equitable mortgagee who does not have the title deeds should protect their interests by registration.

Redemption

Under the so-called **equity of redemption**, the mortgagor is allowed to redeem the property at any time on payment of the loan together with interest and costs, which may include a penalty for early redemption; any provisions in a mortgage deed to prevent redemption (known as **clogs**) are void.

Repossession and foreclosure

In theory, the mortgagee always has the right to take possession of mortgaged property even if there has been no default. However, this right is usually excluded by building-society mortgages until default, and its exclusion may be implied in any instalment mortgage. Where residential property is concerned, the court has power to delay the recovery of possession if there is a realistic possibility that the default will be remedied in a reasonable time. In case of default, the mortgagee has a statutory right to sell the property, but this will normally be exercised after obtaining possession first. Any surplus left after the debt and the mortgagee's expenses have been met must be paid to the mortgagor. The mortgagee also has a statutory right to appoint a *receiver to manage mortgaged property in the event of default; this power is useful where business property is concerned. As a final resort, a mortgage may be brought to an end by *foreclosure, in which the court orders the transfer of the property to the mortgagee. This is not common in times of rising property prices, as the mortgagor would lose more than the value of the debt, so the court will not order foreclosure where a sale would be more appropriate.

lying pool of mortgages. They are very widely used in the USA.

mortgage bond In the USA, a bond in which a debt is secured by a real asset (land or property). **Senior mortgage bonds** have first claim on assets and **junior mortgage bonds** are subordinate. A mortgage bond may have a closed-end provision, which prevents an organization issuing further bonds of a similar nature on the same asset or open-end provision, which permits further issues with the same status.

mortgage debenture A loan made to a company by an investor, secured on the real property of the company. *See* DEBENTURE.

mortgagee *See* MORTGAGE.

mortgage interest relief at source (MIRAS) Formerly, an arrangement allowing income tax relief to be given to a mortgagor on the first £30,000 of a loan taken out to purchase a main residence. MIRAS was progressively restricted from 1994 and abolished in 2000.

mortgagor *See* MORTGAGE.

Mosaic *See* GEOGRAPHIC INFORMATION SYSTEM.

most-favoured-nation clause A clause in a trade agreement between two countries stating that each will accord to the other the same treatment as regards tariffs and quotas as they extend to the most favoured nation with which each trades. Both the World Trade Organization and the EU have used this concept.

motion A proposal put before a meeting for discussion. Usually members of a company who attend a meeting of the company receive a **notice of motion** to enable them to consider the motion before the meeting. If the motion is passed by a majority of the members of the company it becomes a *resolution. If the meeting decides to amend the motion, the amended motion, known as the **substantive motion**, is then discussed and voted upon.

motivation The mental processes that arouse, sustain, and direct human behaviour. Motivation may stem from processes taking place within an individual (*intrinsic motivation) or from the impact of factors acting on the individual from outside (*extrinsic motivation); in most cases these two influences are continually interacting.

The vocabulary associated with motivation is large; such terms as purpose, desire, need, goal, preference, perception, attitude, recognition, achievement, and incentive are commonly used. Many of these drives can act on an individual simultaneously, causing varying degrees of conflict. A consumer deciding between buying chocolate and buying ice cream is in conflict. An employee who wants to disagree with the boss but also wants to keep his or her job is in conflict.

In a business context, an understanding of human motivation is crucial to understanding *consumer buying behaviour. It is also vital to the design of organizational norms and structures, including reward structures, that encourage effort and achievement on the part of employees. In the realm of theory considerable importance has been given to the hierarchy of needs investigated by Abraham Maslow (1908–70; *see* MASLOW'S MOTIVATIONAL HIERARCHY), which places the basic needs of human survival at the bottom of the scale of human motivation and *self-actualization at the top. The more flexible *ERG theory focuses on three groups of needs that form a hierarchy: existence needs (physical and material wants); relatedness needs (the desire for interpersonal relationships); and growth needs (desires to be creative and productive).

Although most psychologists now believe that human needs and motives are too variable to be confined to a fixed hierarchy, these theories have the merit of emphasizing that, besides goals, ambitions, and rewards, there is a need for success to be recognized by others and a need to develop and progress. A person in an organization never works in a vacuum: there can be a real conflict between different motivations that relate to the organization: Would I be worse paid working elsewhere? But would I be more secure/better trained/more appreciated elsewhere? *See* ACHIEVEMENT MOTIVATION THEORY; ALIENATION; THEORY X AND THEORY Y; THEORY Z; VALENCY-INSTRUMENTALITY-EXPECTANCY THEORY.

motivational research A form of

*marketing research in which the motivations for consumers preferring one product rather than another are studied. It may form the basis of a plan to launch a competitive product or of a campaign to boost sales of an existing product.

motivators In the two-factor theory of *motivation proposed by Frederick Herzberg (1923–2000), those aspects of the work situation that can motivate employees by providing positive *job satisfaction (as opposed to a mere absence of dissatisfaction). They include responsibility, autonomy, variety, and the *intrinsic rewards arising from the work itself. *Compare* HYGIENE FACTORS.

motor insurance A form of insurance covering loss or damage to motor vehicles and any legal liabilities for bodily injury or damage to other people's property. Drivers have a legal obligation to be covered against third-party claims (*see* THIRD-PARTY INSURANCE), but most drivers or owners of vehicles have a **comprehensive insurance**, providing wide coverage of all the risks involved in owning a motor vehicle. An intermediate cover is known as third-party, fire, and theft. *See also* NO-CLAIM BONUS.

moving average A series of *arithmetic means calculated from data in a time series, which reduces the effects of temporary seasonal variations. For example, a moving average of the monthly sales figures for an organization might be calculated by averaging the 12 months from January to December for the December figure, the 12 months from February to January for the January figure, and so on.

MPC *See* MONETARY POLICY COMMITTEE.

MPS Abbreviation for *master production schedule.

MRP 1. Abbreviation for manufacturers' recommended price. *See* RECOMMENDED RETAIL PRICE. **2.** Abbreviation for *material requirements planning.

MRS Abbreviation for *Market Research Society.

MSA Abbreviation for *metropolitan statistical area.

MS-DOS *Trademark* Abbreviation for *Mi*crosoft *D*isk *O*perating *S*ystem. Designed originally for the IBM Personal Computer,

it became the standard operating system for larger *personal computers. Earlier versions of *Windows ran on MS-DOS.

MSF Abbreviation for *multisource feedback.

MSP Abbreviation for *matched sale–purchase agreement.

MTN Abbreviation for *medium-term note.

multibrand strategy A strategy in which a seller develops two or more brands in the same product category.

multichannel marketing Marketing one's products or services using two or more marketing channels, often to reach more than one market segment (*see* MARKET SEGMENTATION). Retail chains, for example, besides using the shops to distribute their products, quite often also use catalogue selling.

multi-component euronote facility A *euronote issued in a variety of currencies.

multi-dimensional scaling (MDS) A technique used to assist understanding of a consumer's perception of competing brands or products. A 'perceptual map' is often drawn showing how consumers perceive competitive products along certain dimensions or attributes. For example, respondents may be asked to rank pairs of brands in terms of their perceived similarities, so that some understanding can be gained of their choice criteria.

multifunctional card A plastic card issued by a bank or building society to its customers to function as a *cheque card, *debit card, and *cash card. Multifunctional cards operate in conjunction with a *personal identification number.

Multilateral Investment Guarantee Agency (MIGA) An affiliate of the *International Bank for Reconstruction and Development (IBRD) established in 1988 to encourage foreign investment in developing countries by providing investors with guarantees and developing countries with an advisory service.

multilateral netting 1. The centralizing of international payments of a group of companies so that payments and receipts in different currencies can be offset, thus reducing transaction and hedging costs. **2.** A method of reducing bank charges in which the subsidiaries of a group offset their receipts and payments with each other, usually monthly, resulting in a single net intercompany payment or receipt made by each subsidiary to cover the period concerned. This saves both on transaction costs and paperwork. *See also* BILATERAL NETTING; NETTING.

multilateral trade agreement A trading arrangement between a number of nations in which there is agreement to abolish quotas and tariffs or to accept that there will be a surplus or deficit on the balance of payments.

multimedia The integration of text, graphics, pictures, and sound in the storing and presentation of information by computers. Computers are increasingly able to present information in a wide variety of forms from a wide variety of sources. Networked systems are able to transfer live TV pictures together with text and graphics. However, the ability of many organizations to exploit this technology, e.g. for conferencing, is restricted by the *bandwidth of their systems.

multinational enterprise (MNE) A corporation that has production operations in more than one country for various reasons, including securing supplies of raw materials, utilizing cheap labour sources, servicing local markets taking advantage of tax differences, and bypassing protectionist barriers. Multinationals may be seen as an efficient form of organization, making effective use of the world's resources and transferring technology between countries. On the other hand, some have excessive power, are beyond the control of governments (especially weak governments), and are able to exploit host countries, especially in the developing world, where they are able to operate with low safety levels and inadequate control of pollution. *See* GLOBALIZATION.

multiple *See* PRICE–EARNINGS RATIO.

multiple application The submission of more than one application form for a new issue of shares that is likely to be oversubscribed. In many countries it is illegal to do so either if the applications are made in the same name or if false names are used.

multiple-choice question A question requiring a respondent to select an answer from a list of answers provided with the question. For example, the respondent may be asked to name the brand of cigarettes purchased in the last week from a list of major brands. *Compare* OPEN-ENDED QUESTION.

multiple exchange rate An exchange rate quoted by a country that has more than one value, depending on the use to which the currency is put. For example, some countries have quoted a specially favourable rate for tourists or for importers of desirable goods.

multiple market segmentation *See* DIFFERENTIATED MARKETING.

multiple niching A marketing strategy in which several independent offers of a product are made, which are intended to appeal to several different types of customer.

multiple shops (chain stores) A large chain of shops (usually ten or more) owned by the same *retailer. Compared with *independent retailers, they benefit from *economies of scale and so can charge lower prices to consumers. Multiple shops have therefore become dominant in many areas of retailing, such as packaged groceries.

multiple taxation Taxation of the same income by more than two countries. *Compare* DOUBLE TAXATION.

multiple-unit pricing Selling more than one unit of a product at a lower price than twice the unit price. 'Buy two, get one free' is an example.

multisource feedback (MSF) A system of *employee evaluation that involves collecting performance *feedback from multiple sources, including manager, subordinates, colleagues, and possibly clients and customers. This is sometimes extended to a system of *360° feedback.

multitasking Describing a computer system that can run more than one program at the same time.

multivariate analysis A statistical procedure that simultaneously analyses multiple measurements on each individual or object under study in a marketing-research enquiry. Examples of the procedures used include multiple regression, factor analysis, cluster analysis (*see* CLUSTER THEORY), and *conjoint analysis.

municipal bond A bond issued by a local government authority, especially one in the USA.

muqarada *See* ISLAMIC FINANCE.

murabaha *See* ISLAMIC FINANCE.

musharaka *See* ISLAMIC FINANCE.

mutual A company that is owned by its members or depositors. In the UK *building societies used to have this structure, but most have now demutualized, becoming *public limited companies. **Mutual life-assurance** companies developed out of the *Friendly Societies. There are no shareholders and apart from benefits and running expenses there are no other withdrawals from the fund; thus any profits are distributed to policyholders.

mutual fund The US name for a *unit trust.

mutually exclusive projects A number of alternative projects being considered for appraisal, in which no one project can be pursued in conjunction with any of the other projects. For example, a parcel of land may be used to build a factory, an office block, or a mixture of the two. Each alternative is mutually exclusive because the choice of one alternative automatically excludes the others. Mutually exclusive projects arise when there is a scarce resource, in this case land.

mutual mistake *See* MISTAKE.

mystery shoppers People employed by retailers to pose as customers at their own or their competitors' stores to compare prices, offers, displays, staff attitude, etc.

m

NAFTA Abbreviation for *North American Free Trade Agreement.

naira (ɲaira;) The standard monetary unit of Nigeria, divided into 100 kobo.

naive quantitative methods Techniques used to forecast future trends, e.g. the demand for a product, using historical data to calculate an average of past demand. When this data is plotted against time, it is known as a **time series**. It is usually assumed that a time series will consist of a number of separate elements, such as an underlying trend, seasonal variations, cyclic variations relating to the economy, and a random element. The accuracy of a time series as a forecasting tool is enhanced by identifying and separating these elements by the process known as **decomposition**. *Compare* CAUSAL QUANTITATIVE MODELS.

Nakasone bond A bond issued by the Japanese government in a foreign currency. It is named after the prime minister in office when it was introduced (1982).

naked call writing Selling (writing) a call *option on equities that one does not own. A person may do this if he or she expects the price of a particular share to fall or remain unchanged. It is, however, a dangerous strategy because if the price rises the shares will have to be purchased at the market price in order to deliver them, thus involving an unlimited risk.

naked debenture An unsecured *debenture.

naked position *See* OPEN POSITION.

nakfa The standard monetary unit of Eritrea.

name *See* LLOYD'S; SYNDICATE.

narrow money An informal name for M0, or sometimes M1: the part of the *money supply that can directly perform the function of a *medium of exchange. *Compare* BROAD MONEY.

National Association of Securities Dealers Automated Quotations System (NASDAQ) In the USA, a computerized system for trading in over-the-counter securities that began operations in 1971. Owned and operated by the National Association of Securities Dealers, it is the largest stock market in the USA, listing more than 5000 companies. **NASDAQ International** is an international system providing screen-based quotations for US-registered equities that came into operation in 1992.

national banks US commercial banks established by federal charter (approved by the *Comptroller of the Currency), which requires them to be members of the *Federal Reserve System. They were created by the National Bank Act 1863 and formerly issued their own banknotes.

National certificates and diplomas *See* VOCATIONAL TRAINING.

National Chamber of Trade (NCT) A non-profit making organization founded in 1897, with headquarters in Henley-on-Thames, that links and represents local *chambers of trade and *chambers of commerce, national trade associations, and individual businesses in the UK. It maintains lobbies scrutinizing legislation in both Westminster and Brussels and provides expert advice for affiliated chambers and members.

National Consumer Council An organization set up by the UK government in 1975 to watch over consumer interests and speak for the consumer to the government, industry, and commerce. Funded mainly by the Department of Trade and Industry, it deals only with issues of policy (i.e. it does not issue consumer advice or deal with complaints).

National Insurance contribution (NIC) Payments made by those with earned income that contribute to the National Insurance Fund, from which benefits are paid. These benefits include retirement pensions, unemployment pay, widow's benefits, invalidity benefit, and certain sickness and maternity benefits. There are six different classes of National Insurance contributions; the class applicable to a person depends on the type of earned income received by that person.

Class 1 is paid by those with earnings from employment. There are two parts to class 1, primary contributions paid by the employee and secondary contributions paid by the employer. The rates of contributions depend on the level of earnings and also whether or not the employee is a member of a contracted-out occupational, personal, or stakeholder pension scheme; for employees the standard rate is 11% on weekly earnings between £95 and £630 and 1% on weekly earnings thereafter (2005–06 figures).

Class 2 is a flat-rate contribution paid by the self-employed; it is £2.10 per week for 2005–06.

Class 3 is voluntary, and is also at a flat rate – £7.35 per week for 2005–06. It is paid by those wishing to maintain their contribution record even though they may be unemployed or their level of earnings is below that for mandatory contributions.

Class 4 is paid by the self-employed at a rate of 8% on income between a lower limit of £4895 per year and an upper limit of £32,760 per year and 1% on yearly income thereafter.

Class 1A was introduced in 1991 and is payable by employers who provide cars for private as well as business use for their employees. The level of payment depends on the cost and age of the car and the number of business miles travelled. It is based on the list price of the vehicle, on the day it was first registered as brand new.

Class 1B is payable by employers in value of any items included in a PAYE settlement with HM Revenue and Customs.

nationalization The process of bringing the assets of a business into the ownership of the state. Examples of industries nationalized in the past in the UK include the National Coal Board and British Rail. Historically, nationalization has been achieved through compulsory purchase, although this need not necessarily be the case. Nationalization has often been pursued as much for political as economic ends and the economic justifications themselves are varied. One argument for nationalization is that if a company possesses a natural monopoly, then it should not be run for private profit; another is that certain industries are strategically important for the nation. In the 1980s and 1990s Conservative governments reversed the nationalizations of the post-war Labour governments with a series of *privatization measures, on the grounds that competition would increase efficiency and reduce prices. Even where this has arguably not proved to be the case Labour administrations since 1997 have been reluctant to renationalize.

National Savings A wide range of schemes for personal savers, administered by National Savings and Investments, a government agency established in 1969 as the Post Office Savings Department. They include *premium bonds, guaranteed equity bonds, Children's Bonus Bonds, and inflation-linked savings certificates. The Department also offers *Individual Savings Accounts (ISAs) and (since January 2004) Easy Access Savings Accounts. The **National Savings Bank** (**NSB**; formerly the Post Office Savings Bank) was founded in 1861.

National Savings Stock Register An organization run by *National Savings and Investments from the Bonds and Stock Office in Blackpool. It enables members of the public to buy certain Treasury stocks and other *gilt-edged securities without going through a stockbroker; it thus provides an alternative to the main *Bank of England Stock Register. Purchases and sales are made by post and the interest paid is taxable, but is paid before deduction of tax (unlike the Bank of England Register). Because transactions are carried out by post, this method does not provide the maximum flexibility in a moving market.

National Vocational Qualification (NVQ) *See* VOCATIONAL TRAINING.

natural justice The minimum standard of fairness to be applied by a court when resolving a dispute. The main rules of natural justice include: (1) the right to be heard – each party to the dispute should be given an opportunity to answer any allegations made by the other party; (2) the rule against bias – the person involved in settling the dispute should act impartially, in particular by disclosing any interest in the outcome of the dispute. The rules of natural justice apply equally in judicial as well as in administrative proceedings. Alleging a breach of natural justice is the method commonly used to challenge an administrative decision before the courts.

natural rate of interest *See* INTEREST.

natural wastage The method by which an organization can contract without making people redundant, relying on resignations, retirements, or deaths. If the time is available, this method of reducing a workforce causes the least tension. *See also* REDUNDANCY.

NAV Abbreviation for net asset value. *See* ASSET VALUE (PER SHARE); BOOK VALUE.

navigation On the Internet, the process of finding and moving between different information and pages on a website. It is governed by menu arrangements, site structure, the layout of individual pages, and, sometimes, searching facilities.

NBA Abbreviation for *Net Book Agreement.

NBV Abbreviation for *net book value.

NCI Abbreviation for *New Community Instrument.

NCT Abbreviation for *National Chamber of Trade.

NDP Abbreviation for *net domestic product.

near money (quasi money) An asset that is immediately transferable and may be used to settle some but not all debts, although it is not as liquid as banknotes and coins. *Bills of exchange are examples of near money. Near money is not included in the *money supply definitions.

need recognition The first stage of *consumer buying behaviour, in which the consumer recognizes a problem or need.

negative cash flow A *cash flow in which the outflows exceed the inflows.

negative equity 1. The difference between the value of a property (usually residential) and the outstanding amount borrowed against it where the latter is the greater. For example, if a property's current market value is £200,000 and the borrowing against it is £210,000, there is a negative *equity to the extent of £10,000. Negative equities were common in the mid-1990s when the economic recession had an adverse effect on property prices. House owners who paid more for their houses than their current market value were unable to sell without realizing the loss. **2.** More generally, any asset that has a market value below the sum of money borrowed to purchase it.

negative income tax (NIT) A means of targeting social security benefits to those most in need using the income-tax system. After submitting an income-tax return showing an income level below a set minimum, an individual would receive a direct subsidy from the tax authorities bringing income up to that level.

negative interest A charge made by a bank or other deposit taker for looking after a sum of money for a given period.

negative net worth The value of a company whose liabilities exceed its assets.

negative pledge A *covenant in a loan agreement in which a borrower promises that no secured borrowings will be made during the life of the loan or will ensure that the loan is secured equally and ratably with any new borrowings as specifically defined.

negligence In law, a tort in which a breach of a **duty of care** results in damage to the person to whom the duty is owed. Such a duty is owed by manufacturers to the consumers who buy their products, by accountants, solicitors, doctors, and other professional persons to their clients, by a director of a company to its shareholders, etc. A person who has suffered loss or injury as a result of a breach of the duty of care can claim *damages in tort. The risk of being sued for negligence makes it essential for partners in firms that are not *limited liability partnerships to obtain *professional indemnity insurance.

negotiability The ability of a document

that entitles its owner to some benefit to change hands, so that legal ownership of the benefit passes by delivery or endorsement of the document. For a document to be negotiable it must also entitle the holder to bring an action in law if necessary. *See* NEGOTIABLE INSTRUMENT.

negotiable instrument A document of title that can be freely negotiated (*see* NEGOTIABILITY). Such documents are *cheques and *bills of exchange, in which the stated payee of the instrument can negotiate the instrument by either inserting the name of a different payee or by making the document 'open' by endorsing it (signing one's name), usually on the reverse. Holders of negotiable instruments cannot pass on a better title than they possess. Bills of exchange, including cheques, in which the payee is named or that bear a restrictive endorsement, such as 'not negotiable', are **non-negotiable instruments**.

negotiable order of withdrawal (NOW) A type of cheque used in US savings accounts that are interest-bearing and from which sums can be withdrawn. If no interest is paid the account is called a NINOW.

negotiate 1. To confer with a view to arriving at mutually acceptable terms for a contract or agreement. **2.** To transfer a *bill of exchange or cheque to another for consideration (*see* NEGOTIABILITY; NEGOTIABLE INSTRUMENT).

negotiated transfer prices *Transfer prices set by negotiation between the supplying and receiving divisions of an organization. Negotiated transfer prices are appropriate when there is an imperfect market for the goods and services that are bought and sold between divisions. Negotiation may be seen as a way of reducing conflicts between managers. The relative bargaining power of the divisions is important; a mediator may be used to help the negotiations.

nem con (abbreviation of Latin *nemine contradicente*: no-one disagreeing) These words are often used in the minutes of a meeting when no-one has voted against a proposition.

nested-ad content Related advertising material on the same website to which a person is directed by clicking on an advertisement (rather than being redirected to a corporate or brand site).

net Denoting an amount remaining after specific deductions have been made. For example, **net profit before taxation** is the profit made by an organization after the deduction of all business expenditure but before the deduction of the *taxation charge.

net assets The assets of an organization less its *current liabilities. The resultant figure is equal to the *capital of the organization. Opinion varies as to whether long-term liabilities should be treated as part of the capital and are therefore not deductible in arriving at net assets, or whether they are part of the liabilities and therefore deductible. The latter view is probably technically preferable and is more common. A further practice is to split long-term liabilities and to treat those described as the 'finance element' as part of the capital. *Compare* NET CURRENT ASSETS. *See also* BOOK VALUE; NET WORTH.

net asset value (NAV) *See* ASSET VALUE (PER SHARE); BOOK VALUE.

net basis The basis upon which the *earnings per share of a company is calculated, taking into account both constant and variable elements in the company's tax charge. According to *Statement of Standard Accounting Practice 3, 'Earnings per Share', a *listed company must show the earnings per share on the net basis on the face of the *profit and loss account. *Compare* NIL BASIS.

Net Book Agreement (NBA) A former agreement between publishers and booksellers according to which booksellers did not offer trade books to the public below the price marked on the cover of the book. It was registered under the Restrictive Trade Practices Act (1956) and the Resale Prices Act (1964) as being in the public interest, but it collapsed in 1995.

net book value (NBV; book value) The value at which an asset appears in the books of an organization (usually as at the date of the last balance sheet). This is the purchase cost or latest revaluation less any depreciation applied since purchase or revaluation. The net book value is also known as the **depreciated value** or **depreciated cost**. *See* BALANCE-SHEET ASSET VALUE.

net current assets *Current assets less *current liabilities. The resultant figure is also known as *working capital, as it represents the amount of the organization's capital that is constantly being turned over in the course of its trade. *See also* NET ASSETS.

net dividend The *dividend paid by a company to its shareholders, after excluding the *tax credit received by the shareholders.

net domestic product (NDP) The *gross domestic product of a country less *capital consumption (i.e. depreciation).

net income **1.** The income of a person or organization after the deduction of the appropriate expenses incurred in earning it. **2.** *Gross income from which tax has been deducted.

net interest Interest paid into a savings or current account at a UK bank or building society after the deduction of tax at source. Interest on bank and building society accounts is currently taxed at 20%.

net investment The addition to the stock of capital goods in an economy during a particular period (the **gross investment**) less *capital consumption (i.e. depreciation).

net margin *See* NET PROFIT.

net margin ratio *See* NET PROFIT PERCENTAGE.

net national product (NNP) The *gross national product less *capital consumption (i.e. depreciation) during the period. NNP is therefore equal to the national income, i.e. the amount of money available in the economy for expenditure on goods and services. However, NNP cannot be considered a very accurate measure, as it is difficult to calculate depreciation reliably.

net position The difference between a dealer's long and short *positions in the same security or market.

net present value (NPV) A method of *capital budgeting in which the value of an investment is calculated as the total *present value of all *cash inflows and *cash outflows minus the cost of the initial investment. If the net present value is positive the investment should be considered. A negative net present value indicates that the investment should be rejected. *See also* DISCOUNTED CASH FLOW.

net price The price a buyer pays for goods or services after all discounts have been deducted.

net profit (net margin; net profit margin) The *gross profit less all the other costs of an organization in addition to those included in the *cost of sales. It is shown before and after taxation in the *profit and loss account.

net profit percentage (net margin ratio) A ratio of financial performance calculated by expressing the *net profit as a percentage of sales revenue. *Compare* GROSS PROFIT PERCENTAGE. *See also* MARGIN; MARK-UP.

net realizable value (NRV) **1.** The sales value of the stock of an organization less the additional costs likely to be incurred in getting the stocks into the hands of the customer. It is the value placed on the closing stock according to the requirements of *Statement of Standard Accounting Practice 9, when the NRV is lower than cost. **2.** The amount at which any asset could be disposed of, less any direct selling costs.

net receipts The total amount of money received by a business in a specified period after deducting costs, raw materials, taxation, etc. *Compare* GROSS RECEIPTS.

net relevant earnings A person's non-pensionable earned income before *personal allowances have been deducted but after deduction of expenses, capital allowances, losses, or any stock relief agreed with HM Revenue and Customs. It forms income from which any tax relief on pension contributions can be calculated.

net reproduction rate The number of female children in a population divided by the number of female adults in the previous generation. This figure gives a good guide to population trends; if it exceeds unity the population is expanding.

net residual value (disposal value) The

expected proceeds from the sale of an asset, net of the costs of sale, at the end of its estimated useful life. It is used for computing the *straight-line method and *diminishing-balance method of depreciation, and also for inclusion in the final year's cash inflow in a *discounted cash flow appraisal.

net return The profit made on an investment after the deduction of all expenses, either before or after deduction of *capital gains tax.

Netscape One of the first *web browsers. Introduced in 1994, it became the chief rival to Microsoft *Internet Explorer.

net tangible assets The *tangible assets of an organization less its current liabilities. In analysing the affairs of an organization the net tangible assets indicate its financial strength in terms of being solvent, without having to resort to such nebulous (and less easy to value) assets as *goodwill.

netting The process of setting off matching sales and purchases against each other, especially sales and purchases of futures, options, and forward foreign exchange. This service is usually provided for an exchange or market by a *clearing house. It also provides a means by which a firm can deal with its risks, notably *exchange-rate exposure. *See* BILATERAL NETTING; MULTILATERAL NETTING. *See also* NOVATION.

net tonnage (net register tonnage) *See* TONNAGE.

net weight *See* GROSS WEIGHT.

network *See* LOCAL AREA NETWORK.

network computer A simple access device designed for use on a computer network; it depends on a powerful central server for programs and storage.

network modelling Techniques that enable complex projects to be scheduled, taking into account the precedence of each activity.

Critical-path analysis (CPA) involves identifying all the activities that constitute the project to be modelled, determining their sequence or order of precedence, and estimating the time required for each activity. This information is used to build a graphical representation of the whole project and to establish the chain of activities that defines its overall length, i.e. the critical path. As well as being a powerful analytical tool, the visual qualities of CPA charts make them extremely useful aids to communications. With computer-based CPA programmes, managers can produce rapid updates when unexpected changes occur (e.g. the failure to complete an activity on time). These programmes also enable the appropriate resources to be allocated to the activities and detailed costings to be produced. The key to their successful use is that they should be updated continuously. Considerable resources are required to produce a CPA; if changes, postponements, etc., are not noted the chart quickly becomes irrelevant.

Programme evaluation and review technique (PERT) was developed in 1958 by the US Navy to assist in the construction of the first Polaris submarines. It is based on the same principles as CPA but uses statistical techniques to project optimistic, most probable, and pessimistic times for each activity.

net worth The value of an organization when its liabilities have been deducted from the value of its assets. Often taken to be synonymous with *net assets, net worth so defined can be misleading in that balance sheets rarely show the real value of assets. *See* BOOK VALUE.

New Community Instrument (NCI) Loans organized on the international money market by the *European Investment Bank.

new entrants 1. Those looking for work for the first time. The main group comprises school leavers but housewives are also important, especially with the recent opportunities for job sharing. 2. Firms entering an industry for the first time. They may be new organizations or established organizations entering a new field.

new for old The basis for household insurance policies in which payments of claims are not subject to a deduction for wear and tear. As a result, a claim for an old and worn-out table would be met by the payment of the price of a new table of a similar type.

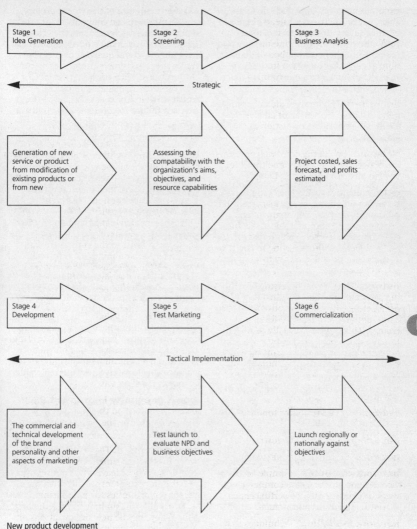

New product development

new issue Any new security, but especially a share being offered on a *stock exchange for the first time. *See* FLOTATION.

new product development (NPD) A *marketing procedure in which new ideas are developed into viable new products or extensions to existing products or product ranges. New ideas, which are generated either internally (e.g. by scientific research) or by feedback from consumers, are first screened for prima facie viability; the few that remain are further reduced by *concept tests and detailed analysis of their potential profitability. Any ideas that survive these obstacles are subjected to extensive product development. Prototypes are made and tested within the company and among consumers, and improvements made. This cycle is repeated until satisfactory marketing research results are obtained, when the new product will be launched (possibly at first in a restricted area; *see* TEST MARKETING). *See also* NEW-PRODUCTS COMMITTEE.

new-products committee A group within an organization assigned to creating new-product policies, evaluating options, and deciding whether to commercialize new products. Membership usually includes the heads of the organization's functional departments and the new-products director (if there is one).

new sol (S/.) The standard monetary unit of Peru, divided into 100 céntimos.

news release A brief written statement sent to the press describing a company's new product, product improvement, price change, or some other development of interest. The release will only be published if it is sufficiently newsworthy.

New York Stock Exchange (NYSE) The main US stock exchange. It was founded in 1792 under the Buttonwood Agreement (the name of the tree under which 24 merchants agreed to give each other preference in their dealings); it moved to Wall Street in 1793. The New York Stock & Exchange Board was formally established in 1817; it was renamed the New York Stock Exchange in 1983.

next-in-first-out cost (NIFO cost) A method of valuing units of raw material or finished goods issued from stock by using the next unit price at which a consignment will be received for pricing the issues. It is effectively using *replacement cost as a stock valuation *method, which is not normally acceptable as a stock valuation system in the UK when computing profits for taxation purposes. *Compare* FIRST-IN-FIRST-OUT COST; LAST-IN-FIRST-OUT COST.

N-form Describing a type of organizational structure in which several smaller companies representing different stages in the production process establish informal links with one another rather than joining together in vertical *integration. The 'N' stands for 'network'. Recent years have seen a trend towards N-form and *M-form structures.

NGT Abbreviation for *nominal group technique.

ngultrum (Nu) The standard monetary unit of Bhutan, divided into 100 chetrum.

ngwee A monetary unit of Zambia, worth one hundredth of a *kwacha.

NIC Abbreviation for *National Insurance contribution.

niche marketing *See* CONCENTRATED SEGMENTATION.

NIF Abbreviation for *note issuance facility.

NIFO cost Abbreviation for *next-in-first-out cost.

night safe A service provided by commercial banks, enabling customers to deposit cash with the bank after banking hours. By using this service shopkeepers, etc., can avoid keeping large sums overnight. A special wallet provided by the bank is inserted into a safe in the outside wall of the bank to which customers are given the key. The following day the wallet is opened, either by the customer or by a bank clerk, and the customer's account is credited accordingly.

Nikkei Stock Average An index of prices on the *Tokyo Stock Exchange. It was originally known as the **Nikkei Dow Jones Index** and first calculated on 16 May 1949, based at 176.21. The Nikkei Stock Average is a price-weighted index of 225 Japanese companies representing 19% of first section issues, and accounting for about 51% of market value. It was restructured for the first time in its history in late 1991 by its administrator, the Nikon Keizai Shimbun financial newspaper group, to try to reduce the impact of futures-related trading on the index (Nikkei is a shortening of the full name of the newspaper group). Membership of the index is now reviewed annually, when up to six members can be replaced if their shares become illiquid or unrepresentative. Previous changes only occurred when companies were taken over or liquidated.

nil basis The basis upon which the *earnings per share of a company is calculated taking into account only the constant elements in the company's tax charge. *Compare* NET BASIS.

NIT Abbreviation for *negative income tax.

NL Abbreviation for no liability. It appears after the name of an Australian company, being equivalent to the British abbreviation *plc (denoting a public limited company).

NMS Abbreviation for *Normal Market Size.

NNP Abbreviation for *net national product.

no-arbitrage condition *See* ARBITRAGE-FREE CONDITION.

no-claim bonus A reward, in the form of a premium discount, given to policyholders if they complete a year or more without making a claim. The system is mostly used in motor insurance. In every case, the bonus is allowed for remaining claim-free and is not dependent on blame for a particular accident.

node *See* LOCAL AREA NETWORK.

noise **1.** In communication theory, any interference or distraction that disrupts the communication process. **2.** In statistics, random fluctuations in data.

nominal account A ledger *account that is not a *personal account in that it bears the name of a concept, e.g. light and heat, bad debts, investments, etc., rather than the name of a person. These accounts are normally grouped in the *nominal ledger. *See also* REAL ACCOUNT.

nominal capital (**authorized capital**) *See* SHARE CAPITAL.

nominal group technique (**NGT**) A group problem-solving technique in which each member of the group is asked to write down a list of ideas without talking to their colleagues. The ideas elicited in this way are then discussed and criticized by the group, who are not told which members contributed which ideas. Similar ideas are grouped or merged; when the discussion has finished the panel ranks the remaining ideas, again without discussion. The individual rankings are then combined mathematically to find the favoured solution, which is adopted. The NGT is intended to eliminate such problems of group decision making as *groupthink, deference to authority, political manoeuvring, and personal likes or dislikes.

nominal interest rate **1.** An interest rate not adjusted for inflation. **2.** The interest rate on a fixed-interest security calculated as a percentage of its par value rather than its market price.

nominal ledger The *ledger containing the *nominal accounts and *real accounts necessary to prepare the accounts of an organization. This ledger is distinguished from the personal ledgers, such as the *sales and *purchase ledgers, which contain the accounts of customers and suppliers respectively.

nominal partner *See* PARTNERSHIP.

nominal price **1.** A minimal price fixed for the sake of having some *consideration for a transaction. It need bear no relation to the market value of the item. **2.** The price given to a security when it is issued. This is the maximum amount the holder can be required to contribute to the company. *See* PAR VALUE.

nominal value *See* PAR VALUE.

nominal yield *See* YIELD.

nomination The person to whom the proceeds of a life-assurance policy should be paid as specified by the policyholder. *See* ASSIGNMENT OF LIFE POLICIES.

nominee A person named by another (the **nominator**) to act on his or her behalf, often to conceal the identity of the nominator. *See* NOMINEE SHAREHOLDING.

nominee shareholding A shareholding held in the name of a bank, stockbroker, company, individual, etc., that is not the name of the beneficial owner of the shares. A shareholding may be in the name of nominees to facilitate dealing or to conceal the identity of the true owner. Although this cover was formerly used in the early stages of a *takeover bid, to enable the bidder clandestinely to build up a substantial holding in the target company, this is now prevented by the Companies

Act (1985), which makes it mandatory for anyone holding 5% or more of the shares in a public company to declare that interest to the company. The earlier Companies Act (1967) made it mandatory for directors to openly declare their holdings, and those of their families, in the companies of which they are directors.

non-acceptance The failure by the person on whom a *bill of exchange is drawn to accept it on presentation.

non-adjusting events Any events occurring between the balance-sheet date and the date on which the *financial statements of an organization are approved that relate to conditions that did not exist at the balance-sheet date. If they are sufficiently material for their non-disclosure to affect a user's understanding of the financial statements, non-adjusting events should be disclosed in the notes to the accounts. If a non-adjusting event suggests that the *going-concern concept is no longer applicable to the whole, or a material part, of the company, changes in the amounts to be included in the financial statements should be made. For example, if serious industrial action has occurred, which if it continues could threaten the continued existence of the business, an appropriate provision should be made in the accounts. *Compare* ADJUSTING EVENTS.

non-adopter A member of the group of consumers who never buys a particular new product or adopts a certain new style. *See* ADOPTION OF INNOVATIONS.

non-assented stock *See* ASSENTED STOCK.

non-business days *See* BANK HOLIDAYS.

non-contributory pension A *pension in which the full premium is paid by an employer or the state and the pensioner makes no contribution. *Compare* CONTRIBUTORY PENSION.

non-cumulative preference share A *preference share that does not have the right to *dividends unpaid in previous years. *Compare* CUMULATIVE PREFERENCE SHARE.

non-cumulative quantity discount A price discount determined by the size of

an individual purchase order. The larger the order, the larger the discount.

non-domiciled Denoting a person whose country of *domicile is not the same as his or her country of residence for tax purposes.

non-durables Consumer non-durables. *See* CONSUMER GOODS.

non-equity share A *share in a company having any of the following characteristics:
- any of the rights of the share to receive payments are for a limited amount that is not calculated by reference to the company's assets or profits or the dividends on any class of equity share;
- any of the rights of the share to participate in a surplus on *liquidation are limited to a specific amount that is not calculated by reference to the company's assets or profits;
- the share is redeemable either according to its terms or because the holder, or any party other than the issuer, can require its redemption.

This definition is based on that contained in *Financial Reporting Standard (FRS) 4, Capital Instruments. A number of changes to FRS 4 were introduced by FRS 25, Financial Instruments: Disclosure and Presentation, which was issued in late 2004 (*see* PREFERENCE SHARE CAPITAL).

non-executive director A director of a company who is not involved in the day-to-day management of the business but who is appointed to bring independent judgement on issues of strategy, performance, resources, and standards of conduct. The Cadbury Report on corporate governance recommended the appointment of non-executive directors (*see* CADBURY CODE). Such directors are often employed for their prestige, experience, contacts, or specialist knowledge.

non-marketable securities Securities that are not sold on financial markets, notably (in the UK) savings bonds and National Savings Certificates.

non-monetary advantages and disadvantages Those aspects of an employment that are not connected with its financial remuneration. They include the employees' subjective opinion of their working environment, the stimulation or boredom of the work itself, the companionship or isolation experienced in their place of work, the distance travelled to reach work, etc. These aspects of an employment, together with the salary, bonuses, commission, and fringe benefits, make employees decide either to stay in their present jobs or seek another. *See* INTRINSIC REWARD; JOB SATISFACTION.

non-negotiable instruments *See* NEGOTIABLE INSTRUMENT.

non-participating preference share A *preference share that does not carry a right to participate in the profits of a company beyond a fixed rate of *dividend. This is the most common type of preference share.

non-personal communication channel A channel of communication that carries messages without personal contact or feedback, including the media, radio, TV, etc.

non-price competition A form of competition in which two or more producers sell goods or services at the same price but compete to increase their share of the market by such measures as advertising, sales promotion campaigns, improving the quality of the product or service, delivery time, and (for goods) improving the packaging, offering free servicing and installation, or giving free gifts of unrelated products or services.

non-probability sampling A sampling procedure in which the sample is chosen on the basis of convenience, personal judgement (*see* JUDGEMENTAL SAMPLING), quota controls (*see* QUOTA SAMPLING), or some other principle, rather than on the basis of random selection from a population. *Compare* PROBABILITY SAMPLING.

non-production overhead costs The *indirect costs of an organization that are not classified as *manufacturing overhead. They include administration overheads, *selling overhead, *distribution overhead, and (in some cases) *research and development costs.

non-profit marketing (social marketing) Organized marketing used by non-profit-making organizations, including those involved in education, culture, health care, charity, social causes, politics, and religious doctrines.

non-qualifying policy A UK life-assurance policy that does not satisfy the qualification rules contained in Schedule 15 of the Income and Corporation Taxes Act (1988).

non-resident The status of an individual who has never lived in a particular country for fiscal purposes or who has moved to another country, either for employment or permanently. This person's liability to tax in the first country is restricted to income from sources within that country. Interest on all British government stocks is exempt from UK tax for non-residents. *See also* RESIDENT; DOUBLE TAXATION.

non-revolving bank facility A loan from a bank to a company in which the company has a period (often several years) in which to make its *drawdowns, as well as flexibility with regard to the amount and timing of the drawdowns, but once drawn an amount takes on the characteristics of a *term loan. *Compare* REVOLVING BANK FACILITY.

non-sampling errors All the errors that can occur in *marketing research other than the *sampling error. These can include a badly phrased questionnaire, an error made by the interviewer, an error made by the respondent, etc.

non-statutory accounts Any financial statement issued by a company that does not form part of the statutory *annual accounts. Prior to the Companies Act (1989) they were known as **abridged accounts**. Under this legislation a company has to make a statement on any non-statutory accounts it issues to the effect that they are not the statutory accounts. Such accounts are often reported in the media.

non-systematic risk *See* SPECIFIC RISK.

non-tariff office *See* TARIFF OFFICE.

non-tariff trade barrier A non-monetary barrier to a foreign product or service, such as a bias against a foreign company's product standards or a rejection of a foreign country's political record.

non-taxable income Income that is

specifically exempt from tax. Examples of such income include:

- income received under a maintenance agreement or court order in cases of divorce or separation;
- income from National Savings Easy Access Savings Accounts;
- income from *Individual Savings Accounts (ISAs);
- up to £4250 annually from a 'rent-a-room' scheme;
- income from scholarships;
- winnings from betting (including the National Lottery) and competition prizes.

no par value capital stock In the USA and Canada, stock (shares) that have no *par value printed on the stock certificate. An advantage of such stock is that it avoids a *contingent liability to stockholders in the event of a stock discount. For accounting purposes, on the issue of no par value capital stock, cash is debited and a capital stock account credited with the total proceeds received. No premium account is required. No par value shares are not permitted under UK law.

normal distribution (Gaussian distribution) The symmetrical bell-shaped frequency curve formed when the frequency of a range of values is plotted on the vertical axis against the value of a random variable on the horizontal axis. The bell shape indicates that extreme values (both large and small) occur infrequently, while the more frequent occurrences are clustered around the *arithmetic mean value, which in a normal distribution is also equal to the *median and the **mode** (the value that occurs most frequently in a set of data).

A wide variety of natural, social, and economic phenomena fall approximately into a normal distribution, which is therefore an important concept in statistical analysis. From Figure 1 it can be seen that if a population is investigated, the **range**

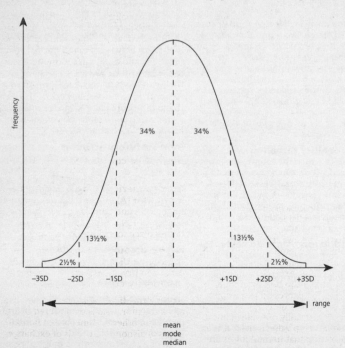

Normal distribution curve. Figure 1: the bell-shaped normal distribution curve

of values is six times the *standard deviation (SD), i.e. almost all the values from the population lie within three SDs either side of the mean. For a normal distribution, one SD either side of the mean can be seen to cover 68% (34% + 34%) of observed values (or the area under the curve); for two SDs it covers 95%; and for three SDs it covers 99%.

The SD is important in marketing research as it provides the researcher with some idea of the range of answers to a question. In Figure 2, two sample populations, A and B, have the same mean, but population B has a greater SD than population A (indicated by the spread of the curve). While the researcher may have asked both populations the same questions, with both populations on average agreeing (i.e. the same mean), there is a greater dispersion in population B, indicating a greater variation of opinion than in A.

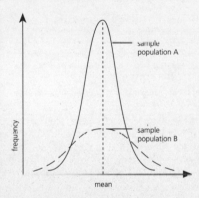

Figure 2: normal distribution curves having the same mean but different standard deviations.

normal loss The loss arising from a manufacturing or chemical process through waste, seepage, shrinkage, or spoilage that can be expected, on the basis of historical studies, to be part of that process. It may be expressed as a weight or volume or in other units appropriate to the process. It is usually not valued but if it is, a notional scrap value is used. It is axiomatic in costing that normal losses are part of the normal *manufacturing cost, whereas the cost of abnormal losses

should not be borne by the good output. *See also* WASTE.

Normal Market Size (NMS) A classification system for trading in securities, which replaced the alpha, beta, gamma, and delta classification used on the *London Stock Exchange in January 1991. The old system had developed in a way that, contrary to the original intention, had made it a measure of corporate virility. NMS is the minimum size of the package of shares in a company traded in normal-sized market transactions; there are 12 categories. The main purpose of the system is to fix the size of transactions in which *market makers are obliged to deal, and to set a basis on which the bargains should be published.

normal retirement age The age at which an individual is expected to retire. At present this is normally 65 for a man and 60 for a woman in the UK. It is at these ages that state pensions begin. However, other policies can nominate other pre-agreed dates, which HM Revenue and Customs will accept in certain cases. The inequality between a man's normal retirement age and a woman's retirement age in the UK will be phased out from 2010, so that both sexes qualify for state pensions at 65.

normal yield curve A *yield curve in which the yield rises in proportion to the length of time the security has to run until maturity.

normative contract *See* PSYCHOLOGICAL CONTRACT.

North American Free Trade Agreement (NAFTA) A free trade treaty signed by the USA and Canada in 1988, and by Mexico in 1993. Negotiations are currently taking place to include Chile.

nostro account A bank account conducted by a UK bank with a bank in another country, usually in the currency of that country. *Compare* VOSTRO ACCOUNT.

notary public A legal practitioner, usually a solicitor, who is empowered to attest deeds and other documents and notes (*see* NOTING) dishonoured *bills of exchange.

note 1. A *promissory note. **2.** A negotiable record of an unsecured loan (*see*

COMMERCIAL PAPER). The word 'note' is now used in preference to *bond when the principal sum is repayable in less than five years. **3.** A *banknote. **4.** An inscription on an unpaid *bill of exchange (*see* NOTING) made by a *notary public.

notebook computer *See* LAPTOP COMPUTER.

note issuance facility (NIF; note purchase facility**)** A means of enabling short-term borrowers in the *eurocurrency markets to issue euronotes, with maturities of less than one year, when the need arises rather than having to arrange a separate issue of euronotes each time they need to borrow. A **revolving underwriting facility** (RUF) achieves the same objective.

notes to the accounts (notes to financial statements) Information supporting that given on the face of a company's *financial statements. Many notes are required to be given by law, including those detailing *fixed assets, investments, *share capital, *debentures, and *reserves. Other information may be required by accounting standards or be given to facilitate the users' understanding of the company and its current and future performance.

notice day The day on which notice must be given that goods will be supplied to fulfil a commodity-market contract, rather than having it cancelled out by a matching contract.

notice in lieu of distringas *See* STOP NOTICE.

notice of abandonment *See* ABANDONMENT.

notice of motion *See* MOTION.

noting 1. The procedure adopted if a *bill of exchange has been dishonoured by non-acceptance or by non-payment. Not later than the next business day after the day on which it was dishonoured, the holder has to hand it to a *notary public to be noted. The notary re-presents the bill; if it is still unaccepted or unpaid, the circumstances are noted in a register and also on a **notarial ticket**, which is attached to the bill. The noting can then, if necessary, be extended to a *protest. **2.** In advertising research, noticing a particular

advertisement when first looking through a newspaper or magazine in which it appears. *See* NOTING SCORE.

noting score The average number of readers *noting a particular advertisement or editorial item in a newspaper or magazine, expressed as a percentage of the total readership.

not negotiable Words marked on a *bill of exchange indicating that it ceases to be a *negotiable instrument, i.e. although it can still be negotiated, the holder cannot obtain a better title to it than the person from whom it was obtained, thus providing a safeguard if it is stolen. A cheque is the only form of bill that can be crossed 'not negotiable'; other forms must have it inscribed on their faces.

novation The replacement of one legal agreement by a new obligation, with the agreement of all the parties. For example, on exchanges using the *London Clearing House (LCH.Clearnet), transactions between members are novated by LCH, so that one contract is created between the buyer and LCH while a matching contract is created between the seller and LCH (*see* COUNTERPARTY RISK).

NOW Abbreviation for *negotiable order of withdrawal.

NPD Abbreviation for *new product development.

NPV Abbreviation for *net present value.

NRV Abbreviation for *net realizable value.

nudum pactum (Latin: nude contract) An agreement that is unenforceable in British law because no *consideration is mentioned. *See* CONTRACT.

numbered account A bank account identified only by a number. This service, offered by some Swiss banks at one time, encouraged funds that had been obtained illegally to find their way to Switzerland. A numbered account is now more frequently used to ensure legitimate privacy.

numerically controlled machine tools Computer-controlled machine tools that store within their built-in memories the parameters of the components they are producing. This enables them to produce work to consistent standards using relatively unskilled labour.

NV Abbreviation for *Naamloze Vennootschap*. It appears after the name of a Dutch company, being equivalent to the British abbreviation Ltd (i.e. denoting a limited liability company). *Compare* BV.

NVQ Abbreviation for National Vocational Qualification. *See* VOCATIONAL TRAINING.

NYSE Abbreviation for *New York Stock Exchange.

O & M *See* ORGANIZATION AND METHODS.

objective and task method A method of setting a promotional budget in which the marketer decides the objective to be accomplished and the tasks necessary to achieve the objective. The budget is decided by estimating the costs of carrying out the tasks.

objectivity An accounting concept attempting to ensure that any subjective actions taken by the preparer of accounts are minimized. The aim of the rules and regulations required to achieve objectivity is that users should be able to compare *financial statements for different companies over a period with some confidence that the statements have been prepared on the same basis (*see* COMPARABILITY). One of the major advantages claimed for *historical-cost accounting is that it is objective, but necessarily some subjective decisions will have been made.

objects clause A clause contained in the *memorandum of association of a company setting out the objects for which the company has been formed. If the activities undertaken by a company are not included in the objects clause, the company is said to be acting beyond its powers, i.e. *ultra vires.

obligation **1.** The duty of a borrower to repay a loan and that of the lender to ensure that repayment is made. **2.** A bond or other promise to pay a sum of money.

obligatory expenditure The spending of the European Union, governed by such treaties as the *Common Agricultural Policy and the *European Regional Development Fund. The European Parliament can add to the amount spent but if it wishes to reduce it, it must obtain the agreement of the Council of Ministers, or reject the whole of the Union Budget in that year.

observation research Marketing research in which a respondent's actions are monitored without direct interaction, without using an interviewer.

OBSF Abbreviation for *off-balance-sheet finance.

obsolescence A fall in the value of an asset as a result of its age. For example, plant and equipment may not have actually worn out but may have become out of date because technology has advanced and more efficient plant has become available. It also applies to consumer durables (*see* CONSUMER GOODS), in which a change of style may render a serviceable piece of equipment, such as a car or washing machine, out of date. In accounting, obsolescence is an important factor both for *depreciation of fixed assets and for valuation of stock.

   Built-in obsolescence or **planned obsolescence** is a deliberate policy adopted by a manufacturer to limit the durability of a product in order to encourage the consumer to buy a replacement more quickly than he or she otherwise might have to. The morality of this policy has been frequently questioned but is usually defended on two grounds. Firstly, in the modern world, the pace of technological improvement is such that many consumers will choose to buy new computers, CD players, etc., before their existing models have worn out. In these circumstances, it makes sense for manufacturers to produce cheap products that will function well for a fairly short period rather than more expensive ones that will function long after they have become technically obsolete. Secondly, Western economies depend on strong consumer demand; if such consumer durables as cars and washing machines were built to last for their purchaser's lifetime, demand would be reduced to a level that would create enormous unemployment.

occasion segmentation Dividing a market into groups according to the occasions on which buyers get the idea to buy, actually make their purchase, or use the purchased item.

occupational hazard A risk of accident or illness at one's place of work. Dangerous jobs usually command higher salaries than those involving no risks, the increase being known as **danger money**. *See also* HEALTH AND SAFETY COMMISSION.

occupational pension scheme (superannuation) A pension scheme open to employees within a certain trade or profession or working for a particular firm. An occupational pension scheme can either be insured or self-administered. If it is insured, an insurance company pays the benefits under the scheme in return for having the premiums to invest. In a self-administered scheme, the pension-fund trustees are responsible for investing the contributions themselves. In order to run an occupational pension scheme, an organization must satisfy the Occupational Pension Board that the scheme complies with the conditions allowing employers to contract out of the State Second Pension (*see* STATE EARNINGS-RELATED PENSION SCHEME). *See also* DEFINED-BENEFIT PENSION SCHEME; DEFINED-CONTRIBUTION PENSION SCHEME.

OCR Abbreviation for *optical character recognition.

OD Abbreviation for *organizational development.

odd-even pricing The pricing of a product so that the price ends in an odd number of pence, which is not far below the next number of pounds. For example, £4.99 might be used in preference to £5.00 in order to make the product appear cheaper.

odd lot *See* ROUND LOT.

OECD Abbreviation for *Organization for Economic Cooperation and Development.

OEIC Abbreviation for *open-ended investment company.

Ofcom *See* OFFICE OF COMMUNICATIONS.

off-balance-sheet finance (OBSF) A method of financing a company's activities so that some or all of the finance and the corresponding assets do not appear on the *balance sheet of the company. By making

use of OBSF a company can enhance its *accounting ratios, such as the *gearing ratio and *return on capital employed, and also avoid breaking any agreements it has made with the banks in respect of the total amount it may borrow. It has been possible for companies, by drawing up complex legal agreements, to conduct off-balance-sheet finance and thus mislead the user of the accounts. The accounting profession has attempted to counter these practices by emphasizing that accounting should reflect the commercial reality of transactions and not simply their legal form. *Financial Reporting Standard 5, Reporting the Substance of Transactions, provides specific guidance for certain transactions, such as *factoring and *consignment stock, for which companies have previously used off-balance-sheet finance.

In the USA, off-balance-sheet finance was identified as a major factor in the scandal surrounding the collapse of the energy-trading giant Enron in 2002 – the largest business scandal in US history. *See* CREATIVE ACCOUNTING; HIDDEN RESERVE.

off-balance-sheet reserve *See* HIDDEN RESERVE.

off-card rate An advertising charging rate that is different from that shown on the *rate card, having been separately negotiated.

offer The price at which a seller makes it known that he is willing to sell something. If there is an *acceptance of the offer a legally binding *contract has been entered into. In law, an offer is distinguished from an **invitation to treat**, which is an invitation by one person or firm to others to make an offer. An example of an invitation to treat is to display goods in a shop window. *See also* FIRM OFFER; OFFER PRICE; QUOTATION.

offer by prospectus An offer to the public of a new issue of shares or debentures made directly by means of a *prospectus, a document giving a detailed account of the aims, objects, and capital structure of the company, as well as its past history. The prospectus must conform to the provisions of the Companies Act (1985). *Compare* OFFER FOR SALE.

offer document A document sent to

the shareholders of a company that is the subject of a *takeover bid. It gives details of the offer being made and usually provides shareholders with reasons for accepting the terms of the offer.

offer for sale An invitation to the general public to purchase the stock of a company through an intermediary, such as an issuing house or *merchant bank (*compare* OFFER BY PROSPECTUS); it is one of the most frequently used means of *flotation. An offer for sale can be in one of two forms: a *public issue (the more usual), in which stock is offered at a fixed price and some form of balloting or rationing is required if the demand for the shares exceeds supply; or an *issue by tender, in which individuals offer to purchase a fixed quantity of stock at or above some minimum price and the stock is allocated to the highest bidders. *Compare* INTRODUCTION; PLACING.

offer price 1. The price at which a security is offered for sale by a *market maker. *Compare* BID PRICE. **2.** The price at which an institution will sell units in a *unit trust.

offer to purchase *See* TAKEOVER BID.

Office for National Statistics The UK government's statistical unit, formed by a merger of the **Central Statistical Office** and the Office of Population Censuses and Surveys in 1996. It is an executive agency of the Treasury responsible for collecting economic statistics for the government. Among its publications are *UK National Accounts* (the *Blue Book*), *UK Balance of Payments* (the *Pink Book*), and the *Annual Abstract of Statistics*. *See also* BUSINESS STATISTICS OFFICE.

Office of Fair Trading (OFT) A government department that reviews commercial activities in the UK and aims to protect the consumer against unfair practices. It was established in 1973 and has three main operational areas: competition enforcement, consumer regulation enforcement, and markets and policies initiatives. It also runs advice and information services and liaises with the relevant departments of the European Commission.

Office of Communications (Ofcom) A UK government body set up in 2003 to supervise the communications industries. It was formed from a merger of the Office for Telecommunications (Oftel) and the various regulatory bodies for radio and television broadcasting. It is responsible for issuing licences, regulating competition, and protecting the interests of the consumer.

Office of Thrift Supervision (OTS) An agency of the US Treasury, founded in 1989, that supervises the country's *savings and loan associations.

officer of a company A person who acts in an official capacity in a company. Company officers include the directors, managers, the company secretary, and in some circumstances the company's auditors and solicitors. The Companies Act (1985) empowers a court dealing with a *liquidation to investigate the conduct of the company's officers with a view to recovering any money they may have obtained illegally or incorrectly.

Official List 1. A list of all the securities traded on the *main market of the *London Stock Exchange. *See* LISTED SECURITY; LISTING REQUIREMENTS. **2. (Daily Official List)** A list prepared daily by the London Stock Exchange, recording all the bargains that have been transacted in listed securities during the day. It also gives dividend dates, rights issues, prices, and other information.

official rate The rate of exchange given to a currency by a government. If the official rate differs from the market rate, the government has to be prepared to support its official rate by buying or selling in the open market to make the two rates coincide.

official receiver (OR) A person appointed by the Secretary of State for Trade and Industry to act as a *receiver in *bankruptcy and winding-up cases. The High Court and each county court that has jurisdiction over insolvency matters has an official receiver, who is an officer of the court. Deputy official receivers may also be appointed. The official receiver commonly acts as the *liquidator of a company being wound up by the court.

official strike *See* STRIKE.

off-line 1. Not connected to a computer

or the Internet. **2.** Denoting computer equipment that is not usable, either because it is not connected to a computer or because the system has been forbidden to use it. *Compare* ON-LINE.

offprint A reprint or photocopy of an article from a periodical or paper.

offset **1.** The right that enables a bank to seize any bank-account balances of a guarantor or debtor if a loan has been defaulted upon (*see also* GARNISHEE ORDER). **2.** A code on the magnetic strip of a plastic card that, together with the *personal identification number (PIN), verifies that the user of the card is entitled to use it. **3.** To cancel a futures contract or options contract by entering into a reverse agreement.

offsetting swap (mirror swap) A *swap in which cash flows exactly offset those of an existing swap.

offshore banking *See* OFFSHORE FINANCIAL CENTRES.

offshore company **1.** A company not registered in the same country as that in which the persons investing in the company are resident. **2.** A company set up in a foreign country or *tax haven by a financial institution with the object of benefiting from tax laws or exchange control regulations in that country.

offshore financial centres Centres that provide advantageous deposit and lending rates to non-residents because of low taxation, liberal exchange controls, and low reserve requirements for banks. Some countries have made a lucrative business out of **offshore banking**; the Cayman Islands is currently one of the world's largest offshore centres. In Europe, Switzerland, the Channel Islands, and the Isle of Man are very popular. Such locations are often described as *tax havens because they can reduce customers' tax liabilities in entirely legal ways. The USA and Japan have both established domestic offshore facilities enabling non-residents to conduct their business under more liberal regulations than domestic transactions. Their objective is to stop funds moving outside the country.

offshore fund **1.** A fund that is based in an *offshore financial centre outside the

UK to avoid UK taxation. Offshore funds operate in the same way as *unit trusts but are not supervised by the Department of Trade and Industry. **2.** Any fund held outside the country of residence of the holder.

off-the-peg research Marketing research that uses existing data, rather than a fresh investigation of a market. *See also* DESK RESEARCH.

off-the-shelf company A company that is registered with the *Registrar of Companies although it does not trade and has no directors. It can, however, be sold and reformed into a new company with the minimum of formality and expense. Such companies are easily purchased from specialist brokers.

OFR Abbreviation for *operating and financial review.

OFT Abbreviation for *Office of Fair Trading.

Old Lady of Threadneedle Street An affectionate name for the *Bank of England, coined by the English politician and dramatist R B Sheridan (1751–1816). The street in which the Bank stands (since 1734 in a Renaissance building by George Sampson) probably takes its name from the thread and needle used by the Merchant Taylors, a guild whose hall is in the same street.

oligopoly A market in which relatively few sellers supply many buyers. Each seller recognizes that prices can be controlled to a certain extent and that competitors' actions will influence profits. *See also* MONOPOLY.

Ombudsman *See* FINANCIAL OMBUDSMAN SERVICE.

OMLX *See* LONDON SECURITIES AND DERIVATIVES EXCHANGE.

omnibus research *Marketing research surveys based on multipart questionnaires sent out regularly to a panel of respondents. Space on the questionnaire is available to companies that have specific marketing research needs, especially those having a limited number of questions to ask, which would not alone justify setting up a separate research study.

OMV Abbreviation for open market value. *See* MARKET VALUE.

on approval (on appro) The practice of allowing potential buyers to take possession of goods in order to decide whether or not they wish to buy them. The potential buyer is a bailee (*see* BAILMENT) and is obliged to return the goods in perfect condition after deciding not to purchase them. Many department stores and mail-order firms allow their customers to take goods on appro.

on consignment *See* CONSIGNMENT.

oncost 1. The additional costs incurred as a consequence of employing personnel, i.e. **wages oncost**, or the additional costs incurred by storing and handling direct materials, i.e. **materials oncost** or **stores oncost. 2.** A rarely used alternative name for *overheads.

on demand Denoting any liability that may be subject to immediate repayment.

one-month money Money placed on the *money market for one month, i.e. it cannot be withdrawn without penalty during this period.

one-to-one marketing A form of marketing in which dialogue occurs directly between a company and individual customers (or, less strictly, with groups of customers with similar needs). The dialogue involves a company listening to the needs of a customer and responding with services to meet these needs.

one-year money Money placed on the *money market for one year, i.e. it cannot be withdrawn without penalty for one year.

on-line 1. Of, relating to, or connected to the Internet. **2.** Denoting computer equipment that is connected to a computer system and is usable by it. *Compare* OFF-LINE.

on-line advertising Advertising on the Internet, typically by *banner advertisements or by pop-up pages, which appear when a user opens a particular page.

on-line banking *See* HOME BANKING.

on-line brand *See* DIGITAL BRAND.

on-line focus groups A form of Inter-

net research in which participants attend a virtual *focus group meeting held at a website. It is particularly useful if collecting all the group participants in one location is difficult.

on-line incentive schemes *See* LOYALTY TECHNIQUES.

on-line marketing Direct marketing conducted through interactive on-line computer services that provide two-way systems, electronically linking consumers with sellers.

on-line service provider (OSP) An *Internet service provider (ISP) having a large amount of specially developed *content available to subscribers. The distinction between an ISP and an OSP is blurred as the distinction depends on the amount of premium content (only available to customers) offered as part of the service.

on stream Denoting that a specified investment or asset is providing the expected revenues.

OPEC Abbreviation for *Organization of the Petroleum Exporting Countries.

open auction An *auction in which each participant is aware of the value of the others' bids.

open charter *See* CHARTERING.

open cheque *See* CHEQUE.

open cover (open policy) A marine cargo insurance policy in which the insurer agrees to cover any voyage undertaken by the policyholder's vessel(s) or any cargo shipped by a particular shipper. A policy condition requires a declaration to be completed on a weekly, monthly, or quarterly basis indicating the vessels involved, the commodities carried, and the voyages undertaken. Insurers use the declaration to calculate the premium. The main advantage of a policy of this kind is that the insurer can be confident that all cargos have insurance cover without the need to notify insurers of the details before the voyage. In some cases there may be a policy limit above which the insurance ceases. On such policies it is necessary to keep a running total of the sums insured to make sure that the policy limit is not exceeded.

open credit Unlimited credit offered by a supplier to a trusted client.

open-door policy An import policy of a country in which all goods from all sources are imported on the same terms, usually free of import duties.

open economy An economy in which a significant percentage of its goods and services are traded internationally. The degree of openness of an economy usually depends on the amount of overseas trade in which the country is involved or the political policies of its government. Thus the UK economy is relatively open, as the economy is significantly dependent on foreign trade, while the US economy is relatively closed as overseas trade is not as important to its economy.

open-ended investment company (OEIC) An *investment trust that operates an *open-end trust. The size of its fund depends on the number of units sold.

open-ended question A question that requires respondents to provide answers in their own words, rather than 'yes', 'no', or 'don't know'. Such questions as Why…? What…? When…? are asked without providing answers from which to choose. Open-ended questions are often used in *exploratory research. Compare MULTIPLE-CHOICE QUESTION; STRUCTURED INTERVIEW.

open-end trust A form of unit trust in which the managers of the trust may vary the investments held without notifying the unit holders. Open-end trusts are used in the USA.

open general licence An import licence for goods on which there are no import restrictions.

open indent An order to an overseas purchasing agent to buy certain goods, without specifying the manufacturer. If the manufacturer is specified this is a **closed indent**.

opening prices The *bid prices and *offer prices made at the opening of a day's trading on any security or commodity market. The opening prices may not always be identical to the previous evening's *closing prices, especially if any significant events have taken place during the intervening period.

opening stock The inventory held by an organization at the beginning of an accounting period as *raw materials, *work in progress, or *finished goods. The *closing stocks of one period become the opening stocks of the succeeding period and it is necessary to establish the level of closing stocks so that the cost of their creation is not charged against the profits of that period but brought forward as opening stocks to be charged against the profits of the succeeding period.

open-market operations The purchase or sale by a central bank of bonds (gilt-edged securities) in exchange for money, with the aim of influencing monetary policy. Buying debt provides liquidity and selling debt reduces liquidity in the private banking sector.

open market value (OMV) *See* MARKET VALUE.

open outcry Quoting prices, making offers, bids, and acceptances, and concluding transactions by word of mouth in a financial market, usually in a trading *pit. *See also* CALLOVER; DOUBLE AUCTION.

open policy *See* OPEN COVER.

open position (naked position) A trading position in which a dealer has commodities, *securities, or currencies bought but unsold or unhedged (*see* HEDGE), or sales that are neither covered nor hedged. In either case the dealer is vulnerable to market fluctuations until the position is closed or hedged.

open-pricing agreement An agreement between firms operating in an oligopolistic market in which prices and intended price changes are circulated to those taking part in the agreement in order to avoid a *price war.

open shop *See* CLOSED SHOP.

open standards Software protocols and operations on the Internet that are readily available, widely documented, and not controlled by a private company.

open system A system that is affected by influences from outside its system boundary and that is able to affect other systems. *Compare* CLOSED SYSTEM.

operating and financial review (OFR)
A statement published with a company's
*annual accounts and *directors' report in
which the directors discuss the business's
performance, giving both positive and
negative points. It is broadly similar to the
*management discussion and analysis
statement issued by US companies. For
financial years beginning on or after 1 January 2005, listed companies are required
to prepare a statutory OFR; this should include key performance indicators and,
where appropriate, information on employees and the company's environmental
record.

operating budget A forecast of the
financial requirements for the future trading of an organization, including its
planned sales, production, cash flow, etc.
An operating budget is normally designed
for a fixed period, usually one year, and
forms the plan for that period's trading activities. Any divergences from it are usually monitored and, if appropriate,
changes can then be made to it as the period progresses. *See* BUDGETARY CONTROL.

operating costs *See* OVERHEAD.

operating doctrine Stock-control policies that specify when and how much
stock should be reordered.

operating lease A lease under which
an asset is hired out to a lessee or lessees
for a period that is substantially shorter
than its useful economic life. Under an operating lease, the ownership of the leased
asset remains with the lessor. *Statement
of Standard Accounting Practice 21, Accounting for Leases and Hire Purchase
Contracts, defines an operating lease as a
lease other than a *finance lease.

operating profit/loss The profit or loss
made by a company as a result of its principal trading activity. This is arrived at by
deducting its **operating expenses** from its
*trading profit, or adding its operating ex-
penses to its trading loss; in either case
this is before taking into account any *extraordinary items.

operating statement A financial and
quantitative statement provided for the
management of an organization to record
the performance achieved by that area of
the operation for which the management

is responsible, for a selected budget period. An operating statement may include
production levels, costs incurred, and
(where appropriate) revenue generated, all
compared with budgeted amounts and the
performance in previous periods.

operating system 1. The collection of
programs that controls the basic operation
of a *computer. Usually purchased with
the computer, it controls such tasks as
start-up routines, input and output, and
memory allocation. It is also responsible
for loading and executing programs. In
small systems, the operating system loads
a program and then gives it control of the
machine. In larger *multitasking systems,
the operating system always retains control of the machine, ensuring that the separate programs do not interfere with each
other and controlling the amount of processing time each receives. **2.** The
configuration of the activities concerned
with transforming resources within an organization. The way in which a particular
organization arranges the components of
its operating system will be a product of
its *operations strategy. While there may
be areas of similarity between successful
organizations, there is no single right way
to set up an operating system. Each system is an attempt to achieve the optimum
match between organizational capabilities
and perceived environmental conditions.

operational flexibility *See* FLEXIBILITY.

**operational gearing (operational lever-
age)** The ratio of a company's *fixed costs
to its total costs. The higher the level of
operational gearing, the greater the risk,
since fixed costs have to be covered before
a profit can be recorded.

operational indicators *See* PERFOR-
MANCE MEASUREMENT.

**operational research (operations re-
search)** A scientific method of approaching industrial and commercial problems
in order to arrive at the most efficient and
economic method of achieving the desired
objective. It basically consists of making a
clear statement of the problem, designing
a model to represent the possible solutions using different strategies, and applying the solutions obtained from the
analysis of the model to the real problem.

It makes use of *game theory, critical-path analysis, *simulation techniques, etc.

operational risk The risk of direct or indirect loss resulting from inadequate or failed internal processes and systems, or from a wide variety of external events. The control of operational risk has been the object of much attention in recent years, for example in the 2004 *Basle Two accord concerning the *capital adequacy of banks and in the *Turnbull Report in the UK. It has also led to changes in the regulation of financial institutions and the requirements for the listing of public companies (*see* LISTING REQUIREMENTS).

operation job card A card or form on which an employee writes up the details of a particular task and the length of time it took to complete. It is used in *work studies.

operations A set of activities concerned with transforming resource inputs into desired outputs, i.e. goods or services. Every purposeful organization has desired outputs and, as every output requires inputs of some sort, all purposeful organizations are involved in operations. Traditionally, the word has been used to refer exclusively to manufacturing processes, but it applies equally to the service sector and to non-profit-making organizations. In some organizations it is possible to identify a single coherent sub-system as performing the operations function. In others, responsibility for various elements may be split between different linked departments.

operations management The management of an *operating system to achieve the desired organizational outputs within an optimum balance of economy, efficiency, and effectiveness.

operations manager A manager with responsibility for running the resource inputs that constitute an *operating system. Most managers have an operational function within their overall job description, e.g. a human resource manager (*see* HUMAN-RESOURCE MANAGEMENT) has to make use of inputs consisting of cash, skilled personnel, documentation, etc., to produce an output consisting of an appropriately skilled workforce.

operations strategy A plan to transform an organization's overall strategic objectives into operational deliverables. It involves the design of the product or service and the processes by which the product or service is produced; the way in which production is managed and controlled; and the design of processes for the constant improvement of the operation. If, at the strategic level, the organization decides to compete in the market on the basis of superior quality, the operations strategy has to plan to produce a package incorporating the specified quality within stated financial constraints. If the strategy is to compete on cost, the plan must produce the product cheaply within the limits of acceptable quality.

opinion giver *See* RELATIONSHIP ROLES.

opinion leaders *See* CONSUMER GROUPS.

opinion poll A poll using marketing research techniques that is specifically concerned with political opinion. Public opinion polls are usually commissioned by the media (especially television and newspapers) in order to keep their readers or viewers informed. Private opinion polls are usually commissioned by the political parties in order to help develop campaign strategies.

opinion seeker *See* RELATIONSHIP ROLES.

opportunities to see The number of times a member of the public (or an audience) may, on average, be expected to see a particular advertisement.

opportunity cost The economic cost of an action measured in terms of the benefit foregone by not pursuing the best alternative course of action. The cost of funds, for example, must be measured in terms of the returns they could earn in the capital markets for taking the same degree of risk. Opportunity cost is an important factor in decision making (*see* COST-BENEFIT ANALYSIS), although it represents costs that are not recorded in the accounts of the relevant organization.

OPT Abbreviation for *optimized production technology.

optical character recognition (OCR) The recognition of printed characters by a light-sensitive optical scanner. The scanner recognizes the shape of a letter by scanning it with a very fine point of light. It then uses a computer to compare the pattern of reflected light with the patterns of the letters of the alphabet stored in its memory. OCR is often used to read responses on questionnaires, thus reducing human error and increasing the speed of analysis.

optical scanner A light-sensitive optical device used to capture photographs, diagrams, printed characters, etc. in a digitized form so that they can be stored electronically.

optimized production technology (OPT) A computer-based system for planning production and the allocation of resources. In contrast to other methods that aim to use machines to their full capacity, for OPT the management of bottlenecks is the key to efficient and effective plant utilization. Maximization of throughput in areas that are not bottlenecks only increases the build-up of work in these areas, and thus locks up capital in work in progress. While an appropriate quantity of work is necessary, too much is counterproductive. *See* THEORY OF CONSTRAINTS.

opt-in A customer or potential customer who chooses to give permission for use of personalized information or to receive solicitation, particularly via *direct marketing and the Internet. *Compare* OPT-OUT.

opt-in e-mail An e-mail sent to a customer only when he or she has explicitly asked for information to be sent (usually when filling in an on-screen form).

option The right to buy or sell a fixed quantity of a commodity, currency, *security, etc., at a particular date at a particular price (the *exercise price). Unlike futures, the purchaser of an option is not obliged to buy or sell at the exercise price and will only do so if it is profitable; the purchaser may allow the option to lapse, in which case only the initial purchase price of the option (the option money or premium) is lost.

An option to buy is known as a **call option** and is usually purchased in the expectation of a rising price; an option to sell is called a **put option** and is bought in the expectation of a falling price or to protect a profit on an investment. Options, like futures, allow individuals and firms to

*hedge against the risk of wide fluctuations in prices; they also allow dealers and speculators to gamble for large profits with limited initial payments.

Professional traders in options make use of a large range of potential strategies, often purchasing combinations of options that reflect particular expectations or cover several contingencies. A **traded option** is one that can be bought or sold on an exchange at any time, as opposed to a **traditional option**, which once bought cannot be resold. There is a further distinction between **European options**, in which the buyer can only exercise the right to take up the option or let it lapse on the expiry date, and **American options**, in which this right can be exercised at any time up to the expiry date. American options are generally worth more than European options because the option holder has more chance of buying or selling at a favourable price. American options are also more difficult to value. *See also* REAL OPTION.

option money The price paid for an *option. The cost of a call option is often known as the **call money** and that for a put option as the **put money**.

option period The time during which an option remains open, i.e. before the final choice as to exercise has to be made.

option to double 1. An *option by a seller to sell double the quantity of securities for which he or she has sold an option, if it is so desired. In some markets this is called a **put-of-more option**. **2.** An option by a buyer to buy double the quantity of securities for which he or she has bought an option, if desired. In some markets this is called a **call-of-more option**.

option to purchase 1. A right given to shareholders to buy shares in certain companies in certain circumstances at a reduced price. **2.** A right purchased or given to a person to buy something at a specified price on or before a specified date. Until the specified date has passed, the seller undertakes not to sell the property to anyone else and not to withdraw it from sale.

opt-out A customer who chooses to receive no solicitation, particularly via *direct marketing or the Internet. *Compare* OPT-IN.

opt-out e-mail An e-mail sent to a customer who will not be contacted again if he or she expresses a wish not to be contacted in future. Opt-out or *unsubscribe options are usually available within the e-mail itself.

OR Abbreviation for *official receiver.

order cheque See CHEQUE.

order driven Denoting a market in which prices are determined by the publication of orders to buy or sell shares, with the objective of attracting a counterparty. Compare QUOTE DRIVEN.

order of business The sequence of the items on the *agenda of a business meeting. It is usual to adopt the following order: apologies for absence; reading and signing of the minutes of the last meeting; matters arising from these minutes; new correspondence received; reading and adoption of reports, accounts, etc.; election of officers and auditors; any special motions; any other business; date of next meeting. See also ANNUAL GENERAL MEETING; EXTRAORDINARY GENERAL MEETING.

order-qualifying criteria (entry-level criteria) The characteristics that a product or service has to have before customers will consider buying it, i.e. before it can gain entry to the market.

order-routine specification The stage of the business buying process in which the buyer writes the final order with the chosen supplier(s), listing the technical specifications, quantity needed, expected time of delivery, and warranties.

order-winning criteria The characteristics of a product or service that are most important in deciding whether or not a customer will make a purchase. These are the characteristics that positively differentiate a particular product from similar products in the market. Clearly order-winning criteria vary from customer to customer. Compare ORDER-QUALIFYING CRITERIA.

ordinary activities Any activities undertaken by an organization as part of its business and any related activities in which it engages in furtherance of, incidental to, or arising from, these activities. This definition is based on that given in *Financial Reporting Standard 3, Reporting Financial Performance. Ordinary activities include the effects on the reporting entity of any event in the various environments in which it operates, including the political, regulatory, economic, and geographical environments, irrespective of the frequency or unusual nature of the events. See also EXTRAORDINARY ITEMS.

ordinary resolution A resolution that is valid if passed by a majority of the votes cast at a general meeting of a British company. No notice that the resolution is to be proposed is required.

ordinary share A fixed unit of the *share capital of a company. Shares in publicly owned quoted companies (see PLC; QUOTATION) are usually traded on *stock exchanges and represent one of the most important types of security for investors. Shares yield dividends, representing a proportion of the profits of a company (compare FIXED-INTEREST SECURITY; PREFERENCE SHARE). In the long term, ordinary shares, by means of *capital growth, yield higher rewards, on average, than most alternative forms of securities, which compensates for the greater element of risk they entail. See also CONVERTIBLE; GROWTH STOCKS.

ordinary share capital The total *share capital of a company consisting of *ordinary shares.

öre A monetary unit of Sweden, worth one hundredth of a *krona.

øre A monetary unit of Denmark, the Faeroe Islands, Greenland, and Norway, worth one hundredth of a *krone.

organic growth See INTERNAL GROWTH.

organic organization An organization characterized by roles that are not well defined, tasks being redefined as individuals interact; there is little reliance on authority, with control and decision making decentralized, and communication is both lateral and vertical. This type of organization, which is a feature of the computer software industry, is appropriate if the external environment is uncertain. Compare MECHANISTIC ORGANIZATION.

organizational behaviour The ways in which people behave, individually and collectively, when working together in organizations. The study of organizational behaviour involves attention to such issues as *organizational commitment, *organizational culture, and group decision making. *See* INDUSTRIAL AND ORGANIZATIONAL PSYCHOLOGY.

organizational buying The way in which an organization (as opposed to an individual consumer) identifies, evaluates, and chooses the products it buys. *See* DECI-SION-MAKING UNIT.

organizational commitment An individual's psychological attachment to an organization and desire to remain part of it. It is normally measured by attitudinal dimensions, e.g. identification with the goals and values of the organization; desire to belong to the organization; and willingness to display effort on behalf of the organization. A distinction is sometimes made between **affective commitment**, which involves a sense of loyalty and shared values, and mere **continuance commitment**, which arises from inertia or the problems of finding alternative employment. *Compare* ALIENATION.

organizational culture (corporate culture) The values, customs, rituals, attitudes, and norms shared by members of an organization, which have to be learnt and accepted by new members of the organization. It is argued that there are at least three different types of organizational culture:

- In an **integrative culture** the objective is to obtain a consensus regarding the values and basic assumptions of the organization and to produce consistent actions. This integration brings unity, predictability, and clarity to work experiences.
- In a **differentiated culture**, subcultures develop that have internal consensus about values and basic assumptions but differ greatly between each subculture; this produces inconsistencies throughout the organization.
- In a **fragmentation culture** there are multiple interpretations of values and assumptions, which produce great ambiguity. This can arise from fast changes within the organization, the growing diversity of the workforce, and the in-

creasingly global environment with which organizations are faced.

organizational design The way in which managers structure their organization in order to achieve the organization's goals. The formal design of an organization is laid out in an *organization chart, which indicates the duties, tasks, and responsibilities of both individuals and departments. Reporting relationships and the number of levels in the organization's hierarchy are other elements in the design. Organizational design has two basic functions:

- to ensure that information reaches the appropriate person to enable effective decisions to be made;
- to assist in the coordination of the interdependent parts of the organization.

organizational development (OD) A long-term, systematic, and prescriptive approach to planned organizational change. It applies the concepts of the social and behavioural sciences to the problem of changing an organization; in doing do it treats the organization as a complex social and technical system, which should have enough flexibility to change its design according to the nature of its tasks and external environment.

Its purpose is to derive strategies and initiatives for improving the effectiveness of an organization, largely by making the best use of the qualities and capabilities of its human resources. To be effective, organizational development should pervade the whole organization, forming part of the strategy that informs all the activities within it. It requires a total corporate commitment, requiring full understanding and acceptance by everyone in the organization. Inherent in organizational development is an overall purpose to address issues and solve problems in a way that is consistent with the *organizational culture. *See also* ORGANIZATIONAL BEHAVIOUR; ORGANIZATIONAL DESIGN; ORGANIZATIONAL THEORY.

organizational psychology *See* INDUS-TRIAL AND ORGANIZATIONAL PSYCHOLOGY.

organizational theory The study of the design, structure, and process of decision making in organizations (*see* ORGANI-ZATIONAL DESIGN). The sociology of organizational systems, and the structure of relationships within them, are central to organizational theory.

Considerable work has been carried out on the way in which decisions are made, both by individuals and groups (committees) within organizations. The extent to which managers are influenced by organizational politics, rather than being guided by reason and economics, in making their decisions is an aspect of considerable importance.

organization and methods (O & M) A form of *work study involving the organization of procedures and controls in a business and the methods of implementing them in management terms. It is usually applied to office procedures rather than factory production.

organization chart A chart illustrating the structure of an organization; in particular it will show for which function of the business each manager is responsible and the chain of responsibility throughout the organization. Some organization charts include managers by name; others show the management positions in the structure.

Organization for Economic Cooperation and Development (OECD) An organization formed in 1961, replacing the Organization for European Economic Cooperation (OEEC), to promote cooperation among industralized member countries on economic and social policies. Its objectives are to assist member countries in formulating policies designed to achieve high economic growth while maintaining financial stability, contributing to world trade on a multilateral basis, and stimulating members' aid to developing countries. Members are Australia, Austria, Belgium, Canada, the Czech Republic, Denmark, Finland, France, Germany, Greece, Hungary, Iceland, Ireland, Italy, Japan, South Korea, Luxembourg, Mexico, The Netherlands, New Zealand, Norway, Poland, Portugal, Slovakia, Spain, Sweden, Switzerland, Turkey, UK, and the USA. Its headquarters are in Paris.

Organization of the Petroleum Exporting Countries (OPEC) An organization created in 1960 to unify and coordinate the petroleum policies of member countries and to protect their interests, individually and collectively. Present members are Algeria, Indonesia, Iran, Iraq, Kuwait, Libya, Nigeria, Qatar, Saudi Arabia, UAE, and Venezuela.

organized market A formal market in a specific place in which buyers and sellers meet to trade according to agreed rules and procedures. Stock exchanges, financial futures exchanges, and commodity markets are examples of organized markets.

origin **1.** The country from which a commodity originates. **Shipment from origin**

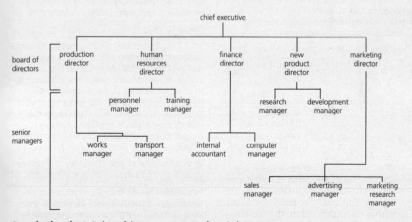

Organization chart. A chart of the top management of a typical company.

denotes goods that are shipped directly from their country of origin, rather than from stocks in some other place. *See also* CERTIFICATE OF ORIGIN. **2.** The country from which a person comes. A person's country of origin is not necessarily his country of *domicile or residence (*see* RESIDENT).

original cost The cost of an item at the time of purchase or creation. This applies particularly to *fixed assets in which depreciation by the *straight-line method uses the original cost as a basis for the calculation. *See also* HISTORICAL COST.

original-entry book *See* BOOK OF PRIME ENTRY.

original goods Natural products that have no economic value until factors of production are applied to them. They include virgin land, wild fruit, natural waterways, etc.

OSP Abbreviation for *on-line service provider.

OTE Abbreviation for on-target earnings, which represents the salary and commission a salesman should be able to earn.

OTS Abbreviation for *Office of Thrift Supervision.

ouguiya (UM) The standard monetary unit of Mauritania, divided into 5 khoums.

out-barrier option An *option that is eliminated when the value of the *underlying reaches a certain level, at which point the initial premium is partly refunded. *Compare* IN-BARRIER OPTION.

outdoor training programme An intervention in which employees are taken to a remote location, often in a National Park or similar area, and presented with a series of challenging physical exercises, which typically involve an element of group problem solving. The aim is usually to develop leadership potential, boost confidence, and build a sense of belonging to a team (*see* TEAM-BUILDING EXERCISES).

outlay cost The expenditure incurred as the initial cost of a project or activity. The outlay cost may include both *capital expenditure and expenditure on working capital, such as stocks of raw material.

outlay tax *See* SALES TAX.

out-of-control process *See* STATISTICAL PROCESS CONTROL.

out-of-pocket costs The additional costs that will be incurred as the result of a particular decision. In some circumstances, these costs will be more relevant to decision making than the total differential cash flows. For example, an organization with limited cash resources may make a decision to pursue an investment alternative that would not have been the first choice had it not offered the lowest level of out-of-pocket costs. *See also* RELEVANT COST.

out-of-the-money option *See* IN-THE-MONEY OPTION.

outplacement counselling Helping employees who are made redundant to come to terms with the situation and find jobs elsewhere. When faced with making workers redundant, progressive employers will often arrange for their employees to receive psychological support as well as career advice and assistance in seeking alternative work.

output tax The VAT that a trader adds to the price of the goods or services he supplies. He or she must account for this output tax to HM Revenue and Customs, having first deducted the *input tax.

outside broker A stockbroker who is not a member of a stock exchange but acts as an intermediary between the public and a stockbroker who is a member.

outside director A US term for a *nonexecutive director.

outsourcing The buying in of components, sub-assemblies, finished products, and services from outside suppliers rather than by supplying them internally. A firm may decide to buy in rather than supply internally because it lacks the expertise, investment capital, or physical space required to do so. It may also be able to buy in more cheaply or more quickly than manufacturing in-house. More recently this decision may be taken in the process of *business process re-engineering or *downsizing, when specific activities have been redefined as noncore activities. In certain instances, computer, legal, and personnel services have been outsourced as well as the more traditional manufactured components.

outwork Work carried out in a person's own home, office, or workshop rather than on a company's premises. The use of outworkers declined in the earlier part of the 20th century but has risen again with the advent of personal computers and information technology (*see* TELECOMMUTING). *See also* OUTSOURCING.

overbought **1.** Having purchased more of a good than one needs or has orders for. **2.** Having purchased more securities or commodities than are covered by margins deposited with a broker or dealer. In a falling market, for example, a bull speculator can become overbought without having made a fresh purchase. **3.** Denoting a market that has risen too rapidly as a result of excessive buying. An overbought market is unstable and likely to fall if unsupported. *Compare* OVERSOLD.

overcapacity The situation that arises when a firm or industry has greater capacity than the market demand. It may be caused by a temporary downturn in the economy or *business cycle, overinvestment in capacity by existing or new entrants, or a permanent decline in demand for a product or service. In the last case, it is likely to be followed by restructuring throughout the industry, resulting in capacity being reduced through merger and closure in order to bring it into line with demand.

overcapitalization A condition in which an organization has too much *capital for the needs of its business. If a business has more capital than it needs it is likely to be overburdened by interest charges or by the need to spread profits too thinly by way of dividends to shareholders. Businesses can now reduce overcapitalization by repaying long-term debts or by buying their own shares. *Compare* UNDERCAPITALIZATION.

overdraft A loan made to a customer with a cheque account at a bank or building society, in which the account is allowed to go into debit, usually up to a specified limit (the **overdraft limit**). Interest is charged on the daily debit balance. This is a less costly way of borrowing than taking a *bank loan (providing the interest rates are the same) as, with an overdraft, credits are taken into account.

over-entry certificate A document issued by HM Revenue and Customs stating that imported goods have paid excessive duty on entry into the country, which may be reclaimed. If too little duty has been paid, **post-entry** duty is claimed.

overhead (overhead cost) An *indirect cost of an organization. Overheads are usually classified as *manufacturing overheads, administration overheads, *selling overheads, *distribution overheads, and *research and development costs.

overheating The state of an economy during a boom, with increasing *aggregate demand leading to rising prices rather than higher output. Overheating reflects the inability of some firms to increase output as fast as demand; they therefore choose to profit from the excess demand by raising prices.

overinsurance The practice of insuring an item for a greater amount than its value. This is pointless as insurers are only obliged to pay the full value (usually the replacement value) of an insured item and no more, even if the sum insured exceeds this value. If insurers find a policyholder has overinsured an item, the premium for the cover above the true value is returned.

overinvestment Excessive investment of capital, especially in the manufacturing industry towards the end of a boom as a result of over-optimistic expectations of future demand. When the boom begins to fade, the manufacturer is left with surplus capacity and can therefore make no further capital investments, which itself creates unemployment and fuels the imminent recession. It is often seen with new technology investment booms.

overnight loan A loan made by a bank to a *bill broker to enable the broker to take up *bills of exchange. Initially the loan will be repayable the following day but it is usually renewable. If it is not, the broker must turn to the *lender of last resort, i.e. the Bank of England in the UK.

overnight position An *open position held overnight.

overpositioning A *positioning error

in which too narrow a picture of a company, its product, or a brand is communicated to target customers.

overseas company A company incorporated outside the UK that has a branch or a subsidiary company in the UK. Overseas companies with a place of business in the UK have to make a return to the *Registrar of Companies, giving particulars of their *memorandum of association, directors, and secretary as well as providing an annual balance sheet and profit and loss account.

overseas-income taxation Taxation of income that has been subject to taxation outside the jurisdiction of the UK tax authorities. When the same income is subject to taxation in more than one country, relief for the double tax is given either under the provisions of the *double taxation agreement with the country concerned or unilaterally.

overseas investment Investment by the government, industry, or members of the public of a country in the industry of another country. For members of the public this is often most easily achieved by investing through foreign stock exchanges.

overseas joint ownership A *joint venture in which a company joins investors in a foreign market to create a local business in which the company shares ownership and control.

overshooting A jump in the value of an asset followed by a slow adjustment to equilibrium. Overshooting has been used as an explanation of exchange-rate movements arising from adjustment problems in economies.

overside delivery The unloading of a cargo over the side of a ship into *lighters.

oversold 1. Having sold more of a product or service than one can produce or purchase. **2.** Denoting a market that has fallen too fast as a result of excessive selling. It may therefore be expected to have an upward reaction.

oversubscription A situation that arises when there are more applications for a *new issue of securities than there are securities available. In these circumstances, applications have to be scaled down according to a set of rules devised by the company issuing the shares or their advisors. Alternatively some companies prefer to allocate the shares by ballot (see ALLOTMENT). Oversubscription usually occurs because of the difficulty in arriving at an issue price that will be low enough to attract sufficient investors to take up the whole issue and yet will give the company the maximum capital. Speculative purchases by *stags also make it difficult to price a new issue so that it is neither oversubscribed nor undersubscribed. In the case of **undersubscription**, which is rare, the *underwriter has to take up that part of the issue that has not been bought by the public. Undersubscription can occur if some unexpected event occurs after the announcement of the issue price but before the issue date.

over-the-counter market (OTC market) A market in which financial obligations are bought and sold outside the jurisdiction of a recognized financial market; it was originally so named in the 1870s, from the practice of buying shares over bank counters in the USA. OTC markets are used for trading in specific tailor-made *derivative products. The world's largest OTC market is the US *National Association of Securities Dealers Automated Quotations System (NASDAQ).

overtime Hours worked in excess of an agreed number per week or per day. The payment made for overtime work is usually higher than the basic rate of pay. Unions therefore have an interest in making the basic working week as short as possible, so that those working longer hours earn as much as possible. Employers, on the other hand, want to make the working week as long as possible.

overtime ban A form of *industrial action in which employees refuse to work *overtime, thus causing considerable dislocation to normal working but clearly less than would occur in a total *strike. Overtime bans are usually supported and often organized by unions. See also WORK-TO-RULE.

overtrading Trading by an organization beyond the resources provided by its existing capital. Overtrading tends to lead to *liquidity problems as too much stock is bought on credit and too much credit is extended to customers, so that ultimately there is not sufficient cash available to pay the debts as they arise. The solution is either to cut back on trading or to raise further permanent capital.

own-account transaction A transaction undertaken by a broker/dealer for his or her own benefit rather than that of a client.

own brand (own label; distributor brand; private brand; house brand) A product sold under a distributor's own name or trademark through its own outlets. These items are either made specially for the distributor or are versions of the manufacturer's equivalent *brand. Own-brand goods are promoted by the distributor rather than the manufacturer and are typically 10–20% cheaper to the distributor than an equivalent brand. Own brands are sold principally by *multiple shops.

owners' equity The funds of an organization that have been provided by its owners, i.e. its total assets less its total liabilities. The balance-sheet or *book value of the owners' equity is unlikely to be equal to its *market value. *See also* NET ASSETS; NET WORTH.

ownership Rights over property, including rights of possession, exclusive enjoyment, destruction, etc. In UK common law, land cannot be owned outright, as all land belongs to the Crown and is held in tenure by the 'owner'. However, an owner of an estate in land in fee simple is to all intents and purposes an outright owner. In general, ownership can be split between different persons. For example, a trustee has the legal ownership of trust property but the beneficiary has the equitable or beneficial ownership. If goods are stolen, the owner still has ownership but not possession. Similarly, if goods are hired or pledged to someone, the owner has ownership but no immediate right to possession.

own label *See* OWN BRAND.

own shares purchase The purchase or redemption of its own shares by a company; this is permitted subject to certain legal restrictions. For example, in the UK redeemable shares may only be redeemed if they are fully paid. If the redemption or purchase of a company's own shares would lead to a reduction of its capital, a *capital redemption reserve will need to be created. In certain cases private companies may reduce their capital in this way (*see* PERMISSIBLE CAPITAL PAYMENT).

O

PA **1.** Abbreviation for personal account, used to denote a transaction made by a professional investment adviser for his own account rather than for the firm for which he or she works. **2.** Abbreviation for *personal assistant. **3.** Abbreviation for *power of attorney. **4.** Abbreviation for particular average. *See* AVERAGE.

pa'anga (T$) The standard monetary unit of Tonga, divided into 100 seniti.

Paasche's index *See* INDEX NUMBER.

PACE Abbreviation for price, assortment, convenience, entertainment. A summary of the benefits available to customers using e-commerce.

package *See* BUSINESS SOFTWARE PACKAGE.

package deal An agreement that encompasses several different parts, all of which must be accepted. A package deal may have involved either or both parties in making concessions on specific aspects of the package in order to arrive at a compromise arrangement.

packaging **1.** The design of wrappers or containers for a product. **2.** The wrappers or containers themselves. **3.** An activity that combines several operations and enables the packager to deliver a finished or near-finished product to a selling organization. For example, many non-fiction books are produced by **book packagers**, who write, illustrate, typeset, and print books, which they deliver to publishers, who sell them to the public under their own imprint.

paid-up policy An *endowment assurance policy in which the assured has decided to stop paying premiums before the end of the policy term. This results in a *surrender value, which instead of being returned in cash to the assured is used to purchase a single-premium *whole life policy. In this way the life assurance protection continues (for a reduced amount), while the policyholder is relieved of the need to pay further premiums. If the original policy was a *with-profits policy, the bonuses paid up to the time the premiums ceased would be included in the surrender value. If it is a unit-linked policy, capital units actually allocated would be allowed to appreciate to the end of the term.

paid-up share capital The *issued share capital of a company when this consists of *fully paid shares, payment for which has been received. *Compare* CALLED-UP SHARE CAPITAL.

paired comparisons **1.** A technique used in marketing research in which consumers are presented with pairs of competing products and asked to choose the one they prefer. This technique can be used to compare, say, a number of brands of soap, giving respondents two at a time to compare. The number of times each brand is selected as a preference in a large number of such tests will reveal an order of brand preference. *Compare* MONADIC TESTING. **2.** A method of *employee evaluation in which each worker in a group is compared with each other worker on one or more performance measures. Employees are then ranked according to the number of favourable comparisons they receive.

paisa (*plural* **paise**) A monetary unit of Bangladesh, Bhutan, India, Nepal, and Pakistan, worth one hundredth of a *rupee.

pallet A wooden frame on which certain goods are stacked in warehouses and during transport. Pallets are designed to be lifted by fork-lift trucks or pallet trucks.

palmtop computer A very small hand-held personal computer with a small screen and a compressed keyboard. They usually provide a personal organizer, diary, calculator, and address list. *See also* LAPTOP COMPUTER; PDA.

P & L account *See* PROFIT AND LOSS ACCOUNT.

Panel on Takeovers and Mergers *See* CITY CODE ON TAKEOVERS AND MERGERS.

paper An informal name for securities that can be bought and sold or held as an investment. It is used particularly on the *money market for *debt instruments maturing in less than 90 days. *See* COMMERCIAL PAPER; EURO-COMMERCIAL PAPER.

paper bid *See* SHARE-FOR-SHARE OFFER.

paper profit A profit shown by the books or accounts of an organization that is not a *realized profit. This is usually for one of three reasons:
• because the value of an asset has fallen below its book value;
• because the asset, although nominally showing a profit, has not actually been sold;
• because some technicality of bookkeeping shows an activity to be profitable when it is not.
For example, a share that has risen in value since its purchase might show a paper profit but this would not be a real profit since the value of the share might fall again before it is sold.

paper sizes See feature INTERNATIONAL PAPER SIZES on p. 287.

paper trail *See* AUDIT TRAIL.

par *See* PAR VALUE.

para A monetary unit of Serbia, worth one hundredth of a *dinar.

paradox of community size The observation that small groups produce more active members and stimulate individual contributions, but that large group sizes are necessary to produce enough committed members. The paradox is often cited in connection with Internet communities but has many wider applications.

parallel hedge A *hedge in which exposure to fluctuation in one foreign currency is matched by a purchase or sale of another currency, which is expected to move in sympathy with the first currency.

parallel processing A method of computing in which two or more parts of a program are executed simultaneously rather than sequentially. Strictly, parallel processing is only possible on computers with more than one arithmetic and logical

unit in the central processing unit, but it is often simulated on other machines by such techniques as *time sharing.

par banking The US practice of one bank paying the full face value of a cheque drawn on another bank, without imposing a charge for encashment. Members of the *Federal Reserve System are obliged to comply with the rules of par banking.

par bond A security or financial instrument that is bought and sold at its face value, rather than at a discount or premium.

parent company (parent undertaking) *See* HOLDING COMPANY.

parenting The way in which the directors of the main *holding company of a large group manage their relationships with the subsidiary companies or business units. The method by which control is exercised varies, with some firms concentrating on financial control and others on the broader strategic targets. *See* STRATEGIC STYLES.

Pareto's Rule (80/20 rule) A rule originally applied by the economist Vilfredo Pareto (1848–1923) to income distribution, i.e. 80% of a nation's income is earned by 20% of the population. It can be widely extended; for example: 80% of value is locked up in 20% of inventory; 80% of car breakdowns can be fixed by 20% of the spare parts range; 80% of a company's profits will come from 20% of its product range; and 80% of system failures will be caused by 20% of possible causes. The rule can be used as a guide to managers: in deciding how to spend limited funds, priority should be given to the most significant 20% of problems. Once they are eliminated the 80/20 rule will again apply to the remainder.

pari passu (Latin: with equal step) Ranking equally. When a new issue of shares is said to rank *pari passu* with existing shares, the new shares carry the same dividend rights and winding-up rights as the existing shares. A *pari passu* loan is one in which the borrower agrees that this new loan will rank equally with other existing debts.

Paris Bourse From January 1991, the

only stock exchange in France, incorporating the six provincial stock exchanges in Bordeaux, Lille, Lyons, Marseilles, Nancy, and Nantes. The merger recognized the dominance of the Paris Bourse, which accounted for 95% of all trading in French securities. The CAC (Cotation Assistée en Continue) electronic trading system was introduced in 1988 and the Relit five-day rolling settlement system was launched in 1990, based on delivery against payment. Trading is carried out through broker members of the exchange; the market's main indicators are now the SBF-250 index, based on the prices of 250 shares, and its subset, the CAC-40.

Paris Club *See* GROUP OF TEN.

parity **1.** An equality between prices of commodities, currencies, or securities on separate markets. **2.** A fixed exchange rate. **3.** Another term for *par value.

parking **1.** Putting company shares that one owns in the name of someone else or of nominees in order to hide their real ownership. This is often illegal. *See also* WAREHOUSING. **2.** Holding assets in a short-term riskless form pending an investment decision.

Parkinson's laws The propositions made by the British writer Cyril Northcote Parkinson (1909–93) in his book *Parkinson's Law.* Facetious but true, they include such aphorisms as: work expands to fill the time available in which to do it; expenditure rises to meet income; and subordinates multiply at a fixed rate that is independent of the amount of work produced. They were devised with large organizations in mind and it is to such organizations that they apply, unless managers take steps to ensure that they do not.

Parliamentary Ombudsman (Parliamentary Commissioner for Administration) An ombudsman responsible for investigating complaints about maladministration by government departments and certain public bodies that have been referred to him or her by MPs. *See also* FINANCIAL OMBUDSMAN SERVICE.

par of exchange The theoretical *rate of exchange between two currencies in which there is equilibrium between the

supply and demand for each currency. The par value lies between the market buying and selling rates. *See also* MINT PAR OF EXCHANGE.

partial loss *See* AVERAGE.

participated loan (participation financing) A large loan, exceeding the lending limit of an individual bank, that is shared among a group of lenders.

participating interest An interest held by one organization in the shares of another organization, provided these shares are held on a long-term basis for the purpose of exercising some measure of control or influence over the organization's activities. The UK Companies Act (1985) lays down that a holding of 20% or more of the shares of an organization constitutes a participating interest, unless contrary indications are given. Options to buy shares are normally treated as an interest in these shares. *See also* CONTROLLING INTEREST; MINORITY INTEREST; SIGNIFICANT INFLUENCE.

participating preference share *See* PREFERENCE SHARE.

participation financing *See* PARTICIPATED LOAN.

participative decision making The inclusion of employees (or their representatives) in the process of management decision making. This can range from a fairly limited form of consultation to a situation in which workers take responsibility for major decisions. *See* INDUSTRIAL DEMOCRACY.

participator Any person having an interest in the capital or income of a company, e.g. a shareholder, loan creditor, or any person entitled to participate in the *distributions of the company.

particular average (PA) *See* AVERAGE.

partly paid share A share the full *par value of which has not been paid by the shareholder. Formerly, partly paid shares were issued by some banks and insurance companies in the knowledge that they could always call on their shareholders for further funds if necessary. Shareholders, however, did not like the liability of being called upon to pay out further sums on demand and the practice largely died out. It has been revived for large new share issues, especially in *privatizations, in which shareholders pay an initial sum for their shares and subsequently pay one or more calls on specified dates. *Compare* FULLY PAID SHARE. *See also* CALLED-UP SHARE CAPITAL; PAID-UP SHARE CAPITAL.

partnership An association of two or more people (**partners**) formed for the purpose of carrying on a business. Partnerships are governed by the Partnership Act (1890). Unlike an incorporated *company, a partnership does not have a legal personality of its own and therefore, as a general rule, partners are liable for the debts of the firm. **General partners** are fully liable for these debts, **limited partners** only to the extent of their investment. A **limited partnership** is one consisting of both general and limited partners and is governed by the Limited Partnership Act (1907). The *Limited Liability Partnership Act (2000) now enables some categories of business partnership to claim limited liability in a similar fashion to that enjoyed by *limited companies. A **partnership-at-will** is one for which no fixed term has been agreed. Any partner may end the partnership at any time provided that notice of the intention to do so is given to all the other partners. **Nominal partners** allow their names to be used for the benefit of the partnership, usually for a reward but not for a share of the profits. They are not legal partners. Partnerships are usually governed by a *partnership agreement.

partnership accounts The accounts kept by a *partnership. They include an *appropriation account in which the profit is shared between the partners in accordance with the *partnership agreement. This may be in the form of salaries, interest on capital, and a share of the profit in the appropriate *profit-sharing ratio. Each partner also has a *capital account and a *current account. The former is used to account for capital contributions, *goodwill, and revaluations; the latter for all other transactions, such as appropriations of profit and *drawings.

partnership agreement (articles of partnership) An agreement made between the partners of a *partnership. In the absence of either an express or an implied agreement the provisions of the Partnership Act (1890) apply. These provisions are also applicable if an agreement is silent on a particular point. The provisions are:

- partners share equally in the profits or losses of the partnership;
- partners are not entitled to receive salaries;
- partners are not entitled to interest on their capital;
- partners may receive interest at 5% per annum on any advances over and above their agreed capital;
- a new partner may not be introduced unless all the existing partners consent;
- a retiring partner is entitled to receive interest at 5% per annum on his or her share of the partnership assets retained in the partnership after his or her retirement;
- on dissolution of the partnership the assets of the firm must be used first to repay outside creditors, secondly to repay partners' advances, and thirdly to repay partners' capital. Any residue on dissolution should be distributed to the partners in the *profit-sharing ratio.

See also LIMITED LIABILITY PARTNERSHIP.

partnership-at-will *See* PARTNERSHIP.

par value (face value; nominal value) The *nominal price of a share or other security. If the market value of a security exceeds the nominal price it is said to be **above par**; if it falls below the nominal price it is **below par**. Gilt-edged securities are always repayed **at par** (usually £100), i.e. at the par value.

passing a name The disclosure by a firm of brokers of the name of the principal for whom they are acting. In some commodity trades, if brokers disclose the names of their buyers to the sellers, they do not guarantee the buyers' solvency, although they may do so in some circumstances. However, if brokers do not pass their principals' names, it is usual for them to guarantee their solvency. Thus, to remain anonymous, a buyer may have to pay an additional brokerage.

passing off Conducting a business in a manner that misleads the public into thinking that one's goods or services are those of another business. The commonest form of passing off is marketing goods with a design, packaging, or trade name that is very similar to that of someone else's goods. It is not necessary to prove an intention to deceive; innocent passing off is actionable.

passing the book Transferring the management of a financial *position from one office of a business to another in a different time zone to take advantage of *24-hour trading.

passive management A style of *portfolio management that involves holding assets over the long term and, in many cases, tracking a market index. *Compare* ACTIVE MANAGEMENT.

past-due loan A banking loan on which the interest is more than 90 days overdue. After this grace period has elapsed, the borrower becomes liable for late charges.

pataca (MOP) The standard monetary unit of Macao, divided into 100 avos.

patent The grant of an exclusive right to exploit an invention. In the UK patents are granted by the Crown through the *Patent Office, which is part of the Department of Trade and Industry. An applicant for a patent (usually from the inventor or the inventor's employer) must show that the invention is new, is not obvious, and is capable of industrial application. An expert known as a **patent agent** often prepares the application, which must describe the invention in considerable detail. The Patent Office publishes these details if it grants a patent. A patent remains valid for 20 years from the date of application (the **priority date**) provided that the person to whom it has been granted (the **patentee**) continues to pay the appropriate fees. During this time, the patentee may assign the patent or grant licences to use it. Such transactions are registered in a public register at the Patent Office. If anyone infringes the monopoly, the patentee may sue for an *injunction and *damages or an *account of profits. However, a patent from the Patent Office gives exclusive rights in the UK only: the inventor must obtain a patent from the European Patent Office in Munich and patents in other foreign countries if the invention is to be protected elsewhere.

patent agent A member of the Chartered Institute of Patent Agents, who gives advice on obtaining *patents and prepares patent applications.

Patent Office A UK government office that administers the Patent Acts, the Registered Designs Act, and the Trade Marks Act. It also deals with questions relating to the Copyright Acts, and provides an information service about *patent specifications.

paternity rights *See* MATERNITY RIGHTS.

pathfinder prospectus An outline *prospectus concerning the flotation of a new company in the UK; it includes enough details to test the market reaction to the new company but not its main financial details or the price of its shares. Pathfinder prospectuses are known in the USA as **red herrings**.

path-goal leadership model A theory of leadership suggesting that a leader needs to influence followers' perceptions of work goals, self-development goals, and paths to goal attainment. A leader will be successful to the extent that he or she creates an expectancy that effort will lead to accomplishment and that accomplishment will produce valued rewards. The *leadership style best suited to achieve this will depend on the characteristics of followers and the nature of the work setting. The model is a development of the *valence-instrumentality-expectancy theory of motivation.

patronage rewards Cash or other rewards for the regular use of a certain company's products or services.

pawnbroker A person who lends money against the security of valuable goods used as collateral. Borrowers can reclaim their goods by repaying the loan and interest within a stated period. However, if the borrower defaults the pawnbroker is free to sell the goods. The operation of pawnbrokers is governed by the Consumer Credit Act (1974).

payable to bearer Describing a *bill of exchange in which neither the payee or endorsee are named. A holder, by adding his name, can make the bill *payable to order.

payable to order Describing a *bill of exchange in which the payee is named and on which there are no restrictions or endorsements; it can therefore be paid to the endorsee.

pay and file A former procedure for paying *corporation tax introduced in the UK in 1993. Under the pay-and-file system, the company had to file a detailed return within twelve months of the end of the accounting period. For accounting periods ending after 1 July 1999 *self-assessment for companies has replaced pay and file.

pay-as-you-earn *See* PAYE.

payback period method A method of *capital budgeting in which the time required before the projected cash inflows for a project equal the investment expenditure is calculated; this time is compared to a required payback period to determine whether or not the project should be considered for approval. If the projected cash inflows are constant annual sums, after an initial capital investment the following formula may be used:

> payback (years) = initial capital investment/annual cash inflow.

Otherwise, the annual cash inflows are accumulated and the year determined when the cumulative inflows equal the investment expenditure. The method is sometimes seen as a measure of the risk involved in the project.

The two major weaknesses of the payback method are:
- the *time value of money is not considered;
- the cash flows after the investment is recovered are not considered.

However, payback is a relatively simple technique for managers to use and for this reason it remains popular. Often managers use payback and *discounted cash flow techniques at the same time, even though they are very different methods of capital budgeting (*see* DISCOUNTED PAYBACK METHOD).

PAYE Pay-as-you-earn. The UK scheme by which both income tax and *National Insurance contributions due from employees are collected by employers and paid over to the *Collector of Taxes. Because it is often difficult to collect tax at the end of the year from wage and salary earners, the onus is placed on employers to collect the tax from their employees as payments are

made to them. There is an elaborate system of administration to ensure that broadly the correct amount of tax is deducted week by week or month by month and that the employer remits the tax collected to HM Revenue and Customs very quickly. The amount of tax due is calculated using *income tax codes and tax tables supplied to employers by the Revenue (now usually in the form of computer software). Although technically called pay-as-you-earn, the system would be better called 'pay-as-you-get-paid'.

payee A person or organization to be paid. In the case of a cheque payment, the payee is the person or organization to whom the cheque is made payable.

payer A person or organization who makes a payment.

paying agent A bank or other organization that contracts under a **paying agency agreement** to pay the interest and capital sums due on a *bearer security.

paying banker The bank on which a *bill of exchange (including a cheque) has been drawn and which is responsible for paying it if it is correctly drawn and correctly endorsed (if necessary).

paying-in book A book of slips used to pay cash, cheques, etc., into a bank account. The counterfoil of the slip is stamped by the bank if the money is paid in over the counter.

payment by results A system of payment in which an employee's pay is directly linked to his performance. The majority are *premium bonus schemes. *See also* PIECE RATE; LUMP SUM.

payment for honour *See* ACCEPTANCE SUPRA PROTEST.

payment in advance (prepayment) Payment for goods or services before they have been received. In company accounts, this often refers to rates or rents paid for periods that carry over into the next accounting period.

payment in due course The payment of a *bill of exchange when it matures (becomes due).

payment in kind A payment that is not made in cash but in goods or services. It is often in the form of a discount or an allowance, e.g. cheap fares for British Airways employees, staff prices for food at supermarkets, etc. Now regarded as a bonus or *fringe benefit, payment in kind in the 19th century was widespread; the Truck Acts (1831) were passed to discourage employers who insisted on paying their employees in goods instead of cash (as often the cash value of goods bought in bulk by the employer was much less than their value to the employee).

payment on account 1. A payment made for goods or services before the goods or services are finally billed. *See also* DEPOSIT. **2.** A payment towards meeting a liability that is not the full amount of the liability. The sum paid will be credited to the account of the payer in the books of the payee as a part-payment of the ultimate liability.

payment supra protest *See* ACCEPTANCE SUPRA PROTEST.

payment terms The agreed way in which a buyer pays the seller for goods. The commonest are cash with order or cash on delivery; prompt cash (i.e. within 14 days of delivery); cash in 30, 60, or 90 days from date of invoice; *letter of credit; *cash against documents; *documents against acceptance; or *acceptance credit.

payoff The value of a portfolio or a single financial obligation at a particular date or at the expiry of an instrument. The value is sometimes calculated in absolute terms and sometimes in terms of the gain made over a given time period.

payroll tax A tax based on the total of an organization's payroll. The main function of such a tax would be to discourage high wages or over-employment. The current employers' Class 1 *National Insurance contributions constitute such a tax.

PBGC Abbreviation for *Pension Benefit Guaranty Corporation.

PC Abbreviation for *personal computer.

PCP Abbreviation for *permissible capital payment.

PDA Abbreviation for personal digital assistant; a small hand-held device that allows the user to store and retrieve information, such as addresses, telephone numbers, dates, etc. PDAs are used as personal organizers and can usually transfer data to or from a personal computer. Many now also combine other functions, such as cellphones, paging systems, and wireless e-mail. *See also* PALMTOP COMPUTER.

PDE Abbreviation for *prepared data entry.

PDF Abbreviation for portable document format. *See* ACROBAT.

PDR (P/D ratio) Abbreviations for *price–dividend ratio.

peaceful picketing *See* PICKETING.

peak time The period of television airtime, usually the middle part of the evening, for which the highest advertising rate is charged as during this period the highest number of people are viewing.

peering arrangement A formal or informal agreement made between independent networking companies governing the way in which Internet traffic moves between their networks.

pegging 1. (pegging the exchange) The fixing of the value of a country's currency on foreign exchange markets. *See* CRAWLING PEG; FIXED EXCHANGE RATE. **2. (pegging wages)** The fixing of wages at existing levels by government order to prevent them rising during a period of *inflation. The same restraint may be applied to prices (**pegging prices**) in order to control inflation.

penalty An arbitrary prearranged sum that becomes payable if one party breaches a contract or undertaking. It is usually expressly stated in a **penalty clause** of the contract. Unlike liquidated *damages, a penalty will be disregarded by the courts and treated as being void. Liquidated damages will generally be treated as a penalty if the amount payable is extravagant and unconscionable compared with the maximum loss that could result from the breach. However, use of the words 'penalty' or 'liquidated damages' is inconclusive as the legal position depends on the interpretation by the courts of the clause in which they appear.

penetration *See* MARKET PENETRATION.

penni (*plural* **penniä**) A former monetary unit of Finland, worth one hundredth of a *markka (until 2002).

penny (p) **1.** A monetary unit of the UK, worth one hundredth of a *pound. **2.** A former monetary unit of the Republic of Ireland, worth one hundredth of a *punt (until 2002).

penny shares Securities with a very low market price (although they may not be as low as one penny) traded on a stock exchange. They are popular with small investors, who can acquire a significant holding in a company for a very low cost. Moreover, a rise of a few pence in a low-priced share can represent a high percentage profit. However, they are usually shares in companies that have fallen on hard times and may, indeed, be close to bankruptcy. The investor in this type of share is hoping for a rapid recovery or a takeover.

pension A specified sum paid regularly to a person who has reached a certain age or retired from employment. It is normally paid from the date of reaching the specified age or the retirement date until death. A widow may also receive a pension from the date of her husband's death.

In the UK, contributory **retirement pensions** are usually paid by the state from the normal retirement age (currently 65 for men and 60 for women, gradually adjusting from 2010 to 65 for both) irrespective of whether or not the pensioners have retired from full-time employment. A non-working wife or widow also receives a state pension based on her husband's contributions.

Since 1978 state pensions have been augmented by the *State Earnings-Related Pension Scheme (SERPS); this is now gradually being replaced by a non-earnings-related scheme, the State Second Pension. Employers can contract out of this additional state pension scheme provided that they replace it with an approved *occupational pension scheme, *personal pension scheme, or *stakeholder pension scheme.

The private sector of the insurance industry also provides a wide variety of pensions, *annuities, and *endowment assurances. Financial analysts predict a major pensions crisis in the mid-21st century, since demographic trends will produce an ever-growing number of people beyond retirement age drawing on insufficient state and personal provision.

pensionable earnings The part of an employee's salary that is used to calculate the final pension entitlement. Unless otherwise stated, overtime, commission, and bonuses are normally excluded.

Pension Benefit Guaranty Corporation (PBGC) A US federal agency that insures *defined-benefit pension schemes of companies.

pensioneer trustee A person authorized to oversee the management of a *pension fund in accordance with the provisions of the Pension Trust Deed.

pension funds State and private pension contributions invested to give as high a return as possible to provide the funds from which pensions are paid. In the UK, pension funds managed by individual organizations work closely with insurance companies and investment trusts, being together the *institutional investors that have a dominant influence on many securities traded on the London Stock Exchange. An enormous amount of money is accumulated by these pension funds, which grows by weekly and monthly contributions; real estate and works of art are often purchased for investment by pension funds in addition to stock-exchange securities.

Pensions Ombudsman *See* FINANCIAL OMBUDSMAN SERVICE.

PEP Abbreviation for *personal equity plan.

PEP mortgage A *mortgage in which the borrower repays only the interest on the loan to the lender, but at the same time puts regular sums into a *personal equity plan (PEP). When the PEPs mature they are used to repay the capital. The PEP mortgage is similar to an endowment mortgage, except that the PEP mortgage does not provide any life-assurance cover and that PEP funds are untaxed.

peppercorn rent A nominal rent. In theory one peppercorn (or some other nominal sum) is payable as a rent to indicate that a property is leasehold and not *freehold, the peppercorn representing the *consideration. In practice it amounts to a rent-free lease.

P/E ratio Abbreviation for *price–earnings ratio.

per capita income The average income of a group, obtained by dividing the group's total income by its number of members. The **national per capita income** is the ratio of the national income to the population.

percent of sales method A method of setting a promotional budget in which the amount budgeted is a set percentage of the sales revenue, often a standard percentage for a given industry. Car companies are known to use a fixed percentage for promotion, based upon the final price of the car.

perceptual mapping The use of mathematical psychology to understand the structure of a market. Consumer images of different brands of a product are plotted on a graph or map; the closer two brands are on the map, the closer they are as competitors. Perceptual mapping is also used in the development of a new product; the closer a new product appears on a map to an ideal product, the more likely the new product is to succeed. It can be useful in determining competitors' positions and what opportunities there are in unoccupied positions.

per contra Denoting a book-keeping entry of a particular amount on the opposite side of an *account. It is often used when two entries, a debit and a credit, are on opposite sides of the same page, as, for example, a transfer from cash to bank or vice versa, both recorded in the same cash book.

per diem (Latin: per day) Denoting a fee charged by a professional person who is paid a specified fee for each day that he is employed.

perfecting the sight See BILL OF SIGHT.

performance appraisal A formal review of the performance of an employee. The results of the appraisal may be used in deciding an employee's pay or other rewards, career prospects, or training requirements. It usually involves an interview between the employee and his or her immediate manager, although in some cases there may be an element of self-appraisal.

In most organizations, appraisal consists of assessing the employee's ability (or otherwise) to meet expected standards and his or her general demeanour as a member of the workforce. See also EMPLOYEE EVALUATION.

performance measurement The process of (a) developing indicators to assess progress towards certain predefined goals and (b) reviewing performance against these measures. Performance measures can be applied to the whole organization or to particular departments, branches, or individuals. They are often divided into:

- **strategic indicators** – related to successful and effective performance over the lifetime of an organization;
- **operational indicators** – related to the success and profitability of products and services; product mixes and portfolios; and productivity and output;
- **specific indicators** – including organization income or profit per member of staff, per customer, per offering, per outlet, per square foot; returns on investment; speed of response; product durability and longevity of usage; volume and quality targets;
- **behaviourial indicators** – related to staff management aspects; prevailing attitudes and values; the extent of strikes, disputes, absenteeism, labour turnover, and accidents; harmony/discord, cooperation/conflict; the general aura of well-being;
- **confidence indicators** – reflecting the relationship between the organization and its environment, its backers, its stakeholders, its customers, and its communities;
- **ethical indicators** – reflecting the standards of behaviour and performance that an organization sets for itself and its acceptance in both markets and communities.

A distinction is also made between **financial measures**, such as *return on capital employed, *residual income, and *Economic Value Added, and **non-financial measures**, such as delivery time or customer retention. Management accountants will be particularly interested in identifying how the use of different financial and non-financial measures influences the behaviour of managers. For example, using return on capital employed as a measure will probably encourage managers to reduce investment; this may improve short-term performance figures but will damage the long-term performance of the company. Another problem may arise if managers improve delivery times to meet targets but significantly increase costs in the process. These two examples emphasize the importance of understanding the behavioral aspects of management accounting. Another issue is how to link non-financial and financial measures. The *balanced scorecard is a recent development that connects non-financial and financial performance measures to a company's overall strategy. *See also* GOODHART'S LAW.

performance standard In *standard costing, the standard level of performance to be achieved during a period. For example, a standard performance for direct labour of two standard hours to complete a task would be combined with the *rate per standard hour for labour to create the *standard direct labour cost for the task.

peril *See* RISK. *See also* EXCEPTED PERIL.

period bill (term bill) A *bill of exchange payable on a specific date rather than on demand.

period of grace *See* DAYS OF GRACE.

perks An informal word for **perquisites**, the benefits arising as a result of employment, in addition to regular renumeration. Perks are privileges that are expected mainly by senior employees (e.g. a company car, private health insurance, an executive dining room). *See* BENEFITS IN KIND.

permanent diminution in value A fall in the value of an asset that is unlikely to be reversed. The *fixed asset must be shown in the *balance sheet at the reduced amount, which will be the estimated *recoverable amount. A provision has to be made through the *profit and loss account; if this is subsequently found to be no longer required, it should be written back to the profit and loss account.

permanent establishment A fixed

place of business that a taxpayer of one country has in another country, thus rendering the taxpayer liable to that second country's taxation. It will include a place of management, branch, office, factory or workshop, and long-term construction projects but it may exclude some sales offices and storage depots. The concept is important in *double-taxation treaties.

permanent health insurance (PHI) A form of health insurance that provides an income (maximum 75% of salary) up to normal retirement age (or pension age) to replace an income lost by prolonged illness or disability in which the insured is unable to perform any part of his or her normal duties. Premiums are related to age and occupation and normally are fixed; benefits, which are not paid for the first 4–13 weeks of disability, are tax free for one year and thereafter are taxed. *Compare* SICKNESS AND ACCIDENT INSURANCE.

permanent interest bearing share (PIBS) A non-redeemable security, usually issued by a building society, that pays interest at a rate fixed at issue. This is often 10–13.5%, giving investors a high yield for perpetuity. However, these shares carry the risks associated with fixed-interest securities, being the last to be paid out should an issuing building society go into liquidation. Moreover, the second-hand market for PIBS is small (approximately £800 million), making it difficult to find a buyer at any particular price.

per mille (per mill; per mil) (Latin: per thousand) Denoting that the premium on an insurance policy is the stated figure per £1000 of insured value. Per mille is also used to mean 0.1% in relation to interest rates.

permissible capital payment (PCP) A payment made out of *capital when a company is redeeming or purchasing its own *shares and has used all available distributable profits as well as the proceeds of any new issue of shares. *See* OWN SHARES PURCHASE.

permission to deal Permission by the *London Stock Exchange to deal in the shares of a newly floated company. It must be sought three days after the issue of a *prospectus.

perpetual annuity The receipt or payment of a constant annual amount in perpetuity. Although the word annuity refers to an annual sum, in practice the constant sum may be for periods of less than a year. The *present value of an annuity is obtained from the formula:

$P = (a \times 100)/i,$

where P is the present value, a is the annual sum, and i is the interest rate.

perpetual debenture 1. A bond or *debenture that can never be redeemed. *See* IRREDEEMABLE SECURITIES. **2.** A bond or debenture that cannot be redeemed on demand.

perpetual FRN A *floating-rate note that is never redeemed. *See also* FLIP-FLOP FRN.

perpetual inventory A method of continuous *stock control in which an account is kept for each item of stock; one side of the account records the deliveries of that type of stock and the other side records the issues from the stock. Thus, the balance of the account at any time provides a record of either the number of items in stock or their values, or both. This method is used in large organizations in which it is important to control the amount of capital tied up in the running of the business. It also provides a means of checking pilferage. Less sophisticated organizations rely on annual *stocktaking to discover how much stock they have.

perpetual succession The continued existence of a corporation until it is legally dissolved. A corporation, being a separate legal person, is unaffected by the death or other departure of any member but continues in existence no matter how many changes in membership occur.

per proc (per pro; p.p.) Abbreviations for *per procurationem* (Latin: by procuration): denoting an act by an agent, not acting on his own authority but on that of his principal. The abbreviation is often used when signing letters on behalf of a firm or someone else, if formally authorized to do so. The firm or person giving the authority accepts responsibility for documents so signed.

perquisites *See* PERKS.

persistent misdeclaration penalty A penalty used in the collection of *value added tax. It applies when there has been a material inaccuracy in a VAT return, being the lower of £500,000 and 10% of the total true amount of VAT due for the quarter. The trader must also have received a *surcharge liability notice resulting from a previous error within the 15 months prior to the current VAT period. In these circumstances a penalty for repeated errors of 15% of the VAT lost will be charged.

personal accident and sickness insurance *See* SICKNESS AND ACCIDENT INSURANCE.

personal account 1. An *account in a *ledger that bears the name of an individual or of an organization; it records the state of indebtedness of the named person to the organization keeping the account or vice versa. Personal accounts are normally kept in the sales (or total debtors) ledger and the purchases (or total creditors) ledger. **2.** *See* PA.

personal allowance The allowance to which every individual resident in the UK is entitled in calculating their *taxable income for *income tax. The allowance depends on the age of the taxpayer (*see* AGE ALLOWANCE). For 2005–06 the personal allowance for those under 65 is £4895, for those between 65 and 74 the allowance is £7090, and for those aged 75 and over it is £7220. *See also* INCOME TAX ALLOWANCES.

personal assistant (PA) A person who is appointed to help a manager or director and who has wider responsibilities than a secretary.

personal communication channels Channels through which two or more people communicate directly with each other, including face to face, person to audience, or by telephone, fax, Internet, or mail.

personal community An Internet *community of users organized around a small network of individuals. The members of a personal community usually know each other.

personal computer (PC) A microcomputer suitable for a single user, with a localized hard storage disk and a *microprocessor. Although microcomputers have limited abilities compared with the larger *mainframes, they are sufficiently powerful to meet the needs of many small businesses; their uses include producing accounts and payrolls, invoicing, word-processing, and compiling mailing lists. More powerful systems can be obtained by linking several small computers by a *local area network. *See also* LAPTOP COMPUTER; PALMTOP COMPUTER.

personal equity plan (PEP) A UK government scheme introduced in 1987 under the Finance Act (1986) to encourage individuals to invest directly in UK quoted companies, offering investors certain tax benefits. The investment is administered by an authorized plan manager. PEPs were superseded by *Individual Savings Accounts (ISAs) in 1999 but arrangements for existing PEPs continue unaltered. **General PEPs** invest in the shares of more than one company. They may be **managed PEPs**, in which the plan manager makes the investment decisions; **self-select PEPs**, in which the investor makes the decisions; or **advisory PEPs**, in which the plan manager (usually a stockbroker) advises the investor about investment decisions. Investors may put in a lump sum or regular monthly amounts. Re-invested dividends are free of *income tax and *capital gains tax is not incurred, as long as the investment is retained in the plan for at least a complete calendar year. There is a limit of £6000 on the amount an individual can invest in a general PEP in any year. However, an additional £3000 may be invested in a **single-company PEP** (containing the shares of only one, EU-based company), which may be a self-select PEP or a **corporate PEP**, sponsored by the company issuing the shares. A few corporate PEPs are general PEPs, with an investment limit of £6000.

personal financial planning Financial planning for individuals, which involves analysing their current financial position, predicting their short-term and long-term needs, and recommending a financial strategy. This may involve advice on pensions, the provision of independent school fees, mortgages, life assurance, and investments.

personal identification number (PIN) A number memorized by the holder of a

*cash card, *credit card, or *multifunctional card and used in *automated teller machines and *electronic funds transfer at point of sale to identify the card owner. The number is given to the cardholder in secret and is memorized so that if the card is stolen it cannot be used. The number is unique to the cardholder. *See* PHANTOM WITHDRAWALS.

personal influence The effect of statements made by one person on another person's attitude or decision to purchase.

Personal Investment Authority (PIA) A *Self-Regulating Organization that took over most of the responsibilities of the Financial Intermediaries, Managers and Brokers Regulatory Association (FIMBRA) and the Life Assurance and Unit Trust Regulatory Organization (LAUTRO) in 1994. Its remit was to regulate investment business carried out mainly with or for private investors. The PIA was absorbed into the *Financial Services Authority in December 2001.

personality tests *See* PSYCHOLOGICAL TESTS. *See also* INTEREST FACTORS.

personalization Creating a specialized form of a product tailored for an individual customer.

personal ledger A *ledger containing *personal accounts, for example the debtors' ledger and the creditors' ledger.

personal loan A loan to a private person by a bank or building society for domestic purposes, buying a car, etc. There is usually no security required and consequently a high rate of interest is charged. Repayment is usually by monthly instalments over a fixed period. This is a more expensive way of borrowing from a bank than by means of an *overdraft.

personal pension scheme An arrangement in which an individual contributes part of his or her salary to a pension provider, such as an insurance company or a bank. The pension provider invests the funds so that at retirement a lump sum is available to the pensioner. This is used to purchase an *annuity to provide regular pension payments. In the UK the system is that an employee who chooses a personal pension instead of the Second State Pension, or their employer's pension scheme, must pay National Insurance contributions at the full ordinary rate and the employer's share must be paid at the same rate. The state pays the difference between the lower contracted-out rate and the full ordinary rate direct to the personal pension scheme. The administration of pensions is scrutinized by the *Financial Ombudsman Service, which is empowered to deal with complaints relating to personal pension schemes. *See also* STAKEHOLDER PENSION SCHEME.

personal property (personalty) Any property other than *real property (realty). This distinction is especially used in distinguishing property for *inheritance tax. Personal property includes money, shares, chattels, etc.

personal representative A person whose duty is to gather in the assets of the estate of a deceased person, to pay his liabilities, and to distribute the residue. Personal representatives of a person dying testate are known as *executors; those of a person dying intestate are known as his *administrators.

personal selling Person-to-person interaction between a buyer and a seller in which the seller's purpose is to persuade the buyer of the merits of the product, to convince the buyer of his or her need for it, and to develop with the buyer an ongoing customer relationship.

personalty *See* PERSONAL PROPERTY.

personnel management *See* HUMAN-RESOURCE MANAGEMENT.

personnel selection The process of choosing the most suitable applicant for a vacancy within an organization. Normally, a *job description is written, stating the purpose of the job and the tasks, duties, and responsibilities it entails. This enables a *personnel specification to be created, listing the qualifications, experience, and personal attributes that will be required in the successful candidate (*see* KSAOS). A search for the right person then begins, using advertisements in newspapers, trade papers, or employment agencies; if the vacancy is sufficiently senior a head hunter may be employed. Initial selection is then made by inviting letters of application (or using application forms) supported by a

*curriculum vitae and listing the applicants that most closely match the job specification. Screening interviews may then be held, which may include practical tests so that a short list of final candidates can be drawn up. Second interviews are sometimes required and, when appropriate, *psychological tests are used. The number of interviews and the extent of testing will depend on the organization and the level of the position within it. *See* ASSESSMENT CENTRE; SELECTION INTERVIEW.

personnel specification A document used in the recruitment process for a job that lists the skills, experience, and other qualities needed in order to perform it successfully. The specification may include general personality traits as well as more objective criteria, such as qualifications. *See also* KSAOS.

person–job fit The extent to which an individual's skills, interests, and personal characteristics are consistent with the requirements and rewards of their work.

person–organization fit The extent to which an individual's values, interests, and behaviour are consistent with the culture of an organization as a whole, rather than with a specific role or task.

persuasive advertising Advertising used to build selective demand for a brand by persuading consumers that it offers the best quality for their money.

PERT Acronym for programme evaluation and review technique. *See* NETWORK MODELLING.

peseta (Pta) Formerly, the standard monetary unit of Spain and one of the two standard monetary units of Andorra (*see also* FRANC), divided into 100 céntimos. It was subsumed into the *euro for all purposes other than cash transactions in January 1999 and abolished in 2002.

pesewa A monetary unit of Ghana, worth one hundredth of a *cedi.

peso 1. The standard monetary unit of Argentina ($), Chile (Ch$), Colombia (Col$), Cuba (CUP), the Dominican Republic (RD$), Mexico (Mex$), and the Philippines; it is divided into 100 centavos.

2. (NUr$) The standard monetary unit of Uruguay, divided into 100 centésimos.

PESTLE analysis Analysis of the external influences on a firm: the acronym stands for *p*olitical, *e*conomic, *s*ocial, *t*echnological, *l*egal, and *e*nvironmental, i.e. issues that could significantly affect the strategic development of a firm. The former acronym, **PEST**, has been expanded to include the legal and environmental aspects.

PET Abbreviation for *potentially exempt transfer.

petrodollars Reserves of US dollars deposited with banks as a result of the steep rises in the price of oil in the 1970s. The export revenues of the oil-exporting nations increased rapidly in this period, leading to large current-account surpluses, which had an important impact on the world's financial system.

petroleum revenue tax (PRT) A tax on the profits from oil and gas extraction in the UK first imposed in 1975. This tax was the principal means enabling the UK government to obtain a share in the profits made from oil in the North Sea. It has been abolished for oilfields getting development consent on or after 16 March 1993.

petty cash The amount of cash that an organization keeps in notes or coins on its premises to pay small items of expense. This is to be distinguished from cash, which normally refers to amounts held at banks. Petty-cash transactions are normally recorded in a **petty-cash book**, the balance of which should agree with the amounts of petty cash held at any given time.

Pfennig (*plural* **Pfennige**) A former monetary unit of Germany, worth one hundredth of a *Deutschmark (until 2002).

phantom withdrawals The removal of funds from bank accounts through *automated teller machines (ATMs) by unauthorized means and without the knowledge or consent of the account holder. Banks have generally maintained that such withdrawals are not possible so long as account holders take proper steps to keep their *personal identification numbers secret.

PHI 1. Abbreviation for *permanent health insurance. **2.** Abbreviation for *private health insurance.

physical capital Items such as *plant and machinery, buildings, and land that can be used to produce goods and services. It is compared to financial capital, i.e. money, and *human capital.

physical delivery The settlement of an *option or *futures contract by the delivery of the *underlying rather than an equivalent cash settlement.

physical distribution The tasks involved in planning, implementing, and controlling the flow of materials and final goods from their points of origin to their final destinations to meet the requirements of customers at a profit. Warehousing, transportation, and other firms that enable a company to stock and move goods are known as **physical distribution firms**.

physical distribution management *See* SUPPLY-CHAIN MANAGEMENT.

physical price The price of a commodity that is available for delivery. In most forward contracts (*see* FORWARD DEALING) and *futures contracts the goods are never actually delivered because sales and purchases are set off against each other.

physicals *See* ACTUALS.

PI *See* PROFITABILITY INDEX.

PIA Abbreviation for *Personal Investment Authority.

piastre A monetary unit of Egypt, Lebanon, and Syria, worth one hundredth of a *pound.

PIBS Abbreviation for *permanent interest bearing share.

PIC Abbreviation for *product innovation charter.

picketing A form of *industrial action in which employees gather outside a workplace in which there is a trade dispute, usually a strike. The pickets so gathered often form a **picket line**, past which they attempt to discourage other workers, delivery lorries, and customers' collection lorries from passing. The purpose is to reinforce the effects of the strike and to encourage the maximum number of employees to join it. The right to **peaceful picketing** at one's own place of work was established by the Trade Union Act (1975). It is not lawful if it has not first been authorized by a ballot of the union involved and if the reason for the action is because the employer involved is employing a non-union employee. **Secondary picketing**, picketing other people's place of work (i.e. picketing employers not otherwise involved in the dispute), is a civil offence under the Employment Acts (1980; 1982). **Flying pickets**, pickets who join a picket line although they are neither employees of the organization being picketed nor union representatives of employees, have no immunity from civil action.

pictogram A diagram providing quantitative information, using stylized drawings of people and things, in which the number of such individual drawings represents the actual number of people or things involved.

piece rate A payment scheme in which an employee is paid a specific price for each unit made. The rate is therefore directly related to output and not to time (*compare* TIME RATE). This method is often combined with a basic salary and takes the form of a productivity bonus, in which individual effort is rewarded. In modern factories, many tasks have been mechanized, making this method of payment less common, although it is simple to operate and popular with employees. Piece rate, to be attractive to workers, depends on speed of production, therefore the standard of quality and safety may suffer if adequate precautions are not taken. *See also* PAYMENT BY RESULTS; PREMIUM BONUS.

pie chart A diagram providing a visual representation of the proportions into which something is divided. It consists of a circle divided in sectors, the area of each sector representing the proportion of a specified component.

piggyback service A distribution service in which loaded truck trailers, or other sealed containers, are carried by rail to destinations from which they can be taken by truck to their final destination. Similar services are **fishyback service**, involving transport of containers by water, and **birdyback service**, involving transport of containers by air.

PII Abbreviation for *professional indemnity insurance.

pilot production The small-scale production of a new product in a **pilot plant**. The object is to check and, if necessary, improve the production method. The product itself is often used in a marketing exercise to monitor its reception by the market and, in some cases, to improve it.

pilot study A small-scale *marketing research study conducted as a trial so that any problems can be eliminated before a full study is undertaken. For example, a pilot study might show that changes are needed in a questionnaire because questions are ambiguous, miss the point, etc.

PIMS (profit impact of market strategies) An extensive database giving details of the performance of over 7000 businesses in Europe and North America. The details include sales, market share, investment, research and development budget, etc. PIMS examines the relationship between expenditure, market performance, and profitability and has provided explanations for nearly 80% of the variations in profitability among the businesses in the database.

PIN Abbreviation for *personal identification number.

PINC Abbreviation for *property income certificate.

Pink Book *See* UK BALANCE OF PAYMENTS.

pink form (preferential form) An *application form in a flotation that is printed on pink paper and usually distributed to employees of the company to give them preference in the allocation of shares. Up to 10% of a share issue can be set aside under London Stock Exchange rules for applications from employees or from shareholders in a parent company that is floating a subsidiary.

Pinpoint *See* GEOGRAPHIC INFORMATION SYSTEM.

pip *See* TICK.

pipeline inventory *See* INVENTORY.

piracy 1. An illegal act of violence, detention, robbery, or revenge committed on a ship or aircraft. It excludes acts committed for political purposes and during a war. In marine insurance it extends to include any form of plundering at sea. **2.** Infringement of copyright. The usual remedy is for the copyright holder to obtain an injunction to end the infringement. This may not be possible in a foreign country and many British and American books are pirated in foreign countries by copying them photographically and printing them cheaply.

pit (trading pit) An area of a stock market, financial futures and options exchange, or commodity exchange in which a particular stock, financial future, or commodity is traded, especially one in which dealings take place by *open outcry. Authorized dealers in these markets are called **pit traders**. In recent years the practice of pit trading has been increasingly replaced by that of screen trading (*see* INTERNATIONAL PETROLEUM EXCHANGE; LONDON INTERNATIONAL FINANCIAL FUTURES AND OPTIONS EXCHANGE). *See also* CALLOVER; FLOOR.

placing The selling of shares in a company to a selected group of individuals or institutions. Placings can be used either as a means of *flotation or to raise additional capital for a listed company (*see also* PRE-EMPTION RIGHTS; RIGHTS ISSUE). Placings are usually the cheapest way of raising capital and they also allow the directors of a company to influence the selection of shareholders. Placings of private companies (**private placings**) are often carried out without the intermediary of a stockbroker. A **public placing** is the placing of a public company. In the USA a placing is called a **placement**. *Compare* INTRODUCTION; OFFER FOR SALE.

planned economy *See* COMMAND ECONOMY.

planned location of industry Government intervention in the location of new industries in an area or country. As old industries in a region, such as shipbuilding, gradually decrease, new industries are required to take their place to avoid high unemployment and skilled workers moving away. Many governments provide assistance to those wishing to set up new industries in these areas.

planned obsolescence *See* OBSOLESCENCE.

planning One of the functions of *management accounting in which plans for the future activities and operations of an organization are incorporated into its *budgets, etc. *See also* BUSINESS PLAN.

planning blight Difficulty in selling or developing a site, building, etc., because it is affected by a government or local-authority development plan. Planning blight may be ended by a compulsory purchase by the government or local authority, but it may continue indefinitely if the government plans fail to mature or if the site itself is not required by the development but is rendered unsaleable or less valuable by its proximity to a development.

planning permission Permission that must be obtained from a local authority in the UK before building on or developing a site or before changing the use of an existing site or building, in accordance with the Town and Country Planning Act (1971).

plant and machinery The equipment required to operate a business. No formal definition is given in the tax legislation. However, from the tax point of view the definition often used is that given in the taxation case *Yarmouth* v *France* (1887). This defines plant and machinery as "whatever apparatus is used by a businessman for carrying on his business – not his stock in trade which he buys – or makes for resale: but all goods and chattels, fixed or moveable, live or dead, which he keeps for permanent employment in the business". Subsequent cases have been concerned with the distinction between plant actively used in a business, and so qualifying as plant and machinery for *capital allowances purposes, and expenditure on items that relate to the setting up of the business, which do not qualify for capital allowances.

plastic money A colloquial name for a *credit card, *cash card, *debit card, or *multifunctional card. It is often shortened to **plastic**.

playing the yield curve An investment strategy designed to take advantage of differences in yield for different terms, for example by funding short term and investing longer term on a *normal yield curve.

plc Abbreviation for *public limited company. This (or its Welsh equivalent *c.c.c.) must appear in the name of a public limited company. Compare LTD.

pledge An article given by a borrower (**pledgor**) to a lender (**pledgee**) as a security for a debt. It remains in the ownership of the pledgor although it is in the possession of the pledgee until the debt is repaid. See also PAWNBROKER.

Plimsoll line See LOAD LINE.

ploughed-back profits See RETAINED EARNINGS.

pluvial insurance (**pluvius insurance**) An insurance policy covering loss of income or profits caused by rain or other weather conditions. The main demand comes from the organizers of outdoor summer events, who could suffer financially if rain caused the event to be curtailed or abandoned. For events in which any profits would be uncertain, e.g. a summer fete, the policy specifies that claims are to be based on the number of millimetres of rain that fall in an agreed period at an agreed weather station near to the site of the event. If the amount of lost revenue can be easily calculated from ticket sales at an event, such as a cricket test match or tennis match, a policy paying for lost profit can be arranged.

PM Abbreviation for *preventative maintenance.

PMTS Abbreviation for *predetermined motion-time standards.

point See BASIS POINT.

point method An analytical method of *job evaluation in which jobs are scored on a number of different features (e.g. skills, effort, level of responsibility, working conditions, etc.). The scores are then summed and used to create a graded pay structure. The method, which is very widely used, is essentially a refinement of the *factor-comparison method. See also CLASSIFICATION METHOD; HAY METHOD; JOB-COMPONENT METHOD; RANKING METHOD.

point-of-purchase promotion (**POP promotion**) A promotional display or demonstration that takes place at the point of sale.

point of sale (**POS**) The place at which a consumer makes a purchase, usually a retail shop. It may, however, also be a doorstep (in door-to-door selling), a market stall, or a mail-order house.

poisha A monetary unit of Bangladesh, worth one hundredth of a *taka.

poison pill A tactic in which a company discourages unwanted *takeover bids by ensuring that a successful bid will trigger some event that substantially reduces the value of the company. Examples of such tactics include the sale of some prized asset to a friendly company or bank or the issue of securities with a conversion option enabling the bidder's shares to be bought at a reduced price if the bid is successful. Poison pills are used all over the world but were developed in the USA. See also PORCUPINE PROVISIONS; STAGGERED DIRECTORSHIPS.

polarization The distinction made in the *Financial Services Act (1986) between intermediaries who give advice on investments and act as a representative of one company (a tied agent) and those who are fully independent (see INDEPENDENT FINANCIAL ADVISER) and able to advise on the full range of products offered by different companies. This polarization has caused some controversy and confusion amongst consumers. It has also raised doubts about the impartiality of advice provided by fully independent intermediaries. Due to the costs associated with maintaining a fully independent status, the majority of High-Street banks and building societies are now tied to one particular company, prompting concerns over the extent to which, at the retail level, the resulting limited consumer choice contributes towards the original objective of investor protection.

policy See INSURANCE POLICY.

policy proof of interest (**PPI**) An insurance policy (usually *marine insurance) in which the insurers agree that they will not insist on the usual requirement that the insured must prove an *insurable interest existed in the subject matter before a claim is paid. The possession of the policy is all that is required. These policies are a matter of trust between insurer and insured as they are not legally enforceable. They are issued for convenience in cases in which an insurable interest exists but is extremely difficult to prove or in which an insurable interest might come into existence later in the voyage.

political and charitable contributions Donations for political or charitable purposes made by an organization. Under the Companies Act a disclosure of such a donation has to be made by companies that are not *wholly owned subsidiariess of another British company and which have on their own or with their subsidiaries given in the financial year in aggregate more than £200. Charitable purposes is taken to mean purposes that are exclusively charitable. A donation for political purposes is taken to mean the giving of money either directly or indirectly to a political party of the UK or any part of it, or to a person who is carrying on activities likely to affect support for a political party. The total amounts given for both political and charitable purposes must be separately disclosed. If the payments are for political purposes, where applicable, the following information must be provided: (a) the name of each person to whom money exceeding £200 in amount has been given for those purposes and the amount given; and (b) if more than £200 has been given as a donation or subscription to a political party, the identity of the party and the amount given must be disclosed.

political credit risk (sovereign risk) The *credit risk arising from the fact that a foreign government may decide not to honour its financial obligations or other business commitments. Compare TRANSFER CREDIT RISK. See also COUNTRY RISK.

poll tax A tax that is the same for each individual, i.e. a lump sum per head (from Middle Low German *polle*: head). The benefits of such taxes are that they do not distort choices, being an equal levy from everyone's resources whatever their circumstances; however, poll taxes are sometimes criticized as being regressive in that they do not take account of *ability to pay.

The **community charge**, an alternative to domestic rates, was a poll tax introduced in 1990 (1989 in Scotland) and replaced by council tax in 1993. See also FLAT TAX.

pollution The disposal into the environment of substances that cannot be made harmless by normal biological processes. As part of a wider and increasing concern for environmental issues, the costs of industrialization are being assessed in terms of discharges into the air and water, the disposal and long-term effects of wastes, recycling, energy efficiency, land use and degradation, and the depletion of raw materials. Legislation has been enacted, increasingly, to limit levels of pollution and in 1996 an Environmental Agency was established in the UK to coordinate the previously separate activities of various agencies. Most other advanced industrial countries have introduced legislation and similar agencies. International targets have been agreed to eliminate the use of CFCs in aerosols and as a refrigerant (because they deplete the ozone layer). The adoption of the 'Polluter Pays Principle' (the fining of major companies for pollution incidents) and increasing awareness of green consumerism has meant that many leading companies have now issued environmental policy statements and some publish annual *environmental audits. See ENVIRONMENTAL COSTS.

pollution permits Permits issued by a government that allow the owner to pollute the environment legally. These permits may be bought and sold; firms that improve their environmental efficiency would reduce their need for permits and be in a position to sell them to less environmentally efficient rivals. In the USA, as part of the Clean Air Act, trading in these permits has cut sulphur dioxide emissions faster and more cheaply than expected. The use of pollution permits appears to have two main advantages over traditional environmental regulations. First, it gives firms a financial incentive to reduce emissions for less than it would cost to buy permits, and secondly, by leaving it to companies to decide how and when to reduce emissions, it reduces not only the cost of compliance but also the bureaucracy required to enforce environmental regulations.

POP promotion Abbreviation for *point-of-purchase promotion.

population (universe) In marketing research, any complete group of entities sharing a common set of characteristics. For example, a population could be all the companies in the car-supplying industries or all the consumers in the South West of England. A population is the group from which a *sample is taken. **Population specification error** is the error that results from an incorrect definition of the population from which the sample is chosen. For example, a population of consumers defined as buyers of Brand X may contain some non-buyers in the sample.

population hypotheses In marketing research, assumptions made by a researcher or manager about some characteristic of a *population being reviewed. Typical hypotheses could be that for a particular population one method of advertising (e.g. TV) is more effective than another (e.g. radio) or that one brand of cereal was more popular in a selected area of the country than in other areas. On the basis of such a hypothesis, data is collected, evaluated, and accepted or rejected according to the probability that it is true.

population pyramid A diagram that illustrates the distribution of a population by age. The youngest and most numerous age group forms a rectangle at the base of the pyramid; the oldest and least numerous is a small rectangle at its apex.

porcupine provisions (shark repellents) Provisions made by a company to deter *takeover bids. They include *poison pills, *staggered directorships, etc.

portal presence Significant references to a website in search-engine indexes and directories. Good portal presence can increase traffic to a site.

portal site A site that provides general Internet capabilities and serves as a gateway to additional information.

portfolio 1. The set of holdings in securities owned by an investor or institution. In building up an investment portfolio an institution will have its own investment analysts, while an individual may make use of the services of a *merchant bank that offers **portfolio management**. The choice of portfolio will depend on the mix of income and capital growth its owner expects, some investments providing good income prospects while others provide good prospects for capital growth. **2.** A list of the loans made by an organization. Banks, for example, attempt to balance their portfolio of loans to limit the risks.

portfolio analysis 1. An analysis enabling management to identify and evaluate the various business units that make up a diversified company. Various techniques are used, the best known being the *Boston matrix. **2.** An analysis of the assets in an investment *portfolio.

portfolio insurance (portfolio protection) The use of a *financial futures and *options market to protect the value of a portfolio of investments. For example, a fund manager may expect the general level of prices to fall on the stock exchange. The manager could protect the portfolio by selling the appropriate number of *index futures, which could then be bought back at a profit if the market falls. Alternately, the manager could establish the value of the portfolio at current prices by buying put options, which would provide the opportunity to benefit if there was a rise in the general level of prices.

portfolio theory The theory developed by H. M. Markowitz that rational investors are averse to taking increased risk unless they are compensated by an adequate increase in expected return. The theory also assumes that for any given expected return, most rational investors will prefer a lower level of risk and for any given level of risk they will prefer a higher return than a lower return. A set of efficient *portfolios can be calculated from which the investor will choose the one most appropriate for their risk profile. The practical conclusions of the theory are that investors should diversify widely and determine their levels of risk by lending a proportion of their assets or borrowing to buy more risky assets. *See also* MARKOWITZ MODEL; PORTFOLIO INSURANCE.

port mark The markings on the packages of goods destined for export, giving the name of the overseas port to which they are to be shipped or sent by air freight.

POS Abbreviation for *point of sale.

position The extent to which an investor, dealer, or speculator has made a commitment in the market by buying or selling securities, currencies, commodities, or any financial obligation. See LONG POSITION; OPEN POSITION; SHORT POSITION.

position audit A systematic assessment of the current situation of an organization. This normally involves drawing up a report (either internally or through external consultants) of the strengths and weaknesses of the organization and the opportunities or threats that it faces (see SWOT). The position audit is a vital tool in designing the future strategies of a large organization.

positioning A marketing strategy that will position a company's products and services against those of its competitors in the minds of consumers. To achieve positioning success it is suggested that there are four basic competitive strategies that a company can follow. The three winning strategies are:

- **cost leadership** – the company tries to achieve lowest costs of production and distribution;
- **differentiation** – making use of specific *marketing mixes (see DIFFERENTIATED MARKETING);
- **focus** – paying attention to a few market segments.

The fourth strategy is a losing strategy in which a company pursues a middle-of-the-road path. Companies that try to be good at everything are rarely particularly good at anything.

position limit **1.** A limit placed by a financial exchange on the *exposure that any single transactor may undertake. **2.** An internal risk-management limit imposed on *positions to be held by traders, desks, etc. within an organization. See also INTRADAY LIMIT; LIMIT.

position trading In finance, the holding of an *open position for a long period of time with an eye to achieving long-term profits from calculated risks.

possession Actual physical control of goods or land. Possession has a wide variety of meanings in English law, depending on the nature of the property and the circumstances. For example, a person may still have possession of goods that have been lost or mislaid, provided that they are not abandoned and that no-one else has physical possession of them. It is sometimes used in the sense of a right to possession, e.g. the right of a person who has pledged goods to get them back. Possession may be divorced from *ownership; for example, a thief has legal possession of stolen goods but not ownership. Possession usually requires intention to possess – a person cannot possess something without knowing that he or she does so.

postal account A savings account with a bank or a building society that can only be operated by letter or (sometimes) by *automated teller machine (i.e. not over the counter or by telephone or over the Internet). Postal accounts usually pay a higher rate of interest than those that can be operated in person because of their cost structure.

post-balance-sheet events See ADJUSTING EVENTS; NON-ADJUSTING EVENTS.

post-completion audit A comparison of the actual cash flows resulting from an investment project with the forecast cash flows. A post-completion audit should identify bad investments made in the past and encourage managers to use more realistic forecasts for future investment projects.

post-date To insert a date on a document that is later than the date on which it is signed, thus making it effective only from the later date. A **post-dated** (or **forward-dated**) **cheque** cannot be negotiated before the date written on it, irrespective of when it was signed. Compare ANTE-DATE.

post-entry duty See OVER-ENTRY CERTIFICATE.

poster A placard or bill exhibited in a public place as an advertisement. Although there are over 200 000 legal poster sites in the UK, poster advertising accounts for less than 10% of the total advertising expenditure. Illegal attachment of posters or bills to empty shop windows, company hoardings, etc., is called **flyposting**. Flyposting is often undertaken at night by a small number of companies, all of whom jealously guard their regular territories. Flyposting is particularly popular with record companies, underground magazines, and some film companies.

post hoc segmentation The process of segmenting a market or markets empirically. *See* MARKET SEGMENTATION.

postpurchase behaviour The stage in *consumer buying behaviour in which the consumer takes further action after purchase, based on his or her satisfaction or dissatisfaction.

post-testing Testing that takes place after an advertisement has appeared to determine whether or not it has met the objectives set for it by the company that paid for it.

potential entrant An organization that is poised to enter a market and would do so if there was a small price rise or a reduction in *barriers to entry.

potentially exempt transfer (PET) A lifetime gift made by an individual to another individual, or into an *interest-in-possession trust that does not attract a liability to *inheritance tax at the date of the gift. No charge occurs if the donor survives seven years after the date of the gift. If death occurs within seven years of the gift, the total lifetime gifts in the seven years preceding death are reviewed. The gifts are taken in chronological order with the first £275,000 (2005–06) worth of gifts being covered by the nil-rate band. Gifts in excess of this sum are charged at a flat rate of 40% with graduated relief for gifts made between three and seven years before death. HM Revenue and Customs provides detailed rules for PETs in the Inheritance Tax Manual. *See also* EXEMPT TRANSFERS.

potential market The consumers who profess some level of interest in a particular product or service.

pound **1.** (£) The standard monetary unit of the UK, divided into 100 pence. It dates back to the 8th century AD when Offa, King of Mercia, coined 240 pennyweights of silver from 1 pound of silver. When *sterling was decimalized in 1971 it was divided into 100 newly defined pence. The pound is also the currency unit of the Falkland Islands (Fk£), Gibraltar (Gib£), the Channel Islands, and the Isle of Man.

2. The standard monetary unit of Egypt (LE), Lebanon (LL), and Syria (LS), divided into 100 piastres. **3.** (£C) The standard monetary unit of Cyprus, divided into 100 cents.

pound cost averaging A method of accumulating capital by investing a fixed sum of money in a particular share every month (or other period). When prices fall the fixed sum will buy correspondingly more shares and when prices rise fewer shares are bought. The result is that the average purchase price over a period is lower than the arithmetic average of the market prices at each purchase date (because more shares are bought at lower prices and fewer at higher prices).

power of attorney (PA) A formal document giving one person the right to act for another. A power to execute a *deed must itself be given by a deed. An attorney may not delegate these powers unless specifically authorized to do so.

power styles The characteristic ways in which different managers attempt to influence the behaviour of employees and others, overcome resistance, and achieve their goals. Styles can be characterized as either competitive or collective.

- **Impression management** is a competitive power style in which information is controlled and manipulated in order to influence peoples' attitudes to events, policies, or personalities. This reliance on presentation and 'spin' may at times amount to actual deceit.

- **Consensus** and **charismatic power styles** are forms of the collective use of power. The consensus power style involves *participative decision making and joint problem solving, whereas the charismatic style makes use of the manager's personality to inspire the members of an organization to work together for a common purpose (*see* CHARISMATIC LEADER; TRANSFORMATIONAL LEADERSHIP).

- A **transactional power style** involves the use of negotiation and *contingent reinforcement (rewards and penalties) to influence others; it can be either competitive or collective, depending on the decision maker. Cooperation is needed for any transaction to take place: if that transaction involves the use and allocation of scarce resources it could become very competitive. *See* TRANSACTIONAL LEADERSHIP.

See also LEADERSHIP STYLE; SOURCES OF POWER.

p.p. Abbreviation for *per procurationem*. *See* PER PROC.

PPI 1. Abbreviation for *policy proof of interest.* **2.** Abbreviation for *producer price index.

PPP 1. Abbreviation for *purchasing power parity. **2.** Abbreviation for *public–private partnership.

PR Abbreviation for *public relations.

preacquisition profit The *retained earnings of one company before it is taken over by another company. Preacquisition profits should not be distributed to the shareholders of the acquiring company by way of dividend, as such profits do not constitute income to the parent company but a partial repayment of its capital outlay on the acquisition of the shares.

preapproach A step in the industrial selling process in which a salesperson learns as much as possible about a prospective customer before making a sales call.

preautomation analysis An analysis that should precede the replacement of a manual system by automation. Research suggests that large-scale investments in automation frequently fail to provide the expected benefits, because they are not used as an opportunity to eliminate unnecessary elements of the process. *See* BUSINESS PROCESS RE-ENGINEERING; VALUE-ADDED MANUFACTURING.

preceding-year basis (PYB) A basis for assessing profits in which the assessment in any given *fiscal year is based on the accounts that ended during the previous tax year. In the UK, the PYB was replaced by the *current-year basis of assessment from 1997–98 onwards.

precept A command by HM Revenue and Customs to a taxpayer to make certain relevant documents available, usually by a specified date.

precious metals The metals silver, gold, and platinum. *Compare* BASE METALS.

predatory pricing strategy 1. The pricing of goods or services at such a low level that other firms cannot compete and are forced to leave the market. While it has long been accepted that some firms resort to predatory pricing on occasions, the application of *game theory to *strategic behaviour has shown that predatory pricing is unlikely to occur very often as it is at least as painful for the predator as for the victim. This encourages most potential predators to look for a more cooperative plan. *See also* PRICE WAR. **2.** An illegal pricing strategy in which a product is offered at a low price to eliminate competition and the price is subsequently raised after the competition has been eliminated.

predetermined motion-time standards (PMTS) A *work measurement technique using libraries of pre-established times for basic human motions, to construct standard times for jobs or processes.

predetermined overhead rate An overhead *absorption rate computed in advance of operations. In practice, most absorption rates are computed from budgeted figures and are therefore predetermined overhead rates, which usually cover one year.

pre-emption First refusal: the right of a person to be the first to be asked if he or she wishes to enter into an agreement at a specified price; for example, the right to be offered a house at a price acceptable to the vendor before it is put on the open market.

pre-emption rights A principle, established in company law, according to which any new shares issued by a company must first be offered to the existing shareholders as the legitimate owners of the company. To satisfy this principle a company must write to every shareholder (see RIGHTS ISSUE), involving an expensive and lengthy procedure. Newer methods of issuing shares, such as *vendor placings or *bought deals, are much cheaper and easier to effect, although they violate pre-emption rights. In the USA pre-emption rights have now been largely abandoned but controversy is still widespread in the UK.

pre-empt spot An advertising spot for a

particular period of airtime on television, bought in advance at a discount for use only if another advertiser does not offer to take up that time at the full rate.

preference dividend A *dividend payable to the holders of *preference shares. Preference dividends not paid in previous periods will only be due to the holders of *cumulative preference shares.

preference share A share in a company yielding a fixed rate of interest rather than a variable dividend. A preference share is an intermediate form of security between an *ordinary share and a *debenture. Preference shares usually confer some degree of ownership of the company. However, in the event of liquidation, they are paid off after *loan capital but before *ordinary share capital.

Participating preference shares carry additional rights to dividends, such as a further share in the profits of the company, after the ordinary shareholders have received a stated percentage. *See also* PREFERRED ORDINARY SHARE.

preference share capital *Share capital consisting of *preference shares. Under *Financial Reporting Standard 4, Capital Instruments, preference share capital was classified as *non-equity share capital. However, FRS4 has now been replaced by FRS25, Financial Instruments: Disclosure and Presentation, which states that from 1 January 2005 preference shares should be classified as *liabilities rather than *shareholders' equity.

preferential creditor A creditor whose debt will be met in preference to those of other creditors and who thus has the best chance of being paid in full on the bankruptcy of an individual or the winding-up of a company. Preferential creditors, who are usually paid in full after *secured liabilities and before ordinary creditors, include the trustees of occupational pensions schemes and employees in respect of any remuneration outstanding. The status of the Crown (i.e. HM Revenue and Customs) as a preferential creditor was abolished from 2003.

preferential debt A debt that will be repaid in preference to other debts. *See* PREFERENTIAL CREDITOR.

preferential duty A specially low import duty imposed on goods from a country that has a trade agreement of a certain kind with the importing country. For example, in the days of the British Empire, imports from member countries were granted Imperial Preference on imported materials, which later became Commonwealth Preference.

preferential form *See* PINK FORM.

preferential payment A payment made to a *preferential creditor.

preferred ordinary share A share issued by some companies that ranks between a *preference share and an *ordinary share in the payment of dividends.

preferred position A desirable position for an advertisement in a publication, for which a premium is charged.

preferred stock The US name for a *preference share.

preliminary announcement An early announcement of their profit or loss for the year that *listed companies are required to make under *London Stock Exchange Regulations. The minimum information is a summarized *profit and loss account, although there has been a trend for companies to provide other information, such as *balance sheets. Companies must lodge their preliminary announcement with the Stock Exchange, but there is no requirement to send the information to shareholders. A number of companies publish some of the information in national newspapers and provide *investment analysts and journalists with substantial information, which receives considerable comment in the press.

preliminary expenses Expenses involved in the formation of a company. They include the cost of producing a *prospectus, issuing shares, and advertising the flotation.

pre-market Denoting any trading that takes place before the official opening of a market.

premium **1.** The consideration payable for a contract of *insurance or life assurance. **2.** An amount in excess of the nominal value of a share, bond, or other security. **3.** An amount in excess of the issue price of a share or other security. When dealings open for a new issue of shares, for instance, it may be said that the market price will be at a premium over the issue price (*see* STAG). **4.** The price paid by a buyer of an *option contract to the seller for the right to exercise the option. In general, the premium asked for an option consists of two components, its *intrinsic value and its *time value. **5.** The difference between the spot price for a commodity or currency and the forward price. **6.** A bonus given to bank customers as an inducement to open an account.

premium bonds UK government securities first issued in 1956 and now administered by *National Savings and Investments, an agency of HM Treasury. No regular income or capital gain is offered but bonds enter monthly draws for a range of tax-free prizes, winners being drawn by ERNIE (electronic random number indicating equipment). Bonds are in £1 denominations with a minimum purchase of £100 and a maximum holding of £30 000. Bonds are repaid at their face value at any time.

premium bonus A *payment by results method of paying workers, in which a standard time is set for the production of each unit and bonuses are paid related to the actual time taken. Depending on the needs of the organization, this scheme can be varied to achieve a balance between quality and speed of production; it also provides an incentive for employees. The standards were formerly set by experienced staff but more scientific attempts at classifying work units have resulted in the introduction of systematic *work-study techniques. These schemes can lead to friction between employee and employer as standard times are a permanent source of conflict. *See also* PIECE RATE.

premium currency Of two currencies, the one whose exchange rate is higher in the forward market.

premium income The total income of an insurance company from insurance policy *premiums.

premium offer A special offer of a domestic product advertised on the package of some other product. The purchaser sends a set number of package tops or labels with a small cash payment to an address given and receives the domestic product by post. Premium offers are handled by **premium houses**, who provide all the services required to distribute the products.

pre-packaged bankruptcy Bankruptcy proceedings that incorporate in advance an already agreed reorganization plan.

prepared data entry (PDE) In marketing research, a method of rapid data collection in which the respondent interacts directly with a computer instead of through the medium of an interviewer. A major advantage is the elimination of *interviewer error.

prepayment **1.** The settlement of a debt before it is due, for example by the early repayment of a mortgage. **2.** *See* PAYMENT IN ADVANCE.

prepayment risk The *risk associated with early payments of obligations. A prime example is the risk that a borrower will repay a fixed-rate mortgage early at a time when interest rates are falling, leaving the lender with a lower interest income than anticipated. To offset this risk, lenders sometimes impose a **prepayment penalty** on loans.

presentation **1.** A verbal report, often supported by explanatory and illustrative material, in which something, such as a balance sheet, new product, etc., is presented to an audience. **2.** A step in the industrial selling process in which a salesperson explains a product to the buyer, giving a detailed description of the way in which the product will make or save money for the buyer.

present value (discounted value) The result arrived at in a *discounted cash flow calculation by multiplying a projected annual cash flow figure by a *discount factor derived from a *hurdle rate of interest and a time period.

present-value factor *See* DISCOUNT FACTOR.

president **1.** The chief executive of a US company, equivalent to the chairman of the board of a UK company. **2.** A title sometimes given to a past chairman or managing director of a UK company, usually for an honorary position that carries little responsibility for running the company.

press conference A meeting called by an organization to announce a newsworthy event to the press. The public relations or press departments of a large organization will often prepare a **press kit**, consisting of press releases and supporting material, to provide the press with accurate information.

prestige price A high price charged for a product to convey an impression of high quality. The underlying assumption is that if a product has a low price it must be inferior to competitive products that are being sold at higher prices.

pre-tax profit The profit of a company before deduction of corporation tax.

pretesting 1. Conducting limited trials of a questionnaire, or other study document, to determine its suitability for a planned marketing research project. **2.** In the context of advertising, marketing research on the effectiveness of an advertisement; it begins at the earliest stage of development and continues until the advertisement is ready for use.

preventative maintenance (PM) An approach to the maintenance of plant, which is central to *just-in-time techniques; it emphasizes frequent proactive inspection and repair in order to reduce downtime and to extend its working life.

prevention costs See COST OF QUALITY. See also ENVIRONMENTAL COSTS.

price The amount of money charged for a product or service, or the value that a consumer exchanges for the benefits of having or using a product or service.

price-bundling strategy A pricing strategy in which the price of a set of products is lower than the total of the individual prices of the components. For example, a car with a set of optional extras may be priced in this way. See BUNDLING.

price competition Competition based on the price at which a product or service is offered. It is especially important in the marketing of products that are not distinc-

tive, such as raw materials. Because *price wars reduce profits, sellers prefer other forms of competition, based on quality, packaging, advertising, etc.

price control Restrictions by a government on the prices of consumer goods, usually imposed on a short-term basis as a measure to control inflation. See also PRICES AND INCOME POLICY.

price discrimination The sale of the same product at different prices to different buyers. Usually practised by monopolists, it requires that a market can be subdivided to exploit different sets of consumers and that these divisions can be sustained. Pure price discrimination rarely exists, since sellers usually differentiate the product slightly (as in first-class rail travel and different types of theatre seat).

price–dividend ratio (PDR; P/D ratio) The current market price of a company share divided by the dividend per share for the previous year. It is a measure of the investment value of the share.

price–earnings ratio (P/E ratio) The current market price of a company share divided by the *earnings per share (eps) of the company. The P/E ratio usually refers to the annual eps and is expressed as a number (e.g. 5 or 10), often called the **multiple** of the company. Loosely, it can be thought of as the number of years it would take the company to earn an amount equal to its market value. High multiples, usually associated with low *yields, indicate that the company is growing rapidly, while a low multiple is associated with dull no-growth stocks. The P/E ratio is one of the main indicators used by fundamental analysts to decide whether the shares in a company are expensive or cheap, relative to the market.

price index See RETAIL PRICE INDEX.

price leadership The setting of the price of a product by a dominant firm in an industry in the knowledge that competitors will follow this lead in order to avoid the high cost of a *price war. This practice is often found in *oligopolies and has the effect of a *cartel. As the price leader is as anxious as the other members of the industry to achieve a stable market, it is in their interest to set the price at a sensible level; a price leader who fails to do so will soon be replaced as leader by another member of the group. *Compare* PRICE RING.

price level The average level of prices of goods and services in an economy, usually calculated as a figure on a price index. *See* RETAIL PRICE INDEX.

price-lining strategy A pricing strategy in which a seller prices individual products in a product line in accordance with certain price points that are believed to be attractive to buyers.

price method The US term for *piece rate.

price packs Products sold at a reduced price that is marked by the producer directly on the label or package of the product.

price ring A group of firms in the same industry that have agreed amongst themselves to fix a minimum retail price for their competing products, thus forming a *cartel. Price rings are illegal in many countries unless they can be shown to be in the public interest. *See* CONSUMER PROTECTION; PRICE LEADERSHIP.

prices and income policy A government policy to curb *inflation by directly imposing wage restraint (*see* WAGE FREEZE) and *price controls.

price-sensitive information Information (usually unpublished) about a company that is likely to cause its share prices to move. *See* INSIDER DEALING.

price stabilization A pricing policy aimed at avoiding widely fluctuating prices. The marketer with this objective sets prices to match competitors' prices or to maintain existing price differentials.

price support A government policy of providing support for certain basic, usually agricultural, products to stop the price falling below an agreed level. Support prices can be administered in various ways: the government can purchase and stockpile surplus produce to support the price or it can pay producers a cash payment as a *subsidy to raise the price they obtain through normal market channels. *See also* COMMON AGRICULTURAL POLICY.

price theory A theory that, at the microeconomic level, defines the role of prices in consumer demand and the supply of goods by firms. At a broader level, it explains the role of prices in markets as a whole. At the macroeconomic level it treats wages and interest rates as the prices of particular goods, thus implying that governments must take market forces into account when formulating such policies as incomes policy and monetary policy.

price war Competition between two or more firms in the same industry that are seeking to increase their shares of the market by cutting the prices of their products. Although this can give short-term advantages in some circumstances to one participant, in the longer run it is a situation from which no one profits. To avoid the perils of selling products at a loss in order to outdo the competition, in most industries prices are not allowed by competitors to fall below a certain level, competition being restricted to other methods, such as advertising, improving the packaging, etc.

pricing The setting of selling prices for the products and services supplied by an organization. In many cases selling prices will be based on market prices but in other circumstances pricing will be based on costs, using information provided by the *management accounting system.

prima facie (Latin: *prima facies* first appearance) At first appearances. **Prima facie evidence** is evidence that appears to be conclusive on first appearances but is not necessarily conclusive.

primage 1. A percentage added to a freight charge to cover the cost of loading or unloading a ship. **2.** An extra charge for handling goods with special care when they are being loaded or unloaded from a ship, aircraft, etc.

primary demand *See* GENERIC DEMAND.

primary-demand advertising Advertising aimed at stimulating *generic demand.

primary domain name *See* DOMAIN NAME.

primary earnings per share *See* FULLY DILUTED EARNINGS PER SHARE.

primary market The market into which a *new issue of securities is launched. *Compare* SECONDARY MARKET.

primary production *See* PRODUCTION.

prime cost *See* DIRECT COSTS.

prime rate The rate of interest at which US banks lend money to first-class borrowers. It is similar in operation to the *base rate in the UK. Competitive markets have forced many banks, both in the USA and the UK, to offer business customers credit at below prime rates. The main difference between US and UK practice is that the US prime rate is approximately equal to the dollar three-month *London Inter Bank Offered Rate (LIBOR) plus 1%, whereas the UK base rate is approximately equivalent to the sterling three-month LIBOR.

prime time The time of the day when radio and TV audiences are expected to be at a peak and therefore advertising rates are highest.

PRINCE Acronym for *Projects in con*trolled *environments. A method of project management, used by government *information technology departments, that provides a shell within which to control a project throughout its life cycle. To the extent that this enables standardized procedures to be used, it allows managers to concentrate on content rather than process. It also permits a more structured and comparative evaluation of a process to be made.

principal **1.** The sum on which interest is paid. **2.** A person who has given express or implied authority for another person to act as an *agent on his or her behalf. *See* AGENCY RELATIONSHIP.

principles of motion economy (characteristics of easy movement) Guidelines that focus on efficient and effective use of the human body, arrangements of the workplace, and design of tools and equipment. *See also* ERGONOMICS; WORK STUDY.

priority date *See* PATENT.

priority percentage (prior charge) The proportion of any profit that must be paid to holders of fixed-interest capital (*preference shares and loan stock; *see* DEBENTURE) before arriving at the sums to be distributed to holders of *ordinary shares. These percentages help to assess the security of the income of ordinary shareholders and are related to the *gearing of the company's capital.

priority sequencing *See* SEQUENCING.

prior-period adjustments Material adjustments applicable to prior *accounting periods arising from changes in *accounting policies or from the correction of fundamental errors. They do not include normal recurring adjustments or corrections of accounting estimates made in prior periods. Under *Financial Reporting Standard 3, if prior-period adjustments fall within these definitions, the *financial statements for the current period should not be distorted, but the prior periods should be restated with an adjustment to the opening balance of the *retained earnings.

privacy statement A statement provided to a customer that makes clear what type of information is collected about him or her and how it is used.

private bank **1.** A *commercial bank owned by one person or a partnership (*compare* JOINT-STOCK BANK). Popular in 19th-century Britain, they have been superseded by joint-stock banks. They still exist in the USA. **2.** A bank that is not a member of a *clearing house and therefore has to use a clearing bank as an agent. **3.** A bank that is not owned by the state.

private brand *See* OWN BRAND.

private carrier *See* CARRIER.

private enterprise (free enterprise) An economic system in which citizens are allowed to own capital and property and to run their own businesses with a minimum of state interference. The free-enterprise system encourages *entrepreneurs and the making of profits by private individuals and firms. *See* FREE MARKET.

private health insurance (PHI) A form of insurance that covers all the normal costs associated with private medical treatment. PHI enables those who wish to do so to choose their own consultants, choose when and where they are hospitalized, and to have private rooms (with private telephones) in hospitals. Because these facilities are often important for managers and executives, businesses often offer PHI to senior employees as a fringe benefit. Many companies offer group schemes at discounted premiums.

private ledger A *ledger containing confidential accounts. A *control account may be used to link it to the general ledger.

private limited company Any *limited company that is not a *public limited company. Such a company is not permitted to offer its shares for sale to the public and it is free from the rules that apply to public limited companies.

private placing See PLACING.

private sector The part of an economy that is not under government control. In a *mixed economy most commercial and industrial firms are in the private sector, run by *private enterprise. Compare PUBLIC SECTOR.

private-sector liquidity See MONEY SUPPLY.

private treaty Any contract made by personal arrangement between the buyer and seller or their agents, i.e. not by public *auction.

privatization (denationalization) The process of selling a publicly owned company or asset (see NATIONALIZATION) to the private sector. Privatization may be pursued for political as well as economic reasons. The economic justification for privatization is that a company will be more efficient under private ownership, although most economists would argue that privatization will only achieve this if it is accompanied by increased competition. Politically, privatization in the form of share offers to the general public is seen as a means of widening the share-owning public and thus increasing the commitment of working people to the capitalist system.

PRO Abbreviation for public relations officer. See PUBLIC RELATIONS.

probability The likelihood that an event or a particular result will occur. It can be

represented on a scale by a number between 0 (zero probability of the event happening, i.e. it is certain not to) and 1 (certainty that it will occur). It is treated mathematically on this basis in statistics.

probability sampling (random sampling) A sampling procedure in which each element of a *population has a known chance of being selected for the *sample. Apart from simple random sampling, this includes certain forms of *stratified sampling and *systematic sampling. The process depends upon up-to-date lists of the population being available; without such lists a probability sample cannot be chosen. Compare NON-PROBABILITY SAMPLING.

probate A certificate issued by the Family Division of the High Court, on the application of *executors appointed by a will, to the effect that the will is valid and that the executors are authorized to administer the deceased's estate. When there is no apparent doubt about the will's validity, probate is granted in **common form** on the executors filing an *affidavit. Probate granted in common form can be revoked by the court at any time on the application of an interested party who proves that the will is invalid. When the will is disputed, probate in **solemn form** is granted, but only if the court decides that the will is valid after hearing the evidence on the disputed issues in a **probate action**.

probate price The price of shares or other securities used for *inheritance-tax purposes on the death of the owner. The price is taken as either one quarter of the interval between the upper and lower quotations of the day on which the owner died added to the lower figure or as half way between the highest and lowest recorded bargains of the day, whichever is the lower.

probate value The value of the assets at the time of a person's death, agreed with HM Revenue and Customs for the purposes of calculating *inheritance tax.

problem child See BOSTON MATRIX.

problem definition The first stage in *marketing research. It consists of a clear definition of the problem to be solved and the precise objectives of the research.

problem recognition The first stage in the business buying process (*see* BUSINESS BUYER BEHAVIOUR) in which someone in a company recognizes a problem or need that can be met by acquiring a good or a service.

process 1. A specific, structured, and managed set of work activities, with known inputs, designed to produce a specified output, e.g. product development, order management, and performance monitoring. **2.** A particular configuration of the workplace, with a related set of operational capabilities and restrictions. *See* PROCESS CHOICE.

process choice The selection of the type of process to be used to provide a product or service. Options range from a one-off project approach (e.g. custommade furniture by a craftsperson), through *batch production, to *continuous processing that produces large volumes over long periods, e.g. a cement kiln. The process decision usually commits an organization to significant capital expenditure. Each option involves a different combination of workforce skills and jobdesign issues, planning and control problems, inventory, and scheduling criteria. The option chosen must therefore fit with the method used by the organization to win orders. For example, a decision to compete in a large-volume low-cost market suggests the need for a mass-production line-flow process.

process costing A costing system sometimes applied to production carried out by a series of chemical or operational stages or processes. Its characteristics are that costs are accumulated for the whole production process and that average unit costs of production are computed at each stage (*see* AVERAGE COST). Special rules are applied in process costing to the valuation of *work in progress, *normal losses, and abnormal losses. In process costing it is usual to distinguish between the *main product of the process, *by-products, and joint products. *Compare* CONTINUOUS-OPERATION COSTING.

process innovation *See* BUSINESS PROCESS RE-ENGINEERING.

process layout (process-oriented layout) A factory, office, or other workplace layout in which work stations and transforming resources are grouped together. The resources to be transformed move from process to process and each product or service may follow a completely unique route, according to its needs. Typical process layouts include small engineering workshops that produce medium to high volumes of similar items. *See also* BATCH PRODUCTION; PROCESS CHOICE. *Compare* PRODUCT LAYOUT.

procuration *See* PER PROC.

produce *See* COMMODITY.

produce broker *See* COMMODITY BROKER.

producer price index (PPI) A measure of the rate of *inflation among goods purchased and manufactured by UK industry (replacing the former **wholesale price index**). It measures the movements in prices of about 10 000 goods relative to the same base year. *Compare* RETAIL PRICE INDEX.

product 1. Anything that can be offered to a market for attention, acquisition, use, or consumption that might satisfy a need. It includes physical objects and services. **2.** Any item, sub-assembly or *cost unit manufactured or sold by an organization.

product adaptation The adaptation of a standard product to meet local conditions or needs, especially in foreign markets.

product assortment *See* PRODUCT MIX.

product category A subset of a *product class (e.g. cars) containing products of a certain type, e.g. sports cars.

product-category extension A new item or new line of items in a *product category new to the company offering it.

product class A broad group of *products that perform similar functions or provide similar benefits but differ in the way in which they do so; for example, all cars made for personal use form a product class.

product concept The idea that consumers will favour products that offer the best quality, performance, and features and that an organization marketing products should therefore devote its energy to making continuous improvements.

product costs The costs of production when charged to the *cost units and expressed as costs of individual products. Product costs may include both *direct costs and *indirect costs (overhead); many different costing methods, such as *absorption costing, *activity-based costing, and *process costing, are used in computing product costs.

product design The process of designing the function and style of a product to ensure that it is both effective and attractive, as well as easy, safe, and inexpensive to use and service. It must also be simple and economical to produce and distribute.

product development A strategy for company growth that relies on offering modified or new products to market segments currently being served. *See* PRODUCT–MARKET STRATEGY. *See also* NEW PRODUCT DEVELOPMENT.

product differentiation The creation of a distinction between products that fulfil the same purpose but are made by different producers and therefore compete with each other. The distinction may be real (i.e. one product is better than others) or largely illusory. Producers in a competitive market use packaging, advertising, etc., to enhance the idea that significant differences exist where none in fact do.

product diversification The strategy of marketing new products to a new set of customers. *See* PRODUCT–MARKET STRATEGY.

product elimination The process used to withdraw a product from a market in an orderly fashion so that it does not disrupt the sale of other products marketed by the same organization.

product enhancement The introduction of a new and improved version of an existing product, in order to extend the *product life cycle by keeping it in the growth stage.

product idea An idea for a possible product that the company can see itself offering to the market. If the idea is pursued, the product enters its *development stage.

product innovation charter (PIC) A statement formalizing a company's new-product strategy and giving management's rationale behind the search for innovation opportunities, the product, market, and technology upon which to focus, as well as the goals and objectives to be achieved. The charter indicates the priority managers should place on developing the search for new products, changing existing ones, and imitating competitors products.

production The *cost units manufactured by an organization. Production may be measured in units, *direct labour hours, *machine hours, or *direct labour cost.

production cost (total cost of production) The total of all the costs incurred in producing a product or *cost unit. In a *manufacturing account the production cost is represented by the total of the *direct costs and the *manufacturing overhead. *See* COST OF GOODS MANUFACTURED.

production cost centre An area of an organization, such as a function, department, section, individual, or any group of these, in which production is carried out. *See also* COST CENTRE.

production cost variance In *standard costing, the *variance arising when the standard cost of the actual production is compared with the actual cost incurred. If the standard cost is higher than the actual cost a favourable variance arises, while if the actual cost exceeds the standard cost an adverse variance occurs. The production cost variance is usually analysed into the direct materials variances, the direct labour variances, and the fixed and variable overhead variances, each of which can be further analysed within such parameters as expenditure and efficiency. *See* ANALYSIS OF VARIANCE.

production department A section of an organization in which production is carried out.

production order (manfacturing requisition) A form issued to the production department of an organization specifying the production to be carried out by the department. A production order gives, inter alia, a description of the operations to be carried out, the quantities to be produced, the time allowed, and the completion times.

production overhead *See* MANUFAC-TURING OVERHEAD.

production planning The administrative operations ensuring that the material, labour, and other resources necessary to carry out production are available when and where they are required in the necessary quantities.

production profit *See* PROFIT ON MANUFACTURE.

production-unit method (units of production method of depreciation) A method of computing the *depreciation charge for a period on a piece of machinery in which the depreciation charge is based on the number of production units manufactured by the machine. When the machinery to be depreciated is purchased an estimate is made of the total number of units of production that will be made by the machine over its lifetime. A rate per production unit is then computed and applied to the production over the life of the machinery. The formula per production unit is as follows:

original cost – estimated residual value/ estimated number of production units.

Unlike the *straight-line method of depreciation, which treats depreciation as a *fixed cost, the production-unit method treats it as a *variable cost.

productivity A measure of the output of an organization or economy per unit of input (labour, raw materials, capital, etc.). *See also* UNIT LABOUR COSTS.

productivity agreement An agreement between an employer and a union in which an increase in wages is given for a measured increase in *productivity. To arrive at such an agreement, **productivity bargaining** is needed to reach a compromise between the increase in wages demanded by the unions and the increase in productivity demanded by the employers.

product layout (product-oriented layout) A factory, office, or other workplace layout in which the position of all the work stations, machines, etc., is optimized to suit the product (e.g. a car assembly line). The resources to be transformed flow along a line of transforming resources in a logical sequence, which is controlled by the requirements of the product. *Compare* PROCESS LAYOUT.

product life cycle The course of a *product's sales and profitability over its lifetime. The model describes five stages,

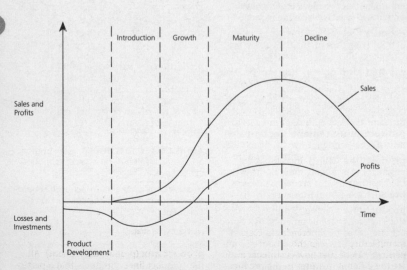

Product life cycle. Sales and profits rise during the growth and maturity stages but subsequently decline.

each of which represents a different opportunity for the marketer. A new product starts in the **development stage**, during which the original idea is transformed into a prototype and its marketing strategy is worked out. This is followed by the **introduction stage**, characterized by low sales: buyers are unsure about the product and it is not stocked by all distributors. In this stage the product is adapted as customers provide feedback. Sales can be increased by introductory price offers and advertising support. If purchasers are satisfied with the product, its reputation will spread and it will enter the **growth stage**: the product will become more widely available and sales will increase. Competitors' versions will then appear and eventually the **maturity stage** will be reached, in which supply and demand are matched and sales stabilize. The maturity stage is the longest period, characterized by intense competition. In this stage there will be an operational emphasis on reducing the costs of production in order to maximize returns, but eventually a better way of satisfying consumers' needs will almost certainly be provided by another new product and the **decline stage** will be entered. The important skill in this stage is to know when to leave the market. The duration of each stage is unique to each product. In practice, many new products will not survive beyond the introduction stage. The concept of product life cycle underpins the strategic management concept of product portfolios.

product line A group of products that are closely related because they function in a similar manner, are sold to the same customer groups, are marketed through the same types of outlets, or fall within particular price ranges. *See also* FAMILY BRAND.

product-line filling Increasing the product line by adding more items within the existing range of products. *Compare* PRODUCT-LINE STRETCHING.

product-line pricing Setting the price steps between various products in a *product line, based on differences in costs of manufacture between the products, competitors' prices, and how customers evaluate the different features in the product line.

product-line stretching Increasing the product line by lengthening it beyond its current range. *Compare* PRODUCT-LINE FILLING.

product manager *See* BRAND MANAGER.

product–market strategy (Ansoff matrix) A *marketing planning model. Companies can either sell existing or new products; and they can sell them either in markets familiar to them (existing markets) or in new markets. The resulting two-by-two matrix gives four alternative strategies for increasing sales. One is to concentrate on selling more existing products into existing markets (**market penetration**), by such means as price reductions and increased advertising. This is regarded as a low-risk low-gain strategy offering few prospects of sustained growth in the longer term. Alternatively, an organization can modify or improve its existing products and sell these to current customers (**product development**); for example, a lawn-mower manufacturer might install a more powerful motor in its products. The third option is to sell existing products to a new market (**market development**) – for example, to export the current range of lawn mowers to America. These two strategies are medium-risk with good prospects for growth in the medium term. The highest-risk strategy is to develop new products for new markets (**product diversification**) – for example, for the lawn-mower manufacturer to develop printing machinery for the publishing industry. Despite the higher risk, this is considered the best strategy for long-term growth. *See also* DEFENDER STRATEGY; PROSPECTOR STRATEGY.

Products	Old/Existing Markets	New Markets
old products	market penetration	market development
new products	product development	product diversification

Product-market strategy

product mix (product assortment) All the *product lines and items that a particular seller offers for sale.

product obsolescence A condition that occurs when an existing product becomes out of date as a result of the introduction of a new or improved product or changes in taste or fashion. *See* OBSOLESCENCE.

product orientation The attitude of a company that believes the product comes first and persuading customers to buy it follows. **Market orientation** typifies the attitude of a company that will only produce what it believes it can sell.

product portfolio A collection of products marketed by one company. An analysis of a product portfolio focuses on the interrelationships of products within a *product mix. The performance of the mix of products is emphasized rather than the performance of individual products.

product position The way a product is seen by consumers in terms of its important attributes, i.e. the place the product occupies in consumers' minds, relative to competing products. *See* PERCEPTUAL MAPPING; POSITIONING.

product prototype tests Tests conducted to obtain the reactions of target customers to working versions of new products in their *development stage to assess marketability. *See* NEW PRODUCT DEVELOPMENT.

product quality The ability of a product to perform its advertised functions in the minds of the consumer. A product's quality includes its durability, reliability, precision, ease of operation, and its ability to be repaired if it goes wrong. Some of these quality attributes can be measured objectively, while others can only be assessed in terms of consumers' perceptions. It is important that companies should achieve consistency of quality. *See* TOTAL QUALITY MANAGEMENT.

product salesforce structure The structure of a company's salesforce in which salespeople specialize in selling only a portion of the company's *product lines.

products-guarantee insurance An insurance policy covering financial loss as a consequence of a fault occurring in a company's product. A product-guarantee claim would be made, for example, to pay for the cost of recalling and repairing cars that are found to have a defective component. This type of policy would not pay compensation to customers or members of the public injured as a result of the defect. Such claims would be met by a *products-liability insurance.

products liability The liability of manufacturers and other persons for defective products. Under the Consumer Protection Act (1987), passed to conform with the requirements of EU law, the producer of a defective product that causes death or personal injury or damage to property is strictly liable for the damage. A claim may only be made for damage to property if the property was for private use or consumption and the value of the damage caused exceeds £275. The persons liable for a defective product are the producer (i.e. the manufacturer, including producers of component parts and raw materials), any persons who hold themselves out to be producers by putting their names or trade marks on the product, a person who imports the product into the EU, and a supplier who fails, when reasonably requested to do so by the person injured, to identify the producer or importer of the product.

The purchaser of a defective product may sue the seller for *breach of contract in failing to supply a product that conforms to the contract. Under the same Act suppliers of consumer goods must ensure that the goods comply with the general safety requirement. Otherwise they commit a criminal offence. *See also* CONSUMER PROTECTION.

products-liability insurance An insurance policy that pays any compensation the insured is legally liable to pay to customers who are killed, injured, or have property damaged as a result of a defect in a product that they have manufactured or supplied. Costs incurred as a consequence of the defect that are not legal *damages would not be covered by a policy of this kind. *Products-guarantee insurance is intended to cover these costs.

product-sustaining-level activities *See* ACTIVITY.

professional indemnity insurance (PII) A form of third-party insurance that covers a professional person, such as a solicitor, surveyor, or accountant, against paying compensation in the event of being sued for *negligence. This can include giving defective advice if the person professes to be an expert in a given field. There have been a number of very high awards made to plaintiffs (especially in the USA where PII is known as **malpractice insurance**) and this has greatly increased the cost of obtaining cover.

professional service technology The type of processing technology used in service industries, which are typified by high customer contact and professional service providers (e.g. legal advice, medical general practice). The service providers are constrained by the practices of their professions as much as by the needs of their organizations; the relationship between the client and the professional is central to the service. *Compare* MASS SERVICE TECHNOLOGY.

professional valuation An assessment of the value of an asset (share, property, stock, etc.) in the balance sheet or prospectus of a company, by a person professionally qualified to give such a valuation. The professional qualification necessary will depend on the asset; for example, a qualified surveyor may be needed to value property, whereas unlisted shares might best be valued by a qualified accountant.

profit 1. (margin; profit margin) For a single transaction or set of transactions, the excess of sales revenue over the costs of providing the goods or services sold. *See* GROSS PROFIT; NET PROFIT. **2.** For a period of trading, the surplus of net assets at the end of a period over the net assets at the start of that period, adjusted where relevant for amounts of capital injected or withdrawn by the proprietors. As profit is notoriously hard to define, it is not always possible to derive one single figure of profit for an organization from an accepted set of data.

profitability The capacity or potential of a project or an organization to make a *profit. Measures of profitability include *return on capital employed and the ratio of net profit to sales.

profitability index (PI) A method used in *discounted cash flow for ranking a range of projects under consideration in which *standard cash flow patterns are projected. It is based on the ratio:

total present values of cash inflows/
initial investment,

the value of which is compared for each project.

The projects with a PI of less than 1 are not expected to earn the required *rate of return and are rejected. The projects with a PI in excess of 1 are ranked according to the magnitude of the PI.

profitable customer A person, household, or company providing long-term revenues that exceed, by an acceptable amount, the company's costs of attracting, selling, and servicing that customer. *See* CUSTOMER PROFITABILITY ANALYSIS.

profit and loss account (P & L account) 1. An *account in the books of an organization showing the profits (or losses) made on its business activities with the deduction of the appropriate expenses. **2.** A statement of the profit (or loss) of an organization over a financial period. It is one of the statutory accounts that, for most limited companies, has to be filed annually with the UK Registrar of Companies (*see* ANNUAL ACCOUNTS). The profit and loss account explains what has happened since the previous *balance sheet; the users of financial statements require information on the progress and future prospects of the company.

The P & L account typically consists of three parts. The first is a trading account, showing the total sales income less the costs of production, etc., and any changes in the value of stock or work in progress from the last accounting period. This gives the *gross profit (or loss). The second part gives any other income and lists administrative and other costs to arrive at a *net profit (or loss). From this net profit before taxation the appropriate corporation tax is deducted to give the net profit after taxation. In the third part, the net profit after tax is appropriated to dividends or to reserves (retained profit). The UK Companies Act (1985) gives a choice of four formats, one of which must be used to file a profit and loss account for a registered company.

profit centre A section or area of an organization to which revenue can be traced, together with the appropriate costs, so that profits can be ascribed to that area. Profit centres may be divisions, subsidiaries, or departments.

profiteer A person who makes excessive profits by charging inflated prices for a commodity that is in short supply, especially during a war or national disaster.

profit forecast A forecast by the directors of a public company of the profits to be expected in a stated period. If a new flotation is involved, the profit forecast must be reported on by the reporting accountants and the sponsor to the share issue. An existing company is not required to make a profit forecast with its *accounts, but if it does it must be reported on by the company's auditors.

profit margin See PROFIT. See also MARGIN.

profit on manufacture (production profit) The margin obtained when manufactured items or finished goods are transferred from the factory at a price in excess of the cost of production. The technique is used in organizations wishing to submit the production departments to market prices and therefore credit production according to some formula; for example, at a price per unit. The system may also create a **loss on manufacture**. See also MANUFACTURING ACCOUNT; MANUFACTURING PROFIT/LOSS.

profit-pool concept The identification of a constellation of minor purchases surrounding a major purchase, and the identification of the money value and profitability of each of these related sales.

profit-related pay (PRP) 1. The situation in which the pay of employees is related to the profit made by the employer. The purpose is to increase motivation, commitment, and effort by the workforce by ensuring that all staff have a positive stake in the commercial success of the company. For such a scheme to be a success it must be believed in, valued, and understood by all concerned. Staff must clearly understand that a bonus payment will be forthcoming if the organization has a good year but will not be if the organization does not make profits. Above all,

profit-related pay should never be used as a means of cutting wage and salary bills. Its general effect is to put up wage and salary bills and this legitimately raises the expectations of the individuals concerned.

Profit-related rewards are usually offered in one of two ways. The simplest of these is to allocate an amount from the surplus generated by the organization and to share this out among employees. For maximum equality, this will be as a percentage increase in all employees' salaries. The other approach is to offer shares in the organization; the employees will thus become investors in their own future. In the UK, the Bell-Hanson Report (1989), researching 113 publicly quoted companies, found that profit-sharing companies outperformed others by an average of 27% on returns on capital, earnings per share, and profit and sales growth. See also GAIN SHARING; PROFIT-SHARING SCHEME. **2.** A former UK scheme enabling employees to be paid part of their salary tax-free; it was phased out in 2000–01. Payments to employees under a registered scheme could be tax-free up to the maximum for the year.

profits available for distribution See DISTRIBUTABLE PROFITS.

profit-sharing ratio (PSR) The ratio in which the profits or losses of a business are shared. For a partnership, the profit-sharing ratios will be set out in the *partnership agreement. This will show the amount, usually given as a percentage of the total profits, attributable to each partner. In some agreements there is a first charge on profits, which is an allocation of the first slice of the profits for the year. The remainder will then be split in the profit-sharing ratios as specified in the agreement. The profit-sharing ratios can also apply to the capital of the partnership, but this does not always follow. The partnership agreement can specify a different capital-sharing ratio. If no specific agreement has been made, profits and losses will be shared equally in accordance with the Partnership Act (1890).

profit-sharing scheme A scheme by which employees share in the profits of a business, usually through some type of share ownership. See EMPLOYEE SHARE OWNERSHIP PLAN; EMPLOYEE SHARE OWNERSHIP TRUST; SAVINGS RELATED SHARE OP-

TION SCHEME; SHARE OPTION. *See also* GAIN SHARING; PROFIT-RELATED PAY.

profits tax Any tax on the profits of a company. *Corporation tax in the UK is a form of profits tax.

profit variance In *standard costing, the variance consisting of the difference between the *standard operating profit budgeted to be made on the items sold and the actual profits made. The analysis of the profit variance into its constituent sales, direct labour, direct material, and overhead variances provides the management of the organization with information regarding the source of the gains and losses compared to the predetermined standard. *See* ANALYSIS OF VARIANCE.

profit–volume chart (PV chart) A graph showing the profits and losses to be made at each level of activity. The profit/loss line is usually plotted as a linear function, and the graph shows the total fixed cost level as the loss at zero activity, the *breakeven point activity level, and the profits or losses at each level of production or sales. See diagram below.

profit warning An announcement by a company that its future profits will be significantly lower than previously announced or forecast.

proforma financial statements *Financial statements for a period prepared before the end of the period, which therefore contain estimates.

proforma invoice A *sales invoice sent in certain circumstances to a buyer, usually before some of the invoice details are known. For example, in commodity trading a proforma invoice may be sent to the buyer at the time of shipment, based on a notional weight, although the contract specifies that the buyer will only pay for the weight ascertained on landing the goods at the port of destination. When the missing facts are known, in this case the landed weight, a *final invoice is sent.

programme evaluation and review technique (PERT) *See* NETWORK MODELLING.

program trading Trading on financial markets using computer programs. The programs used trigger trading automatically once certain limits are reached. It was said to account for some 10% of the daily turnover on the New York Stock Exchange in the late 1980s and has been partly blamed for the market crash in October 1987. Subsequently the New York Stock Exchange imposed limits on program trading.

progress chaser A person who is responsible for following the progress of work being done in a factory or office and for seeing that it is completed on time.

progressive tax A tax in which the rate of tax increases with increases in the *tax base. In the UK, the most obvious such tax is *income tax but progressive rates are also applied to *National Insurance contributions, *inheritance tax, and to a limited extent *corporation tax. Such taxes are generally justified on the *ability-to-pay principle. *Compare* FLAT TAX; REGRESSIVE TAX.

progress payment An instalment of a total payment made to a contractor, when a specified stage of the operation has been completed.

project A set of activities intended to produce a specific output, which has a

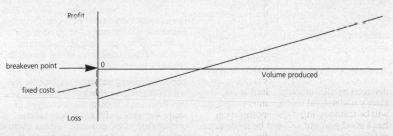

Profit–volume chart

definite beginning and end. The activities are interrelated and must be brought together in a particular order, based on precedence relationships between the different activities. Examples of projects include the building of the Channel Tunnel and the design of a computer system for an ambulance service. Projects are usually based on bringing together teams of specialists within relatively temporary management structures. Project management techniques are increasingly being used to manage such tasks as the introduction of *total quality management within organizations.

project financing (limited recourse financing) Money or loans put up for a particular project (often a major property development), which are secured on that project and its foreseen earnings rather than forming part of the general borrowing of the company carrying out the development. In case of default, the lender has no recourse to the other assets of the company.

projective techniques Methods of exploring respondents' deepest feelings in marketing research, by asking them to project these feelings into an unstructured situation. This technique, which has been borrowed from clinical psychology, encourages respondents to reveal their unconscious feelings and *attitudes, without realizing that they are doing so. Projective techniques used include: word association tests, sentence completion tests, story completion tests, and cartoons with blank balloons to fill in.

project progress reporting The monitoring and reporting of progress on projects, in particular time and cost variations. The successful use of project planning tools, such as critical-path analysis and PERT (see NETWORK MODELLING), is dependent on a regular comparison between planned and actual performance and the consequent updating of the data used in the models. Modern project-control computer packages can calculate the impact of individual variations and the synergistic effects of multiple variations and are able to update all forms of output. Typical outputs include: actual costs of work completed, budgeted costs of work completed, and budgeted costs of work scheduled.

promissory note A document that is a *negotiable instrument and contains a promise to pay a certain sum of money to a named person, to that person's order, or to the bearer at a specified time in the future. It must be unconditional, signed by the maker, and delivered to the payee or bearer. They are widely used in the USA but are not in common use in the UK. A promissory note cannot be reissued, unless the promise is made by a banker and is payable to the bearer, i.e. unless it is a banknote.

promoter A person involved in setting up and funding a new company, including preparing its *articles of association and *memorandum of association, registering the company, finding directors, and raising subscriptions. The promoter is in a position of trust with regard to the new company and may not make an undisclosed profit or benefit at its expense. A promoter may be personally liable for the fulfilment of a contract entered into by, or on behalf of, the new company before it has been formed.

promotion See SALES PROMOTION.

promotional allowance A payment or price reduction to reward dealers for participating in advertising programmes and sales-support programmes.

promotional mix An organization's total promotional effort, including personal selling, advertising, publicity, public relations, and *sales promotion. The promotional mix attempts to attain *integrated marketing communications.

promotional pricing Temporarily setting the price of products below the list price, and sometimes even below cost, to increase sales in the short term.

prompt cash Payment terms for goods or services in which payment is due within a few days (usually not more than 14) of delivery of the goods or the rendering of the service.

prompt day (prompt date) **1.** The day (date) on which payment is due for the purchase of goods. In some commodity spot markets it is the day payment is due and delivery of the goods may be effected. **2.** The date on which a contract on a commodity exchange, such as the *London Metal Exchange, matures.

proper accounting records *Accounting records that are sufficient to show and explain an organization's transactions. For a company, the Companies Act requires that these records should be able to disclose with reasonable accuracy, at any time, the financial position of the company and enable the directors to ensure that the *balance sheet and *profit and loss account comply with the statutory regulations. In particular, the accounting records shall contain entries of all money received and spent and a record of the *assets and *liabilities of the company. If goods are being bought and sold, stock records must also be sufficient. In forming an *audit opinion an auditor performing a *statutory audit under the Companies Act will consider whether proper accounting records have been kept and proper returns adequate for audit have been received from branches not visited. Furthermore, the auditor will consider whether the accounts are in agreement with the accounting records and returns. See also STATUTORY BOOKS.

property Something capable of being owned (see PERSONAL PROPERTY; REAL PROPERTY). It may be tangible, such as a building or work of art, or intangible, such as a right of way or an *intellectual property, such as a copyright.

property bond A bond issued by a life-assurance company, the premiums for which are invested in a fund that owns property.

property income certificate (PINC) A certificate giving the bearer a share in the value of a particular property and a share of the income from it. PINCs can be bought and sold.

property insurance Insurance covering loss, damage, or destruction of any form of item from personal computers to industrial plant and machinery. Property-insurance policies are a form of *indemnity in which the insurer undertakes to make good the loss suffered by the insured. The policy may state the specific compensation payable in the event of loss or damage; if it does not, the policy will normally pay the intrinsic value of the in-

sured object, taking into account any appreciation or depreciation on the original cost. Such policies usually have a maximum sum for which the insurers are liable.

property register See LAND REGISTRATION.

property tax A tax based on the value of property owned by a taxpayer. In the UK, council tax or *business rates are charged on the value of a property, as defined by a series of value bands, which depend on the region of the UK in which the property is situated.

proportional tax See FLAT TAX.

proportional treaty (quota share reinsurance treaty) A *reinsurance agreement in which the risks are transferred in direct proportion to the premiums paid over.

proportionate stratified sampling A *probability sampling method in which different strata in a *population are identified and in which the number of elements drawn from each stratum is proportionate to the relative number of elements in each stratum. Compare DISPROPORTIONATE STRATIFIED SAMPLING. See STRATIFIED SAMPLING.

proposal solicitation The stage in the business buying process (see BUSINESS BUYER BEHAVIOUR) in which the buyer invites qualified suppliers to submit proposals.

proposed dividend A *dividend that has been recommended by the directors of a company but not yet paid.

proprietary company See PTY.

proprietary network A network of *automated teller machines (ATMs) available for use only by the customers of a specific bank or financial institution or some other limited group. Proprietary networks have been supplanted by ATM networks that allow the customers of a bank to use free of charge the withdrawal facilities of several other banks with which it has entered a reciprocal agreement.

proprietary standard A software protocol owned and controlled by a specific company. Microsoft Windows is an example of a proprietary standard.

proprietorship register *See* LAND REGISTRATION.

pro rata (Latin: in proportion) Denoting a method of dividing something between a number of participants in proportion to some factor. For example, some of the profits of a company are shared, pro rata, among the shareholders, i.e. in proportion to the number of shares each shareholder owns.

prospect fee *See* CLICKTHROUGH FEE.

prospecting In sales, the process of identifying likely customers by searching lists of previous customers, lists of trade associations, government publications, and a variety of other sources.

prospector strategy A competitive strategy that emphasizes product innovation and the search for new market opportunities. Such an approach requires creativity and organizational flexibility; it is most likely to succeed in an area characterized by fast-developing technology. *Compare* DEFENDER STRATEGY.

prospect theory A theory, developed by the economists Daniel Kahneman and Amos Tversky, that seeks to explain how individuals make decisions when faced with uncertainty. It is central to the growing area of research known as behavioural finance, which posits that psychology plays a major part in financial decision making. In essence, prospect theory has three components, which concern the role played by decision frames, mistakes in relation to evaluating probabilities, and a *risk preference structure. To help them make a decision individuals use a framework, which has a strong influence on the decision made. Individuals believe that improbable events are more likely to occur than they are in practice, and conversely that probable events are less likely to occur than they are in practice. Moreover, they define outcomes in terms of gains and losses, with the latter having a more important impact on their welfare than the former. *See also* UTILITY THEORY.

prospectus A document that gives details about a new issue of shares and invites the public to buy shares or debentures in the company. A copy must be filed with the Registrar of Companies.

The prospectus of a *listed company must comply with Stock Exchange regulations; that of an unlisted company must conform to the provisions of the Financial Services and Markets Act (2000). In either case, it will describe the aims, capital structure, and any past history of the venture, and may contain future *profit forecasts. There are heavy penalties for knowingly making false statements in a prospectus.

protean career A career that involves frequent changes of organization, work setting, and job content, as opposed to one that involves commitment to a single organization or line of work. Such a career will be shaped by the individual's own needs, goals, and values rather than by organizational structures or received ideas of professional development. Success will depend on adaptability, self-motivation, and a willingness to learn new skills. It has been argued that the increasing trend towards protean career patterns has radically altered the nature of *psychological contracts between organizations and their employees.

protective duty A tariff imposed on an import to protect domestic manufacturers from foreign competition.

protest A certificate signed by a *notary public at the request of the holder of a *bill of exchange that has been refused payment or acceptance. It is a legal requirement after *noting the bill (*see also* ACCEPTANCE SUPRA PROTEST). The same procedure can also be used for a *promissory note that has been dishonoured.

protocol The rules governing the communications between different computers or computer peripherals. The protocol is a formal statement of how data is to be set out when messages are exchanged, the order and priority of various messages, and so on.

prototype A preproduction model developed to evaluate the feasibility of new ideas, materials, technology, and design techniques as part of *new product development. In addition to the technological evaluation, consumer clinics may be used to establish the opinion of potential customers on the acceptability of the product.

provider-based revenue Fees paid to a website owner by other businesses to gain access to the website's visitors. Examples include advertising fees and *clickthrough fees.

provision An amount set aside out of profits in the accounts of an organization for a known liability (even though the specific amount might not be known) or for the diminution in value of an asset. Common examples include *provisions for bad debts, for *depreciation, and for *accruals. According to the UK Companies Act (1981) notes must be given to explain every material provision in the accounts of a limited company. Because of abuses in the use of provision, *Financial Reporting Standard 12 was issued in September 1998, in which a provision was defined as a liability that is of uncertain timing or amount, to be settled by the transfer of economic benefits.

provisional liquidator A person appointed by a court after the presentation of a winding-up petition on a company (*see* COMPULSORY LIQUIDATION). The provisional liquidator, whose powers are limited, has to protect the interests of all the parties involved until the winding-up order is made. The *official receiver is normally appointed to this post. *See also* LIQUIDATOR.

provision for bad debts A provision calculated to cover the debts during an *accounting period that are not expected to be paid. A **general provision**, e.g. 2% of debtors, is not allowed as a deduction for tax purposes. A **specific provision**, in which specific debts are identified, is allowed if there is documentary evidence to indicate that these debts are unlikely to be paid. A **provision for doubtful debts** (or **allowance for doubtful accounts**) is treated in the same way for tax purposes.

provision for depreciation *See* DEPRECIATION.

proximate cause The dominant and effective cause of an event or chain of events that results in a claim on an insurance policy. The loss must be caused directly, or as a result of a chain of events initiated, by an insured peril. For example, a policy covering storm damage would also pay for items in a freezer that deteriorate because of a power cut caused by the storm, which is the proximate cause of the loss of the frozen food.

proximo *See* INSTANT.

proxy A person who acts in the place of a member of a company at a company meeting at which one or more votes are taken. The proxy need not be a member of the company but it is quite common for directors to offer themselves as proxies for shareholders who cannot attend a meeting. Notices calling meetings must state that a member may appoint a proxy and the appointment of a proxy is usually done on a form provided by the company with the notice of the meeting; it must be returned to the company not less than 48 hours before the meeting. A **two-way proxy form** is printed so that the member can state whether the proxy should vote for or against a particular resolution. A **special proxy** is empowered to act at one specified meeting; a **general proxy** is authorized to vote at any meeting.

PRP Abbreviation for *profit-related pay.

PRT Abbreviation for *petroleum revenue tax.

prudence concept The *accounting concept that insists on a realistic view of business activity and stresses that anticipated revenues and profits have no place in a *profit and loss account until they have been realized in the form of cash or other assets for which the ultimate cash value can be assessed with reasonable certainty. However, provision should be made for all known expenses and losses whether the amount of these is known with certainty or is a best estimate in the context of the information available.

The prudence concept was recognized as a fundamental accounting concept in *Statement of Standard Accounting Practice (SSAP) 2, Disclosure of Accounting Policies, the UK Companies Act (1985), and the EU's *Fourth Accounting Directive. However, *Financial Reporting Standard 18, which superseded SSAP 2 from 2000, recognized the prudence concept as a desirable rather than a fundamental quality of financial information.

prudent insurer A theoretical insurer who needs to know all the *material facts before entering into a contract of insurance. The insured must not conceal any information that a prudent insurer would need to know in assessing a risk.

prudent-man rule A US criterion for managing investments, especially in relation to pensions, that is designed to avoid reckless speculation. It requires that a *fiduciary behave as a notional prudent man or woman would when making an investment.

PSBR Abbreviation for *Public Sector Borrowing Requirement.

PSR Abbreviation for *profit-sharing ratio.

psychographic segmentation Dividing a market into different groups, based on social class, lifestyle, and personality characteristics. *See also* GEODEMOGRAPHIC SEGMENTATION; MARKET SEGMENTATION.

psychological contract The psychological nature of a contract between an organization and its staff. This encompasses the implications and expectations that arise as a result of the relationship. Psychological contracts can take various forms:

- A **coercive contract** is one in which the relationship between an organization and its staff, or between an organization and its customers, is based on coercion. An example of this occurs if sections of the community are forced into using a monopoly or near-monopoly for an essential commodity or service (electricity, telecommunication, or fuel). It can occur with institutions, such as schools and colleges, where the students attend because they are required to do so by society.
- In an **alienative contract** the relationship between staff and the employing organization is negative. This traditionally applied to large sophisticated organizations, especially to staff working on production lines and in administrative hierarchies, in which they have very little control over the quality and output of work.
- A **remunerative contract** is one in which the relationship between staff and the employing organization is clearly drawn up in terms of money paid in return for the time spent at work. It is normally used when there is a low level of mutual identity between the staff and the organization.
- A **calculative contract** is one in which the staff have a low commitment to the goals of the employing organization and a high commitment to earnings and satisfaction. It is a key feature of the wage–work bargain for production and administrative staff. For those with professional and technical expertise, the calculative relationship is based on the ability to practise, the need to find an outlet for these skills, and individual drives to serve and become expert.
- In a **normative contract** the individual is highly committed to the objectives of the employing organization. This is usually found in religious organizations, political parties, and trade unions, and also occurs with some business organizations if the wage–work bargain is sound and the organization accepts a range of obligations and responsibilities to ensure that it is maintained.

See also ORGANIZATIONAL COMMITMENT; PROTEAN CAREER.

psychological pricing An approach to pricing that reflects the psychological impact of prices and not simply the economics of the situation. There is evidence that in some instances consumers can associate higher prices with better quality. *See* PRESTIGE PRICE.

psychological tests (personality tests) Tests designed to assess the personalities and abilities of individuals to determine their suitability for a particular job and to make best use of their talents. With the increasing use of computers to analyse information, the tests used in *personnel selection have become increasingly complex; choosing the wrong person for a senior job can be costly and have far-reaching effects in a competitive market. *See also* ASSESSMENT CENTRE; INTEREST FACTORS.

Pty Abbreviation for proprietary company, the name given to a *private limited company in Australia and the Republic of South Africa. The abbreviation Pty is used after the name of the company as Ltd is used in the UK. It is also used in the USA for an insurance company owned by outside shareholders.

public company A company whose shares are available to the public through a stock exchange. *See* PUBLIC LIMITED COMPANY.

public corporation A state-owned organization set up either to provide a national service (such as the British Broadcasting Corporation) or to run a nationalized industry. The chairman and members of the board of a public corporation are usually appointed by the appropriate government minister. The public corporation attempts to reconcile public accountability for the use of public finance, freedom of commercial operation on a day-to-day basis, and maximum benefits for the community.

public debts The debts of the *public sector of the economy, including the national debt.

public deposits The balances to the credit of government departments held at the Bank of England.

public issue (public offering) An *offer for sale in which the public are invited, through advertisements in the national press, to apply for a new issue of shares or other securities at a price fixed by the company. *Compare* ISSUE BY TENDER. *See also* INITIAL PUBLIC OFFERING.

publicity The technique of attracting the attention of the public to a product, organization, or event by the mass media. Publicity involves a third party, such as a newspaper editor or TV presenter, who determines whether the message is sufficiently newsworthy to publish and what the nature of the message should be.

public-liability insurance An insurance policy that pays compensation to a member of the public and court costs in the event of the policyholder being successfully sued for causing death, injury, or damage to property by failing to take reasonable care in his or her actions or those of any employees. A business whose work brings it into contact with the public must have a public-liability policy. *Compare* PRODUCTS-LIABILITY INSURANCE. *See also* EMPLOYERS' LIABILITY INSURANCE; PROFESSIONAL INDEMNITY INSURANCE.

public limited company (plc) A company registered under the Companies Act as a public company. Its name must end with the initials 'plc' (or its Welsh equivalent, c.c.c.). It must have an authorized share capital of at least £50,000, of which at least £12,500 must be paid up. The company's memorandum must comply with the format in Table F of the Companies Regulations (1985). It may offer shares and securities to the public. The regulation of such companies is stricter than that of private companies. Most public companies are converted from private companies, under the re-registration procedure in the Companies Act.

public offering *See* PUBLIC ISSUE. *See also* INITIAL PUBLIC OFFERING.

public policy The interests of the community. If a *contract is (on common-law principles) contrary to public policy, this will normally make it an *illegal contract. In a few cases, however, such a contract is void but not illegal, and is treated slightly more leniently (for example, by *severance). Contracts that are illegal because they contravene public policy include any contract to commit a crime or a tort or to defraud the revenue, any contract that prejudices national safety or the administration of justice, and any immoral contract. Contracts that are merely void include contracts in *restraint of trade.

public–private partnership (PPP) In the UK, any of various schemes devised to bring private-sector investment and expertise into the provision of public services. Examples include the **private-finance initiative** (PFI) hospital-building programme in the National Health Service, the sale of local authority housing stock to housing associations, and the controversial plan to modernize and refurbish the London Underground. Advocates of the policy claim that it will result in better services and lower costs; sceptics argue that the real attraction to government is the fact that PPPs enable upfront borrowing costs to be passed to the private sector, thus improving the Treasury balance sheet.

public relations (PR) Influencing the public so that they regard an individual, firm, charity, etc., in a favourable light in comparison to their competitors. In business a good corporate image is an important asset. Some media personalities, large companies, and national charities employ their own **public relations officers** (**PROs**) to deal with the media, provide information in the form of handouts, and to represent their principals at *press conferences, etc. Others use **public relations agencies** to fulfil these functions. PR does not involve paid advertising, which is a quite separate activity. While an advertising agent will plan an advertising campaign, charging a percentage of the money spent, PR agencies, for a flat fee (plus expenses), will seek to promote their principals by persuading newspapers to feature them in articles, by obtaining publicity for their products, by arranging for TV and radio personalities to interview them, and by lobbying. PR agencies also handle unfavourable reports and rumours.

public sector The part of an economy in a *mixed economy that covers the activities of the government and local authorities. This includes education, the National Health Service, the social services, the services, the police, local public services, etc., as well as state-owned industries and *public corporations. *Compare* PRIVATE SECTOR.

Public Sector Borrowing Requirement (**PSBR**) The amount by which UK government expenditure exceeds its income (i.e. the **public sector deficit**); this must be financed by borrowing (e.g. by selling gilt-edged securities) or by printing money. As an indicator of government fiscal policy the PSBR has acquired increased status since the late 1970s. By that time many economists had come to accept that a high PSBR is inflationary or leads to the crowding out of private expenditure; this remains a widely held view. While printing money simply causes prices to rise, selling gilts has the effect of raising interest rates, reducing private investment, and curbing private expenditure.

public trustee A state official in charge of the Public Trust Office, a trust corporation set up for certain statutory purposes. Being a *corporation sole, the office exists irrespective of the person performing it. He or she may act as *administrator of small estates, as *trustee for English trusts where required, and as *receiver when directed to do so by a court. Another duty is

to hold funds of registered *Friendly Societies and trade unions.

public warehouse *See* WAREHOUSE.

published accounts Accounts of organizations published according to UK law. The most common are the accounts of *limited companies, which must be provided for their shareholders and filed with the Registrar of Companies at Companies House, Cardiff. Companies often include additional documents for shareholders that are not required by company law. *See* ANNUAL ACCOUNTS; ANNUAL RETURN.

puffery The practice of exaggerating a product's good points (while avoiding misleading claims) in advertising or other promotional media.

puisne mortgage A legal *mortgage of unregistered land that is not protected by the deposit of title deeds. It should instead be protected by registration.

pul (*plural* **puli**) A monetary unit of Afghanistan worth one hundredth of an *afghani.

pula (P) The standard monetary unit of Botswana, divided into 100 thebe.

pull manufacturing systems Systems, such as *just in time, in which production only takes place when there is a demand from the next stage in the process or from the customer.

pull strategy A strategy that requires high spending on advertising and consumer promotion to build up consumer demand for a product. If the strategy is successful, consumers will ask their retailers for the product, the retailers will ask the wholesalers, and the wholesalers will ask the producers. Thus, the product will be pulled through the *distribution channel. *Compare* PUSH STRATEGY.

pulsing The scheduling of advertisements in short bursts, over a certain period.

pumping The colloquial name for the injection of money into the US banking system by the *Federal Reserve Bank to force down interest rates.

punt (Ir£) The Irish pound: formerly the standard monetary unit of the Republic of Ireland, divided into 100 pence. It was subsumed into the *euro for all purposes except cash transactions in January 1999 and abolished in 2002.

punter A speculator on a financial market, especially one who hopes to make quick profits.

purchase day book (bought day book; purchases journal) The *book of prime entry in which invoice amounts for purchases are entered.

purchase decision *See* CONSUMER BUYING BEHAVIOUR.

purchased goodwill *Goodwill acquired when a business is purchased as opposed to that which has been internally generated.

purchased life annuity An *annuity in which a single premium purchases an income to be paid from a specified future date for the rest of the policyholder's life.

purchase fund A fund used to purchase bonds that have fallen below *par value.

purchase intent scales Scales used in marketing research to measure a respondent's intention to buy or not buy a product. They are most often used when a company is testing a new product and is attempting to gauge the potential sales of the product.

purchase ledger (creditors' ledger) The *ledger in which the personal accounts of an organization's suppliers are recorded. The total of the balances in this ledger represents the organization's *trade creditors.

purchase ledger control account An account in the *nominal ledger to which the totals of the entries in the *purchase day book are posted at regular intervals. With this procedure the balance on the purchase ledger control account should, at any time, equal the aggregate of the balances on all the individual accounts in the ledger. The balance also represents the total of *trade creditors.

purchase method In the USA, a method of accounting for business combinations in which cash and other assets are distributed or liabilities incurred. The purchase method is used if the criteria are not met for the pooling-of-interests method.

With the purchase method, the acquirer records the net assets acquired at the fair value on the market. Any excess of the purchase price over fair market value is recorded as *goodwill. The net income of the acquired company is recognized from the date of acquisition.

purchases budget A budget set for the purchasing function of an organization under a system of *budgetary control, which plans the volumes and cost of the purchases to be made in a budget period. It will usually provide an analysis of the budgets by material and by *accounting period.

purchasing and supply management *See* SUPPLY-CHAIN MANAGEMENT.

purchasing officer An employee of a manufacturer, who is responsible for purchasing the raw materials used in the manufacturing process. If these include raw materials that fluctuate in price, the purchasing officer has to show that the average purchase price for the year is not excessive. The purchasing officer is also responsible for maintaining adequate stocks to tide the company over any break in the continuity of supply, without tying up excessive amounts of capital.

purchasing power The ability to purchase goods and services. In times of inflation a loss of purchasing power occurs when *monetary assets are held because of the decline in the purchasing power of the currency. If a company has monetary liabilities, a purchasing power gain will arise because the absolute sum of the loans will be repaid with currency with less purchasing power.

purchasing power parity (PPP) The theory that, after adjusting for the exchange rate, the cost of a good should be the same in all countries. In other words, the rate of exchange between two currencies should be such that each currency has exactly the same purchasing power in its own economy. This is never actually the case, although over the long term exchange rates do appear to adjust to differences in national inflation. This latter proposition is referred to as the **relative purchasing power parity theory**.

pure competition A market in which

many buyers and sellers trade in the same commodity, so that no single buyer or seller has much effect on the market price.

pure endowment assurance An assurance policy that promises to pay an agreed amount if the policyholder is alive on a specified future date. If the policyholder dies before the specified date no payment is made and the premium payments cease. The use of the word 'assurance' for this type of contract is questionable as there is no element of life-assurance cover.

pure monopoly A market in which there is a single seller. It may be a government *monopoly, a private regulated monopoly, or a private non-regulated monopoly.

pure play A company that is dedicated to a single narrowly defined activity, as opposed to one that has diverse interests. Investing in a pure play is therefore much the same as investing in the commodity or product that the company deals in.

pure research See RESEARCH AND DEVELOPMENT COSTS.

pure risk See RISK.

push manufacturing systems Systems, such as *material requirements planning (MRP), in which production is driven by a schedule derived from anticipated demand.

push money A cash inducement given to a retailer by a manufacturer or wholesaler to be used to reward sales personnel who are particularly successful in selling specified products.

push programming See WEBCASTING.

push strategy A strategy that makes use of a company's salesforce and trade promotion activities to create consumer demand for a product. The producer promotes the product to wholesalers, the wholesalers promote it to retailers, and the retailers promote it to consumers. Thus, the product will be pushed through the *distribution channel. Compare PULL STRATEGY.

put-of-more option See OPTION TO DOUBLE.

put option See OPTION.

puttable bonds Bonds issued with a provision that the holder is entitled to redeem the bond before the final maturity date. Compare CALLABLE BONDS.

put through Two deals made simultaneously by a *market maker on the London Stock Exchange, in which a large quantity of shares is sold by one client and bought by another, the market maker taking a very small turn.

PV chart See PROFIT–VOLUME CHART.

pya A monetary unit of Myanmar (Burma), worth one hundredth of a *kyat.

PYB Abbreviation for *preceding-year basis.

pyramiding The snowballing effect that derives from a *holding company acquiring a number of subsidiary companies.

pyramid selling A method of selling to the public using a hierarchy of part-time workers. Usually a central instigator (at the apex of the pyramid) sells a franchise to regional organizers for a certain product, together with an agreed quantity of the goods. These organizers recruit district distributors, who each take some of the stock and, in turn, recruit door-to-door salesmen, who take smaller proportions of the stock, which they attempt to sell. In some cases the last stage consists of people who sell the goods to their friends. As the central instigator can sell more goods by this means than are likely to be bought at the base of the pyramid, and someone on the way down is liable to be caught with unsaleable stock, the system is illegal in the UK.

QCA Abbreviation for *Quoted Companies Alliance.

QFD Abbreviation for *quality function deployment.

qindar (*plural* **qindarka**) A monetary unit of Albania, worth one hundredth of a *lek.

QLF Abbreviation for *quality loss function.

Q ratio (Tobin's Q) A ratio devised by the US economic analyst James Tobin to measure the impact of *intangible assets on business value. It is the ratio of the market value of a business to the *replacement cost of its assets.

qualified acceptance An *acceptance of a *bill of exchange that varies the effect of the bill as drawn. If the holder refuses to take a qualified acceptance, the drawer and any endorsers must be notified or they will no longer be liable. If the holder takes a qualified acceptance, all previous signatories who did not assent from liability are released.

qualified available market The consumers who have the interest, income, access, and qualifications to buy a particular product or service.

qualifying The process of evaluating a prospective business customer's potential interest in buying a product. Key questions are whether the customer needs the product, can pay for it, and has the authority to make, or at least contribute to, a decision to purchase it.

qualifying distribution Formerly, a distribution from a company that resulted in *advance corporation tax being paid. Qualifying distributions included dividends and distributions from any company assets to shareholders (except for capital repayments). Advance corporation tax was abolished in 1999.

qualifying loss A trading loss arising in a current accounting period as a result of computing the profits and losses of an organization in accordance with accepted *corporation-tax principles. *See* LOSS RELIEFS.

qualitative forecasting techniques Techniques used to forecast future trends, e.g. the demand for a product, when there is little meaningful data to use as the basis of statistical techniques, or when it is considered necessary to triangulate the results of statistically based projections. Typical techniques include making use of salesforce estimates, juries of executives, and surveys of user expectations. *See also* DELPHI TECHNIQUE.

qualitative marketing research *Marketing research techniques that use small *samples of respondents to gain an impression of their beliefs, motivations, perceptions, and opinions. Such unstructured methods of data collection as *depth interviews and *group discussions are used to explore topics in considerable detail. Qualitative marketing research is frequently used to test an advertisement's effectiveness or to explore new products. *See also* CONCEPT TEST. In general, it is used to show why people buy a particular product, whereas *quantitative marketing research reveals how many people buy it.

quality The totality of the features and characteristics of a product or service that bear on its ability to satisfy stated or implied needs.

quality assurance The design and implementation of systematic activities aimed at preventing quality problems; British Standard 5750 provides a classic example. The approach lies somewhere between the process performance orientation of *quality control and the overall approach of *total quality management.

quality circles A technique that brings together members of a workforce to solve problems and to put forward ideas for improving a process or product. It aims to develop employee participation and process ownership at the same time as exploiting employees' creativity and expertise. Participation is voluntary, employees are paid for participating in such groups, and training is given in analytical and problem-solving techniques. Success is frequently related to whether or not senior management appears to take the recommendations of the groups seriously.

quality control The activities and techniques used to achieve and maintain a high standard of quality in a transformation process. They may include systematic inspection of inputs and outputs, or a sample of inputs and outputs at various stages in their transformation to ensure that acceptable tolerances are not being exceeded. They may also involve a statistical analysis of the data produced by this sampling (particularly in *line production); in this case, in traditional organizations, management has to balance the costs incurred against the customer's goodwill (*see* COST OF QUALITY). Quality control is also concerned with finding, and eliminating, the causes of quality problems. *See also* CONTROL CHART; STATISTICAL PROCESS CONTROL; TOTAL QUALITY MANAGEMENT.

quality cues Indicators or signs that help users gauge the quality of a website or Internet service.

quality function deployment (QFD) A technique for ensuring that a new product or service meets the customer requirement that gave rise to the original concept. *See* VALUE ENGINEERING.

quality loss function (QLF) A measure of the effectiveness of *quality control techniques, which reflects the economic losses incurred by the customer as a result of:
• maintenance and failure costs;
• damage to the environment;
• the costs of operating a product.
QLF was developed by Genichi Taguchi; it differs from other quality approaches that accept *random variation within limits. QLF recognizes that any deviation from the designed specification involves extra cost for the consumer.

quango Acronym for *qu*asi-*auto*nomous government organization. Such bodies, some members of which are likely to be civil servants and some not, are appointed by a minister to perform some public function at the public expense. Examples are the *Advisory Conciliation and Arbitration Service and the *Health and Safety Commission. While not actually government agencies, they are not independent and are usually answerable to a government minister.

quantitative forecasting techniques Techniques used to forecast future trends, e.g. the demand for a product, based on manipulation of historical data. *See* CAUSAL QUANTITATIVE MODELS; NAIVE QUANTITATIVE METHODS. *Compare* QUALITATIVE FORECASTING TECHNIQUES.

quantitative marketing research *Marketing research techniques that use large *samples of respondents to quantify behaviour and reactions to marketing activities. Typically, a structured questionnaire is used to obtain data that quantifies the numbers and proportions of respondents falling into each predetermined category; for example, a study might show how many people per thousand of the population buy a particular product. *Compare* QUALITATIVE MARKETING RESEARCH.

quantity discount *See* DISCOUNT.

quantum meruit (Latin: as much as has been earned) **1.** Denoting a payment for goods or services supplied in partial fulfilment of a contract, after the contract has been breached. **2.** Denoting a payment for goods or services supplied and accepted, although no price has been agreed between buyer and seller.

quarter days Four days traditionally taken as the beginning or end of the four quarters of the year, often for purposes of charging rent. In England, Wales, and Northern Ireland they are Lady Day (25 March), Midsummer Day (24 June), Michaelmas (29 September), and Christmas Day (25 December). In Scotland they are Candlemas (2 February), Whitsuntide (15 May), Lammas (1 August), and Martinmas (11 November).

quarterly report In the USA, a financial report issued by a company every three months. The usual contents are an *income statement, *balance sheet, *statement of changes in financial position, and a narrative overview of business operations.

quarter up The means of arriving at the *probate price of a share or other security.

quasi-contract A legally binding obligation that one party has to another, as determined by a court, although no formal *contract exists between them.

quasi-loan An arrangement in which a creditor agrees to meet some of the financial obligations of a borrower, on condition that the borrower reimburses the creditor.

quasi-manufacturing technology
The type of process technology used in service industries in which there is high capital investment and relatively low customer contact, e.g. postal services. These industries involve a limited range of standardized services with a high level of reliability.

quasi money See NEAR MONEY.

quasi-subsidiary A company, trust, partnership, or other arrangement that does not fulfil the definition of a *subsidiary undertaking but is directly or indirectly controlled by the reporting entity and gives rise to benefits for that entity that are in substance no different from those that would arise if it was a subsidiary. This definition is based on that given in *Financial Reporting Standard 5, Reporting on the Substance of Transactions. If a reporting entity has a quasi-subsidiary, the substance of the transactions entered into by the quasi-subsidiary should be reported in *consolidated financial statements.

Quattro Pro *Trademark* A widely used *spreadsheet supplied by Novell.

Queen's Awards for Enterprise
Awards to British industry instituted by royal warrant in 1976 to replace the Queen's Award to Industry, which was instituted in 1965. The **Queen's Award for International Trade** is given for a sustained increase in overseas earnings to an outstanding level for the products or services concerned and for the size of the applicants' organizations. The **Queen's Award for Innovation** is given for outstanding or

continuous innovation in the production, development, or distribution of goods or the performance of services. There are also two more recent categories: the **Queen's Award for Sustainable Development** and the **Queen's Award for Enterprise Promotion**. The awards are announced on the Queen's actual birthday (21 April). Awards are held for five years and entitle the holders to fly a special flag and display on their packages, stationery, etc., the emblem of the award.

query expansion The ability of a *search engine to retrieve documents that contain related items and synonyms of search terms in addition to documents containing the search terms themselves.

question mark See BOSTON MATRIX.

questionnaire A structured set of questions designed to generate the information required for a specific purpose, especially in *marketing research. The preparation of the questionnaire requires considerable expertise. The questionnaire can make use of *multiple-choice questions, with a series of formal questions designed to produce limited responses; alternatively it can use more *open-ended questions, giving respondents an opportunity to air their views. The latter type of questions are often used with small samples to provide the basis of questionnaires for larger samples.

quetzal (*plural* **quetzales**; Q) The standard monetary unit of Guatemala, divided into 100 centavos.

queuing theory An approach to simulating the way that work arrives in a system (e.g. the rate at which components queue to be processed by a machine) or customers require service, enabling the most effective process for handling these inputs to be designed and evaluated.

quick assets See LIQUID ASSETS.

quick-succession relief Relief available when the same property is assessed for *inheritance-tax purposes in the estates of two separate individuals, the second of whom dies within 5 years of the first. For example, B inherits property from A, which was subject to inheritance tax on A's death of £X. If B dies within one year of the date of the gift, the inheritance tax,

q

£X, that was paid on A's estate will be allowed in full against the inheritance-tax liability on B's estate. If B dies within 1–2 years after the date of A's death the relief is 80% of £X, within 2–3 years relief is 60% of £X, within 3–4 years relief is 40% of £X, and within 4–5 years relief is 20% of £X. The relief is deducted from the whole estate, not simply a particular part of it.

Further details are available in the Inheritance Tax Manual, which is available online from HM Revenue and Customs.

quid pro quo (Latin: something for something) Something given as compensation for something received. *Contracts require a quid pro quo; without a *consideration they would become unilateral agreements.

quorum The smallest number of persons required to attend a meeting in order that its proceedings may be regarded as valid. For a company, the quorum for a meeting is laid down in the *articles of association.

quota **1.** A limit on the import or export of a particular product imposed by a government. Import quotas may be imposed for protectionist reasons (i.e. to shield domestic manufacturers from foreign competition); export quotas may be imposed in countries that depend on the export of a particular raw material, as a means of stabilizing prices. Quotas are usually controlled by the issue of licences. **2.** Any proportional share of a whole allocated to a particular person, organization, or country.

quota sampling A method of *nonprobability sampling in which the selection of the respondents is based upon some stratification and the setting of quota controls on each strata (sub-group). The respondents to be sampled are divided into strata, according to the requirements of the survey; the strata could be determined by age, gender, social class, ownership of a particular product, etc. The interviewer chooses which persons to interview and allocates them to a quota until each quota is filled. This form of sampling tends to be the most frequent form used in *marketing research. *See* SAMPLE.

quotation **1.** The representation of a security on a recognized *stock exchange (*see* LISTED COMPANY). A quotation allows the shares of a company to be traded on the stock exchange and enables the company to raise new capital if it needs to do so (*see* FLOTATION; LISTING REQUIREMENTS; RIGHTS ISSUE). **2.** An indication of the price at which a seller might be willing to offer goods for sale. A quotation does not, however, have the status of a firm *offer. **3.** A bid and offer price indicated by a dealer in financial obligations.

Quoted Companies Alliance (QCA) A pressure group formed in 1992 (as the City Group for Smaller Companies) to represent the interests of smaller companies on the London Stock Exchange. It was instrumental in setting up the *Alternative Investment Market in 1995.

quoted company *See* LISTED COMPANY.

quoted price The last price at which a security or commodity was traded. On the London Stock Exchange, quoted prices are given daily in the *Official List. Quoted prices of commodities are given by the relevant markets and recorded in the financial press.

quote driven Denoting a financial market in which prices are determined by the quotations made by *market makers or dealers. The London *Stock Exchange Automated Quotations System and the US *National Association of Securities Dealers Automated Quotations System use quote-driven arrangements. *Compare* ORDER DRIVEN.

qursh A monetary unit of Saudi Arabia, worth one twentieth of a *riyal.

race discrimination *See* DISCRIMINATION.

rack rent *See* RENT.

RAFT Abbreviation for *revolving acceptance facility by tender.

raider An organization or person that attempts to exploit a company with undervalued assets by making a hostile *takeover bid.

rally A rise in prices in a financial market, after a fall. This is usually brought about by a change of market sentiment. However, if the change has occurred because there are more buyers than sellers, it is known as a **technical rally**. For example, unfavourable sentiment might cause a market to fall, in turn causing sellers to withdraw at the lower prices. The market will then be sensitive to the presence of very few buyers, who, if they show their hand, may bring about a technical rally.

ramping The practice of trying to boost the image of a security and the company behind it by buying the securities in the market with the object of raising demand; if the price rises, the ramper may be able to make a quick profit by selling.

rand (R) The standard monetary unit of South Africa, divided into 100 cents.

random-digit dialling A method of identifying the households to be contacted for a telephone interview. Either all the digits of the telephone number are randomly generated, or numbers are randomly selected from a directory and the last one or two digits are replaced by random numbers.

random number generator A computer program that produces numbers by a random process. It is often used to provide an input to financial *simulation models, notably those using a *Monte Carlo simulation.

random sampling *See* PROBABILITY SAMPLING.

random variations Unplanned and uncontrollable variations from a planned level of performance. They may arise from external influences (e.g. abnormal weather conditions) or they may be inherent in some element of the process (e.g. slight variations in the raw materials delivered). From a quality control point of view, it is important to distinguish between a random variation and one that means that the process is going out of control. *See* STATISTICAL PROCESS CONTROL.

random-walk theory The theory that prices on a financial market move, for whatever reason, without any memory of past movements and that the movements therefore follow no pattern. This theory is used to dispute the predictions of *chartists, who do rely on past patterns of movements to predict present and future prices.

range branding strategy A broad strategy in which a firm develops separate product range names for different families of product.

ranking method 1. A simple method of *job evaluation in which jobs are ranked according to an informal assessment of their overall importance to the organization. This method is fast and inexpensive but becomes difficult to sustain as organizations get larger and more complex. *Compare* CLASSIFICATION METHOD; FACTOR-COMPARISON METHOD; JOB COMPONENT METHOD; POINT METHOD. **2.** A method of *employee evaluation in which a group of employees are ranked on the basis of relevant performance criteria.

rank-order scale A technique used in marketing research in which a respondent is asked to rank various products or brands in terms of *attitude, belief, perception, or some performance criterion. The respondent ranks the products or brands in order of the best, most important, etc.

RAROC Abbreviation for *risk-adjusted return on capital.

rate anticipation swap An *interest-rate swap in which the swap is related to predicted interest-rate changes. *See also* SWAP.

rate card A list of prices charged for advertising space, TV or radio time, etc. *See also* OFF-CARD RATE.

rate of exchange (exchange rate) The price of one currency in terms of another. It is usually expressed in terms of how many units of the home country's currency are needed to buy one unit of the foreign currency. However, in some cases, notably in the UK, it is expressed as the number of units of foreign currency that one unit of the home currency will buy. Two rates are usually given, the buying and selling rate; the difference is the profit or commission charged by the organization carrying out the exchange.

rate of interest *See* INTEREST RATE.

rate of return The annual amount of income from an investment, expressed as a percentage of the original investment. This rate is very important in assessing the relative merits of different investments. It is therefore important to note whether a quoted rate is before or after tax, since with most investments, the after-tax rate of return is most relevant. Also, because some rates are payable more frequently than annually, it may be important, in order to make true comparisons, to consider the *annual percentage rate (APR), which most investment institutions are required to state by law. *See also* RISK-FREE RATE.

rate of turnover (turnover ratio) The frequency, expressed in annual terms, with which some part of the assets of an organization is turned over (i.e. replaced by others of the same class). In order to calculate how frequently stock is turned over, the total sales revenue (or if a more accurate estimate is needed the *cost of sales) is divided by the average value of the stock. This provides a reasonable measure in terms of *current assets. Some accountants also divide the sales figure by

the value of the *fixed assets to arrive at turnover of fixed assets. This is hardly realistic, although it does express the relationship of sales to the fixed assets of the organization, which in some organizations could be significant. *See also* CAPITAL TURNOVER; LABOUR TURNOVER RATE.

rate per direct labour hour A basis used in *absorption costing for absorbing the *manufacturing overhead into the *cost units produced. The formula is:

> budgeted manufacturing overhead/budgeted direct labour hours.

A different approach to *cost allocation is used in *activity-based costing.

rate per machine hour A basis used in *absorption costing for absorbing the *manufacturing overhead into the *cost units produced. The formula is:

> budgeted manufacturing overhead/ budgeted machine hours.

This rate may not be very useful for managers if overheads do not increase or decrease as machine hours increase or decrease. *Activity-based costing systems can provide a more accurate *cause-and-effect allocation of costs.

rate per standard hour A basis used in *absorption costing for absorbing the *manufacturing overhead into the *cost units produced. The formula is:

> budgeted manufacturing overhead/budgeted standard hours.

A different basis of *cost allocation is used in *activity-based costing systems.

rate per unit A basis used in *absorption costing for absorbing the *manufacturing overhead into the *cost units produced. The formula is:

> budgeted manufacturing overhead/budgeted units.

A different basis of *cost allocation is used in *activity-based costing systems.

rates *See* BUSINESS RATES.

rating A *work measurement technique for adjusting data from a series of time studies against a common level of performance, corresponding to *standard performance.

rating agency An organization that

monitors the credit backing of institutions and of bond issues and other forms of public borrowings. It may also give a rating of the risks involved in holding specific stocks. The two best known are Standard & Poor and Moody, both of which have been in existence for over 100 years. *See also* CREDIT RATING.

ratio analysis The use of *accounting ratios to evaluate a company's operating performance and financial stability. Such ratios as *return on capital employed and *gross profit percentage can be used to assess profitability. The *liquid ratio can be used to examine solvency and *gearing ratios to examine the financial structure of the company. In conducting an analysis comparisons will be made with other companies and with industry averages over a period of time. The analysis of ratios can indicate how well a company is run, the risks of financial insolvency, and the financial returns provided. *See also* FINANCIAL-STATEMENT ANALYSIS.

ratio covenant A form of *covenant in a loan agreement that includes conditions relating to such ratios as the *gearing ratio and *interest cover. Breaching such a covenant could indicate significant deterioration in the company's business or a major change in its nature; this will usually empower the lender to request repayment of any of the loan then outstanding, and the loan then becomes null and void.

rational appeal An appeal in an advertisement to the audience's self-interest. The advertisement shows that the product will produce the claimed benefits by, for example, appeals of product quality, economy, value, or performance.

rational expectations The theory, developed by the economist John Muth, that economic transactors make unbiased forecasts on the basis of all the information available. They thus do not make systematic forecasting errors.

rationalization A reorganization of a firm, group, or industry to increase its efficiency and profitability. This may include closing some manufacturing units and expanding others (horizontal *integration), merging different stages of the production process (vertical integration), merging support units, closing units that

are duplicating effort of others, etc. A firm may also rationalize its product range to reflect changes in demand, concentrating its sales and marketing effort on its best sellers. *See also* DOWNSIZING; RIGHTSIZING.

raw materials *Direct materials used in a production process, which are at a low level of completion compared to the final product or *cost unit. Examples include steel plate, wood, and chemicals.

RBV Abbreviation for *resource-based view.

RCH Abbreviation for *Recognized Clearing House.

reach The proportion of a total market that an advertiser hopes to reach at least once within a given period in an advertising campaign.

reaction A reversal in a market trend as a result of overselling on a falling market (when some buyers are attracted by the low prices) or overbuying on a rising market (when some buyers are willing to take profits).

reader service card *See* BINGO CARD.

real (cruzeiro real; R$) The standard monetary unit of Brazil, divided into 100 centavos.

real account A *ledger account for some types of property (e.g. land and buildings, plant, investments, stock) as distinct from a *nominal account, which would be for revenue or expense items (e.g. sales, motor expenses, discount received, etc.). This distinction is now largely obsolete and both sets of accounts are maintained in the same ledger, usually referred to as the *nominal ledger.

real estate The US name for *real property.

real interest rate The actual interest rate less the current rate of inflation. For example, if a building society is paying 5% interest and the rate of inflation is 3%, the real growth of a deposit held for a year in the building society is 2% – this is the real rate of interest. Real interest rates are used to calculate more accurate pre-tax returns on investment, i.e. by discounting inflation.

real investment Investment in capital

equipment, such as a factory, plant and machinery, etc., or valuable social assets, such as a school, a dam, etc., rather than in such paper assets as securities, debentures, etc.

realizable account An account drawn up on the dissolution of a *partnership. The account is debited with the assets of the partnership and any expenses on realization; it is credited with the proceeds of any sales made. The difference between the total debits and credits is either a *profit or loss on realization and must be shared between the partners in the *profit-sharing ratio.

realizable asset *See* LIQUID ASSETS.

realization account An *account used to record the disposal of an asset or assets and to determine the profit or loss on the disposal. The principle of realization accounts are that they are debited with the book value of the asset and credited with the sale price of the asset. Any balance therefore represents the profit or loss on disposal.

realized profit/loss A profit or loss that has arisen from a completed transaction (usually the sale of goods or services or other assets). In accounting terms, a profit is normally regarded as having been realized when an asset has been legally disposed of and not when the cash is received, since if an asset is sold on credit the asset being disposed of is exchanged for another asset, a debtor. The debt may or may not prove good but that is regarded as a separate transaction. *Compare* PAPER PROFIT.

realized yield The total return obtained on a security, including that from the investment of any interest paid.

real option An *option that arises naturally in the course of business activities rather than one purchased on a financial market. A common example of a real option is early investment in a technology, which will enable a firm to exploit the new technology should it prove successful.

real property (realty) Any property consisting of land or buildings as distinct from *personal property (personalty).

real terms A representation of the value of a good or service in terms of money, taking into account fluctuations in the *price level.

real terms accounting A system of accounting in which the effects of changing prices are measured by their effect on a company's financial capital (i.e. *shareholders' equity) to see if its value is maintained in real terms. Assets are measured at *current cost. Profit is defined as any surplus remaining after the shareholders' funds (determined by reference to the current cost of *net assets) have been maintained in real terms. The unit of measurement may be either the nominal pound or the unit of constant purchasing power.

real-time control *See* CONCURRENT CONTROL.

real-time marketing The ability of customized goods and services to update themselves continuously and track changing customer needs, often without input from corporate personnel or conscious input from the customer.

real-time pricing Pricing that reflects current conditions and can therefore change in real time.

real-time processing The processing of data by a computer as soon as it is input so that the results can be output almost immediately.

realtor The US name for an estate agent or land agent.

realty *See* REAL PROPERTY.

real value A monetary value expressed in *real terms.

rebalancing 1. The adjustment of a *hedge in order to improve its effectiveness as circumstances change. **2.** The adjustment of a portfolio over time to better reflect its underlying strategy. For example, a market-tracking hedge will require changes over time in order to reflect the differing importance of particular securities.

rebate 1. A discount offered on the price of a good or service, often one that is paid back to the payer, e.g. a tax rebate is a refund to the taxpayer. **2.** A discount allowed on a *bill of exchange that is paid before it matures.

recall test A test used in marketing research to ascertain how much consumers can remember about an advertisement. **Spontaneous tests** reveal which advertisements a respondent can remember without guidance or assistance. **Prompted** (*or* **aided**) **tests** indicate which advertisements respondents can remember from a series they have seen in a campaign.

recapitalization In the USA, the process of changing the balance of *debt and *equity financing of a company without changing the total amount of *capital. Recapitalization is often required as part of reorganization of a company under bankruptcy legislation.

receipt A document acknowledging that a specified payment has been made. For payments made by cheque, the cheque itself functions as the receipt. *See also* DOCK RECEIPT; MATE'S RECEIPT.

receivables Sums of money due to a business from persons or businesses to whom it has supplied goods or services in the normal course of trade.

received bill A *bill of lading that has been stamped "Goods received for shipment". This does not imply that they have been loaded but that they have been received for loading (*compare* SHIPPED BILL).

receiver A person exercising any form of *receivership. In bankruptcy, the *official receiver becomes receiver and manager of the bankrupt's estate (*see* BANKRUPTCY). Where there is a floating *charge over the whole of a company's property and a crystallizing event has occurred, an **administrative receiver** may be appointed to manage the whole of the company's business. An administrative receiver has wide powers under the Insolvency Act to carry on the business of the company, take possession of its property, commence *liquidation, etc. A receiver appointed in respect of a fixed charge can deal with the property covered by the charge only, and has no power to manage the company's business.

receivership A situation in which a lender holds a mortgage or *charge (especially a floating charge) over a company's property and, in consequence of a default by the company, a receiver is appointed to realize the assets charged in order to repay the debt.

receiving inspection Quality inspections carried out on inputs as they are received into a transformation system. The alternative is a contract with the suppliers that commits them to a guaranteed level of quality, thus transferring the cost of quality control to the supplier. *See also* ACCEPTANCE SAMPLING.

recession A slowdown or fall in the rate of economic growth. A recession is defined by the US National Bureau of Economic Research as a decline in *gross domestic product in two successive quarters. A severe recession is called a *depression. Recession is associated with falling levels of *investment, rising unemployment, and (sometimes) falling prices. *See also* BUSINESS CYCLE.

reciprocal costs Costs apportioned from a *service cost centre to a *production cost centre that carries out work for the original service cost centre. Consequently, a proportion of the production cost centre costs should also be reapportioned to the service cost centre. Cost apportionment can be calculated either by the use of simultaneous equations or by a continuous apportionment method, until all the costs are charged to the production cost centre.

reciprocal exchange rate *See* DIRECT QUOTE.

recognition tests The *post-testing procedure used in advertising to investigate the ability of respondents to recognize advertisements to which they were previously exposed in an interview.

Recognized Clearing House (RCH) A *clearing house that organizes the settlement of transactions on recognized investment exchanges. There are currently two: The *London Clearing House (LCH.Clearnet) and *CREST. LCH guarantees and clears derivatives transactions while CREST clears and settles securities transactions.

Recognized Investment Exchange (RIE) A body authorized in the UK under the Financial Services Act (1986) to sell financial instruments, with the approval of the *Financial Services Authority. The seven RIEs are the *London Stock Exchange, *London International Financial Futures and Options Exchange (LIFFE), *International Petroleum Exchange, *London Metal Exchange, European Derivatives Exchange (EDX) London, *virt-x, and *London Securities and Derivatives Exchange (OMLX).

Recognized Professional Body (RPB) An organization registered with the *Securities and Investment Board as having statutory recognition for regulating their professions. The RPBs are the Chartered Association of Certified Accountants, Institute of Actuaries, Institute of Chartered Accountants in England and Wales, Institute of Chartered Accountants in Ireland, Institute of Chartered Accountants for Scotland, the Insurance Brokers Registration Council, the Law Society, the Law Society of Northern Ireland, and the Law Society of Scotland.

Recognized Supervisory Body In the UK, a body recognized as supervising and maintaining the conduct and technical standards of auditors performing *statutory audits. Currently the *Institute of Chartered Accountants in England and Wales, the Institute of Chartered Accountants of Scotland, and the Institute of Chartered Accountants in Ireland are recognized, together with the *Association of Chartered Certified Accountants; in effect, the Association of Authorized Public Accountants is also recognized.

recommended retail price (RRP) The price that a manufacturer recommends as the retail price for his product. Under the Competition Act (1998) the manufacturer has no legal power to enforce this recommendation. The RRP is also called the **manufacturers' recommended price** (MRP). *See also* RESALE PRICE MAINTENANCE.

reconciliation *See* ACCOUNT RECONCILIATION; BANK RECONCILIATION STATEMENT.

reconciliation of movements in shareholders' funds (statement of movements in shareholders' funds) A *financial statement bringing together the performance of an organization in a financial period, as shown in the *statement of total recognized gains and losses, with all other changes in *shareholders' equity in the period, including capital contributed by or repaid to shareholders.

recontracting The renegotiation of contracts between a company in *financial distress and its creditors.

recorded delivery A postal service offered by the UK Post Office that provides a record of posting and delivery of inland letters for an extra fee; advice of delivery is also offered for a further fee. *Compare* REGISTERED POST.

recourse The right of redress should the terms of a contract not be fulfilled. *See* WITHOUT RECOURSE.

recourse agreement An agreement between a hire-purchase company and a retailer, in which the retailer undertakes to repossess the goods if the buyer fails to pay his regular instalments.

recoverable amount The value of an *asset treated as the greater of its *net realizable value and its *net present value. The value of an asset to a business can be regarded as the lower of the recoverable amount and the current *replacement cost.

recovery *See* TURNAROUND.

recovery stock A share that has fallen in price but is believed to have the potential of climbing back to its original level.

rectification of register 1. An alteration to any of the land registers (*see* LAND REGISTRATION), where it is thought necessary by the registrar or the court. Examples include a mistake that has been made as to the ownership of land or an entry obtained by fraud. Anyone suffering loss because of rectification or anyone who has suffered loss as a result of a refusal to rectify a mistake in the register may be entitled to state compensation. **2.** An alteration of the register of the members of a company by the court if any members have been omitted, a person's name has been wrongly entered, or delay has occurred in removing the name of a former member. The court may award damages as well as rectifying the register.

redeemable gilts *See* GILT-EDGED SECURITY.

redeemable shares *Shares (either *ordinary shares or *preference shares) that the issuing company has the right to redeem, under terms specified on issue. Redemption may be funded from *distributable profits or from a fresh issue of shares.

redeemable trust certificate *See* UNIT TRUST.

redemption The repayment of *shares, *stocks, *debentures, or *bonds. The amount payable on redemption is usually specified on issue. The **redemption date**, or dates, may or may not be specified on issue. *See also* GILT-EDGED SECURITY; MATURITY DATE.

redemption yield *See* GROSS REDEMPTION YIELD; YIELD.

rediscounting The discounting of a *bill of exchange or *promissory note that has already been discounted by someone else, usually by a *discount house. A *central bank, acting as *lender of last resort, may be said to be rediscounting securities submitted to it by brokers in the money market, as the securities will have already been discounted in the market. In some cases the US *Federal Reserve Bank will rediscount a financial instrument that has already been discounted by a local bank.

red-tape syndrome *See* BUREAUPATHOLOGY.

reducing-balance method *See* DIMINISHING-BALANCE METHOD.

reduction of capital A reduction in the *issued share capital of a company. The Companies Act states that, subject to confirmation by the court, a company may, if authorized by its *articles of association, pass a *special resolution to reduce its issued share capital. It may (a) cancel any *paid-up share capital that is lost or no longer represented by available assets, (b) extinguish or reduce the liability on any of its shares in respect of share capital not paid up, (c) pay off any paid-up capital that is in excess of its *warrants.

redundancy **1.** The loss of a job by an employee because the job has ceased to exist or because there is no longer work available. It involves dismissal by the employer, with or without notice, for any reason other than a breach of the contract of employment by the employee, provided that no reasonable alternative employment has been offered by the same employer. In the UK, if the employee has been continuously employed in the business for at least two years, a **redundancy payment** must be made by the employer according to the Employment Rights Act (1996), the amount of which will depend on the employee's age, length of service, and rate of pay. **2.** *See* COMPENSATION FOR LOSS OF OFFICE.

re-exports Goods that have been imported and are then exported without having undergone any material change while in the exporting country. Countries with a major re-export or *entrepôt trade distinguish re-exports from domestic exports in their balance of payments accounts. Any import duty paid on goods imported for re-export can be reclaimed (*see* DRAWBACK).

referee **1.** A person who will, if asked, give an applicant for a job a **reference**. An approach to a referee can be in writing or by telephone and the referee should be given a brief job description of the job the applicant is trying to secure. **2.** A person appointed by two arbitrators, who cannot agree on the award to be made in a dispute to be settled by *arbitration. The procedure for appointing a referee in these circumstances is usually laid down in the terms of arbitration. **3.** A person or organization named on some *bills of exchange as a **referee** (*or* **reference**) in case of need. If the bill is dishonoured its holder may take it to the referee for payment.

reference *See* BANKER'S REFERENCE; REFEREE.

reference bank A bank nominated under the terms of a loan agreement to provide the marker rates for the purposes of fixing interest charges on a variable rate loan.

reference groups *See* CONSUMER GROUPS.

reference prices Prices that buyers carry in their minds and refer to when they look at a given product.

reference rate **1.** An interest rate relative to which financial markets price their products, for example the *London Inter

Bank Offered Rate (LIBOR). **2.** An interest rate relative to which a bank prices its products, sometimes referred to as its *base rate.

referring site The website from which a user reached the site currently being visited. *See also* CLICKTHROUGH; DESTINATION SITE.

refer to drawer Words written on a *cheque that is being dishonoured by a bank, usually because the account of the person who drew it has insufficient funds to cover it and the manager of the bank is unwilling to allow the account to be overdrawn or further overdrawn. Other reasons for referring to the drawer are that the drawer has been made bankrupt, that there is a *garnishee order against the drawer, that the drawer has stopped it, or that something in the cheque itself is incorrect (e.g. it is wrongly dated, words and figures don't agree, etc.). The words 'please re-present' may often be added, indicating that the bank may honour the cheque at a second attempt.

refinance bill *See* THIRD-COUNTRY ACCEPTANCE.

refinance credit A credit facility enabling a foreign buyer to obtain credit for a purchase when the exporter does not wish to provide it. The buyer opens a credit at a branch or agent of his bank in the exporting country, the exporter being paid by sight draft on the buyer's credit. The bank in the exporting country accepts a *bill of exchange drawn on the buyer, which is discounted and the proceeds sent to the bank issuing the credit. The buyer only has to pay when the bill on the bank in the exporting country matures.

refinancing The process of repaying some or all of the loan capital of a firm by obtaining fresh loans, usually at a lower rate of interest.

reflation A policy aimed at expanding the level of output of the economy by government stimulus, either fiscal or monetary policy. This could involve increasing the money supply and government expenditure on investment, public works, subsidies, etc., or reducing taxation and interest rates.

refugee capital *Hot money belonging to a foreign government, company, or individual that is invested in the country offering the highest interest rate, usually on a short-term basis.

regenerative method A procedure applied at regular intervals to the data that forms the basis of *material requirements planning (MRP). All the data is reprocessed to provide a new MRP.

registered auditor An *auditor eligible to carry out *statutory audits in any member state of the European Union, in accordance with the European Community Eighth Directive. This was brought into UK legislation by the Companies Act (1989), which gave the *Recognized Supervisory Bodies power to approve such auditors. Registers of individuals and firms eligible to act as registered auditors are kept.

registered capital *See* AUTHORIZED SHARE CAPITAL.

registered company A *company incorporated in England and Wales or Scotland by registration with the *Registrar of Companies. It may be a *limited company or an *unlimited company, a private company or a public company.

registered land Land the title to which has been registered under the Land Registration Act (1925). *See* LAND REGISTRATION; RECTIFICATION OF REGISTER.

registered land certificate The document that has replaced title deeds for *registered land. It provides proof of ownership of the land and will be in the possession of the land owner unless the land is subject to a mortgage, in which case it will be retained by the *Land Registry.

registered name (business name) The name in which a UK company is registered. The name, without which a company cannot be incorporated, will be stated in the *memorandum of association. Some names are prohibited by law and will not be registered; these include names already registered and names that in the opinion of the Secretary of State for Trade and Industry are offensive. The name may be changed by special resolution of the company and the Secretary of State may order a company to change a misleading name. Unless the name is simply that of the proprietor, it must be displayed at each place of business, on stationery, and on bills of exchange, etc.

registered office The official address of a UK company, to which all correspondence can be sent. Statutory registers are kept at the registered office, the address of which must be disclosed on stationery and in the company's annual return. Any change must be notified to the *Registrar of Companies within 14 days and published in the *London Gazette*.

registered post A postal service offered by the UK Post Office in which letters can be registered (a certificate of posting given and a receipt signed on delivery); the fee is related to the compensation given if the letter is lost. *Compare* RECORDED DELIVERY.

registered stock *See* INSCRIBED STOCK.

registered trader A *taxable person who has complied with the *registration for value added tax regulations.

register of charges **1.** The register maintained by the *Registrar of Companies on which certain *charges must be registered by companies. A charge is created when a company gives a creditor the right to recover his debt from specific assets. The types of charge that must be registered in this way, and the details that must be given, are set out in the Companies Act (1985). Failure to register the charge within 21 days of its creation renders it void, so that it cannot be enforced against a liquidator or creditor of the company. The underlying debt remains valid, however, but ranks only as an unsecured debt. **2.** A list of charges that a company must maintain at its *registered office or principal place of business. Failure to do so may render the directors and company officers liable to a fine. This register must be available for inspection by other persons during normal business hours. **3.** *See* LAND CHARGES REGISTER.

register of companies *See* COMPANY; COMPANIES HOUSE; REGISTRAR OF COMPANIES.

register of debenture-holders A list of the holders of *debentures in a UK company. There is no legal requirement for such a register to be kept but if one exists it must be kept at the company's registered office or at a place notified to the *Registrar of Companies. It must be available for inspection, to debenture-holders and shareholders free of charge and to the public for a small fee.

register of directors and secretaries A statutory register listing the directors and the secretary of a UK company, which must be kept at its *registered office. It must state the full names of the directors and the company secretary, their residential addresses, the nationality of directors, particulars of other directorships held, the occupation of directors, and in the case of a public company, their dates of birth. If the function of director or secretary is performed by another company, the name and registered office of that company must be given. The register must be available for inspection by members of the company free of charge and it may be inspected by the public for a small fee.

register of directors' interests A statutory register in which a company must detail the interests of its *directors in the shares and debentures of the company. The register must be available for inspection during the *annual general meeting of the company.

register of interests in shares A statutory register required to be maintained by *public companies. Interests in shares disclosed to the company by those persons knowingly interested in 3% or more of any class of the voting share capital must be disclosed in the register. Investments held by a spouse, children under 18 years, and corporate bodies over which the person has control are added to the person's own interests.

register of members (share register) A list of the *members of a company, which all UK companies must keep at their *registered office or some other address notified to the *Registrar of Companies. It contains the names and addresses of the members, the dates on which they were registered as members, and the dates on which any ceased to be members. If the company has a share capital, the register must state the number and class of the shares held by each member and the amount paid for the shares. Entry in the register constitutes evidence of ownership. Thus, a shareholder who loses a share certificate can obtain a replacement from the company provided proof of identity is supplied. However, as legal rather than beneficial ownership is registered, it is not always possible to discover from the register who controls the shares. The register must be available for inspection by members free of charge for at least two normal office hours per working day. Others may inspect it on payment of a small fee. The register may be rectified by the court if it is incorrect.

registrar The appointed agent of a company whose task is to keep a register of share and stock holders of that company. The functions of registrar are often performed by a subsidiary company of a bank.

Registrar of Companies An official charged with the duty of registering all the companies in the UK. There is one registrar for England and Wales and one for Scotland. The registrar is responsible for carrying out a wide variety of administrative duties connected with registered companies, including maintaining the **register of companies** and the *register of charges, issuing certificates of incorporation, and receiving annual returns.

registration **1.** The process in which an individual subscribes to a website or requests further information from it by filling in contact details and his or her needs using an electronic form. **2.** The process of reserving a unique web address that can be used to refer to a company website. *See also* DOMAIN NAME; UNIFORM RESOURCE LOCATOR.

registration fee A small fee charged by a company whose shares are quoted on a stock exchange when it is requested to register the name of a new owner of shares.

registration for value added tax An obligation on a person making taxable supplies to register for *value added tax if at the end of any month the amount of taxable supplies in the period of 12 months ending in that month exceeds the **registration threshold** of £60,000, according to the Finance Act (2005–06).

registration statement In the USA, a

lengthy document that has to be lodged with the *Securities and Exchange Commission. It contains all the information relevant to a new *securities issue that will enable an investor to make an informed decision whether or not to purchase the security.

regression analysis A statistical technique that attempts to measure the extent to which one variable is related to two or more other variables, often with the aim of predicting future values of the dependent variable. It is used extensively in financial economics and marketing theory. *See* CAUSAL QUANTITATIVE MODELS.

regressive tax A tax in which the rate of tax decreases as income increases. Indirect taxes fall into this category. Regressive taxes are said to fall more heavily on the poor than on the rich; for example, the poor spend a higher proportion of their incomes on VAT than the rich. *Compare* PROGRESSIVE TAX. *See also* FLAT TAX.

regulated company *See* COMPANY.

reinstatement of the sum insured The payment of an additional premium to return the sum insured to its full level, after a claim has reduced it. Insurance policies are, in effect, a promise to pay money if a particular event occurs. If a claim is paid, the insurance is reduced by the claim amount (or if a total loss is paid, the policy is exhausted). If the policyholder wishes to return the cover to its full value, a premium representing the amount of cover used by the claim must be paid. In the case of a total loss the whole premium must be paid again.

reinsurance The passing of all or part of an insurance risk that has been covered by an insurer to another insurer in return for a premium. The contract between the parties is usually known as a **reinsurance treaty**. The policyholder is usually not aware that reinsurance has been arranged as no mention is made of it on the policy. Reinsurance is a similar process to the bookmaker's practice of laying off bets with other bookmakers when too much money is placed on a particular horse. Very often an insurer will only accept a risk with a high payout if a total loss occurs (e.g. for a jumbo jet) in the sure knowledge that the potential loss can be reduced by reinsurance. *See also* FACULTATIVE REINSURANCE.

reintermediation 1. *See* DISINTERMEDIATION. **2.** The creation of a new *intermediary between customers and suppliers to provide such services as supplier search and product evaluation.

reinvestment rate The interest rate at which an investor is able to reinvest income earned on an existing investment.

relatedness needs *See* ERG THEORY.

related party An individual, partnership, or company that has the ability to control, or exercise significant influence over, another organization.

related-party transaction A transfer of resources or obligations between *related parties, regardless of whether a price is charged.

relationship banking The establishment of a long-term relationship between a bank and its customers. The main advantage is that it enables the bank to develop in-depth knowledge of a customer's business, which improves its ability to make informed decisions regarding loans to the customer. The customer expects to benefit by increased support during difficult times. *See also* BILATERAL BANK FACILITY; SYNDICATED BANK FACILITY.

relationship capital *See* INTELLECTUAL CAPITAL.

relationship marketing (relationship management) Marketing activities aimed at building long-term relationships with parties (especially customers) that contribute to a company's success. The goal is to ensure long-term value to customers, producing enduring customer satisfaction.

relationship-motivated (person-oriented) Describing a *leadership style that is concerned with maintaining positive relationships within the group, removing causes of friction, and lifting morale. A relationship-motivated leader will demonstrate trust of subordinates, respect for their ideas, and consideration for their feelings. *Compare* TASK-MOTIVATED. *See* CONTINGENCY THEORIES OF LEADERSHIP; LEAST PREFERRED CO-WORKER SCALE.

relationship roles A set of coherent, socioemotional roles that are often adopted by the different members of a group in order to sustain good working relationships within the group. Some commonly identified roles of this kind include the **encourager**, who provides praise and reassurance; the **harmonizer**, who mediates between those with opposing views; the **gatekeeper**, who maintains the channels of communication and makes sure that everyone's view is heard; and the **comedian**, who uses humour to relieve stress and lift morale. *Compare* TASK ROLES.

relaunch To reintroduce an existing product or brand into the market after changes have been made to it.

relevance 1. The accounting principle that the financial information provided by a company should (a) be of such a nature that it is capable of influencing the decisions of users of that information, and (b) be provided in time to influence those decisions. To be relevant, information must either have predictive value or act as confirmation or correction of earlier expectations. The concept is defined in the Accounting Standards Board's Statement of Principles and in *Financial Reporting Standard 18, Accounting Policies. **2.** The principle in decision making that the impact of a particular decision on the performance of an organization can only be determined by identifying those elements of cost or revenue that are relevant to the decisions made. *See* RELEVANT COST.

relevant cost An expected future cost that varies with alternative courses of action. Decision making involves choosing between such alternatives and to make the best choice a manager needs to identify the future cash flows for each decision. Costs that have already been incurred as a result of past decisions (*sunk costs) are not relevant for decision making. Likewise, a future cost that will not be changed by a decision is irrelevant to that decision. *See* DIFFERENTIAL ANALYSIS.

An understanding of relevant costs is particularly important for the following types of decision:
- special selling-price decisions;
- product-mix decisions when capacity constraints exist;
- decisions on replacement of equipment;

- outsourcing (make or buy) decisions;
- decisions on whether to drop a product or close a department.

relevant transfer A situation that may arise when a business or part of a business changes ownership and staff transfer to the new owner. If the change of ownership falls within the scope of the Transfer of Undertakings Protection of Employment Regulations 1981 (TUPE), there is an automatic transfer of an employee's contract of employment. TUPE was the UK government's response to EC Directive 77/187, known as the Acquired Rights Directive, the main objective of which was to safeguard employees' rights in the event of a change of employer. The situations in which a relevant transfer governed by TUPE occurs are numerous. The simplest situation is where one company acquires another and staff transfer. More complex situations include contracting out services, the transfer of contracts and franchises, and the transfer of leases. TUPE operates in each of these situations if staff have followed the transfer or have lost employment as a consequence. The scope of the Acquired Rights Directive was expanded in 2001 but the changes have yet to be implemented in the UK.

releveraging Increasing the level of debt in the *capital structure of a business. See GEARING.

reliability The accounting principle that the financial information provided by a company should have the characteristics of faithful representation, neutrality, completeness, freedom from material error, and caution when prepared in uncertain conditions. The concept is defined in the Accounting Standards Board's Statement of Principles and in *Financial Reporting Standard 18, Accounting Policies.

relocation The removal of an office, factory, or other place of work from one place to another, often as a result of a merger, takeover, etc. Sometimes employees are offered a **relocation allowance**, as an incentive for them to remain with the organization.

reminder advertising Advertising in which the purpose is to remind consumers about a product and to keep them thinking about it.

remitting bank See COLLECTING BANK.

remoteness of damage Loss or injury that has resulted from unforeseen or unusual circumstances. In the law of *negligence, a person is presumed to intend the natural consequences of his acts. A person who is negligent will be liable for all the direct and immediate consequences of the negligence. If, however, the consequences of the acts could not be reasonably foreseen or anticipated, the resulting damage is said to be too remote. Similarly, in the law of contract, damage resulting from breach of contract will be deemed too remote unless it arises directly from the breach complained of. No *damages will be awarded for damage the courts deem to be too remote.

remuneration 1. A sum of money paid for a service given. For auditors' remuneration, see AUDIT FEE. **2.** A salary.

remuneration committee In UK public companies, a committee of *non-executive directors who decide the pay of executive directors. Many such bodies were set up as a result of the *Greenbury Report of 1995.

remunerative contract See PSYCHOLOGICAL CONTRACT.

rendu See FRANCO.

renewal notice An invitation from an insurer to continue an insurance policy that is about to expire by paying the **renewal premium**. The renewal premium is shown on the notice; it may differ from the previous premium, either because insurance rates have changed or because the insured value has changed. Many insurers increase the insured value of certain objects automatically, in line with inflation.

renounceable documents Documents that provide evidence of ownership, for a limited period, of unregistered shares. An allotment letter (see ALLOTMENT) sent to shareholders when a new issue is floated is an example. Ownership of the shares can be passed to someone else by *renunciation at this stage.

rent A payment for the use of land, usually under a *lease. The most usual kinds are *ground rent and **rack rent**. Rack rent is paid when no capital payment (premium) has been made for the lease and the rent therefore represents the full value of the land and buildings. The amount of rent may be regulated by statute in certain cases. *See also* PEPPER-CORN RENT.

rentes Non-redeemable government bonds issued by several European governments, notably France. The interest, which is paid annually, for ever, is called **rente**.

rentier A person who lives on income from *rentes or on receiving rent from land. The meaning is sometimes extended to include anyone who lives on the income derived from his assets rather than a wage or salary.

renting back *See* LEASEBACK.

renunciation 1. The surrender to someone else of rights to shares in a rights issue. The person to whom the shares are allotted by allotment letter (*see* ALLOT-MENT) fills in the **renunciation form** (usually attached) in favour of the person to whom the rights are to be renounced. 2. The disposal of a unit-trust holding by completing the renunciation form on the reverse of the certificate and sending it to the trust managers.

reorder level The number of units of a particular item of stock to which the balance can fall before an order for replenishment is placed. A **reorder-level system** is a stock-control system based on the principle that orders for the replenishment of items of stock are only placed when the balance of stock for a particular item falls to a predetermined level. The **reorder quantity** is the quantity ordered to replenish stock when the stock level falls to the reorder level.

reorder point The point at which stock should be reordered. It is usually based on an optimum balance of the costs of holding stock, the costs of running out of stock, the costs of ordering stock, and the time required for the stock to arrive.

reorganization 1. In the US, the process of restructuring a company that is in financial difficulties. Protection against creditors can be sought under *chapter 11 of the Bankruptcy Reform Act (1978) while such a reorganization back to profitability

is being undertaken. If creditors cannot agree on a plan, the company's assets are liquidated and the proceeds distributed by the Bankruptcy Court. 2. The restructuring of a larger organization without the formation of a new company.

repackaged security A *new issue that uses an existing security as its backing.

repairing lease *See* LEASE.

repatriation The return of capital from a foreign investment to investment in the country from which it originally came.

replacement cost The cost of replacing an asset, either in its present physical form or as the cost of obtaining equivalent services. If the latter is lower in amount than the former, the conclusion is that the assets currently used by the company are not those it would choose to acquire in the market place. Replacement cost may be used to value tangible *fixed assets and in some circumstances such *current assets as stock.

replacement cycle The period over which a product or *fixed asset will need to be replaced owing to *obsolescence.

repo 1. Short for *repurchase agreement. 2. Short for *repossession.

reporting accountant 1. An accountant or firm of accountants who report on the financial information provided in a *prospectus. They may or may not be the company's own auditors. It is usual for reporting accountants to have had previous experience of new issues and the preparation of prospectuses. 2. An accountant or firm of accountants who submit a report to accompany the *annual accounts of a *small company stating that (a) the accounts are consistent with the accounting records of the company and the provisions of the Companies Act and (b) that the company is exempt from *statutory audit on the basis of its size. The reporting accountant may not be an officer or employee of the company in question. *See* AUDIT EXEMPTION.

reporting entity *See* ACCOUNTING ENTITY.

reporting partner The partner in a firm of auditors who forms an *audit opinion on the *financial statements of a client company and signs and dates the *auditors' report after the financial statements have been formally approved by the directors of the company.

report of the auditor(s) *See* AUDITORS' REPORT.

report of the directors *See* DIRECTORS' REPORT.

repositioning Changing a product's design, formulation, packaging, price, brand image, or brand name to reposition it in the minds of the customer and in relation to its competitors. *See* PERCEPTUAL MAPPING; POSITIONING.

repossession 1. The taking back of something purchased, for nonpayment of the instalments due under a *hire-purchase agreement. **2.** The situation in which a mortgagee (lender) takes vacant possession of the property occupied by a mortgagor (borrower), usually because the latter has defaulted on payments due. See feature MORTGAGE LAW on p. 352.

representation and warranty A clause in a loan agreement in which the borrower gives a contractual undertaking confirming certain fundamental facts. These will include the borrower's power to borrow and to give guarantees, as well as confirmation that it is not involved in any major litigation.

representations 1. Information given by a person wishing to arrange insurance about the nature of the risk that is to be covered. If it contains a *material fact it must be true to the best knowledge and belief of the person wishing to be insured. *See* UTMOST GOOD FAITH. **2.** Information given by one party in furtherance of a deal.

repudiation 1. The refusal of one party to pay a debt or honour a contract. It often refers to the refusal by the government of a country to settle a national debt incurred by a previous government. **2.** *See* BREACH OF CONTRACT.

repurchase 1. The purchase from an investor of a unit-trust holding by the trust managers. **2. (repurchase agreement; repo)** An agreement (in full a **sale and repurchase agreement**) in which one party sells a financial asset to another on terms

that provide for the seller to buy it back later at an agreed price. The seller is paid in full and makes the agreement to raise ready money without losing the holding. The buyer negotiates a suitable repurchase price to enable a profit to be earned equivalent to interest on the money involved. Repurchase agreements originated in arrangements between the US *Federal Reserve Bank and the *money market, but are now widely used by large companies in the USA and also in Europe. Repos may have a term of only a few days – or even overnight. *See also* RETAIL REPO.

repurchase of own debt The buying back by a company of its own *debt at an amount different from the amount of the liability shown in the *balance sheet.

repurchase transaction A form of discounting in which a corporation raises funds from a bank by selling negotiable paper to it with an undertaking to buy the paper when it matures (*see* NEGOTIABLE INSTRUMENT).

reputational capital The value of an organization's good name and standing. *See also* INTELLECTUAL CAPITAL.

reputed owner A person who acts as the owner of certain goods, with the consent of the true owner. If that person becomes bankrupt, the goods are divided among the creditors and the true owner may be estopped (*see* ESTOPPEL) from claiming them.

requisition A form that requires the recipient department or organization to carry out a specified procedure. Examples are purchase requisition, materials requisition, and manufacturing requisition (*see* PRODUCTION ORDER).

requisitioning The taking possession of property by a government, usually during a national emergency, with or without the consent of the owner. When the emergency has ended, the property may be **derequisitioned**, i.e. returned to its owner. A requisition differs from a *compulsory purchase in that ownership does not pass in a requisition as it does in a compulsory purchase.

resale price maintenance (RPM) Formerly, an agreement between a manufacturer, wholesaler, or retailer not to sell a specified product below a fixed price, usually one given by the manufacturer. The purpose was to ensure that all parties were allowed to make a reasonable profit without cut-throat competition. Such an agreement, however, is not in the public interest as it stifles competition; RPM contracts are now illegal in the UK. *See* RECOMMENDED RETAIL PRICE.

rescission The right of a party to a contract to have it set aside and to be restored to the position he was in before the contract was made. This is an equitable remedy, available at the discretion of the court. The usual grounds for rescission are mistake, misrepresentation, undue influence, and unconscionable bargains (i.e. those in which the terms are very unfair). No rescission will be allowed where the party seeking it has taken a benefit under the contract (affirmation), or where it is not possible to restore the parties to their former position (*restitutio in integrum*), or where third parties have already acquired rights under the contract.

research and development costs
The costs to a company of its research and development. *Statement of Standard Accounting Practice 13, Accounting for Research and Development, distinguishes between pure research, applied research, and development.

- **Pure research** is original investigation undertaken to gain new scientific or technical knowledge and understanding, but without any specific applications.
- **Applied research** is original investigation undertaken to gain new scientific or technical knowledge with a specific practical aim or objective.
- **Development** is the use of scientific or technical knowledge to produce new or substantially improved materials, devices, products, processes, systems, or services prior to the commencement of commercial production.

Under this Statement the costs of pure and applied research should be written off in the year in which they were incurred. In the case of development expenditure, if there is reasonable expectation that the product or process involved is likely to create future income, then the company has the option of capitalizing the development costs, thereby creating an *intangible asset to be shown on the *balance sheet. In all other circumstances development expenditure must be written off to the profit and loss account as soon as it is incurred.

research brief A document that defines the objectives of a *marketing research study before the research is undertaken.

reservation of title A sale of goods in which the seller retains title to the goods sold, or any products made from them, or the resulting sale proceeds, until the buyer pays for the goods. *See also* ROMALPA CLAUSE.

reserve Part of the *capital of a company, other than the share capital, largely arising from retained profit or from the issue of share capital at more than its nominal value. Reserves are distinguished from *provisions in that for the latter there is a known diminution in value of an asset or a known liability, whereas reserves are surpluses not yet distributed and, in some cases (e.g. *share premium account or *capital redemption reserve), not distributable. The directors of a company may choose to earmark part of these funds for a special purpose (e.g. a reserve for obsolescence of plant). However, reserves should not be seen as specific sums of money put aside for special purposes as they are represented by the general net assets of the company. Reserves are subdivided into *retained earnings (revenue reserves), which are available to be distributed to the shareholders by way of dividends, and *undistributable reserves, which for various reasons are not distributable as dividends, although they may be converted into permanent share capital by way of a bonus issue.

reserve assets 1. Money held by a bank that is not required or committed to outstanding loans, and is therefore available to cover shortfalls. In the USA banks must place reserve assets with the *Federal Reserve System. **2.** Gold and foreign currency held by a central bank for intervention in foreign-exchange markets.

Reserve Bank *See* FEDERAL RESERVE BANK.

reserve capital (uncalled capital) When

the *issued share capital of a company consists of *partly paid shares, that part of the share capital that has not been requested from subscribers but is held in reserve until it is required (often only if the company is wound up). *Compare* CALLED-UP SHARE CAPITAL; PAID-UP SHARE CAPITAL.

reserve currency A foreign currency that is held by a government because it has confidence in its stability and intends to use it to settle international debts. The US dollar and the pound sterling fulfilled this role for many years but the Japanese yen and the euro are now also widely used.

reserve price The lowest price a seller is willing to accept for an article offered for sale by public *auction. If the reserve price is not reached by the bidding, the auctioneer is instructed to withdraw the article from sale.

reserve tranche The 25% of its quota to which a member of the *International Monetary Fund has unconditional access, for which it pays no charges, and for which there is no obligation to repay the funds. The reserve tranche corresponds to the 25% of quota that was paid not in the member's domestic currency but in *Special Drawing Rights (SDRs) or currencies of other IMF members. It counts as part of the member's foreign reserves. As before 1978 it was paid in gold, it was known as the **gold tranche**. Like all IMF facilities it is available only to avert balance of payments problems, although for the reserve tranche the IMF has no power either to challenge the member's assessment of need or to impose a corrective policy. Further funds are available through credit tranches but these are subject to certain conditions (*see* CONDITIONALITY).

resident A person living or based in the UK to whom one of the following applies for a given tax year:

• the person is present in the UK for 183 days or more during that year;
• the person pays substantial visits to the UK, averaging 90 days or more for four or more consecutive years;
• the person has accommodation available for use in the UK and one visit is made during the year. This does not apply if the taxpayer is working abroad

full-time nor to individuals who come to the UK for a temporary purpose only.

A UK resident or resident company is subject to UK tax on income or capital gains arising anywhere in the world (unless this is disapplied by a *double taxation agreement). From 15 March 1988 companies incorporated in the UK are regarded as resident in the UK for corporation-tax purposes, irrespective of where the management and control of the company is exercised. HM Revenue and Customs has an International Manual that provides more details. *See also* DOMICILE.

residual income (residual return) The net income that a *subsidiary undertaking or division of an organization generates after being charged a percentage return for the book value of the net assets or resources deemed to be under its control. The headquarters or holding company of the organization will require the subsidiary or division to maximize its profits after the charge for the use of those assets. This approach is very similar to the *Economic Value Added technique. Residual income is often compared with *return on capital employed when measuring the performance of divisions.

residual risk *See* SYSTEMATIC RISK.

residual unemployment The number of people in an economy that remain unemployed, even when there is full employment. They consist largely of people whose physical or mental disabilities are such that they are virtually unemployable; they therefore do not usually feature in unemployment statistics.

resistance level In technical analysis, a level of prices for a security or commodity that is repeatedly reached but not exceeded. Any move beyond this ceiling (*see* BREAKOUT) is regarded as signalling a significant shift to higher prices. *Compare* SUPPORT LEVEL. *See also* DOUBLE TOP.

resistance to change Antagonism towards change among the employees in an organization. The reasons for resistance include a misunderstanding of the goal of the change, having a low tolerance for change (particularly through fear), and perceiving that something of value will be lost. In general, people will only change if they feel it will be in their interests to do so. *See also* CHANGE AGENT; CHANGE MANAGEMENT.

resolution A binding decision made by the members of a company. If a motion is put before the members of a company at a general meeting and the required majority vote in favour of it, the motion is passed and becomes a resolution. A resolution may also be passed by unanimous informal consent of the members.

UK company law recognizes several different types of resolution, each of which has different requirements in terms of the number of days' notice given to members and the required voting majority. The type of resolution required to make a particular decision may be prescribed by the Companies Acts or by the company's articles. For example, an *ordinary resolution is required to remove a director, an *extraordinary resolution is required to wind up a company voluntarily, and a *special resolution is required to change the company's articles of association. *See also* ELECTIVE RESOLUTION; WRITTEN RESOLUTION.

resource-based view (RBV) The view that a company's business strategy should be determined by its internal strengths, including particularly its human resources, rather than by external factors, such as market opportunity.

respondentia bond *See* HYPOTHECATION.

response bias An error that results from the tendency of people to answer a marketing research question falsely, either through deliberate misrepresentation or unconscious falsification.

restitution The legal principle that a person who has been unjustly enriched at the expense of another should make restitution, e.g. by returning property or money. This principle is not yet fully developed in English law but has a predominant place in the law of Scotland and the USA.

restraint of trade A term in a contract that restricts a person's right to carry on his or her trade or profession. An example, in a contract covering the sale of a business, would be a clause that attempts to restrict the seller's freedom to set up in competition to the buyer. Such clauses are illegal, unless they can be shown not to be contrary to the public interest.

restricted surplus *See* UNDISTRIBUTABLE RESERVES.

restrictive covenant **1.** A clause in a contract that restricts the freedom of one of the parties in some way. Employment contracts, for example, sometimes include a clause in which an employee agrees not to compete with the employer for a specified period after leaving the employment. Such clauses may not be enforceable in law. *See* RESTRAINT OF TRADE; RESTRICTIVE TRADE PRACTICES. **2.** A clause in a contract affecting the use of land. *See* COVENANT.

restrictive endorsement An endorsement on a *bill of exchange that restricts the freedom of the endorsee to negotiate it.

restrictive trade practices Agreements between traders that are not considered to be in the public interest. Under the Competition Act (1998) any agreement between two or more suppliers of goods or services restricting prices, conditions of sale, quantities offered, processes, areas and persons to be supplied, etc., must be registered with the Office of Fair Trading and, where appropriate, investigated by the *Office of Fair Trading. Such agreements are presumed to be contrary to the public interest unless the parties are able to prove to the court that the agreement is beneficial.

result node The end point on a web chain.

retailer A *distributor that sells goods or services to consumers (*compare* WHOLESALER). There are, broadly, three categories of retailer: *multiple shops, *co-operative retailers, and *independent retailers.

retailer co-operative organization *See* CO-OPERATIVE.

retailing accordion The manner in which the width of a retailer's product assortment or operation changes over its lifetime: there tends to be a general specific–general cycle, although some retailing businesses evolve over a specific–general–specific cycle.

Retail Price Index (RPI) An index of the prices of goods and services in retail shops purchased by average households, expressed in percentage terms relative to a base year, which is taken as 100. For example, if 1987 is taken as the base year for the UK (i.e. average prices in January 1987 = 100), then in 1946 the RPI stood at 7.4, and in November 2005 at 193.6. The RPI is published by the Office for National Statistics on a monthly basis and includes the prices of some 650 goods and services in 11 groups. The prices of the goods are checked every month and individual items and groups are weighted to reflect their relative importance. Weightings are regularly updated by the Family Expenditure Survey. The RPI can be used to calculate the real change in earnings and expenditure by deflating financial data, and is one of the standard measures of the rate of *inflation. *Compare* CONSUMER PRICE INDEX.

retail repo A *repurchase agreement involving a loan to a bank rather than to a company or an individual.

retail tender An application to buy a substantial number of shares in a privatization offer. The application is made through a **retail tender broker**. Usually the investor either decides on the price to bid for the shares (which may or may not be successful) or bids on a 'strike price only' basis, in which case shares will be allocated to the investor at the price paid by like institutions. Generally a retail tender will not attract the special incentives available to purchasers using a *share shop. Retail tender brokers are often also share shops.

retained earnings (retained profits; ploughed-back profits; retentions) The *net profit available for *distribution, less any distributions made, i.e. the amount kept within the company. Retained earnings are recorded in the profit and loss reserve.

retentions *See* RETAINED EARNINGS.

retirement relief Formerly, a relief from *capital gains tax given to persons disposing of business assets at or over 50 years of age, or earlier if retiring due to ill-health. In 1999–2003 it was phased out in favour of *taper relief.

retiring a bill The act of withdrawing a *bill of exchange from circulation when it has been paid on or before its due date.

return The income from an investment, frequently expressed as a percentage of its cost. *See also* RETURN ON CAPITAL EMPLOYED.

returned cheque A *cheque on which payment has been refused and which has been returned to the bank on which it was drawn. If the reason is lack of funds, the bank will mark it *refer to drawer; if the bank wishes to give the customer an opportunity to pay in sufficient funds to cover it, they will also mark it "please represent". The collecting bank will then present it for payment again, after letting his customer know that the cheque has been dishonoured.

return on assets An *accounting ratio expressing the amount of *profit for an *accounting period as a percentage of the *assets of a company.

return on capital employed (ROCE) An *accounting ratio expressing the *profit of an organization for an *accounting period as a percentage of the capital employed. It is one of the most frequently used ratios for assessing the performance of organizations. In making the calculation, however, there are a number of differing definitions of the terms used. Profit is usually taken as profit before interest and tax, while capital employed refers to fixed assets plus *current assets minus *current liabilities. Sometimes the expression **return on investment** (ROI) is used, in which case even greater care must be used in understanding the calculation of the separate items. Management may consider that profit before interest and tax, expressed as a percentage of total assets, is a useful measure of performance. Shareholders, however, may be more interested in taking profit after interest and comparing this to total assets less all liabilities. The ratio can be further analysed by calculating profit margins and *capital turnover ratios.

For managers, ROCE highlights the benefits that can obtain by reducing investments in current or fixed assets. However, it is important to emphasize that relying on a single *performance measure is not desirable and managers should use

ROCE in conjunction with other measures. For example, ROCE is often compared to *residual income.

return on equity (ROE) The net income of an organization expressed as a percentage of its equity capital.

return on investment (ROI) *See* RETURN ON CAPITAL EMPLOYED.

returns inwards (sales returns) Goods returned to an organization by customers, usually because they are unsatisfactory.

returns outwards Goods returned by an organization to its suppliers, usually because they are unsatisfactory.

Reuters A worldwide agency dealing in news, financial information, and trading services. It was founded in 1851 as a subscription information service for newspapers. It now provides a wide range of financial prices and dealing services.

revalorization of currency The replacement of one currency unit by another. A government often takes this step if a nation's currency has been devalued frequently or by a large amount. The practice is usually associated with high rates of inflation. *Compare* REVALUATION OF CURRENCY.

revaluation account In a *partnership to which a new partner is admitted or if an existing partner dies or retires, assets and liabilities must be revalued to their current market value. The differences between historical values and the revaluations are debited or credited to the revaluation account. The balance on the revaluation account will represent a profit or loss on revaluation, which must be shared between the partners in the *profit-sharing ratio.

revaluation method A method of determining the *depreciation charge on a *fixed asset against profits for an accounting period. The asset to be depreciated is revalued each year; the fall in the value is the amount of depreciation to be written off the asset and charged against the profit and loss account for the period. It is often used for such depreciating assets as loose tools or a mine from which materials are extracted.

revaluation of assets A revaluation of the assets of a company, either because they have increased in value since they were acquired or because *inflation has made the balance-sheet values unrealistic. The Companies Act (1985) makes it obligatory for the directors of a company to state in the directors' report if they believe the value of land differs materially from the value in the balance sheet. The Companies Act (1980) lays down the procedures to adopt when fixed assets are revalued. The difference between the net book value of a company's assets before and after revaluation is shown in a revaluation reserve account or, more commonly in the USA, an **appraisal-surplus account** (if the value of the assets has increased).

revaluation of currency An increase in the value of a currency in terms of gold or other currencies. It is usually made by a government that has a persistent balance of payments surplus. It has the effect of making imports cheaper but exports become dearer and therefore less competitive in a country; revaluation is therefore unpopular with governments. *Compare* DEVALUATION; REVALORIZATION OF CURRENCY.

revenue 1. Any form of income. **2.** Cost and income items that are either charged or credited to the *profit and loss account for an accounting period.

revenue account 1. An *account recording the income from trading operations or the expenses incurred in these operations. **2.** A budgeted amount that can be spent for day-to-day operational expenses, especially in public-sector budgeting. *Compare* CAPITAL ACCOUNT.

revenue bonds Loans in which the *principal and *interest are payable from the earnings of the project financed by the loan. They are sometimes issued in the USA by municipalities, to finance such projects as toll bridges.

revenue expenditure Expenditure written off to the *profit and loss account in the *accounting period in which it is made. Such expenditure is deemed to have been incurred by the revenue generated within that financial period.

revenue reserve A reserve that is not a *capital reserve, i.e. a reserve that is distributable.

reverse takeover 1. The buying of a larger company by a smaller company. **2.** The purchasing of a public company by a private company. This may be the cheapest way that a private company can obtain a listing on a stock exchange, as it avoids the expenses of a *flotation and it may be that the assets of the public company can be purchased at a discount. The majority of reverse takeovers in the UK are now transacted on the *Alternative Investment Market.

reverse yield gap See YIELD GAP.

reversible lay days See LAY DAYS.

reversionary annuity See CONTINGENT ANNUITY.

reversionary bonus A sum added to the amount payable on death or maturity of a *with-profits policy. The bonus is added if the life-assurance company has a surplus or has a profit on the investment of its life funds. Once a reversionary bonus has been made it cannot be withdrawn if the policy runs to maturity or to the death of the insured. However, if the policy is cashed, the bonus is usually reduced by an amount that depends on the length of time the policy has to run.

revocable letter of credit See LETTER OF CREDIT.

revolving acceptance facility by tender (RAFT) An underwritten facility from a bank to place sterling *acceptance credits through the medium of a tender panel of eligible banks.

revolving bank facility (standby revolving credit) A loan from a bank or group of banks to a company in which the company has flexibility with regard to the timing and the number of *drawdowns and repayments; any loan repaid can be reborrowed subject to fulfilment of the conditions of the *committed facility. The facility can be a *bilateral bank facility or a *syndicated bank facility.

revolving credit A bank credit that is negotiated for a specified period; it allows for *drawdown and repayment within that period. Repaid amounts can be redrawn up to the agreed limit of the credit. At the end of the loan period there is a *bullet repayment of the principal and any outstanding interest; alternatively, a repayment schedule is negotiated for the outstanding principal and interest. In the USA a revolving credit is called an **open-end credit**. See also CONVERTIBLE REVOLVING CREDIT.

revolving underwriting facility (RUF) See NOTE ISSUANCE FACILITY.

rial 1. (Rls) The standard monetary unit of Iran. **2.** (RO) The standard monetary unit of Oman, divided into 1000 baizas.

rich pictures A pictorial technique used in *soft systems methodology enabling individuals and groups to compare their views of the key entities, structures, processes, relationships, and issues involved in a problem situation.

RIE Abbreviation for *Recognized Investment Exchange.

riel (KHR) The standard monetary unit of Cambodia, divided into 100 sen.

rigging a market An attempt to make a profit on a market, usually a security or commodity market, by overriding the normal market forces. This often involves taking a *long position or a *short position in the market that is sufficiently substantial to influence price levels, and then supporting or depressing the market by further purchases or sales.

right of resale The right that the seller in a contract of sale has to resell the goods if the buyer does not pay the price as agreed. If the goods are perishable or the seller tells the buyer that the goods will be resold and the buyer still does not pay within a reasonable time, the seller may resell them and recover from the first buyer damages for any loss.

rights issue A method by which listed companies on a stock exchange raise new capital, in exchange for new shares. The name arises from the principle of *preemption rights, according to which existing shareholders must be offered the new shares in proportion to their holding of old shares (a **rights offer**). For example in a 1 for 4 rights issue, shareholders would be asked to buy one new share for every four they already hold. As rights are usually issued at a discount to the market price of existing shares, those not wishing to take up their rights can sell them in the market. *Compare* BOUGHT DEAL; VENDOR PLACING; SCRIP ISSUE.

rightsizing The restructuring and *rationalization of an organization to improve effectiveness and cut costs, without involving a full *downsizing operation, which can often be overdone. Rightsizing could include increasing the size of an organization to meet increased demand, but it is more often used as a euphemism for moderate and controlled downsizing.

rights letter A document sent to an existing shareholder of a company offering him shares in a *rights issue on advantageous terms. If the recipient does not wish to take advantage of the offer himself he can sell the letter and the attendant rights on the stock exchange (*see* RENUNCIATION).

ring 1. A number of manufacturers, dealers, or traders who agree among themselves to control the price or conditions of sale of a product for their own benefit. Such agreements are illegal in most countries, unless they can be shown to be in the public interest. *See* RESTRICTIVE TRADE PRACTICES. **2.** An association of dealers in an auction sale, especially a sale of antiques or paintings, who agree not to bid against each other but to allow one of their number to buy an article being auctioned at an artificially low price, on the understanding that it will be auctioned again, exclusively to members of the ring. The difference between the purchase price and the final price paid is shared among the members of the ring. This is an illegal practice.

Ringelmann effect The finding that the output of groups increases as they grow larger but that the gain in productivity becomes less for each new member added. The effect is named after Max Ringelmann (1861–1931), a French agricultural engineer who studied the output of men, animals, and machines in various combinations. It can be explained by the lower levels of efficiency and motivation characteristic of large groups. *See* COLLECTIVE EFFORT MODEL; SOCIAL LOAFING; SUCKER EFFECT.

ring-fence 1. To allow one part of a company or group to go into receivership or bankruptcy without affecting the viability of the rest of the company or group. **2.** To assign a sum of money to a particular purpose so that it does not become part of the general resources of an organization.

ringgit (M$) The Malaysian dollar: the standard monetary unit of Malaysia, divided into 100 sen.

ring trading *See* CALLOVER.

riot and civil commotion A risk not usually covered in householders' insurance policies or commercial policies, unless a special clause has been added to cover loss or damage due to riot or civil commotion.

rising bottoms A pattern in which the price lows within market fluctuations display a steady upward trend over time. In *chartist analysis such a pattern is seen as a sign of a *bull market. *Compare* ASCENDING TOPS.

risk 1. (speculative risk) A possibility of financial loss (whether in absolute terms or relative to expectations) that is inseparable from the opportunity for financial gain. Some of the major categories are *market risk, *credit risk, *liquidity risk, and *operational risk. Market risk arises from changes in prices in financial markets. Credit risk relates to non-payment of obligations or credit impairment. Liquidity risk is that of running out of cash or problems with asset enhancement. Operational risk is a catch-all category that covers a firm's internal systems and processes, as well as external events. *See also* COUNTERPARTY RISK; EXCHANGE-RATE EXPOSURE; INTEREST-RATE RISK; SPECIFIC RISK; SYSTEMATIC RISK. **2. (peril; pure risk)** The possibility of suffering some form of loss or damage where there is no corresponding opportunity for gain. Risks of this kind – e.g. fire, theft, or accident – are the proper domain of insurance cover. *See* INSURABLE RISK.

risk-adjusted discount rate In *capital budgeting and portfolio management, the *discount rate used in calculations of *present value; it will reflect the level of risk embodied in the cash flows being considered.

risk-adjusted return on capital (RAROC) A measure of the performance of units within a bank or financial organization, be they managerial units, products, distributional units, or such treasury-based units as trading desks. It was developed by Bankers' Trust and the Bank of America in the 1980s. In its most common form RAROC allocates *capital at risk to a unit and divides that into the return obtained from the unit. The capital is allocated in terms of a *value-at-risk methodology. A refinement of this system is known as **RAROC 2020**.

risk analysis The consideration of *risk in a business, project, or decision. It involves the identification of risk, the classification of risks in regard to their impact and likelihood, and a consideration of how they might best be managed. See RISK MANAGEMENT.

risk-averse Describing a *risk preference in which a decision maker's attraction to an investment or other economic choice rises with higher average returns and falls with greater *standard deviations of returns. Compare RISK-NEUTRAL; RISK-SEEKING. See also PORTFOLIO THEORY; UTILITY THEORY.

risk capital (venture capital) Capital invested in a project in which there is a substantial element of risk, especially money invested in a new venture or an expanding business. It is also commonly used in employee or *management buy-outs (see BIMBO). Risk capital is normally invested in the equity of the company in the hope of a high return; it is not a loan.

risk-free rate The *rate of return on an investment that has no risk. The return on US and UK Treasury bills is often regarded as a very close approximation to this rate. The risk-free rate is an important concept in the *capital asset pricing model.

risk management A process that aims to help organizations understand, evaluate, and take action on all their risks. A private-sector organization will need to identify and evaluate the trade-off between risk and expected return and to choose the course of action that will help it to maximize its value. Risk management is also relevant to the public sector. Common forms of risk management include taking out insurance against possible losses and the use of *derivatives to

*hedge against changes in interest rates, exchange rates, or other economic variables. A bank will always try to manage the risks involved in lending by adjusting the level of charges and interest rates to compensate for a percentage of losses.

risk matrix A method of *risk analysis customized for businesses from a basic framework developed by the US military in the identification of *operational risk. It is in essence a brainstorming technique. When applied to a business, the two dimensions of the matrix relate to those assets at risk in the business and how these assets are at risk. When considering what is at risk, the assets of the business are defined as widely as possible, including both *tangible assets and such *intangible assets as reputation and branding.

risk-neutral Describing a *risk preference in which the decision maker is influenced only by the average return on an investment or other choice and not by the *standard deviation of returns. Compare RISK-AVERSE; RISK-SEEKING.

risk preference The attitude of an investor or decision maker to risks. See RISK-AVERSE; RISK-NEUTRAL; RISK-SEEKING.

risk premium (market-risk premium) **1.** The difference between the expected *rate of return on an investment and the *risk-free rate of return over the same period. If there is any risk element at all, the rate of return should be higher than if no risk were involved. See CAPITAL ASSET PRICING MODEL. **2.** An addition to the normal price of a transaction to reflect any extra risk involved.

risk-seeking Describing a *risk preference in which the decision maker's attraction to an investment or other economic choice rises with higher average returns and a higher *standard deviation of returns. Compare RISK-AVERSE; RISK-NEUTRAL.

risky effect See CHOICE-SHIFT EFFECTS.

riyal **1.** (SRIs) The standard monetary unit of Saudi Arabia, divided into 20 qurush and 100 halala. **2.** (QR) The standard monetary unit of Qatar, divided into 100 dirhams. **3.** (YRIs) The standard monetary unit of Yemen, divided into 100 fils.

road haulage The transport of goods by

road vehicles. With the advent of the European Union, the network of motorways throughout Europe, *roll-on roll-off ferries, and the Channel Tunnel, much freight is now carried throughout Europe by road vehicles.

Robinson–Patman Act (1936) A US federal law intended to halt discriminatory pricing policies by specifying certain limited conditions under which a seller is permitted to charge different prices to different buyers.

robot A machine, usually controlled by computer, that is capable of performing routine and repetitive tasks without human intervention.

ROCE Abbreviation for *return on capital employed.

ROE Abbreviation for *return on equity.

ROI Abbreviation for return on investment. *See* RETURN ON CAPITAL EMPLOYED.

rolled-up coupon A certificate of interest (*see* COUPON) on a bond or other security, in which the interest is ploughed back to increase the capital value of the original bond, rather than being drawn as cash.

rolling budget A budget that is regularly updated by adding a further budget period, such as a month or a quarter, while at the same time dropping out the earliest month or quarter as appropriate.

rolling launch The process of gradually introducing a new product into the market.

rolling position A financial *position that is maintained, although the instruments comprising the position are changed over time.

roll-on roll-off ferry (RORO) A ferry that loads motor vehicles by allowing them to drive on and drive off. Such ferries are widely used for transporting road haulage vehicles across the English Channel.

roll-over CD A *certificate of deposit in which the maturity is divided into short periods to make it easier to sell on the secondary market. They are sometimes known as **roly-poly CDs**.

roll-over credit A medium- or long-

term bank loan in which the rate of interest varies with short-term money-market rates (such as LIBOR) because the bank has raised the loan by short-term money-market or *interbank market borrowing.

roll-over relief (replacement of business asset relief) A relief from *capital gains tax available on certain disposals in which the proceeds from the disposal of the asset are reinvested in a new business asset. Both the old and new asset must be business assets, but they do not have to belong to the same category. For example, the proceeds on disposal of land (the old asset) could be rolled over into the acquisition of plant and machinery (the new asset). The disposal of the old asset and the acquisition of the new asset must take place within specified time limits. Detailed regulations are available from HM Revenue and Customs.

roll-up funds An offshore investment fund using securities with *rolled-up coupons designed to avoid *income tax. However, these funds are now assessed for income tax as if the coupons were paid in cash.

roly-poly CD *See* ROLL-OVER CD.

Romalpa clause A clause included in a contract of sale in which the seller retains the title of the goods sold until they have been paid for. This is of importance to accountants as it may affect the ownership of *stocks; it is essential to determine whether the commercial substance of a transaction rests ownership of an *asset in the purchaser, irrespective of any legal agreement. This clause derives its name from the case of *Aluminium Industrie Vasseen BV* v. *Romalpa Aluminium Ltd* (1976), which was concerned with the practice of selling goods subject to *reservation of title.

RORO Abbreviation for roll-on roll-off. *See* ROLL-ON ROLL-OFF FERRY.

rotation of directors Under the *articles of association of most UK companies, the obligatory retirement of one third of the directors each year (normally at the *annual general meeting, so that each director retires by rotation every three years. Retiring directors may be re-elected.

rouble (Rub) **1.** The standard monetary unit of Russia and Belarus, divided into

100 kopeks. **2.** The standard monetary unit of Tajikistan, divided into 100 tanga.

round lot A round number of shares or a round amount of stock for which market makers will sometimes offer better prices than for **odd lots**.

round tripping An opportunity to make a profit by making use of a bank overdraft facility to deposit funds in the money market at rates that exceed the cost of the overdraft. The practice is frowned upon by banks because they may be having to use the money market to fund their customers' overdrafts. This accounts for the name 'round tripping'.

route sheet A document showing the succession of processes through which a product passes. Computer-based scheduling systems make it possible to track individual components and products in situations that would be too complex with manual systems.

Royal Institution of Chartered Surveyors (RICS) An institution, founded in 1868 and given a Royal Charter in 1881, that aims to provide education and training for surveyors and to define and control their professional conduct. Qualification as a Chartered Surveyor can be achieved by passing the Institution's own examinations or through recognized academic or professional experience in the field. A Chartered member of RICS can use the initials MRICS after his or her name; after 12 years' further experience he or she may apply for a Fellowship (FRICS). The Institution also has technical members who qualify by a more vocational route and use the initials TechRICS.

Royal Mint The organization in the UK that has had the sole right to manufacture English coins since the 16th century. Controlled by the Chancellor of the Exchequer, it was formerly situated in the City of London but moved to Llantrisant in Wales in 1968. It also makes banknotes, UK medals, and increasing quantities of foreign coins (now about 65% of the Mint's total output).

royalty A payment made for the right to use the property of another person for gain. This is usually an *intellectual property, such as a copyright (e.g. in a book) or a patent (e.g. in an invention). A royalty may also be paid to a landowner, who has granted mineral rights to someone else, on sales of minerals extracted from the land. A royalty is regarded as a *wasting asset as copyrights, patents, and mines have limited lives.

RPB Abbreviation for Recognized Professional Body. *See* DESIGNATED PROFESSIONAL BODY.

RPI Abbreviation for *Retail Price Index.

RPM Abbreviation for *resale price maintenance.

RRP Abbreviation for *recommended retail price.

RUF Abbreviation for revolving underwriting facility. *See* NOTE ISSUANCE FACILITY.

rufiyaa (Rf) The standard monetary unit of the Maldives, divided into 100 laari.

rule-based system A software system using criteria that a company develops to determine the kinds of special offers, promotions, and information that it should provide for visitors to its website.

rummage A search of a ship or aircraft by customs officers looking for contraband, illegal drugs, etc.

running-account credit A personal credit agreement that enables a person to receive loans from time to time from a bank or other lender provided that a specified credit limit is not exceeded. Interest is charged on the amount loaned during any period.

running broker A bill broker who does not himself discount *bills of exchange but acts between bill owners and discount houses or banks on a commission basis.

running costs The expenditure incurred in order to carry out the operations of a fixed asset. Examples are power, maintenance, and consumable materials for a machine or fuel, oil, tyres, and servicing for motor vehicles.

running days Consecutive days including Saturdays, Sundays, and Bank Holidays. In chartering a vessel the period of the charter is given in running days, rather than working days.

PRODUCT	CURRENT STOCK (UNITS)	DEMAND RATE (UNITS/WEEK)	RUN-OUT TIME (WEEKS)
A	1000	200	5
B	500	150	3.3
C	2000	500	4
D	600	300	2

Run-out time. The run-out times of four products as calculated from current stock levels and demand rates.

running-down clause A clause in a *hull insurance policy covering a shipowner against liability for compensation as a result of a collision with another vessel.

running yield *See* YIELD.

run of paper Denoting an advertisement in a paper, magazine, etc., in which the publisher decides where the advertisement shall be placed. This is offered at a lower rate than an advertisement set in a specified position in the publication.

run-out time The time that will elapse before an item in stock runs out. The concept is essential for scheduling the reordering of a range of goods. The run-out time for a product i is defined as:

$$r_i = l_i/d_i,$$

where r_i is run-out time in weeks, l_i is units in stock, and d_i is demand in units per week.

The table above gives a number of examples.

run to settlement Denoting a *futures contract in a commodity that has run to its settlement day without being set off by a corresponding sales or purchase contract so that delivery of the physical goods must be made or taken.

rupee 1. The standard monetary unit of India (Re, *plural* Rs), Pakistan (PRs), Nepal (NRs), and Bhutan (BRs), divided into 100 paisa. 2. The standard monetary unit of Sri Lanka (SLRs), Mauritius (Mau Re; *plural* Mau Rs), and the Seychelles (SR), divided into 100 cents.

rupiah (Rp) The standard monetary unit of Indonesia, divided into 100 sen.

SA 1. Abbreviation for *société anonyme*. It appears after the name of a French, Belgian, or Luxembourg company, being equivalent to the British abbreviation plc (i.e. denoting a public limited company). **2.** Abbreviation for *sociedad anónima*. It appears after the name of a Spanish public company. **3.** Abbreviation for *sociedade anónima*. It appears after the name of a Portuguese public company. *Compare* SARL.

SAB Abbreviation for *standard application blank.

safe custody A service offered by most UK commercial banks, in which the bank holds valuable items belonging to its customers in its strong room. These items are usually documents, such as deeds and bearer bonds, but they may also include items of value. The bank is a bailee for these items and its liability will depend on whether or not it has charged the customer for the service and the terms of the customer's own insurance (in the case of items of value). In a **safe deposit** the customer hires a small lockable box from the bank or safe-deposit company, to which access is provided during normal banking hours.

sagacity segmentation A form of *market segmentation developed to improve the discriminating power of income and demographic classifications. This form of segmentation combines life-cycle, income, and socio-economic information with *JICNAR data. The underlying theme is that as people pass through the various stages of their lives they have different aspirations and patterns of behaviour, which are reflected in their consumption of goods and services.

saitori Members of the Tokyo Stock Exchange who act as intermediaries between brokers. They cannot deal on their own account or for non-members of the exchange; they may only be allowed to deal in a limited number of stocks.

salaried partner A partner in a *partnership who by agreement draws a regular salary.

salary A regular payment, usually monthly, made by an employer, under a contract of employment, to an employee.

sale and leaseback A transaction in which the owner of an *asset sells it and immediately purchases back from the buyer the right to use the asset under a *lease. The lease may be a *finance lease or an *operating lease.

sale and repurchase agreement *See* REPURCHASE.

sale as seen A sale made on the basis that the buyer has inspected the goods and is buying them as a result of this inspection and not on any guarantee of quality or condition by the seller. The seller does not guarantee or imply that the goods are suitable for any particular purpose. *Compare* SALE BY DESCRIPTION; SALE BY SAMPLE.

sale by description A sale made on the basis that the quality of the goods sold will correspond to the description given of them in the contract of sale. *Compare* SALE AS SEEN; SALE BY SAMPLE.

sale by instalments *See* HIRE PURCHASE.

sale by sample A sale made on the basis of *sample, i.e. that the quality and condition of the bulk of the goods will be at least as good as that of the selling sample. In contracts in which goods are sold by sample, the contract may stipulate how and by whom the bulk should be sampled and what tests should be used to compare it to the selling sample. The contract will also usually lay down the procedure to be adopted if the bulk sample is not as good as the selling sample. *Compare* SALE AS SEEN; SALE BY DESCRIPTION.

sale by tender *See* ISSUE BY TENDER.

sale or return Terms of trade in which the seller agrees to take back from the buyer any unsold goods, usually in a specified period. Some retail shops buy certain of their goods on sale or return.

sales account An *account used to record cash and credit sales transactions resulting from the sale of goods or services.

sales analysis A detailed study of an organization's sales records, including a detailed breakdown of all sales information, to reveal patterns that can be used to evaluate the effectiveness of the marketing efforts.

sales day book (sales journal; sold day book) The *book of prime entry in which an organization records the invoices issued to its customers for goods or services supplied in the course of its trade. Postings are made from this book to the personal accounts of the customers, while the totals of the invoices are posted to the sales account in the *nominal ledger.

salesforce management The planning, organization, direction, recruitment, training, and motivation of the salesforce within a planned marketing strategy. It includes setting *sales objectives and evaluating the results obtained by the salesforce. In very large markets, such as the USA, there might be a hierarchy of sales managers and district managers, reporting to regional managers, who in turn report to a national sales manager.

salesforce promotion A sales promotion designed to motivate the salesforce and make its selling efforts more effective. The promotion may include bonuses, contests, prizes, or sales rallies.

sales forecast An estimate of future sales volumes and revenue. It is usually based on past trends and takes into account current and future directions, such as government regulations, economic forecasts, and industry conditions.

sales function The section of an organization responsible for selling its products and services. See FUNCTION.

sales invoice A document sent by the seller of goods or services to the buyer, detailing the amounts due, discounts available, payment dates, and such administrative details as the account numbers and credit limits.

sales ledger (debtors' ledger) The *ledger that records the personal accounts of an organization's customers. The total of the balances in this ledger represents the organization's trade debtors.

sales mix The relative proportions of individual products that make up the total units sold.

sales objectives The specific objectives that an organization's sales effort will attempt to meet. Sales objectives should be precise and quantifiable; they should include a time frame and should be attainable in terms of the organization's resources.

sales orientation A strategy that concentrates on selling existing products, whether or not they meet consumer needs, often by means of aggressive sales techniques and advertising. It is regarded as a strategy with a limited long-term future.

sales presentation *See* PRESENTATION.

sales promotion An activity designed to boost the sales of a product or service. It may include an advertising campaign, increased PR activity, a free-sample campaign, offering free gifts or trading stamps, arranging demonstrations or exhibitions, setting up competitions with attractive prizes, temporary price reductions, door-to-door calling, telephone selling, personal letters, etc.

sales quota A target set by *salesforce management for a specific area or *sales representative. Since the earnings of sales representatives are often directly related to the sales achieved, the setting of realistic quotas is imperative.

sales representative A person who sells the goods and services of an organization, either as an employee of that organization or as part of a contractual salesforce. Additional responsibilities might include generating new sales leads (see COLD CALLING), publicizing changes in products or prices, gathering information about competitors' activity, and *merchandising products. Sales representatives often receive a commission on what they sell.

sales response function The relationship between the likely sales of a particular product during a specified period and the level of marketing support it receives. The more advertising, sales promotion, or public-relations support for a product, the higher the sales are likely to be.

sales returns 1. *See* RETURNS INWARDS. 2. A report on sales made in a period.

sales tax (expenditure tax; outlay tax) A tax based on the selling price of goods. Such taxes are not now generally favoured, since they have a cascade effect, i.e. if goods are sold on from one trader to another the amount of sales tax borne by the ultimate buyer becomes too great. *Value added tax was largely designed to meet this objection.

sales territory The unit of organization of a salesforce within a company. Each *sales representative is usually assigned a geographical area, market segment, or product group in which to develop sales, and accordingly accepts the credit for the success (or otherwise) of the product within that area.

sales trend The long-term, underlying pattern of sales growth or decline for a product or service resulting from basic changes in population, capital formation, or technology.

salvage 1. Goods, property, etc., saved from a shipwreck or from a fire. If a cargo is treated as a total loss for insurance purposes, there still may be salvagable items that have a **salvage value**; these may be sold by the insurers or allowed for in the settlement of their claim. 2. A reward paid to persons who help to save a ship, goods, etc., voluntarily and at some danger to themselves. **Salvage money** cannot be paid to anyone responsible for the care of the ship. The reward is paid by the owners of the ship or the cargo and the **salvors** have a lien on the property rescued for the salvage money.

salvage value (scrap value) The *net realizable value of an asset at the end of its useful life, when it is no longer suitable for its original use. Fixed assets, stock, or waste arising from a production process can all have a salvage value.

sample 1. A small quantity of a commodity, etc., selected to represent the bulk of a quantity of goods. *See* SALE BY SAMPLE. 2. A small quantity of a product, given to potential buyers to enable them to test its suitability for their purposes. 3. A group of items or individuals selected from a *population to represent the characteristics of the population as a whole. Samples are often used in *marketing research because it is not feasible to interview every member of a particular market; however, conclusions about a market drawn from a sample always contain a *sampling error and must be used with caution. The larger the sample, in general, the more accurate will be the conclusions drawn from it. In *quota sampling the composition of the sample reflects the known structure of the market. Thus, if it is known that 60% of purchasers of household DIY products are men, any sample would reflect this. An alternative sampling procedure is random or *probability sampling, which ensures that everyone in a particular market has an equal probability of being selected. Although more rigorous than quota sampling, it is also more expensive and difficult to implement. *See also* CLUSTER SAMPLING; JUDGEMENTAL SAMPLING; STRATIFIED SAMPLING; SYSTEMATIC SAMPLING.

Sampling is also important in auditing, as it is not usually feasible to inspect all the available documentation.

sampling error Any difference between the true parameters of a *population and a conclusion about these parameters based on a *sample of the population. Sampling errors are of two kinds. The first, which is inevitable, arises from the laws of statistics and probability. The second, which is preventable, arises from inadequate or unrepresentative sampling techniques (*see* SELECTION ERROR). *Compare* NON-SAMPLING ERRORS.

Samurai bond A *bond issued in Japan by a foreign institution. It is denominated in yen and can be bought by non-residents of Japan.

sanctions *See* ECONOMIC SANCTIONS.

sandbag A stalling tactic used by an unwilling target company in a *takeover bid. The management of the target company agrees to have talks with the unwelcome bidder, which it protracts for as long as possible in the hope that a *white knight will appear and make a more acceptable bid.

S&L Abbreviation for *savings and loan association.

santim (*plural* **santimi**) A monetary unit of Latvia, worth one hundredth of a *lats.

S&P 500 Abbreviation for *Standard and Poor's 500 Stock Index.

sandwich course A course of study in the UK for a diploma or degree in which periods of academic study in an institution of higher education are sandwiched between periods of supervised work experience in a factory or industrial organization. The course usually lasts for five years, with six-monthly periods in both college and industry.

sans recours *See* WITHOUT RECOURSE.

Sarl. 1. Abbreviation for *società a responsabilità*. It appears after the name of an Italian company, being equivalent to the British abbreviation Ltd (i.e. denoting a private limited liability company). **2.** Abbreviation for *société à responsibilité limitée*. It appears after the name of a French private limited company. *Compare* SA.

SAS Abbreviation for *Statement of Auditing Standards.

satang A monetary unit of Thailand, worth one hundredth of a *baht.

satisficing behaviour Behaviour by a company or an individual that is aimed at achieving satisfactory returns rather than optimum profit or growth. Given the limitations on any individual's knowledge of the total market situation, this is often a more rational approach than an abstract commitment to maximizing returns. *See* BOUNDED RATIONALITY.

save-as-you-earn (SAYE) A method of making regular savings (not necessarily linked to earnings), which carries certain tax privileges. This method has been used to encourage tax-free savings in building societies or *National Savings and also to encourage employees to acquire shares in their own organizations.

savings Money set aside by individuals, either for some special purpose or to provide an income at some time in the future (often after retirement). Money saved can be placed in a *savings account with a bank or building society or an *Individual Savings Account (ISA), invested in *National Savings, or used to purchase *securities. Savings are also used to buy *pensions, *annuities, and *endowment assurance.

savings account A bank or building-society account designed for the investment of personal savings. The rates tend to be higher than old-fashioned *deposit accounts and interest-bearing *current accounts. Some accounts offer instant access to funds, while others require that notice be given, typically 30, 60, or 90 days.

savings and loan association (S&L) The US equivalent of a UK *building society. It usually offers loans with a fixed rate of interest and has greater investment flexibility than a UK building society.

savings bank A bank that specializes in setting up *savings accounts for relatively small deposits. In the UK the *National Savings Bank and *building societies perform this function. In the USA, *savings and loan associations do so.

savings certificate *See* NATIONAL SAVINGS.

savings related share option scheme An approved *share option scheme established by an employer for the benefit of executives or other employees. HM Customs and Revenue has detailed rules regarding the income tax and capital gains tax chargeable to individuals benefiting from such a scheme. *See also* EMPLOYEE SHARE OWNERSHIP PLAN; EMPLOYEE SHARE OWNERSHIP TRUST; SHARE INCENTIVE SCHEME.

SAYE Abbreviation for *save-as-you-earn.

SBU Abbreviation for *strategic business unit.

scale effect *See* ECONOMIES OF SCALE.

scalpers Traders in financial obligations who deal very frequently for small gains and may only hold a position for a few minutes.

scatter diagram A graph on which observations are plotted on the *y*-axis for events on the *x*-axis. For example, the wages incurred (*y*-axis) for each level of activity (*x*-axis) would produce a scatter graph from which a relationship can be established between the two variables, as an aid to predicting *cost behaviour.

scenario analysis A means of attempting to forecast developments in an industry by using expert opinion to formulate a qualitative view of the future. It should identify major trends and analyse long-term environmental influences. Many factors need to be balanced against each other to produce a range of possible scenarios. From the final scenario managers should be able to examine the strategic options and challenge existing assumptions and practices. *See also* DELPHI TECHNIQUE; STRATEGIC CHOICE.

Schatzwechsel A German government Treasury bill, usually repayable in three months.

schedule 1. A plan of activities that uses the resources made available by *aggregate planning and allocates them to individual jobs, activities, or customers over a particular period. A schedule shows what has to be done, when, by whom, and with what resources. If the output of the system is being made to order, the schedule provides detailed timings for each order. If the output is being made to stock, it provides detailed timings for products. **2.** The part of legislation that is placed at the end of a UK Act of Parliament and contains subsidiary matter to the main sections of the act. **3.** In the UK, one of several schedules formerly used to classify various sources of income for *income-tax purposes and still applicable for *corporation tax. Before reform of the income-tax system in 2003–05 the broad classification was: Schedule A, rents from property in the UK; Schedule D, Case I, profits from trade; Case II, profits from professions or vocations; Case III, interest not otherwise taxed; Case IV, income from securities outside the UK; Case V, income from possessions outside the UK; Case VI, other annual profits and gains; Schedule E,

Cases I, II, and III, emoluments of offices or employments (the cases depending on the residential status of the taxpayer); Schedule F, dividends paid by UK companies. From April 2003 Schedule E was replaced by the three headings (i) employment income, (ii) pensions income, and (iii) social security income. From April 2005 the remaining schedules were replaced by the four headings (i) trading income, (ii) property income, (iii) savings and investment income, and (iv) miscellaneous income. Schedules A, D, and F were, however, retained for corporation tax purposes. **4.** Working papers submitted with tax returns or tax computations.

scheme of arrangement *See* ARRANGEMENT.

Schilling (S) Formerly, the standard monetary unit of Austria, divided into 100 Groschen. It was subsumed into the *euro for all purposes except cash transactions in January 1999 and abolished in 2002.

science park An industrial estate located on or near a university or research centre, in which high-technology firms are located to encourage the transfer of technical knowledge and research results between the academic institution and the commercial user.

scientific management (Taylorism) One of the classic approaches to management theory, which emphasizes the rationality of organizational systems and holds that operational efficiency can be optimized by applying the appropriate scientific management principles. Developed by Frederick Taylor in the late 19th and early 20th centuries, the theory forms the basis for the techniques now known as *work study. The key principles were:

• Managers should take full responsibility for the planning of work and should use scientific methods to specify precisely how the job should be done to achieve the maximum efficiency.

• Managers should select the most appropriate person for the job, train them to do the job efficiently, and monitor their performance to ensure conformity to the specification.

Scientific management is credited with increasing productivity enormously, but only at the cost of *deskilling many areas of work. The boring, repetitive, and alienating nature of the jobs created using scientific management methods causes demotivation in staff and can lead to an extreme emphasis on pay rates as the primary form of motivation.

scope economies (economies of scope) The increases in efficiency and sales that can result from producing, distributing, and marketing a range of products, as opposed to a single product or type of product. *Bancassurance is often seen as an example of scope economies.

scorched earth policy An extreme form of *poison pill in which a company that believes it is to be the target of a *takeover bid makes its balance sheet or profitability less attractive than it really is by a reversible manouevre, such as borrowing money at an exorbitant rate of interest.

scorekeeping One of the functions of *management accounting in which the performance of the managers and operators is monitored and reported in accounting statements to the appropriate levels of management.

SCOUT Acronym for Shared Currency Option Under Tender: a currency *option especially designed for companies who are tendering for the same overseas job in a foreign currency. To save each of them having to *hedge the currency risk separately, SCOUT enables them to share the cost of a single option.

scrambled merchandising The selling of certain products in a retail outlet that is not traditionally associated with these products. Many retailers have extended their product width and depth in this way. For example, most supermarkets now sell books and CDs and many offer financial services.

scrap 1. What is left of an asset at the end of its useful life, which may have a *salvage value. **2.** The waste arising from a production process, which may also have a salvage value.

scrap value See SALVAGE VALUE.

screening stage The stage in *new product development that involves an analysis of new ideas to determine their appropriateness in relation to an organization's goals and objectives.

screen trading See AUTOMATED SCREEN TRADING.

scrip The certificates that demonstrate ownership of *stocks, *shares, and *bonds (capital raised by subscription), especially the certificates relating to a *scrip issue.

scrip issue (bonus issue; capitalization issue; free issue) The issue of new share certificates to existing shareholders to reflect the accumulation of profits in the reserves of a company's balance sheet. The shareholders do not pay for the new shares and appear to be no better off. However, in a 1 for 3 scrip issue, say, the shareholders receive 1 new share for every 3 old shares they own. This automatically reduces the price of the shares by 25%, catering to the preference of shareholders to hold cheaper shares rather than expensive ones; it also encourages them to hope that the price will gradually climb to its former value, which will, of course, make them 25% better off. In the USA this is known as a **stock split**.

script A section of programming code used in web pages to add functionality. The script may run on the *web server (server-side script). Commonly, scripts written in Javascript are included in the HTML (see HYPERTEXT) of the web page and are interpreted by the *web browser when the page is opened (client-side script).

SDDE Abbreviation for *simultaneous direct data entry.

SDR Abbreviation for *Special Drawing Rights.

SEAQ See STOCK EXCHANGE AUTOMATED QUOTATIONS SYSTEM.

search engine A service provided on the Internet that enables the user to search for items of interest. Some, such as the widely used search engines Google, Yahoo, and Alta Vista, are free and attempt to capture information from the whole range of material available on the net. Others are subscription-based but in return provide access to specialist publications, full-text retrieval capabilities, or other added-value services.

search order A court injunction ordering the defendant to allow the plaintiff to enter named premises to search for and take copies of specified articles and documents. These orders are obtained by the plaintiff 'ex parte' (without the other party being present in court) to allow evidence to be preserved in cases in which there are grounds to think it will be destroyed. It is especially useful in 'pirating' cases. The order is not a search warrant, so entry cannot be forced, but the defendant will be in contempt of court if entry is refused. A solicitor must serve the order. It was formerly called an **Anton Piller order**, after an order made in the High Court in 1976 against Anton Piller KG.

seasonality The seasonal variability of certain economic or financial factors, for example unemployment or commodity prices.

seasonal rate A rate of charging that varies according to the time of the year. This is quite common in *advertising, for example the *Radio Times* charges a higher page rate for its Christmas issue than for any other issue. **Seasonal discounts** are also common, especially in advertising, when sellers wish to encourage business in a slack period.

seasonal unemployment *Unemployment that occurs as a result of the seasonal nature of some jobs. The building trade, for example, employs more people in the summer months than the winter months. Much of the seaside holiday trade is seasonal and a considerable amount of agricultural work is seasonal. It is for this reason that UK unemployment figures are usually **seasonally adjusted**, i.e. adjusted to flatten the peaks and troughs of unemployment in certain seasons.

SEATS Abbreviation for *Stock Exchange Alternative Trading Service.

SEC Abbreviation for *Securities and Exchange Commission.

secondary bank **1.** A name sometimes given to *finance houses. **2.** Any organization that offers some banking services, such as making loans, offering secondary mortgages, etc., but that does not offer the usual commercial-bank services of cheque accounts, etc.

secondary data Marketing research information available to researchers that they have not gathered themselves. Examples include data provided by a government department or extracted from company records.

secondary domain name *See* DOMAIN NAME.

secondary market (after market) A market in which existing securities are traded, as opposed to a *primary market, in which securities are sold for the first time. In most cases a *stock exchange largely fulfils the role of a secondary market, with the flotation of *new issues representing only a small proportion of its total business. However, it is the existence of a flourishing secondary market, providing liquidity and the spreading of risks, that creates the conditions for a healthy primary market.

secondary picketing *See* PICKETING.

secondary production *See* PRODUCTION.

Second Banking Directive The most important of the EU directives on banking regulation, introduced in 1989. It stipulates *capital adequacy requirements for banks in member states. The directive also regulates the licensing and operation of banks based in one member state in other EU countries.

second-hand goods scheme An arrangement in which the *value added tax due on second-hand goods sold is calculated on the trader's margin, rather than the total selling price of the goods. This applies regularly with sales of second-hand cars. In order to qualify, the trader must retain detailed records of car purchases and sales, which must be available for inspection at a VAT control visit.

second mortgage A *mortgage taken out on a property that is already mortgaged. Second and subsequent mortgages can often be used to raise money from a *finance house (but not a commercial bank or building society) if the value of the property has increased considerably since the first mortgage was taken out. See feature MORTGAGE LAW on p. 352.

second of exchange *See* BILLS IN A SET.

second-tier market A market for investors to buy and sell shares in new and developing companies. Companies have access to new sources of finance and do not have to follow the complex rules that the main market requires. The *Alternative Investment Market of the *London Stock Exchange is an example of a second-tier market.

secret reserve Funds accumulated by a company but not disclosed on the *balance sheet. They can arise when an *asset has been deliberately undervalued or a method has been used to account for a transaction with the intention of not showing the effect on the balance sheet. *Financial Reporting Standard 5, Reporting the Substance of Transactions, is aimed at such *off-balance-sheet finance.

secular Denoting a long-term trend or development, in contrast to seasonal or cyclical phenomena.

secured creditor A creditor who holds a fixed or floating *charge over the assets of a debtor.

secured debenture A *debenture secured by a *charge over the property of a company, such as mortgage debentures (secured on land belonging to the company). Usually a trust deed sets out the powers of the debenture holders to enforce their security in the event of the company defaulting in payment of the principal or the interest. It is usual to appoint a *receiver to realize the security.

secured liability A debt against which the borrower has provided sufficient assets as security to safeguard the lender in case of non-repayment.

secure electronic transaction (SET) A standard for the secure *encryption of e-commerce transactions. It was developed by Mastercard and Visa.

secure HTTP *HTTP that has been encrypted.

secure sockets layer (SSL) A commonly used *encryption technique for scrambling data, such as credit card numbers, as they are passed across the Internet from a *web browser to a *web server.

Securities and Exchange Commission (SEC) A US government agency established in 1934 to protect investors by regulating behaviour in the securities markets. Each year the SEC brings between 400–500 civil enforcement actions against individuals and companies that break the securities laws. The SEC is also responsible for monitoring and controlling corporate financial reporting and auditing practices.

Securities and Futures Authority Ltd (SFA) The *Self-Regulating Organization formed from the merger of The Securities Association Ltd (TSA) and the Association of Futures Brokers and Dealers Ltd (AFBD) in April 1991. It was responsible for regulating the conduct of brokers and dealers in securities, options, and futures, including most of those on the *London Stock Exchange and the *London International Financial Futures and Options Exchange. Its responsibilities were taken over by the *Financial Services Authority in December 2001.

Securities and Investment Board (SIB) A regulatory body set up by the *Financial Services Act (1986) to oversee London's financial markets. Each market (e.g. the stock exchange, life assurance, unit trusts) had its own *Self-Regulating Organization (SRO), which reported to the SIB. It was superseded by the *Financial Services Authority in December 2001.

Securities Industry Association (SIA) A US trade association for the brokerage industry.

securitization An arrangement in which one party (the originator) sells a portfolio of high-quality assets, such as house mortgages, to a special-purpose vehicle (the issuer), who issues loan notes to finance the purchase. The arrangement may be a form of *off-balance-sheet finance and now falls under the regulations of *Financial Reporting Standard 5, Reporting the Substance of Transactions.

security 1. An asset or assets to which a lender can have recourse if the borrower defaults on the loan repayments. In the case of loans by banks and other money-lenders the security is sometimes referred to as *collateral.
2. A financial asset, including shares, government stocks, debentures, bonds, unit trusts, and rights to money lent or deposited. It does not, however, include in-

surance policies. *See also* BEARER SECURITY; DATED SECURITY; FIXED-INTEREST SECURITY; GILT-EDGED SECURITY; LISTED SECURITY; MARKETABLE SECURITY.
3. Precautions taken in e-commerce to ensure that the following attributes are safeguarded:

- **Authentication**. Are parties to a transaction who they claim to be? This is achieved by using digital certificates.

- **Privacy and confidentiality**. Is transaction data protected? The consumer may want an anonymous purchase. Are all non-essential traces of a transaction removed from the public network and have all intermediary records been eliminated?

- **Integrity**. Are the messages sent complete? Checks are needed to ensure that messages have not been corrupted.

- **Non-repudiability**. Could the sender deny sending the message? It is essential measures are in place to protect against repudiation.

- **Availability**. How can threats to the continuity and performance of the system be eliminated?

seed capital The small amount of initial capital required to fund the research and development necessary before a new company is set up. The seed capital should enable a persuasive and accurate *business plan to be drawn up.

segmental reporting 1. The disclosure in the *annual accounts and report of certain results of major business and geographic segments of a diversified group of companies. Segmental reporting is required by company law, the stock exchange, and *Statement of Standard Accounting Practice (SSAP) 25. The argument for segmental reporting is that the disclosure of profitability, risk, and growth prospects for individual segments of a business will be of use to investors. Under SSAP 25 companies should disclose, for both *business segments and geographic segments, turnover, profit or loss before tax, minority interests, extraordinary items, and net assets. **2.** The approach in *management accounting in which the financial and quantitative performance of each definitive part of an organization is reported to both the management of the business segment and of the organization as a whole.

seigniorage The profits accruing to the issuer of legal tender, mainly as a result of the difference between the material costs of producing currency and its face value. The term is frequently used in reference to the US Treasury's earnings from producing coins and notes; as the producer of the world's major reserve currency and black market currency, the USA can obtain considerable gains from printing money.

selection error The type of *sampling error that results from following an incomplete or improper selection process in sampling (*see* SAMPLE). Often, respondents who are not relevant to the study are used in surveys. For example, ownership of a car may be a prerequisite for an interview, but a respondent may be selected who merely has the use of a car, rather than owning one.

selection interview (job interview) An interview with a candidate for a job in which a manager or personnel worker attempts to form a judgement of the applicant's suitability for the position in question. As basic biographical information about the candidate will already have been obtained (*see* BIODATA), the main purpose of the interview is usually to get an idea of his or her personality, demeanour, motivation, and interpersonal skills. The interview may be highly structured, with a large number of set questions, or virtually unstructured, to provide the candidate with more opportunity to reveal his or her qualities. The interviewer will also use the occasion to provide more information about the job, the company, and its activities.

selective demand A demand for a given brand of a product or service.

selective distribution The use of more than one but less than all of the intermediaries willing to carry a company's products.

selective retention The tendency of people to retain only part of the information to which they are exposed; usually they retain the information that supports their own attitudes or beliefs.

self-actualization The drive people

have to realize their potential and to find fulfilment. Self-actualization encompasses the human need for challenge, responsibility, creativity, and variety at work, enabling employees to take pride in their achievements, as well as in their technical or professional expertise. An integral part of the concept is for their worth to be recognized and valued by those with, and for, whom they work. *See also* MASLOW'S MOTIVATIONAL HIERARCHY; MOTIVATION.

self-administered questionnaire (self-complete questionnaire) A marketing research questionnaire filled out by a respondent with no interviewer involvement.

self-assessment A system that enables taxpayers to assess their own *income tax and *capital gains tax liabilities for the year. Major changes to the UK system occurred in the year 1996–97, since when a self-assessment section has been contained in the *tax return, in addition to the part requiring details of *taxable income, *chargeable gains, and claims for *personal allowances. At present the self-assessment is voluntary; if the taxpayer prefers to let HM Revenue and Customs calculate his or her liability, then the tax return must be submitted by September 30 following the end of the year of assessment, rather than the usual January 31. The introduction of self-assessment was accompanied by the *Board of Inland Revenue being granted extensive audit powers to enquire into any tax return.

self-assessment for companies A scheme for the self-assessment of tax by companies. In the UK, self-assessment of *corporation tax was introduced for all companies with an accounting period ending after 1 July 1999. Tax returns must be completed and filed within 12 months of the end of the accounting period. Smaller companies must pay their tax liability within nine months of the end of the accounting period; large companies must make payments on account in advance of this date.

self-complete questionnaire *See* SELF-ADMINISTERED QUESTIONNAIRE.

self-employed taxpayers Persons who are not employees and who trade on their own account. They are taxed on the profits of their trades rather than by

*PAYE and their *National Insurance contributions differ from those of employees.

self-financing Denoting a company that is able to finance its capital expenditure from undistributed profits rather than by borrowing.

self-liquidating 1. Denoting an asset that earns back its original cost out of income over a fixed period. **2.** Denoting a loan in which the money is used to finance a project that will provide sufficient yield to repay the loan and its interest and leave a profit. **3.** Denoting a *sales-promotion offer that pays for itself. For example, if a seller of tea bags offers a free tea mug in exchange for a specified number of vouchers, each taken from a box of tea bags, the seller expects the extra number of tea-bag boxes sold during the promotion to pay for the costs of buying and despatching the mugs.

Self-Regulating Organization (SRO) One of several organizations set up in the UK under the *Financial Services Act (1986) to regulate the activities of investment businesses and to draw up and enforce specific codes of conduct. By 1995 the SROs recognized by the *Securities and Investment Board, to whom they reported, had been reduced to three: the *Securities and Futures Authority Ltd (SFA), the *Investment Management Regulatory Organization (IMRO), and the *Personal Investment Authority (PIA). All regulatory functions of SROs were taken over by the *Financial Services Authority as of December 2001.

self-select PEP *See* PERSONAL EQUITY PLAN.

self-service A method of retailing goods in which the customer serves himself and pays at a cash point before leaving. Widely used in food supermarkets, petrol stations, and cafés, self-service greatly reduces labour costs but offers increased opportunities for shoplifters.

self supply The *value added tax charge on a commercial building, which is used for an exempt purpose, on the grant of an interest in the building. *Output tax is charged on the land and the building costs. *Input tax is allowed on the building costs. The self supply is due to be assessed and paid within three months of the initial occupation.

self-tender A *tender offer in which a company approaches its shareholders in order to buy back some or all of its shares. There are two circumstances in which this operation can be of use. One is in the case of a hostile bid: the directors may wish to buy back shares in their company in order to reduce the chances of the bidder being able to buy a controlling interest in the company. The other circumstance is that the board may wish to show increased earnings per share; if they are unable to increase their profits it may be appropriate for them to reduce the number of shares in the company.

sellers' market A market in which the demand exceeds the supply, so that sellers can increase prices. At some point, however, buyers will cease to follow the price rises and the sellers will be forced to drop prices in order to make sales, i.e. the supply will have exceeded the demand. *See* BUYERS' MARKET.

sellers over A market in commodities, securities, etc., in which buyers have been satisfied but some sellers remain. This is clearly a weak market, with a tendency for prices to fall. *Compare* BUYERS OVER.

selling agent *See* AGENT.

selling concept The idea that consumers will not buy enough of an organization's products unless the organization undertakes a large-scale selling and promotion effort.

selling out The selling of securities, commodities, etc., by a broker because the original buyer is unable to pay for them. This invariably happens after a fall in market price (the buyer would take them up and sell them at a profit if the market had risen). The broker sells them at the best price available and the original buyer is responsible for any difference between the price realized and the original selling price, plus the costs of selling out. *Compare* BUYING IN.

selling overhead (selling costs) The expenses incurred by an organization in carrying out its selling activities. These would include salaries of sales personnel, advertising costs, sales commissions, etc.

selling process The steps that a salesperson may follow when selling. These include *prospecting and *qualifying potential customers, a *preapproach, approach, *presentation and demonstration, handling objections, closing, and *follow-up.

selling short *See* SHORT SELLING.

semantic differential A method of comparing the strengths and weaknesses of a product or company image with the competition by asking respondents to describe the product or company by choosing one of a pair of words or phrases that would best describe it, e.g. innovative or traditional, modern or old-fashioned. The mean of the responses is then plotted as a profile or image, usually using a 7-point scale.

semi-fixed cost (stepped cost) An item of expenditure that increases in total as activity rises but in a stepped, rather than a linear, function (*see* LINEAR COST FUNCTION). For example, the costs of one supervisor may be required for a particular range of activity, although above this level the cost of an additional supervisor would be incurred.

semisolus An advertisement that appears on a page in a publication containing another advertisement but is not placed adjacent to it. *Compare* SOLUS POSITION.

semi-variable cost An item of expenditure that contains both a *fixed-cost element and a *variable-cost element. Consequently, when activity is zero, the fixed cost will still continue to be incurred. For example, in the UK the cost of gas is made up of a standing charge plus a cost per unit consumed; therefore while the consumption of gas varies with production the fixed standing charge will still be incurred when production is zero.

sen **1.** A monetary unit of Cambodia, worth one hundredth of a *riel. **2.** (cent) A monetary unit of Malaysia, worth one hundredth of a *ringgit. **3.** A monetary unit of Indonesia, worth one hundredth of a *rupiah. **4.** A former monetary unit of Japan (still used as a unit of account), worth one hundredth of a *yen.

sene A monetary unit of Samoa, worth one hundredth of a *tala.

senior capital Capital in the form of secured loans to a company (*see* SECURED CREDITOR; SECURED LIABILITY). In the event of a liquidation, the senior capital is repaid before the *shareholders' equity.

seniti A monetary unit of Tonga, worth one hundredth of a *pa'anga.

sense-of-mission marketing A principle of marketing holding that a company should define its mission in broad social terms, rather than narrow product terms.

sensitive market A market in commodities, securities, etc., that is sensitive to outside influences because it is basically unstable. For example, a poor crop in a commodity market may make it sensitive, with buyers anxious to cover their requirements but unwilling to show their hand and risk forcing prices up. News of a hurricane in the growing area, say, could cause a sharp price rise in such a sensitive market.

sensitivity analysis A method of analysing the sensitivity of a decision to a change in one or more of the assumptions used in making it. For instance, a company might analyse how its future performance might be affected by changing its level of advertising or by lowering the price of a product, to enable it to estimate the likely impact on sales and profitability. Similarly, in considering an investment decision, it could investigate the impact of changing assumptions regarding the life of an asset, the cost of borrowing, and the end value of the asset.

sent (*plural* senti) A monetary unit of Estonia, worth one hundredth of a *kroon.

separable assets and liabilities *See* IDENTIFIABLE ASSETS AND LIABILITIES.

separate-entity concept *See* ACCOUNTING ENTITY.

separation point (split-off point) In *process costing, the point at which the *by-products or the joint products separate and are subsequently processed independently of each other.

sequencing (priority sequencing) Establishing an exact order for jobs, taking into account job interference and queuing times. Priority sequencing specifies the order in which waiting jobs are to be processed. It requires the adoption of a rule to decide the basis upon which priorities are to be allocated. *See* DISPATCHING RULES.

sequential product development An approach to *new product development in which one department of a company completes its stage of the process before passing the new product to the next department. *Compare* SIMULTANEOUS PRODUCT DEVELOPMENT.

sequestration The confiscation of the property of a person or organization who has not complied with a court order. This is a very drastic remedy, and will be ordered in serious cases only. It is most commonly used against companies, trade unions, and in matrimonial cases.

Serious Fraud Office (SFO) A body established in 1987 to be responsible for investigating and prosecuting serious or complex frauds in England, Wales, and Northern Ireland. The Attorney General appoints and superintends its director. Serious and complex fraud cases can go straight to the Crown Court without committal for trial. That court can hold preparatory hearings to clarify issues for the jury and settle points of law.

SERPS Abbreviation for *State Earnings-Related Pension Scheme.

served market *See* TARGET MARKETING.

server (file server) A computer that makes services available to users on a wider network.

service Any activity or benefit that one party can offer to another that is intangible and does not result in the transfer of ownership of any physical object. See feature THE SERVICE ECONOMY on p. 475.

service contract (service agreement) An employment contract between an employer and employee, usually a senior employee, such as a director, executive manager, etc. Service contracts must be kept at the registered office of a company and be open to inspection by members of the company. The Companies Acts (1980; 1985) prohibit service contracts that give

Servqual

an employee guaranteed employment for more than five years, without the company having an opportunity to break the employment as and when it needs to. This measure prevents directors with long service agreements from suing companies for loss of office in the event of a takeover or reorganization. *See also* COMPENSATION FOR LOSS OF OFFICE; GOLDEN PARACHUTE.

service cost centre (indirect cost centre; service department; support cost centre) A *cost centre to which costs are allocated or apportioned in *absorption costing; though the service cost centre is necessary to carry out the production process, it is incidental to it and does not handle the *cost unit. Examples of service cost centres are stores, canteens, and boiler houses.

service industry *See* SERVICE.

service level A comparison between what a customer expects from a service and the actual service received.

service package A collection of facilities, goods, and services put together. These can be tangible, e.g. the decor and fittings of a hotel, or intangible, e.g. the feeling of confidence imparted by an efficient hospital.

servicing a loan Paying the interest on a loan.

servqual The provision of high-quality products together with a high quality of customer service. It can be identified by a number of factors:

• **tangibles**, i.e. physical evidence of the service;

• **reliability**, i.e. consistency of performance and dependability;

• **responsiveness**, i.e. a readiness on the part of employees to provide a prompt service;

• **assurance**, i.e. competence, credibility, and access to those employees providing the service;

• **empathy**, i.e. understanding the customers' needs as well as communicating with them considerately and respectfully.

Servqual provides an important *differentiated marketing strategy. It has been repeatedly shown that providing consumers with a high level of service, combined with high-quality products, affects consumer satisfaction, which is reflected in their buying behaviour. Companies providing outstanding servqual undoubtedly achieve greater sales and profits. While servqual is difficult to quantify, many companies are anxious to know how consumers assess it, especially in terms of comparing their expectations with actual performance. If consumers' expectations do not match the actual level of service provided, a 'gap' is created. If the gap is negative it can be the cause of serious consumer dissatisfaction. On the other hand, a 'positive gap' implies that consumers' expectations are exceeded by the servqual provided, which should be the objective of every company. "We exceed your expectations" is a slogan often used in advertising. Similarly, management's perception of the consumers' expectations, rather than the consumers' actual expectations, can create a further gap.

THE SERVICE ECONOMY

Economic activity has traditionally been divided into extractive, constructive, manufacturing, and service sectors. With the decline of heavy engineering and the rise of the knowledge-based economy, the **service industries** make up an ever-increasing proportion of the national income in nearly all developed countries.

Essentially, services can be classified into three categories:

• **Services to trade** include banking, insurance, transport, etc.

• **Professional services** encompass the advice and skill of accountants, lawyers, doctors, architects, business consultants, etc.

• **Consumer services** include those given by caterers, cleaners, mechanics, plumbers, etc.

Service providers need to define exactly what service they are providing, who they are competing with, and where their markets are. For example, does the Channel Tunnel provide a fast link to Paris for business people in competition with the airlines, or a holiday route to France in competition with the ferries?

Crucially, they also need to be aware of those characteristics of services that make their management different from the production of goods. These can be summarized as:

• **Intangibility** – the exact nature of a service is often difficult to define, the product cannot be handled, and ownership of an object is not transferred. The service is experiential rather than concrete and thus quality is difficult to define and measure.

• **Customer participation** – normally the customer is directly involved in the delivery of the service; e.g. hospital treatment cannot be given if the patient is absent.

• **Simultaneity** – production and consumption of a service are usually simultaneous and therefore not storable.

• **Perishability** – because a service is perishable, stocks cannot be built up; e.g. a seat on the 9 a.m. London to Glasgow train is gone forever as soon as the train departs.

• **Heterogeneity** – because the interaction between the customer and the provider is a unique experience, the same service can be perceived differently by different customers and by the same customer on different occasions. Other customers can affect the experience of a service, e.g. a quiet weekend at a small hotel can be ruined if two rival football teams are also staying in the hotel.

• **Indivisibility of operations and marketing** – frequently the same people do the selling and the delivery of the service. This has implications for training and the efficiency of the operation. Process design needs to ensure a smooth flow from one stage to the next.

• **Geographical dispersion** – most services need to be reasonably near to the customer. However, use of telecommunications and *information technology is increasingly allowing major service organizations to centralize large parts of their process, while retaining an interface with the customer; e.g. the use of national (or international) *call centres and the provision by banks of *automated teller machines and *home banking facilities.

SET Abbreviation for *secure electronic transaction.

set-off An agreement between the parties involved to set off one debt against another or one loss against a gain. A banker is empowered to set off a credit balance on one account against a debit balance on another if the accounts are in the same name and in the same currency. It is usual, in these circumstances, for the bank to issue a **letter of set-off**, which the customer countersigns to indicate agreement. A letter of set-off is also needed if the accounts are not in the same name, e.g. differently named companies in the same group.

SETS Abbreviation for *Stock Exchange Trading System.

settlement **1.** The payment of an outstanding account, invoice, charge, etc. **2.** A disposition of land, or other property, made by deed or will under which a *trust is set up by the settlor. The settlement names the beneficiaries and the terms under which they are to acquire the property. **3.** The document in which such a disposition is made. **4.** The voluntary conclusion of civil litigation or an industrial dispute, as a result of agreement between the parties.

settlement day The day on which trades are cleared by the delivery of the securities or foreign exchange.

settlement price The price at which an *index futures or option contract is settled on the *London International Financial Futures and Options Exchange. Officially known as the **Exchange Delivery Settlement Price (EDSP)**, the settlement price is calculated on the last day of the delivery month and forms the basis for the cash settlement.

settlement risk The *risk that a transaction will not be settled as expected (i.e. that an agreed delivery or payment will not be made). It is sometimes referred to as **Herstatt risk** after a bank of that name, which failed to honour its foreign-exchange transactions in 1974. *See also* COUNTERPARTY RISK.

settlor A person declaring or creating a *settlement or *trust. For tax purposes any person providing money or property

for a settlement will be regarded as the settlor.

set-up reduction (SUR) An approach to operations management that seeks to reduce the *set-up time of a process by better process or product design, by using parallel rather than sequential operations, or by undertaking at least some of the set-up while the process is running, e.g. refuelling nuclear power stations on-line. *See also* JUST IN TIME.

set-up time **1.** The time taken to prepare a machine, process, or operation to carry out production. It may involve such operations as tool setting, calibration, and the initialization of the production process. **2.** The time that elapses between the production of the last acceptable piece in one batch and the first acceptable piece in the next batch. This unproductive time is a cost that should be minimized. *See* SET-UP REDUCTION.

seven-day money Money that has been invested in the *money market for a term of seven days. Special interest rates are quoted for seven-day money.

Seventh Accounting Directive A directive approved by the European Commission in 1983 and implemented in the UK by the Companies Act (1989); it concerns *consolidated financial statements prepared by *groups.

severance The separation of the good parts of a contract from the bad; it applies to contracts that are not illegal but are void by statute or common law. Courts will, if possible, save contracts from complete invalidity by severance of the parts that are void.

severance payment *See* COMPENSATION FOR LOSS OF OFFICE; REDUNDANCY.

sex discrimination *See* DISCRIMINATION.

SFA Abbreviation for *Securities and Futures Authority Ltd.

SFAS Abbreviation for *Statement of Financial Accounting Standards.

SFO Abbreviation for *Serious Fraud Office.

shadow director A person in accordance with whose instructions the directors of a company are accustomed to act although that person has not been appointed as a director. A shadow director influences the running of the company and some provisions of the Companies Acts, including wrongful trading and the regulation of loans to directors, relating to directors also extend to shadow directors.

shamrock organization A type of organizational structure described by the British human-resources expert Charles Handy, who predicts that it will become predominant in the near future. The shamrock organization consists of four 'leaves': the professional core; the contractual fringe; a flexible labour force; and customers, who are regarded as part of the organization. Of these groups only the professional core will enjoy anything like traditional permanent employment.

share One of a number of titles of ownership in a company. Most companies are limited by shares, enabling investors to limit their liability if the company fails to the amount paid for (or owing on) the shares. A share is a *chose in action, conferring on its owner a legal right to the part of the company's profits (usually by payment of a *dividend) and to any voting rights attaching to that share (see VOTING SHARES; A SHARES). Companies are obliged to keep a public record of the rights attaching to each class of share. The common classes of shares are: *ordinary shares, which have no guaranteed amount of dividend but carry voting rights; and *preference shares, which receive dividends (and/or repayment of capital on winding-up) before ordinary shares, but which have no voting rights. Shares in public companies may be bought and sold in an open market, such as a stock exchange. Shares in a private company are generally subject to restrictions on sale, such as that they must be offered to existing shareholders first or that the directors' approval must be sought before they are sold elsewhere. See also CUMULATIVE PREFERENCE SHARE; DEFERRED ORDINARY SHARE; FOUNDERS' SHARES; FULLY PAID SHARE; PARTLY PAID SHARE; PREFERRED ORDINARY SHARE; REDEEMABLE SHARES; SUBSCRIPTION SHARES; TERM SHARES.

share account 1. In the UK, a building society deposit account with no fixed investment period that confers a share of ownership in the society. It entitles the holder to vote at shareholders' meetings and to an allocation of free shares if the society is demutualized. **2.** In the USA, an account with a credit union (a non-profit making co-operative institution) that pays dividends rather than interest.

share capital That part of the *capital of a company received from its owners (i.e. its members or shareholders) in return for *shares. Every company must commence with some share capital (a minimum of two shares). See AUTHORIZED SHARE CAPITAL; CALLED-UP SHARE CAPITAL; ISSUED SHARE CAPITAL; PAID-UP SHARE CAPITAL; RESERVE CAPITAL.

share certificate A document that provides evidence of ownership of shares in a company. It states the number and class of shares owned by the shareholder and the serial number of the shares. It is stamped by the common seal of the company and usually signed by at least one director and the company secretary. It is not a negotiable instrument. See BEARER SECURITY.

shared-cost effect The consequence that a market in which one person chooses the product and another person pays for it will be less price sensitive than a market in which the same person both chooses and pays.

share exchange A service offered by most unit-trust managements and life assurance companies, in which the trust or company takes over a client's shareholding and invests the proceeds in unit-trust funds, etc., of the client's choice. The client is thereby saved the trouble and expense of disposing of his shares and if the shares are absorbed into the trust's or company's own portfolio he may receive a better price than he would on the market (i.e. he may receive the offer price rather than the bid price).

share-for-share offer (paper bid) A *takeover bid in which the directors of one company offer shares in that company as the payment for acquiring the shares in the target company. If the offer is accepted the shareholders of both companies will become the owners of the newly formed combination.

shareholder An owner of shares in a

limited company or limited partnership. A shareholder is a member of the company. In the USA, the more usual word is **stockholder**.

shareholders' equity (shareholders' funds) The *share capital and *reserves of a company. *Financial Reporting Standard (FRS) 4, Capital Instruments, requires that share capital be split into *equity capital and *non-equity shares. The latest regulations are found in FRS 25, Financial Instruments: Disclosure and Presentation.

shareholders' perks Benefits offered by a company to its shareholders as a reward for their loyalty. The benefits are given in addition to dividends and are tax-free. For example, if you enjoy reading the adventures of Harry Potter you can become a shareholder in Bloomsbury Publishing Ltd and get 35% off the recommended retail price of the next book.

shareholder value An approach to business that places the maximization of the value of shares to those who hold them above other business objectives. Normally, shareholder value can be increased in three ways: dividend payments, appreciation in the value of the shares, and cash repayments. However, this focus has been widened by companies buying back shares to increase earnings and the demerging of parts of a group in order to unlock the value of individual components by means of a separate flotation. Shareholder value can also be influenced by maximising *economic value, either by undertaking positive *present-value decisions or by running the business in such a way as to create a surplus above the market costs of funding. The shareholder-value objective has sometimes been criticized as being too narrow and contrary to the longer-term interests of other *stakeholder groups.

shareholder value analysis (SVA) A method for valuing the entire *equity in a company. SVA assumes that the value of a business is the *net present value of its future cash flows, discounted at the appropriate *cost of capital. Once the value of a business has been calculated in this way, the next stage is to calculate shareholder value using the equation:

shareholder value = value of business – debt.

This method was first developed by Alfred Rappaport in the 1980s. The key difference between traditional financial accounting and SVA is that the latter recognizes the *time value of money. The traditional *balance sheet and *profit and loss account report on the past performance of a company is not helpful when measuring the change in value of the company. *See also* VALUE DRIVER.

share incentive scheme Any scheme in which employees who achieve personal or group performance targets are rewarded with shares in the company. There are many different types of scheme. In recent years, some companies have been severely criticized by shareholders for setting up share incentive schemes that are considered too generous. *See also* EMPLOYEE SHARE OWNERSHIP PLAN; EMPLOYEE SHARE OWNERSHIP TRUST; SAVINGS RELATED SHARE OPTION SCHEME; SHARE OPTION.

share index An index formed by selecting a number of prominent shares traded on a *stock exchange and comparing the value of these shares with their value on a stated date in the *base year. The daily value of the shares takes into account the volume of shares traded (*see* WEIGHTED AVERAGE). *See* DOW JONES INDUSTRIAL AVERAGE; FINANCIAL TIMES SHARE INDEXES; NIKKEI STOCK AVERAGE; HANG SENG INDEX. See also feature THE FINANCIAL TIMES SHARE INDEXES on p. 352.

share issued at a discount A share issued at a price (the *issue price) below its *par value. The discount is the difference between the par value and the issue price. It is illegal to issue shares at a discount in the UK.

share of wallet The share of a customer's business that is obtained by a particular company.

share option (stock option) 1. A benefit sometimes offered to employees, especially new employees, in which they are given an option to buy shares in the company for which they work at a favourable fixed price or at a stated discount to the market price. An **approved share option scheme** is one that meets certain conditions imposed by the HM Revenue and Customs. Under such a scheme there are no income tax charges on the grant or exercise of the option or on the growth in value of the shares; the only charge will be to *capital gains tax when the shares are sold. *See* SAVINGS RELATED SHARE OPTION SCHEME. **2.** *See* OPTION.

share premium The amount payable for shares in a company and issued by the company itself in excess of their nominal value (*see* NOMINAL PRICE). Share premiums received by a company must be credited to a *share premium account.

share premium account The account to which any *share premium must be credited. The balance on the share premium account may be used for specified purposes:
• the issue of *bonus shares;
• the writing-off of preliminary expenses;
• the writing-off of underwriting commissions;
• the provision of a premium to be paid on the redemption of *debentures;
• the provision of a premium to be paid on the redemption or purchase of *share capital, subject to certain limits.
The share premium account may not be used to write off *goodwill on consolidation. Relief from the creation of a share premium account is given in section 131 of the Companies Act; this is known as *merger relief and is available in specified circumstances.

share register *See* REGISTER OF MEMBERS.

share shop A stockbroker, bank, building society, or other financial intermediary appointed by the government to promote and handle applications for shares in a *privatization issue. The purpose of these share shops is to enable those members of the public who do not usually buy shares to purchase publicly offered shares without difficulty. Share shops act on behalf of members of the public but members of the public pay no commission. Commission is paid to the share shops by the government on successful share applications. Share shops exist only for the duration of the public share offer. *See also* RETAIL TENDER.

share splitting The division of the share capital of a company into smaller units. The effect of a share split is the same as a *scrip issue although the techni-

calities differ. Share splits are usually carried out when the existing shares reach such a high price that trading in them becomes difficult.

share transfer (stock transfer) A change in the ownership of a share or stock. On the *London Stock Exchange a **stock transfer form** has to be executed by the seller of registered securities to legalize the transaction. This can now be done in electronic form, rather than on paper, using the *CREST system. *See also* STAMP DUTY.

share warehousing *See* WAREHOUSING.

share warrant A certificate giving the holder the right to purchase a security at a particular price at a particular date or dates in the future.

shark repellents *See* PORCUPINE PROVISIONS.

shark watcher A business consultant who specializes in helping companies to identify raiders and to provide early warning of share *warehousing and other manoeuvres used as preliminaries to takeovers.

sharpbender A firm that has been underperforming its rivals in an industry, but suddenly improves and maintains its performance at above the average. Sharpbending may be caused by a new management team, significant new product success, or other major changes in its *business strategy. *See* TURNAROUND.

SHEEP Acronym for *sky-high earnings expectations possibly*: applied to investments that appear to offer an unusually high return but that may prove very unreliable.

shell company 1. A non-trading company, with or without a stock-exchange listing, used as a vehicle for various company manoeuvres or kept dormant for future use in some other capacity. **2.** A company that has ceased to trade and is sold to new owners for a small fee to minimize the cost and trouble of setting up a new company. Some business brokers register such companies with the sole object of selling them to people setting up new businesses. The name and objects of such a company can be changed for a small charge. **3.** A name-plate company set up in a tax haven.

sheqel The standard monetary unit of Israel, divided into 100 agorot.

Shibosai bond A *Samurai bond sold direct by a company to investors, without using a stockbroker.

shilling The standard monetary unit of Kenya (KSh), Somalia (So.Sh.), Tanzania (TSh), and Uganda (USh), divided into 100 cents.

Shingo's Seven Wastes The seven ways that wastage can occur in industrial processes, put forward by Shigeo Shingo, an engineer at Toyota and a noted authority on *just-in-time techniques. They are:
- waste of overproduction – make only what is needed now;
- waste of waiting;
- waste of transportation;
- waste of processing – does this product or part need to be made?;
- waste of stocks;
- waste of motion – first improve, then mechanize or automate;
- waste of making defective products – accept no defects and make no defects.

shipbroker A broker who specializes in arranging charters, cargo space, and sometimes passenger bookings, in return for a brokerage on the business obtained.

shipowner's lien The lien a shipowner has on cargo being carried, if the freight charges are not paid.

shipped bill A *bill of lading confirming that specified goods have been loaded onto a specified ship.

shipper **1.** An organization that exports goods, which it usually owns, to a foreign country by sea or by air. **2.** In some trades, the importer who sells on to merchants or users, especially one that buys FOB port of shipment and pays the freight cost.

shipping and forwarding agent An organization that specializes in the handling of goods sent by sea, air, rail, or road, especially if the goods are being exported or imported. They advise on the best method of transport, book freight, cover insurance, and arrange custom clearance at both ends, if necessary. They usually do all the required paperwork and documentation. They also arrange inland transport in the exporting or importing country, arranging factory-to-factory transport, if it is required.

shipping bill A form used by HM Revenue and Customs before goods can be exported from the UK. It is also required when removing goods from a bonded warehouse before *drawback can be claimed.

shipping conference An association of shipowners whose liners ply the same routes. They combine to fix freight rates, passenger rates, and terms of contracts. Not all liners belong to conferences; those that do are called **conference line ships**.

shipping documents The documents that an exporter of goods delivers to a bank in the exporting country in order to obtain payment for the goods. The bank sends them to its branch or agents in the importing country, who only release them to the importer against payment. Once the importer has these documents, the goods can be claimed at the port of destination. The documents usually consist of a commercial invoice, *bill of lading, insurance policy or certificate, weight note, quality certificate, and, if required, a certificate of origin, consular invoice, and export licence.

shipping ton *See* TON.

ship's certificate of registry A document that the master of a ship must always carry. It records the ship's country of registration, home port, owner's name, registered tonnage, permitted number of passengers, master's name, etc.

ship's papers The documents that the master of a ship must always have available for inspection if required. They include the *ship's certificate of registry, bill of health, log book, the ship's articles (muster roll), the charterparty if the ship is on charter (*see* CHARTERING), cargo *manifest and bills of lading, and passenger manifest if it is carrying passengers.

ship's report A report that the master of a ship must make to the port authorities on arrival at a port. It lists details of the ship, crew, passengers, and cargo.

shirkah *See* ISLAMIC FINANCE.

Shogun bond A bond sold on the Japanese market by a foreign institution and denominated in a foreign currency. *Compare* SAMURAI BOND.

shopping on demand The ability of the Internet to enable customers to shop at any time, day or night, without being curtailed by time or place. This is sometimes referred to as 24/7 access.

shopping product A consumer product that a customer, in the process of selection and purchase, characteristically compares with others taking into account its suitability, quality, price, and style.

shop steward An employee of a firm, who works in a factory or office and is the representative of a trade union. The shop steward is responsible for negotiating with the employers on behalf of the other members of the same union in the factory or office.

short bill A *bill of exchange that is payable at sight, on demand, or within ten days.

short covering The purchasing of goods that have been sold short (see SHORT POSITION) so that the *open position is closed. The dealer in commodities, securities, or foreign exchanges, hopes to cover the shorts at below the price at which they were sold in order to make a profit. Dealers cover their shorts when they expect the market to turn.

short-dated gilt *See* GILT-EDGED SECURITY.

short delivery A delivery of goods that has fewer items than invoiced or a smaller total weight than invoiced. This may be due to accidental loss, which could give rise to an insurance claim, or it may be due to some normal process, such as drying out during shipment, in which case the weight on arrival will be used in a *final invoice. It may also be an attempt by the seller to make an extra profit, in which case the buyer would be well advised to make a claim for short delivery.

short hedging *See* HEDGE.

short interest In marine insurance, the difference between the insured value of goods and their market value, when the insured value exceeds the market value. In these circumstances any excess premium paid can be reclaimed.

short lease A lease that has less than 50 years to run, as defined by the Companies Act (1985). *Compare* LONG LEASE.

short position A position held by a dealer in securities, commodities, currencies, etc., in which sales exceed holdings because the dealer expects prices to fall, enabling the shorts to be covered at a profit. *Compare* LONG POSITION.

shorts 1. *See* GILT-EDGED SECURITY. **2.** Securities, commodities, currencies, etc., of which a dealer is short, i.e. has a *short position.

short selling Selling commodities, securities, currencies, etc., that one does not have. A short seller expects prices to fall so that the short sale can be covered at a profit before the goods have to be delivered. A short seller is a *bear.

short-term capital Capital raised for a short period to cover an exceptional demand for funds over a short period. A bank loan, rather than a debenture, is an example of short-term capital.

short-term instrument A *negotiable instrument that matures in three months or less.

short-termism Any policy that aims to maximize current profits rather than long-term development and wealth. For example, cutting back on research and development reduces immediate costs but may lead to products becoming obsolescent in the future. A company may well experience problems of this kind if managers' salaries or bonuses are linked too closely to short-term results. Similarly, institutional and individual shareholders often overreact to a company's short-term results and policies, causing the company to lose the longer-term focus that is ultimately in the interests of all *stakeholders.

short ton *See* TON.

show stopper A legal action in which the target firm in an unwelcome *takeover bid seeks a permanent injunction to prevent the bidder from persisting in its attempt, on the grounds that the bid is legally defective in some way.

shrinkage The goods that disappear from a retail outlet without being registered as sales. This includes goods that are broken, damaged, stolen, or – in the case of foodstuffs – past their sell-by date and therefore thrown away or given away.

SHRM Abbreviation for *strategic human-resource management.

shut-down cost The costs to be incurred in closing down some part of an organization's activities.

SIA Abbreviation for *Securities Industry Association.

SIB Abbreviation for *Securities and Investment Board.

SIC Abbreviation for *Standard Industrial Classification.

sickness and accident insurance A form of health insurance in which the benefits are paid for a fixed time after the onset of an illness or accident that prevents the insured from working. Premiums can increase each year and renewal can be refused if a claim has been made. *Compare* PERMANENT HEALTH INSURANCE.

side deal A private deal between two people, usually for the personal benefit of one of them, as a subsidiary to a transaction between the officials of a company, government, etc. For example, the chairman of a public company may agree to encourage the board to welcome a takeover bid, provided that a personal profit can be made in some side deal with the bidder. Side deals are rigorously investigated by the Panel on Takeovers and Mergers (*see* CITY CODE ON TAKEOVERS AND MERGERS).

sight bill *See* AT SIGHT.

sight deposit Money deposited in a bank account that can be withdrawn without notice, e.g. money withdrawn by cheque from a current account. In the USA it is known as a *demand deposit.

sight draft Any *bill of exchange that is payable on sight, i.e. on presentation, irrespective of when it was drawn.

signalling hypothesis In investment strategy, the idea that certain decisions made by business organizations reveal their actual position and prospects more accurately than published accounts or other public statements. Thus, dividend policy is often interpreted as a signal of management's view of the firm's future prospects. The signalling hypothesis recognizes a mismatch between the information available to shareholders and managers (*see* ASYMMETRIC INFORMATION) and differences between the interests of these parties (*see* AGENCY RELATIONSHIP).

simple interest *See* INTEREST.

simplified financial statements Simplified versions of the *annual accounts and report intended for readers who do not possess sophisticated financial knowledge. The financial information may be made easier to understand by using simple terminology, showing the information in the forms of graphs and diagrams, providing fuller explanations, and reducing the amount of information. One form of simplified financial statement is the *employee report, which is intended for employees and not covered by legislation; another form is the *summary financial statement intended for shareholders and subject to legislation. *See also* UNDERSTANDABILITY.

simulated test market (Hall test) A laboratory-based marketing research technique for forecasting product sales; it is based upon pretest interviews, forced advertising exposures, simulated store shopping, product trials, and follow-up interviews to measure the repurchase rate.

simulation Recreating or modelling a hypothetical situation in order to consider its likely outcomes and to develop problem-solving strategies. In **computer simulation** all the available data is fed into a computer, which enables a range of possible strategies to be compared. Uncertainty may be modelled by the use of random numbers, as in a *Monte Carlo simulation, or worst cases by the use of *stress testing. In **laboratory simulation** situations are realistically recreated in order to assess possible results or responses. Simulation is widely used in *risk analysis, financial modelling, and marketing.

simultaneous development *See* CONCURRENT ENGINEERING.

simultaneous direct data entry (SDDE) A method used in *computer-assisted telephone interviewing in which questions are displayed on a monitor and the responses (pre-coded) are keyed by the interviewer directly into the computer. It is a relatively fast method of data collection.

simultaneous engineering *See* CONCURRENT ENGINEERING.

simultaneous product development An approach to *new product development in which various departments in a company work closely together so that there is some overlap in the development stages in order to save time and increase effectiveness. *Compare* SEQUENTIAL PRODUCT DEVELOPMENT.

sine die (Latin: without a day) Denoting an adjournment of an action, arbitration, etc., indefinitely.

single-capacity system *See* DUAL-CAPACITY SYSTEM.

single column centimetre A unit used in selling advertising space in printed publications.

single-company PEP *See* PERSONAL EQUITY PLAN.

single-life pension A pension or *annuity that is paid for the lifetime of the beneficiary only, rather than for the lifetime of a surviving spouse. *Compare* JOINT-LIFE AND LAST-SURVIVOR ANNUITIES.

Single Market The concept of a single integrated market that underlies trading in the European Union, as codified in the **Single European Act** (1986), which was introduced in 1987 with a target date of 31 December 1992 for completion. The Single Market came into force on 1 January 1993 with between 90% and 95% of the necessary legislation enacted by all member countries. In practice, however, some of its terms have taken considerably longer to implement. The measures covered by the legislation include:

• the elimination of frontier controls (the full measures have been repeatedly delayed);
• the acceptance throughout the market of professional qualifications;

• the acceptance of national standards for product harmonization;
• open tendering for public supply contracts;
• the free movement of capital between states;
• a reduction of state aid for certain industries;
• the harmonization of VAT and excise duties throughout the market.

single-premium assurance A life-assurance policy in which the insured pays only one capital sum rather than regular premiums. *See also* INVESTMENT BOND.

single-product strategy A strategy that involves a company offering only one product or one product version with very few options. Few companies or organizations find themselves using this strategy because the risks are too high (if the single product fails).

single property ownership trust (SPOT) A single property trust; shares in the trust entitle their holder to a direct share of the property's income and capital. A form of *securitization, a share in a SPOT is similar to a *property income certificate (PINC).

single-source data systems Electronic monitoring systems that link consumers' exposure to television advertising and promotion (measured using television meters) with what they buy in stores (measured using store checkout scanners).

single-tax system A system of taxation in which there would be only one major tax, usually a *comprehensive income tax, instead of several taxes, such as income tax, capital gains tax, and National Insurance, as in the UK. Arguments in favour of such taxes are that they should be less avoidable and should simplify administration. On the other hand the present variety of taxes is designed for a variety of purposes and flexibility may be lost in a single-tax system. *See also* FLAT TAX.

sinking fund A fund set up to replace a *wasting asset at the end of its useful life. Usually a regular annual sum is set aside to enable the fund, taking into account interest at the expected rate, to replace the exhausted asset at a specified date. Some have argued that amounts set aside for *depreciation of an asset should be equal to the annual amounts needed to be placed in a notional sinking fund.

SI Statement *See* WRITTEN STATEMENT OF TERMS OF EMPLOYMENT.

sister-ship clause A clause used in marine insurance policies, enabling the insurer to make a claim as a result of a collision between two ships both owned by the same insurer. Without this clause, the insurer may have no claim as it is not possible to sue oneself.

sit-down strike A strike in which workers come to their place of work, but refuse to either work or to go home. In a **work-in**, the workers refuse to leave the place of work and continue working, usually in spite of management instructions not to do so.

site availability An indication of the ease with which a user can be connected to a website. In theory this figure should be 100%, but for technical reasons, such as failures in the server hardware or upgrades to software, users cannot always access the site and the figure can fall below 90%.

site stickiness An indication of how long a visitor stays on a website. *Log file analysers can be used to assess average visit times.

situational analysis The process of analysing the past and future situations facing an organization in order to identify problems and opportunities. *See* SWOT.

situational leadership theory A *contingency theory of leadership holding that *leadership style should be varied according to the maturity of followers, which encompasses such factors as experience in the job and willingness to take responsibility. Where maturity is low, leaders should be *task-motivated and directive; as maturity increases, leaders should be increasingly *relationship-motivated and supportive.

SI units Système International d'Unités: an international metric system of units used in science and increasingly for commercial purposes. It is based on the seven basic units: metre, kilogram, second, ampere, kelvin, candela, and mole. Derived units with special names include the hertz (frequency), joule (energy), volt (potential), and watt (power). They are used with a standard set of multiples and submultiples, including hecto- ($\times$ 100), kilo- ($\times$ 1000), centi- ($\times$ 1/100), and milli- ($\times$ 1/1000).

six-month money Money invested on the *money market for a period of six months. If it is withdrawn before the six months have elapsed there may be a heavy penalty, although if the market has moved in favour of the recipient of the funds, this penalty may be negligible.

skip-day The two-day period allowed before payment has to be made for a security purchased on the US *money market.

SL Abbreviation for *specification limits.

slack time (float) The difference between the amount of time an activity takes and the amount of time allocated to it in *network modelling. Activities that constitute the critical path in a project are those for which there is no slack time. Activities not on the critical path have an earliest and a latest possible start and finish time. The difference between the two is the slack time.

sleeping partner A person who has capital in a *partnership but takes no part in its commercial activities. He or she has all the legal benefits and obligations of ownership and shares in the profits of the partnership in accordance with the provisions laid down in the partnership agreement.

sliding peg *See* CRAWLING PEG.

slump *See* DEPRESSION.

slush fund A fund that is used by an individual, political organization, or company for illegal purposes. For example, a company may have a slush fund for bribing potential customers.

small company Under UK company law, a private company that satisfies at least two of the following criteria for the current and preceding financial year:
• its *net worth does not exceed £2.8 million;
• its *turnover does not exceed £5.6 million;
• the average number of employees does not exceed 50.

A company that is in its first financial year may still qualify as a small company if it falls within these limits. Alternatively, if the company has qualified in the two preceding financial years, it may qualify. If a company is a member of a *group containing a public company, a banking or insurance company, or an authorized person under the Financial Services Act (1986), it is not eligible for the exemptions for small companies.

Certain small companies may prepare accounts for their members under the special provisions of sections 246 and 246A of the Companies Act (1985). In addition, they may prepare and deliver *abbreviated accounts to the Registrar of Companies.

Some small companies with a turnover of less than £1 million (£250,000 for companies that are charities) and assets of less than £1.4 million can also claim total exemption from *statutory audit. A company with a turnover of between £1 million and £5.6 million (and balance-sheet total of not more than £2.8 million) may also take advantage of the small company *audit exemption, but will need an audit exemption report.

Further details of filing exemptions are available at the Department of Trade and Industry website at www.dti.gov.uk There is a link to the *Companies House website. *Compare* MEDIUM-SIZED COMPANY.

small group A *group that meets two out of three of the following criteria for the current and preceding year, or the two preceding financial years:
- its *net worth should not exceed £2.8 million net or £3.6 million gross;
- its *turnover should not exceed £5.6 million net or £6.72 million gross;
- the average number of employees should not exceed 50.

If a group is in its first financial year, it may still qualify if it falls within these limits.

A group containing a public company, a banking or insurance company, or an authorized person under the Financial Services Act (1986) is ineligible for the exemptions for small groups.

Under the Companies Act, a parent company is not required to prepare *group accounts for a financial year in which the group headed by that parent

qualifies as a small group. A small group may file *abbreviated accounts instead of full accounts with the *Registrar of Companies. Further details of filing exemptions can be obtained from the Department of Trade and Industry website at www.dti.gov.uk There is a link to the *Companies House website. *Compare* MEDIUM-SIZED GROUP.

small print Printed matter on a document, such as a life-assurance policy or hire-purchase agreement, in which the seller sets out the conditions of the sale and the mutual liabilities of buyer and seller. The use of a very small type size and unintelligible jargon is often intended to obscure the buyer's legal rights and safeguards. This unfair practice has largely been remedied by the various Acts that provide *consumer protection. *See also* COOLING-OFF PERIOD.

smart ad An advertisement targeted to specific users of a product or service, based on their observable characteristics and behaviour.

smart card A plastic card that contains a microprocessor that stores and updates information, typically used in performing financial transactions. Unlike an ordinary *debit card or *cash card, a smart card memorizes all transactions in which the card is used. Other uses include storing a person's medical records.

smart money Money invested by experienced and successful people, especially those with inside information about a particular project or investment opportunity.

smart offer A dynamic presentation of an offer to an individual on a website, based on that visitor's history.

smokestack industries An informal name for traditional British industries, especially heavy engineering manufacturers, as opposed to modern industries, such as electronics, etc.

SMP Abbreviation for statutory maternity pay. *See* MATERNITY RIGHTS.

snowball sampling In *marketing research, a sampling technique in which the selection of additional respondents is based on referrals from the initial respondents. Thus, the interviewer might ask the respondents if they know someone else who owned brand X. Clearly, the danger is that interviews are conducted with similar persons.

social accounting issues Issues that concern the impact of an entity on society, both within the organization and externally. Social accounting issues may include charitable donations of equipment and time, education initiatives (such as sponsorships and research funding), product safety, community involvement, employment of disadvantaged groups, and the provision of sports equipment or sponsorship. Environmental issues that are often also included under this heading include energy conservation and control of pollution. *See* SOCIAL RESPONSIBILITY REPORTING.

social audit An *audit of the non-financial impact of an organization on society. For example, an *environmental audit is one kind of social audit. Other aspects may be of interest to other stakeholder groups, such as customers, employees, and the wider community. The object is to enable a firm to assess its performance in relation to society. *See also* SOCIAL RESPONSIBILITY REPORTING.

Social Chapter The section of the founding treaty of the *European Union that reflects the agreement of member states with respect to social policy. The objectives of the Social Chapter are to promote employment, improve living and working conditions, establish dialogue between management and workers by means of works councils, implement proper social protection, and develop human resources with a view to lasting high employment. After much resistance, the British government finally agreed to the incorporation of these social aims and objectives into the main body of the treaty in 1997. This has led to a number of changes to UK law, including the implementation of unpaid parental leave and new rights for part-time workers (who are now entitled to be treated no less favourably than comparable full-time workers in their contractual terms and conditions).

social classes A system for classifying the population according to social status. According to the classification issued by

the UK *Office for National Statistics, there are seven classes for those in work and an eighth class for those on benefit:

- 1A — Large employers, senior managers, senior police and service officers, etc.;
- 1B — Professional people, including teachers, airline pilots, etc.;
- 2 — Journalists, nurses, actors, lower managers, NCOs, etc.;
- 3 — Professional sportspeople, secretaries, etc.;
- 4 — Small employers and the nonprofessional self-employed (e.g. plumbers);
- 5 — Skilled workers, train drivers, foremen, etc.;
- 6 — Caretakers, gardeners, assembly-line workers, etc.;
- 7 — Cleaners, dockers, road workers, etc.;
- 8 — The long-term unemployed and the sick.

social cost The cost of a product that is not paid by its producer but is paid by society in general. An example would be the environmental cost involved in a production process that involves the discharge of pollutants into the environment (i.e. into the sea or the atmosphere). *See also* EXTERNALITY.

social loafing The general tendency for people to expend less effort on a task when working as part of a group than when working individually. There have been various attempts to explain this phenomenon. *See* COLLECTIVE EFFORT MODEL; RINGELMANN EFFECT; SUCKER EFFECT.

socially responsible investment *See* ETHICAL INVESTMENT.

social marketing *See* NON-PROFIT MARKETING.

social overhead capital *See* INFRASTRUCTURE.

social responsibility reporting (corporate social reporting) The reporting of *social accounting issues by a business. These may be discussed in the *annual accounts and report or form the basis of a separate report. Social responsibility costs are the costs to the business of e.g. equipment donated, sponsorship given, or charitable donations. The monetary quantification of social benefits is much harder to measure and necessarily subjective. Owing to the concerns of consumers, investors, and other stakeholders, companies are increasingly obliged to be environmentally and socially conscious. *See also* GREEN REPORTING; SOCIAL AUDIT.

social security A government system for paying allowances to the sick and the unemployed, as well as maternity benefits and retirement pensions. Other low-income members of society are also eligible, such as the disabled and single-parent families. In the UK this is now (since 2001) the responsibility of the Department for Work and Pensions; the *National Insurance scheme that funds the social security payments is now administered by an agency of HM Treasury.

sociedad anónima *See* SA.

sociedade anónima *See* SA.

società a responsabilità limitata *See* SARL.

societal marketing concept **1.** A form of marketing that takes into consideration the long-term welfare of society. For many years the individual needs of consumers dominated the practice of marketing. For example, two cars might be compared in terms of their acceleration. It is now recognized, however, that both cars may have jeopardized the long-term welfare of society as a result of the pollution they cause. Adapting both cars to run on lead-free petrol is an example of the way in which societal marketing concepts are being used. **2.** Marketing techniques applied to a social cause, such as an anti-pollution campaign or an anti-smoking campaign.

società per azioni *See* SPA.

societas Europea A business entity created by the merger of two or more companies resident in different member states of the European Union.

société anonyme *See* SA.

société à responsabilité limitée *See* SARL.

sociogram A diagrammatical representation of patterns of interpersonal relationships amongst group members (likes or dislikes, communication links, etc.).

Usually, each member is represented by a letter or symbol and the various links are shown by arrows. The use of sociograms to analyse intergroup relationships is known as **sociometry**.

socio-technical system A system involving the interaction of *hard systems and human beings, in ways that either cannot be separated or are thought to be inappropriate to separate.

soft benefits Such benefits as improved quality and customer satisfaction that are hard to measure but have indirect benefits to the firm.

soft commodities (softs) Commodities, other than metals. They include cocoa, coffee, grains, potatoes, and sugar.

soft currency A currency that is not freely convertible and for which there is only a *thin market. *Compare* HARD CURRENCY.

soft landing The situation in which an economy slows down but does not go into a recession. The term was first used in astronautics journals of the late 1950s to describe a safe moon landing.

soft loan A special type of government loan in which the terms and conditions of repayment are more generous (or softer) than they would be under normal finance circumstances. For example, the interest rate might be less and the repayment term might be for a longer period.

soft sell The use of unobtrusive methods of selling as opposed to those employed in a *hard sell. Implication, rather than forceful statement and relentless repetition, form the basis of a soft sell.

soft systems methodology (SSM) A method for intervening in problem situations that have a human or social component, as opposed to being purely technological. The method suggests that systems capable of producing desired outputs frequently fail because the participants in these systems have differing views of the world, based on differing values and standards. SSM involves the widest possible research into the nature of the problem, the production of root definitions and conceptual models, the identification of feasible and desirable changes, and, finally, recommendations for action.

software The programs used with a computer, together with their documentation, as opposed to the physical parts of the computer system (*hardware). A distinction is made between systems software, or those programs that control the functioning of the computer itself, and *applications software, such as accounting or *audit software, which is designed to serve a particular specialized function. *See* BUSINESS SOFTWARE PACKAGE.

Sogo Shosa The Japanese word for large overseas trading companies that have a wide spread of commercial and industrial activities.

sol *See* NEW SOL.

sold day book *See* SALES DAY BOOK.

sold note *See* CONTRACT NOTE.

sole agency An agreement between an agent and a principal that gives the agent exclusive rights to sell a product or service in a particular territory for a specified period.

sole proprietor An individual who runs an unincorporated business on his or her own. Generally, a sole proprietor of a business is known as a **sole trader** and a sole proprietor of a professional practice, such as an accountant or solicitor, as a **sole practitioner**.

solicitor's letter A letter written by a solicitor, usually threatening to take a matter to court.

solo (sola) A single *bill of exchange of which no other copies are in circulation.

solus position An isolated position for a poster or press advertisement, so that it is separated from any competitive announcement. *Compare* SEMISOLUS.

solus site A retail outlet, such as a petrol station, that carries the products of only one company.

solvency **1.** The financial state of a person or company that is able to pay all debts as they fall due. **2.** The amount by which the assets of a bank exceed its liabilities.

solvency ratio **1.** The ratio of a bank's own assets to its liabilities. **2.** A ratio used by the UK Department of Trade and Industry to evaluate the stability of insurance companies; it is the ratio of the company's net assets to its non-life premium income.

som (*plural* **somy**; KGS) The standard monetary unit of Kyrgyzstan, divided into 100 tyiyn.

sort code A sequence of numbers on a cheque or a bank card that serves to identify the branch holding the account.

source and application of funds (source and disposition of funds) A statement describing how a business has raised and used its funds for a specified period. Sources of funds are typically trading profits, issues of shares or loan stock, sales of fixed assets, and borrowings. Applications are typically trading losses, purchases of fixed assets, dividends paid, and repayment of borrowings. Any balancing figure represents an increase or decrease in *working capital. Formerly, a statement of source and application of funds (a **funds flow statement**) was required by *Statement of Standard Accounting Practice 10, Statements of Source and Application of Funds, to be produced by a company if its turnover or gross income was above a specified threshold. However, this is now obsolete since SSAP 10 has been withdrawn and replaced by *Financial Reporting Standard 1, Cash Flow Statements.

source document The first document to record a transaction.

sources of power The six major areas that can be used to build a power base by a person or unit working in a large organization:

• **Political network** – support is built up by communication with peers, subordinates, and those not in direct authority. This method is dependent on the person's communication channels within an organization.

• **Perception of dependence** – support comes from the belief that the person controls scarce resources and has the power to allocate them.

• **Work unit power** – power deriving from a department's ability to deal with uncertainty, the uniqueness of its functions, changes in its external environment, etc.

- **Work activities** – power arising by exploiting the visible and necessary differences within the organization.
- **Charisma** – a person who is continuously successful, especially one who takes high risks, often comes to be highly regarded by others, who become inspired by his or her ideas and committed to implement them (*see* CHARISMATIC LEADER; TRANSFORMATIONAL LEADERSHIP). This in turn strengthens the person's knowledge, reputation, and credibility.

See also POWER STYLES.

sovereign risk *See* POLITICAL CREDIT RISK.

SpA Abbreviation for *società per azioni*. It appears after the name of a public limited company in Italy, being equivalent to the British abbreviation plc. *Compare* SARL.

spamming Sending unsolicited and unwanted e-mails in bulk for advertising purposes. The proliferation of such material has become a serious nuisance to many business users.

SPC Abbreviation for *statistical process control.

special clearing The clearing of a cheque through the UK banking system in less than the normal three days, for a small additional charge. A cheque for which a special clearing has been arranged can usually be passed through the system in one day.

Special Commissioners A body of civil servants who are specialized tax lawyers appointed by the Lord Chancellor to hear appeals against assessments to income tax, corporation tax, capital gains tax, and inheritance tax. Hearings are informal and appellants may present their own case or be represented. *See also* GENERAL COMMISSIONERS.

special crossing A crossing on a *cheque in which the name of a bank is written between the crossing lines. A cheque so crossed can only be paid into the named bank.

special deposits Deposits that the UK government may instruct the clearing banks to make at the Bank of England, as a means of restricting credit in the econ-omy. The less money the clearing banks have at their disposal, the less they are able to lend to businesses. A similar system has been used by the Federal Reserve System in the USA.

special dividend (extra dividend) A single irregular *dividend payment. It is usually made after an especially profitable year but is sometimes associated with the restructuring of companies.

Special Drawing Rights (SDRs) The standard unit of account used by the *International Monetary Fund (IMF). In 1970 members of the IMF were allocated SDRs in proportion to the quotas of currency that they had subscribed to the fund on its formation. There have since been further allocations. SDRs can be used to settle international trade balances and to repay debts to the IMF itself. On the instructions of the IMF a member country must supply its own currency to another member, in exchange for SDRs, unless it already holds more than three times its original allocation. The value of SDRs was originally expressed in terms of gold, but since 1974 it has been valued in terms of its members' currencies. SDRs provide a credit facility for IMF members in addition to their existing credit facilities (hence the name); unlike these existing facilities they do not have to be repaid, thus forming a permanent addition to members' reserves and functioning as an international reserve currency.

specialized industry An industry in which there are many opportunities for a firm to create a competitive advantage that gives a high pay-off.

special manager A person appointed by the court in the liquidation of a company or bankruptcy of an individual to assist the *liquidator or *official receiver to manage the business of the company or individual. The special manager's powers are decided by the court.

special notice *See* RESOLUTION.

special resolution A *resolution of the members of a company that must be approved by at least 75% of the members to be valid. Members must have been given at least 21 days' notice of the meeting at which the resolution is proposed and the notice of the meeting must give details of the special resolution. *See also* ORDINARY RESOLUTION; EXTRAORDINARY RESOLUTION.

specialty goods Consumer goods with unique characteristics or a strong brand identification for which a significant number of buyers is willing to make a special purchase effort. For example, if a store is out of stock of this brand, the consumer will go to another store to find it; if it is not available there, they will wait until new supplies become available.

specialty store A retail store that carries a narrow *product line with a wide assortment within that line. Specialty stores include specialist record shops, PC retail outlets, etc.

specie Money in the form of coins, rather than bank notes or bullion.

specification limits (SL) The limits of acceptable variation in the characteristics of a component or product. Outside those limits the item is not fit for use. *See* STATISTICAL PROCESS CONTROL.

specific bank guarantee An unconditional guarantee from the *Export Credits Guarantee Department to a UK bank enabling that bank to finance an exporter's medium-term credit to an export customer without recourse; the arrangement is known as **supplier credit** in contrast to the buyer credit under which the bank finances the overseas buyer to pay the exporter on cash terms.

specific charge *See* CHARGE; FIXED CHARGE.

specific indicators *See* PERFORMANCE MEASUREMENT.

specific performance An equitable legal remedy requiring the parties to carry out the contract they have entered into. This will be granted by a court only if damages are an inadequate remedy and if it is possible to perform the contract. It is the usual remedy in cases in which there is a breach of contract for the sale of land.

specific risk (non-systematic risk) The *risk associated with each of the individual assets in a *portfolio, as opposed to the *systematic risk associated with the market as a whole. It can be eliminated by *diversification. *Portfolio theory holds

that investors should maintain a diversified portfolio in order to maximize the utility of their investments. Because specific risk can be eliminated in this way, there is no requirement for a *risk premium for taking specific risks. This is an important underlying principle of the *capital asset pricing model and *arbitrage pricing theory. Specific risk is measured by the *alpha coefficient.

speculation The purchase or sale of something for the sole purpose of making a capital gain. For professional speculators the security, commodity, and foreign exchange markets are natural venues as they cater for speculation as well as investment and trading. Indeed, speculators help to make a viable market and thus smooth out price fluctuations. This is particularly true of commodity futures and option markets (*see* LONDON INTERNATIONAL FINANCIAL FUTURES AND OPTIONS EXCHANGE).

speculative risk *See* RISK.

spin-off A commercially valuable product or process that emerges as an unexpected benefit from a research project in another field. For example, the non-stick saucepan coating Teflon (trademark) came from the US space programme.

splash page A preliminary page that precedes the normal *home page of a website. Site users can either wait to be redirected to the home page or can follow a link to do so. Splash pages are now less commonly used than formerly as they slow down the process by which customers find the information they need.

split *See* SHARE SPLITTING.

split-capital investment trust (split-level trust; split trust) An *investment trust with a limited life in which the equity capital is divided into various classes of income shares and capital shares. Holders of income shares receive all or most of the income earned plus a predetermined capital value on liquidation. Holders of capital shares receive little or no income but are entitled to all of the assets remaining after repayment of the income shares.

spoilage *See* WASTE.

sponsor 1. The financial institution, usually a merchant bank or investment bank, that handles the *flotation of a company. It will supervise the preparation of the *prospectus and make sure that the company is aware of the benefits and obligations of being a public company. **2.** The lender in a *project financing agreement.

sporadic problem A short-term nonrandom problem that may cause a process to deviate from its control limits. *See* STATISTICAL PROCESS CONTROL.

SPOT Abbreviation for *single property ownership trust.

spot goods Commodities that are available for immediate delivery, as opposed to futures (*see* FUTURES CONTRACT) in which deliveries are arranged for named months in the future. The price of spot goods, the **spot price**, is usually higher than the forward price, unless there is a glut of that particular commodity but an expected shortage in the future.

spot market A market that deals in commodities or *foreign exchange for immediate delivery. Immediate delivery in foreign currencies usually means within two business days. For commodities it usually means within seven days. *Compare* FORWARD DEALING; FUTURES CONTRACT.

spot month The month during which goods bought on a futures contract will become available for delivery.

spot price *See* SPOT GOODS.

spread **1.** The difference between the buying and selling price made by a *market maker on the stock exchange. **2.** The diversity of the investments in a *portfolio. The greater the spread of a portfolio the less volatile it will be. **3.** The simultaneous purchase and sale of commodity futures (*see* FUTURES CONTRACT) in the hope that movement in their relative prices will enable a profit to be made. This may include a purchase and sale of the same commodity for the same delivery, but on different commodity exchanges (*see* STRADDLE), or a purchase and sale of the same commodity for different deliveries.

spreadsheet A computer application used for tabular calculations. A spreadsheet display consists of a large number of cells arranged in rows and columns. Gen-

erally, columns are labelled by a letter, or combination of letters, and rows are labelled by numbers. Each cell in the array has a unique identification: A1, A2, etc., B1, B2, etc. The user can enter text, numbers, or formulas into individual cells. The formulas can be used to perform calculations on values in other cells. For example, A1*100/B1 gives the value in cell A1 and expresses it as a percentage of the value in cell B1. A formula of the type sum (A1:A20) adds all the values in the cells from A1 to A20. Values and formulas can be copied from a single cell to a block of cells. In this way it is possible to set up complex calculations for accounting or financial modelling purposes. Spreadsheet programs generally have a facility for producing graphs and charts automatically from the data. Widely used spreadsheets include Excel, Lotus 1-2-3, and Quattro Pro.

Square Mile *See* CITY.

squeeze **1.** Controls imposed by a government to restrict inflation. An income (pay) squeeze limits increases in wage and salaries, a *credit squeeze limits the amounts that banks and other moneylenders can lend, a dividend (profits) squeeze restricts increases in dividends. **2.** Any action on a market that forces buyers to come into the market and prices to rise. In a bear squeeze (*see* BEAR) dealers holding a *short position are forced to cover in order to deliver. It may be restricted to a particular commodity or security or a particular delivery month may be squeezed, pushing its price up against the rest of the market.

SRO Abbreviation for *Self-Regulating Organization.

SSAP Abbreviation for *Statement of Standard Accounting Practice.

SSL Abbreviation for *secure sockets layer.

SSM Abbreviation for *soft systems methodology.

SSP **1.** Abbreviation for *statutory sick pay. **2.** Abbreviation for State Second Pension. *See* STATE EARNINGS-RELATED PENSION SCHEME.

staff management *See* LINE AND STAFF MANAGEMENT.

stag A person who applies for shares in a *new issue in the hope that the price when trading begins will be higher than the *issue price. Often measures will be taken by the issuers to prevent excessive stagging; it is usually illegal for would-be investors to attempt to obtain large numbers of shares by making multiple applications. Issuers will often scale down share applications to prevent such quick-profit taking, e.g. by ballot.

stagflation A combination of slow economic growth with rising prices. The UK and the USA experienced stagflation for the first time in the 1970s.

staggered directorships A measure used as a defence against unwanted *takeover bids. If the company concerned resolves that the terms of office served by its directors are to be staggered and that no director can be removed from office without due cause, a bidder cannot gain control of the board for some years, even if he has a controlling interest of the shares. *See* POISON PILL.

STAGS Acronym for Sterling Transferable Accruing Government Securities. These European sterling bonds are backed by a holding of Treasury stock. They are *deep-discount bonds paying no interest.

stakeholder pension scheme In the UK, a type of low-cost pension available since April 2001. Employers with five or more employees have to make a stakeholder pension available to their staff. Stakeholder pensions are bought from authorized financial institutions, such as insurance companies, banks, and building societies. The pension providers can only charge a maximum of 1% of the value of the pension fund each year to manage the fund, plus costs and charges. Any extra services and any extra charges not provided for by law, such as advice on choosing a pension or life assurance cover, must be optional. All stakeholder schemes will accept contributions of as little as £20, payable weekly, monthly, or at less regular intervals. The scheme must be run by trustees or by an authorized stakeholder manager.

stakeholders All those with interests in an organization; for example, as *shareholders, employees, suppliers, customers, or members of the wider community (who could be affected by environmental consequences of an organization's activities). **Stakeholder theory** is an approach to business that attempts to incorporate the interests of all stakeholders in a business, as opposed to the view that a firm is responsible only to its owners (*see* SHAREHOLDER VALUE). It thus attempts to adopt an inclusive rather than a narrow approach to business responsibility.

stale bull A dealer or speculator who has a *long position in something, usually a commodity, which is showing a *paper profit but which the dealer cannot realize as there are no buyers at the higher levels. Being fully committed financially and therefore unable to increase the bull position, the dealer may be unable to trade.

stale cheque A cheque that, in the UK, has not been presented for payment within six months of being written. The bank will not honour it, returning it marked 'out of date'.

stalemate industry An industry whose products are characterized by few opportunities to create competitive advantages against existing products.

stamp duty A UK tax collected by stamping the legal documents giving effect to specific transactions. Stamp duty was formerly levied on a wide range of instruments. However, the only transactions that now give rise to stamp duty proper are those in which traditional stampable documents are used to effect the transfer of securities. Since 1999 paperless transactions in shares or other securities have been taxed by **stamp duty reserve tax**. The majority of transactions on UK exchanges are now of this kind.

In 2003 the stamp duty on transfers of land was replaced by **stamp duty land tax**. The rate is 1% of the purchase price of properties sold for between £120,000 and £250,000, and 3% of the price of those between £250,000 and £500,000. Above this figure it is 4%.

Standard and Poor's 500 Stock Index (S&P 500) The widest general-market index of stocks produced by the US credit-rating agency Standard and Poor; it is made up of 425 shares in US industrial companies and 75 stocks in railway and public-utility corporations.

standard application blank (SAB) A standardized application form used to obtain *biodata on the candidates for a job. This enables objective scoring of the candidates according to the information supplied. In a **weighted application blank (WAB)** different weightings are applied to the various categories of data according to their importance as predictors of success in the job.

standard cash flow pattern In a *discounted cash flow calculation, the situation in which the projected cash flows are made up of an initial cash outflow followed by subsequent cash inflows over the life of the project, there being no net cash outflows in subsequent years. Such patterns are rare in practice.

standard cost In *standard costing systems, a predetermined unit cost of a product or service. It is important to emphasize that standard cost is a unit cost concept.

standard cost allowance Under a *standard costing system, the level of expenditure allowed to be incurred for *variable costs, taking into account the actual levels of activity achieved. For example, the standard cost allowance for *direct materials is obtained from the actual number of units produced multiplied by the *standard direct materials cost per unit.

standard costing A system of cost ascertainment and control in which predetermined *standard costs and income for products and operations are set and periodically compared with actual costs incurred and income generated in order to establish any *variances. Standard costing systems are very expensive to develop and maintain; they were also designed for traditional manufacturing systems in which direct labour and direct materials are the most important costs. Recent years have seen a decline in the use of such systems as companies become less labour intensive.

standard deviation A measure of the dispersion of statistical data. For a series of

n values x_1, x_2, x_n, it is given by the formula

$$\sqrt{[(1/n) \sum (x_i - x)]}$$

where x is the average of the n values. The standard deviation of the returns from an investment can be used as a measure of the risk associated with that investment.

standard direct labour cost In *standard costing, a standard cost derived from the *standard time allowed for the performance of an operation and the *standard direct labour rate for the operators specified for that operation.

standard direct labour rate A predetermined rate of pay for *direct labour operators used for establishing *standard direct labour costs in a *standard costing system; it provides a basis for comparison with the actual direct labour rates paid.

standard direct materials cost In *standard costing, a standard cost derived from the standard quantity of materials allowed for the production of a product and the *standard direct materials price for the materials specified for that product.

standard direct materials price In *standard costing, a predetermined price for *direct materials used for establishing *standard direct materials costs in order to provide a basis for comparison with the actual direct material prices paid.

standard fixed overhead cost In *standard costing, a standard cost derived from the standard time allowed for the performance of an operation or the production of a product and the standard fixed overhead *absorption rate per unit of time for that operation or product.

standard hour A measure of production (not time) that represents the amount of work, number of units produced, etc., that can be achieved within an hour under normal conditions. It is used to calculate the *efficiency ratio and a range of *variances that measure the more or less efficient use of *direct labour or production time.

Standard Industrial Classification (SIC) A system developed by the UK and US governments for classifying various industries in order to produce official industrial statistical information. The basis of the classification is an industry's supply characteristic. The British classification follows the principles of the International Standard Industrial Classification.

standardization strategy *See* GLOBALIZATION STRATEGY.

standardized marketing mix A marketing strategy adopted by multinational companies for using basically the same products, advertising, distribution channels, and other elements of the *marketing mix in all the company's international markets. *See* GLOBALIZATION STRATEGY.

standard marginal costing In a *marginal costing system, a system of cost ascertainment and control in which predetermined standards for marginal costs and income generated for products and operations are set and periodically compared with actual marginal costs incurred and income generated in order to establish any *variances.

standard materials usage In *standard costing, a predetermined quantity of materials to be used in the manufacture of a product; this is compared with actual usage of *direct materials to calculate any *variance.

standard mix **1.** The predetermined proportions in which a mixture of different materials are intended to be used in a manufacturing process. It is set as a standard for the purposes of calculating any *variances arising from differences in the proportions or quantity of direct materials used. **2.** The budgeted total volume of sales of an organization expressed in predetermined proportions of its range of related products. It is set as a standard for the purposes of calculating any variances arising from differences in the actual *sales mix or volume of sales achieved.

standard operating cost The total of all the *standard cost allowances for the actual level of activity achieved by an organization.

standard operating profit The *budgeted revenue from an operation less the *standard operating cost.

standard overhead cost A standard cost for the fixed and/or variable overhead of an operation derived from the standard time allowed for the performance of the operation or the production of a product and the standard overhead *absorption rate per unit of time for that operation or product.

standard performance (standard operator performance) A concept used in *work measurement to achieve comparability between a range of observations, for determining standard overhead costs, and as the basis for the calculation of some performance-related bonus schemes. Standard performance is defined as the rate of output that a qualified worker achieves as an average over the working day, shift, or hour provided that the worker adheres to the specified work method and is well motivated. This performance is denoted as 100 on the standard rating and performance scales.

standard production cost The *production costs of products and operations calculated from predetermined levels of performance and cost in order to provide a yardstick against which actual production costs can be compared for the purposes of cost ascertainment and control.

standard purchase price A predetermined price set for each commodity of *direct material for a specified period. These prices are compared with the actual prices paid during the period in order to establish *direct materials price variances in a system of *standard costing.

standard rate **1.** The rate of *value added tax applied to all items sold by *taxable persons that are not specified as either *exempt supplies, *zero-rated goods and services, or taxable at a special rate. The rate for 2004–05 is 17.5%, which has been the rate since 1 April 1991. Previously the standard rate was 15%. **2.** The marginal rate of tax for most taxpayers. *See* BASIC RATE OF INCOME TAX.

standard rate of pay A predetermined rate of pay set for each classification of labour for a period. These rates are compared with the actual rates paid during the period in order to establish *direct labour rate of pay *variances in a system of *standard costing.

standard selling price A predetermined selling price set for each product sold for a specified period. In *standard costing, these prices are compared with the actual prices obtained during the period in order to establish any *variance.

standard time The time allowed to carry out a production task in a *standard costing system. It may be expressed as the standard time allowed or alternatively, when expressed in *standard hours, as the output achieved.

standard variable overhead cost A standard cost derived from the standard time allowed for the performance of an operation or the production of a product and the standard variable overhead *absorption rate per unit of time for that operation or product.

standby agreement An agreement between the *International Monetary Fund and a member state, enabling the member to arrange for immediate drawing rights in addition to its normal drawing rights in such cases of emergency as a temporary balance of payments crisis.

standby credit A *letter of credit that guarantees a loan or other form of credit facility. The bank that issues it promises to refund the amount borrowed if the borrower defaults on repayment. It calls for a certificate of default by the applicant. In a *note issuance facility a standby credit is a third-party guarantee to honour an issue to an investor who may have a low credit rating. See also REVOLVING BANK FACILITY.

standing order An instruction by a customer to a bank (**banker's order**) or building society to pay a specified amount of money on a specified date or dates to a specified payee. Standing orders are widely used for such regular payments as insurance premiums, subscriptions, etc. See also CREDIT TRANSFER.

standstill agreement 1. An agreement between two countries in which a debt owed by one to the other is held in abeyance until a specified date in the future. **2.** An agreement between an unwelcome bidder for a company and the company, in which the bidder agrees to buy no more of the company's shares for a specified period. **3.** An arrangement between banks who have loans to a company in trouble, in which they each agree to maintain their existing credit facilities

and not to force the company into receivership by acting alone.

star See BOSTON MATRIX.

starting rate of income tax A rate of *income tax below the *basic rate of income tax; it was reintroduced in the UK in 1999 to replace the *lower rate of income tax. The starting rate is currently 10%, which is charged on taxable income up to £2090 (2005–06).

start-up A new business or other project, especially one seeking finance.

start-up costs The initial expenditure incurred in the setting up of an operation or project. The start-up costs may include the capital investment costs plus the initial revenue expenditure prior to the start of operations.

state banks Commercial banks in the USA that were established by state charter rather than federal charter (*compare* NATIONAL BANKS). The rules governing their trading are controlled by state laws and there are therefore differences in practices from state to state. State banks are not compelled to join the *Federal Reserve System, although national banks are. State banks are regulated by state banking departments and by the *Federal Deposit Insurance Corporation (FDIC). Even if they choose not to join the Federal Reserve System, they must abide by its rules, particularly on consumer credit protection.

State Earnings-Related Pension Scheme (SERPS) A scheme, started in 1978, run by the UK government to provide a pension for every employed person in addition to the basic state flat-rate pension. The contributions are paid from part of the National Insurance payments made by employees and employers. Payment of the pension starts at the state retirement age and the amount of pension received is calculated using a formula based on a percentage of the person's earnings. Persons who wish to contract out of SERPS may subscribe to an *occupational pension scheme, a *personal pension scheme, or a *stakeholder pension scheme. From 2003 SERPS will be slowly phased out in favour of the **State Second Pension** (**SSP** or **S2P**), a flat-rate scheme targeted at those on lower incomes.

S

statement of account A document recording the transactions of an organization with its customer for a specified period and normally showing the indebtedness of one to the other. Many firms issue statements to their customers every month to draw attention to any unpaid invoices.

statement of affairs A statement showing the assets and liabilities of a person who is bankrupt or of a company in liquidation.

Statement of Auditing Standards (SAS) 1. Any of the statements issued by the Auditing Practices Board (APB) on basic principles and essential procedures in auditing. Auditors are required to comply with an SAS, except where otherwise stated in the SAS concerned, in the conduct of any audit of *financial statements. **2.** Any of the statements laying down accepted US auditing standards issued by the Auditing Standards Board of the American Institute of Certified Public Accountants (AICPA). Members of the AICPA have to explain any deviation from SAS principles in their audit reports.

statement of changes in financial position A US term for a statement of *source and application of funds or *cash flow.

Statement of Financial Accounting Standards (SFAS) In the USA, any of the statements detailing the *financial accounting and reporting requirements of the Financial Accounting Standards Board. These accounting standards are *generally accepted accounting principles and should be followed by accountants responsible for the preparation of *financial statements.

statement of movements in shareholders' funds See RECONCILIATION OF MOVEMENTS IN SHAREHOLDERS' FUNDS.

Statement of Standard Accounting Practice (SSAP) Any of the accounting standards prepared by the *Accounting Standards Board and issued by the six members of the *Consultative Committee of Accountancy Bodies. The first SSAP was issued in 1971 and in total 25 SSAPs were issued. Before a SSAP was issued a discussion document known as an exposure draft was circulated for comment. The SSAPs issued are given in the box opposite, although some of these were withdrawn by the ASC, amended, or superseded by the later *Financial Reporting Standards.

statement of terms of employment See WRITTEN STATEMENT OF TERMS OF EMPLOYMENT.

statement of total recognized gains and losses A *financial statement showing the extent to which *shareholders' equity has increased or decreased from all the various gains and losses recognized in the period. It includes profits and losses for the period, together with all other movements on *reserves reflecting recognized gains and losses attributable to shareholders. Such a statement has been required of UK companies since 1993. The statement is dealt with under *Financial Reporting Standard 3, Reporting Financial Performance.

state ownership See NATIONALIZATION; PUBLIC SECTOR.

State Second Pension (SSP; S2P) See STATE EARNINGS-RELATED PENSION SCHEME.

static risk See INSURABLE RISK.

Stationery Office (TSO) A UK company that supplies all printing, binding, office supplies, and office machinery for the home and overseas public services. It also publishes and sells government publications, such as White Papers, Acts of Parliament, Central Statistical Office information, Hansard, etc., at its own bookshops in London, Edinburgh, Cardiff, Manchester, Bristol, Birmingham, and Belfast. The Stationery Office was founded as **His Majesty's Stationery Office (HMSO)** in 1786. Its name was changed when it was privatized in 1996.

statistical demand analysis A set of statistical procedures used to discover the most important real factors affecting sales and their relative influence; the most commonly analysed factors are prices, income, population, and promotion.

statistical process control (SPC) A technique for checking whether or not a product or service is conforming to its design specification, by means of sampling during production or delivery. Small variations in the output of a process are in-

STATEMENTS OF STANDARD ACCOUNTING PRACTICE

1. Accounting for the Results of Associated Companies
2. Disclosure of Accounting Policies
3. Earnings per Share
4. The Accounting Treatment of Government Grants
5. Accounting for Value Added Tax
6. Extraordinary Items and Prior Year Adjustments
7. Accounting for the Changes in the Purchasing Power of Money (provisional)
8. The Treatment of Taxation under the Imputation System
9. Stocks and Work in Progress
10. Statement of Sources and Application of Funds
11. Accounting for Deferred Taxation
12. Accounting for Depreciation
13. Accounting for Research and Development
14. Group Accounts
15. Accounting for Deferred Taxation
16. Current Cost Accounting
17. Accounting for Post Balance Sheet Events
18. Accounting for Contingencies
19. Accounting for Investment Properties
20. Foreign Currency Translation
21. Accounting for Leases and Hire Purchase Contracts
22. Accounting for Goodwill
23. Accounting for Acquisitions and Mergers
24. Accounting for Pension Costs
25. Segmental Reporting

evitable. For example, when cutting a machine part slight changes in material hardness, operating temperature, etc., will cause dimensions to vary very slightly. Using statistical techniques, SPC defines the limits of these variations that can be accepted. Provided sampled outputs stay within this range the process is in control. *See* CONTROL CHART.

statistics 1. The branch of mathematics concerned with the collection, classification, and presentation of information in numerical form. It is based on the assumption that if a group is sufficiently large, it will, unlike an individual, behave in a regular and reproducible manner. For groups that are not large enough for this assumption to be true, a measure of the likelihood of an event happening is its *probability. Much of statistics is concerned with calculating and interpreting probabilities. *See also* DISTRIBUTION; STANDARD DEVIATION. **2.** The numbers by which information is expressed. *See also* OFFICE FOR NATIONAL STATISTICS.

status enquiry *See* BANKER'S REFERENCE.

statute-barred debt A debt that has not been collected within the period allowed by law. *See* LIMITATION OF ACTIONS.

statutory accounts Accounts required

by law, for example by the Companies Act. *See also* STATUTORY BOOKS.

statutory audit An *audit of a company as required by the Companies Act (1985), subject to *small company exemptions. The auditors are required to report to the company's members on all accounts of the company, copies of which are laid before the company in general meeting. Companies with a *turnover of not more than £5.6 million and a *balance sheet total of not more than £2.8 million may be exempt from the statutory audit. Companies with a turnover of £1 million or less and a balance sheet total of not more than £1.4 million do not need to have any form of accountant's or auditor's report. Companies with a turnover of between £1 million and £5.6 million need a *reporting accountant's *audit exemption report. The government has increased the audit threshold significantly in recent years to reduce costs for small companies.

statutory books The *books of account that the Companies Act (1985) requires a company to keep. They must show and explain the company's transactions, disclose with reasonable accuracy the company's financial position at any time, and enable the directors to ensure that any accounts prepared therefrom comply with the provisions of the act. They must also include entries from day to day of all money received and paid out together with a record of all assets and liabilities and statements of stockholding (where appropriate). *See also* PROPER ACCOUNTING RECORDS.

statutory company *See* COMPANY.

statutory maternity pay (SMP) *See* MATERNITY RIGHTS.

statutory meeting A meeting held in accordance with the Companies Act (1985). This normally refers to the *annual general meeting of the shareholders, although it could refer to any other meeting required to be held by statute.

statutory sick pay (SSP) A compulsory scheme operated by an employer. Payments are made to an employee for up to 28 weeks of absence as a result of sickness. There are two rates of statutory sick pay, the applicable level being determined

by the employee's earnings. The two qualifying conditions for SSP are:
- there must be a period of incapacity for work,
- there must be one or more qualifying days.

The first three days do not count and so it is only on the fourth consecutive day that an entitlement to SSP begins.

stealth tax (hidden tax) A tax, the incidence of which may be hidden from the person who is suffering it. An example could be a tax levied on goods at the wholesale level, which increases the retail price in such a way that the final customer cannot detect either that it has happened or the amount of the extra cost. The term is also applied to various mechanisms by which the government can increase the tax paid by individuals without raising tax rates, notably the abolition or restriction of tax allowances and the adjustment of thresholds.

stepped costs *See* SEMI-VARIABLE COST.

stepped preference share A *preference share that earns a predetermined income, which rises steadily by a set amount each year to the winding-up date; there is also a predetermined capital growth.

stereotyping Making assumptions about individuals or groups based on information (which may or may not be valid) obtained before the individual or group has been encountered. Once encountered, opinions formed may be based on dress, speech, gender, ethnic origin, nationality, and gestures. Unfortunately, human beings are liable to have selective prejudices towards their fellows, seeing only what they want to see and ignoring factors that do not fit in with their preconceived beliefs. They also tend to assume that all the individuals of a group have the same, or similar, characteristics. Thus:
- all graduates are clever
- all unemployed people are lazy

are two of the stereotypes that have to be resisted in carrying out job selection interviews. *See also* HORNS AND HALO EFFECT.

sterling The UK *pound, as distinguished from the pounds of other countries. The name derives from the small star *steorra* (Old English) that appeared on early Norman pennies.

Sterling Transferable Accruing Government Securities *See* STAGS.

stock 1. In the UK, a fixed-interest security (*see* GILT-EDGED SECURITY) issued by the government, local authority, or a company in fixed units, often of £100 each. They usually have a *redemption date on which the *par value of the unit price is repaid in full. They are dealt in on stock exchanges at prices that fluctuate, but depend on such factors as their *yield and the time they have to run before redemption. *See also* TAP STOCK. **2.** The US name for an *ordinary share. **3.** The stock-in-trade of an organization. *See* INVENTORY. **4.** Any collection of assets, e.g. the stock of plant and machinery owned by a company.

stock appreciation/depreciation The amount by which the value of the *inventory of an organization has increased or decreased over any given period. This may be owing to inflation, in which case the increase in value will be recorded in the accounts as a profit, although it is not a real profit as when the goods are sold they will need to be replaced at an inflated price. Stock-in-trade may also appreciate or depreciate genuinely as a result of market fluctuations, especially of raw materials.

stockbroker An agent who buys and sells securities on a stock exchange on behalf of clients and receives remuneration for this service in the form of a commission. Before October 1986 (*see* BIG BANG), stockbrokers on the *London Stock Exchange were not permitted to act as principals (*stockjobbers) and worked for a fixed commission laid down by the Stock Exchange. Since October 1986, however, many London stockbrokers have taken advantage of the new rules, which allow them to buy and sell as principals, in which capacity they are now known as *market makers. This change has been accompanied by the formal abolition of fixed commissions, enabling stockbrokers to vary their commission in competition with each other. Stockbrokers have traditionally offered investment advice, especially for their institutional investors.

stock control (inventory control) Regulation of the *inventory (stock-in-trade) of a company so that all components or items are available without delay but without tying up unnecessarily large sums of money. Stock control is a discipline well suited to computerization. Many large manufacturers, retailers, etc., have a computerized stock-control system with automatic reordering when the stock of an item reaches a predetermined low level. In retail supermarkets, for example, the act of registering a sale at the check-out reduces the quantity of that item on the computer-held stock record; new deliveries are entered as they arrive. Thus, the stock at any instant can be read from the computer. A periodic check of the actual stock reveals the extent of pilfering. *See also* PERPETUAL INVENTORY.

stock cover The time for which a company's stock of raw materials would last, without replenishment at the current rate of sale or use.

stock depreciation *See* STOCK APPRECIATION/DEPRECIATION.

stock exchange (stock market) A *market in which *securities are bought and sold, prices being controlled by supply and demand. Stock markets have developed hand in hand with *capitalism since the 17th century, constantly growing in importance and complexity. The basic function of a stock exchange is to enable public companies, governments, and local authorities to raise *capital by selling securities to investors. The secondary market function of a stock exchange is to enable these investors to sell their securities to others, providing liquidity and reducing the risks attached to investment. Most countries have stock exchanges. *See* LONDON STOCK EXCHANGE; NEW YORK STOCK EXCHANGE.

Stock Exchange Alternative Trading Service (SEATS) A computerized system used on the *London Stock Exchange for trading on the *Alternative Investment Market and for stocks of restricted liquidity. A screen-based service showing current prices and orders, it runs alongside the *Stock Exchange Automated Quotations System (SEAQ).

Stock Exchange Automated Quotations System (SEAQ) A computerized system used on the *London Stock Exchange to record the prices at which trans-

S

actions in securities have been struck, thus establishing the market prices for these securities; these prices are made available to brokers through *TOPIC. When a bargain is concluded, the details must be notified to the central system within certain set periods during the day. **SEAQ International** is the system used on the London Stock Exchange for non-UK equities; it operates on similar lines to SEAQ. *See also* SETS; STOCK EXCHANGE ALTERNATIVE TRADING SERVICE.

Stock Exchange Automatic Execution Facility (SAEF) A computerized system used on the *London Stock Exchange to enable a broker to execute a transaction in a security through an SAEF terminal, which automatically completes the bargain at the best price with a *market maker, whose position is automatically adjusted. The price of the transaction is then automatically recorded on a trading report and also passes into the settlement system. The system has greatly reduced the administrative burden on brokers and market makers but has been criticized for eliminating the personal element between brokers and market makers on the floor of the exchange.

Stock Exchange Trading System (SETS) The London Stock Exchange order-driven electronic trading system that came into operation in 1997. It partly replaced the existing quote-driven system (*see* STOCK EXCHANGE AUTOMATED QUOTATIONS SYSTEM). Buyers and sellers enter their orders, which are matched by computer. It covers the 100 shares of the FT-SE 100 index and other *blue chip securities.

stockholder The usual US name for a *shareholder.

stock-in-trade 1. *See* INVENTORY. *See also* STOCK APPRECIATION/DEPRECIATION; STOCK CONTROL; STOCK TURNOVER. 2. The goods or services that an organization normally offers for sale.

stockjobber (jobber) A wholesale dealer on the *London Stock Exchange prior to the *Big Bang (October, 1986). Stockjobbers were only permitted to deal with the general public through the intermediary of a *stockbroker. This single capacity system was replaced by the *dual-capacity

system of *market makers after the Big Bang.

stockless production system A production system that does not permit stocks to be held in the process. *See* JUST IN TIME.

stock market 1. *See* STOCK EXCHANGE. 2. A market in which livestock are bought and sold.

stock of money *See* MONEY SUPPLY.

stock option 1. *See* SHARE OPTION. 2. *See* OPTION.

stock-out costs The extra costs incurred when stocks are not available to meet demand. These extra costs result from lost sales, overtime spent trying to make up the deficiency, and penalty clauses.

stockpile 1. An unusually large stock of a raw material held by an organization in anticipation of a shortage, transport strike, planned production increase, etc. 2. A large stock of strategic materials, food, etc., built up by a government in anticipation of a war, a break in trading relations with a supplier nation, etc.

stock policy An insurance policy covering the goods stocked and sold by a commercial company for specified risks or for all risks (*see* ALL-RISKS POLICY). Policies of this kind are usually based on the price paid for the stock, not the price at which it might be sold, i.e. the insurance does not cover loss of profit or mark-up on the stock.

stock split *See* SCRIP ISSUE.

stocktaking The process of counting and evaluating inventory (stock-in-trade), usually at an organization's year end in order to value the total stock for preparation of the accounts. In more sophisticated organizations, in which permanent stock records are maintained, stock is counted on a random basis throughout the year to compare quantities counted with the quantities that appear in the, usually, computerized records.

stock turnover The number of times in a year that the *stock-in-trade of an organization is deemed to have been sold. This is best found by dividing the total cost of the goods sold in a year by an average value of the stock-in-trade (*see* RATE OF TURNOVER). The faster the stock is turned over, the more opportunities there are to make profits on it and therefore the lower the margins that are required; for example a supermarket, in which the stock is turned over frequently, makes lower margins than a jeweller's shop, in which high-priced goods are sold infrequently.

Stock Watch The unit of the New York Stock Exchange that monitors share dealing to identify irregular or illegal behaviour.

stock valuation *See* INVENTORY VALUATION.

stock watering The creation of more new shares in a company than is justified by its *tangible assets, even though the company may be making considerable profits. The consequences of this could be that the dividend may not be maintained at the old rate on the new capital and that if the company were to be liquidated its shareholders may not be paid out in full.

stop-loss order An order placed with a broker in a security or commodity market to close an *open position at a specified price in order to limit a loss. It may be used in a volatile market, especially by a speculator, if the market looks as if it might move strongly against his position.

stop notice A court procedure available to protect those who have an interest in shares but have not been registered as company members. The notice prevents the company from registering a transfer of the shares or paying a dividend upon them without informing the server of the notice. It was formerly known as **notice in lieu of distringas**.

stop order An order placed with a broker in a security or commodity market to buy if prices rise to a specified level or sell if they fall to another specified level.

stoppage *in transitu* A remedy available to an unpaid seller of goods when the buyer has become insolvent and the goods are still in course of transit. If the seller gives notice of stoppage to the carrier or other bailee of the goods, the seller is entitled to have them redelivered and may then retain possession of them until the

price is paid. If the right is not exercised, the goods will fall into the insolvent buyer's estate and go towards satisfying the creditors.

store card A plastic card issued by a store or retail chain that entitles the holder to purchase goods or services up to a prescribed limit from that store or outlets in the chain. Customers receive monthly statements from the retailer, or a finance company appointed by the retailer; they may settle the bill in full without interest, or make a specified minimum payment and pay interest on the outstanding balance. *See also* CHARGE CARD.

store image The image formed by a consumer of a particular store. It is affected by the personnel, the range of merchandise, the external and internal appearance of the store, the level of prices, and the standard of service provided.

storyboard A sequence of sketches and cartoons to show the main elements in a television or cinema advertisement.

stotin A monetary unit of Slovenia, worth one hundredth of a *tolar.

stotinka (*plural* **stotinki**) A monetary unit of Bulgaria, worth one hundredth of a *lev.

stowage plan A plan of a ship showing where all the cargo on a particular voyage was stowed.

straddle A strategy used by dealers in *options or *futures contracts. In the option market it involves simultaneously purchasing put and call options; it is most profitable when the price of the underlying security is very volatile. *Compare* BUTTERFLY. In commodity and currency futures a straddle may involve buying and selling options or both buying and selling the same commodity or currency for delivery in the future, often on different markets. Undoing half the straddle is known as *breaking a leg.

straight *See* EUROBOND.

straight bond A *bond issued in the *primary market that carries no equity or other incentive to attract the investor; its only reward is an annual or biannual interest coupon together with a promise to repay the capital at par on the redemption date.

straight-line method A method of calculating the amount by which a *fixed asset is to be depreciated in an accounting period, in which the *depreciation to be charged against income is based on the original cost or valuation, less the asset's estimated *net residual value, divided by its estimated life in years. This has the effect of a constant annual depreciation charge against profits year by year. In some circumstances the net residual value is ignored.

straight product extension Marketing a product in a foreign market without any change to the product sold in the home market.

straight rebuy *Business buyer behaviour characterized by automatic and regular repurchasing of familiar products from regular suppliers.

stranding The running aground of a ship as a consequence of an unusual event. For the purposes of *marine insurance, stranding does not include running aground and being refloated; it might involve being driven onto rocks when taking avoiding action or a similar event.

strap A triple *option on a share or commodity market, consisting of one put option and two call options at the same price and for the same period. *Compare* STRIP.

strapline A slogan often used in conjunction with a brand's name in advertising and other promotions.

strategic alliance (strategic partnership) An agreement between two or more firms to engage in an activity on a shared basis. The outside activities of each partner are not affected by the alliance, which is designed to build on the expertise of each member and the way in which they complement each other. Strategic alliances are generally less formal and far-ranging than *joint ventures and may often be designed to last for a limited time. *See also* CONSORTIUM.

strategic asset A source of competitive advantage derived from factors outside a firm rather than from its own competence. Such sources could include proximity to raw materials and government policy on the exchange rates. *See also* ABSOLUTE COST ADVANTAGE.

strategic behaviour The behaviour of firms or individuals that is aimed at influencing the structure of a *market. In traditional economics, such situations as *monopoly or *oligopoly were seen as the outcome of technological conditions and the state of demand. More recently, it has been observed that a particular firm or individual can influence its competitors in the market in various ways, for example by threatening a *price war if other firms attempt to enter the market; this will clearly influence the structure of the market. *See also* GAME THEORY; PREDATORY PRICING STRATEGY.

strategic business unit (SBU) An autonomous division within some large companies that is responsible for planning the marketing of a particular range of products.

strategic choice The alternative strategic plans available to an organization. The degree of choice in formulating a firm's *business strategy is likely to be determined by its resources and by such external factors as competition and environmental issues. Managerial competence, in terms of a firm's ability to manage a new area of activity or an acquisition, will also influence the choice and, therefore, a firm's future strategic development. *See* DIVERSIFICATION; EXTERNAL GROWTH; INTERNAL GROWTH.

strategic drift The limitations placed on *strategic choice by assumptions made in the past and the application of previously tried remedies. It may restrict a firm from making the radical strategies required to deal with a changing environment.

strategic financial management An approach to management that applies financial techniques to strategic decision making. *See also* STRATEGIC MANAGEMENT ACCOUNTING

strategic fit The extent to which *diversification into another field fits with the future scope of a firm. To evaluate whether or not the proposed action would fit strategically with a firm's plans requires the strategic logic to be examined in detail and the extent to which integration could be achieved to be evaluated. *See* SYNERGY.

strategic gap analysis A method of examining a business strategy and establishing whether or not it will meet a desired objective. If a failure to achieve this objective is predicted, there is a performance gap between the hoped-for and expected states. This gap can be closed by means of a modified strategy, which will need to be formulated.

strategic group A group of firms within a market or industry that is examined to determine the position each holds in terms of range, coverage, and national or international distribution. Analysis of a strategic group shows which companies are the closest competitors and can be used to identify potential gaps or opportunities in a market sector.

strategic human-resource management (SHRM) A systematic attempt to integrate the use of human resources with the wider long-term business strategy of an organization. *See* HUMAN-RESOURCE MANAGEMENT.

strategic indicators *See* PERFORMANCE MEASUREMENT.

strategic intent A clearly understood statement of the direction in which a firm intends to develop. It should be both understood and interpreted by each employee in relation to their work and is a crucial element in the strategic management of a firm. *See also* MISSION STATEMENT.

strategic investment appraisal An appraisal of an investment decision based on wider grounds than that provided by a purely financial appraisal. It is also necessary to evaluate possible long-term strategic benefits and any intangible factors that may be relevant to the decision, particularly if advanced manufacturing technology is concerned.

strategic management accounting A *management accounting system organized so that it is capable of providing the information needed for long-term strategic decision making, as opposed to the more traditional approach of providing short-term costs. Strategic management

accounting, for example, provides information that will assist in the pricing strategy for new products and decisions relating to the expansion of capacity.

strategic plan A plan describing how a firm will adapt to take advantage of opportunities in its constantly changing environment, in order to maintain a *strategic fit between the firm's goals and capabilities and these market opportunities.

strategic styles The ways in which large diversified businesses control their subsidiary companies. Broadly, three strategies have been defined:

- **strategic planning**, in which the central organization develops a detailed overall masterplan with specified targets for the subsidiaries;
- **financial control**, in which the central organization acts as banker to the subsidiaries, setting tight financial targets and regularly monitoring performance;
- **strategic control**, in which the central organization sets an overall strategy, but agrees a *business plan with each subsidiary and monitors each one against the agreed plan.

See also PARENTING.

stratified sampling A sampling procedure in which a population is divided into two mutually exclusive and collectively exhaustive strata and a *probability sample is drawn from each stratum. *See also* DISPROPORTIONATE STRATIFIED SAMPLING.

street-name stocks The US name for nominee stocks (*see* NOMINEE SHAREHOLDING).

stress reduction A decrease in the number of situations that cause a person stressful experiences. Personal strategies that achieve this end include avoiding situations that cause distress and planning ahead. Organizational strategies include training programmes and job redesign. Individuals can also increase their ability to endure stress, without experiencing dysfunctional results; this stress resilience is helped by exercise, diet, and weight control.

stress testing A method of *risk analysis in which *simulations are used to estimate the impact of worst-case situations.

It is commonly used by regulators, rating agencies, and financial institutions, which base their simulations on both historical and hypothetical crises.

strike An organized refusal on the part of a group of employees to work, in an attempt to force their employers to concede to their demands for higher pay, shorter hours, better working conditions, etc. An **official strike** is one that takes place on the instructions of a trade union, whereas an **unofficial strike** is one that takes place without union backing. A **wildcat strike** is called at short notice in contravention of an agreement not to strike and it does not have union backing. A **sympathetic strike** is one in which one union calls its members out on strike to support another union, although it is not in dispute with its own employers. A **token strike** is a short withdrawal of labour, e.g. for an hour or two or even for one day, to threaten employers of more serious action to come if the employees' demands are not met. In a **general strike** most of the trade unions in a country call out their members, virtually bringing the country to a standstill.

Under UK law, a trade union cannot call its members out on strike unless a majority has voted for the action in a secret ballot.

strike price (striking price) **1.** *See* EXERCISE PRICE. **2.** The price fixed by the sellers of a security after receiving bids from would-be buyers in an *issue by tender. Usually, those who bid below the strike price receive nothing, while those who bid at or above it receive some proportion of the amount they have bid for.

string diagrams A technique employed in *work study that uses string wrapped around points on a scale layout diagram to calculate movement. Computerized methods are replacing manual methods, but the generic name is still used.

strip A triple *option on a share or commodity market, consisting of one call option and two put options at the same price and for the same period. *Compare* STRAP.

stripped bond 1. A bond in which payments are sold as a set of 300 coupon bonds. **2.** A bond or stock that has been subjected to *dividend stripping.

structural capital *See* INTELLECTUAL CAPITAL.

structured finance The creation of debt instruments by *securitization or the addition of *derivatives to existing instruments.

structured interview An interview used in *marketing research in which the interviewer asks the questions exactly as they appear on the questionnaire, adding and explaining nothing to the respondent. The questions can only be answered 'yes', 'no', or 'don't know'. Although this type of marketing research produces easily tabulated data quickly, it places a heavy burden on the designer of the questionnaire to ensure that the data is not misleading.

Structured questionnaires and (less rigidly) structured interviews are also sometimes used in *personnel selection.

sub-agent A person or firm that is employed to buy or sell goods as an *agent of an agent. A firm may hold the agency for certain goods in a particular country, for example, and employ sub-agents to represent it in outlying districts of that country.

subjective goodwill The *goodwill of an enterprise calculated by deducting its net tangible assets from the *net present value of its estimated future *cash flows.

sub-lease *See* HEAD LEASE.

suboptimization A situation that arises when the individual components of a system fail to work together to achieve maximum *synergy. This can result from:
- the failure of one or more elements to produce their own outputs to a sufficient standard;
- poor communication of objectives at a strategic level, so that there is no shared understanding of those objectives;
- poor communication across component boundaries, either through ineffective use of the available tools or through deliberate control and manipulation of information;
- the development of subcultures that do not share the overall objectives of the organization.

Most organizations recognize that individual members have a range of personal needs that may not be entirely compatible with the organization's aims. Desired outputs are necessarily a compromise between personal needs and the ideals of an organization. *See also* GOAL DIVERGENCE.

subordinated debt A debt that can only be claimed by an unsecured creditor, in the event of a liquidation, after the claims of *secured creditors have been met. In **subordinated unsecured loan stocks** loans are issued by such institutions as banks, in which the rights of the holders of the stock are subordinate to the interests of the depositors. Debts involving *junk bonds are always subordinated to debts to banks, irrespective of whether or not they are secured.

subpoena (Latin: under penalty) An order made by a court instructing a person to appear in court on a specified date to give evidence, or to produce specified documents. The party calling for the witness must pay all reasonable expenses. Failure to comply with a subpoena is *contempt of court.

subrogation The principle that, having paid a claim, an insurer has the right to take over any other methods the policyholder may have for obtaining compensation for the same event. For example, if a neighbour is responsible for breaking a person's window and an insurance claim is paid for the repair, the insurers may, if they wish, take over the policyholder's legal right to claim the cost of repair from the neighbour.

subscribed share capital *See* ISSUED SHARE CAPITAL.

subscriber A person who signs the *memorandum of association of a new company and who joins with other members in paying for a specified quantity of shares in the company, signing the *articles of association, and appointing the first directors.

subscription shares 1. Shares in a building society that are paid for by instalments; they often pay the highest interest rates. 2. The shares bought by the initial *subscribers to a company.

subsidiary undertaking (group undertaking) An undertaking that is controlled by another undertaking (the parent or *holding company). The extent of the control needed to define a subsidiary is given in the Companies Act (1985). The financial statements of a subsidiary undertaking are normally included in the *consolidated financial statements of the group. *See also* QUASI-SUBSIDIARY; WHOLLY OWNED SUBSIDIARY.

subsidy A payment by a government to producers of certain goods to enable them to sell the goods to the public at a low price, to compete with foreign competition, to avoid making redundancies and creating unemployment, etc. In general, subsidies distort international trade and are unpopular but they are sometimes used by governments to help to establish a new industry in a country. *See also* COMMON AGRICULTURAL POLICY.

subsistence crop A crop grown by a farmer for consumption by himself and his family, rather than for sale. *Compare* CASH CROP.

substance over form An important concept in accounting, according to which transactions and other events are accounted for by their commercial reality rather than their legal form. *Off-balance-sheet finance and *creative accounting depend on acounting according to the legal form, often established in complex agreements. The purpose of *Financial Reporting Standard 5, Reporting the Substance of Transactions, has been to give more strength to the substance aspect as well as guidance in specific transactions.

substantiality The extent to which a market segment is sufficiently large or profitable to provide a worthwhile attempt to service it.

substantive motion *See* MOTION.

substitute awareness effect An effect that depends on the relation between a customer's price sensitivity and his or her awareness of the existence of alternatives. The substitute awareness effect usually lowers a customer's willingness to pay high prices.

sucker effect The finding that some individuals will reduce their individual effort when working on a group task because they fear becoming, or being seen as, a 'sucker', i.e. someone who contributes more to the group than others but receives the same reward. *See also* COLLEC-

TIVE EFFORT MODEL; RINGELMANN EFFECT; SOCIAL LOAFING.

sue and labour clause A clause in a *marine insurance policy extending the insurance to cover costs incurred by the policyholder in preventing a loss from occurring or minimizing one that could not be avoided. Without this clause the policy would only cover damage that had actually occurred.

sugging (survey under the guise of research) The unethical practice of deliberate deception by telemarketers masquerading as market researchers. Respondents are often invited to take part in a survey as a lead-in to a sales presentation or as an attempt to get information that could be used for sales leads or mailing lists. *Compare* FRUGGING.

sum insured The maximum amount the insurers will pay in the event of a claim.

summarizer *See* TASK ROLES.

summary financial statement An abbreviated form of the *annual accounts and report that, providing certain conditions are met, may be sent by *listed companies to their shareholders instead of the full report. Summary financial statements were introduced by section 251 of the Companies Act (1989), which took effect from 1 April 1990. *See also* ABBREVIATED ACCOUNTS; SIMPLIFIED FINANCIAL STATEMENTS.

sum-of-the-digits method A method of calculating the amount by which a *fixed asset is depreciated in an accounting period. The estimated life is expressed in years, and the digits for each year of its life are totalled. The proportion of the asset's cost or valuation less residual value to be written off as depreciation in a particular year is determined by the number of years remaining before the asset's removal from commission, expressed as a proportion of the sum of the years; the greatest amount is therefore written off in the early years of the asset's life. For example, for an asset with an estimated life of 5 years, the sum of the digits is 5 + 4 + 3 + 2 + 1 = 15. Thus 5/15 is written off in the first year, 4/15 in year 2, 3/15 in year 3,

and so on. In some circumstances the *net residual value is ignored.

sundry expenses Costs incurred as small items of expenditure, which do not lend themselves to easy classification under any other heading. Sometimes they refer to a specific area, such as sundry office expenses or sundry production costs.

sunk capital The amount of an organization's funds that has been spent and is therefore no longer available to the organization, frequently because it has been spent on either unrealizable or valueless assets.

sunk costs 1. Expenditure, usually on capital items, that once having been incurred can be included in the *books of account as an asset, although this value cannot be recovered. **2.** In *management accounting, expenditure that has already been incurred and that cannot be recovered. Such costs are not relevant to any subsequent decisions. An example of a sunk cost is the original cost of a machine when the decision is whether or not to replace this machine. *Compare* RELEVANT COST.

superannuation *See* OCCUPATIONAL PENSION SCHEME.

supermajority provisions Provisions in the byelaws of a company that call for more than a simple majority of its members when voting on certain *motions, such as the approval of a merger or whether or not to agree to a takeover. In these circumstances the provisions may call for a supermajority of between 70% and 80% of the votes cast.

supermarket A large self-service store that carries a wide variety of food, household products, and other goods, which it sells in high volumes at relatively low prices. *See also* HYPERMARKET.

superstore A store usually about twice the size of a regular *supermarket, which is often found on the edge of a town. It carries a large assortment of food and nonfood items and offers such services as dry cleaning, a pharmacy, lunch counters, car care, etc.

supervisory board A board of *non-

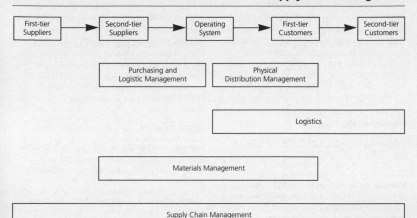

Supply chain management

executive directors who appoint and oversee the members of the executive boards of many companies in Continental Europe. *See* TWO-TIER BOARD.

supplementary costs *See* OVERHEAD.

supplier A firm or individual that provides the resources needed by a company and its competitors to produce goods and services.

supplier credit *See* SPECIFIC BANK GUARANTEE.

supplier search The stage of the business buying process (*see* BUSINESS BUYER BEHAVIOUR) in which the buyer tries to find the best vendors.

supplier selection The stage of the business buying process (*see* BUSINESS BUYER BEHAVIOUR) in which the buyer reviews proposals from suitable vendors and selects a supplier or suppliers.

supply and demand *See* MARKET FORCES.

supply chain The series of linked stages in a supply network along which a particular set of goods or services flows; it usually consists of: suppliers, vendors of the suppliers, producers, distribution partners, and customers. *See* SUPPLY-CHAIN MANAGEMENT.

supply-chain management The man-

agement of the links between an organization and its suppliers and customers to achieve strategic advantage. Many specialist companies now offer to manage the whole of the supply chain, on behalf of manufacturers. Supply-chain management covers:

- **Materials management** – the management of the flow of materials through an organization's supply chain, including first-tier suppliers, inventory management, operations planning and control, and distribution to first-tier customers.
- **Logistics** – the management of materials and information flows from an organization to its customers. (Sometimes 'logistics' is also used as a synonym for 'supply-chain management'.)
- **Physical distribution management** – the management of the process that connects the producer and the first-tier customers, including storage and transport.
- **Purchasing and supply management** – the management of an organization's interface with suppliers, ensuring that the right quantity is bought at the right time, at the right price, to the right quality specification, and from the right sources.
- **Information flow management** – the management of the flow of information between an organization and both its suppliers and its customers. For every

unit of material flow in one direction through the supply chain, there should be at least one corresponding information flow in the opposite direction. Many of the more recent improvements in materials management have come from the use of computers and information technology in the flow of information.

supply-chain support A network of vendors, dealers, and distribution partners linked on-line so that queries in one category can lead to related information in another.

supply risk 1. The inherent risk in *project financing that the raw materials necessary for the operation of the plant to be constructed may become unavailable. *Compare* COMPLETION RISK; TECHNOLOGICAL RISK. **2.** The risk of disruption of inputs into a firm.

support level In technical analysis, a floor level of prices for a security or commodity at which the price tends to stop falling and begin to rebound. A fall below this level is regarded as marking a significant shift to lower prices. *Compare* RESISTANCE LEVEL. *See also* DOUBLE BOTTOM.

supra protest *See* ACCEPTANCE SUPRA PROTEST.

SUR Abbreviation for *set-up reduction.

surcharge liability notice A notice issued when a trader is late with a *value added tax return or with the payment of the tax. The surcharge period is specified on the notice and it will run to the anniversary of the end of the period in which the default occurred. Any default in the liability notice period will result in a further notice extending the notice period to the anniversary of the end of the VAT period in which the second default occurred.

surety 1. A guarantor for the actions of someone. **2.** A sum of money held as a *guarantee or as evidence of good faith.

surfer An undirected seeker of information on the Internet. Some surfers, however, are looking for an experience rather than information.

surrender value The sum of money given by an insurance company to the in-

sured on a life policy that is cancelled before it has run its full term. The amount is calculated approximately by deducting from the total value of the premiums paid any costs, administration expenses, and a charge for the life-assurance cover up to the cancellation date. There is little or no surrender value to a life policy in its early years. Not all life policies acquire a surrender value; for example, term assurance policies have no surrender value.

survey research Any form of *marketing research in which data is gathered systematically from a sample of people by means of a questionnaire. Surveys are usually conducted by means of face-to-face interviews, telephone interviews, or mailed questionnaires.

sushi bond A bond issued by a Japanese-registered company in a currency other than yen but targeted primarily at the Japanese institutional investor market.

suspense account A temporary account in the books of an organization to record balances to correct mistakes or balances that have not yet been finalized (e.g. because a particular deal has not been concluded).

SVA Abbreviation for *shareholder value analysis.

swap A means by which a borrower can exchange the type of funds most easily raised for the type of funds required, usually through the intermediary of a bank. For example, a UK company may find it easy to raise a sterling loan when they really want to borrow euros; a German company may have exactly the opposite problem. A swap will enable them to exchange the currency they possess for the currency they need. The other common type of swap is an interest-rate swap, in which borrowers exchange fixed- for floating-interest rates. The essence of a swap is that the parties exchange the net cash flows of different types of borrowing instruments on an *over-the-counter market.

swap line A line of credit between two central banks in different countries, when securities of equal value are exchanged but the borrowing bank repays on a forward contract.

swaption An *option to enter into a *swap contract.

sweep facility A service provided by a bank which automatically transfers funds above a certain level from a current account to a higher-interest earning account. The process can work in reverse when funds in the current account fall below a certain level. The purpose is to provide the customer with the greatest amount of interest, with the minimum personal intervention.

swingline bank facility (swingline loan) A facility that enables a borrower to avail itself of funds at very short notice, usually on a same-day basis, often to cover shortfalls in other credit arrangements. It may form part of a multi-option facility.

switching **1.** Using the cash from the sale of one investment to purchase another. This may, or may not, involve a liability for capital gains tax, depending on the circumstances. **2.** Closing an *open position in a commodity market and opening a similar position in the same commodity but for a different delivery period. For example, a trader may switch a holding of sugar for October delivery FOB to an equal quantity of sugar for March delivery FOB for the next year. **3.** A country's intervention in the international currency market to stop an outflow of its currency. **4.** Exporting and importing through a third nation, where the currency paying for the goods can be easily exchanged into one acceptable to the seller.

switching cost A means of building a *competitive advantage into a product or service by involving buyers in an extra cost if they switch to an alternative supplier. It may form part of the physical characteristics of the product, which make it incompatible with the equipment of alternative suppliers (such as a different computer operating system), or the switching cost may result from the disruption of the quality of service formed by a long-established and close working relationship.

SWOT Acronym for strengths, weaknesses, opportunities, and threats. During the planning of the marketing of a new product a company needs to embark on a SWOT analysis to assess its strengths and weaknesses (internally) and the opportunities and threats facing it (externally). Internal strengths could be a good distribution system and adequate cash flow. Weaknesses might be identified as an already extended product line or poor servicing facilities. Opportunities could be consumer demand for a particular product or the vulnerability of a competitor, while threats might be forthcoming government legislation or diversification by a competitor. A SWOT analysis is also the main feature of an organization's managerial *position audit.

symbol retailer (voluntary retailer) A voluntary group of independent retailers formed to buy in large quantities from *wholesalers at lower prices than they could achieve independently. Originally a defensive move by independents to counter the increasing dominance and expansion of the multiple stores, supermarkets, hypermarkets, etc., these groups can also provide each other with such services as promotional support and management advice. The members of a group often use a common name or symbol to identify themselves.

sympathetic strike *See* STRIKE.

syndicate **1.** A group of bankers, insurers, contractors, etc., who join together to work on a large project. Notable activities undertaken by such a group may include syndicated loans and underwriting (*see also* SYNDICATED BANK FACILITY). **2.** A number of *Lloyd's underwriters who accept insurance risks as a group; each syndicate is run by a syndicate manager or agent. The **names** in the syndicate accept an agreed share of each risk in return for the same proportion of the premium. The names do not take part in organizing the underwriting business but treat their involvement with the syndicate as an investment. Since the reorganization of Lloyd's in the 1990s, limited companies have been allowed to become names. Although a syndicate underwrites as a group, each member is financially responsible for only his or her own share.

syndicated bank facility (syndicated loan) A very large loan made to one borrower by a group of banks headed by one *lead manager, which usually takes only a small percentage of the loan itself, syndicating the rest to other banks and financial institutions. The loans are usually made on a small margin. The borrower can reserve the right to know the names of all the members of the syndicate. If the borrower states which banks are to be included, it is known as a **club deal**. A syndicated bank facility is usually a *revolving bank facility. There is only one loan agreement.

syndicated research A large-scale marketing research project undertaken by market-research companies and subsequently offered for sale to interested parties. It is not therefore undertaken on behalf of a client.

syndicated selling See AFFILIATES PROGRAM.

synergy The added value created by joining two separate firms, enabling a greater return to be achieved than by their individual contributions as separate entities; i.e. the overall return is greater than the sum of its parts. The synergy is usually anticipated and analysed during merger or takeover activities; for example, one firm's strength in marketing would be complementary to the other firm's versatility in new product development. Although synergy is often optimistically sought, it can be hard to achieve in practice owing to resistance to change, particularly after a contested takeover. The corporate culture that each participant may have built up over many years of separate existence may prove too inflexible to enable a productive merger to be achieved without friction. The condition that arises when, far from adding value, a merger produces an outcome that is less than the sum of the parts is known as **anergy**. See also SUBOPTIMIZATION.

synthetic standard times A *work measurement technique that produces standard times for new tasks (see STANDARD PERFORMANCE) by assembling data from previous time studies of component parts of the task.

system An assembly of components or elements connected together in an organized way to produce outputs; the components of the assembly are affected by being in the system and the behaviour of

the system is changed if any component leaves it.

systematic risk (residual risk) The element of *risk in a *portfolio of investments that cannot be reduced by *diversification, because it is common to all securities of the same general class. The compensation that an investor requires for undertaking such risks forms the basis for the *risk premium calculation of the *capital asset pricing model and *arbitrage pricing theory. Systematic risk is measured by the *beta coefficient. *Compare* SPECIFIC RISK.

systematic sampling A type of *cluster sampling in which every kth element is selected from the frame, after a random start somewhere within the first k elements, where k = the sampling interval.

system capacity See CAPACITY.

systems analysis The examination or analysis of the objectives and problems of a system for the purpose of developing and improving the system by the use of computers. Systems analysis entails producing a precise statement of what is to be accomplished, determining the methods of achieving the objectives that are most cost-effective, and preparing a feasibility study. If the study is accepted by the customer, the **systems analysts** will advise on the hardware and software needed, provide programmers with the details they need to write the programs, produce documentation describing the system, plan staff training on it, and monitor the system once it is installed.

systems dynamics A computer-based system, developed at the Massachusetts Institute of Technology, for modelling the behaviour of transient systems. It attempts to unravel the synergistic effects (see SYNERGY) of numerous individual changes being made at various points in a system; it also allows 'what if' questions to be asked.

systems selling The selling of a total system rather than an individual product. For example, some computer manufacturers sell VDUs, keyboards, printers, and the necessary software for their computers, while other companies might only supply the software for these computers.

systems software Computer programs that control the functioning of the computer itself, rather than directly meeting the user's computing needs (*compare* APPLICATIONS SOFTWARE). Examples are *operating systems and utility programs, which perform such tasks as copying *files, checking the integrity of magnetic disks, etc. These programs are usually supplied with the computer and may even be built into it (*see* FIRMWARE).

system utilization *See* UTILIZATION.

tachistoscope A projection device used in studies of visual perception and memory. In advertising and marketing research it is used to measure the extent to which the features of an advertisement or brand are registered by consumers. The tachistoscope shows a package or advertisement for a brief period (which can be varied), enabling researchers to test the effectiveness of the design, colour, lay-out, or name. Tachistoscope tests are often undertaken before the product or advertisement is released. Various methods of achieving the same effect on a computer screen are being explored.

tactical asset allocation An attempt to increase *portfolio returns in the short term by altering the asset composition of the portfolio. The academic literature is sceptical as to whether this will result in higher returns for any reason other than chance.

Taguchi methods Methods of testing the design of a new product or service in the most extreme circumstances likely to occur. In theory, all possible design variables and combinations are investigated to achieve the optimum combination. In reality, this would be impossible; therefore a range of statistical techniques are used to determine the best combinations, leading to the lowest cost and the highest degree of uniformity. The methods were devised by Genichi Taguchi.

taka (Tk) The standard monetary unit of Bangladesh, divided into 100 oisha.

takeover bid (offer to purchase) An offer made to the shareholders of a company by an individual or organization to buy their shares at a specified price in order to gain control of that company. In a welcome takeover bid the directors of the company will advise shareholders to accept the terms of the bid. This is usually known as a *merger. If the bid is unwelcome, or the terms are unacceptable, the board will advise against acceptance. In

the ensuing **takeover battle**, the bidder may improve the terms offered and will usually write to shareholders outlining the advantages that will follow from the successful takeover. In the meantime bids from other sources may be made (*see* GREY KNIGHT; WHITE KNIGHT) or the original bidder may withdraw as a result of measures taken by the board of the *target company (*see* POISON PILL; PORCUPINE PROVISIONS). In an **unconditional bid**, the bidder will pay the offered price irrespective of the number of shares acquired, while the bidder of a **conditional bid** will only pay the price offered if sufficient shares are acquired to provide a controlling interest. Takeovers in the UK are subject to the rules and disciplines of the *City Code on Takeovers and Mergers.

Takeover Panel *See* CITY CODE ON TAKEOVERS AND MERGERS.

taker The buyer of a traded *option. *Compare* WRITER.

tala (WS$) The standard monetary unit of Samoa, divided into 100 sene.

TALISMAN Acronym for Transfer Accounting Lodgement for Investors and Stock Management. This was the *London Stock Exchange computerized transfer system, covering most UK securities, until 1997, when the Bank of England *CREST system replaced it.

tallyman (tallyclerk) A worker at a port or airport, who checks that the goods unloaded from a ship or aircraft tally with the documents covering them and the ship's or aircraft's manifest.

talon A printed form attached to a *bearer bond that enables the holder to apply for a new sheet of *coupons when the existing coupons have been used up.

tambala A monetary unit of Malawi, worth one hundredth of a *kwacha.

tanga A monetary unit of Tajikistan, worth one hundredth of a *rouble.

tangible assets Literally, *assets that can but touched, i.e. physical objects such as land, buildings, or machinery. However, tangible assets may also include leases and company shares. They are therefore best defined as the *fixed assets of an organization excluding such *intangible assets as goodwill, patents, and trademarks, which are even more intangible than leases and shares.

tanker A ship designed to carry liquids in bulk in large storage tanks. Most carry oil but some carry wine, sugar products, and liquified gases.

Tannenbaum-Schmidt continuum (leadership continuum theory) A model of leadership that sees *leadership style as a continuum varying from leader-centred (autocratic) to subordinate-centred (democratic). The type of leadership that is practical and desirable in any given situation will depend on three types of force: forces in the leader (e.g. self-confidence, personal philosophy); forces in the followers (e.g. experience, willingness to take responsibility); and forces in the situation (e.g. the complexity of the problem, time pressures). *See also* CONTINGENCY THEORIES OF LEADERSHIP.

tape A reporting system for stock-market information, primarily prices. It was formerly known as **tickertape**, before the process was computerized.

taper relief In the UK, a tax relief that can be set against a liability to *capital gains tax arising from the disposal of chargeable assets. The amount of taper relief depends on the type of asset (business or non-business) and the number of complete years of ownership after 5 April 1998. The rules governing the extent of the relief are complex and have been changed several times since it was introduced in 1998. The maximum reduction in the chargeable gain is 75% for business assets and 40% for non-business assets. In the case of a capital gain made by a company, *indexation is applied rather than taper relief.

tap issue The issue of UK government securities or bills to selected market makers, usually to influence the price of gilts. The government can control their volume and price, like turning a tap on or off.

tap stock A gilt-edged security from an issue that has not been fully subscribed and is released onto the market slowly when its market price reaches predetermined levels. **Short taps** are short-dated stocks and **long taps** are long-dated taps.

TAR Abbreviation for throughput accounting ratio. *See* THROUGHPUT ACCOUNTING.

tare *See* GROSS WEIGHT.

target company A company that is subject to a *takeover bid.

target costing A method of costing products or services to reflect the price that customers are willing to pay. Target costing has four stages:
(1) Identify the **target price** that customers will pay for the product. This involves market research to identify competitors' products and prices.
(2) Identify the **target cost** by deducting a target profit margin from the target price. The target profit margin will vary from company to company. Sony is an example of a company that would require a high profit margin to cover the investment in new technology.
(3) Forecast the **actual cost** of the product.
(4) If the forecast actual cost is greater than the target cost, the company will have to identify ways of lowering the forecast actual cost. Product designers may have to change the design so that it is cheaper to manufacture. Manufacturing engineers may also look into ways of making the production processes more efficient. If the company cannot bring actual costs down to the target cost, then the product should not be manufactured.
This approach to pricing is very different from *cost-plus pricing.

Target Group Index (TGI) An annual marketing research report compiled from the returned questionnaires of a random sample of thousands of respondents on their use of hundreds of products and thousands of brands. The questionnaires, which are completed with no interviewer present, also collect information on respondents' demographics, attitudes and values, leisure activities, and exposure to the media. TGI was originated in the UK in

1969 but is now operated in some 50 countries.

target marketing The selection of one or more segments of an available market as a target for marketing a product or service. This is known as the **target market** or **served market**. Since it has become almost impossible to market products that will satisfy everyone, target marketing enables companies to aim the products at specific groups of consumers.

target population A *population of interest in *marketing research. It is from this population that the *samples to be researched are drawn.

tariff 1. Any list of charges for goods or services. **2.** A tax or customs duty payable on imports or exports, or a list detailing such duties. The Customs and Excise issue tariffs stating which goods attract duty and what the rate of duty is. **3.** A list of charges in which the charging rate changes after a fixed amount has been purchased or in which a flat fee is imposed in addition to a quantity-related charge, as in two-part tariffs for gas or telephone services.

tariff office An insurance company that bases its premiums on a tariff arranged with other insurance companies. A **non-tariff office** is free to quote its own premiums.

task identity *See* CORE JOB CHARACTERISTICS.

task-motivated (task-oriented) Describing a *leadership style that is concerned with setting goals, structuring tasks, and measuring performance. A task-motivated leader will focus on such activities as planning, scheduling, defining roles and responsibilities, and providing performance-related feedback. *Compare* RELATIONSHIP-MOTIVATED. *See* CONTINGENCY THEORIES OF LEADERSHIP; LEAST PREFERRED CO-WORKER SCALE.

task roles A set of coherent roles that are often adopted by the different members of a group in order to solve problems, make decisions, and meet targets. Some commonly identified roles of this kind include the **initiator**, who defines goals, recognizes problems, and initiates procedures; the **opinion giver**, who provides

ideas and information; the **opinion seeker**, who elicits the ideas or expertise of others; and the **summarizer**, who clarifies and sums up the ideas of the group. *Compare* RELATIONSHIP ROLES.

task significance *See* CORE JOB CHARACTERISTICS.

taxable income Income liable to taxation. It is calculated by deducting *income tax allowances and any tax-deductible expenses from the taxpayer's gross income. *Compare* NON-TAXABLE INCOME. *See also* TOTAL INCOME.

taxable person In the UK *value added tax legislation, an individual, partnership, limited company, club, association, or charity that makes regular *taxable supplies above a certain annual value. Value added tax is charged on taxable supplies made by taxable persons in the course or furtherance of a business.

taxable supply In *value added tax legislation, any supply of goods or services made in the UK other than an *exempt supply. As well as straightforward sales, taxable supplies include rentals, hirings, the granting of rights, and the distribution of promotional gifts.

taxation A levy on individuals or corporate bodies by central or local government in order to finance the expenditure of that government and also as a means of implementing its fiscal policy. Payments for specific services rendered to or for the payer are not regarded as taxation. In the UK, an individual's income is taxed by means of an *income tax (*see also* PAYE), while corporations pay a *corporation tax. Increases in individual wealth are taxed by means of *capital gains tax and by *inheritance tax. *See also* DIRECT TAXATION; INDIRECT TAXATION; VALUE ADDED TAX.

taxation brackets Figures between which taxable income or wealth is taxed at a specified rate. In the UK there are three main brackets of income tax: the *starting rate of income tax, the *basic rate of income tax; and the *higher rate of income tax. *See also* CAPITAL GAINS TAX.

tax avoidance (tax planning) Minimizing tax liabilities legally and by means of full disclosure to the tax authorities. *Compare* TAX EVASION.

tax base The specified domain on which a tax is levied, e.g. an individual's income for *income tax, the estate of a deceased person for *inheritance tax, the profits of a company for *corporation tax.

tax break A tax advantage for a particular activity.

tax burden The amount of tax suffered by an individual or organization. This may not be the same as the tax actually paid because of the possibility of shifting tax or the normal *incidence of taxation. As an example of the latter case, *inheritance tax is paid by the personal representatives of the deceased but the tax burden falls on the heirs, since their inheritance is reduced.

tax clearance An assurance, obtained from HM Revenue and Customs, that a proposed transaction, for example the reorganization of a company's share capital, will, if executed, not attract tax.

tax code 1. *See* INCOME TAX CODE. **2.** The body of tax law applicable in a country, in which the tax law is codified rather than laid down by statute.

tax credit 1. The tax allowance associated with the *dividend paid by a company. The shareholder is given allowance for the tax paid at source by the tax credit, at the same rate, 10/90; i.e. a dividend of £90 received by the shareholder has an associated tax credit of £10. For those whose taxable income does not exceed £32,400 there is no further tax to pay. For those whose income is higher, the excess is chargeable at a rate of 32.5%. **2.** Any other allowance against a tax liability. **3.** In the UK, a social security payment such as the Working Tax Credit or Child Tax Credit that is administered by HM Revenue and Customs. Despite their titles, neither of these payments affects the amount of tax that is payable.

tax-deductible Denoting an amount that can be deducted from income or profits, in accordance with the tax legislation, before establishing the amount of income or profits that is subject to tax.

tax-deferred Describing a financial instrument in which tax is paid at maturity.

tax deposit certificate A certificate issued by HM Revenue and Customs to a taxpayer who has made an advance payment in anticipation of future income tax, capital-gains tax, or corporation tax. The initial payment must not be less than £2000 and has to be made to a tax-collection office. The certificates bear interest, which is liable to tax. The interest rate depends on whether the certificate is withdrawn for cash or surrendered to meet a tax demand. A higher rate is paid on the latter. Interest normally runs to the date of encashment but if the certificate is used to pay tax, it runs only to the due date of payment of the liability, not the actual date of payment.

tax-effective Denoting a procedure that is in accordance with the tax legislation and results in a reduction in the tax charge.

tax evasion Minimizing tax liabilities illegally, usually by not disclosing that one is liable to tax or by giving false information to the authorities. Evasion is liable to severe penalties. *Compare* TAX AVOIDANCE.

Tax Exempt Special Savings Account (Tessa) A UK savings account with a bank or building society, introduced in January 1991, in which savers were allowed to invest up to £9000 over a five-year period with no tax to pay on their interest, provided that special conditions were met. Savers investing in a Tessa for the first time could deposit up to £3000 in the first year and £1800 in any subsequent year (the maximum of £1800 could only be invested in the fifth year if a reduced amount was invested in one of the previous years). Savers with a matured Tessa could invest all the capital (i.e. up to £9000) from this account in a new Tessa during the first year, provided the new account was opened within six months of the maturity date of the old Tessa. The tax exemption was lost if: (a) capital was withdrawn at any time; (b) withdrawals of interest or bonuses exceeded 80% of the total amount of these credited to the account prior to the withdrawal; (c) the account holders' rights were assigned or used as security for a loan. Tessas were replaced by *Individual Savings Accounts (ISAs) in April 1999; however, existing Tessas were allowed to continue under the same arrangements until their term expired.

tax exile A person with a high income or considerable wealth who chooses to live in a *tax haven in order to avoid the high taxation of his or her native country.

tax-free Denoting a payment, allowance, benefit, etc., on which no tax is payable.

tax harmonization The process of increasing the compatibility of various taxation systems by limiting the variations between them. The main areas of difference in taxation are the *tax base and the rates of tax applicable. There is often strong resistance to tax harmonization between independent states as, by setting limits within which the tax rates can be set, the authority of individual governments is eroded.

tax haven A country or area that has a low rate of tax and therefore offers advantages to retired wealthy individuals or to companies that can arrange their affairs so that their tax liability falls at least partly in the low-tax haven. In the case of individuals, the cost of the tax saving is usually residence in the tax haven for a majority of the year (*see* TAX EXILE). For multinational companies, an office in the tax haven, with some real or contrived business passing through it, is required. Monaco, Liechtenstein, the Bahamas, and the Cayman Islands are examples of tax havens. *See also* OFFSHORE FINANCIAL CENTRES.

tax holiday A period during which a company, in certain countries, is excused from paying corporation tax or profits tax (or pays them on only part of its profits) as an export incentive or an incentive to start up a new industry.

tax invoice A detailed *value added tax invoice that must be provided by a *taxable person to another taxable person when the *taxable supply is made for over £100. The tax invoice must show:
- the supplier's name, address, and VAT registration number;
- the tax point and invoice number;
- the name and address of the customer;
- a description of the transaction and the goods supplied;

- the amount of VAT and the amount excluding VAT.

A less detailed invoice is required for a supply of less than £100.

tax loss A loss made by an organization in one period, that can be carried forward to another period to reduce the tax payable by that organization in the subsequent period. *See* LOSS RELIEFS.

tax month Under the UK taxation system, the month running from the 6th day of one month to the 5th day of the following month. This ensures that there are 12 complete tax months in the *fiscal year.

tax planning *See* TAX AVOIDANCE.

tax point The date on which goods are removed or made available to a customer or the date on which services to a customer are completed. The tax point determines the tax period for which the *output tax must be accounted for to the *Board of Customs and Excise.

tax rebate A repayment of tax paid. A repayment claim must be made and approved by an *Inspector of Taxes and the refund due to the taxpayer will be made by the *Collector of Taxes following the Inspector's instructions.

tax relief A deduction from a taxable amount, usually given by statute. In the UK, income-tax reliefs are given in respect of income from tax-exempt sources (e.g. ISAs), as well as tax-deductible expenses, personal allowances, tax credits, and *gift aid. *See* INCOME TAX ALLOWANCES.

The reliefs against *capital gains tax include an annual exemption, exemption from the proceeds of the sale of an only or a principal private residence, and *taper relief. For *inheritance tax there is an annual relief as well as relief in respect of gifts between spouses and gifts to political parties and charities; agricultural and business reliefs are also available.

tax return A form upon which a taxpayer makes an annual statement of income and personal circumstances enabling claims to be made for personal allowances. In the UK an income tax return also requires details of *capital gains in the year. The onus is on the taxpayer to provide HM Revenue and Customs with the appropriate information even if the taxpayer receives no tax return. Categories of tax payer who can expect to receive a tax return include the self-employed, company directors, people with a high investment income, and those acting as trustees or personal representatives. Since 1996–97 income tax returns have included a section for *self-assessment, in which the tax payer calculates his or her own liability for income tax. Separate returns are required for *inheritance tax purposes and by the *Board of Customs and Excise in respect of VAT and excise duties. It is now possible to complete and send back a tax return over the Internet.

tax schedules *See* SCHEDULE.

tax shelter (tax shield) Any financial arrangement made to lower a person's or a company's tax liabilities.

tax tables Tables issued by HM Revenue and Customs to employers to assist them in calculating the tax due from their employees under the pay-as-you-earn system (*see* PAYE). The tables are provided either for weekly or monthly payments. In practice, most employers now calculate salaries, wages, and tax deductions by computer, using a program into which the tax tables are incorporated.

tax treaty An agreement between two countries, identifying the treatment of income, profits, or gains that are subject to tax in both countries. The amount of *double taxation relief will be specified in the treaty.

tax year *See* FISCAL YEAR.

Taylorism *See* SCIENTIFIC MANAGEMENT.

team building exercises Various interventions designed to increase the extent to which a work group functions as a team; that is, as a cohesive, united, emotionally bonded group in which individual inputs (skills, effort, personal characteristics) are combined to maximum effect in pursuit of the common goal. Such exercises usually involve an element of group problem solving, which may or may not be related to the usual professional activities of the group. *See* BUSINESS GAMES; OUTDOOR TRAINING PROGRAMME.

team selling The use of teams of people drawn from a number of departments in a company to service large and complex accounts. The team may include personnel from sales, marketing, production, finance, and technical support departments; it may also be headed by a member of the upper management.

technical analysis *See* INVESTMENT ANALYST.

technical rally *See* RALLY.

technical reserves The assets held by an insurance company against future claims or losses.

technological change An increase in the level of output resulting from automation and computerized methods of production. Apart from increasing output, technological change can affect the ratio of capital to labour used in a factory. If it involves reducing the labour force it can lead to **technological unemployment** in an area or industry.

technological risk **1.** The *risk to a business from changing technology. **2.** The inherent risk in *project financing schemes that the newly constructed plant will not operate to specification. *Compare* COMPLETION RISK; SUPPLY RISK.

technology transfer The transfer of technological knowledge to a third party, which often occurs when a patent holder grants a licence to another firm to use a technology, process, or product. In many instances this transfer takes place between countries, when a firm establishes an overseas subsidiary or grants a licence to a local producer. It is therefore a means by which countries gain new technology or update their existing technological base, enabling them to build up their industrial infrastructure. *See* MULTINATIONAL ENTERPRISE.

telecommuting (teleworking) A work arrangement in which employees work at remote locations, usually at home, using computers and telecommunications links to carry out their responsibilities and communicate with others as necessary.

teleconferencing *See* VIDEOCONFERENCING.

telegraphic transfer (TT) A method of transmitting money overseas by means of a cabled transfer between banks. The transfer is usually made in the currency of the payee and may be credited to his account at a specified bank or paid in cash to the payee on application and identification.

telemarketing *See* TELEPHONE SELLING.

telenet A computer program that provides remote access to data and text-based programs on other computer systems at a different location. For example, a retailer could check to see whether or not an item was in stock in a warehouse using a telenet application.

telephone banking A *home banking facility enabling customers to use banking services by means of a telephone link.

telephone focus groups *Focus groups that are conducted by means of *audioconferencing or *videoconferencing.

telephone research A marketing research technique in which **telephone interviews** are conducted. It is cheaper than personal interviewing and, perhaps because it avoids face-to-face confrontations, seems to be more popular with respondents.

telephone selling (telemarketing) A method of *direct marketing in which the telephone is used to contact potential customers in order to reduce the time spent in making personal visits. Certain products, such as double glazing and central heating, are frequently marketed using this technique. Orders may be taken over the phone, or arrangements are made for sales representatives to visit interested clients. *See also* COLD CALLING.

teletext An information service in which pages of text are transmitted to the home or office for display on a television set. The information is given under various headings, with a *menu call-up system, and includes latest stock exchange prices. The two systems originally developed in the UK were Ceefax, provided by the BBC, and Oracle, provided by the IBA. Oracle was replaced by a new system provided by Teletext Ltd in 1992 and Ceefax was phased out in favour of a digital text service from 2001. *See also* VIEWDATA.

television home shopping A cable or digital television shopping service in which consumers see a product on their home TV screens and are able to place orders by telephone. *See also* HOME SHOPPING CHANNELS.

television rating (TVR) The measurement of the popularity of a television programme based on survey research. Equipment attached to sets in selected homes records which channel the set is tuned to, while *diary panels are used to determine how many people are watching the set. In this way ratings can be calculated for each programme and expressed as a percentage of the total households that can receive TV. Survey research is undertaken in the UK by the Broadcasters Audience Research Board (*BARB).

Telex A method of communicating written messages over the international telephone network, using a Telex (teleprinter) machine. Although *fax and *e-mail have replaced Telex in virtually all business applications it is still used by shipping, news services, and the military.

teller The US name for a bank or building society cashier, i.e. someone who accepts deposits and pays out cash over the counter to customers.

temporal method A method of converting a foreign currency involved in a transaction in which the local currency is translated at the exchange rate in operation on the date on which the transaction occurred. If rates do not fluctuate significantly, an average for the period may be used as an approximation. Any exchange gain or loss on translation is taken to the *profit and loss account. This contrasts with the closing rate or net-investment method of translation, which uses the exchange rate ruling at the balance-sheet date for translation and takes exchange differences to *reserves. *Statement of Standard Accounting Practice (SSAP) 20, Foreign Currency Translation, allows either method to be adopted. This area is now governed by the detailed regulations in *Financial Reporting Standard 23, The Effects of Change in Foreign Exchange Rates, which replaced SSAP 20 in 2004.

temporary assurance *See* TERM ASSURANCE.

tenancy agreement An agreement to let land. See LEASE.

tenancy in common Two or more persons having an interest in the same piece of land. Each person can bequeath his or her interest by will, although the land itself has not been physically divided. Trustees must hold the legal estate and the tenancy in common exists in equity. See also JOINT TENANTS.

tender **1.** A written offer to purchase something at a stated price. **2.** A means of auctioning an item of value to the highest bidder. Tenders are used in many circumstances, e.g. for allocating valuable construction contracts, for selling shares on a stock market (see OFFER FOR SALE; ISSUE BY TENDER), or for the sale of government securities (see GILT-EDGED SECURITY).

tender offer **1.** An offer by one company to buy the shares of another from the shareholders at a stated price (usually at a premium above the market price). It is normally made as part of a *takeover bid. See also SELF-TENDER; TWO-TIER TENDER OFFER. **2.** See ISSUE BY TENDER.

tender panel A group of banks who are asked to subscribe as a syndicate for the issue of *euronote facilities.

tenesi A monetary unit of Turkmenistan, worth one hundredth of a *manat.

tenge (T) The standard monetary unit of Kazakhstan, divided into 100 tiyn.

tenor The time period elapsing between the issue of a security (such as a *bill of exchange) and its maturity.

Ten Windows Ten institutions in the People's Republic of China that are authorized to borrow abroad.

terabyte A billion kilobytes, i.e. a million megabytes, a thousand gigabytes, or a trillion bytes.

term **1.** The period of time before a security expires or is redeemed. **2.** See TERM ASSURANCE. **3.** A clause in a contract that refers to a particular obligation between the contracting parties.

term assurance (temporary assurance) A life-assurance policy that operates for a specified period of time. No benefit is paid if the insured person dies outside the period. This form of insurance is often used to cover the period of a loan, mortgage, etc. If the insured person dies before the loan has been repaid, it is settled by the insurance company. See also DECREASING TERM ASSURANCE.

term bill See PERIOD BILL.

terminable annuity See CERTAIN ANNUITY.

terminal A computer input and output device. It commonly consists of a keyboard and display screen, connected to the computer. Terminals that are distant from the computer and connected to it by a communications link are called remote terminals. Terminals with some computing power, often incorporating a *microprocessor, are called *intelligent terminals. Specialized terminals have been developed for use in banking and retailing.

terminal bonus An additional amount of money added to payments made on the maturity of an insurance policy or on the death of an insured person, because the investments of the insurer have produced a profit or surplus. Bonuses of this kind are paid at the discretion of the life office and usually take the form of a percentage of the sum assured.

terminal date The date on which a *futures contract expires.

terminal-loss relief Relief for a loss made by a company, partnership, or sole trader during the last 12 months of trading. The business or profession must be permanently discontinued. For partnerships and sole traders, the loss of the last 12 months can be set against the profits of the three years prior to the final tax year, taking the most recent year first. For companies, the trading loss arising in the accounting period in which the trade ceases may be carried back and offset against the profits of the three years ending immediately before the commencement of the final period of trading. See LOSS RELIEFS.

terminal market A commodity market in a trading centre, such as London or New York, rather than a market in a producing centre, such as Calcutta or Singapore. The trade in terminal markets is predominantly in *futures, but *spot goods may also be bought and sold.

terminal value (TV) The value of an investment at the end of an investment period taking into account a specified rate of interest over the period. The formula is the same as that for compound *interest, i.e.

$$TV = P(1 + r)^t,$$

where TV is the final amount at the end of period, P is the principal amount invested, r is the interest rate, and t is the time in years for which the investment takes place.

term loan A loan from a bank to a company. The term of the loan is fixed and it is drawn down (see DRAWDOWN) immediately or within a short period of signing the loan agreement as set out in the *amortization schedule.

term shares Shares that cannot be sold for a given period (term). They are usually shares in a building society that cannot be cashed on demand and consequently carry a higher rate of interest.

terms of trade A measure of the trading prospects of a country expressed as an index of export prices divided by an index of import prices. A country's terms of trade improve if this ratio rises, because it can purchase more imports for a particular volume of exports.

term structure of interest rates A set of discount rates for each year to maturity, applied to fixed-rate securities such as government bonds. The term structure of interest rates is related to the *yield curve, but differs from this in that it gives a discount rate appropriate for individual years to maturity, rather than the discount rate for all years on a bond to maturity.

terotechnology The branch of technology that involves the use of management, financial, and engineering skills in installing, operating, and maintaining plant and machinery. See LIFE-CYCLE COSTING.

territorial salesforce structure A salesforce organization that assigns an exclusive geographic territory to a particular salesperson, who carries the company's full line.

territorial waters The part of the sea around a country's coastline over which it has jurisdiction according to international law. Historically, it was the sea within three miles of the coast, a practical distance determined by the range of a cannon ball. Since disputes have arisen over fishing rights, off-shore oil mining, and mineral rights below the ocean, the universal three-mile rule has been abrogated and various nations have made different claims, some, but not all, of which have been accepted internationally. Ten to fifteen miles is now quite common in definitions of territorial waters. The Territorial Sea Act (1987) fixes the UK territorial waters at 12 nautical miles. A UN convention proposes a new 200-mile **exclusive economic zone**, which would give a country sovereign rights over all the resources of the sea, seabed, and subsoil within this zone. Fishing rights extending to 200 miles are also claimed by many nations, including the UK.

tertiary production See PRODUCTION.

Tessa Abbreviation for *Tax Exempt Special Savings Account.

testimonial advertisement An advertisement that makes use of the implied or explicit patronage of a product by a well-known person or organization.

test marketing (market testing) A procedure for launching a new product in a restricted geographical area to test consumers' reactions. If the product is unsuccessful, the company will have minimized its costs and can make the necessary changes before a wider launch. Test marketing is typically undertaken in large towns or in areas served by a particular commercial television company. Test marketing has the disadvantage that competitors learn about the new product before its full launch. See also NEW PRODUCT DEVELOPMENT.

tetri A monetary unit of Georgia, worth one hundredth of a *lari.

TGI Abbreviation for *Target Group Index.

thebe A monetary unit of Botswana, worth one hundredth of a *pula.

theory of constraints (TOC) An approach to the planning of production that focuses attention on the capacity constraints or bottlenecks that occur in the process, rather than attempting to maximize loading across the whole system.

Examples of TOC solutions include:
- providing additional training for employees to improve working speeds;
- replacing an existing bottleneck machine with a faster one;
- changing the design of a product to reduce manufacturing time.

See also OPTIMIZED PRODUCTION TECHNOLOGY.

theory of games *See* GAME THEORY.

Theory X and Theory Y Two conflicting theories regarding the human motivation to work, put forward by the US psychologist Douglas McGregor (1906–64), which have relevance in *human-resource management.

Theory X is based on the premise that people are inherently lazy, dislike work, and will avoid it if they can. They prefer being directed to accepting responsibility; their only use for creativity is in getting round the rules of an organization. Because they are motivated to work only by money, they require coercion and tight control to make them function adequately.

Theory Y, on the other hand, assumes that people wish to be interested in their work and, given the right conditions, will enjoy it. Motivated by the wish to achieve, and to have their achievements recognized, most people will work to the best of their capabilities, creativity, and ingenuity. They accept responsibility and the rules of the organization they work for, imposing self-discipline on their work, given accepted targets.

The generally accepted view is that if management follow Theory Y they will achieve better operational performance. *See also* THEORY Z.

Theory Z An alternative approach to *human-resource management put forward by William Ouchi, as a way of enabling US companies to integrate aspects of the Japanese approach to human resource management (*compare* THEORY X AND THEORY Y). The theory proposes: more secure employment, better career prospects, greater employee participation in decision making, greater emphasis on the team spirit, recognition of the contributions of employees, and the development of greater mutual respect between managers and employees. The implementation of this theory requires a commitment to consultation and to training by top management.

thin capitalization An arrangement in which a company is incorporated with a small share capital and financed with a large loan from its parent company, usually in order to benefit from tax relief or the interest payment on the loan. Some countries, including the UK, reserve the right in such cases to treat some of the interest on the loan stock as if it were a dividend, thus denying the right to a tax deduction.

thin market A market in which the price of the underlying commodity, currency, or financial instrument may change if sizable transactions are carried out. *Compare* DEEP MARKET.

third-country acceptance (refinance bill) An international trade *time draft drawn on a country other than that of the importer or exporter. *See also* BANKER'S ACCEPTANCE.

third-line forcing Forcing a buyer to take a supply of something unwanted as a condition of supplying him or her with a desired product. The practice is deprecated by the Restrictive Practices Court (*see* RESTRICTIVE TRADE PRACTICES).

third-party insurance Insurance of a person's legal liabilities to others. The insurer and the policyholder are the two parties to the insurance contract, any other person to whom there is a legal obligation is therefore a third party. Some forms of third-party insurance are compulsory, e.g. motorists must have third-party cover for any loss or damage suffered by members of the public as a result of their driving and employers must cover against any results of injury to employees at work. Professional indemnity insurance is a form of third-party insurance that is optional.

360° feedback A system that provides employees with all-round performance *feedback from colleagues, manager(s), customers, and others. Crucially, it also compares the individual's self-perception with performance ratings supplied by others.

threshold agreement An agreement between an employer and employees (or their union) that pay will increase by a specified amount if the rate of inflation exceeds a specified figure in a specified period. Threshold agreements are seen by some as providing an inflationary pressure of their own but others claim that they reduce inflation by making it unnecessary for unions to press for excessive settlements to protect their members against inflation.

threshold effect The point at which advertising begins to show signs of increasing sales. As advertising is expensive, the threshold effect is important because it sets the minimum level for an advertising budget.

threshold price *See* COMMON AGRICULTURAL POLICY.

throughput accounting An approach to short-term decision making in manufacturing in which all *conversion costs are treated as though they were fixed and products are ranked if a particular *constraint or scarce resource exists. Decisions are made using the **throughput accounting ratio** (**TAR**) as follows:

return per factory hour/cost per factory hour,

where return per factory hour =

(sales price – material cost)/hours on scarce resource;

and cost per factory hour =

total factory cost/total available hours of constraint.

More recently, throughput accounting has been applied in more general areas of *management accounting.

tick The smallest possible price movement on a financial market; this is usually a single *basis point (0.01%). In foreign-exchange trading, the term **pip** is often preferred.

tickertape *See* TAPE.

tied loan A loan made by one nation to another on condition that the money loaned is spent buying goods or services in the lending nation. It thus helps the lending nation, by providing employment, as well as the borrowing nation.

tied outlet A retail outlet that is obliged to sell only the products of one producer (and possibly other noncompeting products). The outlet is usually owned by the producer; in other cases the outlet agrees to become tied in return for financial concessions.

tie-in A collaboration between two or more organizations, working as partners in a promotional effort.

tiger markets The colloquial name for the four most important markets in the Pacific Basin after Japan. They are Hong Kong, South Korea, Singapore, and Taiwan. *Compare* DRAGON MARKETS.

tight money *See* DEAR MONEY.

TIGR Abbreviation for Treasury Investors Growth Receipt. These *zero-coupon bonds are linked to US Treasury bonds. They are denominated in dollars and are usually referred to as **Tigers**.

time and motion study A method of finding the best way of performing a complex task by breaking the task into small steps and measuring the time taken to perform each step. This enables standards of performance to be set. These standards can then be used to plan and control production, estimate prices and delivery times, and devise incentive schemes. Time and motion studies are associated with the school of *scientific management.

time bargain A contract in which securities have to be delivered at some date in the future.

time card (clock card) A card on which is recorded the time spent by an employee at the place of work or the time spent on a particular job. The card is usually marked by mechanical or electronic means by recording the starting and ending times, enabling the elapsed time to be calculated.

time charter The hire of a ship or aircraft for a specified period of time rather than for a specified number of voyages (*compare* VOYAGE CHARTER).

time deposit A deposit of money in an

interest-bearing account for a specified period. In the USA, a time deposit requires at least 30 days' notice of withdrawal.

time draft A *bill of exchange drawn on and accepted by a US bank. *See also* BANKER'S ACCEPTANCE.

time fence A period during which a *master production schedule (MPS) must not be changed, to enable the *material requirements planning to stabilize. Once the system is stable, the MPS can change.

time pacing The practice of producing, or introducing, new products according to a given schedule.

time rate A rate of pay expressed as a sum of money paid to an individual for the time worked, rather than for a specified output (*compare* PIECE RATE).

time-series analysis A marketing research technique for forecasting sales, in which past sales are broken down into trends, cycles, seasons, and erratic components; these components are then recombined to produce a sales forecast. *See also* NAIVE QUANTITATIVE METHODS.

time sharing A method of operating a computer in which several programs apparently run at the same time. Although the computer actually divides its time between the programs, it is fast enough to allow each program to operate at an acceptable speed. Most *multitasking and multiuser systems are time sharing systems.

time sheet A form on which is recorded the employee time or machine time spent on each activity during a period. It is used for costing jobs, operations, or activities.

time to market (TTM) The time taken to bring a new product or service from the initial concept stage to its introduction to the market. Shortening TTM can often deliver a substantial competitive advantage. *See* CONCURRENT ENGINEERING.

time value The market value of an *option over and above its *intrinsic value, representing the value of the possibility that the price of the *underlying will shift significantly in a favourable direction before the option expires. Clearly, this value declines with the passage of time; the option's value at expiry will be nil if it is not

*in the money. At expiry the value of an option, if any, consists solely of its intrinsic value.

time value of money The concept, used as the basis for *discounted cash flow calculations, that cash received earlier is worth more than a similar sum received later, because the sum received earlier can be invested to earn interest in the intervening period. For the same reasons, cash paid out later is worth less than a similar sum paid at an earlier date.

title deed A document proving the ownership of land. The document must go back at least 15 years to give a good root of title. If the land is registered, the *land certificate now takes the place of the title deed. *See* ABSTRACT OF TITLE.

tiyn A monetary unit of Kazakhstan, worth one hundredth of a *tenge.

TLF Abbreviation for *transferable loan facility.

Tobin's Q *See* Q RATIO.

Tobin tax A proposed low-level tax on foreign-exchange dealings. It has been suggested that such a tax could have the effect of restraining destabilizing currency speculation while also raising large sums that could be used to aid developing nations. The tax was proposed by the US economist John Tobin.

TOC Abbreviation for *theory of constraints.

toea A monetary unit of Papua New Guinea, worth one hundredth of a *kina.

toehold An initial stake in a company obtained as a prelude to an acquisition attempt.

token strike *See* STRIKE.

tokkin A special investment fund on the Japanese stock markets owned by companies using their cash surpluses to generate extra income, although their main business is not in the financial markets.

Tokyo Stock Exchange (TSE) The largest and most important of the eight stock exchanges in Japan. There are three sections. The first lists some 1200 of the largest issues in the market. The second has around 400 stocks, with less stringent listing requirements, similar to the *Alternative Investment Market in the UK. Foreign shares are traded on the third section. Dealing is now mainly through the Computerized Order Routing and Execution System (CORES). The main market indicator is the *Nikkei Stock Average.

tolar (*plural* **tolarji**; SIT) The standard monetary unit of Slovenia, divided into 100 stotin.

tombstone An advertisement in the financial press giving brief deals of the amount and maturity of a recently completed bank facility. The names of the *lead managers are prominently displayed, as well as the co-managers and the managers. It is customary for the borrower to pay although he or she receives little benefit from the advertisement.

ton The formerly widely used **long ton** of 2240 pounds has now been replaced by the **metric ton** or **tonne** of 1000 kilograms for all purposes of trade and commerce. In the USA the **short ton** of 2000 lbs is still in use (consisting of 20 short hundredweights of 100 lbs each). The **shipping ton** is a measure of cargo-carrying capacity and consists of 100 cubic feet of space (*see* TONNAGE).

tone The sentiment of a market. If a stock exchange or commodity market has a firm or strong tone, prices are tending upwards, whereas if the tone is weak, nervous, unsettled, etc., prices are tending to fall.

tonnage A measure of the volume or cargo-carrying capacity of a ship. The **gross register tonnage** (**GRT**) is the volume of a ship below the upper deck measured in shipping *tons of 100 cubic feet. The **net register tonnage** (**NRT**) is the GRT less the space occupied by engines, fuel, stores, and accommodation for crew and passengers. Harbour and port dues are usually based on the NRT and dry dock dues are usually based on the GRT. In the UK it is now mandatory to measure tonnage in either GRT or NRT, rather than in any of the various alternative ways sometimes used formerly.

Since 2000 a UK shipowning company may elect to pay *corporation tax on the basis of the NRT of its shipping, rather than on the basis of the profit or loss made.

tonne *See* TON.

tontine *See* LAST-SURVIVOR POLICY.

too big to fail The idea that certain banks will always be supported, because their failure would have an unacceptable effect on the stability of the national or international financial system. If such a bank should get into trouble, it is argued, the central bank would be sure to bail it out. It is further contended that this will make such a bank more willing to take risks. The counterargument is that even if it received aid, there might still be serious consequences for the managers and shareholders of the bank. In any case, the theory only applies to the largest financial institutions. For example, in 1995 the London-based merchant bank Barings plc was allowed to fail after sustaining major losses through irregular trading in the Singapore derivatives market, since the Bank of England could identify no systemic risk resulting from its failure.

top-box score A high score in a scale used in marketing research to estimate purchase intentions. When companies are assessing the intention of potential customers to buy a product or service, they often use a 3-, 4-, 5-, 6-, or 7-point scale representing 'very unlikely to buy' (or some similar statement) to 'very likely to buy'. It is argued that companies should only use those percentages in the highest category ('very likely to buy') to estimate purchase intention.

top-down design An approach to product design based on general principles or deductive reasoning, rather than on empirical research or user feedback. *Compare* BOTTOM-UP DESIGN.

top-hat scheme A pension plan for a senior executive of a company. *See* EXECUTIVE PENSION PLAN.

TOPIC Acronym for Teletext Output Price Information Computer. This computerized communication system provides brokers and market makers on the *London Stock Exchange with information about share price movements and bargains as they are transacted. Input is from the *Stock Exchange Automated Quotations System

(SEAQ). It is now run by a private company independently of the stock exchange.

top slicing A method of assessing the taxable gain on a *life-assurance policy. The proceeds of the policy plus all capital withdrawals, less the premiums paid, are divided by the number of years for which the policy has been in force. This amount is added to any other income for the year in which the chargeable event occurred; if this places the taxpayer in a higher tax band, the whole gain is charged at the appropriate marginal rate, i.e. the tax rate in that band less the basic rate of tax. If the sum does not exceed the basic rate tax, no further tax is due.

top up To increase the benefits due under an existing insurance scheme, especially to increase the provision for a pension when a salary increase enables the insured to pay increased premiums.

tort A civil wrong other than one relating to a contract. The law of tort is concerned with providing *damages for personal injury and damage to property resulting from negligence. It is also concerned with protecting against defamation of character and preserving personal freedom, enjoyment of property, and commercial interests. A person who commits a tort is called a **tortfeasor**.

total absorption costing *See* ABSORPTION COSTING.

total income The income of a taxpayer from all sources. This is often referred to as **statutory total income** and comprises income from sources calculated on the basis of the income of the current *fiscal year and income from other sources calculated on the basis of the *accounting period ending in the current fiscal year. This artificial concept is used to calculate a person's income tax for a given year. *See* BASIS OF ASSESSMENT.

total market demand The total volume of a product or service that would be bought by a defined consumer group in a defined geographic area in a defined period in a defined marketing environment under a defined level and mix of industry marketing effort.

total productive management (TPM) An approach to management that empow-

ers the employees operating a piece of equipment to take responsibility for a wide range of routine maintenance tasks, traditionally carried out by a separate engineering function, and to develop a proactive approach to the prevention of failure. Integral to *total quality management, TPM is an essential part of *just-in-time techniques. The overall objective is to optimize the effectiveness of plant by eliminating downtime, less-than-maximum speed of throughput, and process-generated defects.

total profits Profits chargeable to *corporation tax (PCTCT), including profits from trading, property, investment income, overseas income, and chargeable gains, less charges.

total quality management (TQM) An approach to management that seeks to integrate all the elements of an organization in order to meet the needs and expectations of its customers. A number of people have pioneered this approach, including W. Edwards Deming, Armand V. Feigenbaum, Kaoru Ishikawa, Joseph M. Juran, and Genichi Taguchi. Some details of their various methods are in conflict, but all share a commitment to ensuring that all the parts of an organization and all the individuals within the organization understand and contribute to the desired outputs. The implementation of TQM involves:

- a systematic and long-term commitment, in particular by senior management;
- a commitment to getting things right the first time;
- a commitment to *continuous improvement;
- an understanding of both internal and external customer–supplier relationships;
- an understanding of the total costs involved in the purchase of products and services, e.g. cheap inputs of low quality can cause serious faults in processes and products;
- a commitment to aligning systems to organizational needs, which may involve a radical redesign of work processes;
- appropriate management and training techniques to improve communications

between sections and between staff and management;

- improved workplace training and a degree of employee *empowerment;
- meaningful measures of performance to enable workers to understand what they are contributing and how they can improve.

TQM as a philosophy should be able to incorporate other programmes of management change. However, many organizations fail to exploit its full potential by abandoning it too soon, either through lack of commitment or because it costs too much.

total return The total income plus the capital growth obtained from an investment.

total standard cost In *standard costing, the *total standard production cost plus the *standard cost allowance for the non-production overhead.

total standard production cost In *standard costing, the total of *standard direct materials cost, *standard direct labour cost, the *standard fixed overhead cost, and the *standard variable overhead cost.

total standard profit The difference between the sales at *standard selling prices and the *standard overhead cost of these sales.

town clearing Formerly, a special same-day clearing service for high value cheques drawn on accounts within the City of London and paid into another City account. All other cheques (known as **country cheques**) went into the general clearing system and took two or more days to clear. From 1995 the town clearing service ceased to be available. To guarantee a same-day transfer of funds, bank customers have to use the *telegraphic transfer service.

TPM Abbreviation for *total productive management.

TQM Abbreviation for *total quality management.

tracker fund *See* INDEX TRACKING.

trade 1. The activity of selling goods or services in order to make a profit. Profits from trade are taxed under *income tax

or *corporation tax on income, rather than under *capital gains tax or corporation tax on capital gains. The concept of trade is difficult to define for taxation purposes (*see* BADGES OF TRADE). **2.** To buy or sell in a market.

trade advertising Advertising that is aimed at members of the distribution channel of a product or service rather than at the consumer. It is sometimes advantageous to draw the attention of the trade to a product either in addition to *consumer advertising or instead of it (usually because it is much cheaper). For example, book publishers rarely go to the great expense of consumer advertising (say, on TV) but usually advertise a new book in the trade journals seen by booksellers, so that the staff in bookshops are kept advised of forthcoming productions.

trade agreement A commercial treaty between two (**bilateral trade agreement**) or more (**multilateral trade agreement**) nations.

trade association An association of companies in the same trade, formed to represent them in negotiations with governments, unions, other trade associations, etc., and to keep members informed of new developments affecting the trade. Trade associations also frequently draw up contracts for their members to use and provide arbitration procedures to settle disputes between members.

trade barrier Any action by a government that restricts free trading between organizations within that country and the world outside. Tariffs, quotas, embargoes, sanctions, and restrictive regulations all present barriers to free trade.

trade bill A *bill of exchange used to pay for goods. They are usually either held until they mature, as they do not command a favourable discount rate compared to bank bills, or they are discounted by banks.

trade bloc A group of nations united by trade agreements between themselves; for example, the European Union.

trade credit Credit given by one company to another; it usually results when a supplier of goods or services allows the customer a period (e.g. 14 days, 90 days) before expecting an invoice to be settled.

trade creditor One who is owed money by an organization for having provided goods or services to that organization.

trade cycle *See* BUSINESS CYCLE.

trade description Any direct or indirect indication of certain characteristics of goods or of any part of them, such as their quantity, size, fitness for their purpose, time or place of origin, method of manufacture or processing, and price. Under the Trade Descriptions Act (1968), it is a criminal offence to apply a false trade description to goods or to supply or offer any goods to which a false description is applied.

trade discount (trade terms) A reduction on the recommended retail price of a product or service that is offered to distributors because they buy regularly in bulk. The difference between the retail price and the discounted price provides the retailer with his overheads and profit. The amount of the trade discount will often depend on the size of an order. Thus, a supermarket chain buying goods in very large quantities expects a higher trade discount than a corner shop buying in small quantities. It is also usual for members of the same trade to offer each other trade terms as a matter of course.

trade dispute (industrial dispute) A dispute between an employer and employees (or their trade union), usually about wages or conditions of working. Under the Trade Union and Labour Relations Act (1974), a person cannot be sued in *tort for an act that is committed in furtherance of a trade dispute on the grounds that it induces or threatens breach of interference with the performance of a contract. Generally, such immunity extends only to the acts of employees against their own employer. Secondary industrial action (*see* PICKETING) may be unlawful when it is directed against an employer who is neither a party to the dispute nor the customer or supplier of the employer in dispute. Moreover, there is no immunity in respect of action taken to enforce a *closed shop.

The Act, as amended by the Employment Acts (1982 and 1988) and the Trade Union Act (1984), gives similar immunity

to trade unions for their acts committed in contemplation or furtherance of a trade dispute provided the act concerned is authorized by a majority vote in favour of the action in a secret ballot of the union's members. Under the Employment Act (1988) a trade union member can obtain a court order preventing industrial action being taken if it has not been authorized by a ballot.

Under the Employment Act (1982), when a trade union's immunity does not apply and it is ordered to pay damages (other than for causing personal injury or for breach of duty concerning the ownership, control, or use of property, or for *products liability under the Consumer Protection Act (1987)), the amount awarded may not exceed specified limits. These limits depend on the number of members in the union.

traded option *See* OPTION.

trade gap The difference between the value of a nation's imports and the value of its exports. *See also* BALANCE OF PAYMENTS.

trade investment Shares in or loans made to another company with a view to facilitating trade with the other company.

trademark A distinctive symbol that identifies particular products of a trader to the general public. The symbol may consist of a device, words, or a combination of these. A trader may register a trademark at the Register of Trade Marks, which is at the Patent Office (*see* PATENT). This authorizes the trader to enjoy the exclusive right to the trademark for which it was registered. Any manufacturer, dealer, importer, or retailer may register a trademark. Registration is initially for seven years and is then renewable. The right to remain on the register may be lost if the trademark is not used or is misused. The owner of a trademark may assign it or, subject to the Registrar's approval, allow others to use it. If anyone uses a registered trademark without the owner's permission, or uses a mark that is likely to be confused with a registered trademark, the owner can sue for an *injunction and *damages or an *account of profits.

The owner of a trademark that is not registered in the Register of Trade Marks but is identified with particular goods through established use may bring an action for *passing off in the case of infringement.

Tradepoint Investment Exchange A former *order-driven electronic market for *blue chip securities in London. It was superseded by *virt-x in 2001.

trade price The price paid for goods to a wholesaler or manufacturer by a retailer. It is usually the recommended retail price less the *trade discount.

trade promotion A sales promotion designed to gain reseller support and to improve reseller selling efforts. These include discounts, allowances, free goods, cooperative advertising, and push money, as well as conventions and trade shows. *See also* TRADE ADVERTISING.

trade reference A reference concerning the creditworthiness of a trader given by another member of the same trade, usually to a supplier. If a firm wishes to purchase goods on credit from a supplier, the supplier will usually ask for a trade reference from another member of the same trade, in addition to a *banker's reference.

trade secret Knowledge of some process or product belonging to a business, disclosure of which would harm the business's interests. In the UK, the courts will generally grant injunctions to prohibit any threatened disclosure of trade secrets by employees, former employees, and others to whom the secrets have been disclosed in confidence. *See also* INDUSTRIAL ESPIONAGE.

trade show A meeting or convention of members of a particular industry, at which business-to-business contacts are routinely made.

Trades Union Congress (TUC) The central UK organization to which most *trade unions belong. It represents the trade-union movement in negotiations with the government and such bodies as the *Confederation of British Industry. It also acts as an arbitrator in disputes between member unions.

trade terms *See* TRADE DISCOUNT.

trade union An organization whose principal purposes include the regulation of relations between employees and employers or employers' associations. A **house** (*or* **company**) **union** is an association of employees all belonging to the same company, which will probably have no connection with the trade-union movement. An **industrial** (*or* **general**) **union** has members who work in the same industry; it is usually very large. A **craft union** is a small union of skilled workers. Unions' affairs are regulated by the Trade Union Act (1984) and the Employment Act (1988). These provide that secret ballots must be held for election of unions' executive committees and before any industrial action backed by the union is taken. The Employment Act (1988) gives a right to trade-union members not to be unjustifiably disciplined by their union (for example for failing to take industrial action). A member can apply to an *employment tribunal for a declaration that he or she has been unjustifiably disciplined.

trading account The part of a *profit and loss account in which the *cost of sales is compared with the money raised by their sale in order to arrive at the *gross profit.

trading estate (industrial estate) An area of land that has been granted planning permission for the development of factories, warehouses, offices, retail outlets, etc. Originating in the late 19th century (e.g. at Trafford Park, Manchester in 1896), they offer land away from residential areas that is well served by transport and services; they also enable premises to be acquired at low rentals. *See also* SCIENCE PARK.

trading floor *See* FLOOR.

trading halt **1.** The cessation of trading on a financial market when price movements reach the permitted *limit. **2.** The halting of trading in a particular security, usually as a result of a major news development or destabilizing rumour.

trading pit *See* PIT.

trading post The base on the trading *floor from which a specialist on a US stock exchange operates.

trading profit The *profit of an organization before deductions for such items as interest, directors' fees, auditors' remuneration, etc.

trading stock *See* STOCK-IN-TRADE.

traditional costing system Any of the systematic costing methods that prevailed before the rise of *activity-based costing in the 1990s. Because they rely on an essentially *arbitrary allocation of *indirect costs, such systems do not give managers accurate product cost information, which means that accurate calculation of product profitability is not possible. The overhead rate in a traditional costing system would typically be calculated using direct labour hours, machine hours, or units. This could lead to accurate product costs when direct costs were high and indirect costs were low, as was usually the case 50 years ago; however, modern organizations typically have low direct costs and higher indirect costs.

The strengths of traditional costing systems are:

- simplicity – the calculation of overhead rates is relatively straightforward;
- they are widely understood in the business;
- they are not expensive to operate;
- until the late 1980s they were seen as fairly accurate;
- they are still being used after many decades.

The weaknesses of traditional costing systems are:

- their reliance on arbitrary rather than *cause-and-effect allocation of overheads;
- their inability to give accurate product costs in multiproduct companies;
- their failure to analyse non-manufacturing costs.

traditional option *See* OPTION.

trait theories of leadership *See* LEADERSHIP THEORIES.

tramp ship A cargo-carrying ship that does not have a planned itinerary but carries its cargo to any ports for which its charterers can find cargo. Tramps are available for *voyage charter or *time charter (the latter is now more common) and many are tankers.

tranche (French: slice) A part or instalment of a large sum of money. In the International Monetary Fund the first 25% of a loan is known as the **reserve** (formerly **gold**) **tranche**. In **tranche funding**, successive sums of money become available on a prearranged basis to a new company, often linked to the progress of the company and its ability to reach the targets set in its *business plan.

tranche CD A *certificate of deposit that has one maturity date but is sold by the issuing bank in portions (*tranches) to other investors.

transactional database A computerized database of the purchases made by a particular customer.

transactional leadership A *leadership style based on the setting of clear goals and objectives for followers and the use of rewards and punishments to encourage compliance. *Compare* TRANSFORMATIONAL LEADERSHIP. *See also* CONTINGENT REINFORCEMENT; POWER STYLES.

transaction costs Costs arising from such transactions as buying and selling.

transfer **1.** The movement of money from one bank account to another. **2.** The movement of funds through the banking system's *clearing house. **3.** A large movement of dollars in the USA through the *fedwire system. **4.** The conveyance of property ownership by the transfer of deeds. **5.** *See* SHARE TRANSFER.

transferable Denoting a deed or other document the ownership of which can be transferred freely, e.g. a *negotiable instrument.

transferable loan facility (TLF) A bank loan facility that can be traded between lenders, in order to reduce the credit risk of the bank that provided the loan. It is a form of *securitization but can have an adverse effect on *relationship banking.

transfer credit risk The *credit risk that arises, especially on long-term contracts, as a result of a foreign debtor's inability to obtain foreign currency from the central bank at the appropriate time. This may occur even when the debtor is able and willing to pay. *Compare* POLITICAL CREDIT RISK.

transferee A person to whom an asset is transferred.

transfer of value The reduction in the value of a person's estate by a gratuitous transfer. Such transfers are subject to *inheritance tax in most cases if made in a given period before the date of the donor's death.

transferor A person who transfers an asset to another (the transferee).

transfer payment (transfer income) A payment made or income received in which no goods or services are being paid for. Pensions, unemployment benefits, subsidies to farmers, etc., are transfer payments; they are excluded in calculating *gross national product.

transfer prices The prices at which goods and services are bought and sold between divisions or subsidiaries within a group of companies.

The transfer price is a cost to the receiving division and revenue to the supplying division: therefore the transfer price will affect the profitability of each division. In a complex organization there may be several buying and selling divisions in a group. Transfer prices can also apply between *cost centres.

Managers need to consider a complex range of issues when setting a transfer price. This is because transfer pricing can be used for several quite different purposes:
- to provide information that motivates managers to make good economic decisions;
- to provide information for evaluating the managerial and economic performance of divisions;
- to maintain divisional autonomy;
- to move profits between divisions, which may involve moving profits from one country to another to minimize tax on profits. (In the UK the scope for doing this has been greatly reduced by legislation passed in 2002.)

As a result, those setting transfer prices may find that they face a conflict of objectives. For example, senior managers of a group may want to maximize profitability even though this will means reducing the autonomy of divisional managers. This may result in short-term increases in profitability but at the expense of the motivation of divisional managers in the long run.

There are six main transfer-pricing methods: *see* COST-PLUS TRANSFER PRICES;

DUAL-RATE TRANSFER PRICES; FULL-COST TRANSFER PRICES; MARGINAL-COST TRANSFER PRICES; MARKET-BASED TRANSFER PRICES; NEGOTIATED TRANSFER PRICES.

transformational leadership A *leadership style that involves generating a vision for the organization and inspiring followers to meet the challenges that it sets. Transformational leadership depends on the leader's ability to appeal to the higher values and motives of followers and to inspire a feeling of loyalty and trust. Successful leadership of this kind usually has four components:
- individualized consideration – each team member is recognized and respected for their individual contribution;
- intellectual stimulation – the free exchange of ideas and opinions is encouraged;
- inspirational motivation – an optimistic but clear and attainable vision is set by the leader;
- charisma – the leader is seen to take responsibility, make personal sacrifices, show determination in the face of setbacks, and share any glory.

Compare TRANSACTIONAL LEADERSHIP.

transformation system A system that takes inputs and converts them into desired outputs. *See* OPERATIONS; TRANSFORMED RESOURCES; TRANSFORMING RESOURCES.

transformed resources Resources input into a *transformation system that are changed or acted upon by the system to produce the desired outputs. Examples include steel rod converted into bolts, survey data converted into market-research forecasts, and passengers transported from A to B. *Compare* TRANSFORMING RESOURCES.

transforming resources Resources input into a *transformation system that act upon, or facilitate action upon, *transformed resources to produce the desired outputs. Examples include machine tools, trained market researchers, and railway stations.

transhipment The shipment of goods from one port to another with a change of ship at an intermediate port. Transhipments are usually made because there is no direct service between the ports of shipment and destination, or because it is necessary for some political reason, e.g. wishing to conceal the port of shipment from the buyers, whose government may have embargoed goods from the country of that port.

transire A two-part document in which the cargo loaded onto a coaster is detailed. It is supplied by the Customs at the port of shipment; one part has to be handed to the Customs at the port of destination to prove that the cargo comes from a home port rather than an overseas port.

transmission lag A network delay in transmission caused by such factors as distance, the level of network congestion, and other variables.

transparency 1. An essential condition of a free market in securities, in which transaction prices and volumes of trade are visible for all to see. **2.** The quality of a financial product that makes clear to the purchaser what the *front-end load and other charges will be.

transparent customization Changes in a product suggested by observed user behaviour rather than a user request.

traveller's cheque A cheque issued by a bank, building society, travel agency, credit-card company, etc., to enable a traveller to obtain cash in a foreign currency when abroad. They may be cashed at banks, exchange bureaus, restaurants, hotels, some shops, etc., abroad on proof of identity. The traveller has to sign the cheque twice, once in the presence of the issuer and again in the presence of the paying bank, agent, etc. Most traveller's cheques are covered against loss.

treasurer 1. A person who is responsible for looking after the money and other assets of an organization. This may include overseeing the provision of the organization's finances as well as some stewardship over the way in which the money is spent. **2.** In more recent times, the manager responsible for an organization's relationship with financial markets.

treasure trove Formerly, gold or silver found on land that had been hidden deliberately and that had no known owner. Treasure trove belonged to the Crown but

the finder was recompensed for its value. Under the Treasure Act (1996) treasure is redefined as any item with no known owner that is at least 300 years old and contains over 5% precious metal (except single coins). All such treasure belongs to the Crown, which will reward the finder.

Treasury The UK government department responsible for the country's financial policies and management of the economy. The First Lord of the Treasury is the Prime Minister, but the Treasury is run by the Chancellor of the Exchequer.

Treasury bill A *bill of exchange issued by the Bank of England on the authority of the UK government that is repayable in three months. They bear no interest, the yield being the difference between the purchase price and the redemption value. The US Treasury also issues Treasury bills.

Treasury bill rate The rate of interest obtainable by buying a *Treasury bill at a discount and selling it at its redemption value.

Treasury bill tender A weekly sale of Treasury bills to UK *discount houses by the Bank of England. The cost of the bills is set by the **Treasury bill tender rate**.

Treasury bond A bond issued by the US Treasury.

Treasury Investment Growth Receipts *See* TIGR.

Treasury stocks *See* GILT-EDGED SECURITY.

treaty 1. Any formal agreement in writing between nations. A **commercial treaty** relates to trade between the signatories. **2.** A transaction in which a sale is negotiated between the parties involved (**by private treaty**) rather than by auction. **3.** An agreement, usually in reinsurance, in which a reinsurer agrees automatically to accept risks from an insurer, either when a certain sum insured is exceeded or on the basis of a percentage of every risk accepted. With such a treaty an insurer has the confidence and capacity to accept larger risks than would otherwise be possible, as the necessary reinsurance is already arranged.

Treaty of Rome The 1957 treaty that

set up the *European Economic Community (EEC), now the *European Union.

Treynor's alpha *See* ALPHA COEFFICIENT.

trial balance A listing of the balances on all the accounts of an organization, with debit balances in one column and credit balances in the other. If the rules of *double-entry book-keeping have been accurately applied, the totals of each column should be the same. If they are not the same, checks must be carried out to find the discrepancy. The figures in the trial balance after some adjustments, e.g. for closing stocks, prepayments and accruals, depreciation, etc., are used to prepare the final accounts (profit and loss account and balance sheet). *See also* EXTENDED TRIAL BALANCE.

trial sampling The distribution as free samples of newly marketed products to consumers to enhance familiarity with the product. If a favourable impression is made by the free sample, consumers are encouraged to place a trial order.

Trinity House A UK corporation granted its first charter in 1514. It is responsible for lighthouses, aids to navigation maintained by local harbours, and dealing with wrecks that present a hazard to navigation in England and Wales and the Channel Islands. A separate authority, the **Northern Lighthouse Board**, is responsible for these matters in Scotland and the Isle of Man.

triple witching hour The third Friday of each March, June, September, and December, when stock-index options, futures, and individual stock options all expire at the same time. This makes for very volatile trading conditions.

true and fair view Auditors of the published accounts of companies are required to form an opinion as to whether the accounts they audit show a 'true and fair view' of the organization's affairs. This is an important concept in the UK and may be used as an override to depart from legal requirements. Despite its importance there is no legal definition of the expression. The meaning of 'true and fair view' develops over time as accounting standards are issued and new accounting issues are debated. The US and *International Accounting Standards

equivalent of the concept is *fair presentation.

trunking Delivering goods by road over long distances, usually by means of a service that has local distribution depots, from which collections and deliveries are made.

trust An arrangement enabling property to be held by a person or persons (the *trustees) for the benefit of some other person or persons (the beneficiaries). The trustee is the legal owner of the property but the beneficiary has an equitable interest in it. A trust may be intentionally created or it may be imposed by law (e.g. if a trustee gives away trust property, the recipient will hold that property as constructive trustee for the beneficiary). Trusts are commonly used to provide for families and in commercial situations (e.g. pensions trusts). *See* DISCRETIONARY TRUST; INTEREST-IN-POSSESSION TRUST.

trust bank A Japanese bank that both lends and accepts savings; it also carries out trust activities, usually involving property or pension funds.

trust deed The document creating and setting out the terms of a *trust. It will usually contain the names of the trustees, the identity of the beneficiaries, and the nature of the trust property, as well as the powers and duties of the trustees. Trusts of land must be declared in writing; trusts of other property need not be although there is often a trust deed to avoid uncertainty.

trustee A person who holds the legal title to property but who is not its beneficial owner. Usually there are two or more trustees of a *trust and for some trusts of land this is necessary. The trustee may not profit from the position but must act for the benefit of the beneficiary, who may be regarded as the real owner of the property. Either an individual or a company may act as trustee. It is usual to provide for the remuneration of trustees in the trust deed, otherwise there is no right to payment. Trustees may be personally liable to beneficiaries for loss of trust property.

trustee investments *See* AUTHORIZED INVESTMENTS.

trust fund A fund consisting of the assets belonging to a *trust, including money and property, that is held by the *trustees for the beneficiaries.

trust letter A document that assigns goods to a bank as security against a loan and enables the borrower to regain title of the goods in order to sell them to pay off the loan.

trust receipt A document given by a bank holding a borrower's goods as security against a loan (see TRUST LETTER), when the borrower takes possession of these goods in order to sell them to pay off the loan.

Truth in Lending Act US consumer protection legislation, dating from 1969, that required lenders to state how they calculated interest on loans and other charges and to express them as an *annual percentage rate. The Act also allows the borrower a 'cooling off' period, authorizing withdrawal from a financial agreement on a mortgage, within three days of signing a consumer credit agreement.

TSE Abbreviation for *Tokyo Stock Exchange.

TT Abbreviation for *telegraphic transfer.

TTM Abbreviation for *time to market.

TUC Abbreviation for *Trades Union Congress.

tugrik (Tug) The standard monetary unit of Mongolia, divided into 100 möngös.

turn The difference between the price at which a *market maker will buy a security (see BID) and the price at which he will sell it (see OFFER PRICE), i.e. the market maker's profit.

turnaround (recovery) A strategy designed to reverse the decline in profitability of a firm or subsidiary, enabling it to achieve a viable and sustainable future. Firms in crisis require drastic action to effect a turnaround, which may involve managerial changes, redundancies (see DOWNSIZING), or closure to avoid receivership. See SHARPBENDER.

Turnbull Report A report (1999) providing a framework of *risk management for UK companies. It was prepared by a working party of the Institute of Chartered Accountants in England and Wales and endorsed by the London Stock Exchange.

turnkey system 1. The planning and execution of a major capital project, in which one company has responsibility for its overall management, so that the client only has to 'turn the key' in order to start the operation. 2. A computer system that is ready to start work as soon as it is installed. All the necessary programs and equipment are supplied with the system.

turnover 1. The total sales figure of an organization for a stated period. Turnover is defined in the UK Companies Act (1985) as the total revenue of an organization derived from the provision of goods and services, less trade discounts, VAT, and any other taxes based on this revenue. 2. More generally, the rate at which some asset is turned over, i.e. sold and replaced by one of the same class. See CAPITAL TURNOVER; LABOUR TURNOVER RATE; STOCK TURNOVER. See also RATE OF TURNOVER. 3. The total value of the transactions on a market or stock exchange in a specified period.

turnover ratio See RATE OF TURNOVER.

turnover tax A tax on the sales made by a business, i.e. on its turnover. See SALES TAX.

turn-round rate The total cost of a transaction on a commodity market, including the broker's commission and the fee charged by the *clearing house.

TV 1. Abbreviation for television. 2. Abbreviation for *terminal value.

TVR Abbreviation for *television rating.

24-hour trading Round-the-clock dealings in securities, bonds, and currency. In practice, it is not normally carried out from any one office of a securities house; instead, the dealers in one time zone pass on their *position to associates in another time zone. Thus, a London office may pass its position to its New York office, which is passed, in turn, to Tokyo, and back to London. Twenty-four-hour trading has been encouraged by the rise in cross-border share trading.

two-factor theory of motivation See HYGIENE FACTORS; MOTIVATION.

two-handed process chart A technique used in *work study to identify the individual movements of both hands. *See* ERGONOMICS.

two-tier board A method of running a large organization in which, in addition to a board of management, there is a *supervisory board. It is claimed that this practice, which is common in Continental Europe, provides an effective method of *corporate governance. In the UK, the normal practice is for a single board to consist of both executive and *non-executive directors.

two-tier tender offer In a *takeover bid, a *tender offer to purchase in which shareholders are offered a high initial offer for sufficient shares to give the bidder a controlling interest in the company, followed by an offer to acquire the remaining shares at a lower price. Bidders use this technique in order to provide an incentive to shareholders to accept the initial offer quickly. Such offers are usually for a combination of cash and shares in the bidder's own company. They are illegal in some countries, notably the UK. *See also* BOOTSTRAP.

tyiyn A monetary unit of Kyrgyzstan, worth one hundredth of a *som.

uberrima fides *See* UTMOST GOOD FAITH.

UBR Abbreviation for Uniform Business Rate. *See* BUSINESS RATES.

UCITS Abbreviation for Undertakings for Collective Investment in Transferable Securities: *unit trusts or *investment trusts that are permitted to operate throughout the EU on the basis of their admission by the domestic regulator in one member state. A set of rules making this possible was drawn up in 1989.

UK Balance of Payments An annual publication of the *Office for National Statistics. It is often known as the **Pink Book**. *See* BALANCE OF PAYMENTS.

UK National Accounts An annual publication of the *Office for National Statistics. It is often known as the **Blue Book**. It provides figures for the *gross domestic product and separate accounts of production, income, and expenditure.

ullage 1. The amount by which the full capacity of a barrel or similar container exceeds the volume of the contents, as a result of evaporation or leakage. **2.** As defined by HM Customs and Excise, the actual contents of a barrel or similar container at the time of importation into the UK. The difference between this volume and the full capacity is called the **vacuity**.

ULS Abbreviation for *unsecured loan stock.

ultimate holding company (ultimate parent company) A *company that is the *holding company of a group in which some of the subsidiary companies are themselves *immediate holding companies of their own groups.

ultimo *See* INSTANT.

ultra vires (Latin: beyond the powers) Denoting an act of an official or corporation for which there is no authority. The powers of officials exercising administrative duties and of companies are limited by the instrument from which their powers are derived. If they act outside these powers, their action may be challenged in the courts. A company's powers are limited by the objects clause in its *memorandum of association. If it enters into an agreement outside these objects, the agreement may be unenforceable, although a third party may have a remedy under the Companies Act (1985) if it was dealing with the company in good faith (or there may be other equitable remedies).

umbrella fund An *offshore fund consisting of a *fund of funds that invests in other offshore funds.

umpire *See* ARBITRATION.

unabsorbed cost The part of the overhead costs of a production process that are not covered by its revenue when the output falls below a specified level. Overheads are sometimes added to the *direct costs of a process and divided by the output to give a *unit cost. The output for this calculation is often set at such a level that the whole of the overheads are absorbed by the unit cost. If, in fact, the output falls below this level, the whole of the overheads will not be absorbed, the deficit being the unabsorbed cost.

unamortized cost 1. The *historical cost of a *fixed asset less the total *depreciation shown against that asset up to a specified date. **2.** The value given to a fixed asset in the accounts of an organization after *revaluation of assets less the total depreciation shown against that asset since it was revalued.

unappropriated profit The part of an organization's *profit that is neither allocated to a specific purpose nor paid out in *dividends. *See* APPROPRIATION.

unbundling 1. The separation of a business into its constituent parts, generally by selling off certain subsidiaries or business lines. **2.** The selling off of separate parts of a security, for example its *coupon.

uncalled capital See RESERVE CAPITAL.

uncertificated units A small number of units purchased for an investor in a *unit trust by reinvestment of dividends. If the number of units is too small to warrant the issue of a certificate they are held on account for the investor and added to the total when the holding is sold.

uncleared effects Financial documents lodged with a bank for collection, still held by the bank pending the completion of the collection.

uncommitted facility An agreement between a bank and a company in which the bank agrees in principle to make funding available to the company but is under no obligation to provide a specified amount of funding; if a loan is made it will be for only a short period. Examples of an uncommitted facility include a *money-market line or an *overdraft. *Compare* COMMITTED FACILITY.

unconditional bid See TAKEOVER BID.

unconfirmed letter of credit See LETTER OF CREDIT.

unconscionable bargain See CATCHING BARGAIN.

unconsolidated subsidiary An undertaking that, although it is a *subsidiary undertaking of a group, is not included in the *consolidated financial statements of the group.

uncontrollable costs (non-controllable costs) Items of expenditure appearing on a manager's *management accounting statement that are not able to be controlled or influenced by that level of management. Costs regarded as uncontrollable by one level of management may, however, be controllable at a higher level of management. There is always potential for disagreement over what is or is not an uncontrollable cost. Correctly identifying such costs is important for *performance measurement. *Compare* CONTROLLABLE COSTS. *See also* CONTROLLABILITY CONCEPT.

uncontrollable turnover See LABOUR TURNOVER RATE.

uncoupling inventory See INVENTORY.

UNCTAD Abbreviation for *United Nations Conference on Trade and Development.

undated security A *fixed-interest security that has no *redemption date. *See* CONSOLS.

underabsorbed overhead (underapplied overhead) In *absorption costing, the circumstance in which the absorbed overhead is less than the overhead costs incurred for a period. This adverse *variance represents a reduction of the budgeted profits of the organization.

undercapitalization The state of a company that does not have sufficient *capital or *reserves for the size of its operations. For example, this may be due to the company growing too quickly. Although such a company may be making profits it may be unable to convert these profits sufficiently quickly into cash to pay its debts. *Compare* OVERCAPITALIZATION.

underlying The asset, measure, or obligation on which a *derivative, such as an option or futures contract, is based.

underpositioning A *positioning error involving a failure to position a company, its product, or brand correctly.

understandability The accounting principle that the financial information provided by a company should be such that its significance is capable of being perceived by a person with a reasonable knowledge of business and accounting and a willingness to study it with reasonable diligence. The information should not leave out anything material, but should not be so comprehensive that the main points of significance are obscured. The concept is defined in the Accounting Standards Board's Statement of Principles and in *Financial Reporting Standard 18, Accounting Policies.

undersubscription See OVERSUBSCRIPTION.

underwriter 1. A person who examines a risk, decides whether or not it can be insured, and, if it can, works out the premium to be charged, usually on the basis of the frequency of past claims for similar risks. Underwriters are either employed by insurance companies or are members of *Lloyd's. The name arises from the early days of marine insurance, when a merchant would, as a sideline, *write* his name *under* the amount and details of the risk he had agreed to cover on a slip of paper. **2.** The firm that issues an insurance policy, thereby accepting liability for specified losses. **3.** A financial institution, usually a *merchant bank, that guarantees to buy a proportion of any unsold shares, bonds, etc. when a new issue is offered to the public. Underwriters usually work for a commission, and a number may combine together to buy all the unsold shares, provided that the minimum subscription stated in the prospectus has been sold to the public. **4.** Any person or enterprise that accepts financial responsibility for a transaction or project.

undifferentiated marketing The marketing of a product aimed at the widest possible market. An early example was the Model T Ford, which was mass-produced, aimed at a very wide market, and only available in black. Ford now produce a wide range of models, with different engine capacities, colours, and prices aimed at attracting a wide variety of tastes and requirements. *Compare* DIFFERENTIATED MARKETING.

undischarged bankrupt A person whose *bankruptcy has not been discharged. Such persons must not obtain credit (above £250) without first informing their creditors that they are undischarged bankrupts, become directors of companies, or trade under another name. Undischarged bankrupts may not hold office as a JP, MP, mayor, or councillor, or sit in the House of Lords.

undisclosed factoring A form of *factoring in which the seller of goods does not wish to disclose the use made of a factor. In these circumstances, the factor buys the goods that have been sold (rather than the debt their sale incurred) and, as an *undisclosed principal, appoints the original seller to act as agent to recover the debt. The factor assumes responsibility in the case of non-payment so that from the point of view of the seller, the factor offers the same service as in normal factoring.

undisclosed principal A person who buys or sells through an agent or broker and remains anonymous. The agent or broker must disclose when dealing on behalf of an undisclosed principal; failure to do so may result in the agent being treated in law as the principal and in some circumstances the contract may be made void.

undistributable reserves *Reserves that may not be distributed according to the Companies Act (1985). They include *share capital, *share premium account, *capital redemption reserve, certain *unrealized profits, or any other reserve that the company may not distribute according to some other act or its own articles of association. In the USA such reserves are known as **restricted surplus**. *Compare* DISTRIBUTABLE PROFITS.

undistributed profit Profit earned by an organization but not distributed to its shareholders by way of *dividends. Such sums are available for later distribution but are frequently used by companies to finance their activities. *See* RETAINED EARNINGS.

undiversifiable risk *See* SYSTEMATIC RISK.

undue influence Unfair pressure exerted on a person to sign a contract that is not a true expression of that person's aims or requirements at the time, but is to the advantage of another party (either a party to the contract or a third party). Such a contract may be set aside by a court.

unearned income Income not derived from trades, professions or vocations, or from the emoluments of office. In the UK, until 1984, it was taxed more heavily than earned income, incurring an investment-income surcharge of 15%. Both earned and unearned income are now taxed at essentially the same rates.

unemployment An inability to find work although it is actively sought. Theoretically the unemployed are those members of the active labour force who are out of work, although in most cases statistics are based on the number of people claiming unemployment benefit. Unemployment has been a persistent problem in industrial economies during *recession over the last 200 years. *See also* FRICTIONAL

UNEMPLOYMENT; HIDDEN UNEMPLOYMENT; RESIDUAL UNEMPLOYMENT; SEASONAL UNEMPLOYMENT.

unexpired cost The balance of an item of expenditure, recorded in the books of account of an organization, that has not been written off to the profit and loss account. For example, the *net book value of an asset represents the unexpired cost of that asset.

unfair contract terms Contractual terms relating to the exclusion or restriction of a person's liability that, under the Unfair Contract Terms Act 1977 and Unfair Terms in Consumer Contracts Regulations 1999, are either ineffective or effective only so far as is reasonable.

unfair dismissal The dismissal of an employee that the employer cannot show to be fair. Under the Employment Protection (Consolidation) Act (1978) employees have the right not to be unfairly dismissed, provided they have served the required period of continuous employment (52 weeks for full-time employment) and are not over 65 or the normal retirement age for an employee in that particular job. Employees who consider that they have been unfairly dismissed can apply within three months after the effective date of termination of their employment contract to an *employment tribunal for reinstatement, re-engagement, or compensation. The tribunal will make an award unless the employer shows that the principal reason for the dismissal was the employee's incapability, lack of qualifications, or conduct; redundancy; the fact that it would be illegal to continue employing the person; or some other substantial reason. The employer must also show that he acted reasonably in dismissing the employee. The statutory protection does not apply to members of the police and armed forces and certain other employees. *Compare* WRONGFUL DISMISSAL. *See also* DISMISSAL PROCEDURE.

unfair prejudice Conduct in the running of a company's affairs that may entitle members to a remedy under the Companies Act (1985). In small companies, the unfairness may consist of a failure by some members to honour a common understanding reached when the company

was formed, e.g. that a member be allowed to assist in the management and be paid accordingly. The usual remedy sought is for the purchase of the member's shares at a fair price. *See also* MINORITY PROTECTION.

unfair trading *See* CONSUMER PROTECTION.

unfavourable balance A *balance of trade or *balance of payments deficit.

Unicode In computing, a coding standard in which one or more bytes are used to represent each character. Unicode allows unique definition of symbols, foreign alphabets, Chinese ideographs, etc. To date over 90 000 have been defined.

UNIDO Abbreviation for *United Nations Industrial Development Organization.

Uniform Business Rate (UBR) *See* BUSINESS RATES.

uniform delivered pricing A geographic pricing strategy in which a company charges the same price, including freight charges, to all its customers, regardless of their location.

uniform load scheduling (level scheduling) An approach to scheduling work that aims to produce small quantities of each product each day, throughout the day. *Just-in-time techniques are designed to work on the basis of level scheduling.

uniform resource locator (universal resource locator; URL) An address for a specific resource on the Internet. The URL always starts with the protocol for data transfer (http for web pages and ftp for file transfer protocol). A web page has a URL of the form

 http://www.domain-name.extension/
  filename.html

See also DOMAIN NAME.

unilateral contract A *contract in which one party (the promisor) undertakes to do or refrain from doing something if the other party (the promisee) does or refrains from doing something, but the promisee does not undertake to do or refrain from doing that thing. An example of a unilateral contract is one in which the promisor offers a reward for the giving of information. *Compare* BILATERAL CONTRACT.

unilateral relief Relief against *double taxation given by the UK authorities for tax paid in another country with which the UK has no double-taxation agreement.

uninsurable risk *See* INSURABLE RISK.

unique selling proposition (USP) A product benefit that can be regarded as unique and therefore can be used in advertising to differentiate it from the competition. The concept is not now as popular as it was as not every product can have a USP.

unique value effect Features and benefits of a product that make it unique in its field, thereby lowering the price sensitivity of potential customers. The unique value effect raises consumers' willingness to pay higher prices.

unissued share capital The difference between the *authorized share capital of a company and the *issued share capital.

unit banking A system of banking in which a bank must be a single enterprise without branches. This was once common practice in the USA, but regulators have turned against this form of bank, following the collapse of the Continental Illinois Bank.

unit cost Expenditure incurred by an organization expressed as a rate per unit of production or sales. It may be difficult to make valid comparisons of unit costs between organizations. The main problem is the *arbitrary allocation of *fixed overhead costs.

United Nations Common Fund for Commodities (CFC) *See* UNITED NATIONS CONFERENCE ON TRADE AND DEVELOPMENT.

United Nations Conference on Trade and Development (UNCTAD) A permanent organization set up by the UN in 1964 to encourage international trade, particularly to help developing countries to finance their exports. Under its auspices the **UN Common Fund for Commodities (CFC)** was established in 1989 to provide finance for international commodity organizations to enable *buffer stocks to be maintained and to carry out research into the development of *commodity markets.

United Nations Industrial Development Organization (UNIDO) An international organization that became a specialized agency of the UN in 1986, having developed from the Centre for Industrial Development, set up in 1961. With headquarters in Vienna, its aim is to promote the industrialization of developing countries, with special emphasis on the manufacturing sector. It provides planning policies and technical advice and assistance for third world countries.

unitization The process of changing an *investment trust into a *unit trust.

unit labour costs The total expenditure on labour per unit of output. A comparison between changes in *productivity and unit labour costs in different countries enables economists to make predictions about changes in their *competitiveness. For example, if unit labour costs and productivity both rise by the same amount in the UK, UK producers do not have to change the prices of their goods; if, however, Japanese unit labour costs rise by less than productivity, Japanese prices could fall, making them increasingly competitive.

unit-level activities *See* ACTIVITY.

unit-linked policy A *life-assurance policy in which the benefits depend on the performance of a portfolio of shares. Each premium paid by the insured person is split: one part is used to provide life-assurance cover, while the balance (after the deduction of costs, expenses, etc.) is used to buy units in a *unit trust. In this way a small investor can benefit from investment in a *managed fund without making a large financial commitment. As they are linked to the value of shares, unit-linked policies can go up or down in value. Policyholders can surrender the policy at any time and the *surrender value is the selling price of the units purchased by the date of cancellation (less expenses). Recent decades have also seen a widespread increase in **unit-linked savings plans**, both with and without life-assurance cover.

unit of account 1. A function of *money enabling its users to calculate the value of their transactions and to keep accounts. **2.** The standard unit of currency of a country. **3.** An artificial currency used only for accounting purposes.

unit price The price paid per unit of item purchased or charged per unit of product sold.

unit pricing The practice of showing the price of a single unit of a product in order that shoppers can compare the price against the cost of a multipack. A single bag of crisps in a supermarket might cost 30p. A larger bag containing six single bags could be offered at £1.50, i.e. a unit price of 25p each. The shopper can therefore see at a glance that the larger purchase is the more economical.

unit profit (*or* **loss**) The profit (or loss) attributable to one unit of production. *See* UNIT COST.

unit standard operating profit The *standard operating profit, expressed as a rate per unit of production or sales.

unit standard production cost The *standard production cost, expressed as a rate per unit of production or sales.

unit trust 1. In the UK, an investment fund shared by a large number of different investors. A unit trust is an 'open-ended fund', which means that the fund gets bigger as more people invest and smaller as people withdraw their money. A fund manager is responsible for the fund and makes the investment decisions. The fund is divided into segments called 'units'. Investors take a stake in the fund by buying these units, the price of which will vary as the value of the investments the trust has invested in increase or decrease. The *Financial Services Authority (FSA) authorizes firms that sell unit trusts, most of which belong to the Investment Management Association (IMA). Investors should always look carefully at the charges associated with unit trusts. Basic-rate tax is deducted from the dividends paid by unit trusts and capital gains on the sale of a holding are subject to capital gains tax. In the USA unit trusts are called **mutual funds. 2.** A trust scheme (also called a **unit investment trust**) in the USA in which investors purchase **redeemable trust certificates**. The money so raised is used by the trustees to buy such securities as bonds, which are usually held until they mature. Usually

both the number of certificates issued and the investments held remain unchanged during the life of the scheme, but the certificates can be sold back to the trustees at any time.

Unit Trusts Ombudsman Scheme *See* FINANCIAL OMBUDSMAN SERVICE.

univariate statistics *See* DESCRIPTIVE STATISTICS.

universal banking Banking that involves not only services related to loans and savings but also those involved in making investments in companies. Universal banking is most common in Germany, Switzerland, and the Netherlands. The *Glass–Steagall Act (1933) prohibited universal banking in the USA, but the restrictions placed on it have now been removed. In the UK, it has been largely avoided.

universal product code (UPC) The *bar code found on most products for sale in retail outlets.

universe *See* POPULATION.

UNIX A computer operating system, largely used by universities and service providers, that was significant in the development of the Internet.

unlimited company A *company whose *shareholders do not benefit from limited liability (*compare* LIMITED COMPANY). Such companies are exempt from filing accounts with the *Registrar of Companies.

unlimited liability A liability to pay all the debts incurred by a business. For a *sole proprietor or general partner (*see* PARTNERSHIP), liability is not limited to the amount he or she has agreed to invest. All debts of the business must not only be paid out of the assets of the business but also, if necessary, out of personal assets.

unliquidated damages *See* DAMAGES.

unlisted securities (unquoted securities) Securities (usually *equities) in companies that are not on an official stock-exchange list. They are therefore not required to satisfy the standards set for listing (*see* LISTED SECURITY). Unlisted securities are usually issued in relatively small companies and their shares usually carry a high degree of risk. In London, unlisted securities were traded on the **Unlisted Securities Market** (**USM**) until 1995, when it was replaced by the *Alternative Investment Market. Other exchanges have similar markets.

unofficial strike *See* STRIKE.

unpaid cheque A cheque that has been sent to the payee's bank and then through the clearing process only to be returned to the payee because value cannot be transferred. If the reason is lack of funds the bank will mark the cheque 'refer to drawer'.

unquoted securities *See* UNLISTED SECURITIES.

unrealized profit/loss A profit or loss that results from holding *assets rather than using them; it is therefore a profit or loss that has not been realized in cash.

unsecured creditor A person who is owed money by an organization but who has not arranged that in the event of non-payment specific assets would be available as a fund out of which he or she could be paid in priority to other creditors. *Compare* SECURED CREDITOR.

unsecured debt A debt that is not covered by any kind of collateral.

unsecured loan stock (**ULS**; **unsecured debenture**) A loan stock or *debenture in which no specific assets have been set aside as a fund out of which the debenture holders could be paid in priority to other creditors in the event of non-payment. *Compare* SECURED DEBENTURE.

unsocial hours Working hours, other than normal office or factory hours, that prevent an employee from enjoying family life and the usual social activities. Shift workers and workers who have to work unsocial hours are often paid at higher rates than 9–5 workers.

unsubscribe To *opt out from an e-mail newsletter, mailing list, on-line discussion group, etc.

unvalued policy An insurance policy for property that has a sum insured shown for each item although the insurers do not acknowledge that this figure is its actual value. As a result, if a claim is made the insured must provide proof of the value of the item lost, damaged, or stolen before a payment will be made. The policy may have a maximum specified payment. *Compare* VALUED POLICY.

UPC Abbreviation for universal product code. *See* BAR CODE.

upload To transfer a copy of a file from a local computer to a remote server. It is usually achieved using *FTP.

upstream Denoting a loan from a subsidiary company to its parent, for example a loan from a subsidiary of a bank to its holding company to enable the holding company to pay its dividends.

URL Abbreviation for *uniform resource locator, i.e. an address on the Internet.

URL placement Integrating the address of a website into manuals, warranty cards, and software programs, enabling them to help direct traffic to the website of the placing company.

usance **1.** The time allowed for the payment of short-term foreign *bills of exchange. It varies from country to country but is often 60 days. **2.** Formerly, the rate of interest on a loan.

US Customary units The units of measurement in use in the USA. They are based on *Imperial units but the US gallon is equal to 0.8327 Imperial gallons and the hundredweight is taken as 100 lbs, making the *ton 2000 lbs (instead of the Imperial 2240 lbs). The USA has fallen behind Europe in converting to metric units but intends to do so.

useful economic life The period for which the present owner of an *asset will derive economic benefits from its use. Under *Statement of Standard Accounting Practice 12, Accounting for Depreciation, an asset should be depreciated over its useful economic life.

USENET (**user's network**) A very large network of on-line newsgroups, run very informally to discuss particular topics, such as a sport, hobby, or business area. USENET predates the *Internet, although some Internet hosts do not subscribe to USENET and some USENET hosts are not on the Internet.

user *See* CONSUMER BUYER BEHAVIOUR. *See also* DECISION-MAKING UNIT.

user-friendly Denoting a computer system that is intended to be easy to use by people who are not computer specialists.

USP Abbreviation for *unique selling proposition.

usury An excessively high rate of interest. In Christian countries the term was formerly used to condemn all forms of lending on interest, a prohibition that has been maintained by Islam. *See* ISLAMIC FINANCE.

utility theory A class of theory concerned with the behaviours, strategies, and mental processes adopted by individuals faced with making a risky choice or decision. Utility is usually taken as the subjective value to the individual of a particular outcome or attribute. The main applications of utility theory in business and finance are in relation to consumer and investment choices. Different structures of utility and *risk preference are considered in *portfolio theory. *See also* CONJOINT ANALYSIS; PROSPECT THEORY.

utilization (system utilization) The ratio of the actual output of an *operating system to its designed capacity. For example, if the designed capacity of a plant is 4000 units per week and the output is 3000 units per week, the utilization is 75%. However, it is important to remember that 75% represents the utilization of the most restricted part of the operating system, i.e. the bottleneck. If other parts of the plant are capable of more than 4000 units per week their utilization will be lower.

utmost good faith (uberrima fides) The fundamental principle of insurance practice, requiring that a person wishing to take out an insurance cover must provide all the information the insurer needs to calculate the correct premium for the risk involved. Nothing must be withheld from the insurers, even if they do not actually ask for the information on an application form. The principle is essential because an insurer usually has no knowledge of the facts involved in the risk they are being asked to cover; the only source of information is the person requiring the insurance. If an insured person is found to have withheld information or given false information, the insurer can treat the policy as void and the courts will support a refusal to pay claims.

u

vacuity *See* ULLAGE.

valence-instrumentality-expectancy theory (VIE theory) A theory of *motivation stating that the level of effort individuals will exert in any task can be computed from three variables: expectancy, or the belief that action or effort will lead to a successful outcome; instrumentality, or the belief that success will bring rewards; and valence, or the desirability of the rewards on offer. The theory, which was proposed by Victor H. Vroom in 1964, inspired the *path-goal theory of leadership.

valium holiday (valium picnic) A colloquial name for a non-trading day on a stock exchange or other commercial market; i.e. a market holiday.

valorization The raising or stabilization of the value of a commodity or currency by artificial means, usually by a government. For example, if a government wishes to increase the price of a commodity that it exports it may attempt to decrease the supply of that commodity by encouraging producers to produce less, by stockpiling the commodity itself, or, in extreme cases, by destroying part of the production.

VALS *See* LIFESTYLE.

valuation risk The *risk that arises from problems of valuation. For example, it can be difficult to value a business during the acquisition process or to put an accurate value on an option on the *over-the-counter market.

value added (added value) The value added to goods or services by a step in the chain of original purchase, manufacture or other enhancement, and retail. *See* VALUE-ADDED STATEMENT; VALUE CHAIN. *See also* ECONOMIC VALUE ADDED.

value-added manufacturing A method of optimizing the efficiency of a process by eliminating any element that

does not add value to the product or service.

value-added statement (added-value statement) A *financial statement showing how much wealth (value added) has been created by the collective effort of capital, employees, and others and how it has been allocated for an *accounting period. Value added is normally calculated by deducting materials and bought-in services from *turnover. The value added is then allocated to employees in the form of wages, to shareholders and lenders in the form of dividends and interest, and to the government in the form of taxes, with a proportion being retained in the company for reinvestment.

value added tax (VAT) A charge on *taxable supplies of goods and services made in the UK by a *taxable person in the course or furtherance of a business. Where appropriate, each trader adds VAT to sales and must account to HM Revenue and Customs for the *output tax. The *input tax paid on purchases can be deducted from the output tax due. VAT, indirect taxation that falls on the final customer, was introduced in 1973 when the UK joined the European Economic Community. Unless they are *zero-rated goods and services, *exempt supplies, or taxed at a special rate, all goods and services in the UK now bear VAT at a rate of 17.5%.

value analysis An examination of every feature of a product to ensure that its cost is no greater than is necessary to carry out its functions. Value analysis can be applied to a new product idea at the design stage and also to existing products. *See also* VALUE ENGINEERING.

value-at-risk (VAR) A measure of risk developed at the former US bank J. P. Morgan Chase in the 1990s, now most frequently applied to measuring *market risk and *credit risk. It is the level of losses over a particular period that will only be exceeded in a small percentage of cases. A cut-off value for gains and losses is established that excludes a certain proportion of worst-case results (e.g. the bottom 1% of outcomes); the value-at-risk is then measured relative to that cut-off value. VAR was initially designed to measure the overnight risk in certain highly diversified *portfolios. It has since developed into a finance industry standard and has been incorporated into the regulatory requirements applying to financial institutions.

value-based pricing Setting the price for a product or service on the basis of the buyer's perception of its value, rather than its cost.

value chain The chain of activities by which a good or service is produced, distributed, and marketed. Each step of the chain (which may consist of the activities of one company or of several) creates different amounts of value for the consumer. There are five value-creating activities:
• inbound distribution
• operations
• outbound distribution
• marketing
• after-sales service;
and four supporting activities:
• buying
• research and development
• human resource management
• infrastructure of the firm.
For management, the main application of the value-chain concept is that a company should examine its costs and performance at each stage, and decide, among other things, whether it is best to carry out a particular stage in house or externally. The value chain can provide the basis for a strategic analysis in terms of the search for competitive advantage.

value date 1. The date on which specified funds become available for use. **2.** The date on which a transaction actually takes place. **3.** The date on which foreign exchange is due to be delivered.

valued policy An insurance policy in which the value of the subject matter is agreed when the cover starts. As a result, the amount to be paid in the event of a total-loss claim is already decided and does not need to be negotiated.

value driver Any variable that significantly affects the value of an organization. In his development of *shareholder value analysis, Alfred Rappaport identified seven key drivers of value:
• sales growth rate
• operating profit margin
• tax rate
• fixed capital investment
• working capital investment
• planning period
• cost of capital.
Of these, the first five can be used to forecast the future cash flows of a business, whereas the remaining two can be used to calculate the *present value of these cash flows.

In practice, different companies will have different value drivers. For example, Sony is a company that produces high-quality products for which customers are prepared to pay a relatively high price. Maintaining a high operating profit margin is therefore more important for Sony than sales growth. For another company, however, sales growth may well be the more important factor.

value engineering Designing a product to eliminate any costs that do not contribute to the value of the product, i.e. the performance (or some other attribute) that leads the customer to purchase the product in preference to other similar products.

value for money audit An audit of a government department, charity, or other non-profit-making organization to assess whether or not it is functioning efficiently and giving value for the money it spends.

value marketing A principle of enlightened marketing holding that a company should put most of its resources into value-building marketing investments.

value positioning A range of *positioning alternatives based on the value and price a product offers.

value received Words that appear on a *bill of exchange to indicate that the bill is a means of paying for goods or services to the value of the bill. However, these words need not appear on a UK bill as everyone who has signed a UK bill is deemed to have been a party to it for value.

value to the business The value of an *asset taken as the lower of the *replacement cost and the *recoverable amount. The latter is the greater of the *net realizable value and *net present value. It is claimed that generally an asset should never be worth more to a business than its replacement cost, because if the business were deprived of the asset it would replace it. If an asset is not worth replacing it would be sold (net realizable value), unless the net present value were higher. The concept is also known as the **deprival value** and was a feature of *current-cost accounting as set out in *Statement of Standard Accounting Practice 16.

value transferred The amount by which a donor's estate is diminished by making a *transfer of value. The term is used in the computation of *inheritance tax.

VAR Abbreviation for *value-at-risk

variable A characteristic of a product or service that can be measured on a continuously variable scale, e.g. length, weight, time, price. *Compare* ATTRIBUTE.

variable cost An item of expenditure that, in total, varies directly with the level of activity achieved. For example, *direct materials cost will tend to double if output doubles, a characteristic being that it is incurred as a constant rate per unit. In practice, there are few examples of true variable costs or true *fixed costs, most costs being *semi-variable costs.

variable costing *See* MARGINAL COSTING.

variable cost ratio The ratio of *variable cost to sales revenue, expressed as a percentage.

variable life assurance A *unit-linked policy in which the policyholder can vary the amount of life assurance cover provided.

variable output plan *See* CHASE DEMAND STRATEGY.

variable overhead cost The elements of an organization's indirect costs for a product that vary in total in proportion to changes in the levels of production or sales. Examples can include power, commission earned by sales personnel, and consumable materials.

variable production overhead The elements of an organization's indirect manufacturing costs that vary in total in proportion to changes in the level of production or sales. Examples can include factory power and depreciation of machinery using the *production-unit method.

variable-rate mortgage A *mortgage in which the rate of interest is varied from time to time by the mortgagee (lender) according to market conditions.

variable-rate note (VRN) A *bond, usually with a fixed maturity, in which the interest coupon is adjusted at regular intervals to reflect the prevailing market rate (usually a margin over the *London Inter Bank Offered Rate). A VRN differs from a *floating-rate note in that the margin is not fixed and will be adjusted to take into account market conditions at each coupon setting date.

variable-rate security A *security in which the interest rate varies with market rates. *Floating-rate notes, *eurobonds, and 90-day *certificates of deposit are examples of variable-rate securities.

variance **1.** In *standard costing and *budgetary control, the difference between the standard or budgeted levels of cost or income for an activity and the actual costs incurred or income achieved. If the actual performance is better than standard then a **favourable variance** results, while if actual performance is worse than standard there is an **adverse variance**. **2.** In statistics, a measure of the dispersion of a distribution of outcomes. It is the square of the *standard deviation. *See* ANALYSIS OF VARIANCE.

variation margins The gains or losses on open contracts in future markets, calculated on the basis of the closing price at the end of each day. They are credited by the *clearing house to its members' accounts and by its members to their customers' accounts.

variety-seeking buying behaviour *Consumer buying behaviour in situations characterized by low consumer involvement, but significant perceived brand differences.

VAT Abbreviation for *value added tax.

vatu (VT) The standard monetary unit of Vanuatu.

VCT Abbreviation for *venture capital trust.

velocity of circulation The average number of times that a unit of money is used in a specified period, approximately equal to the total amount of money spent in that period divided by the total amount of money in circulation. The **income velocity of circulation** is the number of times that a particular unit of currency forms part of a person's income in a specified period. It is given by the ratio of the gross national product to the amount of money in circulation. The **transactions velocity of circulation** is the number of times that a particular unit of currency is spent in a money transaction in a specified period, i.e. the ratio of the total amount of money spent in sales of goods or services to the amount of money in circulation.

vendor A person who sells goods or services.

vendor placing A type of *placing used as a means of acquiring another company or business. For example, if company X wishes to buy a business from company Y, it issues company X shares to company Y as payment with the prearranged agreement that these shares are then placed with investors in exchange for cash. Vendor placings have been popular with companies in recent years as a cheaper alternative to a *rights issue. *See also* BOUGHT DEAL.

venture capital *See* RISK CAPITAL.

venture capital trust (VCT) An *investment trust that provides *risk capital for businesses. The trust managers accept sums of money from investors who wish to share in the profits of the trust. This form of investment has certain tax advantages in the UK, in that any profits are free of *capital gains tax and income is untaxed. They have the additional advantages that up to £100,000 can be invested in any year; 20% of any investment in a VCT can be claimed back from previously paid tax, provided the VCT is held for three years. By investing a taxable gain in a VCT that is held for three years, the payment of the capital gains tax is deferred

until the VCT investment is sold (and the annual exemptions from capital gains tax can be carried forward).

vertical integration *See* INTEGRATION.

vertical job enlargement *See* JOB ENLARGEMENT.

vertical marketing system (VMS) A *distribution channel structure in which producers, wholesalers, and retailers act as a unified system. One channel member owns the others, has contracts with them, or has so much power that they all have to cooperate. *See* ADMINISTERED VMS; CONTRACTUAL VMS; CORPORATE VMS.

vertical mobility *See* MOBILITY OF LABOUR.

vertical spread A strategy used with *options, consisting of buying a long call option and a short call option with the same exercise date.

vested benefit A benefit owing to a member of a pension scheme, whether or not the member is employed by the organizers of the scheme.

vested interest **1.** In law, an interest in property that is certain to come about rather than one dependent upon some event that may not happen. For example, a gift to 'A for life and then to B' means that A's interest is **vested in possession**, because A has the property now. B's gift is also vested (but not in possession) because A will certainly die sometime and then B (or B's estate if B is dead) will inherit the property. A gift to C 'if C reaches the age of 30' is not vested, because C may die before reaching that age. An interest that is not vested is known as a **contingent interest**. **2.** An involvement in the outcome of some business, scheme, transaction, etc., usually in anticipation of a personal gain.

vestibule training A form of training in which new employees learn the job in a setting that approximates as closely as is practicable to the actual working environment. An example is the training of airline pilots in a simulated cockpit. This type of training is generally used when the use of actual equipment by untrained employees would be too risky or when the actual work setting would be unconducive to learning (e.g. because of noise levels).

videoconferencing (teleconferencing) A system available in the UK and internationally enabling groups of people at various locations to see and speak to each other, making it possible to hold meetings, seminars, etc., without the expense and time wasted in travel. Special studios are not required; information is available from British Telecom. In **Confravision**, public videoconferencing facilities, with studios in several major cities, are offered by British Telecom.

videotex An information system in which information from a distant computer is displayed on a television screen. There are two types: in *viewdata the information is sent to the television set using telephone lines or cables; in *teletext, the information is broadcast as a part of the normal signal from a television station.

VIE theory Abbreviation for *valence–instrumentality–expectancy theory.

viewdata A *videotex system in which information from a distant computer is sent along telephone wires to a television set in the receiving home or office. Viewdata provides a vast amount of general information, such as news, stock-exchange prices, and travel information, as well as access to specialist databases. The system also allows users to shop, book theatre tickets, and conduct their banking from home.

view to resale The grounds on which a *subsidiary undertaking is excluded from the *consolidated financial statements of a group, because the group's interest in the subsidiary is held exclusively with a view to subsequent resale. *Financial Reporting Standard 2, Accounting for Subsidiary Undertakings, defines the circumstances appropriate for this exclusion as if a purchaser has been identified or is being sought for a subsidiary and it is reasonably expected that the interest will be disposed of within approximately one year of its date of acquisition. The subsidiary undertaking should not previously have been consolidated in group accounts prepared by the *holding company. Where a subsidiary undertaking is excluded on these grounds, it should be recorded in the consolidated financial statements as a *cur-

rent asset at the lower of cost and *net realizable value.

vigilance A person's ability to perform a task at a constant level of efficiency and effectiveness over a period.

vigilance decrement A decline in a person's ability to perform a task at a constant level of efficiency and effectiveness as that person becomes tired or less able to respond due to psychological factors.

vigilantibus non dormientibus jura subveniunt (Latin: the law will not help those who sleep on their rights) *See* LACHES.

vineyard organization A model of organizational structure in which the company's mission is pictured as a vine and the various units of employees as 'clusters' of grapes. The major clusters will include a team of core management, a series of largely autonomous business units, staff units providing back-up services, and a range of project teams assembled for specific short-term purposes.

viral marketing 1. A marketing strategy in which various unconventional techniques are used to generate word-of-mouth excitement about a product. Conventional media outlets may be deliberately avoided in order to create an air of mystery or exclusivity. **2.** More specifically, a form of *direct marketing in which a company encourages Internet users to forward its material in e-mails, usually by including jokes, games, or other entertaining features. The aim is that publicity for the company will spread in the manner of a computer virus.

virement The practice allowed in some systems of *budgetary control in which overspending under one budget expenditure head may be offset by underspending under another budget expenditure head. If virement is not allowed, each head of expenditure must be treated individually.

virtual auction An auction conducted completely on-line, with no physical location. Virtual auctions are conducted on the Internet by such auction houses as *Ebay.

virtualization A process by which a

company develops some of the characteristics of a *virtual organization.

virtual mall (electronic mall) A website that brings together different electronic retailers at a single on-line location. The term derives from the traditional shopping mall in which retail stores operate from fixed locations.

virtual organization An organization that uses information and communications technology to enable it to operate without clearly defined physical boundaries. It usually provides customized services by outsourcing production and other functions to third parties.

virtual reality (VR) A computer modelling system capable of creating three-dimensional images that give the user the experience of being with, or inside, the object being modelled. Used as part of *computer-aided design systems, VR enables customers to view new products without the expense of creating prototypes. Building layouts, for example, can be optimized by allowing customers to 'walk through' the VR model. Advanced systems allow them to move elements of the design, with any modifications (e.g. repositioned doors) being translated into new drawings and blueprints. VR can also be used to train staff without exposing them to hazardous conditions.

virtual trade show An on-line site that shows new products, technologies, and services to current or potential buyers.

virtual value activities The strategies that firms use to make website information more valuable.

virtuous cycle A cycle of growth that produces positive returns. Each success in the loop promotes another success in another part of the loop.

virt-x An *order-driven electronic market for pan-European *blue-chip securities, created in 2001 from London's *Tradepoint Investment Exchange with the involvement of the SWX Swiss Exchange. Clearing is through LCH.Clearnet (*see* LONDON CLEARING HOUSE) and SIS x-clear and the deals are settled through *CREST, *Euroclear, and Sega Inter Settle. virt-x is a *Recognized Investment Exchange under the UK *Financial Services Authority.

visible control A technique used in *total quality management to make defects visible to employees so that resources can be focused on removing the source of the problem. For example, flashing lights, called *andon*, can be linked to electronic sensors that detect a failure to complete all stages of a process.

visibles Earnings from exports and payments for imports of goods, as opposed to services (such as banking and insurance). The *balance of trade is made up of visibles and is sometimes called the **visible balance**.

vision statement *See* MISSION STATEMENT.

visit duration The length of time a user spends on a website during a visit, or the number of pages viewed during a visit.

Visual Basic *See* BASIC.

visual load profile A graph that compares work loads with available capacity against time (see diagram opposite).

vital statistics Statistics relating to a nation's or region's population, including its birth rate, death rate, marriage rate, etc.

vitamin model A model that compares the effect of certain factors on *job satisfaction to the effect of vitamins on the body. Nine 'vitamins' are identified, and the employee will require a minimum level of each if he or she is to remain satisfied. Of these nine, three (money, security, and social position) can be taken in very large amounts with no ill effects. However, an excess of the other six factors (externally set goals, clarity, variety, control, use of skills, and contact with others) can be problematic.

VMS Abbreviation for *vertical marketing system.

Voca Ltd *See* ASSOCIATION FOR PAYMENT CLEARING SERVICES.

vocational training Training in a trade or occupation. In the UK, the Business and Technology Education Council (BTEC) was set up in 1983 to develop a national system of vocational training. National Vocational Qualifications (NVQs) recognize ability in a particular trade or occupation; a General National Vocational Qualification (GNVQ) for those considering a number of employments was introduced in 1992.

volatile Denoting a market, commodity, share, bond, etc., that may be expected to fluctuate greatly and frequently in value.

volume **1.** The space occupied by something. **2.** A measure of the amount of trade that has taken place, usually in a specified period. On the *London Stock Exchange, for example, the number of shares traded in a day is called the volume and the value of these shares is called the **turnover**. In commodity markets, the daily volume is usually the number of lots traded in a day.

voluntary arrangement A procedure provided for by the Insolvency Act (1986), in which a company may come to an arrangement with its creditors to pay off its debts and to manage its affairs so that it resolves its financial difficulties. This arrangement may be proposed by the directors, an administrator acting under an *administration order, or a *liquidator. A qualified insolvency practitioner must be appointed to supervise the arrangement. This practitioner may be the administrator or liquidator, in which case a meeting of the company and its creditors must be called to consider the arrangement. The proposals may be modified or approved at this meeting but, once approved, they bind all those who had notice of the meeting. The court may make the necessary orders to bring the arrangement into effect. The arrangement may be challenged in court in the case of any irregularity. The aim of this legislation is to assist the company to solve its financial problems without the need for a winding-up (*see* LIQUIDATION).

voluntary liquidation (voluntary winding-up) *See* CREDITORS' VOLUNTARY LIQUIDATION; MEMBERS' VOLUNTARY LIQUIDATION.

voluntary registration Registration for *value added tax by a *taxable person whose taxable turnover does not exceed the registration threshold.

voluntary retailer *See* SYMBOL RETAILER.

volunteer A person who, in relation to

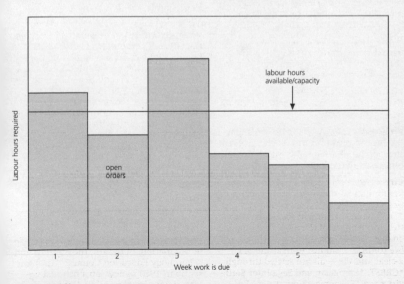

labour hours available/capacity

open orders

Labour hours required

Week work is due

Visual load profile

any transaction, has not given valuable *consideration.

vostro account A bank account held by a foreign bank with a UK bank, usually in sterling. *Compare* NOSTRO ACCOUNT.

voting shares Shares in a company that entitle their owner to vote at the annual general meeting and any extraordinary meetings of the company. Shares that carry **voting rights** are usually *ordinary shares, rather than *A shares or *debentures. The company's articles of association will state which shares carry voting rights.

voucher A receipt for money or any document that supports an entry in a book of account.

voyage charter A charter of a ship or of cargo space for a fixed number of voyages rather than for a fixed period (*compare* TIME CHARTER). The shipowner usually warrants that the ship will arrive at an agreed port on an agreed day, will be in seaworthy condition, and will be properly equipped. The charterer agrees to load and unload in the agreed number of *lay days.

VR Abbreviation for *virtual reality.

VRN Abbreviation for *variable-rate note.

Vroom–Yetton–Jago model A *contingency theory of leadership holding that leaders should vary the extent to which they allow followers to participate in decision making according to certain key factors in the situation. These include the nature of the task, the extent to which followers can be expected to disagree over the best solution, and the extent to which followers will accept decisions they personally disagree with. A *decision tree is used to assess these factors and to decide which of a range of *leadership styles is most appropriate.

V

WA Abbreviation for with average. *See* AVERAGE.

WAB Abbreviation for weighted application blank. *See* STANDARD APPLICATION BLANK.

WACC Abbreviation for *weighted average cost of capital.

wafer seal A modern form of seal used on such documents as deeds. It is usually a small red disc stuck onto the document to represent the seal. Almost any form of seal agreeable to all the parties concerned is now acceptable in place of sealing wax.

wage differential The difference in earnings between workers with similar skills in different industries or between workers with different skills in the same industry. There may also be differentials between urban and non-urban wages or between regions (wages in the UK are highest in the Southeast, where the cost of living is highest). The Equal Pay Act (1970) makes it illegal for a differential to exist between the pay of men and women doing like work in the same employment.

wage freeze An attempt by a government to counter inflation by fixing wages at their existing level for a specified period. For various reasons, including the use of overtime and bonuses to defeat the measure, this is no longer considered an effective policy. **Wage restraint** is a less rigidly applied attempt to control prices by obtaining union agreement to make only modest and essential claims for wage increases.

wagering contract *See* GAMING CONTRACT.

wages The remuneration paid to hourly paid employees for the work done, usually based on the number of hours spent at the place of work.

waiter An attendant at *Lloyd's, who carries messages and papers, etc. The name goes back to the 17th-century London coffee houses from which this institution grew, in which the waiters also performed these functions.

waiting time The period during which the operators of a machine or the machinery itself are idle or waiting for work, material, or repairs. *See also* IDLE TIME.

waiver The setting aside or non-enforcement of a right. This may be done deliberately or it may happen by the operation of law. For example, if a tenant is in breach of a covenant in a lease and the landlord demands rent in spite of knowing of the breach, the landlord may be held to have waived the right to terminate the lease.

walk-through test An *audit test that takes a few transactions from the records of a business and follows them through every stage of the accounting system. For example, a walk-through test of a purchases system would follow through from the material requisition to settlement of the supplier's invoice.

Wall Street **1.** The *New York Stock Exchange, which stands on Wall Street in New York. **2.** The financial institutions, collectively, of New York, including the stock exchange, banks, money markets, commodity markets, etc.

WAP Abbreviation for *wireless application protocol.

warehouse Any building in which goods are stored; a **public warehouse** is one at or near a port in which goods are stored after being unloaded from a ship or before being loaded onto a ship (*see also* BONDED WAREHOUSE). When goods are taken into a public warehouse a warehouse *warrant is issued, which must be produced before the goods can be removed.

warehouse club (**wholesale club**; **membership warehouse**) A cut-price retailer that sells a limited selection of brand-name grocery items, appliances, clothing, and other goods at substantial discounts to members, who pay an annual membership fee.

warehouse keeper The person in charge of a warehouse. A *bonded warehouse also has a **warehouse officer**, employed by HM Customs and Excise, to inspect goods entering and leaving the warehouse.

warehousing 1. The storage of goods in a warehouse. **2.** Building up a holding of shares in a company prior to making a *takeover bid, by buying small lots of the shares and 'warehousing' them in the name of nominees. The purpose is for the bidder to remain anonymous and to avoid having to make the statutory declaration of interest. This practice is contrary to the *City Code on Takeovers and Mergers.

war loan A government stock issued during wartime; it has no redemption date, pays only 3½% interest, and stands at less than half its face value.

warrant 1. A security that offers the owner the right to subscribe for the *ordinary shares of a company at a fixed date, usually at a fixed price. Warrants are themselves bought and sold on *stock exchanges and are equivalent to stock options. Subscription prices usually exceed the market price, as the purchase of a warrant is a gamble that a company will prosper. They have proved increasingly popular in recent years as a company can issue them without including them in the balance sheet. **2.** A document that serves as proof that goods have been deposited in a public *warehouse. The document identifies specific goods and can be transferred by endorsement. Warrants are frequently used as security against a bank loan. Warehouse warrants for warehouses attached to a *wharf are known as **dock warrants** or **wharfinger's warrants**.

warranty 1. A statement made clearly in a contract (**express warranty**) or, if not stated clearly, understood between the parties to the contract (**implied warranty**). An unfulfilled warranty does not invalidate the contract (as it would in the case of an unfulfilled *condition) but could lead to the payment of damages. *See also* FLOAT-ING WARRANTY. **2.** A condition in an insurance policy that confirms that something

will or will not be done or that a certain situation exists or does not exist. If a warranty is breached, the insurer is entitled to refuse to pay claims, even if they are unconnected with the breach. For example, if a policy insuring the contents of a house has a warranty that certain locks are to be used on the doors and windows and these are found not to have been used, the insurers could decline to settle a claim for a burst pipe. In practice, however, this does not happen as insurers have agreed that they will only refuse to pay claims if the breach of warranty has affected the circumstances of the claim. **3.** A manufacturer's written promise to repair or replace a faulty product, usually free of charge, during a specified period subsequent to the date of purchase. This is often called a **guarantee**.

wash sale A US name for the sale and purchase by a single investor, or a group in collusion, of a block of securities either simultaneously or in a short space of time to establish a loss or a gain; it may also be used to create the impression that the security in question is trading actively. It is similar to the practice known in the UK as *bed and breakfast.

waste (spoilage) The amount of material lost as part of a production process. Acceptable levels of waste, known as a *normal loss, are part of the cost of production and as such are allowed for in the product costs. *See also* PROCESS COSTING.

wasting asset An *asset that has a finite life; for example, a lease may lose value throughout its life and become valueless when it terminates. It is also applied to such assets as plant and machinery, which wear out during their life and therefore lose value.

watered stock *See* STOCK WATERING.

waybill 1. *See* CONSIGNMENT NOTE. **2.** *See* AIR WAYBILL.

WDA Abbreviation for *writing-down allowance.

WDV Abbreviation for *written-down value.

wealth tax A tax used in some European countries, not including the UK, consisting of an annual levy on wealth. In practice, the implementation of a wealth tax requires a clear identification of the assets to be charged and an unassailable valuation of these assets.

wear and tear A diminution in the value to an organization of a fixed asset due to the use and damage that it inevitably sustains throughout its working life. It is one of the causes of *depreciation.

weather insurance *See* PLUVIAL INSURANCE.

weather working days *Working days on which the weather permits work to be carried out. This often refers to the days allowed in a charter for loading or unloading a ship. *See* LAY DAYS.

web address *See* UNIFORM RESOURCE LOCATOR.

web browser A computer program, such as Netscape Navigator or Microsoft Internet Explorer, that provides an easy method of accessing and viewing information stored as HTML web documents on different *web servers.

webcasting (push programming) A process in which an on-line marketer of a product or service sends advertisements or information over the Internet, directly to the desktops of target customers. Companies can also sign on with a webcasting service provider, who will automatically download customized information to the personal computers of subscribers to their service.

webmaster A person responsible for ensuring the quality of a website. This means achieving suitable availability, speed, working links between pages, and connections to company databases. In small companies the webmaster may also be responsible for graphic design and *content development.

web server A store of web pages that can be accessed by a *web browser. Web servers may also contain databases of customer or product information, which can be queried and retrieved using a web browser.

website *Content accessible on the *World Wide Web created by a particular organization or individual. The location

and identity of a website is indicated by its web address (*see* UNIFORM RESOURCE LOCATOR). It may be stored on a single server in a single location, or on a cluster of servers.

website brand impact The benefits to a particular brand that result from a website visit.

website reach The fraction of the total number of web users that visit a specified website during a specified time interval.

weighted aggregate indices *See* INDEX NUMBER.

weighted application blank (WAB) *See* STANDARD APPLICATION BLANK.

weighted average (weighted mean) An arithmetic average that takes into account the importance of the items making up the average. For example, if a trader buys a commodity on three occasions, 100 tonnes at £70 per tonne, 300 tonnes at £80 per tonne, and 50 tonnes at £95 per tonne, his or her purchases total 450 tonnes; the simple average price would be $(70 + 80 + 95)/3 = £81.7$. The weighted average, taking into account the amount purchased on each occasion, would be $[(100 \times 70) + (300 \times 80) + (50 \times 95)]/450 = £79.4$ per tonne.

weighted average cost of capital (WACC) A method for calculating the average cost of a company's different sources of finance. The WACC is calculated on the assumption that the company will maintain the same *debt–equity ratio. Managers should only use the WACC as an appropriate *discount rate for a project when the project has about the same level of risk as the company. The most difficult part of the calculation is the estimate for the cost of equity.

In theory, a company can lower its weighted average cost of capital by increasing the proportion of debt. However, this could become a problem for shareholders, who may feel that higher levels of debt will increase the risk of their investment. *See also* COST OF CAPITAL.

weighted ballot A *ballot held if a new issue of shares has been oversubscribed, in which the allocation of shares is based on the number of shares applied for and biased towards either the smaller investor or the larger investor.

W

weightless **1.** Denoting a business that has very few *tangible assets, especially one involved in *Internet trading. **2.** Denoting that part of the economy that is based on ideas and information rather than trade in physical goods.

weight note A document produced by a seller of goods in which the *gross weights of the packages are listed. It also gives the marks and numbers of the packages and an indication of the average tare.

weight or measurement *See* FREIGHT.

wharf The quay at which ships dock in a port, together with the adjacent warehouses in which goods are stored before loading or after unloading. The **wharfinger** is the firm or individual responsible for running the wharf.

wharfage The charge made by a wharfinger for the use of a wharf for loading or unloading cargo onto or from a ship.

wharfinger's receipt *See* DOCK RECEIPT.

wharfinger's warrant *See* WARRANT.

wheel of retailing concept A retailing concept assuming that new-style retailers usually begin as low-margin, low-price, and low-status operations but later evolve into higher-priced higher-service operations, eventually resembling the conventional retailers they attempted to replace.

whipsawing **1.** A procedure in which individual employees or groups of employees are made to compete with one another on a task, usually with the aim of increasing productivity. Employers have sometimes used whipsawing as a means of undermining trade unions. **2.** A bargaining tactic employed by trade unions in which there is an attempt to spread wage and other concessions from one employer to another using 'coercive comparisons'.

white-collar worker Any non-manual office worker, including clerical, administrative, managerial, and professional personnel. *Compare* BLUE-COLLAR WORKER.

white goods A class of consumer durables that includes washing machines, dishwashers, refrigerators, tumble-dryers, deep-freezers, and cookers; they are so named because they are usually finished in white enamel paint, although browns

and other colours are now being used to make them fit less starkly into modern kitchens. *Compare* BROWN GOODS.

white knight A person or firm that makes a welcome *takeover bid for a company on improved terms to replace an unacceptable and unwelcome bid from a *black knight. If a company is the target for a takeover bid from a source of which it does not approve or on terms that it does not find attractive, it will often seek a white knight, whom it sees as a more suitable owner for the company, in the hope that a more attractive bid will be made. *Compare* GREY KNIGHT.

whole life policy (whole of life policy) A *life-assurance policy that pays a specified amount on the death of the life assured. Benefits are not made for any other reason and the cover continues until the death of the life assured, provided the premiums continue to be paid, either for life or until a specified date. They may be *with-profits policies or *unit-linked policies.

wholesale banking Interbank lending as well as lending to or by other large financial institutions, pension funds, and government agencies. *See* INTERBANK MARKET; MONEY MARKET. In the USA, wholesale banking also refers to the provision of banking services to large corporate businesses at special rates.

wholesale club *See* WAREHOUSE CLUB.

wholesale deposit A large deposit obtained by a bank, financial institution, or large corporate business.

wholesale market *See* MONEY MARKET.

wholesale price index *See* PRODUCER PRICE INDEX.

wholesaler A *distributor that sells goods in large quantities, usually to other distributors. Typically, a wholesaler buys and stores large quantities of several producers' goods and breaks into the bulk deliveries to supply *retailers with smaller amounts assembled and sorted to order.

wholesaler-sponsored voluntary chain A *vertical marketing system initiated by a *wholesaler, in which a group of independent retailers participate in a relationship linked to the wholesaler supplier.

wholly owned subsidiary A *subsidiary undertaking that is owned 100% by a holding company (i.e. there is no *minority interest).

wildcat strike *See* STRIKE.

windbill *See* ACCOMMODATION BILL.

windfall gains and losses Gains and losses arising from actual or prospective receipts that differ from those originally predicted or from changes in the *net present value of the receipts as a result of differences in discount rates.

winding-up *See* LIQUIDATION.

winding-up order An order given by a British court, under the Insolvency Act (1986), compelling a company to be wound up.

windmill *See* ACCOMMODATION BILL.

window 1. An opportunity to borrow or invest that may be only temporary and should therefore be taken while it is available. **2.** A period during the day during which interbank transfers and clearance may be enacted.

window dressing Any practice that attempts to make a situation look better than it really is. It has been used extensively by accountants to improve the look of balance sheets. For example, banks used to call in their short-term loans and delay making payments at the end of their financial years, in order to show spuriously high cash balances. Another example is when a company borrows cash from an associated undertaking to disguise a short-term liquidity problem. These practices now fall within the remit of the *Accounting Standards Board. *See* CREATIVE ACCOUNTING; OFF-BALANCE-SHEET FINANCE.

Windows *Trademark* A *graphical user interface developed by Microsoft for *microprocessors. It is the most widely used operating system on personal computers. There have been a number of versions. It was originally based on *MS-DOS.

WIP Abbreviation for *work in progress.

wireless application protocol (WAP) A standard that enables mobile phones to access text from websites.

with average (WA) *See* AVERAGE.

withholding tax Tax deducted at source from *dividends or other income paid to non-residents of a country. If there is a *double-taxation agreement between the country in which the income is paid and the country in which the recipient is resident, the tax can be reclaimed.

without prejudice Words used as a heading to a document or letter to indicate that what follows cannot be used in any way to harm an existing right or claim, cannot be taken as the signatory's last word, cannot bind the signatory in any way, and cannot be used as evidence in a court of law. For example, a solicitor may use these words when making an offer in a letter to settle a claim, implying that the client may decide to withdraw the offer. It may also be used to indicate that although agreement may be reached on the terms set out in the document on this occasion, the signatory is not bound to settle similar disputes on the same terms.

without-profits policy A life-assurance or pension policy that does not share in the profits of the life-assurance office that issued it. *Compare* WITH-PROFITS POLICY.

without recourse (sans recours) Words that appear on a *bill of exchange to indicate that the holder has no recourse to the person from whom it was bought, if it is not paid. It may be written on the face of the bill or as an endorsement. If these words do not appear on the bill, the holder does have recourse to the drawer or endorser if the bill is dishonoured at maturity.

with-profits bond An investment bond that has a cash-in value to some extent protected by the payment and accrual of bonuses.

with-profits policy A life-assurance policy that has additional amounts added to the sum assured, or paid separately as cash bonuses, as a result of a surplus or profit made on the investment of the fund or funds of the life-assurance office. *Compare* UNIT-LINKED POLICY.

won (W) The standard monetary unit of North Korea and South Korea, divided into 100 chon.

word association A technique used in

*marketing research in which a series of words is presented to a respondent, who is asked to respond to each one with the first word that comes to mind. The researcher seeks to interpret the results.

word-of-mouth advertising (word-of-mouth influence) The process in which the purchaser of a product or service tells friends, family, neighbours, and associates about its virtues, especially when this happens in advance of media advertising. *See* VIRAL MARKETING.

word processor (WP) A computerized text-processing system consisting of a computer unit with a keyboard, display screen, printer, and hard disk. Modern wordprocessors enable text to be justified and correctly hyphenated, a variety of fonts and typefaces to be used, tables and footnotes to be automatically generated, and graphics to be incorporated. Most word processors are now capable of producing documents that are equivalent in quality to a printed book.

work breakdown structure A preliminary stage in producing a project network model (*see* NETWORK MODELLING) in which the work to be done is broken down into broad categories, the resources required are identified, and details of the deliverables expected at each stage are listed.

work centre A machine, set of machines, or a work station that performs a transformation or provides a service as part of a job. A product may pass through several such work centres in the course of manufacture.

workers' participation *See* INDUSTRIAL DEMOCRACY.

work-in *See* SIT-DOWN STRIKE.

working capital The part of the capital of a company that is employed in its day-to-day trading operations. It consists of *current assets (mainly trading stock, debtors, and cash) less *current liabilities (mainly trade creditors). In the normal trade cycle – the supply of goods by suppliers, the sale of stock to debtors, payments of debts in cash, and the use of cash to pay suppliers – the working capital is the aggregate of the net assets involved, sometimes called the **working assets**. The

management of working assets is very important to a company. Holding sufficient levels of finished goods to meet customer requirements is important, but managers must also be aware of the cost of holding these goods.

working days In commerce, the days of the week excluding Sunday and, in some cases, Saturday (depending on the custom of the trade). Public holidays (*see* BANK HOLIDAYS) are also excluded from working days. In shipping and some other trades it is usual to distinguish *weather working days. *See also* LAY DAYS.

working director *See* EXECUTIVE DIRECTOR.

working hours The EU **Working Time Directive** of 1993 required all member states to limit the working week of employees to 48 hours (except when employees have agreed otherwise). The provisions of this directive were enacted by the British government in the Working Time Regulations (1998). Key elements of the Regulations require a maximum working week of 48 hours, daily rest breaks, weekly rest periods, and annual paid leave of four weeks in each holiday year. They are enforced by the Health and Safety Executive.

work in progress (WIP) Materials, parts, and unfinished products within an *operating system, in which they represent locked-up capital. *Just-in-time techniques aim to minimize WIP, while more traditional systems see WIP as necessary to provide a head of work. WIP is normally valued at the lower of cost or *net realizable value, using either the *first-in-first-out cost, the *last-in-first-out cost, or the *average cost method of valuation. In the USA, **work in process** is the more common term.

workload approach An approach to setting the size of a salesforce in which a company groups accounts into classes of different sizes in order to determine how many salespeople are needed to call on the members of each class the desired number of times.

work measurement The application of techniques to establish the time required for a qualified worker to carry out a specified task at a defined level of performance. *See* WORK STUDY.

work-sample tests In *personnel selection, an assessment procedure that requires candidates to carry out tasks sampled from the job(s) in question. For example, an applicant may be required to use actual or simulated equipment or to make a decision based on complex financial data. An **in-basket test** is a work-sample test in which the candidate is presented with a typical manager's in-basket full of memos, letters, etc. and is asked to prioritize and deal with these items.

work sampling *See* ACTIVITY SAMPLING.

workstation *See* LOCAL AREA NETWORK.

work study A systematic examination of human work processes, designed to identify the ways in which the efficiency and effectiveness of these processes can be improved. It usually consists of a *method study to compare existing methods with proposed methods and *work measurement to establish the time required by a qualified worker to do the job to a specified standard. Traditionally, work study techniques have been associated with the school of *scientific management and applied by specialists known as *industrial engineers (or more colloquially as time-and-motion experts), working in *management services departments. The introduction of such approaches as *total quality management has enabled managers and staff to take responsibility for the design and management of their own systems. Recent techniques, such as *business process re-engineering, share many of the same objectives as work study but exploit *information technology, which was not available to earlier industrial engineers.

work-to-rule A form of *industrial action in which employees pay a slavish obedience to employers' regulations in order to dislocate working procedures, without resorting to a *strike. A work-to-rule usually involves an *overtime ban.

World Bank The name by which the *International Bank for Reconstruction and Development combined with its affiliates, the *International Development As-sociation and the *International Finance Corporation, is known.

World Trade Organization (WTO) The world trading system founded at the Uruguay round of the *General Agreement on Tariffs and Trade (GATT) in 1994, and superseding GATT in the following year. WTO's aims are to continue the work of GATT in agreeing international trading rules and furthering the liberalization of international trade. WTO has wider and more permanent powers than GATT and extends its jurisdiction into such aspects of trading as *intellectual property rights. The highest authority of WTO is the Ministerial Conference, held at least every two years. As at May 2005 there were 148 members of WTO. Recent meetings of WTO have been met with violent anti-capitalist demonstrations in several countries.

World Wide Web (WWW; Web) *See* INTERNET.

WP Abbreviation for *word processor.

writ An order issued by a court. A **writ of summons** is an order by which an action in the High Court is started. It commands the defendant to appear before the court to answer the claim made in the writ by the plaintiff. It is used in actions in *tort, claims alleging *fraud, and claims for *damages in respect of personal injuries, death, or infringement of *patent. A **writ of execution** is used to enforce a judgement; it is addressed to a court officer instructing that officer to carry out an act, such as collecting money or seizing property. A **writ of delivery** is a writ of execution directing a sheriff to seize goods and deliver them to the plaintiff or to obtain their value in money, according to an agreed assessment. If the defendant has no option to pay the assessed value, the writ is a writ of specific delivery.

write To cover an insurance risk, accepting liability, under an insurance contract as an *underwriter.

write off 1. To reduce the value of an asset to zero in a balance sheet. An expired lease, obsolete machinery, or an unfortunate investment would be written off. **2.** To reduce to zero a debt that cannot be collected (*see* BAD DEBT). Such a loss will be shown in the *profit and loss account of an organization.

writer The seller of a traded option. *Compare* TAKER.

writing-down allowance (WDA) A *capital allowance available to a UK trader; from 1 November 1993 it became the only allowance generally available for *plant and machinery used in trade, although *first-year allowances have at times been reintroduced for specific types of equipment or types of business. Any additions to plant and machinery are added to the *written-down value of assets acquired in previous years and the writing-down allowance is calculated as 25% of the total. For cars the allowance is restricted to £3000, for vehicles whose initial cost is in excess of £12,000. For *industrial buildings the allowance is calculated at 4% of the initial cost, on the *straight-line method. For certain long-life assets it is calculated at 6% in the same way.

written-down value (WDV) The value of an asset for tax purposes after taking account of its reduction in value below the initial cost, as a result of its use in the trade. An asset acquired for a trade is eligible for *capital allowances. A *writing-down allowance of 25% is available in the year of purchase, which is deducted from the initial cost to establish the written-down value. In the following year the written-down value is subject to the 25% writing-down allowance, which is deducted to arrive at the written-down value at the end of the second year. The table shows the WDA and WDV for an asset acquired for £1000. The written-down value of the asset, for tax purposes, at the end of year 2 is £563.

		£
YEAR 1	Cost	1000
	WDA 25%	(250)
	WDV	750
YEAR 2	WDA 25%	(187)
	WDV	563

Written-down value

written resolution A *resolution signed by all company members and treated as effective even though it is not passed at a properly convened company meeting. Under the Companies Act (1985) private companies can, in some circumstances, pass resolutions in this way; other companies may have power to do so under their *articles of association.

written statement of terms of employment A statement in writing that an employer must give to certain employees under the terms of the Employment Rights Act (1996), which aims to comply with the EU Proof of Employment Relationship Directive. Not later than two months after the beginning of employment, the employer must give to every employee who works for eight or more hours a week a written statement (known as an **SI Statement**) setting out the following information:

- the names of employer and employee;
- the date employment began;
- the date when the employee's continuous employment began;
- the scale or rate of remuneration or method of calculating remuneration;
- the intervals at which remuneration is paid;
- the hours of work;
- the holiday entitlement;
- the procedure to be adopted in the event of incapacity for work as a result of sickness or injury (including sick pay provisions, if any);
- pensions and pension schemes;
- the length of notice the employee is obliged to give and entitled to receive to terminate the contract;
- the title of the job the employee is employed to do or a brief description of the work;
- if the employment is not intended to be permanent, the period for which it is expected to continue or, if it is for a fixed term, the date it is intended to end;
- either the place of work or, if the employee is required to work at various places, an indication that this is the case;
- any collective bargaining agreements that directly affect the terms and conditions of employment.

If any amendment is made to these terms after the statement has been issued, the employer must give the employee a written statement setting out the details of the change. Failure to comply with the requirements set out above gives the employee the right to complain to an *employment tribunal at any time during the employment or within three months of its coming to an end. The written statement, although providing evidence of the terms of employment, is not itself the contract of employment.

wrongful dismissal The termination of an employee's contract of employment in a manner that is not in accordance with that contract. Thus when an employee is dismissed without the correct notice entitlement (in circumstances that do not justify summary dismissal) or when the employer prematurely terminates the employee's fixed-term contract, the employee is entitled to claim *damages in the courts for wrongful dismissal. The court's jurisdiction concerns only the parties' contractual rights and not their statutory rights under the employment protection legislation (*compare* UNFAIR DISMISSAL). The Employment Protection (Consolidation) Act (1978) empowers the Secretary of State for Employment to give industrial tribunals jurisdiction to hear claims of wrongful dismissal.

wrongful trading Trading during a period in which a company had no reasonable prospect of avoiding insolvent *liquidation. The liquidator of a company may petition the court for an order instructing a director of a company that has gone into insolvent liquidation to make a contribution to the company's assets. The court may order any contribution to be made that it thinks proper if the director knew, or ought to have known, of the company's situation. A director would be judged liable if a reasonably diligent person carrying out the same function in the company would have realized the situation: no intention to defraud need be shown. *Compare* FRAUDULENT TRADING.

WTO Abbreviation for *World Trade Organization.

WWW Abbreviation for World Wide Web. *See* INTERNET.

xd Abbreviation for ex-dividend (*see* EX-).

xerography A dry electrostatic process for making photocopies and printing computer output with a *laser printer. In a **plain-paper photocopier** an electrostatic image is formed on a selenium-coated plate or cylinder. This is dusted with a resinous toner, which sticks selectively to the charged areas, the image so formed being transferred to a sheet of paper, on which it is fixed by heating.

xu A monetary unit of Vietnam, worth one hundredth of a *dông.

Yankee bond A *bond issued in the USA by a foreign borrower.

yearling bond A UK local authority bond that is redeemable one year after issue.

year of assessment See FISCAL YEAR.

Yellow Book The colloquial name for *Admission of Securities to Listing*, a book issued by the Council of the *London Stock Exchange that sets out the regulations for admission to the *Official List and the obligations of companies with *listed securities. See LISTING REQUIRE-MENTS.

Yellow Pages See CLASSIFIED DIRECTO-RIES.

yen (¥) The standard monetary unit of Japan, formerly divided into 100 *sen.

yield 1. The income from an investment expressed in various ways. The **nominal yield** of a fixed-interest security is the interest it pays, expressed as a percentage of its *par value. For example, a £100 stock quoted as paying 8% interest will yield £8 per annum for every £100 of stock held. However, the **current yield** (also called **running yield**, **earnings yield**, or **flat yield**) will depend on the market price of the stock. If the 8% £100 stock mentioned above was standing at a market price of £90, the current yield would be 100/90 × 8 = 8.9%. As interest rates rise, so the market value of fixed-interest stocks (not close to redemption) fall in order that they should give a competitive current yield. The capital gain (or loss) on redemption of a stock, which is normally re-deemable at £100, can also be taken into account. This is called the **yield to redemption** (or the **redemption yield**). The re-demption yield consists approximately of the current yield plus the capital gain (or loss) divided by the number of years to re-demption. Thus, if the above stock had 9 years to run to redemption, its redemp-tion yield would be about 8.9 + 10/9 = 10%.

The yields of the various stocks on offer are usually listed in commercial papers as both current yields and redemption yields, based on the current market price. How-ever, for an investor who actually owns stock, the yield will be calculated not on the market price but the price the in-vestor paid for it. The annual yield on a fixed-interest stock can be stated exactly once it has been purchased. This is not the case with *equities, however, where nei-ther the dividend yield (see DIVIDEND) nor the capital gain (or loss) can be forecast, reflecting the greater degree of risk attach-ing to investments in equities. Yields on fixed-interest securities and equities are normally quoted gross, i.e. before deduc-tion of tax. **2.** The income obtained from a tax.

yield curve A curve on a graph in which the *yield of fixed-interest securities is plotted against the length of time they have to run to maturity. The yield curve usually slopes upwards, indicating that in-vestors expect to receive a premium for holding securities that have a long time to run. However, when there are expecta-tions of changes in interest rate, the slope of the yield curve may change (see TERM STRUCTURE OF INTEREST RATES).

yield gap The difference between the average annual dividend yield on *equities and the average annual yield on long-dated *gilt-edged securities. Before the 1960s yields obtained from UK equities usually exceeded the yields provided by long-dated UK gilts, reflecting the greater degree of risk involved in an investment in equities. In the 1960s, however, rising equity prices led to falling dividend yields causing a **reverse yield gap**. This was widely regarded as acceptable, as equities were seen to provide a better hedge against *inflation than fixed-interest secu-rities; thus their greater risk element is compensated by the possibility of higher capital gains.

yield to maturity *See* GROSS REDEMPTION YIELD.

yield to redemption *See* YIELD.

yuan (Y) The standard monetary unit of China, divided into 10 jiao or 100 fen.

yuppie A successful and ambitious young person, especially one from the world of business or finance. The word is formed from *y*oung *u*pwardly-mobile *p*rofessional.

zaibatsu A Japanese conglomerate. It differs from a *keiretsu* in having a bank as its dominant member.

ZBB Abbreviation for *zero-base budget.

Zebra A discounted *zero-coupon bond, in which the accrued income is taxed annually rather than on redemption.

zero-base budget (ZBB) A *cash-flow budget in which the manager responsible for its preparation is required to prepare and justify the budgeted expenditure from a zero base, i.e. assuming that initially there is no commitment to spend on any activity.

zero-coupon bond A type of *bond that offers no interest payments. In effect, the interest is paid at maturity in the redemption value of the bond. Investors sometimes prefer zero-coupon bonds as they may confer more favourable tax treatment. *See also* DEEP DISCOUNT; TIGR; ZEBRA.

zero defects A component of *total quality management aimed at changing workers' attitudes to quality by stressing the goal of error-free performance. In practice, error-free performance is neither economically nor practically realizable. Experience suggests that, while short-term improvements may be achieved by these programs, performance usually returns to previous levels quite quickly. *See* ABSOLUTE PERFORMANCE STANDARD.

zero-rated goods and services Goods and services that are taxable for *value added tax purposes but are currently subject to a tax rate of zero. These include:
- most food items,
- sewerage and water services for non-industrial users,
- periodicals and books,
- certain charitable supplies,
- new domestic buildings,
- transport fares for vehicles designed to carry not less than 10 passengers,
- banknotes,
- drugs and medicines,
- clothing and footwear for children,
- all exports.

zip code The US name for a postcode. It consists of a five- or nine-digit code, the first five digits indicating the state and postal zone or post office, the last four digits the rural route, building, or other delivery location.

zloty (Zl) The standard monetary unit of Poland, divided into 100 groszy.

zone pricing A pricing strategy in which a company delineates two or more zones. All the customers within a zone pay the same price for a product; the more distant the zone from the company's headquarters or warehouse, the higher the price.

Z score (Altman's Z score) A statistic, devised by Edward Altman, that attempts to measure the susceptibility of a business to failure. It is computed by applying *beta coefficients to a number of selected ratios taken from an organization's final accounts using the technique of multiple discriminant analysis.

Appendix

Useful websites

Business and Management

Association of Business Recovery Professionals
www.r3.org.uk

British Chambers of Commerce
www.chamberonline.co.uk

British Exporters Association
www.bexa.co.uk

British Retail Consortium
www.brc.org.uk

BSI Group
www.bsi-global.com

Chartered Institute of Personnel and Development
www.cipd.co.uk

Chartered Institute of Purchasing and Supply
www.cips.org

Chartered Management Institute
www.managers.org.uk

Confederation of British Industry
www.cbi.org.uk

Enterprise Investment Scheme
www.eisa.org.uk

Institute of Chartered Secretaries and Administrators
www.icsa.org.uk

Institute of Directors
www.iod.com

Institute of Management Services
www.ims-productivity.com

Institute of Sales Promotion
www.isp.org.uk

International Chamber of Commerce
www.iccuk.net

London Chamber of Commerce
www.londonchamber.co.uk

Management Consultancies Association
www.mca.org.uk

Queen's Award for Enterprise
www.queensawards.org.uk

Takeover Panel
www.takeoverpanel.org.uk

Advertising and Marketing

Advertising Association
www.adassoc.org.uk

Advertising Standards Authority
www.asa.org.uk

Audit Bureau of Circulation
www.abc.org.uk

British Market Research Association
www.bmra.org.uk

Campaign
www.brandrepublic.com/magazines/campaign

Chartered Institute of Marketing
www.cim.co.uk

Direct Marketing Association UK
www.dma.org.uk

Incorporated Society of British Advertisers
www.isba.org.uk

Institute of Practitioners in Advertising
www.ipa.co.uk

Market Research Society
www.mrs.org.uk

MORI
www.mori.com

Banking

Association for Payment Clearing Services
www.apacs.org.uk

Bank for International Settlements
www.bis.org

Bank of England
www.bankofengland.co.uk

British Bankers' Association
www.bba.org.uk

European Central Bank
www.ecb.int

European Investment Bank
www.eib.org

Federal Reserve Board (USA)
www.federalreserve.gov

International Bank for Reconciliation and Development
www.worldbank.org

Finance

Association of Private Client Investment Managers and Stockbrokers
www.apcims.co.uk

Chicago Mercantile Exchange
www.cme.com

Commodity Exchange Inc. of New York
www.nymex.com

Euronext NV
www.euronext.com

Dow Jones Indexes
www.djindexes.com

Financial Times
www.ft.com

International Petroleum Exchange
www.theipe.com

Euronext NV
www.euronext.com

Investment Management Association
www.investmentuk.org

London Bullion Market
www.lbma.org.uk

London International Financial Futures and Options Exchange
www.liffe.com

London Metal Exchange
www.lme.co.uk

London Stock Exchange
www.londonstockexchange.com

National Association of Securities Dealers (USA)
www.nasd.com

New York Stock Exchange
www.nyse.com

Nikkei Stock Average
www.nikkei.co.jp/CF/FR/MKJ/

Quoted Companies Alliance
www.qcanet.co.uk

Securities and Exchange Commission (USA)
www.sec.gov

Tokyo Stock Exchange
www.tse.org.jp

virt-x
www.virt-x.com

Accountancy

Accounting Standards Board
www.asb.org.uk/asb

Association of Chartered Certified Accountants
www.acca.co.uk

Association of Corporate Treasurers
www.treasurers.org

Auditing Practices Board
www.asb.org.uk/apb

Chartered Institute of Management Accounting
www.cimaglobal.com

Chartered Institute of Public Finance and Accounting
www.cipfa.org.uk

Chartered Institute of Taxation
www.tax.org.uk

Financial Accounting Standards Board (USA)
www.fasb.org

Institute of Chartered Accountants in England and Wales
www.icaew.co.uk

Institute of Chartered Accountants in Ireland
www.icai.org.uk

Institute of Chartered Accountants in Scotland
www.icas.org.uk

Institute of Management Accountants
www.imanet.org

International Accounting Standards Board
www.ifac.org/iasb.org

Insurance

Association of British Insurers
www.abi.org.uk

British Insurance and Investment Brokers Association
www.bsi-global.com

Chartered Insurance Institute
www.cci.co.uk

Institute of Actuaries
www.actuaries.org.uk

Lloyds of London
www.lloyds.com

Government and Public Bodies

Advisory Conciliation and Arbitration Service
www.acas.org.uk

Central Arbitration Committee
www.cac.gov.uk

Companies House
www.companieshouse.gov.uk

Competition Commission
www.competition-commission.org.uk

Customs and Excise
www.hmrc.gov.uk

Department for Education and Skills
www.dfes.gov.uk

Department for Work and Pensions
www.dwp.gov.uk

Department of Trade and Industry
www.dti.gov.uk

Employment Tribunals
www.employmenttribunals.gov.uk

Export Credits Guarantee Department
www.ecgd.gov.uk

Federal Trade Commission (USA)
www.ftc.com

Financial Ombudsman Service
www.financial-ombudsman.org.uk

Financial Services Authority
www.fsa.gov.uk

Health and Safety Commission
www.hsc.gov.uk

Inland Revenue
www.hmrc.gov.uk

Insolvency Service
www.insolvency.gov.uk

Internal Revenue Service (USA)
www.irs.gov

Occupational Pensions Regulatory Authority
www.opra.gov.uk

Office for National Statistics
www.statistics.gov.uk

Office of Fair Trading
www.oft.gov.uk

Patent Office
www.patent.gov.uk

Scottish Enterprise
www.scottish-enterprise.com

Serious Fraud Office
www.sfo.gov.uk

HM Treasury
www.hm-treasury.gov.uk

International

Asia-Pacific Economic Cooperation
www.apecsec.org.sg

Association of South East Asian Nations
www.asean.or.id

Caribbean Community and Common Market
www.caricom.org

European Free Trade Association
www.efta.int

European Parliament
www.europarl.eu.int

International Labour Organization
www.ilo.org

International Monetary Fund
www.imf.org

International Standards Association
www.iso.org

Latin American Integration Association
www.aladi.org

Mercosur
www.mercosur.org.uy

North American Free Trade Association
www.nafta-sec-alena.org

Organization for Economic Cooperation and Development
www.oecd.org

Organization of the Petroleum Exporting Countries
www.opec.com

United Nations Conference on Trade and Development
www.unctad.org

United Nations Industrial Development Organization
www.unido.org

World Trade Organization
www.wto.org

Miscellaneous

Consumers' Association
www.which.net

National Consumer Council
www.ncc.org.uk

Trades Union Congress
www.tuc.org.uk